Multisystemic Resilience

Multisystemic Resilience

Adaptation and Transformation in Contexts of Change

EDITED BY
Michael Ungar

Oxford University Press is a department of the University of Oxford. It furthers
the University's objective of excellence in research, scholarship, and education
by publishing worldwide. Oxford is a registered trade mark of Oxford University
Press in the UK and certain other countries.

Published in the United States of America by Oxford University Press
198 Madison Avenue, New York, NY 10016, United States of America.

© Oxford University Press 2021

All rights reserved. No part of this publication may be reproduced, stored in
a retrieval system, or transmitted, in any form or by any means, without the
prior permission in writing of Oxford University Press, or as expressly permitted
by law, by license, or under terms agreed with the appropriate reproduction
rights organization. Inquiries concerning reproduction outside the scope of the
above should be sent to the Rights Department, Oxford University Press, at the
address above.

You must not circulate this work in any other form
and you must impose this same condition on any acquirer.

Library of Congress Cataloging-in-Publication Data
Names: Ungar, Michael, 1963– editor.
Title: Multisystemic resilience : adaptation and transformation in contexts of change /
edited by Michael Ungar.
Description: New York : Oxford University Press, 2021. |
Includes bibliographical references and index.
Identifiers: LCCN 2020031178 (print) | LCCN 2020031179 (ebook) |
ISBN 9780190095888 (hardback) | ISBN 9780190095901 (epub) |
ISBN 9780197541159
Subjects: LCSH: Resilience (Personality trait) | Resilience (Personality trait)—Social aspects.
Classification: LCC BF698.35.R47 M85 2021 (print) | LCC BF698.35.R47(ebook) |
DDC 155.2/4—dc23
LC record available at https://lccn.loc.gov/2020031178
LC ebook record available at https://lccn.loc.gov/2020031179

DOI: 10.1093/oso/9780190095888.001.0001

9 8 7 6 5 4 3 2

Printed by Marquis, Canada

Contents

Acknowledgments ix
Contributors xi

Introduction: Why a Volume on Multisystemic Resilience? 1
Michael Ungar

1. Modeling Multisystemic Resilience: Connecting Biological, Psychological, Social, and Ecological Adaptation in Contexts of Adversity 6
Michael Ungar

Section 1: Human Biology and Social Environments

2. Bringing a Neurobiological Perspective to Resilience 35
Nicole Bush and Danielle S. Roubinov

3. Risk and Resilience in Pregnancy and Birth 57
Cecily Young and Susan Ayers

4. Promoting Resilience Within Public Health Approaches for Indigenous Communities 78
Christopher Mushquash, Elaine Toombs, Kristy Kowatch, Jessie Lund, Lauren Dalicandro, and Kara Boles

5. Narrative Resilience: Neurological and Psychotherapeutic Reflections 100
Boris Cyrulnik

Section 2: Psychological Processes in Challenging Contexts

6. Resilience in Developmental Systems: Principles, Pathways, and Protective Processes in Research and Practice 113
Ann S. Masten

7. Stressor Appraisal as an Explanation for the Influence of Extra-Individual Factors on Psychological Resilience — 135
   Raffael Kalisch and Miriam Kampa

8. Resilience in the Salutogenic Model of Health — 153
   Maurice B. Mittelmark

9. People, Perceptions, and Process: Multisystemic Resilience in Social-Ecological Systems — 165
   Lilian Alessa and Andrew Kliskey

10. Social Ecology of Police Resilience — 181
    Mehdi Ghazinour and Arian Rostami

Section 3: Education Systems, Arts, and Well-Being

11. Indigenous Education, Well-Being, and Resilience—A Systemic Approach — 199
    Janya McCalman and Roxanne Bainbridge

12. A Transactional, Whole-School Approach to Resilience — 220
    Carmel Cefai

13. Learning About Systemic Resilience From Studies of Student Resilience — 232
    Linda Theron

Section 4: Family and Kinship Systems

14. Family Resilience: A Dynamic Systemic Framework — 255
    Froma Walsh

15. What Does It Take for Early Relationships to Remain Secure in the Face of Adversity? Attachment as a Unit of Resilience — 271
    Ana Berástegui and Carlos Pitillas

Section 5: Community Well-Being

16. Resilience to Violent Extremism and Terrorism: A Multisystemic Analysis — 293
    Michele Grossman

17. The Creation and Recreation of Borderlands Among Indigenous Peoples: A Kamentza's Journey of Resilience — 318
    Pilar Hernández-Wolfe and Santos Jamioy Muchavisoy

18. A Socioecological Developmental Systems Approach for the Study of Human Resilience — 335
    Ingrid Schoon

Section 6: Recovery and Resilience in Humanitarian Settings

19. Resilience Humanitarianism and Peacebuilding — 361
    Catherine Panter-Brick

20. Toward a Multisystemic Resilience Framework for Migrant Youth — 375
    Qiaobing Wu and Ying Ou

21. Psychological Resilience in Response to Adverse Experiences: An Integrative Developmental Perspective in the Context of War and Displacement — 395
    Cassandra M. Popham, Fiona S. McEwen, and Michael Pluess

22. The Assessment of Multisystemic Resilience in Conflict-Affected Populations — 417
    Alexandros Lordos and Daniel Hyslop

Section 7: Organizational Processes

23. The Multisystem Approach to Resilience in the Context of Organizations — 455
    Monique Crane

24. Resilience Engineering for Sociotechnical Safety Management — 477
    Riccardo Patriarca

25. Transformative Social Innovation and Multisystemic Resilience: Three Case Studies — 493
    Katharine McGowan and Francis Westley

Section 8: Legal, Policy, and Economic Systems

26. Resilience of Legal Systems: Toward Adaptive Governance — 509
    J. B. Ruhl, Barbara Cosens, and Niko Soininen

27. Thinking Systemically About Transitional Justice, Legal Systems, and Resilience — 530
    Janine Natalya Clark

28. Understanding Societal Resilience: The Case for Engaged Scholarship — 551
    Rosanne Anholt, Caroline van Dullemen, Juliana Santos de Carvalho, Joris Rijbroek, Stijn Sieckelinck, and Marieke W. Slootman

29. Decolonial Enactments of Human Resilience: Stories of Palestinian Families From Beyond the Wall — 565
    Devin G. Atallah

30. The Economics of Multisystemic Resilience — 584
    Gabriella Conti and Tatiana Paredes

Section 9: Architecture and Urban Design

31. The Embodied Multisystemic Resilience of Architecture and Built Form   603
    Brian McGrath and Dongxue Lei

32. The Social Contexts of Resilient Architecture   625
    Terri Peters

33. Resilience in Postdisaster Reconstruction of Human Settlement:
    An Architectural Perspective   646
    Haorui Wu

Section 10: Technology and Human Systems

34. Design and Engineering of Resilience for Networked Computer Systems   663
    David Hutchison, Mark Rouncefield, Antonios Gouglidis, and Tom Anderson

35. Patterns for Achieving Resilience in Engineered and Organizational Systems   682
    Scott Jackson, Victoria Hailey, Keith D. Willett, Timothy Ferris, and Eric A. Specking

Section 11: Social Ecological Systems

36. Social and Ecological Systems Resilience and Identity   705
    Francois Bousquet, Tara Quinn, Clara Therville, Raphaël Mathevet, Olivier Barreteau, Bruno Bonté, and Chloé Guerbois

37. Adaptive Management of Ecosystem Services for Multisystemic Resilience:
    Iterative Feedback Between Application and Theory   725
    Katharine F. E. Hogan, Kirsty L. Nash, and Elena Bennett

38. Conceptualizing Cascading Effects of Resilience in Human–Water Systems   744
    Li Xu, Feng Mao, James S. Famiglietti, John W. Pomeroy, and Claudia Pahl-Wostl

Conclusion: A Summary of Emerging Trends

39. Multisystemic Resilience: An Emerging Perspective From
    Social-Ecological Systems   771
    Katrina Brown

Name Index   785
Subject Index   793

Acknowledgments

A groundbreaking volume such as this depends on the contributions of many individuals. I am grateful to my many colleagues who, over the years, helped advance my thinking about resilience. Many of these individuals kindly agree to author chapters for this volume.

I would also like to thank a devoted team of research assistants who helped me prepare the final drafts of this manuscript. Igor Pekelny and Daniel Blais, long-time associates of the Resilience Research Centre at Dalhousie University, were instrumental in helping me bring the project to completion.

A special thanks as well to my editor at Oxford University Press, Abby Gross, who from the first contact saw the potential for this innovative work. And to my family, especially my partner Paula, who has been very loving and tolerant as I sequestered myself for long hours in my office editing chapters.

To each of you, my sincere appreciation.

Michael Ungar

Contributors

Lilian Alessa, BSc, PhD, PRegBiol, is President's Professor and Director of the Center for Resilient Communities at the University of Idaho. She has worked as Deputy Chief for Global Strategies at the U.S. Department of Homeland Security, and as a Defense Intelligence Senior Level (DISL) Special Advisor with the U.S. Office of the Director of National Intelligence. Trained as both a physical and social scientist, she currently works as an expert advisor to strengthen security and defense resilience in both Canada and the United States. Among her many achievements, she also pioneered human sensor community-based observing networks (CBONS) and developed the only arctic freshwater resilience assessment index, which is used to enhance infrastructure and resource security, particularly for remote and Indigenous communities. She received her PhDs from the University of British Columbia and sits on several national advisory committees including the Science, Technology and Education Advisory Committee for the National Ecological Observing Network.

Tom Anderson, PhD, is a Senior Research Associate in the School of Computing and Communications, Lancaster University. As an Engineer, Organizational Psychologist, and Consultant, he has held technical, advisory, and strategic roles in safety critical industries, such as nuclear and oil and gas. His particular research interest relates to the human and organizational factors that contribute to, and impact on, safety and resilience in high-risk industries.

Rosanne Anholt, MSc, is Assistant Professor of Public Administration at the Department of Political Science and Public Administration at the Vrije Universiteit Amsterdam, the Netherlands. She is currently finalizing her PhD, which deals with the meaning of resilience in the context of international policies and practices around security, humanitarian aid, and development assistance. She is also a Board Member of the Dutch Foundation for Peace Studies.

Devin G. Atallah, PhD, Assistant Professor of Psychology, Racial/Cultural Focus, with Psychology Department, University of Massachusetts Boston. Atallah aims to engage decolonizing, qualitative, and community-based participatory approaches to critical inquiry. As an activist, scholar, practitioner, and healer, Atallah focuses on better understanding and supporting intergenerational resilience, resistance, healing justice, and decolonization journeys. Atallah aims to honor and anchor his work in local or Indigenous knowledge of communities in struggle contesting racism and settler colonialism, primarily within his long-term partnerships with communities in Boston, Massachusetts, USA; Bethlehem, Palestine; and Santiago de Chile.

Susan Ayers, BSc, MSc, PhD, CPsychol is a psychologist and professor at City, University of London in the Centre for Maternal and Child Health Research. Her research examines women's perinatal mental health, in particular posttraumatic stress disorder and high-risk groups such as parents who have preterm or stillborn babies. She is a founder of the International Network for Perinatal PTSD and author of *Psychology for Medicine and Healthcare*, and an editor of the *Cambridge Handbook of Psychology, Health and Medicine*.

Roxanne Bainbridge, PhD is from the Gunggari/Kunja nations of South-Western Queensland. She is a Professorial Research Fellow in Indigenous Health at Central Queensland University Australia and an inaugural Senior Atlantic Fellow for Social Equity (University of Melbourne/Oxford). With a background in medical anthropology, she focuses on culturally constructive critiques of the biomedical sciences and policymaking to provide new understandings of human health, wellness and illness, and, identify the highest leverage points for change opportunities to improve the health and prosperity of Aboriginal and Torres Strait Islander nations. Roxanne's methodological expertise is in community-driven, high-impact applied research embedded in participatory action-oriented research approaches and improvement and systems sciences. She is committed to improving the integrity and quality of research to maximize its impact and benefit to society.

Olivier Barreteau, PhD is senior water scientist. He has about 25 years of experience of interdisciplinary research at the interface between hydrology, modeling, and management sciences in projects on local water governance, using social simulation with Agent based modeling and role playing games. His recent works focus on joint adaptive management of land and water in the frame of global changes with issues of interdependences between local adaptation plans. He is committed to interdisciplinary research, keeping a strong link between policymakers, water users, and research on the long term.

Elena Bennett, PhD is a professor in the Department of Natural Resource Sciences and McGill School of Environment at McGill University in Montreal, Canada. Her work focuses on multifunctionality and resilience of working landscapes (agriculture, forestry, fisheries, and energy development). Learn more about her work at bennettlab.weebly.com.

Ana Berástegui, PhD is a professor of Psychological Intervention in Contexts of Social Exclusion and a director of University Institute for Family Studies (Pontifical Comillas University). She isalso the Family and Disability Chair at Pontifical Comillas University and is the co-founder of *Primera Alianza: enhancing early attachments*, a brief, group intervention program to enhance parental sensitivity and early attachment among caregivers of preschool children, in the context of social exclusion. Her research interests cover family diversity and child welfare and development including adoption, disability, gender, and social exclusion issues. Berástegui has published five research monographs and over 50 journal articles and book chapters.

Kara Boles is a second-year MA student in the Clinical Psychology program at Lakehead University. Her research interests include parent–child relationships, pediatric health/wellness, parenting practices, resilience, wellness intervention, mental health, and addictions. Her MA thesis is testing a moderation model focused on childhood adversity, executive function, and functional impairment in emerging adults.

Bruno Bonté, PhD has a doctorate in computer science. He is interested in the modeling and simulation of complex systems, using, and participating in the development of, integrative tools at the level of formalisms (based on the Discrete Event System Specification formalism), at the conceptual level (based on the multiagent system paradigm, and at the level of the use of modeling and simulation for collective decision-making (based on the companion modeling approach). His recent research focuses on multiscale simulation of socioecological systems, with applications to the management of water resources and territories subject to global change.

Francois Bousquet, PhD is an environmental social scientist who looks at the interactions among diverse actors for the management of the environment and renewable resources. He is interested in the analysis of multiple perspectives and looks at how dialogues between heterogeneous actors who have different points of views, attachments, and different power can favor desirable trajectories for social and ecological systems.

Katrina Brown is Professor Emerita at the University of Exeter. She has a long-standing commitment to interdisciplinary analysis of environmental change and international development using a social-ecological systems lens. Her research focuses on vulnerability, adaptation and resilience, and poverty and well-being. She is interested in how people understand, perceive, and respond to environmental and other changes, and her work takes a broadly defined political ecology approach. Her widely acclaimed research monograph, *Resilience, Development and Global Change* (Routledge, 2016) proposes a revisioning of resilience to meet contemporary international development challenges and how this might inform deliberate transformative change.

Nicole Bush, PhD is an Associate Professor and the Director of the Division of Developmental Medicine in the University of California–San Francisco Department of Psychiatry and Behavioral Sciences and the Department of Pediatrics. She is a licensed clinical child psychologist and oversees research examining how early social contexts interface with individual differences to affect developmental trajectories of risk and resilience. She also investigates how contextual experiences of adversity become biologically embedded, thereby shaping individual differences that influence the effects of context on mental and physical health. These projects, in conjunction with her intervention work, aim to inform policies to enhance individual and community resilience and reduce population health disparities.

Juliana Santos de Carvalho, LLM is former Research Assistant to the Institute for Societal Resilience at the Vrije Universiteit Amsterdam. She is currently a PhD student in International Law at the Graduate Institute of International and Development Studies. She holds an LLM cum laude in Law and Politics of International Security at the VU Amsterdam. She is a licensed lawyer in Brazil, with a Bachelor of Laws summa cum laude from the Universiade Federal do Rio Grande do Norte.

Carmel Cefai, PhD is the director at the Centre for Resilience and Socio-Emotional Health, and Professor at the Department of Psychology at the University of Malta. He is Honorary Chair of the European Network for Social and Emotional Competence, joint founding editor of the *International Journal of Emotional Education*, and a member of the European Commission Network of Experts on Social Aspects of Education and Training. He has led various local, national, European, and international research projects in social and emotional learning, mental health in schools, and resilience and well-being in children and young people. He has published extensively, including *RESCUR Surfing the Waves: A Resilience Curriculum for Early Years and Primary Schools*.

Janine Natalya Clark, PhD, MA, LLB is a Professor of Gender, Transitional Justice, and International Criminal Law at the University of Birmingham. Her research interests include conflict-related sexual violence, transitional justice, resilience, ethnic conflict, and reconciliation. She is currently the Principal Investigator of a five-year research project, funded by the European Research Council, about resilience and victims/survivors of conflict-related sexual violence. The aim is to develop a new ecological model of transitional justice that fosters resilience. Clark has published three research monographs and over 60 journal articles and book chapters. She has been conducting fieldwork in the former Yugoslavia for more than 15 years.

Gabriella Conti holds a PhD in Economics from the University of Essex, London; Co-Investigator of the 1958 British Birth Cohort; and Research Fellow of the Institute for Fiscal Studies. Her research areas are health economics, the economics of human development, and biology and economics. Her research draws on both the biomedical and the social sciences with the aim of understanding the developmental origins of health inequalities, the role of child development as input in the production of health, and the behavioral and biological pathways through which early life shocks, investments and policies have health consequences throughout the life course. She has published in prestigious journals in different disciplines, such as *Science*, *Lancet*, *PNAS*, *Pediatrics*, *International Journal of Epidemiology*, the *Economic Journal*, and the *Journal of Econometrics*. She has recently been awarded the Nick Hales Award from the International Society for Developmental Origins of Health and Disease, and a five-year ERC Consolidator Award from the European Research Council.

Barbara Cosens, BS, MS, JD, LLM, is a University Distinguished Professor with the University of Idaho College of Law. Her teaching and research expertise is in water law, the law–science interface, and water dispute resolution. She is faculty on the University of Idaho Water Resources IGERT and WSU INFEWS both focused on climate change in the Columbia River Basin. She co-chaired the Adaptive Water Governance project made possible through support from the National Science Foundation–funded National Socio-Environmental Synthesis Center, SESYNC, and spent spring 2015 as the Goyder Institute in Australia comparing water law reform in the western United States and Australia during drought.

Monique Crane, PhD is a senior lecturer at Macquarie University, a registered psychologist, member of the Australian Psychological Society, and academic member of the College of Organisational Psychologists. She directs a program of research seeking to understand human resilience, particularly in the military context and has worked with the Australian Defence Force since 2010. Crane has developed a new generation of resilience training based on accumulating research and theoretical advancements implicating the critical role of self-reflection and coping insight in strengthening resilience.

Boris Cyrulnik, PhD is a neuropsychiatrist and Lecturer at the Marseille Faculty of Medicine, and former Director of Teaching at the University of Toulon. He is renowned for his research on early human interactions and the acquisition of protective or vulnerable factors. Since 1995, he has lead multiple research groups on resilience and in 2004 was the recipient of the Jean Bernard Prize of the Foundation for Medical Research. He has also served as the Dean of the psychological center of the National School of Magistracy (since 2009) and has been awarded several honorary doctorates from the Universities of Mons-Hainaut (2001), Lima (2008), Louvain (2009), and Laval (2010). He is the author of 30 general public essays on resilience (and received the Renaudot Prize in 2008 for this work) and a large number professional books on clinical practice related to this theme.

Lauren Dalicandro, MA is a first-year PhD student in the Clinical Psychology program at Lakehead University. Her research interests include addictions and substance use, with a focus on improving intervention effectiveness and cultural fit. Her master's thesis focused on a program evaluation of a culturally adapted parent management program for Indigenous youth and their families in Thunder Bay, Ontario. Her research work is partially supported by an Ontario Graduate Scholarship.

Caroline van Dullemen, PhD is lecturing public affairs and she is fellow of the Institute of Societal Resilience, an interdisciplinary research institute at the Vrije Universiteit Amsterdam. Her field of expertise is demography and migration. In 2017 she published the *Politics of Aging, the Risk of Old Age Poverty in Emerging Countries*, in which she brings together the analytics of four country studies and the different ways aging is managed. Earlier, she founded World Granny, an organization focused on improving the quality of life of older people in Africa, Latin America, and Asia. As a result, van Dullemen specializes in financial inclusion for older generations and currently assists the United Nations in the Pacific to realize micro pension schemes for the informal sector. Before, she worked for the Ministry of Foreign Affairs for almost 10 years and was Managing Director of the Academic Bureau of the Green Left Party.

James S. Famiglietti, PhD is a hydrologist, a professor and the Executive Director of the Global Institute for Water Security at the University of Saskatchewan, where he holds the Canada 150 Research Chair in Hydrology and Remote Sensing. He is a fellow of the

American Geophysical Union and of the Geological Society of America. Prior to moving to Saskatchewan, he served as the Senior Water Scientist at the NASA Jet Propulsion Laboratory at the California Institute of Technology. From 2013 through 2018, he was appointed by Governor Jerry Brown to the California State Water Boards. Jay and his team have been researching and communicating about water and climate change for over 30 years.

Timothy Ferris, PhD is a Senior Lecturer in systems engineering at Cranfield University. He has been an academic since 1991, having had previous experience in the electricity supply industry and in small scale manufacturing. His research interests include systems engineering education, resilience in systems engineering, research methods, and financial analysis for systems engineering

Mehdi Ghazinour, PhD is professor of Social Work and has studied different dimensions of psychological trauma. He is Medicine Doctor of Sceince, licensed psychotherapist in cognitive behavioral therapy, an approved clinical supervisor and trainer. He has over 20 years of experience working with individuals and families in outpatient clinics with experience of sever traumatic life event and posttraumatic stress disorder. He studied individual strategies for managing stress and trauma to understand and identify the factors that explain why some individuals retain their health despite traumatic life experiences while others develop psychological and psychiatric disorders. For couple of years he was deputy head and director of police research environment at Umeå University. He is at the moment guest professor and head of center for police research and practice in Linne´University in Sweden. His work now focuses on policing and security services to help officers develop and maintain resilience.

Antonios Gouglidis, PhD is a Lecturer in Computing at Lancaster University. His research aims at the integration between theoretical and applied security, toward designing secure and resilient systems. He has published more than 30 papers in international journals, conferences, and workshops. Currently, he investigates security and resilience mechanisms for application in cloud systems and critical infrastructures. More specific topics of research are access control in the cloud, formal verification (model checking) of models and policies, and resilience processes in critical infrastructures.

Michele Grossman, PhD is Professor of Cultural Studies and Research Chair in Diversity and Community Resilience at the Alfred Deakin Institute for Citizenship and Globalisation, Deakin University in Melbourne, Australia, where she also leads the Centre for Resilient and Inclusive Societies and the AVERT (Addressing Violent Extremism and Radicalisation to Terrorism) Research Network. Her research and publications focus on community dimensions of preventing and countering violent extremism. She has held major research grants from Australian, British, Canadian, U.S. and European research councils and funding agencies and is a Robert Schuman Fellow (Distinguished Scholar) at the European University Institute in Florence.

Chloé Guerbois, PhD after obtaining a Master in Ecology in Paris, flew to Zimbabwe in 2009 to do a PhD on the management of protected areas. Living among elephants and subsistence farmers on the edge of Hwange National Park, she started to learn empirically about people and resilience. This undisciplinary journey led her to the Garden Route in 2015 to study adaptation to global change in coastal areas. Since then her research navigates between human–nature relationships, the dynamics of social-ecological systems and transformative conservation.

Victoria Hailey is a Certified Management Consultant. Her organization, VHG (Victoria Hailey Group Corporation; www.vhg.com), helps organizations "engineer trust." Her research includes emerging technologies that close the responsibility gap in achieving ethical and socially-responsible outcomes reflective of healthy triple bottom lines. She is an ISO Lead Auditor/Instructor (including ISO 22301 BCMS) and was international convenor of ISO/IEC 90003 and inaugural chair of IEEE/SSIT/SC.

Pilar Hernández-Wolfe, PhD is Professor in the Marriage, Couple, and Family Therapy program at Lewis and Clark College in Portland, Oregon and guest faculty at the Universidad Javeriana, Cali in Colombia. She is a licensed marriage and family therapist and American Association for Marriage and Family Therapy–approved supervisor. She pioneered the concept of vicarious resilience in the context of torture survivor treatment in the United States and mental health services addressing politically based violence. She is the author of numerous peer reviewed articles, chapters, and the books *A Borderlands' View of Latinos, Latin Americans and Decolonization*; *Rethinking Mental Health*; **and** *La resiliencia vicaria en las relaciones de ayuda* (with Victoria Acevedo). As a consultant, trainer and presenter, she has collaborated with organizations in the United States, Colombia, and México in the areas of clinical supervision, traumatic stress, resilience, equity, and contextually responsive family therapy, the animal human bond, and eco-informed family therapy.

Katharine F. E. Hogan is a PhD student and research assistant at the University of Nebraska–Lincoln within the National Science Foundation research traineeship, Training in Theory and Application of Cross-Scale Resilience in Agriculturally Dominated Social Ecological Systems. Her research focuses on prairie restorations, plant community ecology, and ecosystem services. She enjoys musing on complex systems while on long walks with her dog and designing creative, interdisciplinary approaches to science communication.

David Hutchison, PhD is a Distinguished Professor of Computing at Lancaster University and the founding Director of InfoLab21. He leads a research group that is well known internationally for contributions in a range of areas including quality of service (QoS), active and programmable networking, content distribution networks, and testbed activities. His current research focuses on the resilience of networked computer systems, and the protection of critical infrastructures and services. He has served on the Technical Program Committee of many Association for Computing Machinery (ACM), Institute of Electrical and Electronics Engineers (IEEE), and International Federation for Information Processing (IFIP) conferences; on editorial boards of the Springer-Verlag Lecture Notes in Computer Science (LNCS), Computer Networks Journal, and the IEEE Transactions on Network and Service Management; and as Editor of the Wiley book series Communications Networking and Distributed Systems.

Daniel Hyslop, MEcon, is the Director of Policy and Learning at Interpeace, the International Organisation for Peacebuilding. Previously, he was the Research Director at the Institute for Economics and Peace where he led a wide research agenda on measuring peace, the economic costs of violence and understanding the drivers of positive peace. There, he led development of more than 50 research reports, including seven iterations of the Global Peace Index, a widely read resource on international trends in peace and conflict. He has also contributed to several international flagship studies on peace and fragility with the OECD, United Nations, and World Bank. He holds first-class honors Masters in Economics and Social Science from the University of Sydney.

Scott Jackson, PhD is an INCOSE Fellow and the author of the book *Architecting Resilient Systems: Accident Avoidance, Survival and Recovery from Disruptions* (Wiley, 2010). He is an independent researcher and consultant working with aircraft companies around the world to help them incorporate systems engineering in their organizations. He was awarded a PhD by the University of South Australia for his research and findings into the principles for achieving resilience in engineered systems.

Raffael Kalisch, PhD graduated in Human Biology at the University of Marburg, with a work on molecular-cellular neuroscience performed at Ecole Normale Supérieure, Paris. He subsequently moved into systems neuroscience, obtaining his PhD with a work on a rat model of anxiety at the Max Planck Institute of Psychiatry, Munich. After positions at the Wellcome Department of Imaging Neuroscience, London, and the University Medical Center Hamburg-Eppendorf, he became a professor of Human Neuroimaging at Johannes Gutenberg University Medical Center, Mainz. He is a founding member of Deutsches Resilienz Zentrum and the founding spokesperson of the International Resilience Alliance (intresa).

Miriam Kampa, PhD received her doctoral degree in Psychology from the Johannes Gutenberg University Mainz in 2018. During her time as a PhD student in Raffael Kalisch's laboratory, she established and validated a behavioral and imaging test battery for the Mainz Resilience Project. In her current position as a postdoctoral researcher at the Bender Institute of Neuroimaging, she investigates the timing of extinction learning and supports the development of a multimodal stress reduction intervention. Miriam Kampa has a strong interest in replicability of functional neuroimaging results, contributing to the field with her research on reproducibility of group activations.

Andrew Kliskey, BSurv, MRRP, PhD is President's Professor, Director of the Center for Resilient Communities, and Idaho EPSCoR Director at the University of Idaho. Originally from Aotearoa/New Zealand he trained as a land surveyor, resource planner, landscape behavioral geographer, and landscape ecologist. He has spent the last 20 years working with people in Maori communities in New Zealand, Inupiat communities in northwestern Alaska, Denai'na communities in southcentral Alaska, and rural communities in Idaho examining community and landscape resilience. He is lead of the National Science Foundation Innovations at the Nexus of Food-Energy, and Water Systems project in the Upper Snake River Basin, Idaho.

Kristy Kowatch, MA is a third-year PhD student in Clinical Psychology at Lakehead University. Her research interests include culturally relevant mental health treatments for First Nation people, substance abuse as a form of self-medication, and resilience in childhood and adolescence, as well as responsible gambling in Northern Ontario and Indigenous populations. Her dissertation research examines the development, implementation, and evaluation of a transdiagnostic group intervention for First Nations children, relying on cultural skills and practices. Kristy's work is partially supported by a Canadian Institutes of Health Research Doctoral Award.

Dongxue Lei is a PhD candidate in Architecture at Nanjing University, China, and a Visiting Scholar at Parsons School of Design. Lei's research interests center on design studies, cognitive data visualization, and big interdisciplinarity. For her PhD research, Lei is focusing on the relationship between design interventions and social-ecological resilience in "wet" human-landscape environments within the lower Yangtze River Basin.

Alexandros Lordos, PhD is a Lecturer in Clinical Psychology at the University of Cyprus, and is one of the founders of the Centre for Sustainable Peace and Democratic Development, through which he established research partnerships with several international organizations, including UNICEF, the World Bank, Interpeace, United Nations Development Programme (UNDP), and USAID's Office for Transition Initiatives. He has served as principal investigator in research projects across several conflict-affected countries in Europe, Africa, and Asia, investigating the interplay between individual, community, and institutional factors in the emergence of social cohesion and societal resilience. At the University of Cyprus, he directs the Centre for the Study of Life Skills and Resilience, while contributing to the teaching and supervision of undergraduate and postgraduate students in the Psychology Department.

Jessie Lund, MA is a second-year PhD student in Clinical Psychology at Lakehead University. Her research interests include childhood adversity, sexual violence, and substance use. Her dissertation research examines executive functioning in relation to past adverse childhood experiences in First Nations adults with substance use problems. Jessie's work is partially supported by a Joseph-Armand Bombardier SSHRC Doctoral Scholarship.

Feng Mao, PhD is a lecturer in Environmental and Physical Geography at the School of Earth and Environmental Sciences, Cardiff University. He holds a PhD in Geography from University of Cambridge. His research focuses on interdisciplinary water sciences, with the aim of achieving water sustainability in the Anthropocene through ecological, social, and technical innovations, such as new tools for data collection and environmental modelling, improved knowledge of water-centered dynamics and interactions, and more adaptive governance strategies for global change.

Ann S. Masten, PhD Regents Professor of Child Development at the University of Minnesota, studies resilience in human development, particularly in the context of homelessness, war, disaster, migration, and other severe adversities. She is a past President of the Society for Research in Child Development and Division 7 (Developmental) of the American Psychological Association (APA), and a recipient of APA's Bronfenbrenner Award for

Lifetime Contributions to Developmental Psychology in the Service of Science and Society. She has authored more than 200 publications, including the book, *Ordinary Magic: Resilience in Development*. She offers a massive open online course on Coursera: Resilience in Children Exposed to Trauma, Disaster and War: Global Perspectives.

Raphaël Mathevet, PhD is an ecologist and geographer. He works on the conservation of biodiversity, protected areas and conservation planning tools, adaptive management, and the evaluation of public policies. He applies simulation tools in interdisciplinary and participatory approaches to resolving management conflicts, especially in the context of wetlands. His most recent work focuses on the concepts of ecological solidarity and stewardship, social-ecological resilience and adaptation, social representations, and mental models. During the last decade he focused on environmental history and political ecology of SES.

Janya McCalman, PhD is a Professorial Research Fellow and Program Leader of the Centre for Indigenous Health Equity at Central Queensland University in Australia. She is a National Health and Medical Research Council Fellow, recognized nationally for her contributions to research with schools, health and social services and community groups focused on resilience, empowerment, and mental health research to improve the well-being of Aboriginal and Torres Strait Islander Australians. Research outputs have focused on Aboriginal mental health and well-being, youth health, maternal and child health, health services research, systems integration, health promotion, and implementation research. Her methodological expertise lies in participatory and action-oriented quality improvement research approaches; grounded theory; systematic literature reviews; and research transfer and implementation.

Fiona S. McEwen, PhD is a postdoctoral researcher in developmental psychology and a study coordinator in the Department of Biological and Experimental Psychology at the School of Biological and Chemical Sciences, Queen Mary University of London. McEwen obtained her PhD in Psychology from the Institute of Psychiatry, Psychology and Neuroscience, King's College London, and has conducted research in neurodevelopmental disorders and developmental psychopathology. She currently coordinates two studies focusing on mental health in Syrian refugees living in Lebanon and leads a third project exploring measurement of psychopathology in Syrian refugee children.

Katharine McGowan, PhD is an assistant professor of social innovation at the Bissett School of Business, Mount Royal University in Calgary, Alberta. Her research spans several centuries and continents as she explores social innovation's past and present to understand it relevance to contemporary questions around Indigenous-settler reconciliation and climate change. Previously, Katharine was a postdoctoral fellow at the Waterloo Institute for Social Innovation and Resilience, where she worked on a wide variety of projects, including editing *The Evolution of Social Innovation* (2017). She holds a doctorate in Canadian History from the University of Waterloo.

Brian McGrath, MArch is Professor of Urban Design at Parsons School of Design with expertise in the integration of architecture, ecology, and media. His books include *Urban Design*

Ecologies Reader (2012), *Resilience in Ecology and Urban Design* (2012), *Digital Modeling for Urban Design* (2008), *Cinemetrics* (2007), and *Transparent Cities* (1994). McGrath is a Principle Investigator in the Baltimore Ecosystem Study, served as a Fulbright Senior Scholar in Thailand (1998–1999), was an India China Institute Fellow (2006–2008), and Director of Research, Urbanisms of Inclusion, Atlantis Transatlantic program, funded by the U.S. Department of Education and the European Commission (2010–2014).

Maurice B. Mittelmark, PhD is Professor Emeritus at the University of Bergen. His academic interests include health promotion, community development, participatory action research, resources for health and development, and the salutogenic model of health. He has served as President of the International Union for Health Promotion and Education, as Editor of the journal *Health Promotion International*, and for more than two decades, he directed graduate education in health promotion at the University of Bergen. He is the lead editor of Springer's *The Handbook of Salutogenesis* (2017), as well as the second edition (2021).

Santos Jamioy Muchavisoy, MA is a Kamentza elder or "Taita." He was elected Kamentza governor four times (1994–2010) and was staff consultant for the state of Putumayo (2016–2018). He holds a master's degree in human systems from the Universidad Central de Colombia and diplomates in Law and Indigenous Legislation. He was an adjunct professor at the Technological Institute of Putumayo and at Remington University in Medellín, Colombia. He is a traditional healer based in Sibundoy and travels throughout Colombia as a consultant on Kamentza traditional healing practices.

Christopher Mushquash, PhD, CPsych is Canada Research Chair in Indigenous Mental Health and Addiction, Associate Professor in the Department of Psychology at Lakehead University and the Northern Ontario School of Medicine, Director of the Centre for Rural and Northern Health Research at Lakehead University, and the Associate Vice President Research at the Thunder Bay Regional Health Sciences Centre and Chief Scientist at the Thunder Bay Regional Health Research Institute. In addition to his academic appointments, Mushquash is a registered clinical psychologist providing assessment, intervention, and consultation services for First Nations children, adolescents, and adults at Dilico Anishinabek Family Care.

Kirsty L. Nash, PhD is a Research Fellow at the Centre for Marine Socioecology and the Institute for Marine and Antarctic Studies at the University of Tasmania. Her research focuses on the resilience of marine socio-ecological systems, functional ecology, and facilitating interdisciplinary research. She is also the founder of www.aKIDemicLife.com a website full of resources to support parents and carers working in academia.

Ying Ou, PhD graduated from the Department of Social Work and Social Administration at the University of Hong Kong and currently working as a postdoctoral fellow at the Department of Applied Social Sciences, Hong Kong Polytechnic University. Trained at the intersection of social work and population health, she is keen on exploring how the contexts shape and being shaped by human behavior and well-being. Her current research interests focus on social class, social capital, altruism, and health.

Claudia Pahl-Wostl, PhD is a professor for resources management at the Institute for Environmental Systems Research (USF) in Osnabrück, Germany. She is an internationally leading scholar on governance and adaptive and integrated management of water resources and the role of social and societal learning. Her research program builds on foundations in systems science, which explicitly acknowledge the complex and often-unpredictable dynamics of the systems to be managed. In 2012, she was awarded the Bode Foundation Water Management Prize for her contribution to pioneering interdisciplinary work on governance in times of change and comparative analyses of water governance in large river basins.

Catherine Panter-Brick, PhD is the Bruce A. and Davi-Ellen Chabner Professor of Anthropology, Health, and Global Affairs at Yale University. She is an expert on risk and resilience, having spent three decades working with people affected by war, poverty, and marginalization. A medical anthropologist, she was trained in both human biology and the social sciences. She has extensive experience leading mixed-methods research, having directed over 40 interdisciplinary projects in Afghanistan, Ethiopia, the Gambia, Jordan, Mexico, Nepal, Niger, Pakistan, Saudi Arabia, Tanzania, the United Kingdom, and the United States. For her work in humanitarian areas, she received the Lucy Mair Medal, awarded by the Royal Anthropology Institute to honor excellence in the application of anthropology to the active recognition of human dignity. At Yale University, she directs the Global Health Studies Multidisciplinary Academic Program, the Program on Conflict, Resilience, and Health and the Program on Stress and Family Resilience, and leads research initiatives to develop effective partnerships between scholars, practitioners, and policymakers. She publishes extensively in biomedical and social sciences journals and has co-edited seven books, most recently *Medical Humanitarianism* (Penn Press, 2015) and *Pathways to Peace* (MIT Press, 2014).

Tatiana Paredes, PhD holds her PhD from the London School of Economics and currently works as a Research Fellow in the Department of Economics and in the Department of Social Science at University College London. Her primary areas of research are development economics, health economics, and education. She has conducted research about the long-term effects of cash transfer programs on young people's education and labor market outcomes and the impact of government reforms on physicians' and teachers' performance in developing countries.

Riccardo Patriarca, PhD is a Postdoctoral Researcher and Adjunct Professor in the Department of Mechanical and Aerospace Engineering at Sapienza University, Rome, Italy. His research focuses on the analysis of complex sociotechnical systems, mainly in terms of risk, safety, and resilience management. His research efforts are aimed at developing methods and models to increase safety of modern and future systems, with the ultimate purpose of supporting sustainable societal development. Patriarca has received several research awards, among them, SESAR certificate of scientific excellence for research in air traffic management (2015, 2018), Royal Aeronautical Society Young Person Award (2017), and the Resilience Engineering Association's Young Talent Award (2017). Riccardo is a 2019 Forbes 30 Under 30 Europe list maker in the category Science and Healthcare (2019), and he has been nominated by Forbes Italy (2019) as one of the 100 most influential young Italian leaders of the future.

Terri Peters, PhD is an Assistant Professor at Ryerson University in the Department of Architectural Science in Toronto, Canada. She holds a PhD in Architecture (Aarhus, Denmark), a Professional Diploma in Architecture (UK) and bachelor degrees in Environmental Design (Dalhousie, Canada) and History of Art and Architecture (Victoria, Canada). She has published 20 peer-reviewed journal articles and conference papers on sustainable design, design for daylight, and architectural approaches to building performance. Her area of expertise is the human and social dimensions of green building, and her current research investigates the qualitative and quantitative aspects of daylight and how it can promote well-being.

Carlos Pitillas, PhD is a professor, researcher, and therapist at the University Institute for Family Studies and the Human and Social Sciences Faculty at Pontifical Comillas University. His current teaching covers the general teaching of psychoanalysis, as well as specific training in psychoanalytic psychotherapy and child and child psychotherapy. His research interests cover the intergenerational transmission of relational trauma, principles and methods of attachment-centered intervention, psychological consequences of extreme poverty, or pediatric disease. He is co-founder and coordinator of the project *Primera Alianza: Enhancing Early Attachments* and has recently published a book about this model of intervention in Spanish (with A. Berástegui, *Primera Alianza: Fortalecer y reparar los vínculos tempranos*; Gedisa, 2018). A new book on understanding and approaching the intergenerational transmission of trauma is also on the way (Desclée de Brouwer, in press).

Michael Pluess, PhD is a chartered psychologist and Professor in Developmental Psychology at the Department of Biological and Experimental Psychology at the School of Biological and Chemical Sciences, Queen Mary University of London. Pluess's research focuses on the investigation of individual differences in the capacity for environmental sensitivity, the notion that some people are more affected by negative as well as positive experiences than other people. He is currently leading several studies on resilience and mental health of Syrian refugee children. His research on differential susceptibility and vantage sensitivity has been published in the leading journals of the field.

John W. Pomeroy, PhD is Director of the Global Water Futures programme—the largest university-led freshwater research project in the world. He is a Fellow of the Royal Society of Canada, the American Geophysical Union and the Royal Geographical Society. At the University of Saskatchewan, he is the Canada Research Chair in Water Resources and Climate Change; Distinguished Professor of Geography; Director of the Centre for Hydrology; and Director of the Coldwater Laboratory, Canmore, Alberta. His current research interests are on the impact of land use and climate change on cold regions hydrology and water quality, and improved prediction of climate change impacts, especially floods and droughts.

Cassandra M. Popham is a doctoral student in the Department of Biological and Experimental Psychology at Queen Mary University of London. Her research is on children's mental health and resilience in response to war and displacement, specifically in a sample of Syrian refugees living in informal settlements in Lebanon. Cassandra's PhD thesis aims to explore the concept of resilience and apply this to understanding the multisystemic processes influencing refugee children's mental health over time.

Tara Quinn, PhD is an environmental social scientist who works on the impacts of social and environmental change with a particular focus on the risk perception and adaptation.

Joris Rijbroek, MSc is director of the Institute for Societal Resilience at Vrije Universiteit Amsterdam, the interdisciplinary research institute of the Faculty of Social Sciences. After studying human geography at the University of Amsterdam, he worked as lecturer in Middle Eastern and Mediterranean studies in the Department of Arabic and Islam at Radboud University Nijmegen. In 2002, he started working as a policy advisor and program manager at the municipality of Amsterdam, focusing on diversity, social cohesion, and polarization in Amsterdam. From 2009 until 2015, he was policy advisor to the national government on the policy fields of diversity, integration, radicalization, and polarization.

Arian Rostami, PhD is a researcher at the Police Education Unit, Umeå University. She has considerable experience in preventive interventions in health sciences and has conducted studies on stressful professions such as the medical profession with a special focus on family life and quality of life.

Danielle S. Roubinov, PhD is an Assistant Professor in the University of California–San Francisco Department of Psychiatry and Behavioral Sciences and licensed clinical psychologist. Her research examines the pathways and mechanisms through which exposure to adversity early in life shapes children's trajectories of physical and psychological health. A particular focus of her work is on children's developing stress response systems, with a goal to understand how environmental contexts become "biologically embedded" to influence health outcomes across the lifespan. By understanding the *how, when, and for whom* of early trauma and its effects on children's development, she aims to help develop tailored prevention and intervention program to promote resilience among at-risk children and families.

Mark Rouncefield, PhD is a Reader in Social Informatics in the School of Computing and Communications, Lancaster University. His research interests are in Computer Supported Cooperative Work and Computer Human Interaction and involve the study of various aspects of the empirical study of work, organization, human factors, and interactive computer systems design, working across traditional disciplinary boundaries to address challenging sociotechnical problems. He is particularly associated with the development of ethnography as a method for informing design and evaluation. His empirical studies of work and technology have contributed to important debates concerning the relationship between social and technical aspects of IT systems design and use.

J. B. Ruhl, BA, JD, LLM, PhD is the David Daniels Allen Distinguished Chair of Law at the Vanderbilt University Law School in Nashville, Tennessee, where he also serves as Director of the Program on Law and Innovation and the Co-Director of the Energy, Environment, and Land Use Law Program. His work has focused on the application of complexity science, resilience theory, and adaptive governance theory to environmental and natural resources policy contexts. He is an elected member of the American Law Institute and the American

College of Environmental Lawyers, and has served in officer positions in the American Bar Association.

Ingrid Schoon has a PhD in Psychology (Unversity of Leiden, The Netherlands). She is Professor of Human Development and Social Policy at University College London, Institute of Education and a Fellow at the Social Science Centre (WZB) in Berlin. She is currently President elect of the European Association for Research on Adolescents and past President of the Society for Longitudinal and Lifecourse Studies. Her research focuses on the study of risk and resilience, in particular during the transition from dependent childhood to independent adulthood, asking (a) to what extent and how do social conditions, in particular socioeconomic adversity, affect individual thinking, feeling and behavior; (b) to what extent and in what circumstances can individuals succeed against the odds and steer their own life course; and (c) what can be done to improve the life chances of the most vulnerable?

Stijn Sieckelinck, PhD is senior researcher at the Institute for Societal Resilience at Vrije Universiteit Amsterdam, The Netherlands, where he coordinates the expert lab on Resilient Identities. He holds a PhD in Social Educational Theory and is a board member of the Radicalisation Awareness Network (EU). Research and consultancy interests lie in the broad field of education, governance, and professionalization, but with a particular focus on radicalization, conflict resolution, and citizenship education.

Marieke W. Slootman, PhD works as an Assistant Professor at the Department of Sociology at the Vrije Universiteit Amsterdam. In addition, she is Diversity Officer Education at the Vrije Universiteit Amsterdam. She was Vice-Chair of the Commission Diversity that studied diversity and inclusion at the University of Amsterdam in 2016. In 2014, she earned her PhD (cum laude) from the University of Amsterdam for her dissertation about identification of social climbers with ethnic minority backgrounds, which was rewarded the prize for best sociological dissertation by the Dutch Sociological Association (NSV). Slootman's research focuses on processes of minoritization and exclusion, processes of identification and social mobility, and on diversity in educational institutions.

Niko Soininen, BS, MS, LLD, is a Professor of Environmental Law at University of Eastern Finland Law School, Center for Climate, Energy and Environmental Law. His research focuses on the governance of complex social-ecological systems with a particular emphasis on freshwater and marine systems. In his recent work, he has studied the resilience and adaptive capacity of European Union (EU) and Finnish law in regulating complex phenomena, such as the ecological condition of fresh and marine waters in a policy environment geared toward economic growth. Outside of academia, he has worked as a consultant for HELCOM, the World Bank, and for several ministries in Finland.

Eric A. Specking, PhD serves as the Assistant Dean of Enrollment Management and Retention for the College of Engineering at the University of Arkansas. Specking received a BS in Computer Engineering, an MS in Industrial Engineering, and a PhD in Engineering from the University of Arkansas. His research interest includes decision quality, resilient design, set-based design, engineering and project management, and engineering education.

During his time at the University of Arkansas, Eric has served as Principal Investigator, Co-Principal Investigator, or Senior Personnel on over 40 research projects totaling over $6.6 million, which produced over 50 publications (journal articles, book chapters, conference proceedings, newsletters, and technical reports). He is an active member of the American Society for Engineering Education (ASEE) and International Council on Systems Engineering (INCOSE) where he has served in various leadership positions.

Linda Theron, DEd, is an educational psychologist by training. She is a full professor in the Department of Educational Psychology/Centre for the Study of Resilience, Faculty of Education, University of Pretoria and an extraordinary professor in Optentia Research Focus Area, North-West University, South Africa. Her research focuses on the resilience processes of South African young people challenged by chronic adversity and accounts for how sociocultural contexts shape resilience. She is lead editor of *Youth Resilience and Culture: Complexities and Commonalities* (Springer, 2015). She is also an associate journal editor of *Child Abuse and Neglect* (Elsevier) and of *School Psychology International* (SAGE).

Clara Therville, PhD is a social geographer interested in the governance of environment–society interactions, mostly regarding biodiversity issues. Mobilizing theoretical tools from SES resilience thinking and institutional analysis, she worked on a diversity of social-ecological issues such as protected areas, adaptation to global change along coastlines and agroforestry systems.

Elaine Toombs, MA is a fourth-year PhD student in Clinical Psychology at Lakehead University. Her research primarily focuses on First Nations mental health, resilience, and parenting using community-based methods. Her dissertation research examines how adverse childhood experiences may affect psychological and physical health outcomes within a First Nations population seeking treatment for substance use. Elaine's work is partially supported by a Canadian Institutes of Health Research Doctoral Award.

Michael Ungar, PhD is a Family Therapist and Professor of Social Work at Dalhousie University where he holds the Canada Research Chair (Tier 1) in Child, Family, and Community Resilience. Since 2002, Ungar has directed the Resilience Research Centre, designing multisite longitudinal research and evaluation projects in more than two dozen low-, middle-, and high-income countries, with much of that work focused on the resilience of marginalized children and families and adult populations experiencing mental health challenges. Building on his work as both a researcher and clinician, Ungar has published over 180 peer-reviewed articles and book chapters on the subject of resilience and is the author of 15 books for mental health professionals, researchers, and lay audiences. He is a Fellow of the Royal Society of Canada and former recipient of the Canadian Association of Social Workers National Distinguished Service Award.

Froma Walsh, PhD is Mose and Sylvia Firestone Professor Emerita, School of Social Service Administration and Department of Psychiatry, University of Chicago, and Co-Founder and Co-Director, Chicago Center for Family Health. Walsh, a leader in the field of family therapy, is the foremost authority on family resilience; with 120+ scholarly publications, notably her book,

Strengthening Family Resilience (third edition, 2016). She is Past President, American Family Therapy Academy; past Editor, *Journal of Marital and Family Therapy*; recipient of numerous professional awards; and a respected consultant internationally in clinical and community-based applications of a family resilience framework.

Francis Westley, PhD is Professor Emeritus and J. D. McConnell Chair of Social Innovation at University of Waterloo. There she led a 10 year project on Social Innovation Generation and founded the Waterloo Institute of Social Innovation and Resilience. She has published, lectured, and presented widely on social innovation, resilience, and transformative change. Previously she held the position of Director of the Nelson Centre, an interdisciplinary environmental center at University of Wisconsin Madison, and the James McGill Professorship in Strategy at McGill University, Montreal, Quebec. She holds a PhD in Sociology from McGill University and Honorary Doctorate from University of Stockholm. She has recently been awarded the 2019 World Thought Leader Award from the Schwab Foundation for Social Entrepreneurship.

Keith D. Willett, PhD currently supports the U.S. Department of Defense as a Data Scientist. He holds a PhD in Systems Engineering from Stevens Institute of Technology (2017). Willett is co-chair of the INCOSE System Security Engineering Working Group and has (ISC)^2 CISSP and ISSAP certifications and over 35 years' experience in technology and security.

Haorui Wu, PhD is an assistant professor in the School of Social Work at the Dalhousie University. With an interdisciplinary background (social work, architecture, urban planning, and urban design), his community-based interdisciplinary teaching, research, and emerging practice examine postdisaster reconstruction, recovery, and rehabilitation initiatives through the lens of environmental justice and social justice. He seeks to employ community-engaged planning strategies to strengthen built environment social missions, build social capital, enhance holistic well-being, and advance community resiliency in the context of global climate change, disaster, and other world crises. His research consists of (a) empowering local resident leadership and supporting overall well-being by advancing non-discriminatory civic engagement in community-based planning and architecture design and (b) enhancing the humanitarian quality of postdisaster built environment to support community resiliency and sustainability.

Qiaobing Wu, PhD is Associate Professor and Associate Head at the Department of Applied Social Sciences, Hong Kong Polytechnic University. She received her PhD in Social Work from University of Southern California. Her primary area of research centers on the health and well-being of children and youth, particularly in the context of migration, including the rural–urban migration in China, the cross-border migration between Hong Kong and the mainland, and international migration. Her research has been funded by various grant agencies such as the National Science Foundation of the United States and the Research Grants Council of HKSAR, and her publications appear widely in the fields of migration, health, and youth studies.

Li Xu, PhD holds a PhD in Environmental Science and Sustainability from Curtin University, Australia. Prior to joining the current institute, he worked as a postdoctoral researcher at the School of Environment and Society in Tokyo Institute of Technology. His research interests generally lie in the field of resilience and sustainability of water systems. His previous paper entitled "Resilience Thinking: A Renewed System Approach for Sustainability Science" in *Sustainability Science* won the 2015 Best Paper Award of the journal. Recently, he published a paper which integrated, for the first time, resilience thinking across all research fields into a general framework.

Cecily Young, BPsych(Hons), Grad Dip(Jung), MPsych(Clin), MAPS is a clinical psychologist specializing in perinatal mental health and doctoral candidate at the University of Adelaide School of Psychology. Her research examines resilience in the transition to parenthood with a focus on preventative intervention and community engagement.

Introduction

Why a Volume on Multisystemic Resilience?

Michael Ungar

Across diverse disciplines, the term *resilience* is appearing more and more often. However, while each discipline has developed theory and models to explain the resilience of the systems they study (e.g., a natural environment, a community postdisaster, the human mind, a computer network, or the economy), there is a lack of overarching theory that describes (i) whether the principles that underpin the resilience of one system are similar or different from the principles that govern resilience of other systems; (ii) whether the resilience of one system affects the resilience of other co-occurring systems; and (iii) whether a better understanding of resilience can inform the design of interventions, programs, and policies that address "wicked" problems that are too complex to solve by changing one system at a time. In other words (and as only one example among many), are there similarities between how a person builds and sustains psychological resilience and how a forest, community, or the business where he or she works remains successful and sustainable during periods of extreme adversity? Does psychological resilience in a human being influence the resilience of the forests (through a change in attitude toward conservation), community (through a healthy tolerance for differences), and businesses (by helping a workforce perform better) with which a person interacts? And finally, does this understanding of resilience help build better social and physical ecologies that support individual mental health, a sustainable environment, and a successful economy at the same time?

In response to such questions, the many contributing authors to this volume have shown that multisystemic thinking about resilience is growing in disciplines ranging from genetics to community development, family therapy, aviation, and dozens more. In the first chapter of the volume, I survey emerging discourses of resilience found across disciplines and the definitions that have followed. Whatever the focus of the discipline, the study of multisystemic resilience shifts the focus from breakdown and disorder to deepening our understanding of processes like recovery, adaptation, and transformation that occur before, during, and after exposure to an atypical stressor. In this way, studies of resilience are distinguished from fields like positive psychology (where adversity is not a requirement for the study of systemic change) and materials science (where human interactions, such as the process of observation, account for only a small amount of the change in the material). Although this volume covers a lot of conceptual ground, to maintain a cohesive focus, each author was tasked with exploring resilience in a similar way. They all looked at how coping occurs when a system experiences adversity, although their explanations for why and how systems recover, adapt, and transform are disciplinarily diverse.

Given the range of disciplines represented, this volume is a first of its kind, an innovative endeavor that positions side by side very different ways of using the concept of resilience. I have clustered the chapters by topic area to make it easier for readers to contrast and compare theories and models and their application through the case studies each author included in their chapter. Although no one system is more important or influential than another, the sections of this volume move from smaller human systems to larger social, then built (engineered), and finally ecological systems. A closing chapter by Katrina Brown reflects on what can be learned from the volume as a whole. I encourage you to read her reflections.

Taken together, the sum of the chapters is greater than just the individual contributions. While each chapter alone only advances a theory of multisystemic resilience slightly (every chapter deals with more than one system and their interactions), the entire collection of papers suggests many different ways that the resilience of one system can influence the resilience of other systems. Thus, my goal is to rebut those who say resilience is an ambiguous concept that is difficult to operationalize in research and practice. I suggest, instead, that resilience is better understood as a multisystemic process that is extremely useful when thinking about how complex systems function under stress.

Readers will, therefore, want to approach this volume much as they would a buffet. While you may be drawn to one or two chapters that most suit your current interests (or tastes), I would encourage you to also sample chapters that explore content with which you are less familiar.

My hope is that you will be just as inspired by this collection of papers as I have been during my meetings with resilience scholars around the world and across disciplines. Although I am a social scientist by training, I have had opportunities to learn from geneticists and engineers, psychiatrists and ecologists, all of whom have sparked my imagination with their descriptions of systems that deal with adversity. Through hundreds of conversations I have come to see more similarities in our theories than differences. For example, those concerned with how humans overcome genetic susceptibility (see Chapter 3) and those thinking about how to design better computer systems (Chapter 34) to avoid latent vulnerabilities are likely to find they share many fundamental principles of resilience design.

The initial impulse for this specific work began when I read the exhaustive network citation analysis by Xu and Kajikawa (2017) who identified at least 10 disciplinary siloes concerned with the study of resilience, but very few examples of disciplines referencing each other's work. It is for this reason that most publications on resilience are concerned with just one discipline, even though the leading scholars in the field, such as Michael Rutter (in developmental psychiatry) and Katrina Brown (who studies social ecological systems—see Chapter 39) have been arguing for more work to be done to build bridges between disciplines.

To help build these bridges, this volume draws together the world's foremost resilience researchers and an emerging next generation of scholars to answer questions such as

1. How can we better understand and develop theoretical models that explain the dynamic interplay of resilience processes across systems (and at different scales within systems)?
2. How do we assess, measure, and study the resilience of multiple systems across scales and over time?
3. How does an emerging science of systemic resilience help us generate scalable solutions to human-environment interactions that threaten the health of individuals, communities, and the planet?

Despite the need for cross-disciplinary, multilevel modeling of resilience to tackle these problems, most of the work focused on resilience has remained siloed.

An Urgent Need to Understand Resilience

The world is changing faster than ever before. Rapid and unprecedented social and environmental change, accompanied by heightened uncertainties and novel and diverse risks are broadly recognized as a feature of contemporary life (Anderies, Folke, Walker, & Ostrom, 2013; Reid et al., 2010). Regardless of discipline, research shows that these disruptions to human and ecological systems are triggering new responses and adaptations, but it is also clear that these require profound and transformative action in order to be sustainable and equitable. As a recent special feature of *Science* observed, "Resilience is on many peoples' minds these days" (Couzin-Frankel, 2018). Indeed, research on recovery after Hurricane Katrina, adaptation to sea level rise in Bangladesh, and interventions to support refugees fleeing from war, are all examples of new research insights informed by the science of resilience. However, despite the ubiquity of the concept, we still know little about the mechanisms that produce resilience. And yet, with time our understanding of resilience is finding common ground across disciplines. Ann Masten (2014a), a world-renowned developmental psychologist who studies resilience defines the concept as "the capacity of a dynamic system to adapt successfully to disturbances that threaten system function, viability, or development" (p. 10). This definition is remarkably similar to that of the leading systems ecologist Carl Folke (2016) who describes resilience as "the capacity of a system to absorb disturbance and reorganize while undergoing change so as to still retain essentially the same function, structure, and feedbacks, and therefore identity" (p. 44). Both definitions, from very different fields of study, emphasize the need to account for the way human and nonhuman systems deal successfully with shocks and disturbances to thrive despite exposure to adversity. A new science of multisystemic resilience that is advanced by this volume offers an innovative way to understand these changes and to approach problems in paradigmatically different transdisciplinary ways (Alexander,

2013; Brown, 2016; Masten, 2014b). For example, a multisystemic approach to resilience is likely to improve services in contexts of humanitarian aid by reminding us that when providing emergency aid to beneficiaries, they are seldom powerless victims, but instead individuals and communities with local resources and the potential for long-term ability to cope with future stressors. What we lack, however, is ways to document these strengths and the tools required to measure sometimes intangible traits and ambiguous processes that make the difference between successful and unsuccessful recovery, adaptation, and transformation after a major disaster.

For all these reasons, a siloed approach to the study of resilience needs to be challenged and a bridging concept across systems and disciplines introduced. Arguably, we need far less research on why things break down and far more on the way systems improve functioning and the principles that predict success. To accomplish this, we will need to shift our focus from one that conventionally deals with pathology—how the environment harms people, or how people harm the environment—to the ability of multiple human and ecological systems to reciprocally and positively interact in ways that respond to perturbations in ways that lead to health and sustainability. We also need to increase the breadth of resilience research to fully integrate the many different disciplines studying resilience to produce a transdisciplinary approach to understanding the processes that enhance the capacity of systems to experience resilience over time. Finally, and just as important, we need to confront the hegemony of Western scientific discourse in the study of resilience. More attention is required to account for the diverse sources of knowledge and world views about resilience, including those that indigenize and decolonize knowledge, as well as those that challenge discourses that privilege specific genders, abilities, or racial biases.

This volume, then, is riding the crest of an emerging trend. This is evidence from national policy forums, research investments, political rhetoric, and public discourse that greater resilience is going to be needed if people and our planet are going to survive. At the highest level, resilience underpins the Sustainable Development Goals and the UN's Global Agenda 2030 and was the focus of the 2018 High Level Political Forum, *Transformation Towards Sustainable and Resilient Societies*. But these calls must be supported by the highest caliber of science and new and novel approaches that take resilience beyond "business as usual" to address the complex problems and challenges of knowledge co-production for sustainable development (Folke, Biggs, Norström, Reyers, & Rockström, 2016). While definitions of resilience may be contested, there is plenty of agreement among scholars that further research that is bold and new is needed. Thinking about resilience multisystemically, as is the focus in this volume, is one way to find better solutions to persistent and challenging problems that have yet to be solved.

References

Alexander, D. E. (2013). Resilience and disaster risk reduction: An etymological journey. *Natural Hazards and Earth System Sciences, 13*(11), 2707–2716.

Anderies, J. M., Folke, C., Walker, B., & Ostrom, E. (2013). Aligning key concepts for global change policy: Robustness, resilience, and sustainability. *Ecology and Society, 18*(2), 8. doi:10.5751/ES-05178-180208

Brown, K. (2016). *Resilience, development and global change*. New York, NY: Routledge.

Couzin-Frankel, J. (2018, February 27). The science of resilience: What are the ingredients that help people cope? *Science Magazine News*. Retrieved from http://www.sciencemag.org/news/2018/02/science-resilience-what-are-ingredients-help-people-cope

Folke, C. (2016). Resilience (Republished). *Ecology and Society, 21*(4), 44. doi:10.5751/ES-09088-210444

Folke, C., Biggs, R., Norström, A. V., Reyers, B., & Rockström, J. (2016). Social-ecological resilience and biosphere-based sustainability science. *Ecology and Society, 21*(3), 41. doi:10.5751/ES-08748-210341

Masten, A. S. (2014a). *Ordinary magic: Resilience in development*. New York, NY: Guilford Press.

Masten, A. S. (2014b). Global perspectives on resilience in children and youth. *Child Development, 85*, 6–20. doi:10.1111/cdev.12205

Reid, W. V., Chen, D., Goldfarb, L., Hackmann, H., Lee, Y. T., Mokhele, K., . . . Whyte, A. (2010). Earth system science for global sustainability: Grand challenges. *Science, 330*(6005), 916–917.

Xu, L., & Kajikawa, Y. (2017). An integrated framework for resilience research: A systematic review based on citation network analysis. *Sustainability Science, 13*(1), 235–254.

Modeling Multisystemic Resilience

Connecting Biological, Psychological, Social, and Ecological Adaptation in Contexts of Adversity

Michael Ungar

Introduction

Although resilience has been studied across a great number of scientific disciplines with a substantive body of knowledge established in fields like psychology and systems ecology, transdisciplinary approaches to studying resilience are still lacking. This situation can be attributed to a range of problems such as definitional ambiguity of the construct, disciplinary blinders, difficulty funding multisystemic research, methodological challenges designing good studies, and problems with analyzing complex sources of data that are typically not included in the same models. Despite these challenges, there is growing interest in thinking about resilience as a multisystemic concept.

The term *resilience* enjoys many different definitions, although all emphasize the same shift in focus from breakdown and disorder to processes of recovery, adaptation, or systemwide transformation before, during, and after exposure to adversity (Masten, 2014; for exception, see Brown, 2016; Xu & Kajikawa, 2017). Even when focused on a single organism (i.e., a human being or a coral reef), the process of resilience is concerned with the changing condition of one or more systems when they are exposed to an atypical amount of stress. A child, for example, demonstrates resilience when she shows positive developmental outcomes despite early exposure to adversity related to extreme neglect often associated with abusive parents or placement in substandard institutional care (Masten, 2006). By its very nature, then, resilience implies an interaction between nested or contingent and co-occurring systems (e.g., a child's individual strengths, a foster placement that compensates for a difficult start in life, and human services that address a child's developmental delays) that help one or more of these systems do better than expected when disturbed.

To glimpse how complicated a systemic understanding of resilience can be, one has only to try to define a system itself. In general, a system is "a group or set of related or associated things perceived or thought of as a unity or complex whole" ("System," 2018). Defining a system by its internal relations and distinction from other systems, however, creates its own problems. The medical, psychological, and social sciences, for example, tend to think about systems as having easily perceived boundaries that distinguish one from the other even as they interact. To illustrate, our neurological stress response system, the hypothalamic–pituitary–adrenal axis, is distinct from, but interacts with, our microbiome and our genome at a biological level; likewise, our response to stress depends on the quality of our interactions with our family, peers, and other social systems like online communities and the economy, as well as the toxicity of our natural and built environments (Böbel et al., 2018; Doan et al., 2016; Ungar & Perry, 2012). Social ecological systems scholars, meanwhile, tend to view a system as embracing all the elements that interact at different scales of a single, unified system. Whereas the medical anthropologist might see an intricate weave of *different* systems, the ecologists sees a *single* system with many different layers, or scales (Figure 1.1). The distinction is subtle but significant when developing theory as, depending on one's perspective, multiple systems could be seen holistically as a single system with multiple scales or as multiple systems in their own right that are contingent on one another's actions. For ease of discussion (and because I am more a social scientist than social ecologist), I will talk about mutually dependent supraordinate and subordinate *systems* (rather than scales) whenever there is a reasonable assumption that a cluster of "related or associated things" work closely together. Regardless of how a system is defined, the science of resilience

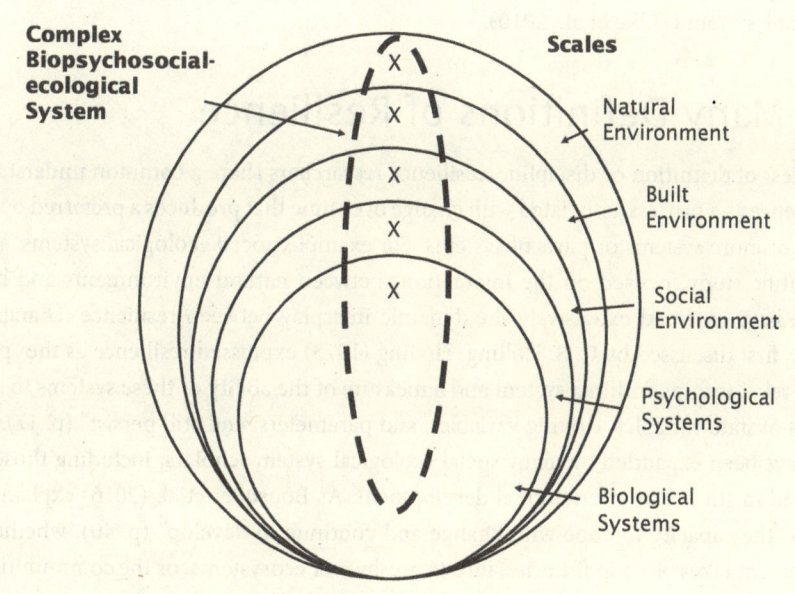

FIGURE 1.1 A system comprised of interacting scales.

requires that multiple systems (and scales of systems) are accounted for as no single variable can be wholly responsible for the complexity of the processes associated with resilience and the outcomes that result. System variables can, in fact, look very different from one another. They might be the neurons of the parasympathetic system of the brain that moderates trauma, the economic and political aspects of a community recovering from a hurricane, or the interacting flora and fauna of a forest rejuvenating after a fire. With the term *system* defined (albeit arbitrarily), it becomes easier to see a shift in thinking occurring from single system explanations for complex social and biological processes (like resilience) to more contingent models that account for the way systems cope with external and internal threats to their sustainability.

When brought together, systemic thinking and theories of resilience produce new ways of understanding processes of change that involve human and nonhuman systems and their many parts. In the area of trauma research, for example, we now understand the need to stop asking individuals who have been traumatized, "What is wrong with you?" and instead ask, "What happened to you that is causing you to behave the way you do?" This second question shifts attention away from a single system's (i.e., the individual) responsibility for recovery, adaptation, or transformation and focuses instead on the environmental triggers that influence patterns of change (i.e., in the case of human resilience after exposure to war, protective factors include being resettled in a host country as a refugee, access to health care, and family reunification; Ott & Montgomery, 2015). When studying the resilience of human populations under stress, the most pertinent question is, "What happened to individual lives that made them different from what would be expected given the amount of stress they have experienced?" This pattern of inquiry reflects a change in thinking from simple explanations for complex behaviors to a multisystemic understanding of interactions between two or more systems (i.e., people and their environments), with as much emphasis on the interactions between systems as the pattern of adaptation evidenced by any one system (Folke et al., 2010).

The Many Definitions of Resilience

Regardless of definition or discipline, resilience researchers share a common understanding of resilience as a process associated with change over time that produces a preferred outcome for one or more systems or parts of systems. For example, social ecological systems, an area of scientific study focused on the interactions between natural environments and human activity, have explored extensively the dynamic interplay between resilience (change) and stability, first discussed by C. S. Holling. Holling (1973) expressed resilience as the "persistence of relationships within a system and a measure of the ability of these systems to absorb changes of state variables, driving variables, and parameters, and still persist" (p. 17). These ideas have been expanded by many social ecological system scholars, including those most interested in studies of international development. As Bousquet et al. (2016) explain, resilience is "the capacity to cope with change and continue to develop" (p. 40), whether that development takes place in fisheries, forests, freshwater ecosystems, or the communities that depend on each of these natural ecologies for their survival.

In other areas, including the physical sciences, these same themes of sustainability and change are becoming commonplace. For example, in architecture, the term *resilience* is synonymous with "a process for creating sustainable, successful places that promote wellbeing, by understanding what people need from the places they live and work" (Woodcraft, Bacon, Caistor-Arendar, & Hackett, 2012, p. 16). In computing science, the resilience of networked systems produces a "system that continues to offer an acceptable level of service even in the face of challenges" (Hutchison & Sterbenz, 2018, p. 1).

The term *resilience* has also become well recognized in the psychological sciences where there has been intense scrutiny of promotive and protective processes that function when human biological, psychological, social, economic, and political systems become stressed. Masten (2014), a developmental psychologist, is known for her definition of resilience that has evolved to take a more systemic approach. She writes:

> Resilience can be broadly defined as the capacity of a dynamic system to adapt successfully to disturbances that threaten system function, viability, or development. The concept can be applied to systems of many kinds at many interacting levels, both living and nonliving, such as a microorganism, a child, a family, a security system, an economy, a forest, or the global climate. (p. 6)

The study of human psychology has shown that this pattern of adaptation can appear in many different ways, ranging from persistence in one's behavior when confronting stress to forcing systems to transform themselves in ways that result in entirely new regimes of behavior to avoid a stressor altogether. For example, victims of sexual abuse may choose a number of viable strategies to cope with their abuse. Where they perceive the consequences of disclosure as too high (e.g., stigma or being blamed for the abuse), a possible coping strategy may be to avoid the abuser and persist with previous patterns of behavior, sublimating potentially traumatizing thoughts and feelings. This is not an optimal strategy for the individual victim or society as a whole, but it is a contextually reasonable adaptation in contexts where victims of abuse may risk further abuse if they disclose (Priebe & Svedin, 2008). When social movements give victims a collective voice (e.g., the #MeToo movement), a different pattern of resilience becomes possible, one that transforms broader social institutions and the individual's identification of himself or herself as a victim with rights. In this sense, manifestations of psychological resilience are a reflection of how broader systems interact with individual choices to produce patterns of coping that are more or less effective.

It is becoming increasingly clear (as the chapters in this volume show) that there is a synergy in how resilience is defined when describing the functioning of different systems. Masten's definition, for example, shares much in common with those in distantly related fields like disaster resilience, where the focus is on "the ability to prepare and plan for, absorb, recover from or more successfully adapt to actual or potential adverse events" (Cutter, 2016a, p. 742). My own work on the resilience of human systems that accounts for changes in multiple psychological, sociocultural, and institutional systems integrates dimensions of social justice, defining resilience as the capacity of systems (whether that system is an individual, a community, or an institution) in contexts of adversity to navigate to the resources necessary to sustain well-being and the ability of these human systems to negotiate for promotive and protective resources to be provided in contextually and culturally meaningful ways (Ungar, 2011).

Although these definitions all focus on the functioning of different systems or parts of systems, they share a number of similarities. First, resilience only exists where there has been a perturbation that is unusual and stressful for one or more interdependent systems. The result is destabilization that threatens the capacity of the system to maintain its functioning. Second, all resilient systems engage in processes of one kind or another that give them opportunities to persist, resist, recover, adapt, or transform (I will discuss each of these processes later). What these contextually specific processes look like, however, is always a reflection of the stressors placed on a system, the resources that are available to protect the system's functioning, and the desirable outcomes that are sought. In this sense, resilience is contextually specific, much as evolving thinking in the field of public health now emphasizes "precision public health" that identifies localities most at risk and then targets interventions to their unique contexts, rather than always looking for generalizable mechanisms that sustain the well-being of entire populations (Dowell, Blazes, & Desmond-Hellmann, 2016). The third quality of resilience reflects this need for sensitivity to the local context, acknowledging the different levels of power each system (or part of a system) has and its capacity to influence the individual or collective well-being of a system (or systems) as a whole. This expression of power is always a matter of negotiation that leads to trade-offs as different parts of systems compete for the resources each needs to cope with internal and external stressors. A system is perceived as showing resilience only when it functions in ways that are valued positively by its constituent parts or co-occurring systems. In practice, this means that a family that embraces criminal behavior as a way of managing social marginalization or an economy that resists modernization to preserve the livelihoods of a few individuals may both be described as resilient from the perspective of those who benefit from these patterns of adaptation (Ungar, 2016).

While these three aspects of resilience (i.e., exposure to an atypical perturbation, contextual specificity of the protective processes, and negotiated outcomes) may seem abstract, in practice, resilience in response to a disturbance that produces patterns of adaptation that benefit some parts of a system more than others has been the basis for voluminous amounts of study in many different disciplines. For example, Annarelli and Nonino (2016) have adapted Hollings's work on social ecological systems to examine the resilience of supply chains, linking their resilience to the functioning of the multiple systems upon which they depend. These include both distal environmental systems (e.g., disruptive weather and political strife can be disruptive to supply chains) and the everyday practices used by management (e.g., labor strikes and poor financial decisions can affect the planned production of goods and services). While it may seem that the only desirable outcome of supply chain resilience is stable production (recovery), a return to business as usual is too narrow an understanding of what resilience can look like. A system that recovers may, in fact, be one that has failed to account for changes in its environment or adapted to mismanagement when it resumes doing what it did before a crisis. While resilience may in such circumstances be synonymous with recovery, with recovery comes a trade-off if ineffective management systems are allowed to persist at the expense of the entire business adapting to changing market conditions. Seen from the perspective of the long-term viability of the enterprise, a better outcome might be the removal of the current management and their replacement with a new system of governance that prepares a business for the next unanticipated stressors in the marketplace, diversifying the goods and services it produces, finding new markets, or sourcing new inputs.

Whether such a broad definition of a process that characterizes so many systems is useful is a point of debate (Brown, 2016). What is likely most useful about a more systemic understanding of resilience is the potential it brings to discern patterns across systems that explain how the resilience of one system might influence the resilience of other co-occurring systems. The more we know about how resilience works, the better we will be able to influence systems to change in ways that are desirable to different parts of those same systems. Seldom, however, have researchers in the natural and human sciences explored collaboratively the full extent of the links between the resilience of one system and the resilience of mutually dependent, co-occurring supraordinate and subordinate systems (for exception, see Brown, 2016; Xu & Kajikawa, 2017).

In this chapter, I propose an algebraic expression to conceptually guide studies of systemic resilience as a way to account for all the complex reciprocal interactions that make resilience contextually responsive. Elaboration of the model is followed by the presentation of seven principles common to the resilience of different systems. In the final part of the chapter, I explore the implications of systemic resilience for the design of interventions and social policies that have the greatest potential to make the resilience of human, built, and natural systems more likely to occur.

A Model of Multisystemic Resilience

All systems have the potential to show resilience, but that resilience will reflect the capacity of multiple co-occurring systems to interact well together under stress. Patterns of resilience are always responses to the quality of the stressors that a system experiences. This is one way in which the study of resilience is distinguished from fields like positive psychology, population health, and ecology, all of which include research on the factors that maintain normative functioning associated with expected patterns of change and growth. For example, while adults need a sense of self-worth, efficacy, and problem-solving skills, under conditions of war or forced displacement due to climate change these aspects of cognitive functioning may look quite different as individuals adapt how they think about themselves and to whom they attribute the locus of control for change (Tol, Song, & Jordans, 2013). There may also be protective psychological processes like social withdrawal that are functional only in contexts of exposure to overwhelming amounts of external stress (Obradović, Bush, Stamperdahl, Adler, & Boyce, 2010). Resilience, then, always occurs in contexts where the amount of stress a system experiences is above that which is accepted as optimal for the system's functioning (some stress is, after all, necessary and can inform the development of healthy coping strategies for all systems). Expressed algebraically, there must be above-normal levels of exposure to adversity to trigger resilience. This can be summarized as $\Sigma A >$ average A for a population where A is adversity.

The assessment of risk, then, is a precondition for understanding resilience. Risk, however, is seldom contained to one or two narrowly defined proximal systems but instead occurs in mixtures of risk factors at different systemic levels. The Centers for Disease Control and Prevention in the United States, for example, describe the exposome as the measure of all the exposures an individual experiences over his or her lifetime and how these exposures influence the individual's health. The study of resilience is not about understanding these risks or their negative sequelae that follow risk exposure, such as disorder, dysfunction, or disease. The study of resilience (in contexts of adversity) focuses attention on the factors that prevent a potentially traumatizing event from causing a system to function poorly.

The challenge when theorizing resilience is to address the complexity of resilience across interrelated systems and create models to capture the interactions between systems (Adger, Barnett, Brown, Marshall, & O'Brien, 2013). The expression in Figure 1.2 is one such effort to account for the many dimensions of resilience as they co-occur within and between systems, whether that system is biological, psychological, social, mechanical, or environmental.

Figure 1.2 is an expression of resilience that adapts the work of famed social psychologist Kurt Lewin. Lewin (1951) suggested that behavior is a function of a person's interaction with his or her environment, expressed as $B = f(P,E)$. Expanding that simple expression produces a succinct story of interacting resilience systems and their component parts. The resilience of any single system (Rsystem) is mutually dependent upon the resilience of other co-occurring, supraordinate and subordinate systems at a particular moment in time (Rsystem$_{1,2,3,...}$), whether those systems are as small as a gene or as large as a family, computer network, government, or biosphere. This reciprocity is captured by the left-hand side of the expression. At the level of each system, resilience is first a function of the system's capacities (S_c) and vulnerabilities (S_v; this includes factors like gender, physiology, and genetics of human systems; social and built capital of community systems; and biodiversity and chemical composition of ecological systems). These interact with aspects of a system's distal and proximal physical and social environment (E) in ways that either sustain a system's current regime of behavior or compel it to change.

$$\left.\begin{array}{c} Rsystem_a \\ \updownarrow \\ Rsystem_b \\ \updownarrow \\ Rsystem_c... \end{array}\right\} Rsystem_{1,2,3} \left\{ \frac{(O_{av} O_{ac})(M)}{f(S_{cv}E)} \right.$$

Recovery/Adaptation/Transformation*

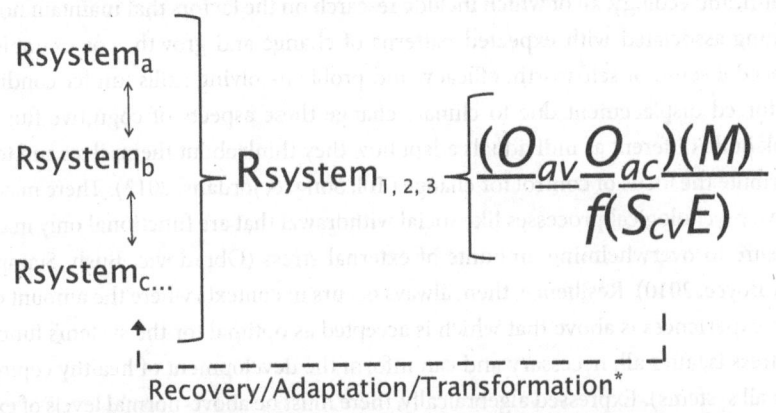

FIGURE 1.2 An expression of resilience (in contexts where a population is exposed to above-normal levels of adversity). R = resilience; O = opportunity; M = meaning; E = environment; av = availability of resources; ac = accessibility of resources; cv = capacities and vulnerabilities. Adapted from Ungar (2011).

These interactions, however, will have a greater or lesser impact on the system's resilience based on the opportunities (O) that are more or less available (O_{av}) and accessible (O_{ac}) to the system, which limit the system's expression of its purpose or function. Available resources may be near at hand but not accessible due to barriers occurring across scales (e.g., a sanctuary for orphaned elephant calves may be available, but weaknesses in funding or transportation infrastructure make it inaccessible to animals that need care and protection). Opportunities are, in turn, influenced by meaning systems (M), which are expressed through the relative power of each part of the system to privilege solutions of one kind over another (Adger et al., 2013). Finally, as systems go through the process of coping with adversity, they exert an influence on other mutually dependent systems (returning again to the left-hand side of the expression). These coping processes can appear as a recovery to a previous regime of behavior, as an adaptation to ongoing adversity through engagement in new coping strategies, or can force the transformation of contingent systems that decreases or buffers exposure to adversity in the future.

A comprehensive model of resilience like this is intended to broaden the scope of research that focuses on patterns of recovery, adaptation, and transformation of any system. The enhanced breadth of factors that should be accounted for may also help to better inform sustainable solutions to "wicked" problems, whether those are the high rates of suicide among racially marginalized and structurally disadvantaged indigenous peoples or ecological problems caused by the Anthropocene era, such as climate change and the decreasing diversity of ecological systems. Besides helping guide the design of resilience research, the expression is also useful for interpreting research findings where multiple systems have been implicated in the successful development of one or more focal systems.

Co-occurring Systems and Resilience

There are many studies in both the human and natural sciences that suggest that a long list of variables must be accounted for to understand developmental processes that result in changes to behavioral regimes of contingent systems under stress that help these systems to remain viable. To date, most studies have only accounted for a small number of factors that explain how the resilience of one system might affect the resilience of other co-occurring systems. A new generation of studies that include far more scope to their data collection, however, is showing that when systems are described in sufficient detail, correlations can be found between conditions in one system and performance of other contingent systems (Kaplan, Collins, & Tylavsky, 2017; Noble, Norman, & Farah, 2005). For example, a U.S.-based study of pediatric neuroimaging and genetics found strong correlations between childhood socioeconomic factors and different aspects of brain structure among 10-year-olds (Noble et al., 2015). Parental educational attainment and family income accounted for individual variation in brain structural development in regions associated with the development of language, executive functions, and memory. While the study was focused on explaining the factors that inhibit brain development rather than those that facilitate positive development in stressed environments, the results are useful in demonstrating that economic systems affect biological systems (brain development) through the moderating effect of parental educational attainment, family income, and social marginalization related to class structure. Given these findings, it is very likely possible (although as yet relatively unstudied) that as opportunity structures change and economically marginalized families are better resourced, they are more likely to raise children with better neurological functioning and improved ability to break cycles of poverty. This is a hypothesis that still needs to be tested, although longitudinal studies of child development without neurological testing have shown that the cumulative effect of multiple resilience factors at different systemic levels are likely to contribute to better than expected outcomes among children who experience early disadvantage (Beckett et al., 2006; Boivin et al., 2013; Werner & Smith, 2001). In this sense, the resilience of one system (e.g., the education system, social welfare system, or political system) can mean that other systems or scales are more resistant to problems and better able to recover, adapt, or transform. Simpler models of resilience that seek to explain resilience as change in just one or two systems are unlikely to produce sufficiently robust accounts for why resilience does or does not occur when problems are complex and solutions unsustainable in contexts where there are multiple forms of disadvantage and stress.

It is not surprising, then, that increasingly complex models are being proposed to account for reciprocity between systems as they change, with empirical evidence that show that processes like recovery, adaptation, and transformation by one system contributes to concurrent or sequential change in other subordinate and superordinate systems or scales. To illustrate this pattern with an example that reaches beyond the human sciences, Hutchison and Sterbenz (2018) have shown that the design of resilient computer architecture is dependent upon the resilience of the critical infrastructure that it needs to function, like the Internet; management structures in the corporation that hosts it; and the capacity of end-users to exploit the technology in ways that are meaningful and improve their lives. If one thinks, for example, of handheld devices as a networked computing system, then it is clear that their sustainability as a communication tool relies on software systems, especially social media platforms, and mobile phone companies to ensure handheld devices continue to fulfill a meaningful function for consumers. The technology, then, is a system networked to other systems, even the biology of the users (e.g., the production of stress hormones like cortisol is influenced by the use of handheld devices) and the political environment created by humans (e.g., election meddling and the proliferation of "fake news" on social media). Much has been made of the cascading negative effects of a technology like handheld devices or the potential for negative outcomes when these computer networks are stressed by outside agents.

The resolution of risk and enhancement of resilience to sustain connectivity and convenience depend on more than their hardware and software (two important, mutually dependent technical systems). Hutchison and Sterbenz (2018) propose the formula D^2R^2+DR (defend, detect, remediate, recover; then diagnose, refine) as the stages in a recurring process by which the architecture of a computer system evolves its capacity to withstand attacks. Each part of the process is reliant on contingent systems like government regulation (that prevent security breaches), financial markets (that monetize these networks and support their proliferation), and psychological systems (that create favorable attitudes toward new forms of communication). Together, these and many other systems create recursive environments that respond to expanding computer networks.

In this regard, resilient systems (whether biological, psychological, social, or engineered) are malleable over time. When they work well, they benefit multiple systems at once with fewer negative trade-offs, while still being responsive to the exigencies of systems coping under stress. There is, however, always a danger that strategies to make one system more resilient can inadvertently compromise the capacity of other co-occurring systems. One example of this pattern is found in discussions of regrettable substitutions (Scherer, Maynard, Dolinoy, Fagerlin, & Zikmund-Fisher, 2014), which are solutions to complex problems that result in adaptations that make one system better but compromise the functioning of other contingent systems. This concept has been used to explain the unintended consequences of interventions like chemical coatings on household objects that retard fire or make plastics more durable but that are later proven to be toxic to humans. A solution that appears to enhance resilience of one system may compromise the resilience of others.

Examples like these suggest that resilience has both trade-offs and a potential "pay forward" function, with the resilience of one system likely to influence negatively or positively the resilience of other systems. This pattern can be seen in all systems, whether biological, built, or natural. Therefore, the capacity for systems to withstand stress (to demonstrate resilience) is unlikely to be a function of a single system's self-righting capacity. As Hutchison and Sterbenz (2018) explain in regard to computing networks:

> [Because] attacks can happen at any layer of the communication stack (e.g., hidden attacks exploiting vulnerabilities of web application in legitimate network packets), various detection and protection mechanisms usually co-exist at different levels to mitigate security threats. However, if security management is localized only to corresponding layers, the security related information will be fragmented, which fails to give a big picture for situation awareness and prompt and correct responses. (p. 3)

The better integrated resilient systems are, the more likely they are to benefit from each system's efforts to remain sustainable.

The downside to this systemic understanding of resilience is that no one study is likely to account for every dimension of resilience found in Figure 1.2. The science, however, is continuing to build toward a comprehensive understanding of recovery, adaptation, and transformation under stress through incremental research that investigates more than one system at a time (this trend is evident in the chapters that are included in this volume). This incrementalism is, for example, demonstrated by many multidisciplinary studies, such as those by Böbel and his colleagues (2018) in the field of molecular psychosomatics and Dinan and Cryan's (2013) work on immunology. Both programs of research have proven a link between the diversity of the human microbiome (e.g., gut bacteria) and the ability of the human immune system to suppress inflammation and reduce the incidence of a range of psychiatric disorders including depression and anxiety. For example, in a recent study of the potential protective function of exposure to a more diverse natural biome, healthy young men who spent the first 15 years of their lives on farms with animals were compared with those who grew up in an urban environment without animals (Böbel et al., 2018). A number of characteristics distinguished the two samples. First, when given the Trier Social Stress Test in a laboratory setting (a test of public speaking skills and stress reactivity), urban participants raised in the absence of animals showed increases in stress-related immune system secretion of the interleukin 6 and suppressed anti-inflammatory secretion of interleukin 10. These two types of cytokines, or proteins, help cells signal one another and have been linked to different levels of inflammation that affect neurological and psychological functioning. This pattern of biological response suggests that urban participants had more immunoregulatory deficits when stressed. Participants were also subjected to a number of psychological tests and had samples of their plasma cortisol and salivary α-amylase (a protein enzyme) assessed, all of which showed that rural participants experienced the Trier Social Stress Test as more difficult. Although the results are still preliminary due to the relatively small sample size and use of a nonclinical population, studies like this are providing an interesting clue to the potential benefits of exposure to a healthy and diverse natural environment and its positive influence on human biological and psychological processes, particularly the "missing-microbes" or "old friends" (Rook, Lowry, & Raison, 2013) as some bacteria have come to be known. From an evolutionary point of view, the presence of these microbes likely helped establish regulatory (i.e., protective) immune pathways that are now lacking in urban environments because of increased sanitation, water treatment, the overuse of antibiotics, lower rates of breastfeeding, and cesarean sections (it is believed that during the birthing process the mother's microbiome is transferred, like a baton, to the child during a vaginal birth). Once again, systems that potentiate greater resilience of one system, like better sanitation, may inadvertently compromise the resilience of other systems, just as the resilience of co-occurring systems can also create cascades of positive change.

These theories have been proven in laboratory experiments and through careful sampling of populations with differential rates of exposure to more diverse ecosystems. Combined, they suggest that exposure to the right amount and type of stressors (such as bacteria) can produce a "steeling effect" (Rutter, 2012) that make systems more robust when exposed to future stressors. For example, children from more traditional Amish communities in the United States had better immune system activation than Hutterite farm children where the farm work is more mechanized (Rook & Lowry, 2008). Thus, Stanford, Stanford, and Grange (2001) proposed the "hygiene hypothesis," which attributes recent spikes in psychiatric disorders and diseases to compromised immune systems among people in industrialized and heavily urbanized settings where there is minimum contact with natural environments. It appears to be a truism of resilience research that the right amount of stress is required for successful development of all systems. Stress a system too much, however, and it fails. Stress a system the right amount, and it will demonstrate increased capacity for resilience when dealing with future disturbance.

This understanding of resilience as a systemic process is found in numerous other studies of very different systems. Looking outward toward the quality of the natural environment (rather than its component microbial parts), Lederbogen and his colleagues (2011) were able to show that a 90-minute walk in a natural, but not urban, setting was able to decrease self-reported rumination and concurrent neural activity in the subgenual prefrontal cortex of human subjects. The findings indicate a heightened capacity of people to withstand stress following contact with nature. In this example, an externally diverse, natural environment is able to enhance the capacity of neurological resilience to stress, which makes the placement of green spaces contiguous to urban environments a potentially important buffer against the physiological changes that follow from urbanization. Not only might these enhanced spaces increase neurological capacity to cope with stress, they might also permit greater access to microbial diversity that could produce yet another positive influence on the human biological system. It is these complex and reciprocal relationships between resilient systems that justify the need to account for multiple systems at the same time when studying resilience.

Returning to Figure 1.2, there is plenty of evidence from studies of multiple systems (from the microbiome to the engineered systems like computer networks) that by strengthening any one system, other co-occurring and contingent systems will also benefit, although the lines of causality are far from linear. That is because it remains difficult to privilege any single behavioral regime of one or more systems as a resilience ideal. Every behavioral regime benefits some portion of an entire ecosystem (Holling, 1973). Change opportunity structures, meaning systems, or the context in which a system operates and what resilience looks like will also change. Indeed, one always needs to ask, "Resilience to what? Resilience for whom?" (Cutter, 2016b). Even when a system is not anthropomorphic, the same question can be adapted to ask, "Resilience to what, and for which part of a system's benefit?" Researchers of human resilience, however, have tended to privilege certain outcomes over others, positing resilience as a process of recovery to a previous level of functioning, adaptation to new ways of coping with stress, or the forced transformation of one or more systems to ensure that individual and social systems thrive in ways that are socially constructed (Cutter et al., 2008). There is typically a bias, however, in the psychological and social sciences toward positive (socially desirable) outcomes that benefit human systems as a whole over those that benefit natural systems or subsystems (Rutter, 1987). An increasingly complex story of systemic resilience is showing that the teleological view, which sees some systems as worthwhile only if they serve the needs of human beings in the short-term, is being challenged as we come to realize that even systems with the potential to threaten human health may, in the long-term, be in our best interest to maintain. Thus, a less anthropocentric understanding of resilience leads to the conclusion that a resilient system does not always function for the benefit of humans and that even behavioral regimes of human systems that are labeled as suboptimal can sometimes protect contingent systems. For example, social withdrawal after a traumatic event like child abuse may help to maintain lower levels of cortisol and preserve biological homeostasis, even if that coping strategy compromises long-term social development (Alink, Cicchetti, Kim, & Rogosch, 2012).

Resilience cannot, therefore, be understood as a linear set of causal relationships without accounting for trade-offs. Where ecological and human understandings of resilience intersect, the resilience of ecological and human systems has been found to be mutually dependent (Quinlan, Berbés-Blázquez, Haider, & Peterson, 2015). In the example of the "old friends" discussed earlier, protective factors like access to antibiotics, which enhance opportunities for health and improve the resilience of human beings to debilitating diseases, may actually compromise the viability of other systems necessary for the resilience of the same organism they are meant to sustain.

Seven Principles

Despite this potential for cross-disciplinary modeling, there has been little effort to synthesize our diverse conceptualizations of resilience. Ecologists have remained largely focused on patterns of resilience in the ecosphere, although social ecological systems theorists like Folke (2006), Brown (2016), and Gunderson (Gunderson, Allen, & Holling, 2010) point to the impact of humans on the resilience of natural environments, and vice versa. Ecopsychologists and epigeneticists, meanwhile, talk about environmental triggers, but their conceptualizations of resilience focus mostly on individual human processes (Ellis & Del Giudice, 2014). Some authors have suggested that despite a common lexicon, the fields are fundamentally too different to bring together into a single model (Olsson, Jerneck, Thoren, Persson, & O'Byrne, 2015). There is plenty of resilience-related research that suggests otherwise. A recent review of the principles that govern resilience across diverse bodies of research (Ungar, 2018) identified seven common principles that can account for much of what we understand about how resilience functions when a system (human, built, or natural) is stressed. These include (1) resilience occurs in contexts of adversity; (2) resilience is a process; (3) there are trade-offs between systems when a system experiences resilience; (4) a resilient system is open, dynamic, and complex; (5) a resilient system promotes connectivity; (6) a resilient system demonstrates experimentation and learning; and (7) a resilient system includes diversity, redundancy, and participation.

Resilience Occurs in Contexts of Adversity

Studies of resilience can be distinguished from related research on mental health, social capital and even ecology by their explicit focus on systems under stress. While systems show periodic changes in behavioral regimes due to maturation, or adjustments to expected and normal changes in the environment over time (e.g., animals experience seasonal changes; children must adjust when they are first sent to school; communication systems grow as the number of users increases), a system shows resilience when it is able to recover, adapt, or transform under conditions of *atypical* stress.

To illustrate with an example from the psychological sciences, Oshri, Duprey, Kogan, Carlson, and Liu (2018) studied changes in the future orientation of abused children over a three-year period starting in early adolescence. Rather than focus on normative developmental processes, however, they put an unusual amount of effort into assessing children's social environments to better understand how children's anticipation of future consequences and their beliefs that they could influence their futures are associated with the shifting balance between exposure to contextually specific risk factors (e.g., caregiver–child closeness, peer relations, school engagement, positive community environment, and access to services) and the internal and external resources the children experience over time. Findings show that as the equilibrium between risk and resources changes and children are able to cope with an abnormally high burden of expectations placed on them by their families and communities, their level of future orientation steadily increases despite, and possibly as a consequence of, stress exposure. To model this association, Oshri et al. (2018) used growth mixture modeling to distinguish three developmental trajectories for future orientation as a cognitive coping strategy: low start/increasing; high start/decreasing; and high persistent. Each trajectory was explained by the quality of the child's experience with external conditions, including the degree of physically abusive discipline they received, the quality of their peer relationships, their level of engagement in school, the disorganization of children's communities, and their gender. As access to supportive resources improved, children's future orientation (a protective factor against psychological problems) also improved. By disaggregating the data by gender, it was further shown that girls (who are, statistically, more at risk for depression) tended to more consistently report high future orientation. All of this raises questions with regard to how children's experiences of the proximal systems that influence them shape internal cognitive coping strategies. In this example, a commonly assumed metric of personal resilience, children's ability to use cognitive strategies to solve problems and maintain optimism, depends on the capacity of both internal and external systems to manage both proximal and distal stressors. As the example illustrates, resilience only exists when a system is under stress but exhibits a desirable behavioral regime.

Resilience is a Process

Drawing together models of resilience from ecological and human sciences is fraught with ontological and epistemological problems. Ecologists tend to describe resilience as a system state in which equilibrium is reached (Folke et al., 2010), while psychologists lean toward resilience as a process. For example, researchers concerned with ecological systems talk about a system's resilience as its capacity to maintain homeostasis while under threat (Gunderson & Holling, 2002). Psychologists, however, dating back half a century have come to see resilience as a set of protective processes that contribute to positive developmental goals (Rutter, 1987). To reconcile this difference, scholars are concluding that resilience is a process that increases the capacity of a system to withstand or adapt to a present or future insult. A system that shows resilience is one that is able to optimize its capacity to successfully cope under stress.

Resilience-promoting processes can look very different depending on the context in which they occur. At least five processes have been found to be associated with resilience: persistence, resistance, recovery, adaptation, and transformation.

a. *Persistence.* Persistence is a system's ploddingly regular behavior that is only possible if outside threats are dealt with by other co-occurring systems that insulate it enough to allow the focal system to continue unchanged. In ecology, a nature preserve with armed guards creates the conditions for rare species of mammals like rhinos to persist with relatively little change in their behavior despite the threats posed to them. In psychology, children who have been described as "orchids" (Ellis & Boyce, 2011) are genetically susceptible to stress but excel in conditions where their social environments protect them (i.e., a child susceptible to anxiety, but also a gifted artist, will thrive in an alternative school where she can avoid bullying). In each example, the resilience of a system under threat is only possible if co-occurring systems protect the focal system from stressors that would force the system to change.

b. *Resistance.* Resistance may look the same as persistence, but the focal system maintains its behavioral regime by actively pushing back against outside threats (i.e., an immune system is activated to avoid infection of the host organism, maintaining the host's health). Most systems will demonstrate a pattern of resistance before they recover, adapt, or transform. For example, communities facing the loss of a large employer may seek government intervention to subsidize an industry that might otherwise fail. In each instance, the focal system is only as resilient as the subordinate and supraordinate systems it can actively mobilize to avoid change.

c. *Recovery.* The process of recovery means that a system's defenses, whether internal or external, were insufficient to resist perturbation and the system's capacity to cope has been compromised temporarily. Recovery is a description of a system's return to a previous level of functioning, although in actual fact systems are changed by their experience of insult and recovery. Hutchison and Sterbenz (2018), for example, suggest that a computing system's recovery is never a return to a previous state, but usually results in an improvement in its engineering as it learns to avoid the same breakdown twice. Likewise, a forest may recover from a fire with increased nutrients in the soil (e.g., potassium, calcium, and magnesium). In each instance, the recovered system may look and function similar to its previous state but is likely to have new capacities as a result of having survived a disturbance.

d. *Adaptation.* Adaptation refers to a system changing in ways that make it possible for it to accommodate itself to stress. For example, an invasive species imposes the need for adaptation on an ecosystem, which may lose some of its diversity—species—to accommodate the intruder or develop compensatory means of coping with the invader (e.g., weaker parts of the system may die off, leaving the remaining parts more genetically robust). In humans, adaptation is particularly common in studies of resilience. For example, O'Brien and Hope (2010) found that elderly persons who live mostly on their own or in substandard nursing homes are more vulnerable to centralized energy systems, which are likely to fail during extreme weather events. Once stressed, elderly people who are socially isolated are more likely to die from heat stroke when air conditioning fails or from exposure or carbon monoxide poisoning when heating systems do not work. One possible adaptation is to provide these people with more localized energy solutions (like home-based solar units that feed energy into the grid) that have more capacity to withstand catastrophic weather events. This change in energy policy facilitates the adaptation of energy systems to the needs of vulnerable elderly even though it does not fundamentally change the conditions that predispose elderly persons to health problems.

e. *Transformation.* A resilient system that transforms under stress must find a new behavioral regime that allows it to continue its previous functions (or perform new functions) by taking advantage of new strategies and resources. All systems have this capacity, whether it is advances to energy storage systems that have allowed renewable energy to transform the energy sector or personal transformation of a heart attack victim who makes dramatic changes to his lifestyle after discharge from hospital. In each instance, systems (human, built, or natural) are fundamentally changed by their exposure to stress, finding a different behavioral regime better suited to the internal and external threats the system faces.

These five processes are not agentic. Systems do not "choose" one coping strategy over another. They, instead, optimize their functioning by exploiting co-occurring systems for resources that make different strategies more or less feasible. Change the resources available, and the meaning of those resources to the system (i.e., their value), and the process a system uses to improve its resilience will also change. In this sense, the locus for change that explains which process a system uses depends as much on the condition of the environment that surrounds a system as it does the system's own resources to cope with unusually high amounts of stress.

There Are Trade-Offs Between Systems When a System Experiences Resilience

The resilience of one system has the potential to influence the resilience of other co-occurring systems (e.g., a biologically diverse natural environment has the potential to enrich the human microbiome, which in turn affects the immune system and mental health). However, resilience cannot be understood as a linear set of causal relationships without accounting for the trade-offs between systems. In the example of the "old friends" discussed earlier, protective factors like better sanitation and antibiotics, which enhance opportunities for human health, compromise the viability of other external systems like one's natural environment, and internal systems like the microbiome where more diverse bacteria (i.e., dirt) would actually be more useful to overall human well-being. By making the environment less rich in bacteria, one could say that the human organism is protected from harmful pathogens and therefore more resilient to diseases like cholera. However, the trade-off is that those same measures to sanitize the environment also compromise access to helpful bacteria. Without accounting for all aspects of system change at multiple systemic levels, there is greater likelihood for unintended (iatrogenic) consequences to interventions that are meant to increase system capacity.

A Resilient System Is Open, Dynamic, and Complex

Systems that show resilience integrate new information when necessary, adding to their complexity in ways that increase the resources available to cope with disruption. For example, a rich literature is emerging that connects threats to environmental sustainability like climate change with reciprocal, bidirectional chains of causality with human aspects of the problem, specifically culture. Adger et al. (2013) deconstruct the complexity of cultural narratives and practices that define the relationships between humans and their environments. As they show through a review of the literature, cultural narratives about the relationship between people and the natural environment interact with beliefs and cultural practices in ways that may prevent rational response to a scientifically demonstrable threat (e.g., the reluctance of some adherents of fundamentalist religions to acknowledge climate change occurring as a result of our exploitive relationship with nature). In such cases, systems are unable to change (to show resilience) because they remain closed, stable, and simple. In such contexts, even advocates for responsible social policy are likely to fail if the changes they propose conflict with the dominant discourse that defines "business as usual" as sustainable. A more resilient system shows openness to new explanations for human experience, is nimble enough to change, and is capable of integrating new technologies and ideologies to effectively address threats to the system's long-term viability. This nod to complexity, and the multiple ways in which resilience is manifest, reflects emerging science across many disciplines, not just ecology. Current thinking in the field of human psychological resilience is also moving from more deterministic and simplified models of human behavior to more complex explanations (Cutuli & Herbers, 2018).

A Resilient System Promotes Connectivity

Resilient systems are connected systems. While connections can also threaten a system's sustainability (as connected systems are vulnerable to contamination, infection, and misinformation), this appears to be a necessary trade-off for systems to share resources and seed growth. The better connected systems are, the more likely they are to provide access to the resources systems need to overcome disruption when the system's own resources become overwhelmed. To illustrate, restorative justice provides an alternative means of dealing with offenders through a community process that keeps those who commit crimes living in their own communities (Ward & Langlands, 2009). Rather than separation through incarceration, and the risks that accompany imprisonment and discharge afterwards, restorative justice maintains offenders in their communities but holds them accountable to those they have harmed through a structured process of healing that strengthens community connectivity. Likewise, returning to the previous example of vulnerable elderly and energy distribution systems, countering both industrial gigantism and the trend toward seniors living on their own, changes to energy infrastructure could make both power companies and elderly persons who are socially marginalized more resilient by connecting small-scale power systems. One could say that decentralized but locally networked power generation through initiatives like rooftop solar power ensure a diversity of resources are available that can become active during a crisis. Connected systems tend to be better at working together to make both energy and human systems resilient.

A Resilient System Demonstrates Experimentation and Learning

Systems that show resilience experiment with innovative solutions to stressors as they occur, learning from each trial and integrating failure and success into future strategies. This praxis of reflection and action can be observed in all systems. For example, Alt and Raichel (2017) have shown that the experience of citizenship and media literacy are protective factors that contribute to personal attitudes that endorse national accountability, reinforce participatory democracy, and support institutional practices like voting. In turn, these protective factors enhance the efficacy of political and legal systems that ensure responsive governance. Each of these systems is, in turn, most effective when they learn from earlier efforts to adapt, and the lessons learned in one system (e.g., providing people with opportunities to be lifelong learners through educational reform) leads to sustained change in many different dimensions of citizenship. For example, digital literacy implicates a number of contingent systems, including cognitive capacities and values (a psychological system), and cultural systems that must be robust enough to help voters distinguish important issues from manipulation by those in power. Alt and Raichel (2017) argue that well-connected people (principle 5) with access to the technology required to connect and a cognitive mindset to seek out opposing points of views (cognitive disruptions) can be created through a personal learning network, which includes information already handy in the environment and social media. The better a system is at learning from past efforts to stabilize and able to be influenced positively by other systems, the more likely that system is to thrive when confronted with an atypical stressor.

A Resilient System Includes Diversity, Redundancy, and Participation

Systems, whether human, built, or natural, do better when they are more diverse and have sufficiently complex coping strategies to create redundancies. In the event of system overload and partial failure, a diverse system with plenty of its components engaged is more likely to be capable of generating new coping strategies to compensate for those that have failed. It is easy to see these traits in the design of airplanes where multiple system backups exist in case of catastrophic failure of any single system (Jackson & Ferris, 2013) or a small-holding farmer who diversifies her crop to ensure that changing weather patterns do not threaten every part of the harvest at once. These examples suggest that resilient systems are those designed with these characteristics in mind.

A good illustration of this principle in action is ride-sharing applications like Uber, where there is direct participation from drivers and riders, sufficient capacity to ensure cars are available (and incentives by way of spike demand pricing to put more cars on the road when they are needed), and a diversity of products to make use of the capacity Uber has created (e.g., Uber Eats). Combined, Uber has been able to withstand regional setbacks and maintain corporate resilience without threatening the viability of the entire company, as well as provide a more efficient use of resources (Cramer & Krueger, 2016).

The Resilience Tangram

Understanding resilience multisystemically, with numerous trade-offs and complex patterns of interaction within and between systems, means that the factors that predict resilience are seldom fixed or predictable across all environments. Visually, resilience is an interwoven set of relationships that look more like a tangram than a picture puzzle (Figure 1.3). Picture puzzles are sets of printed pieces with predictable patterns of association that snap together in only one predetermined way. Each edge of a puzzle piece is intended to properly lock with only one other. Arguably, much of the empirical research on resilience has searched for these "pieces" and their relationship with other pieces. Complexity is introduced by including more and more parts of the puzzle, but the assumption is that the pieces will come together in some orderly way. This approach to empiricism is well-reflected in much of the research cited so far in this paper. Change a mouse's environment and the pattern of resilience changes in a predictable way. Change an elderly person's access to energy, and she is less vulnerable to social isolation. Protect a computer system from hacks, and it better fulfils its function for users.

The metaphor of the picture puzzle, however, is not theoretically sound when it comes to explaining the principles of resilience. What we observe through research is an artifact

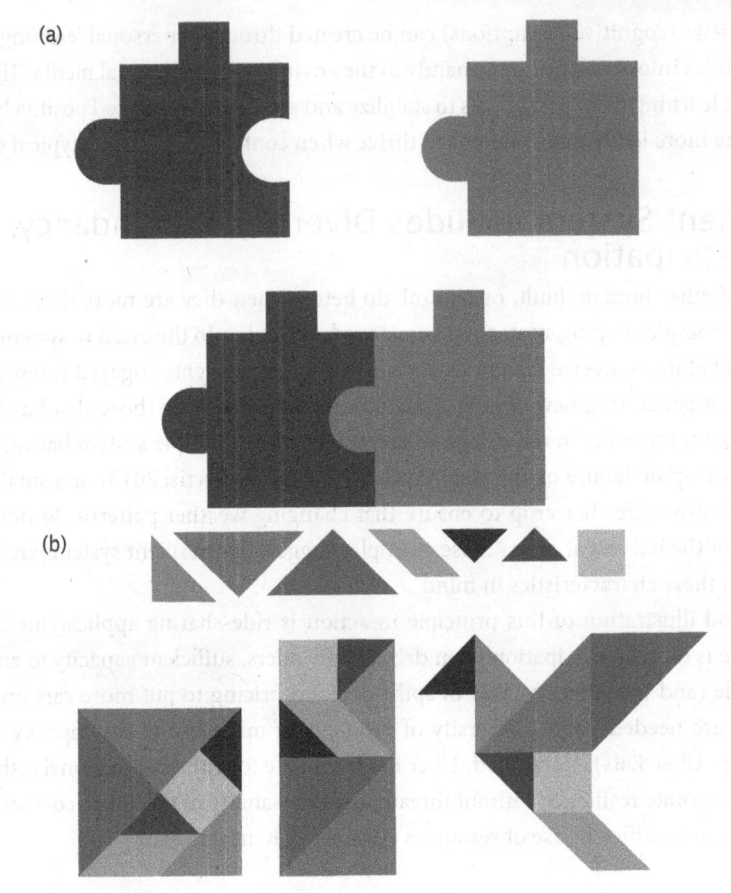

FIGURE 1.3 Visual representations of resilience as puzzle (a) and tangram (b).

of observation and study design. Patterns of adaptation and transformation look predictable because researchers control the conditions of study to select for predetermined patterns. A better metaphor for systemic resilience is the tangram. A tangram is comprised of a set of unique geometric shapes that can associate together to form one shape (a square) or many shapes (a triangle, a bird, etc.). Thinking about resilience as a tangram allows us to appreciate both the equifinality and multifinality of the patterns that predict resilience of one or more systems at the same time. Equifinality is defined as multiple means to a single outcome. Multifinality means there are multiple means to many different outcomes, all of which may be desirable to a system under stress. In the case of the tangram (and unlike a puzzle), there are many different ways of using the pieces in the set to form either the same shape (a square) or using the same pieces to create a number of other imaginative designs.

Studies of family resilience are an illustration of these patterns of resilience and the multiple systems involved (Ungar, 2016). *Family*, and related terms like *clan* or *kinship network*, tends to be defined as a group of people united by sexual and/or affective bonds or legal and/or economic ties, structured as an open, socially recognized, culturally normative system that fulfils a series of fundamental functions for the survival and development of its members and the society of which each family is a part. These functions (much like puzzle pieces) include a long list of possible outcomes, such as procreation and the raising of children; mutual support; or collection, consumption, and distribution of wealth. These outcomes are assumed to be part of one cohesive whole and reflect normative family functioning within a single cultural space (Walsh, 2012). Broader cultural forces (meaning systems) and economic opportunities are often controlled for through purposeful or randomized sampling, which makes it possible to describe families much like puzzles. Each family, depending on sociohistorical factors, seeks to achieve a more or less similar set of outcomes regardless of their form. In this sense, there is equifinality. Many culturally nuanced patterns of behavior are assumed to fulfill the same roles required of families in every context.

Other research, however, suggests that families can also show patterns of multifinality. A study by Hordge-Freeman (2015) on racial diversity within families and the "Russian roulette of genetics" that produces varying skin tones among Afro-Brazilian populations, documented the variability in how families fulfill their basic functions. As an example of multifinality, Hordge-Freeman found that families employ coping strategies that are expedient in the racially marginalizing context they and their children live. Through qualitative research with 116 families, Hordge-Freeman discovered that how love is expressed between parent and child has much to do with a child's phenotype. Parents adapt their child-rearing practices to enhance a child's ability to withstand racism, often using harsher discipline with children who are darker skinned to protect them against future social stigma. Hordge-Freeman does not argue that this strategy is socially just or even effective, but her work, like that of Ungar (2016), documents how many different, contextually relevant patterns of family resilience are associated with the many different outcomes that families strive for in contexts of adversity.

This same multifinality can be found in other domains of research such as community resilience. A community's resilience is the capacity of its human, institutional, built, and natural capital to withstand stress (Hobfoll, 2011; Longstaff, Armstrong, Perrin, Parker, & Hidek, 2010; Norris, Sherrieb, & Pfefferbaum, 2011). Although the factors that produce community resilience are many, there have been very few studies that have looked at the interactions between psychological protective factors, ecological protective factors, and the many different ways a community's resilience is manifested. Furthermore, the many different ways communities show resilience have tended to be overlooked in favor of a narrow set of outcomes such as employment, safety, and good governance. Cox and Perry (2011), however, suggest that resilience may be far more heterogeneous. Writing about the McClure fire in western Canada in 2003, they found that the disorientation that comes from catastrophic events like this are long-lasting, challenge identities, destroy social capital, and undermine community cohesion. However, such events sometimes bring unintended positive outcomes (such as improvements in family functioning) and many new regimes of social interaction that have the potential to improve a community in unanticipated ways over the long-term. This tension between predetermined expressions of resilience and multifinality was reflected in their finding of an opening for creative expressions of resilience that was caused by the disaster's disruption. In this example, there are multiple patterns to recovery (a tangram of possible forms that community resilience can take), but very few are privileged. Those that are preferred (like puzzle pieces already printed and ready to assemble) tend to occur fast and celebrate a community's normal capacity to recover. Atypically slower patterns of growth, and new patterns of community social and economic well-being that may be more sustainable, can be just as viable but have not received the attention they deserve. Examples such as this demonstrate that the processes associated with the resilience of systems, whether a community, a family, the human genome, or a natural environment, all exhibit diverse patterns of coping that are influenced by factors within and between systems.

Application to Research and Intervention

These emerging ways of understanding resilience are not only intriguing; they also have the potential to inform both research and intervention. With regard to research, the expression of resilience provided in Figure 1.2 suggests the need to account for many different factors and multiple systems when studying patterns of persistence, resistance, recovery, adaptation, and transformation. Single system analysis of growth in stressed environments is unlikely to show the complexity of the processes that systems use to survive under stress.

The shift from narrow models of resilience that focus on just a few factors to systemic processes is noteworthy but has been fraught with problems. It can be extremely challenging to conduct research on more than one (or perhaps two) systems at a time. For example, it is typical in the biological sciences to identify highly specific molecular processes, such as the influence of telomeres on aging, or to investigate the relationship between the aging process and exposure to toxic stress resulting from intimate partner violence experienced by pregnant mothers. Better and more complicated research designs are showing that exposure to violence during pregnancy not only affects the mother's aging process; its effects are also passed along to her child in utero, affecting the fetus's telomeres (Drury et al., 2014). Preventing family violence, then, is likely to also be a protective factor against shortened life expectancy. However, while human biologists have identified the minutest qualities of DNA to advance theories like this, these studies tend to assume a high degree of homogeneity in the stressors that influence negative developmental outcomes (i.e., stress on the mother is measured as a single, sometimes dichotomous variable). The assumption seems to be that exposure to intimate partner violence is experienced by all women in much the same way (ignoring differences by class, education, or proximity to family supports), while DNA is assumed to be sensitive to a large number of factors, which biologists account for in their designs. Social scientists make a similar error when they control for a single biological marker like salivary or hair cortisol as a proxy for stress while explaining in great detail the psychosocial, political, and economic aspects of a person's life when coping with political violence, war, or a natural disaster. While it goes without saying that no study can account for all the variations in biological, psychological, social, and environmental factors that contribute to risk and resilience (at least not yet), emerging approaches to research, greater capacity to analyze large amounts of data, and the still nascent preference for multidisciplinary teams and transdisciplinary perspectives are introducing more complexity to how resilience is modeled.

A model of multisystemic resilience also has value when designing interventions. Modeling resilience systemically reminds practitioners and policymakers to consider the interrelationships between systems when developing and implementing interventions targeted at increasing the coping capacity of multiple systems at the same time. Narrow thinking about the dynamics of a single system is unlikely to account for such things as trade-offs or encourage the kind of complexity that is required to promote resilience of one system without doing harm to the resilience of contingent systems. To illustrate, in the area of agroecological resilience (the capacity of food systems to withstand perturbations and develop new regimes that ensure continuous supply), many interventions to enhance sustainability target highly tangible, but essentially weak, leverage points (i.e., they use interventions that are easy, like introducing drought-resistant seeds, which increases system adaptability but has limited potential for transformational change; Fabricus & Currie, 2015). In contrast, Cabell and Oelofse (2012) argue for interventions that increase the distributive capacity of agricultural systems, such as expanding local food sources to make systems more resilient. Such change is similar to calls for whole school approaches and improved social support to combat bullying, rather than individually focused treatment for children who are victims (Mishna et al., 2016).

There is, then, an urgent need to focus on less obvious but potentially far more powerful areas of intervention, regardless of the systems that need influencing. All of this suggests that resilience can be a complicated concept to explain and work with. The ontological and epistemological barriers to studying resilience and applying it to practice are not, however, insurmountable. They are a symptom of the lack of communication between disciplines and the difficulty juxtaposing complementary descriptions of resilience for analysis. When effort is made to compare and contrast models of resilience that account for the behavior of multiple systems at once, our understanding of how systems can successfully cope with change is likely to be vastly improved.

Conclusion

This chapter has demonstrated that there is synergy in how the concept of resilience is theorized across disciplines. Each system's resilience is mutually dependent upon the resilience of co-occurring superordinate and subordinate systems. The quality of these interactions is patterned but not necessarily predictable. Constantly changing environments cause systems to enjoy differing access to the resources they need to sustain themselves or be transformed. While it is possible to identify the broad categories of factors that affect a system's expression of resilience, what resilience looks like will always depend on the variability in risk exposure, the availability of resources, and the desired outcomes of competing systems. A set of seven principles is evident in the way systems manage stress and become more resilient. These principles help to explain whether a system will demonstrate resilience when it experiences a disruption to its functioning. They also show that there are useful commonalities across resilient systems that could be used to better understand and model processes of recovery, adaptation, and transformation. When understood this way, resilience processes show both equifinality and multifinality. Furthermore, as this chapter has shown, the more the concept of resilience is described multisystemically, with all its complexity, the more the concept will be of use to scholars, policymakers, and those designing individual, institutional, and environmental interventions.

Key Messages

1. A multisystemic understanding of resilience explains how the resilience of co-occurring systems are mutually dependent.
2. How a system (whether biological, psychological, social, built, or natural) experiences resilience depends on the variability in the system's exposure to adversity, the availability of resources, and the desired outcomes of competing systems.
3. There are seven principles and five processes that account for the patterns that systems show when maintaining their functioning during periods of disruption and stress.
4. The more the concept of resilience is described multisystemically, the more useful it is when designing research and interventions that address the "wicked" problems that individuals and environments face.

References

Adger, W. N., Barnett, J., Brown, K., Marshall, N., & O'Brien, K. (2013). Cultural dimensions of climate change impacts and adaptation. *Nature Climate Change, 3*, 112–117. doi:10.1038/nclimate1666

Alink, L. R., Cicchetti, D., Kim, J., & Rogosch, F. A. (2012). Longitudinal associations among child maltreatment, social functioning, and cortisol regulation. *Developmental Psychology, 48*(1), 224–236. doi:10.1037/a0024892

Alt, D., & Raichel, N. (2017). *Lifelong citizenship*. Leiden, The Netherlands: Brill.

Annarelli, A., & Nonino, F. (2016). Strategic and operational management of organizational resilience: Current state of research and future directions. *Omega, 62*, 1–18. doi:10.1016/j.omega.2015.08.004

Beckett, C., Maughan, B., Rutter, M., Castle, J., Colvert, E., Groothues, C., . . . Sonuga-Barke, E. J. S. (2006). Do the effects of early severe deprivation on cognition persist into early adolescence? Findings from the English and Romanian Adoptees Study. *Child Development, 77*(3), 696–711. doi:10.1111/j.1467-8624.2006.00898.x

Böbel, T. S., Hackl, S. B., Langgartner, D., Jarczok, M. N., Rohleder, N., Rook, G. A., . . . Reber, S. O. (2018). Less immune activation following social stress in rural vs. urban participants raised with regular or no animal contact, respectively. *PNAS, 115*(20), 5259–5264. doi:10.1073/pnas.1719866115

Boivin, M., Hertzman, C., Barr, R., Boyce, T. Fleming, A., MacMillan, H., . . . Trocmé, N. (2013). *Early childhood development: Adverse experiences and developmental health*. Ottawa, ON: Royal Society of Canada-Canadian Academy of Health Sciences Expert Panel.

Bousquet, F., Botta, A., Alinovi, L., Barreteau, O., Bossio, D., Brown, K., . . . Staver, C. (2016). Resilience and development: Mobilizing for transformation. *Ecology and Society, 21*(3), 40. doi:10.5751/ES-08754-210340

Brown, K. (2016). *Resilience, development and global change*. New York, NY: Routledge.

Cabell, J. F., & Oelofse, M. (2012). An indicator framework for assessing agroecosystem resilience. *Ecology and Society, 17*(1), 18. doi:10.5751/ES-04666-170118

Cox, R. S., & Perry, K. M. E. (2011). Like a fish out of water: Reconsidering disaster recovery and the role of place and social capital in community disaster resilience. *American Journal of Community Psychology, 48*(3–4), 395–411. doi:10.1007/s10464-011-9427-0

Cramer, J., & Krueger, A. B. (2016). Disruptive change in the taxi business: The case of Uber. *American Economic Review, 106*(5), 177–182. doi:10.1257/aer.p20161002

Cutter, S. L. (2016a). The landscape of disaster resilience indicators in the USA. *Natural Hazards*, *80*(2), 741–758. doi:10.1007/s11069-015-1993-2

Cutter, S. L. (2016b). Resilience to what? Resilience for whom? *Geographical Journal*, *182*(2), 110–113. doi:10.1111/geoj.12174

Cutter, S. L., Barnes, L., Berry, M., Burton, C., Evans, E., Tate, E., & Webb, J. (2008). *Community and regional resilience: Perspectives from hazards, disasters, and emergency management* (CARRI Research Report 1). Oak Ridge, TN: Community and Regional Resilience Initiative, National Security Directorate.

Cutuli, J. J., & Herbers, J. E. (2018). Resilience in the context of development: Introduction to the special issue. *Journal of Early Adolescence*, *38*(9), 1205–1214. doi:10.1177/0272431618757680

Dinan, T. G., & Cryan, J. F. (2013). Melancholic microbes: A link between gut microbiota and depression? *Neurogastroenterology and Motility*, *25*(9), 713–719. doi:10.1111/nmo.12198

Doan, S. N., Tardif, T., Miller, A., Olson, S., Kessler, D., Felt, B., & Wang, L. (2016). Consequences of "tiger" parenting: A cross-cultural study of maternal psychological control and children's cortisol stress response. *Developmental Science*, *20*(3), e12404. doi:10.1111/desc.12404

Dowell, S. F., Blazes, D., & Desmond-Hellmann, S. (2016). Four steps to precision public health. *Nature*, *540*(7632), 189–191. doi:10.1038/540189a

Drury, S. S., Mabile, E., Brett, Z. H., Esteves, K., Jones, E., Shirtcliff, E. A., & Theall, K. P. (2014). The association of telomere length with family violence and disruption. *Pediatrics*, *134*(1), e128–137.

Ellis, B. J., & Boyce, W. T. (2011). Differential susceptibility to the environment: Toward an understanding of sensitivity to developmental experiences and context. *Development and Psychopathology*, *23*, 1–5. doi:10.1017/S095457941000060X

Ellis, B. J., & Del Giudice, M. (2014). Beyond allostatic load: Rethinking the role of stress in regulating human development. *Development and Psychopathology*, *26*, 1–20. doi:10.1017/S0954579413000849

Fabricus, C., & Currie, B. (2015). Adaptive co-management. In C. R. Allen & A. S. Garmestani (Eds.), *Adaptive management of social-ecological systems* (pp.147–179). Dordrecht, The Netherlands: Springer.

Folke, C. (2006). Resilience: The emergence of a perspective for social-ecological systems analyses. *Global Environmental Change*, *16*(3), 253–267. doi:10.1016/j.gloenvcha.2006.04.002

Folke, C., Carpenter, S. R., Walker, B., Scheffer, M., Chapin, T., & Rockström, J. (2010). Resilience thinking: Integrating resilience, adaptability and transformability. *Ecology and Society*, *15*(4), 20. http://www.ecologyandsociety.org/vol15/iss4/art20/

Gunderson, L. H., Allen, C. R., & Holling, C. S. (2010). *Foundation of ecological resilience*. Washington, DC: Island Press.

Gunderson, L. H., & Holling, C. S. (Eds.). (2002). *Panarchy: Understanding transformations in human and natural systems*. Washington, DC: Island Press.

Hobfoll, S. (2011). Conservation of resources theory: Its implication for stress, health, and resilience. In S. Folkman (Ed.), *The Oxford handbook of stress, health, and coping* (pp. 127–147). New York, NY: Oxford University Press.

Holling, C. S. (1973). Resilience and stability of ecological systems. *Annual Review of Ecology and Systematics*, *4*(1), 1–23.

Hordge-Freeman, E. (2015). *The color of love: Racial features, stigma, and socialization in black Brazilian families*. Austin, TX: University of Texas Press.

Hutchison, D., & Sterbenz, J. P. G. (2018). Architecture and design for resilient networked systems, computer communications. *Computer Communications*, *131*, 13–21. doi:10.1016/j.comcom.2018.07.028

Jackson, S., & Ferris, T. L. J. (2013). Resilience principles for engineered systems. *Systems Engineering*, *16*(2), 152–164. doi:10.1002/sys.21228

Kaplan, E. K., Collins, C. A., & Tylavsky, F. A. (2017). Cyclical unemployment and infant health. *Economics and Human Biology*, *27*(Part A), 281–288. doi:10.1016/j.ehb.2017.08.001

Lederbogen, F., Kirsch, P., Haddad, L., Streit, F., Tost, H., Schuch, P., . . . Meyer-Lindenberg, A. (2011). City living and urban upbringing affect neural social stress processing in humans. *Nature*, *474*(7352), 498–501. doi:10.1038/nature10190

Lewin, K. (1951). Defining the "field at a given time." In D. Cartwright (Ed.), *Field theory in social science* (pp. 43–59). New York, NY: Harper & Brothers.

Longstaff, P. H., Armstrong, N. J., Perrin, K., Parker, W. M., & Hidek, M. A. (2010). Building resilient communities: A preliminary framework for assessment. *Homeland Security Affairs, 6*(3). https://www.hsaj.org/articles/81

Masten, A. S. (2006). Promoting resilience in development: A general framework for systems of care. In R. J. Flynn, P. M. Dudding, & J. G. Barber (Eds.), *Promoting resilience in child welfare* (pp. 3–17). Ottawa, ON: University of Ottawa Press.

Masten, A. S. (2014). Global perspectives on resilience in children and youth. *Child Development, 85*(1), 6–20. doi:10.1111/cdev.12205

Mishna, F., Khoury-Kassabri, M., Schwan, K., Wiener, J., Craig, W., Beran, T., . . . Daciuk, J. (2016). The contribution of social support to children and adolescents' self-perception: The mediating role of bullying victimization. *Children and Youth Services Review, 63*(C), 120–127. doi:10.1016/j.childyouth.2016.02.013

Noble, K. G., Houston, S. M., Brito, N. H., Bartsch, H., Kan, E., Kuperman, J. M., . . . Sowell, E. R. (2015). Family income, parental education and brain structure in children and adolescents. *Nature Neuroscience, 18*(5), 773–778. doi:10.1038/nn.3983.

Noble, K. G., Norman, M. F., & Farah, M. J. (2005). Neurocognitive correlates of socioeconomic status in kindergarten children. *Developmental Science, 8*(1), 74–87.

Norris, F. H., Sherrieb, K., & Pfefferbaum, B. (2011). Community resilience: Concepts, assessment, and implications for intervention. In S. M. Southwick & B. T. Litz (Eds.), *Resilience and mental health: Challenges across the lifespan* (pp. 162–175). Cambridge, England: Cambridge University Press.

Obradović, J., Bush, N. R., Stamperdahl, J., Adler, N. E., & Boyce, W. T. (2010). Biological sensitivity to context: The interactive effects of stress reactivity and family adversity on socioemotional behavior and school readiness. *Child Development, 81*(1), 270–289. doi:10.1111/j.1467-8624.2009.01394.x

O'Brien, G., & Hope A. (2010). Localism and energy: negotiating approaches to embedding resilience in energy systems. *Energy Policy, 38*, 7550–7558.

Olsson, L., Jerneck, A., Thoren, H., Persson, J., & O'Byrne, D. (2015). Why resilience is unappealing to social science: Theoretical and empirical investigations of the scientific use of resilience. *Science Advances, 1*(4), e1400217. doi:10.1126/sciadv.1400217

Oshri, A., Duprey, E. B., Kogan, S. M., Carlson, M. W., & Liu, S. (2018). Growth patterns of future orientation among maltreated youth: A prospective examination of the emergence of resilience. *Developmental Psychology, 54*(8), 1456–1471. doi:10.1037/dev0000528

Ott, E., & Montgomery, P. (2015). Interventions to improve the economic self-sufficiency and well-being of resettled refugees: A systematic review. *Campbell Systematic Reviews, 11*(4), 1–53. doi:10.4073/csr.2015.4

Priebe, G., & Svedin, C. G. (2008). Child sexual abuse is largely hidden from the adult society: An epidemiological study of adolescent's disclosures. *Child Abuse & Neglect, 32*(12), 1095–1108. doi:10.1016/j.chiabu.2008.04.001

Quinlan, A., Berbés-Blázquez, M., Haider, J. L., & Peterson, G. D. (2015). Measuring and assessing resilience: Broadening understanding through multiple disciplinary perspectives. *Journal of Applied Ecology, 53*(3), 677–687. doi:10.1111/1365-2664.12550

Rook, G. A., & Lowry, C. A. (2008). The hygiene hypothesis and psychiatric disorders. *Trends in Immunology, 29*(4), 150–158. doi:10.1016/j.it.2008.01.002

Rook, G. A., Lowry, C. A., & Raison, C. L. (2013). Microbial "old friends," immunoregulation and stress resilience. *Evolution Medicine and Public Health, 2013*(1), 46–64. doi:10.1093/emph/eot004

Rutter, M. (1987). Psychosocial resilience and protective mechanisms. *American Journal of Orthopsychiatry, 57*(3), 316–331. doi:10.1111/j.1939-0025.1987.tb03541.x

Rutter, M. (2012). Resilience as a dynamic concept. *Development and Psychopathology, 24*(2), 335–344. doi:10.1017/S0954579412000028

Scherer, L. D., Maynard, A., Dolinoy, D. C., Fagerlin, A., & Zikmund-Fisher, B. J. (2014). The psychology of "regrettable substitutions": Examining consumer judgements of bisphenol A and its alternatives. *Health, Risk & Society, 16*(7–8), 649–666, doi:10.1080/13698575.2014.969687

Stanford, J. L., Stanford, C. A., & Grange, J. M. (2001). Environmental echoes. *Science Progress, 84*(2), 105–124. doi:10.3184%2F003685001783239014

System. (2018). *Oxford English Dictionary*. Retrieved from http://www.oed.com.ezproxy.library.dal.ca/view/Entry/196665?redirectedFrom=system#eid

Tol, W. A., Song, S., & Jordans, J. D. (2013). Annual research review: Resilience and mental health in children and adolescents living in areas of armed conflict—A systemic review of findings in low- and middle-income countries. *Journal of Child Psychology and Psychiatry, 54*(4), 445–460. doi:10.1111/jcpp.12053

Ungar, M. (2011). The social ecology of resilience: Addressing contextual and cultural ambiguity of a nascent construct. *American Journal of Orthopsychiatry, 81*(1), 1–17. doi:10.1111/j.1939-0025.2010.01067.x

Ungar, M. (2016). Which counts more? The differential impact of the environment or the differential susceptibility of the individual? *British Journal of Social Work, 47*(5), 1279–1289. doi:10.1093/bjsw/bcw109

Ungar, M. (2018). Systemic resilience: Principles and processes for a science of change in contexts of adversity. *Ecology and Society, 23*(4), 34. doi:10.5751/ES-10385-230434

Ungar, M., & Perry, B. (2012). Violence, trauma and resilience. In C. Vine & R. Alaggia (Eds.), *Cruel but not unusual* (2nd ed., pp. 119–146). Waterloo, ON: Wilfrid Laurier University Press.

Walsh, F. (2012). Facilitating family resilience: Relational resources for positive youth development in conditions of adversity. In M. Ungar (Ed.), *The social ecology of resilience: A handbook of theory and practice* (pp. 173–185). New York, NY: Springer.

Ward, T., & Langlands, R. L. (2009). Repairing the rupture: Restorative justice and the rehabilitation of offenders. *Aggression and Violent Behavior, 14*(3), 205–214. doi:10.1016/j.avb.2009.03.001

Werner, E. E., & Smith, R. S. (2001). *Journeys from childhood to midlife: Risk, resilience, and recovery*. Ithaca, NY: Cornell University Press.

Woodcraft, S., Bacon, N., Caistor-Arendar, L., & Hackett, T. (2012). *Design for social sustainability: A framework for creating thriving new communities*. London, England: Social Life/Young Foundation.

Xu, L., & Kajikawa, Y. (2017). An integrated framework for resilience research: A systematic review based on citation network analysis. *Sustainability Science, 13*(1), 235–254. doi:10.1007/s11625-017-0487-4

SECTION 1

Human Biology and Social Environments

Bringing a Neurobiological Perspective to Resilience

Nicole Bush and Danielle S. Roubinov

Introduction

The concept of resilience has become remarkably popular in recent years, across a range of academic fields and within the media. This popularity stems, in part, from a culture shift toward wanting to focus on positive outcomes. Understanding within the psychological and social sciences has been based largely upon the rich conceptualization and articulation of leaders such as Ann Masten (2015; Masten & Barnes, 2018; Masten, Best, & Garmezy, 1990) and Michael Rutter (1987, 2012), and more recently, Michael Ungar (2006, 2015). In this chapter, we leverage those expert frameworks and describe their application to children's mental and physical health outcomes, with a predominant focus on describing the growing literature on *neurobiological* indicators of risk, protection, and resilience across early development.

Brief Introduction to Resilience

Our review of neurobiological resilience must be couched in the larger framework of resilience theory and research, briefly reviewed here. Although definitions vary, many social scientists agree that resilience can be defined as the capacity of a dynamic system to withstand or recover from significant disturbances that threaten its adaptive function, viability, or development (Masten, 2014). Key to this definition within our fields is that a challenging or threatening disturbance must occur, which can be an acute or chronic adversity or an accumulation of risk factors that becomes threatening. Others have emphasized that when explicitly considering a child's capacity to resist the effects of adverse exposures, one must evaluate the capacity of that child's formal and informal social ecological networks to facilitate positive development after stress; importantly, individuals and their environments interact to optimize development and individuals' capacity, within the constraints of opportunities and resources in their communities (Ungar, 2011). These definitions and conditions highlight the role of micro- and macrolevel factors in culture and society, in addition to individual agency, in different constellations that contribute to the chances for resilience (Ungar, 2013).

After an individual experiences adversity, a range of potential patterns of outcomes reflecting resilience can occur. First, one may experience a major adversity without any change in functioning, which would be considered "buffered" from the adversity. High-visibility studies of adverse childhood experiences (ACEs) have focused on how many individuals experience trauma and the negative outcomes that ensue (Hughes et al., 2017). However, a significant proportion (sometimes even the majority) of children who experienced trauma are without the poor outcomes examined, suggesting resilience to the experience of ACEs, at least in the measured domains. Second, one may have an initial decline in functioning or increase in problems, but a later return to pre-adversity levels; such a recovery response suggests the individual became resilient to the adversity after some time. Importantly, resilience may not just be the absence of a "bad" outcome in the context of adversity, but can also be reflected in the presence of "good" outcomes, such as positive health and well-being. Thus, third, one may also demonstrate increased positive outcomes or higher-than-previous functioning after an adversity either as an immediate response to the threat or after time, often referred to as "posttraumatic growth."

Resilience is not a trait—it is dynamic, arising from the interaction of many systems across many levels (Gottlieb & Halpern, 2002; Waddington, 1966) and the capacity for adaptation to adversity is distributed across systems. Within a system, main effects of factors that are risks, assets, and promoters can accumulate in a summative fashion to influence a child's developmental outcome. However, in the remarkable symphony of human social processes, interactions can matter more than main effects. Social or biological factors within a system can enhance vulnerability to the effects of adversity or confer protection, moderating the effects of exposure. In line with this chapter's focus on biological factors, we emphasize biological moderators. For example, biological sensitivity to context (BSC; Boyce, 2015; Bush & Boyce, 2016; Ellis, Boyce, Belsky, Bakermans-Kranenburg, & van Ijzendoorn, 2011) and differential susceptibility (DS; Belsky & Pluess, 2009, 2013; also see Popham, McEwen, & Pluess, 2020) theories articulate how individual differences in stress-relevant biology can make children more or less sensitive to both positive and negative influences in the environment, with "more sensitive" children demonstrating the worst outcomes in contexts of adversity but the best outcomes in advantaged environments. In contrast, "less sensitive" children are more likely to be buffered from adversity and demonstrate greater resilience, but they also do not demonstrate advantage in more optimal contexts. Empirical tests of BSC and DS have demonstrated that such sensitivity to context can be reflected in a variety of physiological systems and genomic markers. We provide highlights of this influential work later in the chapter. Importantly, even though this BSC or DS framework can imply a trait-like susceptibility to environment, each circumstance of sensitivity is system and environmentally dependent, will vary by outcome considered, and thus does not reflect a cross-situation or system trait of biological resilience.

How Resilience Can Be Understood Systemically

Advances in the study of childhood resilience are not the product of a single discipline. Rather, formative resilience research has spanned fields of genetics, biology, and neuroscience as well as psychology, sociology, and public health. Moreover, it is arguably not simply the additive products of various disciplines, but the *interdisciplinary* collaborations across fields that have yielded the greatest progress in understanding the factors that promote and sustain processes of resilience early in life.

The perspective of childhood resilience as a multisystemic construct has its theoretical roots in broader frameworks that have recognized the interactive influences of multiple contexts on human development. One of the most highly regarded and well-referenced of these frameworks is Bronfenbrenner's bioecological model of human development, which describes how systems ranging from the individual and the microsystem (e.g., family, peers, school) to the macrosystem (e.g., social attitudes and ideologies) guide human development (see Figure 2.1). Bronfenbrenner posited that human development occurs not through the independent activities within these subsystems, but through "complex reciprocal interactions between an active, evolving biopsychological human organisms and the persons, objects, and symbols in its immediate external environment" (Bronfenbrenner & Morris, 1998, p. 996; Masten & Monn, 2015). Guided by this framework, research has provided evidence of how such interactive effects may operate to promote children's resilience. In several empirical examinations of a diverse community sample of kindergarten children (the Peers and Wellness Study), multilevel variables have emerged as powerful protective factors for children reared under conditions of risk. For example, children were buffered from the negative physical health consequences of low family socioeconomic status (SES) by higher quality, more resourced neighborhoods (Roubinov, Hagan, Boyce, Adler, & Bush, 2018) and lower levels of negativity in the parent–child relationship (Hagan, Roubinov, Adler, Boyce, & Bush, 2016). Across the sample, offspring exposed to harsh parenting were more likely to exhibit hostile, aggressive behavior; however, risk was reduced if children had warmer, more positive relationships with their peers and teachers (Roubinov, Boyce, & Bush, 2018). In these examples, the poor physical or health outcomes that would be expected on the basis of early family adversity were significantly diminished by processes originating within another developmental context (e.g., neighborhood, school, peer).

As illustrated by the aforementioned examples, resilience research has mainly focused on the contribution of psychosocial and environmental factors, with limited attention to the potential role of intraindividual biological factors (Curtis & Cicchetti, 2003), perhaps owing to the once prevalent, but largely superficial distinction between biological and psychological domains (Cicchetti & Rogosch, 2009). An abundance of literature has documented for decades how varied biological factors interact with environmental exposures to elevate the risk for psychopathology (Shonkoff, Boyce, & McEwen, 2009); a logical extension of such work would suggest that the pathways to resilient functioning are similarly multiply influenced by the dynamic activity of biological and environmental systems across many levels of analysis. Yet, it is only in recent years that research has adopted a more integrative perspective in which physiological and neurobiological systems (and their interactions with each other

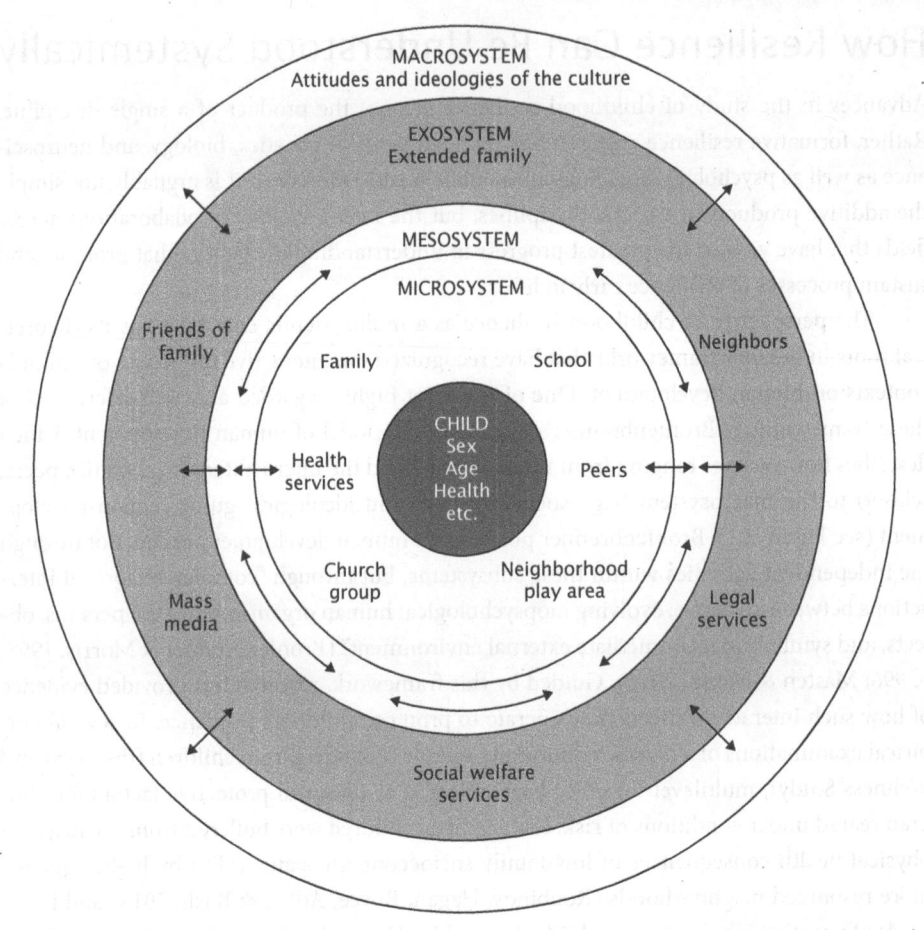

FIGURE 2.1 Bronfenbrenner's bioecological model. From sociocultural risk: Dangers to competence, by J. Garbarino. In C. B. Kopp & J. B. Krakow (Eds.), *The child: Development in a social context* (pp. 630–685). Copyright © 1982 by Addison-Wesley Longman Publishing Company, Inc. Reprinted with permission.

and the environment) are viewed as integral to processes of psychological resilience. Notably, indicators of biological functioning may be viewed as not only predictors or promoters of resilient processes, but reflections of resilient functioning.

There are several potential advantages of examining biological indicators of risk and resilience. Self- or proxy reports of symptoms and functioning are heavily influenced by the reporter's awareness, biases, and social desirability, whereas physiology is more precisely quantified in a standardized manner across individuals, regions, and cultures. Another advantage is that a focus on physiological changes and their recovery allows neutrality regarding whether resilience is achieved via automatic, unconscious processes or intentional, conscious efforts of the individual, which can provide opportunities for tracking markers of resilience that are agnostic to theoretical or political goals. Evidence of the biological impact of adversity can minimize perceptions of psychological weakness and victim blaming, and policymakers may be motivated to promote biological resilience for its potential to improve healthcare costs and economic opportunities at a population level. Certain biological outcomes may be considered intermediary variables that predict longer term physical and psychological health, thus it is possible to consider neural, physiological, and other biological factors as indicative of the degree to which resilient processes are occurring. In this manner, biomarkers of risk and resilience can be "canaries in the coalmine" or, more positively, migrating birds whose return predicts the coming spring, allowing communities to intervene early to prevent trajectories of decline and poor health and create the conditions for positive development as children age.

Brief Overview of Stress-Relevant Neurobiological Systems and their Indicators

Although a comprehensive review is outside the scope of the current chapter, we briefly describe the primary biological systems that are involved in stress responsivity (and by extension, resilience). The autonomic nervous system (ANS) is comprised of two branches: the parasympathetic nervous system (PNS), which is conventionally described in terms of its role in reducing arousal and promoting restoration ("rest and digest") and the sympathetic nervous system (SNS), which is known for its capacity to mobilize the body to respond to stress through physiological activation ("flight or fight"; Gunnar & Vazquez, 2006; Lovallo & Sollers, 2007). Individuals' reactivity (change from baseline) and recovery (time it takes to return to baseline levels) within their ANS can be assessed in response to standardized challenges by attaching noninvasive electrodes that measure indices of activation at rest, during the stressors, and after the stressor has ended (for video example, see Bush, Caron, Blackburn, & Alkon, 2016). Compared to the faster acting PNS and SNS, the hypothalamic–pituitary–adrenal (HPA) axis enacts a more delayed, longer-term response to stress through a cascade of hormonal processes that culminates in the release of cortisol (Del Giudice, Ellis, & Shirtcliff, 2011). Key functions of cortisol include mobilizing energy, enhancing alertness, facilitating memory formation, and deploying the physiological resources needed to adequately respond to stress (Sapolsky, Romero, & Munck, 2000). Cortisol can be assessed in circulating blood or, less invasively, in saliva samples collected before and after stressors (Gunnar, Talge, & Herrera, 2009). More recently, cortisol levels in hair have been used to reflect HPA axis activity over the three months prior to hair collection, allowing for indication of more chronic levels of activation or blunting/suppression (Gray et al., 2018).

In addition to well-studied effects of adversity and resilience with the PNS, SNS, and HPA axis, increasingly evidence is pointing to the utility of other biomarkers, including indicators of immune functioning (Dantzer, Cohen, Russo, & Dinan, 2018; Segerstrom & Miller, 2004), cellular aging (Shalev et al., 2013), epigenetic modifications to DNA that can alter gene activity (Boyce & Kobor, 2015; Choi, Stein, Dunn, Koenen, & Smoller, 2019; Provençal & Binder, 2015; Romens, McDonald, Svaren, & Pollak, 2015), and brain structure and activity (Bick & Nelson, 2016; Carnevali, Koenig, Sgoifo, & Ottaviani, 2018; Miller et al., 2018). Interested readers are referred to various reviews for a deeper discussion on the myriad of biological systems involved in the neurobiology of resilience to stress (e.g., Charney, 2004; Osório, Probert, Jones, Young, & Robbins, 2017) and to more lay-accessible reviews such as those in social work (Hunter, Gray, & McEwen, 2018). A recent review in the adult psychiatry literature (Walker, Pfingst, Carnevali, Sgoifo, & Nalivaiko, 2017) suggests that immune system responses to laboratory challenges (e.g., cytokines) and lab-based in vitro immune cell assay are some of the most promising resilience biomarker candidates, yet both require blood draws and complex laboratory efforts, which may inhibit their realistic use in samples of young children, low-income communities, or developing countries. However, this is shifting as the science advances, alternative collection methods are developed, and cultural uptake around the value of biology increases. One example of this is reflected by the increasing use of biomarkers by anthropologists, such as using dried blood spots for population-based research, even in remote, undeveloped regions (McDade, Williams, & Snodgrass, 2007).

Although stress response systems are often studied in isolation of each other, the well-supported concept of *allostasis* describes how multiple biological systems work together in a complex, integrated manner to promote the body's adaptation to threat or challenge (McEwen, 2007). Allostasis functions to achieve stability through change and is an essential, life-supporting process that underlies physiological homeostasis. Allostasis can be achieved quickly, via automatic processes, or more slowly through intentional adaptations, such as cognitive reappraisal or meditation after a stressor—both types of responses promote resilience in the face of challenge to achieve allostasis. However, exposure to repeated or chronic stressors may lead to a state of dysregulated physiological responses termed *allostatic load* that is associated with elevated risk for disease and poor health across the lifespan (McEwen, 2017; McEwen & Wingfield, 2010).

Evidence for the Role of Neurobiology in Resilience Processes

A limited, but growing body of research has incorporated biological measures into multilevel analyses of resilience. We highlight exemplars of such research in the following section, although we recognize that several may fall short of the most optimal representations of resilience, given the scarcity of research in this area.

Family

Attachment relationships are likely the most primary source of neurobiological resilience for young children, as development regulatory systems are dependent on the primary caregiver (Bowlby, 1988; Thompson, Kiff, & McLaughlin, 2018) and stress-buffering social influences reside most proximally within the family and childcare context (Hostinar & Gunnar, 2015). A large body of animal research has established the remarkable causal effects of higher quality parenting practices on offspring biological, behavioral, and emotional outcomes (Meaney, 2001) and the manner in which postnatal care can buffer offspring from risk (Fish et al., 2004). Although ethics prohibit experimental manipulation of parenting and care provision, well-designed observational studies in humans also demonstrate that parenting behaviors can promote child resilience. For example, more sensitive and responsive parenting buffers infants from the effects of prenatal stress (Conradt & Ablow, 2010), with effects that may persist to ameliorate the effects of childhood adversity on a range of adult health outcomes (Farrell, Simpson, Carlson, Englund, & Sung, 2017). Parent–child attachment has also been found to associate with epigenetic profiles of late adolescents within genes related to stress reactivity (Jones-Mason, Allen, Bush, & Hamilton, 2016). As another example, kindergarten children with better parental relationships were protected from the negative effects of socioeconomic adversity on their physical health (Hagan et al., 2016). Although research of the potential protective effects of high-quality parental relationships predominantly focuses on mothers, emerging work highlights the importance of studying the father role. In a sample of low-income, Mexican origin families, infants with higher PNS activity at rest exhibited more behavior problems at two years of age in the context of lower father engagement. However, behavior problems did not vary by infant resting PNS levels among those exposed to higher levels of father engagement (Luecken, Somers, & Roubinov, 2020). Current societal shifts toward increasing paternal time in childcare activities (Hofferth & Lee, 2015) obligate future research to explore dynamic interactions between fathering and children's biological functioning in the prediction of developmental outcomes.

Temperament/Personality

Individual differences in temperament, biologically based behavioral, and emotional differences in reactivity and regulation that are present at birth but shaped over time (Rothbart, Ahadi, & Evans, 2000), have been shown to meaningfully alter trajectories of risk and resilience for child outcomes. For example, children higher in self-regulation are less likely to demonstrate disruptive behaviors and emotional dysregulation in the context of family adversity (Lengua, Bush, Long, Kovacs, & Trancik, 2008) and less likely to report symptoms of depression and anxiety in the presence of negative parenting (Kiff, Lengua, & Bush, 2011). Children high in negative emotionality (e.g., fearfulness, difficult temperament) are prone to depression or anxiety and demonstrate elevated biological risk factors (Goldsmith & Lemery, 2000); however, as a striking example of the need to consider all individual differences in context and system, such children are also less likely to engage in antisocial activities and display conduct disorder (Nigg, 2006), even when raised in families/neighborhoods with many risk factors. This contrasting pattern of findings reveals how one individual factor might be considered a "resilience trait" but is highly situation-dependent.

Physiology

Physiological reactivity demonstrates risk and protective effects that parallel temperament. For example, children who show lower ANS or HPA axis reactivity to standardized stress-evoking challenges are often buffered from risk and show protection from the effects of family adversity or low SES on physical health, socioemotional behavior, and school readiness, whereas their more reactive counterparts demonstrate worse outcomes in those adverse contexts (Conradt, Measelle, & Ablow, 2013; Hagan et al., 2016; Obradovic, Bush, Stamperdahl, Adler, & Boyce, 2010; Rudolph, Troop-Gordon, & Granger, 2011). Although physiology may interact with environmental contexts to exacerbate or buffer risk, it may also be the case that physiological factors are the product of dynamic factors across multiple resilience-related systems. As an example of such cross-system resilience, research has observed that "risky child temperaments" in kindergarten (high negative affect, overcontrolled) were associated with elevated levels of children's daily cortisol, but children within classrooms where teachers provided high levels of motivational support were buffered from this potentially harmful association between temperament and stress physiology (Roubinov, Hagan, Boyce, Essex, & Bush, 2017).

Brain Structure and Function

As brain imaging techniques become more accessible and understanding of brain structure and function relevant to the study of resilience advances, evidence points to the growing value of examining resilience within the brain. The capacity for social support to buffer children from the effects of adversity increasingly appears to operate through neural substrates associated with effective self-regulation (Hostinar & Gunnar, 2015). Miller et al. (2018) recently found that urban adolescents who displayed greater brain connectivity (assessed by functional magnetic resonance imaging) within an area of the brain that facilitates self-control, reinterpretation of threatening events, and suppression of unwanted emotional imagery were protected from the harmful cardiometabolic effects of living in high-violence neighborhoods. These findings suggest functional connectivity in specific brain regions may be a neurobiological contributor to resilience. In a compelling study of high-neglect conditions within Romanian orphanages, children were randomized to either high-quality foster care or continued care in the institution. At age eight, children in the early intervention condition demonstrated more normative brain development (white matter microstructure), showing resilience to the effects of early deprivation on their brains' structural development (Bick et al., 2015).

Genetics

Individual differences in genetic make-up have also been shown to promote resilience for children. One of the most robust associations in the health disparities literature is that children of low SES are at increased risk, in a linear fashion, for being overweight or obese. Among children with a specific genotype related to oxytocin hormone regulation however, there was no relation between SES and body mass index, revealing likely metabolic and behavioral-emotional genomic pathways for protection from that risk (Bush, Adler, & Boyce, 2011). Genetic differences have also been shown to buffer adolescents from the effects of unsupportive parenting on their self-regulatory abilities (Belsky & Beaver, 2011). An increasing wealth of evidence shows that children's variation in specific genes, such as those regulating dopamine and serotonin, can enhance their sensitivity to intervention and promote resilient outcomes (Belsky & van Ijzendoorn, 2015). For example, behavioral benefit for Romanian orphans who were randomized to the foster care condition described earlier appears to differ depending upon children's genetic sensitivity, promoting greater resilience in some children (Drury et al., 2012). In another example, adolescents' cumulative counts of specific "sensitivity" genetic variants (polygenic scores) predicted who would benefit most from a smoking prevention and cessative intervention (Musci et al., 2015). The lure of genomics for explanations about who may be buffered most from adversity or benefit most from interventions is strong, yet issues around placing emphasis on this immutable individual difference factor are controversial (Belsky & van Ijzendoorn, 2015), and this work should be considered with caution as genetics are one of myriad factors influencing systemic resilience.

Across all these systems, or layers of context or process, it is important to note that none can be considered in isolation. A child lacking protective factors in her HPA axis functioning may have resilience-promoting differences in her ANS response to stress, nutritional advantages that influence the expression of her genes related to stress regulation, or an exceptionally supportive classroom environment that offsets her risk for neurobiological deficits and subsequent mental and physical health risks related to chronic adversity. We have attempted to highlight various layers of a child's internal biology that might be affected by adversity or protective/promotive against risk, yet it is typically only examined at one cross-section of the complex system within and external to the child. Emerging multisystem physiology models hold promise for advancing understanding in this realm (see, e.g., Roubinov, Boyce, Lee, & Bush, 2020).

Issues of Developmental Timing and Domain

Beyond the examination of various layers and systems, it is critical to consider the additional influence of time. First, timing in development affects a child's sensitivity to the influence of adversity or factors promoting neurobiological resilience (Hunter et al., 2018; Masten & Barnes, 2018). Data from the intervention with Romanian orphans highlight how critical earlier timing of adoption placement was for children to demonstrate beneficial effects on their biology and behavioral and cognitive functioning (Almas et al., 2012; Bick et al., 2015; Nelson et al., 2007). A second key factor is that development involves the progressive changing and growth of systems, with processes at one time point having cascading effects and influences on trajectories of later functioning and well-being. There has been a tendency in the resilience literature to overinterpret findings at one period of development (and in one system). Given the considerable variation in trajectories of development, and the ever-changing social/environmental exposures with which a child interacts as he or she matures, it is critical to consider development and timing as co-dependent dimensions of resilience. Factors might promote resilience in the short term, but have long-term trade-offs that are maladaptive for other, later outcomes—for example, the body's physiological adaptation to stress in the short term that leads to allostatic load later is one version of this (McEwen, 2007). Another example comes from work showing children with high cortisol and blood pressure exhibited lower concurrent internalizing symptoms than peers; however, the same physiological pattern was associated with greater symptomatology two years later (Hastings et al., 2011). In a third manner, there are specific windows of risk or opportunity across development, or sensitive periods when plasticity is surging, when conditions converge for change, and when systems are in flux or unstable (Shonkoff et al., 2009). In light of these issues, the understanding and promotion of biological resilience requires addressing unique needs by developmental period. A small body of evidence informs this area. For example, prenatal stress effects on offspring physiology may be best mitigated by social support for mothers (Racine et al., 2018; also see Chapter 3 of this volume on perinatal mental health) or early postnatal sensitive parenting (Conradt & Ablow, 2010; Ham & Tronick, 2006). Concerns during early to middle childhood may benefit from a focus on peer support (Roubinov, Boyce, et al., 2018) and promotive classroom environments (Roubinov et al., 2017), whereas promotion of resilience to trauma in adolescence requires developmentally-sensitive approaches that incorporate adolescents needs for confidentiality and emerging independence (Soleimanpour, Geierstanger, & Brindis, 2017). More longitudinal research is needed for a richer understanding of the role of developmental timing in biological resilience.

It is also critical for readers to understand that factors promoting resilience in one domain (e.g., psychological) may not promote resilience in another/all other domain/s (e.g., physiological). This is one reason to carefully consider biomarkers of resilience. A key illustration of this is the idea of "skin-deep resilience." Brody et al. (2013) found that rural Black youth from high-cumulative-risk backgrounds who showed positive psychosocial functioning at 19 also displayed higher "allostatic load," the multisystem biological "wear and tear" described earlier. This group later found that, although certain Black individuals from disadvantaged backgrounds showed successful psychosocial functioning in terms of educational attainment, symptoms of depression, and quality of relationships, they were more likely to contract infectious illness in an experimental exposure paradigm, revealing a "double-edged sword" to their apparent resilience (Miller, Cohen, Janicki-Deverts, Brody, & Chen, 2016). They also found that Black and White high-striving adolescents were more likely to report positive psychosocial outcomes at age 29 than their lower-striving counterparts; however, among those identified as high-strivers, Black adolescents from disadvantaged backgrounds had greater risk for physical health problems in adulthood than Black adolescents from lower-risk backgrounds (Brody, Yu, Miller, & Chen, 2016). This is in line with the long-standing weathering hypothesis (Geronimus, 1992), which argues that Black Americans exposed to high rates of chronic stress, such as that related to racism, must engage in sustained high-effort coping, which although protective in the short run, increases wear and tear on physiological systems. A key examination from this perspective demonstrated that in the American context, the health biomarker profile of accomplished Blacks was worse than for Whites or less-accomplished Blacks, particularly for females, providing evidence for disparities in chronic disease risk that were dependent upon outcome and which biological system was examined (Geronimus, Hicken, Keene, & Bound, 2006). Evidence that resilience in psychosocial outcomes does not necessarily extend to skin-deep resilience is a core finding supporting the value of examining biology in those who have experienced significant adversity, particularly early in life.

Biological Resilience in a Culturally Sensitive Framework

Social and cultural values assume a key role in Bronfenbrenner's bioecological model and are represented by the most encompassing layer of nested environmental influences on child development. More recently, Ungar's work has articulated the manner in which culture is core to defining and promoting resilience (e.g., Ungar, 2013). Others provide a comprehensive introduction to the newly emerging field of "cultural neurobiology," with a specific focus on psychophysiological stress systems (Doane, Sladek, & Adam, 2018). Here, we introduce select examples of culturally salient resilience processes in biological markers.

Empirical studies have identified values unique to particular communities that may operate to promote resilience processes. For example, familism is conceptualized as one of the defining Latino cultural values, representing a strong identification with and attachment to immediate and extended family (Sabogal et al., 1987). Familism values may operate in a protective fashion by espousing the provision of economic and emotional support to family members and a sense of loyalty and respect within family relations (Germán, Gonzales, & Dumka, 2008). Illustratively, bicultural adolescents who endorse high orientation to both Anglo and Mexican orientation have been shown to exhibit a stronger, more adaptive cortisol response to a laboratory stressor compared to adolescents who endorsed high levels of Anglo orientation only (Gonzales et al., 2018). Similar values emphasize the primacy of family/social ties that exist in other cultural contexts (e.g., communalism among African Americans and filial piety among Asian Americans) and may also operate to buffer minority individuals from the negative consequences of physiological stress response systems that are chronically activated by discriminatory practices, racism, neighborhood violence, and other daily stressors disproportionally experienced by individuals of nonmajority culture groups (Doane et al., 2018).

In addition to defining unique factors that promote resilience within a particular community, social and cultural values may *redefine* a particular construct as contributing to resilience in a given environment when it may otherwise operate in a risk-promoting fashion. For example, greater levels of restrictive, controlling parenting have been positively associated with early behavior problems among White offspring; however, this relation has been negative or nonsignificant among African American children (Deater-Decker & Dodge, 1997). More restrictive parenting has also been associated with fewer upper respiratory and febrile illnesses among minority, but not White children (Roubinov, Bush, Adler, & Boyce, 2018). Differences in children's appraisal of such parental behaviors and what is considered normative or functional within varied sociocultural contexts may help explain the mechanisms underlying these cultural differences (Soenens, Vansteenkiste, & Van Petegem, 2015).

Finally, the long reach of the cultural context may extend to influence the very way in which purported resilience-promoting factors relate to health outcomes within different communities. As previously discussed, a growing body of research finds evidence of skin-deep resilience among at-risk African American youth who were followed longitudinally from childhood through adulthood (Brody et al., 2016; Miller, Yu, Chen, & Brody, 2015). These studies observed that factors traditionally conceptualized as promoting resilience (e.g., high educational aspirations, persistence, optimism) were associated with poorer physiological and physical health despite more adaptive psychosocial health, perhaps due to the unique features of the cultural context. More specifically, it was hypothesized that maintaining positive *outward* functioning amid the systematic adversities associated with poverty and racial inequities may have exacted an *internal* toll on physiological functioning, possibly via excessive activation of stress response systems (Brody et al., 2013). This interpretive framework is also informed by John Henryism, a construct named for an African

American railroad worker of that name who exerted remarkable physical strength to beat a mechanical drill, only to die soon after from mental and physical exhaustion (James, Hartnett, & Kalsbeek, 1983).

Intervention/Reversibility

The dynamic and rapidly changing nature of early developmental periods may make it difficult to use sharply defined diagnostic classifications of psychopathology to assess and identify children in need of intervention (Boyce et al., 1995), and stress-related diseases do not typically manifest in childhood, although their initial roots may be laid during this period. For this reason, elucidating intermediate, presyndromal neurobiological risk factors offers utility for predicting the onset—and intervening in the development—of adversity-induced physical and mental health problems. Moreover, although it is preferable to prevent harm from occurring, it is critical that resilience science focuses on how we might reverse biological or psychosocial risk trajectories/harms through intervention (resilience after the fact). Understanding the biological processes that influence pathology and moderate intervention effects can contribute to tailored programs, answering questions of *for whom* and *which treatment* enhances or promotes resilience (Cicchetti & Curtis, 2007). However, intervention research has predominantly focused upon bolstering the supportive factors that are *external* to the child. Early Head Start and Head Start are some of the largest and most highly researched examples of such programming, which have been shown to improve developmental outcomes for infants, toddlers, and preschool children from economically disadvantaged backgrounds through home visits, parent education, case management, and other supportive services (Anderson et al., 2003; Love et al., 2005). There is some good evidence for the "reversibility" of harm in biological systems, although much more research is needed. An early harbinger is the work of Phil Fisher and colleagues who found that maltreated children who were in a randomized foster care intervention, compared to foster care as usual, were protected from expected cortisol dysregulation after placement in a new home (Fisher, Van Ryzin, & Gunnar, 2011). Their intervention trial also produced evidence that it is possible to impact many areas that have been negatively affected by early stress beyond the child's HPA axis activity, including child problem behavior, attachment to caregivers, and caregiver stress, all of which affect multiple systems/levels.

Informed by theoretical and empirical research on early neurobiological functioning and attachment relationships, Mary Dozier and colleagues developed the Attachment and Biobehavioral Catch-Up (ABC) program for infants and toddlers in high-risk family environments. The intervention focuses on improving parental sensitivity, responsivity, and other environmental inputs to children's developing stress physiology. In a series of randomized controlled trials, children who received ABC were shown to demonstrate more adaptive regulatory activity within the ANS (Tabachnick, Raby, Goldstein, Zajac, & Dozier, 2019) and HPA axis (Bernard, Dozier, Bick, & Gordon, 2015; Bernard, Hostinar, & Dozier, 2015), as well as more normative patterns of neural functioning (Bick, Palmwood, Zajac, Simons, & Dozier, 2019) compared to children in a control condition.

Another notable illustration of how an intervention can affect multiple systems/levels comes from the MAMAS study, a longitudinal trial examining the effects of a mindfulness-based stress reduction intervention during pregnancy on maternal well-being and health. Compared to a matched comparison group of low-income pregnant women, women in the intervention group showed decreases in stress and depression during pregnancy that were sustained through 18-months postpartum (Epel et al., 2019; Felder et al., 2018). This finding showed highly stressed women could fare better, in terms of mental health, in response to an intervention. Impressively, resilience for maternal mental health was also associated with a women's level of healthcare utilization for her infant in its first year of life (Roubinov, Felder, et al., 2018).

Importantly, the aforementioned intervention examples all focused on dyadic or family factors even though that their impacts ranged across multiple levels of outcomes and systems. Investigation of intervention programs to promote reversibility of biological vulnerabilities for health problems later in life is a remarkably promising current area of research (Bush & Aschbacher, 2019).

Challenges and Tension in Understandings of Resilience Processes Moving Ahead

One challenge for the field is the inconsistent use of the term *resilience* and confusion about related constructs. Social scientists have used the term to refer to an individual's "ability" to succeed, a style or way of being in the world (a "resilient personality"), and a process (our definition). As previously noted, we emphasize that resilience is not a trait and differs markedly from trait constructs such as "grit" (Duckworth & Gross, 2014), which is defined as the tendency to sustain interest and effort toward long-term goals and defer short-term gratification. Trait definitions are least systemic in their thinking because labels of *resilient type* or *high in a resilience-factor* do not consider the myriad outcomes across development and contexts with potential divergent functioning, the manner in which a child reaches a successful outcome at the cost of burdening a parent in its system, or ignoring the time-course issue that may bring resilience now but put the child at risk for later health problems.

Another core challenge for the field involves measurement. In social sciences, some have used a single questionnaire item (Bethell, Newacheck, Hawes, & Halfon, 2014), whereas others have developed cross-cultural questionnaires to assess resilience processes (Liebenberg, Ungar, & LeBlanc, 2013; Ungar & Liebenberg, 2011). Others have developed models outlining steps necessary to determine resilience (Masten, 2011; Masten & Obradovic, 2006; Rutter, 2012). Just as has been done with ACEs where children receive a score for each adversity type they have experienced, researchers have created counts of "resilience assets" using a cumulative exposure-type count. For example, one group quantified cumulative counts of community assets, including being treated fairly, supportive childhood friends, being given opportunities to use your abilities, and access to a trusted adult and having someone to look up to, and found that children with higher counts demonstrated better outcomes vs. children with assets in a single domain (Bellis et al., 2018). Paralleling efforts in the questionnaire domain, researchers have begun to move beyond single-system, single biomarker indicators and are attempting to create biological indices of neurobiological resilience. Although the previously reviewed data points to promising biological indicators, there are currently no established robust biomarkers of resilience, as all proposed biomarkers currently lack evidence for consistent discriminative power (Walker et al., 2017). For these reasons, we need more research that explores relations between these potential indicators of biological resilience and psychosocial/psychological resilience. Even more so, there are not multisystem indices of resilience that would reflect the complexity of the myriad of layers and systems required to understand vulnerability and recovery or biological thriving. Of course, substantial economic and public health advantages would come from identifying individuals susceptible to risk or intervention prospectively to target resilience-enhancing interventions, however such identifying neurobiological profiles are yet to be determined (Bush & Aschbacher, in press).

Another major deficit in the field is the typical lack of measurement of positive factors to ascertain what multi-level conditions promote resilience, as well as resilience reflected by greater levels of positive outcomes (rather than the absence of risky ones), such as social competence, although this is shifting (Bush & Bibbins-Domingo, 2019). A comprehensive view of multisystem resilience requires knowing that although an adversity-exposed child may show a risky profile of stress biomarkers and behavioral outcomes, she may exhibit resilience in other systems, such as better expression of anti-inflammatory markers, greater circulating oxytocin (bonding hormone) and better academic competence.

Confronting the origins of disparities in neurobiology or physical and mental health problems early in life is more likely to produce desired positive outcomes than attempting to modify health-related behaviors or improve access to healthcare in adulthood (Shonkoff et al., 2009). Policymakers can play a major role in advancing neurobiological resilience early in life at the population level. For example, the American Academy of Pediatrics has recently emphasized the need to screen children for early social determinants of health during primary care visits (American Academy of Pediatrics, 2016), and subsequently their organization and others have provided recommendations for pediatric practitioners to leverage modifiable factors that can promote resilience (American Academy of Pediatrics, 2019; Traub & Boynton-Jarrett, 2017).

Principles to Guide Future Research

Our goal for the current chapter was to review and provide evidence for the inclusion of biology as part of a comprehensive, systemic understanding of resilience. The extant evidence is promising, but very limited, and future resilience research is tasked to integrate the complexities of biological functioning in a sophisticated manner that will advance the field. With this in mind, we offer the following guidelines for ongoing studies of biological resilience:

1. In recognition of rapid developmental change that occurs in the early years of life, biological functioning should be measured at multiple timepoints, particularly before, during,

and after periods of transition. It is important to remember that the implications of a biomarker may shift over time such that short-term adaptive functioning or purported biological resilience at any given stage may be associated with longer-term poor outcomes.
2. Consider the ways in which biological functioning may be operating to predict resilience in the context of adversity (direct relation), shape the nature of relations between another environmental/biological system and an outcome (moderated relation), and/or serve as an indicator of resilient functioning in and of itself.
3. Unlike established medical biological indicators such as blood pressure or hemoglobin A1C, to date, there are not established cut points or "thresholds" within the biomarkers described here that indicate a particular child is suffering, adapting, or thriving; a value that is atypically high for one child may be normative or reflect health for a different child. When research includes samples across the early life course developmental stages and represents children of all races, ethnicities, and SES, clarity on optimal values may be achieved. Until then, major changes within children will be helpful to indicate impact, and values relative to other same aged children in their communities may be useful.
4. Interpretation of any single measure of biological functioning requires careful consideration of context—environmental, social, cultural, and the interactions therein. Even a biological value conventionally be interpreted as dysregulated may reflect an adaptive response within a given context.
5. There is no single measure of biological functioning that can serve as an indicator or predictor of resilient functioning. In addition to the need to consider context, biological systems are optimally studied in terms of their relations to and interactions with other biological systems (i.e., allostasis, multisystem resilience).
6. The absence of adaptive or resilience-promoting biological functioning is neither the fault of the individual nor is it immutable. Biological systems that promote adaptive responses to stress do not arise solely from internal factors and can develop through social environmental contexts related to families, schools, and neighborhoods. They can also be responsive to well-researched, theoretically and empirically sound interventions.

Conclusion

In sum, we suggest that a holistic approach to resilience science must include a neurobiological perspective. The considerable complexity this adds to the field is offset by wide-reaching benefits. Beyond simply understanding resilience on a much more comprehensive level, the incorporation of neurobiological factors offers the opportunity to identify early markers of risk prior to the development of detectable behavioral, emotional, or physical health disorders and provide targets of prevention/intervention previously believed to be immutable. Resilience cannot be determined by a single process, indicator, or outcome—biological or otherwise. Rather, resilience emerges through complex interactions of factors both internal and external to the individual. Thus, we may be most optimally positioned to promote successful adaptation with efforts that integrate factors across the many micro- and macrosystems in which human development unfolds.

Key Messages

1. A comprehensive understanding of resilience science requires interdisciplinary collaboration across multiple fields, including (but not limited to) psychology, sociology, and public health, genetics, biology, and neuroscience.
2. In the context of risk and resilience, biological factors may be considered intermediary variables that predict longer term physical and psychological health. Biological factors may also interact with factors across multiple other systems (e.g., environmental, social, familial) to predict adjustment to adversity.
3. There is no single measure of biological functioning that can serve as an indicator or predictor of resilient functioning. Interpretation of any single measure of biological functioning also requires careful consideration of context—environmental, social, cultural, and the interactions therein.
4. Biological factors are not immutable. Emerging research suggests such indicators may be targeted in novel prevention and intervention programs to promote resilience under conditions of risk.

References

Almas, A. N., Degnan, K. A., Radulescu, A., Nelson, C. A., III, Zeanah, C. H., & Fox, N. A. (2012). Effects of early intervention and the moderating effects of brain activity on institutionalized children's social skills at age 8. *PNAS, 109*(Suppl 2), 17228–17231. doi:10.1073/pnas.1121256109

American Academy of Pediatrics. (2016). Poverty and child health in the United States. *Pediatrics, 137*(4), e20160339. doi:10.1542/peds.2016-0339

American Academy of Pediatrics. (2019). The resilience project: We can stop toxic stress. Retrieved from https://www.aap.org/en-us/advocacy-and-policy/aap-health-initiatives/resilience/Pages/Resilience-Project.aspx

Anderson, L. M., Shinn, C., Fullilove, M. T., Scrimshaw, S. C., Fielding, J. E., Normand, J., . . . Task Force on Community Preventive Services. (2003). The effectiveness of early childhood development programs: A systematic review. *American Journal of Preventive Medicine, 24*(3), 32–46. doi:10.1016/S0749-3797(02)00655-4

Bellis, M. A., Hughes, K., Ford, K., Hardcastle, K. A., Sharp, C. A., Wood, S., . . . Davies, A. (2018). Adverse childhood experiences and sources of childhood resilience: A retrospective study of their combined relationships with child health and educational attendance. *BMC Public Health, 18*(1), 792. doi:10.1186/s12889-018-5699-8

Belsky, J., & Beaver, K. M. (2011). Cumulative-genetic plasticity, parenting and adolescent self-regulation. *Journal of Child Psychology and Psychiatry, 52*(5), 619–626. doi:10.1111/j.1469-7610.2010.02327.x

Belsky, J., & Pluess, M. (2009). Beyond diathesis stress: Differential susceptibility to environmental influences. *Psychological Bulletin, 135*(6), 885–908. doi:10.1037/a0017376

Belsky, J., & Pluess, M. (2013). Beyond risk, resilience and dysregulation: Phenotypic plasticity and human development. *Development and Psychopathology, 25*, 1243–1261. doi:10.1017/S095457941300059X

Belsky, J., & van Ijzendoorn, M. H. (2015). What works for whom? Genetic moderation of intervention efficacy. *Development and Psychopathology, 27*(1), 1–6. doi:10.1017/S0954579414001254

Bernard, K., Dozier, M., Bick, J., & Gordon, M. K. (2015). Intervening to enhance cortisol regulation among children at risk for neglect: Results of a randomized clinical trial. *Development and Psychopathology, 27*(3), 829–841. doi:10.1017/S095457941400073X

Bernard, K., Hostinar, C., & Dozier, M. (2015). Intervention effects on diurnal cortisol rhythms of CPS-referred infants persist into early childhood: Preschool follow-up results of a randomized clinical trial. *JAMA Pediatrics, 169*(2), 112–119. doi:10.1001/jamapediatrics.2014.2369

Bethell, C., Newacheck, P., Hawes, E., & Halfon, N. (2014). Adverse childhood experiences: Assessing the impact on health and school engagement and the mitigating role of resilience. *Health Affairs, 33*(12), 2106–2115. doi:10.1377/hlthaff.2014.0914

Bick, J., & Nelson, C. A. (2016). Early adverse experiences and the developing brain. *Neuropsychopharmacology, 41*(1), 177–196. doi:10.1038/npp.2015.252

Bick, J., Palmwood, E. N., Zajac, L., Simons, R., & Dozier, M. (2019). Early parenting intervention and adverse family environments affect neural function in middle childhood. *Biological Psychiatry, 85*(4), 326–335. doi:10.1016/j.biopsych.2018.09.020

Bick, J., Zhu, T., Stamoulis, C., Fox, N. A., Zeanah, C., & Nelson, C. A. (2015). Effect of early institutionalization and foster care on long-term white matter development: A randomized clinical trial. *JAMA Pediatrics, 169*(3), 211–219. doi:10.1001/jamapediatrics.2014.3212

Bowlby, J. (1988). *A secure base: Parent-child attachment and healthy human development.* New York, NY: Basic Books.

Boyce, W. T. (2015). Differential susceptibility of the developing brain to contextual adversity and stress. *Neuropsychopharmacology, 41*(1), 142–162. doi:10.1038/npp.2015.294

Boyce, W. T., Chesney, M., Alkon, A., Tschann, J. M., Adams, S., Chesterman, B., . . . Wara, D. (1995). Psychobiologic reactivity to stress and childhood respiratory illnesses: Results of two prospective studies. *Psychosomatic Medicine, 57*(5), 411–422.

Boyce, W. T., & Kobor, M. S. (2015). Development and the epigenome: The "synapse" of gene-environment interplay. *Developmental Science, 18*(1), 1–23. doi:10.1111/desc.12282

Brody, G. H., Yu, T., Chen, E., Miller, G. E., Kogan, S. M., & Beach, S. R. (2013). Is resilience only skin deep? Rural African Americans' socioeconomic status-related risk and competence in preadolescence and psychological adjustment and allostatic load at age 19. *Psychological Science, 24*(7), 1285–1293. doi:10.1177/0956797612471954

Brody, G. H., Yu, T., Miller, G. E., & Chen, E. (2016). Resilience in adolescence, health, and psychosocial outcomes. *Pediatrics, 138*(6), e20161042. doi:10.1542/peds.2016-1042

Bronfenbrenner, U., & Morris, P. A. (1998). The ecology of developmental processes. In W. Damon & R. M. Lerner (Eds.), *Handbook of child psychology: Theoretical models of human development* (pp. 993–1028). Hoboken, NJ: John Wiley.

Bush, N. R., Adler, N., & Boyce, W. T. (2011). *Mechanisms for socioeconomic health disparities: SES predicts longitudinal change in children's ANS reactivity.* Unpublished manuscript.

Bush, N. R., & Aschbacher, K. (2019). Immune biomarkers of early-life adversity and exposure to stress and violence—searching outside the streetlight. *JAMA Pediatrics*, 1–3.

Bush, N. R., & Bibbins-Domingo, K. (2019). Power of the positive: Childhood assets and future cardiometabolic health. *Pediatrics, 143*(3), e20184004. doi:10.1542/peds.2018-4004

Bush, N. R., & Boyce, W. T. (2016). Differential sensitivity to context: Implications for developmental psychopathology. In D. Cicchetti (Ed.), *Developmental psychopathology: Developmental neuroscience* (pp. 107–137). Hoboken, NJ: John Wiley.

Bush, N. R., Caron, Z. K., Blackburn, K. S., & Alkon, A. (2016). Measuring cardiac autonomic nervous system (ANS) activity in toddlers: Resting and developmental challenges. *Journal of Visualized Experiments, 108*, e53652. doi:10.3791/53652

Carnevali, L., Koenig, J., Sgoifo, A., & Ottaviani, C. (2018). Autonomic and brain morphological predictors of stress resilience. *Frontiers in Neuroscience, 12*(228). doi:10.3389/fnins.2018.00228

Charney, D. S. (2004). Psychobiological mechanisms of resilience and vulnerability: Implications for successful adaptation to extreme stress. *American Journal of Psychiatry, 161*(2), 195–216. doi:10.1176/appi.ajp.161.2.195

Choi, K. W., Stein, M. B., Dunn, E. C., Koenen, K. C., & Smoller, J. W. (2019). Genomics and psychological resilience: A research agenda. *Molecular Psychiatry.* doi:10.1038/s41380-019-0457-6

Cicchetti, D., & Curtis, W. J. (2007). Multilevel perspectives on pathways to resilient functioning. *Development and Psychopathology, 19*(3), 627–629. doi:10.1017/S0954579407000314

Cicchetti, D., & Rogosch, F. A. (2009). Adaptive coping under conditions of extreme stress: Multilevel influences on the determinants of resilience in maltreated children. *New Directions for Child and Adolescent Development, 2009*(124), 47–59. doi:10.1002/cd.242.

Conradt, E., & Ablow, J. (2010). Infant physiological response to the still-face paradigm: Contributions of maternal sensitivity and infants' early regulatory behavior. *Infant Behavior & Development, 33*(3), 251–265. doi:10.1016/j.infbeh.2010.01.001

Conradt, E., Measelle, J., & Ablow, J. C. (2013). Poverty, problem behavior, and promise: Differential susceptibility among infants reared in poverty. *Psychological Science, 24*(3), 235–242. doi:10.1177/0956797612457381

Curtis, W. J., & Cicchetti, D. (2003). Moving research on resilience into the 21st century: Theoretical and methodological considerations in examining the biological contributors to resilience. *Development and Psychopathology, 15*(3), 773–810.

Dantzer, R., Cohen, S., Russo, S. J., & Dinan, T. G. (2018). Resilience and immunity. *Brain, Behavior, and Immunity, 74*, 28–42. doi:10.1016/j.bbi.2018.08.010

Deater-Decker, K., & Dodge, K. A. (1997). Externalizing behavior problems and discipline revisited: Nonlinear effects and variation by culture, context, and gender. *Psychological Inquiry, 8*(3), 161–175. doi:10.1207/s15327965pli0803_1

Del Giudice, M., Ellis, B. J., & Shirtcliff, E. A. (2011). The adaptive calibration model of stress responsivity. *Neuroscience & Biobehavioral Reviews, 35*(7), 1562–1592. doi:10.1016/j.neubiorev.2010.11.007

Doane, L. D., Sladek, M. R., & Adam, E. K. (2018). An introduction to cultural neurobiology: Evidence from physiological stress systems. In J. M. Causadias, E. H. Telzer, & N. A. Gonzales (Eds.), *The handbook of culture and biology* (pp. 227–254). Hoboken, NJ: John Wiley.

Drury, S. S., Gleason, M. M., Theall, K. P., Smyke, A. T., Nelson, C. A., Fox, N. A., & Zeanah, C. H. (2012). Genetic sensitivity to the caregiving context: The influence of 5httlpr and BDNF val66met on indiscriminate social behavior. *Physiology & Behavior, 106*(5), 728–735. doi:10.1016/j.physbeh.2011.11.014

Duckworth, A., & Gross, J. J. (2014). Self-control and grit: Related but separable determinants of success. *Current Directions in Psychological Science, 23*(5), 319–325. doi:10.1177/0963721414541462

Ellis, B. J., Boyce, W. T., Belsky, J., Bakermans-Kranenburg, M. J., & van Ijzendoorn, M. H. (2011). Differential susceptibility to the environment: An evolutionary-neurodevelopmental theory. *Development and Psychopathology, 23*(1), 7–28. doi:10.1017/s0954579410000611

Epel, E., Laraia, B., Coleman-Phox, K., Leung, C., Vieten, C., Mellin, L., Kristeller, J. L., Thomas, M., Stotland, N., Bush, N., Lustig, R. H., Dallman, M., Hecht, F. M., & Adler, N. (2019). Effects of a mindfulness-based intervention on distress, weight gain, and glucose control for pregnant low-income women: a quasi-experimental trial using the ORBIT model. *International Journal of Behavioral Medicine, 26*(5), 461–473.

Farrell, A. K., Simpson, J. A., Carlson, E. A., Englund, M. M., & Sung, S. (2017). The impact of stress at different life stages on physical health and the buffering effects of maternal sensitivity. *Health Psychology, 36*(1), 35–44. doi:10.1037/hea0000424

Felder, J. N., Roubinov, D. S., Bush, N. R., Coleman-Phox, K., Vieten, C., Laraia, B., . . . Epel, E. (2018). Effect of prenatal mindfulness training on depressive symptom severity through 18-months postpartum: A latent profile analysis. *Journal of Clinical Psychology, 74*(7), 1117–1125. doi:10.1002/jclp.22592

Fish, E. W., Shahrokh, D., Bagot, R., Caldji, C., Bredy, T., Szyf, M., & Meaney, M. J. (2004). Epigenetic programming of stress responses through variations in maternal care. *Annals of the New York Academy of Sciences, 1036*, 167–180.

Fisher, P. A., Van Ryzin, M. J., & Gunnar, M. R. (2011). Mitigating HPA axis dysregulation associated with placement changes in foster care. *Psychoneuroendocrinology, 36*(4), 531–539. doi:10.1016/j.psyneuen.2010.08.007

Germán, M., Gonzales, N. A., & Dumka, L. (2008). Familism values as a protective factor for Mexican-origin adolescents exposed to deviant peers. *The Journal of Early Adolescence, 29*(1), 16–42. doi:10.1177/0272431608324475

Geronimus, A. T. (1992). The weathering hypothesis and the health of African-American women and infants: Evidence and speculations. *Ethnicity & Disease, 2*(3), 207–221.

Geronimus, A. T., Hicken, M., Keene, D., & Bound, J. (2006). "Weathering" and age patterns of allostatic load scores among Blacks and Whites in the United States. *American Journal of Public Health, 96*(5), 826–833. doi:10.2105/AJPH.2004.060749

Goldsmith, H. H., & Lemery, K. S. (2000). Linking temperamental fearfulness and anxiety symptoms: A behavior-genetic perspective. *Biological Psychiatry, 48*(12), 1199–1209.

Gonzales, N. A., Johnson, M., Shirtcliff, E. A., Tein, J. Y., Eskenazi, B., & Deardorff, J. (2018). The role of bicultural adaptation, familism, and family conflict in Mexican American adolescents' cortisol reactivity. *Development and Psychopathology, 30*(5), 1571–1587. doi:10.1017/S0954579418001116

Gottlieb, G., & Halpern, C. T. (2002). A relational view of causality in normal and abnormal development. *Developmental Psychopathology, 14*(3), 421–435.

Gray, N. A., Dhana, A., Van Der Vyver, L., Van Wyk, J., Khumalo, N. P., & Stein, D. J. (2018). Determinants of hair cortisol concentration in children: A systematic review. *Psychoneuroendocrinology, 87*, 204–214. doi:10.1016/j.psyneuen.2017.10.022

Gunnar, M. R., Talge, N. M., & Herrera, A. (2009). Stressor paradigms in developmental studies: What does and does not work to produce mean increases in salivary cortisol. *Psychoneuroendocrinology, 34*(7), 953–967. doi:10.1016/j.psyneuen.2009.02.010

Gunnar, M. R., & Vazquez, D. (2006). Stress neurobiology and developmental psychopathology. In D. Cicchetti & D. J. Cohen (Eds.), *Developmental psychopathology* (Vol. 2, pp. 533–577). Hoboken, NJ: John Wiley.

Hagan, M. J., Roubinov, D. S., Adler, N. E., Boyce, W. T., & Bush, N. R. (2016). Socioeconomic adversity, negativity in the parent child-relationship, and physiological reactivity: An examination of pathways and interactive processes affecting young children's physical health. *Psychosomatic Medicine, 78*(9), 998–1007. doi:10.1097/psy.0000000000000379

Ham, J., & Tronick, E. (2006). Infant resilience to the stress of the still-face: Infant and maternal psychophysiology are related. *Annals of the New York Academy of Sciences, 1094*, 297–302. doi:10.1196/annals.1376.038

Hastings, P. D., Shirtcliff, E. A., Klimes-Dougan, B., Allison, A. L., Derose, L., Kendziora, K. T., . . . Zahn-Waxler, C. (2011). Allostasis and the development of internalizing and externalizing problems: Changing relations with physiological systems across adolescence. *Developmental Psychopathology, 23*(4), 1149–1165. doi:10.1017/s0954579411000538

Hofferth, S., & Lee, Y. (2015). Family structure and trends in US fathers' time with children, 2003-2013. *Family Science, 6*(1), 318–329. doi:10.1080/19424620.2015.1082805

Hostinar, C. E., & Gunnar, M. R. (2015). Social support can buffer against stress and shape brain activity. *AJOB Neuroscience, 6*(3), 34–42. doi:10.1080/21507740.2015.1047054

Hughes, K., Bellis, M. A., Hardcastle, K. A., Sethi, D., Butchart, A., Mikton, C., . . . Dunne, M. P. (2017). The effect of multiple adverse childhood experiences on health: A systematic review and meta-analysis. *The Lancet Public Health, 2*(8), e356–e366. doi:10.1016/S2468-2667(17)30118-4

Hunter, R. G., Gray, J. D., & McEwen, B. S. (2018). The neuroscience of resilience. *Journal of the Society for Social Work and Research, 9*(2), 305–339. doi:10.1086/697956

James, S. A., Hartnett, S. A., & Kalsbeek, W. D. (1983). John Henryism and blood pressure differences among Black men. *Journal of Behavioral Medicine, 6*(3), 259–278.

Jones-Mason, K., Allen, I. E., Bush, N. R., & Hamilton, S. (2016). Epigenetic marks as the link between environment and development: Examination of the associations between attachment, socioeconomic status, and methylation of the SLC6A4 gene. *Brain and Behavior, 6*(7), e00480. doi:10.1002/brb3.480

Kiff, C. J., Lengua, L. J., & Bush, N. R. (2011). Temperament variation in sensitivity to parenting: Predicting changes in depression and anxiety. *Journal of Abnormal Child Psychology, 39*(8), 1199–1212. doi:10.1007/s10802-011-9539-x

Lengua, L. J., Bush, N. R., Long, A. C., Kovacs, E. A., & Trancik, A. M. (2008). Effortful control as a moderator of the relation between contextual risk factors and growth in adjustment problems. *Development and Psychopathology, 20*(2), 509–528. doi:10.1017/s0954579408000254

Liebenberg, L., Ungar, M., & LeBlanc, J. C. (2013). The CYRM-12: A brief measure of resilience. *Canadian Journal of Public Health, 104*(2), e131–e135. doi:10.1007/bf03405676

Lovallo, W. R., & Sollers, J. J., III. (2007). Autonomic nervous system. In G. Fink (Ed.), *Encyclopedia of stress* (2nd ed., pp. 282–292). Cambridge, MA: Academic Press.

Love, J. M., Kisker, E. E., Ross, C., Raikes, H., Constantine, J., Boller, K., . . . Vogel, C. (2005). The effectiveness of early head start for 3-year-old children and their parents: Lessons for policy and programs. *Developmental Psychology, 41*(6), 885. doi:10.1037/0012-1649.41.6.885

Luecken, L. J., Somers, J. A., & Roubinov, D. S. (2020). Infant biological sensitivity to context in low-income Mexican American families. *unpublished manuscript*.

Masten, A. S. (2011). Resilience in children threatened by extreme adversity: Frameworks for research, practice, and translational synergy. *Developmental Psychopathology, 23*(2), 493–506. doi:10.1017/s0954579411000198

Masten, A. S. (2014). Global perspectives on resilience in children and youth. *Child Development, 85*(1), 6–20. doi:10.1111/cdev.12205t

Masten, A. S. (2015). *Ordinary magic: Resilience in development*. New York, NY: Guilford Press.

Masten, A. S., & Barnes, A. J. (2018). Resilience in children: Developmental perspectives. *Children, 5*(7), 98. doi:10.3390/children5070098

Masten, A. S., Best, K. M., & Garmezy, N. (1990). Resilience and development: Contributions from the study of children who overcome adversity. *Development and Psychopathology, 2*(4), 425–444. doi:10.1017/S0954579400005812

Masten, A. S., & Monn, A. R. (2015). Child and family resilience: A call for integrated science, practice, and professional training. *Family Relations, 64*(1), 5–21. doi:10.1111/fare.12103

Masten, A. S., & Obradovic, J. (2006). Competence and resilience in development. *Annals of the New York Academy of Sciences, 1094*, 13–27. doi:10.1196/annals.1376.003

McDade, T. W., Williams, S., & Snodgrass, J. J. (2007). What a drop can do: Dried blood spots as a minimally invasive method for integrating biomarkers into population-based research. *Demography, 44*(4), 899–925. doi:10.1353/dem.2007.0038

McEwen, B. S. (2007). Physiology and neurobiology of stress and adaptation: Central role of the brain. *Physiological Reviews, 87*(3), 873–904. doi:10.1152/physrev.00041.2006

McEwen, B. S. (2017). Neurobiological and systemic effects of chronic stress. *Chronic Stress, 1*. doi:10.1177/2470547017692328

McEwen, B. S., & Wingfield, J. C. (2010). What's in a name? Integrating homeostasis, allostasis and stress. *Hormones and Behavior, 57*(2), 105–111. doi:10.1016/j.yhbeh.2009.09.011

Meaney, M. J. (2001). Maternal care, gene expression, and the transmission of individual differences in stress reactivity across generations. *Annual Review of Neuroscience, 24*, 1161–1192. doi:10.1146/annurev.neuro.24.1.1161

Miller, G. E., Chen, E., Armstrong, C. C., Carroll, A. L., Ozturk, S., Rydland, K. J., . . . Nusslock, R. (2018). Functional connectivity in central executive network protects youth against cardiometabolic risks linked with neighborhood violence. *Proceedings of the National Academy of Sciences of the United States of America, 115*(47), 12063–12068. doi:10.1073/pnas.1810067115

Miller, G. E., Cohen, S., Janicki-Deverts, D., Brody, G. H., & Chen, E. (2016). Viral challenge reveals further evidence of skin-deep resilience in African Americans from disadvantaged backgrounds. *Health Psychology, 35*(11), 1225–1234. doi:10.1037/hea0000398

Miller, G. E., Yu, T., Chen, E., & Brody, G. H. (2015). Self-control forecasts better psychosocial outcomes but faster epigenetic aging in low-SES youth. *Proceedings of the National Academy of Sciences of the United States of America, 112*(33), 10325–10330. doi:10.1073/pnas.1505063112

Musci, R. J., Masyn, K. E., Uhl, G., Maher, B., Kellam, S. G., & Ialongo, N. S. (2015). Polygenic score × intervention moderation: An application of discrete-time survival analysis to modeling the timing of first tobacco use among urban youth. *Development and Psychopathology, 27*(1), 111–122. doi:10.1017/S0954579414001333

Nelson, C. A., Zeanah, C. H., Fox, N. A., Marshall, P. J., Smyke, A. T., & Guthrie, D. (2007). Cognitive recovery in socially deprived young children: The Bucharest early intervention project. *Science, 318*(5858), 1937–1940. doi:10.1126/science.1143921

Nigg, J. T. (2006). Temperament and developmental psychopathology. *Journal of Child Psychology and Psychiatry, 47*(3–4), 395–422. doi:10.1111/j.1469-7610.2006.01612.x

Obradovic, J., Bush, N. R., Stamperdahl, J., Adler, N. E., & Boyce, W. T. (2010). Biological sensitivity to context: The interactive effects of stress reactivity and family adversity on socioemotional behavior and school readiness. *Child Development, 81*(1), 270–289. doi:10.1111/j.1467-8624.2009.01394.x

Osório, C., Probert, T., Jones, E., Young, A. H., & Robbins, I. (2017). Adapting to stress: Understanding the neurobiology of resilience. *Journal of Behavioral Medicine, 43*(4), 307–322. doi:10.1080/08964289.2016.1170661

Popham, C., McEwen, F. S., & Pluess, M. (2020). Psychological resilience in response to adverse experiences: An integrative developmental perspective in the context of war and displacement. In M. Ungar (Ed.), *Multisystemic resilience: Adaptation and transformation in changing contexts*. Oxford, UK: Oxford University Press.

Provençal, N., & Binder, E. B. (2015). The effects of early life stress on the epigenome: From the womb to adulthood and even before. *Experimental Neurology, 268*, 10–20. doi:10.1016/j.expneurol.2014.09.001

Racine, N., Madigan, S., Plamondon, A., Hetherington, E., McDonald, S., & Tough, S. (2018). Maternal adverse childhood experiences and antepartum risks: The moderating role of social support. *Archives of Women's Mental Health, 21*(6), 663–670. doi:10.1007/s00737-018-0826-1

Romens, S. E., McDonald, J., Svaren, J., & Pollak, S. D. (2015). Associations between early life stress and gene methylation in children. *Child Development, 86*(1), 303–309. doi:10.1111/cdev.12270

Rothbart, M. K., Ahadi, S. A., & Evans, D. E. (2000). Temperament and personality: Origins and outcomes. *Journal of Personality and Social Psychology, 78*(1), 122–135. doi:10.1037//0022-3514.78.1.122

Roubinov, D. S., Boyce, W. T., & Bush, N. R. (2018). Informant-specific reports of peer and teacher relationships buffer the effects of harsh parenting on children's oppositional defiant disorder during kindergarten. *Developmental Psychopathology*, 1–12. doi:10.1017/s0954579418001499

Roubinov, D. S., Boyce, W. T., Lee, M. R., & Bush, N. R. (2020). Evidence for discrete profiles of children's physiological activity across three neurobiological system and their transitions over time. *Developmental Science*, e12989. https://doi.org/10.1111/desc.12989

Roubinov, D. S., Bush, N. R., Adler, N. E., & Boyce, W. T. (2018). Differences in febrile and respiratory illnesses in minority children: The sociodemographic context of restrictive parenting. *Academic Pediatrics, 19*(5), 534–541. doi:10.1016/j.acap.2018.09.012

Roubinov, D. S., Felder, J. N., Vieten, C., Coleman-Phox, K., Laraia, B., Adler, N., . . . Bush, N. R. (2018). Maternal depressive symptoms and infant healthcare utilization: The moderating role of prenatal mindfulness. *General Hospital Psychiatry, 53*, 82–83. doi:10.1016/j.genhosppsych.2018.01.001

Roubinov, D. S., Hagan, M. J., Boyce, W. T., Adler, N. E., & Bush, N. R. (2018). Family socioeconomic status, cortisol, and physical health in early childhood: The role of advantageous neighborhood characteristics. *Psychosomatic Medicine, 80*(5), 492–501. doi:10.1097/psy.0000000000000585

Roubinov, D. S., Hagan, M. J., Boyce, W. T., Essex, M. J., & Bush, N. R. (2017). Child temperament and teacher relationship interactively predict cortisol expression: The prism of classroom climate. *Development and Psychopathology, 29*(5), 1763–1775. doi:10.1017/S0954579417001389

Rudolph, K. D., Troop-Gordon, W., & Granger, D. A. (2011). Individual differences in biological stress responses moderate the contribution of early peer victimization to subsequent depressive symptoms. *Psychopharmacology, 214*(1), 209–219. doi:10.1007/s00213-010-1879-7

Rutter, M. (1987). Psychosocial resilience and protective mechanisms. *American Journal of Orthopsychiatry, 57*(3), 316–331.

Rutter, M. (2012). Resilience as a dynamic concept. *Developmental Psychopathology, 24*(2), 335–344. doi:10.1017/s0954579412000028

Sabogal, F., Marin, G., Otero-Sabogal, R., Vanoss Marin, B., & Perez-Stable, E. (1987). Hispanic familism and acculturation: What changes and what doesn't? *Hispanic Journal of Behavioral Sciences, 9*(4), 397–412. doi:10.1177/07399863870094003

Sapolsky, R. M., Romero, L. M., & Munck, A. U. (2000). How do glucocorticoids influence stress responses? Integrating permissive, suppressive, stimulatory, and preparative actions. *Endocrine Reviews, 21*(1), 55–89. doi:10.1210/edrv.21.1.0389

Segerstrom, S. C., & Miller, G. E. (2004). Psychological stress and the human immune system: A meta-analytic study of 30 years of inquiry. *Psychological Bulletin, 130*(4), 601–630. doi:10.1037/0033-2909.130.4.601

Shalev, I., Entringer, S., Wadhwa, P. D., Wolkowitz, O. M., Puterman, E., Lin, J., & Epel, E. S. (2013). Stress and telomere biology: A lifespan perspective. *Psychoneuroendocrinology, 38*(9), 1835–1842. doi:10.1016/j.psyneuen.2013.03.010

Shonkoff, J. P., Boyce, W. T., & McEwen, B. S. (2009). Neuroscience, molecular biology, and the childhood roots of health disparities: Building a new framework for health promotion and disease prevention. *JAMA, 301*(21), 2252–2259. doi:10.1001/jama.2009.754

Soenens, B., Vansteenkiste, M., & Van Petegem, S. (2015). Let us not throw out the baby with the bathwater: Applying the principle of universalism without uniformity to autonomy-supportive and controlling parenting. *Child Development Perspectives, 9*(1), 44–49. doi:10.1111/cdep.12103

Soleimanpour, S., Geierstanger, S., & Brindis, C. D. (2017). Adverse childhood experiences and resilience: Addressing the unique needs of adolescents. *Academic Pediatrics, 17*(7S), S108–S114. doi:10.1016/j.acap.2017.01.008

Tabachnick, A. R., Raby, K. L., Goldstein, A., Zajac, L., & Dozier, M. (2019). Effects of an attachment-based intervention in infancy on children's autonomic regulation during middle childhood. *Biological Psychology, 143*, 22–31. doi:10.1016/j.biopsycho.2019.01.006

Thompson, S. F., Kiff, C. J., & McLaughlin, K. H. (2018). The neurobiology of stress and adversity in infancy. In C. H. Zeanah (Ed.), *The handbook of infant mental health* (Vol. 4, pp. 81–94). New York, NY: Guilford Press.

Traub, F., & Boynton-Jarrett, R. (2017). Modifiable resilience factors to childhood adversity for clinical pediatric practice. *Pediatrics, 139*(5), e20162569. doi:10.1542/peds.2016-2569

Ungar, M. (2006). Resilience across cultures. *The British Journal of Social Work, 38*(2), 218–235. doi:10.1093/bjsw/bcl343

Ungar, M. (2011). The social ecology of resilience: Addressing contextual and cultural ambiguity of a nascent construct. *American Journal of Orthopsychiatry, 81*(1), 1–17. doi:10.1111/j.1939-0025.2010.01067.x

Ungar, M. (2013). Resilience, trauma, context, and culture. *Trauma, Violence, & Abuse, 14*(3), 255–266. doi:10.1177/1524838013487805

Ungar, M. (2015). Practitioner review: Diagnosing childhood resilience—A systemic approach to the diagnosis of adaptation in adverse social and physical ecologies. *Journal of Child Psychology and Psychiatry, 56*(1), 4–17. doi:10.1111/jcpp.12306

Ungar, M., & Liebenberg, L. (2011). Assessing resilience across cultures using mixed methods: Construction of the child and youth resilience measure. *Journal of Mixed Methods Research, 5*(2), 126–149. doi:10.1177/1558689811400607

Waddington, C. H. (1966). *Principles of development and differentiation.* New York, NY: Macmillan.

Walker, F. R., Pfingst, K., Carnevali, L., Sgoifo, A., & Nalivaiko, E. (2017). In the search for integrative biomarker of resilience to psychological stress. *Neuroscience & Biobehavioral Reviews, 74*(Part B), 310–320. doi:10.1016/j.neubiorev.2016.05.003

Risk and Resilience in Pregnancy and Birth

Cecily Young and Susan Ayers

Introduction

Pregnancy, birth, and becoming a parent involves substantial changes at biological, psychological, social, and broader cultural levels. As such, it is a continuing process of adaptation to change and new demands. In most societies pregnancy and childbirth are not typically thought of as being associated with adversity, risk, and resilience. However, adversity can arise for women, their partners, and infants during this time. The World Health Organization (2018) estimated that about 830 women die every day from pregnancy- or childbirth-related complications around the world. Physical illness and morbidity can also occur, such as postpartum hemorrhage or preterm birth, with potential long-term consequences for women and their families.

The experience of adversity, stress, and trauma during pregnancy, birth, and postpartum is particularly important because of the potential impact on women and their infants. Pregnancy and birth are associated with increased risk of mental illness, which may be due to exacerbation or recurrence of pre-existing mental health problems or the onset of new mental health problems. In particular, research shows the events of labor and birth can be traumatic for some women and result in posttraumatic stress disorder (PTSD). Reviews show PTSD after birth affects approximately 4% of women in community samples and up to 18% of women in high-risk groups, such as those with severe complications or a history of sexual abuse (Dekel, Stuebe, & Dishy, 2017; Dikmen-Yildiz, Ayers, & Phillips, 2017a). Men can also experience stress and psychological problems during this time (Leach, Poyser, Cooklin, & Giallo, 2016; Philpott, Leahy-Warren, FitzGerald, & Savage, 2017).

There is increasing evidence that anxiety and trauma in pregnancy may also have a long-term impact on the child. A review of prospective studies found children of women who were stressed in pregnancy were at greater risk of emotional and cognitive problems, language delay, and adverse outcomes like attention-deficit hyperactivity disorder and anxiety (Talge, Neal, & Glover, 2007). Similarly, epidemiological evidence suggests PTSD in pregnancy may be associated with poor outcomes such as preterm birth (Rogal et al., 2007; Yonkers et al., 2014). Stress hormones and epigenetic mechanisms are thought to underlie the effect of stress in pregnancy on the developing baby (Wadhwa, 2005).

Although stress and trauma in pregnancy puts infants at increased risk of poor outcomes, not all children will be affected. A child's long-term risk of poor outcomes is also shaped by psychological and social factors in childhood like parental mental health, parenting, attachments, and exposure to adversity. For example, the importance of women's mental health is evidenced by research showing that depression is associated with poorer maternal sensitivity to the infant's state and more negative patterns of parenting (Field, 2010).

The potential impact of adversity on women and their infants during the perinatal period highlights the importance of examining both risk and resilience in pregnancy, birth, and postpartum. The first part of this chapter provides an overview of experiences of pregnancy and birth and risks that arise, in particular trauma experienced during birth. The second part looks at resilience in pregnancy and birth, what we know, and what we still need to know in this area. The third part looks at theories of resilience in the perinatal period and how it is important to look at resilience at different systemic levels. We conclude with key considerations for future research and theory in this area.

Pregnancy and Birth

Different perspectives on health determine how women's experiences of pregnancy and birth are understood. Medicine has traditionally adopted a biomedical perspective where the focus is on physiological processes and risk. The biopsychosocial model put forward by Engel (1979) challenged this to argue that psychological and social factors also need to be considered when investigating health and illness related to pregnancy and birth. More recently, researchers have argued the biopsychosocial model should be expanded further to include systemic factors such as macrocultural factors (e.g., ethnicity, socioeconomic status, income) and the rise in digital health (Ahmadvand, Gatchel, Brownstein, & Nissen, 2018; Suls & Rothman, 2004).

In pregnancy, birth, and motherhood, women's experiences are framed by the culture they live in. In high-income countries access to contraception and healthcare means women have more choice, autonomy, and less risk. Healthcare is largely predicated on the medical model, which focuses on detecting and treating risk, disease, and abnormality. Women have regular checks throughout pregnancy to screen for physical risk or problems (e.g., fetal ultrasounds, genetic screening, maternal checks for physical complications). Reduced morbidity and mortality in high-income countries means there is more emphasis on women's experiences of pregnancy and birth, particularly in individualistic cultures.

In low- and middle-income countries (LMIC), however, reduced access to contraception and healthcare means women face greater risk of morbidity and mortality and have less choice and autonomy. The World Health Organization estimates that 99% of maternal deaths occur in LMIC, predominantly sub-Saharan Africa and South Asia. Poor, young women in remote areas are at greatest risk, with complications of pregnancy and birth being the leading cause of death of adolescent girls in many LMIC countries (World Health Organization, 2018). However, there are social and cultural benefits to having children in LMIC countries. For example, a qualitative study of women in Gambia found childbirth was viewed as a rite of passage that all women must experience to show their womanhood. Becoming pregnant and having children guaranteed marital security. Conversely, not getting pregnant could lead to insecurity and maltreatment from family (Sawyer et al., 2011).

Risk and Adversity in Pregnancy and Birth

Risk and adversity during pregnancy and birth can be caused by physical, psychological, or social factors. Physically, there is increased risk of maternal or infant morbidity and mortality. It is worth noting that although maternal mortality is greatest in LMIC countries, it does still occur in high-income countries and is even increasing in some countries. For example, in the U.S. pregnancy-related mortality increased from 7 to 18 deaths per 100,000 births from 1987 to 2014 (Centers for Disease Control and Prevention, 2014). Major complications of pregnancy and birth that cause maternal morbidity include pre-eclampsia, severe perineal tears, and postpartum hemorrhage or infection. Infant morbidity and mortality can also arise in pregnancy or birth, including congenital abnormalities, preterm birth, or birth complications resulting in lack of oxygen to the infant.

Psychologically there is also increased risk. Mental illness affects up to one in five women during pregnancy and after birth (O'Hara & Wisner, 2014). Depression and anxiety are most common but other anxiety and stress-related disorders such as obsessive-compulsive disorder and PTSD are also reported. Postpartum psychosis is a rare but severe disorder that affects 1 woman in every 1,000 and has a high risk of maternal suicide and/or infanticide. A number of risk factors make it more likely women will develop mental health problems, some of which are remarkably consistent across different disorders and cultures. For example, mental health problems are more likely to occur if women live in circumstances of social adversity (e.g., deprivation, low socioeconomic status), have a history of psychological problems, have experienced childhood or current adversity (e.g., domestic violence, child sexual abuse), and have poor support (e.g., isolated, single parent, poor family support). In addition, if women are anxious or depressed during pregnancy, this is likely to continue or worsen postpartum (Bayrampour, Tomfohr, & Tough, 2016; Denckla et al., 2018).

Socially, the changes associated with having a baby may increase risk of family dysfunction, breakdown, and adversity, particularly for vulnerable populations. The evidence suggests that for some women having a baby can have a negative impact on marital functioning (Doss, Rhoades, Stanley, & Markman, 2009), the quality of a couple's relationship (Ahlborg, Misaver, & Möller, 2009), and satisfaction with the relationship (Mortensen, Torsheim, Melkevik, & Thuen, 2012) in the first year after birth. For vulnerable or disadvantaged women the risks may be more severe. For example, the highest rates of intimate partner violence (IPV) are found among women of reproductive age (aged 18–34) with rates of between 3% and 9% (Hahn, Gilmore, Aguayo, & Rheingold, 2018). However, there is wide variation between countries with, for example, a study in South Africa finding 42% of women experienced at least one act of IPV during pregnancy and nine months after birth (Groves et al., 2015).

Traumatic Birth

Labor and birth is an intense and challenging experience that can be empowering for women but also traumatic for some. Research suggests between 20% and 30% of women experience birth as traumatic. However, it is important to distinguish between women appraising birth as traumatic (commonly referred to as "birth trauma"), women having PTSD symptoms, and women meeting all the criteria for a diagnosis of PTSD. Not all women who report birth as traumatic will have PTSD symptoms or meet diagnostic criteria. Similarly, women may experience some PTSD symptoms but not meet all diagnostic criteria. This has been labeled "partial PTSD" or "subclinical PTSD" and the range of women affected varies widely according to how it is defined or measured. A review of this literature estimated an average prevalence of 9% of women have partial PTSD (Dekel et al., 2017), and it is possible these women may still benefit from treatment or find symptoms resolve spontaneously over time. In terms of diagnostic PTSD, research has predominantly been conducted using diagnostic criteria from the American Psychiatric Association (2000). A meta-analysis of 59 studies using diagnostic criteria found an average prevalence of PTSD of 3% in pregnancy and 4% postpartum (Dikmen-Yildiz et al., 2017b). However, it is worth noting that the majority of this research was conducted in high-income countries. There is some indication the prevalence of PTSD after birth may be greater in LMIC countries. For example, a study in Iran found 54% of women experienced birth as traumatic and 20% had PTSD (Modarres, Afrasiabi, Rahnama, & Montezeri, 2012). PTSD is also highly comorbid with depression with up to 71% of women also reporting depression (Dikmen-Yildiz et al., 2017a).

Understanding of birth trauma and PTSD has to account for the fact that the causes are multifactorial. Conceptual frameworks of the etiology of postpartum PTSD outline various vulnerability, risk, and maintaining factors thought to be important in birth-related PTSD (Ayers, Bond, Bertullies, & Wijma, 2016; Slade, 2006). For example, a diathesis-stress framework was used by Ayers et al. (2016) to summarize the potential interaction between key vulnerability factors in pregnancy, risk factors during birth, and possible maintaining/recovery factors postpartum, which were identified in a review and meta-analysis of 50 studies.

However, it is also clear that many women who have operative births do not develop PTSD and, conversely, that some women with obstetrically normal births do develop PTSD. This is illustrated by a review of the association between severe maternal morbidity and PTSD that concluded the evidence is inconsistent (Furuta, Sandall, & Bick, 2012). This illustrates a few critical points. First, the *subjective experience* of birth is more important in determining whether a woman develops PTSD than obstetric events. Second, we need to consider potential moderating factors, such as whether a woman has a history of trauma, depression or other vulnerabilities. Alongside this, we should also consider resilience factors that can help to explain why women do or do not develop PTSD. Third, social or contextual factors can reduce or buffer against adverse events during birth to influence outcomes.

Unlike vulnerability and birth factors, the role of postpartum factors such as additional stress or support in the maintenance or recovery from PTSD has been less examined. A prospective population-based study of 950 women in Turkey found that symptoms of PTSD six months after birth were predicted by poor satisfaction with health professionals during birth and poor support after birth. Other factors that contributed to PTSD in this study were vulnerability factors (anxiety and PTSD symptoms in pregnancy), complications during birth, and postpartum comorbid depression, postpartum fear of childbirth, and further traumatic events after birth (Dikmen-Yildiz et al., 2017b).

Thus, there is a substantial body of evidence identifying the risk factors for birth trauma and PTSD, as well as models proposing how these factors might interact to cause postpartum PTSD. These risk factors for postpartum PTSD are broadly consistent with the literature on risk factors for PTSD in other populations (Brewin, Andrews, & Valentine, 2000; Ozer, Best, Lipsey, & Weiss, 2003). However, a few issues need to be considered. For example, models that have been proposed are mainly psychosocial in their approach and do not consider underlying physiological mechanisms or social and environmental influences on trauma. For example, although the importance of social support in birth trauma is evident (Ayers et al., 2016), broader social and environmental factors associated with resilience such as how healthcare system are organized or societal views of birth have not been examined in relation to the prevention of birth trauma and PTSD. Thus, there are likely to be other factors that are important, such as environmental and organizational factors, although there is not enough research for these to be included in reviews and models at this time.

Resilience in Pregnancy and Birth

The literature on resilience in pregnancy and birth is small and emerging. A thematic analysis of published articles in the area (Young, Roberts, & Ward, 2018) found that researchers describe resilience in pregnancy and birth as a multifaceted process, active in multiple different systems including individual (self-esteem, optimism, attachment), social (positive family relationships, access to peers), and environmental (financial resources, child care, transport) systems as shown in Figure 3.1. Similar to the general literature on resilience, it is defined as being able to (a) protect against (b) minimize the impact of, and/or (c) promote recovery from a crisis or stressor event. Most definitions of resilience describe it as a dynamic process that involves activation of coping techniques to manage or recover from a stressor event (Davydov, Stewart, Ritchie, & Chaudieu, 2010). Definitions diverge, however, in the type and severity of stressor under consideration, outcomes that are considered to show resilience, specific risk and protective factors involved, and the focal actor or actors of the model.

A few specific definitions have been put forward in relation to perinatal resilience. Baraitser and Noack (2007) defined maternal resilience as the mother's ability to accept fluctuations in parenting satisfaction, negative affective experiences within this role, and imperfection in her performance while maintaining emotional connectedness with her child and investment in the parenting role. Gavidia-Payne, Denny, Davis, Francis and Jackson (2015)

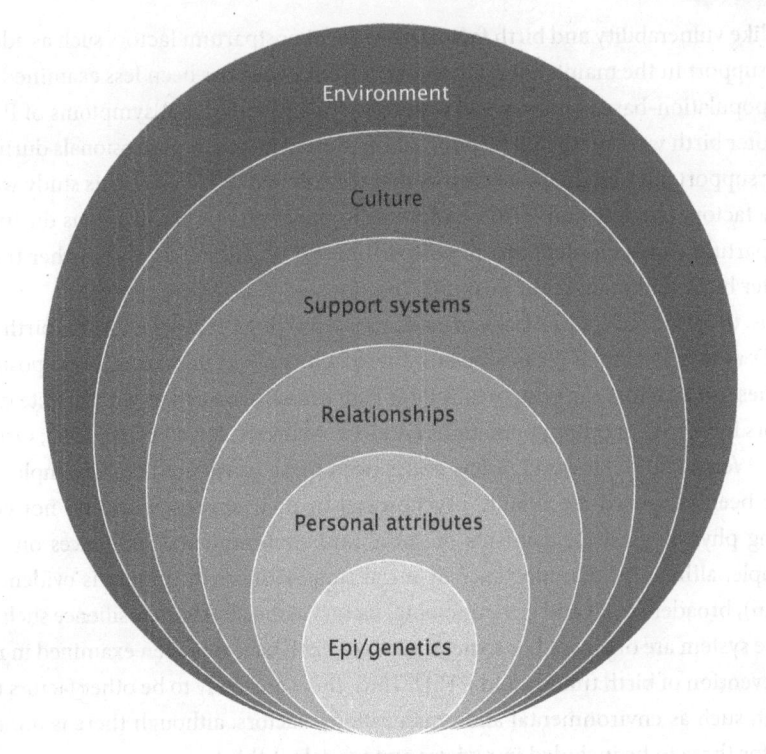

FIGURE 3.1 The multisystemic nature of perinatal resilience.

defined parental resilience as the delivery of appropriate parental care despite the presence of significant risk factors.

A few qualitative studies have examined the way that parents themselves define resilience. Gagnon and Stewart (2014) interviewed 10 women who had experienced violence in pregnancy and found most participants were unfamiliar with resilience as a term but offered content that reflected related concepts. Such content included "to be able to get through situations," "continuing to go in a positive direction," "not giving up," "cope and bounce back," "find balance and solution," and "overcome problems and move forward."

Constructs of Posttraumatic Growth and Salutogenesis

A number of related constructs have also been applied to birth processes and outcomes. Posttraumatic growth refers to a positive change in one's belief or functioning as a result of the struggle with highly challenging life circumstances (Tedeschi, Park, & Calhoun, 1998). This goes beyond resilience and includes changes in self-perception (e.g., a greater sense of personal strength, improved self-concept), philosophy of life (e.g., a greater appreciation for each day, spiritual development), and relationships (e.g., deepening of relationships, compassion; Tedeschi & Calhoun, 2004). Posttraumatic growth is conceptualized as a possible, but not necessary, outcome of trauma and may present in some individuals but not others (Michael & Cooper, 2013). It is now acknowledged that developmental events that are not necessarily traumatic or negative also have the potential to promote personal growth (Aldwin & Levenson, 2004). Evidence suggests up to 50% of women experience at least a moderate amount of personal growth following childbirth (Sawyer & Ayers, 2009). Qualitative studies also support this. For example, a qualitative study with 15 women who had experienced a traumatic birth found four themes of personal growth, which were "opening oneself up to a new present," "achieving a new level of relationship nakedness," "fortifying spiritual-mindedness," and "forging new paths" (Beck & Watson, 2016).

Salutogenesis is a concept from public health that positions health along a continuum and advocates health promotion through supporting well-being rather than analysis of disease (Antonovsky, 1979). It is a systemic model charting health promoting factors in context and across multiple systems. The central component of salutogenesis is sense of coherence, which refers to the belief that (a) challenges experienced are structured, predicable and explicable, (b) adequate resources exist to meet these challenges, and (c) the challenges are worthy of investment and engagement (Mittelmark & Bauer, 2017). Salutogenesis charts a balance between generalized resistance resources (such as social support, coping skills, and ego identity) and generalized resource deficits (such as significant changes of circumstance, developmental crises, and social relational conflict). The concept of salutogenesis has been used in midwifery to challenge the dominant risk avoidance approach to maternity care (Meier Magistretti, Downe, Lindstrøm, Berg, & Schwarz, 2016). While there is a great deal of commonality between salutogenesis and resilience, the most prominent difference is that salutogenesis is a general principle of good health and does not require a significant stressor to become active (Lindstrøm & Eriksson, 2005).

Resilience During Pregnancy and Birth

Findings that clearly relate to resilience concepts can be seen throughout the broader literature of pregnancy and birth but conscious application of resilience concepts to investigation of pregnancy and birth outcomes is relatively new. For example, research examining resilience to traumatic birth suggests the majority of women are resilient. A longitudinal study of women whose births met DSM-IV criteria for a traumatic event found that only 14% of these women had chronic PTSD one month and six months after birth (Dikmen-Yildiz, Ayers, & Phillips, 2018). Women who were resilient reported more social support and satisfaction with healthcare professionals, less severe PTSD symptoms, less depression, fear of childbirth, and fewer additional traumas since birth. However, this study used diagnostic criteria as an indicator of illness so it is possible that women who did not meet diagnostic criteria (i.e., classed as resilient) still experienced significant symptoms, distress, and disability.

A number of protective factors that buffer against stressors in the transition to parenthood, or mediate the impact of stressors on well-being, have been suggested. Table 3.1 shows a truncated summary of factors (selected to give an overview of the area) reported in the transition to parenthood literature mapped onto the range of systems shown in Figure 3.1.

TABLE 3.1 Systems Contributing to Resilience in Pregnancy, Birth, and New Parenthood

Systemic Level	Definition	Suggested Attributes
Epi/genetics	Transgenerational heritable factors related to genetic code and gene expression	Vulnerability to anxiety, depression and other psychological challenges
		Family history of breastfeeding
		Family history of trauma
		Fertility
		Sensitivity to stress
		General health
Personal attributes	Individual qualities and characteristics	Disposition
		Psychological flexibility
		Meaning making
		Attachment style
		Humor
		Self-efficacy
		Coping style
		Locus of control
		Positive self-esteem
		Hope
		Curiosity
		Reflective functioning
Relationships	Connections with valued others (mediated by availability, attunement, and responsivity)	Child
		Intimate partner
		Other children
		Family of origin
		Peer network
		Mentors
		Work
		Religious institution
Support systems	Groups and institutions with varying degrees of formality providing assistance for pregnant women and new parents	Childcare
		Financial aid
		Parenting groups
		Midwifery
		Obstetrics
		Pediatric medicine
		Playgroups
		Parenting helplines and websites
		The legal system
		Health insurance and access initiatives
		Workplace participation and leave policy
		Language lessons and cultural inclusion

TABLE 3.1 Continued

Systemic Level	Definition	Suggested Attributes
Culture	Dominant social behavior and norms in which the parent is immersed	Parenting narratives
		Traditional postpartum practices
		Gender norms
		Media content
		Normalized health behaviors (diet, smoking, exercise)
Environment	Natural conditions, circumstances, resources, and stressors	Transport
		Neighborhood safety
		Parenting rooms
		Natural disasters
		Food quality and security
		Water sources
		Exposure to toxins (e.g. pesticides, heavy metals)
		Air pollution

A number of personal skills and abilities that play a protective role in resilience outcomes have been identified including meaning making, dispositional optimism, psychological flexibility, and an active coping style. Meaning making is the process of attributing coherence and value to life experiences. This has been found to have a protective effect on parents' resilience particularly when related to the changes in identity and relationship that they experience during the process of become a parent (e.g., Fletcher & Sarkar, 2013; Garcia-Dia, Di Napoli, Garcia-Ona, Jakubowski, & O'Flaherty, 2013; Gardner & Harmon, 2002). Parents with optimistic dispositions may feel more hopeful that good outcomes will eventuate in the future (even when the present is characterized by difficulty) and demonstrate flexible application of coping skills (Baldwin, Kennedy, & Armata, 2008; Nes & Segerstrom, 2006). For example, a study of 37 working mothers found those who scored higher on optimism reported less distress and scored higher on resilience (Baldwin et al., 2008). This was true even for those women who reported more objective stressor events.

Interestingly, both psychological flexibility and an active coping style have been identified as protective factors although these two skills are different approaches to challenges. Psychological flexibility refers to the ability to let go of what was expected, accept what is, and formulate new understandings and responses to demand (Skowron, Fingerhut, & Hess, 2014). Active coping refers to approaching problems with a sense of agency and using active problem-solving skills to advocate for needs, utilize resources, and make change in the situation (Brodsky & De Vet, 2000; Gardner & Harmon, 2002). There is a need for future research to refine whether both types of coping confer an advantage or whether resilient parents are employing them both in different contexts and for different needs. For example, acceptance may be the most useful response to a child with a difficult temperament or to a disrupted birth plan, whereas advocacy and linking in with available supports may be more useful when trying to manage a high needs pregnancy or access help for postpartum depression or birth trauma.

Perhaps the most robust finding about resilience in pregnancy and birth is the importance of social support. It is well established that continuous support during labor is important in birth outcomes (Bohren, Hofmeyr, Sakala, Fukuzawa, & Cuthbert, 2017) and, conversely, that poor support or interpersonal difficulties during birth are a risk factor for postpartum PTSD (Ayers et al., 2016; Harris & Ayers, 2012). Reviews of clinical trials show that continuous support during labor is associated with less pain medication, shorter labors, fewer caesarean births, and greater satisfaction with birth (Bohren et al., 2017). Prospective studies show support can potentially buffer women against traumatic birth events and is particularly important for women with a history of trauma or who have complications or high levels of intervention during birth (Ford & Ayers, 2011). Support during labor and birth is therefore likely to be critical in terms of reducing risk and increasing resilience. Research has found associations between PTSD symptoms and a range of support variables, such as poor interaction with medical personnel, perceptions of inadequate care during birth, low support from partner and staff, and being poorly informed or not listened to (Czarnocka & Slade, 2000; Soet, Brack, & Dilorio, 2003; Creedy, Shochet, & Horsfall, 2000). Specific support needs include validation of negative and ambivalent emotions, challenging unreasonable expectations, provision of practical information and support, listening and emotional nurturing, financial aid, distraction, and social engagement (Darvill, Skirton, & Farrand, 2010; Deave, Johnson, & Ingram, 2008). For example, a study of over 1,300 women in the United States examined what characterized women with resilient, moderate or vulnerable psychosocial profiles after birth. Results showed that women who were resilient were characterized by high support and self-efficacy and reported less depression and stress. In contrast, vulnerable women were characterized by high depression and stress and poor support and self-efficacy. Vulnerable women were more likely to have an unintended pregnancy, engage in risky health behaviors, and give birth preterm (Maxson, Edwards, Valentiner & Miranda, 2016).

Qualitative research has shown that parents often perceive their intimate partner to be their first and most important source of social support and that one parent's adjustment influences the other's (Porat-Zyman, Taubman-Ben-Ari, & Spielman, 2017). Some of the key findings in this area have been the importance of effective communication and conflict resolution strategies, open negotiation about the distribution of household chores, shared caregiving, and managing changing sexual dynamics (Cohen, Pentel, Boeding, & Baucom, 2019; Shockley, & Allen, 2018; Vannier, Adare, & Rosen, 2018). Supportive family of origin also contributes to resilience outcomes, especially for the mother, as does access to peers, friends, and parenting communities (Darvill et al., 2010; Lois, 2016).

A number of broader protective factors from community, cultural, and environmental systems have also been identified. These include social connectedness, midwifery and child health services, traditional postpartum practices, and neighborhood safety (Nelson, Kushlev, & Lyubomirsky, 2014; Pistella & Synkewecz, 1999). Goodness of fit between the individual's personal and cultural needs and available community and environmental resources are also important. The parenting narratives present in media and cultural discourse, particularly with regard to gendered parenting roles and division of labor/workforce participation, have also been found to influence resilience outcomes (Welch, Rouleau-Mitchell, Farero, Lachmar, & Wittenborn, 2019).

Factors Associated With Poor Perinatal Resilience

There are a variety of factors that reduce resilience that are common during pregnancy and the transition to parenthood. These include relationship strain, social isolation, community disengagement, fear of judgment, and low self-esteem. New and expecting parents are also more susceptible to additional life stress due to the greater demand on their coping resources and skills (Dunkel-Schetter, 2011). Relationship strain between parenting partners has been shown to undermine parental resilience (Harville, Xiong, Buekens, Pridjian, & Elkind-Hirsch, 2010; Lennon & Heaman, 2015). Specifically, nonresilient parents scored more highly on marital conflict and dissatisfaction with division of labor in the home (De Haan, Hawley, & Deal, 2002) and IPV, drinking behavior, and anger management difficulties are key concerns for new mothers experiencing poor resilience (Gagnon & Stewart, 2014; Baraitser & Noack, 2007).

Poor support and/or social isolation has also been linked to lower resilience (Lennon & Heaman, 2015; Harville et al., 2010; Hynie et al., 2015) and higher levels of postpartum depression (Miranda et al., 2012). In particular, women who had poor relationships with or were unable to access their mothers due to migration reported greater distress than those who had access to this resource (Miranda et al., 2012; Schlager, 2014). Community disengagement in the form of lack of knowledge about or access to community services has also been identified as a key hindrance to resilience after the birth of a child (Gagnon & Stewart, 2014; Harville et al., 2010). Specifically, new migrant mothers experienced additional difficulties in utilizing systemic supports (Gress-Smith, 2015; Schlager, 2013), and rural women struggled with lack of privacy and limited resources (Shaikh & Kauppi, 2010). Women who lived in the context of poor financial support and unaffordable healthcare perceived strong pressure to return to work as soon as possible following a difficult or traumatic birth despite the risks to their own health and impact on their ability to provide care for their babies (Kaye et al., 2014).

Theoretical Approaches to Resilience During Pregnancy and Birth

A recent scoping study of resilience theory in the transition to parenthood (Young et al., 2018) found that over half of the published studies did not identify a theoretical framework for their research. Instead, they defined resilience through narrative literature review and then inferred its presence either through low scores on a distress measure or high scores on measures of positive outcomes such as self-efficacy. This approach is problematic and confounds integration of findings. Resilience is a multilevel process involving numerous interacting systems and operationalizing it through inference on a single measure obscures this complexity and may lead to misclassification of participants. For example, a resilient parent may have a low score on a measure of self-efficacy because, within that parent's unique psychosocial context, self-efficacy is not salient to mobilizing a resilience response.

Cross-sectional research relying on distress as a measure of resilience may assess individuals prior to them regaining psychological equilibrium and therein erroneously classify them as non-resilient. Unfortunately, even in studies where a clear theoretical framework has been applied there has been no consensus on which theory should be used. Different frameworks have different emphases on family stress and coping, pathways of resilience to particular outcomes (e.g., low anxiety), or resilience in terms of parenting and child outcomes. Three theoretical frameworks are outlined in this chapter, which were selected because they are explicit theories of resilience and/or specifically pertain to the perinatal period. The list is far from exhaustive. Other less often used theoretical approaches in the area have included application of feminist critical theory, positive psychology, and existentialism.

Dunkel Schetter's Model of Pregnancy Anxiety

Dunkel Schetter's (2011) model of pregnancy anxiety is a conscious effort to elucidate some of the unique factors related to coping during pregnancy and provide a more specialized theoretical framework. Dunkel Schetter positions pregnancy as a distinct time in the lifespan that potentiates revitalization of coping resources as well as revealing developmental vulnerability. She described pregnancy-related stress as chronic in nature and questioned the applicability of resilience models that are built on research about single-impact trauma.

Dunkel Schetter's model presents stress factors as predictors of pregnancy anxiety, biological processes, and resilience resources as mediators, with preterm birth and adverse developmental outcomes as potential outcomes. The model takes a systemic approach, incorporating individual, relational, sociocultural, and community systems and plotting a variety of mechanisms including neuroendocrine, immune, behavioral, sociorelational, and cultural processes. It charts a selection of stress and protective factors based on a synthesis of available literature representing the most robust findings linking pregnancy anxiety and preterm birth. Stressors include maternal hypothalamic–pituitary–adrenal axis, placental corticotropin-releasing hormone, fetal hypothalamic–pituitary axis, and uteroplacental dysfunction as well as disruptive life experiences, predisposition to anxiety, and medical complications. Protective factors include mastery, self-esteem, dispositional optimism, conscientiousness, relaxation, problem-solving, childhood socioeconomic status, presence of an available and effective social support network, familism, spirituality, and communalism.

While Dunkel Schetter's model could, in its entirety, be understood as a model of resilience, it is specifically focused on tracing the trajectory of adverse birth outcomes and child health. The mother's broader psychosocial well-being is not an explicit outcome within this model and the father or alternative parenting partner is not included (other than as a source of support for the mother).

The Preconception Stress and Resiliency Pathways Model

Following from Dunkel Schetter's (2011) investigation of pregnancy anxiety, the preconception stress and resiliency pathways (PSRP) model describes differential outcomes for pregnancy, fetal programming, and child health (Ramey et al., 2015). This model is novel in that it is the result of a community-based participatory research process that coordinated input from numerous transdisciplinary academics, clinicians, and community representatives over an extended period of time. The PSRP model is systemic and multilevel in nature combining biomedical and psychosocial indicators and outcomes. The model charts a progression over time from (a) the parenting partnership relationship and home environment to (b) the interpregnancy interval (preconception period), then (c) prenatal development and birth outcomes, and finally (d) the child's outcomes, health behavior, and neurocognitive development. Both mother and father appear in the model but, while their well-being is charted as a direct contributor to child outcomes, it is not explicitly positioned as an outcome of the pathway process.

The resilience processes chart each parent's social support in juxtaposition against their stress and stressors. Allostatic load is also charted, which refers to a composite score of biomarkers that may impact on pregnancy health and outcomes including systolic and diastolic blood pressure, heart rate, body mass index, waist-to-hip ratio, glycosylated hemoglobin, cholesterol, c-reactive protein, and salivary cortisol level. These, along with parental mental and physical health, health behaviors, and parenting, are positioned as causal contributors to resilient child outcomes. The social and environmental variables healthcare, education, work, recreation, spiritual resources, neighborhood, and community contexts are also included and conceptualized as an encompassing framework in which these processes occur.

The PSPR model identifies social attitudes, community well-being, and environmental resources, as having a direct impact on the biology of the individual and the family. Many of the variables are depicted in reciprocal relationships with each other, acknowledging that these influences are not static or unidirectional. For example, the mother's balance of stress versus support will influence the health of the parental relationship and the nature of the home environment, but the relationship and environmental will also influence the mother's level of stress and perceived support. Other novel contributions include tracking the impact of the parental relationship and home environment on the mother's physical health during pregnancy, father's stress and resilience factors positioned as direct contributors rather than moderating variables, and positioning community level variables as causal agents rather than mediating variables.

Parental Resilience Model

Gavidia-Payne et al. (2015) offer a theory of parental resilience informed by a review of the existing literature, noting that the weight of inquiry lies in family resilience and maternal resilience. Parental resilience is described as both a process in and of its own right and a system that contributes to family and child well-being during crisis. As such, they position parental resilience as an independent concept and a subsystem within family and child resilience. Here, resilient parents are defined as being able to deliver an appropriate level of parental care to children despite the presence of significant risk factors.

Gavidia-Payne et al. (2015) describe parenthood as a seminal stage in human development and thus a time of heightened vulnerability and propensity for resilience behavior. They highlight that factors are rarely inherently risky or protective and instead must be understood in the specific context of each parent. For example, new parents often traverse a period of social withdrawal where their attentions are largely focused on the parent–child dyad to the exclusion of other pre-existing social connections. While in the long term this can cause stress due to social disconnection and alterations in self-concept, in the short term it is understood as a protective mechanism supporting bonding between parent and child as well as ensuring plenty of stimulation for the parent to learn how to effectively understand and meet the child's needs. Thus provision of social support in the form of increased participation in social groupings outside of the parent–child dyad may not be a beneficial intervention during this time.

Gavidia-Payne et al. (2015) consider child and family characteristics (such as infant temperament and family socioeconomic status), parental well-being, parental self-efficacy, family functioning, and social connectedness as contributing factors to resilience. Notably, they recommend family functioning be assessed in the context of the individual family's everyday routines in cooperation with the parents and children involved. In such a way they hope to build opportunities to operationalize each family's unique personal and cultural context into the model. These contributing factors are charted as mediating against stressor events to facilitate resilient outcomes.

In sum, while a number of models have been used within the literature, there is no one model that fully reflects resilience in pregnancy and birth. This makes meaningful synthesis of findings from studies applying such different conceptualizations of resilience challenging. Researchers cannot be sure they are, in fact, talking about the same thing. Certainly, the heterogenous way in which resilience is conceptualized within this small literature remains a serious challenge to meaningful comparison of results.

Key Principles for Future Research and Theory Development

Consideration of the literature on perinatal resilience highlights a few key principles that need to be examined with further research. First, resilience in this period rests on the assumption that pregnancy, birth, and the transition to parenthood is a period of challenges and adaptation with the potential for resilience and growth. While this is broadly accepted in the perinatal literature, it is inconsistent with cultural stereotypes of pregnancy and birth as positive. This paradox needs further explanation.

Second, it is important to take a systems approach to perinatal resilience that considers the role of factors at epi/genetic, personal, relationship, support structures, cultural, and environmental levels. Resilience processes in pregnancy and after birth are highly complex because of the impact of pregnancy and birth on so many of these systems. Thus, research needs to consider how factors from different systems may interact to increase or reduce resilience.

Third, there are key areas of research and theory that have the potential to change how we care for women and families during this time. While an array of factors that contribute to resilience have been identified, the evidence from different areas of study is that relational and support factors are critical in the adjustment to parenthood generally as well as more specifically in relation to birth trauma. This is an area where it is relatively easy to intervene in maternity care systems, healthcare professionals, family relationships, and communities to improve communication and support.

Fourth, there is no one-size-fits-all answer to increasing perinatal resilience. Resilience during pregnancy and after birth will vary across individual contexts and cultures. This is illustrated by examples throughout this chapter of how a woman's culture can affect her risk of exposure to birth trauma and other stressors, as well as the resources available to her and the way in which the same factor can present as either stressor or resource depending on the individuals' unique biopsychosocial context.

Finally, the literature on perinatal resilience is developing. Heterogenous and often atheoretical approaches to research mean results are tentative. Furthermore, the lack of consensus on the best theoretical conceptualization of perinatal resilience hinders comparison and synthesis of available evidence.

Conclusion

In this chapter, we have outlined how pregnancy, birth, and becoming a parent involves substantial changes at physical, psychological, social, and broader cultural levels. During this time women are at increased risk of poor physical, psychological, and social outcomes, such as obstetric complications, psychological problems, and relationship difficulties. Examining adversity, risk, and resilience during pregnancy, birth, and postpartum is important because of the potential impact on women and their infants.

Resilience can be examined in terms of specific trauma events, such as birth trauma, or more widely in relation to the transition to parenthood. While a few relevant theories can be drawn on to study resilience, there is no one model that fully reflects resilience in pregnancy and birth. It is important, therefore, that future research and theory examines resilience across different systems. Theoretical development and consensus on how we understand perinatal resilience is also essential to move the field forward.

While some risk and protective factors involved in resilience throughout pregnancy and birth have been identified, meaningful investigation of these factors needs to take into account that the same resource, relationship, or personal ability can be helpful or unhelpful depending on context. For example, community supports and father participation are both protective factors and so it may be assumed that families would benefit from a universal parenting group that both mothers and fathers are expected to attend. However, in some communities involving fathers in a group that some women might attend alone or where topics such as breastfeeding or postpartum care will be discussed might be seen as inappropriate precluding attendance from both the father and the mother. A thorough understanding of nuances is needed to design effective interventions in this area. Particular attributes or relationships are not, in and of themselves, wholly helpful or unhelpful. Instead, the distribution of protective and risk factors plays out within a unique context that must be understood if we are to intervene effectively.

With regard to context, one of the most significant limitations to the current research body is the absence of information about fathers. The majority of studies either limit inclusion to mothers only or examine the experiences of couples as a unit. Parenting constellations that are not cisgender mother–father dyads or single mothers have also received little attention. There is a lack of research exploring resilience in queer, nonbinary, and transgender parenting communities although there has been some work done within the broader transition to parenthood literature (e.g., see Cao, Mills-Koonce, Wood, & Fine, 2016; Tornello, Riskind, & Babic, 2019).

Another prominent limitation is the focus on parents considered "at risk" in some way (such as IPV or premature birth). Researchers have largely focused on parents who are managing an extra stressor or crisis factor to justify the use of resilience concepts, but some theorists have argued that parents who do not meet additional at risk criteria also experience compromised well-being and must navigate personal and relational distress throughout pregnancy and new parenthood (Cowan et al., 1985; Feinberg et al., 2016).

Factors loading onto community and environment systems are also not well explored, and there is a need for longitudinal research that measures resilience at different points in the process beginning with a baseline measurement where possible (e.g., before birth). Pathway models using configural frequency analysis (a statistical technique that uses a priori data categorization to detect patterns in data sets across a number of variables and points in time; see De Haan et al., 2002) or similar techniques are also worth exploring further. Some studies (Gress-Smith, 2015; Ramey et al., 2015) have incorporated biological correlates of resilience into the research design, but more work incorporating environmental and neurological/biological factors would be beneficial and create opportunities for cross disciplinary collaboration (Rutten et al., 2013).

Key Messages

1. Pregnancy, birth, and becoming a parent involves substantial changes at biological, psychological, social, and cultural levels. As such, it is a continuing process of adaptation to change and new demands.
2. The experience of adversity, stress, and trauma during pregnancy, birth, and postpartum is particularly important because of the potential impact on women and their infants.
3. Resilience in pregnancy and after birth can be examined in terms of specific trauma events, such as birth trauma or IPV, or more widely in relation to the transition to parenthood.
4. Research and theory in this area is developing so understanding and conclusions are limited. A few relevant theories can be drawn on but there is no one model that fully reflects resilience in pregnancy and birth.
5. Future research and theory needs to examine resilience at different levels (e.g., epi/genetic, personal attributes, relationships, support systems, culture, and environment).

References

Ahlborg, T., Misvaer, N., & Möller, A. (2009). Perception of marital quality by parents with small children: A follow-up study when the firstborn is 4 years old. *Journal of Family Nursing, 15*(2), 237–263. doi:10.1177/1074840709334925

Ahmadvand, A., Gatchel, R., Brownstein, J., & Nissen, L. (2018). The biopsychosocial-digital approach to health and disease: Call for a paradigm expansion. *Journal of Medical Internet Research, 20*(5), e189. doi:10.2196/jmir.9732

Aldwin, C. M., & Levenson, M. (2004). Post-traumatic growth: A developmental perspective. *Psychological Inquiry, 15*(1), 19–22.

American Psychiatric Association. (2000). *Diagnostic and statistical manual of mental disorders* (4th ed., Text Revision). Washington, DC: Author.

Antonovsky, A. (1979). *Health, stress and coping*. San Francisco, CA: Jossey-Bass.

Ayers, S., Bond, R., Bertullies, S., & Wijma, K. (2016). The aetiology of post-traumatic stress following childbirth: A meta-analysis and theoretical framework. *Psychological Medicine*, *46*(6), 1121–1134. doi:10.1017/S0033291715002706

Baldwin, D. R., Kennedy, D. L., & Armata, P. (2008). De-stressing mommy: Ameliorative association with dispositional optimism and resiliency. *Stress and Health*, *24*(5), 393–400. doi:10.1002/smi.1189

Baraitser, L., & Noack, A. (2007). Mother courage: Reflections on maternal resilience. *British Journal of Psychotherapy*, *23*(2), 171–188. doi:10.1111/j.1752-0118.2007.00016.x

Bayrampour, H., Tomfohr, L., & Tough, S. (2016). Trajectories of perinatal depressive and anxiety symptoms in a community cohort. *Journal of Clinical Psychiatry*, *77*(11), 1467–1473. doi:10.4088/JCP.15m10176

Beck, C. T., & Watson, S. (2016). Posttraumatic growth after birth trauma: I was broken, now I am unbreakable. *American Journal of Maternal and Child Nursing*, *41*(5), 264–271. doi:10.1097/NMC.0000000000000259

Bohren, M. A., Hofmeyr, G., Sakala, C., Fukuzawa, R. K., & Cuthbert, A. (2017). Continuous support for women during childbirth. *Cochrane Database of Systematic Reviews*, *2017*(7). doi:10.1002/14651858.CD003766.pub6

Brewin, C. R., Andrews, B., & Valentine, J. D. (2000). Meta-analysis of risk factors for posttraumatic stress disorder in trauma-exposed adults. *Journal of Consulting and Clinical Psychology*, *68*(5), 748–766. doi:10.1037//0022-006x.68.5.748

Brodsky, A. E., & De Vet, K. A. (2000). "You have to be real strong": Parenting goals and strategies of resilient, urban, African American, single mothers. *Journal of Prevention and Intervention in the Community*, *21*(1–2), 159–178. doi:10.1300/J005v20n01_11

Cao, H., Mills-Koonce, W. R., Wood, C., & Fine, M. A. (2016). Identity transformation during the transition to parenthood among same-sex couples: An ecological, stress-strategy-adaptation perspective. *Journal of Family Theory and Review*, *8*(1), 30–59. doi:10.1111/jftr.12124

Centers for Disease Control and Prevention. (2014). *Pregnancy mortality surveillance system*. Retrieved from https://www.cdc.gov/reproductivehealth/maternalinfanthealth/pregnancy-mortality-surveillance-system.htm

Cohen, M. J., Pentel, K. Z., Boeding, S. E., & Baucom, D. H. (2019). Postpartum role satisfaction in couples: Associations with individual and relationship well-being. *Journal of Family Issues*, *40*(9), 1181–1200. doi:10.1177/0192513X19835866

Cowan, C. P., Cowan, P. A., Heming, G., Garrett, E., Coysh, W. S., Curtis-boles, H., & Boles, A. J. (1985). Transitions to parenthood: His, hers, and theirs. *Journal of Family Issues*, *6*(4), 451–481. doi:10.1177/019251385006004004

Creedy, D. K., Shochet, I. M., & Horsfall, J. (2000). Childbirth and the development of acute trauma symptoms: Incidence and contributing factors. *Birth*, *27*(2), 104–111. doi:10.1046/j.1523-536x.2000.00104.x

Czarnocka, J., & Slade, P. (2000). Prevalence and predictors of post-traumatic stress symptoms following childbirth. *British Journal of Clinical Psychology*, *39*(1), 35–51.

Darvill, R., Skirton, H., & Farrand, P. (2010). Psychological factors that impact on women's experiences of first-time motherhood: A qualitative study of the transition. *Midwifery*, *26*(3), 357–366. doi:10.1016/j.midw.2008.07.006

Davydov, D. M., Stewart, R., Ritchie, K., & Chaudieu, I. (2010). Resilience and mental health. *Clinical Psychology Review*, *30*(5), 479–495. doi:10.1016/j.cpr.2010.03.003

De Haan, L., Hawley, D. R., & Deal, J. E. (2002). Operationalizing family resilience: A methodological strategy. *American Journal of Family Therapy*, *30*(4), 275–291. doi:10.1080/01926180290033439

Deave, T., Johnson, D., & Ingram, J. (2008). Transition to parenthood: The needs of parents in pregnancy and early parenthood. *BMC Pregnancy Childbirth*, *8*(1), 30. doi:10.1186/1471-2393-8-30

Dekel, S., Stuebe, C., & Dishy, G. (2017). Childbirth induced posttraumatic stress syndrome: A systematic review of prevalence and risk factors. *Frontiers in Psychology*, *8*, 560. doi:10.3389/fpsyg.2017.00560

Denckla, C. A., Mancini, A. D., Consedine, N. S., Milanovic, S. M., Basu, A., Seedat, S., . . . Bonanno, K. C. (2018). Distinguishing postpartum and antepartum depressive trajectories in a large population-based cohort: The impact of exposure to adversity and offspring gender. *Psychological Medicine*, *48*(7), 1139–1147. doi:10.1017/S0033291717002549

Dikmen-Yildiz, P., Ayers, S., & Phillips, L. (2017a). The prevalence of posttraumatic stress disorder in pregnancy and after birth: A systematic review and meta-analysis. *Journal of Affective Disorders, 208*, 634–645. doi:10.1016/j.jad.2016.10.009

Dikmen-Yildiz, P., Ayers, S., & Phillips, L. (2017b). Factors associated with post-traumatic stress symptoms (PTSS) 4-6 weeks and 6 months after birth: A longitudinal population-based study. *Journal of Affective Disorders, 221*, 238–245. doi:10.1016/j.jad.2017.06.049

Dikmen-Yildiz, P., Ayers, S., & Phillips, L. (2018). Longitudinal trajectories of post-traumatic stress disorder (PTSD) after birth and associated risk factors. *Journal of Affective Disorders, 229*, 377–385. doi:10.1016/j.jad.2017.12.074

Doss, B. D., Rhoades, G. K., Stanley, S. M., & Markman, H. J. (2009). The effect of the transition to parenthood on relationship quality: An 8-year prospective study. *Journal of Personality and Social Psychology, 96*(3), 601–609. doi:10.1037/a0013969

Dunkel-Schetter, C. (2011). Psychological science on pregnancy: Stress processes, biopsychosocial models, and emerging research issues. *Annual Review of Psychology, 62*(1), 531–558. doi:10.1146/annurev.psych.031809.130727

Engel, G. L. (1979). The biopsychosocial model and the education of health professionals. *Annals of the New York Academy of Sciences, 310*(1), 169–181. doi:10.1111/j.1749-6632.1978.tb22070.x

Feinberg, M. E., Jones, D. E., Hostetler, M. L., Roettger, M. E., Paul, I. M., & Ehrenthal, D. B. (2016). Couple-focused prevention at the transition to parenthood, a randomized trial: Effects on coparenting, parenting, family violence, and parent and child adjustment. *Prevention Science, 17*(6), 751–764. doi:10.1007/s11121-016-0674-z

Field, T. (2010). Postpartum depression effects on early interactions, parenting, and safety practices: A review. *Infant Behavior and Development, 33*(1), 1–6. doi:10.1016/j.infbeh.2009.10.005

Fletcher, D., & Sarkar, M. (2013). Psychological resilience: A review and critique of definitions, concepts, and theory. *European Psychologist, 18*(1), 12–23. doi:10.1027/1016-9040/a000124

Ford, E., & Ayers, S. (2011). Support during birth interacts with trauma history and birth intervention to predict postnatal post-traumatic stress symptoms. *Psychology & Health, 26*(12), 1553–1570. doi:10.1080/08870446.2010.533770

Furuta, M., Sandall, J., & Bick, D. (2012). A systematic review of the relationship between severe maternal morbidity and post-traumatic stress disorder. *BMC Pregnancy and Childbirth, 12*(1), 125. doi:10.1186/1471-2393-12-125

Gagnon, A. J., & Stewart, D. E. (2014). Resilience in international migrant women following violence associated with pregnancy. *Archives of Women's Mental Health, 17*(4), 303–310. doi:10.1007/s00737-013-0392-5

Garcia-Dia, M. J., Di Napoli, J. M., Garcia-Ona, L., Jakubowski, R., & O'Flaherty, D. (2013). Concept analysis: Resilience. *Archives of Psychiatric Nursing, 27*(6), 264–270. doi:10.1016/j.apnu.2013.07.003

Gardner, J., & Harmon, T. (2002). Exploring resilience from a parent's perspective: A qualitative study of six resilient mothers of children with an intellectual disability. *Australian Social Work, 55*(1), 60–68. doi:10.1080/03124070208411672

Gavidia-Payne, S., Denny, B., Davis, K., Francis, A., & Jackson, M. (2015). Parental resilience: A neglected construct in resilience research. *Clinical Psychologist, 19*(3), 111–121. doi:10.1111/cp.12053

Gress-Smith, J. L. (2015). *Resilience profiles and postpartum depression in low-income Mexican American women*. Available from Dissertation Abstracts International: Section B: The Sciences and Engineering. (UMI No. 3631533)

Groves, A. K., Moodley, D., McNaughton-Reyes, L., Martin, S. L., Foshee, V., & Maman, S. (2015). Prevalence, rates and correlates of intimate partner violence among South African women during pregnancy and the postpartum period. *Journal of Maternal and Child Health, 19*(3), 487–495. doi:10.1007/s10995-014-1528-6

Hahn, C. K., Gilmore, A. K., Aguayo, R. O., & Rheingold, A. A. (2018). Perinatal intimate partner violence. *Obstetric and Gynecological Clinics of North America, 45*(3), 535–547. doi:10.1016/j.ogc.2018.04.008

Harris, R., & Ayers, S. (2012). What makes labour and birth traumatic? A survey of intrapartum "hotspots." *Psychology & Health, 27*(10), 1166–1177. doi:10.1080/08870446.2011.649755

Harville, E. W., Xiong, X., Buekens, P., Pridjian, G., & Elkind-Hirsch, K. (2010). Resilience after hurricane Katrina among pregnant and postpartum women. *Womens Health Issues, 20*(1), 20–27. doi:10.1016/j.whi.2009.10.002

Hynie, M., Umubyeyi, B., Gasanganwa, M., Bohr, Y., McGrath, S., Umuziga, P., & Mukarusanga, B. (2015). Community resilience and community interventions for post-natal depression: Reflecting on maternal mental health in Rwanda. In N. Khanlou & F. B. Pilkington (Eds.), *Women's mental health* (pp. 343–356). Cham, Switzerland: Springer International.

Kaye, D. K., Kakaire, O., Nakimuli, A., Mbalinda, S. N., Osinde, M. O., & Kakande, N. (2014). Survivors' understanding of vulnerability and resilience to maternal near-miss obstetric events in Uganda. *International Journal of Gynaecology and Obstetrics, 127*(3), 265–268. doi:10.1016/j.ijgo.2014.05.019

Leach, L. S., Poyser, C., Cooklin, A. R., & Giallo, R. (2016). Prevalence and course of anxiety disorders (and symptom levels) in men across the perinatal period: A systematic review. *Journal of Affective Disorders, 15*(190), 675–686. doi:10.1016/j.jad.2015.09.063

Lennon, S. L., & Heaman, M. (2015). Factors associated with family resilience during pregnancy among inner-city women. *Midwifery, 31*(10), 957–964. doi:10.1016/j.midw.2015.05.007

Lindström, B., & Eriksson, M. (2005). Salutogenesis. *Journal of Epidemiology and Community Health, 59*(6), 440–442. doi:10.1136/jech.2005.034777

Lois, D. (2016). Types of social networks and the transition to parenthood. *Demographic Research, 34*(1), 657–688. doi:10.4054/DemRes.2016.34.23

Maxson, P. J., Edwards, S. E., Valentiner, E. M., & Miranda, M. L. (2016). A multidimensional approach to characterizing psychosocial health during pregnancy. *Maternal & Child Health Journal, 20*(6), 1103–1113. doi:10.1007/s10995-015-1872-1

Meier Magistretti, C., Downe, S., Lindstrøm, B., Berg, M., Schwarz, K. T. (2016). Setting the stage for health: Salutogenesis in midwifery professional knowledge in three European countries. *International Journal of Qualitative Studies on Health and Well-Being, 11*(1). doi:10.3402/qhw.v11.33155

Michael, C., & Cooper, M. (2013). Post-traumatic growth following bereavement: A systematic review of the literature. *Counselling Psychology Review, 28*(4), 18–33.

Miranda, A. M., Soares, C. N., Moraes, M. L., Fossaluza, V., Serafim, P. M., & Mello, M. F. (2012). Healthy maternal bonding as a resilience factor for depressive disorder. *Psychology & Neuroscience, 5*(1), 21–25. doi:10.3922/j.psns.2012.1.04

Mittelmark, M. B., & Bauer, G. F. (2017). The meanings of salutogenesis. In M. B. Mittelmark, S. Sagy, M. Eriksson, G. Bauer, J. M. Pelikan, B. Lindstrom, & G. A. Espnes (Eds.), *The handbook of salutogenesis* (pp. 7–13). Berlin, Germany: SpringerLink Press.

Modarres, M., Afrasiabi, S., Rahnama, P., & Montazeri, A. (2012). Prevalence and risk factors of childbirth-related post-traumatic stress symptoms. *BMC Pregnancy and Childbirth, 12*(1), 88–93. doi:10.1186/1471-2393-12-88

Mortensen, Ø., Torsheim, T., Melkevik, O., & Thuen, F. (2012). Adding a baby to the equation: Married and cohabiting women's relationship satisfaction in the transition to parenthood. *Family Process, 51*(1), 122–139. doi:10.1111/j.1545-5300.2012.01384.x

Nelson, S. K., Kushlev, K., & Lyubomirsky, S. (2014). The pains and pleasures of parenting: When, why, and how is parenthood associated with more or less well-being? *Psychological Bulletin, 140*(3), 846–895. doi:10.1037/a0035444

Nes, L. S., & Segerstrom, S. C. (2006). Dispositional optimism and coping: A meta-analytic review. *Personality and Social Psychology Review, 10*(3), 235–251. doi:10.1207/s15327957pspr1003_3

O'Hara, M. W., & Wisner, K. L. (2014). Perinatal mental illness: Definition, description and aetiology. *Best Practice in Research and Clinical Obstetrics and Gynaecology, 28*(1), 3–12. doi:10.1016/j.bpobgyn.2013.09.002

Ozer, E. J., Best, S. R., Lipsey, T. L., & Weiss, D. S. (2003). Predictors of posttraumatic stress disorder and symptoms in adults: A meta-analysis. *Psychological Bulletin, 129*(1), 52–73. doi:10.1037/0033-2909.129.1.52

Philpott, L. F., Leahy-Warren, P., FitzGerald, S., & Savage, E. (2017). Stress in fathers in the perinatal period: A systematic review. *Midwifery, 55*, 113–127. doi:10.1016/j.midw.2017.09.016

Pistella, C. Y., & Synkewecz, C. A. (1999). Community postpartum care needs assessment and systems development for low income families. *Journal of Health and Social Policy, 11*(1), 53–64. doi:10.1300/J045v11n01_04

Porat-Zyman, G., Taubman—Ben-Ari, O., & Spielman, V. (2017). Dyadic transition to parenthood: A longitudinal assessment of personal growth among parents of pre- and full-term infants. *Stress and Health, 33*(1), 24–34. doi:10.1002/smi.2669

Ramey, S. L., Schafer, P., DeClerque, J. L., Lanzi, R. G., Hobel, C., Shalowitz, M., . . . Raju, T. N. (2015). The preconception stress and resiliency pathways model: A multi-level framework on maternal, paternal, and child health disparities derived by community-based participatory research. *Journal of Maternal and Child Health, 19*(4), 707–719. doi:10.1007/s10995-014-1581-1

Rogal, S. S., Poschman, K., Belanger, K., Howell, H. B., Smith, M. V., Medina, J., & Yonkers, K. A. (2007). Effects of posttraumatic stress disorder on pregnancy outcomes. *Journal of Affective Disorders, 102*(1–3), 137–143. doi:10.1016/j.jad.2007.01.003

Rutten, B. P., Hammels, C., Geschwind, N., Menne-Lothmann, C., Pishva, E., Schruers, K., . . . Wichers, M. (2013). Resilience in mental health: Linking psychological and neurobiological perspectives. *Acta Psychiatrica Scandinavica, 128*(1), 3–20. doi:10.1111/acps.12095

Sawyer, A., & Ayers, S. (2009). Post-traumatic growth in women after childbirth. *Psychology and Health, 24*(4), 457–471. doi:10.1080/08870440701864520

Sawyer, A., Ayers, S., Smith, H., Sidibeh, L., Nyan, O., & Dale, J. (2011). Women's experiences of pregnancy, childbirth, and the postnatal period in The Gambia: A qualitative study. *British Journal of Health Psychology, 16*(3), 528–541. doi:10.1348/135910710X528710

Schlager, E. A. (2014). *Resiliency and vulnerability to post-partum depression in acculturating new mothers* (Doctoral dissertation). Retrieved from Dissertation Abstracts International: Section B: The Sciences and Engineering, 75. (UMI No. 3601168)

Shaikh, A., & Kauppi, C. (2010). Coping strategies as a manifestation of resilience in the face of postpartum depression: Experiences of women in northern Ontario. *International Journal of Interdisciplinary Social Sciences, 5*(6), 261–273. doi:10.18848/1833-1882/CGP/v05i06/51770

Shockley, K. M., & Allen, T. D. (2018). It's not what I expected: The association between dual-earner couples' met expectations for the division of paid and family labor and well-being. *Journal of Vocational Behavior, 104*, 240–260. doi:10.1016/j.jvb.2017.11.009

Skowron, A., Fingerhut, R., & Hess, B. (2014). The role of assertiveness and cognitive flexibility in the development of postpartum depressive symptoms. *Journal of Reproductive and Infant Psychology, 32*(4), 388–399. doi:10.1080/02646838.2014.940518

Slade, P. (2006). Towards a conceptual framework for understanding post-traumatic stress symptoms following childbirth and implications for further research. *Journal of Psychosomatic Obstetrics and Gynecology, 27*(2), 99–105. doi:10.1080/01674820600714582

Soet, J. E., Brack, G. A., & Dilorio, C. (2003). Prevalence and predictors of women's experience of psychological trauma during childbirth. *Birth, 30*(1), 36–46. doi:10.1046/j.1523-536X.2003.00215.x

Suls, J., & Rothman, A. (2004). Evolution of the biopsychosocial model: Prospects and challenges for health psychology. *Health Psychology, 23*(2), 119–125. doi:10.1037/0278-6133.23.2.119

Talge, N. M., Neal, C., & Glover, V. (2007). Antenatal maternal stress and long-term effects on child neurodevelopment: How and why? *Journal of Child Psychology and Psychiatry, 48*(3–4), 245–261. doi:10.1111/j.1469-7610.2006.01714.x

Tedeschi, R. G., & Calhoun, L. G. (2004). Target article: Posttraumatic growth: Conceptual foundations and empirical evidence. *Psychological Inquiry, 15*(1), 1–18. doi:10.1207/s15327965pli1501_01

Tedeschi, R. G., Park, C., & Calhoun, L. G. (Eds.). (1998). *The LEA series in personality and clinical psychology. Posttraumatic growth: Positive changes in the aftermath of crisis.* Mahwah, NJ: Lawrence Erlbaum.

Tornello, S. L., Riskind, R. G., & Babić, A. (2019). Transgender and gender non-binary parents' pathways to parenthood. *Psychology of Sexual Orientation and Gender Diversity, 6*(2), 232–241. doi:10.1037/sgd0000323

Vannier, S. A., Adare, K. E., & Rosen, N. O. (2018). Is it me or you? First-time mothers' attributions for postpartum sexual concerns are associated with sexual and relationship satisfaction in the transition to parenthood. *Journal of Social and Personal Relationships, 35*(4), 577–599. doi:10.1177/0265407517743086

Wadhwa, P. D. (2005). Psychoneuroendocrine processes in human pregnancy influence fetal development and health. *Psychoneuroendocrinology, 30*(8), 724–743. doi:10.1016/j.psyneuen.2005.02.004

Welch, T., Rouleau-Mitchell, E., Farero, A., Lachmar, E. M., & Wittenborn, A. K. (2019). Maintaining relationship quality during the transition to parenthood: The need for next generation interventions. *Contemporary Family Therapy, 41*(2), 211–218. doi:10.1007/s10591-018-9481-y

World Health Organization. (2018). *Fact sheets: Maternal mortality*. Retrieved from https://www.who.int/news-room/fact-sheets/detail/maternal-mortality

Yonkers, K. A., Smith, M. V., Forray, A., Epperson, C. N., Costello, D., Lin, H., & Belanger, K. (2014). Pregnant women with posttraumatic stress disorder and risk of preterm birth. *JAMA Psychiatry, 71*(8), 897–904. doi:10.1001/jamapsychiatry.2014.558

Young, C., Roberts, R., & Ward, L. (2018). Application of resilience theories in the transition to parenthood: A scoping review. *Journal of Reproductive and Infant Psychology, 37*(2), 139–160. doi:10.1080/02646838.2018.1540860

4

Promoting Resilience Within Public Health Approaches for Indigenous Communities

Christopher Mushquash, Elaine Toombs,
Kristy Kowatch, Jessie Lund, Lauren Dalicandro,
and Kara Boles

Introduction

Public health is "the science of protecting and improving the health of people and their communities" (Centers for Disease Control and Prevention, 2019, p. 1). Primary initiatives in public health are rooted in the research, prevention, and promotion of community wellness. These initiatives typically take place in four domains: social determinants of health, healthy behaviors, healthy communities, and population health assessment (Ministry of Health and Long-Term Care, 2018). These public health prevention and intervention initiatives can serve as a means to foster resilience at the individual, community, and systemic level. Within public health, resilience is recognized as the capacity for a community to "endure, adapt, and generate new ways of thinking and functioning in the context of change, uncertainty, or adversity" (Seaman, McNeice, Yates, & McLean, 2014, p. 23). Rather than theorizing resilience as an individual or collective trait, resilience in the public health sector is conceptualized as an interconnected process that involves many system inputs that contribute to success in the face of adversity. Many public health institutions around the world, such as the Public Health Agency of Canada (2014), have highlighted the need for research on resilience as a protective factor within a number of different areas including mental health outcomes, health security, and emergency preparedness and response. Resilience in public health goes beyond aiming to reduce negative outcomes when populations face predictable challenges, such as high levels of diabetes. A focus on resilience allows for the development of a system that, ideally,

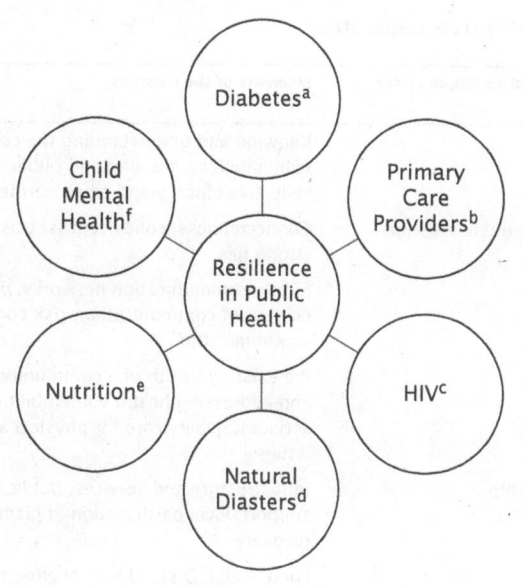

FIGURE 4.1 Examples of research areas addressed in public health resilience research.

can resist a multitude of stressors (Figure 4.1) including those that are unpredictable, such as natural disasters (Seaman et al., 2014).

This chapter will discuss the role of resilience in public health and how resilience can be identified and promoted through individual, community, and systemic assets. In particular, multisystemic approaches will be reviewed to describe how public health intervention in communities can use contemporary resilience models to promote primordial, primary, secondary, and tertiary prevention. Indigenous approaches to identifying and fostering resilience will be described, as such approaches may exemplify diverse contextual and cultural needs within a range of public health settings.

Public Health Promotes Community Resilience Across Levels of Care

Given that the goals of the public health sector are to promote broader health and well-being through primary, secondary, and tertiary care processes, efforts to enhance resilience can inform each level of care. Communities may utilize context-dependent methods to promote resilience; however, the broader presence of resilience may be identified in a similar manner across communities. Nine core adaptive capacities required for community resilience include: local knowledge, community networks and relationships, communication, health, governance and leadership, resources, economic investment, preparedness, and mental outlook (Patel, Rogers, Amlôt, & Rubin, 2017). Subcapacities exist within each of the core adaptive traits required for community resilience (See Table 4.1). Individually and collaboratively, these capacities create resilience within a community.

TABLE 4.1 Core Adaptive Capacities

Nine Core Adaptive Capacities Required for Community Resilience	Elements of the Capacity
Local knowledge	Knowing and understanding the community's vulnerabilities, training and public disaster education, collective efficacy and empowerment
Community networks and relationships	Connectedness, cohesiveness, trust, shared values, strong ties
Communication	Strong communication networks, diversity of mode and context of communication, risk communication, crisis communication
Health	Pre-existing health of a community, understanding and addressing health vulnerabilities, access to health services, quality care for physical and mental health issues
Governance and leadership	Infrastructure and services, public involvement and support, local participation in planning, response and recovery
Resources	Food, water, first-aid kits, shelter, transportation, essential machinery, financial and social resources
Economic Investment	Distribution of financial resources, economic programming, cost-effective interventions, economic development of postdisaster infrastructure
Preparedness	Risk assessment, drills, planning, mitigation measures
Mental Outlook	Attitudes toward uncertainty, hope, adaptability

Adapted from Patel et al. (2017).

Individual Assets

Individual factors contribute to resilience as they enable individuals to endure challenges with a higher likelihood of adaptability than those who do not possess those same traits (Hu, Zhang, & Wang, 2015). For example, higher levels of executive functioning, extraversion, spirituality, intellectual and cognitive abilities, and self-efficacy have been shown to act as protective qualities that increase resilience at an individual level (Campbell-Sills, Cohan, & Stein, 2006; Elliott et al., 2006; Kasen, Wickramaratne, Gameroff, & Weissman, 2012; Masten & Obradović, 2006; Windle, Markland, & Woods, 2008). While some of these qualities (i.e., cognitive ability and personality traits) can be genetically linked, there are other qualities that are developed due to experiences in early childhood, such as through secure relationships with a primary caregiver. Schore (2014), for example, demonstrated the necessity of early secure attachments in fostering self-regulation across the lifespan, which is a known precursor for resilience (Luthar & Eisenberg, 2017). While these traits are an important feature of resilience in individuals, having resources at the community level remains necessary for resilience to be fostered or demonstrated at the population level (Liebenberg, Joubert, & Foucault, 2017).

Community Assets

Ungar (2013) has suggested that resilience is better understood as "both the capacity of individuals to navigate their way to the psychological, social, cultural, and physical resources that sustain their well-being, and their capacity individually and collectively to negotiate for these resources to be provided in culturally meaningful ways" (p. 14). According to the U.S. Department of Health and Human Services (2009), a resilient *community* is composed of healthy individuals who have knowledge about, as well as access to, necessary resources (i.e., food, water, hospitals, shelter) in both routine and emergency situations. Resilience definitions, however, can differ based on the population. For example, Indigenous communities in Canada (First Nations, Métis, and Inuit) have unique histories to be considered in relation to public health systems and resilience. Long-standing assimilation policies and practices (e.g., the reserve system, residential school system, "sixties scoop," etc.) have influenced, and continue to influence, the development, delivery, and utilization of services in many Indigenous communities (Health Canada, 2015). Even across Indigenous communities within Canada, individuals have varying experiences with regard to these assimilation policies and their impact on health systems (Health Canada, 2015). Knowledge of larger social and political influences suggests that communities may have different priorities when assessing or addressing community resilience within public health models. Protective factors within a community may mitigate the negative effects of adversity, and there are varying risks of adversity for different communities. Thus, so-called one-size-fits-all approaches have limitations in terms of their potential for effectiveness.

Many characteristics promote community resilience, including social cohesion, education, policy, and engagement with cultural practices (Cost, 2015; Kapucu & Sadiq, 2016; Raich, Lorenzoni, Stummer, & Nöhammer, 2017). Factors that foster community resilience are interconnected and often interdependent, with one factor alone not sufficiently preparing a community for any given disaster (Toombs, Kowatch, & Mushquash, 2016). Rather, a resilient community often demonstrates community cohesion, routine and structure, good social policies, and equity, as well as cultural and civic engagement opportunities prior to, or as a consequence of, exposure to adversity (Patel et al., 2017). For this level of resilience to be exemplified, there are efforts that must be put forth within the community. In Canada, public health initiatives and programs such as Healthy Babies Healthy Children are in place to foster resilience in newborns and their families (Ontario Ministry of Children, Community and Social Services, 2019). Programs such as this can improve early environmental conditions by encouraging attentive parenting or connecting parents with community resources when needed. Resilient babies grow up to be resilient children, and those children develop into resilient adults who eventually make up a resilient community. Strategies used in programs such as Healthy Babies Healthy Children aim to strengthen a child's traits associated with resilience (e.g., ability to verbally express needs, develop positive interpersonal connections, etc.), while also fostering characteristics of the child's environment that support the child's optimal psychosocial development (i.e., positive family relationships, supportive parenting behaviors, and prosocial educational settings; Ontario Ministry of Children, Community and Social Services, 2019). Similar programs, such as Aboriginal Head Start (2006), also a Canadian program, are tailored to building resilience in Indigenous children. These programs demonstrate how public health initiatives conceptualize resilience as a multifaceted process that requires a harmonious interaction between individuals, their communities, and their natural or built environments.

More broadly, many public health efforts facilitate resilience within a community. Community-based and governmental organizations measure base rates to recognize risk. This can help inform the development of organizations' abilities not only to identify risk, but also to measure the influence of such risk within the broader organizational system. This can facilitate more effective decision-making processes and may create novel solutions to previous health concerns. For example, broad social initiatives such as employment assistance programs, safe injection sites, and emergency planning can be implemented to reduce initial risk to an individual, but also prevent further harm from re-occurring. Such services are in place to not only prevent, but to also adequately prepare for hardship (Frieden, 2014). The level of community resilience is indicated by the capability of a community to adapt and function adequately in the face of adversity (Patel et al., 2017). For example, adversity experienced within and/or between Indigenous communities can vary, affecting the way communities respond to ongoing stress. Elevated rates of historical residential school attendance of Indigenous children may influence the capacity of a community to respond to distress (Truth and Reconciliation Commission of Canada [TRCC], 2015). Attending a residential school has been noted to have negative intergenerational effects on health and well-being of both those attendees and their current offspring (Hackett, Feeny, & Tompa, 2016). Indigenous children were legally required to attend a residential school, and many were removed from their communities without consent from their families and were forbidden access to cultural or traditional activities. Ongoing and frequent physical, emotional, and sexual abuse at these institutions resulted in overall low well-being and disrupted overall psychosocial health long term in many of the children who attended (Hackett et al., 2016; Health Canada, 2015; McQuaid et al., 2017). The effect of these experiences on generations of Indigenous individuals, families, and communities may influence ongoing community response to current crises (Health Canada, 2015).

Differing historical contexts influence the level of resources that are required within a community to adequately address any health concerns. Indigenous communities that have reported self-government, greater involvement in land claims, and greater resources (including health, police, and cultural) have reported lower levels of suicide (Chandler & Lalonde, 1998). Cultural continuity, such as identifying strongly with a culture or engaging in cultural activities, has also been identified as promoting resilience (Toombs et al., 2016). For example, in communities where abuse was experienced by many members, a higher level of resources to address the resultant mental health concerns may be required, specifically as greater levels of adversity are experienced by future generations (Health Canada, 2015). Some suggestions on how mental health professionals can implement initiatives to support wellness with consideration of historical contexts of Indigenous communities, are provided by Boksa, Joober, and Kirmayer (2015). These include strategies such as recognizing long-term effects of historical trauma, understanding current challenges within a community, incorporating Indigenous concepts of wellness, and continuous support for sustainable program funding (Boksa et al., 2015). When a group of people have the ability to identify and direct resources to the areas with the greatest need within their communities, they experience greater levels of success (Health Canada, 2015; Maar et al., 2009).

Systemic Assets

There are particular assets that work collaboratively within a system to promote resilience. For example, Sherrieb, Norris, and Galea (2010), outlined four factors that most commonly influence community resilience, identified as economic development, community competence, information and communication, and social capital. Within the system of a community, these factors were identified to promote the adaptive capacity to foster resilience. Of these factors, economic development and social capital were identified to influence community resilience the most (Sherrieb et al., 2010). Economic development encompassed the availability of community resources as well as the distribution and diversity of these resources. More diverse, equally distributed resources allow for more opportunity within the community, which can cultivate more resilience for that community. Economic development can open up opportunity for a community to gain social capital. Social capital, defined as the process by which individuals invest, access, and use resources embedded within social networks for the purpose of gaining returns, can be seen as a systemic asset for resilience in public health (Lin, Fu, & Hsung, 2001). Social capital fosters interpersonal relationships among community members and brings about trust, shared norms, shared values, cooperation, and reciprocity within a community (Aldrich & Meyer, 2014). These factors work congruently within a community system to promote how well that system can adapt to adversity.

Resilience-promoting policy in public health practice also cultivates systemic resilience. The resilience of a community can be affected through policy decisions, also known as primordial prevention, which incorporates procedures that influence social and economic health while also promoting physical resilience through building codes, engineering standards, land use planning, and assessing environmental threats (Morton & Lurie, 2013; National Academies of Sciences, Engineering, & Medicine, 2017). The development of policy and how policies are implemented within a community can also affect how adversity influences the broader community but also individual community members (Chandler & Lalonde, 1998).

Procedural aspects of community resilience can be found in the tools used to measure resilience within populations and display shared knowledge that are measured across populations systematically (Mitchell & Harris, 2012). Measuring the needs of a community in preparation for disaster can provide an important buffer against adverse events. However, the resources available vary between populations, and not every community enjoys adequate resources needed for disaster preparedness. Thus, efforts that leverage equality and maximize a shared research agenda across disciplines can be important for a community's overall resilience. Creating a shared research agenda, by incorporating various discipline perspectives, may generate more useful results across disciplines. Such partnerships can then be extended to a broader community and may incorporate international conceptualizations of resilience within a larger public health sector. Given the potential for high resources required to successfully engage in research within the public health sectors, future studies pertaining to resilience must be designed to best meet the needs of multiple fields. Interdisciplinary research can be particularly complex, given the tendency for many researchers to operate within specific research silos of their areas of expertise, and thus capacity-building within disciplines may be required (Allen-Scott, Buntain, Hatfield, Meisser, & Thomas, 2015). Further, "translating" results away from discipline-specific jargon when disseminating research may also improve the uptake of results between sectors, thus improving the accessibility of results.

Resilience as Multisystemic

Public health approaches suggest that there are multiple points for intervention that can be targeted for any presenting concern (see Figure 4.2). These areas of intervention can be broadly conceptualized as primordial prevention, primary prevention, secondary prevention, and tertiary prevention. These concepts will be elaborated within an Indigenous context, with relevant examples provided.

Primordial Prevention

Primordial prevention efforts refer to programs that target social and economic policies that influence communities' or individuals' health (Snair, Nicholson, & Giammaria, 2017). Integrative models of knowledge, such as the two-eyed seeing approach, have emphasized mutual respect and prioritization of various Indigenous and non-Indigenous health-based teachings (Bartlett, Marshall, & Marshall, 2012). The most effective public health

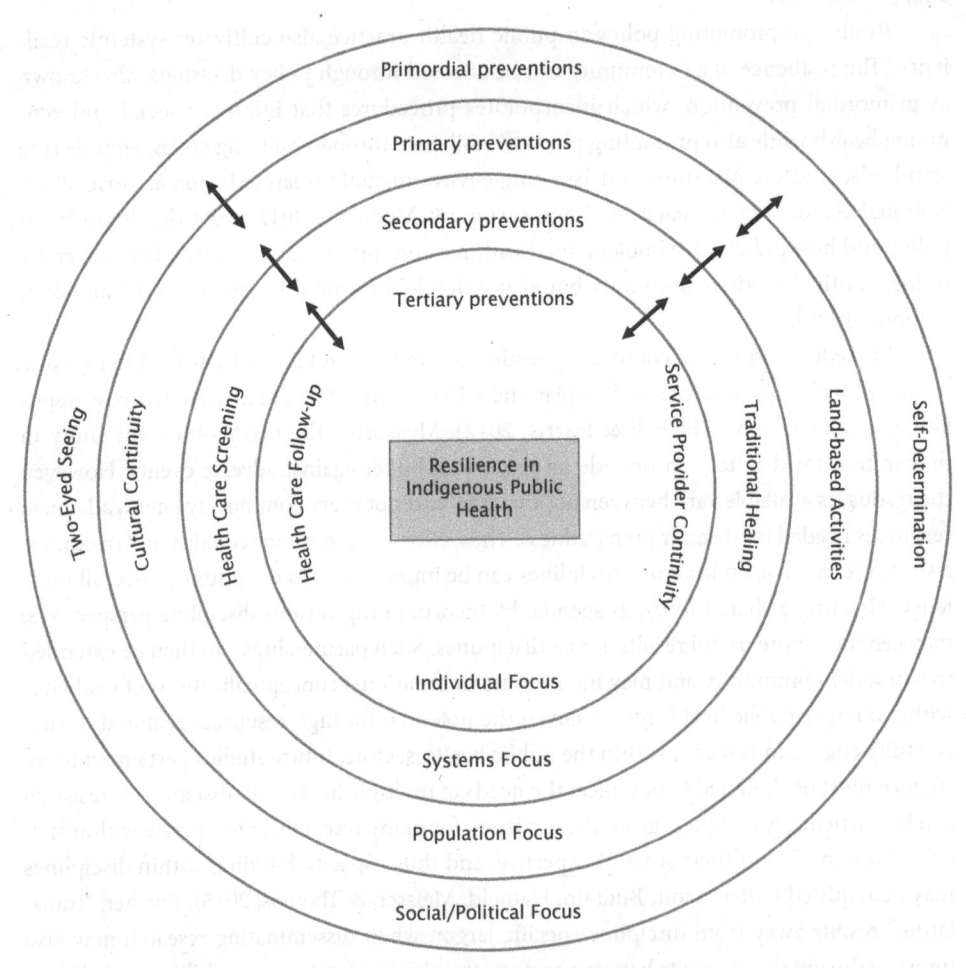

FIGURE 4.2 Broad public health factors for Indigenous people in Canada.

interventions are those that continue to bring together both knowledge systems in complimentary, respectful, and mutually beneficial ways. Integration and access to traditional practices and knowledge can influence the resilience of health systems for Indigenous people.

Community-level systems can demonstrate culturally appropriate care by integrating traditional knowledge keepers and spiritual advisors within a healthcare center. Such practices have been shown to increase resilience and overall beneficial outcomes for Indigenous healthcare users (Maar et al., 2009). Culturally appropriate care can emphasize holistic approaches that incorporate mental, physical, spiritual, and emotional health (Health Canada, 2015). Further, having these resources available and accessible in the same physical space emphasizes the complimentary nature of Indigenous knowledge and non-Indigenous medical practices (Maar et al., 2009). Although beneficial to healthcare users, implementation of these best practices can be challenging, as the resources required to develop and sustain such a health system is influenced by the capacity of community members to write grants or applications, obtain funding for services and employ a sufficient number of qualified staff to successfully implement these services.

Primary Prevention

The next level of interventions within a public health approach is primary prevention, which consists of population-based interventions intended to address the underlying causes of risk factors associated with poor outcomes. Within Indigenous populations, developing a sense of positive cultural identity and connection to culture acts as protective factors (Fanian, Young, Mantla, Daniels, & Chatwood, 2015; Hansen & Antsanen, 2016; Kral, Salusky, Inuksuk, Angutimarik, & Tulugardjuk, 2014). For example, Chandler, Lalonde, Sokol, and Hallett (2003), found that cultural continuity served as a protective factor among Indigenous children in British Columbia, Canada. Cultural continuity was deemed to be present when Indigenous communities retained control over government, education, police and fire protection services, and health services, as well as cultural facilities and land claims. Youth who resided in the communities with greatest numbers of these cultural continuity indicators were less likely to attempt suicide than youth in communities that had control over fewer services (Chandler et al., 2003). Although a replication of similar findings in other geographical areas is needed to suggest how these findings may apply to other Indigenous peoples, this study reinforces the long-held view that Indigenous-directed services within communities will benefit overall community well-being when services are implemented in ways that align best with cultural understandings.

Secondary and Tertiary Prevention

Secondary and tertiary prevention efforts both involve attempts to address adverse outcomes that have already occurred. Secondary prevention focuses on reducing the effect of an adverse outcome (e.g., detecting and treating a disease) or programs to return individuals to a previous level of functioning. Meanwhile, tertiary prevention refers to reducing the complications or harms of adverse outcomes (e.g., safe injection sites) as well as preventing reoccurrence (Baumann & Ylinen, 2017). For a public health system to be resilient, it needs to have the resources available at each level of intervention to address a population's needs appropriately. If the system is focused solely on one area of intervention (e.g., secondary or tertiary prevention), then the resilience within the entire system remains limited. This was demonstrated in a study of three remote Indigenous communities in Northern Ontario (Minore, Boone, Katt, Kinch, & Birch, 2004). When patients presented to community health clinics with diabetes, they were referred to specialists (i.e., tertiary prevention) and subsequently received relatively consistent follow-up (i.e., secondary prevention). In contrast, patients who were identified as being suicidal were also referred to specialists (i.e., tertiary prevention) but often returned to their communities without consistent follow-up treatment (i.e., secondary prevention). Without such secondary prevention efforts, health services can become stuck in a crisis–response pattern, as exemplified by suicidality and mental health concerns within a community ultimately leading to ineffective use of all levels of care. It is acknowledged that the lack of capacity to develop a more resilient health system stems from funding systems that are short-term focused, as well as staffing deficits.

Barriers to Systemic Resilience

The ability of Indigenous communities to secure financial and human resources that can help to further the success of community members is influenced by diverse factors, including the written and oral literacy abilities of community members. Thus, the education available, and how it is delivered, within a community is a contributing factor to the resilience of public health systems for Indigenous people. When children and community members receive education that demonstrates a respect and consideration for multiple knowledge systems (i.e., non-Indigenous thought and Indigenous knowledge), children may be better able to identify where these systems can come together to be beneficial. This complimentary knowledge helps Indigenous children find success, which may influence later educational attainment (Sutherland, 2005). Demonstrating this complimentary knowledge may be penalized if the educational system does not value Indigenous knowledge at the same level as non-Indigenous knowledge. Nevertheless, retention of this complimentary knowledge can assist in developing community resources by allowing grant writers to speak the language of the granting agency, increasing the likelihood of being successful while presenting an argument for how different systems can benefit from one another.

Having an educational system that respects and values Indigenous culture may also potentially contribute to higher levels of engagement in schooling (Sutherland, 2005). Indigenous populations within Ontario, Canada, have a lower rate of educational obtainment as evidenced by fewer Indigenous people having completed high school or any other degree in comparison to non-Indigenous Ontarians (Kelly-Scott, 2016). In one Cree community, students reported that they were more likely to attend school if family members attend school (Sutherland, 2005). However, the ability of children to attend and succeed in school is influenced by the community's level of access to consumer goods, including food. When children have greater access to nutritious food, they are better able to concentrate on lessons and find greater academic success. In Northern communities where the delivery of food is dependent upon air transportation, the resulting costs of fresh fruit and vegetables can make nutritionally sound foods inaccessible (Skinner, Hanning, & Tsuji, 2006; Socha, Zahaf, Chambers, Abraham, & Fiddler, 2012).

It is possible that when communities have the ability to secure enough food for the year through traditional means such as hunting and fishing during the summer, a greater ability to engage in activities such as schooling and resource development may take place. Success within such land-based activities are often influenced by the level of traditional knowledge of animal patterns within the geographical area (Socha et al., 2012). Thus, if communities retain strong oral traditions about hunting practices and reside in an area that is similar to their traditional lands, it can be postulated that greater individual and community outcomes will be demonstrated. These can include increased social support, greater abstinence from problematic substance use, increased physical activity, and reduced stress (Liebenberg, Ikeda, & Wood, 2015; Rowan et al., 2014; Tang & Jardine, 2016). The practice of being on the land and obtaining necessary resources is also tied to spiritual health that affects an individual's overall well-being (Health Canada, 2015). The ability to obtain food through hunting is also influenced by the community's access to aides, such as firearms and transportation (i.e., boats and all-terrain equipment), as well as social and political influences that affect where, when, and what community members can hunt or fish (Socha et al., 2012).

Resilience is often a process that leads to growth and development of new knowledge and practices. An example of a community that is addressing the influence of food on the overall well-being of the community is Opaskwayak, a Cree Nation in Ontario, Canada, where a hydroponic garden provides residents with fresh produce throughout the year (Laychuck, 2018). Notably, the ability to sustain such as system relies on people who are knowledgeable about maintaining a hydroponic system, as well as access to clean and reliable water. This is an example of how community level resilience which is fostered through infrastructure and programming can be an attribute of an Indigenous community that also influences individual resilience. Having access to fresh fruits and vegetables can reduce the negative health effects of chronic diseases such as diabetes (Laychuck, 2018), which in turn can release funds to be used in other areas such as primary prevention programs.

The ability for communities to obtain and retain knowledgeable health specialists also contributes to their resilience. Indigenous communities in remote locations often have limited access to healthcare professionals such as nurses and physicians who provide services to for only short periods of time. These practitioners often experience isolation in their rural positions, making these less desirable positions to hold (Minore et al., 2004). The inclusion of Elders and knowledge keepers can help to lessen the emphasis on non-Indigenous models of health that are unapproachable for some while integrating a holistic model of wellness that is focused on balance between mental, physical, spiritual, and emotional health appropriate for Indigenous populations (Anonson, Desjarlais, Nixon, Whiteman, & Bird, 2008).

The conceptualization of resilience in public health as multisystemic is further complicated when urban Indigenous populations are considered. In the Canadian context, the majority of Indigenous people live within urban centers; however, they comprise less than 10% of the overall Canadian population (Kelly-Scott, 2016). Accessing and coordinating culturally appropriate services may be more difficult for these groups as urban Indigenous communities are wider spread and most services that are available tend to be embedded in non-Indigenous healthcare systems. Taken together, the examples presented within this section demonstrate how many systems influence the health outcomes for Indigenous people within Canada. The political, education, ecological, and transportation systems have direct and indirect impacts on health systems.

Resilience Measurement

The preceding section discussed the various structural levels that define resilience from a public health perspective, providing insight into how interventions can be implemented in a multisystemic fashion. To further guide decision-making around what preventative actions and interventions are needed, accurate measurement of resilience is required. Public health institutions deploy public health surveillance, or the continuous systematized collection, analysis, and interpretation of health-related data, that is then used for planning, implementing, and evaluating public health practices (Thacker & Berkelman, 1988). The measurement tools used in public health surveillance can be used to discern how resilience is conceptualized and measured at a macrolevel. Further, an evaluation of existing measures can provide insight into what facets of resilience ought to be expanded on in public health surveillance and initiatives.

In the Canadian public health sector, for example, resilience is referenced as a method to support positive mental health outcomes (Orpana, Vachon, Dykxhoorn, Mcrae, & Jayaraman, 2016). There have been recent efforts to support the measurement of positive mental health outcomes and, as a result, the Mental Health Strategy for Canada developed the Positive Mental Health Surveillance Indicator Framework (PMSIF; Orpana et al., 2016). The PMSIF is a framework and affiliated list of indicators and measures of positive health associated with positive health outcomes. The PMISF can be utilized to inform public health programs and policies on the state of these outcomes. Within the framework, there are five broad positive mental health outcomes (self-rated mental health, happiness, life satisfaction, psychological well-being, and social well-being) and 25 related indicators at individual, family, community, and society levels. Individual level factors include resiliency, control, coping, and violence; family level factors encompass health status, income, and parenting style; community level factors describe aspects related to community involvement and social networks; and society level factors were inequality, political participation, and experiences of discrimination. At the individual level, a measure of resilience is incorporated conceptually, although this is currently indicated as "under development" with no information on how resilience will be defined or measured. While individual positive mental health outcomes used by public health institutions can serve as one way to measure the positive adaptation facet of resilience, this narrow view of the construct confines measurement of resilience.

Positive Outcomes in Comparison to Context-Specific Outcomes

By measuring resilience through positive mental health outcome data, there is the implication that positive outcomes are needed for resilience to be identified or accurately measured. This conceptualization can limit marginalized populations' measured levels of resilience. While individuals in marginalized communities may experience significant negative mental health outcomes, they may be exceeding beyond what is expected given the level of adversities experienced (Kirmayer, Dandeneau, Mashall, Phillips, & Williamson, 2011). Rather than only relying on the presence of positive outcomes when measuring resilience, incorporation of additional indicators, including how a system or an individual adapts to adversity, can be included at the public health surveillance level. As an example, in the face of significant adversities that put individuals at risk for mental illnesses, the lack of significant emotional or behavioral problems may define successful adaptation, rather than high levels of positive functioning (Luthar & Cicchetti, 2000).

Indigenous peoples in Canada have endured chronic and pervasive effects of intergenerational trauma as a result of colonization (TRCC, 2015). These outcomes have put Indigenous peoples at risk for various negative health outcomes. The measures of positive mental health outcomes of the PMSIF may not capture the extent of resilience exerted for Indigenous individuals, as they can establish resilience through more diverse culturally-specific avenues. For example, culturally-specific programming and healthcare initiatives have been found to promote better psycho-social outcomes than interventions that were tailored for non-Indigenous people (Clifford, McCalman, Bainbridge, & Tsey, 2015). Within public health resilience promotion, further recognition of community perseverance, particularly for those regions facing widespread health difficulties, must also be considered when recognizing resilience.

Positive Mental Health in Comparison to Holistic Well-Being

Considering only positive mental health outcomes as a measure of successful adaptation limits our understanding of resilience to individual dimensions of mental health. As an example, individual resilience has been associated with overall improved self-reported health, nutrition, and sleep behaviors, as well as better outcomes associated with chronic illnesses and lower rates of healthcare utilization (Denisco, 2011; Ezeamama et al., 2016; Lavoie, Pereira, & Talwar, 2016). Success in such health outcomes, among many others, can be used to define levels of successful adaptation observed in individuals. Indigenous views of resilience often reflect not only resilience as a function of mental health outcomes but also spiritual, physical, and emotional outcomes (King, Smith, & Gracey, 2009). The intersecting nature of these aspects of well-being is recognized, and a balance between all four constructs is promoted for well-being to be realized (Assembly of First Nations & Health Canada, 2014). Using Indigenous measures to explore these facets can provide a more comprehensive view of resilience measurement, not only for Indigenous communities but also for non-Indigenous populations. The Native Wellness Assessment (NWA) serves as an example of a way to measure wellness as it considers wellness across the four directions in the Sacred Medicine Wheel, where a healthy person establishes balance of spirit, heart, mind, and body (Fiedeldey-Van Dijk et al., 2016). The NWA recognizes that engagement in distinct cultural activities may foster broader spiritual, social, and psychological well-being, thus expanding conceptualizations of health and prosocial activities. For example, individuals can self-report on dimensions related to hope, belonging, meaning, and purpose, through statements such as "I want to learn about the meaning of my life," "I pay attention to my physical well-being," and "My connection to Mother Earth makes the land I come from feel like home." These types of items can separate the NWA from other measures of well-being and may further understanding in facets that promote well-being within an individual, as well as what type of constructs foster resilience.

Case Study of Indigenous Assessment of Resilience Within a Public Health Service

Through an ongoing collaboration between a community-based mental health provider and researchers at Lakehead University, First Nations communities in Northwestern Ontario, Canada, requested information describing the current mental health status of local children and adolescents. Although many youth experience adversities, many are able to adapt and/or thrive across domains of functioning (Kowatch, 2017). Researchers aimed to understand current rates of mental health concerns and predictors of future mental health needs in these youth.

To meet these goals, Kowatch (2017) evaluated youth with the Child and Adolescent Needs and Strengths (CANS) assessment tool. In contrast to many commonly used instruments, the CANS is a broadband measure that assesses factors beyond specific deficits experienced by the individual. The CANS scale includes assessments of individual needs and strengths, caregiver needs and strengths, acculturation, language abilities, and wider domains, such as family, community, and education. The individual strengths domain, most notably, assesses established individual level indicators of resilience, such as talents or interests, participation in community events, and community involvement. Through an evaluation of the individual within other contexts (e.g., familial, community, education), there is an acknowledgement of the wider contributing factors to resilience and well-being. The CANS tool also allows the assessor to draw upon knowledge of specific community contexts (e.g., what services are available; the overall climate of the community; etc.) and incorporate these into an overall assessment of the individual. This specific measure thus incorporates some aspects of Indigenous conceptualizations of wellness, as it measures more holistic facets of an individual's well-being. Research outcomes supported the conclusion that individual resilience factors, level of functioning, and social determinants of health (including family and caregiver strengths and needs) are integral to assessments of youth and adolescents in an Indigenous community. Past research has also supported this multilevel view of wellness indicating that positive peer and family relationships, engagement in culture, and community support and connectedness were all aspects that promoted positive outcomes with Indigenous youth (Toombs et al., 2016).

This research holds Indigenous conceptualizations of wellness at the forefront, while applying research techniques to understand pockets of need within the community. It is an example of how resilience conceptualized within a multisystemic model attentive to cultural variation can be used to develop intervention plans that are sensitive to individual, familial, and community needs.

Process Measures in Comparison to Outcome Measures

Existing literature on resilience considers positive adaptation from a developmental perspective, highlighting that it should be viewed as an interactive process, rather than an outcome

(Egeland, Carlson, & Sroufe, 1993; Masten, 2001; Ungar, 2011). Measuring resilience through developmental processes, rather than specific outcomes, may be informative with regards to understanding how adversity may be acknowledged and managed within a system. When disruption of status quo or the generalized equilibrium within a broader health system occurs, public health initiatives can implement intervening methods or future preventative ones to foster resilience. The process by which resilience is generated needs to be explored and subsequently measured. This can exist systematically in a dose–response fashion, when one "amount" of a specific action can increase one "unit" of measured outcome variable. For example, preventative risk assessment of cause–effect relationships may be completed to reduce the initial likelihood of an adverse event occurring within a system. The "dose" of the intervention required to reduce the "response" of the adverse event can foster a more resilient system. If an incremental number of handwashing tutorials provided to staff systematically reduced rates of disease within a public health setting (such as one session reducing rates by 10%, two sessions by 20%, and so on), this could be a dynamic process measure of resilience using a dose–response relationship.

The First Nations Mental Wellness Continuum Framework

One model of how resilience for Indigenous communities has been visually portrayed as multisystemic capacity is through the First Nations Mental Wellness Continuum Framework (FNMWCF; Figure 4.3). The FNMWCF provides a model of holistic wellness conceptualized from a First Nations perspective (Assembly of First Nations and Health Canada, 2014). The FNMWCF reflects this view through a focus on resilience across a continuum of interacting levels of wellness, moving away from a strict dichotomy of sick or well. Presenting multiple levels of wellness allows for a nuanced approach and acknowledges the multitude of items both within and outside each system that contribute to Indigenous individuals' thriving. Bidirectional forms of influence are present between the levels of the model as is the acknowledgement of the interactions between levels of resilience. Some key components that are critical to resilience provided in the FNMWCF (including culture, social determinants of health, essential services, governmental organizations, community relationships, and individual factors) will be discussed to provide a greater understanding of the diversity of components that contribute to this multisystemic conceptualization of wellness.

Culture
Culture is the outermost layer of the model and supports all other areas of the FNMWCF in promoting wellness. Depending on the community, culture may expand to a connection with the land, a sense of connection with a broader Indigenous culture, or connection with the familial structure. The benefits of integrating culture and cultural practices into services and interventions has been noted across several studies (Leske et al., 2016; Minore et al., 2004; Rowan et al., 2014).

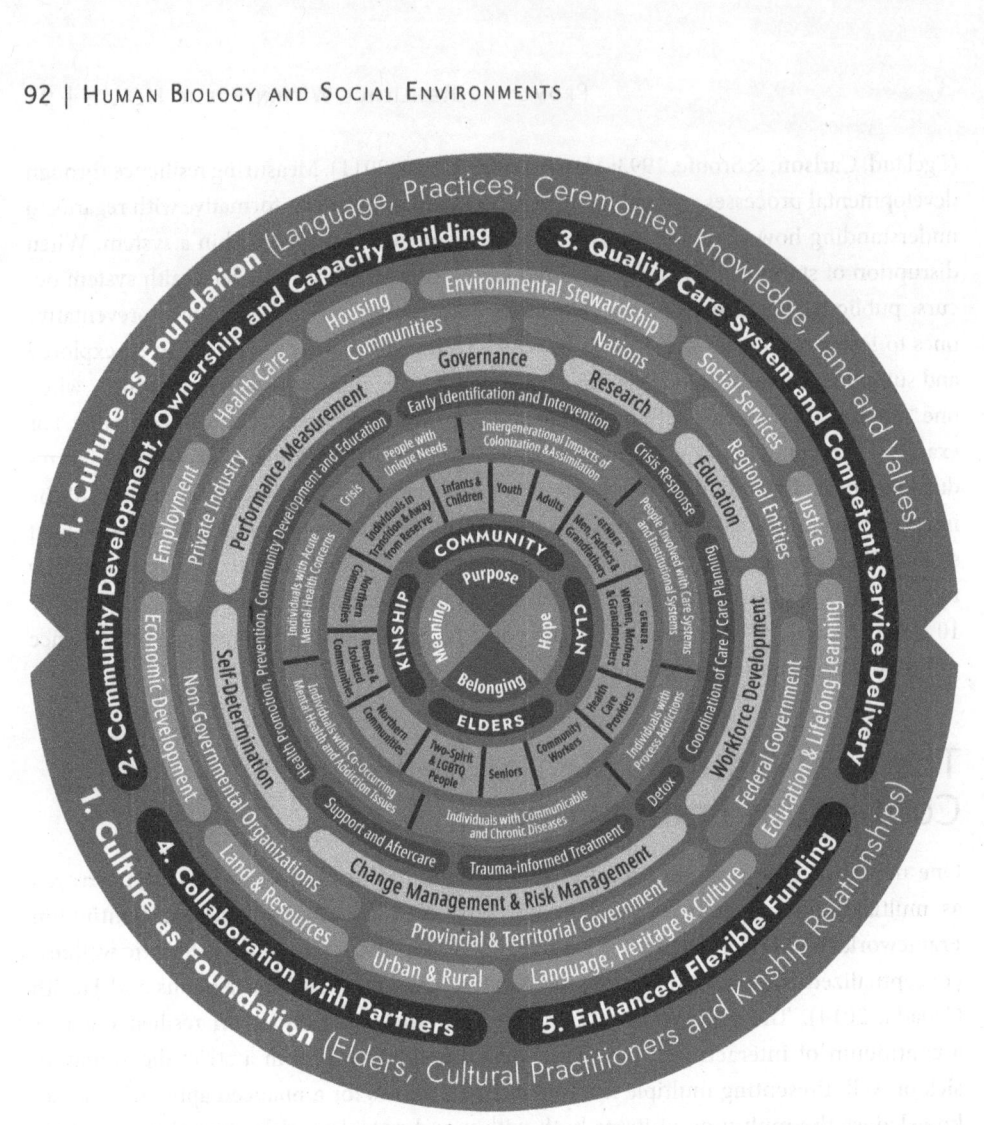

FIGURE 4.3 The First Nations Mental Wellness Continuum Framework. Reprinted from *First Nations mental wellness continuum framework* (Health Canada Publication No. 140358), by Health Canada, 2015. Copyright 2018 by Carol Hopkins, Executive Director of the Thunderbird Partnership Foundation. Reprinted with permission.

Indigenous Social Determinants of Health

Social determinants of health are environmental conditions, structures, systems, and institutions that influence health outcomes of individuals and communities (Reading & Wien, 2009). Social determinants, such as social services, justice, education, land and resources, employment, healthcare, and housing, are included in the FNMWCF. Each of these factors can be uniquely understood within the context of Indigenous communities. For example, 24% of First Nations people in Canada live in housing in need of major repairs, in comparison to 6% of non-Indigenous people (Statistics Canada, 2018). There is an overrepresentation of Indigenous victims within the Canadian justice system. For example, in 2015, Indigenous people accounted for 25% of all homicide victims in Canada, while representing approximately 5% of the Canadian population (Statistics Canada, 2018). Finally, within educational settings there may be unique considerations for best supporting scholarly success among Indigenous youth, including encouraging self-reflection by students of current lessons, promoting learning through community engagement such as incorporating Elders, and teaching with open-mindedness and flexibility (Oskineegish, 2015). It is vital to consider these social determinants of health as important contextual features of wellness and resilience.

Government and Organizational Partners

To promote communitywide wellness, support from government and organizational partners is a necessity to create change and to support individual and community autonomy. Government and organizational partners can include private industry; nongovernmental organizations; communities; nations; regional entities, and federal, provincial, and territorial government systems. Policy change, research, and monetary support from these sources can increase access to resources which can promote resilience across multiple sectors. For example, in 2007, the Canadian federal government approved a motion entitled "Jordan's Principal," which was a child-first principle intended to prioritize access First Nations access to healthcare regardless of jurisdiction. This funding applies to all health services, including those that are considered to be beyond normative standards of care across federal, provincial, and territorial jurisdictions (Blackstock, 2012).

Essential Services

As in many other countries with histories of colonization, Indigenous communities in Canada are influenced by the repercussions of a history of the government's attempts to force assimilation (TRCC, 2015). Recognizing the impact of historical trauma (Wilk, Maltby, & Cooke, 2017) allows us to conceptualize the essential services individuals may need to foster wellness and resilience. For example, trauma-informed treatment, support and aftercare, early identification and interventions, and crisis response are all components of these necessary essential services. Active and appropriate essential services can combat fears of healthcare systems (Denison, Varcoe, & Browne, 2014) that some Indigenous people may develop as a result of past negative experiences with service providers (Goodman et al., 2017; Tang, Browne, Mussell, Smye, & Rodney, 2015). These supports should also promote individual help-seeking behaviors and increase the capacity for self-advocacy on an individual and community level.

Relationships and Roles in the Community

At a microlevel, the FNMWCF recognizes that each Indigenous person will have individual characteristics that will create specific strengths and challenges for moving toward holistic wellness. For example, Two-Spirit and LGBTQ people have a unique history, and some individuals may have close community involvement, in combination with commonly reported discriminatory experiences (Brotman, Ryan, Jalbert, & Rowe, 2002; Meyer-Cook & Labelle, 2004).

Individuals

At the core of the FNMWCF is a focus on the wellness of the individual, encompassed by concepts of purpose, hope, belonging, and meaning. These four components are shared across many Indigenous cultures, although they may be described in different ways by different communities (Assembly of First Nations & Health Canada, 2014). At the individual level, these concepts represent the interconnection between physical, mental, spiritual, and emotional behavior (Assembly of First Nations & Health Canada, 2014). The wellness of any individual is complex, involving physical and mental health, safety, education, food security, connections with community and culture, and many other components.

The FNMWCF helps to visualize the interwoven components of individual wellness. Communities and organizations can derive the largest positive benefit through approaches at multiple systemic levels that improve individual resilience and wellness.

Conclusion

Public health approaches to resilience with sensitivity to Indigenous culture warrant further discussion and research, especially in the nonphysical domains of mental, emotional, interpersonal/community or spiritual health. To date, population level, public health approaches to resilience in the physical domain, such as vaccination programs, have been better understood. However, when it comes to public health approaches to resilience in nonphysical domains, it is not obvious how to intervene. What is clear is that for resilience to be fostered, individuals within populations require their capacity for adaptation in the face of adversity to be challenged within a developmentally appropriate range, but not be so overwhelmed as to result in maladaptive responses. This means that multisystemic approaches will be essential, particularly in the case of populations for which differential access to social determinants exist and for those who have experienced ongoing stressors that overwhelm the capability for individual adaptive responses in the context of limited resources for support in their communities. Conceptualizing individual-level resilience alone may absolve policy- and decision makers from making necessary investments in each of the domains that contribute to the overall resilience of individuals, families, communities, and nations. This need to think about resilience multisystemically is especially important for public health initiatives with Indigenous peoples.

Key Messages

1. Promoting resilience in public health prioritizes approaches that use multisystemic integration of primary, secondary, and tertiary interventions across public heath settings. These approaches may best reflect individual needs of various populations.
2. For Indigenous communities in Canada, resilience should be measured using both process and outcome-based indicators across public health sectors that reflect specific contextual needs.
3. Using community-based and culturally relevant conceptualizations of wellness and health, such as models used within the NWA and the FNMWCF can generate useful strategies to build resilience within Indigenous communities.

Acknowledgments

Christopher J. Mushquash's involvement in this work is partially supported by the Canada Research Chairs Program and the Canada Foundation for Innovation.

References

Aboriginal Head Start. (2006). *Aboriginal Head Start in urban and northern communities: Closing the gap in health and education outcomes for Indigenous children in Canada*. Public Health Agency of Canada. Retrieved from https://www.canada.ca/content/dam/hc-sc/documents/services/publications/healthy-living/aboriginal-head-start/closing-the-gap-fact-sheet-en.pdf

Aldrich, D. P., & Meyer, M. A. (2014). Social capital and community resilience. *American Behavioral Scientist*, 59(2), 254–269. doi:10.1177/0002764214550299

Allen-Scott, L. K., Buntain, B., Hatfield, J. M., Meisser, A., & Thomas, C. J. (2015). Academic institutions and one health: Building capacity for transdisciplinary research approaches to address complex health issues at the animal-human-ecosystem interface. *Academic Medicine*, 90(7), 866–871. doi:10.1097/ACM.0000000000000639

Anonson, J. M., Desjarlais, J., Nixon, J., Whiteman, L., & Bird, A. (2008). Strategies to support recruitment and retention of First Nations youth in baccalaureate nursing programs in Saskatchewan, Canada. *Journal of Transcultural Nursing*, 19(3), 274–283. doi:10.1177/1043659608317095

Assembly of First Nations & Health Canada. (2014). The First Nations mental wellness continuum framework (Health Canada Publication Number 140358). Retrieved from https://www.canada.ca/en/indigenous-services-canada/services/first-nations-inuit-health/reports-publications/health-promotion/first-nations-mental-wellness-continuum-framework-summary-report.html

Bartlett, C., Marshall, M., & Marshall, A. (2012). Two-eyed seeing and other lessons learned within a co-learning journey of bringing together Indigenous and mainstream knowledges and ways of knowing. *Journal of Environmental Studies and Sciences*, 2(4), 331–340. doi:10.1007/s13412-012-0086-8

Baumann, L. J., & Ylinen, A. (2017). Prevention: Primary, secondary, tertiary. In M. Gellman (Ed.), *Encyclopedia of behavioral medicine* (pp. 1–3). New York, NY: Springer. doi:10.1007/978-1-4614-6439-6_135-2

Blackstock, C. (2012). Jordan's principle: Canada's broken promise to First Nations children? *Paediatrics & Child Health*, 17(7), 368–370.

Boksa, P., Joober, R., & Kirmayer, L. J. (2015). Mental wellness in Canada's Aboriginal communities: Striving toward reconciliation. *Journal of Psychiatry & Neuroscience*, 40(6), 363–365. doi:10.1503/jpn.150309

Brotman, S., Ryan, B., Jalbert, Y., & Rowe, B. (2002). Reclaiming space-regaining health: The health care experiences of Two-Spirit people in Canada. *Journal of Gay & Lesbian Social Services*, 14(1), 67–87. doi:10.1300/J041v14n01_04

Campbell-Sills, L., Cohan, S. L., & Stein, M. B. (2006). Relationship of resilience to personality, coping, and psychiatric symptoms in young adults. *Behaviour Research and Therapy*, 44(4), 585–599. doi:10.1016/j.brat.2005.05.001

Centers for Disease Control and Prevention. (2019). *What is public health?* Retrieved from https://www.cdcfoundation.org/what-public-health

Chandler, M. J., & Lalonde, C. E. (1998). Cultural continuity as a hedge against suicide in Canada's First Nations. *Transcultural Psychiatry*, 35(2), 191–219. doi:10.1177/136346159803500202

Chandler, M. J., Lalonde, C. E., Sokol, B. W., & Hallett, D. (Eds.). (2003). Personal persistence, identity development, and suicide: A study of Native and non-Native North American adolescents. *Monographs of the Society for Research in Child Development*, 68(2), 1–138. Retrieved from http://www.jstor.org/stable/1166217

Clifford, A., McCalman, J., Bainbridge, R., & Tsey, K. (2015). Interventions to improve cultural competency in health care for Indigenous peoples of Australia, New Zealand, Canada and the USA: A systematic review. *International Journal for Quality in Health Care*, 27(2), 89–98. doi:10.1093/intqhc/mzv010

Cost, D. S. (2015). The role of public education in governance for resilience in a rapidly changing Arctic. *Ecology and Society, 20*(3). doi:10.5751/ES-07757-200329

DeNisco, S. (2011). Exploring the relationship between resilience and diabetes outcomes in African Americans. *Journal of the American Academy of Nurse Practitioners, 23*(11), 602–610. doi:10.1111/j.1745-7599.2011.00648.x

Denison, J., Varcoe, C., & Browne, A. J. (2014). Aboriginal women's experiences of accessing health care when state apprehension of children is being threatened. *Journal of Advanced Nursing, 70*(5), 1105–1116. doi:10.1111/jan.12271

Egeland, B., Carlson, E., & Sroufe, L. A. (1993). Resilience as process. *Development and Psychopathology, 5*(4), 517–528. doi:10.1017/s0954579400006131

Elliott, D. S., Menard, S., Rankin, B., Elliott, A., Wilson, W. J., & Huizinga, D. (2006). *Good kids from bad neighborhoods: Successful development in social context*. Cambridge, UK: Cambridge University Press. doi:10.1017/CBO9780511499746

Ezeamama, A. E., Elkins, J., Simpson, C., Smith, S. L., Allegra, J. C., & Miles, T. P. (2016). Indicators of resilience and healthcare outcomes: Findings from the 2010 health and retirement survey. *Quality of Life Research, 25*(4), 1007–1015. doi:10.1007/s11136-015-1144-y

Fanian, S., Young, S. K., Mantla, M., Daniels, A., & Chatwood, S. (2015). Evaluation of the Kò̵ts'iìhtła ("We light the fire") project: Building resiliency and connections through strengths-based creative arts programming for Indigenous youth. *International Journal of Circumpolar Health, 74*, 27672. doi:10.3402/ijch.v74.27672

Fiedeldey-Van Dijk, C., Rowan, M., Dell, C., Mushquash, C., Hopkins, C., Fornssler, B., . . . Shea, B. (2016). Honoring Indigenous culture-as-intervention: Development and validity of the Native wellness assessment. *Journal of Ethnicity in Substance Abuse, 16*(2), 181–218. doi:10.1080/15332640.2015.1119774

Frieden, T. R. (2014). Six components necessary for effective public health program implementation. *American Journal of Public Health, 104*(1), 17–22. doi:10.2105/ajph.2013.301608

Goodman, A., Fleming, K., Markwick, N., Morrison, T., Lagimodiere, L., Kerr, T., & Western Aboriginal Harm Reduction Society. (2017). "They treated me like crap and I know it was because I was Native": The healthcare experiences of Aboriginal peoples living in Vancouver's inner city. *Social Science & Medicine, 178*, 87–94. doi:10.1016/j.socscimed.2017.01.053

Hackett, C., Feeny, D., & Tompa, E. (2016). Canada's residential school system: Measuring the intergenerational impact of familial attendance on health and mental health outcomes. *Journal of Epidemiology in Community Health, 70*(11), 1096–1105. doi:10.1136/jech-2016-207380

Hansen, J. G., & Antsanen, R. (2016). Elders' teachings about resilience and its implications for education in Dene and Cree communities. *International Indigenous Policy Journal, 7*(1), 1–17. doi:10.18584/iipj.2016.7.1.2

Health Canada. (2015). *First Nations mental wellness continuum framework* (Health Canada Publication No. 140358). Retrieved from https://thunderbirdpf.org/first-nations-mental-wellness-continuum-framework/

Hu, T., Zhang, D., & Wang, J. (2015). A meta-analysis of the trait resilience and mental health. *Personality and Individual Differences, 76*, 18–27. doi:10.1016/j.paid.2014.11.039

Kapucu, N., & Sadiq, A.-A. (2016). Disaster policies and governance: Promoting community resilience. *Politics and Governance, 4*(4), 58–61. doi:10.17645/pag.v4i4.829

Kasen, S., Wickramaratne, P., Gameroff, M. J., & Weissman, M. M. (2012). Religiosity and resilience in persons at high risk for major depression. *Psychological Medicine, 42*(3), 509–519. doi:10.1017/S0033291711001516

Kelly-Scott, K. (2016). *Aboriginal peoples: Fact sheet for Ontario* (Publication No. 89-656-X2016007). Retrieved from https://www150.statcan.gc.ca/n1/pub/89-656-x/89-656-x2016007-eng.htm

King, M., Smith, A., & Gracey, M. (2009). Indigenous health part 2: The underlying causes of the health gap. *The Lancet, 374*(9683), 76–85. doi:10.1016/s0140-6736(09)60827-8

Kirmayer, L. J., Dandeneau, S., Marshall, E., Phillips, M. K., & Williamson, K. J. (2011). Rethinking resilience from Indigenous perspectives. *The Canadian Journal of Psychiatry, 56*(2), 84–91. doi:10.1177/070674371105600203

Kowatch, K. R. (2017). *Analysis of the Child and Adolescent Needs and Strengths assessment in a First Nation population* (Unpublished master's thesis). Lakehead University, Thunder Bay.

Kral, M., J., Salusky, I., Inuksuk, P., Angutimarik, L., & Tulugardjuk, N. (2014). Tunngajuq: Stress and resilience among Inuit youth in Nunavut, Canada. *Transcultural Psychiatry*, *51*(5), 673–692. doi:10.1177/1363461514533001

Lavoie, J., Pereira, L. C., & Talwar, V. (2016). Children's physical resilience outcomes: Meta-analysis of vulnerability and protective factors. *Journal of Pediatric Nursing*, *31*(6), 701–711. doi:10.1016/j.pedn.2016.07.011

Laychuck, R. (2018, April 3). Year-round garden provides free fresh vegetables to hundreds on Manitoba's Opaskwayak Cree Nation. *CBC News*. Retrieved from https://www.cbc.ca/news/canada/manitoba/manitoba-first-nation-indoor-farm-1.4600746

Leske, S., Harris, M. G., Charlson, F. J., Ferrari, A. J., Baxter, A. J., Logan, J. M., . . . Whiteford, H. (2016). Systematic review of interventions for Indigenous adults with mental and substance use disorders in Australia, Canada, New Zealand and the United States. *Australian & New Zealand Journal of Psychiatry*, *50*(11), 1040–1054. doi:10.1177/0004867416662150

Liebenberg, L., Ikeda, J., & Wood, M. (2015). "It's just part of my culture": Understanding language and land in the resilience processes of Aboriginal youth. In L. C. Theron, L. Liebenberg, & M. Ungar (Eds.), *Youth resilience and culture* (pp. 105–116). Dordrecht, The Netherlands: Springer.

Liebenberg, L., Joubert, N., & Foucault, M.-L. (2017). *Understanding core resilience elements and indicators: A comprehensive review of the literature* (Public Health Agency of Canada Resilience Report). Retrieved from http://lindaliebenberg.com/wp-content/uploads/2017/11/PHAC-Resilience-Report-Final-Version-November-2017.pdf

Lin, N., Fu, Y.-C., & Hsung, R.-M. (2001). The position generator: Measurement techniques for investigations of social capital. In N. Lin, K. Cook, & R. S. Burt (Eds.) *Social capital: Theory and research* (pp. 57–81). New York, NY: Routledge.

Luthar, S. S., & Cicchetti, D. (2000). The construct of resilience: Implications for interventions and social policies. *Development and Psychopathology*, *12*(4), 857–885. doi:10.1017/s0954579400004156

Luthar, S. S., & Eisenberg, N. (2017). Resilient adaptation among at-risk children: Harnessing science toward maximizing salutary environments. *Child Development*, *88*(2), 337–349. doi:10.1111/cdev.12737

Maar, M. A., Erskine, B., McGregor, L., Larose, T. L., Sutherland, M. E., Graham, D., . . . Gordon, T. (2009). Innovations on a shoestring: A study of a collaborative community-based Aboriginal mental health service model in rural Canada. *International Journal of Mental Health Systems*, *3*(27). doi:10.1186/1752-4458-3-27

Masten, A. S. (2001). Ordinary magic: Resilience processes in development. *American Psychologist*, *56*(3), 227–238. doi:10.1037//0003-066x.56.3.227

Masten, A. S., & Obradović, J. (2006). Competence and resilience in development. In B. M. Lester, A. S. Masten, & B. S. McEwen (Eds.), *Annals of the New York Academy of Sciences, 1094, Issue 1, Resilience in Children* (pp. 13–27). doi:10.1196/annals.1376.003

McQuaid, R. J., Bombay, A., McInnis, O. A., Humeny, C., Matheson, K., & Anisman, H. (2017). Suicide ideation and attempts among First Nations peoples living on-reserve in Canada: The intergenerational and cumulative effects of Indian residential schools. *The Canadian Journal of Psychiatry*, *62*(6), 422–430. doi:10.1177/0706743717702075

Meyer-Cook, F., & Labelle, D. (2004). Namaji: Two-Spirit organizing in Montreal, Canada. *Journal of Gay & Lesbian Social Services*, *16*(1), 29–51. doi:10.1300/J041v16n01_02

Ministry of Health and Long-Term Care. (2018). *Protecting and promoting the health of Ontarians*. Retrieved from http://www.health.gov.on.ca/en/pro/programs/publichealth/oph_standards/docs/protocols_guidelines/Ontario_Public_Health_Standards_2018_en.pdf

Minore, B., Boone, M., Katt, M., Kinch, P., & Birch, S. (2004). Addressing the realities [correction of realties] of health care in northern Aboriginal communities through participatory action research. *Journal of Interprofessional Care*, *18*(4), 360–368. doi:10.1080/13561820400011784

Mitchell, T., & Harris, K. (2012). *Resilience: A risk management approach*. Overseas Development Institute (ODI) Background Note. Retrieved from https://www.odi.org/sites/odi.org.uk/files/odi-assets/publications-opinion-files/7552.pdf

Morton, M. J., & Lurie, N. (2013). Community resilience and public health practice. *American Journal of Public Health*. *103*(7), 1158–1160. doi:10.2105/ajph.2013.301354

National Academies of Sciences, Engineering, and Medicine. (2017). *Preparing for a rapid response to major marine oil spills: Protecting and assessing the health and well-being of communities: Proceedings of a workshop—in brief.* Washington, DC: National Academies Press. doi:10.17226/24924.

Ontario Ministry of Children, Community and Social Services. (2019). *Healthy babies healthy children.* Retrieved from http://www.children.gov.on.ca/htdocs/English/earlychildhood/health/index.aspx

Orpana, H., Vachon, J., Dykxhoorn, J., McRae, L., & Jayaraman, G. (2016). Monitoring positive mental health and its determinants in Canada: The development of the positive mental health surveillance indicator framework. *Health Promotion and Chronic Disease Prevention in Canada: Research, Policy and Practice, 36*(1), 1–10. doi:10.24095/hpcdp.36.1.01

Oskineegish, M. (2015). Are you providing an education that is worth caring about? Advice to non-Native teachers in northern First Nations communities. *Canadian Journal of Education, 38*(3), 1–25.

Patel, S. S., Rogers, M. B., Amlôt, R., & Rubin, G. J. (2017). What do we mean by "community resilience"? A systematic literature review of how it is defined in the literature. *PLOS Currents, 9.* doi:10.1371/currents.dis.db775aff25efc5ac4f0660ad9c9f7db2

Public Health Agency of Canada. (2014). *Public health agency of Canada 2013–2014. Departmental performance report.* Retrieved from http://www.phac-aspc.gc.ca/about_apropos/dpr-rmr/2013-2014/assets/pdf/dpr-rmr-2013-2014-eng.pdf

Raich, M., Lorenzoni, N., Stummer, H., & Nöhammer, E. (2017). Impact of culture on community resilience in natural disaster situations. *European Journal of Public Health, 27*(Suppl. 3), 436–437. doi:10.1093/eurpub/ckx186.103

Reading, C. L., & Wien, F. (2009). *Health inequalities and social determinants of Aboriginal people's health.* Prince George, BC: National Collaborating Centre for Aboriginal Health.

Rowan, M., Poole, N., Shea, B., Gone, J. P., Mykota, D., Farag, M., . . . Dell, C. (2014). Cultural interventions to treat addictions in Indigenous populations: Findings from a scoping study. *Substance Abuse Treatment, Prevention, and Policy, 9*(1), 34. doi:10.1186/1747-597X-9-34

Schore, A. N. (2014). Early interpersonal neurobiological assessment of attachment and autistic spectrum disorders. *Frontiers in Psychology, 5*, 1049. doi:10.3389/fpsyg.2014.01049

Seaman, P., McNeice, V., Yates, G., & McLean, J. (2014). *Resilience and public health.* Glasgow Centre for Population Health. Retrieved from https://www.gcph.co.uk/assets/0000/4198/Resilience_for_public_health_2014.pdf

Sherrieb, K., Norris, F. H., & Galea, S. (2010). Measuring capacities for community resilience. *Social Indicators Research, 99*(2), 227–247. doi:10.1007/s11205-010-9576-9

Skinner, K., Hanning, R., & Tsuji, L. (2006). Barriers and supports for healthy eating and physical activity for First Nation youths in northern Canada. *International Journal of Circumpolar Health, 65*(2), 148–161. doi:10.3402/ijch.v65i2.18095

Snair, J., Nicholson, A., & Giammaria, C. (2017). *Countering violent extremism through public health practice: Proceedings of a workshop.* Washington, DC: National Academies Press. Retrieved from https://www.ncbi.nlm.nih.gov/books/n/nap24638/pdf/

Socha, T., Zahaf, M., Chambers, L., Abraham, R., & Fiddler, T. (2012). Food security in a northern First Nations community: An exploratory study on food availability and accessibility. *Journal of Aboriginal Health, 8*(2), 5–14. Retrieved from https://pdfs.semanticscholar.org/6fb1/802bd0202a82d956ffd0deaf5a11921d88ae.pdf

Statistics Canada. (2018). *First Nations people, Métis and Inuit in Canada: Diverse and growing populations* (Publication No. 89-659-x2018001). Retrieved from https://www150.statcan.gc.ca/n1/pub/89-659-x/89-659-x2018001-eng.htm

Sutherland, D. (2005). Resiliency and collateral learning in science in some students of Cree ancestry. *Science Education, 89*(4), 595–613. doi:10.1002/sce.20066

Tang, S. Y., Browne, A. J., Mussell, B., Smye, V. L., & Rodney, P. (2015). "Underclassism" and access to healthcare in urban centres. *Sociology of Health & Illness, 37*(5), 698–714. doi:10.1111/1467-9566.12236

Tang, K., & Jardine, C. G. (2016). Our way of life: Importance of Indigenous culture and tradition to physical activity practices. *International Journal of Indigenous Health, 11*(1), 211–227. doi:10.18357/ijih111201616018

Thacker, S. B., & Berkelman, R. L. (1988). Public health surveillance in the United States. *Epidemiologic Reviews, 10*(1), 164–190. doi:10.1093/oxfordjournals.epirev.a036021

Toombs, E., Kowatch, K. R., & Mushquash, C. J. (2016). Resilience in Canadian Indigenous youth: A scoping review. *International Journal of Child and Adolescent Resilience, 4*(1), 4–32. Retrieved from https://in-car.ca/ijcar/issues/vol4/2016/IJCAR_Vol4_No1_2016.pdf#page=4

Truth and Reconciliation Commission of Canada. (2015). *Honouring the truth, reconciling for the future: Summary of the final report of the Truth and Reconciliation Commission of Canada* (Publication No. IR4-7/2015E-PDF). Retrieved from http://www.trc.ca/assets/pdf/Honouring_the_Truth_Reconciling_for_the_Future_July_23_2015.pdf

Ungar, M. (2011). The social ecology of resilience: Addressing contextual and cultural ambiguity of a nascent construct. *American Journal of Orthopsychiatry, 81*(1), 1–17. doi:10.1111/j.1939-0025.2010.01067.x

Ungar, M. (2013). Resilience, trauma, context, and culture. *Trauma, Violence, & Abuse, 14*(3), 255–266. doi:10.1177/1524838013487805

United States Department of Health and Human Services. (2009). *National health security strategy*. Retrieved from https://www.phe.gov/preparedness/planning/authority/nhss

Wilk, P., Maltby, A., & Cooke, M. (2017). Residential schools and the effects on Indigenous health and well-being in Canada—A scoping review. *Public Health Reviews, 38*(8). doi:10.1186/s40985-017-0055-6

Windle, G., Markland, D. A., & Woods, R. T. (2008). Examination of a theoretical model of psychological resilience in older age. *Aging and Mental Health, 12*(3), 285–292. doi:10.1080/13607860802120763

Narrative Resilience
Neurological and Psychotherapeutic Reflections

Boris Cyrulnik

Introduction

Western practice separates the body and mind. Modern epistemology tends to integrate heterogeneous data within the same functional set. That is why in this chapter I attempt to associate brain development with the emotional effect of speech (narratives) and to explain the development of a valuable resilience factor.

We human beings are the only species capable of storytelling. By connecting the prefrontal neurons that allow anticipation with the circuits of memory and emotions, our brain enables us to understand time. Throughout our development, these circuits are activated, modified, and shaped by the emotional pressures of both family and social environments.

The words that shape these stories are learned in the early years. As soon as a child has acquired an array of words and some grammar guidelines, he or she has a tool for self-expression and emotional relationships that modify the secretion of neurohormones and impact the functions of the brain. That is why we human beings can suffer twice. The first time, through the sensory world we perceive, and then, a second time, in the world of verbal expression.

The process of developing capacity to understand and contribute to narrative proceeds as follows:

- The preverbal world begins to be built at the time of the fusion of the gametes where epigenetics allows the development of the organism and its capability to see the world. When speech occurs, in the third year, rationalizations give verbal form to a feeling whose origin cannot be understood.

- Around the age of six to eight years, brain maturation makes it possible to conceive time. Children can then recount the events of their memory. They can tell a story whose destiny depends on relationships. When a listener is trustworthy, a child's storytelling sheds light on the past and gives coherence to the world in which the child feels confident. But when the other (most often the primary caregiver) is not trustworthy, the child expresses a reluctant, fragmented, and incoherent story that makes the child feel uncertain and alters his or her relationships.
- When there is a match between the narratives of self, family, and culture, traumatized people feel supported and can undertake the work of building resilience. But when a discrepancy prevents affected persons from expressing themselves because the stories around them silence them or give an interpretation of the facts that is incompatible with that of the subjects, the work of resilience will then be difficult.

Neurological Traces in the Preverbal World

Epigenetics is an old concept. In animal ethology, it has long been known that the same genetic strip is expressed very differently depending on the nature of the environment. In a peaceful environment, a rat becomes a fat, white, and quiet adult. A rat of the same strain, in a stressful environment, will become a small, brown, hyperkinetic adult with a much shorter life expectancy.

Neurobiology today suggests a notion of generational transmission: when a pregnant mother is stressed by difficult living conditions, the substances of stress she secretes cross the placenta barrier, soak the early stages of cell division in the embryo she carries, and produce methyl radicals (CH3) and histone acetylations that stick to and modify the strands. There is no mutation, but the expression of the future baby's genetic profile is modified. It should be noted that what changed the expression of DNA was the mother's living conditions. What is transmitted is not the trauma; it is the biological adaptability of the parent to her existential crash.

Epigenetics explains why children born to traumatized mothers or mothers in socially precarious situations are born with cognitive impairments. Neuroimaging photographs bifrontal hypoactivity, atrophy of limbal circuits, and hyperactivity of rhinencephalic amygdala. These brain dysfunctions are due to stress substances secreted by the mother in existential difficulty (Lupien, King, Meaney, & McEwen, 2000). These cerebral areas were shaped by the mother's sadness. The protective factors that contribute to resilience at this stage of embryo development are to protect the mother to reduce her secretion of cortisol and catecholamines. In a few hours, as soon as the toxic substances are eliminated thanks to the mother's psycho-emotional support, the embryo's brain construction returns to its normal course, which does not mean that there are no traces left circulating in the child's brain due to the mother's difficulty (Geva, Eshel, Leitner, Valevski, & Harel, 2006). In addition to the hereditary parental DNA, there is the inheritance of their sadness. But, as with stem cells, early cell divisions are so vivid and malleable that supporting the mother is enough to trigger almost immediately a process of embryo resilience.

When a baby is born, its brain is already shaped by the developmental conditions in the womb. It is with this neurological acquisition that the brain will continue to weave an attachment bond, extracting from the environment some familiarized sensory information, such as the low frequencies of the mother's voice, the brilliance of her saccade, and her way of handling the newborn when giving care. When the sensory niche of the first few months is stable, regular stimulation can revive synaptic boiling and rewire a previously altered brain. But when the sensory niche is not reorganized, the impoverishment of stimuli reinforces acquired disorders.

The main causes of niche depletion are

- The emotional neglect of a mother who is sick, isolated, impacted by sadness, or has died without putting an emotional substitute in place.
- Domestic violence, which, even if the baby's body is not affected, overwhelms the child's brain with an emotional onslaught that the child does not yet know how to control.
- Social precariousness, as when parents devote their efforts to survival, which means they are less available for their newborn.

The causes of impoverishment are heterogeneous, but the cerebral impact is the same: hypotrophy of the two prefrontal unstimulated lobes, atrophy of the limbal circuits when the isolated baby has nothing to store and hypertrophy of the rhinencephalic amygdala, which are no longer hindered by the prefrontal lobes (Cohen, 2012).

A dysfunctional brain has thus been shaped by an environmental failure (e.g., isolation, marital conflict, or social precariousness). Under such conditions, the baby acquires a particular way of processing the information he or she extracts from his or her environment. The hypertrophy of the amygdala, the neurological foundation of unbearable emotions (e.g., anxiety, rage, panic), explains that, for a child thus shaped, the slightest information will have the effect of an aggression. Any encounter will be, for the child, a hostile relationship, and it is with this way of feeling the world that he or she will arrive, around the 20th month, in the world of words.

Resilience, at this preverbal stage of development, is possible if a stable sensory niche surrounds the child. The child can then create familiarity and weave new attachments that can gradually calm the emotional reactions of the amygdala. Early interactions have a stimulating effect on the prefrontal and temporal lobes. Playing repeated motor games or singing nursery rhymes with the child stimulates the child's ability to anticipate and prepare the child for speech and, later, narrative.

When children reach the sensitive period of language, they acquire a verbal relational tool that facilitates socialization (Nelson et al., 2007). They can form short sentences to establish a relationship ("Nadine is mean") but not yet a story. It will be necessary to wait until brain maturation establishes connections between the prefrontal lobe (the basis for anticipation) and the limbic system (the basis for memory) for the representation of time to be neurologically established. The child, around the age of six to eight years old, can finally collect memories and arrange them into a story for someone else to hear.

If a child is left alone, with his or her acquired brain defect due to a failure of the environment, the work of resilience will not be possible. Isolation can only reinforce the child's feeling of an aggressive world to which he or she responds with inhibition, evasion, or aggression. Such a relational style evokes borderline states, with a very painful intimate world and a disconnected relational style. In this population, suicidal thoughts are common (Bateman & Fonagy, 2010).

The verbal form that these young people give to their bitterness, rejection, and despair is a rationalization and not a reason. It is a process by which the youth seeks to give a coherent explanation from a logical point of view or one that is morally acceptable, to an attitude, an action, or an idea whose true motives are not perceived (Laplanche & Pontalis, 1973, p. 387). The unhappy young person, for example, gives a coherent appearance of verbal form to a feeling whose origin he or she does not know. The young person experiences an unpleasant emotional connotation and assigns a negative attribution to what he or she perceives, but he or she does not have the scientific knowledge that would allow him or her to hold systemic reasoning. Such a young person cannot say: "Everything makes me angry, because my brain is dysfunctional, because of my mother's misfortune, which impoverished the sensory niche of my first months as soon as my father was put in prison." Such reasoning is simply not yet possible.

Narration of Memories

Community support (secular, religious, political, athletic or artistic) is the best way to support a developmental recovery for a child who has early experiences of neglect or violence. In a project-oriented group, these unstructured young people learn to make sense of their rationalizations: "I am unhappy because society is unfair. I will make a political commitment to fight against injustice." You can also hear: "I can't say what happened to me. I will form an association to denounce incest and find ways to get back to living well" (Thomas, 2004). These commitments, by coordinating projected-oriented meetings, eventually form links and provoke reflections that calm the subject and can initiate an evolutionary recovery. It is not uncommon to see these young people in difficulty become educators, political actors, or writers. By using their past dysfunctions to make it a theoretical creation or written work, they rework their memories into a socially shareable narrative. While their spoken words could not establish a peaceful relationship because they were too impulsive or because their entourage could not bear to hear them, written words facilitate impulse control by keeping emotion at a greater distance. For these young people, spoken speech is an act, a blow to which they respond. They give this impulsive reaction a rationalizing form, a logical appearance, a moral argument, and a justification to explain their emotional discharge.

The developmental conditions of these young people do not allow them to acquire the three regulators of emotions:

- The brain dysfunction set up during the emotional failure of early interactions leads them to feel any information as an alert.
- This impulsivity prevents them from acquiring the mastery of speech that controls emotion.

- This kind of "talking-punching" becomes an act that alters their relationships with others.

To restore speech to its function as a mental tool, it is first necessary to provide a sense of security to the speaker (this security is derived from the resources available to the now older child at multiple systemic levels). When the listener (e.g., psychotherapist, priest, confidant, friend) acquires the function of a trusted source, the speaker ends up no longer feeling attacked. The previously abused child's words lose their defensive function to become a tool for reflection (Bowlby, 2011). But when the listener is not trustworthy (e.g., an intimidating police officer who asks intrusive questions or a brutal psychotherapist), the speaker remains on the defensive and may even become worse emotionally. Fortunately, when the person who is listening is a source of trust and safety, the speaker calms down and is better able to elaborate the narrative of his trauma. By searching for words, by arranging the images of his traumatic memories, he creates a narrative of them, a script of images and words that he addresses to the other in a relationship of trust. This work of speaking in a safe relationship calms the emotions and helps reshape a child's representation of past trauma into an experience that is compartmentalized and less of a negative influence on the child's pattern of attributions about the world.

When memory is healthy, the story is not the return of past events; it is a representation or description of past events. It is from the present that we shed light on the past. This evocative and relational work does not bring back the past, as is the case in psychotraumatic syndrome where the past is imposed on the present. It redesigns the representation of this past. Such work sets up a factor of resilience and then, when the process is triggered, is enough to elaborate on and contribute to emotional and psychological progress.

Spoken speech requires a secure relationship to reshape memory to escape the prison of the past. The intentional aspect of memory makes it possible for representations to evolve. Neuroimaging explains this idea. An experimenter asks someone to recall a memory: "What did you do last Sunday?" Quickly, the two prefrontal lobes consume energy. This neurological foundation of anticipation will seek information. When it is found, images "light up" the two occipital lobes that process visual information. "I was fishing by boat," says the subject while the limbal circuits turn red, revealing that this evocation provokes an emotion. Further, when the subject says, "I was fishing by boat," his left temporal lobe also gives off energy.

If then we ask, "What are you going to do next Sunday?" we can see that almost the same circuits light up in the same sequence. This means that the memory of the past requires an effort close to that of the imagination of the future. We anticipate our past to shape our present but the two remain separate, whereas in the case of a psychotraumatic syndrome it is the past that invades the present. We can deduce from this that the work of speech and imagination is opposed to repetition and instead remodels memory.

Emotion is always associated with this work. The experimenter asks a teacher to read a text in a monotonous tone. A month later, he tests the students and finds that they have learned almost nothing. Then he asks the teacher to read the same text, in the same way, but the experimenter adds a ringing tone at irregular intervals. A month later, the students retain many more memories. The simple act of awakening consciousness by provoking a small emotion improves memory (Schacter, 1999, p. 39). In safe psychotherapy, emotions sharpen memory. With a nonsecuring psychotherapist, the patient adapts by fleeing, inhibiting, or assaulting the therapist. Talking, thinking, and being moved in the presence of a security base are not just statements of facts. You must analyze your own reactions, give them meaning, and arrange the words to make a story that can be shared with the person who makes you feel secure to overcome experiences of earlier trauma.

This work, unlike repetition, leads to the activation of new brain circuits (Fontenelle, de Oliveira-Souza, & Moll, 2015) and the resilience required to live a good life despite a difficult beginning. We free ourselves from the past when we organize the safe and stimulating conditions of speech and imagination.

The Surrounding Stories

In the usual conditions of development, a child is immersed every day in family and cultural stories that constantly narrate tragedies and celebrations (Miller & Sperry, 1988). These compelling stories build a moral sense by telling the child who he or she is, where he or she comes from, what the values of his or her group are, and what to expect from life. These stories compose a verbal environment that permeates a feeling in the child's soul. Depending on the context, the child will experience a world of euphoria or despair, confidence or distrust. Preverbal memory can be said to trace unconscious circuits in the brain (Lejeune & Delage, 2017) that create an ability to perceive a type of world, soothing or stressful depending on the surrounding stories. The world is not perceived as it is; what we feel is the impression it gives us. These stories, by being inscribed in memory, compose a hyperconscious mental world that participates in the formation of the person.

When the child grasps the concept of time, the stories presented to her (like fairy tales) tell the child about the existence for which he or she must prepare. To illustrate, if a child is told a story in which every morning a donkey's droppings turn into a golden shield, the child learns that it is possible to metamorphose, to see disgusting things differently. When the same story tells of a princess dressed in a time-colored dress that becomes subject to her father's sexual gaze, the child learns that it is necessary to respect the forbidden and protect herself with donkey skin.

To tell a horror story is to tame it, to control the fear of the unknown, to fill a void with a discovery. This is how creation is opposed to repetition. When his mother disappears, the child loses the familiarity with his world and unknown objects become worrying. Then a scarf, teddy bear, or drawing is put in the mother's place to wait for her return. The creation of a symbol, an object placed there to fill the absences, also fills the distressing void. It is the child who attributes a reassuring effect to the object; he lures himself by inventing a transitional object (Winnicott, 1958).

Is that how works of art evoke emotions? Orphans deprived of real role models experience the anguish of emptiness when left alone, but as soon as they are surrounded, they invent a dream family and write its history to share it with their new family environment. These stories become mechanisms for resilience, protective artifacts of a child's world. Wagner, the 19th-century German composer and musical director, experienced the death of his father when he was just five months old. It may be thought that the child's sensory niche was impoverished when his mother was bereaved. But when Wagner enters the world of stories, he invents an imaginary filiation coming from a model proposed by his culture: "I Richard Wagner, I am the son of Shakespeare the bard." This identification with a cultural model became a grandiose compensatory response to a huge past loss. Wagner is not alone in this trait. By writing our dreams, we put existence where there is nothing left. Mary Shelley invented Frankenstein, a monster who depicts the immense losses of her life. Her mother died giving birth to her at the age of 16. Mary gave birth to three children who died one after the other. By inventing a monster, Shelley gave written form to the four dead who remain in her, as in a living tomb.

When these spoken or written accounts, testimonies or fictions are received, shared with the family and cultural environment, injured persons feel understood. They are no longer alone in the world; they can speak quietly or write a compensatory story. This alignment between the narratives of oneself and the surrounding narratives constitutes a precious factor of resilience since the subject accepts his or her wound and can speak authentically about the pain. People can also make narratives fictions to interest their entourage and invite them to share mental worlds. The shared stories thus take on a basic security effect: "I feel liberated since I wrote." Resilience is on the move.

When there is a discrepancy, however, between what subjects need to say and the cultural portrayal of their experience, the traumatic tear is aggravated. Often, the stories around the wounded can silence them: "The war is over, stop talking about it" or "If this man raped you, it's because you provoked him." Such a discordance induces a divide, not an intrapsychic one, but rather a gap between subjects and their families or cultural environments. The traumatized person can only say what his or her environment expects to hear. This discrepancy puts a tomb in the soul of the wounded. The people around them feel a sense of ambivalence: "Why does he suddenly become dark and silent when moments before he was joyous?"

In such a relationship, resilience is chaotic, the environment has lost its reassuring effect, and the injured suddenly feel betrayed by their silence. They falsely come to believe: "My beliefs are invalidated" (Rimé, 2005, p. 375).

Mature Narration

When we reach the age of reasoning, we look back on our past and finally understand the direction of our lives. But the old memory modifies the representation of past events. A recounted memory is clearer than a memory never expressed (Croisile, 2008, p. 133) because the mere fact of having spoken it increases the poignancy of the memory—the memory of the story that one has made of it. The traumatized person who has developed a trauma by talking to a trusted source or writing to an imaginary reader has altered the representation of his or her past.

Working memory deteriorates from the age of 40, while semantic memory is maintained for a longer time (provided that you do not have Alzheimer's; Eustache & Eustache-Vallée, 2016, p. 47). When the trauma has been encysted without being altered by relationship and speech, it can resurface with age. Some outbursts of delirium can be explained by this phenomenon. An elderly lady suddenly says: "You hear the tanks passing through the street . . . I hear the soldiers' steps on the stairs." Her daughter answers with a logical explanation: "Mom, calm down, the war has been over for 70 years." But the war still exists, buried in the mother's memory as if it had just happened, as a psychotraumatic syndrome that has never been altered. The intense emotion of the trauma of the war has been neurologically imprinted into the elderly woman's brain and this imprint, never altered, reappears when the working memory can no longer bury it beneath daily actions.

This neurological imprint of the past is regularly observed in the case of polyglot aphasia (Botez, 1987, p. 322). As a child, our first language is learned in 10 months, between the 20th and 30th month, without books and without school, because of the sensitive biological period of memory. The determinism of this intellectual prowess is chronobiological since it always occurs at the same time, regardless of the culture, and corresponds to a peak of synthesis of neuromediators of memory, such as acetylcholine. It is not uncommon for a person who has spent his or her life in several languages to forget them in the reverse order of learning. The mother tongue, acquired first, remains the most deeply imbued. That is why we can see immigrants who have spent their entire lives in the United States, becoming unable to speak English from the age of 70, while still speaking Italian or Polish learned in their early childhood years.

This classic phenomenon in neurogeriatrics explains that a trauma is never forgotten; it remains imprinted like a trace in the depths of the self. It can be intentionally reworked, by talking about it, writing it, forming a relationship, or through psychotherapy, but when this work of resilience cannot be done, the past suffering that we thought we had forgotten can arise again.

Discussion

The word *resilience* refers to a natural phenomenon: how to get back to a life lived well after a trauma? The Latin word *re-salire*" gave rise to "projection," and "respill." The flow of life can resume even after it has been obstructed by a trauma. Used in agriculture since the 17th century, this word defines resilient soil when, after a disaster such as a flood or fire, new flora or fauna reappear.

For mental health practitioners, it is important to discover the factors that allow this return to another facet of life. It is therefore a neodevelopmental psychology that is required to understand resilience, where the word *evolution* organizes our thoughts. Some traumatized people easily recover, which defines resilience. But others are unable to do so because of their psychotraumatic alterations. As with any type of development, one that is neodevelopmental lasts as long as life itself. It is constantly retriggered by family pressures, friendships, and the sociocultural environment.

To discover the factors that allow the resumption of resilient development, the method consists of

1. Analyzing the protective factors put in place during development before the trauma. These factors characterize the acquisition of internal resources, imbued in memory by the community. These factors help the subject to cope with the incident. It is more of a resistance than resilience.

2. Analyzing the structure of the trauma, acute or insidious, family or foreign, natural or cultural, short or long lasting. The impact of the event, its traumatic effect, is a result of the person he or she is at this stage of organic development and what is around him or her (at this moment in time).
3. Support and meaning are the main resilience factors that characterize the external resources arranged around the traumatized victim. This developmental recovery can only be new, since the trauma has inflicted a scar that leaves a trace in the implicit memory or in the individual's history.

The process of narrative resilience is the result of the convergence of several heterogeneous narratives that can be combined to form a representation of the self. For example, the earlier, more intense and long-lasting sensory isolation has occurred, the more the baby's brain is altered. The acquired dysfunction explains his inability to plan an action program because of his frontal hypotrophy. The baby can only respond to the stimuli of the context. Since the atrophied prefrontal lobes can no longer inhibit the rhinencephalic tonsil, the slightest information is felt as a real aggression. As the representation of time is impossible, the child can only respond to the world he or she experiences as an aggression.

Resilience would be possible, provided that the child is offered, as soon as possible, an emotional substitute that will stimulate prefrontal neurons and inhibit the amygdala. When the child has been left alone, he cannot tell a story of himself, he can only respond to the violent world with frightened immobility, fearful silence, avoidance, escape, or a violent response against others or against self.

When an emotional substitute is provided later, the partial resilience that results is not of good quality. The child calms down, his emotional responses are less violent, but he keeps in his implicit memory the trace of what was previously lacking. To express the world he feels, he gives a verbal form, a logical appearance to the feelings that invade him and whose origin he ignores: "Everyone is evil. . . . I have rage inside me. . . . I have to defend myself." A sect or a radical commitment that allows him to express himself can exploit this need to defend against a past wound. The French novelist and political activist Jean Genet illustrates the low resilience of his intimate world dominated by the emotional desert he inhabits and his attraction to garbage cans, the pleasure of stealing, and hurting those he loves (White, 1993). Abandoned and isolated from birth, placed in an adorable foster family, he was unable to perceive the warmth of his new parents. His frozen soul, barely warmed, remained attracted by waste, rot, and evil.

Alice Miller, the great psychologist, has also been very helpful to the cause of children. After a traumatic childhood in Poland where anti-Semitic persecution was immense and incessant, she lacked the reassurance of a stable mother and instead experienced an untrustworthy caregiver. Miller opposed the theories of resilience because she had developed a fully explanatory rationalization: men are violent because they have been abused. Hitler is anti-Semitic because his father physically abused him, and the wars in the Middle East will never cease because men are circumcised. Such rationalization gave a logical form to a feeling of a hostile world, imprinted in her memory during her childhood and never terminated.

Each example shows that an organism cannot develop elsewhere than in its environment. A psyche cannot learn to love and think outside its emotional and cultural context.

Such an epistemological attitude cannot be linear; it can only be systemic. It is a convergence of heterogeneous factors, a harmony of endogenous and exogenous pressures that allow or prevent a resilient evolution. This method of collecting information, which is usual for a practitioner (doctor, psychologist, educator), is different from that of a laboratory researcher but is not opposed to it. Scientist must reduce their field of knowledge to make a hypothesis and propose a repeatable and refutable method to validate or invalidate their hypothesis. While a practitioner (e.g., a pulmonologist) will have to analyze how external factors such as oxygen in the air can pass through the solid wall of a pulmonary alveolus and float on the plasma fluid carried by the red blood cells, the respiratory system is composed of totally heterogeneous elements (gaseous, solid, and liquid), which constitute a functional unit. It is enough that only one subsystem is altered (hypoxia, silicosis, anemia) for the whole system to malfunction. But it is also enough to act on a single altered subsystem for the whole system to start working again. This is why the notion of *multisystem* is almost a pleonasm since, in a single functional unit, several subsystems coordinate.

Conclusion

By this logic, the definition of resilience is simple: resilience is a neuropsychosocial process that allows a new development to be resumed after a psychological trauma. The factors of this new evolution are so numerous and heterogeneous that they require teamwork where researchers work together to analyze and harmonize these heterogeneous determinants.

Since this research and this new epistemological attitude entered the realm of the mental health clinic, we can see that trauma is no longer a fatality that cannot be treated.

Key Messages

1. The brain, sculpted by its environment, during early interactions, acquires protective or vulnerable factors.
2. Having acquired a particular sensitivity to the world, rationalization gives a verbal form to a feeling whose origin is unknown.
3. When the stories the traumatized person hears are consistent with his or her memories, resilience is an easy process. However, when they are discordant, the cleaved subject achieves only partial resilience.

References

Bateman, A., & Fonagy, P. (2010). Mentalization based treatment for borderline personality disorder. *World Psychiatry*, 9(1), 11–15. doi:10.1002/j.2051-5545.2010.tb00255.x

Botez, M. I. (1987). *Neuropsychologie clinique et neurologie du comportement*. Montréal, QC: Presses de l'Université de Montréal.

Bowlby, J. (2011). *Le Lien, la psychanalyse et l'art d'être parent* [The link, psychoanalysis and the art of being a parent]. Paris, France: Albin Michel.

Cohen, D. (2012). The developmental being. In M. E. Garralda & J. P. Raynaud (Eds.), *Brain, mind and developmental psychopathology in childhood* (pp. 3–30). New York, NY: Jason Aronson.

Croisile, B. (2008) *Votre mémoire* [Your memory]. Paris, France: Larousse.

Eustache, F., & Eustache-Vallée, M. L. (2016). *La mémoire: En 40 pages*. Paris, France: Éditions UPPR.

Fontenelle L. F., de Oliveira-Souza, R., & Moll, J. (2015). The rise of moral emotions in neuropsychiatry. *Dialogue in Clinical Neuroscience, 17*(4), 411–420.

Geva, R., Eshel, R., Leitner, Y., Valevski, A. F., & Harel, S. (2006). Neuropsychological outcome of children with intrauterine growth restriction: A 9-year prospective study. *Pediatrics, 118*(1), 91–100. doi:10.1542/peds.2005-2343

Laplanche J., & Pontalis, J. B. (1973). Rationalisation. In *Vocabulaire de la psychanalyse* [The language of psychoanalysis] (4th ed.). Paris, France: PUF.

Lejeune, A., & Delage, M. (2017). *La mémoire sans souvenir* [Memory without remembrances]. Paris, France: Odile Jacob.

Lupien, S., King, S., Meaney, M., & McEwen, B. (2000). Child's stress hormone levels correlate with mother's socioeconomic status and depressive state. *Biological Psychiatry, 48*(10), 976–980. doi:10.1016/s0006-3223(00)00965-3

Miller, P., & Sperry L. L. (1988). Early talk about the past: The origins of conversational stories of personal experience. *Journal of Child Language, 15*(2), 293–315.

Nelson, C. A., III., Zeanah, C. H., Fox, N. A., Marshall, P. J., Smyke, A. T., & Guthrie, D. (2007). Cognitive recovery in socially deprived young children: The Bucharest early intervention project. *Science, 318*(5858), 1937–1940. doi:10.1126/science.1143921

Rimé, B. (2005). *Le partage social des émotions* [Social sharing of emotions]. Paris, France: PUF.

Schacter, D. L. (1999). *À la recherche de la mémoire: Le passé, l'esprit et le cerveau* [In search of memory: The past, the mind and the brain]. Brussels, Belgium: De Boeck.

Thomas, E. (2004). *Le sang des mots: Les victimes, l'inceste et la loi* [The blood of words: Victims, incest and the law]. Paris, France: Desclée de Brouwer.

White, E. (1993). *Jean Genet*. Paris, France: Gallimard, 1993.

Winnicott, D. (1958). *La capacité d'être seul* [The capacity to be alone]. Paris, France: Petite Bibliothèque Payot.

SECTION 2

Psychological Processes in Challenging Contexts

6

Resilience in Developmental Systems

Principles, Pathways, and Protective Processes in Research and Practice

Ann S. Masten

Introduction

Research explicitly focused on resilience in human development emerged in the 1970s as pioneering investigators noted the striking variation in adaptive function and outcomes of children identified as high-risk for mental health problems due to their circumstances or experiences (Masten, 2014b). Initially, the research was largely descriptive, as scholars charted patterns of healthy adjustment among children at risk for a wide variety of reasons, including maltreatment, genetic risk (e.g., born to parents with mental disorders), poverty, family conflict, or a combination of multiple known risk factors associated with elevated probabilities of undesirable outcomes (Masten, 2007). Nonetheless, these early investigators were searching for answers to a fundamental question: What makes a difference? In other words, how do we account for the positive life course of some children in the context of exposure to risks or severe adversity? The ultimate goal of answering this question was translational, to inform practice and policy that would prevent problems from arising or support positive development despite the presence of hazardous circumstances.

This chapter highlights the meaning and findings of developmental resilience science, particularly in regard to children and families. Following a brief history on the emergence of resilience research, this chapter presents an overview of the current meaning of resilience in studies of children and families and the developmental systems principles that inform that definition. Key concepts and models that guide this research are described and illustrated by empirical results. Implications of a developmental resilience framework for practice and policy are delineated, with illustrations from research on children at risk due to poverty, homelessness, or forced migration from the violence and chaos of political conflict. The chapter concludes with a discussion of new horizons in developmental research on resilience.

The study of development in the lives of children threatened by negative life experiences was influenced by streams of theory and empirical research in multiple fields of study concerned with normative human and mammalian development, the biology and psychology of stress, the origins of competence and psychopathology in childhood, and human responses to extreme adversity observed in children exposed to violence in families or trauma on the scale of war (Garmezy & Rutter, 1983; Masten, 2014a). It is notable that leading pioneers in the study of resilience in medicine and the social sciences were themselves often survivors of World War II, including Garmezy, Rutter, and Werner (Masten, 2014b). This devastating global conflict gave rise to theory, research, and interventions focused on understanding and mitigating the impact of trauma on child development.

Early research on resilience in children focused on identifying factors associated with better outcomes in children at risk and later research focused on explaining why those factors seemed to matter, shifting attention from "what matters" to "how" questions about the processes involved in resilience. These were the first two waves of resilience science in the behavioral sciences (Masten, 2007, 2014b). Once investigators identified key processes associated with resilience, interventions research ensued to test the causal role of these processes, representing the third wave. We are now in the midst of the fourth wave as scholars tackle multisystem questions and attempt to integrate concepts and findings about resilience across disciplines and levels of analysis.

During the initial decades of research on resilience in children, definitions of the concept varied in their emphasis on the observable patterns of manifested resilience ("doing well despite adversity"), the individual, relational, or sociocultural differences associated with better adjustment in risky conditions (often described as protective factors, assets, or promotive factors), and the processes involved in adapting or coping with the challenges of risk or adversity. Thus, in an early review, my colleagues and I noted that "resilience refers to the process of, capacity for, or outcome of successful adaption despite challenging or threatening circumstance" (Masten, Best, & Garmezy, 1990, p. 426).

As the early research on resilience was emerging, a broad revolution in developmental theory was unfolding, often described as developmental systems theory or relational developmental systems theory (Lerner, 2006; Osher, Cantor, Berg, Steyer, & Rose, 2018; Overton, 2013). This movement integrated theory in multiple disciplines focused on development in living systems, ranging from embryology (e.g., Gottlieb, 2007; Lickliter, 2013) and behavioral genetics (Gottesman & Hanson, 2005) to family systems (Henry, Morris, & Harrist, 2015; Walsh, 2016) and ecological models (e.g., Bronfenbrenner & Morris, 1998). This perspective integrated disparate theory on the roles of multiple interacting systems at multiple levels of analysis in shaping the development of living systems, including the development of children (Masten & Cicchetti, 2016). Zelazo (2013) described the growing prominence of systems theory in developmental psychology as the "new synthesis."

For resilience science, however, the emergence of developmental systems theory as the most prominent unifying theory in developmental science represented only part of the impetus to shift toward a full-blown systems approach. Entirely consistent with the practical focus of resilience science, the other major influence that motivated a powerful shift toward systems theory arose from the growing threat of mass-trauma global adversities in the form of terror attacks, disasters, and pandemics (Masten, Narayan, Silverman, & Osofsky, 2015).

Mass-trauma adversities always played a role in resilience research, beginning with the pioneers, who highlighted observations about the effects of war and disaster on children in addition to the more everyday stressors of family violence, poverty, or oppression (Garmezy, 1983; Masten et al., 1990). Subsequently, a series of mass-casualty events elevated awareness of threats posed by large-scale calamities, such as domestic and international terrorism (e.g., Oklahoma City, 9/11), natural disasters (Hurricane Katrina, the 2004 tsunami in the Indian Ocean), and pandemics (e.g., Ebola, HIV/AIDS). Simultaneously, the number of children threatened by armed conflict also was growing internationally, generating huge numbers of displaced children and refugees (Masten et al., 2015). Concerns also were growing about climate change, as the frequency or intensity of storms and floods appeared to grow (Stott, 2016).

In April 2008, the Resilience Alliance and the Royal Swedish Academy of Sciences hosted a conference on resilience, Resilience 2008, which featured not only numerous presentations on climate change but also a symposium on interdisciplinary perspectives on resilience and natural disasters. This symposium highlighted the work of a research network, including this author, on "Building an Interdisciplinary Study of Resilience," funded by the National Science Foundation under its Human and Social Dynamics Initiative (Masten & Obradović, 2008; NSF 0524157). Our work was subsequently published as a special feature in the journal of the Resilience Alliance, *Ecology and Society*, "Managing Surprises in Complex Systems," edited by Lance Gunderson and Pat Longstaff. Our small network of five senior and five junior investigators met with the goal of integrating perspectives on resilience. As we met to discuss different definitions of resilience in disparate fields (e.g., ecology, human development, and computer science), we found it was easier to communicate and advance our agenda when we focused on the real issues posed by disasters and related mass-trauma calamities. Preparing for and responding to disasters, when many interconnected systems essential to human life collapse or stop functioning at the same time, made it abundantly clear that a multisystem approach was essential.

This interdisciplinary network experience underscored my belief that we needed a common and scalable language to facilitate integration of the many sciences engaged in research on resilience. My own shift to emphasize a systems approach to resilience was accelerated by this experience (Masten, 2007; Masten & Obradović, 2008).

Definition of Resilience from a Developmental Systems Perspective

From a developmental systems perspective, resilience can be defined as the capacity of a dynamic system to adapt successfully to challenges that threaten the function, survival, or development of the system (Masten, 2011, 2014a, 2014b, 2018a). This definition is intended to be scalable across system levels from micro- to macrolevels and also across diverse disciplines. Resilience is relevant to understanding many kinds of complex adaptive systems, including a whole person the immune system within a person, a family, an economy, a business organization or a school, a community or a society, and many dynamic ecosystems across the planet.

The capacity of a complex adaptive system, such as a living person, to respond well to challenges is dynamic because the sources of that capacity are also dynamic and distributed across many interacting systems. Moreover, living systems develop and change over the life course in ways that influence their adaptive capacity. Problem-solving capacities generally expand with development and learning experiences until the organism begins to decline with age. However, at any given time, capacity can be affected by temporary situations, such as illness or overload.

Resilience in a person will reflect important general principles of development drawn from developmental systems theory (Masten & Cicchetti, 2016). Human development arises from the interactions of an individual's genetic inheritance (DNA plus any other heritable epigenetic marks) with many other interacting systems at multiple levels over time (Gottlieb, 2007). A human individual is embedded in other systems, such as a family and later a school, which in turn are embedded in higher order systems, such as a community). The great contribution of Bronfenbrenner's ecological theory (Bronfenbrenner, 1979; Bronfenbrenner & Morris, 1998) to developmental science was highlighting the role of context in the form of these other systems in the development of individuals. A child interacts directly with microsystems such as the family or a set of friends or a team and indirectly with many other systems external to these proximal systems, such as a parent's workplace (an exosystem) or large, distal macrosystems that influence a child or her microsystems indirectly, such as a state government.

Within the individual child there also are many interacting systems at multiple levels, including an immune system, neural systems that support many other adaptive systems, and neuroendocrine systems that regulate arousal and stress responses. Child development also is influenced by a microbiome of non-human organisms that inhabit and surround the individual child (Cho & Blaser, 2012). All of these systems develop as the individual develops, continually influenced by interactions with the "external" context, beginning in the womb and continuing after birth. Development emerges from a complex network of interacting systems that also shape the capacity of the person to adapt to adversity.

The following principles stem from a developmental systems perspective on resilience (adapted from Masten & Cicchetti, 2016):

1. Many interacting systems shape the development of resilience in a living system.
2. Living systems are self-organizing with higher-order emergent capabilities that can be surprising or unpredictable based on knowledge from lower levels of analysis.
3. Resilience develops and changes because all of the systems accounting for resilience are dynamic; thus, human resilience develops and changes as a person develops and changes.

4. The capacity for adapting to challenging circumstances (resilience) depends on many interconnected systems.
5. The capacity for adaptation can be conceptualized at multiple levels.
6. The resilience of an individual extends beyond the individual organism through interactions and connections to other systems.
7. Adaptation of a complex system, such as a person, to major disturbances can take multiple forms: returning to equilibrium through self-stabilizing or external co-regulatory systems, breaking down to lower levels of function, death, or transformation.
8. Human resilience is shaped by the legacy of biological and cultural evolution through the evolution of many systems in the natural and built world and also by individual development.

It follows from these principles that the resilience of an individual child at any given time depends on other systems, and indeed on the resilience of other systems, both within and external to the child, and most especially in relationships and proximal systems, such as the family, school, peer groups, community, and culture. It also follows from these principles that no singular trait could account for resilience. Resilience is not a trait, although many attributes of the individual person many contribute to resilience.

Because so many unique interactions shape the development of a human individual and no two people (even identical twins with the same DNA) can have the same experiences, development is probabilistic and the life course of a person is often described as a *pathway*. The pathways of twins and children in the same family can diverge quite dramatically, and the pathways of two individuals from very different backgrounds can converge if their experiences shape them toward similar directions or outcomes. These possibilities are known as multifinality and equifinality in the developmental literature (Cicchetti & Rogosch, 1996). Trauma exposure can contribute to diverging pathways, particularly when individuals differ in their resilience to adapt to the trauma.

Typically we infer resilience capacity from observed pathways of *manifested resilience*. Manifested resilience refers to observable "good adaptation" in the context of adversity, by whatever criteria are being applied to evaluate the success of meeting a significant challenge. It has been noted for decades of resilience research that manifested resilience requires two fundamental judgments: (a) that there has been a significant challenge or disturbance of some kind that threatens the function of the person and (b) that the person is doing okay by meaningful adaptive criteria (Luthar, 2006; Masten, 2001). These criteria are discussed further later in the chapter. The goal of identifying manifested resilience typically is to advance the search for processes that made it possible for the system to adapt. In other words, it is important to distinguish manifested resilience from the resilience processes that made it possible for the person or other system of interest to adapt to serious challenges.

It was a logical starting point in the early research on resilience to begin the search for resilience by studying individuals who had demonstrated by their successful adaptation to adversity that they had the capacity to cope with or overcome in as yet unknown ways the challenges posed by negative life experiences. The resilience research pioneers hoped that by studying naturally occurring manifested resilience they could identify the resilience factors and processes that accounted for good outcomes under challenging circumstances. Armed with that knowledge, the ultimate goal was to foster better development among children at risk due to adversity by informing interventions to promote resilience.

Key Concepts and Models in Developmental Resilience Science

Three central questions inform the purpose and design of resilience research in systems:

- What are the challenges confronting the system? (What are the risks?)
- How well is the system doing? (What are the criteria for adaptive success?)
- What processes support the adaptive success of the system?

Studies of resilience in human individuals have spanned a wide variety of challenges and adaptive criteria over the years, encompassing a large body of evidence pertinent to resilience in children and youth (see Goldstein & Brooks, 2013; Luthar, 2006; Masten, 2014b), resilience in adults (see Reich, Zautra, & Hall, 2010; Southwick & Charney, 2018), and resilience in families (e.g., Walsh, 2016). There are bodies of literature on specific hazards, such as divorce, death of a parent, or sexual abuse (Garmezy & Rutter, 1983; Masten & Cicchetti, 2016), as well as research on cumulative risk factors or threats, such as studies of adverse childhood experiences (Felitti et al., 1998) and studies of children growing up in poverty or disadvantage characterized by a multiplicity of hazards (e.g., Evans, Li, & Whipple, 2013; Maholmes, 2014). Now, scholarship on the disastrous cascading effects of the global COVID-19 pandemic is beginning to emerge (e.g., Masten & Motti-Sefanidi, 2020).

Criteria for evaluating how well a person is doing have also varied in the resilience literature on children and youth. Developmental researchers often focus on developmental tasks or the expected achievements for children of a given age, culture, and period in history (Masten & Coatsworth, 1998; Masten, 2014b). In modern societies across the world, for example, young children are expected to form attachment bonds to their caregivers and to learn to walk and speak the language of the family, and older children are expected to go to school, learn to read, get along with other people, and follow the rules of the family, classroom, and community. Trauma researchers often have focused on mental health symptoms as their criteria for (not) doing well while other investigators have focused on psychological well-being or happiness. As in the case with risk factors, some investigators focus on a specific criterion of adaptive success (e.g., work success or academic achievement), while others have a broader view of doing well that encompasses multiple indicators (e.g., Masten et al., 1999; Werner & Smith, 2001).

Many resilience factors and processes also have been investigated in answer to the third question, which is directly focused on resilience. These factors, or the processes believed to underlie them, have been divided into two basic groups: *promotive factors or processes* that are associated with better functioning on the criteria for judging adaptive function across risk levels (a main effect) and *protective factors or processes* that are associated with better function or outcomes when threat levels are higher than normal (a moderating effect). Promotive and protective influences vary by situation (Masten & Cicchetti, 2016).

Some of these resilience predictors are very common across diverse situations, perhaps because they reflect very fundamental human adaptive systems and capabilities. From the outset of resilience research, for example, it was clear that the quality of caregiving and support from other attachment relationships played a central role in the resilience of children, as did the individual capabilities of the children, such as problem-solving skills. Other factors and processes were less common or relatively unique to a given culture or situation. Examples include ceremonial forgiveness rituals practiced by a particular community or practice drills at schools for fires, tornadoes, or other threats to school safety common in the regional context. In their article on rethinking resilience from Indigenous perspectives, Kirmayer and colleagues describe a ritual of reconciliation and forgiveness practiced by the Mi'kmaq people of Atlantic Canada (Kirmayer, Dandeneau, Marshall, Phillips, & Williamson, 2011).

Resilience factors and processes have been studied at different levels of analysis, ranging from neurobiological and psychological levels within the individual to relationships at a dyadic or group level (including families) to cultural beliefs and practices and services or policies at the community, state, or national level. Given that systems are interconnected and often embedded in other systems (such as a child whose life is embedded in a family and a classroom), as previously discussed, the resilience capacity of a person may reflect the resilience of other systems that person is connected to. Perhaps the most studied example of this interdependence of system resilience is between the resilience of a child and the resilience of the caregiving system or family caring for that child (Masten & Palmer, 2019). However, there appear to be many parallels in the commonly identified resilience qualities of individuals, families, schools, and communities that suggest vertically integrated human adaptive systems that may have co-evolved socioculturally as a result of the inherent interdependence of individuals and their social ecologies.

In fact, there are striking similarities in the resilience factors or processes identified in different literatures on resilience in children, families, schools, communities, cultures, and religions (Berkes & Ross, 2013; Crawford, Wright, & Masten, 2006; Harrist, Henry, Liu, & Morris, 2019; Masten, 2014b, 2018a, 2018b; Ungar, 2008, 2011; Walsh, 2016). Common protective factors described across levels in these different human systems include the following.

- Social connectedness
- Sense of belonging
- Optimism or a positive outlook
- Meaning
- Agency
- Self-efficacy or collective efficacy
- Problem-solving skills
- Executive function or leadership

These parallels suggest that there are meaningful processes connecting the development of these resilience factors or processes across systems. In the child literature, for example, it is argued that effective families and effective schools have similar qualities and also that both contexts nurture resilience in children by modeling, teaching, and otherwise fostering the development of supportive relationships, problem-solving skills, self-regulation skills, agency, and a sense of belonging (Masten, 2014b, 2018b).

Models Linking Threats, Adaptive Processes, and Functional Adaptive Status

Two basic kinds of models have guided research on resilience in recent decades, sometimes described as person-focused or pathway models and variable-focused models (Masten, 2001, 2014b). Person-focused models include case studies of individuals who show positive patterns of adjustment to adversity over time and also models of life-course pathways that unfold from the interplay of many interacting influences on development. These latter models were rooted in the developmental literature in embryology, behavior genetics, and psychology on the shaping of individual development by the interplay of genes and experience (e.g., Gottesman, 1974; Gottesman & Shields, 1972; Gottlieb, 2007; Waddington, 1957/2014).

My earliest pathway models (e.g., Masten & Reed, 2002) were strongly influenced by the work of Gottesman, one of the faculty who trained the clinical students at the University of Minnesota for many years, including my years of doctoral study. Gottesman famously illustrated the various pathways of individuals with varying genetic diathesis for schizophrenia who developed or avoided this serious mental illness over the life course, depending on their life experiences (Gottesman, 1974).

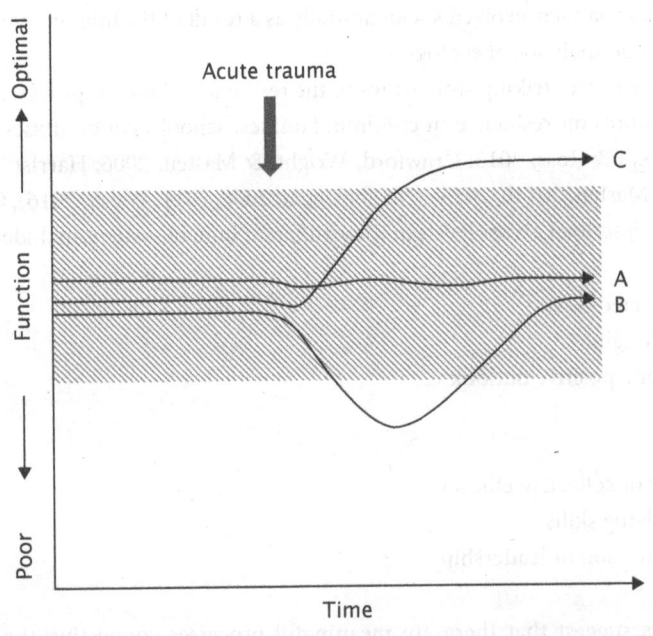

FIGURE 6.1 Resilience pathways following acute onset trauma. Pattern A = stress-resistance; B = breakdown and recovery; C = posttraumatic growth. *Source:* © Ann S. Masten. Reprinted with permission.

Early pathway models described the ups and downs of adaptive function over time in simplified form, illustrating commonly observed or hypothesized responses to acute trauma. A more recent version of responses reflecting resilience to an acute trauma experience is shown in Figure 6.1. This figure illustrates stress-resistance (a), breakdown with recovery (b), and posttraumatic growth (c). Many other patterns are possible, including breakdown patterns where resilience is not evident (at least not yet). Common examples of breakdown are a pathway of immediate breakdown without recovery of function as yet and delayed breakdown or a depletion model (see Masten & Narayan, 2012).

Figure 6.2 illustrates a model of chronic adversity, where conditions are so difficult that functioning deteriorates or remains poor until more favorable conditions occur, either naturally or through intervention. Numerous examples of recovery following chronic, severe adversity have emerged in recent decades, such as the recovery of children exposed to extreme violence or deprivation for prolonged periods, including child soldiers, children rescued from abusive homes, and children adopted from inadequate orphanages (see Masten, 2014b). While not all children recover from prolonged exposure to severe adversity, many do recover when favorable conditions are established or restored.

Recent studies have begun to document distinct pathways of adjustment following acute or chronic adversity, utilizing mixed modeling strategies of analyzing repeated measures of adjustment over time (e.g., Betancourt, McBain, Newnham, & Brennan, 2013; Meijer, Findenauer, Tierolf, Lünnemann, & Steketee, 2019; Osofsky, Osofsky, Weems, King, & Hansel, 2015). More longitudinal data are needed but these observed and measured patterns of adjustment have corroborated expected resilience patterns based on case studies

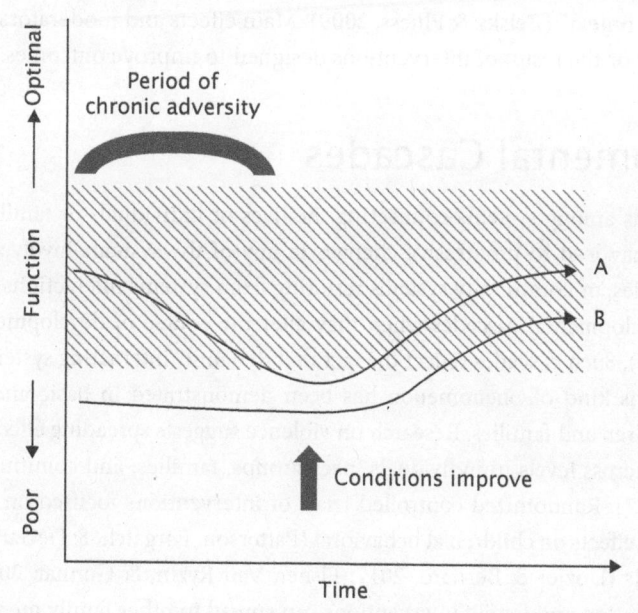

FIGURE 6.2 Resilience pathways following chronic severe adversity. Pattern A = decline with recovery after conditions improve; B = normalization when conditions improve. *Source*: © Ann S. Masten. Reprinted with permission.

or anecdotal observations to a surprising degree. Moreover, similar pathway models of resilience have been proposed and observed in the literature on adults (see Bonanno, 2004; Bonanno, Romero, & Klein, 2015).

It is interesting to note that pathway models also have been proposed in the ecology literature, and these models often take a similar form. The nomenclature varies, but patterns that resemble stress resistance, bouncing back (breakdown with recovery), or breakdown without recovery have been described in the literature on seeds, microorganisms, and soil, to mention a few (e.g., Tugel et al., 2005).

Pathway models are inherently person-focused because they usually chart how the person (or other system) is doing over time. Another kind of model central to resilience science is variable-focused, depicting major expected statistical effects, including main effects, mediating effects, and moderating effects that represent the direct, indirect, and interactional effects of multiple variables on adaptive functioning over time (Masten, 2001; Masten & Cicchetti, 2016). These models often illustrate various theories about the function of risk, vulnerability, and promotive or protective factors on the adaptive criteria of interest. Figure 6.3 illustrates major effects often tested in resilience studies, including main effects of risk factors on adjustment (negative effects), main effects of assets or other resources on adjustment (positive or promotive effects), mediated effects (usually linking intervening variables to risks and outcomes of interest), and moderating effects where one variable alters the effects of another. When a moderator produces better-than-expected outcomes in the context of risk, it is usually designated as protective or a buffer of adversity. When a moderator produces worse than typical effects, it is usually described as a vulnerability. When a moderator has varying effects depending on the nature of the environment (favorable or risky), recent models have described this as "differential susceptibility" or "sensitivity to context" (Belsky & Pluess, 2009). Main effects and moderators may be naturally occurring or the result of interventions designed to improve outcomes.

Developmental Cascades

The interactions among systems connecting the lives of individuals or families with other systems also may lead to progressive changes in any of the systems involved. Changes in children, families, or community systems resulting from systems interactions have been described as developmental cascades when they alter the course of development (Masten & Cicchetti, 2010). Such cascades reflect the fact that dynamic, interacting systems can change each other. This kind of phenomenon has been demonstrated in basic and intervention studies of children and families. Research on violence suggests spreading effects within families and also across levels in individuals, peer groups, families, and communities (Labella & Masten, 2017). Randomized controlled trials of interventions focused on parenting, for example, show effects on children at behavioral (Patterson, Forgatch, & DeGarmo, 2010) and biological levels (Dozier & Bernard, 2017; Fisher, Van Ryzin, & Gunnar, 2011). Effects of successful parenting and family interventions can spread to other family members in unexpected ways. Patterson et al. (2010), for example, observed that their parenting intervention

(a)

- Resource → Outcome
- Risk → Outcome
- Intervention → Outcome

(b)

- Risk → Outcome
- Risk → Risk-activated moderator → Outcome
- Independent moderator → Outcome

(c)

- Adverse Environment → Outcome
- Differential sensitivity moderator → Outcome
- Favorable Environment → Outcome

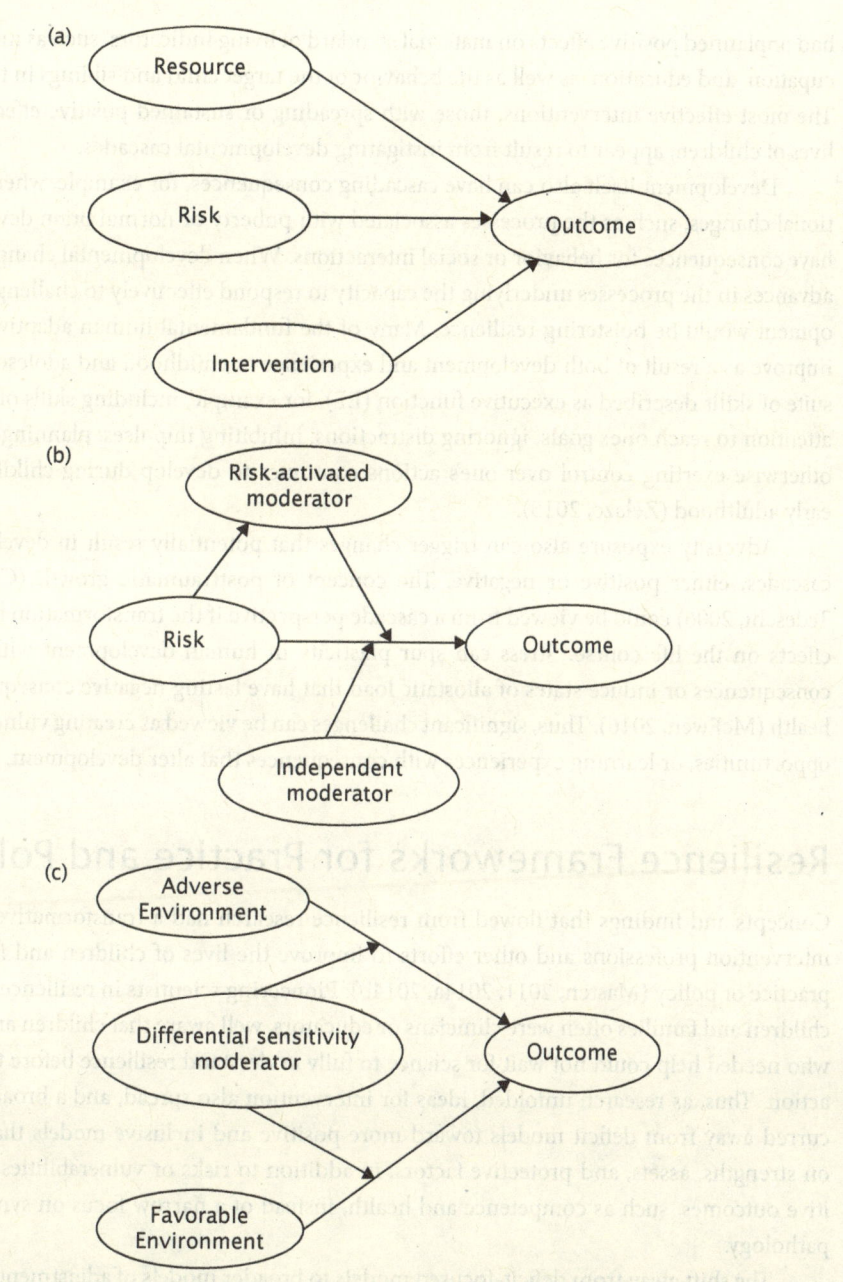

FIGURE 6.3 Common models relating risks, resources, interventions, and moderators in variable-focused models of resilience. A = main effects model. B = moderating effect of a protective factor, showing a risk-activated and an independent moderator. C = moderating effect dependent on the context; differential susceptibility or sensitivity to context. *Sources*: Figures 6.3a and 6.3b were adapted from figures by Ann S. Masten appearing in "Ordinary Magic: Resilience Processes in Development" (*American Psychologist*, 56, p. 229 and p. 231), published by the American Psychological Association. Figure 6.3c source: © Ann S. Masten. Reprinted with permission.

had unplanned positive effects on maternal standard of living indicators, such as income, occupation, and education, as well as the behavior of the target child and siblings in the family. The most effective interventions, those with spreading or sustained positive effects on the lives of children, appear to result from instigating developmental cascades.

Development itself also can have cascading consequences, for example, when maturational changes, such as the processes associated with puberty or normal brain development have consequences for behavior or social interactions. When developmental change leads to advances in the processes underlying the capacity to respond effectively to challenges, development would be bolstering resilience. Many of the fundamental human adaptive systems improve as a result of both development and experience in childhood and adolescence. The suite of skills described as executive function (EF), for example, including skills of directing attention to reach one's goals, ignoring distractions, inhibiting impulses, planning ahead, or otherwise exerting control over one's actions continues to develop during childhood into early adulthood (Zelazo, 2015).

Adversity exposure also can trigger changes that potentially result in developmental cascades, either positive or negative. The concept of posttraumatic growth (Calhoun & Tedeschi, 2006) could be viewed from a cascade perspective if the transformation has lasting effects on the life course. Stress can spur plasticity in human development with positive consequences or induce states of allostatic load that have lasting negative consequences for health (McEwen, 2016). Thus, significant challenges can be viewed as creating vulnerabilities, opportunities, or learning experiences with consequences that alter development.

Resilience Frameworks for Practice and Policy

Concepts and findings that flowed from resilience research had a transformative effect on intervention professions and other efforts to improve the lives of children and families in practice or policy (Masten, 2011, 2014a, 2014b). Pioneering scientists in resilience studies of children and families often were clinicians or educators, well aware that children and parents who needed help could not wait for science to fully understand resilience before taking any action. Thus, as research unfolded, ideas for intervention also spread, and a broad shift occurred away from deficit models toward more positive and inclusive models that focused on strengths, assets, and protective factors, in addition to risks or vulnerabilities, and positive outcomes, such as competence and health, instead of a narrow focus on symptoms or pathology.

The shift away from deficit-focused models to broader models of adjustment reflecting resilience perspectives occurred in multiple domains of practice, including psychology, psychiatry, pediatrics, nursing, school counseling, family therapy, social work, and interdisciplinary prevention (Masten, 2011, 2014b; Masten & Cicchetti, 2016). This profound shift also is evident in global humanitarian efforts to promote positive development and flourishing among children and their families contending with or fleeing conditions of extreme poverty, violence, or marginalization (Ager, 2013; Leckman, Panter-Brick, & Salah, 2014; Lundberg & Wuermli, 2012; Masten, 2014a).

Analyses and testimony by influential economists of the high returns yielded by investing in disadvantaged children, particularly early in their development, offered persuasive and complimentary evidence to policymakers on the cost-effectiveness of building a foundation of competence and health in their future citizens (Heckman, 2006, 2007; Huebner et al., 2016; Rolnick & Grunewald, 2003). Nobel laureate James Heckman has been particularly influential in papers and presentations supporting the Heckman curve (Heckman, 2006, 2019), a figure illustrating higher return on investments earlier rather than later in development. Heckman's views align with developmental theory and research indicating that "competence begets competence" (Masten, 2014b, p. 19).

A Resilience Framework for Action

In a series of publications, I have delineated a resilience framework for practice and policy based on resilience science (Masten, 2011, 2014b; Masten & Powell, 2003). This framework includes the components described in Table 6.1. These components represent my conclusions about the translational implications of resilience research after many years of interactions with practitioners and policymakers. Highlights from three decades of collaborative research on resilience among children and families experiencing homelessness illustrate the application of this model in practice and policy.

It is important to set positive goals for multiple reasons, not the least of which is the appeal to stakeholders, including children and parents themselves (Masten, 2006). The idea of preventing bad outcomes does not engender the same enthusiasm from stakeholders as promoting success. Positive objectives also ensure that positive criteria for evaluating success of a program or policy are included in models and measures. For example, in our collaborative research on risk and resilience among children and families experiencing homelessness, interest and participation rates generally have been high (Masten, Fiat, Labella, & Strack, 2015). Even during a period of uncertainty and high stress, we find parents to be highly interested in healthy brain development, school readiness, and academic achievement of their children and intrigued with research on the development of EF skills and other tools for learning that parents can support.

In a resilience framework for action, models encompass positive influences and outcomes along with risks and problems. Theories of change and logic models that guide

TABLE 6.1 A Resilience Framework for Action

Component	Approach
Mission	Set positive goals
Models	Include positive factors and processes in models of change
Measures	Measure positive factors, processes, and outcomes
Methods	Prevent or mitigate risk, boost resources or access to assets, and mobilize powerful human adaptive systems
Multiple systems	Leverage system interplay to optimize change conditions and generate cascading effects

interventions or policies include promotive or protective factors and processes and positive short- and long-term outcomes. Negative influences are not ignored, but models are broadened to encompass positive elements and change processes. In other words, resilience models for intervention transformed older diathesis-stressor models that originated in medical models of illness, broadening the focus to include assets, strengths, and adaptive processes neglected in deficit-oriented models of adjustment to adversity (Luthar & Cicchetti, 2000; Masten, 2001; Masten & Coatsworth, 1998; Wyman, Sandler, Wolchik, & Nelson, 2000). Many contemporary preventive interventions are designed now to support or protect key protective factors in the lives of children, such as high-quality parenting or caregiving. Accordingly, the logic models and theories of change for these interventions often focus on positive processes.

Our basic studies of children experiencing homelessness repeatedly have implicated EF skills and parenting quality as key promotive or protective factors associated with resilience among these children, particularly with their school success (e.g., Masten et al., 2015; Herbers, Cutuli, Supkoff, Narayan, & Masten, 2014). As a result, we have advocated for policies and practices in shelters and schools to support EF development and parenting. Furthermore, when we developed an intervention to help young children staying in shelters with their families, we targeted EF skills with an intervention that had multiple components, including parent education, family fun nights for learning and practicing EF activities, teacher training and curriculum development to enhance EF-supportive preschool activities, and individual child coaching. This program—called Ready? Set. Go!—showed promise and appeal (Casey et al., 2014; Distefano et al., 2020).

This resilience framework for action also calls for measuring positive inputs, mediators, and outcomes, along with any risk factors or negative processes and outcomes. It is particularly important for interventions targeting adaptive processes to measure those processes directly or the manifested resilience that reflects improvements in resilience. Many interventions for children have targeted parenting quality to boost resilience and improve child outcomes (Masten & Palmer, 2019). Randomized controlled trials provide strong evidence that this strategy has been successful (Sandler, Schoenfelder, Wolchik, & MacKinnon, 2011). To demonstrate change, however, it is essential to have valid measures of parenting, child adjustment, and other targeted variables.

Early resilience researchers were confronted with a paucity of positive measures of inputs and outputs, which fostered a surge of studies on measures and dimensions of child and family competence and well-being, as well as potential promotive or protective factors (Masten, 2014b; Masten & Tellegen, 2012). Resilience investigators had to validate measures developed in narrow segments of the global population for use with high-risk populations from diverse socioeconomic or cultural backgrounds. For example, in our work with highly disadvantaged, mobile families and children, it was important to examine the psychometric properties of measures of EF and parenting for this context. In regard to parenting, our studies have validated methods such as the Family Interaction Tasks developed by the team that created the Oregon model of Parent Management Training (DeGarmo, Patterson, & Forgatch, 2004) as well as the Five Minute Speech Sample (Magaña-Amato, 1993). In contrast, the NIH Toolbox measures of EF (Zelazo et al., 2013) did not work well with disadvantaged children, which led us to create the Developmental Extensions (Dext) of these tasks (Flanker-Dext and Dimensional Change Card Sort–Dext) to improve the usability of these tasks with younger and more disadvantaged children (Kalstabakken et al., 2019; Masten et al., 2011).

Three basic methods or strategies of intervention are suggested by a resilience framework, focused on risk, resources, or resilience systems. The first is preventing or mitigating risk. Actions to reduce exposure to adversity serve to lower the burden for resilience. Many interventions take the form of harm reduction, including efforts to prevent premature birth or homelessness, a crisis nursery to provide respite to desperate parents, digging up landmines, or treating postpartum depression in new mothers.

The second basic strategy is to boost resources or access to resources that support positive adjustment or development of children regardless of risk level. Providing more assets also can take many forms, ranging from cash transfers or food to libraries and childcare. Shelters for families experiencing homelessness often provide food, clothing, childcare, transportation, healthcare, and other resources that these families typically need. Governments have the resources to provide scholarship for children to attend quality preschools and rental subsidies or housing vouchers intended to stabilize the lives of families at risk of homelessness.

A new dimension of our research on homelessness is the Homework Starts With Home Research Partnership, which is a collaboration with state agencies and community partners to evaluate efforts by the Minnesota state government to support housing stability among families with school-aged children. The program funds community programs to provide rental assistance and related supports to families as a strategy for improving education outcomes in their children. The ultimate goal of this program is improving school success in children, mediated by housing, family, and school stability.

The third basic strategy for intervention in this framework is to mobilize or restore powerful adaptive systems that protect or drive positive adaptation in the context of adversity. For children, examples include interventions that support or foster good caregiving and relationships with competent and caring adults (including teachers or mentors) or prosocial friends (peers), strengthen self-regulation or problem-solving skills, provide opportunities or routines that build self-efficacy, and other interventions that focus on bolstering known or hypothesized adaptive systems. The previously described intervention—Ready? Set. Go!—was designed to target self-regulation capacity in mobile children as a strategy for boosting school readiness.

From a multisystem perspective, interventions that support family resilience in diverse ways, through programs, therapy, or policies, would be expected to boost child resilience because their success would protect the capacity for adapting to adversity that is embedded in a child's interactions with the family. Similarly, interventions that build resilience in other systems important to children's lives, such as schools, would be expected to boost resilience of children interacting with those systems.

This resilience framework recognizes that multiple systems are involved in the capacity of any individual to adapt to challenges. The complexity of human adjustment and development provides for multiple levels of analysis and multiple leverage points for change. Knowledge about targeting and timing is in its beginning stages, and it is challenging to identify the best targets and timing for intervening to promote positive change. Nonetheless, there is considerable interest in aligning interventions across sectors and levels to create synergy for change (Masten, 2011). Child welfare outreach and humanitarian interventions often plan for "two generation" programs or packages of intervention that coordinate health and education efforts (Christie et al., 2014; Huebner et al., 2016). Disaster relief and humanitarian interventions for war refugees typically combine multisystem efforts to provide a surge in resilience capacity at multiple levels (Masten et al., 2015), although this approach is not always described from a resilience perspective.

New Horizons in Developmental Resilience Science

Developmental resilience science continues to expand on multiple fronts, reflecting in many respects the growing edges of developmental research and technology. Notable areas of contemporary research include studies of the neurobiology of resilience, including epigenetic processes, developmental timing studies of adversity and resilience and windows of opportunity for intervening to promote resilience, cultural practices and processes that foster resilience, measures of adaptive systems at different levels of analysis (e.g., stress regulation, emotion regulation, social regulation, and community resilience), and methods to capture dynamic change. Advances in technology are making it possible and practical to study adaption in real time through wearable devices, apps for ecological momentary assessment and similar experience sampling methods, and biological parameters of stress response in the field. Progress in field-based measurement is altering the study of resilience in the context of refugee camps and disaster recovery conditions. There also is a promising alignment of researchers with humanitarian agencies and other service providers at the local, state, and international levels (Masten & Barnes, 2018).

The fourth wave of resilience science (which this volume represents) is unfolding as investigators attempt to study the interplay of multiple systems as they shape development and response to the challenges and disturbances engendered by adversity. Formerly distinct research areas are merging in the process of uncovering how systems interact in normative development and response to threats and how policymakers need to align supports and interventions horizontally across sectors and vertically across major system levels (e.g., individuals, families, communities, and governments) to nurture the next generation of citizens and weather current and future storms faced by children and families. Meanwhile, climate change is beginning to alter the ecologies that today's children will inhabit across their lifespans and the concomitant threats posed by a global population adapting to these changes (Sanson, Wachs, Koller, & Salmela-Aro, 2018).

Global threats from political conflict, natural disasters, epidemics, and the challenges of impending climate change appear to be motivating intense interest in resilience across many sectors and sciences concerned with human welfare (Masten, 2019). The scope of these challenges also underscores the importance of integrating knowledge and practice across traditional disciplinary boundaries of training and practice. Multisystem challenges call for integrated knowledge and coordinated multisystem responses. Meeting this challenge also calls for new models of training in collaboration across sectors and disciplines (Masten, 2014a; Masten & Barnes, 2018; Masten & Motti-Stefanidi, 2020). The study of multisystem resilience is still in its infancy, but awareness of the urgency for progress is expanding rapidly.

Conclusion

Research on resilience in children and youth played a central role in the history of resilience science. Now entering its sixth decade, the study of resilience in human development has advanced and aligned with other disciplines to define and study resilience in terms of dynamic and complex adaptive systems. The fourth wave of resilience science in human development is focused on integrating knowledge and disciplines across sectors and disciplines at multiple levels of analysis to understand human capacity for adapting to challenges and to inform efforts to foster present and future resilience through practice and policy. Progress is likely to require new models of training for multisector and multidisciplinary teams to advance the science and application of multisystem approaches to resilience.

Key Messages

1. Resilience in human development depends on many adaptive systems and resources embedded in the person, their relationships, and their connections to many other systems in the environment.
2. Resilience in complex adaptive systems is dynamic because the individuals, contexts, and processes involved are always changing.
3. Resilience develops over time and childhood is an important period for nurturing resilience for the future, both for individuals and societies.
4. There are windows of vulnerability and opportunity during the life course, such as early childhood, early adolescence, and the transition to adulthood, when a confluence of changes in children and their contexts creates high plasticity and potential for transformation.
5. Progress in the science and applications of resilience in human development requires the integration of knowledge from multiple disciplines and sectors across multiple levels of analysis, along with training in multisystem collaboration.

Acknowledgments

The author is grateful to all the mentors, colleagues, students, research participants, and funders who have contributed to the ideas and findings discussed in this chapter. Preparation of this chapter was supported by the Irving B. Harris and Regents Professorships in Child Development.

References

Ager, A. (2013). Annual Research Review: Resilience and child well-being–public policy implications. *Journal of Child Psychology and Psychiatry, 54*(4), 488–500. doi:10.1111/jcpp.12030

Belsky, J., & Pluess, M. (2009). Beyond diathesis stress: Differential susceptibility to environmental influences. *Psychological Bulletin, 135*(6), 885–908. doi:10.1037/a00117376

Berkes, F., & Ross, H. (2013). Community resilience: toward an integrated approach. *Society & Natural Resources, 26*(1), 5–20. doi:10.1080/08941920.2012.736605

Betancourt, T. S., McBain, R., Newnham, E. A., & Brennan, R. T. (2013). Trajectories of internalizing problems in war affected Sierra Leonean youth: Examining conflict and post conflict factors. *Child Development, 84*, 455–470. doi:10.1111/j.14678624.2012.01861.x

Bonanno, G. A. (2004). Loss, trauma, and human resilience: Have we underestimated the human capacity to thrive after extremely aversive events? *American Psychologist, 59*, 20–28. doi:10.1037/0003-066X.59.1.20

Bonanno, G. A., Romero, S. A., & Klein, S. I. (2015). The temporal elements of psychological resilience: An integrative framework for the study of individuals, families, and communities. *Psychological Inquiry, 26*(2), 139–169. doi:10.1080/1047840X.2015.992677

Bronfenbrenner, U. (1979). *The ecology of human development*. Cambridge, MA: Harvard University Press.

Bronfenbrenner, U., & Morris, P. A. (1998). The ecology of developmental processes. In W. Damon, & R. M. Lerner (Eds.), *Handbook of child psychology: Theoretical models of human development* (pp. 993–1028). Hoboken, NJ: John Wiley.

Calhoun, L. G., & Tedeschi, R. G. (2006). The foundations of posttraumatic growth: An expanded framework. In L. G. Calhoun, & R. G. Tedeschi (Eds.), *Handbook of posttraumatic growth: Research and practice* (pp. 1–23). Mahwah, NJ: Lawrence Erlbaum.

Casey, E. C., Finsaas, M., Carlson, S. M., Zelazo, P. D., Murphy, B., Durkin, F., . . . Masten, A. S. (2014). Promoting resilience through executive function training for homeless and highly mobile preschoolers. In S. Prince-Embury, & D. H. Saklofske (Eds.), *The Springer series on human exceptionality: Resilience interventions for youth in diverse populations* (pp. 133–158). New York, NY: Springer Science + Business Media.

Cho, I., & Blaser, M. J. (2012). The human microbiome: At the interface of health and disease. *Nature Reviews Genetics, 13*, 260–270. doi:10.1038/nrg3182

Christie, D. J., Behrman, J. R., Cochrane, J. R., Dawes, A., Goth, K., Hayden, J., . . . Tomlinson, M. (2014). Healthy human development as a path to peace. In J. F. Leckman, C. Panter-Brick, & R. Salah (Eds.), *Pathways to peace: The transformative power of families and child development* (pp. 273–302). Cambridge, MA: MIT Press.

Cicchetti, D., & Rogosch, F. A. (1996). Equifinality and multifinality in developmental psychopathology. *Development and Psychopathology, 8*(4), 597–600. doi:10.1017/S0954579400007318

Crawford, E., Wright, M. O., & Masten, A. S. (2006). Resilience and spirituality in youth. In E. C. Roehlkepartain, P. E. King, L. Wagner, & P. L. Bensen (Eds.), *The handbook of spiritual development in childhood and adolescence* (pp. 355–370). Thousand Oaks, CA: SAGE. doi:10.4135/9781412976657.n25

DeGarmo, D. S., Patterson, G. R., & Forgatch, M. S. (2004). How do outcomes in a specified parenting training intervention maintain or wane over time? *Prevention Science, 5*(2), 73–89.

Distefano, R., Schubert, E. C., Finsaas, M. C., Desjardins, C. D., Helseth, C. K., Lister, M., . . . Masten, A. S. (2020). Ready? Set. Go! A school readiness program designed to boost executive function skills in preschoolers experiencing homelessness and high mobility. *European Journal of Developmental Psychology*. https://doi.org/10.1080/17405629.2020.1813103

Dozier, M., & Bernard, K. (2017). Attachment and biobehavioral catch-up: Addressing the needs of infants and toddlers exposed to inadequate or problematic caregiving. *Current Opinion in Psychology, 15*, 111–117. doi:10.1016/j.copsyc.2017.03.003

Evans, G. W., Li, D., & Whipple, S. S. (2013). Cumulative risk and child development. *Psychological Bulletin, 139*(6), 1342–1396. doi:10.1037/a0031808

Felitti, V. J., Anda, R. F., Nordenberg, D., Williamson, D. F., Spitz, A. M., Edwards, V., . . . Marks, S. (1998). Relationship of childhood abuse and household dysfunction to many of the leading causes of death in adults: The Adverse Childhood Experiences (ACE) study. *American Journal of Preventive Medicine, 14*(4), 245–258. doi:10.1016/S0749-3797(98)00017-8

Fisher, P. A., Van Ryzin, M. J., & Gunnar, M. R. (2011). Mitigating HPA axis dysregulation associated with placement changes in foster care. *Psychoneuroendocrinology, 36*(4), 531–539. doi:10.1016/j.psyneuen.2010.08.007

Garmezy, N. (1983). Stressors of childhood. In N. Garmezy, & M. Rutter (Eds.), *Stress, coping, and development in children* (pp. 43–84). New York, NY: McGraw-Hill.

Garmezy, N., & Rutter, M. (Eds.). (1983). *Stress, coping, and development in children*. New York, NY: McGraw-Hill.

Goldstein, S., & Brooks, R. B. (2013). Why study resilience? In S. Goldstein, & R. B. Brooks (Eds.), *Handbook of resilience in children* (pp. 3–14). Boston, MA: Springer.

Gottesman, I. I. (1974). Developmental genetics and ontogenetic psychology: Overdue détente and propositions from a matchmaker. In A. D. Pick (Ed.), *Minnesota symposium on child psychology* (Vol. 8, pp. 55–80). Minneapolis: University of Minnesota Press.

Gottesman, I. I., & Hanson, D. R. (2005). Human development: Biological and genetic processes. *Annual Review of Psychology, 56*, 263–286. doi:10.1146/annurev.psych.56.091103.070208

Gottesman, I. I., & Shields, A. (1972). *Schizophrenia and genetics: A twin study vantage point*. New York, NY: Academic Press.

Gottlieb, G. (2007). Probabilistic epigenesis. *Developmental Science, 10*(1), 1–11. doi:10.1111/j.1467-7687.2007.00556.x

Harrist, A. W., Henry, C. S., Liu, C., & Morris, A. S. (2019). Family resilience: The power of rituals and routines in family adaptive systems. In B. H. Fiese, M. Celano, K. Deater-Deckard, E. N. Jouriles, & M. A. Whisman (Eds.), *APA handbook of contemporary family psychology: Foundations, methods, and contemporary issues across the lifespan* (pp. 223–239). Washington, DC: American Psychological Association.

Heckman, J. J. (2006). Skill formation and the economics of investing in disadvantaged children. *Science, 312*(5782), 1900–1902. doi:0.1126/science.1128898

Heckman, J. (2019). *The Heckman curve*. Retrieved from https://heckmanequation.org/resource/the-heckman-curve/.

Heckman, J. (2007, June). *Investing in disadvantaged young children is good economics and good public policy* [Testimony before the Joint Economic Committee]. United States Senate Joint Economic Committee Archive. Retrieved from https://www.jec.senate.gov/archive/Hearings/06.27.07%20Early%20Learning/Testimony%20-%20James%20Heckman.pdf.

Henry, C. S., Morris, A. S., & Harrist, A. W. (2015). Family resilience: Moving into the third wave. *Family Relations, 64*(1), 22–43. doi:10.1111/fare.12106

Herbers, J. E., Cutuli, J. J., Supkoff, L. M., Narayan, A. J., & Masten, A. S. (2014). Parenting and coregulation: Adaptive systems for competence in children experiencing homelessness. *American Journal of Orthopsychiatry, 84*(4), 420–430. doi:10.1037/h0099843

Huebner, G., Boothby, N., Aber, J. L., Darmastadt, G. L., Diaz, A., Masten, A. S., . . . Arnold, L. (2016, June). *Beyond survival: The case for investing in young children globally* (Discussion paper). National Academy of Medicine. doi:10.31478/201606b

Kalstabakken, A., Desjardins, C. D., Anderson, J. E., Berghuis, K. J., Hillyer, C. K., Seiwart, M. . . . Masten A. S. (2019). *Executive function measures in early childhood screening: Concurrent and predictive validity*. Unpublished manuscript.

Kirmayer, L. J., Dandeneau, S., Marshall, E., Phillips, M. K., & Williamson, K. J. (2011). Rethinking resilience from Indigenous perspectives. *Canadian Journal of Psychiatry, 56*(2), 84–91. doi:10.1177/070674371105600203

Labella, M. H., & Masten, A. S. (2017). Family influences on the development of aggression and violence. *Current Opinion in Psychology, 19*, 11–16. doi:10.1016/j.copsyc.2017.03.028

Leckman, J. F., Panter-Brick, C., & Salah, R. (Eds.). (2014). *Pathways to peace: The transformative power of children and families* (Vol. 15). Retrieved from https://mitpress.mit.edu/books/pathways-peace

Lerner, R. M. (2006). Developmental science, developmental systems, and contemporary theories of human development. In R. M. Lerner & W. Damon (Eds.), *Handbook of child psychology: Theoretical models of human development* (pp. 1–17). Hoboken, NJ: John Wiley.

Lickliter, R. (2013). Biological development: Theoretical approaches, techniques, and key findings. In P. D. Zelazo (Ed.), *The Oxford handbook of developmental psychology, Vol. 1: Body and mind* (pp. 65–90). New York, NY: Oxford University Press.

Lundberg, M., & Wuermli, A. (Eds.). (2012). *Children and youth in crisis: Protecting and promoting human development in times of economic shocks*. Washington, DC: The World Bank.

Luthar, S. S. (2006). Resilience in development: A synthesis of research across five decades. In D. Cicchetti & D. J. Cohen (Eds.), *Developmental psychopathology, Vol. 3: Risk, disorder, and adaptation* (2nd ed., pp. 739–795). Hoboken, NJ: John Wiley.

Luthar, S. S., & Cicchetti, D. (2000). The construct of resilience: Implications for interventions and social policies. *Development and Psychopathology, 12*(4), 857–885. doi:10.1017/S0954579400004156

Magaña-Amato, A. (1993). *Manual for coding expressed emotion from the five-minute speech sample: UCLA family project*. Los Angeles: University of California.

Maholmes, V. (2014). *Fostering resilience and well-being in children and families in poverty: Why hope still matters*. New York, NY: Oxford University Press.

Masten, A. S. (2001). Ordinary magic: Resilience processes in development. *American Psychologist, 56*(3), 227–238. doi:10.1037/0003-066X.56.3.227

Masten, A. S. (2006). Promoting resilience in development: A general framework for systems of care. In R. J. Flynn, P. Dudding, & J. G. Barber (Eds.), *Promoting resilience in child welfare* (pp. 3–17). Ottawa, Canada: University of Ottawa Press.

Masten, A. S. (2007). Resilience in developing systems: Progress and promise as the fourth wave rises. *Development and Psychopathology, 19*(3), 921–930. doi:10.1017/S0954579407000442

Masten, A. S. (2011). Resilience in children threatened by extreme adversity: Frameworks for research, practice, and translational synergy. *Development and Psychopathology, 23*(2), 141–154. doi:10.1017/S0954579411000198

Masten, A. S. (2014a). Global perspectives on resilience in children and youth. *Child Development, 85*(1), 6–20. doi:10.1111/cdev.12205.

Masten, A. S. (2014b). *Ordinary magic: Resilience in development*. New York, NY: Guilford Press.

Masten, A. S. (2018a). Resilience theory and research on children and families: Past, present, and promise. *Journal of Family Theory and Review, 10*(1), 12–31. doi:10.1111/jftr.12255

Masten, A. S. (2018b). Schools nurture resilience of children and societies. *Green Schools Catalyst Quarterly, 3*(3), 14–19.

Masten, A. S. (2019). Resilience from a developmental systems perspective. *World Psychiatry, 18*(1), 101–102. doi:10.1002/wps.20591

Masten, A. S., & Barnes, A. J. (2018). Resilience in children: Developmental perspectives. *Children, 5*(7), 98. doi:10.3390/children5070098

Masten, A. S., Best, K. M., & Garmezy, N. (1990). Resilience and development: Contributions from the study of children who overcome adversity. *Development and Psychopathology, 2*(4), 425–444. doi:10.1017/S0954579400005812

Masten, A. S., Carlson, S. M., Zelazo, P. D., Wenzel, A. J., Anderson, J. E., Buckner, M., & McGovern, P. (2011, August). *Assessment of executive function for the national children's study*. Poster presented at NCS Research Day, Washington, DC.

Masten, A. S., & Cicchetti, D. (2010). Editorial: Developmental cascades [Special issue on Developmental Cascades, Part 1]. *Development and Psychopathology, 22*(3), 491–495. doi:10.1017/S0954579410000222.

Masten, A. S., & Cicchetti, D. (2016). Resilience in development: Progress and transformation. In D. Cicchetti (Ed.), *Developmental psychopathology, Vol. 4: Risk, resilience, and intervention* (3rd ed., pp. 271–333). New York, NY: John Wiley. doi:10.1002/9781119125556.devpsy406

Masten, A. S., & Coatsworth, J. D. (1998). The development of competence in favorable and unfavorable environments: Lessons from research on successful children. *American Psychologist, 53*(2), 205–220. doi:10.1037/0003-066X.53.2.205

Masten, A. S., Fiat, A. E., Labella, M. H., & Strack, R. A. (2015). Educating homeless and highly mobile students: Implications of research on risk and resilience. *School Psychology Review, 44*(3), 315–330. doi:10.17105/spr-15-0068.1

Masten, A. S., Hubbard, J. J., Gest, S. D., Tellegen, A., Garmezy, N., & Ramirez, M. (1999). Competence in the context of adversity: Pathways to resilience and maladaptation from childhood to late adolescence. *Development and Psychopathology, 11*(1), 143–169. doi:10.1017/S0954579499001996

Masten, A. S., & Motti-Stefanidi, F. (2020). Multisystem resilience for children and youth in disaster: Reflections in the context of COVID-19. *Adversity and Resilience Science, 1*(2), 95–106. doi:10.1007/s42844-020-00010-w

Masten, A. S., & Narayan, A. J. (2012). Child development in the context of disaster, war and terrorism: Pathways of risk and resilience. *Annual Review of Psychology, 63*, 227–257. doi:10.1146/annurevpsych-120710-100356

Masten, A. S., Narayan, A. J., Silverman, W. K., & Osofsky, J. D. (2015). Children in war and disaster. In R. M. Lerner, M. H. Bornstein, & T. Leventhal (Eds.), *Handbook of child psychology and developmental science, Vol. 4: Ecological settings and processes in developmental systems* (7th ed., pp. 704–745). New York, NY: John Wiley.

Masten, A. S., & Obradović, J. (2008). Disaster preparation and recovery: Lessons from research on resilience in human development. *Ecology and Society, 13*(1), 9. doi:10.5751/ES02282-130109

Masten, A. S., & Palmer, A. (2019). Parenting to promote resilience in children. In M. H. Bornstein (Ed.), *Handbook of parenting, Vol. 5: The practice of parenting* (3rd ed., pp. 156–188). New York, NY: Routledge.

Masten, A. S., & Powell, J. L. (2003). A resilience framework for research, policy, and practice. In S. S. Luthar (Ed.), *Resilience and vulnerability: Adaptation in the context of childhood adversities* (pp. 1–25). New York, NY: Cambridge University Press.

Masten, A. S., & Reed, M. G. J. (2002). Resilience in development. In C. R. Snyder & S. J. Lopez (Eds.), *Handbook of positive psychology* (pp. 74–88). New York, NY: Oxford University Press.

Masten, A. S., & Tellegen, A. (2012). Resilience in developmental psychopathology: Contributions of the project competence longitudinal study. *Development and Psychopathology, 24*(2), 345–361. doi:10.1017/S095457941200003X

McEwen, B. (2016). In pursuit of resilience: Stress, epigenetics, and brain plasticity. *Annuals of the New York Academy of Science, 1373*(1), 56–64. doi:10.1111/nyas.13020

Meijer, L., Finkenauer, C., Tierolf, B., Lünnemann, M., & Steketee, M. (2019). Trajectories of traumatic stress reactions in children exposed to intimate partner violence. *Child Abuse & Neglect, 93*, 170–181. doi:10.1016/j.chiabu.2019.04.017

Osher, D., Cantor, P., Berg, J., Steyer, L., & Rose, T. (2018). Drivers of human development: How relationships and context shape learning and development. *Applied Developmental Science*. doi:10.1080/10888691.2017.1398650

Osofsky, J. D., Osofsky, H. J., Weems, C. F., King, L. S., Hansel, T. C. (2015). Trajectories of post-traumatic stress disorder symptoms among youth exposed to both natural and technological disasters. *Journal of Child Psychology and Psychiatry, 56*(12), 1347–1355. doi:10.1111/jcpp.12420

Overton, W. F. (2013). A new paradigm for developmental science: Relationism and relational-developmental systems. *Applied Developmental Science, 17*(2), 94–107. doi:10.1080/10888691.2013.778717

Patterson, G. R., Forgatch, M. S., & Degarmo, D. S. (2010). Cascading effects following intervention. *Development and Psychopathology, 22*(4), 949–970. doi:10.1017/S0954579410000568

Reich, J. W., Zautra, A. J., & Hall, J. S. (2010). *Handbook of adult resilience*. New York, NY: Guilford Press.

Rolnick, A., & Grunewald, R. (2003, March). Early childhood development: Economic development with a high public return. *Fedgazette*, 6–12. Retrieved from https://www.minneapolisfed.org/~/media/files/publications/studies/earlychild/abc-part2.pdf

Sandler, I. N., Schoenfelder, E. N., Wolchik, S. A., and MacKinnon, D. P. (2011). Long-term impact of prevention programs to promote effective parenting: Lasting effects but uncertain processes. *Annual Review of Psychology, 62*, 299–329. doi:10.1146/annurev.psych.121208.131619

Sanson, A. V., Wachs, T. D., Koller, S. H., & Salmela-Aro, K. (2018). Young people and climate change: The role of developmental science. In S. Verma & A. C. Petersen (Eds.), *Developmental science and sustainable development goals for children and youth* (pp. 115–137). Cham, Switzerland: Springer.

Stott, P. (2016). How climate change affects extreme weather events. *Science, 352*(6293), 1517–1518. doi:10.1126/science.aaf7271

Southwick, S. M., & Charney, D. S. (2018). *Resilience: The science of mastering life's greatest challenges.* New York, NY: Cambridge University Press.

Tugel, A. J., Herrick, J. E., Brown, J. R., Mausbach, M. J., Puckett, W., & Hipple, K. (2005). Soil change, soil survey, and natural resources decision making: A blueprint for action. *Soil Science Society of America Journal, 69*(3), 738–747. doi:10.2136/sssaj2004.0163

Ungar, M. (2008). Resilience across cultures. *The British Journal of Social Work, 38*(2), 218–235. doi:10.1093/bjsw/bcl343

Ungar, M. (2011). Community resilience for youth and families: Facilitative physical and social capital in contexts of adversity. *Children and Youth Services Review, 33*(9), 1742–1748. doi:10.1016/j.childyouth.2011.04.027

Waddington, C. H. (1957/2014). *The strategy of the genes: A discussion of some aspects of theoretical biology.* New York, NY: Routledge.

Walsh, F. (2016). *Strengthening family resilience* (3rd ed.). New York, NY: Guilford Press.

Werner, E. E., & Smith, R. S. (2001). *Journeys from childhood to midlife: Risk, resilience, and recovery.* New York, NY: Cornell University Press.

Wyman, P. A., Sandler, I., Wolchik, S., & Nelson, K. (2000). Resilience as cumulative competence promotion and stress protection: Theory and intervention. In D. Cicchetti, J. Rappaport, I. Sandler, & R. P. Weissberg (Eds.), *The promotion of wellness in children and adolescents* (pp. 133–184). Washington, DC: Child Welfare League of America.

Zelazo, P. D. (2013). Developmental psychology: A new synthesis. In P. D. Zelazo (Ed.), *The Oxford handbook of developmental psychology. Vol. 1: Body and mind* (pp. 3–12). New York, NY: Oxford University Press.

Zelazo, P. D. (2015). Executive function: Reflection, iterative reprocessing, complexity, and the developing brain. *Developmental Review, 38,* 55–68. doi:10.1016/j.dr.2015.07.001

Zelazo, P. D., Anderson, J. E., Richler, J., Wallner-Allen, K., Beaumont, J. L., & Weintraum, S. (2013). NIH toolbox cognition battery (CB): Measuring executive function and attention. *Monographs of the Society for Research in Child Development, 78*(4), 16–33. doi:10.1111/mono.12032

Stressor Appraisal as an Explanation for the Influence of Extra-Individual Factors on Psychological Resilience

Raffael Kalisch and Miriam Kampa

Introduction

Individual or, more specifically, psychological resilience has recently been defined as the maintenance and/or quick recovery of mental health during and after times of adversity, such as trauma, difficult life circumstances, challenging life transitions, or physical illness (Kalisch et al., 2017). To understand how this definition overlaps with definitions from other disciplines, a brief history of the concept of resilience is necessary.

At its origins in the 1970s, one strong assumption in individual resilience research was that people stay mentally healthy despite stressor exposure because they have a certain type of personality that protects them against the deleterious influences of negative life events or circumstances (Block & Block, 1980; Kobasa, 1979). For instance, a popular term in the early days of resilience research was *hardy personality*, a character structure including dispositions for high commitment, controllability beliefs, and acceptance of, and appetite for, change and challenge (Kobasa, 1979). It became clear relatively quickly, though, that no single set of traits, let alone any single, unitary individual characteristic, was sufficient to explain, or predict, mental health outcomes in stressor-exposed individuals. Instead, resilience appeared to be linked to a multitude of character-like, less stable traits, skills, behaviors, and beliefs, each of which exert only a limited influence on psychological outcomes (Masten & Garmezy, 1985; Werner & Smith, 1989). Depending on which model of resilience a researcher adhered to, these traits might include self-esteem, optimism, attachment style, communication ability, spirituality, or emotion regulation skills. The lists of potential resilience factors were soon extended to comprise extra-individual factors as well, such as social support or cultural influences (e.g., McCubbin et al., 1998). It was also noted that the characteristics of the stressor itself (e.g., acute versus chronic, interpersonal vs. nonpersonal, direct vs. indirect exposure; Bonanno, Romero, & Klein, 2015) play a role.

Acknowledging the complexity of resilience was a big step forward and also opened the door toward shifting model building from a trait to a process perspective. The mere insight that mental health maintenance may involve spirituality or social support implies that resilience cannot be a stable, fixed phenotype, simply because neither spirituality nor social support are personality traits. They may grow or decline over time, meaning resilience may grow or decline over time as well. More so, if some resilience factors can vary over a life time, they are most likely malleable, meaning one may even learn to become resilient, and it may perhaps even be possible to train resilience.

Resilience researchers have therefore emphasized for at least two decades that resilience involves a process—or processes—of change, or adaptation to adverse life circumstances (Bonanno et al., 2015; Kent, Davis, & Reich, 2014; Luthar, Cicchetti, & Becker, 2000; Rutter, 2012; Sapienza & Masten, 2011). Change obviously occurs whenever an individual acts (outwardly or mentally) in an effort to cope, and such changes at the individual level nearly always co-occur with changes at the level of the environment, to the extent that they constitute person–environment interactions. Observing such changes, however, does not contradict the trait perspective, as even a hardy person would cope with a challenge, for instance, by committing himself or herself more to the new situation or by greeting it with a positive attitude. The point is that, having overcome the challenge, he or she would be just as hardy as before. These types of changes can be considered homeostatic adaptation processes that do not modify an individual's or an environment's capacity for coping.

More relevant from a theoretical point of view are those observations that document long-lasting and more profound changes to an individual's internal make-up. Indeed, the claim of lasting individual adjustment, or allostasis, during and after stress exposure now has a strong empirical foundation (Kalisch et al., 2017). The claim may at first appear trivial, as adversity oftentimes leads to disease (which arguably is a change) but becomes very meaningful if a lasting change is observed in individuals who do not become ill despite adversity (i.e., they do not change or change only temporarily with regard to their mental health). For example, some individuals who are mentally unaffected by a disaster, a serious accident, or severe illness develop a deeper appreciation of life or personal relationships. Some even adopt a more spiritual or religious belief system, a phenomenon that has become known as posttraumatic growth (Johnson & Boals, 2015; Joseph & Linley, 2006; Tedeschi & Calhoun, 2004). Overcoming stressor exposure and remaining in good mental health can also go along with the emergence of new strengths or competencies (Luthar et al., 2000). Furthermore, individuals who were exposed to a moderate number of negative life events in their past have also been found in some studies to be more functional in daily life, to exhibit higher levels of life satisfaction, and to be less reactive to laboratory stressors than individuals with no or negligible exposure (Seery, Holman, & Silver, 2010; Seery, Leo, Lupien, Kondrak, & Almonte, 2013). These latter observations suggest that stressor exposure can immunize against the effects of future stressors, a phenomenon that has since become known as *stress immunization*, *stress inoculation*, or the *steeling effect*. Among the most unexpected finding from longitudinal analyses in stressor-exposed populations, however, is that some individuals even become less depressed, anxious, or stressed when they experience adversity; that is, they adapt to a degree that their mental health improves (Mancini, 2019).

Beyond the psychological level of analysis, it is now also clear from epigenetic and gene expression studies that change in people who show stable mental health can even involve the molecular level (Boks et al., 2015; Breen et al., 2015). For instance, one study analyzing messenger RNA levels in white blood cells drawn from American soldiers before and after exposure to war zone trauma found an increase in the expression of genes presumably involved in wound healing and hemostasis, which was also associated with these soldiers not developing posttraumatic stress disorder (PTSD) as a consequence of their deployment (Breen et al., 2015). Notably, the differential effect relative to the group that did develop PTSD could not be explained by group differences in war zone trauma severity.

None of these empirical studies establish causality between the observed change and the maintenance of mental health. However, there are now numerous studies in rodent stress models in which more or less specific manipulations of nervous system functions have been shown to contribute to the maintenance of normal, adaptive behavior after periods of severe event-like or prolonged stress exposure (Cathomas, Murrough, Nestler, Han, & Russo, 2019; Friedman et al., 2014; Krishnan et al., 2007; Maier, 2015; Russo, Murrough, Han, Charney, & Nestler, 2012). A prominent case is the adjustment in the expression of certain ion channels in midbrain dopamine neurons that only occurs in animals whose dopamine neurons initially react to a repeated social defeat situation with a pronounced increase in their excitability, only to then normalize back to excitability levels comparable to those of nonstressed control animals. This happens precisely because the initial neuronal excitability increases cause changes in ion channel expression that in turn cause reductions in neuronal excitability. After stressor exposure, these animals produce normal hedonic and social behavior. Other animals that reacted to defeat with clearly less pronounced excitability increases never enter the homeostatic excitability readjustment process and also develop anhedonia and social interaction deficits (Friedman et al., 2014). Remarkably, manipulations of ion channel expression can restore normal behavior in these animals.

One commonality between these animal studies and the molecular human studies cited before is the availability of a clear outcome. In Breen et al. (2015), all analyzed soldiers were free from PTSD before deployment, then experienced comparable war zone trauma exposure, and then either did or did not develop PTSD. This allowed for simply comparing those who maintained mental health (resilient, no PTSD) to those showing clear mental health deterioration (nonresilient, PTSD). In the animal studies, animals exposed to, for instance, a well-controlled, standardized form of social defeat could be compared in their postdefeat anhedonic and social behavior to nondefeated control animals, allowing for animals behaving like controls to be classified as resilient and those showing long-term maladaptive behavioral changes as susceptible or nonresilient. Like in the soldier study, stressor exposure was comparable (controlled) between resilient and nonresilient groups. We can, therefore, exclude differences in stressor exposure as a trivial explanation for the observed behavioral differences.

Very surprisingly, there are only a few human resilience studies using a longitudinal mental health outcome and controlling for stressor exposure that identify either resilience factors (in the sense of trait-like or nontrait-like predispositions that are measured at baseline and predict good outcomes) or processes of change (as may occur over the course of the observation period and statistically relate to good outcomes). (For an overview of existing prospective-longitudinal studies, see Kalisch et al., 2017.) The vast majority of human resilience studies uses cross-sectional designs in which one of the many existing resilience questionnaires (Windle, Bennett, & Noyes, 2011) is correlated with some other variable of interest, such as a personality trait, a skill, habit, belief, extra-individual factor, etc. Such cross-sectional resilience questionnaire studies are now also more and more frequently conducted with biological variables of interests, such as gene variants or measures of brain function or structure (Berg et al., 2017; Bradley, Davis, Wingo, Mercer, & Ressler, 2013; Kong, Ma, You, & Xiang, 2018; Kong, Wang, Hu, & Liu, 2015; Shao, Lau, Leung, & Lee, 2018; Shi et al., 2016; Waaktaar & Torgersen, 2012; Waugh, Wager, Fredrickson, Noll, & Taylor, 2008).

There is a stunning circularity in these approaches. The development of a resilience questionnaire usually involves insights from qualitative and sometimes quantitative work that leads the authors to formulate their own resilience model, based on the factors they believe constitute resilience. Accordingly, a resilience questionnaire may include items indexing emotion regulation ability, optimistic outlook, or self-efficacy beliefs, if those constructs figure in the authors' resilience model. If a study using the questionnaire shows a correlation of the questionnaire with another measure of emotion regulation, optimism, or self-efficacy, this is interpreted as support for the tested resilience model. Not much better, if a resilience questionnaire happens to show a correlation with, say, resting-state functional connectivity in a network of brain regions supporting emotion regulation, this is often interpreted as revealing the neurobiological basis of resilience.

There are two additional major problems with the cross-sectional questionnaire approach. First, none of the existing questionnaires has yet been found to be a reliable and strong predictor of good mental health despite adversity. That is, even if a study were to identify a new variable whose correlation with the questionnaire is not just the result of circular reasoning (say, a gene polymorphism), it would still be entirely unclear if this newly identified resilience factor has any role in how people overcome adversity. The second additional problem is a deeper one and ultimately the cause of the first. As pointed out by Mancini and Bonanno (2009), cross-sectional application of resilience questionnaires is based on the assumption that resilience can be measured in the absence of stressors and an individual's reaction to the stressor. If, however, staying mentally healthy despite adversity involves processes of change; if these processes presumably vary from individual to individual; if they most likely affect, or occur at, the biological, psychological, social, and cultural levels (given the complex picture of the previously described resilience factors); and, finally, if stressor exposure itself can be experienced individually very differently, then it is simply highly unlikely that it will ever be possible to predict long-term mental health outcomes following adverse events or life phases with very high accuracy. Complex dynamic systems are notoriously difficult to predict (e.g., the weather[1]). Together, this means that findings from cross-sectional correlations with resilience questionnaires cannot be interpreted as representing resilience factors. And this in turn means that individual resilience research has a serious problem.

We would like to emphasize that we are not arguing here against attempts to predict mental health outcomes, which, if successful, may have enormous benefit for disease prevention. We also believe that even prediction tools with only moderate or good prediction accuracy would be of great value, given the very poor predictions afforded by existing methods in psychiatry and clinical psychology. We are also confident that prediction accuracy will soon increase massively due to progress in the fields of digital phenotyping, machine learning, and other areas of data science as well as in the fields of biology and neuroscience. Encouraging examples can be found in the PTSD literature (Schultebraucks & Galatzer-Levy, 2019). Apart from their practical value for medicine, the more sophisticated prediction tools that are anticipated may at some point even be useful for resilience research by providing much better surrogate markers for mental health outcomes under adversity than resilience questionnaires. Nevertheless, a correlation of a variable of interest with whatever prediction instrument or surrogate marker can in principle never provide more than a starting hypothesis that that variable may be related to resilience. To show this, it is inevitable to test the influence of the variable in an observational or, if possible, a longitudinal data set following an intervention.

Such longitudinal testing must necessarily include a difficult period in the lives of the subjects and an observation of what this does to their mental health. This is because one wants to know what helps people stay healthy *despite* adversity, which logically requires the existence of adversity (Kalisch et al., 2017; Mancini & Bonanno, 2009). Further, longitudinal testing must include an as-good-as-possible characterization and, ideally, quantification of the experienced adversity or stressor exposure. This is because if one person gets a tooth pulled and then jumps 10 points on a PTSD scale, that person is surely less resilient than a person that loses his or her family in a car accident and ends up in a wheel-chair and also jumps 10 points on the same scale. Both show the same mental health change, but if one did not in some way normalize mental health changes to stressor exposure, that outcome would not be informative about resilience in any way. Another illustration of the importance of normalizing mental health changes to stressor exposure is the example of a two times as large mental health deterioration in person A than person B, while person A has experienced two times as much stressors. Here, the explanation for the individual differences in mental health change is a trivial one and consists in the individual's different levels of stressor exposure but does not reflect differences in resilience (Kalisch et al., 2017; Kalisch, Müller, & Tüscher, 2015).

As a consequence of all these different considerations, it may be prudent to abandon definitions of resilience based on any particular trait or traits (which surely do not predict resilient outcomes) or on any nontrait-like resilience factor or factors (whose predictive power we currently do not know) and also on presumed processes of change (which most likely play an important role but which we are only beginning to understand). We propose, instead, an outcome-based definition that simply looks at mental health changes over the course of a difficult time and relates them to the amount or level of difficulty experienced. Hence, resilience defined as the maintenance or quick recovery (because anyone can have a temporary emotional setback) of mental health during and after adversity or, in other words, long-term mental health stability despite adversity (Kalisch et al., 2017). (We note that this definition can interchangeably be applied to other outcomes than mental health, such as personal functioning, performance, or developmental achievements. We here restrict ourselves to mental health outcomes for the sake of simplicity.)

This definition is a purely pragmatic one that emphasizes operationalization in longitudinal measurement. (For a more detailed discussion on practical implications and the requirements the definition poses on longitudinal testing, as well as for more details about how to quantify resilience in longitudinal studies, see Kalisch et al., 2015, 2017, 2019). The deliberately technical nature of the definition also means that it is entirely atheoretical (i.e., it does not propose any specific factor or mechanism as being resilience). Basing a definition of resilience on a specific factor or mechanism would not only be premature given our current knowledge (see previous discussion), but it would also unnecessarily divide the community and lead, mutually, to exclusion of researchers with different mechanistic models. In the absence of an objectively measurable outcome, different models could never be pitched against each other to decide which one explains the outcome better. Instead, a resilience definition based on, for example, model 1, but not model 2, would necessarily always confirm model 1 and disconfirm model 2. Next to producing circularity, such a definition would also preclude new discoveries.

The future of resilience research, as we see it, consists of longitudinal studies in which mental health and stressor exposure are monitored repeatedly and at high temporal resolution, to thus quantify the influence of stressors on mental health. The same methodology is required to identify potential resilience factors, which also need to be measured repeatedly and at high sampling frequency to thus describe and quantify how they affect (dampen) negative influences of stressors on mental health in a time-variant fashion. Mathematical–statistical approaches harnessing dynamic systems theory may be particularly suited to analyze the data generated by these studies and to eventually identify key processes of adjustment to adversity (Kalisch et al., 2019). The entire focus of this approach is on detecting and understanding beneficial processes of adaption. It is entirely possible, or even likely given current knowledge, that these processes will differ from individual to individual and also depend on the type of adversity and type of mental health outcome studied. A youth with a history of childhood maltreatment (an extra-individual factor) may achieve a depression-free life through different processes than the processes that protect a soldier traumatized in war against PTSD. Nevertheless, it can be hoped that over the course of time a certain pattern, or systematology of processes, may be discovered. That is, certain generic or typical pathways of successful adaptation may emerge, at least within categories of individuals, adversity and outcomes. Along the way, the shift described in this chapter from the trait to the outcome perspective constitutes a complete abandonment of the idea that resilience is a unitary construct or common cause for mental health under strain. Resilience is better conceptualized as a range of protective processes that results in maintained mental health in response to many different external stressors that can occur at many different systemic levels (Kalisch et al., 2019).

Can a Multisystemic Approach Benefit Psychological Resilience Research? The Case for Reductionism

Even a perfectly happy and relaxed human being is a system complex enough to defy understanding. Understanding how human beings successfully respond to adversity would appear an even more daunting task. When considering the methodological demands to contemporary resilience research that we have discussed previously, one would be tempted to argue that, before even trying to integrate psychological resilience research into a broader context of other systems that affect human resilience and are affected by human resilience, it should be a priority to understand the laws that, in the first instance, govern psychological resilience. One system at a time is a sober and pragmatic position of reductionism that we believe is necessary to advance the field.

Reductionism, although intuitively appealing to researchers that struggle not to despair of the complexity of human resilience, is not, however, typically used as a orienting principle in a research area that is defined by studying how a system (the human mind) defends itself against an extra-systemic challenge (a natural disaster, an act of violence, a disease of the body, etc.). Reductionism may even appear a hopeless position, if one adds into the picture the social and cultural influences that may facilitate resilience.

We will nevertheless defend a position of reductionism in the remainder of this chapter. We will argue that, at least at the present moment, psychological resilience research is well advised to focus on intra-individual mechanisms of resilience (those that occur within the mind) and that it should only include extra-individual factors (those extraneous to the mind, including those occurring within the body) where this is absolutely necessary. Opening up to the wide range of extra-individual factors that arguably affect human mental health under adverse conditions would do nothing to clarify the key determinants of human resilience, but would instead only lead to further confusion in a field that already suffers from confusion regarding definitions, measures, and levels of analysis. To make this more than an emotional rejection of complexity, we will propose a theoretical framework that affords an integration of the effects of extra-individual factors on resilient outcomes via intra-individual (mental, cognitive, neural) mediators. Extra-individual factors, while important even in this reductionistic model, only impact resilience to the extent that their effects are transmitted via intra-individual effect paths. Because intra-individual factors exert a more proximal causal influence on resilience than extra-individual factors, the framework is justified to ignore extra-individual influences altogether, where the goal of a given study is to contribute to a truly mechanistic understanding of resilience. In other words, a reductionistic framework aims at a parsimonious explanation of resilience. Further, the approach we propose here has the potential to lead to the identification of targets for efficient and effective intervention based on the reasoning that manipulating proximal factors is likely to have a stronger influence on mental health outcomes than manipulating distal factors.

Before outlining in more detail our reductionist proposal, we will argue first that the inclusion of extra-individual factors is not only not necessary to understand resilience but in one specific case even undermines the very idea of resilience. The argument starts with an analysis of the role of stressors in resilience. Because, as pointed out, most stressors are extra-systemic influences, the case of stressors is the one instance where the defense line of reductionism apparently has its weakest spot. How can one ignore extra-systemic influences on resilience when resilience is about adapting to extra-systemic influences?

In our historical overview of the development of the resilience concept from a trait construct to an outcome, we have emphasized how crucial it is for the measurement of resilience as an outcome to characterize and quantify stressor exposure. Resilience cannot be measured in the absence of stressors and mental health changes have to be normalized somehow to stressor exposure for none or only moderate mental health deterioration in a stressed individual to still count as mental health despite adversity (i.e., resilience).

To illustrate, let us assume a financially strained single mother who receives financial support through a government program aimed at underprivileged members of society. Under the influence of year-long financial restrictions (the stressor), the woman has begun to show first signs of depression (the mental health variable), a downward path that comes to a halt when she is moved to a better apartment with her child and provided the means to finance some of her child's social activities. The government might claim it has installed a resilience-promoting program for single parents and that the money provided from the public is a resilience factor. From a resilience point of view, however, the government has simply allowed the mother to reduce her stressor exposure. For example, by changing neighborhood, mother (and child) may witness or experience less criminality, and by now being able to afford a cinema visit or a school trip for her child, mother and child may have fewer strenuous conflicts. In the overall equation, the mother's improvement in mental health may simply be commensurate with her reduction in stressor load. There would be no reason to classify her as now more resilient. What would be right to say, though, is (provided a systematic effect, of course) that the government program is a mental health program.

The scenario is more than a hypothetical one. For instance, several studies have provided evidence that financial assets predict maintenance of mental health despite onset of physical disability (McGiffin, Galatzer-Levy, & Bonanno, 2019). In line with psychosocial resource models of mental health and resilience (Hobfoll, 2002), these data can be interpreted to show that wealth and related socioeconomic variables are resilience factors. Wealth, however, is essentially a means to buffer against stressors, providing relief. A wealthy disabled individual may afford better medical treatment, may be able to better equip his household or to pay for domestic help to compensate for loss of functioning, and may still be able to take part in social life because he has the money to pay for transportation. In sum, there is less stressor exposure. If, however, resilience is to do well despite adversity, then taking away stressors can by no means count as a resilience measure. If anything, reducing overall stressor exposure reduces the individual's need to withstand and adjust. In its extreme, complete absence of stressor exposure may even be associated with poorer mental health and other desirable outcomes (such as psychosocial function, life satisfaction, or stress reactivity in laboratory conditions) than moderate exposure, as is evidenced by the previously discussed steeling effect.

A similar logic can be applied to other presumed resilience factors that can be more straightforwardly classified as extra-individual than financial resources. Social support, for instance, can consist in a neighbor doing the shopping for a sick person, a group of colleagues defending an employee against false allegations from a superior, or a family member making an interest-free loan during a financial crisis. All of these are effectively stressor exposure reductions. On an instrument that measures stressors, the supported individual would score lower. Actions or circumstances that improve housing or environmental conditions, reduce crime, or boost the economy could only then rightfully qualified as resilience factors if they were shown to improve the ratio between mental health burden and stressor burden, that is, to moderate the effects of stressors on mental health. In other words, resilience is to be mentally healthy if conditions are poor.

A Parsimonious Intra-Individual Theory of Resilience

The previous example of social support as a protective factor for mental health will serve us as an entry point into a brief presentation of an intra-individual, mechanistic theory of resilience, which we believe can both guide psychological resilience research and potentially explain the effects of extra-individual factors on resilience (provided these effects exist and do not merely reflect stressor buffering). Social support most likely benefits mental health not only by providing material resources. It also may shape cognitions. In the biblical story of Job, the critical turning point back to mental health is reached when the words of Job's friend Elihu help Job to change his perspective on what happened to him and why it happened. Elihu does nothing to improve Job's material or physical condition. He acts exclusively through passionate argumentation. Eventually, Elihu's intervention (and subsequently God's) changes the way Job reacts to his calamity. Because Job returns to mental health after temporary disturbance even though his external circumstances do not improve (immediately), Job's story meets all the criteria for being a resilience story. (It is also a nice example of resilience resulting from a process of change, in this case, a change in mindset.)

There is another potential effect path through which social support may promote resilience. Following failure to demonstrate a positive role of social support in various studies and evidence that social support can sometimes have no or negative effects on mental health, resilience researchers have worked out an apparently comparatively more important positive role of perceived social support. Perceived social support is the belief or conviction that one is embedded in a strong supportive network and may be able to fall back on family or friends if needed. Thereby, high social support perceptions presumably allow one to adopt a more relaxed perspective on many difficult situations. (For a concise overview of the social support literature, but also a nuanced perspective on the effectiveness of perceived social support, see Nickerson et al., 2017).

In both scenarios, an extra-individual factor's effect on resilience is mediated by an intra-individual factor, namely by how an individual perceives, and reacts to, a threat. The extra-individual factor (Elihu's intervention, the social support network) is distal; the intra-individual factor is proximal in its causality. The examples can also be used to illustrate why relying on proximal intra-individual factors afford more explanatory power than relying on distal extra-individual factors. Job did get quite some social support already before Elihu entered the scene. Numerous friends provided Job advice, but they were either too selfish or too unwise or Job was simply not open to their arguments. In any case, things for Job only got worse. Social support that does not meet the needs of the stressed person or is more of a burden than a help (for instance, because one feels one has to be grateful to the helper or because the helper makes demands or criticizes the victim or uses the situation for self-enhancement) is unlikely to promote resilience. Rather, social support furthers resilience if and only if it helps the victim of bad fortune better cope with the bad situation. This means that statistical relationships between social support and resilience can only be moderate at best. By contrast, good measures of the mediating intra-individual factor or factors (to be defined more precisely in the remainder of the section) should explain considerably more variance in resilience.

This is not to say that an intervention from another person may not be *the* decisive event in a process of adjustment to adversity. To the contrary, from qualitative and quantitative studies, there is enough evidence indicating the important role played in many lives by trusted others (Werner & Smith, 1989). This argument can be extended to the presumably very important role for cultural influences, such as inspiring works of religion, philosophy, or art, encouraging traditions and belief systems and contact with role models. It would be short-sighted to dismiss these influences on resilience, but at the same time it would also be short-sighted to ignore that these influences impact different individuals very differently. A holy scripture that inspires one person to bear torture and execution with a song on her lips can be the source of fear of eternal damnation for the other. Music that uplifts the teenager is usually a hassle for his parents. And the example of a resilient public person may motivate one person to follow in her path and make another feel weak and worthless in comparison.

So what is the common denominator? What is the final end-path to resilience? The same question needs to be answered not only with regards to resilience factors located outside the individual but also to those factors inside the person that may well affect resilience but are unlikely to do so directly. For instance, there is initial evidence that a certain composition of the gut microbiome may protect mental health and perhaps even promote resilience (Reber et al., 2016). (In a way, gut bacteria could also be seen as extra-individual, of course, at least if they are incorporated through diet.) Other studies indicate an important contribution of the immune system (Cathomas et al., 2019). However, any peripheral bodily function and even any gene expressed in our brains can only affect resilience if it somehow affects those systems or functions in our brain/mind that make us more or less sad, anxious, desperate, or hypervigilant.

To provide a classification of distal versus proximal resilience factors and to guide our own research toward those factors with a high likelihood to have a strong impact on resilient outcomes, the first author (Raffael Kalisch) together with Marianne Müller and Oliver Tüscher have proposed that various resilience factors converge in how individuals regulate their stress responses (Kalisch et al., 2015). Individuals who either learn over the course of a process of adjustment to stressors or who already are able to more or less optimally regulate stress reactions are likely to overcome difficult circumstances with minimal mental health impairments.

This basic tenet is derived from a functional analysis of stress, according to which stress responses are primarily adaptive reactions to potential threats to an organism's needs and goals that serve to protect the organism from harm and to preserve physiological homeostasis (Sterling & Eyer, 1988; Weiner, 1992). Albeit in principle protective, stress responses are also costly by consuming energy, time, and cognitive capacity, by interfering with the pursuit of other important goals and by placing a burden on an individual's social, financial, and health resources. This implies that, if very intense, repeated, or chronic stress responses can become harmful themselves, as exemplified in the concept of "allostatic load" (McEwen & Stellar, 1993). For these reasons, the organism needs regulatory mechanisms or "brakes" that fine-tune stress responses to optimal levels and, thus, preserve their primary adaptive function while at the same time assuring efficient deployment of resources. Stress-regulatory mechanisms prevent a response overreaction in amplitude or duration; they shut off stress responses once a threat has vanished (i.e., response termination or recovery occurs), and they counteract response generalization. Rather than acting on the acute stress response, stress-regulatory mechanisms may also have an influence on how individuals respond to future exposures to the same or other stressors, by affecting, for instance, postexposure evaluation or memory formation processes. Such flexible and adjustable responses to stressors (Ragland & Shulkin, 2014) limit resource consumption and maintains general functioning, thereby allowing for the concurrent pursuit of other goals. Ultimately, optimized stress responses prevent the accumulation of allostatic costs and reduce the likelihood of developing lasting dysfunctions under stressor exposure (Kalisch et al., 2015). Hence, any biological, psychological, social, and cultural adaptation processes most likely promote resilience in so far as they promote optimal stress response regulation. While some individuals may enter adverse life situations with already efficient regulation capacities, most individuals presumably still improve or even develop such capacities through their confrontation with stressors.

Optimal Stress Response Regulation via Positive Appraisal

This functional analysis permits us to focus investigation of protective adaptation processes on adaptations in the cognitive and neural mechanisms that underpin stress response regulation. A useful theoretical framework to approach these mechanisms is appraisal theory, which holds that the type, extent, and temporal evolution of emotional reactions, including acute and chronic stress responses, are not determined by simple, fixed stimulus–response relationships but by subjective and context-dependent appraisal (evaluation, analysis, interpretation) of the relevance of a stimulus or situation for the needs and goals of the organism (Arnold, 1960; Lazarus & Folkman, 1984; Scherer, 2001). Stress or threat responses, in particular, result from the appraisal of a situation as potentially harmful and as exceeding coping resources (Lazarus & Folkman, 1984). Both unconscious and conscious processes can contribute to this "meaning analysis." Unconscious, nonverbal appraisal is presumably at the heart of phylogenetically old threat processing that also exists in animals. Conscious and explicit appraisal may be more dominant in unfamiliar and ambiguous situations and is restricted to humans (Leventhal & Scherer, 1987; Robinson, 1998). Regardless of human or nonhuman, appraisal processes have a neurobiological foundation (Kalisch & Gerlicher, 2014; Sander, Grandjean, & Scherer, 2005).

Combining these general considerations on stress and appraisal, our theory, termed "positive appraisal style theory of resilience" (PASTOR), proposes that individuals with a generalized tendency to appraise potentially threatening stimuli or situations in a non-negative (nonpessimistic, noncatastrophizing) fashion are less likely to produce exaggerated, repeated, inflexible, and persistent stress responses and may thus be better protected against many long-term deleterious effects of trauma or chronic stressors (Kalisch et al., 2015). A positive appraisal style, on average, reduces the values that an individual attributes to stressors on the key threat appraisal dimensions threat magnitude or cost, threat probability, and coping potential to levels that realistically reflect the threat or even slightly underestimate it. In mildly aversive situations, positive appraisal is easily achieved by a class of neurocognitive processes or mechanisms that we have termed "positive situation classification," consisting of the comparison of a current situation with earlier, successfully managed ones ("I have been there before—and I survived."). It may also refer to the recurrence of a positive cultural stereotype that eventually leads to the relatively effortless activation of pre-existing positive appraisal patterns. For instance, grown up in a family that cultivates optimism and self-efficacy, one may be inclined to respond to a challenge with the assumption that the worst things usually never happen or that one will find a way to deal with it. However, in many aversive situations, negative appraisals are triggered automatically and are therefore largely unavoidable, presumably reflecting an evolutionarily determined preference for protection and defense. In such situations, positive appraisal and concomitant stress response regulation depend on the individual's ability to positively reappraise (re-evaluate) a situation. Reappraisal processes/mechanisms can range from unconscious, automatic/effortless, implicit, nonverbal, and nonvolitional to conscious, effortful, explicit, verbal, and volitional. They may reflect decreases in the actual threat value of a situation, for example in fear extinction, when a fear-conditioned stimulus (CS) that originally predicted threat (the unconditioned stimulus) is no longer followed by the unconditioned stimulus. Two other such "safety learning" processes are discrimination (e.g., between a threat-predictive CS+ and a nonpredictive and hence non-dangerous CS−) and recovery after stressor termination. The function of these processes is to avoid unnecessary, costly stress responses. Another class of reappraisal processes changes the relative weighting of the negative and positive aspects present in any situation toward a more positive interpretation. One example is volitional (cognitive) reappraisal (Gross, 1998). Reappraisals do not necessarily have to occur at the time of stressor exposure but may also be achieved in retrospect, thereby counteracting the consolidation or overgeneralization of aversive memories or generating competing positive memories. Finally, the positive adjustment of appraisals in strongly aversive situations (reappraisal proper) also requires a capacity to inhibit the interference resulting from competing negative appraisals and from the accompanying aversive emotional reactions. Hence, in addition to positive situation classification, positive reappraisal (proper) and interference inhibition are two other broad classes of neurocognitive processes whose efficiency and effectiveness together shape an individual's appraisal style.

In the context of this current volume, it may be worth pointing out that human stress responses are multifaceted, and since humans are social animals, adaptive stress responses often include efforts of help-seeking, affiliation, negotiation, and cooperation. Stress responses may also involve changing, or even exchanging, one's goals, if maintaining them would lead to disaster. Successfully recruiting social support and negotiating social interactions is evidently dependent on the responsiveness and resourcefulness of the social environment; changing one's goals can hardly be thought of without reference to the possibilities provided and the norms defined by one's society and culture. At the same time, assessing the possibilities for coping available in a given sociocultural context and calculating their potential costs and benefits, while taking into account one's own assets, competencies, and resources, are again just an inherent part of the stress response. Catastrophizing (i.e., overestimating threat magnitude/cost), pessimism (overestimating threat probability), and helplessness (underestimating coping potential) all lead to biased calculations that undermine any adaptive responding, including where responding involves exploitation of sociocultural resources. Others may be seen as a source of threat or burden rather than help, the benefits coming from social interactions may be neglected, or one's own ability to interact positively or to negotiate successfully may be misjudged. Avoiding a negative appraisal style is thus paramount for benefiting from extra-individual resilience factors. On the other hand, realistic or perhaps even slightly too positive appraisal will facilitate and energize adaptive social behavior (as well as any nonsocial ways of coping) that may include learning and benefiting from others, finding friends, and building networks.

To summarize, then, an appraisal style is first determined (a) by the efficacy and efficiency of certain neurocognitive processes that produce appraisal outputs (i.e., appraisal contents or values on the different dimensions of threat appraisal) in situations of potential threat and (b) by an individual's memory of her own threat experiences and extra-individually determined norms that commend particular appraisal outputs in particular situations. Second, an appraisal style is malleable and may change over time as the efficacy and efficiency of the underlying neurocognitive processes change (e.g., by training) and as new memories of one's own experiences accumulate and other sociocultural norms and reaction patterns are integrated into one's memory schemata. And, third, an appraisal style governs an individual's typical appraisal outputs, but it does not determine each appraisal output in each particular threat situation. (I may generally believe I am a good coper, but I may well come to the conclusion in a specific situation that I cannot cope with the situation at all.) Appraisal style is a subjective bias that colors appraisal and therefore probabilistically determines the likelihood of breakdown from allostatic load costs that accumulate over extended periods of time when individuals produce stress reactions. A positive appraisal style reduces this likelihood except if stressor exposure is so overwhelming that lasting stress reactions are unavoidable. In that case, any organism will eventually break down (Neuner et al., 2004).

PASTOR theoretically affords a way to explain both extra-personal and noncognitive (bodily) intrapersonal influences on resilience via a common end-path. Noncognitive biological factors (the gut microbiome, the immune system, genes, etc.) are likely to affect appraisal style by affecting the working of neurocognitive appraisal processes. As an example, there is first evidence suggesting that the immune system may interact with the function of the nucleus accumbens, a brain region important for generating positive evaluations (Menard et al., 2017). Extra-individual social or cultural factors may predominantly shape typical appraisal output patterns through memory. Examples may be when the culture of a family predisposes its children to produce benign threat estimates (see previous discussion) or when individuals with long-term stable, supportive social networks tend to appraise their coping potential as high because they have experienced many times that they can rely on others. Because PASTOR is a probabilistic theory that focuses on average effects, it is not optimally suited to explain the sometimes pronounced effects on resilience of single extra-individual interventions (like Elihu from the biblical story of Job), but even those are considered to be transmitted via appraisal. After all, Job finally realizes that he had been proud and self-righteous and adopts a much more humble identity, for which loss, defeat, and disease are no longer vital threats. The latter is a reminder that threat appraisal is necessarily always in relation to the individual's needs and goals that may be threatened in a given situation.

Conclusion

At its very essence, resilience needs to be qualified by words like *despite* or *although*. One stays well despite adversity, although life is conjuring up new challenges. There is a leitmotiv of independence and autonomy, even self-empowerment, inherent in resilience. Even if others may help me gain, or persevere, it is still *my* independence that defines my resilience. If multisystemic resilience research wants to understand how the (personal or nonpersonal) "other" can provide effective help, it must understand the pathways through which that help translates into benefits for mental health. Since mental health itself is an inherently individual construct, those pathways must at some point converge within the individual. PASTOR is an attempt to identify this intra-individual point of convergence.

Key Messages

1. Psychological resilience is the maintenance and/or quick recovery of mental health during and after times of adversity. Thus, psychological resilience is defined as an outcome.
2. Psychological resilience cannot be determined in the absence of adversity.
3. Staying mentally healthy despite adversity (i.e., a resilient outcome) involves processes of change or adaptation. To describe these processes, prospective longitudinal studies are required in which mental health, adversity, and potential resilience factors are measured repeatedly and with high temporal resolution.
4. Extra-individual resilience factors are assumed to only impact resilience to the extent that their effects are transmitted via intra-individual effect paths. Hence, intra-individual resilience factors exert a comparatively more proximal causal influence on resilience.
5. Positive stressor appraisal is a potential key intra-individual resilience mechanism.

Acknowledgments

This project has received funding from the European Union's Horizon 2020 research and innovation program under grant agreement No 777084 (DynaMORE project), from the Deutsche Forschungsgemeinschaft (DFG grant CRC 1193, subprojects B01, C01), and from the State of Rhineland-Palatinate (DRZ program).

Note

1. The weather is probably a less complex system compared to a human brain/mind in a human body in a human society in a natural environment.

References

Arnold, M. B. (1960). *Emotion and personality*. New York, NY: Columbia University Press.

Berg, C. J., Haardörfer, R., McBride, C. M., Kilaru, V., Ressler, K. J., Wingo, A. P., . . . Smith, A. (2017). Resilience and biomarkers of health risk in black smokers and nonsmokers. *Health Psychology, 36*(11), 1047–1058. doi:10.1037/hea0000540

Block, J. H., & Block, J. (1980). The role of ego-control and ego-resiliency in the organization of behavior. In W. A. Collins (Ed.), *Development of cognition, affect and social relations: The Minnesota Symposia on Child Psychology* (Vol. 13, pp. 39–101). New York, NY: Lawrence Erlbaum.

Boks, M. P., van Mierlo, H. C., Rutten, B. P. F., Radstake, T. R. D. J., De Witte, L., Geuze, E., . . . Vermetten, E. (2015). Longitudinal changes of telomere length and epigenetic age related to traumatic stress and post-traumatic stress disorder. *Psychoneuroendocrinology, 51*, 506–512. doi:10.1016/j.psyneuen.2014.07.011

Bonanno, G. A., Romero, S. A., & Klein, S. I. (2015). The temporal elements of psychological resilience: An integrative framework for the study of individuals, families, and communities. *Psychological Inquiry, 26*(2), 139–169. doi:10.1080/1047840X.2015.992677

Bradley, B., Davis, T. A., Wingo, A. P., Mercer, K. B., & Ressler, K. J. (2013). Family environment and adult resilience: Contributions of positive parenting and the oxytocin receptor gene. *European Journal of Psychotraumatology, 4*. doi:10.3402/ejpt.v4i0.21659

Breen, M. S., Maihofer, A. X., Glatt, S. J., Tylee, D. S., Chandler, S. D., Tsuang, M. T., . . . Woelk, C. H. (2015). Gene networks specific for innate immunity define post-traumatic stress disorder. *Molecular Psychiatry, 20*, 1538–1545. doi:10.1038/mp.2015.9

Cathomas, F., Murrough, J. W., Nestler, E. J., Han, M.-H., & Russo, S. J. (2019). Neurobiology of resilience: Interface between mind and body. *Biological Psychiatry, 86*(6), 410–420. doi:10.1016/j.biopsych.2019.04.011

Friedman, A. K., Walsh, J. J., Juarez, B., Ku, S. M., Chaudhury, D., Wang, J., . . . Han, M.-H. (2014). Enhancing depression mechanisms in midbrain dopamine neurons achieves homeostatic resilience. *Science, 344*(6181), 313–319. doi:10.1126/science.1249240

Gross, J. J. (1998). Antecedent- and response-focused emotion regulation: Divergent consequences for experience, expression, and physiology. *Journal of Personality & Social Psychology, 74*(1), 224–237.

Hobfoll, S. E. (2002). Social and psychological resources and adaptation. *Review of General Psychology, 6*(4), 307–324. doi:10.1037/1089-2680.6.4.307

Johnson, S. F., & Boals, A. (2015). Refining our ability to measure posttraumatic growth. *Psychological Trauma: Theory, Research, Practice, and Policy, 7*(5), 422–429. doi:10.1037/tra0000013

Joseph, S., & Linley, P. A. (2006). Growth following adversity: Theoretical perspectives and implications for clinical practice. *Clinical Psychology Review, 26*(8), 1041–1053. doi:10.1016/j.cpr.2005.12.006

Kalisch, R., Baker, D. G., Basten, U., Boks, M. P., Bonanno, G. A., Brummelman, E., . . . Kleim, B. (2017). The resilience framework as a strategy to combat stress-related disorders. *Nature Human Behaviour, 1*(11), 784–790. doi:10.1038/s41562-017-0200-8

Kalisch, R., Cramer, A. O. J., Binder, H., Fritz, J., Leertouwer, I., Lunansky, G., . . . van Harmelen, A.-L. (2019). Deconstructing and reconstructing resilience: A dynamic network approach. *Perspectives on Psychological Science, 14*(5), 765–777. doi:10.1177/1745691619855637

Kalisch, R., & Gerlicher, A. M. V. (2014). Making a mountain out of a molehill: On the role of the rostral dorsal anterior cingulate and dorsomedial prefrontal cortex in conscious threat appraisal, catastrophizing, and worrying. *Neuroscience & Biobehavioral Reviews, 42*, 1–8. doi:10.1016/j.neubiorev.2014.02.002

Kalisch, R., Müller, M. B., & Tüscher, O. (2015). A conceptual framework for the neurobiological study of resilience. *Behavioral and Brain Sciences, 38*. doi:10.1017/S0140525X1400082X

Kent, M., Davis, M. C., & Reich, J. W. (2014). Introduction. In M. Kent, M. C. Davis, & J. W. Reich (Eds.), *The resilience handbook* (pp. xii–xix). New York, NY: Routledge.

Kobasa, S. C. (1979). Stressful life events, personality, and health: An inquiry into hardiness. *Journal of Personality and Social Psychology, 37*(1), 1–11.

Kong, F., Ma, X., You, X., & Xiang, Y. (2018). The resilient brain: Psychological resilience mediates the effect of amplitude of low-frequency fluctuations in orbitofrontal cortex on subjective well-being in young healthy adults. *Social Cognitive and Affective Neuroscience, 13*(7), 755–763. doi:10.1093/scan/nsy045

Kong, F., Wang, X., Hu, S., & Liu, J. (2015). Neural correlates of psychological resilience and their relation to life satisfaction in a sample of healthy young adults. *NeuroImage, 123*, 165–172. doi:10.1016/j.neuroimage.2015.08.020

Krishnan, V., Han, M.-H., Graham, D. L., Berton, O., Renthal, W., Russo, S. J., . . . Nestler, E. J. (2007). Molecular adaptations underlying susceptibility and resistance to social defeat in brain reward regions. *Cell, 131*(2), 391–404. doi:10.1016/j.cell.2007.09.018

Lazarus, R. S., & Folkman, S. (1984). *Stress, appraisal and coping*. New York, NY: Springer.

Leventhal, H., & Scherer, K. R. (1987). The relationship of emotion to cognition: A functional approach to a semantic controversy. *Cognition and Emotion, 1*, 3–28.

Luthar, S. S., Cicchetti, D., & Becker, B. (2000). The construct of resilience: A critical evaluation and guidelines for future work. *Child Development, 71*(3), 543–562.

Maier, S. F. (2015). Behavioral control blunts reactions to contemporaneous and future adverse events: Medial prefrontal cortex plasticity and a corticostriatal network. *Neurobiology of Stress, 1*, 12–22. doi:10.1016/j.ynstr.2014.09.003

Mancini, A. D. (2019). When acute adversity improves psychological health: A social-contextual framework. *Psychological Review, 126*(4), 486–505. doi:10.1037/rev0000144

Mancini, A. D., & Bonanno, G. A. (2009). Predictors and parameters of resilience to loss: Toward an individual differences model. *Journal of Personality, 77*(6), 1805–1832. doi:10.1111/j.1467-6494.2009.00601.x

Masten, A. S., & Garmezy, N. (1985). Risk, vulnerability, and protective factors in developmental psychopathology. In B. B. Lahey & A. E. Kazdin (Eds.), *Advances in clinical child psychology* (pp. 1–52). doi:10.1007/978-1-4613-9820-2_1

McCubbin, H. I., Fleming, W. M., Thompson, A. I., Neitman, P., Elver, K. M., & Savas, S. A. (1998). Resiliency and coping in "at risk" African-American youth and their families. In H. I. McCubbin, E. A. Thompson, A. I. Thompson, & J. A. Futrell (Eds.), *Resiliency in African-American families* (pp. 287–328). Thousand Oaks, CA: SAGE.

McEwen B. S., & Stellar, E. (1993). Stress and the individual: Mechanisms leading to disease. *Archives of Internal Medicine, 153*(18), 2093–2101. doi:10.1001/archinte.1993.00410180039004

McGiffin, J. N., Galatzer-Levy, I. R., & Bonanno, G. A. (2019). Socioeconomic resources predict trajectories of depression and resilience following disability. *Rehabilitation Psychology, 64*(1), 98–103. doi:10.1037/rep0000254

Menard, C., Pfau, M. L., Hodes, G. E., Kana, V., Wang, V. X., Bouchard, S., . . . Russo, S. J. (2017). Social stress induces neurovascular pathology promoting depression. *Nature Neuroscience, 20*(12), 1752–1760. doi:10.1038/s41593-017-0010-3

Neuner, F., Schauer, M., Karunakara, U., Klaschik, C., Robert, C., & Elbert, T. (2004). Psychological trauma and evidence for enhanced vulnerability for posttraumatic stress disorder through previous trauma among West Nile refugees. *BMC Psychiatry, 4*(1), 34. doi:10.1186/1471-244X-4-34

Nickerson, A., Creamer, M., Forbes, D., McFarlane, A. C., O'Donnell, M. L., Silove, D., . . . Bryant, R. A. (2017). The longitudinal relationship between post-traumatic stress disorder and perceived social support in survivors of traumatic injury. *Psychological Medicine, 47*(1), 115–126. doi:10.1017/S0033291716002361

Ragland, G. B., & Shulkin, J. (2014). Introduction to allostasis and allostatic load. In M. Kent, M. C. Davis, & J. W. Reich (Eds.), *The resilience handbook: Approaches to stress and trauma* (pp. 44–52). New York, NY: Routledge.

Reber, S. O., Siebler, P. H., Donner, N. C., Morton, J. T., Smith, D. G., Kopelman, J. M., . . . Lowry, C. A. (2016). Immunization with a heat-killed preparation of the environmental bacterium Mycobacterium vaccae promotes stress resilience in mice. *Proceedings of the National Academy of Sciences of the United States of America, 113*(22), E3130–E3139. doi:10.1073/pnas.1600324113

Robinson, M. D. (1998). Running from William James' bear: A review of preattentive mechanisms and their contributions to emotional experience. *Cognition and Emotion, 12*, 667–696. doi:10.1080/026999398379493

Russo, S. J., Murrough, J. W., Han, M.-H., Charney, D. S., & Nestler, E. J. (2012). Neurobiology of resilience. *Nature Neuroscience, 15*(11), 1475–1484. doi:10.1038/nn.3234

Rutter, M. (2012). Resilience as a dynamic concept. *Development and Psychopathology, 24*(2), 335–344. doi:10.1017/S0954579412000028

Sander, D., Grandjean, D., & Scherer, K. R. (2005). A systems approach to appraisal mechanisms in emotion. *Neural Networks, 18*(4), 317–352. doi:10.1016/j.neunet.2005.03.001

Sapienza, J. K., & Masten, A. S. (2011). Understanding and promoting resilience in children and youth. *Current Opinion in Psychiatry, 24*(4), 267–273. doi:10.1097/yco.0b013e32834776a8

Scherer, K. R. (2001). Appraisal considered as a process of multilevel sequential checking. In K. R. Scherer, A. Schorr, & T. Johnstone (Eds.), *Appraisal processes in emotion: Theory, methods, research* (pp. 92–120). New York, NY: Oxford University Press.

Schultebraucks, K., & Galatzer-Levy, I. R. (2019). Machine learning for prediction of posttraumatic stress and resilience following trauma: An overview of basic concepts and recent advances. *Journal of Traumatic Stress, 32*(2), 215–225. doi:10.1002/jts.22384

Seery, M. D., Holman, E. A., & Silver, R. C. (2010). Whatever does not kill us: Cumulative lifetime adversity, vulnerability, and resilience. *Journal of Personality and Social Psychology, 99*(6), 1025–1041. doi:10.1037/a0021344

Seery, M. D., Leo, R. J., Lupien, S. P., Kondrak, C. L., & Almonte, J. L. (2013). An upside to adversity?: Moderate cumulative lifetime adversity is associated with resilient responses in the face of controlled stressors. *Psychological Science, 24*(7), 1181–1189. doi:10.1177/0956797612469210

Shao, R., Lau, W. K. W., Leung, M.-K., & Lee, T. M. C. (2018). Subgenual anterior cingulate-insula resting-state connectivity as a neural correlate to trait and state stress resilience. *Brain and Cognition, 124*, 73–81. doi:10.1016/j.bandc.2018.05.001

Shi, L., Sun, J., Wei, D., & Qiu, J. (2019). Recover from the adversity: Functional connectivity basis of psychological resilience. *Neuropsychologia, 122*, 20–27. doi:10.1016/j.neuropsychologia.2018.12.002

Sterling, P., & Eyer, J. (1988). Allostasis: A new paradigm to explain arousal pathways. In S. Fisher & J. Reason (Eds.), *Handbook of life stress, cognition and health* (pp. 629–649). New York, NY: John Wiley.

Tedeschi, R. G., & Calhoun, L. G. (2004). Posttraumatic growth: Conceptual foundations and empirical evidence. *Psychological Inquiry, 15*(1), 1–18. doi:10.1207/s15327965pli1501_01

van Rooij, S. J. H., Stevens, J. S., Ely, T. D., Fani, N., Smith, A. K., Kerley, K. A., . . . Jovanovic, T. (2016). Childhood trauma and COMT genotype interact to increase hippocampal activation in resilient individuals. *Frontiers in Psychiatry, 7*, 156. doi:10.3389/fpsyt.2016.00156

Waaktaar, T., & Torgersen, S. (2012). Genetic and environmental causes of variation in trait resilience in young people. *Behavior Genetics, 42*(3), 366–377. doi:10.1007/s10519-011-9519-5

Waugh, C. E., Wager, T. D., Fredrickson, B. L., Noll, D. C., & Taylor, S. F. (2008). The neural correlates of trait resilience when anticipating and recovering from threat. *Social Cognitive and Affective Neuroscience, 3*(4), 322–332. doi:10.1093/scan/nsn024

Weiner, H. (1992). *Perturbing the organism: The biology of stressful experience.* Chicago, IL: University of Chicago Press.

Werner, E. E., & Smith, R. S. (1989). *Vulnerable but invincible: A longitudinal study of resilient children and youth.* New York, NY: Adams Bannister Cox.

Windle, G., Bennett, K. M., & Noyes, J. (2011). A methodological review of resilience measurement scales. *Health and Quality of Life Outcomes, 9,* 8. doi:10.1186/1477-7525-9-8

Resilience in the Salutogenic Model of Health

Maurice B. Mittelmark

Introduction

This chapter discusses the question, how does the salutogenic model of health (Antonovsky, 1979, 1987) address the concept resilience? Others have raised this question. Looking for links between resilience and a salutogenic orientation to health, Eriksson and Lindström (2006, 2010) summarized that (a) both are understood as processes (rather than personal attributes); (b) in both, resources/assets play key roles in coping; (c) they are both meaningful at multiple levels (individual, group, community); and (d) a strong sense of coherence (the key construct of salutogenesis) is a resource for resilience. Others have concluded that salutogenesis is a relevant framework for therapy and counseling to promote resilience (Langeland & Vinje, 2016; Vossler, 2012). It is not surprising, then, that the ideas of human resilience and sense of coherence, which is a key construct in salutogenesis, fit within a broad family of concepts that have assets/resources for well-being in common. Other concepts include hardiness, self-efficacy, optimism, hopefulness, and action competence, among other human strengths (Eriksson & Lindström, 2010).

Since resilience and salutogenesis share so many features, it may seem strange that the scientific literature on one hardly refers to the other. Alternatively, perhaps the lack of connection is not so strange. The main academic fields concerned with the study of human resilience are social work, psychiatry, clinical psychology, developmental psychology, and disaster preparedness. The main fields concerned with the study of salutogenesis are health promotion, community development, organizational psychology, and nursing science. As we shall see, resilience and salutogenesis researchers address different research problems at slightly different systemic levels. Suffice it to note for the moment that the two fields touch, and even overlap, but they remain distinctive. How they relate is the main subject of this chapter.

I turn first, however, to a discussion of the meaning of the concepts resilience and salutogenesis. Both terms—and especially *resilience*—have a range of meanings and usage in science, so that a meaningful discussion of resilience depends on a meticulous paring down of the term (Kaplan, 2013; Ungar, 2012; van Breda, 2018; Wright & Masten, 2015).

Resilience

Here, the term *resilience* refers to transdisciplinary theory and research aiming to develop, test, and disseminate interventions that increase the coping capacity of individuals, households, and groups that experience significant and atypical adversity or deprivation. Adversity in this sense means significant hardship forged by social conditions (Dagdeviren, Donoghue, & Promberger, 2016). Theory and research on structural interventions to assist society in coping with disaster and catastrophe is excluded for present purposes, even if the term *resilience* is used in this arena. Also excluded is resilience scholarship focused on living systems without an anthropocentric focus (e.g., animals and plants).

The delimitation of individuals, households, and groups who experience atypical adversity or deprivation is essential. As Ungar (2012) expresses it in his ecological model, resilience is a set of observable behaviors associated with adaptive outcomes in contexts of *exposure to significant adversity*. The study of resilience defined this way is the investigation of biopsychosocial-ecological processes (the interplay of intrapersonal factors and one's ecological context) that give expression to particular behaviors that signal resilience. For example, resilience may be inferred when a young person does not drop out of schooling despite living under conditions of deprivation in which dropping out of school is a notable risk. In research on humans, resilience is inferred from observation of living conditions and behaviors in particular circumstances. It cannot be assessed directly, though, and its expression is fluid, depending on the conditions of the study.

Attention to the individual, as previously described, is, however, an oversimplification. Resilience, as understood here, has three components: (a) exposure to significant adversity; (b) a set of behaviors (outcomes) that signal coping; and (c) a set of multilevel processes that result in degrees of coping.

Resilience processes are the main subject of two recent systematic analyses of theory on human resilience: Ungar's (2018) principles of systemic human–environment resilience and Shean's (2015) comparative analysis of mainline theories focused on resilience in young people.

Ungar's (2018) analysis has the aim of identifying resilience principles that emerge from the theoretical and empirical transdisciplinary literature. Ungar understands systemic resilience in a particular way that is crucial to the present analysis: resilience in a given subsystem may confer resilience in another subsystem. Such interventions are themselves a resilience subsystem, and their influence may be reciprocal: children staying in school may contribute to the quality of family life. This idea of subsystem interrelatedness is important, as a similar idea underlies the salutogenic model of health. The following are principles of resilience theory, followed by an overview of salutogenesis theory to demonstrate points of agreement and disagreement between the two concepts.

Ungar's analysis of resilience processes aims to identify a set of principles that explain resilience among co-occurring systems (Ungar, 2018). The analysis has as its starting point previously published syntheses (and related material and experts' comments).

Shean's (2015) analysis is a comparative examination of the work of six theorists in the field of human resilience: Michael Rutter, Norman Garmezy, Emmy Werner, Suniya Luthar, Ann Masten, and Michael Ungar. She identifies several points of convergence (and also of divergence) that seem evident amongst the main resilience models/theories she examined. The points of convergence are in synchrony with several of Ungar's principles. Resilience, as addressed by Ungar and by Shean, includes six key features. An abbreviated synthesis of their conclusions follows:

- The study of resilience focuses on several processes of coping with adversity/deprivation, involving the person and her environment (more so than on characteristics of people or of groups, or outcomes of coping):
  - A persistence process by which a system may undertake change to maintain functioning in the face of stressors;
  - A resistance process whereby a system at risk of being overcome by stressors may use resources to continue functioning;
  - A recovery (bounce back) process whereby a system may undergo rebuilding, repair, and adaptation to return to normal functioning;
  - An adaptation process whereby a system under stress may learn new ways of functioning to be sustainable; and
  - A transformation process whereby a system under stress changes in a fundamental way, as compared to adaptation for sustainability (adapted from Ungar, 2018).
- The study of resilience focuses on the experience of individuals, groups and communities experiencing atypically severe adversity/deprivation. Resilience is, therefore, *not* a population-level phenomenon.
- In the study of resilience, a person who does well in life (copes well) despite experiencing atypical adversity/deprivation is considered to be resilient. Doing well is defined diversely, in concert with researchers' study questions.
- The influences of one's social context and one's cultural context are critically important determinants of one's resilience.
- The study of resilience has the primary aim of informing interventions to increase the coping capacity of person's who experience atypical adversity/deprivation.
- Resilience scholarship addresses multilevel systems that contribute to individuals' experience of coping with atypical adversity/deprivation. Multilevel systems are open, dynamic, and complex and exhibit redundancy, connectivity, adaptation, and experimentation (Chapter 1 of this volume explains these concepts further).

The term *resilience* does not have a formal place among the concepts of the salutogenic model of health. Therefore, to address the question posed at the beginning, one must search for concepts in the salutogenesis theory literature that correspond to resilience processes.

Salutogenesis

Aaron Antonovsky, the originator of the salutogenesis concept, viewed the concept of resilience to be compatible with salutogenesis (Antonovsky, 1987, p. xv). In his earliest exposition of salutogenesis, Antonovsky wrote: "[S]alutogenesis asks . . . how can it be explained that a given individual, in this miserable world of ours, has not broken down? Or, in a group version, how come this group has such a relatively low proportion of people who have broken down?" (Antonovsky, 1979, pp. 55–56). His research and theorizing were motivated initially by the impressive coping capacity of individuals who experienced extraordinary adversity. When it came to the explication of salutogenesis as formal theory, he contended that we are all, always, in the rough and tumble river of life. The salutogenic model of health, to which I now turn, was formulated to explain the origins and progression of health in every human being, not just those experiencing atypical adversity/deprivation.

The salutogenic model of health is presented in detail in two books authored by Antonovsky published in 1979 and 1987, and further developed by him in many published papers until his passing in 1994, including the posthumous publication in which Antonovsky proposed salutogenesis as a theory for health promotion (Antonovsky, 1996). There is no doubt that momentum in salutogenesis's development as a theory of health faltered somewhat with his untimely death in 1994. In the decades since, the momentum has been recovered. The community of scholars working with the salutogenic model of health has grown appreciably, contributing to a burgeoning theoretical and empirical literature (Bauer et al., 2019).[1]

The salutogenic model of health is a systems theory, drawing on an eclectic range of biological, psychological, sociological, anthropological, and measurement theories that Antonovsky considered essential to his developing idea about the origins of health (Antonovsky, 1979, 1987). He understood coping resources as properties of the ecosystem and not just the individual. Furthermore, his delineation of the theory of salutogenesis was undertaken as a systems analysis.

The starting point is the proposition that experience throughout life (but especially the earliest years) shapes one's orientation to life, one's sense of coherence. The sense of coherence, which is one of two key constructs of the theory, is a subjective viewing/interpreting lens, through which life may be experienced as more or less comprehensible, manageable, and meaningful. A strong sense of coherence facilitates the adaptive use of resources to tackle life's ubiquitous stressors. Expounding on the concept of resources, Antonovsky coined the term "generalized resistance resources," which is the other key construct in the salutogenic model of health (Antonovsky, 1979). These are properties/characteristics of a person, group, or community that facilitate an individuals' or group's ability to cope effectively with stressors and contribute to the development of the sense of coherence (Idan, Eriksson, & Al-Yagon, 2017). Examples of generalized resistance resources are knowledge, skills, coping strategies, materials, social relationships and support, cultural stability, and genetic and constitutional factors.

The relationship between the sense of coherence and generalized resistance resources is reciprocal, the one strengthening or weakening the other. A strong sense of coherence mobilizes resources to confront potentially serious stressors through processes including evaluating them as not serious, avoiding them, or actively managing them (tension management). Successful tension management strengthens the sense of coherence and helps one stay-in-place along ease/dis-ease continua (e.g., health, good social functioning, well-being). Ease/dis-ease continua (not *disease*) indicate a sliding range of functioning from good to poor, contra the dichotomous medical diagnostic classification "ill–not ill."

Many in the field of health promotion have embraced the salutogenesis model as a framework for intervention to help people gain control over the own health. The application of salutogenesis has been described in settings as diverse as neighborhoods, schools, workplaces, prisons, hospitals, and residential care facilities (Mittelmark et al., 2017). Thus, the salutogenic model of health, initially a descriptive model, has evolved into an intervention model. Like resilience scholarship, much of salutogenesis scholarship is today oriented to the study of social change to improve quality of life.

Comparing Resilience Scholarship and the Salutogenic Model of Health

Processes

The study of processes characterizes both traditions, as Eriksson and Lindström (2010) observed, yet there are important differences. Resilience scholarship is focused on transactional processes involving person and environment, which Ungar (2018) terms *persistence, resistance, recovery, adaptation*, and *transformation*. Absent is an emphasis on mental processes involved in appraisal, judgement, and reaction to potentially stressful stimuli, processes associated with neurological functioning. In explaining how one person does well under fundamentally the same adverse circumstances under which another person does less well, resilience scholarship pays little attention to how intrapersonal factors affect the unfolding of those processes. The focus is, instead, on environmental factors. As Hadfield and Ungar (2018) put it, the focus is on coping resources in proximal (family) and distal (community) systems. This is understandable in applied mental health fields where the aim is to intervene to help people living in adverse situations do well. Social and physical environment that offers opportunities for intervention and change. Intrapersonal (individual) differences are admitted but offer no intervention opportunities except individually focused therapy. In other words, the emphasis in much of the resilience literature is not on altering intrapersonal factors, but on altering the person's living situation.

This is in contrast to counseling research applying salutogenesis, which aims to strengthen a particular intrapersonal factor: the sense of coherence. Clinical interventions to strengthen the sense of coherence in people with mental health challenges have been used to achieve outcomes such as increasing tolerance for disturbing feelings, experiencing oneself more positively as a person, improving one's self-identity, increasing one's perception of the quality of social support, and developing one's perceptions of life's comprehensibility, manageability, and meaningfulness (Langeland & Vinje, 2016). These changes in cognitions and emotions distinguish salutogenic interventions from the environmental interventions promoted by resilience researchers. This is not to underplay that much intervention stimulated by salutogenesis aims, as resilience interventions do, to increase the availability and quality of environmental coping resources (creating supportive environments).

Severe Adversity

Resilience scholarship focuses on the needs of individuals, groups, and communities experiencing atypically severe adversity/deprivation. It does not, therefore, address whole populations. Resilience researchers seek to understand the needs and challenges of especially vulnerable people and groups and help them to cope. Children living in disadvantaged conditions that put them at risk of school dropout, for example, exemplifies the concern at the heart of resilience scholarship. School dropout among disadvantaged children is a serious aberration of societal aspirations. It is to be prevented. The task of building at-risk children's resilience to dropout through effective interventions is an example of the challenge that motivates resilience research. The focus of intervention is not so much the at-risk child herself as her home, community, and societal environments. Yet the raison d'etre of intervention should be to help particular at-risk children cope better.

Salutogenesis, on the other hand, has as its starting point the idea of "the river of life." It is a misconception, in salutogenic eyes, that most people are safely ashore, and it is therefore sufficient to erect barriers to prevent people from falling into the river and provide rescue services to save those who do stumble in. Salutogenesis takes the perspective that all people are born into the river of life and must learn to swim and to navigate and tackle the dangers and obstacles that are unavoidable aspects of life (Antonovsky, 1987). No one is on the shore, yet the river is not uniformly challenging. Some people do find themselves situated at particularly hazardous parts of the river, they are at alarming risk of foundering, and they need urgent help. Resilience and salutogenesis thus have complementary but not indistinguishable concern with the struggle for survival. It is this distinction, between concern for at-risk subgroups and attention to the population as a whole, which most cogently illustrates the fundamental divide between the interests of resilience and salutogenesis scholarship. From a salutogenesis perspective, one could consider that resilience interventions, and the entire field of resilience scholarship, are concerned with providing effective and *specific* resistance resources that match a person's needs at particular times (Mittelmark, Bull, Daniel, & Urke, 2017).

Doing Well Despite Adversity

The outcomes of interest in resilience research are varied, but they share the characteristic that they are indicators of "doing well" under adverse conditions. In the child development arena, for example, resilience under adverse conditions is recognized by a child's achievement of positive developmental outcomes and the avoidance of maladaptive outcomes (Rutter, 2006). Doing well for such children is no different from doing well for all children, meaning that the goal of resilience-promoting interventions is, according to Wright, Masten, and Narayan (2013), to meet

> the expectations for children of a given age and gender in their particular sociocultural and historical context. Competence is typically assessed by how well the

child has met, and continues to meet, the expectations explicitly or implicitly set in the society for children as they grow up. This is often referred to as the child's track record of success in meeting developmental tasks, age-related standards of behavior across a variety of domains, such as physical, emotional, cognitive, moral, behavioral, and social areas of achievement or function. (p. 18)

While the concept of doing well is relevant to all people, the special interest of resilience scholarship is to assist people living in particularly adverse conditions to do well. Adverse conditions in this sense are exemplified by the experience of poverty, unemployment, violence, crime, family breakdown, and substance abuse. In salutogenesis scholarship, extreme conditions like this cause deep consternation, but the main thrust of the theory is the notion that *all* people live in the rough and tough river of life from birth to death. In the spirit of the salutogenic model of health, resilience (when the term is used) is the essence of every human life, the entire process of experiencing life whether one is at-risk or not, acquiring resources, meeting stressful conditions, coping, building a sense of coherence, and having one's health and well-being affected positively.

As to the concept of "doing well," salutogenesis scholars have evolved ideas about what it may mean. In Antonovsky's (1979) exposition of the theory, doing well meant moving toward the ease end of an ease/dis-ease continua. His interest was focused on a health continuum defined by the degrees to which one experiences pain, has functional limitations, has a medical condition with prognostic implications, and whether one needs medical treatment. However, he was open to other continua having relevance to positive functioning, flourishing, and well-being (Antonovsky, 1996).

Cultural Contexts

Social and cultural contexts play an important role in conferring resilience. As put by Ungar (2012), resilience scholars aim to "explore the context in which the individual experiences adversity, making resilience first a quality of the broader social and physical ecology, and second a quality of the individual" (p. 27). The implications of this viewpoint are profound. It calls for intervention to create (and treat as outcomes in research) supportive social and physical environments, and not just intervention to change the individual (Ungar, 2011). It urges caution in generalizing findings from any particular context to other contexts. It acknowledges the possibility that coping may be manifest in atypical and unexpected ways. It calls for scholars to seek understanding of resilience from the perspective of nondominant cultural groups who are at heightened risk compared to dominant cultural groups.

Thus, resilience scholarship is called to be highly sensitive to the role of cultural context in resilience processes. This is in complete synchrony with the salutogenic model of health, in which culture is understood to be a constant force on health, from conception to death. This is especially evident among people who confront the challenge of engaging with several distinct cultures at once as Riedel, Wiesmann, and Hannich (2011) point to in their work on salutogenesis, acculturative stress, and mental health.

The explicit starting point in Antonovsky's (1979) model is the person's sociocultural and historical context. Antonovsky theorized that cultural context influences the development of health at every phase of the salutogenic process (Benz, Bull, Mittelmark, & Vaandrager, 2014). First, while stressors are ubiquitous in all cultural contexts, they are differently distributed and perceived between cultures. Second, stressors connected explicitly to culture include minority background, rapid culture change, and gaps between aspirations and achievements that are exacerbated by culture. Third, cultures generate (more or less) general resistance resources following from degree of cultural stability, being valued for one's culture, and being integrated into society. Fourth, life experience is shaped in part by cultural stability, consistency, and personal and social achievement. Fifth, a sense of coherence is shaped by all the aforementioned cultural factors (but is not culture-bound). Finally, one's understanding of the concept of well-being is influenced by culture. For example, one's religiosity may play an important role in how one defines what is meant by the idea of the "good and worthy life."

In more recent formulations of salutogenesis, the level of analysis has expanded to include the family and the community, with key variables like the sense of coherence measured at several levels (Mana, Sagy, & Srour, 2016). Research on social relations at the community level has had a decidedly cultural orientation, as in the study of in- and out-groups' community sense of coherence and their degree of openness to other cultures. Recall from the previous discussion of resilience that due to contextual factors, coping may be manifest in atypical and unexpected ways: the possibility for this is startlingly obvious in research with Palestinian Muslims and Christians in Israel where a strong community sense of coherence was correlated with higher levels of acceptance of the in-group's collective narratives and with lower levels of acceptance of the out-group collective narratives, which were often stigmatizing or otherwise threatened well-being (Mana et al., 2016). Ungar (2011) has written about the complexity of resilience due to contextual factors, and the complexity of salutogenesis due to culture is correspondingly evident. For example, the roles of personal and of community sense of coherence in influencing well-being may differ significantly in Western-oriented societies compared to collectivist societies (Braun-Lewensohn & Sagy, 2011).

Whatever factors may differentiate resilience and salutogenesis, one thing is clear: these two areas of study are in complete agreement that coping is complex and culturally and contextually bounded. As a consequence of this insight, both bodies of research are committed to socioecological (multilevel) approaches to descriptive and intervention research. While a discussion between a resilience researcher and a salutogenesis researcher might reveal a number of areas of misapprehension, they would quickly come to agreement about the core roles of context and culture in shaping coping phenomena.

Conclusion

I now turn to the question this chapter is meant to address: How does the salutogenic model of health address the concept resilience? A too facile answer is that it does not, or that the term *resilience* has no place in the model. Yet, when resilience is characterized in terms of its main principles, it is evident that several features of the salutogenic model of health map on to resilience with a high degree of complementarity.

Regarding consideration of social and cultural contexts, resilience, and salutogenesis scholarship could hardly be in closer kinship. Both are systems oriented, and cognizant that the social challenges they address are complex and multilevel. Both are keenly sensitive to cultures as the cauldrons of life experience. Both encounter the complexity and frustration of attempting to do quality social research, wherein simple cause–effect analyses are wholly inadequate. Both face the challenge that arises when the need to tackle complexity across systems with a degree of specificity triumphs the wish to achieve broader generalizability.

Regarding social change, both bodies of research are incontrovertibly committed to informing intervention, while still recognizing that high-quality intervention development and dissemination depends on a bedrock of descriptive research that establishes the dimensions and contours of complex social problems.

Are resilience and salutogenesis siblings or cousins? *Cousins* seems to be the better response as the concepts differ significantly on two important dimensions. First, while both are concerned with the study of processes and not just associations, resilience scholarship deals in an almost piecemeal way with a range of coping processes having relevance to multiple stages/phases/aspects of coping—persistence, resistance, recovery, adaptation, and transformation. There is as yet no formal theory that accounts for these processes in an integrated manner. Readers of the resilience literature might be able to piece together a serviceable, integrated understanding of resilience-as-process, but no theoretician has yet undertaken the task, as far as I am aware. It is also noteworthy that resilience scholarship has not evidenced discipline-wide interest in how the human brain is the mediator of environment–person interaction (for an exception, see Kalisch, Müller, & Tüscher, 2015), that experience is therefore forged in the brain and that understanding how the brain creates experience is essential to understanding resilience and individual and community levels. In other words, resilience scholarship seems to eschew cognition in its research on resilience processes. Probably all resilience researchers would agree that "something is happening up there" that influences resilience, but they do not prioritize studying it.

Salutogenesis does have a formal theory, the salutogenic model of health. It postulates one main mediator in the link between environment and coping behavior—the sense of coherence. It elaborates pathways in which experience from the cradle to the grave gives meaning to life and imparts deeply held impressions about life's comprehensibility and manageability. It postulates that one's life orientation influences one's perceptions of coping resources, how stressors are experienced and appraised, and what coping actions/adjustments are possible/desirable/inevitable under the labile circumstances of one's own life.

Finally, resilience and salutogenesis scholarship differ sharply regarding the social situations they are concerned with. Resilience scholarship aims to help particular people do well despite living in risky life situations characterized by atypical adversity/deprivation. Salutogenesis considers that all people live in risky conditions—the river of life. Salutogenic processes are thereby equally relevant to those living lives of atypical adversity *and* those having all other manifestations of experience.

What opportunities for mutual enrichment might there be? Might salutogenesis research benefit from examining the resilience processes of persistence, resistance, recovery, adaptation, and transformation, to shed additional light on mechanisms by which potential stressors are managed? Might resilience research benefit from examining the sense of coherence, to shed additional light on the mediating processes by which environment and person interact to develop or weaken resilience? Future efforts to draw these fields of study closer together can only be of benefit to the health sciences.

Key Messages

1. Resilience scholarship focuses on coping processes in persons and groups who experience severe adversity and deprivation, while salutogenic processes are posited to be descriptive of coping in all persons.
2. Resilience scholarship has always had a focus on developing interventions to help people do well in life despite barriers, while salutogenesis has until recently been more concerned with descriptive research.
3. Resilience and salutogenesis share the perspective that coping is culturally and contextually bounded.
4. Resilience scholarship is principled, but no single, articulated theory is dominate. Salutogenesis is well developed as theory, following the scholarship of Aaron Antonovsky.
5. The concept resilience does not have a formal place in salutogenesis theory, yet when salutogenesis scholars focus on coping under conditions of severe adversity, they apply resilience approaches and strategies, even if the concept resilience is not explicit.

Note

1. As of this writing, salutogenesis' advancement is buoyed by a recently inaugurated scientific organisation, The Society for Theory and Research on Salutogenesis—STARS, at https://www.stars-society.org. The Center of Salutogenesis at the University of Zurich play a key global coordinating role in advancing salutogenesis scholarship. Annual salutogenesis scientific meeting and conferences attract scholars worldwide, and several thousand papers and books populate a rapidly expanding literature. The Handbook of Salutogenesis (Mittelmark, et al., 2016) describes the history of salutogenesis and recent developments in theory and practice in community and healthcare settings in many countries.

References

Antonovsky, A. (1979). *Health, stress, and coping*. San Francisco, CA: Jossey-Bass.
Antonovsky, A. (1987). *Unraveling the mystery of health. How people manage stress and stay well*. San Francisco, CA: Jossey-Bass.
Antonovsky, A. (1996). The salutogenic model as a theory to guide health promotion. *Health Promotion International*, *11*(1), 11–18. doi:10.1093/heapro/11.1.11
Bauer, G. F., Roy, M., Bakibinga, P., Contu, P., Downe, S., Eriksson, M., . . . Vinje, H. F. (2019). Future directions for the concept of salutogenesis: A position article. *Health Promotion International*, 1–9. doi:10.1093/heapro/daz057

Benz, C., Bull, T., Mittelmark, M., & Vaandrager, L. (2014). Culture in salutogenesis: The scholarship of Aaron Antonovsky. *Global Health Promotion, 21*(4), 16–23. doi:10.1177/1757975914528550

Braun-Lewensohn, O., & Sagy, S. (2011). Salutogenesis and culture: Personal and community sense of coherence among adolescents belonging to three different cultural groups. *International Review of Psychiatry, 23*(6), 533–541. doi:10.3109/09540261.2011.637905

Dagdeviren, H., Donoghue, M., & Promberger, M. (2016). Resilience, hardship and social conditions. *Journal of Social Policy, 45*(1), 1–20. doi:10.1017/S004727941500032X

Eriksson, M., & Lindström, B. (2006). Antonovsky's sense of coherence scale and the relation with health: A systematic review. *Journal of Epidemiology & Community Health, 60*(5), 376–381. doi:10.1136/jech.2005.041616

Eriksson, M., & Lindström, B. (2010). Bringing it all together: The salutogenic response to some of the most pertinent public health dilemmas. In A. Morgan, M. Davies, & E. Ziglio (Eds.), *Health assets in a global context* (pp. 339–351). New York, NY: Springer. doi:10.1007/978-1-4419-5921-8

Hadfield, K., & Ungar, M. (2018). Family resilience: Emerging trends in theory and practice. *Journal of Family Social Work, 21*(2), 81–84. doi:10.1080/10522158.2018.1424426

Idan, O., Eriksson, M., & Al-Yagon, M. (2017). The salutogenic model: The role of generalized resistance resources. In M. B. Mittelmark, S. Sagy, M. Eriksson, G. F. BauerJürgen, M. Pelikan, B. Lindström, & G. Arild Espnes (Eds.), *The handbook of salutogenesis* (pp. 57–69). New York, NY: Springer. doi:10.1007/978-3-319-04600-6

Kalisch, R., Müller, M. B., & Tüscher, O. (2015). A conceptual framework for the neurobiological study of resilience. *Behavioral and Brain Science, 38*, 1–21. doi:10.1017/S0140525X1400082X

Kaplan, H. B. (2013). Reconceptualising resilience. In S. Goldstein & R. B. Brooks (Eds.), *Handbook of resilience in children* (pp. 39–55). New York, NY: Springer. doi:10.1007/978-1-4614-3661-4

Langeland, E., & Vinje, H. F. (2016). The application of salutogenesis in mental healthcare settings. In M. B. Mittelmark, S. Sagy, M. Eriksson, G. F. BauerJürgen, M. Pelikan, B. Lindström, & G. Arild Espnes (Eds.), *The handbook of salutogenesis* (pp. 299–305). New York, NY: Springer. doi:10.1007/978-3-319-04600-6

Mana, A., Sagy, S., & Srour, A. (2016). Sense of community coherence and inter-religious relations. *Journal of Social Psychology, 156*(5), 469–482. doi:10.1080/00224545.2015.1129302

Mittelmark, M. B., Sagy, S., Eriksson, M., Bauer, G. F., Pelikan, J. M., Lindström, B., & Espnes, G. A. (Eds.). (2017). *The handbook of salutogenesis*. New York, NY: Springer. doi:10.1007/978-3-319-04600-6

Mittelmark, M. B., Bull, T., Daniel, M., & Urke, H. (2017). Specific resistance resources in the salutogenic model of health. In M. B. Mittelmark, S. Sagy, M. Eriksson, G. F. BauerJürgen, M. Pelikan, B. Lindström, & G. Arild Espnes (Eds.), *The handbook of salutogenesis* (pp. 71–76). New York, NY: Springer. doi:10.1007/978-3-319-04600-6

Riedel, J., Wiesmann, U., & Hannich, H. (2011). An integrative theoretical framework of acculturation and salutogenesis. *International Review of Psychiatry, 23*(6), 555–564. doi:10.3109/09540261.2011.637912

Rutter, M. (2006). Implications of resilience concepts for scientific understanding. *Annals of the New York Academy of Sciences, 1094*(1), 1–12. doi:10.1196/annals.1376.002

Shean, M. (2015). *Current theories related to resilience and young people: A literature review*. Melbourne, Australia: Victorian Health Promotion Foundation. Retrieved from https://evidenceforlearning.org.au/assets/Grant-Round-II-Resilience/Current-theories-relating-to-resilience-and-young-people.pdf

Ungar, M. (2011). The social ecology of resilience: Addressing contextual and cultural ambiguity of a nascent construct. *American Journal of Orthopsychiatry, 81*(1), 1–17. doi:10.1111/j.1939-0025.2010.01067.x

Ungar, M. (2012). *The social ecology of resilience: A handbook of theory and practice*. New York, NY: Springer. doi:10.1007/978-1-4614-0586-3

Ungar, M. (2018). Systemic resilience: Principles and processes for a science of change in contexts of adversity. *Ecology and Society, 23*(4), 34. doi:10.5751/ES-10385-230434.

van Breda, A. D. (2018). A critical review of resilience theory and its relevance for social work. *Social Work, 54*(1), 1–18. doi:10.15270/54-1-611

Vossler, A. (2012). Salutogenesis and the sense of coherence: Promoting health and resilience in counselling and psychotherapy. *Counselling Psychology Review, 27*(3), 68–78.

Wright, M. O. D., Masten, A. S., & Narayan, A. J. (2013). Resilience processes in development: Four waves of research on positive adaptation in the context of adversity. In M. Goldstein & R. B. Brooks (Eds.), *Handbook of resilience in children* (pp. 15–37). Boston, MA: Springer. doi:10.1007/978-1-4614-3661-4_2

Wright M. O., & Masten A. S. (2015) Pathways to resilience in context. In L. C. Theron, L. Liebenberg, & M. Ungar (Eds.), *Youth resilience and culture: Commonalities and complexities* (pp. 3–22). New York, NY: Springer. doi:10.1007/978-94-017-9415-2_1

People, Perceptions, and Process

Multisystemic Resilience in Social-Ecological Systems

Lilian Alessa and Andrew Kliskey

Introduction

A growing community of practice has treated human and biophysical systems as linked and has characterized them as a social-ecological system (SES), that is, complex, integrated systems of humans within the ecosystem (Berkes & Folke, 1998; Kliskey et al., 2016; Alessa, Kliskey & Altaweel, 2009; Young et al., 2006). An SES is characterized by feedbacks, which occur between human values, perceptions, and behaviors and the biophysical components of the ecosystems in which people exist resulting in a resilient or vulnerable trajectory leading to sustainability or collapse (Gallopin, 2006). When technology is factored in, these feedbacks result in markedly different outcomes depending on the type of SES; factors include whether a community is able to afford and maintain the technologies that support them as well as how human skills and cognitive abilities are degraded or lost due to an overreliance on technology (Alessa, Kliskey, & Williams, 2010). This is due to the phenomenon through which technology is viewed as no longer a tool to enhance human organization, dynamics, and skills but rather as a solution, and consequently at the expense of all of these facets. Such a phenomenon is particularly marked in the U.S. intelligence and military communities (Bolia, Vidulich, Nelson, & Cook, 2007; Roper, 1997).

SESs are an instance of complex adaptive systems (CAS). In this chapter we make the case for multisystemic resilience in SESs being considered as a social process predicated on accurate perception of constantly changing social and ecological conditions, rather than the conventional notion of resilience as a static configuration or condition. First, we set out key principles of complexity theory and CAS as a foundation for understanding multisystemic resilience in SES. Second, we explore multisystemic resilience in SES as a social process. Third, we examine the role of human perceptions and group dynamics as the key underpinning of the social process of multisystemic resilience. Fourth, we consider how technology factors into multisystemic resilience as a social process and its impact on perception of change in SES. We conclude by providing some suggestions for advancing multisystemic resilience as a social process.

Complexity Theory: The Origins of Resilience

We live in an era where the fabric of society is comprised of an enormous number of variables that collide to form supportive and destructive actions at multiple scales. The core science governing much of what we see on Earth stems from the science of complexity that is also known as complex systems science. A common miscommunication is that the field of complexity was born at the Santa Fe Institute in the 1980s, but it was first described by Schrödinger (1944) as "order out of chaos." At its most basic definition *complexity* can be defined as a set of emergent structures, processes, or outcomes that arise from the interaction of two or more entities (molecules, organisms, structures, processes) that give rise to new structures, functions, and/or regime shifts at larger scales (Bar-Yam, 2003). Complexity can be framed into disciplinary silos ranging from computer science to societal governance. For example, an illustration of complexity in computer science is the NP versus P problem, a computational efficiency class of problems where P is known as polynomial time and refers to efficient algorithms that use a fixed polynomial of the input size (Fortnow, 2009). However, many related problems cannot be solved using the P efficient algorithm, and instead use NP or nondeterministic polynomial time (Fortnow, 2009). Consequently P = NP refers to problems that have efficiently verifiable solutions (i.e., NP) and where the solution can be found efficiently, (i.e., P). Likewise, an example of complexity in sociology and political science is the way governance affects equity and social justice (Mercier, 2014). In cell biology an example of resilience predicated on perception comes from the establishment of the developmental axis in zygotes of *Pelvetia compressa*, an alga: successful tissue differentiation, necessary for a healthy organism, begins with the organism's perception of which way is up and which way is down to respond by reorganizing its F-actin cytoskeleton (Alessa & Kropf, 1998); in human organizations such as the U.S. intelligence community, which is comprised of 16 member agencies, the ability to accurately respond to threats requires detection of signals hidden in noise, something the intelligence community has repeatedly failed to accomplish (Shelton, 2011; Zegart, 2019).

Complex systems science is a nuance of complexity defined as "collections of simple units or agents interacting in a system" (Jennings, 2000, p. 286) with a *complex system* being one that is derived from the interactions of agents to establish a system that is both emergent (possessing design) and complicated (many pieces). Systems ranging from chemical reactions, biological cells, neurological systems, ecological systems, human societies, and military systems may be described as complex, emergent systems. The underlying mathematics and physics have given rise to a range of technologies such as genetic and evolutionary algorithms that are used on distributed computing systems to drive artificial intelligence and machine learning (M'Hamdi et al., 2017; Nemiche, M'Hamdi, Chakraoui, Cavero, & Pla-Lopez, 2013). Related to this are CASs in which one or more components within a complex system adjusts its form and/or behavior in response to a perturbation whether negative or positive is the applied form of complexity science. Since this adjustment in behavior occurs in parallel with changes across other components the resulting system features can be described as complex and emergent (Dekker, 2016). Thus responsiveness, and hence resilience, to change is more accurately described as an ongoing process rather than a steady state.

The resilience literature (e.g., Anderies, Janssen, & Ostrom, 2007; Resilience Alliance, 2010) tends to reduce SESs to "neat" systems, that is, as systems in which humans and their resources are simplified to a single resource system, group of users, and governance system (Anderies et al., 2007). One of the more well-known approaches for analyzing the resilience of SESs is Ostrom's (2009) multilevel, nested framework that recognizes the multiple levels of SES at varying spatial and temporal scales. The framework adopts complex systems thinking and applies it to common pool resources. Common pool, or common property, resources refer to family, tribal, or community commons (e.g., pasture, forest, or fisheries) with unrestricted local availability and use of the resource (Ostrom, 1999). Control or management of common property is typically achieved through social checks (e.g., cultural or religious practices). The tragedy of the commons is a well-known case of resource overuse (e.g., overgrazing, overfishing, overhunting) that common property resources can be susceptible to (Hardin, 1968) and is in essence a social and economic trap involving competing individual interests versus the common good when using a finite resource (Ostrom, 1999).

The Ostrom (1999) SES framework characterizes common-property resources as decomposed into resource systems, resource units, governance systems, users, and the interactions between these elements. It has been shown to be generalizable for many community-based common property resources in specific locales, for example, coastal fisheries in Mexico's Sea of Cortez (Basurto, Gelcich, & Ostrom, 2013). However, this describes a relatively neat system; other SES approaches build from this generalized framework for common pool resources but incorporate more robust data that reflect SESs as complex and messy systems. Complex SESs are typically less easily framed and less compliant with the theoretical descriptions of the "ball and basin" analogy (e.g., Berkes & Folke, 1998).

To move from CAS to the concept of resilience we must look at its multisystemic origins. Resilience, in part derived from physics, is defined in materials science as the ability of a material to absorb energy when it is deformed elastically and release that energy upon unloading (Motamedi, Iranmanesh, & Nazari, 2018). Proof *resilience* is defined as the maximum energy that can be absorbed up to the elastic limit, without creating a permanent distortion (O'Brien & Hope, 2010). Other definitions took this analogy and applied it to a range of settings, for example, in psychology and social work resiliency and resilience theory is presented as three waves of inquiry. The identification of resilient qualities was the first wave characterized through phenomenological identification of developmental assets and protective factors. The second wave described resilience as a disruptive and reintegrative process for accessing resilient qualities. The third wave exemplified the postmodern and multidisciplinary view of resilience, which is the force that drives a person to grow through adversity and disruptions (Richardson, 2002). This construct was subsequently adopted by ecologists to describe disturbance in habitats and vegetation patterns (Chapin, Kofina, & Folke, 2009).

Resilience in messy SESs can be characterized as a set of processes that map to systemic resilience (Ungar, 2018). It is notable that resilience as a systemic process does not have a single corresponding match in messy SESs since the set of processes in messy SESs taken in toto denote resilience as a process. As dynamic, complex systems, the resilience of messy SES is inherently process-based. This is analogous to ends and means in planning, where ends refers to an end goal or end state as the focus of planning, while means refers to the approach or the process for achieving an objective as the focus of planning (Banfield, 1959). Consequently, resilience in messy SESs describe a means for examining and understanding resilience, rather than an ends (Alessa et al., 2009; Sem, 2013) comprising a complex set of interactions (Table 9.1).

Messy SESs involve the simultaneous use of multiple resources by diverse users and the technologies they employ. Each of these facets must be explicitly considered as both related and independent (Alessa et al., 2009). Such a viewpoint can more readily accommodate the inherent complexity of SESs than strictly neat SESs. For example, an SES comprising a

TABLE 9.1 Comparison of Characteristics of Resilience as a Process in Messy SESs

Messy SES Resilience	Ostrom SES Resilience	Ungar Systemic Resilience
Development of diverse options	Property rights system; resource unit mobility	Diversity
Interactions across landscape	Clarity and size of resource system; Interaction and spatial distribution of resource units	Open, dynamic, complex
Retention	Productivity of resource system	Trade-offs between systems
Distribution over space	Spatial and temporal distribution of resource units	Promotion of connectivity
Persistence over time	History of use	Learning
Collectivism in community	Government organizations; collective choice rules	Participation
Variability	Number of users	Diversity
Directionality of trajectory	Growth rate of resource	Experimentation and learning
Identifying substitutability	Dependence on resource	Redundancy
Communicating across networks	Information sharing among users; networking activities; network structure	Promotion of connectivity
Minimization of risks	Frequency of long-term hazards (e.g., economic, major and large-scale environmental catastrophes)	Contexts of adversity

Based on Alessa et al. (2009) and Altaweel et al. (2015), with elements in common pool resource systems (Ostrom, 2009), and systemic resilience (Ungar, 2018).

town in the American West and the mountain landscape in which it exists (e.g., Altaweel, Virapongse, Griffith, Alessa, & Kliskey, 2015) is not only subject to the consequences of regional, national, and global economies and global climate change effects on precipitation and temperature; it is also influenced by policies governing resource use and conservation, with norms and cultural idiosyncrasies that shape and affect perceptions. Regardless of the example the resilience process in messy SESs begins and continues through the ability to accurately perceive change. Accurate perception (P) determines the types of information and means needed to successfully respond to changes.

Resilience as a Process

Writ large, resilience as a field of inquiry is essentially a social construct built within individual disciplines with a range of descriptors and there has been a great deal of effort to reconcile these disciplinary constructs toward a unifying foundation (Olsson, Jerneck, Thoren, Persson, & O'Byrne, 2015; Ungar, 2018). In other words, resilience is often portrayed as a state or configuration (a static thing). A person or a society is said to be resilient when a certain number of indicators, variables, traits, and/or features are present (Cutter, Barnes, Berry, Burton, & Evans, 2008; Scheffer, Dakos, & van Nes, 2015). Conversely, in the absence of these a system is described as vulnerable (Beroya-Eitner, 2016; Hinkel, 2011). Since so many constructs assign resilience as a "thing," the search for unity may not only be unnecessarily complicated but also misleading.

In messy SES resilience is a process that implicates people, perception, and place—the communities and the landscapes in which communities reside and includes the built and technological environments that support them. Resilience as a process is predicated on the ability to accurately sense, perceive, and/or evaluate change trajectories, frequency, and magnitude (Williams et al., 2018). Social-ecological resilience refers to the ability of communities and landscapes to detect physical, social, or economic changes; identify their nature; and respond to it while retaining core social and physical functionality (Alessa et al., 2015). This establishes the adaptive capacity of communities through a measure of their ability to respond proactively, versus reactively, to slower changes and maintain a level of functionality and cohesion during acute or catastrophic ones (Alessa et al., 2009; Altaweel et al., 2015).

As a process resilience shares three ubiquitous phases: perception of environment and change (e.g., sensing [cells, tissues], perception [organisms], communication [populations] and calibration), responses (actions), and outcomes (consequences; see Figure 9.1). With each cycle, n, the environment (milieu) is altered and these changes feed back to the first, and most critical, phase (perception of change in the milieu). Perceptions are fundamental to understanding multisystemic resilience as a social process. Using a standard degrees of belief algorithm based on three meta analyses (Lee et al., 2013; Ungar, 2018; Xu & Marinova, 2013), combined with input from several resilience experts in SES science, three interacting processes that affect resilience as a process were derived. The assumptions made here is that technologies and built environments are inseparable from SESs in the current Anthropocene. In messy SESs, the interacting processes are

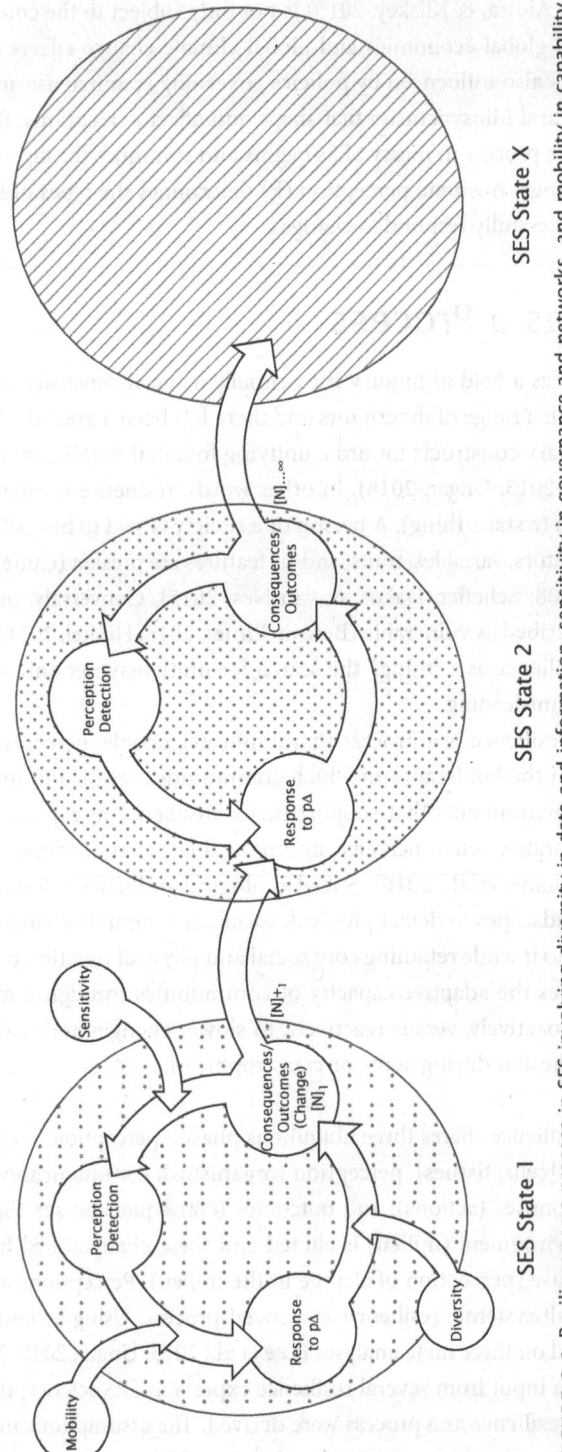

FIGURE 9.1 Resilience as a process in SES involving diversity in data and information, sensitivity in governance and networks, and mobility in capability and response to change.

1. Diversity (D) of sensors to generate both a breadth and depth of data and information since few decisions are made on scientific data themselves.
2. Sensitivity (S) in the ability of institutions, networks, and governance structures, both informal and formal, to respond in a timely manner to a perceived change requiring response(s).
3. Mobility (M) or the fluidity of responses and the ability to maintain function during sudden, adverse change.

Figure 9.1 illustrates the three interactions defining resilience as a process in the context of a changing environment where resilience is an iterating process that integrates diversity, sensitivity, and mobility. The process represents a continual sequence that may lead to successive and different states of resilience (State 1, State 2, etc.) and the transition to a new state is in part governed by the perception of the community that a transition has occurred (Figure 9.1).

Perceptions of Change in Messy Social Ecological Systems

Perceptions of the environment held by people are an important filter in human behavior and decision-making with respect to the environment in which they exist (e.g., Golledge, 2008; Golledge & Stimson, 1997). Our attitudes, beliefs, culture, skills (both inherent and taught), and values inform the way we perceive the world around us, not least the environment, and as a consequence perceptions heavily influence adaptive responses to social-environmental change (Williams et al, 2018). This notion can be extended to social-ecological resilience on the basis that resilience as a process, particularly as a human process, is in large part governed by our perceptions of social and physical change affecting communities and landscapes and by our perceptions of perturbations that generate adversity for those communities and landscapes. Thus, perceptions of change are a fundamental part of multisystemic resilience, especially when viewed as a dynamic process.

While some resilience research has focused on technological, demographic, and economic factors that are associated with changing landscapes and adaptive responses, less attention has been given to identifying determinants of decisions and behavior by individuals (Adger & Vincent, 2005; Adger et al., 2009; Engle, 2011; Mimura et al., 2014). There appear to be individual and social characteristics, such as risk perception that, in tandem with values, form subjective limits to adaptive responses. Consideration of social cognition and its influence upon the perception of environmental change can contribute to a better understanding of the subjective limits to adaptation facilitating the communication of science-based information to improve adaptive capacity (Clayton et al., 2015; Grothmann & Patt, 2005; Kunda, 1990; Marx et al., 2007; Spence, Poortinga, & Pidgeon, 2012). The impact of environmental change can be considered a vague risk as those consequences are generally future oriented, uncertain, and frequently detached from individual relevance (Grunblatt & Alessa 2016; Hulme, 2009). Given these cognitive uncertainties, risk perception suggests that individuals may tend toward exploratory interpretations that bypass cognitive processes of logic and data assessment. Consequentially, perception may be based more on simplified representations that are formed through fast, intuitive, and unconscious information processing than on rational logic, probability, and utility (Slovic, Finucane, Peters, & MacGregor, 2004; Marx et al., 2007). Under this paradigm, an individual acquires general understanding of environmental change from diverse sources such as personal experience along with social media and networks (Myers et al., 2013). These diverse sources form an "affective pool" that contribute to heuristic decision making and replaces more deliberative and rational cognitive processes (Slovic et al., 2004). Accurate, fast intuitive perception is heavily modified, often degraded, through exposure to digital technology (Underwood, 2009). This is particularly pronounced in communities such as law enforcement, resource planning, and military and national intelligence (Roper, 1997).

The mental and perceptual processes that shape the way a person extracts information has been expressed in construal level theory (CLT; Liberman, Trope, McCrea, & Sherman, 2007). CLT establishes four dimensions of psychological distance (temporal, spatial, social, and certainty) and proposes that psychological distance contributes to how a person mentally forms perception. A larger psychological distance supports a more general and abstract construal while a smaller psychological distance supports more concrete construal and specific detail (Spence et al., 2012). Focusing on far-off concepts and abstract goals emphasizes the processing of psychologically distant information. As a consequence, a larger psychological distance promotes consideration of high-level abstractions and may lead to perceptions that are defined distinctively by an individual and that individual's values (Spence et al., 2012). Perception of change in the local environment can also be subject to cognitive biases due to an individual's attitudes and values (Kunda, 1990; Nickerson, 1998). CLT and cognitive biases suggest that rational cognition is typically circumvented in risk assessment and decision-making. An additional element is the Dunning–Kruger effect, whereby perception is eroded due to the inability to improve the accuracy of perception through seeking and incorporating diverse inputs into decision-making (Dunning, 2011). The influence of Dunning–Kruger is apparent, for example, in the U.S. intelligence community where a lack of qualifications makes individuals more susceptible to inaccurate perception (Alessa, Moon, Griffith, & Kliskey, 2018). Grothmann, Grecksch, Winges, & Siebenhuner, (2013) incorporate adaptation motivation (threat appraisal or risk perception) and adaptation belief (coping appraisal) to explain subjective human responses to natural hazard assessment in a model of institutional adaptive capacity. Adaptive motivation and adaptation belief are intended to represent psychological factors of adaptive capacity that result from the subjective perception of objective conditions.

One example in which the role of perceptions is manifested in systemic resilience as a process can be found in the manner in which the perceptions of environmental change held by natural resource managers correspond with documented measures of environmental change. Accurate perception of system change is considered a prerequisite for adaptive response in resilient systems (Weber, 1997). When there is disparity between perceptions of change and measured change there is a likelihood of an inappropriate or even maladaptive response to social-ecological changes—a condition termed the *difference*, or *delta*, between perceptions of environmental change and instrumented measures of environmental change, or P Δ I (Williams et al., 2018). This has been demonstrated in groups of natural resource managers with respect to changes in Pacific salmon fisheries in Alaska. Natural resource managers do not always accurately perceive change in the environment that is consistent with instrumented measures of change. While managers' perceptions of change were aligned with measured change for summer rainfall, land use development, and Chinook salmon size, their perceptions of change in summer and winter air temperature, stream temperature, and Chinook salmon abundance were disparate (Williams et al., 2018). Well-informed decisions and policies that are intended to support adaptive responses, and consequently enhance system resilience, are contingent on decision-makers accurately perceiving change. To the contrary, decisions are frequently made on perceptions rather than data (Robbins & Judge, 2013; Weber, 1997). The more accurately a change is perceived (P Δ I), the smaller the delta (Figure 9.2). Smaller deltas generally result in more accurate responses and thus better resilience outcomes. The process of perception and responses to environmental changes and the feedback of the consequences of these

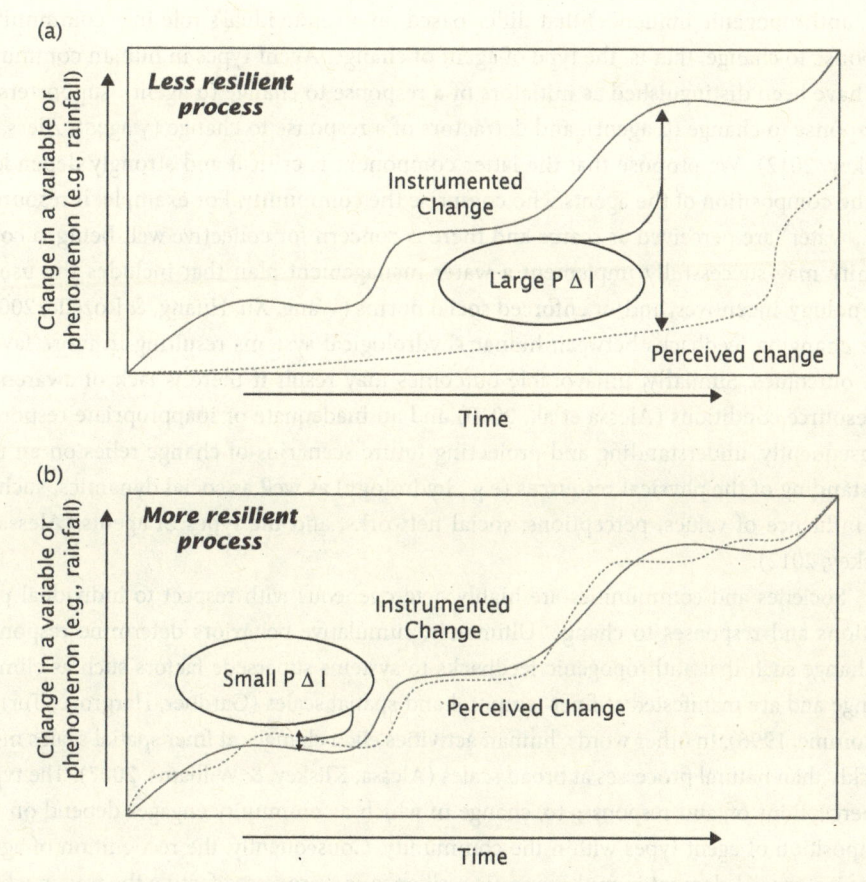

FIGURE 9.2 Difference between perceived change and measured change (P Δ I) as a factor in resilience as a process depicting: (a) Less resilient process and (b) more resilient process. Adapted from Williams et al. (2018).

actions constitutes a stable process. Thresholds of change, sometimes referred to as tipping points, can be avoided when P Δ I is small (Figure 9.2). When P Δ I is large response to environmental change is likely to be either delayed or nonexistent (Figure 9.2) giving rise to maladaptive responses (Williams et al., 2018).

Agent Types and Perceptions of Change

Historical and contemporary relationships between people and the changing environment in which they live can offer insights for anticipatory environmental modeling and management that promote social-ecological resilience, even under unfamiliar conditions of change. Changes in resource use patterns by people responding to their environments may affect feedbacks in resource availability and quality. Such feedbacks offer lessons on adaptive responses and have the potential to impact the resource use patterns of human communities (Wilbanks & Kates, 1999). The outcomes of adaptive responses are determined not only by inherent environmental conditions (Alessa et al., 2010), but also by social responses arising from perceptions about the need to adapt to environmental conditions (i.e., anthropogenic influence) that differ based on an individual's role in a community's response to change, that is, the type of agent of change. Agent types in human communities have been distinguished as initiators of a response to change (α agent), supporters of a response to change (β agent), and detractors of a response to change (γ agent; Alessa & Kliskey, 2012). We propose that the latter component is critical and strongly dependent on the composition of the agents who comprise the community. For example, if resources (e.g., water) are perceived as scarce and there is concern for collective well-being, a community may successfully implement a water management plan that includes the use of technology, incentives, and/or enforced social norms (Wang, Xu, Huang, & Rozelle, 2005), thus changing feedbacks between human–hydrological systems resulting in more favorable outcomes. Similarly, unfavorable outcomes may result if there is lack of awareness of resource conditions (Alessa et al., 2010) and an inadequate or inappropriate response. Consequently, understanding and projecting future scenarios of change relies on an understanding of the physical resources (e.g., hydrology) as well as social dynamics, such as the influence of values, perceptions, social networks, and the types of agents (Alessa & Kliskey, 2012).

Societies and communities are highly heterogeneous with respect to individual perceptions and responses to change. Ultimately, cumulative behaviors determine responses to change such that anthropogenic feedbacks to systems supersede factors such as climate change and are manifested at finer temporal and spatial scales (Gardner, Hargrove, Turner, & Romme, 1996). In other words, human activities elicit changes at finer spatial scales more quickly than natural processes at broad scales (Alessa, Kliskey, & Williams, 2007). The types of perceptions of, and responses to, change in which a community engages depend on the composition of agent types within the community. Consequently, the recognition of agent types is a crucial element in multisystemic resilience as a process, affecting the way in which adaptive responses develop and are implemented.

Technology-Induced Environmental Distancing

A further consequence of the role of perceptions on multisystemic resilience is found in the way in which technology affects perceptions. Overreliance on technology, whether it be GPS or water infrastructure, can impact the awareness of a person or a community to change in the environment (Alessa et al., 2007). For example, evidence suggests that community members in rapidly modernizing resource-dependent communities became desensitized to awareness, or perception, of change in river flow and water availability as a consequence of the installation of water technology (Alessa et al., 2007, 2009). This phenomenon is termed technology-induced environmental distancing (TIED). The ability to turn on a tap to have water reduces the effort involved in acquiring and using it and effectively increases the distance between the user and the water resource. This is tantamount to Aldo Leopold's caution on the "spiritual dangers . . . of supposing that breakfast comes from the grocery, and . . . that heat comes from the furnace" (Leopold, 1949, p. 12). That is, a decreased awareness of a resource, or distancing, can result from the adoption and use of technology. This TIED effect encumbers trade-offs between short- and long-term system resilience.

Testing the Resilience Process Using Technology as an Inhibitor

For all these reasons, human decision-making to promote resilience in SESs relies on a complex set of neurocognitive functions that have evolved through the need to integrate a range of complex landscape, situational, and social-emotional variables using both simple and advanced tools. Several studies are building a body of knowledge that support the hypothesis that technologies affect spatial reasoning (Iqbal & Lim, 2008) and our own studies and real-time, on-the-ground games have revealed that the use of digital technologies distances individuals from their environments, the TIED effect, and results in a larger delta and less accurate perception of change (Alessa et al., 2007; Williams et al., 2018). This process means that our increasing use of technology to sense our environment (perception phase of the resilience process; Figure 9.2) may exhibit an equilibrium where the very tools we use surpass their capacity to support accurate perception. Instead, they reduce our ability to make appropriate decisions in an on-the-ground context, particularly in noisy SESs. Several other studies have made correlations between exposure to unbuilt environments (e.g., natural and wilderness settings) and mental health and personal resilience (e.g., Bratman, Hamilton, & Daily, 2012). Our own pioneering work has demonstrated community-scale effects of the introduction of technologies into primarily subsistence-based social groups both in real and modeled worlds (Alessa et al., 2007, 2010). We propose that, in SESs, resilience as a process can be tested to (a) assess the range and types of TIED; (b) potential consequences of TIED in different populations (e.g., vulnerable); (c) reveal possible interventions that could mitigate and/or eliminate the TIED effect; and (d) protect and evolve the advantages of technologies that assist, rather than hinder, the resilience process (e.g., community-based observing networks and systems coupled with instrumented observing systems).

The concepts of P Δ I and TIED are both manifestations of the role of human perception in connoting awareness of the state of an SES and, consequently, in conferring multisystemic resilience. While there is still much that is not known about how perceptions held by individuals scale up to communities and other societal groups, perceptions are fundamental to the social fabric that engenders resilience as a dynamic process.

Conclusion

Resilience in SES is a multifaceted process that is derived from complexity theory—notably the idea of emergent behaviors that are an outcome of the network interactions that occur in the landscapes and communities of an SES. As a CAS, SESs operate near the threshold between complexity and chaos. SESs undergo three phases in the resilience process, affected by three factors: diversity, sensitivity, and mobility. These are exhibited as diversity in the means for sensing change, sensitivity of institutions to respond to perceived change, and the fluidity in responses by institutions to perceived change. Fundamental in this view of multisystemic resilience as a social process is the role of human perception and awareness of change in the environment. Perceptions of change held by individuals and communities are manifested in at least three effects. First, the P Δ I effect suggests that accurate perception of change with respect to measured change is a condition for appropriate response to change and decision-making. The limited studies to date on P Δ I indicate variability in the magnitude of P Δ I for individuals and groups highlighting how understanding multisystemic resilience as a process can contribute to different outcomes in response to change in SESs. Second, agent types presuppose that the collective ability of a community to perceive and respond to change is a consequence of the ratio of different roles assumed by individuals with respect to their capacity to perceive change and institute appropriate behaviors as a response. Third, the TIED effect shows how overdependence on technological tools and solutions may also afford a reduced ability to perceive change in the environment and consequently contribute to maladaptive responses and behavior. The TIED effect is potentially significant and should be incorporated into resilience research in the future. Technology is inherent in SESs and can lead to a transition in the trajectory of that SESs subject to accurate perception and decision-making, that is, the P Δ I effect. In summary, resilience is a social process rather than a state.

Key Messages

1. Resilience in SESs is a process governed by human perceptions rather than data, per se.
2. Perceptions in SESs are manifested in individual and group differences between the perceived change in the environment and the measured change in the environment.
3. Perceptions contribute to resilience in SESs through technology, particularly when technology acts as a barrier to awareness of, and response to, change.
4. Multisystemic resilience in SESs can be characterized as an iterative process involving consequences and outcomes of environmental change, the perception of those changes, and the detection and response to perceived change.

Acknowledgments

The authors acknowledge the support of the University of Idaho through the Center for Resilient Communities. The work was funded by the National Science Foundation (award numbers SES-1639524, PLR-1642847, SES-1856059, and PLR-1927713). Any opinions, findings, or recommendations expressed in this paper are those of the authors and the Center for Resilient Communities, and do not reflect the views of NSF.

References

Adger, W., & Vincent, K. (2005). Uncertainty in adaptive capacity. *Comptes Rendus Geoscience, 337*(4), 399–410. doi:10.1016/j.crte.2004.11.004

Adger, W., Dessai, S., Goulden, M., Hulme, M., Lorenzoni, I., Nelson, D., Naess, L., Wolf, J., & Wreford, A. (2009). Are there social limits to adaptation to climate change? *Climate Change, 93,* 335–354.

Alessa, L. & Kliskey, A. (2012). The role of agent types in detecting and responding to environmental change. *Human Organization, 71*(1), 1–10. doi:10.17730/humo.71.1.y7692065g232w1g1

Alessa, L., Kliskey, A., & Altaweel, M. (2009). Toward a typology of social-ecological systems. *Sustainability: Science, Practice, & Policy, 5*(1), 31–34. doi:10.1080/15487733.2009.11908026

Alessa, L., Kliskey, A., Gamble, J., Fidel, M., Beaujean, G., & Gosz, J. (2015). The role of Indigenous science and local knowledge in integrated observing systems: Moving toward adaptive capacity indices and early warning systems. *Sustainability Science, 11*(1), 91–102. doi:10.1007/s11625-015-0295-7

Alessa, L., Kliskey, A., & Williams, P. (2007). The distancing effect of modernization on the perception of water resources in Arctic communities. *Polar Geography, 30*(3-4), 175–191. doi:10.1080/10889370701742761

Alessa, L., Kliskey, A., & Williams, P. (2010). Forgetting freshwater: The effect of modernization on water values in remote Arctic communities. *Society and Natural Resources, 23*(3), 254–268. doi:10.1080/08941920802454813

Alessa, L., & Kropf, D. (1998). Role of F-actin in the establishment of developmental polarity in pelvetia compressa zygotes. *Development, 126*(1), 201–209.

Alessa, L., Moon, S., Griffith, D., & Kliskey, A. (2018). Operator driven policy: Deriving action from data using the quadrant-enabled Delphi (QED) method. *Homeland Security Affairs Journal, 14*(6). Retrieved from https://www.hsaj.org/articles/14586

Altaweel, M., Virapongse, A., Griffith, D., Alessa, L., & Kliskey, A. (2015). A typology for complex social-ecological systems in mountain communities. *Sustainability: Science, Practice and Policy, 11*(2), 1–13. doi:10.1080/15487733.2015.11908142

Anderies, J. M., Janssen, M. A., & Ostrom, E. (2007). A framework to analyze the robustness of social-ecological systems from an institutional perspective. *Ecology and Society, 9*(1), 18. Retrieved from http://www.ecologyandsociety.org/vol9/iss1/art18/

Banfield, E. (1959). Ends and means in planning. *International Social Science Journal, 11*(3), 1–8.

Bar-Yam, Y. (2003). *Dynamics of complex systems (Studies in nonlinearity).* Boulder, CO: Westview Press.

Basurto, X., Gelcich, S., & Ostrom, E. (2013). The social-ecological system framework as a knowledge classificatory system for benthic small-scale fisheries. *Global Environmental Change, 23*(6), 1366–1380. doi:10.1016/j.gloenvcha.2013.08.001

Berkes, F., & Folke, C. (1998). *Linking social and ecological systems: Management practices and social mechanisms for building resilience.* Cambridge, UK: Cambridge University Press.

Beroya-Eitner, M. (2016). Ecological vulnerability indicators. *Ecological Indicators, 60,* 329–334. doi:10.1016/j.ecolind.2015.07.001

Bolia, R., Vidulich, M., Nelosn, T., & Cook, M. (2007). A history lesson on the use of technology to support military decision making and command and control. In J. Noyes, M. Cook, & Y. Masakowski (Eds.), *Decision making in complex environments* (pp. 191–200). Aldershot, UK: Ashgate.

Bratman, G., Hamilton, J., & Daily, G. (2012). The impacts of nature experience on human cognitive function and mental health. *Annals of the New York Academy of Sciences, 1249*(1), 118–136. doi:10.1111/j.1749-6632.2011.06400.x

Chapin, F., Kofina, G., & Folke, C. (Eds.). (2009). *Principles of ecosystem stewardship: Resilience-based natural resources management in a changing world*. New York, NY: Springer.

Clayton, S., Devine-Wright, P., Stern, P., Whitmarsh, L., Carrico, A., Steg, L., . . . Bonnes, M. (2015). Psychological research and global climate change. *Nature Climate Change, 5*(7), 640–646. doi:10.1038/nclimate2622

Cutter, S., Barnes, L., Berry, M., Burton, C., & Evans, E. (2008). A place-based model for understanding community resilience to natural disasters. *Global Environmental Change, 18*(4), 598–606. doi:10.1016/j.gloenvcha.2008.07.013

Dekker, S. (2016). *Drift into failure: From hunting broken components to understanding complex systems*. London, UK: CRC Press.

Dunning, D. (2011). The Dunning-Kruger effect: On being ignorant of one's own ignorance. *Advances in Experimental Social Psychology, 44*, 247–296. doi:10.1016/B978-0-12-385522-0.00005-6

Engle, N. L. (2011) Adaptive capacity and its assessment. *Global Environmental Change, 21*(2), 647–656. doi:10.1016/j.gloenvcha.2011.01.019

Fortnow, L. (2009). The status of the P vs NP problem. *Communications of the ACM, 52*(9), 78–86. doi:10.1145/1562164.1562186

Gallopin, G. C. (2006). Linkages between vulnerability, resilience, and adaptive capacity. *Global Environmental Change, 16*(3), 293–303. doi:10.1016/j.gloenvcha.2006.02.004

Gardner, R., Hargrove, W., Turner, M., & Romme, W. (1996). Climate change, disturbances, and landscape dynamics. In B. H. Walker & W. L. Steffen (Eds.), *Global change and terrestrial ecosystems* (pp. 149–172). Cambridge, UK: Cambridge University Press.

Golledge, R. G. (2008). Behavioral geography and the theoretical/quantitative revolution. *Geographical Analysis, 40*(3), 239–257.

Golledge, R. G., & Stimson, R. J. (1997). *Spatial behavior: A geographic perspective*. New York, NY: Guilford Press.

Grothmann, T., Grecksch, K., Winges, M., & Siebenhüner, B. (2013). Assessing institutional capacities to adapt to climate change: Integrating psychological dimensions in the adaptive capacity wheel. *Natural Hazards and Earth System Science, 13*(12), 3369–3384.

Grothmann, T., & Patt, A. (2005). Adaptive capacity and human cognition: The process of individual adaptation to climate change. *Global Environmental Change, 15*(3), 199–213. doi:10.1016/j.gloenvcha.2005.01.002

Grunblatt, J., & Alessa, L. (2016). Role of perception in determining adaptive capacity. *Sustainability Science, 12*(1), 3–13. doi:10.1007/s11625-016-0394-0

Hardin, G. (1968). The tragedy of the commons. *Science, 162*(3859), 1243–1248.

Hinkel, J. (2011). Indicators of vulnerability and adaptive capacity: Towards a clarification of the science-policy interface. *Global Environmental Change, 21*(1), 198–208. doi:10.1016/j.gloenvcha.2010.08.002

Hulme, M. (2009). *Why we disagree about climate change: Understanding controversy, inaction and opportunity*. Cambridge, UK: Cambridge University Press.

Iqbal, M., & Lim, S. (2008). Legal and ethical implications of GPS vulnerabilities. *Journal of International Commercial Law and Technology, 3*(3), 178–187.

Jennings, N. (2000). On agent-based software engineering. *Artificial Intelligence, 117*(2), 277–296. doi:10.1016/S0004-3702(99)00107-1

Kliskey, A., Alessa, L., Wandersee, S., Williams, P., Powell, J., Wipfli, M., & Grunblatt, J. (2016). A science of integration: Frameworks, processes, and products in a place-based, integrative study. *Sustainability Science, 12*(2), 293–303. doi:10.1007/s11625-016-0391-3

Kunda, Z. (1990). The case for motivated reasoning. *Psychology Bulletin, 108*(3), 480–498. doi:10.1037/0033-2909.108.3.480

Lee, J., Nam, S., Kim, A., Kim, B., Lee, M., & Lee, S. (2013). Resilience: A meta-analytic approach. *Journal of Counseling & Development, 91*(3), 269–279. doi:10.1002/j.1556-6676.2013.00095.x

Leopold, A. (1949). *Sand County Almanac, and sketches here and there*. New York, NY: Oxford University Press.

Liberman, N., Trope, Y., McCrea, S., & Sherman, S. (2007). The effect of level of construal on the temporal distance of activity enactment. *Journal of Experimental Social Psychology, 43*(1), 143–149. doi:10.1016/j.jesp.2005.12.009

Marx, S., Weber, E., Orlove, B., Leiserowitz, A., Krantz, D., Roncoli, C., & Phillips, J. (2007). Communication and mental processes: Experiential and analytic processing of uncertain climate information. *Global Environmental Change, 17*(1), 47–58. doi:10.1016/j.gloenvcha.2006.10.004

Mercier, J. (2014). Equity, justice, and sustainable urban transportation in the twenty-first century. *Administrative Theory & Praxis, 31*(2), 145–163. doi:10.2753/ATP1084-1806310201

M'Hamdi, A., Memiche, M., Pla-Lopez, R., Ezzahra, F., Sidati, K., & Baz, O. (2017). A generic agent-based model of historical social behaviors change. In M. Nemiche & M. Essaidi (Eds.), *Advances in complex societal, environmental and engineered systems* (Series 18, pp. 31–49). Cham, Switzerland: Springer. doi:10.1007/978-3-319-46164-9_2

Mimura, N., Pulwarty, R., Duc, D., Elshinnawy, I., Redsteer, M., Huang, H., . . . Sanchez-Rodriguez, R. (2014). Climate change 2014: Impacts, adaptation, and vulnerability. In *Part A: global and sectoral aspects. Contribution of working group ii to the fifth assessment report of the intergovernmental panel on climate change* (pp. 869–898). Cambridge, UK: Cambridge University Press.

Motamedi, M., Iranmanesh, A., & Nazari, R. (2018). Quantitative assessment of resilience for earthen structures using coupled plasticity-damage model. *Engineering Structures, 172*(1), 700–711. doi:10.1016/j.engstruct.2018.06.050

Myers, T., Maibach, E., Roser-Renouf, C., Akerlof, K., & Leiserowitz, A. (2013). The relationship between personal experience and belief in the reality of global warming. *Nature Climate Change, 3*(4), 343–347. doi:10.1038/nclimate1754

Nemiche, M., M'Hamdi, A., Chakraoui, M., Cavero, V., & Pla-Lopez, R. (2013). A theoretical agent-based model to simulate an artificial social evolution. *Systems Research & Behavioral Science, 30*(6), 693–702. doi:10.1002/sres.2238

Nickerson, R. (1998). Confirmation bias: A ubiquitous phenomenon in many guises. *Review of General Psychology, 2*(2), 175–220.

O'Brien, G., & Hope, A. (2010). Localism and energy: Negotiating approaches to embedding resilience in energy systems. *Energy Policy, 38*(12), 7550–7558. doi:10.1016/j.enpol.2010.03.033

Olsson, L., Jerneck, A., Thoren, H., Persson, J., & O'Byrne, D. (2015). Why resilience is unappealing to social science: Theoretical and empirical investigations of the scientific use of resilience. *Science Advances, 1*(4), e1400217. doi:10.1126/sciadv.1400217

Ostrom, E. (1999). *Governing the commons: The evolution of institutions for collective action*. New York, NY: Cambridge University Press.

Ostrom, E. (2009). A general framework for analyzing sustainability of social-ecological systems. *Science, 325*(5939), 419–422. doi:10.1126/science.1172133

Resilience Alliance. (2010). *Assessing resilience in social-ecological systems: Workbook for practitioners* (Version 2.0). Retrieved from: https://www.resalliance.org/files/ResilienceAssessmentV2_2.pdf

Richardson, G. E. (2002). The metatheory of resilience and resiliency. *Journal of Clinical Pyschology, 58*(3), 307–321. doi:10.1002/jclp.10020

Robbins, S. P., & Judge, T. A. (2013). *Organizational behavior* (15th ed.). Boston, MA: Pearson Education.

Roper, D. (1997). Technology: Achilles heel or strategic vision. *Military Review, 77*(2), 87–92.

Scheffer, M., Dakos, V., & van Nes, E. (2015). Generic indicators of ecological resilience: Inferring the chance of a critical transition. *Annual Review of Ecology, Environment, & Systematics, 46*(1), 145–167. doi:10.1146/annurev-ecolsys-112414-054242

Schrodinger, E. (1944). *What is life? The physical aspect of the living cell*. Cambridge, UK: Cambridge University Press.

Sem, A. (2013). The ends and means of sustainability. *Journal of Human Development and Capabilities, 14*(1), 6–20. doi:10.1080/19452829.2012.747492

Shelton, C. (2011). The roots of analytic failures in the U.S. intelligence community. *International Journal of Intelligence and CounterIntelligence, 24*(4), 637–655. doi:10.1080/08850607.2011.598779

Slovic, P., Finucane, M., Peters, E., & MacGregor, D. (2004). Risk as analysis and risk as feelings: Some thoughts about affect, reason, risk, and rationality. *Risk Analysis*, 24(2), 311–322. doi:10.1111/j.0272-4332.2004.00433.x

Spence, A., Poortinga, W., & Pidgeon, N. (2012). The psychological distance of climate change: Psychological distance of climate change. *Risk Analysis*, 32(6), 957–972. doi:10.1111/j.1539-6924.2011.01695.x

Underwood, D. (2009). *The impact of digital technology: A review of the evidence of the impact of digital technologies on formal education*. Coventry, UK: Becta.

Ungar, M. (2018). Systemic resilience: Principles and processes for a science of change in contexts of adversity. *Ecology and Society*, 23(4), 36. doi:10.5751/ES-10385-230434

Wang, J., Xu, Z., Huang, J., & Rozelle, S. (2005). Incentives in water management reform: Assessing the effect on water use, production, and poverty in the Yellow River Basin. *Environment and Development Economics*, 10(6), 769–799. doi:10.1017/S1355770X05002524

Weber, E. U. (1997). Perception and expectation of climate change: Precondition for economic and technological adaptation. In M. Bazerman, D. Messick, A. Tenbrunsel, & K. Wade-Benzoni (Eds.), *Psychological perspectives to environmental and ethical issues in management* (pp. 314–341). San Francisco, CA: Jossey-Bass.

Wilbanks, T., & Kates, R. (1999). Global change in local places: How scale matters. *Climatic Change*, 43(3), 601–628.

Williams, P., Alessa, L., Kliskey, A., Rinella, D., Trammell, J., Powell, J., . . . Abatzoglou, J. (2018). The role of perceptions versus instrumented data of environmental change in decision-making: Implications for increasing adaptive capacity. *Environmental Science & Policy*, 90, 110–121. doi:10.1016/j.envsci.2018.09.018

Xu, L., & Marinova, D. (2013). Resilience thinking: A bibliometric analysis of socio-ecological research. *Scientometrics*, 96(3), 911–927. doi:10.1007/s11192-013-0957-0

Young, O. Berkhout, F., Gallopin, G., Janssen, M. A., Ostrom, E., & van der Leeuw, S. (2006). The globalization of socio-ecological systems: An agenda for scientific research. *Global Environmental Change*, 16(3), 304–316. doi:10.1016/j.gloenvcha.2006.03.004

Zegart, A. (2019). U.S. Intelligence Needs Another Reinvention. *The Atlantic*, September 11, 2019. https://www.theatlantic.com/ideas/archive/2019/09/us-intelligence-needs-another-reinvention/597787/

10
Social Ecology of Police Resilience

Mehdi Ghazinour and Arian Rostami

Introduction

Most of the research in the police field focuses on stress and traumatic events in policing as a predictive factor for developing negative outcomes (e.g., emotional disorder or alcohol abuse) in police officers' work. However, a underdeveloped field in police research focuses on positive and adaptive consequences, such as posttraumatic growth and resilience. Resilience on an individual level can act as a shield for police officers in dealing with the stressful environment of police work, thereby providing more effective police services. Fortunately, the literature on police resilience is increasing within the growing field of police science and researchers are exploring the police working environment, community policing, police training, and other related fields of police work (Andersen, Papazoglou, Arnetz, & Collins, 2015; Janssens, van der Velden, Taris, & van Veldhoven, 2018; Pandey, 2014). However, despite the interest in the construct of resilience within police research, there is still a lack of theoretical and operational models. In this chapter, we start by giving a brief overview of the context of police work and later the definition of police resilience. Thus far, the definition of resilience in policing has been strongly influenced by the disciplines of physiology and psychology. We attempt to go one step further and argue for a systemic model of police resilience, not only including individual physiology and psychology but also the organizational level and community policing.

The Context of Police Work

The first pioneering studies of policing by Banton (1964) and Rubinstein (1973) highlighted that the police officer acts not as a law enforcement officer but as a "peacekeeper," using discretion and by being problem-solving oriented. The picture of a police officer being a "philosopher" or "friend and guide" has changed over the years. Today, the main task of police forces is crime prevention and the safety and the security of citizens. Dijk, Hoogewoning, and Punch (2015) state that police organizations not only assume responsibility for crime prevention, but the police is also charged with other duties of a more social nature. Regulating traffic, keeping a watchful eye on unsafe buildings, administering first aid at accident sites, and school attendance duties are just a few examples of their many tasks on a small or large scale. The police are involved in international missions and must collaborate with other international agencies in combating drugs, smuggling, trafficking, and other crimes (Dijk et al., 2015). However, there are other processes involved in police work that are not visible at the first glancelike use of power, decision-making, or affect regulation. All of these examples and many other factors play an important role in how police officers manage everyday stress and conflicts.

Nowadyas stress represents a common experience in nearly all professions and the variety of sources, intensity, and frequency of stressors vary from job to job. Police work is recognized as being one of the most stressful professions, and the consequences of long-term stress among police officers has been well documented (Hartley, Burchfiel, Fekedulegn, Andrew, & Violanti, 2011; Violanti et al., 2006; Webster, 2013). Police officers' working conditions unually imply being on duty 24 hours a day. This means that police officers have to act in many different situations, whereas some situations require police officers to encounter potentially traumatic events such as involvement of firearm in crime situation or other type of violent confrontation with citizens.

Police Work and Stressors

Sources of possible stressors in Police work can be categorized as follows: (a) operational/situation-inherent stressors (e.g., interacting with vulnerable, abusive or hostile citizens, encountering danger, threats, or traumatic events) and (b) management/organizational stressors (e.g., bureaucratic policies and procedures, inadequate training, equipment and supervision, lack of organizational support, insufficient pay; Collins & Gibbs, 2003; Patterson, 2001; Violanti, 2014; Violanti et al., 2016). In their study, Violanti and Aron (1995) found that shooting a person in the line of duty, witnessing the loss of a fellow officer, exposure to physical/verbal attacks, and dealing with child abuse and violence were the most highly rated stressors by police officers. In another study by Gershon, Barocas, Canton, Li, and Vlahov (2009), exposure to critical incidents, workplace discrimination, lack of cooperation among co-workers, and job dissatisfaction significantly correlate with perceived work stress.

Both intensity and frequency of stressors are crucial in assessing the stressors and stress consequences of policing. The previously mentioned studies have reported highly rated stressors in police officers, although not their frequency. Violanti e al. (2016) indicated that the most highly rated and frequently occurring stressors in police officers were dealing with family disputes, responding to a felony in progress, lack of fellow officers' cooperation, making critical on-the-spot decisions, and insufficient manpower. Also, police officers indicated that exposure to battered or dead children, killing someone in the line of duty, a fellow officer killed in the line of duty, situations requiring the use of force, and physical attacks were perceived as most stressful. It is noteworthy that some of the top-rated stressors such as dealing with crimes related to children, killing someone in the line of duty, and losing a fellow officer had low prevalence, which shows the importance of considering the intensity and prevalence of stressors together. This finding also clarifies why different studies have demonstrated organizational stressors as being the main source of stress reported by police officers.

The organizational challenges and stressful job environment that police officers have to deal with can increase the risk of job burnout and negative consequences on different aspects of life such as psychological well-being (e.g., depression, anxiety, psychosomatic complaints, posttraumatic stress symptoms), physical health (e.g., cardiovascular disease, fatigue, back pain, insomnia, migraine), and behavioral aspects (e.g., aggression, alcohol use, family conflicts, spouse abuse, suicide attempts; Gershon et al., 2009; Kurtz, 2008). Besides other job characteristics such as shift work, long working hours, and absence from family, these negative effects can influence the interpersonal relationships of police officers, especially intimate relationships with their families (Roberts & Levenson, 2001; Taris, Kompier, Geurts, Houtman, & Van Den Heuvel, 2010). Research suggested that critical incidents and work-related stressors can lead officers to adopt dysfunctional behaviors such as avoidance (Pasillas, Follette, & Perumean-Chaney, 2006) and dissociation (Aaron, 2000) and suffer negative outcomes such as alcohol misuse (Swatt, Gibson, & Piquero, 2007), suicidal thoughts, or other psychiatric disorders (Stanley, Hom, & Joiner, 2016). Police officers are reported to have a high rate of alcohol consumption (Ballenger et al., 2011) and binge drinking (Weir, Stewart, & Morris, 2012), and their mortality rate resulting from alcoholic liver diseases is twice that of the general population (McNeill, 1996). Looking at research on police well-being, we can understand why the construct of resilience is psychologically oriented since the literature highlights the vulnerability of police officers.

Police Resilience: Toward a Multisystemic Definition

Summarizing the physio-psychological definition of resilience, two definitions of the construct are frequently used. Psychological resilience has been defined as the ability of an individual to rebound or recover from adversity (Leipold & Greve, 2009) or as the ability to maintain psychological and physical health despite exposure to a traumatic event. The definition of resilience in police work suggests enhancing the experience of well-being among individuals who face significant and chronic exposure to adversity and stressful events through, for example, physical training and self-awareness (Bonanno, 2004; de Terte, Stephens, & Hudleston, 2014). Resilience also includes the capacity of agencies and officers to "draw upon their own individual, collective, and institutional resources and competencies to cope with, adapt to, and develop from the demands, challenges, and changes encountered during and after a critical incident, mass emergency, or disaster" (Paton et al., 2008, p. 96). Paton and his colleagues are influenced by Antonovsky's definition of resilience. Based on Antonovsky's definition, they developed the stress shield police resilience model. The model assumes that the resilience of a person or group reflects the extent to which they can call upon their psychological and physical resources and competencies in ways that allow them to reduce challenging events in a coherent, manageable, and meaningful manner. The model suggests that a police officer's capacity to render challenging experiences meaningful, coherent, and manageable reflects the interaction of person, team, and organizational factors. This model is one step further toward a systems theory of police resilience, moving from an individual perspective to a multisystemic holistic lens. Ungar, Ghazinour and Richter (2013), drawing upon the work of Bronfenbrenner (1979) and Ungar (2008, 2011), developed a social-ecological interpretation of resilience that shifts focus from the invulnerable individual to the social-ecological factors that facilitate the development of well-being under stress.

Research examining the impact of societal, community, and other support systems on well-being has consistently shown that environments count more than individual biology or temperament with regards to psychosocial outcomes, especially when risk exposure is high (Ungar, 2018). The role of the environment in individual well-being is highly relevant to police officers and their profession, and we take this as our point of departure in proposing a systemic model of resilience in policing. An ecological approach to police resilience helps to conceptualize the police officers' social and physical ecologies, from individual support to workplace support, as well as the role of society's perceptions of the police—a system of factors that all account for successful development under adversity (Armeli, Eisenberger, Fasolo, & Lynch, 1998; Bartone, 2006; Goerling, 2012; Kamphuis & Delahaij, 2014; Paton et al., 2008).

The Social-Ecology of Resilience in Police Work

Ungar (2016) states that resilience of one system might be at the expense of the resilience of another system. Thus, applying a systemic resilience perspective in police work indicates how police officers influence their working environment and are influenced by simultaneous processes within the police organization and from the political level. In the following section, we focus on the three main levels of ecological police resilience presented in Figure 10.1.

Individual-Level Psychological and Physiological Factors

Studies reveal that constant and intense stress has physiological effects on the brain that cause psychophysiological, cognitive, and behavioral disorders (Pole, 2007; Yehuda, 2002). With regards to policing, resilience constitutes both *psychological* and *physiological* flexibility in the face of adversity (i.e., a conscious awareness of the best course of action and the best moment to take action), self-awareness, and control over one's physiological stress responses to threat and recovery from exposure beyond one's own control (Andersen, Gustafsberg, et al., 2015; Andersen, Papazoglou, Koskelainen, et al., 2015; Arnetz, Arble, Backman, Lynch, & Lublin, 2013; Arnetz, Nevedal, Lumley, Backman, & Lublin, 2009; Masten, 2014; McCraty & Atkinson, 2012). Importantly, police resilience includes the recognition of one's

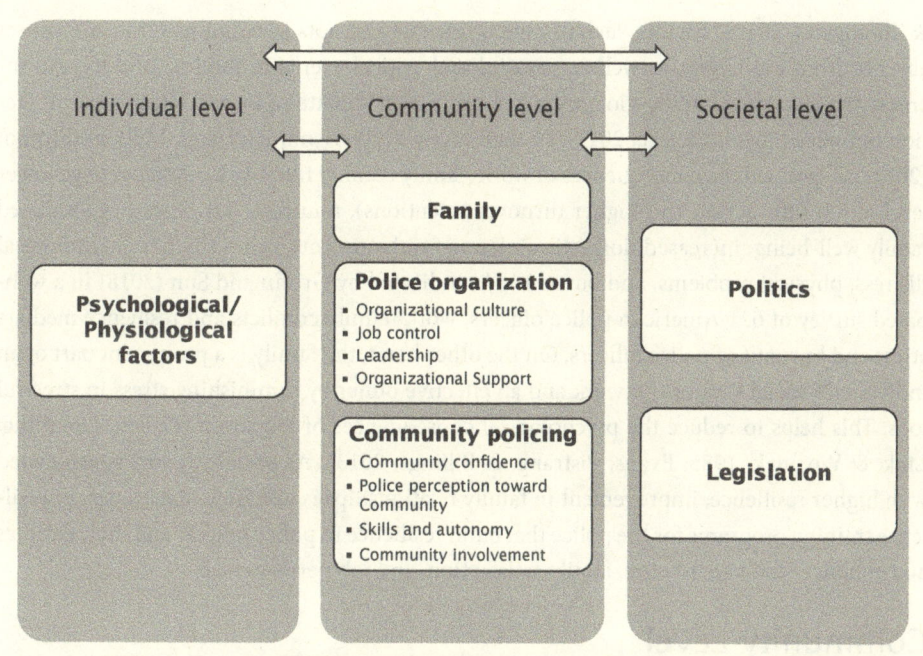

FIGURE 10.1 Main levels of ecological police resilience.

A diagram showing three levels: Individual level (Psychological/Physiological factors), Community level (Family; Police organization: Organizational culture, Job control, Leadership, Organizational Support; Community policing: Community confidence, Police perception toward Community, Skills and autonomy, Community involvement), and Societal level (Politics, Legislation).

limitations—both physical and mental; the reality-based awareness of one's strengths and weaknesses and the knowledge of when to ask for support and assistance and when to soldier on alone (Andersen, Papazoglou, Arnetz, et al., 2015).

However, because police officers are constantly asked to deal with increasingly complex and threatening incidents, it is appropriate to expand the scope of this definition to include the development of a police officer's capacity to deal with future events. Consequently, the definition adopted here embodies the notion of "adaptive capacity" (Klein, Nicholls, & Thomalla, 2003). According to this definition, some activities—including imagery exposure to potential stressors, practicing adaptive responses when facing stressful events, and the frequent practice of both exposure and skills—can prevent stressful psychological outcomes and increase resilience to trauma and improve behavioral performance (Arnetz et al., 2013).

The Family

Job stress and demands at home have direct and indirect effects on the well-being and performance of police officers (Peeters, Montgomery, Bakker, & Schaufeli, 2005). Family-based conflicts have a significant relationship to burnout in police officers. Also, police work pressure and burnout increase the level of conflict within the family and reduces police officers' interest in family issues, spent time with the family, and marital satisfaction (Jackson & Maslach, 1982; Roberts & Levenson, 2001). A longitudinal study of 257 Australian police officers at two points, 12 months apart, delineated the relationship between work demands, emotional exhaustion, and work–family conflicts. The demands of police work and emotional exhaustion can cause work–family conflicts; also job demands can lead to emotional exhaustion as mediated by work–family conflicts (Hall, Dollard, Tuckey, Winefield,

& Thompson, 2010). Factors such as shift work that disrupts sleeping patterns and causes absence from the family, as well as stressful and critical events in the line of duty, can increase the level of domestic violence, alcoholism, suicide attempts, and family overprotection in police officers (Burke, 2017). In their study, Culbertson, Huffman, Mills, and Imhof (2017) categorized the consequences of work–family conflict into work outcomes (e.g., lower level of job satisfaction and higher turnover intentions), nonwork outcomes (e.g., reduced family well-being, increased domestic violence), and stress outcomes (higher psychological distress, physical problems, and burnout). As indicated by Griffin and Sun (2018) in a web-based survey of 621 American police officers, work–family conflicts and resilience mediate stress and burnout of police officers. On the other hand, the family is a prominent part of an individual's social support network and an effective buffer by diminishing stress in stressful jobs. This helps to reduce the psychological consequences of job strain (Cullen, Lemming, Link, & Wozniak, 1985; Evans, Pistrang, & Billings, 2013). As social support is associated with higher resilience, improvement in family relationships is therefore a main part of resilience training programs for the police that build resilience in police officers and their families and enhances their well-being, family satisfaction, and job performance.

Community Level

According to our proposed model, the mesosystem of police work comprises of two components whereby each relates to individual resilience and, in another direction, are also influenced by macro level factors. These two components are organizational factors and community policing. We start by giving a brief description of police organization and then about police community resilience.

Several studies have determined that organizational stressors are a more significant source of stress than operational stressors and critical incidents in police work (Biggam, Power, Macdonald, Carcary, & Moodie, 1997; Falconer, Alexander, & Klein, 2013; Kop, Euwema, & Schaufeli, 1999; Shane, 2010). The interaction between workplace environment and well-being of police officers influences the function of both sides and has consequences for effective policing. Thus, building resilience in police officers and the policing organization is crucial for surviving and thriving amid growing changes and disturbances in police work.

The concept of a healthy organization was introduced by Lim and Murphy (2010) as "one whose culture, climate and practices create an environment that promotes employee health and safety as well as organizational effectiveness" (p. 64). Lowe (2010) described positive cultures, inclusive leadership, vibrant workplaces, and inspired employees as the four fundamental building blocks of a healthy organization.

Thus, we categorize the main effective elements in interactions between organization and police officers as follows. *Organizational culture* is defined as the shared values and norms within the police force, such as traditions of the organization, moral norms of the staff, positive or negative experiences, relationships between individuals in the organization, work atmosphere, relationship between leaders and officers, and other invisible elements that shape the culture (Elekes, 2014). Organizational culture affects the level of trust through interpersonal and organizational relationships and consequently increases the effectiveness of personal and organizational interactions and teamwork, which is associated with empowerment of the police officers (Dirks, 1999; Siegrist & Cvetkovich, 2000). Working in a trusting and fostering environment increases organizational effectiveness, has positive impacts on job satisfaction, commitment (Laschinger, Finegan, Shamian, & Casier, 2000; Laschinger, Finegan, & Shamian, 2002) and the physical and mental health of the organizational members (Tănase, Manea, Chraif, Anței, & Coblaș, 2012).

According to the job demands-resources model (Bakker & Demerouti, 2007; Demerouti, Bakker, Nachreiner, & Schaufeli, 2001), job resources such as equality, social support of colleagues, job security and participation in decision-making are job characteristics that are functional in achieving work goals, reducing job demands, improving personal development, well-being and life satisfaction (Bakker & Demerouti, 2007; Demerouti et al., 2001; Salmela-Aro, & Upadyaya, 2018).

Job security and participation in decision-making are two of the most important aspects of work-related resources (Bakker, Demerouti, & Verbeke, 2004; Crawford, LePine, & Rich, 2010), under the broad conceptual framework of "job control" (Schieman & Reid, 2009). Job control has been defined as an individual's potential control over the pace and content of work tasks (Karasek & Theorell, 1990). In line with Karasek and Theorell (1990), disparity between perceived job demands and job control can lead to emotional stress and illness. A low level of job control, particularly in combination with high job demands (demanding job), negatively impacts the mental health of employees (Bentley, Kavanagh, Krnjacki, & LaMontagne, 2015; Dalgard et al., 2009). Police officers have broad discretionary powers to achieve the goals and accomplish the tasks that the police are supposed to perform (Lipsky, 2010). Stress and poor mental health influence the judgment and decision-making of police officers by affecting their cognitive functions and capacities (Gutshall, Hampton, Sebetan, Stein, & Broxtermann, 2017; Starcke & Brand, 2012), which can lead to maladaptive behaviors or police misconduct.

Police management plays a key role in empowering the work environment by translating organizational culture into daily values and procedures. Management based on supportive and officer-centered leadership practices creates an empowering environment (Liden, Wayne, & Sparrowe, 2000; Quinn, & Spreitzer, 1997). In highly demanding professions where individuals have to deal with extreme work-related stressors and hazards, leaders play a pivotal role in the way in which stressful experiences are perceived and interpreted by team members (Bartone, 2006). Based on the model of psychological resilience for the Netherlands Armed Forces, Kamphuis and Delahaij (2014) indicate that organizational leadership and information provision by the organization are the most important factors before and during operations that affect the resilience of armed forces officers. Schafer (2010) studied the characteristics of effective leadership among 1,042 police supervisors attending the Federal Bureau of Investigations National Academy in Virginia. According to their findings, honesty and integrity, communication skills, leadership by example, delegation and empowerment, promoting innovation and growth, taking appropriate action, establishing and maintaining trust and fairness, and organizational justice were reported as being the main characteristics of effective leadership. The organizational stressors that need to be considered by police managers include authoritarian management, lack of administrative support, inept and apathetic supervision, inappropriate work schedules, excessive paperwork, insufficient wages and resources, and race and gender issues (Kyle & Schafer, 2017). The application of an appropriate stress management approach to identify stressors in the work environment and reduce them to create a healthy organizational environment are necessary for effective leadership (Ayres & Flanagan, 1990; Kyle & Schafer, 2017) that contributes to a more resilient police workforce.

Organizational support is a crucial resource that influences the performance, effectiveness, and socioemotional needs of officers (Adebayo, 2005; Armeli et al., 1998; Currie & Dollery, 2006). Perceived organizational support is the degree to which employees believe their organization values their contribution and cares about their well-being and needs (Eisenberger, Huntington, Hutchison, & Sowa, 1986). Organizational support can reduce the general level of stress and psychological and psychosomatic reactions to stressors through the availability of tangible and emotional support when facing pressure at work. With this regard, organizational support is very useful in reducing severe consequences of stressors at work (George, Reed, Ballard, Colin, & Fielding, 1993; Rhoades & Eisenberger, 2002). In a quantitative study in the Indian state of Haryana on job demands and resources among 827 police officers, Frank, Lambert, and Qureshi (2017) concluded that organizational support represent a main job resource for mitigating work stress.

Community Policing

Community policing is a philosophy for reducing conflict and crime in communities by promoting trust, respect, and collaboration between the police and the members of a community (Nicholl, 2000). In community policing, the combination of police expertise and community knowledge and resources has been applied to define, prioritize, and address crime problems (Weisburd & McElroy, 1998). By collaborating with the community, the police focus on the main concerns of the community and underlying causes of problems to find a solution and act proactively. Studies show the important benefits of community policing for communities and the police (Roh & Oliver, 2005; Xu, Fielder, & Flaming, 2005). Police–community relations and public confidence have been improved through the implementation of community policing (Cordner, 2000; Kuo & Shih, 2018; Skogan, 2006). Several studies indicated that officers who are involved in community policing have a more positive perception of the community and residents. The positive view can be explained by day-to-day collaboration with individuals from the general public rather than dealing with problematic individuals, as well as the community's trust and positive perception of the police (Skolnick & Bayley, 1988; Trojanowicz & Bucqueroux, 1998). Thus, complete and consistent implementation of community policing was associated with higher job satisfaction in police officers (Brody, DeMarco, & Lovrich, 2002; Kuo & Shih, 2018). Community policing encourages police officers to apply their skills and experiences creatively and perceive their role as more valuable (Pelfrey, 2004; Skolnick & Bayley, 1988). Although there is a lack of evidence regarding the impact of community policing on police officers' well-being, a higher level of job satisfaction, collaborative relationship with the community, perceived support from the community, and a positive community attitude toward the role of police and legitimacy can influence different aspects of police officers' health and promote their well-being (Basinska & Dåderman, 2019; Deschênes, Desjardins, & Dussault, 2018; Kohan & O'Connor, 2002). Community involvement and active participation in community-oriented policing empowers the police and the community to recognize and respond to concerns and to develop a resilient community (Pandey, 2014).

Community-oriented policing also helps to promote community cohesion. Community cohesion has been defined as the extent to which community members bond with shared common interests and goals, a sense of belonging and collective identity, collective knowledge, understanding, and trust. In a cohesive community, people from diverse backgrounds and circumstances are valued and respected, people from different backgrounds have the same life opportunities, and community members share a sense of belonging and have strong relationships with each other (Local Government Association, 2002). Community cohesion leads to mobilization and prepares community members to collaborate in interventions against common problems such as conflicts and tensions between different groups, crime, or environmental issues. Various studies show that higher levels of community cohesion are associated with a lower risk of individual violent victimization and crime rates (Hirschfield & Bowers, 1997; Lee, 2000; Olutola & Bello, 2016). In addition, a number of studies demonstrated the significant link between the community cohesion and resilience (Ludin, Rohaizat, & Arbon, 2019; Patel & Gleason, 2018). Community resilience refers to the capacity of a community to survive, respond to, and recover from adverse events and community cohesion plays a key role in this process.

Law and Police Resilience

The police are key actors in the security sector and the only actor with the legitimacy to use power in the public context. Legislation and constant control mechanisms from legislative and regulatory sections are necessary to supervise the police (Council of Europe, 2002; United Nations Office on Drugs and Crime, 2011). Thus, we believe that beyond individual, team, and organizational factors, there is a need to add societal factors such as laws and regulations to the police resilience model.

At the macrosystem level, the government establishes the missions, general priorities, regulations and police budget and has control over police actions (Reiner, 2010). Political and social changes and/or establishing new legislation on a governmental level from judicial, administrative, and legislative authorities affect police actions on both organizational and individual levels. A few studies on police stress have considered broader aspects of job stress and described societal and political changes as being important sources of stress in police officers, which influence them through altering organizational policies and rules (Kara, Sunger, & Kapti, 2015; Saunders, Kotzias, & Ramchand, 2019).

Indeed, police forces have the legal authority to intervene directly in citizens' lives and defend or attack citizens' freedom or even their lives. Maintaining public order and security, ensuring public protection, providing assistance, preventing crime, solving crimes, monitoring public order and safety, conducting reconnaissance, and carrying out criminal investigations are other types of police work in which legitimacy and the use of power and discretion take place (Hansson, Ghazinour, & Wimelius, 2015). According to Lipsky's (2010) framework, street-level bureaucrats are "public service workers who directly interact with citizens in the course of their jobs, and who have substantial discretion in their execution of their work" (p. 3). He argued that discretion involves a balance between implementing societal rules and legislation and being sensible and flexible to the needs of citizens and the general public. Operationalizing discretion means that the police make independent priorities and interpretations, disregard rules, and invent praxises (Hansson et al., 2015). Finding a balance between police professionalism and serving the state and serving the public is crucial to appropriate policing (United Nations Office on Drugs and Crime, 2011). Keeping this balance might place extra pressure on police organization and police officers, especially if there is a contradiction between the organizational policy and individuals' principles.

Conclusion

Our point of departure is that three main systems interact with each other to maintain equilibrium in the face of adversity as overall terms of resilience in the police force: (a) each system influences the other, and there is a reciprocal relationship between them; (b) each of the systems comprises a certain level of resilience; and (c) each system comprises a number of visible and invisible processes that create a synergy effect in the other systems.

Research showed that police work is one of the most stressful professions in the world and officers often suffer from a variety of physiological, psychological, and behavioral symptoms (Manzella & Papazoglou, 2014; McCraty & Atkinson, 2012). For this reason, the need to develop a resilience-building program is crucial for this professional group. McCraty and Atkinson (2012) conducted a resilience training study on police officers and determined effectiveness of the program by assessing well-being, stress coping skills, work performance, family relationships, and physiological changes (heart rate and blood pressure) following severe stressors in police officers. Their results indicated that a resilience-building training can improve officers' reactions to stressors from different sources. Applying practical stress and emotion self-regulation skills by police officers can decrease negative physiological and psychological consequences of stress and positively influence both personal and occupational aspects of their lives. However, enhancing the capacity of individual resources through a resilience program without accessing working environment resources and policies that protect police officers reduces the ability to negotiate for resources to be provided in culturally meaningful ways. Therefore, a multisystemic social-ecological theory should be applied to resilience programs to increase police officers' resilience by empowering police officers, their families, and police organization, as well as considering police-related policies and laws.

Key Messages

- There is a great emphasis on psychological and physiological resilience in the police profession. There is a great need for a transformation from an individual perspective toward a multisystem approach.
- Multisystem resilience in police work requires balancing the demands of different systems on police officers and their organizations.

- A multisystemic resilience perspective should be applied to the development of resilience-promoting programs for police officers.

References

Aaron, J. D. (2000). Stress and coping in police officers. *Police Quarterly, 3*(4), 438–450.

Adebayo, D. O. (2005). Ethical attitudes and prosocial behavior in the Nigerian police: Moderator effects of perceived organizational support public recognition. *Policing: An International Journal of Police Strategies & Management, 28*(4), 684–705. doi:10.1108/13639510510628767

Andersen, J. P., Gustafsberg, H., Papazoglou, K., Nyman, M., Koskelainen, M., & Pitel, M. (2015, August). *A potentially lifesaving psychophysiological intervention for special forces officers.* Poster presented at the annual conference of the American Psychosomatic Society, Savannah, GA.

Andersen, J. P., Papazoglou, K., Arnetz, B. B., & Collins, P. (2015). Mental preparedness as a pathway to police resilience and optimal functioning in the line of duty. *International Journal of Emergency Mental Health and Human Resilience, 17*(3), 624–627.

Andersen, J. P., Papazoglou, K., Koskelainen, M., Nyman, M., Gustafsberg, H., & Arnetz, B. B. (2015). Applying resilience. Promotion training among special forces police officers. *Journal of Police Emergency Response, 5*(2), 1–8. doi:10.1177/2158244015590446

Armeli, S., Eisenberger, R., Fasolo, P., & Lynch, P. (1998). Perceived organizational support and police performance: The moderating influence of socioemotional needs. *Journal of Applied Psychology, 83*(2), 288–297. doi:10.1037//0021-9010.83.2.288

Arnetz, B. B., Nevedal, D. C., Lumley, M. A., Backman, L., & Lublin, A. (2009). Trauma resilience training for police: Psychophysiological and performance effects. *Journal of Police and Criminal Psychology, 24*(1), 1–9. doi:10.1007/s11896-008-9030-y

Arnetz, B. B., Arble, E., Backman, L., Lynch, A., & Lublin, A. (2013). Assessment of a prevention program for work-related stress among urban police officers. *International Archives of Occupational and Environmental Health, 86*(1), 79–88. doi:10.1007/s00420-012-0748-6

Ayres, R., & Flanagan, G. (1990). *Preventing law enforcement stress: The organization's role.* Washington, DC: Bureau of Justice Assistance, U.S. Department of Justice.

Bakker, A. B., & Demerouti, E. (2007). The job demands-resources model: State of the art. *Journal of Managerial Psychology, 22*(3), 309–328. doi:10.1108/02683940710733115

Bakker, A. B., Demerouti, E., & Verbeke, W. (2004). Using the job demands-resources model to predict burnout and performance. *Human Resource Management, 43*(1), 83–104. doi:10.1002/hrm.20004

Ballenger, J. F., Best, S. R., Metzler, T. J., Wasserman, D. A., Mohr, D. C., Liberman, A., . . . Marmar, C. R. (2011). Patterns and predictors of alcohol use in male and female urban police officers. *The American Journal on Addictions, 20*, 21–29. doi:10.1111/j.1521-0391.2010.00092.x

Banton, M. (1964). *The policeman in community.* London, UK: Tavistock.

Bartone, P. T. (2006). Resilience under military operational stress: Can leaders influence hardiness? *Military Psychology, 18*(Suppl.), 131–148. doi:10.1207/s15327876mp1803s_10

Basinska, B. A., & Dåderman, A. M. (2019). Work values of police officers and their relationship with job burnout and work engagement. *Frontiers in Psychology, 10*, 442. doi:10.3389/fpsyg.2019.00442

Bentley, R. J., Kavanagh, A., Krnjacki, L., & LaMontagne, A. D. (2015). A longitudinal analysis of changes in job control and mental health. *American Journal of Epidemiology, 182*(4), 328–334. doi:10.1093/aje/kwv046

Biggam, F. H., Power, K. G., Macdonald, R. R., Carcary, W. B., & Moodie, E. (1997). Self-perceived occupational stress and distress in a Scottish police force. *Work & Stress, 11*(2), 118–133. doi:10.1080/02678379708256829

Bonanno, G. A. (2004). Loss, trauma, and human resilience: Have we underestimated the human capacity to thrive after extremely aversive events? *American Psychologist, 59*(1), 20–28. doi:10.1037/0003-066X.59.1.20

Brody, D. C., DeMarco, C., & Lovrich, N. P. (2002). Community policing and job satisfaction: Suggestive evidence of positive workforce effects from a multijurisdictional comparison in Washington State. *Police Quarterly, 5*(2), 181–205. doi:10.1177/109861102129198093

Bronfenbrenner, U. (1979). *The ecology of human development: Experiments by nature and design.* Cambridge, MA: Harvard University Press.

Burke, R. J. (2017). Stress in policing: An overview. In R. J. Burke (Ed.), *Stress in policing* (pp. 3–27). New York, NY: Routledge.

Collins, P. A., & Gibbs, A. C. C. (2003). Stress in police officers: A study of the origins, prevalence and severity of stress-related symptoms within a county police force. *Occupational Medicine, 53*(4), 256–264. doi:10.1093/occmed/kqg061

Cordner, G. (2000). Community policing: Elements and effects. In G. Alpert & A. Piquero (Eds.), *Community policing: Contemporary readings* (pp. 401–418). Chicago, IL: Waveland Press.

Council of Europe. (2002). *The European code of police ethics.* Strasbourg, France: Council of Europe Publishing.

Crawford, E. R., LePine, J. A., & Rich, B. L. (2010). Linking job demands and resources to employee engagement and burnout: A theoretical extension and meta-analytic test. *Journal of Applied Psychology, 95*(5), 834–848. doi:10.1037/a0019364

Culbertson, S. S., Huffman, A. H., Mills, M. J., & Imhof, C. B. (2017). Balancing the badge: Work-family challenges within policing and recommended supports and interventions. In R. J. Burke (Ed.), *Stress in policing* (pp. 66–94). New York, NY: Routledge.

Cullen, F. T., Lemming, T., Link, B. G., & Wozniak, J. F. (1985). The impact of social supports on police stress. *Criminology, 23*(3), 503–522.

Currie P., & Dollery B. (2006). Organizational commitment and perceived organizational support in the NSW police. *Policing: An International Journal of Police Strategies & Management, 29*(4), 741–756. doi:10.1108/13639510610711637

Dalgard, O. S., Sorensen, T., Sandanger, I., Nygård, J. F., Svensson, E., & Reas, D. L. (2009). Job demands, job control, and mental health in an 11-year follow-up study: Normal and reversed relationships. *Work & Stress, 23*(3), 284–296. doi:10.1080/02678370903250953

Demerouti, E., Bakker, A. B., Nachreiner, F., & Schaufeli, W. B. (2001). The job demands-resources model of burnout. *Journal of Applied Psychology, 86*(3), 499–512. doi:10.1037/0021-9010.86.3.499

Deschênes, A. A., Desjardins, C., & Dussault, M. (2018). Psychosocial factors linked to the occupational psychological health of police officers: Preliminary study. *Cogent Psychology, 5*(1), 1426271. doi:10.1080/23311908.2018.1426271

de Terte, I., Stephens, C., & Huddleston, L. (2014). The development of a three part model of psychological resilience. *Stress and Health, 30*(5), 416–424. doi:10.1002/smi.2625

Dijk, A., Hoogewoning, F., & Punch, M. (2015). *What matters in policing? Change, values and leadership in turbulent times.* Chicago, IL: Bristol University Press.

Dirks, K. T. (1999). The effects of interpersonal trust on work group performance. *Journal of Applied Psychology, 84*, 445–455.

Eisenberger, R., Huntington, R., Hutchison, S., & Sowa, D. (1986). Perceived organizational support. *Journal of Applied Psychology, 71*, 500–507. doi:10.1037/0021-9010.71.3.500

Elekes, E. (2014). An examination of the organizational culture at the policing. *APSTRACT: Applied Studies in Agribusiness and Commerce, 8*, 43–50. doi:10.22004/ag.econ.187527

Evans, R., Pistrang, N., & Billings, J. (2013). Police officers' experiences of supportive and unsupportive social interactions following traumatic incidents. *European Journal of Psychotraumatology, 4*(1), 19696. doi:10.3402/ejpt.v4i0.19696

Falconer, M., Alexander, D. A., & Klein, S. (2013). *Resilience and wellbeing in a Scottish police force.* Scottish Institute for Policing Research, SIPR Report-November 2013.

Frank, J., Lambert, E. G., & Qureshi, H. (2017). Examining police officer work stress using the job demands-resources model. *Journal of Contemporary Criminal Justice, 33*(4), 348–367.

George, J. M., Reed, T. F., Ballard, K. A., Colin, J., & Fielding, J. (1993). Contact with AIDS patients as a source of work-related distress: Effects of organizational and social support. *Academy of Management Journal, 36*(1), 157–171. doi:10.5465/256516

Gershon, R. R., Barocas, B., Canton, A. N., Li, X., & Vlahov, D. (2009). Mental, physical, and behavioral outcomes associated with perceived work stress in police officers. *Criminal Justice and Behavior, 36*(3), 275–289. doi:10.1177/0093854808330015

Goerling, R. J. (2012). Police officer resilience and community building. *ASBBS Proceedings, 19*(1), 394–397.

Griffin, J. D., & Sun, I. Y. (2018). Do work-family conflict and resiliency mediate police stress and burnout: A study of state police officers. *American Journal of Criminal Justice, 43*(2), 354–370. doi:10.1007/s12103-017-9401-y

Gutshall, C. L., Hampton, D. P., Jr., Sebetan, I. M., Stein, P. C., & Broxtermann, T. J. (2017). The effects of occupational stress on cognitive performance in police officers. *Police Practice and Research, 18*(5), 463–477. doi:10.1080/15614263.2017.1288120

Hall, G. B., Dollard, M. F., Tuckey, M. R., Winefield, A. H., & Thompson, B. M. (2010). Job demands, work-family conflict, and emotional exhaustion in police officers: A longitudinal test of competing theories. *Journal of Occupational and Organizational Psychology, 83*(1), 237–250. doi:10.1348/096317908X401723

Hansson, J., Ghazinour, M., & Wimelius, M. E. (2015). Police officers' use of discretion in forced repatriations of unaccompanied, asylum-seeking refugee children—Balancing efficiency and dignity. *International Journal of Social Work and Human Services Practice, 3*(3), 101–108. doi:10.13189/ijrh.2015.030301

Hartley, T. A., Burchfiel, C. M., Fekedulegn, D., Andrew, M. E., & Violanti, J. M. (2011). Health disparities in police officers: Comparisons to the US general population. *International Journal of Emergency Mental Health, 13*(4), 211.

Hirschfield, A., & Bowers, K. J. (1997). The effect of social cohesion on levels of recorded crime in disadvantaged areas. *Urban Studies, 34*(8), 1275–1295. doi:10.1080/0042098975637

Jackson, S. E., & Maslach, C. (1982). After-effects of job-related stress: Families as victims. *Journal of Organizational Behavior, 3*(1), 63–77. doi:10.1002/job.4030030106

Janssens, K. M., van der Velden, P. G., Taris, R., & van Veldhoven, M. J. (2018). Resilience among police officers: A critical systematic review of used concepts, measures, and predictive values of resilience. *Journal of Police and Criminal Psychology*, 1–17. doi:10.1007/s11896-018-9298-5

Kamphuis, W., & Delahaij, R. (2014, January). *The relevance of resources for resilience at different organizational levels within the military deployment cycle*. Paper presented at the 5th Symposium on Resilience Engineering: Managing Trade-Offs, Soesterberg, Netherlands.

Kara, H. B., Sunger, E., & Kapti, A. (2015). Police stress factors among law enforcement agencies: A comparison study of US and Turkish police. *European Scientific Journal, 11*(4), 82–94.

Karasek, R., & Theorell, T. (1990). *Healthy work: Stress, productivity, and the reconstruction of working life*. New York. NY: Basic Books.

Klein, R. J., Nicholls, R. J., & Thomalla, F. (2003). Resilience to natural hazards: How useful is this concept? *Global Environmental Change Part B: Environmental Hazards, 5*(1), 35–45. doi:10.1016/j.hazards.2004.02.001

Kohan, A., & O'Connor, B. P. (2002). Police officer job satisfaction in relation to mood, wellbeing, and alcohol consumption. *The Journal of Psychology, 136*(3), 307–318. doi:10.1080/00223980209604158

Kop, N., Euwema, M., & Schaufeli, W. (1999). Burnout, job stress and violent behaviour among Dutch police officers. *Work & Stress, 13*(4), 326–340. doi:10.1080/02678379950019789

Kuo, S. Y., & Shih, Y. C. (2018). An evaluation of a community-oriented policing program in Taiwan. *International Journal of Offender Therapy and Comparative Criminology, 62*(7), 2016–2044. doi:10.1177/0306624X17703719

Kurtz, D. L. (2008). Controlled burn: The gendering of stress and burnout in modern policing. *Feminist Criminology, 3*(3), 216–238. doi:10.1177/1557085108321672

Kyle, M. J., & Schafer, J. A. (2017). Effective leadership in policing. In R. J. Burke (Ed.), *Stress in policing* (pp. 295–308). New York, NY: Routledge.

Laschinger, H. K. S., Finegan, J., & Shamian, J. (2002). The impact of workplace empowerment, organizational trust on staff nurses' work satisfaction and organizational commitment. In *Advances in health care management* (pp. 59–85). Bingley, UK: Emerald Group. doi:10.1016/S1474-8231(02)03006-9

Laschinger, H. K. S., Finegan, J., Shamian, J., & Casier, S. (2000). Organizational trust and empowerment in restructured healthcare settings: Effects on staff nurse commitment. *Journal of Nursing Administration, 30*(9), 413–425.

Lee, M. R. (2000). Community cohesion and violent predatory victimization: A theoretical extension and cross-national test of opportunity theory. *Social Forces, 79*(2), 683–706. doi:10.1093/sf/79.2.683

Leipold, B., & Greve, W. (2009). Resilience: A conceptual bridge between coping and development. *European Psychologist, 14*(1), 40–50. doi:10.1027/1016-9040.14.1.40

Liden, R. C., Wayne, S. J., & Sparrowe, R. T. (2000). An examination of the mediating role of psychological empowerment on the relations between the job, interpersonal relationships, and work outcomes. *Journal of Applied Psychology, 85*(3), 407–416. doi:10.1037/0021-9010.85.3.407

Lim, S. Y., & Murphy, L. R. (1999). The relationship of organizational factors to employee health and overall effectiveness. *American Journal of Industrial Medicine, 36*(Suppl. 1), 64–65. doi:10.1002/(SICI)1097-0274(199909)36:1+<64::AID-AJIM23>3.0.CO;2-1

Lipsky, M. (2010). *Street-level bureaucracy: Dilemmas of the individual in public services*. New York, NY: Russell Sage Foundation.

Local Government Association. (2002). *Guidance on community cohesion*. Retrieved from http://www.tedcantle.co.uk/publications/006%20Guidance%20on%20Community%20Cohesion%20LGA%202002.pdf

Lowe, G. (2010). *Healthy organizations: How vibrant workplaces inspire employees to achieve sustainable success*. Toronto, ON: University of Toronto Press.

Ludin, S., Rohaizat, M., & Arbon, P. (2019). The association between social cohesion and community disaster resilience. *Health & Social Care in the Community, 27*(3), 621–631. doi:10.1111/hsc.12674

Manzella, C., & Papazoglou, K. (2014). Training police trainees about ways to manage trauma and loss. *International Journal of Mental Health Promotion, 16*(2), 103–116. doi:10.1080/14623730.2014.903609

Masten, A. S. (2014). Global perspectives on resilience in children and youth. *Child Development, 85*(1), 6–20. doi:10.1111/cdev.12205

McCraty, R., & Atkinson, M. (2012). Resilience training program reduces physiological and psychological stress in police officers. *Global Advances in Health and Medicine, 1*(5), 44–66. doi:10.7453/gahmj.2012.1.5.013

McNeill, M. (1996). *Alcohol and the police workplace: Factors associated with excessive intake* (Report Series No. 119.1). Retrieved from http://www.anzpaa.org.au/ArticleDocuments/239/ACPR-RS-119.1.pdf.aspx

Nicholl, C. G. (2000). *Community policing, community justice and restorative justice: Exploring the links for the delivery of a balanced approach to public safety*. Washington, DC: University of Michigan Library.

Olutola, A. A., & Bello, P. O. (2016). Exploring the association between community cohesion and crime in the republic of South Africa. *International Journal of Social Sciences and Humanity Studies, 8*(1), 133–151.

Pandey, V. (2014). Community policing for conflict resolution and community resilience. *International Journal of Social Work and Human Services Practice, 2*(6), 228–233. doi:10.13189/ijrh.2014.020604

Pasillas, R. M., Follette, V. M., & Perumean-Chaney, S. E. (2006). Occupational stress and psychological functioning in law enforcement officers. *Journal of Police and Criminal Psychology, 21*(1), 41–53. doi:10.1007/BF02849501

Patel, R. B., & Gleason, K. M. (2018). The association between social cohesion and community resilience in two urban slums of Port au Prince, Haiti. *International Journal of Disaster Risk Reduction, 27*, 161–167. doi:10.1016/j.ijdrr.2017.10.003

Paton, D., Violanti, J. M., Johnston, P., Burke, K. J., Clarke, J., & Keenan, D. (2008). Stress shield: A model of police resiliency. *International Journal of Emergency Mental Health, 10*(2), 95–108.

Patterson, G. T. (2001). Reconceptualizing traumatic incidents experienced by law enforcement personnel. *Australasian Journal of Disaster and Trauma Studies, 5*(2).

Peeters, M. C., Montgomery, A. J., Bakker, A. B., & Schaufeli, W. B. (2005). Balancing work and home: How job and home demands are related to burnout. *International Journal of Stress Management, 12*(1), 43–61. doi:10.1037/1072-5245.12.1.43

Pelfrey, W. V., Jr. (2004). The inchoate nature of community policing: Differences between community policing and traditional police officers. *Justice Quarterly, 21*(3), 579–601. doi:10.1080/07418820400095911

Pole, N. (2007). The psychophysiology of posttraumatic stress disorder: A meta-analysis. *Psychological Bulletin, 133*(5), 725–746. doi:10.1037/0033-2909.133.5.725

Quinn, R. E., & Spreitzer, G. M. (1997). The road to empowerment: Seven questions every leader should consider. *Organizational Dynamics, 26*(2), 37–49. doi:10.1016/S0090-2616(97)90004-8

Reiner, R. (2010). *The politics of the police* (4th ed.). Oxford, UK: Oxford University Press.

Rhoades, L., & Eisenberger, R. (2002). Perceived organizational support: A review of the literature. *Journal of Applied Psychology, 87*(4), 698–714. doi:10.1037//0021-9010.87.4.698

Roberts, N. A., & Levenson, R. W. (2001). The remains of the workday: Impact of job stress and exhaustion on marital interaction in police couples. *Journal of Marriage and Family, 63*, 1052–1067. doi:10.1111/j.1741-3737.2001.01052.x

Roh, S., & Oliver, W.M. (2005). Effects of community policing upon fear of crime: Understanding the causal linkage. *Policing: An International Journal of Police Strategies & Management, 28*(4), 670–683. doi:10.1108/13639510510628758

Rubinstein, J. (1973). *City police*. New York, NY: Farrar, Strauss & Giroux.

Salmela-Aro, K., & Upadyaya, K. (2018). Role of demands-resources in work engagement and burnout in different career stages. *Journal of Vocational Behavior, 108*, 190–200. doi:10.1016/j.jvb.2018.08.002

Saunders, J., Kotzias, V., & Ramchand, R. (2019). Contemporary police stress: The impact of the evolving socio-political context. *Criminology, Criminal Justice, Law & Society, 20*(1), 35–52.

Schafer, J. A. (2010). Effective leaders and leadership in policing: Traits, assessment, development, and expansion. *Policing: An International Journal of Police Strategies & Management, 33*(4), 644–663. doi:10.1108/13639511011085060

Schieman, S., & Reid, S. (2009). Job authority and health: Unraveling the competing suppression and explanatory influences. *Social Science & Medicine, 69*(11), 1616–1624. doi:10.1016/j.socscimed.2009.08.038

Shane, J. M. (2010). Organizational stressors and police performance. *Journal of Criminal Justice, 38*(4), 807–818. doi:10.1016/j.jcrimjus.2010.05.008

Siegrist, M., & Cvetkovich, G. (2000). Perception of hazards: The role of social trust and knowledge. *Risk Analysis, 20*, 713–719. doi:10.1111/0272-4332.205064

Skogan, W. G. (2006). *Police and community in Chicago: A tale of three cities*. New York, NY: Oxford University Press.

Skolnick, J. H., & Bayley, D. H. (1988). *Community policing: Issues and practices around the world*. Washington, DC: U.S. Department of Justice, National Institute of Justice, Office of Communication and Research Utilization.

Stanley, I. H., Hom, M. A., & Joiner, T. E. (2016). A systematic review of suicidal thoughts and behaviors among police officers, firefighters, EMTs, and paramedics. *Clinical Psychology Review, 44*, 25–44. doi:10.1016/j.cpr.2015.12.002

Starcke, K., & Brand, M. (2012). Decision making under stress: A selective review. *Neuroscience & Biobehavioral Reviews, 36*(4), 1228–1248. doi:10.1016/j.neubiorev.2012.02.003

Swatt, M. L., Gibson, C. L., & Piquero, N. L. (2007). Exploring the utility of general strain theory in explaining problematic alcohol consumption by police officers. *Journal of Criminal Justice, 35*(6), 596–611. doi:10.1016/j.jcrimjus.2007.09.005

Tănase, S., Manea, C., Chraif, M., Anței, M., & Coblaş, V. (2012). Assertiveness and organizational trust as predictors of mental and physical health in a Romanian oil company. *Procedia—Social and Behavioral Sciences, 33*, 1047–1051. doi:10.1016/j.sbspro.2012.01.282

Taris, T. W., Kompier, M. A., Geurts, S. A., Houtman, I. L., & Van Den Heuvel, F. F. (2010). Professional efficacy, exhaustion, and work characteristics among police officers: A longitudinal test of the learning-related predictions of the demand–control model. *Journal of Occupational and Organizational Psychology, 83*(2), 455–474. doi:10.1348/096317909X424583

Trojanowicz, R. C., & Bucqueroux, B. (1998). *Community policing: How to get started*. Cincinnati, OH: Anderson.

Ungar, M. (2008). Resilience across cultures. *The British Journal of Social Work, 38*(2), 218–235. doi:10.1093/bjsw/bcl343

Ungar, M. (2016). Which counts more: Differential impact of the environment or differential susceptibility of the individual? *The British Journal of Social Work, 47*(5), 1279–1289. doi:10.1093/bjsw/bcw109

Ungar, M. (2018). The differential impact of social services on young people's resilience. *Child Abuse & Neglect, 78*, 4–12. doi:10.1016/j.chiabu.2017.09.024

Ungar, M. (2011). The social ecology of resilience. Addressing contextual and cultural ambiguity of a nascent construct. *American Journal of Orthopsychiatry, 81*, 1–17. doi:10.1111/j.1939-0025.2010.01067.x

Ungar, M., Ghazinour, M., & Richter, J. (2013). Annual research review: What is resilience within the social ecology of human development? *Journal of Child Psychology and Psychiatry, 54*(4), 348–366. doi:10.1111/jcpp.12025

United Nations Office on Drugs and Crime. (2011). *Handbook on police accountability, oversight and integrity*. Retrieved from https://www.unodc.org/pdf/criminal_justice/Handbook_on_police_Accountability_Oversight_and_Integrity.pdf

Violanti, J. M., & Aron, F. (1995). Police stressors: Variations in perception among police personnel. *Journal of Criminal Justice, 23*(3), 287–294. doi:10.1016/0047-2352(95)00012-F

Violanti, J. M., Burchfiel, C. M., Miller, D. B., Andrew, M. E., Dorn, J., Wactawski-Wende, J., . . . Sharp, D. S. (2006). The Buffalo Cardio-Metabolic Occupational Police Stress (BCOPS) Study: Methods and participant characteristics. *Annals of Epidemiology, 16*(2), 148–156. doi:10.1016/j.annepidem.2005.07.054

Violanti, J. M., Fekedulegn, D., Hartley, T. A., Charles, L. E., Andrew, M. E., Ma, C. C., & Burchfiel, C. M. (2016). Highly rated and most frequent stressors among police officers: Gender differences. *American Journal of Criminal Justice, 41*(4), 645–662. doi:10.1007/s12103-016-9342-x

Violanti, J. M. (2014). Police suicide: A detrimental outcome of psychological work exposures. In J. M. Violanti (Ed.), *Dying for the job: Police work exposure and health* (pp. 115–123). Springfield, IL: Charles C Thomas.

Webster, J. H. (2013). Police officer perceptions of occupational stress: The state of the art. *Policing: An International Journal of Police Strategies & Management, 36*(3), 636–652. doi:10.1108/PIJPSM-03-2013-0021

Weir, H., Stewart, D. M., & Morris, R. G. (2012). Problematic alcohol consumption by police officers and other protective service employees: A comparative analysis. *Journal of Criminal Justice, 40*(1), 72–82. doi:10.1016/j.jcrimjus.2011.11.007

Weisburd, D., & McElroy, J. (1998). Enacting the CPO role: Finding from the New York City pilot program in community policing. In J. R. Greene & S. D. Mastrofski (Eds.), *Community policing: Rhetoric or reality* (pp. 89–101). New York, NY: Praeger.

Xu, Y., Fielder, M. L., & Flaming, K. H. (2005). Discovering the impact of community policing: The broken windows thesis, collective efficacy, and citizens' judgement. *Journal of Research in Crime and Delinquency, 42*(2), 147–186. doi:10.1177/0022427804266544

Yehuda, R. (2002). Current status of cortisol findings in post-traumatic stress disorder. *Psychiatric Clinics of North America, 25*(2), 341–368. doi:10.1016/s0193-953x(02)00002-3

SECTION 3

Education Systems, Arts, and Well-Being

11

Indigenous Education, Well-Being, and Resilience— A Systemic Approach

Janya McCalman and Roxanne Bainbridge

Introduction

All children need opportunities to strengthen their resilience and enjoy supportive environments. But resilience is particularly important for promoting flourishing and educational and life outcomes for Indigenous students, who are more likely to experience high levels of cumulative and co-occurring risks that can lower their resilience, engagement, and participation in education and increase their risks of social exclusion. In turn, education can play a vital role in improving the overall socioeconomic and cultural prosperity and positioning of Indigenous nations in colonized countries.

Alongside individual asset development (Masten Cutuli, Herbers, & Reed, 2009), accounting for the interactions between the innate qualities of children and their environments that critically influence how they develop and learn is imperative to improving student outcomes. Schools and school systems strive to achieve better student learning outcomes— academic outcomes, better engagement, greater enjoyment of learning, and improved student health and well-being—as their core business (Masters, 2016). However, fundamental to learning outcomes and engagement is good health and well-being and resilience— the capacity of students to navigate to resources that sustain their well-being in the face of life challenges and the capacity of their environment to provide these resources in meaningful ways (Ungar, 2008). Understanding how Indigenous students' sociocultural and historical environments and contexts interact to influence their learning, psychosocial development, and well-being is imperative as a change strategy if we are to meet benchmark educational standards.

While a focus on children's resilience and well-being is an intrinsic part of the early childhood education curriculum in Australia, it is often a neglected aspect of school improvement efforts once students move past the early years. Early childhood frameworks take an ecological pedagogical approach to learning and recognize the important role educators, parents, other children, and the physical environment play in a child's learning and development (Department of Education and Training, 2010). But in the later years of education, strengthening resilience and other targeted well-being activities are often ad hoc at best, and where resilience activities are implemented, they frequently emphasize individual student development. The absence of coordinated systemic and ecological approaches to achieving improved educational outcomes for Indigenous students limits their opportunities and quality of life.

In this chapter, we offer suggestions for how resilience thinking across systems could help to inform better education practices and policies, with a specific focus on our work with Indigenous Australian students. It is written by a non-Indigenous Australian researcher and Gungarri/Kunja Aboriginal researcher. We will (a) define resilience; (b) map Australia's education system and describe what has been done to date to improve resilience at different levels of the system, as it pertains to Indigenous students; (c) propose the use of systems thinking and continuous quality improvement (CQI) approaches to assess, measure, and study the resilience of the education system across levels; (d) describe a case study of an exploratory systems approach in our Resilience Research Program with remote Indigenous community primary schools and regional/urban secondary boarding schools; and (e) explore how emerging systemic resilience research can help us generate scalable solutions to the education and well-being of Indigenous students. Concluding remarks speculate on the type of resilience practices and research that are needed to improve Indigenous education in the future. The chapter is also relevant for considering how resilience thinking across systems could help to inform better education practices and policies for all children, including children from other populations that are structurally marginalized.

What Is Resilience?

Definitions of resilience are important because they guide the operationalization of interventions and measurement of cumulative and co-occurring risks and protective factors (Luthar & Cicchetti, 2000). A vast international body of literature has resulted from 50 years and four waves of international resilience research factors (Masten et al., 2009). Schools and other educational institutions have been embraced as ideal sites for resilience research because they are places in which children and adolescents spend so much of their time (Condly, 2006). Hence, a Google search of the term *resilience and education* produced an enormous 86 million results (searched February 20, 2019), and an overwhelming variance in, and ambiguity of, definitions of resilience (Luthar, 2006). Despite this breadth of resilience research, however, Australian educational policy is still adhering to first-wave definitions of resilience as an individualized concept. Individualized definitions do not acknowledge the effects of complex interactions between internal factors and external determinants in students' social and physical environments, including families, communities, schools, and other systems that shape their outcomes (Bottrell, 2009; Jongen, McCalman, & Bainbridge, in press; Wright, Masten, & Narayan, 2013). Australia's recent education policy, for example, defined resilience as "the ability to cope and bounce back after encountering negative events, and to return to almost the same level of emotional well-being" (Australian Catholic University & Erebus International, 2008, p. 29).

From a systems perspective, we define resilience as being concerned with the capacity of the education system to adapt through stronger feedback loops and continuous improvement to better meet the needs of Indigenous students (Sonnemann & Goss, 2018). As well, it involves the capacity and choice of Indigenous students, family, and community members; teachers; and other school personnel to navigate toward resources to meet the needs of Indigenous students in their personal, social, and physical ecologies and to negotiate to use those resources in ways that make sense to them (Domitrovich, Durlak, Staley, & Weissberg, 2017; Ungar, 2008). Thus, since resilience entails a broad-based exploration of the interactions between resources, characteristics, and processes that operate from the student right through to the structural levels, it can be applied at multiple levels to drive change (Barankin & Khanlou, 2007; Bottrell, 2009; Ungar, 2004; van Breda, 2017; Waller, 2001). Different contexts shape different meanings; hence, having choice is important with the most promising interventions reflecting Indigenous students' aspirations and values.

Why Resilience?

Achieving systemic shifts in the education system is complex and requires multifaceted structured and informal strategies at different levels that align with the needs and aspirations of Indigenous students and families. At the broadest level, improving resilience of the education system entails adaptation of the system to support improvements in Indigenous students' educational outcomes (e.g., student engagement and participation, academic achievement and school completion) and well-being (e.g., lower health risks and fewer mental health problems; Australian Catholic University & Erebus International, 2008; Jongen et al., in press). The process usefully encompasses acknowledgement of adversity, which for Indigenous students is well documented (e.g., Hopkins, Taylor, & Zubrick, 2018; McCalman et al., 2016), but works toward enhancement of well-being (Ungar, 2008; Ungar & Liebenberg, 2011). Munford and Sanders (2017), for example, argue that adopting integrated resilience approaches in educational practice with high-risk young people, including working at multiple levels, has transformative potential. When high-risk students were able to continue with their education at age-appropriate educational levels, they experienced higher levels of resilience and well-being (Munford & Sanders, 2017).

Resilience interventions targeting Indigenous students have proven outcomes. Our systematic review of resilience interventions targeting Indigenous students in Canada, Australia, New Zealand, and the United States (Jongen, Langham, Bainbridge, & McCalman,

2019) found group workshops, cultural engagement and participation, education, training, mentoring, and community capacity-building aimed at increasing student well-being and resilience produced outcomes at the levels of individual students, communities/culture, and schools. For example, families and community Elders and leaders contributed to Indigenous educational strategies for supporting students to navigate the differences in their community and school cultures and identity. Such strategies include engaging students in cultural events or cultural excursions in the community; culturally grounded, enhanced, or tailored curricula; leading a specific cultural program or class; teaching Indigenous languages; leading outdoor/nature-based activities; participating in program delivery or other school activities; linking with schools to provide community contact/support for adolescents; developing local language around mental health and well-being; and engaging students in art, music, film and media, and dance.

Consistent with outcomes that are now considered as universal promotive and protective factors, we found that individual Indigenous students gained peer support/social inclusion and/or social connection/involvement, coping skills and communication/conflict resolution skills, self-esteem and/or confidence, self-reliance and acceptance of seeking support, analytical and reflective skills, the ability to set goals, leadership capacity, personal power and autonomy, and sense of purpose (Domitrovich et al., 2017; Roffey & McCarthy, 2013). We also found improvements in social and psychiatric functioning, reduced risk of clinically significant mental health concerns, decreased depression symptoms; improvements in overall health; increased knowledge and awareness/understanding of alcohol, drugs, and suicide; reduced anxiety for students with elevated anxiety (Domitrovich et al., 2017; Fleming, Dixon, Frampton, & Merry, 2011; Morsillo & Prilleltensky, 2007; Roffey & McCarthy, 2013); and behavioral outcomes such as reduced substance use, suicidality, and self-harm. Outcomes at the level of communities/culture included a stronger sense of Indigenous identity (Blignault, Haswell, & Pulver, 2016; Dobia et al., 2014), development of local language, increased understandings of mental health and well-being, and the promotion of resources in the local Indigenous language. For schools, outcomes from resilience interventions included increased adolescent training and leadership opportunities (Cahill Beadle, Farrelly, Forster, & Smith, 2014; Domitrovich et al., 2017), increased student retention rates, an increase in academic proficiency, less teasing and bullying, anecdotal evidence of reduced violence, increased graduations, and a decrease in money spent on external mental health services (LaFromboise & Howard-Pitney, 1995; Spears, Sanchez, Bishop, Rogers, & DeJong, 2006).

Furthermore, systemic resilience enhancement approaches are consistent with calls by Indigenous Australian leaders for a strengths-based, human rights approach to Indigenous development rather than the current focus on the persistently lower educational achievements of Indigenous learners compared to their non-Indigenous counterparts. The United Nations' (2007) Declaration on the Rights of Indigenous Peoples Article 14 states: "Indigenous peoples have the right to establish and control their educational systems and institutions providing education in their own languages, in a manner appropriate to their cultural methods of teaching and learning" (p. 7). In his 2011 Social Justice Report, for example, former Aboriginal and Torres Strait Islander Australian Social Justice

Commissioner Mick Gooda (2011) advocated for a shift to a more emancipatory narrative, stating: "Unfortunately, governments continue to see Aboriginal and Torres Strait Islander disadvantage from a deficit-based approach—addressing the 'Indigenous problem.' Governments need to move to seeing us as capable and resilient" (p. 9). Despite such promising evidence and advocacy, the Australian federal government has been slow to consider the utility of resilience, with the concept not appearing explicitly in educational policy until 2018.

The Education System in Australia

As an example of the need to think about educational systems from a multisystemic perspective, the Australian education system as it pertains to Indigenous students can be depicted as in Figure 11.1. At the center of this education system are its students; 207,852 Indigenous students (who comprise 5.5% of all Australian students) were enrolled full- or part-time in primary and secondary schools in 2016 (Australian Bureau of Statistics, 2014); 83.9% were enrolled in free government schools, 10.5% in Catholic and 5.6% in independent schools that usually charge attendance fees. Seven percent of Indigenous males and 12% of females aged 18 to 24 years went on to attend a university or other tertiary educational institution in 2016. Australia's six state and two territory governments are responsible for ensuring the day-to-day regulation of the education system and delivery of public school education (Sonnemann & Goss, 2018); Catholic and independent schooling sectors are also accountable for students' educational progress and expenditure of funding. The federal government exerts some control over the education system through conditions on commonwealth funding to state and territory governments.

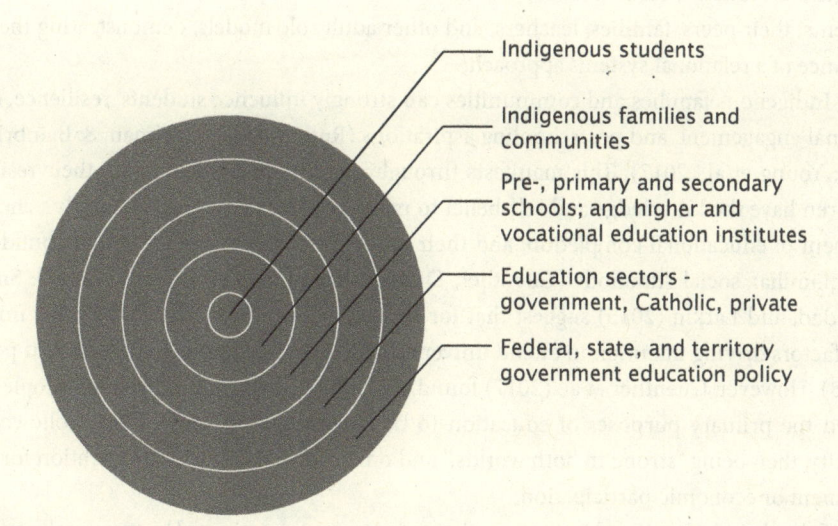

FIGURE 11.1 The multiple layers of the Australian education system as it pertains to Indigenous education.

The Context of Education for Indigenous Students

We argue that a shift is necessary from the current approach that attempts to prepare Indigenous children to become more resilient at school, to one that also prepares schools, other educational institutions, and policy *for* Indigenous students (Krakouer, 2016a). While the education system is multilayered, efforts to improve Indigenous education to date have been highly siloed, uncoordinated, and most often focused only on the student, with each component of the system working independently. Shifting the paradigm to prepare *for* Indigenous students will require integrated strategies at multiple layers of the system. The contributions of each layer will be discussed in turn with our belief that educational systems improve results for other marginalized populations, too, if they approach student success and well-being with systemwide and multiscale transformation.

International evidence suggests that students themselves become more resilient if they have at least one secure attachment relationship with a supportive adult; access to competent, prosocial adults (role models) in the wider community; and positive school, religious organizations, and other community networks involving the broader cultural context (Glover, 2009; Khanlou & Wray, 2014; Luthar & Cicchetti, 2000; Wright et al., 2013). A study of Indigenous children and adolescents from Western Australia, for example, found that prosocial friendships and the likelihood of living near extended family members in areas with low-level socioeconomic status protected those from high-risk families from the effects of harsh parenting, low nurturing parenting, and exposure to family violence (Hopkins et al., 2018). A study from New South Wales suggested that low risk was associated with family encouragement to attend school, having someone to talk to if there was a problem, and regular strenuous exercise (Young, Craig, Clapham, Banks, & Williamson, 2019). However the context-specific findings of these and other studies (Jongen et al., in press; Langham et al., 2018) show that for Indigenous students, resilience may not be situated internally within students but between students, their peers, families, teachers, and other adult role models, demonstrating the importance of a relational systems approach.

Indigenous families and communities can strongly influence students' resilience, educational engagement, and postschooling aspirations (Rutherford, McCalman, & Bainbridge, 2019; Young et al., 2017). This manifests through a family's confidence that their resilient children have the knowledge and self-belief to make positive decisions, the family's encouragement of educational completion, and their modeling of behaviors that build confidence in unfamiliar social situations (Guenther, Disbray, Benveniste, & Osborne, 2017). Smith, Trinidad, and Larkin (2015) suggest that for Indigenous children "one of the most important factors driving intention to attend university are the expectations of parents and peers" (p. 18). However, Guenther et al. (2017) found that remote-dwelling Indigenous people perceived the primary purposes of education to be language, land, and culture, followed by identity, then being "strong in both worlds," and only as fourth priority, preparation for employment or economic participation.

Schools and educational institutions themselves can be experienced by structurally and socially marginalized students as either risky or protective environments. There is evidence, for example, that educational engagement is likely to be enhanced by a school environment that affirms culture and identity and seeks to engage positively with students and their families (Bottrell, 2009; Munford & Sanders, 2017; Sanders, Munford, & Thimasarn-Anwar, 2015; Theron, Liebenberg, & Malindi, 2013; Ungar, 2004). To create support environments for Indigenous students, schools can serve to reduce discriminatory and exclusionary practices through high teacher expectations; understanding or valuing of Indigenous cultures, world views and perspectives, and issues; sensitivity to Aboriginal English; a culturally inclusive curriculum, pedagogy, and supportive teaching and learning strategies; and strategies to improve Indigenous student success and resilience (Doyle & Hill, 2008; Krakouer, 2016b; Ministerial Council for Education Early Childhood Development and Youth Affairs, 2014). But educational systems have been critiqued for often not adapting to the needs of Indigenous children (Krakouer, 2016b).

Finally, government structures, policies, and practices require a focus on Indigenous education as something that can be achieved not simply through the persistence and robustness of student, family, and school/educational institution staff, but through the engagement and resourcing of integrated cross-sectoral approaches to learning (Bottrell, 2009). At a policy level, the current approach by all Australian governments is driven by the national policy paper, *Closing the Gap*, which targets reductions in the disparities between Indigenous and other Australians' life expectancy, health, education, training, and employment. Three of these targets address educational disadvantage: to ensure access to and participation in early childhood education; halve the gap in reading, writing, and numeracy achievement; and halve the gap in Indigenous school completion rates (Department of Education and Training, 2018). The targets were developed in response to the situation noted by Fogarty and Schwab (2012) who argued that for a range of complex reasons, "it is fair to say that the constants in Indigenous education over the last 50 years have been poor attendance, low retention rates, and literacy and numeracy outcomes well below those of other groups within Australian society" (p. 7). A series of funding agreements and action plans outline governments' strategies and initiatives, but there are continued gaps in each of these indicators, with targets for school attendance, reading, writing, and numeracy not being on track (Department of the Prime Minister and Cabinet, 2019). On the one hand, there is value in the *Closing the Gap* narratives that attempt to raise the persistently lower educational achievements of Indigenous learners compared to their non-Indigenous counterparts (Department of Education and Training, 2018). On the other hand, adopting a strengths and resilience approach needs to be founded on Indigenous aspirations and values and a realistic analysis of social inequality and the fundamental causes of those disparities (Bottrell, 2009). In contexts of limited educational and employment opportunity such as in remote communities, *Closing the Gap* targets are often not met (Munford & Sanders, 2017). As such, the targets risk further alienating and disengaging those students who cannot see how education relates to their world outside of school (Altman & Fogarty, 2010; Guenther et al., 2017).

Methods and Measures

There is a lack of clarity about which measurement instruments most adequately capture and assess the (often culturally specific) complex, dynamic, adaptive, and unpredictable risk and protective factors that are part of resilience processes (Langham et al., 2018; Ungar, Ghazinour, & Richter, 2013) for diverse Indigenous Australians (Jongen et al., 2019). Our systematic review of measures of resilience constructs used with Indigenous adolescents in Canada, Australian, New Zealand, and the United States identified 20 mainstream and Indigenous-specific instruments. These measured both individual assets and environmental resources ($n = 7$), only environmental resources ($n = 6$), only individual assets ($n = 3$), or constructs of cultural resilience ($n = 5$; Jongen et al., 2019). However, there was no consistency regarding the critical factors that constituted resilience for Indigenous students and no consensus on appropriate instruments. While national surveys in Australia collect well-being indicators for happiness, stressful life events, connection to traditional homelands or country and cultural events, and psychological distress, it is not clear whether these are indicators that are most meaningful to children or adolescents (Australian Institute of Health and Welfare, 2018), how the different combinations of factors shape the ways in which both risk and resilience manifest in specific contexts, or any correlations between them (Masten, 2014; Panter-Brick et al., 2018; Ungar, 2008; Ungar et al., 2007; Ungar & Liebenberg, 2011). International researchers have even critiqued the construct of resilience itself because limited correlation among the domains of resilience suggests that aggregated domains are likely to be weakly correlated with outcomes (Luthar & Cicchetti, 2000; Tusaie & Dyer, 2004). Furthermore, there is very limited evidence about how the pathways from adversity to resilience are navigated by Indigenous Australian students or what constitutes best practice educational interventions for Indigenous students. In the absence of basic understandings, governments, schools and tertiary education institutions, families, and communities struggle to determine where or how to most appropriately invest their energies to engage, promote resilience, or avert risk for Indigenous students (Jongen et al., 2019; Munford & Sanders, 2017; Ralph & Ryan, 2017; Sanders, Munford, & Liebenberg, 2016; Toland & Carrigan, 2011). Given the multitude of challenges and complexity of situational factors, contexts, and levels of resilience in Indigenous education, we need to augment past methods, theories, and models that have often been linear and reductionist in nature (Rutter et al., 2017) and develop new systems approaches to account for complexity (Masten et al, 2009; Masten & Coatsworth, 1998).

To address these shortcomings, quantitative and qualitative methods that assess systems are needed to understand and improve resilience by pulling together data and knowledge, models, and theories for as many relevant protective and risk factors and their interrelationships as practically possible. The goal is to form an overall picture to improve our understanding of how changes at one level impact the system at other levels (van Beek & McCalman, 2018). By doing this, systems thinking develops understanding that is both broad, including many factors and their interactions, and deep, moving between the levels within a system (van Beek & McCalman, 2018). For example, Hopkins, Zubrick, and Taylor (2014), in the study previously mentioned, unexpectedly found that cultural indicators were not significantly associated with psychosocial function, and that only Indigenous students in low-risk family settings self-reported that exposure to racism reduced their psychosocial functioning. For generic student populations, Aldridge et al. (2016) found that a school's efforts to affirm diversity across the school had a negative influence on students' resilience (the authors hypothesized that this may have resulted from a lack of knowledge, skills, and attitudes in the school community to meaningfully harmonies student diversity—thereby creating an additional stressor for marginalized students). These unexpected findings are consistent with conceptualizations of resilience as a dynamic process that differs across contexts and cultures, but suggest a need to explore systems at multiple levels.

Case Study: Supporting the Resilience of Indigenous Students at Boarding Schools

Our five-year resilience research project has explored the concept of resilience in relation to Indigenous students from remote Cape York communities who are compelled to attend boarding schools for secondary education because there is no, or limited, secondary schooling available in their home communities (McCalman et al., 2016). Nationally, 22,391 Indigenous secondary school students in Australia make such transitions annually at age 11 (Australian Bureau of Statistics, 2011). This study was developed in response to a concern about increased suicide risk held by the Queensland Department of Education's Transition Support Service (TSS), which supports students academically and in the practicalities of accessing and attending boarding schools across Queensland (McCalman et al., 2016). Our findings suggest a theoretical framework for conceptualizing systemic resilience research in Indigenous education.

The study aimed to build individual student resilience by strengthening our understanding and practice of TSS, schools and boarding houses, family/community, health services, and policymakers in relation to student resilience. An immediate challenge, however, related to the logistics (including cost) of working across the discrete and geographically and culturally disparate "systems" that are navigated by the students. As depicted in Figure 11.2, students come from 11 remote north Queensland home communities (red dots on map). They transition to 18 boarding schools that can be up to 2000 kilometers away (black squares), with most being generalist private schools and a few being Indigenous-specific or state schools (Pearson, 2011).

For students, transitions involve negotiating not only the logistics of shifting from one location to another, but also changes in cultures, including language, autonomy, educational standards, roles, responsibilities and expectations, parental influence, personal freedom, relationships, and, at times, confrontation with institutional discrimination and racism (Mellor & Corrigan, 2004). As an exploratory study, we outline the research we conducted with the students, families/communities, school, education sectors, policymakers, and health services engaged in the transitions of students from their remote Indigenous home communities to boarding schools (Figure 11.3). We attempted to create stronger linkages between levels of the system to better support student resilience and well-being.

Using a tailored survey instrument developed collaboratively with TSS (McCalman et al., 2017), we found, as expected, that most of the remote community Indigenous primary school students reported high levels of resilience, but somewhat unexpectedly, two-thirds reported moderate-high levels of psychological distress. Upon transition to boarding schools, secondary students reported lower scores on resilience and higher psychological distress; those excluded from boarding schools reported even poorer scores (Redman-MacLaren et al., 2017).

FIGURE 11.2 Map of students' home communities and destination boarding schools. From M. Redman-MacLaren, T. Benveniste, J. McCalman, K. Rutherford, A. Britton, E. Langham, . . . R. Bainbridge, 2019, Through the eyes of students: The satisfaction of remote Indigenous boarding students' with a transition support service in Queensland, Australia. *The Australian Journal of Indigenous Education*, 1–12. doi:10.1017/jie.2019. Reproduced with permission.

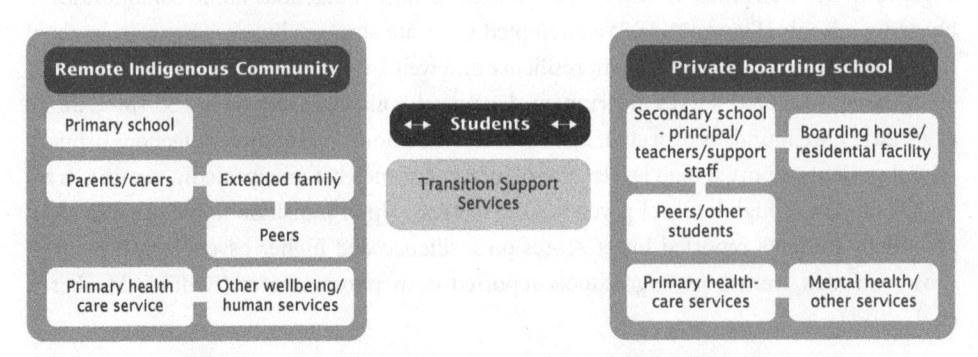

FIGURE 11.3 Students' transitions from community to boarding schools systems.

Figure 11.4 depicts a multilevel theoretical model for enhancing the resilience of Indigenous boarding school students. At the center, the sources and expressions of students' resilience were identified through our confirmatory factor analysis of the internationally validated subscales of the Child and Youth Resilience Measure (Liebenberg, Ungar, & de Vijver, 2011). The key sources of students' resilience were relational: caring and supportive friendships, role models, connection with family, connection with culture, and safe home with plenty of good food to eat. The key expressions of their resilience were staying on task, helping out others, robust interpersonal social skills, knowing how to behave in different situations, and celebrating culture. The process of resilience for students was captured through qualitative research. The core process was one of carrying through: being held by an integrated ecology of support. Carrying through was the process of successfully making it through each term, and each year, due to the web of supports provided by the different processes and stakeholders across home and school environments. The subprocesses for strengthening students' capacity to navigate tensions as student's educational and home lives changed encompassed both their innate capabilities and relationships at school and at home. Factors included (a) friends keeping you strong—feeling supported, belonging; (b) being with mob (peer)—being understood, belonging; (c) understanding, caring, and helping—trusting, feeling respected, and cared for; (d) having a say, being listened to—feeling heard,

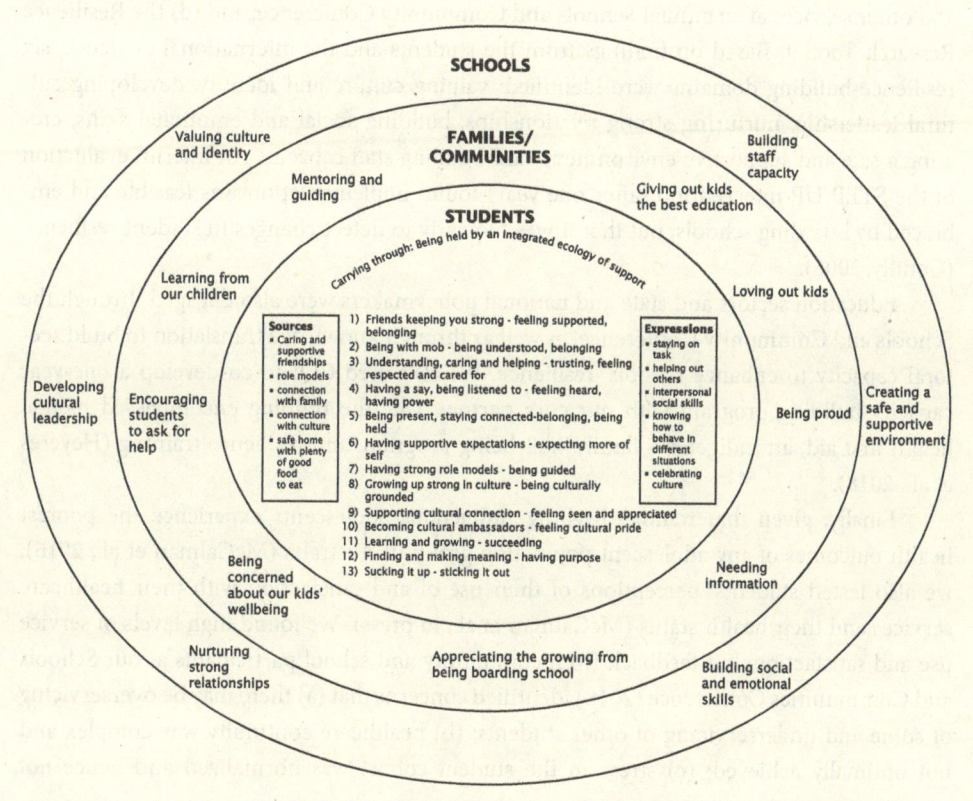

FIGURE 11.4 A theoretical model of resilience enhancement for Indigenous boarding students.

having power; (e) being present, staying connected—belonging, being held; (f) having supportive expectations—expecting more of self; (g) having strong role models—being guided; (h) growing up strong in culture—being culturally grounded; (i) supporting cultural connection—feeling seen and appreciated; (j) becoming cultural ambassadors—feeling cultural pride; (k) learning and growing—succeeding; (l) finding and making meaning—having purpose; and (m) sucking it up—sticking it out.

Contributions were also made by caregivers and parents who expressed a number of preferred strategies to support Indigenous students during this period of transition. These included loving our kids, mentoring and guiding, encouraging students to ask for help, learning from our children, being proud, being concerned about our kids' well-being, appreciating their growing from being at boarding school, and needing information and resources about how to best support our children at boarding schools. As found in previous resilience research (Evans & Pinnock, 2007), there is a need for further research that engages the whole family as a fundamental part of students' environments and with a central role in supporting resilience (Burnette & Figley, 2016).

Participating boarding schools were also engaged in co-developing a CQI STEP UP intervention to strengthen the resilience of their Indigenous students. The intervention encompassed four key strategies: (a) a site-based STEP UP action plan in each school; (b) school staff capacity development through a community of practice and the provision of professional development; (c) linking with parents/community representatives, students, TSS staff, and other services at an annual Schools and Community Conference; and (d) the Resilience Research Toolkit. Based on findings from the students and the international evidence, six resilience-building domains were identified: valuing culture and identity, developing cultural leadership, nurturing strong relationships, building social and emotional skills, creating a safe and supportive environment, and building staff capacity. An interim evaluation of the STEP UP intervention (after one year) found implementation was feasible and embraced by boarding schools, but that it was too early to detect changes in student resilience (Condly, 2006).

Education sectors and state and national policymakers were also engaged through the Schools and Community Conference, as well as through knowledge translation to build sectoral capacity to enhance schools' resilience. We also used CQI to co-develop a one-year capacity-building program with our core partner TSS; the training encompassed mental health first aid, an Indigenous family well-being program, and resilience training (Heyeres et al., 2018).

Finally, given that remote-dwelling Indigenous adolescents experience the poorest health outcomes of any adolescent population group in Australia (McCalman et al., 2016), we also tested students' perceptions of their use of and satisfaction with their healthcare services and their health status (McCalman et al., in press). We found high levels of service use and satisfaction, but feedback from community and school participants at our Schools and Communities Conference (2018) identified concerns that (a) there may be overservicing of some and underservicing of other students; (b) healthcare continuity was complex and not optimally achieved; (c) stress in the student cohort was normalized and hence not acknowledged; and (d) schools adopted diverse models of healthcare, with no clear "best practice" model available (McCalman et al., in press).

The study thus modeled students' resilience and psychological distress, theorized their pathways to resilience, and attempted to enhance the awareness and supportiveness of family/community, boarding school, TSS, policymakers, and health services. Yet it is challenging to capture the effects of such multisystemic interventions on students' levels of risk and resilience or the effects of incremental boarding school and TSS quality improvement decisions on the system as a whole. Despite this shortcoming, we see evidence that enhancing resilience has the potential to improve the educational and well-being outcomes of these students, enabling them not only to withstand the considerable challenges they encounter but also to grow stronger and flourish.

Discussion

Systemic resilience research in education is just emerging but offers potential for generating solutions at different systemic levels to improve the education and well-being of Indigenous Australian students and other structurally and socially marginalized children globally. Given variation in understanding resilience factors across different cultures and risk contexts and the diverse ways that they are negotiated (Fleming & Ledogar, 2008; Ungar et al., 2007; Ungar & Liebenberg, 2011), flexible systemic approaches are needed that respond to and account for the specific meanings of resilience with specific populations. CQI approaches can be used at each level of the system, using evidence of what works in other Indigenous contexts and available local data to plan and implement reforms, study their effects, and incrementally improve interventions. Not all of the contributing factors to resilience hold the same importance, however, and it is challenging to know where and how to intervene to impact the different combinations of factors by which both risk and resilience manifest in different cultures and contexts at different times (Masten, 2014; Panter-Brick et al., 2018; Ungar, 2008; Ungar et al., 2007; Ungar & Liebenberg, 2011). Thus, systems thinking is useful for determining, for each setting or population group, the relationship between risk and protective factors and for identifying individual and environmental aspects of resilience (Pessoa, Coimbra, Murgo, van Breda, & Baker, 2018). These may include not only the complex, intersecting influences that cause personal adversities, the trauma experienced by students, and their coping strategies, but also the social and structural inequalities that initiate and perpetuate a child's experience of stress (Bottrell, 2009; Sanders, 2013).

Schools are at the hub of interventions that engage Indigenous students in resilience-enhancement interventions. As a body of international evidence shows, schools have the capacity to link vertically with students' families and communities and with education sector and government policymakers. They also have the capacity for horizontal integration with best practice Indigenous education guidelines and intersectorally with health, mental health, child protection, juvenile justice, and other services that are also engaged in mitigating Indigenous students' risk and strengthening their resilience. Interventions that are more likely to promote resilience in educational settings are those that not only prepare

Indigenous children to become more resilient at school, but also those that prepare schools and educators *for* Indigenous students (Krakouer, 2016a). Implementing CQI processes and reflective practice can attend to cultural bias and provide a means of using data to review current school practices and outcomes, set goals for improvement, design and implement school improvement strategies based on evaluated evidence, monitor changes in student outcomes, and review and reflect on the effectiveness of the schools' improvement efforts (Masters, 2016).

Figure 11.5 proposes a comprehensive framework for understanding and conceptualizing quality in education systems and facilitating development of reform strategies for achieving it. Using CQI processes, there is a role for participation of leaders at each level of the education system: the students, families and communities, schools and education sectors, and policymakers. Such interventions require innovation and flexibility; sustained investment; strong collaboration and work across levels; ground–up resourcing, drive, and effort; school leadership; and a broad and deep approach to problem solving (Acil Allen Consulting, 2014; van Beek & McCalman, 2018).

In the evaluation of Australia's *Aboriginal and Torres Strait Islander Education Action Plan 2010–2014*, school leaders identified that productive strategies are likely to respond to local contextual needs, share learnings of practices that have been proven elsewhere, be multifaceted and build capacity (Acil Allen Consulting, 2014). CQI strategies, as illustrated in Figure 11.5, provide an effective process for planning and implementing these priority strategies. At the bottom of Figure 11.5, family engagement activities are vital, such as through

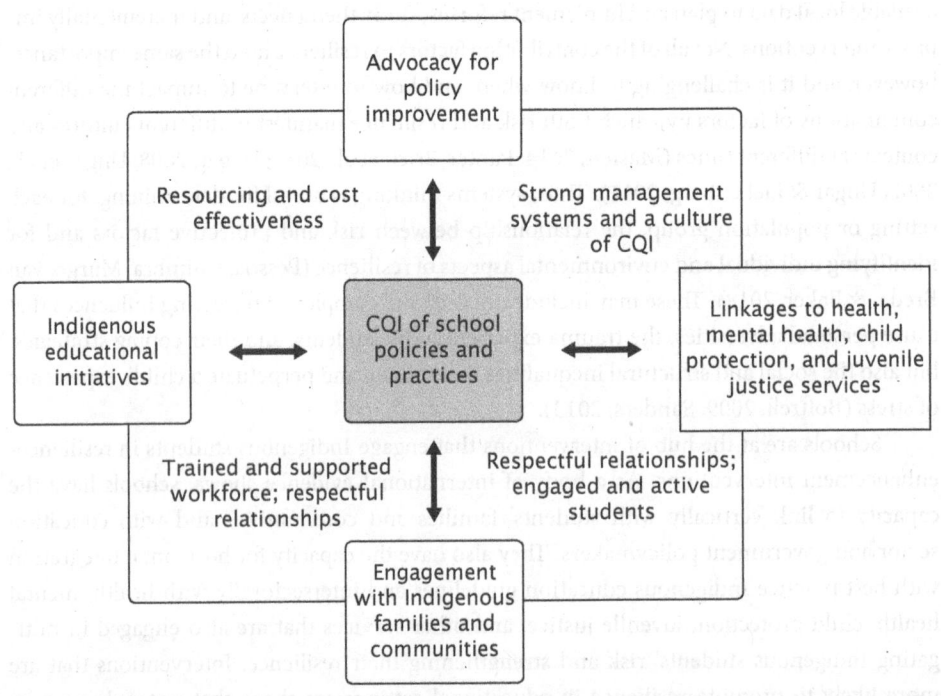

FIGURE 11.5 Vertical and horizontal integration by schools to strengthen Indigenous students' resilience.

holding Indigenous events at schools and school staff engaging in community events. On the left of Figure 11.5, Indigenous educational initiatives include the promotion of language, culture, high expectations, Indigenizing the curriculum, continuing to push for improved literacy and numeracy programs for students, promotion of postschool options, a continued emphasis on attendance, and promotion of role models and tutoring (Acil Allen Consulting, 2014). At the top of Figure 11.5, school leaders advocated that rather than responding to an ongoing plethora of new policy initiatives that have led them to a sense of "drowning in a sea of fads and disjointed innovations" (Driese & Thomson, 2014, p. 3), there is a need for closer alignment between policy, schools, and Indigenous communities in ways that align with the values and aspirations of Indigenous communities (Gooda, 2011). On the right of Figure 11.5, linking with health and other sectors is also shown to be critical for improving well-being, which plays a vital role in educational participation and outcomes (McCalman et al., in press). The conditions that support such CQI innovations are workforce development, including for Indigenous teachers and support staff; developing strong and respectful relationships between teachers, other school staff, and students to extend the coping capacities of students and foster teachers' positive relationships with students and key stakeholders and allow professionals to learn about what young people are capable of doing to scaffold opportunities for personal problem-solving and development of life skills (Bottrell, 2009); resourcing and cost effectiveness; strong management systems and a culture of CQI in the school; and engaged and active students.

The responsibility for educational reform, however, does not lie solely with schools. For students themselves, the evidence suggests the importance of adopting at least one secure attachment relationship with a supportive adult, prosocial peers, and adults (role models), and positive school and other community networks (Glover, 2009; Khanlou & Wray, 2014; Luthar & Cicchetti, 2000; Wright et al., 2013). Along the education pathway, these protective factors can mitigate against risk factors such as family adversities, higher psychological distress, and perceptions of a lack of further education or employment in their local areas that contribute to their early discontinuation from education (Australian Bureau of Statistics, 2011; Mission Australia, 2014). They can prevent students from experiencing inadequate support at school and subsequent exclusion and the self-blame that can accompany feelings of not making the most of opportunities or making the wrong decisions (Sanders et al., 2017). Students' access to valuable family and community networks and resources also means that school professionals can more effectively harness many resources at multiple systemic levels to support the positive engagement and development of Indigenous students, even when they are being educated beyond their home communities (Sanders et al., 2017).

Conclusion

For policymakers, shifting the education system to focus on preparing schools and educators *for* Indigenous students through interventions that support resilience and well-being protective and promotive factors would offer an alternative to the focus on developmental deficits that has saturated Indigenous policy and practice in the past and failed to produce social change (Bainbridge, 2011; Bainbridge et al., 2015; Salmon et al., 2018; Walter & Andersen, 2013). Achieving such a systemic shift of the education system requires acknowledgement of the values and aspirations of Indigenous communities (Gooda, 2011), moving beyond reductionist thinking about individual resilience factors to exploring how the interdependent elements of the system affect each other and how changes potentially reverberate throughout the system (Rutter et al., 2017). Researchers such as Bottrell (2009) also suggest that an analysis of inequalities and power relations (historic and present) must be taken into account.

Globally, Indigenous nations have long viewed the world as complex ecological adaptive systems that change across the life course (Bainbridge, McCalman, Redman-MacLaren & Whiteside, 2019). Reductionist paradigms of Western knowledge systems have never accounted for these holistic interrelated dynamic understandings of the world. However, contemporaneous movement in the Western sciences is beginning to recognize that simplistic ways of viewing the world are no longer valid in attempts to understand the experiences of humanity and implement effective change in the 21st century. Systems approaches in resilience research and practice have the potential to strengthen the simplistic interventions that have saturated Indigenous education research in the past and failed to produce impact (Bainbridge et al., 2015). They can contribute by engaging those in the situation in context- and population-adapted strategies, using the available evidence in cycles of planning, doing, studying, and acting for improvements at different levels of the education system, within different contexts, and across different time scales (Sollecito & Johnson, 2013). These strategies can involve families and communities, schools and tertiary educational institutions, educational sectors, and linkages with health, mental health, and other services in developing local, culturally appropriate knowledge and resources targeted to better enable educators to enhance Indigenous student resilience (Osborne, 2013). In times of limited resources, system approaches enable services to make smarter decisions about providing support for Indigenous resilience in meaningful ways and investing where need is greatest.

Key Messages

1. A shift is needed from the current Australian education policy approach that largely ignores student health and well-being to one that embeds pedagogical processes that support Indigenous children to become more resilient at school and prepares school cultures and environments and educators *for* Indigenous students.
2. Interventions work best when they focus on the protective factors that are most meaningful to Indigenous students and focus at multiple levels: the students, their families and communities, schools and education sectors, and the policy level.
3. A relational approach that considers resilience across the life course and attends to risks, promotes assets, and is process-focused for students is imperative.
4. Reflective CQI approaches provide a methodology for attending to cultural bias and provides a means for using data to review current school practices and outcomes, set goals for improvement, design and implement school improvement strategies based on evaluated evidence, monitor changes in student outcomes, and review and reflect on the effectiveness of improvement efforts.

Acknowledgments

This manuscript was funded by the National Health and Medical Research Council Project GNT1076774, and NHMRC early career fellowship GNT1113392. The funding body played no role in design, collection, analysis, or interpretation of data; writing of the manuscript; or the decision to submit the manuscript for publication.

We wish to thank the students that participated in the Resilience Research project and their families who provided consent. We also wish to acknowledge and thank our partner organizations—the Queensland Department of Education and Training's Transition Support Service and 18 boarding schools across Queensland. Finally, we wish to acknowledge the contributions of our Resilience Research Project team: Dr Tessa Benveniste, Amelia Britton, Erika Langham, Katrina Rutherford, Cassi-Ann Seden, and Alexandra van Beek.

References

Acil Allen Consulting. (2014). *Evaluation of the Aboriginal and Torres Strait Islander education action plan 2010–2014*. Retrieved from http://www.educationcouncil.edu.au/site/DefaultSite/filesystem/documents/ATSI%20documents/ATSI%202010-2014%20Final%20Evaluation%20Report/0Appendices_ATSIEAP_ACILAllenConsulting.pdf

Aldridge, J. M., Fraser, B. J., Fozdar, F., Ala'i, K., Earnest, J., & Afari, E. (2016). Students' perceptions of school climate as determinants of wellbeing, resilience and identity. *Improving Schools, 19*(1), 5–26. doi:10.1177/1365480215612616

Altman, J. C., & Fogarty, W. (2010). Indigenous Australians as "no gaps" subjects: Education and development in remote Australia. In I. Snyder & J. Nieuwenhuysen (Eds.), *Closing the gap in education? Improving outcomes in Southern world societies* (pp. 109–128). Melbourne, Australia: Monash University Publishing.

Australian Bureau of Statistics. (2011). *Australian social trends. Education and Indigenous wellbeing*. Canberra: Author. Retrieved from http://www.abs.gov.au/AUSSTATS/abs@.nsf/Lookup/4102.0Main+Features50Mar+2011.

Australian Bureau of Statistics. (2014). *NSSC Table 42b: Full-time and part-time students 2006-2012*. Canberra: Author.

Australian Catholic University, & Erebus International. (2008). *Scoping study into approaches to student wellbeing*. Retrieved from https://docs.education.gov.au/system/files/doc/other/scoping_study_into_approaches_to_student_wellbeing_final_report.pdf

Australian Institute of Health and Welfare. (2018). *Aboriginal and Torres Strait Islander adolescent and youth health and wellbeing 2018*. Canberra: Australian Bureau of Statistics. Retrieved from https://www.aihw.gov.au/reports/indigenous-australians/atsi-adolescent-youth-health-wellbeing-2018/contents/summary.

Bainbridge, R. (2011). Becoming empowered: A grounded theory study of Aboriginal women's agency. *Australasian Psychiatry, 19*, S26–S29. doi:10.3109/10398562.2011.583040

Bainbridge, R., Tsey, K., McCalman, J., Kinchin, I., Saunders, V., Watkin Lui, F., . . . Lawson, K. (2015). No one's discussing the elephant in the room: Contemplating questions of research impact and benefit in Aboriginal and Torres Strait Islander health research. *BMC Public Health, 15*, 696.

Bainbridge, R., McCalman, J., Redman-MacLaren, M., & Whiteside, M. (2019). Grounded theory as systems science: Working with Indigenous nations for social justice. In A. Bryant, K. Charmaz (Eds.), *The Sage Handbook of Grounded Theory*. Sage, Thousand Oaks.

Barankin, T., & Khanlou, N. (2007). *Growing up resilient: Ways to build resilience in children and youth*. Toronto, ON: CAMH.

Blignault, I., Haswell, M., & Pulver, L. J. (2016). The value of partnerships: Lessons from a multi-site evaluation of a national social and emotional wellbeing program for Indigenous youth. *Australian and New Zealand Journal of Public Health, 40*(Suppl. 1), S53–S58. doi:10.1111/1753-6405.12403

Bottrell, D. (2009). Understanding "marginal" perspectives: Towards a social theory of resilience. *Qualitative Social Work, 8*(3), 321–339. doi:10.1177/1473325009337840

Burnette, C. E., & Figley, C. R. (2016). Risk and protective factors related to the wellness of American Indian and Alaska Native youth: A systematic review. *International Public Health Journal, 8*(2), 137–154.

Cahill, H., Beadle, S., Farrelly, A., Forster, R., & Smith, K. (2014). *Building resilience in children and young people: A literature review for the Department of Education and Early Childhood Development (DEECD)*. Retrieved from https://www.education.vic.gov.au/documents/about/department/resiliencelitreview.pdf

Condly, S. J. (2006). Resilience in children: A review of literature with implications for education. *Urban Education, 41*(3), 211–236. doi:10.1177/0042085906287902

Department of Education and Training. (2010). *Early years learning framework for Australia: Belonging, being and becoming*. Canberra, Australia: Author. Retrieved from https://docs.education.gov.au/system/files/doc/other/belonging_being_and_becoming_the_early_years_learning_framework_for_australia_0.pdf

Department of Education and Training. (2018). *Indigenous education*. Canberra, Australia: Author. Retrieved from https://www.education.gov.au/indigenous-schooling

Department of the Prime Minister and Cabinet. (2019). *Closing the gap report 2019*. Retrieved from https://ctgreport.pmc.gov.au/sites/default/files/ctg-report-2019.pdf

Dobia, B., Bodkin-Andrews, G., Parada, R., O'Rourke, V., Gilbert, S., Daley, A., & Roffey, S. (2014). *Aboriginal girls circle: Enhancing connectedness and promoting resilience for aboriginal girls: Final pilot report*. Sydney, Australia.

Domitrovich, C. E., Durlak, J. A., Staley, K. C., & Weissberg, R. P. (2017). Social-emotional competence: An essential factor for promoting positive adjustment and reducing risk in school children. *Child Development, 88*(2), 408–416. doi:10.1111/cdev.12739

Doyle, L., & Hill, R. (2008). Unlocking improved outcomes for disadvantaged students. *Australian Philanthropy, 70*, 20–21.

Driese, T., & Thomson, S. (2014). Unfinished business: PISA shows Indigenous youth are being left behind. *ACER Occasional Essays—February 2014*. Australian Council for Educational Research, Camberwell, Victoria.

Evans, R., & Pinnock, K. (2007). Promoting resilience and protective factors in the children's fund: Supporting children's and young people's pathways towards social inclusion? *Journal of Children and Poverty, 13*(1), 21–36. doi:10.1080/10796120601171211

Fleming, J., & Ledogar, R. J. (2008). Resilience, an evolving concept: A review of literature relevant to aboriginal research. *Pimatisiwin, 6*(2), 7–23.

Fleming, T., Dixon, R., Frampton, C., & Merry, S. (2011). A pragmatic randomized controlled trial of computerized CBT (Sparx) for symptoms of depression among adolescents excluded from mainstream education. *Behavioural and Cognitive Psychotherapy, 40*(5), 529–541. doi:10.1017/S1352465811000695

Fogarty, W., & Schwab, R. (2012). *Indigenous education: Experiential learning and learning through country*. Retrieved from http://caepr.anu.edu.au

Glover, J. (2009). *Bouncing back: How can resilience be promoted in vulnerable children and young people?* Retrieved from https://www.barnardos.org.uk/bouncing_back_resilience_march09.pdf

Gooda, M. (2011). *Social justice report 2011*. Sydney, Australia.

Guenther, J., Disbray, S., Benveniste, T., & Osborne, S. (2017). "Red dirt" schools and pathways into higher education. In S. L. J. Frawley & J. A. Smith (Eds.), *Indigenous pathways, transitions and participation in higher education: From policy to practice* (pp. 251–272). Singapore: Springer Open.

Hattie, J. (2008). *Visible Learning: A synthesis of over 800 metaanalyses relating to achievement*. London, UK: Routledge.

Heyeres, M., McCalman, J., Langham, E., Bainbridge, R., Redman-MacLaren, M., Britton, A., . . . Tsey, K. (2018). Strengthening the capacity of education staff to support the wellbeing of Indigenous students in boarding schools: A participatory action research study. *The Australian Journal of Indigenous Education, 48*(1), 79–92. doi:10.1017/jie.2017.42

Hopkins, K. D., Zubrick, S. R., & Taylor, C. L. (2014). Resilience amongst Australian Aboriginal youth: An ecological analysis of factors associated with psychosocial functioning in high and low family risk contexts. *PLoS ONE, 9*(7), e102820. doi:10.1371/journal.pone.0102820

Hopkins, K., Taylor, C., & Zubrick, S. (2018). Psychosocial resilience and vulnerability in Western Australian Aboriginal youth. *Child Abuse & Neglect, 78*, 85–95. doi:10.1016/j.chiabu.2017.11.014

Jongen, C., Langham, E., Bainbridge, R., & McCalman, J. (2019). Instruments to measure the resilience of Indigenous adolescents: An exploratory review. *Frontiers in Public Health: Special Resilience Edition, 7*, 1–14. doi:10.3389/fpubh.2019.00194

Jongen, C., McCalman, J., & Bainbridge R. (2020). A systematic scoping review of school-based resilience interventions for Indigenous adolescents in CANZUS nations. *Frontiers in Public Health*, 10 January 2020. https://doi.org/10.3389/fpubh.2019.00351

Khanlou, N., & Wray, R. (2014). A whole community approach toward child and youth resilience promotion: A review of resilience literature. *International Journal of Mental Health and Addiction, 12*(1), 64–79. doi:10.1007/s11469-013-9470-1

Krakouer, J. (2016a). *Aboriginal early childhood education: Why attendance and true engagement are equally important*. Retrieved from https://research.acer.edu.au/indigenous_education/44

Krakouer, J. (2016b). *Literature review relating to the current context and discourse surrounding indigenous early childhood education, school readiness and transition programs to primary school*. Retrieved from https://research.acer.edu.au/indigenous_education/43

LaFromboise, T., & Howard-Pitney, B. (1995). The Zuni life skills development curriculum: Description and evaluation of a suicide prevention program. *Journal of Counseling Psychology, 42*(4), 479–486. doi:10.1037/0022-0167.42.4.479

Langham, E., McCalman, J., Redman-MacLaren, M., Hunter, E., Wenitong, M., Britton, A., . . . Bainbridge, R. (2018). Validation and factor analysis of the child and youth resilience measure for Indigenous Australian boarding school students. *Frontiers in Public Health, 6*(299). doi:10.3389/fpubh.2018.00299

Liebenberg, L., Ungar, M., & de Vijver, F. V. (2011). Validation of the Child and Youth Resilience Measure-28 (CYRM-28) among Canadian youth. *Research on Social Work Practice, 22*(2), 219–226. doi:10.1177/1049731511428619

Luthar, S. (2006). Resilience in development: A synthesis of research across five decades. In D. Cicchetti & D. J. Cohen (Eds.), *Developmental psychopathology: Risk, disorder, and adaptation* (pp. 739–795). New York, NY: Wiley.

Luthar, S., & Cicchetti, D. (2000). The construct of resilience: Implications of interventions and social policies. *Developmental Psychopathology, 12*(4), 857–885. doi:10.1017/s0954579400004156

Masten, A. S. (2014). Global perspectives on resilience in children and youth. *Child Development, 85*(1), 6–20. doi:doi:10.1111/cdev.12205

Masten, A. S., & Coatsworth, J. D. (1998). The development of competence in favorable and unfavorable environments: Lessons from research on successful children. *American Psychologist, 53*(2), 205–220. doi:10.1037/0003-066X.53.2.205

Masten, A. S., Cutuli, J. J., Herbers, J. E., & Reed, M. G. J. (2009). Resilience in development. In C. R. Snyder & S. J. & Lopez (Eds.), *Oxford handbook of positive psychology* (2nd ed., pp. 117–131). New York, NY: Oxford University Press.

Masters, G. (2016). *Schools as learning organisations*. Retrieved from https://research.acer.edu.au/cgi/viewcontent.cgi?article=1126&context=eppc.

McCalman, J., Bainbridge, R. G., Redman-MacLaren, M., Russo, S., Rutherford, K., Tsey, K., . . . Hunter, E. (2017). The development of a survey instrument to assess Aboriginal and Torres Strait Islander students' resilience and risk for self-harm. *Frontiers in Education, 2*(19). doi:10.3389/feduc.2017.00019

McCalman, J., Bainbridge, R., Russo, S., Rutherford, K., Tsey, K., Wenitong, M., . . . Jacups, S. (2016). Psychosocial resilience, vulnerability and suicide prevention: Impact evaluation of a mentoring approach to modify suicide risk for remote Indigenous Australian students at boarding school. *BMC Public Health, 16*, 98. doi:10.1186/s12889-016-2762-1

McCalman, J., Langham, E., Benveniste, T., Wenitong, M., Rutherford, K., Britton, A., Stewart, R., & Bainbridge, R. (2020). Integrating healthcare services for Indigenous Australian students at boarding schools: A mixed-methods sequential explanatory study. *International Journal of Integrated Care, 20*(1), 8, 1–16. doi:https://doi.org/10.5334/ijic.4669.

Mellor, S., & Corrigan, M. (2004). *The case for change: A review of contemporary research on Indigenous education outcomes.* Australian Council for Educational Research. Retrieved from https://research.acer.edu.au/cgi/viewcontent.cgi?article=1006&context=aer

Ministerial Council for Education Early Childhood Development and Youth Affairs. (2014). *Aboriginal and Torres Strait Islander education action plan 2010-2014.* Canberra: Australian Government.

Mission Australia. (2014). *Indigenous aspirations Employment & educational opportunities for Aboriginal & Torres Strait Islander youth.* Retrieved from https://www.missionaustralia.com.au/annual-reports-page/doc_download/274-indigenous-aspirations-report

Morsillo, J., & Prilleltensky, I. (2007). Social action with youth: Interventions, evaluation, and psychopolitical validity. *Journal of Community Psychology, 35*(6), 725–740. doi:10.1002/jcop.20175

Munford, R., & Sanders, J. (2017). Harm, opportunity, optimism: Young people's negotiation of precarious circumstances. *International Social Work, 62*(1), 185–197. doi:10.1177/0020872817717322

Osborne, S. (2013). Kulintja Nganampa Maa-kunpuntjaku (strengthening our thinking): Place-based approaches to mental health and wellbeing in Anangu schools. *The Australian Journal of Indigenous Education, 42*(2), 182–193. doi:10.1017/jie.2013.25

Panter-Brick, C., Hadfield, K., Dajani, R., Eggerman, M., Ager, A., & Ungar, M. (2018). Resilience in context: A brief and culturally grounded measure for Syrian refugee and Jordanian host-community adolescents. *Child Development, 89*(5), 1803–1820. doi:10.1111/cdev.12868

Pearson, N. (2011). *Radical hope: Education and equality in Australia.* Melbourne, Australia: Black.

Pessoa, A. S. G., Coimbra, R. M., Murgo, C. S., van Breda, A., & Baker, A. (2018). Resilience processes of Brazilian young people: Overcoming adversity through an arts program. *Pesquisas e Práticas Psicossociais, 13*(3), e2565.

Ralph, S., & Ryan, K. (2017). Addressing the mental health gap in working with Indigenous youth. *Australian Psychologist, 52*(4), 288–298. doi:10.1111/ap.12287

Redman-MacLaren, M. L., Klieve, H., Mccalman, J., Russo, S., Rutherford, K., Wenitong, M., & Bainbridge, R. G. (2017). Measuring resilience and risk factors for the psychosocial well-being of Aboriginal and Torres Strait Islander boarding school students: Pilot baseline study results. *Frontiers in Education, 2*(5), 1–22. doi:10.3389/feduc.2017.00005

Roffey, S., & McCarthy, F. (2013). Circle solutions, a philosophy and pedagogy for learning positive relationships: What promotes and inhibits sustainable outcomes? *International Journal of Emotional Education, 5*(1), 36–55.

Rutherford, K., McCalman, J., & Bainbridge, R. (2019). The post-schooling transitions of remote Indigenous secondary school graduates: A systematic scoping review of support strategies. *International Journal of Rural and Remote Education, 29*(2), 8–25.

Rutter, H., Savona, N., Glonti, K., Bibby, J., Cummins, S., Finegood, D. T., . . . White, M. (2017). The need for a complex systems model of evidence for public health. *The Lancet, 390*(10112), 2602–2604. doi:10.1016/S0140-6736(17)31267-9

Salmon, M., Doery, K., Dance, P., Chapman, J., Gilbert, R., Williams, R., & Lovett, R. (2018). *Defining the indefinable: Descriptors of Aboriginal and Torres Strait Islander peoples' cultures and their links to health and wellbeing.* A literature review. Aboriginal and Torres Strait Islander Health Team, Research School of Population Health, The Australian National University, Canberra.

Sanders, J. (2013). *Conceptual development of the Pathways to Resilience Study.* The Pathways to Resilience Research Project (New Zealand):Whāia to huanui kia toa. Technical Report 1.

Sanders, J. R., Munford, R., & Liebenberg, L. (2016). The role of teachers in building resilience of at risk youth. *International Journal of Educational Research, 6*(80), 111–123. doi:10.1016/j.ijer.2016.10.002

Sanders, J., Munford, R., & Boden, J. (2017). Pathways to educational aspirations: Resilience as a mediator of proximal resources and risks. *Kōtuitui: New Zealand Journal of Social Sciences Online, 12*(2), 205–220. doi:10.1080/1177083X.2017.1367312

Sanders, J., Munford, R., & Thimasarn-Anwar, T. (2015). Staying on-track despite the odds: Factors that assist young people facing adversity to continue with their education. *British Educational Research Journal, 42*(1), 56–73. doi:org/10.1002/berj.3202

Smith, J., Trinidad, S., & Larkin, S. (2015). Participation in higher education in Australia among underrepresented groups: What can we learn from the Higher Education Participation Program to better support Indigenous learners? *Learning Communities: International Journal of Learning in Social Contexts*, *17*(Special Issue: Indigenous Pathways and Transitions into Higher Education), 12–28. doi:10.18793/LCJ2015.17.02

Sollecito, W., & Johnson, J. (2013). *McLaughlin and Kaluzny's continuous quality improvement in health care* (4th ed). Burlington, MA: Jones & Bartlett Learning.

Sonnemann, J., & Goss, P. (2018). *The commonwealth's role in improving schools*. Retrieved from https://grattan.edu.au/wp-content/uploads/2018/02/898-the-Commonwealths-role-in-improving-schools.pdf

Spears, B., Sanchez, D., Bishop, J., Rogers, S., & DeJong, J. A. (2006). Level 2 therapeutic model site. *American Indian and Alaska Native Mental Health Research*, *13*(2), 52–78.

Theron, L., Liebenberg, L., & Malindi, M. (2013). When schooling experiences are respectful of children's rights: A pathway to resilience. *School Psychology International*, *35*(3), 253–265. doi:10.1177/0142723713503254

Toland, J., & Carrigan, D. (2011). Educational psychology and resilience: New concept, new opportunities. *School Psychology International*, *32*(1), 95–106. doi:10.1177/0143034310397284

Tusaie, K., & Dyer, J. (2004). Resilience: A historical review of the construct. *Holistic Nursing Practice*, *18*(1), 3–8.

Ungar, M. (2004). The importance of parents and other caregivers to the resilience of high-risk adolescents. *Family Process*, *43*(1), 23–41.

Ungar, M. (2008). Resilience across cultures. *British Journal of Social Work*, *38*(2), 218–235. doi:10.1093/bjsw/bcl343

Ungar, M., & Liebenberg, L. (2011). Assessing resilience across cultures using mixed methods: Construction of the Child and Youth Resilience Measure. *Journal of Mixed Methods Research*, *5*(2), 126–149. doi:10.1177/1558689811400607

Ungar, M., Brown, M., Liebenberg, L., Othman, R., Kwong, W., & Armstrong, M. (2007). Unique pathways to resilience across cultures. *Adolescence*, *42*, 287–310.

Ungar, M., Ghazinour, M., & Richter, J. (2013). Annual research review: What is resilience within the social ecology of human development? *Journal of Child Psychology and Psychiatry*, *54*(4), 348–366. doi:10.1111/jcpp.12025

United Nations. (2007). *United Nations declaration on the rights of Indigenous people article 14: Right to education*. New York, NY: Author. Retrieved from https://www.humanrights.gov.au/united-nations-declaration-rights-indigenous-peoples-human-rights-your-fingertips-human-rights-your.

van Beek, A., & McCalman, J. (2018). *From research to impact: The Resilience Study. Research Translation in an Indigenous Student Resilience Project*. Retrieved from https://www.nhmrc.gov.au/sites/default/files/documents/attachments/symposium/alexandra_van_beek.pdf

van Breda, A. (2017). A comparison of youth resilience across seven South African sites. *Child & Family Social Work*, *22*(1), 226–235. doi:10.1111/cfs.12222

Waller, M. (2001). Resilience in ecosystemic context: Evolution of the concept. *American Journal of Orthopsychiatry*, *71*(3), 290–297.

Walter, M., & Andersen, C. (2013). *Indigenous statistics: A quantitative research methodology*. Los Angeles, CA: Left Coast Press.

Wright, M. O., Masten, A. S., & Narayan, A. J. (2013). Resilience processes in development: Four waves of research on positive adaptation in the context of adversity. In S. Goldstein & R. B. Brooks (Eds.), *Handbook of resilience in children* (pp. 15–37). New York, NY: Springer Science+Business Media.

Young, C., Craig, J. C., Clapham, K., Banks, S., & Williamson, A. (2019). The prevalence and protective factors for resilience in adolescent Aboriginal Australians living in urban areas: A cross-sectional study. *Australian and New Zealand Journal of Public Health*, *43*(1), 8–14. doi:10.1111/1753-6405.12853

Young, C., Tong, A., Nixon, J., Fernando, P., Kalucy, D., Sherriff, S., . . . Williamson, A. (2017). Perspectives on childhood resilience among the Aboriginal community: An interview study. *Australian and New Zealand Journal of Public Health*, *41*(4), 405–410. doi:10.1111/1753-6405.12681

12

A Transactional, Whole-School Approach to Resilience

Carmel Cefai

Introduction

When he was young, teachers thought that he was "too stupid to learn anything." He was fired from his first two jobs. His repeated electricity experiments were met with never-ending failure. After 1,000 failed attempts, he finally succeeded at inventing the light bulb.

The story of Thomas Edison and other famous people like Walt Disney, Nelson Mandela, Steve Jobs, Steve Hawking, and Albert Einstein are frequently used as role models for resilience and eventual success in the face of adversity and disadvantage. Resilience in these success stories, however, resides more in the individual himself or herself, construed as individual strengths like stress resistance, determination, grit, persistence, and hardiness. This conceptualization reflects the first generation of resilience research which led to the notion of "invulnerability" in the face of adverse life circumstances (Anthony, 1987; Garmezy & Nuechterlein, 1972). This linear, within-child model, however, did not endure in the face of more recent research, which suggests that like any other aspect of human development, resilience is best understood as the interaction between the individual and his or her environment, with both influencing one another (Luthar, 2006; Masten, 2001). Resilience depends on how individual psychological qualities interact with social systems such as the family, the community, and school as well as broader sociocultural systems (Masten, 2014; Ungar, 2012). The biopsychosocial perspective (Sameroff, 1995) defines resilience in terms of three key processes: biological processes such as predisposition and temperament; psychological processes such as coping skills, self-concept, and resourcefulness; and social processes such as healthy relationships and social support. It varies according to individual characteristics, age, context, and the nature of adversity, making it a unique experience for each individual

(Bonanno, 2012). In this chapter, I explore these transactional processes in the context of educational systems. After briefly discussing the ecological, transactional approach to resilience, I will present a resilience framework for educational systems informed by the research evidence. I conclude with a case study of a recently developed resilience program.

From Individual Invulnerability to Transactional Processes and Ecological Protection

Developmental outcomes are determined by complex patterns of interaction and transaction. Masten's (2014) more recent definition refers to the "capacity of a dynamic system to adapt successfully to disturbances that threaten system function, viability, or development" (p. 10) while Ungar (2008) defines resilience as "the capacity of individuals to navigate their way to the psychological, social, cultural, and physical resources that sustain their wellbeing, and their capacity individually and collectively to negotiate for these resources to be provided in culturally meaningful ways" (p. 225). Developmental systems theory (Lerner et al., 2013) construes resilience as a dynamic attribute of the relationship between an individual and his or her multilevel and relational developmental systems and how the fit between the individual and the features of the ecology reflect either adjustment or maladjustment in the face of threats. Ungar (2012) has developed a specific ecological perspective of resilience, shifting the understanding of resilience to a more socially embedded understanding of wellbeing, with resilience more likely to occur when society provides the services, support, and resources required to make it possible for every child to enjoy positive development.

In contrast to earlier understandings of resilience as a quality of the select, invulnerable few, the ecological perspective provides the opportunity for all children to develop resilience given resilience-enhancing, protective social contexts. Rather than an extraordinary process for some children possessing stress-resistant qualities, resilience is about "ordinary" responses focusing on individual and contextual strengths and assets (Masten, 2001; Ungar, 2012). A broad brush, ecological view avoids the danger of neoliberal approaches that put the onus of responsibility for successful adaptation on the individual in place of social structures and support services (Hart & Heaver, 2015). It is also more likely to yield interpretive models of resilience that can explain how people navigate through negative environments (Ungar, 2012, 2019). An evaluation of preventive resilience programs in fact shows that effective interventions are more likely when based on a developmental, ecological systems approach (O'Dougherty, Masten, & Narayan, 2013).

A Transactional, Whole-School, Resilience Framework

In line with the transactional model of resilience, multiple lines of research have identified various processes at both individual and contextual levels that protect children exposed to adversity. These include personal qualities like self-regulation, social competence, sense of control and self-efficacy, cognitive flexibility, goal-setting, and problem-solving. Protective contexts are characterized by a stable and supportive relationship with a significant adult, a stable and caring family environment, authoritative parenting, prosocial peer group, safe and prosocial community, and a caring school community (Cicchetti & Garmezy, 1993; Rutter, 1998; Werner & Smith, 1992). Schools are one of the most important and influential social systems in children's lives, having access to practically all children, including those coming from adverse environments. Various school processes have been found to promote resilience in children and young people, including a nurturing safe environment that reduces the stress in children's lives while providing opportunities for caring relationships, social connectedness, and active engagement in learning and social activities (Garmezy, Masten, & Tellegen, 1984; Rutter, 1998; Ungar, 2008, 2018; Werner & Smith, 1992). The identification of these protective processes has led to the development of various school-based interventions that seek to nurture the resilience of children and young people facing adversity. Such interventions focus on the whole school population (universal interventions) or on groups of children or individual children considered to be at risk in their development (targeted interventions). Proportional universal interventions seek to integrate universal interventions with targeted ones, presenting interventions to the whole school or class but with a specific focus on children at risk or experiencing developmental and social difficulties (Hart & Heaver, 2015).

Successful interventions are theory-driven, informed by a developmental, ecological systems approach, culturally relevant, comprehensive across multiple settings; occur at key transitional points; and maximize positive resources (O'Dougherty et al., 2013). In a qualitative review of systemic resilience Ungar (2018) concludes that systemic resilience occurs as a result of a sequence of multisystemic, interdependent interactions through which actors, whether individuals or systems, secure the resources required for sustainability in stressed environments. Resilience enhancing systems are those that are open, dynamic, and complex; promote connectivity; demonstrate experimentation and learning; and include diversity and participation. In a review of international studies of school-based resilience interventions for 12- to 18-year-olds, Hart and Heaver (2013) reported that effectiveness (prevention and reduction in emotional and behavior difficulties) resulted from teaching problem-solving skills, building relationships, and working at multiple system levels (individual, home, school, community). In the case of young people with complex needs, more intense and individualized interventions and continuity in the strategies employed to help children in both school and home contexts were found to predict better child development and academic outcomes.

One of the key components of many school-based interventions is the direct instruction in resilience skills. Rutter (2015) argues that resilience is not a quality that can be taught or measured since it is an interactive process that can only be identified as a response to adversity. He agrees, however, that children may be provided with experiential learning opportunities that provide them with the competencies that make them better prepared to face adversity and to function optimally despite challenges. Having the tools to deal effectively with manageable stressors strengthens the child's resolve and ability to overcome adversity and keep thriving, a process Rutter (2015) calls "steeling." One of the most effective programs that bolsters resilience is the FRIENDS program (Barrett, Lowry-Webster, & Turner, 1999). The program was developed in Australia with the aim of building resilience and social skills to address anxiety and depression through a whole school cognitive-behavioral therapy approach. It consists of four age-based programs: Fun Friends (4–7 years), Friends for Life (8–11 years), My Friends Youth (12–15 years), and Adult Resilience (16+ years). Each program includes activities that seek to promote social skills, self-esteem, problem-solving, resilience, emotional regulation, and building healthy relationships. Various large-scale studies, making use of randomized control trials, have reported that FRIENDS have been found to reduce anxiety in school children and increase their self-esteem, particularly in late childhood and early adolescence (Barrett et al., 2006; Bernstein et al., 2005; Lowry-Webster, Barrett, & Dadds, 2001; Stallard et al., 2007). In an randomized control trial carried out with 453 students aged 7 to 11 from three U.S. schools, Bernstein et al. (2005) reported significantly decreased anxiety levels in the FRIENDS group when compared with controls, with the best outcomes found among those who received the version of the intervention that also included a parent training component. Various reviews of studies provide evidence for the effectiveness of school-based, universal interventions like FRIENDS in improving self-confidence and social skills and reducing anxiety and depression among school children (Brunwasser, Gillham, & Kim 2009; Dray et al., 2017; Stockings et al., 2016; Werner-Seidler et al., 2017).

Universal social and emotional learning (SEL) programs have also been found to operate as resilience-enhancing interventions with children from more challenging environments (Durlak et al., 2011; Taylor et al., 2017, Weare & Nind, 2011). Taylor et al.'s (2017) meta-analyses of SEL programs reported that SEL not only helps to prevent internalizing and externalizing problems but also increases positive social attitudes and prosocial behavior as well as academic achievement. Other SEL reviews, such as those by Wilson and Lipsey (2009), Weare and Nind (2011) and Clarke et al. (2015) found that SEL was particularly effective for students at risk. Wilson and Lipsey's review of the effectiveness of both universal and targeted programs on the prevention of aggressive behaviors concluded that the most effective approaches included both universal and targeted aspects to the interventions. Clarke et al. found that interventions aimed at increasing social and emotional skills and reducing problem behaviors such as violence and substance misuse were particularly effective with children and youth who are most at risk of developing such behaviors. Weare and Nind reported that most universal approaches had a positive impact on the mental health of all children but were particularly effective for children most at risk.

The resilience literature, supported by closely related areas such as SEL and interventions to improve school climate indicate that a whole school, systems approach is one of the most effective ways to promote resilience in educational settings. Such an approach would include the following core components.

- *A skills based, universal resilience curriculum*, including building such competences as healthy relationships, problem-solving, decision-making, growth mindset, and self-determination (Elamé, 2013; Hart & Heaver, 2013; Hutchinson & Dorsett, 2012; National Scientific Council on the Developing Child, 2015; Porcelli, Ungar, Liebenberg, & Trepanier, 2014; Rutter, 2015). Research suggests that universal programs are more likely to be effective if they are integrated into standard curriculum (rather than presented as additions); are focused, skills-based, and experiential with the active participation of students; and

are embedded with other areas of the curriculum and improve classroom climate (Durlak et al., 2011; Rutter, 2015).
- *Targeted interventions:* Universal programs focused on interventions like SEL may not provide equal access to programs and services, particularly for children facing poverty, abuse, and neglect (Boivin & Hertzmanet, 2012). On their own they may not be as effective for students experiencing difficulties as programs with a targeted component (Weare & Nind, 2011). Proportional universal interventions integrate universal interventions with targeted ones, presenting interventions to the whole school or a single class, but with a specific focus on children at risk or experiencing difficulties, at a scale and intensity proportionate to the level of children's disadvantage (Boivin & Hertzman, 2012). Weare and Nind (2011) suggest universal interventions need to be accompanied by parallel targeted interventions for those with additional needs, while Werner et al. (2017) suggest a staged approach, with universal interventions followed by targeted interventions for students at risk.
- *Early intervention*: Resilience building needs to start at a young age when the child's brain and personality are still developing (Diamond & Lee, 2011). Early interventions, particularly during the early school years, are more likely to be effective than interventions begun later (Durlak et al., 2011; Jones, Greenberg & Crowley, 2015). In a longitudinal study of students coming from low income, multiethnic, and mixed rural/urban communities in the United States, Jones, Greenberg, and Crowley (2015) reported statistically significant associations between social-emotional skills in early years education and important positive outcomes in adulthood related to education, employment, criminal activity, substance use, and mental health.
- *Contextual processes:* Resilience-enhancing classrooms and schools are characterized by caring and supportive teacher–student relationships, supportive and inclusive peer networks, equal access to necessary resources, active and meaningful learner engagement, and positive beliefs and high expectations for all learners, particularly those from marginalized and disadvantaged backgrounds (Cicchetti & Garmezy, 1993; Garmezy et al., 1984; Pianta & Stuhlman, 2004; Rutter, 1998; Ungar, 2018; Werner & Smith, 1992).
- *Multiple systems interventions:* Resilience thrives when multiple social systems interact such as classrooms, schools (as a whole), peer groups, families, communities and cultural practices, with one system supporting and reinforcing processes occurring in other systems (Ungar, 2018). In their review of effective resilience interventions, O'Dougherty, Masten, and Narayan (2013) reported that successful programs are framed within a developmental, ecological systems approach; are culturally relevant; and comprehensive across multiple settings. This means that all influential adults in a child's life have a role to play in developing the child's resilience.
    - Parents are one of the most important systems in the promotion of resilience among school children. School-based programs are more likely to be effective when they are supported by complementary home-based interventions (Downey & Williams, 2010; Luthar, 2006; Weare & Nind, 2011). The active participation of parents not only helps to reinforce the resilience-related competencies being learned at school, but also enables the transfer of these competencies to different contexts such as the home, peer group, and community. Empowering parents to address their own well-being and

resilience, is another important component in a whole-school approach to resilience building (Bryan & Henry, 2012; Weare & Nind, 2011). The school may provide opportunities for parents for their own education and resilience, making accessible culturally sensitive information and resources, links to community services and facilities, and parent-led family learning and personal development courses (Cefai & Cavioni, 2014).

- When teachers' own interpersonal needs are addressed, they are more likely to pay attention to the social and emotional needs of their students and to do so effectively (Beltman, Mansfield, & Price, 2011; Day & Gu, 2010; Johnson & Down, 2013). Cefai and Cavioni (2014) suggest an integrated framework of teacher resilience, underlining teachers' psychological resources such as self-efficacy and agency on the one hand and a caring and supportive context such as collegiality and supportive administration on the other, with these two sets of processes complementing and supporting one another.

Interactions between these elements are critical to effective program delivery that bolsters resilience. A case study follows.

Case Study: *RESCUR Surfing the Waves*

RESCUR Surfing the Waves (Cefai et al., 2015) is a resilience program for early years and primary school children developed to support the education and well-being of marginalized and vulnerable children from ethnic, migrant, and low socioeconomic communities and children with special educational needs or disability. The program consists of an evidence-informed curriculum for children aged 4 to 12 making use of a "taught and caught approach," that is, direct instruction in resilience skills with sufficient program intensity and duration and experiential, skills-based learning, within resilience enhancing contexts at classroom, school, and family levels (Durlak et al., 2011; Weare & Nind, 2011).

Approach. RESCUR Surfing the Waves has been designed as a universal program for all students, but with various activities tailored according to the needs of marginalized and vulnerable children. It consists of skills-based activities based on six major themes, delivered regularly by the classroom teacher as part of the curriculum within a spiral approach, building the key competencies from the early years to the infant and the junior years in the primary school, with increasing complexity at each developmental level. The activities address the diversity of learners, and are presented at basic, intermediate and advanced levels to be adapted according to the developmental level of the learners. In line with the program's proportional universalism perspective, each theme addresses the challenges faced by vulnerable and marginalized children, such as bullying, prejudice, discrimination, isolation, language barriers, difficulty in accessing learning, and exclusion.

The Six Themes

The program covers a range of resilience competencies such as self-awareness, problem-solving, growth mindset, optimism, adaptability, self-determination, empathy, collaboration, and caring relationships (Elamé, 2013; Hart & Heaver, 2013; Hutchinson & Dorsett, 2012; National Scientific Council on the Developing Child, 2015; Porcelli, Ungar, Liebenberg, & Trepanier, 2014; Rutter, 2015; Ungar, 2012). These concepts are embedded within six broad themes. The first theme aims to develop the learners' *communication skills*, balancing self-expression and standing up for oneself with listening to and understanding others. The second theme seeks to develop social competencies like making friends, seeking and providing support, enhancing cooperative skills, and engaging in empathic, ethical, and responsible behavior. In the third theme, learners develop positive and optimistic thinking and identify and make use of such qualities as hope, happiness, and humor. In the fourth theme, developing self-determination, learners are supported to develop problem-solving skills, as well as a sense of purpose, agency, and self-advocacy. The fifth theme focuses on developing a positive self-concept while making use of strengths in academic and social engagement. The sixth and final theme develops the competency of turning challenges into opportunities for growth, such as how to deal effectively with adversity, discrimination, rejection, loss, family conflict, bullying, and change.

Pedagogy

RESCUR Surfing the Waves makes use of the SAFE (sequenced, active, focused, explicit) approach (Durlak et al., 2011) in skills development. The activities follow a step-by-step structure, are experiential and interactive, are focused on resilience building as part of the curriculum and have clear learning goals. Pedagogically, the curriculum makes use of a multisensory approach, including mindfulness, storytelling, drama, role play, physical activities, and art and crafts, among others. Among all these techniques, story-telling is one of the most important tools, giving learners the opportunity to gain insight into their own and others' behavior (Hankin, Omer, Elias, & Raviv, 2012). The stories for the younger children are based on animals, focused on the adventures of Sherlock the squirrel (representing diversity) and Zelda the hedgehog (representing disability). The late primary school activities make use of resilience fables and real-life stories, such as the stories of Nelson Mandela, Walt Disney, Steve Jobs, and Malala, among others. Each activity includes a take-home activity where the learners and members of their family complete a related home-based task. To enable the transfer of learning, teachers are encouraged to embed the resilience competencies being taught into other academic subjects and the daily life of the classroom, while providing learners with the opportunity to practice their newly learned skills both in the classroom and outside. At the end of each theme teachers and learners (primary school years only) complete a formative checklist evaluating the development of the respective learning goals and outcomes. The checklist also includes qualitative information on the learners' strengths, needs and targets for improvement.

A Systemic, Ecological Approach

RESCUR Surfing the Waves was developed as a whole school, systemic program, with the curriculum being supported by the entire school community, including the active participation of parents and caregivers (Weare & Nind, 2011). Each classroom activity includes a take-home task, while the Learners' Portfolio serves as a home–school channel of communication. Parents and caregivers are also provided with a Parents' Guide, which describes their role in the program and includes activities they can do with their own children at home on each of the six themes. The program recommends close collaboration between home and school, including training workshops for parents.

Teachers' education and their own resilience are also a key component of RESCUR Surfing the Waves. Before the start of the implementation, classroom teachers are expected to attend a workshop on how to implement the program. Workshops include training in mindfulness, storytelling, and use of puppets (including processing discussions); organization of practical activities; working with parents; creating a resilience-enhancing classroom climate; dealing with sensitive issues; quality adaptation according to context; use of assessment checklists; completing the implementation index; and finally promoting teachers' own well-being and resilience. The Teachers' Guide includes a chapter on how the teachers may organize the classroom as a caring community built on warm and caring relationships, collaboration, inclusion, meaningful engagement, and participation in decision-making. The teaching of resilience competencies itself is set to impact the teachers' overall practice, with resilience becoming embedded within the classroom climate (Jennings & Greenberg, 2009). The program addresses the school staff's own social and emotional needs (Beltman, Mansfield, & Price, 2011; Mansfield et al., 2012), and the Teachers' Guide includes a chapter on how teachers can maintain their own resilience through such strategies as mindfulness, connectedness, collegiality, mentoring, education, and support.

Evaluation

Although RESCUR Surfing the Waves is heavily influenced by the existing research on resilience (evidence-informed), evaluations of the program itself are ongoing. A small-scale pre–post study of the early years program (Milković, 2017) evaluated two themes with 173 children aged three to seven years over a three-month period in Croatia. It reported an improvement in children's resilience skills and behaviors for children both with and without risk factors. Another study of the early years program was carried out in five kindergarten centers in Malta over a one-year period (Cefai et al., 2018). A preintervention–post intervention study in 20 classrooms (97 children; no control groups) showed an improvement in resilience skills, prosocial behavior, and learning engagement, but no significant decrease in internalizing and externalizing problem behaviors. In a series of evaluations of the programme in Portuguese schools, making use of semi-randomised control trial as well as a qualitative design, Simoes et al. (2020) reported an increase in students' social and emotional competence and decrease in social, emotional and behaviour difficulties, particularly in young children, as well as a positive impact on teachers' social and emotional competence and resilience. A study on Greek parents' perspectives, Matsopoulos, Govogiannaki and Griva (2020) found that parents of primary school children exposed to the programme reported an increase in their children's social and emotional competence, with benefits also for the family.

Conclusion

A resilience perspective has brought about a paradigm shift in our understanding of children's healthy development and well-being, moving away from a deficit model of human development to strengths-based, positive development of marginalized and vulnerable children. The field itself has been undergoing a process of transformation in recent decades through a series of "waves" of research and theory development, from the initial notion of individual invulnerability to systems resilience, and from linear models based on resilience factors to the integration of transactional processes within and between multiple systems. Current research points to a comprehensive, multilayered ecosystems approach to resilience, focusing both on microprocesses such as listening to and including children's own voices in the development, implementation, and evaluation of interventions to the consideration of the contextual, cultural, and political influences of broad ecosystems on positive human development. Such an approach is contributing to the creation of more effective resilience-enhancing systems such as schools, families, and communities, as well as broader social, cultural, and political systems, thus serving as a medium for the promotion of equity, social inclusion, and well-being. Programs that foster changes across all these levels are those most likely to have the greatest impact on children's psychosocial outcomes, although evidence for the effectiveness of such programs is still emerging.

Key Messages

1. Resilience is not about invulnerability but about growth and success in the face of vulnerability, a result of the interaction between the individual and his or her environment.
2. Resilience is more about ecology than individuality. In contrast to the earlier understandings of resilience for the select, invulnerable few, the ecological perspective provides the opportunity for all children to develop resilience given resilience-enhancing, protective social contexts. This perspective avoids the danger of putting the onus of responsibility for change on the individual in place of social structures and support services.
3. Resilience building needs to start early in children's development, with interventions occurring across multiple settings, informed by a developmental, ecological systems approach, and it must be culturally relevant.

References

Anthony, E. J. (1987). Risk, vulnerability and resilience: An overview. In E. J. Anthony & B. Cohler (Eds.), *The invulnerable child* (pp. 3–48). New York, NY: Guilford Press.

Barrett, P. M., Lowry-Webster, H., & Turner, C. M. (1999). *FRIENDS for children group leader manual*. Brisbane: Australian Academic Press.

Barrett, P. M., Farrell, L. I., Ollendick, T. H., & Dadds, M. (2006). Long-term outcomes of an Australian universal prevention trial of anxiety and depression symptoms in children and youth: An evaluation of the friends program. *Journal of Clinical Child and Adolescent Psychology, 35*(3), 403–411. doi:10.1207/s15374424jccp3503_5

Beltman, S., Mansfield, C. F., & Price, A. (2011). Thriving not just surviving: A review of research on teacher resilience. *Educational Research Review, 6*(3), 185–207. doi:10.1016/j.edurev.2011.09.001

Bernstein, G. A., Layne, A. E., Egan, E. A., & Tennison, D. M. (2005). School-based interventions for anxious children. *Journal of the American Academy of Child & Adolescent Psychiatry, 44*(11), 1118–1127. doi:10.1097/01.chi.0000177323.40005.a1

Boivin, M., & Hertzman, C. (2012). *Early childhood development: Adverse experiences and developmental health*. Ottawa, ON: Royal Society of Canada.

Bonanno, G. A. (2012). Uses and abuses of the resilience construct: Loss, trauma, and health-related adversities. *Social Science & Medicine, 74*(5), 753–756. doi:10.1016/j.socscimed.2011.11.022

Brunwasser, S. M., Gillham, J. E., & Kim, E. S. (2009). A meta-analytic re-view of the Penn Resiliency Program's effect on depressive symptoms. *Journal of Consulting and Clinical Psychology, 77*(6), 1042–1054. doi:10.1037/a0017671

Bryan, J., & Henry, L. (2012). A model for building school-family-community partnerships: Principles and process. *Journal of Counseling and Development, 90*, 408–420. doi:10.1002/j.1556-6676.2012.00052.x

Cefai, C., & Cavioni, V. (2014). *Social and emotional education in primary school. Integrating theory and research into practice*. New York: NY: Springer.

Cefai, C., Miljević-Riđički, R., Bouillet, D., Pavin Ivanec, T., Matsopoulous, A., Gavogiannaki, M., . . . Eriksson, C. (2015). *RESCUR Surfing the Waves. A resilience curriculum for early years and primary schools. A teachers' guide*. Malta: Centre for Resilience and Socio-Emotional Health, University of Malta.

Cefai, C., Arlove, A., Duca, M., Galea, N., Muscat, M., & Cavioni, V. (2018) RESCUR Surfing the Waves: An evaluation of a resilience program in the early years. *Pastoral Care in Education, 36*(3), 189–204. doi:10.1080/02643944.2018.1479224

Cicchetti, D., & Garmezy, N. (1993). Milestones in the development of resilience. *Development and Psychopathology, 5*(4), 497–774.

Clarke, A. M., Morreale, S., Field, C. A., Hussein, Y., & Barry, M. M. (2015). *What works in enhancing social and emotional skills development during childhood and adolescence? A review of the evidence on the effectiveness of school-based and out-of-school programs in the UK*. WHO Collaborating Centre for Health Promotion Research, National University of Ireland Galway.

Day, C., & Gu, Q. (2010). Resilience counts. In C. Day & Q. Gu (Eds.), *The new lives of teachers* (pp. 156–176). London, UK: Routledge.

Diamond, A., & Lee, K. (2011). Interventions shown to aid executive function development in children 4-12 years old. *Science, 333*, 959–964. doi:10.1126/science.1204529

Downey, C., & Williams, C. (2010). Family SEAL—A home-school collaborative program focusing on the development of children's social and emotional skills. *Advances in School Mental Health Promotion, 3*(1), 30–41. doi:10.1080/1754730X.2010.9715672

Dray, J., Bowman, J., Campbell, E., Freund, M., Wolfenden, L., Hodder, R., . . . Wiggers, J. (2017). Systematic review of universal resilience interventions targeting child and adolescent mental health in the school setting. *Journal of the American Academy of Child & Adolescent Psychiatry, 56*(10), 813–824. doi:10.1016/j.jaac.2017.07.780

Durlak, J. A., Weissberg, R. P., Dymnicki, A. B., & Taylor, R. D. (2011). The impact of enhancing students' social and emotional learning: A meta-analysis of school-based universal interventions. *Child Development, 82*(1), 474–501. doi:10.1111/j.1467-8624.2010.01564.x

Elamé, E. (2013). *Discriminatory bullying: A new intercultural dialogue*. Berlin, Germany: Springer Verlag.

Garmezy, N., & Nuechterlein, K. (1972). Invulnerable children: The fact and fiction of competence and disadvantage. *The American Journal of Orthopsychiatry, 42*, 328–329.

Garmezy, N., Masten, A. S., & Tellegen, A. (1984). The study of stress and competence in children: A building block for developmental psychopathology. *Child Development, 55*, 97–111. doi:10.2307/1129837

Hankin, V., Omer, D., Elias, M. J., & Raviv, A. (2012). *Stories to help build emotional intelligence and resilience in young children*. Champaigne, IL: Research Press.

Hart, A., & Heaver, B. (2013). Evaluating resilience-based programs for schools using a systematic consultative review. *Journal of Child and Youth Development, 1*(1), 27–53.

Hart, A., & Heaver, B (2015). *Resilience approaches to supporting young people's mental health appraising the evidence base for schools and communities*. Brighton, UK: University of Brighton/Boingboing.

Hutchinson, M., & Dorsett, P. (2012). What does the literature say about resilience in refugee people? Implications for practice. *Journal of Social Inclusion, 3*, 55–78. doi:10.36251/josi.55

Jennings, P. A., & Greenberg, M. T. (2009). The prosocial classroom: Teacher social and emotional competence in relation to child and classroom outcomes. *Review of Educational Research, 79*(1), 491–525. doi:10.3102/0034654308325693

Johnson, B., & Down, B. (2013). Critically re-conceptualising early career teacher resilience. *Discourse: Studies in the Cultural Politics of Education, 34*(5), 703–715. doi:10.1080/01596306.2013.728365

Jones, D. E., Greenberg, M., & Crowley, M. (2015). Early social-emotional functioning and public health: The relationship between kindergarten social competence and future wellness. *American Journal of Public Health, 105,* 2283–2290. doi:10.2105/AJPH.2015.302630

Lerner, R. M., Agans, J. P., Arbeit, M. R., Chase, P. A., Weiner, M. B., Schmid, C. L., & Warren, A. E. A. (2013). Resilience and positive youth development: A relational developmental systems model. In S. Goldstein & R. B. Brooks (Eds.), *Handbook of resilience in children* (pp. 293–308). New York, NY: Springer.

Lowry-Webster, H. M., Barrett, P. M., & Dadds, M. R. (2001). A universal prevention trial of anxiety and depressive symptomatology in childhood: Preliminary data from an Australian study. *Behaviour Change, 18*(1), 36–50. doi:10.1375/bech.18.1.36

Luthar, S. (2006). Resilience in development: A synthesis of research across five decades. In D. Cicchetti & D. J. Cohen (Eds.), *Developmental psychopathology: Risk, disorder and adaptation* (2nd ed., pp. 739–795). New York, NY: Wiley.

Mansfield, C. F., Beltman, S., Price, A., & McConney, A. (2012). "Don't sweat the small stuff:" Understanding teacher resilience at the chalkface. *Teaching and Teacher Education, 28,* 357–367. doi:10.1016/j.tate.2011.11.001

Masten, A. S. (2001). Ordinary magic: Lessons from research on resilience in human development. *Education Canada, 49*(3), 28–32.

Masten, A. S. (2014). Global perspectives on resilience in children and youth. *Child Development, 85*(1), 6–20. doi:10.1111/cdev.12205

Matsopoulos, A., Gavongiannaki, M., & Griva, A.M. (2020) Parents' perceptions and evaluation of the implementation of a resilience curriculum in Greek schools. *International Journal of School & Educational Psychology, 8*(2), 104–118.

Milković, M. (2017, June). *Evaluation of RESCUR's effects on resilience of children in kindergarten in Croatia.* Presentation at the sixth ENSEC conference, Stockholm, Sweden.

National Scientific Council on the Developing Child. (2015). *Supportive relationships and active skill-building strengthen the foundations of resilience: Working paper 13.* Cambridge, MA: Centre for the Developing Child, Harvard University.

O'Dougherty, M., Masten, A., & Narayan, A. (2013). Resilience processes in development: Four waves of research on positive adaptation in the context of adversity. In S. Goldstein & R. B. Brooks (Eds.), *Handbook of resilience in children* (pp. 15–37). New York, NY: Springer.

Pianta, R. C., & Stuhlman, M. W. (2004). Teacher-child relationships and children's success in the first years of school. *School Psychology Review, 33*(3), 444–458.

Porcelli, P., Ungar, M., Liebenberg, L., & Trepanier, N. (2015). (Micro)mobility, disability and resilience: Exploring well-being among youth with physical disabilities. *Disability & Society, 29*(6), 863–876. doi:10.1080/09687599.2014.902360

Rutter, M. (1998). Developmental catch-up, and deficit, following adoption after severe global early privation. English and Romanian Adoptees (ERA) Study Team. *Journal of Child Psychology and Psychiatry, 39*(4), 465–476. doi:10.1111/1469-7610.00343

Rutter, M. (2015). Resilience: Concepts, findings, and clinical implications. In A. Thapar, D. S. Pine, J. F. Leckman, S. Scott, M. J. Snowling, & E. A. Taylor (Eds.), *Rutter's child and adolescent psychiatry* (pp. 341–351). Oxford, UK: Wiley-Blackwell.

Sameroff, A. J. (1995). General systems theories and developmental psychopathology. In D. Cicchetti & D. J. Cohen (Eds.), *Wiley series on personality processes. Developmental psychopathology, Vol. 1. Theory and methods* (pp. 659–695). John Wiley & Sons.

Simões, C., Lebre, P., Santos, A., Fonseca, A. M., Simões, A., Branquinho, C., Gaspar, T., & Gaspar De Matos, M. (2020). Resilience Promotion In Portugal: Rescur In Action. In C. Cefai and R. Spiteri (Eds.), *Resilience in Schools: Research and Practice* (pp. 109–126). Malta: Centre for Resilience and Socio-Emotional Health, University of Malta.

Stockings, E. A., Degenhardt, L., Dobbins, T., Lee, Y. Y., Erskine, H. E., Whiteford, H. A., & Patton, G. (2016). Preventing depression and anxiety in young people: A review of the joint efficacy of universal, selective and indicated prevention. *Psychological Medicine, 46*(1), 11–26. doi:10.1017/S0033291715001725

Stallard, P., Simpson, N., Anderson, S., Hibbert, S., & Osborn, C. (2007). The FRIENDS emotional health programme: Initial findings from a school-based project. *Child and Adolescent Mental Health, 12*(1), 32–37. doi:10.1111/j.1475-3588.2006.00421.x

Taylor, R., Oberle, E., Durlak, J. A., & Weissberg, R. P. (2017). Promoting positive youth development through school-based social and emotional learning interventions: A meta-analysis of follow-up effects. *Child Development, 88*(4), 1156–1171. doi:10.1111/cdev.12864

Ungar, M. (2008). Resilience across cultures. *The British Journal of Social Work, 38*(2), 218–235. doi:10.1093/bjsw/bcl343

Ungar, M. (2012). Researching and theorizing resilience across cultures and contexts. *Preventive Medicine, 55*(5), 387–389. doi:10.1016/j.ypmed.2012.07.021

Ungar, M. (2018). Systemic resilience: Principles and processes for a science of change in contexts of adversity. *Ecology and Society, 23*(4), 34. doi:10.5751/ES-10385-230434

Ungar, M. (2019). *Change your world: The science of resilience and the true path to success.* Toronto, ON: Sutherland House.

Weare, K., & Nind, M. (2011). Mental health promotion and problem prevention in schools: What does the evidence say? *Health Promotion International, 26*(Suppl. 1), i29–i69. doi:10.1093/heapro/dar075

Werner, E., & Smith, R. (1992). *Overcoming the odds: High-risk children from birth to adulthood.* New York, NY: Cornell University Press.

Werner-Seidler, A., Perry, Y., Calear, A. L., Newby, J. M., & Christensen, H. (2017). School-based depression and anxiety prevention programs for young people: A systematic review and meta-analysis. *Clinical Psychology Review, 51*, 30–47.

Wilson, S. J., & Lipsey, M. J. (2009). Effectiveness of school-based intervention programs on aggressive behavior: Update of a meta-analysis. *American Journal of Preventive Medicine, 33*(Suppl. 2), S130–S143. doi:10.1016/j.amepre.2007.04.011

13

Learning About Systemic Resilience From Studies of Student Resilience

Linda Theron

Introduction

Significant stressors, such as family or school dysfunction, poor physical and mental health, sociopolitical conflict, disasters, and structural disadvantage, have the potential to jeopardize human development and learning. Moreover, these stressors are pervasive (Masten, 2018). Even so, many students whose learning and development are challenged engage in education (Kabiru, Beguy, Ndugwa, Zulu, & Jessor, 2012; Theron & Van Rensburg, 2018), demonstrate academic buoyancy and/or academic achievement (Martin & Marsh, 2008; Motti-Stefanidi, 2015; Obradović et al., 2009), and/or attain or sustain mental health (Dray et al., 2017; Sharp, Penner, Maraïs, & Skinner, 2019).

To explain and facilitate the previously mentioned positive outcomes, studies of student resilience have proliferated (see Table 13.1). Following Ungar (2011) and other similarly prominent social scientists' emphasis on a social ecology's (e.g., a school ecology) shared responsibility for youth resilience, accounts of student resilience do not hold vulnerable students solely responsible for positive learning and developmental outcomes. Instead, student resilience is defined as a dynamic interaction between a student and a school ecology that facilitates her or his positive adaptation to current and historic stressors that have, or previously had, the potential to obstruct learning and/or development (Theron & Donald, 2013; Toland & Carrigan, 2011).

A school ecology comprises multiple systems that are primarily relational and organizational (Waters, Cross, & Shaw, 2010). The relational systems include a school's major role players—its students, staff, and parents—and the interactions between these role players.

TABLE 13.1 Microsystemic Competencies/Processes/Resources Associated With Resilient Learning and Development

Microsystem	Competencies/Processes/Resources	Sample Sources
Student	Agency, autonomy	Berridge (2017), Deakin Crick et al. (2015), Doll (2013), Truebridge (2014)
	Cognitive capacity	Cinkara (2017), Malekan and Hajimohammadi (2017), Willner et al. (2015)
	Self-regulation	Ainscough et al. (2018), Fried and Chapman (2012), Kim et al. (2018), Portilla et al. (2014)
	Social/emotional competencies	Alessandri et al. (2017), Bailey and Baines (2012), Khambati et al. (2018), Truebridge (2014), Wilson (2016)
	Engagement in school	Irvin (2012), Khambati et al. (2018), Jones and Lafreniere (2014), Motti-Stefanidi and Masten (2013), Venta et al. (2018)
Educational institution	**Whole school level**	
	Compliance with enabling district/national policy	Cornell and Limber (2015), Crawford and Burns (2015), Freeman and Simonsen (2015), Snelling et al. (2017)
	Community-congruent, positive values	Cohen (2013), Reyes et al. (2013)
	Competent leadership	Day and Gu (2013), Sardar and Galdames (2018)
	Curricula; prevention and/or intervention programs	Corcoran et al. (2018), Dray et al. (2017), Fenwick-Smith et al. (2018), Henderson (2012), Hodder et al. (2017), Mirzah and Arif (2018), Obradović et al. (2009), Siu (2009)
	Green school yards/opportunities to play	Chawla et al. (2014), Doll and Brehm (2010)
	Infrastructure/furniture that support the physical safety of students/staff; safe schools	Cluver et al. (2019), Hewitt et al. (2001), Sheffield et al. (2017), Shiwaku et al. (2016), Sweet and Tucker (2018)
	Positive organizational climate	Aldridge et al. (2016), Cohen (2013), Henderson (2012), Mampane and Bouwer (2011), Peguero et al. (2019), Yablon (2015)
	Relevant school-based services	Höjer and Johansson (2013 Kumpulainen et al. (2016), Masten (2014)
	School family connections/partnerships	Esquivel et al. (2011), Nichols et al. (2016), Motti-Stefanidi (2015), Shute et al. (2011), Tzuriel and Shomron (2018)
	Supportive and/or prosocial peers	Delgado et al. (2016), Espinoza et al. (2014), Furrer et al. (2014), Im et al. (2016), Maunder and Monks (2018), Oldfield et al. (2018), Sapouna and Wolke (2013), Tatlow-Golden et al. (2016), Wentzel et al. (2004)
	Classroom level	
	Resilient teachers	Beltman (Mansfield (and Price (2011), Papatraianou et al. (2018), Soulen and Wine (2018), Wosnitza et al. (2018)
	Warm, respectful classroom relationships [including teacher↔student and student↔peer relationships]	Cefai (2007), Doll (2013), Doll et al. (2014), Hall and Theron (2016), Harðardóttir et al. (2015), Nolan et al. (2014), Papatraianou et al. (2018), Roorda et al. (2011), Sharkey et al. (2008), Theron and Theron (2014), Trieu and Jayakody (2018), Venta et al. (2018)
	Adaptive teaching and/or assessment approaches	Hadas-Lidor and Weiss (2014), Harðardóttir et al. (2015), Howell et al. (2018), Tull et al. (2017)

The organizational systems, meanwhile, comprise structural (e.g., the size of a school or the sector it represents), functional (e.g., policies and procedures), and built (e.g., a school's buildings or recreational facilities) dimensions. Waters et al. (2010) expressed concern that studies of positive student outcomes (e.g., school connectedness) have marginalized the role of organizational impacts (particularly the built environment). However, organizational systems (including the built school environment) are surfacing in studies relating to school capacity for disaster resilience (e.g., Shiwaku, Ueda, Oikawa, & Shaw, 2016).

As presaged by Bronfenbrenner (1979), students, their families, and the human and organizational systems associated with a school ecology are themselves nested in a wider ecology. For instance, school implementation of enabling policies (e.g., policies that support healthy nutrition or physical safety) implies that the school is embedded in a macrosystem (such as a school district or state) that is sensitive to its duty to support young citizens' well-being and has the necessary capitals to support policy compliance (Snelling et al., 2017). In other words, as illustrated in Figure 13.1, student resilience needs to be understood in systemic context that includes micro- and macrolevel influences (Theron & Donald, 2013). From this systemic perspective, student resilience is intertwined with proximal and distal human and organizational systems that are interdependently and iteratively facilitative of positive student outcomes (Roffey, 2016).

In this chapter I draw on studies of student resilience, and their attention to the multiple and co-occurring systems that facilitate a student's positive adaptation to significant stressors, to distill a set of propositions that promotes a multisystemic conceptualization of human resilience. To arrive at these propositions, I first reflect on resilience-enabling transactions between students and school ecologies and argue that these transactions are (a) complex, (b) scaffolded by resilient school ecologies, and (c) imply trade-offs at the expense of teacher well-being. I conclude the chapter by considering the value of the three propositions for future investigations and applications of resilience in educational settings.

Resilience-Enabling Transactions Between Students and School Ecologies Are Complex

Inter- and cross-disciplinary inquiry has supported a comprehensive understanding of how students and their school ecologies contribute to the process of successful learning and development under stress (Alexander, 2018; Noltemeyer & Bush, 2013). Essentially, each facilitates successful learning and development via various adaptive capacities, processes, or supports (see Table 13.1). For instance, much attention has been paid to students' capacity to regulate their emotion, behavior, and cognition and how this capacity shapes positive learning and developmental outcomes, particularly in the face of threats to their learning and development (Masten, 2014; Masten & Wright, 2010). Similarly, much attention has also been paid to teacher capacity to champion the resilience of vulnerable children and youth (Ungar, Russell, & Connelly, 2014). Teachers' capacity to work supportively with students and their families, communicate realistic expectations, inspire agency and mastery, and teach competently are associated with students' successful learning and development (Theron, 2016a). Even though

Diagram

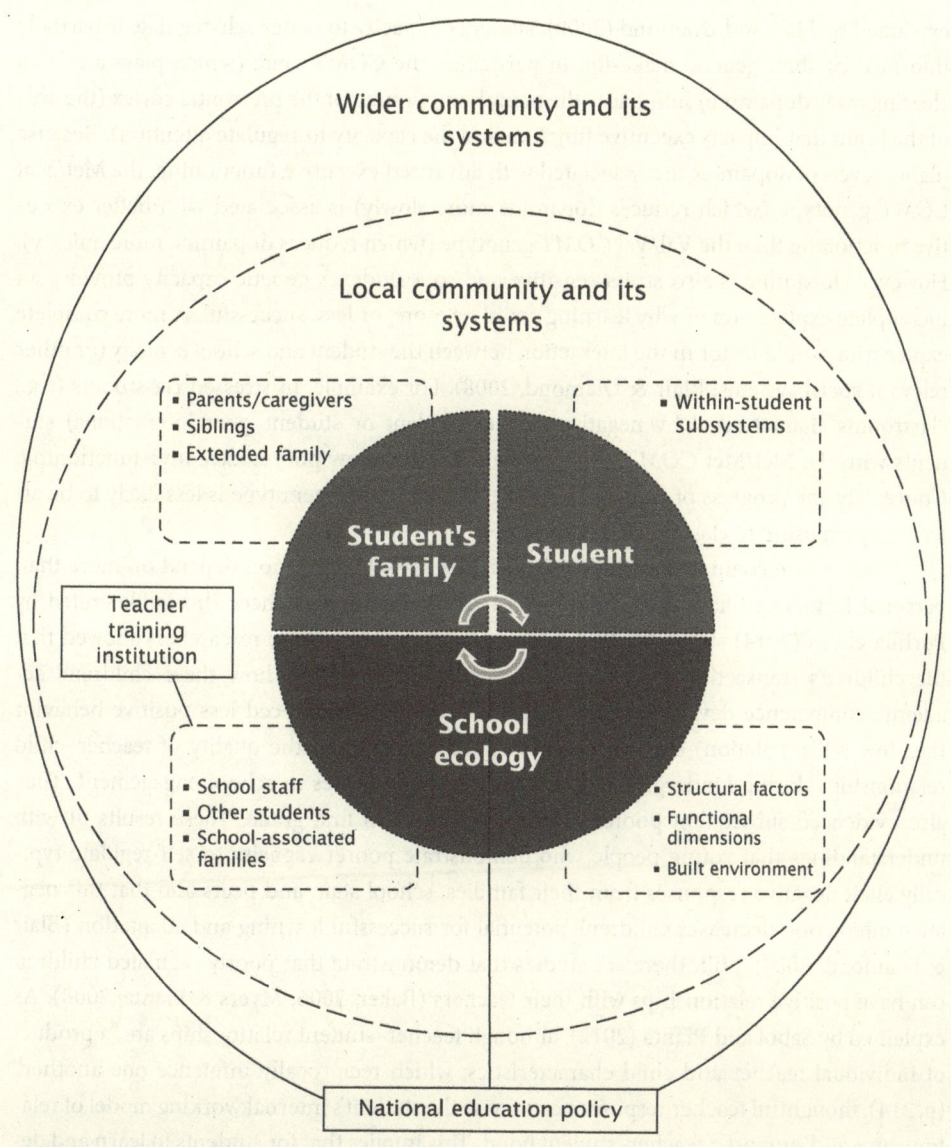

- Wider community and its systems
  - Local community and its systems
    - Student's family
      - Parents/caregivers
      - Siblings
      - Extended family
    - Student
      - Within-student subsystems
    - School ecology
      - School staff
      - Other students
      - School-associated families
      - Structural factors
      - Functional dimensions
      - Built environment
    - Teacher training institution
    - National education policy

FIGURE 13.1 The multiple systems implicated in vulnerable young people's learning and development. Adapted from Donald et al. (2010) and Masten (2014).

these capacities often come at a cost to teachers themselves (e.g., teacher burnout; Fleming, Mackrain, & LeBuffe, 2013), they are considered pivotal to student resilience.

In interaction, however, adaptive capacities, processes, or supports are strengthened or weakened (e.g., Baker, 2006; Mitchell, 2017; Portilla, Ballard, Adler, Boyce, & Obradović, 2014; Rimm-Kaufman, Baroody, Larsen, Curby, & Abry, 2015; Rudasill & Rimm-Kaufman, 2009; Vanlaar et al., 2016). Studies on self-regulation offer a meaningful illustration of the aforementioned. Better executive functioning and associated self-regulation skills (traditionally considered a within-person subsystem) advance students' capacity to learn effectively. As explained by Blair and Diamond (2008), students' capacity to better self-regulate is partially informed by their genetic make-up. In particular, the COMT gene (which plays a role in clearing away dopamine) influences the neural functioning of the prefrontal cortex (the area of the brain that impacts executive function and the capacity to regulate attention). Because higher levels of dopamine are associated with advanced executive functioning, the Met/Met *COMT* genotype (which reduces dopamine more slowly) is associated with better executive functioning than the Val/Val *COMT* genotype (which reduces dopamine more quickly). However, dopamine is also stress-sensitive and so a student's genetic capacity provides an incomplete explanation of why learning could be more, or less, successful. A more complete explanation would factor in the interaction between the student and school ecology (or other relevant social systems; Blair & Diamond, 2008). For example, in stressed classrooms (e.g., classrooms characterized by negative teacher–student or student–peer interactions) students with the Met/Met *COMT* genotype would likely show poorer executive functioning. Conversely, the progress of students with the Val/Val *COMT* genotype is less likely to be affected by exposure to classroom-related stress.

Failure to recognize that students' capacities for self-regulation depend on more than personal factors can have dire consequences for academic resilience. This is illustrated by Portilla et al.'s (2014) study of 338 American five-year-olds. These researchers showed that the children's transactional relationships with teachers shaped how these children's academic competence developed over time. Children who evidenced less positive behavior (i.e., low self-regulation) experienced associated decreases in the quality of teacher–child relationships during kindergarten and concomitant decreases in school engagement. They also evidenced subsequent poorer academic progress in first grade. These results fit with understandings that young people who demonstrate poorer capacity to self-regulate typically elicit negative responses from their families, school staff, and peers and that this negative interaction decreases children's potential for successful learning and adaptation (Blair & Diamond, 2008). Still, there are studies that demonstrate that poorly regulated children can have positive relationships with their teachers (Baker, 2006; Myers & Pianta, 2008). As explained by Sabol and Pianta (2012), although teacher–student relationships are "a product of individual teacher and child characteristics, which reciprocally influence one another" (p. 214), thoughtful teacher responses can revise the student's internal working model of relationships and support a teacher–student bond. This implies that for students to learn and develop well, the capacity of teachers (and other adults) to regulate their responses to students who are poorly self-regulated is at least as important as students' capacity to self-regulate. The same applies to the other microsystems (e.g., families or peers) implicated in successful learning and development.

Despite growing understandings that adult capacity to self-regulate intersects with students' regulatory capacities, interventions to support self-regulation are typically aimed at students; parents, teachers, and others with whom students might interact regularly are routinely excluded (Haslam, Mejia, Thomson, & Betancourt, 2019). Moreover, as Haslam and colleagues (2019) showed in their empirical work documenting the benefits of self-regulation to resilience and how best to advance this skill, most of this research has been conducted in high-income countries that value individualism. This has fueled concerns about whether self-regulation manifests similarly or differently in low- and middle-income countries where interdependence is valued and self-regulation is often a function of the collective. These concerns illustrate the complexity of truly understanding, and facilitating, resilience-enabling student↔school transactions across contexts.

Further, how school ecologies transact with students to support resilience can be influenced by schools'/students' interactions with other important microsystems (e.g., the at-risk student's family). For instance, teacher interactions with parents, and vice versa, are associated with vulnerable young people's constructive engagement in education (Doll, 2013). A case in point is a phenomenological study of the resilience of 16 South African university students from structurally disadvantaged contexts (Theron & Theron, 2014). During high school, their academic success was frequently threatened by a lack of basic resources that complicated payment of mandatory school fees, punctuality, and/or regular school attendance. Once the students' family had communicated the reasons for these complications to school staff, the staff were supportive and found creative ways to accommodate these young people in the school system. The students reported that teachers' positive responses to family-mediated information fueled their determination to succeed academically. Importantly, Theron and Theron (2014) drew attention to the role of teacher approachability in family disclosures about hardship and linked such openness to teachers' understanding of the socioeconomic and historical context of the schools they worked in and how this impacted local families and students. Many South African parents, particularly those from disadvantaged communities, avoid interacting with their children's school. This relates to South Africa's historic political inequities and ongoing structural inequality that have translated into significant numbers of poorly educated or illiterate parents and concomitant parental reticence to be involved in children's schooling. In addition to teachers acting on this knowledge, some South African schools have chosen to purposefully educate parents about the value of family involvement in children's education and to implement interventions to support parent involvement (Okeke, 2014). Implicit in the results of studies such as that by Okeke (2014) is that one system implicated in young people's successful learning and development may need to prompt and enable another implicated system to facilitate young people's resilience. Put differently, even though systemic support of student resilience is usually reactive, it is possible to proactively scaffold student resilience (Theron, 2016a).

Such proactivity would be helpful at the macro level, particularly given how a social ecology's functioning, norms, and values shape student resilience (Phasha, 2010). This is well illustrated in a South African study with 503 adolescents from disadvantaged and violent communities (Herrero Romero, Hall, Cluver, Meinck, & Hinde, 2018). This study showed that exposure to multiple types of violence heightened the chances that young people's academic progress would be delayed (e.g., via grade failure or disrupted schooling). Ironically, even though their academic progress was obstructed, the adolescent participants from the Herrero Romero et al. (2018) study continued to report academic aspirations. In and of themselves, these aspirations are not significant, given that disadvantaged but high-functioning South African youth regularly report a desire to complete secondary schooling and obtain a tertiary qualification (Dass-Brailsford, 2005; Phasha, 2010; Theron, 2016b). What is significant, however, is Herrero Romero et al.'s conclusion that macrosystemic influences (i.e., living in a community characterized by high rates of violence) have the power to impact young people's capacity to realize academic aspirations. Put differently, a dysfunctional macrosystem has the power to compromise resilience-enabling school ecology↔student transactions.

Finally, the protective effects of student↔school transactions may not endure over time or apply equally to all students. This compounds the complex nature of resilience-enabling transactions between students and school ecologies. A case in point is the longitudinal study of the resilience of 269 school-attending African American adolescents exposed to violence (DiClemente et al., 2018). This study showed that school cohesion facilitated students' self-esteem and ethnic identity when the students were in Grade 7. Thereafter (i.e., in Grade 8 and subsequently) school cohesion did not yield similar protective effects. Moreover, the protective effects only applied to boys. Sex/gender and age differences are not the only reasons for differential protective effects. As theorized by Ungar (2018b), the level of risk that students are exposed to can translate into protective student↔school transactions being differentially impactful. In this regard, a longitudinal study of 571 classes across six European countries showed that teacher practices and school factors (e.g., accessible resources) were differentially supportive of student achievement in mathematics and science (Vanlaar et al., 2016). Low-achieving students benefitted more than high-achieving students from teacher practices, thereby pointing to the importance of placing the most competent teachers in schools with the greatest numbers of low-achieving students.

In summary, this section has illustrated that interactions between students and their school ecologies are multifaceted and account for the strengthening or weakening of the adaptive capacities, processes, and supports that scaffold student resilience. Other co-occurring systems—specifically the quality of their functioning and, in the case of co-occurring human systems, their willingness to co-facilitate student resilience in contextually appropriate ways—ratchet up the complexity of resilience-enabling student↔school ecology transactions. Dysfunctional co-occurring systems do more than jeopardize resilience-enabling student↔school ecology transactions; they jeopardize the functioning of school ecologies too. For this reason there is increasing attention to the resilience of school ecologies.

Resilient School Ecologies Scaffold Resilience-Enabling School-Student Transactions

As alluded to in the aforementioned study by Herrero Romero et al. (2018), vulnerable students often attend schools in disadvantaged and/or violent communities. There is a risk that the odds that characterize these communities will seep into the schools and jeopardize school functioning and/or that high numbers of high-risk students will compromise school effectiveness (Day & Gu, 2013). Schools that function well despite such systemic risks to their functioning have become known as resilient schools (Day & Gu, 2013; Hewitt, Epstein, Leonard, Mauthner, & Watkins, 2001; Masten, 2014; Pinskaya et al., 2018). School resilience is typically deduced from indicators of organizational efficacy, such as student pass rates, reputation for academic excellence, or capacity to control within-organization violence. For instance, in her study of the education-facilitated resilience of vulnerable girls from an all-girls school in Sierra Leone, Sharkey (2008) described a school system that appeared to not only tolerate the pervasive violence against girls that characterized the wider Sierra Leone ecology at that time, but also enact violence against girls. Girls were harassed in the streets surrounding the school, but the school apparently did nothing to prevent this. Within the school, physical and verbal violence seemed to be normalized (i.e., staff routinely humiliated and beat the girls). In short, the school system failed to protect its students or to optimize their development. In contrast, Naicker et al. (2016) described a no-fee, poorly resourced school (Wembibona) located in a disadvantaged South African neighborhood characterized by risks that routinely undermine a school's capacity to function well. Despite these risks, Wembibona outperformed schools facing similar threats. It kept its members safe with the help of a full-time security guard. Staff and students were known for their motivation to achieve and their curricular and extracurricular success. In short, its capacity to resist the neighborhood risks contagion led to Wembibona being described as a school "performing against the odds" (Naicker, Grant, & Pillay, 2016, p. 1).

Although resilient schools hold benefits for staff and the local community (Day & Gu, 2013), benefits to students are more typically reported. For instance, a large-scale American study showed that students who are at greater risk for school attrition (i.e., ethnically or racially marginalized students from disadvantaged families or communities) are less likely to disengage from schooling if their school functions well and if they perceive it to be well-functioning (Peguero, Merrin, Hong, & Johnson, 2019). One implication of these findings is that resilient schools are perhaps even more important to the developmental outcomes of ethnically and racially marginalized students than students made vulnerable by nonstructural risks.

Increasingly, school resilience also denotes the capacity of a school to protect staff and students from physical harm. For instance, awareness of the harmful effects of specific pollutants (e.g., lead) has meant that the construction and upkeep of schools purposefully avoids student and staff exposure to pollutants (e.g., preferences for lead-free paint; Sheffield, Uijttewaal, Stewart, & Galvez, 2017). Also, in the face of the growing incidence of disasters, resilient schools are those schools that are designed, or adapted, to withstand disaster (Gedey et al., 2018). To this end, primary schools in New Zealand have investigated how best to adapt school furniture (e.g., school desks) to offer protection to students and staff in the face of earthquakes (Sweet & Tucker, 2018). Elsewhere, earlier understandings of how green schoolyards enabled student resilience (Chawla, Keena, Pevec, & Stanley, 2014) have been expanded to include their potential protection against localized flooding (Gedey et al., 2018).

Japanese researchers have drawn attention to the multiple systems, at both the micro- and macrolevel, implicated in the capacity of schools to be disaster resilient. For example, Shiwaku and colleagues (2016) surveyed the resilience of schools in Kesennuma (a city that was devastated by the 2011 East Japan Earthquake and Tsunami). They measured the schools' physical conditions (i.e., buildings, facilities, and equipment, environmental conditions), human resources (i.e., teachers, students, parents), institutional resources (i.e., management, budget, disaster planning), external relationships (i.e., collaboration with local government and board of education, relationship to local community, mobilizing funds from local, government, and other stakeholders), and natural conditions (i.e., severity and frequency of natural disasters and the natural environment surrounding the school). Although the aforementioned were all important to the schools' capacity for disaster resilience, study results urged improved relationships between schools and systems external to a school. Such results draw attention to the important role that macrosystems (such as communities and governments) can play in a school's disaster resilience, particularly when the natural ecology (also a macrosystem) of the school is characterized by higher potential for natural disasters. In this regard, the World Bank's (2018) willingness to fund the construction of earthquake-resistant schools in various seismically active areas in Turkey is both exemplary and far-seeing of the facilitative value of constructive macro/microsystem relationships.

These systemic advances are crucial as disasters that strike schools can be criminal in origin. For instance, students and school staff are frequently the victims of lethal attacks that take place on school premises (e.g., shootings at American schools [Coughlan, 2018], stabbings at South African schools [Grobler, 2018]). While these disasters probably reflect microsystemic pathology and macrosystemic disorder (e.g., lax firearm laws; normalization of violence), they nevertheless signal that school capacity to be disaster resilient should go beyond so-called natural disasters. The impact of criminal disasters is often profound for teachers; their lives are potentially imperiled and in addition they frequently have to support traumatized students. This calls teacher resilience into question.

Resilience-Enabling Transactions Between Students and School Ecologies Imply Trade-Offs at the Expense of Teacher Well-Being

Continuously caring for and about children, particularly children who are disadvantaged or otherwise challenged, fatigues teachers (Day & Hong, 2016; Day & Gu, 2013; Muijs, Harris, Chapman, Stoll, & Russ, 2004). It is, therefore, not surprising that championing student resilience could have costs for teachers' well-being and long-term commitment to the profession (Fleming et al., 2013; Wosnitza et al., 2018). Resilient teachers, however, neither burn out nor quit the profession. Instead, they evidence "positive adaptation and ongoing professional commitment and growth in the face of challenging circumstances" (Beltman & Mansfield, 2018, p. 4). In addition to personal benefits, teacher resilience holds advantages for students (Briner & Dewberry, 2007; Roffey, 2012) and for schools and their immediate communities (Beltman, Mansfield, & Harris, 2016; Wosnitza et al., 2018). Accordingly, some tertiary institutions offer teacher resilience training programs at pre- and in-service levels (Beltman, Mansfield, Wosnitza, Weatherby-Fell, & Broadley, 2018; Jennings, Frank, Snowberg, Coccia, & Greenberg, 2013; Mansfield, Beltman, Broadley, & Weatherby-Fell, 2016; Peixoto et al., 2018). Additionally, schools (particularly resilient schools; see Day & Gu, 2013) can deploy resources to enable and/or sustain teacher well-being (Mathur, Gehrke, & Kim, 2013; Soulen & Wine, 2018). For instance, a study by Beltman et al. (2016) reported that rural Australian teachers' interaction with support services (such as those provided by educational psychologists or chaplains) facilitated the resilience of teachers challenged by difficult or needy students.

The work by Acevedo and Hernandez-Wolfe (2014) suggests that student resilience can serve as a vicarious pathway of teacher resilience, particularly when the schools in which teachers work demand that teachers care for vulnerable young people. Their study with 21 teachers from Colombia showed that student resilience can inspire teachers toward personal and professional resilience. In witnessing their students' capacity to adjust well, Colombian teachers experienced a reciprocal benefit from their care-demanding work (Hernandez-Wolfe, 2018). Conversely, studies of the resilience of South African adolescents have explicated that teachers who come from the same or similar disadvantaged contexts as their students have inspired resilience in these students (e.g., Dass-Brailsford, 2005; Theron, 2007). Just as the Colombian teachers were enabled by the example of their students, the South African students were enabled by the example of their teachers who had risen above the odds of structural inequality. Taken together these studies suggest that teacher resilience prompts student resilience vicariously, and vice versa.

Despite the apparent value of teacher resilience, and systemic efforts to enable and sustain teacher resilience, Ungar's (2018a) reference to the trade-offs that one system experiences when the resilience of another system (e.g., a student) is prioritized comes to mind. Expectations of teachers to care continuously (e.g., Day & Gu, 2013; Day & Hong, 2016; Gu, 2018) elevate the chances of teachers experiencing emotional exhaustion (Day & Hong, 2016; Hernandez-Wolfe, 2018). In contrast, when teachers are not expected to care, there is apparently no trade-off to teacher well-being, but there is limited evidence of resilience-enabling student↔school ecology transactions (Sharkey, 2008).

Three Propositions

The studies of student resilience that I included in the preceding parts of this chapter support Ungar's (2018a) theorizing that the resilience of a stressed system (such as a student at risk) manifests as a complex adaptive process to which multiple systems and subsystems co-contribute. Via their appreciation of the multiple, co-occurring systems—human *and* organizational—that co-facilitate vulnerable students' positive adaptation to significant stressors, the previously referenced studies discourage mono-systemic or simplistic accounts of human resilience, particularly ones that ignore the role of nonhuman systems. Likewise they signpost that resilience goes beyond psychological resources. To date, most studies of human resilience have emphasized adaptive psychological processes and associated systems (Masten, 2014). Whereas psychological inputs (such as self-regulation) remain important, the student resilience studies compel attention to how various human and nonhuman systems strengthen or weaken psychological inputs. Further, the included studies suggest that it is plausible that co-contributing systems (human and organizational) are themselves resilient, so to speak, and that their co-contribution could involve an immediate or long-term trade-off (i.e., come at a cost to the co-contributing system). In the case of a trade-off, interventions or rewards (even vicarious ones) may be necessary to maintain the resilience of

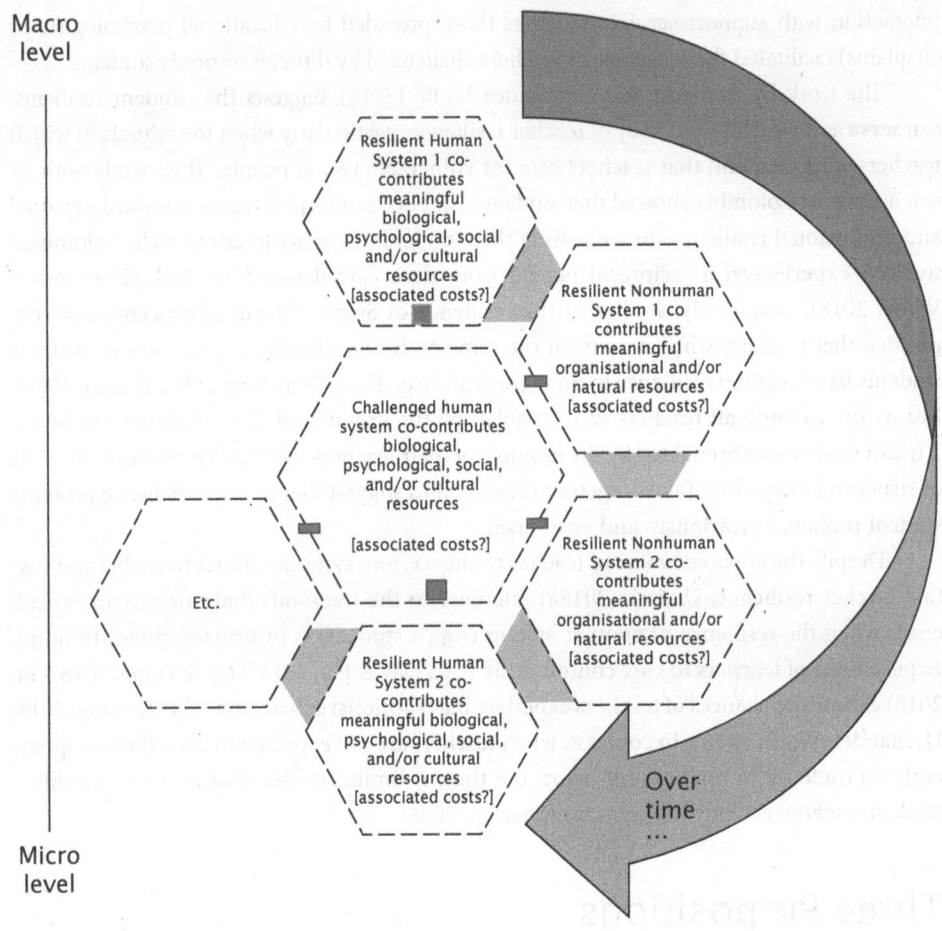

FIGURE 13.2 The multisystemic underpinnings of human resilience at a given point in time and over time.

the co-contributing system. Taken together then, and as illustrated in Figure 13.2, studies of systemic student resilience prompt three propositions:

1. The resilience of a challenged human system (or subsystem) is meaningfully co-facilitated by co-occurring human and nonhuman systems at the micro through to macro level.
    a. Meaningful implies that the co-facilitation is not a random response. Instead, it is purposefully supportive of the adaptive capacity of a vulnerable system in ways that align with that system's particulars (e.g., its biological/chronological characteristics; its contextual, sociocultural, and/or temporal positioning). The response, which can be proactive or reactive, fits the type and severity of the risk that resulted in the human system in question being vulnerable.
    b. Co-facilitation implies that the challenged human system is not a passive recipient of systemic support. Instead, the challenged human system contributes actively to the

process of resilience. Further, co-facilitation implies no sequence. Co-facilitation of resilience could be initiated by the challenged system or the facilitative one.

    c. The co-occurring human and nonhuman systems are not specified as they are likely to vary, depending on risk specifics. For example, in instances where disasters have challenged the learning or development of a student the human and nonhuman systems could include school–community partnerships and the built and natural environment (as in the study by Shiwaku et al., 2016). In comparison, when structural disadvantage and communicable disease challenge the learning or development of students, the human and nonhuman systems may well be supportive parents, safe schools, and welfare (i.e., cash transfers), as in the study by Cluver et al. (2019).

2. The co-occurring, co-facilitative systems are functional (i.e., resilient) systems.

    a. The resilience of co-occurring systems is indicated by their capacity to be functional despite the presence and history of risks that predict impaired system functioning and to champion the resilience of co-occurring challenged systems regardless of the aforementioned risks.

3. There might be a cost to the co-facilitative system or subsystem, but this potential cost can be moderated by the provision of relevant interventions and/or rewards.

    a. Much like the reference to "meaningful" in Proposition 1, relevant implies a purposeful response that is designed to enable and sustain a co-facilitating system's functionality when that functionality is compromised by a system or subsystem championship of the resilience of a challenged system or multiple systems. The moderating response can be proactive or reactive.

    b. Functional co-occurring systems provide the relevant interventions.

    c. The rewards, which could be vicarious, intangible, and/or reciprocal, could be provided by functional co-occurring systems or the challenged system or systems (e.g., as in the case of the Colombian teachers who were enabled by the example of their vulnerable students; Hernandez-Wolfe, 2018).

Implications of the Three Propositions for Resilience Research and Intervention

The three propositions promote a complex systemic understanding of resilience that cautions against a business-as-usual approach to future resilience research or intervention. Forthcoming resilience research will need to be more attentive to the roles of interdependent systems and the complexity of resilience. In particular, advanced understandings of human resilience will require prospective consideration of protective systems and subsystems and systemic interactions that matter most for specific human systems at lower and higher levels of risk (Theron, 2018). Similarly, it will be important to identify what level (or threshold) of adaptation could be used to judge the resilience of a system or the need for resilience-enabling interventions (Sattler & Gershoff, 2019). Further, Masten's (2018) certainty that the resilience of various systems is informed by similar processes encourages scrutiny of the similarities in the resilience of co-occurring systems. For instance, resilient schools are characterized by an enabling set of beliefs about the school's capacity and vision and by facilitative organizational patterns (Naicker et al., 2016); a resilient family shares a set of enabling beliefs about its capacity to solve problems and is flexible in its organization (Walsh, 2003). Such apparent similarities (and potential differences) should be explored empirically before being assimilated in the support of system resilience.

Understanding that co-occurring human and nonhuman systems co-facilitate human resilience means that future studies of human resilience, including student resilience, will require multidisciplinary research teams and a transdisciplinary appetite to drive these studies. For instance, Sheffield et al. (2017) have contended that schools' capacity to protect and enable students transcends "the instruction, relationships, and other significant experiences that occur in school" to also encompass "building infrastructure, grounds, neighborhood and surroundings" (p. 1). Similarly, Sun and Stewart (2008) have argued that enabling physical and social contexts—also at schools—are key to the promotion of resilience. To draw attention to the complexity of these insights, and to leverage them, requires education scientists and educational psychologists to collaborate with scholars specializing in disaster recovery, architecture and design, ecological systems, and the prevention of violent crime.

Conclusion

Globally, the study of resilience remains relevant (Masten, 2014, 2018). However, if the study of resilience is to generate scalable solutions to the escalating threats to humans and natural ecologies then it must pay systematic, sophisticated attention to the multiple human and other systems that scaffold the resilience of multiple systems at a given point in time and over time. Moreover, attention is needed to how human and nonhuman systems interact in ways that advance or ameliorate risk and to their differential impacts (see Ungar, 2018b). The advent of modern scientific tools (e.g., geospatial mapping and tracking, bio-scanners, DNA sequencers, neurological scans) will do much to facilitate such an advanced study, so long as resilience researchers and their funders suspend studies that fail to define, investigate, and account for resilience systemically. If not, the field will most certainly research itself into irrelevance and the next generation of practitioners and policymakers will fail to make a meaningful difference to the systems they serve, including the very educational systems which must produce the next generation of researchers.

Key Messages

1. The science of resilience—including student resilience—is popular. Nevertheless, simplistic or mono-systemic accounts of resilience are likely to jeopardize the long-term usefulness of resilience science.
2. Student resilience—like other human forms of resilience—is a dynamic process that is grounded in interacting human and non-human systems and associated subsystems.
3. Resilient school ecologies (and associated relational and organizational subsystems) are fundamental to student resilience. Even so, the resilience of other co-occurring systems

(e.g., resilient families, resilient neighborhoods, resilient natural ecologies, resilient governments) also matter for student resilience.
4. There are costs to resilient systems championing the resilience of less resilient systems. These costs can, and should, be moderated.

References

Acevedo, V. E., & Hernandez-Wolfe, P. (2014). Vicarious resilience: An exploration of teachers and children's resilience in highly challenging social contexts. *Journal of Aggression, Maltreatment & Trauma, 23*(5), 473–493. doi:10.1080/10926771.2014.904468

Ainscough, L., Stewart, E., Colthorpe, K., & Zimbardi, K. (2018). Learning hindrances and self-regulated learning strategies reported by undergraduate students: Identifying characteristics of resilient students. *Studies in Higher Education, 43*(12), 2194–2209. doi:10.1080/03075079.2017.1315085

Aldridge, J. M., Fraser, B. J., Fozdar, F., Ala'i, K., Earnest, J., & Afari, E. (2016). Students' perceptions of school climate as determinants of wellbeing, resilience and identity. *Improving Schools, 19*(1), 5–26. doi:10.1177/1365480215612616

Alessandri, G., Zuffianò, A., Eisenberg, N., & Pastorelli, C. (2017). The role of ego-resiliency as mediator of the longitudinal relationship between family socio-economic status and school grades. *Journal of Youth & Adolescence, 46*(10), 2157–2168. doi:10.1007/s10964-017-0691-7

Alexander, P. A. (2018). Past as prologue: Educational psychology's legacy and progeny. *Journal of Educational Psychology, 110*(2), 147–162. doi:10.1037/edu0000200

Baker, J. A. (2006). Contributions of teacher-child relationships to positive school adjustment during elementary school. *Journal of School Psychology, 44*(3), 211–229. doi:10.1016/j.jsp.2006.02.002

Bailey, S., & Baines, E. (2012). The impact of risk and resiliency factors on the adjustment of children after the transition from primary to secondary school. *Educational & Child Psychology, 29*(1), 47–63.

Beltman, S., & Mansfield, C. (2018). Resilience in education: An introduction. In M. Wosnitza, F. Peixoto, S. Beltman, & C. F. Mansfield (Eds.), *Resilience in education: Concepts, contexts and connections* (pp. 3–12). Cham, Switzerland: Springer.

Beltman, S., Mansfield, C. F., Wosnitza, M., Weatherby-Fell, N., & Broadley, T. (2018). Using online modules to build capacity for teacher resilience. In M. Wosnitza, F. Peixoto, S. Beltman, & C. F. Mansfield (Eds.), *Resilience in education: Concepts, contexts and connections* (pp. 237–253). Cham, Switzerland: Springer.

Beltman, S., Mansfield, C. F., & Harris, A. (2016). Quietly sharing the load? The role of school psychologists in enabling teacher resilience. *School Psychology International, 37*(2), 172–188. doi:10.1177/0143034315615939

Beltman, S., Mansfield, C., & Price, A. (2011). Thriving not just surviving: A review of research on teacher resilience. *Educational Research Review, 6*(3), 185–207. doi:10.1016/j.edurev.2011.09.001

Berridge, D. (2017). The education of children in care: Agency and resilience. *Children and Youth Services Review, 77*, 86–93. doi:10.1016/j.childyouth.2017.04.004

Blair, C., & Diamond, A. (2008). Biological processes in prevention and intervention: The promotion of self-regulation as a means of preventing school failure. *Development and Psychopathology, 20*(3), 899–911. doi:10.1017/S0954579408000436

Briner, R., & Dewberry, C. (2007). *Staff well-being is key to school success*. London, UK: Worklife Support Ltd/Hamilton House. Retrieved from http://www.teachertoolkit.co.uk/wp-content/uploads/2014/07/5902birkbeckwbperfsummaryfinal.pdf

Bronfenbrenner, U. (1979). *The ecology of human development: Experiments by nature and design*. Cambridge, MA: Harvard University Press.

Cefai, C. (2007). Resilience for all: A study of classrooms as protective contexts. *Emotional & Behavioural Difficulties, 12*(2), 119–134. doi:10.1080/13632750701315516

Chawla, L., Keena, K., Pevec, I., & Stanley, E. (2014). Green schoolyards as havens from stress and resources for resilience in childhood and adolescence. *Health & Place, 28*, 1–13. doi:10.1016/j.healthplace.2014.03.001

Cinkara, E. (2017). The role of L+ Turkish and English learning in resilience: A case of Syrian students at Gaziantep University. *Journal of Language and Linguistic Studies, 13*(2), 190–203.

Cluver, L. D., Orkin, F. M., Campeau, L., Toska, E., Webb, D., Carlqvist, A., & Sherr, L. (2019). Improving lives by accelerating progress towards the UN Sustainable Development Goals for adolescents living with HIV: A prospective cohort study. *The Lancet Child & Adolescent Health, 3*(4), 245–254. doi:10.1016/S2352-4642(19)30033-1

Cohen, J. (2013). Creating a positive school climate: A foundation for resilience. In S. Goldstein & R. B. Brooks (Eds.), *Handbook of resilience in children* (2nd ed., pp. 411–423). New York, NY: Springer.

Corcoran, R. P., Cheung, A. C. K., Kim, E., & Xie, C. (2018). Effective universal school-based social and emotional learning programs for improving academic achievement: A systematic review and meta-analysis of 50 years of research. *Educational Research Review, 25,* 56–72. doi:10.1016/j.edurev.2017.12.001

Cornell, D., & Limber, S. P. (2015). Law and policy on the concept of bullying at school. *American Psychologist, 70*(4). 333–343. doi:10.1037/a0038558

Coughlan, S. (2018, December 12). 2018 "worst year for US school shootings." *BBC News.* Retrieved from https://www.bbc.com/news/business-46507514

Crawford, C., & Burns, R. (2015). Preventing school violence: Assessing armed guardians, school policy, and context. *Policing: An International Journal of Police Strategies & Management, 38*(4), 631–647. doi:10.1108/PIJPSM-01-2015-0002

Dass-Brailsford, P. (2005). Exploring resiliency: Academic achievement among disadvantaged Black youth in South Africa. *South African Journal of Psychology, 35*(3), 574–591. doi:10.1177/008124630503500311

Day, C., & Gu, Q. (2013). *Resilient teachers, resilient schools: Building and sustaining quality in testing times.* London, UK: Routledge.

Day, C., & Hong, J. (2016). Influences on the capacities for emotional resilience of teachers in schools serving disadvantaged urban communities: Challenges of living on the edge. *Teaching and Teacher Education, 59,* 115–125. doi:10.1016/j.tate.2016.05.015

Crick, R. D., Huang, S., Ahmed S. A., & Goldspink, C. (2015). Developing resilient agency in learning: The internal structure of learning power. *British Journal of Educational Studies, 63*(2), 121–160. doi:10.1080/00071005.2015.1006574

Delgado, M. Y., Ettekal, A. V., Simpkins, S. D., & Schaefer, D. R. (2016). How do my friends matter? Examining Latino adolescents' friendships, school belonging, and academic achievement. *Journal of Youth and Adolescence, 45*(6), 1110–1125. doi:10.1007/s10964-015-0341-x

DiClemente, C. M., Rice, C. M., Quimby, D., Richards, M. H., Grimes, C. T., Morency, M. M., . . . Pica, J. A. (2018). Resilience in urban African American adolescents: The protective enhancing effects of neighborhood, family, and school cohesion following violence exposure. *Journal of Early Adolescence, 38*(9), 1286–1321. doi:10.1177/0272431616675974

Doll, B. (2013). Enhancing resilience in classrooms. In S. Goldstein & R. B. Brooks (Eds.), *Handbook of resilience in children* (2nd ed., pp. 399–409). New York, NY: Springer.

Doll, B., & Brehm, K. (2010). *Resilient playgrounds.* New York, NY: Routledge.

Doll, B., Brehm, K., & Zucker, S. (2014). *Resilient classrooms: Creating healthy environments for learning.* New York, NY: Guilford Press.

Donald, D., Lazarus, S., & Lolwana, P. (2010). *Educational psychology in social context: Ecosystemic applications in Southern Africa* (4th ed.). Cape Town, RSA: Oxford University Press.

Dray, J., Bowman, J., Campbell, E., Freund, M., Wolfenden, L., Hodder, R. K., . . . Wiggers, J. (2017). Systematic review of universal resilience-focused interventions targeting child and adolescent mental health in the school setting. *Journal of the American Academy of Child & Adolescent Psychiatry, 56*(10), 813–824. doi:10.1016/j.jaac.2017.07.780

Espinoza, G., Gillen-O'Neel, C., Gonzales, N. A., & Fuligni, A. J. (2014). Friend affiliations and school adjustment among Mexican-American adolescents: The moderating role of peer and parent support. *Journal of Youth and Adolescence, 43*(12), 1969–1981. doi:10.1007/s10964-013-0023-5

Esquivel, G. B., Doll, B., & Oades-Sese, G. V. (2011). Introduction to the special issue: Resilience in schools. *Psychology in the Schools, 48*(7), 649–651. doi:10.1002/pits.20585

Fenwick-Smith, A., Dahlberg, E. E., & Thompson, S. C. (2018). Systematic review of resilience-enhancing, universal, primary school-based mental health promotion programs. *BMC Psychology, 6*, 30. doi:10.1186/s40359-018-0242-3

Fleming, J. L., Mackrain, M., & LeBuffe, P. A. (2013). Caring for the caregiver: Promoting the resilience of teachers. In S. Goldstein & R. B. Brooks (Eds.), *Handbook of resilience in children* (2nd ed., pp. 387–397). New York, NY: Springer.

Freeman, J., & Simonsen, B. (2015). Examining the impact of policy and practice interventions on high school dropout and school completion rates: A systematic review of the literature. *Review of Educational Research, 85*(2), 205–248. doi:10.3102/0034654314554431

Fried, L., & Chapman, E. (2012). An investigation into the capacity of student motivation and emotion regulation strategies to predict engagement and resilience in the middle school classroom. *Australian Educational Researcher, 39*(3), 295–311.

Furrer, C. J., Skinner, E. A., & Pitzer, J. R. (2014). The influence of teacher and peer relationships on students' classroom engagement and everyday motivational resilience. *National Society for the Study of Education, 113*(1), 101–123.

Gedey, S., Barnes, J., Whitaker-Williams, A., de Angel, Y., Poelker, J., Turckes, S., & Penndorf, J. (2018, May 1). 5 considerations for resilience schools. *School Planning and Management*. Retrieved from https://webspm.com/articles/2018/05/01/resilient-schools.aspx

Grobler, R. (2018, November 22). Violence and killing at SA schools: These stories shocked us in 2018. *News24*. Retrieved from https://www.news24.com/news24/southafrica/news/violence-and-killing-at-sa-schools-these-stories-shocked-us-in-2018-20181122

Gu, Q. (2018). (Re)conceptualising teacher resilience: A social-ecological approach to understanding teachers' professional worlds. In M. Wosnitza, F. Peixoto, S. Beltman, & C. F. Mansfield (Eds.), *Resilience in education: Concepts, contexts and connections* (pp. 13–33). Cham, Switzerland: Springer.

Hadas-Lidor, N., & Weiss, P. (2014). Never say never to learning: Dynamic Cognitive Intervention (DCI) for persons with severe mental illness. *Transylvanian Journal of Psychology, Special Issue*, 133–151.

Hall, A. M., & Theron, L. C. (2016). Resilience processes supporting adolescents with intellectual disability: A multiple case study. *Intellectual and Developmental Disabilities, 54*(1), 45–62. doi:10.1352/1934-9556-54.1.45

Harðardóttir, S., Júlíusdóttir, S., & Guðmundsson, H. S. (2015). Understanding resilience in learning difficulties: Unheard voices of secondary school students. *Child & Adolescent Social Work Journal, 32*(4), 351–358. doi:10.1007/s10560-014-0373-1

Haslam, D., Mejia, A., Thomson, D., & Betancourt, T. (2019). Self-regulation in low-and middle-income countries: Challenges and future directions. *Clinical Child and Family Psychology Review, 22*(1), 104–117. doi:10.1007/s10567-019-00278-0

Henderson, N. (2012). Resilience in schools and curriculum design. In M. Ungar (Ed.), *The social ecology of resilience: Culture, context, resources and meaning* (pp. 297–306). New York, NY: Springer.

Hernandez-Wolfe, P. (2018). Vicarious resilience: A comprehensive review. *Revista de Estudios Sociales, 66*, 9–17. doi:10.7440/res66.2018.02

Herrero Romero, R., Hall, J., Cluver, L., Meinck, F., & Hinde, E. (2018). How does exposure to violence affect school delay and academic motivation for adolescents living in socioeconomically disadvantaged communities in South Africa? *Journal of Interpersonal Violence*. doi:10.1177/0886260518779597

Hewitt, R., Epstein, D., Leonard, D., Mauthner, M., & Watkins, C. (2001). *The violence-resilient school: A comparative study of schools and their environments*. London, UK: Economic and Social Research Council.

Hodder, R. K., Freund, M., Wolfenden, L., Bowman, J., Nepal, S., Dray, J., . . . Wiggers, J. (2017). Systematic review of universal school-based "resilience" interventions targeting adolescent tobacco, alcohol or illicit substance use: A meta-analysis. *Preventive Medicine, 100*, 248–268. doi:10.1016/j.ypmed.2017.04.003

Höjer, I., & Johansson, H. (2013). School as an opportunity and resilience factor for young people placed in care. *European Journal of Social Work, 16*(1), 22–36. doi:10.1080/13691457.2012.722984

Howell, J. A., Roberts, L. D., & Mancini, V. O. (2018). Learning analytics messages: Impact of grade, sender, comparative information and message style on student affect and academic resilience. *Computers in Human Behavior, 89*, 8–15. doi:10.1016/j.chb.2018.07.021

Im, M. H., Hughes, J. N., & West, S. G. (2016). Effect of trajectories of friends' and parents' school involvement on adolescents' engagement and achievement. *Journal of Research on Adolescence, 26*(4), 963–978. doi:10.1111/jora.12247

Irvin, M. J. (2012). Role of student engagement in the resilience of African American adolescents from low-income rural communities. *Psychology in the Schools, 49*(2), 176–193. doi:10.1002/pits.20626

Jennings, P. A., Frank, J. L., Snowberg, K. E., Coccia, M. A., & Greenberg, M. T. (2013). Improving classroom learning environments by Cultivating Awareness and Resilience in Education (CARE): Results of a randomized controlled trial. *School Psychology Quarterly, 28*(4), 374–390. doi:10.1037/spq0000035

Jones, G., & Lafreniere, K. (2014). Exploring the role of school engagement in predicting resilience among Bahamian youth. *Journal of Black Psychology, 40*(1), 47–68. doi:10.1177/0095798412469230

Kabiru, C. W., Beguy, D., Ndugwa, R. P., Zulu, E. M., & Jessor, R. (2012). "Making it": Understanding adolescent resilience in two informal settlements (slums) in Nairobi, Kenya. *Child & Youth Services, 33*(1), 12–32. doi:10.1080/0145935X.2012.665321

Khambati, N., Mahedy, L., Heron, J., & Emond, A. (2018). Educational and emotional health outcomes in adolescence following maltreatment in early childhood: A population-based study of protective factors. *Child Abuse & Neglect, 81*, 343–353. doi:10.1016/j.chiabu.2018.05.008

Kim, T.-Y., Kim, Y., & Kim, J.-Y. (2018). A qualitative inquiry on EFL learning demotivation and resilience: A study of primary and secondary EFL students in South Korea. *Asia-Pacific Education Researcher, 27*(1), 55–64. doi:10.1007/s40299-017-0365-y

Kumpulainen, K., Theron, L., Kahl, C., Bezuidenhout, C., Mikkola, A., Salmi, S., ... Uusitalo-Malmivaara, L. (2016). Children's positive adjustment to first grade in risk-filled communities: A case study of the role of school ecologies in South Africa and Finland. *School Psychology International, 37*, 121–139. doi:10.1177/0143034315614687

Malekan, F., & Hajimohammadi, R. (2017). The relationship between Iranian ESP learners' translation ability and resilience in reading comprehension. *International Journal of Education and Literacy Studies, 5*(2), 47–52. doi:10.7575/aiac.ijels.v.5n.2p.47

Mampane, R., & Bouwer, C. (2011). The influence of township schools on the resilience of their learners. *South African Journal of Education, 31*(1), 114–126. doi:10.15700/saje.v31n1a408

Mansfield, C. F., Beltman, S., Broadley, T., & Weatherby-Fell, N. (2016). Building resilience in teacher education: An evidenced informed framework. *Teaching and Teacher Education, 54*, 77–87. doi:10.1016/j.tate.2015.11.016

Martin, A. J., & Marsh, H. W. (2008). Academic buoyancy: Towards an understanding of students' everyday academic resilience. *Journal of School Psychology, 46*(1), 53–83. doi:10.1016/j.jsp.2007.01.002

Masten, A. S. (2014). *Ordinary magic: Resilience in development*. New York, NY: Guilford Press.

Masten, A. S. (2018). Resilience theory and research on children and families: Past, present, and promise. *Journal of Family Theory & Review, 10*(1), 12–31. doi:10.1111/jftr.12255

Masten, A. S., & Wright, M. O. (2010). Resilience over the lifespan: Developmental perspectives on resistance, recovery, and transformation. In J. W. Reich, A. J. Zautra, & J. S. Hall (Eds.), *Handbook of adult resilience* (pp. 213–237). New York, NY: Guilford Press.

Mathur, S. R., Gehrke, R., & Kim, S. H. (2013). Impact of a teacher mentorship program on mentors' and mentees' perceptions of classroom practices and the mentoring experience. *Assessment for Effective Intervention, 38*(3), 154–162. doi:10.1177/1534508412457873

Maunder, R., & Monks, C. P. (2018). Friendships in middle childhood: Links to peer and school identification, and general self-worth. *British Journal of Developmental Psychology, 37*(2), 211–229. doi:10.1111/bjdp.12268

Mirza, M. S., & Arif, M. I. (2018). Fostering academic resilience of students at risk of failure at secondary school level. *Journal of Behavioural Sciences, 28*(1), 33–50.

Mitchell, V. (2017). African-American students in exemplary urban high schools: The interaction of school practices and student actions. In S. F. Arvizu & M. Saravia-Shore (Eds.), *Cross-cultural literacy* (pp. 19–36). London, UK: Routledge.

Motti-Stefanidi, F. (2015). Risks and resilience in immigrant youth adaptation: Who succeeds in the Greek school context and why? *European Journal of Developmental Psychology, 12*(3), 261–274. doi:10.1080/17405629.2015.1020787

Motti-Stefanidi, F., & Masten, A. S. (2013). School success and school engagement of immigrant children and adolescents: A risk and resilience developmental perspective. *European Psychologist, 18*(2), 126–135. doi:10.1027/1016-9040/a000139

Muijs, D., Harris, A., Chapman, C., Stoll, L., & Russ, J. (2004). Improving schools in socioeconomically disadvantaged areas: A review of research evidence. *School Effectiveness and School Improvement, 15*(2), 149–175. doi:10.1076/sesi.15.2.149.30433

Myers, S. S., & Pianta, R. C. (2008). Developmental commentary: Individual and contextual influences on student-teacher relationships and children's early problem behaviors. *Journal of Clinical Child & Adolescent Psychology, 37*(3), 600–608. doi:10.1080/15374410802148160.

Naicker, I., Grant, C. C., & Pillay, S. S. (2016). Schools performing against the odds: Enablements and constraints to school leadership practice. *South African Journal of Education, 36*(4), 1–10. doi:10.15700/saje.v36n4a1321

Nichols, E. B., Loper, A. B., & Meyer, J. P. (2016). Promoting educational resiliency in youth with incarcerated parents: The impact of parental incarceration, school characteristics, and connectedness on school outcomes. *Journal of Youth & Adolescence, 45*(6), 1090–1109. doi:10.1007/s10964-015-0337-6

Nolan, A., Taket, A., & Stagnitti, K. (2014). Supporting resilience in early years classrooms: The role of the teacher. *Teachers and Teaching, 20*(5), 595–608. doi:10.1080/13540602.2014.937955

Noltemeyer, A. L., & Bush, K. R. (2013). Adversity and resilience: A synthesis of international research. *School Psychology International, 34*(5), 474–487. doi:10.1177/0143034312472758

Obradović, J., Long, J. D., Cutuli, J. J., Chan, C.-K., Hinz, E., Heistad, D., & Masten, A. S. (2009). Academic achievement of homeless and highly mobile children in an urban school district: Longitudinal evidence on risk, growth, and resilience. *Development and Psychopathology, 21*(2), 493–518. doi:10.1017/S0954579409000273.

Okeke, C. I. (2014). Effective home-school partnership: Some strategies to help strengthen parental involvement. *South African Journal of Education, 34*(3), 1–9. doi:10.15700/201409161044

Oldfield, J., Stevenson, A., Ortiz, E., & Haley, B. (2018). Promoting or suppressing resilience to mental health outcomes in at risk young people: The role of parental and peer attachment and school connectedness. *Journal of Adolescence, 64*, 13–22. doi:10.1016/j.adolescence.2018.01.002

Papatraianou, L. H., Strangeways, A., Beltman, S., & Schuberg Barnes, E. (2018). Beginning teacher resilience in remote Australia: A place-based perspective. *Teachers and Teaching: Theory and Practice, 18*(4), 893–914. doi:10.1080/13540602.2018.1508430

Peguero, A. A., Merrin, G. J., Hong, J. S., & Johnson, K. R. (2019). School disorder and dropping out: The intersection of gender, race, and ethnicity. *Youth & Society, 51*(2), 193–218. doi:10.1177/0044118X16668059

Peixoto, F., Wosnitza, M., Pipa, J., Morgan, M., & Cefai, C. (2018). A multidimensional view on pre-service teacher resilience in Germany, Ireland, Malta and Portugal. In M. Wosnitza, F. Peixoto, S. Beltman, & C. F. Mansfield (Eds.), *Resilience in education: Concepts, contexts and connections* (pp.73–89). Cham, Switzerland: Springer.

Phasha, T. N. (2010). Educational resilience among African survivors of child sexual abuse in South Africa. *Journal of Black Studies, 40*(6), 1234–1253. doi:10.1177/0021934708327693

Pinskaya, M., Khavenson, T., Kosaretsky, S., Zvyagintsev, R., Mikhailova, A., & Chirkina, T. (2018). Above barriers: A survey of resilient schools. *Educational Studies, 2*, 198–227. doi:10.17323/1814-9545-2018-2-198-227

Portilla, X. A., Ballard, P. J., Adler, N. E., Boyce, W. T., & Obradović, J. (2014). An integrative view of school functioning: Transactions between self-regulation, school engagement, and teacher-child relationship quality. *Child Development, 85*(5), 1915–1931. doi:10.1111/cdev.12259

Reyes, J. A., Elias, M. J., Parker, S. J., & Rosenblatt, J. L. (2013). Promoting educational equity in disadvantaged youth: The role of resilience and social-emotional learning. In S. Goldstein & R. B. Brooks (Eds.), *Handbook of resilience in children* (2nd ed., pp. 349–370). New York, NY: Springer.

Rimm-Kaufman, S. E., Baroody, A. E., Larsen, R. A., Curby, T. W., & Abry, T. (2015). To what extent do teacher-student interaction quality and student gender contribute to fifth graders' engagement in mathematics learning? *Journal of Educational Psychology, 107*(1), 170–185. doi:10.1037/a0037252

Roffey, S. (2012). Pupil wellbeing—Teacher wellbeing: Two sides of the same coin? *Educational and Child Psychology, 29*(4), 8–17.

Roffey, S. (2016). Building a case for whole-child, whole-school wellbeing in challenging contexts. *Educational & Child Psychology, 33*(2), 30–42.

Roorda, D. L., Koomen, H. M., Spilt, J. L., & Oort, F. J. (2011). The influence of affective teacher-student relationships on students' school engagement and achievement: A meta-analytic approach. *Review of Educational Research, 81*(4), 493–529. doi:10.3102/0034654311421793

Rudasill, K. M., & Rimm-Kaufman, S. E. (2009). Teacher-child relationship quality: The roles of child temperament and teacher-child interactions. *Early Childhood Research Quarterly, 24*(2), 107–120. doi:10.1016/j.ecresq.2008.12.003

Sabol, T. J., & Pianta, R. C. (2012). Recent trends in research on teacher-child relationships. *Attachment & Human Development, 14*(3), 213–231. doi:10.1080/14616734.2012.672262

Sapouna, M., & Wolke, D. (2013). Resilience to bullying victimization: The role of individual, family and peer characteristics. *Child Abuse & Neglect, 37*(11), 997–1006. doi:10.1016/j.chiabu.2013.05.009

Sardar, H., & Galdames, S. (2018). School leaders' resilience: Does coaching help in supporting headteachers and deputies? *Coaching: An International Journal of Theory, Research and Practice, 11*(1), 46–59. doi:10.1080/17521882.2017.1292536

Sattler, K., & Gershoff, E. (2019). Thresholds of resilience and within- and cross-domain academic achievement among children in poverty. *Early Childhood Research Quarterly, 46*, 87–96. doi:10.1016/j.ecresq.2018.04.003

Sharkey, D. (2008). Contradictions in girls' education in a post-conflict setting. *Compare: A Journal of Comparative Education, 38*(5), 569–579. doi:10.1080/03057920802351333

Sharkey, J. D., You, S., & Schnoebelen, K. (2008). Relations among school assets, individual resilience, and student engagement for youth grouped by level of family functioning. *Psychology in the Schools, 45*(5), 402–418.

Sharp, C., Penner, F., Marais, L., & Skinner, D. (2019). School connectedness as psychological resilience factor in children affected by HIV/AIDS. *AIDS Care, 30*(Suppl. 4), 34–41. doi:10.1080/09540121.2018.1511045

Sheffield, P. E., Uijttewaal, S. A. M., Stewart, J., & Galvez, M. P. (2017). Climate change and schools: Environmental hazards and resiliency. *International Journal of Environmental Research and Public Health, 14*(11), 1397. doi:10.3390/ijerph14111397

Shiwaku, K., Ueda, Y., Oikawa, Y., & Shaw, R. (2016). School disaster resilience assessment in the affected areas of 2011 East Japan earthquake and tsunami. *Natural Hazards, 82*, 333–365. doi:10.1007/s11069-016-2204-5

Shute, V. J., Hansen, E. G., Underwood, J. S., & Razzouk, R. (2011). A review of the relationship between parental involvement and secondary school students' academic achievement. *Education Research International*. doi:10.1155/2011/915326

Siu, A. F. Y. (2009). Promoting resilience in Hong Kong school children: A critical reflection. *Advances in School Mental Health Promotion, 2*(4), 19–27. doi:10.1080/1754730X.2009.9715713

Snelling, A., Belson, S. I., Watts, E., Malloy, E., Van Dyke, H., George, S., . . . Katz, N. B. (2017). Measuring the implementation of a school wellness policy. *Journal of School Health, 87*(10), 760–768. doi:10.1111/josh.12548.

Soulen, R. R., & Wine, L. D. (2018). Building resilience in new and beginning teachers: Contributions of school librarians. *School Libraries Worldwide, 24*(2), 80–91. doi:10.14265.24.2.006

Sun, J., & Stewart, D. (2008). How can we improve the physical and social environment of the school to promote student resilience? Evidence from the Resilient Children and Communities Project in China. *International Journal of Mental Health Promotion, 10*(2), 45–54. doi:10.1080/14623730.2008.9721762

Sweet, T., & Tucker, R. (2018). Resilient furniture design: A reconceived school table for earthquake safety. *International Journal of Designed Objects, 12*(2), 1–14. doi:10.18848/2325-1379/CGP/v12i02/1-14

Tatlow-Golden, M., O'Farrelly, C., Booth, A., O'Rourke, C., & Doyle, O. (2016). "Look, I have my ears open": Resilience and early school experiences among children in an economically deprived suburban area in Ireland. *School Psychology International, 37*(2), 104–120. doi:10.1177/0143034315613777

Theron, L. C. (2007). Uphenyo ngokwazi kwentsha yasemalokishini ukumelana nesimo esinzima: A South African study of resilience among township youth. *Child and Adolescent Psychiatric Clinics of North America, 16*(2), 357–375. doi:10.1016/j.chc.2006.12.005

Theron, L. C. (2016a). The everyday ways that school ecologies facilitate resilience: Implications for school psychologists. *School Psychology International*, *37*(2), 87–103. doi:10.1177/0143034315615937

Theron, L. C. (2016b). Towards a culturally and contextually sensitive understanding of resilience: Privileging the voices of Black, South African young people. *Journal of Adolescent Research*, *31*(6), 635–670. doi:10.1177/0743558415600072

Theron, L. C. (2018). Championing the resilience of sub-Saharan adolescents: Pointers for psychologists. *South African Journal of Psychology*, *49*(3), 325–336. doi:10.1177/0081246318801749

Theron, L. C., & Donald, D. R. (2013). Educational psychology and resilience in developing contexts: A rejoinder to Toland and Carrigan (2011). *School Psychology International*, *34*(1), 51–66. doi:10.1177/0143034311425579

Theron, L. C., & Theron, A. M. C. (2014). Education services and resilience processes: Resilient Black South African students' experiences. *Child and Youth Services Review*, *47*(3), 297–306. doi:10.1016/j.childyouth.2014.10.003

Theron, L. C., & Van Rensburg, A. (2018). Resilience over time: Learning from school-attending adolescents living in conditions of structural inequality. *Journal of Adolescence*, *67*, 167–178. doi:10.1016/j.adolescence.2018.06.012

Toland, J., & Carrigan, D. (2011). Educational psychology and resilience: New concept, new opportunities. *School Psychology International*, *32*(1), 95–106. doi:10.1177/0143034310397284

Trieu, Q., & Jayakody, R. (2018). Ethnic minority educational success: Understanding accomplishments in challenging settings. *Social Indicators Research*, 1–39. doi:10.1007/s11205-018-1900-9

Truebridge, S. (2014). *Resilience begins with beliefs. Building on student strengths for success in school.* New York, NY: Teachers College Press.

Tull, S., Dabner, N., & Ayebi-Arthur, K. (2017). Social media and e-learning in response to seismic events: Resilient practices. *Journal of Open, Flexible and Distance Learning*, *21*(1), 63–76.

Tzuriel, D., & Shomron, V. (2018). The effects of mother-child mediated learning strategies on psychological resilience and cognitive modifiability of boys with learning disability. *British Journal of Educational Psychology*, *88*(2), 236–260. doi:10.1111/bjep.12219

Ungar, M. (2011). The social ecology of resilience: Addressing contextual and cultural ambiguity of a nascent construct. *American Journal of Orthopsychiatry*, *81*(1), 1–17. doi:10.1111/j.1939-0025.2010.01067

Ungar, M. (2018a). Systemic resilience: principles and processes for a science of change in contexts of adversity. *Ecology and Society*, *23*(4), 34. doi:10.5751/ES-10385-230434

Ungar, M. (2018b). The differential impact of social services on young people's resilience. *Child Abuse & Neglect*, *78*, 4–12. doi:10.1016/j.chiabu.2017.09.024

Ungar, M., Russell, P., & Connelly, G. (2014). School-based interventions to enhance the resilience of students. *Journal of Educational and Developmental Psychology*, *4*(1), 66–83. doi:10.5539/jedp.v4n1p66

Vanlaar, G., Kyriakides, L., Panayiotou, A., Vandecandelaere, M., McMahon, L., De Fraine, B., & Van Damme, J. (2016). Do the teacher and school factors of the dynamic model affect high-and low-achieving student groups to the same extent? A cross-country study. *Research Papers in Education*, *31*(2), 183–211. doi:10.1080/02671522.2015.1027724

Venta, A., Bailey, C., Muñoz, C., Godinez, E., Colin, Y., Arreola, A., . . . Lawlace, S. (2018). Contribution of schools to mental health and resilience in recently immigrated youth. *School Psychology Quarterly*, *34*(2), 138–147. doi:10.1037/spq0000271

Walsh, F. (2003). Family resilience: A framework for clinical practice. *Family Process*, *42*(1), 1–18. doi:10.1111/j.1545-5300.2003.00001.x

Waters, S., Cross, D., & Shaw, T. (2010). Does the nature of schools matter? An exploration of selected school ecology factors on adolescent perceptions of school connectedness. *British Journal of Educational Psychology*, *80*(3), 381–402. doi:10.1348/000709909X484479

Wentzel, K. R., Barry, C. M., & Caldwell, K. A. (2004). Friendships in middle school: Influences on motivation and school adjustment. *Journal of Educational Psychology*, *96*(2), 195–203. doi:10.1037/0022-0663.96.2.195

Willner, C. J., Gatzke-Kopp, L. M., Bierman, K. L., Greenberg, M. T., & Segalowitz, S. J. (2015). Relevance of a neurophysiological marker of attention allocation for children's learning-related behaviors and academic performance. *Developmental Psychology*, *51*(8), 1148–1162. doi:10.1037/a0039311

Wilson, J. T. (2016). Brightening the mind: The impact of practicing gratitude on focus and resilience in learning. *Journal of the Scholarship of Teaching and Learning, 16*(4), 1–13. doi:10.14434/josotl.v16i4.19998

World Bank. (2018, May). *Building safer schools in Turkey: Increasing disaster resilience for school-age children.* Retrieved from https://www.gfdrr.org/sites/default/files/publication/Turkey-final_0.pdf

Wosnitza, M., Delzepich, R., Schwarze, J., O'Donnell, M., Faust, V., & Camilleri, V. (2018). Enhancing teacher resilience: From self-reflection to professional development. In M. Wosnitza, F. Peixoto, S. Beltman, & C. F. Mansfield (Eds.), *Resilience in education: Concepts, contexts and connections* (pp. 275–288). Cham, Switzerland: Springer.

Yablon, Y. B. (2015). Positive school climate as a resilience factor in armed conflict zones. *Psychology of Violence, 5*(4), 393401. doi:10.1037/a0039600

SECTION 4

Family and Kinship Systems

14

Family Resilience

A Dynamic Systemic Framework

Froma Walsh

Introduction

The concept of *resilience*—the capacity to withstand and rebound from disruptive life challenges—has come to the forefront in the social sciences and in healthcare and mental health fields. A growing body of research has expanded our understanding of human resilience as involving the dynamic interplay of multilevel systemic processes fostering positive adaptation in the context of significant adversity (Masten & Cicchetti, 2016). Beyond coping, these strengths and resources enable recovery and positive growth from serious life challenges.

A relational view of resilience assumes the centrality of supportive relationships in positive adaptation to adversity. Early theory and research focused on personal traits and abilities of resilient children and adults who overcame adverse conditions. Yet, the positive influence of a significant dyadic bond with a caregiver or mentor stood out across many studies (Walsh, 1996). Relational processes support individuals' resilience by encouraging their potential to overcome stressful challenges and by supporting their best efforts to make the most of their lives.

A family systems orientation expands our understanding of resilience to the broad relational network, attending to the ongoing mutuality of influences and identifying potential resources for resilience throughout the immediate and extended family. A resilience-oriented family approach (Walsh, 2016b) seeks to identify and involve members who are, or could become, invested in the positive development and well-being of at-risk youth or vulnerable adults. Even in troubled families, positive contributions might be made by parents, stepparents, siblings, and other caregivers (Ungar, 2004). Grandparents and godparents, aunts and uncles, cousins, nephews and nieces, and informal kin can play a vital role. Beyond the influence of family members for individual resilience, a systemic perspective focuses on risk and resilience in the family as a functional unit.

The Concept of Family Resilience

The concept of *family resilience* refers to the capacity of the family, as a functional system, to withstand and rebound from adversity (Walsh, 1996, 2002, 2003, 2016a, 2016b). A basic premise in family systems theory is that serious crises and persistent life challenges have an impact on the whole family, and in turn, key family processes mediate adaptation (or maladaptation) for individual members, their relationships, and the family unit.

The concept of family resilience extended family developmental theory and research on family stress, coping, and adaptation by McCubbin and colleagues (Hawley & DeHaan, 1996; McCubbin & McCubbin, 2013; McCubbin & Patterson, 1983; Patterson, 2002). In the clinical field, a family resilience conceptual framework was developed by Walsh, building on a body of family systems research on transactional processes in well-functioning families (Walsh, 1996, 2003, 2016a, 2016b).

A resilience-oriented lens is distinct because of its focus on family capacities in dealing with situations of adversity. Major stressors or a pile-up of stresses over time can derail family functioning, with ripple effects throughout the relational network. The family's approach and response are crucial for the resilience of all members, from young children to vulnerable adults (Walsh, 2016a, b). For instance, in eldercare, mobilizing a family caregiving team can reduce strains on the primary caregiver as it strengthens family efforts to support the well-being of the elder member (Walsh, 2012a). Key transactional processes enable the family to rally in highly stressful times: to take proactive steps, to buffer disruptions, to reduce the risk of dysfunction, and to support positive adaptation and resourcefulness in meeting challenges.

Resilience entails more than coping, managing stressful conditions, shouldering a burden, or surviving an ordeal. It involves the potential for personal and relational transformation and positive growth that can be forged out of adversity. Many studies have found that couples and families, through suffering and struggle, often emerge stronger, more loving, and more resourceful through collaboration and mutual support. (e.g., see the study by McCubbin, Balling, Possin, Frierdich, & Byrne, 2002, on family resilience with childhood cancer.) While some families are more vulnerable or face more hardships than others, a family resilience perspective is grounded in a conviction that all families have the potential to build resilience in dealing with their challenges. Even those who have experienced severe trauma or very troubled relationships can experience repair and growth over the life course and across the generations (Walsh, 2007, 2016b).

Ecosystemic and Developmental Perspectives

A family resilience framework integrates ecosystemic and developmental dimensions of experience. Effective functioning is contingent on the type, severity, and chronicity of adverse challenges faced and the resources, constraints, and aims of the family in its social context and life passage. Similar to Falicov's (2012) multidimensional approach with immigrant families, each family is considered within a complex ecological niche, sharing borders and common ground with other families, as well as differing positions with the intersection of such variables as gender, economic status, life stage, ethnicity, and location in the dominant society. Each family's experience of adversity will have common and unique features. A holistic assessment includes the varied contexts and aims to understand the constraints and possibilities in each family's position.

Ecosystemic View

From a *biopsychosocial systems orientation*, risk and resilience are contingent upon multiple, recursive influences. Human functioning and dysfunction involve an interaction of individual, family, community, and larger system variables; their interplay affects vulnerability and resilience in dealing with stressful life experiences and chronic conditions. Genetic and neurobiological influences may be enhanced or countered by family processes (Spotts, 2012) and by wider sociocultural resources and constraints. Family distress may result from unsuccessful attempts to deal with an overwhelming crisis, such as traumatic loss of a loved one, or with cumulative stresses, or the wider impact of a major disaster (Walsh, 2007).

From an ecosystems perspective, the family, peer group, community resources, school, work setting, and other social systems can be seen as nested contexts for resilience. Cultural and spiritual resources also support family resilience (McCubbin & McCubbin, 2013; Walsh, 2009), especially for those facing discrimination and socioeconomic barriers (Boyd-Franklin & Karger, 2012; Kirmayer, Dandeneau, Marshall, Phillips, & Williamson, 2011). Powerful social influences are not simply external forces or factors that impact families. Understood in dynamic terms, risks are countered and resources are mobilized through active agency in family transactional processes, as members navigate and negotiate their relationship within their social environment (Ungar, 2010).

Developmental View

A developmental perspective is essential in understanding and fostering resilience. The impact of adversity varies over time, with unfolding conditions and in relation to individual and family life cycle passage.

Emerging Challenges and Resilient Pathways Over Time

Most major stressors are not simply a short-term single event, but rather a complex set of changing conditions with a past history and a future course (Rutter, 1987). For instance, risk and resilience with divorce involve family processes over time: from an escalation of predivorce tensions to separation, legal divorce and custody agreements, reorganization of households, and realignment of parent–child relationships (Greene, Anderson, Forgatch,

DeGarmo, & Hetherington, 2012; Walsh, 2016a). Most children and their families undergo subsequent disruptive transitions, with financial strains, residential changes, parental remarriage/repartnering, and stepfamily formation. Longitudinal studies find that children's resilience depends largely on supportive family processes over time: how both parents and their extended families buffer stress as they navigate these challenges and establish cooperative parenting networks across households.

The psychosocial demands of an adverse situation, such as serious illness, may vary with the evolving course of different conditions (Rolland, 2018). For instance, a medical crisis may be followed by: a full recovery, with normal life resumed; a plateau of persisting disability (e.g., with a stroke); a roller coaster course of remissions and recurrences (e.g., with cancer); or a deteriorating course (e.g., with Alzheimer's disease). Given this complexity, varied strategies may be more or less useful over time depending on their fit with emerging challenges.

In assessing family resilience, it is important to explore how families approach their adverse situation, their immediate response, and long-term coping strategies. Initial efforts that are functional in the short term may rigidify, becoming dysfunctional over time. For instance, with a father's heart attack, a family must rapidly mobilize resources and pull together to meet the crisis, but it may become maladaptive if family members continue to hover over the father long after his recovery. Families need to shift gears to attend to other priorities and other needs. Likewise, a recurrence will require flexible readjustments. Family resilience thus involves varied adaptational pathways extending over time.

Cumulative Stressors

Some families do well with a short-term crisis but buckle under the cumulative strain of multiple, persistent challenges, as with chronic illness, conditions of poverty, unemployment, or ongoing, complex trauma in war and conflict zones. A pile-up of internal and external stressors can overwhelm family functioning, heightening vulnerability and risk for subsequent problems (Patterson, 2002). For instance, the closing of a factory and job loss for wage earners can bring a cascade of problems such as loss of essential family income which triggers prolonged unemployment, which heightens risks for housing insecurity, relational conflict, and family breakup. In one community-based program, workshops were designed for displaced workers and their families to reduce stresses and strengthen worker and family resilience (Walsh, 2016b). The large group sessions focused on overcoming challenges with job transition stresses: sharing effective strategies; reducing relational strains; realigning functional family roles; mobilizing extended kin, social, and financial resources; and increasing family support for displaced workers' reemployment efforts.

Multigenerational Family Life Cycle

Human functioning is assessed in the context of the family system as it moves forward over the life course and across the generations (McGoldrick, Garcia-Preto, & Carter, 2015). No family life course of sequential stages should be regarded as the standard, since family cultures, structures, and gender relations are becoming increasingly diverse, complex, and fluid over an extended life trajectory (Walsh, 2012b). Amid global social, economic, political, and climate disruptions, families are also navigating unprecedented challenges and facing many uncertainties about their future. Abundant research finds that children and families can thrive in varied family structures that are stable, nurturing, and protective (Biblarz & Savci, 2010; Lansford, Ceballo, Abby, & Stewart, 2001). Yet, adults and their children are increasingly likely to experience varied households and family configurations over time, requiring resilience to meet adaptational challenges.

Across the family life cycle, a family resilience lens focuses on adaptation with critical events and major transitions. This includes unexpected complications with predictable, normative transitions, such as the birth of a child with disabilities, and with highly disruptive events, such as the untimely death of a child-rearing parent. The timing of symptoms in a family member is often concurrent with highly stressful family events or transitions (Walsh, 2016b). A resilience-oriented genogram (diagram of family relationships) and a family time line (noting major events and stressors) are useful to organize relationship information, track system patterns, and guide intervention (McGoldrick et al., 2008). Connections are explored, for example, when a son's school dropout follows his father's job loss. Frequently, child emotional or behavior problems coincide with anxiety-provoking disruptions, such as parental separation, incarceration, or military deployment, which also involve family boundary shifts and role redefinition. The impact for children is likely to vary with salient issues at different developmental phases.

Losses for a family are multifaceted (Walsh, 2013, in press), involving not only particular persons and relationships, but also crucial role functioning (e.g., breadwinner, caregiver); financial security, homes, and communities following a major disaster; and future hopes and dreams. Family processes facilitate immediate and long-term adaptation to loss, through shared acknowledgment, meaning-making, and shared grief processes, facilitated by open communication and helpful rituals, family reorganization and relational realignment, and reinvestment in relationships and life pursuits, while sustaining continuing bonds with lost loved ones.

The convergence of developmental and multigenerational strains increases risk for complications when facing adversity (McGoldrick et al., 2015; Walsh, 2016b). Distress is heightened when current stressors reactivate painful memories and emotions from past family experiences, especially those involving trauma and loss (Walsh & McGoldrick, 2013). Family members may lose perspective, conflating immediate and past situations, becoming overwhelmed or cutting off from painful feelings and connections. Experiences of past adversity influence expectations: Catastrophic fears can heighten risk of dysfunction, whereas multigenerational models and stories of resilience can inspire positive adaptation. Families, especially immigrant and transnational families, are more resilient when they are able to balance intergenerational continuity and change and maintain links between their past, present, and future (Falicov, 2007, 2012).

Mapping Key Processes in Family Resilience

The very definition of the family has been expanding with recent social and economic transformations worldwide, growing diversity, and complexity in family life. Systems-oriented family process research over recent decades has provided empirical grounding for assessment of effective couple and family functioning (Lebow & Stroud, 2012). However, family instruments and typologies tend to be static and acontextual, offering a snapshot of interaction patterns but often not considering a family's stressors, resources, and challenges in social and developmental contexts.

When families face adversity, their problem-saturated life situation and the deficit focus in the mental health field can skew attention, making it difficult to identify and build on their strengths and resources. Diagnostic categories that reduce the richness of family life or typologies that propose a "one-size-fits-all" model of "the resilient family" do not fit the many, varied ways that families face their challenges and can pathologize those who differ from a norm. A family resilience framework, by definition, focuses on strengths under stress when dealing with a crisis or prolonged adversity. Yet, it is assumed that no single model of healthy functioning fits all families or their situations. Functioning is assessed in context: relative to each family's values, structural and relational resources, and life challenges. Processes for optimal functioning and the well-being of members may vary over time as challenges emerge and families evolve.

Resilience-oriented maps can be useful to guide family assessment and intervention/prevention approaches. Informed by an extensive review of three decades of research on resilience and family functioning, the Walsh Family Resilience Framework identified nine key transactional processes that facilitate family resilience (Walsh, 2003; see Box 14.1; for greater detail, see Walsh, 2016b). These core processes—shared beliefs and practices—were organized into three domains (dimensions) of family functioning (shared belief systems, organizational resources, and communication processes) to serve as a useful map to guide inquiry in research and practice with families facing varied situations of adversity.

These core transactional processes are mutually interactive and synergistic, both within and across domains. For example, shared meaning-making facilitates communication clarity, emotional sharing, and problem-solving, and reciprocally, effective communication processes facilitate shared meaning-making. A counterbalance of process components is also needed, as in fluid shifts between stability and change in organizational flexibility, as required in a crisis or disruptive transition or in meeting new challenges over time.

Thus, rather than a typology of traits of a "resilient family," *dynamic processes* involve strengths and resources that family members can mobilize within their family system and in transaction with their social environment. Core processes may be expressed in varied ways, related to cultural norms and family preferences, and they may be more (or less) relevant and useful in different situations of adversity and evolving challenges over time. Families forge varying pathways in resilience depending on their resources, challenges, values, and aims.

BOX 14.1. Key Processes: Family Resilience Framework

Belief systems

1. Making meaning of adversity
   - Relational view of resilience
   - Normalize, contextualize distress
   - Sense of coherence: meaningful, comprehensible, manageable challenge
   - Facilitative appraisal: Explanatory attributions; future expectations
2. Positive outlook
   - Hope, optimistic bias; confidence in overcoming challenges
   - Encouragement; affirm strengths, focus on potential
   - Active initiative and perseverance (can-do spirit)
   - Master the possible; accept what can't be changed; tolerate uncertainty
3. Transcendence and spirituality
   - Larger values, purpose
   - Spirituality: Faith, contemplative practices, community; connection with nature
   - Inspiration: Envision possibilities, aspirations; creative expression; social action
   - Transformation: learning, change, and positive growth from adversity

Organizational processes

4. Flexibility
   - Rebound, adaptive change to meet new challenges
   - Reorganize, restabilize: continuity, dependability, predictability
   - Strong authoritative leadership: Nurture, guide, protect
   - Varied family forms: cooperative parenting/caregiving teams
   - Couple/co-parent relationship: Mutual respect; equal partners
5. Connectedness
   - Mutual support, teamwork, and commitment
   - Respect individual needs, differences
   - Seek reconnection and repair grievances
6. Mobilize social and economic resources
   - Recruit extended kin, social, and community supports; models and mentors
   - Build financial security; navigate stressful work/family challenges
   - Transactions with larger systems: Access institutional, structural supports

Communication/Problem-solving Processes

7. Clarity
   - Clear, consistent messages, information
   - Clarify ambiguous situation; truth seeking
8. Open emotional sharing
   - Painful feelings: (sadness, suffering, anger, fear, disappointment, remorse)
   - Positive interactions: (love, appreciation, gratitude. humor, fun, respite)

> **BOX 14.1. Continued**
>
> 9. Collaborative problem-solving
>   - Creative brainstorming; resourcefulness
>   - Share decision making; negotiation & conflict repair
>   - Focus on goals; concrete steps; build on success; learn from setbacks
>   - Proactive stance: preparedness, planning, prevention
>
> From Walsh (2016b).

Broad Range of Practice Applications

A family resilience orientation is finding useful application with a wide range of crisis situations, disruptive transitions, and multistress conditions in clinical and community-based services (Walsh, 2002, 2016b). Interventions utilize principles and techniques common among strength-based family systems practice approaches, but they attend more centrally to the impact of significant stressors and aim to increase family capacities for positive adaptation. A family-centered systems assessment may lead to individual, family, and/or group work with youth, parents, and significant extended family members. Putting an ecological view into practice, interventions may involve collaboration with school, workplace, social service, justice, or healthcare systems. Resilience-oriented family interventions can be adapted to many formats.

- Family consultations, brief intervention, or more intensive family therapy may combine individual and conjoint sessions, including members most affected by stressors and those who can contribute to resilience.
- Psychoeducational multifamily groups provide social support and practical information, offering concrete guidelines for stress reduction, crisis management, problem-solving, and optimal functioning as families navigate through stressful periods and face future challenges.
- Brief, cost-effective "check-ups" can be timed around stressful transitions, milestones, or emerging challenges in long-term adaptation.

To illustrate the wide range of applications of a family resilience framework, Box 14.2 outlines training, clinical services, and community-based partnerships designed and implemented by the Chicago Center for Family Health (CCFH) over 25 years (see Walsh, 2002, 2016b, for program descriptions).

The benefits of multilevel interventions were seen in one community-based partnership to develop and implement a resilience-oriented family component for a gang prevention program sponsored by the Los Angeles mayor's office (Walsh, 2016a, 2016b). The multilevel approach (including individual, peer group, family, and community interventions) aimed to support the positive development of 1,000 youth (aged 10–14) identified at high-risk of gang involvement in neighborhoods with high gang activity. CCFH provided family intervention training for 150 counselors, broadening focus from youth risk factors and problem behaviors

> **BOX 14.2. CCFH Resilience-Oriented, Community-Based Program Applications**
>
> Chicago Center for Family Health (1991–2015)
> Family resilience-oriented training, services, partnerships
>
> - Recover from crisis, trauma, and loss
>   - Family adaptation to complicated, traumatic loss (Walsh)
>   - Mass trauma events; Major disasters (Walsh)
>   - Relational trauma (Barrett, Center for Contextual Change)
>   - Refugee families (Rolland, Walsh, Weine)
>   - War and conflict-related recovery (Rolland, Weine, Walsh)
>   - Navigate disruptive family transitions
> - Divorce, single-parent, stepfamily adaptation (Jacob, Lebow, Graham)
>   - Foster care (Engstrom)
>   - Job loss, transition, and re-employment strains (Walsh, Brand)
> - Overcome challenges of chronic multistress conditions
>   - Serious illness, disabilities, end-of-life challenges (Rolland, Walsh, R. Sholtes, Zuckerman)
>   - Poverty; ongoing complex trauma (Faculty)
>   - LGBT issues, stigma (Koff)
> - Overcome obstacles to success: at-risk youth
>   - Child and adolescent developmental challenges (Lerner, Schwartz, Gutmann, Martin)
>   - Family–school partnership program (Fuerst & Team)
>   - Gang reduction/youth development (Rolland, Walsh & Team)
>
> From Walsh (2016b).

to identify and build strengths and resources in the relational network toward positive aims. A case example follows.

> Eleven-year-old Miguel's family was initially seen only as a negative influence: the (nonresidential) father and older brother were active gang members, and his mother was not at home after school to keep Miguel off the streets and invested in school. An interview with Miguel's mother revealed her loving concern for Miguel, her limited resources, and her dismay that her job and long commute constrained her ability to monitor his activities or support his studies. The intervention team learned that the maternal uncle—the boy's godfather—a former gang member, who had been incarcerated, had turned his life around productively. Invited to a family session, he readily agreed to take a mentoring role with Miguel and to bolster the mother's parenting efforts to strengthen family functioning and reduce obstacles toward a positive future vision for Miguel.
>
> In this multilevel intervention, multiple protective/preventive and promotive influences related to resilience were overlapping and synergistic. An outcome study found that

youth involved in the program over one year scored significantly lower on problems and risk factors than at their entry and compared to a matched control group. In program evaluation (Cahill et al., 2015), separate interviews with youths and their parents found that they experienced prevention services as a whole-family intervention, with positive family impacts such as improved relationships, greater connection across generations, and improved family functioning, communication, and problem-solving.

Resilience-oriented services like this foster family empowerment as they bring forth shared hope, develop new and renewed competencies, and strengthen family bonds. Interventions to strengthen family resilience also have preventive value, building capacities in meeting future challenges. Further, studies have found that in focusing on client resilience, helping professionals working with trauma experienced *vicarious resilience* in their work, countering burnout and yielding greater personal, relational, and spiritual well-being in their own lives (Hernandez, 2002; Hernandez, Gangsei, & Engstrom, 2007).

Advances and Challenges in Family Resilience Research

Over the past decade there has been growing interest internationally in family resilience research. Most studies are based on qualitative or mixed methods and grounded in the previously described conceptual frameworks. Most studies, to date, examine family processes in dealing with a particular type of adversity within the family, such as serious illness (Kazak, 2006), developmental disabilities (Greeff & Nolting, 2013), the death of a child or parent (Greeff & Joubert, 2007; Greeff, Vansteenwegen, & Herbiest, 2011), divorce (Greene et al., 2012), stepfamilies (Coleman, Ganong, & Russell, 2013), foster care (Lietz, Julien-Chinn, Geiger, & Hayes Piel, 2016), and family reunification (e.g., Lietz, 2013). Increasing attention is being directed to family resilience in conditions of extreme poverty, community disasters (Knowles, Sasser, & Garrison, 2010), and war and terrorism (MacDermid, 2010; Saltzman et al., 2016) and with refugees, forced migration, and populations in war-torn regions (Rolland & Weine, 2000; Weine et al., 2005). Only a few studies to date have tracked the evolving challenges and adaptational pathways over time in family resilience (e.g., Greeff & Joubert, 2007; Lietz, et al., 2016). More mixed-methods research and longitudinal studies incorporating a developmental perspective are needed to advance our knowledge of family-focused mental health prevention and intervention.

No Single Model: Subjectivity and Context Matter

The very flexibility of the construct of resilience complicates research efforts (Card & Barnett, 2015). Unlike a static, singular model, typology, or set of traits, human resilience involves dynamic, multilevel, recursive processes over time, which are contingent on the impact and demands of adverse situations and on each family's composition, future aims, and available resources. The diversity and complexity of kinship bonds within and across households require clear yet flexible definitions of "the family" under study.

There is widespread interest in use of a simple questionnaire for a quantitative measure of both individual and family resilience. Yet conceptual and methodological challenges in questionnaire use are vexing, given the contextually contingent nature of the construct of resilience. Further, instruments designed to measure individual resilience have shown unstable psychometric properties across studies and cultures, particularly in factor structures (Windle, Bennett, & Noyes, 2011). The Walsh Family Resilience Questionnaire (Walsh, 2016b) has been translated and validated by researchers in Italy (Rocchi et al., 2017) and elsewhere, with ongoing use in studies of chronic illness, extreme poverty, and other adverse situations. Across cultures, questionnaire adaptation is encouraged to translate and frame questions to fit varied socioeconomic contexts, linguistic differences, target populations, and types of adversity under study. Mindful that different mappings are to be expected, questionnaire use might be thought of as mapping a particular family profile, while being cautious neither to "profile" families in a stereotypic way nor to label families as either resilient or not.

Questionnaires can be useful to rate within-family changes over time, as in immediate- and long-term disaster recovery or changes over the course of a recurrent illness. They can also be used for pre- and postassessment in practice effectiveness research. Similar to scaling questions in systemic practice, questionnaire responses are most useful when explored more fully in interviews. For instance, in several studies, families, whether religious or not, have noted the value of spiritual resources for resilience (e.g., Greeff & Joubert, 2007), which might vary from congregational involvement to prayer or meditation, humanist values, connection with nature, and helping others in need.

In designing research, more attention is needed to clarify important family characteristics, social and developmental contexts, and the adverse situation under study. Specific variables include (a) the family unit (e.g., couple; family structure; household or relational network), (b) respondent's position (e.g., mother, spouse, nonresidential parent, child/adolescent), (c) socioeconomic location, and (d) type and severity of adversity faced and whether it is an acute event (recent or past), recurrent crisis, or ongoing multi-stress condition. Some processes, such as good communication, tend to promote resilience across contexts, while others may be situation-specific. Different strengths might be more or less helpful to deal with the death of a child, a divorce, a parent's recurrent cancer, a major disaster, or ongoing complex trauma in war zones or prolonged refugee situations.

Studies to date tend to be scattered across diverse literatures and remain largely fragmented in focus, identifying a few significant variables, in particular situations and social contexts. More interdisciplinary, mixed-methods approaches are recommended to yield a fuller understanding of family resilience (Criss, Henry, Harrist, & Larzelere, 2015). Flexibility is needed to adapt study methods and interventions to fit the diverse experiences of families in their social and developmental contexts.

Advancing Multilevel Resilience Research and Practice Application

There is a growing impetus to develop multilevel systems research and practice applications linking individual, family, and community risk and resilience. Community approaches are commonly linked with the individual level but leave out the family impact of adversity, the crucial importance of family stability and well-being, and the mediating role families play in positive adaptation for their individual members and their communities.

Masten and Monn (2015) strongly encourage efforts to integrate youth and family resilience approaches. Distelberg, Martin, Borieux, and Oloo (2015) designed a multidimensional tool to assess family resilience in socioeconomic mobility programs for families in poverty. In studies of resilience in indigenous First Nations groups in Canada, who have suffered historical and ongoing trauma, Kirmayer et al. (2011) documented the crucial importance of intertwined family, community, and cultural/spiritual resources, urging their attention in mental health services. Saul and Simon (2016) provide international training to foster family and community resilience in situations of collective trauma. Weine's targeted ethnographic studies with populations in war-torn regions and refugee resettlement (Weine, 2011; Weine et al., 2005) offer a superb model of multilevel systemic research yielding valuable recommendations.

The key processes (facilitative beliefs, organizational resources, and communication processes) summarized in the previously described family resilience framework are consistent with research on individual resilience and can be applied at larger system levels, as in emergency response services in disaster relief (Walsh, 2007, 2016b). Figure 14.1 depicts the dynamic, recursive processes in resilience operating both within and across system levels in the context of stress and over time.

A dynamic process framework for human systems accounts for the complex nature of family life in social and developmental contexts without trying to resolve it using mechanistic concepts and data analysis. Although it is not feasible to directly assess or control all variables, it is advisable to focus on those most relevant to the type of adversity, target population, social and temporal contexts, and study aims. Advancing our understanding of human resilience requires more than robust and measurable indices. A systemic conceptual lens keeps awareness of the many interdependent influences across and within levels. As in family resilience, collaborative team efforts are encouraged, linking research and practice (including practice-informed research) for a more integrative, wholistic approach addressing the dynamic multilevel processes in human resilience.

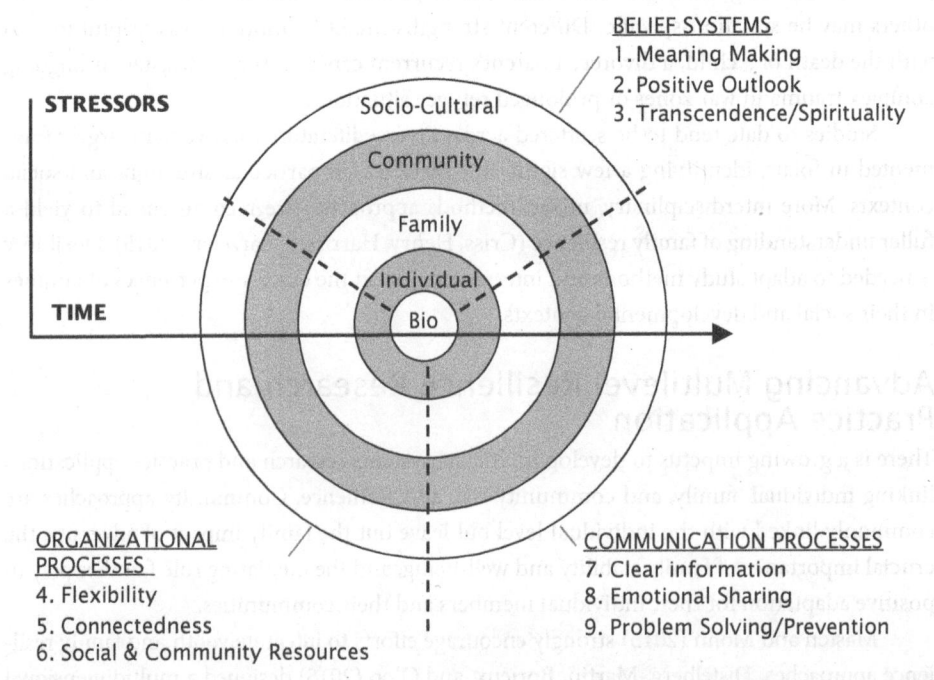

FIGURE 14.1 Dynamic systemic perspective: Multilevel recursive processes in resilience. From Walsh (2016b).

Caution is advised that assessment of family resilience not be misapplied to judge families as "not resilient" if they are unable to rise above serious life challenges. Family processes can strengthen a family's capacities, yet may not be sufficient to overcome devastating biological, social, or environmental conditions. Moreover, the notion of resilience should not be misused in public policy to withhold social supports or to maintain inequities, rationalizing that success or failure is determined by individual or family strengths or deficits—that is, the presumption that those who are resilient will flourish and those who falter simply weren't resilient. It is not enough to bolster the resilience of vulnerable families so that they can "beat the odds"; a multilevel approach requires larger systems supports to change their odds. Attention is also required to address larger societal and global forces that heighten family and community vulnerability, such as the devastating impact of climate change, which in turn fuels mass migration, war, and conflict. Advances in research on human resilience—in individuals, families, and communities—can be transformative for social policy, intervention, and prevention programs with vulnerable and at-risk populations, services that have been largely problem-focused (Waldegrave et al., 2016). Such research can reorient funding and service priorities from how families fail to how families, when challenged, succeed.

Conclusion

In sum, a research-informed family resilience framework can guide research and practice by (a) assessing family functioning on key system variables as they fit each family's values, structure, resources, and challenges and then (b) targeting interventions to strengthen family functioning in overcoming the adverse challenges faced. This collaborative approach strengthens relational, community, cultural, and spiritual resources, grounded in a deep conviction in the human potential for recovery and positive growth forged from adversity.

Key Messages

1. The concept of family resilience refers to the capacity of the family as a functional system in overcoming significant life challenges.
2. Highly stressful and/or traumatic events, persistent stressors, and social contexts impact the whole family; in turn, family processes facilitate the adaptation of all members, their relationships, and the family unit.
3. The broad application of a family resilience framework in clinical and community-based intervention and prevention is discussed and illustrated.

References

Biblarz, T., & Savci, E. (2010). Lesbian, gay, bisexual, and transgender families. *Journal of Marriage and Family, 72*(3), 480–497. doi:10.1111/j.1741-3737.2010.00714.x

Boyd-Franklin, N., & Karger, M. (2012). Intersections of race, class, and poverty. In F. Walsh (Ed.), *Normal family processes: Growing diversity and complexity* (4th ed., pp. 273–296). New York, NY: Guilford Press.

Cahill, M., Jannetta, J., Tiry, E., Lowry, S., Becker-Cohen, M., & Serakos, M. (2015). *Evaluation of the Los Angeles Gang Reduction and Youth Development Program: 4 year evaluation report*. Retrieved from https://www.urban.org/sites/default/files/publication/77956/2000622-Evaluation-of-the-Los-Angeles-Gang-Reduction-and-Youth-Development-Program-Year-4-Evaluation-Report.pdf

Card, N., & Barnett, M. (2015). Methodological considerations in studying individual and family resilience. *Family Relations, 64*, 120–133. doi:10.1111/fare.12102

Coleman, M., Ganong, L., & Russell, L. (2013). Resilience in stepfamilies. In D. Becvar (Ed.), *Handbook of family resilience* (pp. 85–104). New York, NY: Springer.

Criss, M. M., Henry, C. S., Harrist, A. W., & Larzelere, R. E. (2015). Interdisciplinary and innovative approaches to strengthening family and individual resilience: An introduction to the special issue. *Family Relations, 64*(1), 1–4. doi:10.1111/fare.12109

Distelberg, B. J., Martin, A. S., Borieux, M., & Oloo, W. A. (2015). Multidimensional family resilience assessment: The Individual, Family, and Community Resilience (IFCR) profile. *Journal of Human Behavior in the Social Environment, 25*(6), 1–19. doi:10.1080/10911359.2014.988320

Falicov, C. J. (2007). Working with transnational immigrants: Expanding meanings of family, community, and culture. *Family Process, 46*(2), 157–172. doi:10.1111/j.1545-5300.2007.00201.x

Falicov, C. J. (2012). Immigrant family processes: A multidimensional framework. In F. Walsh (Ed.), *Normal family processes* (4th ed., pp. 297–323). New York, NY: Guilford Press.

Greeff, A., & Joubert, A.-M. (2007). Spirituality and resilience in families in which a parent has died. *Psychological Reports, 100*(3), 897–900. doi:10.2466/pr0.100.3.897-900

Greeff, A., & Nolting, C. (2013). Resilience in families of children with developmental disabilities. *Families, Systems and Health, 31*, 396–405. doi:10.1037/a0035059

Greeff, A., Vansteenwegen, A., & Herbiest, T. (2011). Indicators of family resilience after the death of a child. *Omega, 63*, 343–358. doi:10.2190/OM.63.4.c

Greene, S., Anderson, E., Forgatch, M. S., DeGarmo, D. S., & Hetherington, E. M. (2012). Risk and resilience after divorce. In F. Walsh (Ed.), *Normal family processes* (4th ed., pp. 102–127). New York, NY: Guilford Press.

Hawley, D. R., & DeHaan, L. (1996). Toward a definition of family resilience: Integrating life-span and family perspectives. *Family Process, 35*, 283–298. doi:10.1111/j.1545-5300.1996.00283.x

Hernandez, P. (2002). Resilience in families and communities: Latin American contributions from the psychology of liberation. *Journal of Counseling & Therapy for Couples and Families, 10*(3), 334–343. doi:10.1177/10680702010003011

Hernandez, P., Gangsei, D., & Engstrom, D. (2007). Vicarious resilience: A new concept in work with those who survive trauma. *Family Process, 46*(2), 229–241. doi:10.1111/j.1545-5300.2007.00206.x

Kazak, A. (2006). Pediatric Psychosocial Preventative Health Model (PPPHM): Research, practice and collaboration in pediatric family systems medicine. *Families, Systems and Health, 24*(4), 381–395. doi:10.1037/1091-7527.24.4.381

Kirmayer, L. J., Dandeneau, S., Marshall, E., Phillips, M. K., & Williamson, K. J. (2011). Rethinking resilience from indigenous perspectives. *Canadian Journal of Psychiatry, 56*(2), 84–91. doi:10.1177/070674371105600203

Knowles, R., Sasser, D., & Garrison, M. E. B. (2010). Family resilience and resiliency following Hurricane Katrina. In R. Kilmer, V. Gil-Rivas, R. Tedeschi, & L. Calhoun (Eds.), *Helping families and communities recover from disaster* (pp. 97–115). Washington, DC: American Psychological Association Press.

Lansford, J. E., Ceballo, R., Abby, A., & Stewart, A. J. (2001). Does family structure matter? A comparison of adoptive, two-parent biological, single-mother, stepfather, and stepmother households. *Journal of Marriage and Family, 63*(3), 840–851. doi:10.1111/j.1741-3737.2001.00840.x

Lebow, J., & Stroud, C. (2012). Assessment of couple and family functioning: Useful models and instruments. In F. Walsh (Ed.), *Normal family processes* (4th ed., pp. 501–528). New York, NY: Guilford Press.

Lietz, C. A. (2013). Family resilience in the context of high-risk situations. In D. Becvar (Ed.), *Handbook of family resilience* (pp. 153–172). New York, NY: Springer.

Lietz, C. A., Julien-Chinn, F. J., Geiger, J. M., & Hayes Piel, M. (2016). Cultivating resilience in families who foster: Understanding how families cope and adapt over time. *Family Process, 55*(4), 660–672. doi:10.1111/famp.12239

MacDermid, S. M. (2010). Family risk and resilience in the context of war and terrorism. *Journal of Marriage and Family, 72*(3), 537–556. doi:10.1111/j.1741-3737.2010.00717.x

Masten, A. S., & Cicchetti, D. (2016). Resilience in development: Progress and transformation. In D. Cicchetti (Ed.), *Developmental psychopathology, Vol. 4: Risk, resilience, and intervention* (3rd ed., pp. 271–333). New York, NY: Wiley. doi:10.1002/9781119125556.devpsy406

Masten, A. S., & Monn, A. R. (2015). Child and family resilience: A call for integrated science, practice, and professional training. *Family Relations, 64*(1), 5–21. doi:10.1111/fare.12103

McCubbin, L. D., & McCubbin, H. I. (2013). Resilience in ethnic family systems: A relational theory for research and practice. In D. Becvar (Ed.), *Handbook of family resilience* (pp. 175–195). New York, NY: Springer.

McCubbin, H. I., & Patterson, J. M. (1983). The family stress process: The Double ABCX model of adjustment and adaptation. *Marriage and Family Review, 6*(1–2), 7–37. doi:10.1300/J002v06n01_02

McCubbin, M. A., Balling, K., Possin, P., Frierdich, S., & Bryne, B. (2002). Family resiliency in childhood cancer. *Family Relations, 51*(2), 103–111. doi:10.1111/j.1741-3729.2002.00103.x

McGoldrick, M., Garcia-Preto, N., & Carter, B. (Eds.). (2015). *The expanding family life cycle: Individual, family, and social perspectives* (5th ed.). Boston, MA: Pearson.

McGoldrick, M., Gerson, R., & Petry, S. (2008). *Genograms: Assessment and intervention* (3rd ed.). New York, NY: Norton.

Patterson, J. (2002). Integrating family resilience and family stress theory. *Journal of Marriage and Family, 64*(2), 349–360. doi:10.1111/j.1741-3737.2002.00349.x

Rocchi, S., Ghidelli, C., Burro, R., Vitacca, M., Scalvini, S., Vedova, A. M., . . . Bertolotti, G. (2017). The Walsh Family Resilience Questionnaire: The Italian version. *Neuropsychiatric Disease and Treatment, 13*, 2987–2999. doi:10.2147/NDT.S147315

Rolland, J. S., & Weine, S. (2000). Kosovar family professional educational collaborative. *American Family Therapy Academy Newsletter, 79*, 34–36.

Rolland, J. S. (2018). *Helping couples and families navigate illness and disability: An integrated approach.* New York, NY: Guilford Press.

Rutter, M. (1987). Psychosocial resilience and protective mechanisms. *American Journal of Orthopsychiatry, 57*(3), 316–331. doi:10.1111/j.1939-0025.1987.tb03541.x

Saltzman, W. R., Lester, P., Milburn, N., Woodward, K., & Stein, J. (2016). Pathways of risk and resilience: Impact of a family resilience program on active-duty military parents. *Family Process, 55*(4), 633–646. doi:10.1111/famp.12238

Saul, J., & Simon, W. (2016). Building resilience in families, communities, and organizations: A training program in global mental health and psychosocial support. *Family Process, 55*(4), 689–699. doi:10.1111/famp.12248

Spotts, E. (2012). Unraveling the complexity of gene-environmental interplay and family processes. In F. Walsh (Ed.), *Normal family processes* (4th ed., pp. 529–552). New York, NY: Guilford Press.

Ungar, M. (2004). The importance of parents and other caregivers to the resilience of high-risk adolescents. *Family Process, 43*(1), 23–41. doi:10.1111/j.1545-5300.2004.04301004.x

Ungar, M. (2010). Families as navigators and negotiators: Facilitating culturally and contextually specific expressions of resilience. *Family Process, 49*(3), 421–435. doi:10.1111/j.1545-5300.2010.01331.x

Waldegrave, C., King, P., Maniapoto, M., Tamasese, T. K., Parsons, T. L., & Sullivan, G. (2016). Relational resilience in Maori, Pacific, & European sole parent families: From theory and research to social policy. *Family Process, 55*(4), 673–688. doi:10.1111/famp.12219

Walsh, F. (1996). The concept of family resilience: Crisis and challenge. *Family Process, 35*(3), 261–281. doi:10.1111/j.1545-5300.1996.00261.x

Walsh, F. (2002). A family resilience framework: Innovative practice applications. *Family Relations, 51*(2), 130–137. doi:10.1111/j.1741-3729.2002.00130.x

Walsh, F. (2003). Family resilience: A framework for clinical practice. *Family Process, 42*(1), 1–18. doi:10.1111/j.1545-5300.2003.00001.x

Walsh, F. (2007). Traumatic loss and major disasters: Strengthening family and community resilience. *Family Process*, 46(2), 207–227. doi:10.1111/j.1545-5300.2007.00205.x

Walsh, F. (Ed.). (2009). *Spiritual resources in family therapy* (2nd ed.). New York, NY: Guilford Press.

Walsh, F. (2012a). Successful aging and family resilience. In B. Haslip & G. Smith (Eds.), *Emerging perspectives on resilience in adulthood and later life* (pp. 153–172). New York, NY: Springer.

Walsh, F. (2012b). The "new normal": Diversity and complexity in 21st century families. In F. Walsh (Ed.), *Normal family processes* (4th ed., pp. 4–27). New York, NY: Guilford Press.

Walsh, F. (2016a). Applying a family resilience framework in training, practice, and research: Mastering the art of the possible. *Family Process*, 55(4), 616–632. doi:10.1111/famp.12260

Walsh, F. (2016b). *Strengthening family resilience* (3rd ed.). New York, NY: Guilford Press.

Walsh, F. (in press). *Complicated loss, healing, and resilience: A family systems approach*. New York, NY: Guilford Press.

Walsh, F., & McGoldrick, M. (2013). Bereavement: A family life cycle perspective. *Family Science*, 4(1), 20–27. doi:10.1080/19424620.2013.819228

Weine, S. (2011). Developing preventive mental health interventions for refugee families in resettlement. *Family Process*, 50(3), 410–430. doi:10.1111/j.1545-5300.2011.01366.x

Weine, S., Knafl, K., Feetham, S., Kulauzavic, Y., Klebec, A., Sclove, S., . . . Spahovic, D. (2005). A mixed methods study of refugee families engaging in multiple-family groups. *Family Relations*, 54(4), 558–568. doi:10.1111/j.1741-3729.2005.00340.x

Windle, G., Bennett, K. M., & Noyes, J. (2011). A methodological review of resilience measurement scales. *Health and Quality of Life Outcomes*, 9(8), 1–18. doi:10.1186/1477-7525-9-8

15

What Does It Take for Early Relationships to Remain Secure in the Face of Adversity?

Attachment as a Unit of Resilience

Ana Berástegui and Carlos Pitillas

Introduction

It has been at least four decades since the term *resilience* was established within psychology, serving as a lever for overcoming, or complementing deficit models of human development and offering a lens for understanding trauma with a focus on healing mechanisms (Walsh, 2003, 2015; Windle, 2011). Despite the lack of consensus on the definition and scope of resilience, there seems to be some agreement with respect to three dimensions of the concept: the presence of adversity or relative risk, the deployment of resources to face the effects of adversity, and a positive adaptation as a result (including the avoidance of an expected negative result; Windle, 2011).

Our goal in this chapter is to explore resilience as it pertains to attachment relationships. We view early attachment relationships not only as a mediating factor between adversity and its impact or as a source of protection in the face of hardship, but also as a resilient mechanism in itself. This is to say that caregiver–child dyads, as bipersonal, dynamic systems of interaction and meaning-making, may themselves show resilience when exposed to adversity. In our view, a resilient early attachment relationship would be able to maintain a constant level of felt security within these dyadic interactions to regain such security when conflict or harm arises and/or to protect a circuit of connection and mutual recognition. As will be developed throughout this chapter, we believe that resilient attachment relationships may facilitate resilience across development, and promote healthier, more resilient societies at different levels (extended families, schools, neighborhoods, cultures). The first part of this paper will be devoted to a review of attachment relationships in the resilience literature. In its second part, we will develop our concept of attachment resilience and its constituent factors. In the third part, we will delve into the ecological nature of attachment resilience. In the fourth part of this chapter, a set of four principles for the study and enhancement of attachment resilience will be presented. We will conclude with a discussion of the implications of these ideas for family intervention.

Resilience and Early Attachment Relationships

Researches have approached the relationship between attachment and resilience from three different viewpoints: the absence or distortion of attachment as a source of adversity for the child, attachment security as an adaptive result, and attachment as a resource for coping in the face of adversity.

The Absence of Attachment as Adversity: Attachment as Cause

From the beginning of the study of attachment, with Bowlby's (1951) or Spitz's (1945) research on the deleterious consequences of abandonment and loss, a marked relationship between the absence of attachment and experiences of trauma has been established. The absence of attachment figures, the breakdown of early relationships, or abuse and neglect within early attachment relationships have been highlighted from very diverse perspectives as a specific and relevant source of adversity in childhood, with a long-term impact at different levels (physiological, neurological, cognitive, emotional, social) on a child's development. The results of the Bucharest Early Intervention Project, which followed children who were under institutional care during their early years and were subsequently fostered or adopted, point toward changes in brain development, significant cognitive and physical growth delays, and increased risk for psychological disorders, among other negative outcomes when early attachments are compromised (Nelson, Fox, & Zeanah, 2014; Zeanah, Smyke, Koga, Carlson, & Bucharest Early Intervention Project Core Group, 2005).

If we define trauma as any event that entails danger to life or threatens the physical integrity of the person (American Psychiatric Association, 2013), neglect or toxicity in early relationships with caregivers entails a stressful event and a threat to the physical and psychological well-being of a child, as well as a loss of the central mechanism (attachment with a caregiver), which enables a child to face other sources of threat. Thus, we can consider the absence, loss, or the abusive or neglectful nature of early attachment relationships as traumatic events in themselves, which, when marked by chronicity, may function as an antecedent of complex trauma (Cook et al., 2005).

Attachment Security as a Resilient Result: Attachment as Outcome

Attachment and internal working models of attachment are sensitive to conditions of adversity. A greater tendency to develop insecure working models of attachment has been found under adverse conditions, such as chronic illness or disability, migration, poverty, and especially in situations of cumulative risk (Cerezo, Trenado, & Pons-Salvador, 2006; Diener, Nievar, & Wright, 2003). Therefore, security of attachment can be seen as an outcome that indicates whether resilience mechanisms have been activated and successful in preserving a level of health despite risk. For example, one common research finding is the higher prevalence of insecure attachment patterns among children with intellectual disabilities. This can be attributed to a negative impact of disability on the transition to parenthood, which would reduce the capacity of parents to bond securely with their child (Rubio, 2015).

Attachment as a Factor of Resilience: Attachment as Process

Attachment security has also been considered a condition for individual resilience. This can be assessed across the ecological spectrum, from mental health, school adaptation, well-being in adult relationships, or social inclusion. The family in particular, though, has been posed as a protective agent against contextual adversity and as a facilitator for the development of resilient individuals (see Walsh, this volume; Werner, 1992). A set of studies conducted in situations of accumulated risk suggest that the impact of multiple adversities on cognitive and socioemotional development is mediated by the quality of relationships in the family (Treyvaud et al., 2012) or, more specifically, by the quality of parental responsiveness (Wade, Moore, Astington, Frampton, & Jenkins, 2015). On the other hand, much of the research on adoption has been undertaken from this vantage point and has tried to ascertain how the establishment of new family relationships and the development of secure attachments, can mitigate the impact of early psychosocial adversity (Berástegui, 2012; Haugaard & Hazan, 2003; McGuinness & Dyer, 2006; McGoron et al., 2012; Palacios & Brodzinsky, 2010).

Attachment Resilience

Beyond this triple perspective, we believe that early attachment relationships may be considered, in themselves, a subject of resilience. Thus, we conceptualize attachment resilience as the processes by which the attachment relationship between a child and its primary caregivers is capable, when subjected to a certain degree of adversity, of preserving enough levels of affective connection, and of maintaining its functions as a safe and secure base for exploration. Attachment resilience also entails the relationship's capacity to recover such functions after their suspension, and even to see these functions enhanced following exposure to adversity. Therefore, attachment resilience requires a deepening or specification of theories about family resilience (Walsh, 2003), although it is not identical to it. We understand it as a nested dyadic component, an intermediate level between individual and family resilience.

Characteristics of Attachment Resilience

As with all aspects of human resilience, attachment resilience is characterized by a number of qualities evident in a range of studies.

Activation under adversity. At the most basic level, every attachment relationship develops in a context of some adversity, as it is a system that evolves to maintain the child's safety under situations of stress, dysregulation, and potential danger common to all children (Bowlby, 1973; Crittenden, 2016). Thus, by its very definition, the attachment system is set in motion in the face of perceived adversity and must show some capacity to facilitate the child's development. We will, however, refer to attachment resilience when these processes of care and protection take place under circumstances of special adversity that, by their nature (unexpected) and/or their degree (accumulated), interact with or overwhelm the daily strains and challenges associated with natural processes of transition to parenthood and child development. This extraordinary and potentially traumatic adversity can affect attachment by directly impacting upon the child, impacting upon the caregiver (and, through her or him, upon the relationship; Scheeringa & Zeanah, 2001), or impacting upon the family system as a whole. Trauma in the family puts attachment to the test: attachment relationships may amplify suffering or serve as a buffer and a growth-promoting factor in the face of adversity. These "tests" take place in different ways:

- When stress and/or trauma affects the child, it challenges the caregivers' ability to provide security. This would be the case, for example, when a child is diagnosed with a serious, life-threatening illness. Diagnosis not only affects the experience of the family members involved, but may also compromise the parents' capacity to show emotional availability, support the child or read his/her emotional signals accurately during the illness and subsequent treatment (Kazak et al., 2006; Pitillas, 2014).
- When stress and/or trauma affects the family, or one of its members, and compromises security within the child–caregiver relationship. This would be the case, for example, of the impact of maternal depression on attachment (Martins & Gaffan, 2000) or the impact of gender violence on the security of a mother–child relationship (Levendosky, Bogat, & Huth-Bocks, 2011).
- When stress and/or trauma affects the whole family, compromising its natural protective components. Such would be the case of poverty, migration, or displacement (Betancourt et al., 2012; Villacieros, 2017) which distorts availability, communication and regulation witgin the family, and can affect children more strongly than adults.
- When the source of the trauma is the very deterioration of attachment relationships, their absence, or their character as negligent or abusive.

Connection and security. Attachment is not only resilient when it maintains security, but also when it is capable of restoring security after damage or rupture (see following discussion for more details). In daily situations and, more specifically, under adversity, there are many episodes of disconnection, of insensitivity, or intrusion. An attachment relationship is resilient when it is capable of re-establishing connection after disconnection, restoring security when it feels loss, or reactivating the ability to give meaning to the interaction, after a time of misunderstanding or inability to mentalize.

Finally, beyond seeking homeostasis through interactive repair, attachment resilience can also be associated with growth (Triplett, Tedeschi, Cann, Calhoun, & Reeve, 2012), which would entail a more solid sense of interpersonal connection, a reinforcement of the experience of safety and effective interactions.

Procedural character. One of the common debates in the resilience literature is whether it can be thought of as a trait or a set of processes. We believe it is best described as a dynamic mechanism, although we are aware that the practice and success of attachment resilience processes may generate a disposition to respond "resiliently" to new challenges. A relationship's capacity to respond supportively will be put to test repeatedly, depending on the character, the degree, the temporality, and the accumulation of demands that characterize each episode of adversity (Berástegui, 2013; Smith & Pollack, 2020; see our case analysis later in the chapter for reflection on the influence of time on the evolution of attachment resilience in a mother–child dyad). For these reasons, attachment resilience is not only linked to parental responsiveness or caregivers' working models of attachment, nor to the child's working model of a successful relationship, but is an emerging property of each relationship (e.g., attachment can be more secure toward the mother than the father at a particular point in time).

Components of Attachment Resilience

What does it take for early attachment relationships to maintain security in the face of hardship? The following is a list of the most important processes associated with attachment resilience.

Responsiveness and mutual regulation. The concept of parental responsiveness[1] refers to the caregivers' ability to detect, understand, and adequately respond to the child's emotional signals and needs (Ainsworth, 1979). Responsivity is of great importance, since infants and young children are unable to satisfy their physiological and psychological needs autonomously. Caregivers promote security by meeting their children's need for attachment and exploration. Attachment needs are those activated by experiences of distress or vulnerability in the child, who seeks the adult to soothe, protect, and provide emotional containment. Exploration needs relate to the child's tendencies toward growth and differentiation: the child needs a responsive adult to promote separation, offer stimulation, support the child within her zone of proximal development (Vygotsky, 1978), and celebrate her achievements (Powell, Cooper, Hoffman, & Marvin, 2013). Shifts between both systems may take place rapidly, and the child's attachment and exploration signals are usually expressed nonverbally and within a microscopic time frame (seconds and split seconds). This means that caregivers' responsiveness is often a matter of sensitivity to rapid, subtle changes in the child's needs and the child's cues. An immigrant child, for example, who has recently arrived at a new country may show signs of curiosity toward new stimuli and a tendency to explore his physical space (exploration) and, within seconds, shift to a stance of cautiousness and needing his parents to regulate his feelings of uncertainty and fear in the face of novelty (attachment). A resilient attachment relationship would involve the parents' capacity to dynamically perceive and respond to these shifts in the child's motivation. Parental responsiveness may contribute to attachment resilience by generating dynamics of mutual regulation and adjustment between parent and child: "Caregiver and infant learn the rhythmic structure of the other and modify their behavior to fit that structure" (Schore, 2010, p. 20). When this occurs, mutual regulation can be a basic source of agency for both caregiver and child. When involved in this circuit of mutual transformation and adjustment, both participants in the relationship develop a sense of basic trust in their own ability to modify contingencies within the relationship and, extensively, within the social world. This may be especially valuable for the child's emerging experience of self and her future ability to respond to hardship with hope and a sense of self-efficacy.

It is important to note that, despite the interactive, co-constructed dimension of regulation within the attachment dyad, this relationship is also defined by asymmetry: one participant (the caregiver) has a more mature organism and is more powerful than the other (the child). As Bowlby explained, attachment figures are "stronger and wiser" (see Powell et al., 2013) than children, something that enables the first to protect and nurture the second. Attachment relationships are somewhat the seat of a creative tension between mutual influence/reciprocity and the regulating influence provided by a caregiver who is in charge. Part of what characterizes attachment resilience is an ability of the relationship to maintain a balance between both dimensions when the relationship is facing adversity.

Representations and interaction. Attachment relationships are also the result of the relation between two dimensions: interactions (events) and representations (meanings). The interactive dimension of attachment includes the constant exchange of signals and responses between both partners in the relationship and the co-constructive, evolving nature of mutual influence between partners. The representational dimension includes interpretations, expectancies, feelings, reenactments from the past, and mental images that give meaning to interactions. Each aspect of attachment relationships has the potential to exert a transformative power upon the other as the two of them co-evolve. Traditionally, parenting programs and cultural views around infancy have mostly dealt with the behavioral, interactive dimension of attachment. This has brought issues such as behavior and needs management, limit-setting, feeding, sleeping, and toilet training to the fore. Additionally, the preverbal nature of the infant's psychological functioning may contribute to the relative neglect of the mental, representational side of attachment during the first years of life.

We believe, however, that a genuine psychosocial approach to parenting and attachment must include a consideration of the meanings that define, direct, influence, and are influenced by child–parent interactions. In this sense, our consideration of factors related to attachment resilience has a strong focus upon parental representations. Researchers have taken the exploration of attachment security to the realm of parental *states of mind* regarding attachment and parental *reflective functioning* (e.g., see Luyten, Nijssens, Fonagy, & Mayes, 2017; Slade, 2005). How do parents represent the world of affective relationships? What do they expect from significant others? Are they able to retrieve memories of their early attachment experiences and organize them in narratives that promote understanding of the social world of their own child? What do they expect from close relationships, and how do they proceed to minimize relational anxiety and have their emotional needs met while remaining responsive to the emotional needs of their children? These questions pertain to parental mental states regarding attachment. Likewise, are parents able to understand behaviors (especially, the child's behaviors) in terms of underlying mental states? This question is related to parental reflective functioning. A well-known study showed that these dimensions of maternal subjectivity, when measured during pregnancy, strongly predict a child's level of security at one year of age (Fonagy, Steele, Steele, Moran, & Higgitt, 1991). Such findings highlight the fact that the resilience of attachment relationships may not only be influenced by what happens between caregiver and child (interactions) but also by what the caregiver *feels*, *thinks*, and *expects*; his capacity to reflect upon his relational history; and his capacity to *read* his child's states of mind.[2]

This ability to read the child's behavior as a sign of mental states involves a dynamic state of parental attunement with the child, since the meaning of behaviors and signals is not predefined, but related to their place in the interactive sequence. Reflecting upon mother-baby interactions, Tronick (2018) explained:

> Their unique ways of being together cannot be transferred to being with others. No one else shares their configuration of meanings. During feeding, mother and infant implicitly know that a glance with a small smile means "I am ready for more," but at bedtime it means "Don't go yet." No one else could possibly know the meaning of these affects and relational intentions. (p. 36)

Intersubjectivity. The discovery of the influence that mental states and mentalization have upon security shows us that attachment relationships are also a matter of intersubjectivity (Tronick, 2018). From early on, children are able to share mental states with adults and derive a sense of joy and security from experiences of emotional attunement with the adult (Jurist, Slade, & Bergner, 2008). Research shows that children are able to know that they are seen and felt by others while interacting and that when this experience of mental sharing is not achieved (e.g., in cases where parents become emotionally disengaged), children protest and make efforts to regain a sense of intersubjectivity (Beebe & Lachman, 2014). Child–parent intersubjective attunement is highly dependent upon parental states of mind regarding attachment and reflective functioning. For a child to be seen and to feel intersubjectively connected, parental subjectivity must be free of unresolved trauma and excessive levels of anxiety (states of mind regarding attachment need to be secure) and open to have the baby's mind considered (Miller, Kim, Boldt, Goffin, & Kochanska, 2019). Early intersubjectivity is an important source of security for the child and, probably, of flexibility and strength within the attachment relationship. A continuous experience of mutual recognition may help both participants of the interaction to adjust to each other's state of mind, to anticipate each other's responses, to collaborate, and to efficiently absorb interactional conflict. This last point is closely related to the following factor involved in attachment resilience.

Rupture and repair. Decades ago, when thinking about the dynamics of maternal "devotion" and adaptation to a child's needs, Winnicott (1949) advocated for a "good-enough mother", that is, a caregiver who may be imperfect or fail sometimes and who, by this very imperfection, leads a child toward security and growth. Infant research shows that secure mother–infant dyads, far from demonstrating perfect (or even high) levels of attunement, are constantly involved in sequences of interactive rupture and repair (Beebe & Lachmann, 2014). Often, the child's needs or mental states are not evident, or when they are, the caregiver's capacity to adjust her responses in intensity, rhythm, and quality is imperfect. Moments of synchronicity are believed to occur as little as 30% of the time between secure mothers and their children (Tronick, 2018):

> "Thus, a more accurate characterization of the normal interaction, and a better basis for assessment, is that it frequently moves from affectively positive mutually coordinated states to affectively negative, miscoordinated states and back again on a frequent basis" (p. 45)

Early attachment security, and the ability of early relationships to be resilient in the face of adversity, is also a matter of flexibility and the capacity of the dyad to recover from mismatches, by means of interactive repair. In the face of adversity, caregiver–child dyads accustomed to interactive repair may be able to maintain connection and feel a basic sense of competence when misunderstandings or conflicts take place. Rupture-and-repair sequences push the child toward the acquisition and development of communication skills that are increasingly efficient. This may help the child stay connected to the caregiver and maintain trust (vs. withdrawing and/or deploying unregulated demands; Beebe & Lachmann, 2014). Concomitantly, caregivers may maintain a sense of affective connection to a communicative, present child who makes herself progressively more understandable. A virtuous circle of feelings of security in the child and competency in the caregiver may ensue.

The Ecological Construction of Attachment Resilience

When considering attachment relationships as a subject of resilience, we come across several variables that interact to pose a risk to such relationships. Resilience processes are complex, and often, they resist a reduction in terms of linear, simple relationships between protective processes and predictable outcomes (Ungar, 2011).

First, these risks are present across all the ecological levels, although with variable weight (Bronfenbrenner, 1979). For example, the impact of hardship upon attachment relationships will presumably be stronger when risk factors accumulate (e.g., as happens with the cumulative loss of migration; Achotegui, 2009) but also depends largely on the transversal nature of risk or its ability to cross ecological layers. Individuals, as well as caregiver–child dyads, continually interact with their contexts across multiple levels (Osher, Cantor, Berg, Steyer, & Rose, 2018).

As has been already advanced, a second characteristic of attachment resilience consists of its double dimension: an empirical dimension and a semantic dimension, one linked to interactive events and the other to how events are understood or represented. Decades ago, Bronfenbrenner (1979) stressed the importance of addressing both action and perception as a way to promote human development. Cyrulnik (2002) refers to this characteristic as the double dimension of trauma (real and narrative). With regard to attachment resilience, we conceptualize it as the circular and recursive relationship between interaction and representation for family interaction (Pitillas & Berástegui, 2018). This double lens is pertinent across all ecological levels. Thus, children and their parents attribute multiple meanings to their interactions. Institutions create narratives to understand their functioning and the events that have an impact upon them. Finally, large groups (societies, countries, or ethnic groups) use myths and historical narratives to understand their history, interpret their present, and guide adaptation for the foreseeable future (see Volkan, 2013, 2014, for a thorough review of large-group psychology in the face of collective trauma, transition, and loss). Therefore, attention to the dimension of events and interactions should not impede attention to the representational and meaning-making processes, which lead to complex responses to trauma within attachment relationships. In the same way, understanding the representational processes of children and their attachment figures should not keep us away from the observable dynamics that take place between them.

A third characteristic of attachment resilience is its processual nature: time is a key variable in understanding attachment resilience. This pertains to the interaction of different temporal levels of experience, the recursion of the processes, and the impact of the child's and the caregivers' developmental cycle. First, a transversal analysis allows us to see how temporal planes overlap, linking in the past with the present with what is expected in the future (see the following discussion for details). For instance, traumatic experiences of the past, such as situations of loss or impacts that are difficult to overcome, become recursively present (re-edited) within current family life (Fraiberg, Adelson, & Shapiro, 1975; Walsh, 2003). A similar pattern of influence takes place between anticipations and prophecies related to the future and the current sense of security within attachment relationships. Second, a longitudinal view enables us to see how processes of risk and protection tend to interact and feed back into each other, so that vicious or virtuous cycles emerge in the mid- to long-term (see Wachtel, 2017, for a more detailed version of this phenomena in relation to attachment patterns across the life cycle). Negative impacts are expected to be stronger when adversity is persistent (Pynoos, 1994). Besides, adversity may set in motion the use of defensive strategies that, despite being useful in diminishing threat in the short-term, may become personality traits in the mid- to long-term, reducing the child's ability to process social-affective information (Perry, Pollard, Blaicley, Baker, & Vigilante, 1995; Perry & Szalavitz, 2017) and compromising the dyad's ability to engage in cooperative, affective dialogues, which would promote adaptive narratives in the face of stress (Koren-Karie, Oppenheim, & Getzler-Yosef, 2008).[3]

Finally, attachment relationships go through different stages, as a function of the child's and the caregivers' developmental transitions, requiring adjustments that interact with adversity. Vulnerability takes different forms across the different stages of the life cycle, so a family response can be useful at one time and not at another. For example, Rolland (1994) has shown how families facing illness and disability may adapt well to diagnosis by means of repressive adaptation (being practical and avoiding emotional expression), whereas this kind of response could lead to difficulties in the mid- to long term (e.g., children may struggle to express their emotional needs clearly and develop adaptation or behavior problems). Thus, a change from repressive adaptation to more open ways of communicating and collaborative meaning-making within the family may enhance resilience. At the same time, each developmental crisis introduces new opportunities for attachment relationships to reorganize and to reactivate processes linked to resilience. In this sense, early attachment relationships are forged at a very sensitive moment both for the infant and young child (who is extremely vulnerable and laying the foundations for its psychological development; Evangelou, Sylva & Kyriacou, 2009) and for attachment figures (who are in transition to parenthood; Saxbe, Rossin-Slater, & Goldenberg, 2018).

The combination of these four characteristics of attachment relationships yields a complex, rich framework of analysis that allows us to better organize research and practice centered upon resilience during the early years. For example, research that focuses on medical illness in the child as a risk factor for early attachment must consider how the impact of diagnosis is mediated by the meanings given by the child himself (which is partly received from the family), and those "negotiated" with general social views and with health systems. Thus, from the perspective of attachment relationships, an event can work as a risk factor in some contexts and a protective factor in others. For example, research conducted by

García-Sanjuán (2017) found that a diagnosis of disability for an adopted child functioned as a protective factor for those families in which this disability was chosen and accepted before adoption and a risk factor for those families that were surprised by the disability, even though levels of disability were milder in the second group.

Some variables that have shown a relation to early attachment security across different ecological levels, the interaction-representation system, and time are synthesized in Table 15.1.[4]

TABLE 15.1 Most Frequently Studied Variables Involved in Attachment Resilience, Across the Different Levels of Human Ecology of Development

		Interaction (Events)	Representation (Meanings)	Time
Child	Individual resilience	Temperament Chronic illness Disability	Developing internal working models of attachment	Attachment phase Developmental history
Dyad	Attachment resilience	Parental responsivity Parental stress Parenting skills	Mentalization Parental self-efficacy Representations about the child	Intergenerational transmission of care or trauma
Microsystem[a]	Family resilience	Parental physical and mental health Support between spouses Domestic/gender violence Communication Family organization and structure	Positive perspective Sense of coherence (predictability, controllability, worth) Meaning Transcendence Stigma	Family history Family's developmental cycle Family members' developmental cycle Stressful life events
Mesosystem		Attachment networks	Attachment networks	
Exosystem	Community resilience	Institutional environment (prison, hospital protection system, etc.) Instrumental and economic support versus poverty Social support and community bonds versus exclusion Professional and formal support Accumulated risk	Sense of belonging Rituals Racism and stigmatization	Community development History of the community
Macrosystem	Cultural resilience	Laws for the promotion/protection of parenthood Cultural practices and views on parenting Migration	Acculturation/Inculturation Stigma Parental ethnotheories[b]	Historical moment Political and social moment

[a]We consider in this table the family microsystem, although other microsystems of care outside the home and the interaction of these with the family through the attachment networks (Lamb, 2005; Lewis, 2005) constitute a relevant area of analysis. Childcare practices within the zero-to-three period (homecare, group care, kindergarten, nanny, mother, shared mother–father care) vary widely, according to the cultural context in which early development takes place.
[b]The term *parental ethnotheories* refers to internalized cultural theories on parenting (Harkness & Super, 2005).

Principles for Study and Intervention

The following is a set of principles that, we believe, should guide researchers and practitioners in their consideration of attachment resilience and the promotion of it.

Chains of Security

Attachment security is a systemic phenomenon: it takes place and develops within a set of interactive sources of influence. In a very concrete sense, the security that a child is provided with by a caregiver is, to some extent, dependent upon the security the caregiver is provided within his or her couple, family, and social relationships. Those relationships are a source of security to the caregiver as long as they are embedded in wider relational domains defined by basic trust. At the same time, the circulation of trust between individuals and groups across several domains is supported by the structural security that stems from institutions, laws, and culture, among others. Elsewhere (Pitillas & Berástegui, 2018), we have used the concept of "chains of security" to designate the fact that security is, in a sense, a descending phenomenon: it flows down from the wider structures of society (the macrosystem) to its constituent social networks (the exosystem) and, ultimately, to child–caregiver dyads and individuals (microsystem). Inversely, security within attachment dyads may ascend toward the whole society by propelling dynamics of trust within the nuclear family, the extended family, neighborhoods, schools, and communities, a pattern that may finally lead to security-based cultures and social policies. As a result, studies on attachment resilience should be able to move from a dyadic to a multisystems lens. On the other hand, interventions aimed at enhancing attachment security should not only be able to promote safer interactions between caregiver and child but also to promote more effective chains of security between the caregiver–child dyad and the social and educational milieu that envelops the dyad. Finally, relationships between different levels of influence upon the dyad (e.g., the relationship of culture with educational models in schools, with teacher–parent relationships, and with parent–child relationships) should be considered as an essential component of a comprehensive map for the understanding of attachment resilience. As systemic and complex thinking may suggest, solutions to insecurity at a given level may be pursued at a superior logical level. Personal insecurity may be approached by working with the attachment dyad; dyadic insecurity may be approached at the family level; family insecurity may be approached at the extended family and/or community level; and so on. The space where understanding of problems (and their possible solutions) is found is an intermediate space between ecological levels.

From Harm to Resources (and the Other Way Around)

The study of human responses to adversity has traditionally been undertaken from a perspective centered upon *harm*: deficits, risk, and psychopathology. Despite the undeniable usefulness of a vision that considers risks, the study of attachment relationships as a potential unit of resilience adds a focus upon the *resources* that can be found within the dyad and that may be enhanced by intervention. Maintaining a double lens that recognizes harms and resources may be a difficult task for professionals who work within protection systems, where families are prone to display an array of risks and harmful parenting practices. However, dynamics of adjustment, responsiveness, and repair are almost always detectable at the microscopic level of interactions. We may not only move toward a recognition of positive, secure parenting practices but, very importantly, in the direction of questions that are sensitive to the ecological dimension of attachment resilience: *Under what conditions* are positive, secure parenting practices more likely to appear?

Intervention models that integrate harm and resources as essential aspects of attachment relationships incorporate a diversity of ingredients, which involve, among others, corrective/educational approaches, the recognition and support of idiosyncratic parenting practices, clinical strategies, deliberation, and problem-solving. Professional flexibility and a diversity in intervention tools seem especially well-tailored to working in contexts of adversity, where families are under pressure to adapt to complex circumstances.

Detecting and celebrating family resources may help break cycles of insecure interactions: caregivers may feel secure within their relationship with professionals, something that prevents many families from disengaging from treatment. Most important, it may promote the progressive transformation of the parent's view of himself- or herself-as-caregiver. As Stern (1995) brilliantly discussed more than two decades ago, an essential therapeutic ingredient within child–parent treatment is the opportunity that parents are granted to see themselves as caregivers in a different, more positive light in the eyes of the professional. This may push the whole set of ingredients that define the attachment relationship (i.e., parental representations of the child, interactions around attachment and exploration, the child's representation of herself and her caregiver, etc.) in the direction of positive, systemic change.

From Past to Present (and the Other Way Around)

Far from being the result of random, or purely pathological processes, insecure parenting practices are forms of adaptation to a specific history and circumstances. Conducting research and practice around attachment resilience entails the recognition of the history of adaptations that underlies parenting practices (Crittenden, 2016). Parents develop ways of caring that are congruent with the environment in which they grew up and that, somehow, they expect will also be present to the child. A recent proposal for the understanding of mental suffering and adaptation, the Power, Threat, Meaning Framework (Johnstone & Boyle, 2018) has put forth the idea that "dysfunction" is the result of threats that were experienced by the individual within a set of power relationships (with their caregivers, teachers, spouses, and/or wider systems of power or production) and that stimulated processes of meaning-making (e.g., I am trapped in situation of danger without escape; people should not be trusted; intimacy brings pain; etc.), something that ultimately puts adaptation strategies in motion (fight, flight, paralysis, victimization, etc.). According to this perspective, instead of diagnosing people (or families), we may ask: "What happened to you?" (power), "How did it affect you?" (threat), "What did you make of it?" (meaning), and "What have you learned to do, to survive under those circumstances?" (adaptation). This last question may be formulated in terms of caregiving strategies: "What have you learned to do *as a caregiver* to help your child adapt to the threats that you experienced?" Threat-related learnings among parents, and the adaptations derived from them, may be enduring despite changes in external conditions (Crittenden, 2016). In this sense, coercive/corrective approaches in the face of parenting practices may sometimes be misdirected. Conversely, secure parenting practices may have at their core a set of positive meanings that stem from parental history. We should integrate these into our view of attachment relationships if we want to consolidate those strengths when they are present in families.[5] In short, we cannot understand and promote change in parenting practices unless we understand (and honor) the meanings and adaptations that underlie such practices.

Sanata and Badou: A Case Study

Sanata is a 27-year old immigrant woman from Mali, recently arrived in Spain with her husband, Aziz, and her infant son, Badou. Sanata's attachment history is one of severe neglect and abuse. When she was born, she was taken away from her birthmother's hands and secretly delivered to one of her father's wives who, at that time, was not able to conceive. She was raised under strong physical abuse by her adoptive mother, who became pregnant when Sanata was 11. This led to Sanata being informed that her biological mother was another woman and being rejected by her adoptive mother. Sanata was delivered back to her birthmother, who showed an extreme difficulty bonding to her after 11 years of separation.

Years later, Sanata married, became pregnant with Badou, and then migrated with her husband and son to Spain. The marriage between Sanata and Aziz was unsatisfactory, marked by conflict. Even though Aziz provided for Sanata and Badou, he provided no support with child-rearing. Shortly after their arrival in Spain, Sanata was diagnosed with an acute medical condition that lead to a three-month hospitalization. During this time, Badou (a toddler) was separated from her mother without explanation or any contact. Also around Badou's toddlerhood, and during a significant part of his preschool years, Sanata suffered from severe depression and posttraumatic symptoms such as dissociation and affective numbing. These symptoms alternated with sudden outbursts of rage directed at Badou. Within this context, Badou developed attachment strategies characterized by inhibition, the absence of affective expression, and self-sufficiency regarding his needs for protection and comfort. When Badou was four-years old, Sanata started receiving help from a community-based nongovernmental organization.

In Figure 15.1 we apply our ecological model to develop a map of processes that define the development of resilience within Sanata and Badou's relationship under the dialectical tension between events and meanings, harms and resources, across different ecological contexts and levels, and, very importantly, across time.

First, we can observe adversity factors that operate across the ecological systems, characterizing the mother's and the dyad's experience with insecurity, disconnection, and isolation, both in the past and in the present, both in Mali and Spain and from microsystems to macrosystems.

For example, poverty forces the family to illegal immigration, which implies an illegal status at arrival, which increases the probability of being employed in informal jobs (e.g., domestic work) that prevent the creation of social networks and acquisition of the language. Sanata and Badou´s attachment relationship struggles within a framework of disconnection,

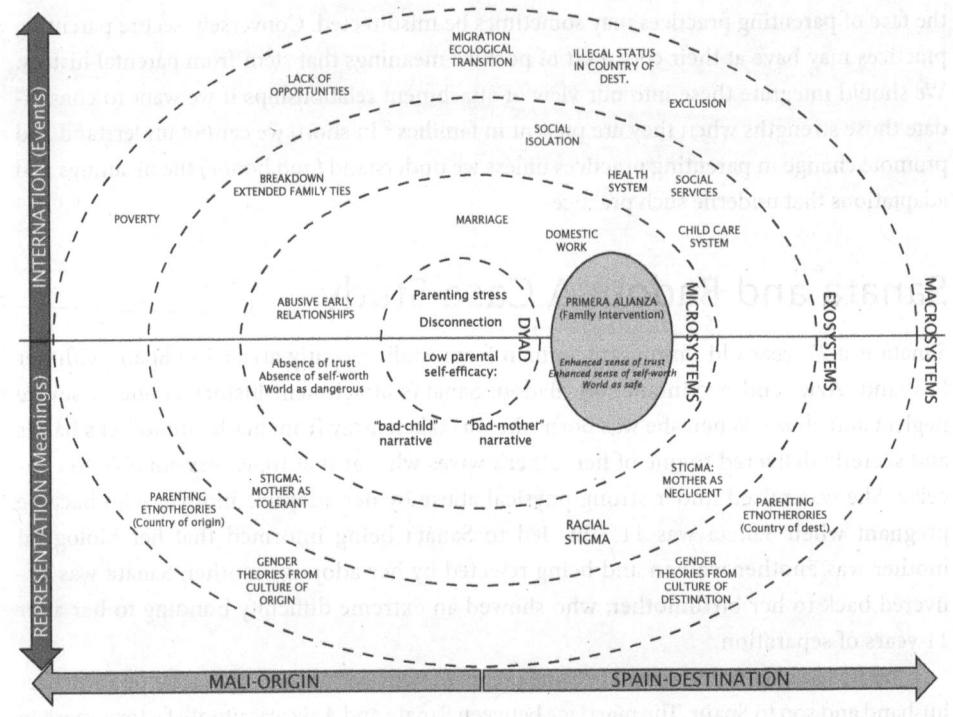

FIGURE 15.1 An ecological map of factors involved in Sanata and Badou's resilience process.

mistrust, resource overwhelm, and absence of support. All this provokes a relative inability to "see" the child and his emotional needs.

Second, on the horizontal axis we find a conflict between pre- and postmigration narratives. This exacerbates the problems that compromise Sanata and Badou's attachment relationship.

1. On the one hand, from Mali´s culture, we find the idea of women as the sole providers of care and a *parental ethnotheory* (Harkness & Super, 2005) focused on raising strong children for a difficult world and neglecting emotional signals because they are considered a sign of fragility. The cultural sanctioning of early trauma (abandonment and abuse) has led to Sanata's inability to process early experience as harm, and to mourn. This idea has marked Sanata's upbringing and how she understands herself and lives her suffering and also her son's behavior. This results in the idea that she has been a bad daughter and that her son is a bad child whenever he cries or is unable to fend for himself. The stigmatization of mothers who are too tolerant of the demands of their children influences the way in which both are seen by Sanata's husband and Badou's father.
2. On the other hand, Spanish parental ethnotheories punish the lack of affection and protection. This idea of parenthood leads to the stigmatization of Sanata as a "typically African negligent mother," as she is evaluated by the health system, the social services system, and specially by the child care system. This results in the idea that she is a bad mother.

Both the bad child and the bad mother narratives feed into parenting-related stress, the sense of disconnection, the lack of self-efficacy, and both Sanata's and Badou's self-esteem. Besides, the tension between pre-/postmigration parenting models, as well as the stigma related to Sanata's African ways of managing behavior and affect expression, provoke confusion related to child-rearing: what is the appropiate way to care for my child and educate him? All of these processes make it hard for Sanata and Badou to attach securely.

In this context, she participated in Primera Alianza, an attachment-centered intervention program developed by the authors (Pitillas & Berástegui, 2018; see the following discussion for details). During this participation in the program, Sanata was provided with

1. *A short but strong experience of security, trust, and connection and a new way of understanding herself and her son.* This corrective emotional experience enabled Sanata to reconstruct her image of herself as caregiver and to see her child under a new, more positive light.
2. *New attachments within the community and a sense of belonging to a social network.* Thus, the previous sense of overwhelm was buffered by social support.
3. A *decrease in the cultural tension between parenting models.* The intervention process helped Sanata build a more integrated, complex model of parenting. Some processes that led to this result were the participation in new cultural beliefs and images about childhood, an opportunity to reconstruct meanings about herself and her child, the detection and validation the meaning and the project that underlay her parenting practices, and the invitation and support in testing new practices and perceptions around attachment.

Sanata's affective state, accompanied by great difficulty with language, led to a mild level of success in this intervention but the change, although discretely, had begun. Five years later, Sanata participated again in Primera Alianza, this time with a focus on her relationship with her 18-month-old son Cheikh. Her use of Spanish had greatly improved, she had developed some important relationships within her community, and, generally, she seemed better acculturated. Her affective state was one of general well-being despite the daily struggles of being an immigrant woman in a low-income family. As a consequence of ongoing tensions within the marriage, Aziz is forced to get more involved in parenting now that they have two children. Badou's avoidant strategies stabilized over the years. Despite important costs to his affective balance, these strategies made him a manageable, "easy" child, thus reducing the former levels of aggression that defined Sanata's relationship with him during his first few years of life.

Sanata's participation on the program this second time activated processes that enhanced her attachment relationship with Cheikh, her image of herself as caregiver, and, significantly, led to a better relationship with Badou. This was expressed as an enhanced ability to understand her eldest son's early traumatic experiences (related to separations, emotional neglect, and intermittent abuse) and a wish to reestablish stronger affective availability.

Conclusion

Historically, attachment has been related to resilience in different ways (as a source of adversity in itself, as a factor of protection against adversity, and as the outcome of resilience/

adaptation processes). But attachment can also be studied as a unit of resilience, as a subject of processes of adaptation, repair, and growth that take place under conditions of hardship. Attachment resilience is characterized by the capacity of an attachment relationship to maintain adequate levels of emotional regulation, connection and intersubjectivity and to entertain processes of rupture and repair in the face of hardship.

A fundamental aspect of this level of resilience is its ecological nature, which entails a processual interaction between different types of impact across ecological levels, events and the meanings that are built upon them, and time as a source of change, recurrence, accumulation of harm, or new developmental opportunities. Our case description was intended to illustrate the complex interaction of these dimensions within a real attachment relationship over a period of years.

Our systemic perspective would entail that, if the caregiver–child relationship is resilient, this would positively impact on other levels of individual and family functioning. Thus, the child would grow with a wider set of resources for adaptation; the parent see his/her sense of competency and purpose reinforced; more positive interactions may take place at the family level; the child may show higher levels of social-affective adjustment at school, something that would bring forth secure relationships with teachers and peers and better acquisition of knowledge; families and children who are adapted and feel well may be more prosocial; and prosocial families may build secure neighborhoods. We believe that incorporating this level of analysis in the work of psychosocial intervention agents may enhance precision, efficacy, and, ultimately, social justice within preventive and therapeutic systems.

Key Messages

1. The study of attachment has been closely linked to that of resilience. Although attachment has been placed at different points in the resilient process (as trigger, mediator, and result), early attachment relationships can be a system or subject of resilience in themselves.
2. Attachment resilience is defined as the processes by which the child-caregiver attachment relationship is capable, when under adversity, of preserving a sense of interpersonal connection, maintaining the relationship's function as a safe haven (for regulating stress) and secure base (for stimulating exploration), to recover those functions after their suspension, and even to grow in the wake of adversity.
3. Attachment resilience is built and develops ecologically. Therefore, to understand attachment resilience processes, a complex view that integrates different ecological levels, the interaction of events and meanings, and time is warranted.
4. Including this level of analysis in the work of psychosocial intervention agents may enhance precision, complexity, and effectiveness.

Acknowledgments

We thank Professor Ungar for his kind and generous invitation to participate in this project, as well as for his enriching feedback and edition, which made the final version of this chapter possible.

Notes

1. Research concerning the precursors of attachment security is somewhat inconsistent when using terms that deal with quality of parental care. Concepts such as parental *availability, responsiveness, sensitivity, involvement, warmth, interactional synchrony,* and others, have been used to highlight aspects of the parental response both to the child's attachment and exploration needs. Here, we have opted for *responsiveness* to designate caregivers' ability to provide care that is consistent and sensitive to different needs in the child.
2. The child's emerging representations of the social world may also play an important role in the determination of attachment security and resilience processes within relationships. Nevertheless, the difficulty of accessing the young child's representational world and the fact that parents are usually the "stronger" part of the relationship have directed researchers and practitioners to focus most of their attention on the parents' representational world.
3. The issue of defenses, their costs and benefits, and their positive or negative effect upon resilience is complex, and warrants a close study of each attachment relationship as well as the circumstances under which each develops. In some cases, the assimilation of defenses into the individual's personality may be helpful in adapting to chronic threats, thus promoting physical/psychological survival. As will be shown in our final case study, the early consolidation of defensive maneuvers, despite their costs, sometimes set the stage for the profitting of new developmental opportunities.
4. See Halty (2017) for a recent revision of this issue in Spanish.
5. Terms such as *angels in the nursery* (Lieberman, Padron, Van Horn, & Harris, 2005) or *kind memories* (Pitillas & Berástegui, 2018) have been coined to designate positive aspects of the caregivers' relational history that sustain positive meanings within the dyad as well as the intergenerational transmission of care.

References

American Psychiatric Association. (2013). *Diagnostic and statistical manual of mental disorders* (5th ed.). Arlington, VA: Author.

Achotegui, J. (2009). Migración y salud mental: El síndrome del inmigrante con estrés crónico y múltiple (Síndrome de Ulises). *Zerbitzuan, 46,* 163–171.

Ainsworth, M. S. (1979). Infant-mother attachment. *American Psychologist, 34*(10), 932–937.

Beebe, B., & Lachmann, F. M. (2014). *The origins of attachment: Infant research and adult treatment.* New York, NY: Routledge.

Berástegui, A. (2013). La postadopción en España: entre el riesgo, la recuperación y la resilencia. In. B. Charro & M. J. Carrasco. (coord.) *Crisis, vulnerabilidad y superación* (pp. 167–180). Madrid: Universidad Pontificia Comillas.

Berástegui, A. (2012). La adaptación familiar y social de los menores adoptados internacionalmente. Seguimiento postadoptivo en la Comunidad de Madrid. *Miscelánea Comillas. Revista de Ciencias Humanas y Sociales, 70*(136), 91–121.

Betancourt, T. S., Newnham, E. A., Layne, C. M., Kim, S., Steinberg, A. M., Ellis, H., & Birman, D. (2012). Trauma history and psychopathology in war-affected refugee children referred for trauma-related mental health services in the United States. *Journal of Traumatic Stress, 25,* 682–690. doi:10.1002/jts.21749

Bowlby, J. (1951). *Maternal care and mental health: A report prepared on behalf of the World Health Organization as a contribution to the United Nations programme for the welfare of homeless children.* Geneva, Switzerland: World Health Organization.

Bowlby, J. (1973). *Attachment and loss: Volume II: Separation, anxiety and anger.* London UK: Hogarth Press.

Bronfenbrenner, U. (1979). *The ecology of human development.* Cambridge, MA: Harvard University Press.

Cerezo, M. A., Trenado, R. M., & Pons-Salvador, G. (2006). Interacción temprana madre-hijo y factores que afectan negativamente a la parentalidad. *Psicothema, 18*(3), 544–550.

Cook, A., Spinazzola, J., Ford, J., Lanktree, C., Blaustein, M., Cloitre, M., … Mallah, K. (2005). Complex trauma in children and adolescents. *Psychiatric Annals, 35*(5), 390–398. doi:10.3928/00485713-20050501-05

Crittenden, P. M. (2016). *Raising parents: Attachment, parenting and child safety.* Abingdon, UK: Routledge.

Cyrulnik, B. (2002). *Los patitos feos: La resiliencia, una infancia infeliz no determina la vida.* Barcelona, Spain: Gedisa.

Diener, M. L., Nievar, M. A., & Wright, C. (2003). Attachment security among mothers and their young children living in poverty: Associations with maternal, child, and contextual characteristics. *Merrill-Palmer Quarterly, 49*(2), 154–182. doi:10.1353/mpq.2003.0007

Evangelou, M., Sylva, K., & Kyriacou, M. (2009). *Early years learning and development: Literature review* (Report No. DCSF-RR176). London, UK: Department for Children, Schools and Families.

Fonagy, P., Steele, M., Steele, H., Moran, G. S., & Higgitt, A. C. (1991). The capacity for understanding mental states: The reflective self in parent and child and its significance for security of attachment. *Infant Mental Health Journal, 12*(3), 201–218. doi:10.1002/1097-0355(199123)12:3<201::AID-IMHJ2280120307>3.0.CO;2-7

Fraiberg, S., Adelson, E., & Shapiro, V. (1975). Ghosts in the nursery: A psychoanalytic approach to the problems of impaired infant-mother relationships. *Journal of the American Academy of Child Psychiatry, 14*(3), 387–421. doi:10.1016/S0002-7138(09)61442-4

García-Sanjuán, N. (2017). *Adopción y acogimiento de niños con discapacidad intelectual: Bienestar familiar y factores asociados* (Doctoral dissertation). Universidad Pontificia Comillas, Madrid, Spain. Retrieved from: https://repositorio.comillas.edu/xmlui/handle/11531/19968

Halty, A. (2017). *La calidad de la responsividad parental: Creación y validación de un instrumento observacional* (Doctoral dissertation). Universidad Pontificia Comillas, Madrid, Spain. Retrieved from https://repositorio.comillas.edu/xmlui/handle/11531/20257

Harkness, S., & Super, C. M. (2005). Themes and variations: Parental ethnotheories in Western cultures. In K. H. Rubin & O.-B. Chung (Eds.), *Parental beliefs, parenting, and child development in cross-cultural perspective.* (pp. 61–79). New York: Psychology Press

Haugaard, J. J., & Hazan, C. (2003). Adoption as a natural experiment. *Development and Psychopathology, 15*(4), 909–926.

Johnstone, L., & Boyle, M. (2018). *The power threat meaning framework: Overview.* London, UK: British Psychological Society.

Jurist, E. L., Slade, A. E., & Bergner, S. E. (2008). *Mind to mind: Infant research, neuroscience, and psychoanalysis.* New York, NY: Other Press.

Kazak, A. E., Kassam-Adams, N., Schneider, S., Zelikovsky, N., Alderfer, M. A., & Rourke, M. (2006). An integrative model of pediatric medical traumatic stress. *Journal of Pediatric Psychology, 31*(4), 343–355. doi:10.1093/jpepsy/jsj054

Koren-Karie, N., Oppenheim, D., & Getzler-Yosef, R. (2008). Shaping children's internal working models through mother-child dialogues: The importance of resolving past maternal trauma. *Attachment and Human Development, 10*(4), 465–483. doi:10.1080/14616730802461482

Lamb, M. E. (2005). Attachments, social networks, and developmental contexts. *Human Development, 48*, 108–112. doi:10.1159/000083222

Levendosky, A. A., Bogat, G. A., & Huth-Bocks, A. C. (2011). The influence of domestic violence on the development of the attachment relationship between mother and young child. *Psychoanalytic Psychology, 28*(4), 512–527. doi:10.1037/a0024561

Lewis, M. (2005). The child and its family: The social network model. *Human Development, 48*, 8–27.

Lieberman, A. F., Padron, E., Van Horn, P., & Harris, W. W. (2005). Angels in the nursery: The intergenerational transmission of benevolent parental influences. *Infant Mental Health Journal, 26*(6), 504–520. doi:10.1002/imhj.20071.

Luyten, P., Nijssens, L., Fonagy, P., & Mayes, L. C. (2017). Parental reflective functioning: Theory, research, and clinical applications. *The Psychoanalytic Study of the Child, 70*(1), 174–199. doi:10.1080/00797308.2016.1277901

Martins, C., & Gaffan, E. A. (2000). Effects of early maternal depression on patterns of infant-mother attachment: A meta-analytic investigation. *Journal of Child Psychology and Psychiatry and Allied Disciplines, 41*(6), 737–746.

McGoron, L., Gleason, M. M., Smyke, A. T., Drury, S. S., Nelson III, C. A., Gregas, M. C., . . . Zeanah, C. H. (2012). Recovering from early deprivation: Attachment mediates effects of caregiving on psychopathology. *Journal of the American Academy of Child & Adolescent Psychiatry, 51*(7), 683–693. doi:10.1016/j.jaac.2012.05.004

McGuinness, T. M., & Dyer, J. G. (2006). International adoption as a natural experiment. *Journal of Pediatric Nursing, 21*(4), 276–288. doi:10.1016/j.pedn.2006.02.001

Miller, J. E., Kim, S., Boldt, L. J., Goffin, K. C., & Kochanska, G. (2019). Long-term sequelae of mothers' and fathers' mind-mindedness in infancy: A developmental path to children's attachment at age 10. *Developmental Psychology, 55*(4), 675–686. doi:10.1037/dev0000660

Nelson, C. A., Fox, N. A., & Zeanah, C. H. (2014). *Romania's abandoned children: Deprivation, brain development, and the struggle for recovery*. Cambridge, MA: Harvard University Press.

Osher, D., Cantor, P., Berg, J., Steyer, L., & Rose, T. (2018). Drivers of human development: How relationships and context shape learning and development. *Applied Developmental Science*, 1–31. doi:10.1080/10888691.2017.1398650

Palacios, J., & Brodzinsky, D. (2010). Adoption research: Trends, topics, outcomes. *International Journal of Behavioral Development, 34*(3), 270–284. doi:10.1177/0165025410362837

Perry, B. D., Pollard, R. A., Blaicley, T. L., Baker, W. L., & Vigilante, D. (1995). Childhood trauma, the neurobiology of adaptation, and "use-dependent" development of the brain: How "states" become "traits." *Infant Mental Health Journal, 16*(4), 271–291.

Perry, B. D., & Szalavitz, M. (2017). *The boy who was raised as a dog: And other stories from a child psychiatrist's notebook*. New York, NY: Basic Books.

Pitillas Salvá, C. (2014). *Funcionamiento parental y estrés postraumático infanto-juvenil. Estudio sobre una muestra de supervivientes de cáncer pediátrico* (Doctoral dissertation). Universidad Pontificia Comillas, Madrid, Spain) Retrieved from:https://dialnet.unirioja.es/servlet/tesis?codigo=72255

Pitillas, C., & Berástegui, A. (2018). *Primera alianza: Fortalecer y reparar los vínculos tempranos*. Barcelona, Spain: Gedisa.

Powell, B., Cooper, G., Hoffman, K., & Marvin, B. (2013). *The circle of security intervention: Enhancing attachment in early parent-child relationships*. New York, NY: Guilford Press.

Pynoos, R. S. (1994). Traumatic stress and developmental psychopathology in children and adolescents. In R. S. Pynoos (Ed.), *Posttraumatic stress disorder: A clinical review* (pp. 65–98). Baltimore, MD: Sidran Press.

Rolland, J. S. (1994). *Families, illness, and disability: An integrative treatment model*. New York, NY: Basic Books.

Rubio, E. M. (2015). *La adaptación de las familias con hijos/as con síndrome de Down: Una aproximación desde el modelo doble ABCX* (Doctoral dissertation). Universidad Pontificia Comillas, Madrid, Spain. Retrieved from https://repositorio.comillas.edu/xmlui/handle/11531/6576

Saxbe, D., Rossin-Slater, M., & Goldenberg, D. (2018). The transition to parenthood as a critical window for adult health. *American Psychologist, 73*(9), 1190–1200. doi:10.1037/amp0000376

Scheeringa, M. S., & Zeanah, C. H. (2001). A relational perspective on PTSD in early childhood. *Journal of Traumatic Stress, 14*(4), 799–815.

Schore, A. N. (2010). Relational trauma and the developing right brain: The neurobiology of broken attachment bonds. In T. Baradon (Ed.), *Relational trauma in infancy: Psychoanalytic, attachment and neuropsychological contributions to parent-infant psychotherapy* (pp. 19–47). New York, NY: Routledge/Taylor & Francis.

Slade, A. (2005). Parental reflective functioning: An introduction. *Attachment & Human Development, 7*(3), 269–281. doi:10.1080/14616730500245906

Smith, K. E., & Pollak, S. D. (2020). Rethinking Concepts and Categories for Understanding the Neurodevelopmental Effects of Childhood Adversity. *Perspectives on Psychological Science*, 1–27.

Spitz, R. A. (1945). Hospitalism: An inquiry into the genesis of psychiatric conditions in early childhood. *The Psychoanalytic Study of the Child, 1*, 53–74.

Stern, D. N. (1995). *The motherhood constellation: A unified view of parent-infant psychotherapy*. London, UK: Karnac Books.

Treyvaud, K., Inder, T. E., Lee, K. J., Northam, E. A., Doyle, L. W., & Anderson, P. J. (2012). Can the home environment promote resilience for children born very preterm in the context of social and medical risk? *Journal of Experimental Child Psychology, 112*(3), 326–337. doi:10.1016/j.jecp.2012.02.009

Triplett, K. N., Tedeschi, R. G., Cann, A., Calhoun, L. G., & Reeve, C. L. (2012). Posttraumatic growth, meaning in life, and life satisfaction in response to trauma. *Psychological Trauma: Theory, Research, Practice, and Policy, 4*(4), 400–410. doi:10.1037/a0024204

Tronick, E. (2018). Emotions and emotional communication in infants. In J. Raphael-Leff (Ed.), *Parent-infant psychodynamics: Wild things, mirrors and ghosts* (pp. 35–53). New York, NY: Routledge.

Ungar, M. (2011). The social ecology of resilience: Addressing contextual and cultural ambiguity of a nascent construct. *American Journal of Orthopsychiatry, 81*(1), 1–17. doi:10.1111/j.1939-0025.2010.01067.x

Villacieros, I. (2017). *Resiliencia familiar: Un acercamiento al fenómeno de las migraciones en la triple frontera Perú-Bolivia-Chile desde la perspectiva de los adolescentes* (Doctoral dissertation).,Universidad Pontificia Comillas, Madrid, Spain. Retrieved from https://repositorio.comillas.edu/jspui/bitstream/11531/18375/1/TD00244.pdf

Volkan, V. D. (2013). *Enemies on the couch: A psychopolitical journey through war and peace.* Durham, NC: Pitchstone.

Volkan, V. D. (2014). *Psychoanalysis, international relations, and diplomacy: A sourcebook on large-group psychology.* New York, NY: Routledge.

Vygotsky, L. S. (1978) *Mind in society: Development of higher psychological processes.* Cambridge, MA: Harvard University Press.

Wachtel, P. L. (2017). Attachment theory and clinical practice: A cyclical psychodynamic vantage point. *Psychoanalytic Inquiry, 37*(5), 332–342. doi:10.1080/07351690.2017.1322431

Wade, M., Moore, C., Astington, J. W., Frampton, K., & Jenkins, J. M. (2015). Cumulative contextual risk, maternal responsivity, and social cognition at 18 months. *Development and Psychopathology, 27*(1), 189–203. doi:10.1017/S0954579414000674

Walsh, F. (2003). Family resilience: A framework for clinical practice. *Family Process, 42*(1), 1–18. doi:10.1111/j.1545-5300.2003.00001.x

Walsh, F. (2015). *Strengthening family resilience* (3rd ed.). New York, NY: Guilford Press.

Werner, E. E. (1992). The children of Kauai: Resiliency and recovery in adolescence and adulthood. *Journal of Adolescent Health, 13*(4), 262–268. doi:10.1016/1054-139X(92)90157-7

Windle, G. (2011). What is resilience? A review and concept analysis. *Reviews in Clinical Gerontology, 21*(2), 152–169. doi:10.1017/S0959259810000420

Winnicott, D. W. (1949). The ordinary devoted mother. In D. W. Winnicott (Ed.), *Babies and their mothers* (pp. 3–14). Reading, MA: Adison-Wesley.

Zeanah, C. H., Smyke, A. T., Koga, S. F., Carlson, E., & Bucharest Early Intervention Project Core Group. (2005). Attachment in institutionalized and community children in Romania. *Child Development, 76*(5), 1015–1028. doi:10.1111/j.1467-8624.2005.00894.x

SECTION 5

Community Well-Being

16
Resilience to Violent Extremism and Terrorism
A Multisystemic Analysis

Michele Grossman

Introduction

This chapter explores the ways in which concepts and discourses of resilience have been taken up and deployed in scholarly and policy work focused on understanding, preventing, and countering violent extremism (P/CVE). It places particular emphasis on the construct of resilience as a multilevel, multisystemic process demonstrating the capacity to adapt successfully to challenges that threaten systems function, viability, or development of systems (Masten, 2016; Ungar, 2018). From the outset, it is worth noting that violent extremism and terrorism[1] are themselves multisystemic phenomena. Terrorist and violent extremist movements, actors, and events are embedded within deeply complex and highly networked co-occurring systems and scales that interact with one another at different levels to support and enable violent extremist narratives, behaviors, actions, and outcomes. They can pose significant challenges and threats to the function and viability of multiple nested and interconnected human (and at times natural) systems.

Studying violent extremism and terrorism thus involves analysis and understanding of how complex multilevel factors (e.g., individual, family, community, national, and transnational) intersect and converge with multiple co-occurring systems (e.g., psychological, educational, social, cultural, local, economic, legal, political, institutional, media, environmental, and global) to create conditions that facilitate and legitimize the use of ideologically based instrumental violence to achieve transformative change in the social and political order.

While Islamist-inspired or -based violent extremist movements have dominated the international policy and political agenda since 9/11 across diverse countries and regions including Europe, North America, Africa, the Asia-Pacific, North Africa, the Middle East, and both South and West Asia, other modes of violent extremism are now emerging that complicate further the landscape in which governments and civil society are attempting to prevent or counter violent extremism. These modes include resurgent transnational right-wing violent extremist movements (Froio & Ganesh, 2018; Hutchinson, 2017; Jones, 2018) that capitalize on the extent to which democracies around the world are increasingly experiencing social and political polarization, "a process whereby the normal multiplicity of differences in a society increasingly align along a single dimension and people increasingly perceive and describe politics and society in terms of 'Us' versus 'Them'" (McCoy, Rahman, & Somer, 2018, p. 16). Although such polarization attempts to reject or flatten the nature and impacts of globalized, heterogeneous social and political systems and increased human and cultural diversity and mobility, from a terrorism analysis perspective, the emergence of multiple, co-occurring vectors and flashpoints of violent extremist ideation and action merely emphasizes the way in which terrorist threats, as well as solutions to these, are now more multisystemic and multiscalar than ever.

Consequently, efforts to prevent or counter violent extremism—which generally adopts "soft power" (Keohane & Nye, 1998, p. 86) models of community and regionally based policy and programming to prevent or address conditions that may enable the take-up or spread of violent extremism (Rosand, Winterbotham, Jones, & Praxl-Tabuchi, 2018)—have increasingly had to develop complex systems-based approaches in tackling radicalization to violence. Violent radicalization feeds on a matrix of social, political and economic influences, networks, resources, and challenges (in different contexts and combinations, and with varying emphases) that are leveraged by violent extremist movements in their recruitment and propaganda strategies.

This has generated increasing recognition in successive iterations of both counterterrorism (CT) and P/CVE[2] theory and policy that co-occurring, multilevel systems across governments, communities, law enforcement, civil society, and the private sector must work collaboratively to develop whole-of-society (Global Counterterrorism Forum, 2012; International Committee of the Red Cross, 2017; Organization for Security and Co-operation in Europe, 2018; Rosand et al., 2018) or whole-of-community (Los Angeles Interagency Coordination Group, 2015; Snair, Nicholson, & Giammaria, 2017) approaches to preventing and countering violent extremism at both individual and community levels. The whole-of-society approach moves well beyond the whole-of-government models that were a mainstay of earlier efforts to develop joined-up countering violent extremism (CVE) frameworks (Executive Office of the President of the United States, 2011) and explicitly distances itself from the more securitized focus of law enforcement and intelligence agencies on detecting, disrupting, and pursuing terrorist actors and plots (Grossman, 2015; Hardy, 2015).

Not all terrorism researchers and analysts support the whole-of-society approach to preventing or countermanding violent extremism. Berger (2016, p. 8), for example, argues against what he terms the "unreasonably wide scope of activity characterized as CVE," suggesting that its lack of definitional clarity and miscellaneous character has weakened the ability of societies to take P/CVE seriously. Instead, he suggests, the field needs to see violent extremism as a narrow problem and, accordingly, limit its efforts to "a narrow process of disrupting extremist recruitment and radicalisation efforts" rather than attempting to engage in broad-scale "'social engineering' that can produce unintended consequences" (p. 34).

How Research and Policy Defines Resilience to Violent Extremism

Berger's argument remains, however, a minority perspective in the current research and policy environment, especially when it comes to the concept of resilience to (or sometimes, against) violent extremism. Identifying and building resilience to violent extremism has for some time been a key concept and key term in both CT and P/CVE research, discourse, and policy (Dalgaard-Nielsen & Schack, 2016; Grossman, Peucker, Smith, & Dellal, 2016; Longstaff, Armstrong, Perrin, Parker, & Hidek, 2010; Spalek & Davies, 2012; Ungar, Hadfield, Amarasingam, Morgan, & Grossman, 2017; Weine, Henderson, Shanfield, Legha, & Post, 2013). The international policy focus on resilience as a core feature of CT and P/CVE strategies has developed significantly in particular over the last decade, so much so that resilience is now considered a "key ingredient to effectively manage terrorism" (Dechesne, 2017, p. 414).

Resilience in CT contexts tends to think about resilience in line with models of disaster and crisis recovery. It prioritizes infrastructure defense, target-hardening, and urban design (Coaffee, Moore, Fletcher, & Bosher, 2008; Sampaio, 2017), along with victim, general population, and systems recovery following a terrorist attack. It is also concerned with the resilience of emergency and first-response workers and organizations that are on the front lines in the immediate aftermath of a critical or catastrophic event (Ranstorp, 2018). However, the centrality of resilience as a P/CVE "keyword" in the sense used by the eminent cultural studies critic Raymond Williams (Bracke, 2016; Williams, 1976) is more pervasive, demonstrated in part by the number of national and international P/CVE policy frameworks that have explicitly referenced *resilience* as a constitutive element of their approach over the last several years. These include Public Safety Canada's (2013) *Building Resilience Against Terrorism: Canada's Counter-Terrorism Strategy*; the Council of Australian Governments'(2015) *Australia's Counter-Terrorism Strategy: Strengthening our Resilience*; the U.S. Strategic Implementation Plan, *Empowering Local Partners to Prevent Violent Extremism in the United States* (Executive Office of the President of the United States, 2011); and the UK's focus on resilience as a foundational organizing concept (Hardy, 2015) in both the Prepare and Prevent streams of its broader antiterrorism CONTEST strategy (HM Government, 2018).

Beyond these nation-specific frameworks, multilateral international bodies and institutions such as the European Commission's (n.d.) Radicalisation Awareness Network, the Global Community Engagement and Resilience Fund (2017), and the Global Counter-Terrorism Forum (2012) have all adopted explicitly resilience-based or focused frameworks and strategies in seeking to prevent and counteract terrorist ideology and action in various global regions and settings.

All of these strategies identify building both individual and community resilience as a critical conceptual and practical element in P/CVE. They also reflect an earlier reorientation of the CT and P/CVE field toward what Coaffee (2006) called "a new lexicon to make sense of the counterterrorist challenge" (p. 389) in which counter-terrorism specialists "adopt[ed] a new vocabulary—centred on *resilience*—which is at once proactive and reactive, with an inbuilt adaptability to the fluid nature of the new security threats challenging states and their urban areas in 'the age of terrorism'" (p. 397).

In practical terms, this pivot has at times meant that the idea of resilience to violent extremism has been reduced to equivalence with P/CVE initiatives in ways that have sometimes harmed efforts to engage communities and desecuritize the language associated with counter-terrorism thinking and practice (Hardy, 2015). To the extent that efforts to rebadge CVE as *resilience* signaled a strategic interest by governments and law enforcement authorities in making P/CVE strategies more palatable and less threatening to communities (and Muslim communities in particular) who felt chronically stigmatized and besieged by conventional CT discourse, the concept of resilience as a desirable social good suffered because it came to be seen as mere camouflage for more sinister, securitized agendas in relation to the monitoring and surveillance of targeted communities. As a consequence, government-led community resilience strategies aimed at countering terrorism have in some contexts come to be perceived as a Trojan horse or proxy for other agendas related to government concerns with security and control, rather than serving to build genuine community resilience to harms and threats in their own right (Coaffee & Fussey, 2015; Council on American-Islamic Relations Minnesota, 2016; Hardy, 2015).

This is of a piece with what some analysts have seen as a more insidious "emergence and proliferation of security-driven resilience logics," which captures a series of intersecting processes and discourses in which "resilience policy becomes increasingly driven by security concerns and, at the same time, security policy adopts the language of resilience" (Coaffee & Fussey, 2015, p. 98). This leads to resilience to violent extremism becoming equated by targeted communities with coercive, opaque, and profiling government measures designed to "hitchhike" onto a broader community safety agenda (Coaffee & Fussey, 2015, p. 98). Others have reached similar conclusions in exploring the resilience dimensions of the Prevent and Prepare strands of the UK's CONTEST strategy, for example, suggesting that resilience remains a "contested and divisive concept . . . in counterterrorism" (Hardy, 2015, p. 84) and that "understandings of resilience cannot be readily separated out from these contexts" given their mobilization within the broader apparatus of the security state (Walklate, Mythen, & McGarry, 2012, p. 185).

However, such security-driven logics and the political exigencies that inform them are not the sole reason for the prominence of resilience concepts within P/CVE discourse. There has also been genuine interest on the part of governments, policymakers, researchers, practitioners, and communities to think creatively about what genuine and effective extremist violence prevention efforts might look like, and whether and how constructs of both individual and community resilience can contribute to this. Some of the thinking about what "resilience to violent extremism" might mean in theory and in practice has been explored through the lens of public health models (Bhui, Hicks, Lashley, & Jones, 2012; Challgren et al., 2016; Ellis & Abdi, 2017; Harris-Hogan, Barrelle, & Zammit, 2015; Weine, Eisenman, Kinsler, Glik, & Polutnik, 2017), while others have turned to theories of resilience and disaster or crisis recovery to start thinking about what paradigms of resilience could mean to communities experiencing the profound stressors of either the aftermath of a terrorist attack or a heightened securitized environment for daily life in the context of intensified terrorist risks and threats (Ranstorp, 2018).

Perhaps because of this multisited genealogy, the deployment of resilience as a concept in the context of P/CVE policy and programming remains polysemous (Bracke, 2016). A pervasive understanding of violent extremism as comprising multilevel and systemic risks, vulnerabilities, and threats, and the need to prepare for and defend against risks and threats by remediating vulnerabilities and strengthening protections, has found a highly resonant correlate in the general emphasis in cross-disciplinary resilience theory on risk and protective factor relationships—what Norris, Stevens, Pfefferbaum, Wyche, and Pfefferbaum (2008) call "resilience as a metaphor" (p. 127).

In some instances, this perceived correlation has resulted in *resilience* becoming a taken-for-granted term with no effort to define or operationalize it other than as a weak byword for P/CVE-think. In others, there has been a conflation of meanings in advancing competing definitions of resilience (e.g., resilience as a simple case of "bouncing back" to a recovered state of equilibrium vs. resilience as a complex process of adaptation and transformation in the context of adversity)—sometimes within the same argument—which has hampered an understanding of the efficacy of resilience theories for P/CVE modeling and practice. However, in more nuanced applications of various resilience constructs to P/CVE, scholars have drawn on existing definitions of resilience from across the interdisciplinary literature and worked critically with these in developing field-specific definitions and meanings.

Resilience to Violent Extremism: Prevention, Resistance, and Recovery

Resilience in CT and P/CVE contexts can mean resilience as resistance, resilience as prevention, resilience as adaptation, or resilience as recovery. All of these dimensions are present in various research articles, policies, programs, and strategies, sometimes in conjunction with one another in either complementary or contradictory ways. As Hardy (2015) notes, two prevailing yet competing paradigms for resilience to violent extremism that feature in different pillars of the UK's CONTEST strategy are resilience as community *recovery from a crisis or disaster* (albeit focused on "reinstating normality" after an attack rather than "transforming in response to crisis"; Hardy, 2015, p. 90), and resilience linked to *community resistance to terrorist ideology*.

The most common construct of resilience for many P/CVE scholars, analysts, and program developers is, however, a concept of resilience allied to *prevention of* and *resistance to* violent extremism. In its simplest form, resilience-as-resistance can mean both "withstand[ing] violent extremist ideologies" and also "challeng[ing] those who espouse them" (Public Safety Canada, 2013, p. 11). Doosje et al. (2016) observe that resilience to violent extremism can mean something similar up until the point that someone becomes radicalized to violence; thereafter, resilience retains its core meaning of "resistance" but the force being resisted shifts, so that the radicalized individual, embedded within ideological frameworks and social networks that reinforce and nurture her or his world view now becomes resilient or resistant to being challenged about or disengaged from violent extremism.

For the most part, definitions of violent extremism focused on resilience as prevention or resistance tend to be very strongly grounded in the social-ecological resilience model (Bronfenbrenner, 1988; Hunter, 2012; Liebenberg, Ungar, & Van de Vijver, 2012; Masten, 2014; Stokols, 1992, 1996; Stokols, Lejano, & Hipp, 2013; Ungar, 2008, 2011, 2015, 2018; Yates & Masten, 2004), which understands resilience as the ability to thrive in contexts of adversity or challenge through positive, prosocial adaptation; the presence and mobilization of protective factors that can offset risks and vulnerabilities; and the ability to access and navigate resources in culturally meaningful ways—all of which rely on complex interrelationships, dynamics, and trade-offs between different levels and systems of humans and their social and natural environments The work of Norris et al. (2008) on resilience in the context of disaster recovery as a "process linking a set of networked adaptive capacities to a positive trajectory of functioning and adaptation" (p. 1321) following a crisis has also been influential.

Individual Resilience to Violent Extremism

Within the prevention/resistance framework of resilience to violent extremism, there has been a focus on both individual and community level features. In terms of individual resilience, P/CVE scholars have concentrated on identifying individual-level social-psychological resilience traits and processes that may serve as protective factors in relation to violent extremism. These include, for example, empathy (Aly, Taylor, & Karnovsky, 2014; BOUNCE, 2018; Lösel, King, Bender, & Jugl, 2018; Stephens, Sieckelinck, & Boutellier, 2019; Taylor, Taylor, Karnovsky, Aly, & Taylor, 2017; Van Brunt, Murphy, & Zedginidze, 2017), self-regulation/self-control and value complexity (Lösel et al., 2018; Sieckelinck & Gielen, 2017), self-esteem and assertiveness (BOUNCE, 2018), intercultural tolerance of diversity (Ellis & Abdi, 2017), and the ability to "overcome a terrorist attack or reject extremist messages" (Ranstorp, 2018, p. 9). While many of these resilience features apply to all forms of violent extremism across an ideological continuum, some research identifies two further individual resilience characteristics related specifically to right-wing extremists: levels of perceived personal discrimination and subjective deprivation, that is, a negative evaluation of one's own socioeconomic status relative to others (Lösel et al., 2018). The European Commission–funded BOUNCE program, which from 2013 to 2015 delivered training and tools to youth, family members, community educators, and youth workers, focuses primarily on individual youth resilience to violent extremism using what they term a "synthesized definition of resilience, including seven elements: (1) self-knowledge, (2) social skills, (3) knowing and understanding others, (4) self-confidence, (5) an open view, (6) making choices and following them, (7) handling diverging situations," as well as aiming to "increase critical thinking, tolerance and empathy" (BOUNCE, 2018, p. 41).

Some definitions of individual resilience to violent extremism, however, share an understanding of the individual-in-context that is more socially-ecologically oriented, seeing individual capacities for development, coping strategies and adaptation taking place within dynamically interactive settings and systems including families, schools, places of employment, communities, and the broader society (Bronfenbrenner & Morris, 2006). For example, Sieckelinck and Gielen (2017) identify 10 features of individual-level resilience protections against violent extremism, almost all of which involve interactions with and interdependencies on multilevel and multisystemic social, political, and institutional processes. These 10 resilience protections include social coping skills through anger management and conflict resolution; democratic citizenship; religious knowledge; counternarratives; internet safeguarding measures; (social and civic) participation; trauma therapy; supportive and warm family environment; autonomy, self-esteem, and sense of self-control (agency); and social and emotional well-being and life skills.

Similarly, Taylor et al. (2017), analyzing an education-based model for building resilience to violent extremism that draws on moral disengagement and moral agency theory, see the program under review as potentially "transformational because it approaches building resilience to violent extremism both externally—through the curriculum materials and community engagement—and internally—through engagement in moral learning" (p. 199). Related to the focus on education, a strong emphasis also emerges on the importance of critical thinking (sometimes referred to as *critical literacy*) as a key feature of individual resilience to violent extremism (BOUNCE, 2018; GCERF, 2017; Ghosh, Chan, Manuel, & Dilimulati, 2017; Royal United Services Institute, 2015; Stephens et al., 2019; Taylor et al., 2017), gesturing toward the multisystemic relationship between resilience, cognition, and education, on the one hand, but also toward the increasingly complex and highly mediated information and discursive environments in which social, political, and cultural messaging and influences are now navigated and negotiated.

Community Resilience to Violent Extremism

Such theorizations and definitions of individual resilience to violent extremism do not, however, reflect the dominant trend within the P/CVE field to the same extent as constructs of community resilience. In many ways, this reflects four continuing emphases in how P/CVE analysts think about resilience:

1. The extent to which terrorist and violent extremist trajectories themselves have been conceptualized as group-level rather than individual-level processes, involving an understanding of individuals who radicalize to violence as embedded within group-level socio-ideological processes and networks of various kinds and to various degrees.
2. Following from this, the extent to which social-ecological paradigms of resilience, which stress the complex interdependency between individuals and their collective social systems, have resonated most strongly in P/CVE thinking and programming to date.
3. The responsiveness of CT and P/CVE scholars to the needs of policymakers and security agencies, which have been interested in what building collective resilience to social harms such as violent extremism might look like in terms of programming, planning, and resourcing by governments.

4. The problematic tendency to attribute terrorist and violent extremist ideologies and behaviors to *communal identity* structures (e.g. Muslims, Whites, men) rather than to *communal ideological or belief* structures (e.g. right-wing, Islamist, ecological, misogynist).

The emphasis on community-level resilience to violent extremism and terrorism is thus driven by a convergence of conceptual, pragmatic, and problematic assumptions that both help and hinder understanding of how multilevel and multisystemic resilience processes in relation to violent extremism may play out in practice. Explorations of community resilience to violent extremism may define *community* as either or both "a physical or geographical area" but also as the "relational aspects of community—the ways in which one's perception of similarity to others or belongingness can provide a psychological sense of community" (Ellis & Abdi, 2017, p. 291; Anderson, 1983). The meanings of community in the context of violent extremism-related resilience discourse thus accommodate strategies and paradigms for community resilience that can be applied both spatially—for example, in geographical areas like Minneapolis-St. Paul (Weine & Ahmed, 2012) or New South Wales, Australia (Multicultural New South Wales, n.d.)—and/or ethnoculturally, for example, among both diaspora and national-majoritarian Muslim communities from diverse ethnic backgrounds in a wide range of countries; Somali diaspora communities in Canada, the United States, Kenya, and Australia (Grossman, Tahiri, & Stephenson, 2014; GCERF, 2017; Weine & Ahmed, 2012), or low socioeconomic status White communities in the United Kingdom (Warrell, 2019).

However, there are both conceptual and practical risks in treating either spatially or relationally constructed communities as homogenous entities, whether in P/CVE or other contexts. As Weine et al. (2013) observe, different communities "often have leadership rivalries and contested meanings, as well as different political, religious and ethnic subgroups" and this means recognizing and engaging with a plurality of local community contexts and partnerships (p. 330).

The Importance of Social Capital to P/CVE Resilience Models

Nevertheless, scholars and practitioners continue to grapple with the concept of community resilience to generate useful policy tools and guidance for understanding and assessing community resilience in various contexts (Grossman et al., 2016; Hardy, 2015; Longstaff et al., 2010; Walklate et al., 2012). Policy guidance in the P/CVE field has most frequently centered on an understanding of community resilience to violent extremism that stresses the relationship between resilience and social capital (Dalgaard-Nielsen & Schack, 2016; Ellis & Abdi, 2017; Grossman et al., 2014, 2017).

For instance, resilience to "militant Islamist" violent extremism has been conceptualized in Denmark as the capacity to "leverage social capital," which has been defined as "stable trust-based relationships and networks among actors (civil society, local government, local businesses)" in addition to resilience at the levels of families, peer and social networks (Dalgaard-Nielsen & Schack, 2016, p. 312). Ellis and Abdi (2017), as do Grossman et al.

(2014), draw on the interrelationship between bonding, bridging, and linking social capital in fostering prosocial engagement and partnerships between both intercultural "others" and also between communities and the systems of regulatory and institutional power and governance in which they are embedded. Weine et al. (2013) propose that the social capital dimension of community resilience to violent extremism involves shared problem-solving, safe community spaces for youth, and investment in community-building activities such as "after school programs, mentoring programs, community policing [and] opportunities for civic dialogue" (p. 331), while Lösel et al. (2018) see basic attachment to or integration into society, informal social control and social bonding as constituent protective factors linked to social capital influencing resilience to violent extremism, along with a variant of linking capital conceived of as "an accepting attitude toward law, society and police legitimacy" (Lösel et al., 2018, p. 98).

Paradigms of community resilience to violent extremism also draw implicitly or explicitly on the social capital dimensions of resilience related to disaster recovery, in particular through the work of Norris and colleagues (2008). Norris et al.'s report on resilience and disaster readiness, which builds its analysis through the critical review of a wide range of theoretical and applied resilience literature (p. 128), emphasizes the importance of social connectedness for resilient communities and proposes three dimensions of community resilience-oriented social capital: sense of trust and community belonging, sense of attachment to place, and civic participation. This framework has informed analyses of resilience that straddle preparedness for crises, resistance to resilience-eroding phenomena, adaptation in the face of adversity, and recovery from disturbances to systemic functioning.

This nexus between social capital and resilience nexus is responsive to an understanding of violent extremism itself as a complex, dynamic, multisited ideological, and behavioral matrix in which multilevel and multisystemic influences, networks, capacities, resources, and vulnerabilities converge to enable a distinctive form of violent social and political threat or attack. If the drivers and attractors of violent extremism are bound up with social conditions, protections, dynamics, and adversities, in whatever proportion, then so too must be the solutions that seek to prevent, divert, or rechannel these factors (Day & Kleinmann, 2017). Community resilience paradigms thus offer a socially attractive, policy-, and investment-friendly way forward in relation to conceptualizing what an integrated multisystemic social and political response might look like, one that draws individuals, communities, governments, and sometimes the private sector together in new collaborative relationships and partnerships.

The social capital–resilience nexus has influenced P/CVE thinking about resilience not only in relation to taking a less securitized, more prosocial approach to anti-violent radicalization agendas. It also has more pragmatic utility as a political project in two ways. First, it helps provide a clear and relatively accessible roadmap for government agencies tasked with developing extremist violence prevention responses who may be familiar with resilience theory and practice from other policy areas such as disaster preparedness and recovery or public health. This offers prospects for synthesizing and streamlining whole-of-government and whole-of-community approaches to policymaking and resource allocation—an especially desirable benefit in times of limited social funding or investment by governments.

Second, it diverges, at least in theory, from more securitized approaches nourished by "risk society" assumptions that target entire communities as suspect, vulnerable, or deficient (Kundnani, 2012; Spalek, 2010; Vermeulen, 2014), moving toward more holistic assessments of sociocultural resilience capital (Grossman et al., 2014) that communities can bring to the challenge of preventing, resisting, or recovering from the influence or impact of violent extremist ideologies and behaviors.

Nevertheless, the models of community resilience taken up by P/CVE scholars and practitioners in different countries reflect uneven awareness that while community resilience can be built or strengthened, it may also be weakened or undermined if risk factors accumulate in the absence of offsetting protective factors or trade-offs (Evans et al., 2013; Obradovic, Shaffer, & Masten, 2012; Wright & Masten, 2015). As Grossman et al. (2016) observe, "this highlights the need for a cumulative and contextual approach to assessing resilience risks at community level" in which a distinction is drawn between "communities that experience acute adversity against the backdrop of persistent resilience threats (such as chronic social conflict, discrimination or lack of resources)" (p. 48) and those that experience acute resilience challenges in an otherwise well-resourced and well-functioning setting (Dalgaard-Nielsen & Schack, 2016).

Is There a Difference Between Community Resilience and Resilience to Violent Extremism?

Such analyses continue to highlight the question of whether we can distinguish readily between more generalized theories or models of community resilience on the one hand and specific theories or models of community resilience to violent extremism on the other. Do the general protective features of social-ecological resilience, for example, guarantee strengthened resilience to violent extremism in particular? Are healthy, functioning communities that are sufficiently resourced, open, dynamic, trusting, and stable the best prophylactic against the appeals of violent ideology and action? Or does the focus on resilience genuinely indicate "a change in paradigms" in the study of terrorism and violent extremism (Weine et al., 2013, p. 28) in which particularized meanings and outcomes for resilience to violent extremism have emerged?

There is no field-based consensus on this issue, but the question has been addressed explicitly within recent terrorism prevention scholarship. Responses include an explicit emphasis in defining resilience to violent extremism as a process of "detect[ing] radicalization risks, prevent[ing] the recruitment of community members into violent extremism, and bounc[ing] back after instances of recruitment via learning and adaptability that permits the community to better limit future recruitment" (Dalgaard-Nielsen & Schack, 2016, p. 312), a definition echoed by Weine et al. (2013). Alternatively, Ellis and Abdi (2017) suggest that resilience specifically to violent extremism leverages social capital capacities to help resolve identity tensions, remediate disadvantage, and build trust to offset vulnerabilities amongst marginalized or fragile individuals and communities. Along similar lines, two studies that explored resilience to violent extremism in Canada (Ungar et al., 2017) and Australia

(Grossman et al., 2014) using a strengths-based, social-ecological approach were used as a springboard to develop a standardized and validated five-factor, 14-item measure of youth resilience to violent extremism. These five factors are cultural identity and connectedness, bridging capital, linking capital, violence-related behaviors, and violence-related beliefs (Grossman et al., 2017, 2020).

Important insights for resilience to violent extremism have also come from the work of Luthar, Cicchetti, and Becker (2000), who move beyond the familiar binary structure of resilience as comprising risk versus protective factors to distinguish between resilience risks, vulnerabilities, and protections. They define risks as adverse circumstances or environments that affect entire groups or communities, vulnerabilities as specific challenges or difficulties that can enhance risks, and protection as factors that can mitigate either or both vulnerabilities and risks. Applied to the P/CVE field, this tripartite structure helps organize an understanding of community resilience to violent extremism that locates broad community-strengthening measures designed to address systemic or group-level challenges under "risks" (building prevention capacity), targeted interventions to address specific identified community-level challenges or adversities under vulnerabilities (building resistance capacity), and harnessing or strengthening existing community assets and resources that redress or mediate risks and vulnerabilities under protection (identifying, creating, or extending resilience capital). As the foregoing discussion makes clear, the risk–vulnerability–protection framework is evident at a number of levels in how P/CVE research, policy and practice has defined and mobilized definitions of resilience. These definitions and mobilizations are, for the most part, social-ecologically attuned and cognizant of both multisystemic and multiscalar complexity. For example, Grossman, Carland, Tahiri, and Zammit (2018) found that in working with young women to build their resilience to online violent extremist social influence, identifying, and building their resilience capacities would involve addressing *risks* related to gender-based lack of self-esteem, social connection, and public voice; *vulnerabilities* related to social influence by others and seeking freedoms online from real-world gendered constraints; and *protections* such as strong relationships with mothers, strong intercultural relationships with peers, and critical literacy in relation to online narratives and propaganda.

Resilience to Violent Extremism: Conceptual Gaps

However, a critical gap in how P/CVE research conceptualizes and applies resilience to violent extremism is its tendency to advance resilience analyses and models that largely stop at the door of individuals and communities, without contemplating the presence or nature of resilience risks, vulnerabilities, and protections at the level of policy and governance. As we have seen, scholarship on resilience to violent extremism and terrorism has tended to focus intensively on mesolevel community level resilience and to a lesser extent on microlevel psychosocial resilience, but hardly at all on the macrolevel resilience of national or international systems (Dechesne, 2017).

This means that risk and vulnerability, especially in First World settings, are often conceptualized and applied only in relation to communities or subsections of communities, with no reference to the risks or vulnerabilities that may be features of government or institutional systems such as those relating to law and justice, education, health, employment, or the media. While the negative impacts of broader systemic social phenomena such as biased global media reporting about Muslims, hostile political and policy environments for immigration and refugees, underfunded and unevenly distributed education and employment opportunities, or the ghettoization of minorities in socially and economically disadvantaged enclaves are often widely discussed as elements that can influence the taking up of violent extremist attitudes and support, there has been no systematic effort to address how these phenomena register within a social-ecological resilience framework as risks or vulnerabilities when it comes to counter-terrorism policy responses.

In effect, this means that the conceptualization of resilience to violent extremism is only partially multisystemic. It accounts for some but not all the co-occurring systems that make up the P/CVE resilience matrix, overprivileging community resilience at the expense of considering other systems that are crucial to the prevention (or alternatively the taking up) of violent extremism but remain exempted from resilience analyses. While these other systems have in some cases been exhaustively studied (e.g., the role and impacts of CT policing models on P/CVE), they have not been studied through a systems-based resilience lens.

How Multisystemic Is Resilience to Violent Extremism?

Terrorism and violent extremism are exemplars of communal stressors with multilevel and multisystem impacts—psychological, social, economic, cultural, and environmental, among others—that can create enormous strain, disturbance, and adversity for individuals, communities, and societies that are exposed to or affected by such movements or events. Stressors at this level can be simultaneously chronic and acute. For example, a terrorist attack and its attendant death, chaos, fear, resource strain, and uncertainty would clearly register as an acute stressor. But living in a more routinely securitized environment—for example, where rubbish bins have been removed from public thoroughfares because of fears they might hide improvised explosive devices, in which random stop-and-search exercises by police routinely occur in local neighborhoods and at airports, where civil liberties have been curtailed, or where both public and private surveillance mechanisms and intrusions have increased—can create an environment characterized by chronic stressors, shifting daily life into a paradoxically less secure, confident, and stable state. Living with the threat and reality of terrorism, in other words, can create both chronic and acute forms of adversity.

It is an axiom of resilience studies across disciplines that resilience becomes activated in contexts of adversity (Ungar, 2018). When thinking about this in the context of violent extremism, it is critical to consider not only the interaction between multiple systems but also the presence and impacts of multiple intersecting adversities. "Adversity" as a singular construct is insufficient to describe the dynamic interplay *between* adversities within different systems and at different levels that can help sustain or erode resilience to violent extremism. Terrorism and violent extremism represent challenges that are scaled all the way from the erosion of individual mental health, social belonging, and the fraying of family and community security and cohesion to trauma experiences (for victims, first responders, and often the families of violent extremists); overtly securitized social policies, information and communication uncertainty or breakdown, collisions between law enforcement responses and human rights, political instability, and systems compromises or failures in health, education, the economy and emergency services, transport, communications, energy, border management, trust, democratic procedures, and the rule of law.

However, these adversities—prospective or actualized—can intersect with a range of co-occurring sociopolitical adversities such as political or economic oppression and disadvantage, social marginalization, and ethnic, racial, cultural, or religious discrimination and victimization that much prevention work in building resilience to violent extremism aims to address. These sociopolitical adversities can prime the pump for the emergence and uptake of violent extremist narratives that offer seemingly definitive solutions to social and political grievances. They are in some sense "enabling" multisystemic adversities that are seen as influential (although not directly causative) in fostering increased vulnerability to violent extremist propaganda and recruitment efforts.

As a result, many government-led resilience strategies accordingly focus simultaneously on three or four multisystemic elements in their approach to tackling terrorism and violent extremism. One example would be the UK's CONTEST strategy, with its four pillars of "Pursue" (investigate and disrupt violent extremist criminal behavior through policing, intelligence, and the courts), "Prevent" (social and government programming and referral through schools, clinics, and local council authorities, sometimes in partnership with civil society), "Protect" (safeguarding human, built environment and infrastructure systems), and "Prepare" (mitigation strategies for recovery after a terrorist attack). Another would be Australia's tripartite Living Safe Together strategy, which advocates prevention, diversion, and disengagement through a combination of preventive resilience-building activities focused on social cohesion (community, social, and political systems); diversion through targeted intervention programs managed by government agencies, including police (law enforcement and social service and welfare systems) (Cherney et al., 2018) and the disengagement from and reintegration of convicted violent extremists when possible (legal, social welfare, and informal community systems).

Yet it is also the case that sometimes programs or policies designed to build resilience to violent extremism can constitute new adversities that undercut the very resilience such strategies are trying to promote. For example, a number of governments have pushed out national or area-based antiterrorist hotlines, sometimes supplemented by web-based reporting systems (e.g., the National Security Hotline in Australia, Anti-Terrorism Hotlines in the United Kingdom and Pakistan, the Canadian Security and Intelligence Service telephone and website reporting mechanisms, and the Public Security Tips Hotline in New York City). These are designed to provide confidential, easy-to-access routes for the reporting of information or suspicions concerning violent extremism that will make it easier for law enforcement and security agencies to investigate, disrupt, or prevent terrorist activity.

However, reporting on terrorism is itself a complex, multisystemic process. As work by Grossman (2015, 2018) and Thomas, Grossman, Miah, and Christmann (2017, 2020) has shown, if the hotline is perceived to be little more than a cipher for security and intelligence gathering, those who may be in the best position to come forward, such as family and close friends, will be reluctant to do so because they fear criticism or shunning by others within their communities; are uncertain or fearful of the consequences of reporting because they do not know what will happen (to them or to the person they are concerned about) after sharing information; and are unlikely to be referred to support structures following what is by any measure a very difficult and confronting disclosure process. Moreover, even when reports are initiated, if the triaging systems that receive such information from communities are unclear about where that information should go or how it should be handled, then the systems cluster involved in the reporting process displays what Grossman (2015, 2018) calls the "leaky pipeline" of P/CVE reporting, in which both people and information drop out of co-occurring systems at various points because of inappropriate or unclear procedures and messaging related to the violent extremism reporting process.

Sustaining resilience in times of adversity also relies on systems' capacity for persistence, resistance, recovery, adaptation, and transformation (Ungar, 2018). Of these, *persistence* can be a double-edged sword when it comes to resilience to violent extremism. In terrorism contexts, persistence may mean maintaining sociopolitical cohesion, functioning systems of civil and human rights, and equitable access to social and economic resources so that social and political systems do not require change, even when faced with the risk of alienated individuals or groups who may advocate or conduct ideologically based violent attacks or when social cohesion fragments because social tensions mount. To a large extent, such persistence is a core feature of government strategies designed to prevent the risk or threat of violent extremism from overwhelming co-occurring government and civil society systems.

However, persistence can have a deleterious impact on resilience to violent extremism when there are legitimate social demands for change—for example, when agitating for violations of human rights or procedural fairness—that are ignored or dismissed by the state. An intriguing example arises in this regard. A number of European countries, including France, Denmark, Austria, Germany, the United Kingdom, the Netherlands and Belgium, have between 2003 and 2018 enacted various bans on Muslim women's culturally prescribed attire, including bans on full or partial facial and body covering such as the niqab, the burqa, and the burkini (a "modesty swimsuit" enabling Muslim women to swim at the beach in public). The burkini ban in France, beginning in 2014 and upheld by many local provincial governments from 2016 onward, is a case in point from a multisystemic resilience perspective.

Originally designed and marketed in Australia (Gerrand, 2016), the burkini (a portmanteau of "burqa" and "bikini") was designed to allow Muslim women who adhered to traditional cultural dress codes to access the public spaces of beaches—which serve as both material and symbolic signifiers in Australian culture—in ways that did not violate these codes. The burkini provided opportunities for Muslim women to feel like they belonged to broader Australian society without creating cultural conflict over issues of dress and modesty; facilitated civic participation and interaction with cultural others through the culturally democratic spaces of beach-going leisure in Australian communities, where many civic as well as recreational activities occur; and provided opportunities for Muslim women to educate others about their cultural and religious beliefs and practices through informal dialogue about the burkini with non-Muslims.

All of these features—civic participation, sense of belonging, and intercultural dialogue—are benchmarks in the literature for building and sustaining resilience to violent extremism—and in general—in culturally pluralist settings. The creation of the burkini still arguably contributes to these outcomes in Australia because it is not banned. In France, however, the banning of the burkini and other elements of Muslim women's visible choices of attire based on the persistence of French *laïcité* (and despite the surmised rise[3] in numbers of practicing Muslim French citizens over recent decades) has not only eroded these opportunities, but created significant angst and alienation among Muslim women who feel they are being discriminated against not as potential security risks (it would be very difficult to hide a weapon or a bomb while wearing a burkini, for instance), but simply as Muslims. In this case, a sociopolitical system (state-based secularism) has undermined the resilience of cultural and social co-occurring systems (leisure in shared public spaces, intercultural contact, religio-cultural diversity) that might otherwise have thrived in this context. In so doing, it creates low-hanging fruit that can be easily plucked by terrorist narratives seeking to escalate a range of sociocultural grievances.

In a related vein, responses to coping with the risks and threats of violent extremism and terrorism have to some extent revealed the limits in how well various social and political systems are able to tolerate heterogeneity, a key feature of multisystemic resilience. Social and cultural heterogeneity is a basic feature of all P/CVE systems, which frequently bring together different sectors (government, community), cultures (religious, secular, ethnic), and social strata (e.g. youth, community leaders, authorities). However, such heterogeneity within P/CVE contexts can be adversely affected by lack of tolerance for heterogeneity at the level of broader social and cultural systems that then adversely impact P/CVE relationships. For example, the current fragility of community cohesion signaled by the rise of and enhanced tolerance for illiberal and far-right political responses to immigration and refugee mobility in pluralist democracies across Europe and North America shows that "sunny days" multiculturalism can fray under conditions of political stress or uncertainty. This then weakens community trust in institutions and authorities who are seen as aligned with political statements that are hostile to the presence of sociocultural diversity.

However, P/CVE can also demonstrate key resilience features such as optimal openness to new information, capacity to integrate environmental shocks and the initiation of new behavioral regimes (Ungar, 2018). P/CVE is inherently built on the basis of complex, reciprocal relationships between different social and institutional domains that seek to strengthen resilience across systems through new (or enhanced) behavioral regimes. Such regimes might include partnerships or programs for reducing social marginalization, creating more opportunities for cross-cultural contact and understanding, or retraining police to think and behave differently in their community engagement roles.

Nevertheless, the same may also be said for various terrorist movements themselves. They have demonstrated their capacity over time to integrate environmental shocks (e.g., financial or territorial losses), initiate new behavioral regimes (e.g., shifting from large-scale high-tech attack strategies to small-scale, low-tech domestic attacks; developing new or adapted digital behaviors and strategies), integrate both internal and co-occurring system stressors (e.g., internal competitions for movement control; military assaults); and negotiate new resources to accommodate these stressors through complex, reciprocal relationships (e.g., decentralizing a terrorist movement's resource base by creating local franchises in a range of different regional and national locations).

Thus the multisystemic resilience of P/CVE must not only contend with its own cross-system dynamics and complexities; it also needs to continuously adapt to and transform its strategies in relation to the resilience demonstrated by the co-occurring systems that nourish and sustain the violent extremist and influences it is attempting to combat and remediate. In this sense, the systems dynamic for P/CVE is always an interaction between both its own cluster of co-occurring systems and also between its own systems and the systems of its opponents, which can both overlap and diverge.

Principles for the Future Study of Multisystemic Resilience to Violent Extremism and Terrorism

As the foregoing analysis demonstrates, both violent extremism and resilience to violent extremism are complex, multilevel, multisystemic processes. The study of resilience to violent extremism to date has tended to focus primarily on community level resilience, with a less dominant focus on individual resilience. The dominance of community-sited models of P/CVE recognizes and works with the multisystemic nature of risk, vulnerability and protective factors involved in preventing and intervening in radicalization to violence at many different levels and across many co-occurring systems.

But the predominant focus on community-level resilience has also arisen as a response to pragmatic demands from governments that want rapid, actionable knowledge that sometimes limits the complexity and nuance required to move beyond what is known about resilience to violent extremism and instead start to explore what may be possible. An intriguing observation in this regard comes from the study of ecological resilience, where a distinction is drawn between "fast" and "slow" variables in relation to feedback loops that influence the growth or degradation of an environment (Walker & Salt, 2012).

A full-blown terrorist event would be an example of a fast variable that produces significant change in a system's regime, as we saw after 9/11 in the United States or in New Zealand following the Christchurch attack. By contrast, P/CVE is a slow variable. Its emphasis on building individual, social, and community resilience through strengthening social cohesion; tackling areas of social disadvantage and marginalization; enhancing the capacity for critical thinking and analysis; developing sustainable and meaningful partnerships at local, regional, and national systems levels; and maintaining democratic openness and responsiveness are all processes that both take time and require longitudinal assessment. Preventing a specific terrorist attack can occur in a highly compressed period of time with intensive resource distribution. P/CVE, on the other hand, spreads out over time, over place, and with a much more diffused resource and investment base. It might be years before the outcomes of a particular P/CVE initiative can be effectively assessed, but the political and funding cycles by which many P/CVE programs and models are framed are often inhospitable to this reality. The result can be superficial or premature assessments of theoretical, program and policy efficacy that do not serve longer-term interests or goals in building multisystemic resilience.

A few principles emerge from this that may serve as guides for future studies of multisystemic resilience to violent extremism:

1. The study of resilience to violent extremism should be able to clearly define the co-occurring systems, the multiple levels—and, where applicable, the scalar implications of how genuinely multisystemic resilience is built, demonstrated, or eroded—and the specific adaptations and transformations that do or don't enable this to occur. This means moving beyond the idea that only communities need to be resilient to violent extremism and including institutional and governance systems within the frame of resilience-based analysis and assessment.
2. In both conceptual and pragmatic terms, however, there is no P/CVE without communities. This means that wherever possible, communities should be engaged and involved as co-researchers when developing, investigating or assessing specific P/CVE initiatives in the context of resilience building (and beyond).
3. Triangulation is essential for the study of multisystemic resilience to violent extremism. The data points available for the study of resilience to violent extremism may be either limited or incomplete for a variety of reasons, making triangulation all the more important to develop a deepened contextual understanding of how resilience can be manifested in diverse ways, and with diverse meanings, across different systems and at different levels.
4. There is a tendency to develop short-term studies of resilience to violent extremism because of policy and funding constraints. However, longitudinal studies of multisystemic resilience to violent extremism are critical if we are to assess capacities and behaviors linked to persistence, adaptation, and transformation across systems in particular.
5. The meanings of "resilience to violent extremism" need to continue to be explored, diversified, and contested. Resilience has been shown to vary its meanings not only across disciplines but also across cultural, organizational, institutional, and ideological systems. The study of resilience discourse in the context of violent extremism is in continuous need of refinement and elaboration.
6. The ways in which resilient systems cope with the risks and threats of violent extremism need to be investigated in tandem with the multisystemic resiliency of violent extremist and terrorist movements themselves. Failing to understand how resilient systems can compete as well as cooperate with each other will result in suboptimal analyses of what resilience means in conflict-defined settings.
7. The reliable measurement of resilience to violent extremism is in its infancy. While a number of measures exist for assessing indicators of radicalization to violence and violent extremism, very few studies have attempted to develop or validate measurements of resilience to violent extremism. Exploratory work in this regard has been conducted by Weine and Ahmed (2012) through the DOVE tool, and Grossman, Ungar, and their colleagues (Grossman et al., 2017, 2020) through the BRAVE measure, but further work to extend

and refine the measurement of resilience to violent extremism in multisystemic and diverse contexts is needed.
8. Finally, the study of multisystemic resilience to violent extremism is already embedded within a co-occurring system of multiple studies drawn from a range of different disciplines and branches of knowledge. The study of resilience to violent extremism should draw creatively and innovatively on multidisciplinary knowledge of how multisystemic resilience functions outside the sphere of violent extremism—as in fact a number of studies have already done—to continue to refresh and expand understanding of what resilience capacities may look like, or need to look like, in relation to violent extremism and terrorism.

Conclusion

The field of resilience has been defined since its inception by multiple genealogies in terms of its disciplinary coordinates, beginning with its elaboration in the fields of engineering and materials sciences through to the human sciences of psychology and the environmental study of ecological systems. The legacy of these multiple genealogies has both enlivened and complicated theoretical and empirical research on resilience in different contexts, largely in exciting ways. Increasingly, resilience as an interdisciplinary field has come to see resilience as a process of adaptation and transformation, in which multiple systems interact, influence, and, at times, compete with, trade off against, or resist one another. The classical idea of resilience as a process of "bouncing back" from trauma or adversity and returning to a state of equilibrium has been superseded by more complex analyses that ask us to think about the different dimensions of resilience capacity and function within complex, messy, dynamic, uncertain, and often volatile multi-system environments.

The study of resilience to violent extremism shares this complexity and uncertainty. The ways in which resilience to violent extremism have been studied to date reflect important advances in understanding the features and dynamics of multiple human, social, technological, cultural, political, and environmental systems as these influence and are in turn shaped by nonstate movements that seek to use violence against populations to achieve ideological or political outcomes. The focus within the field of P/CVE in particular has been alert to the relevance of aspects of resilient systems drawn from outside an immediate concern with social or political violence, such as social capital and connectedness, and the strength of social support and development systems such as the education, health, social welfare, and human rights sectors.

However, the predominant emphasis on community resilience to violent extremism has come at the expense of exploring the dynamics of resilience at the level of those systems of power that govern the way in which policies and practices of building resilience to violent extremism are developed and enacted. These power systems are by and large driven by governments and their institutional coordinates, such as law enforcement and a variety of government-supported or -enabled civil society institutions and systems. To provide a quick concluding example: trust is considered a highly salient variable in the context of resilience to violent extremism (Dalgaard-Nielsen & Schack, 2016; Grossman et al., 2014; Spalek, 2010). Yet the capacity and level of trust in the context of preventing or countering violent extremism tends to be explored only in terms of how much or how little communities experience trust in government; the reverse question, of whether, why, and how much or how little governments trust communities, and the consequences of this, is not canvassed. When we stop thinking about "trust" as a static variable and start thinking about it instead as a multisystemic and dynamic process of flows, what might this tell us about how to advance multisystemic resilience to violent extremism through building transformative relationships that understand the dynamics and distribution of reciprocal trust in new ways?

The emphasis on understanding and sustaining community resilience to violent extremism has also come at the expense of exploring in greater depth the resilience of the very phenomena such approaches are trying to mitigate: violent extremist and terrorist movements and actors themselves. Building resilience to violent extremism means understanding the particular resilience features and capacities of violent extremism itself. For societies and communities it also means a whole-of-systems approach that encompasses all the systems and actors involved in the P/CVE matrix—and not just communities. Responsibilizing communities for demonstrating resilience capacity in this way (Bottrell, 2013; Thomas, 2017) excludes the state from accounting for its own resilience protections and vulnerabilities both within its own co-occurring systems and also in relationship with independent community-based systems.

This goes against the grain of what Gunderson and Holling (2002) describe as "panarchy," a phrase used in the context of resilience in the built environment to denote interconnectedness in the way that systems at different spatial and temporal scales are dynamically influenced by systems at other scales. Working with this fundamental interconnectedness between the scales of individual, community, government, and institutional systems means acknowledging that neither communities nor the state are wholly responsible for P/CVE; it is a shared responsibility. It follows that the task of understanding, building, and assessing multisystemic resilience capacity to violent extremism and terrorism must also be undertaken together as a meaningfully shared and mutually negotiated enterprise, one in which all elements of this complex landscape are able to recognize and strengthen their adaptive and transformative interdependence.

Key Messages

1. The study of resilience to violent extremism needs to move beyond the idea that only communities need to be resilient to violent extremism by including institutional and governance systems within the frame of resilience-based analysis and assessment.
2. There is no P/CVE without communities. This means that wherever possible, communities should be engaged and involved as co-researchers when developing, investigating or assessing specific P/CVE initiatives in the context of resilience-building (and beyond).
3. There is a tendency to develop short-term studies of resilience to violent extremism because of policy and funding constraints. However, longitudinal studies of multisystemic

resilience to violent extremism are critical if we are to assess capacities and behaviors linked to persistence, adaptation, and transformation across systems.
4. The ways in which resilient systems cope with the risks and threats of violent extremism need to be investigated in tandem with the multisystemic resiliency of violent extremist and terrorist movements themselves. Failing to understand how resilient systems can compete as well as cooperate with each other will result in suboptimal analyses of what resilience means in conflict-defined settings.
5. In the context of terrorism and violent extremism, a singular construct of "adversity" when considering how resilience emerges and can be mobilized is insufficient. Multiple, co-occurring adversities need to be understood and addressed if the complex nature of building resilience to violent extremism is to advance both conceptually and empirically.

Acknowledgments

I am grateful to Michael Ungar for a careful and constructive reading of an earlier draft of this chapter and to Vanessa Barolsky for her thoughtful help with research materials and preparation of the bibliography.

Notes

1. *Violent extremism* and *terrorism* are often used interchangeably but they have slightly different meanings. The distinction between these terms that informs the current discussion is as follows: terrorism refers to ideologically based or inspired violent *acts and events* by nonstate actors that are designed to coerce, intimidate, or create fear in populations to achieve particular political or social outcomes. Terrorists are those who plot or commit such acts. Violent extremism, by contrast, is more broadly defined because it can include not only ideologically based acts of nonstate violence themselves, but also the *attitudes, beliefs, and orientations* that justify and legitimate the use of violence to achieve social and political outcomes. Terrorism can be a subset of violent extremist thinking and movements, although not all terrorists are extremists in the way that extremism tends to be defined (Berger, 2017, 2018). Resilience is particularly meaningful in relation to the broader parameters of preventing and addressing violent extremism rather than the narrower phenomenon of terrorism.
2. *Counterterrorism* and *preventing/countering violent extremism* are sometimes used interchangeably in the literature and in public commentary. However, the terms bear different signals in relation to antiterrorism policy and practice. CT tends to align more closely with "hard power," securitized approaches taken by law enforcement and intelligence agencies that focus on investigation, disruption and interdiction of terrorist actors and events. P/CVE, on the other hand, distinguishes itself from CT approaches by adopting "soft power" models that seek to engage, involve, and, at their best, empower communities and civil society in the effort to prevent violent extremist ideologies and narratives from gaining a foothold. CT focuses on preventing actors, networks, plots, and attacks; P/CVE focuses on preventing or addressing the sociocultural drivers and "push" or "pull" factors than serve as enabling conditions for violent extremism to develop and thrive.
3. "Surmised" because, as part of its commitment to *laïcité*, France does not collect any census or other official data on religious beliefs or adherence. For a recent discussion of *laïcité* and Muslim communities in France, see https://www.thenation.com/article/french-secularism-is-in-crisis-what-does-that-mean-for-muslim-youth/.

References

Aly, A., Taylor, E., & Karnovsky, S. (2014). Moral disengagement and building resilience to violent extremism: An education intervention. *Studies in Conflict & Terrorism*, *37*(4), 369–385. doi:10.1080/1057610X.2014.879379

Anderson, B. (1983). *Imagined communities*. London, UK: Verso.

Berger, J. M. (2016). Making CVE work: A focused approach based on process disruption. *The International Centre for Counter-Terrorism—The Hague*, *7*(5). doi:10.19165/2016.1.05

Bhui, K. S., Hicks, M. H., Lashley, M. H., & Jones, E. (2012). A public health approach to understanding and preventing violent radicalization. *BMC Medicine*, *10*(16). doi:10.1186/1741-7015-10-16

Bottrell, D. (2013). Responsibilised resilience? Reworking neoliberal social policy texts. *M/C Journal*, *16*(5). Retrieved from: http://journal.media-culture.org.au/index.php/mcjournal/article/view/708

BOUNCE. (2018). *Resilience Training, Network and Evaluation: STRESAVIORA II (Strengthening Resilience Against Violent Radicalisation) 2015–2018*. Brussels, Belgium: European Commission with the Egmont Institute. Retrieved from https://www.bounce-resilience-tools.eu/sites/default/files/downloads/2018-04/BOUNCE%2520Manual_A4-07.pdf

Bracke, S. (2016). Bouncing back: Vulnerability and resistance in times of resilience. In J. Butler, Z. Gambetti, & L. Sabsay (Eds.), *Vulnerability in resistance* (pp. 52–75). Durham, NC: Duke University Press.

Bronfenbrenner, U. (1988). Interacting systems in human development: Research paradigms: Present and future. In N. Bolger, A. Caspi, G. Downey, & M. Moorehouse (Eds.), *Persons in context: Developmental processes* (pp. 25–49). New York, NY: Cambridge University Press.

Bronfenbrenner, U., & Morris, P. A. (2006). The bioecological model of human development. In R. M. Lerner & W. Damon (Eds.), *Handbook of child psychology: Theoretical models of human development* (6th ed., pp. 793–828). Hoboken, NJ: John Wiley.

Challgren, J., Kenyon, T., Kervick, L., Scudder, S., Walters, M., Whitehead, K., . . . Flynn, C. R. (2016). *Countering violent extremism: Applying the public health model*. Washington, DC: Georgetown Security Studies Review. Retrieved from https://georgetownsecuritystudiesreview.org/wp-content/uploads/2016/10/NSCITF-Report-on-Countering-Violent-Extremism.pdf

Cherney, A., Sweid, R., Grossman, M., Derbas, A., Dunn, K., Jones, C., . . . Barton, G. (2018). Local service provision to counter violent extremism: Perspectives, capabilities and challenges arising from an Australian service mapping project. *Behavioral Sciences of Terrorism and Political Aggression*, *10*(3), 187–206. doi:10.1080/19434472.2017.1350735

Coaffee, J. (2006). From counterterrorism to resilience. *The European Legacy*, *11*(4), 389–403. doi:10.1080/10848770600766094

Coaffee, J., & Fussey, P. (2015). Constructing resilience through security and surveillance: The politics, practices and tensions of security-driven resilience. *Security Dialogue*, *46*(1), 86–105. doi:10.1177/0967010614557884

Coaffee, J., Moore, C., Fletcher, D., & Bosher, L. (2008). Resilient design for community safety and terror-resistant cities. *Proceedings of the Institution of Civil Engineers—Municipal Engineer*, *161*(2), 103–110. doi:10.1680/muen.2008.161.2.103

Council of Australian Governments. (2015). *Australia's counter-terrorism strategy: Strengthening our resilience*. Commonwealth of Australia. Retrieved from https://www.nationalsecurity.gov.au/Media-and-publications/Publications/Documents/Australias-Counter-Terrorism-Strategy-2015.pdf

Council on American-Islamic Relations Minnesota. (2016). *Countering violent extremism program (CVE): What you need to know*. Retrieved from http://www.cairmn.com/civil-rights/cve-toolkit/59-cve.html

Dalgaard-Nielsen, A., & Schack, P. (2016). Community resilience to militant Islamism: Who and what? An explorative study of resilience in three Danish communities. *Democracy and Security*, *12*(4), 309–327. doi:10.1080/17419166.2016.1236691

Day, J., & Kleinmann, S. (2017). Combating the cult of ISIS: A social approach to countering violent extremism. *The Review of Faith & International Affairs*, *15*(3), 14–23. doi:10.1080/15570274.2017.1354458

Dechesne, M. (2017). The concept of resilience in the context of counterterrorism. In U. Kumar (Ed.), *The Routledge international handbook of psychosocial resilience* (pp. 414–423). London, UK: Routledge.

Doosje, B., Fathali, M. M., Kruglanski, A. W., de Wolf, A., Mann, L., & Feddes, A. R. (2016). Terrorism, radicalization and de-radicalization. *Current Opinion in Psychology, 11*, 79–84. doi:10.1016/j.copsyc.2016.06.008

Ellis, H. B., & Abdi, S. (2017). Building community resilience to violent extremism through genuine partnerships. *American Psychologist, 72*(3), 289–300. doi:10.1037/amp0000065

European Commission. (n.d.). *Radicalisation Awareness Network*. Retrieved from https://ec.europa.eu/home-affairs/what-we-do/networks/radicalisation_awareness_network_en

Evans, G. W., Li, D., & Whipple, S. S. (2013). Cumulative risk and child development. *Psychological Bulletin, 139*(6), 1342–1396. doi:10.1037/a0031808

Executive Office of the President of the United States. (2011). *Strategic implementation plan for empowering local partners to prevent violent extremism in the United States*. Washington, DC: The White House.

Froio, C., & Ganesh, B. (2018). The transnationalisation of far right discourse on Twitter. *European Societies, 21*(4), 513–539. doi:10.1080/14616696.2018.1494295

Gerrand, V. (2016, August). No longer afraid to come out of the locker: Going berko for burkinis. *Overland Magazine*. Retrieved from https://overland.org.au/2016/08/no-longer-afraid-to-come-out-of-the-locker-going-berko-for-burkinis/

Ghosh, R., Chan, W. Y. A., Manuel, A., & Dilimulati, M. (2017). Can education counter violent religious extremism? *Canadian Foreign Policy Journal, 23*(2), 117–133. doi:10.1080/11926422.2016.1165713

Global Community Engagement and Resilience Fund. (2017). *Strategy to engage communities and address the drivers of violent extremism 2017–2020*. Geneva, Switzerland: Author. Retrieved from https://www.gcerf.org/wp-content/uploads/GCERF-Strategy-2017-2020.pdf

Global Counterterrorism Forum. (2012). *Ankara memorandum on good practices for a multi-sectoral approach to countering violent extremism*. Retrieved from https://www.thegctf.org/documents/10162/72352/13Sep19_Ankara+Memorandum.pdf

Grossman, M. (2015). *Community reporting thresholds: Sharing information with authorities concerning violent extremist activity and involvement in foreign conflict: A UK replication study*. Canberra: Australia-New Zealand Counter-Terrorism Committee.

Grossman, M. (2018). When the "right thing to do" feels so wrong: Australian Muslim perspectives on "intimates" reporting to authorities about violent extremism. In J. Esposito & D. Iner (Eds.), *Islamophobia and radicalization: Breeding intolerance and violence* (pp. 203–222). London, UK: Palgrave Macmillan.

Grossman, M., Carland, S. J., Tahiri, H., & Zammit, A. (2018). *The roles of women in supporting and opposing violent extremism: Understanding gender and terrorism in contemporary Australia*. Melbourne, Australia: Alfred Deakin Institute for Citizenship and Globalisation, Deakin University.

Grossman, M., Hadfield, K., Jefferies, P., Gerrand, V., & Ungar, M. (2020) Youth resilience to violent extremism: Development and validation of the BRAVE measure. *Terrorism and Political Violence*, https://doi.org/10.1080/09546553.2019.1705283

Grossman, M., Peucker, M., Smith, D., & Dellal, H. (2016). *Stocktake research project: A systematic literature and selected program review on social cohesion, community resilience and violent extremism 2011–2015*. Melbourne, Australia: Victoria University and Australian Multicultural Foundation.

Grossman, M., Tahiri, H., & Stephenson, P. (2014). *Harnessing resilience capital: An investigation of resilience and cultural diversity in countering violent extremism*. Canberra: Australia-New Zealand Counter-Terrorism Committee.

Grossman, M., Ungar, M., Brisson, J., Gerrand, V., Hadfield, K., & Jefferies, P. (2017). *Understanding youth resilience to violent extremism: A standardised research measure: Final research report*. Melbourne, Austalia: Alfred Deakin Institute for Citizenship and Globalisation, Deakin University. doi:10.13140/RG.2.2.21022.79689

Gunderson, L. H., & Holling, C. S. (2002). *Panarchy: Understanding transformations in human and natural systems*. Washington, DC: Island Press.

Hardy, K. (2015). Resilience in UK counter-terrorism. *Theoretical Criminology, 19*(1), 77–94. doi:10.1177/1362480614542119

Harris-Hogan, S., Barrelle, K., & Zammit, A. (2015). What is countering violent extremism? Exploring CVE policy and practice in Australia. *Behavioral Sciences of Terrorism and Political Aggression, 8*(1), 6–24. doi:10.1080/19434472.2015.1104710

HM Government. (2018). *CONTEST: The United Kingdom's strategy for countering terrorism.* London, UK: Her Majesty's Stationery Office. Retrieved from https://assets.publishing.service.gov.uk/government/uploads/system/uploads/attachment_data/file/716907/140618_CCS207_CCS0218929798-1_CONTEST_3.0_WEB.pdf

Hunter, C. (2012). Is resilience still a useful concept when working with children and young people? (CFCA Paper No. 2). *Journal of the Home Economics Institute of Australia, 19*(1), 45–52. Retrieved from https://search.informit.com.au/documentSummary;dn=020407233943460;res=IELIND

Hutchinson, J. (2017). Violent extremism and far-right radicalism in Australia: A psychosocial perspective. *Counter Terrorist Trends and Analyses, 9*(11), 16–19. https://www.rsis.edu.sg/wp-content/uploads/2017/11/CTTA-November-2017.pdf

International Committee of the Red Cross. (2017). *Background note and guidance for National Red Cross and Red Crescent societies on "preventing and countering violent extremism."* Geneva, Switzerland: Author. Retrieved from https://www.icrc.org/en/document/guidance-note-national-societies-preventing-and-countering-violent-extremism-approach

Jones, S. G. (2018). *The rise of far-right extremism in the United States.* CSIS Briefs. Washington, DC: Center for Strategic and International Studies. Retrieved from https://www.csis.org/analysis/rise-far-right-extremism-united-states

Keohane, R. O., & Nye, J. S., Jr. (1998). Power and interdependence in the information age. *Foreign Affairs, 77*(5), 81–94. doi:10.2307/20049052

Kundnani, A. (2012). Radicalisation: The journey of a concept. *Race and Class, 54*(2), 3–25. doi:10.1177/0306396812454984

Liebenberg, L., Ungar, M., & Van de Vijver, F. (2012). Validation of the Child and Youth Resilience Measure-28 (CYRM-28) among Canadian youth. *Research on Social Work Practice, 22*(2), 219–226. doi:10.1177/1049731511428619

Longstaff, P. H., Armstrong, N. J., Perrin, K., Parker, W. M., & Hidek, M. A. (2010). Building resilient communities: A preliminary framework for assessment. *Homeland Security Affairs, 6*(3), Article 6. Retrieved from https://www.hsaj.org/articles/81

Los Angeles Interagency Coordination Group. (2015). *The Los Angeles framework for countering violent extremism.* Retrieved from https://www.dhs.gov/publication/los-angeles-framework-countering-violent-terrorism

Lösel, F., King, S., Bender, D., & Jugl, I. (2018). Protective factors against extremism and violent radicalization: A systematic review of research. *International Journal of Developmental Sciences, 12*(1–2), 89–102. doi:10.3233/DEV-170241

Luthar, S. S., Cicchetti, D., & Becker, B. (2000). The construct of resilience: A critical evaluation and guidelines for future work. *Child Development, 71*(3), 543–562.

Masten, A. S. (2014). Global perspectives on resilience in children and youth. *Child Development, 85*(1), 6–20. doi:10.1111/cdev.12205

Masten, A. S. (2016). Resilience in developing systems: The promise of integrated approaches. *European Journal of Developmental Psychology, 13*(3), 297–312. doi:10.1080/17405629.2016.1147344

McCoy, J., Rahman, T., & Somer, M. (2018). Polarization and the global crisis of democracy: Common patterns, dynamics, and pernicious consequences for democratic polities. *American Behavioral Scientist, 62*(1), 16–42. doi:10.1177/0002764218759576

Multicultural New South Wales. (n.d.). *COMPACT program guidelines.* Sydney, Australia: Multicultural New South Wales. Retrieved from https://multicultural.nsw.gov.au/communities/compact/compact_program/

Norris, F. H., Stevens, S. P., Pfefferbaum, B., Wyche, K. F., & Pfefferbaum, R. L. (2008). Community resilience as a metaphor, theory, set of capacities, and strategy for disaster readiness. *American Journal of Community Psychology, 41*(1–2), 127–150. doi:10.1007/s10464-007-9156-6

Obradovic, J., Shaffer, A., & Masten, A. S. (2012). Risk and adversity in developmental psychopathology: Progress and future directions. In L. C. Mayes & M. Lewis (Eds.), *The Cambridge handbook of environment in human development* (pp. 35–57). New York, NY: Cambridge University Press.

Organization for Security and Co-operation in Europe. (2018). *The role of civil society in preventing and countering violent extremism and radicalization that lead to terrorism: A guidebook for South-Eastern Europe*. Vienna, Austria: OSCE Secretariat. Retrieved from https://www.osce.org/secretariat/400241

Public Safety Canada. (2013). *Building resilience against terrorism: Canada's counter-terrorism strategy* (2nd ed.). Ottawa, ON: Author. Retrieved from https://www.publicsafety.gc.ca/cnt/rsrcs/pblctns/rslnc-gnst-trrrsm/rslnc-gnst-trrrsm-eng.pdf

Ranstorp, M. (2018). *Ex post paper "Research Seminar."* Amsterdam, The Netherlands: RAN Centre of Excellence. Retrieved from https://ec.europa.eu/home-affairs/sites/homeaffairs/files/what-we-do/networks/radicalisation_awareness_network/ran-papers/docs/ran_research_seminar_17102018_en.pdf

Rosand, E., Winterbotham, E., Jones, M., Praxl-Tabuchi, F. (2018). *A roadmap to progress: The state of the global P/CVE agenda*. Prevention Project and Royal United Services Institute. Retrieved from https://organizingagainstve.org/wp-content/uploads/2018/09/GCCS_ROADMAP_FNL.pdf

Royal United Services Institute. (2015). *STRIVE for development: Strengthening resilience to violence and extremism*. Luxembourg: European Commission. Retrieved from https://rusi.org/publication/other-publications/strive-development

Sampaio, A. (2017, December). Resilience gains ground in counter-terrorism strategies. *Jane's Intelligence Review*, 18–21. Retrieved from https://www.academia.edu/37118238/Resilience_gains_ground_in_counter-terrorism_strategies

Snair, J., Nicholson, A., & Giammaria, C. (2017). *Countering violent extremism through public health practice: Proceedings of a workshop*. Washington, DC: National Academies Press. Retrieved from https://www.nap.edu/read/24638/chapter/1

Spalek, B. (2010). Community policing, trust, and Muslim communities in relation to "new terrorism." *Politics & Policy*, *38*(4), 789–815. doi:10.1111/j.1747-1346.2010.00258.x

Spalek, B., & Davies, L. (2012). Mentoring in relation to violent extremism: A study of role, purpose, and outcomes. *Studies in Conflict & Terrorism*, *35*(5), 354–368. doi:10.1080/1057610X.2012.666820

Sieckelinck, S. & Gielen, A. J. (2017). *RAN issue paper: Protective and promotive factors building resilience against violent radicalisation*. Amsterdam, The Netherlands: RAN Centre of Excellence. Retrieved from https://ec.europa.eu/home-affairs/sites/homeaffairs/files/what-we-do/networks/radicalisation_awareness_network/ran-papers/docs/ran_paper_protective_factors_042018_en.pdf

Stephens, W., Sieckelinck, S., & Boutellier, H. (2019). Preventing violent extremism: A review of the literature. *Studies in Conflict & Terrorism*, 1–16. doi:10.1080/1057610X.2018.1543144

Stokols, D. (1992). Establishing and maintaining healthy environments: Toward a social ecology of health promotion. *American Psychologist*, *47*(1), 6–22. doi:10.1037/0003-066x.47.1.6

Stokols, D. (1996). Translating social ecological theory into guidelines for community health promotion. *American Journal of Health Promotion*, *10*(4), 282–298. doi:10.4278/0890-1171-10.4.282

Stokols, D., Lejano, R. P., & Hipp, J. (2013). Enhancing the resilience of human-environment systems: A social-ecological perspective. *Ecology and Society*, *18*(1), 7. doi:10.5751/ES-05301-180107

Taylor, E. L., Taylor, P. C., Karnovsky, S., Aly, A., & Taylor, N. (2017). "Beyond Bali": A transformative education approach for developing community resilience to violent extremism. *Asia Pacific Journal of Education*, *37*(2), 193–204. doi:10.1080/02188791.2016.1240661

Thomas, P. (2017). Changing experiences of responsibilisation and contestation within counter-terrorism policies: The British Prevent experience. *Policy & Politics*, *45*(3), 305–321. doi:10.1332/030557317X14943145195580

Thomas, P., Grossman, M., Christmann, K., & Miah, S. (2020). Community reporting on violent extremism by "intimates": emergent findings from international evidence. *Critical Studies on Terrorism*, https://doi.org/10.1080/17539153.2020.1791389

Thomas, P., Grossman, M., Miah, S., & Christmann, K. (2017). *Community reporting thresholds: Sharing information with authorities concerning violent extremist activity and involvement in foreign conflict: A UK replication study*. Lancaster, UK: Centre for Research and Evidence on Security Threats. Retrieved from https://crestresearch.ac.uk/resources/community-reporting-thresholds-full-report/

Ungar, M. (2008). Resilience across cultures. *British Journal of Social Work*, *38*(2), 218–235. doi:10.1093/bjsw/bcl343

Ungar, M. (2011). The social ecology of resilience: Addressing contextual and cultural ambiguity of a nascent construct. *American Journal of Orthopsychiatry, 81*(1), 1–17. doi:10.1111/j.1939-0025.2010.01067.x

Ungar, M. (2015). Practitioner review: Diagnosing childhood resilience—A systemic approach to the diagnosis of adaptation in adverse social and physical ecologies. *Journal of Child Psychology and Psychiatry, 56*(1), 4–17. doi:10.1111/jcpp.12306

Ungar, M. (2018). Systemic resilience: Principles and processes for a science of change in contexts of adversity. *Ecology and Society, 23*(4), 34. doi:10.5751/ES-10385-230434

Ungar, M., Hadfield, K., Amarasingam, A., Morgan, S., & Grossman, M. (2017). The association between discrimination and violence among Somali Canadian youth. *Journal of Ethnic and Migration Studies, 44*(13), 2273–2285. doi:10.1080/1369183X.2017.1374169

Van Brunt, B., Murphy, M., & Zedginidze, A. (2017). An exploration of the risk, protective, and mobilization factors related to violent extremism in college populations. *Violence and Gender, 4*(3). doi:10.1089/vio.2017.0039

Vermeulen, F. (2014). Suspect communities—Targeting violent extremism at the local level: Policies of engagement in Amsterdam, Berlin, and London. *Terrorism and Political Violence, 26*(2), 286–306. doi:10.1080/09546553.2012.705254

Walklate, S., Mythen, G., & McGarry, R. (2012). States of resilience and the resilient state. *Current Issues in Criminal Justice, 24*(2), 185–204. doi:10.1080/10345329.2012.12035954

Walker, B., & Salt, D. (2012). *Resilience practice: Building capacity to absorb disturbance and maintain function*. Washington, DC: Island Press.

Warrell, H. (2019, July 23). There is no alternative: An artistic critique of the UK's counter-terrorism policy, *Financial Times*. Retrieved from https://www.ft.com/content/88843dae-a977-11e9-984c-fac8325aaa04

Weine, S., & Ahmed, O. (2012). *Building resilience to violent extremism among Somali-Americans in Minneapolis-St. Paul*. College Park, MD: National Consortium for the Study of Terrorism and Responses to Terrorism. Retrieved from: https://www.start.umd.edu/sites/default/files/files/publications/Weine_BuildingResiliencetoViolentExtremism_SomaliAmericans.pdf

Weine, S., Eisenman, D. P., Kinsler, J., Glik, D. C., & Polutnik, C. (2017). Addressing violent extremism as public health policy and practice. *Behavioral Sciences of Terrorism and Political Aggression, 9*(3), 208–221. doi:10.1080/19434472.2016.1198413

Weine, S., Henderson, S., Shanfield, S., Legha, R., & Post, J. (2013). Building community resilience to counter violent extremism. *Democracy and Security, 9*(4), 327–333. doi:10.1080/17419166.2013.766131

Williams, R. (1976). *Keywords: A vocabulary of culture and society*. London, UK: Croom Helm.

Wright, M. O. D., & Masten, A. S. (2015). Pathways to resilience in context. In L. C. Theron, L. Liebenberg, & M. Ungar (Eds.), *Youth resilience and culture: Commonalities and complexities* (pp. 3–22). Berlin, Germany: Springer.

Yates, T. M., & Masten, A. S. (2004). Fostering the future: Resilience theory and the practice of positive psychology. In P. A. Linley & S. Joseph (Eds.), *Positive psychology in practice* (pp. 521–539). Hoboken, NJ: Wiley.

17

The Creation and Recreation of Borderlands Among Indigenous Peoples

A Kamentza's Journey of Resilience

Pilar Hernández-Wolfe and Santos Jamioy Muchavisoy

Introduction

Our epistemic point of departure to discuss processes of survival and resilience for indigenous communities impacted by the enduring effects of colonization and coloniality is grounded in de Sousa Santos's (2012) *Epistemologies of the South*. The framework provided therein recognizes different ways to understand our existence in this world by attending to our own social locations, histories, conditions, and possibilities, yet de Sousa Santos does not claim to have arrived at a new general theory. The framework outlines trajectories for re-engaging with the experiences and knowledges of those whose who can no longer be rendered legible by Eurocentric knowledge. We, Santos Jamioy Michavisoy and Pilar Hernandez-Wolfe, see ourselves within that framework. We locate ourselves within the colonial history of Abya yala—named by the Europeans as Americas—(Consejo Mundial de Pueblos Indígenas, 1977). Jamioy's primary frame of reference is that of a Kamentza Taita (political and spiritual leader), born, raised, and living in the land of Tabanok (named by the Spaniards and Mestizo[1] settlers/Colombians, Valle del Sibundoy). Hernandez's primary frame of reference is that of a Colombian Mestiza who inhabits the borderlands of binguality, binationality, and interculturality. In analyzing resilience, we seek to understand how knowledge and subjectivity are intertwined with modernity/coloniality. We believe that the construction of knowledges and mental health practices must be centered in processes that reorient and sustain communal practices affirming the lives and ways of being of the peoples whose lives were disrupted by the European invasions that began in the 15th century. Herein we discuss what resilience means for the Kamentza people, thus relocating the concept to a borderlands space where Western notions of resilience can dialogue with and be transformed by the local context of this community. In this sense, our work seeks to make resilience a more systemic concept, engaging multiple sources of knowledge and both individual and collective (e.g., cultural) systems into our understanding of what resilience means to one specific indigenous people. We agree with Mendenhall and Wooyoung (2019), who, in discussing their failed attempt to standardize a resilience scale in South Africa, state that in rethinking how we approach the study of suffering and resilience it is imperative that culture be kept at the center of an understanding of how people envision themselves within the world around them. This is key to understanding how they perceive, relate, and respond to challenges from their social world.

We contextualize Ungar's (2011) definition of resilience within the history of colonization and coloniality of Abya Yala, as this point of departure takes the meaning of resilience into other levels of complexity. As researchers, and building on Ungar's work, we believe that understanding resilience in contexts of exposure to significant adversity involves examining the processes by which communities struggle, adapt, and navigate their way to a state of well-being and how they negotiate, recreate, and affirm their way of life. Resilience processes must be anchored in the multiple subjectivities of those who face adversities; embodied voices must be part of the meaning making process, along with access and opportunity for collective coping and an outlook open to possibilities. In this chapter, we will situate our analysis within an epistemology of the South; discuss resilience as a systemic process occurring in borderland spaces; offer a narrative about the Kamentza people of Colombia highlighting their interaction with larger systems, historical processes, and ways of coping with adversity; and finally, offer our view on the type of research/practice that is needed in the future from this perspective.

An Epistemology of the South: Colonization, Coloniality, and Borderlands

Our thinking about resilience is situated in our brown bodies and in the lands we inhabit in Abya Yala, as they are the sites of life that survived the genocide of the indigenous peoples of these lands. This point of departure integrates viewpoints, narratives, and ways of life that exist and develop along the margins of political and economic structures. In this section, we delineate key concepts that inform how we see the Kamentza's trajectory of resilience, as their existence must take into account how their life has changed with colonization, coloniality and the negotiation for survival in borderland spaces.

Colonization has been a key constitutive factor in shaping our world. Abya Yala was likely to have been populated by 60 to 110 million people before Columbus arrived in 1492 (Mann, 2005). According to the modernity/coloniality collective project (Grosfoguel, 2005; Quijano, 2000), colonialism refers to a form of political and judicial domination over the means of production, work, and livelihood that one population assumed over others throughout a historical period that can be marked as ending in 1824 with the independence battles that freed Latin America from Spain. These scholars contend, however, that the end of colonialism did not end the power relationships that produce and legitimize oppressive differences between forms of knowledge, groups of people, and societies. Anibal Quijano (2000) coined the term "coloniality" to refer to the systemic suppression of subordinated cultures and knowledges by the dominant Eurocentric paradigm of modernity and the emergence of knowledges and practices resulting from this experience. However, the emergence of knowledges and practices at the margins has the potential to engender distinct alternatives, thereby fostering a pluriverse of cultural configurations. Mignolo and Walsh (2018) speak of border thinking as resulting from the wound of coloniality; that is, experiences and knowledges have emerged from differing and conflicting epistemologies from the south and Eurocentric thought. For Mignolo (2011) border thinking allows us to draw different paths and to enunciate other knowledges after having recognized inequality and accepted the wound inflicted by coloniality. Two interrelated aspects of coloniality are the systemic suppression of local knowledges and the emergence of alternative knowledges resulting from this oppressive experience. It is within this interstice that we locate the resilience of the Kamentza people who have experienced a constant pulling and loosening of relationships through negotiations with the European and Colombian settlers, as well as protection and affirmation of their territories and culture.

According to Anzaldúa (1987), the borderlands are the places in between; the spaces in which border knowledge and border identities are constructed; the gaps, fissures, and silences of hegemonic narratives; and the overlapping border spaces and cultural representations that those who inhabit these spaces negotiate to exercise personal and collective agency. The borderland concept is transnational; it can be applied to the multiplicity of borders present in Abya Yala, and is consistent with Lionnet and Shih's (2005) view of the transnational "as a space of exchange and participation wherever processes of hybridization occur and where it is still possible for cultures to be produced and performed without necessary mediation from the center" (p. 5). Borderland spaces emerge out of coloniality.

What allowed the survival of the Kamentza people in spite of the deliberate effort to exterminate them? How did border spaces emerge out of their survival? How did resilience develop in these spaces? The answers to these questions are multiple and should be addressed from an interdisciplinary perspective. However, for the purposes of this chapter, we will limit our focus to resilience as a response to colonization and coloniality, as embedded in border spaces, and as possibly operating through autopoiesis and structural coupling (Maturana & Varela, 1980; Varela, Thompson, & Rosch, 2016).

Similar to other indigenous peoples in Abya Yala (Deloria, 2006; Kirmayer, Dandeneau, Marshall, Phillips, & Williamson, 2011; Rocha Vivas, 2012), the Kamentza's notion of community and personal identity is rooted in their connection to the land and the environment as a whole, which includes a recognition of nonhuman beings and a spiritual world. They see being in relationship as the way in which all of us exists, with no opposition between nature and culture because humans and other beings do not simply occupy the world; instead, they constitute each other's conditions for existence. As Escobar (2018) explains, "non-moderns dwell in places by moving along the lines and threads that produce the place" (p. 87). They do not separate themselves to control, take from, and subjugate other beings, but co-exist with them. This view is akin to Bateson's view of the "subject" and "object" as co-arising and of knower and known as standing in relation to each other through mutual co-origination. Escobar argues that nature is a recursive, mind-like system, with information its unit of exchange; mental activity occurs in all living organisms and nonhuman processes. The mind is a set of integrated and interacting parts that can process information by identifying differences that make a difference; it is the totality of conscious and unconscious processes that interact in a recurrent and recursive fashion. Thus the mind can be seen as a process shared by all beings—not only humans. The human mind/brain–body is itself situated within a complex web of life and consciousness, interacting with other mind/brain–bodies and with nature and nonhuman beings. Maturana and Varela (1987) state, "all doing is knowing and all-knowing is doing" (p. 27), to underscore that the world is created through interaction of the senses and through language.

According to Varela (1979), an autopoietic system is a network of processes of transformation in which its components continuously regenerate, maintain, and change while constituting a concrete unit in space. An autopoietic system is a living system that maintains its own organization, that is, the preservation of the relational networks that constitutes its unity. Varela, Thompson, and Rosch (2016) explain that the concept of autopoiesis relies on a conception of the universe as in flux; autopoietic entities are mutually constituted according to their own processes and rules and are actively engaged with other beings. The Kamentza, an autopoietic system, can be seen as an information system and as a material entity (people, land, culture) with its own operational mechanism that folds recursively back upon itself while having to adapt to and cope with historical and structural violence. This process of adaptation is a form of structural coupling in which the Kamentza have had to engage with other systems such as European colonizers, the Colombian state, mestizos migrating into their territory, that have perpetrated violence on them at multiple levels, territorial, physical, psychological, and ontological. The historical trajectory of the Kamentza has been impacted by the constraints placed by colonization and coloniality. As a system, they had to undergo structural changes and adopt various structures in response to interactions with the environment; they had to negotiate their continued existence by letting go of territory, traditions, and ways of being. We argue that, in spite of significant adversity, the Kamentza have maintained themselves as an organized system. The Kamentza constitute an autopoietic system; for them, autonomy means that everything is mutually dependent. Escobar (2018) argues that "Latin American conceptions of autonomy are predicated on relationality" (p. 171). That is, first there is an understanding that we are all related and in relationship; second, the conception of the other is always a part of a relationship, not merely the other. In this relational ontology, territories/communities are seen as whole, living entities with memory. We are not individual systems fundamentally separated from what we commonly think of as external reality; instead, such reality comes into being moment by moment through our participation in the world (Escobar, 2018; Sharma, 2015). Thus, a Latin American indigenous view of autonomy and our understanding of autopoiesis elucidate the conditions that have prepared the Kamentza as a community for relating with each other and to the waves of newcomers into their lands. In the next section we outline key historical events in the history of the

Kamentza while illustrating how the processes of autopoiesis and structural coupling evolved from the colonial wound (coloniality) in borderland spaces.

The Kamentza

The Kamentza indigenous people are among the most resilient peoples in southwestern Colombia. Their ancestral knowledge, leadership, and ability to adapt throughout waves of invasions by Spaniards, Colombians, and other colonizers is a testament to their strength under prolonged adversity. Their resilience draws from traditional knowledges, values, and practices as well as from the ongoing challenges posed by evolving relationships with the dominant society and relationship networks with other indigenous peoples in the area.

The Kamentza inhabit their ancestral territory in Tabanok, or the valley of Sibundoy, in the middle of the eastern mountains of the Colombian Andes, in a space of transition and integration of the Andean and Amazonian worlds. The valley of the Sibundoy and the high mountains that surround it are part of the most important Colombian water source, with rich ecosystems full of flora and fauna and a complex system of lagoons and moors. With the Inga people, who are settled in neighboring municipalities, the Kamentza share territory, culture, and a struggle for identity and survival. In 2014, 6,029 Kamentza people lived in the municipality of Sibundoy, distributed as 1,476 families, comprising 58% of the total Kamentza population, as well as 42% of the municipality's population (Life Plan, 2015). Their self-government is recognized by the Colombian government through the concession of their own councils of Indigenous Traditional Authorities. These councils are the legal representatives and governmental authorities dealing with the affairs of each city or town.

The Kamentza people survived genocide and have suffered various forms of loss of land and displacement over time. Historically, while the colonization of their territory began later than in other parts of Colombia, because of its strategic location it has served as a corridor for different goods, resources, and the transit of peoples from other parts of the country, conquistadors, missionaries, encomenderos,[2] settlers, merchants, and groups outside the law have taken away their lives and lands and disrupted their way of life. They were systematically stripped of their physical and symbolic territory, and other forms of life have been violently imposed since the arrival of the catholic missions in 1542. According to Santos Jamioy, the oral history of the Kamentza documents how community members abandoned their customs, traditions, language, and beliefs to survive. Others chose to take their own lives, hoping to appease the violence to which the elders were subjected. Yet others chose to keep their culture hidden, or moved to distant places that were alien to the settler to preserve their identity and culture.

Augustinian, Dominican, Jesuit, Franciscan, and Capuchino priests stripped the Kamentza of their best lands to build missions and schools. Overall, the strategies used by the Spanish were those of punishment, forced labor, public mockery, excommunication, and exile (Bonilla, 2006). Initially, the Kamentza community resisted colonization from education; there are records of resistance indicating that when the first school in Sibundoy opened around 1902, it did not have students: "It opened with only one student after many announcements and notifications to the parents" (Bonilla, 2006, p. 72). The parents hid their children to prevent them from attending the catholic school and chose to take them to work while doing their daily chores. Later the colonizing establishment used law enforcers to persecute the families and force them to send their children to school. Even in the 1970s when Jamioy attended the local Marista school, he was forbidden from speaking Kamentza and severely punished when he did so. As a child, his own family taught him the Kamentza language, but discouraged him from using it in public spaces after he began elementary school. According to Avila (2004), today, 60% of the population is fluent in the Kamentza language; a smaller group (40%) is able to speak both the formal and informal forms of the language; 20% of the community is able to understand the language, and 20% has no knowledge of it. Today there are different educational spaces such as a Kamentza nursery, a Kamentza/Spanish bilingual school, and Spanish speaking schools.

In the 16th century, the Kamentza fell prey to the consequences of the gold rush and were infected by diseases, such as smallpox, which together with forced labor created a humanitarian crisis that caused their population to decline. According to Córdoba (1982), in 1558 there were 9,000 inhabitants in the valley; in 1582 the population declined to 1,600 inhabitants, and by 1691 there were only 150 survivors in the community. At the end of the 17th century, when the mines were closed and the exploitation of gold moved to the Pacific coast of the country, the region fell into a kind of isolation from the colonial regime and communities slowly began to recover their population and their ancestral traditions (Gómez López, 2005). However, between 1879 and 1912 the rubber rush in the Amazon brought another wave of indentured labor, disease, and hardship. The decline of the rubber rush allowed isolation again and the recovery of the population. In the 1960s Americans arrived in the region through the Alliance for Progress, the Peace Corps, and the Summer Institute of Linguistics. According to Barrera (2011), their presence impacted the local production of arts and crafts, making their products commodities for sale. The artisans were asked to introduce designs suggested by the foreigners and to produce larger quantities of a similar product for commercial purposes that encouraged the adoption of capitalism as a way of living. This generated a loss of the symbols that narrated their local beliefs and stories. In her research on the resistance of the Kamentza to colonization, Barrera (2011) states that while they responded with submission to the decisions of these external actors, they also resisted by slowly neutralizing and erasing designs suggested by the foreigners. Over time, they reclaimed their own designs and brought them back into their arts and crafts.

During the 1980s and 1990s, with the beginning of oil exploitation, the massive arrival of peasants displaced from other parts of Colombia, the proliferation of coca crops, and the presence of guerrillas, paramilitaries and the military brought other forms of disruption and violence to the region. Like many other indigenous groups in Colombia, the Kamentza were in the midst of a violent conflict that was not theirs but that impacted their lives and resources (Gonzalez, 1989; Medina & Tellez, 1994). In the last 20 years the arrival of Colombians and Venezuelans has increased the interdependence of the Colombian urban centers and the countryside; the use of land for cattle raising, meat, and milk production; and extensive bean, tomato, and fruit crops, with high use of agrotoxics (Preciado Beltran, 2003). The traditional farm that fed the community with a diversity of products has been fragmented by the newcomers and their business, impacting the traditional nutritional practices of the Kamentza. In addition, biopiracy has become a tremendous concern, as Spaniards are back looting the Kamentza's plants and knowledge of medicinal plants through business deals with the Colombian government (Jacanamejoy, 2015).

The Interstices of the Kamentza's Resilience: Territory, Ritual, Medicine, and Communal Ways of Living

The continued existence of the Kamentza on this planet is itself an act of resilience. They have faced ongoing structural violence characterized by a systematic effort to take their lands, turn them into indentured labor, kill them through biological warfare, and disrupt the reproduction of their cultural knowledge and traditions across generations by religious suppression and cultural persecution. They have been forced to deal with immediate threats to their survival, as well as the prolonged challenges posed by capitalism and colonization. Notwithstanding the Kamentza's ability to survive, adapt, and generate hybrid spaces has been key to their survival. The Kamentza have affirmed their existence between the Andean and Amazonian worlds while negotiating, fending off and managing the presence of colonizers, the displaced peoples and the newcomers looking for a place to settle have been key to the survival of the Kamentza. For example, the town of Sibundoy was designed with a central square in which a catholic church and school take two sides, and homes and businesses take the other two sides following designs of colonial architecture. In the 1950s, the Kamentza acquired a property near the square's corner as a site for their own house of government, and in the 2000s they negotiated with the major's office for the presence of their culture in the central park of Sibundoy's square; they sculpted the trees with their ancestral art and created additional monuments symbolizing their community's presence and healing traditions. Their world view and spirituality are now standing next to the religion imposed through colonization. Today, the square itself is a testament to the presence, albeit unequal, and co-existence of the Kamentza, the catholic church, and the Colombian settlers.

The Kamentza people call their ancestral territory "Tabanok," a place of departure, arrival, and return. In their view, their birth is linked with the womb of the earth as a living being. Another symbol of their adaptation while retaining their traditions involves the ritual of "shinÿak." This ritual signals the connection of humans with the earth when the placenta and umbilical cord of the newborn is buried next to a stone, or "shachekbé." It also signals that all beings return to the earth and will continue the legacy of the elders relative to work with the land, home building, craft and art making, and the interpretation of nature, dreams, and the cycles of life. In their view, the continuation of these practices is what makes them Kamentza. They see themselves as beings from this territory which they describe as "kamuentsá yentsá, Kamëntšá biya" (people from here with their own thinking and their own language; an education project owned by the Kamentza, 2013). Their resilience is first collective and anchored in the negotiation of identity, land, government, and ways of life, affirmed by their belief systems, self-organization, and problem-solving within the community and with outsiders. Walsh's (2016) view, that relational resilience involves organizational patterns, communication and problem-solving processes, community, resources, and affirming belief systems, only applies if the ecological context of colonization and coloniality is seen as interacting and shaping people's survival and well-being. Only then can their community narrative have coherence, and they will be able to make meaning of their existence.

The Kamentza's struggle for their territory is key to understanding that their pathways to resilience are intrinsically tied to their relationship with the land. According to the Kamentza Life Plan (2015), around the 1700s Inga—another and Kamentza community leaders Carlos Tamabioy (Inga) and Leandro Agreda (Kamentza) "bought" some of their lands back from the Spanish crown for 400 pieces of gold. The territory in question included their ancestral lands in the Sibundoy valley. The community government possesses documents that attest to this deal and provide further proof that since the 1940s both the Colombian State and the catholic church accepted that the lands belonged to these communities. While today the Kamentza have a protected territory within Colombia, the struggle for their ancestral lands is ongoing and essential to their autonomous existence, their decision-making, and the survival of the system of relationships that are created and recreated between them and their environment. Their relationship with the land conditions and transforms the human experience of reality; it frames and structures it. For example, the jajañ or chagra (the farm), involves relationships with plants, including the interactions between medicinal plants, humans, and animals. The Kamentza's knowledge and relationship with their lands are valuable hubs of practice in which indigenous peoples apply and produce knowledge related to the ecological dynamics of their land. According to Fonseca-Cepeda, Idrobo, and Restrepo (2019), a vast body of ecological knowledge is contained in the relationship with the chagra. For example, knowledge related to careful selection of plots, accurate recognition of light intensity, soil nutrients, and diverse vegetation strata evolves in this relationship. Knowledge and management of multiple components of the environment over time and space in chagras make up a cyclical process of intervention that assures continuous and sustainable production of food and the regeneration of the land. Chagras support both the material and the spiritual existence of the community in spaces demarcated by the relationship with the ecological system. According to Santos Jamioy (2019), younger Kamentza generations, like other indigenous groups in the area, move between chagra and school. Borderland spaces are generated as academic knowledge from the colonizers and agricultural wisdom from their elders is utilized. The information gained through formal education and the combination of different knowledge systems has the potential to promote unique pathways for adaptation.

The Kamentza's relationship with time, like their relationship with land, also reflects the experiences of their community and of the quality of their collective lives lived together. While they conceive time as cyclical in some aspects (e.g., agriculture, rituals), there four grand times that mark their relationship with colonization and coloniality: (i) Kaca temp, or time of darkness, mythological entities, and extraordinary occurrences relative to their initial origin; (ii) Kabengbe temp, or time of cultural flourishing and development of the community with its own ways of governance, cultural traditions, and healing practices; (iii) Squenegbe temp, or arrival of the colonizers, a time marked by physical, emotional, and spiritual violence; and (iv) Shenetsa temp, or time of scarcity when all cultures and communities inhabited the lands and had to agree on how to share and survive over time. This general marking of times shows how the Kamentza have organized their world and maintained a sense of coherence (a factor in their resilience) out of the experience of coloniality.

Today, life is marked by risks and possibilities that the Kamentza have to navigate while negotiating their relationships with hostile environments that undermine their efforts via capitalism, expert institutions, a repressive government, and dualist rationalities perpetrated by a larger dominant culture that pushes capitalism and individualism. Bolivian scholars such as Zavaleta (1990), Rivera Cusicanqui (2014), and Tapias Mealla (2002) capture what resilience looks like in these contexts. Pathways to resilience (Wright & Masten, 2015) here involve communities' existence in spaces where there is a disarticulated superimposition of various types of societies, implying various historical times, modes of production, languages, and forms of government, among other factors. In these spaces, communities have developed a capacity to define their own ways of coexisting with modernity, with more conviviality and less competition because of the weaving of indigenous practices with those brought in by outsiders. Some of these spaces have been generated by community work systems based on "jenabuatemban" (lend a hand, accompany and teach each other at work) that preserve the collective character of activities essential to the reproduction of the communal life and "mengay," a community gathering to work on a specific activity targeting communal involvement in harvesting, construction of homes and places for rituals, and preparations for annual community rituals and festivities such as the "Bëtsknaté" (Big Day). Escobar (2018) explains that each communal way of coming together:

> Can be understood only in its relation with the noncomunal exterior; that is the outside spiral: it begins with an external imposition, which unleashes, or not, an internal resistance, and develops into adaptation. This results in lo propio (what is one's own) and the We. (p. 178)

Escobar (2018) cites Oaxacan activist Arturo Guerrero to explain the meaning of making community as an opening to all beings and all forces:

> Because even if the We comes about in the actions of concrete women, men and children, in that same movement, all that is visible and invisible below and on the Land also participates, following the principle of complementarity, among all that is different. The communal is not a set of things, but an integral fluidity. (p. 177)

This intimate connection between the Kamentza and the Land has supported a rich legacy of traditional healing practices involving plant medicine. Jamioy explains that his people hold the view that since the beginning of the human experience, plants have played a role in the evolution of humans, in the provision of food and medicine, and in spiritual experiences and the development of consciousness. For the Kamentza shamans, it was the plants themselves that taught humans how to heal and know their souls. The plants that are central to their culture are used in medicine, religious ceremonies, and rites of passage.

Traditions relative to the relationship with the plant and its curative uses survived within the secret spaces of family homes. Yajé, for example, is a tea made from the vine *Banisteriopsis caapi* and the leaves of the chacruna (*Psychotria viridis*) or chagrapanga (*Banisteriopsis rusbyana*) plants; it is a potent visionary mixture that alters human consciousness and opens the person who drinks it to the experience of other emotions, thoughts, and worlds. The Kamentza and other indigenous peoples believe that a yajé purge releases "spiritual poisons" that can lead to physical illness. By clearing out the system physically and spiritually, the purge restores balance to the soul and empowers the body to fight against disease. This healing practice seems in line with an understanding of human cognition as embodied beyond the head and extending throughout and beyond the living body to encompass the world outside of the organism's physiological boundaries and as emerging through self-organized processes that span and interconnect the brain, body, and environment in reciprocal loops of causation. The curative aspects of this tradition involve personal consciousness as intricately related to neural and somatic activity (Varela et al., 2016). Despite all this, the catholic Church made every possible effort to destroy the Kamentza's healing traditions, shamans, and shamanic rituals (Musalem Nazar, 2017). The survival and thriving of plant knowledge and healing practices amongst the peoples of the Amazon Basin and among the Kamentza is another illustration of how a world view in which plants and humans coexist and collaborate with each other generates borderland spaces and bolsters resilience. In fact, today these practices are protected by the Colombian government and their survival has been symbolized in the monuments erected in the municipal square right in front of the catholic church.

The relationships that the Kamentza in the Andes and other indigenous peoples had in the Amazon Basin with yajé and other plants were almost certainly well-established before the arrival of Europeans in Abya Yala (Wade, 2007). Indigenous peoples believe that the medicinal work they do with yajé goes back to the earliest human inhabitants of the region. Yajé, along with many other medicinal plants, gradually became integrated into the ethnomedical traditions of the mestizo populations through colonization. Adults, young people, and children are integrated into the yagé rituals, which are directed by the "tatšëmbuá," "maestro," "taita," or "curandero," who must have learned for many years next to a teacher and who have a special recognition within the community for their healing arts and communication with the spirits of the jungle. Unlike what has happened in other places in the Amazon, where yagé is known as ayahuasca and where its traditional use has been lost or christianized, among the Kamentza it is part of a medicinal and spiritual practice in which the healer makes use of plants from the chagra that he/she knows and takes care of (Life Plan, 2015). Thus, the circulation of knowledge of life is enacted through a series of practices involving knowledge, sacred sites, seeds, rituals, and customary law. In this context, resilience is both process and outcome resulting from the interweaving of a sophisticated relationship with plants in which the human capacity to perceive the world through sensory capacities developed over evolutionary time have been extended to allow for an ongoing capacity to give rise to other ways to exist in the world (Harrod Buhner, 2014). The example of yajé also demonstrates how community healing practices that promote physical, psychological, and spiritual resilience are closely tied to institutionalized government laws and practices, the codification of morality through religious doctrine (and its oppression of subordinated cultures), and many other social, political, and religious systems that work for or against the promotion of the well-being of indigenous peoples.

In addition to diverse and multiple healing practices that we do not have space to discuss here, the Kamentza have been able to preserve key festivities that encapsulate their identity and history such as the Clestrinye/Cabenge Bëtsknaté. According to Jamioy, Cabenge Bëtsknaté means our Big Day in relation to our surroundings. It marks the end of one span of time and the germination of another; a form of cyclical temporality, based on the restitution of the natural life forces. It is an organized ritual in which specific music, dances, and songs are prepared. Ironically, the festival begins the Monday before the christian holiday of Ash Wednesday and ends on Ash Wednesday. However, preparations and cleanup begin earlier and end later. This carnival is a call from the traditional authorities to re-encounter and to reconcile; it begins within the space of families and moves outside to the larger community and the traditional authorities to the public space. It is a way in which the Kamentza demonstrate their existence as a people and their culture in spite of the past genocide (Jaramillo Guerrero & Davila Zambrano, 2013).

Ontological Resilience

From the standpoint of the Kamentza, the survival and affirmation of their people, way of life, and territory is about being, that is, existing, and re-existing in a relational world in which every being exists because all others exist. The historical expropriation of their territories and the current occupation and continued looting is both material and ontological. Its ontological dimension involves the pressure of individualism, expert knowledge, and a capitalist economy. One strategy for responding to the pressures of the Colombian state, foreign corporations, and globalization has been to develop a place-based Life Plan (Life Plan, 2015) centered in the recovery of their territory, as this is the collective space for existence in which traditions are kept alive. During the last 10 years the Kamentza developed a formal vision for their community, to be disseminated within and outside of the community and to be used as a guide in their own voice. Their Life Plan is a narrative that makes sense of their predicament; it maps possibilities for adaptation and a positive vision for the community. Kirmayer et al. (2011) speaks of narrative resilience as having a collective dimension:

> Maintained by the circulation of stories invested with cultural power and authority, which the individual and groups can use to articulate and assert their identity, arraign core values and attitudes needed to face challenges, and generate creative solutions to new predicaments. (p. 86)

The Life Plan is a narrative affirming the existence of a place-based and communal weave of life.

According to Jacanamejoy (Life Plan, 2015), this life vision is about re-existing, that is, challenging and coping with various ways in which the dominant culture affects the Kamentza while maintaining a way of life that is differentiated from the dominant culture.

It is about sustaining their social, political, cultural, and economic fabric. The community's vision is called "Benge luarents sboachanak mochtaboashents juabin, nemoria and beyan," which means "Let's plant with strength and hope the thought, memory and language in our territory." It seeks through legal and practical efforts to protect their lands, sources of food, and traditional knowledge of ancestral agriculture, education, culture, and artistic and spiritual knowledge and practices.

This vision for the community was created with a methodology faithful to their ways of constructing knowledge, "Jenebtbiaman y Jenoyeunayam," in which community held discussions and generated consensus and decisions, going back to their beginning as a people and through their connection with their territory. This is an example of what Tuhiwai Smith (2012) calls decolonizing methodology; for the Kamentza, it involves the following processes of knowledge building and decision-making:

> 1) JENOJUABOYAN: devising, thinking, organizing, planning, and identifying needs, opportunities and actions; 2) JOTSANAN: taking the step, getting closer to where perspectives and experiences can begin to connect; 3) JENCHUAYAN: the respectful greeting that acknowledges the previous dialogic encounters; 4) JOBJAN or JENOBJAN: attention, invitation to enter, to share; 5) JENEBTBIAMAN: the dialogic encounter where children, youth, and adults have the opportunity to share their knowledge, and experiences; 6) JOUENAN, JOYEUNAYAN: the process of listening to each other, responding spontaneously, and understanding; Jouenan refers not only the human word but also communication between all living beings (plants, animals, rivers, etc.); JOYEUNAYAN: listening with all the senses, sitting with what is heard, and digesting it; 7) JENANJAN: providing food; 8) JENJUAN: allowing conversation on topics where there isn't agreement or disagreement; it is a process that results from spontaneous and ongoing conversation in which the words are heard, interpreted, and reinterpreted in the light of experience, feeling, history, and tradition; 9) JENOYEUNAYAM: agreement between the parties through dialogue outside of the binary good/bad; 10) JTISENOBJAN: the spirit of creating a space and invitation to future dialogue; 11) JTOCHUAYAN: appreciation for the opportunity to share the word (Jacanamejoy, 2015, p. 30).

This methodology gives new meaning to Bakhtin's (1990) understanding of dialogue as a discourse that allows for, encourages, recognizes the appropriation and adaptation of other voices, and is characterized by a polyphony of voices. Here, the act of speaking, naming or articulating one's experience with words is intimately connected with the flow of emotions and experience as the basis for the recursive coordination of behavior. It also shows the self-other co-determination that Varela, Thompson, and Rosh (2016) explain as resulting from open boundaries that exist at all levels through ongoing, dynamic interaction in which self and other create one another at the most fundamental levels.

According to Masten (2011), Theron and Liebenberg (2015), and Ungar (2018), in examining resilience in contexts of high exposure to stress, the impact of social policies, community supports, schools, and families counts more than individual biology or temperament in psychosocial outcomes. Canadian scholars (Kirmayer et al., 2011) proposed a social-ecological view of resilience to address the distinctive cultures, geographic and social settings, and histories of adversity of indigenous peoples. They identified the following processes of resilience: regulating emotion and supporting adaptation through relational, ecocentric, and cosmocentric concepts of self and personhood; revisioning collective history in ways that valorize collective identity; revitalizing language and culture as resources for narrative self-fashioning, social positioning, and healing; and renewing individual and collective agency through political activism, empowerment, and reconciliation. Fikret and Ross (2012), for example, proposed addressing resilience as a systems concept dealing with adaptive relationships and learning in social-ecological systems across nested levels and as a process whereby community strengths are identified and fostered in indigenous communities. In cultural studies, Mohanty (2003) speaks of similar processes in which the sources of connection, support, liberatory meaning-making, and change stem from creating, recreating, and maintaining community. However, she considers these processes to be forms of resistance that are not always identifiable through organized movements and that are encoded in practices of remembering, alternative forms of family life, and in writings such as testimonials. Feminist queer Chicana scholar Pérez (1999, 2003) speaks of the decolonial imaginary as a space in between, where systems of domination are negotiated, a space to inhabit and hold while at the same time challenging those systems. Pérez (1999) explains that social positioning should not be read as a binary, describing, on one end, oppression and victimization and on the other privilege and perpetration. She insists that multiple social positions are always at work, and this creates a liminal identity in which "one negotiates within the imaginary to a decolonizing otherness where all identities are at work in one way or another" (p. 7). However, this position needs to go further to acknowledge and articulate the standpoints of nature and other beings. It is a human articulation of course, but it can express a standpoint from which humans are not the center of the planet but only a component in relationship with everyone and everything else.

Given this standpoint, specific initiatives have been developed within the Kamentza community targeting actions within and outside their territory that can lend themselves to expansion and increased sophistication for the benefit of the community involved. For example, a youth project in which there is a continuous and coordinated set of activities that foster learning, valuing, and affirming material and spiritual connections with the land through film clubs, recreational activities, reading rooms, rituals, and dance and music groups. Jamioy explains that field trips involve observation and dialogue about how their land and livelihood have been negatively impacted and how they can keep and strengthen them by developing a sense of self, belonging, and connection with other beings. These initiatives engage the youth in accompanying the elders such as Taitas and government leaders into negotiations and mobilizations relative to the rights of their people. Reading and conversation with adults designated by the community emphasize recovering the memory of their wisdom and customs. At the same time, the ongoing fight for their territory is the most important site of resilience, as this territory is the living container for life interconnected with all beings:

> For us, the territory goes beyond the occupation itself. That is, if the land with all its life is there, if the earth is there, intact and natural, that is also territory for us. Let it

be there, let no one touch it, if the water is there, let it be there. That if the mountains are there, without being inhabited, if there is not bean cultivated there, corn, whatever, but they are there. Because there, life is being guaranteed. It is as if we were saving for ourselves, for our children. But if that land is paved then it would no longer make sense and it would lose all that spiritual value. . . . For us that has been taught to us by our elders, that is, the fact that you are stepping on the earth, that is more valuable, the direct contact with mother watsana is more important. (Jacanamejoy, 2015, p. 35)

Conclusion

If we think of resilience from the practices of subaltern groups, we have to acknowledge and validate the legacies of colonization and the struggle to keep alive and expand borderland spaces where ontological resilience is at stake today. This involves moving away from purely internal cognitive processes to account for the complexity of environmental influences within models that integrate the impact of colonization, coloniality, and the interstices where resilience dwells. For the Kamentza, this means support from the international community and the academy in recovering and protecting their ancestral lands from private hands and the Colombian government; and an active stance to protect their territory from international corporations mining and destroying their sources of water, and looting their traditional knowledge of medicinal plants; material support to sustain and expand the learning of the Kamentza language and the bilingual and intercultural schools that center their ways of life while addressing how to understand, interact, and negotiate with Colombians and the foreigners who visit and settle in the area and initiatives that generate economic pathways to sustain well-being in relation to the modern world.

Research initiatives should be based in decolonizing methodologies (Glidden, 2011; Kovach, 2010; Tuhiwai Smith, 2012) that claim, reclaim, and name a relational sense of self inclusive of land and all other living beings, testimonials to bring in the memories of their pathways to resilience throughout history, storytelling, and narrative (Denborough, 2014; Jupp, Berumen, & O'Donald, 2018; Polanco, 2011). These projects are key to addressing resilience from the ways in which people narrate their lives, making sense of their own predicaments and mapping possibilities and visions for being. However, they must be integrated with actions involving processes of indigenizing, revitalizing, restoring, and protecting in concrete material ways the lands, homes, schools, native agriculture, and local economy. Resilience scholars can play an important role in calling for the mobilization of accountability from the dwellers of the modern world to take responsibility and extend their respectful support for a way of life to be solely determined by the Kamentza people (Reynolds, 2013).

Key Messages

1. Resilience is local and specific to the intricacies of systems of living of indigenous peoples.
2. An explicit epistemological point of departure is key to understanding the complexities of resilience processes in an ethical and socially just manner that addresses legacies of colonization and conditions of coloniality for indigenous peoples.

3. Understanding resilience in contexts of exposure to significant adversity involves examining the processes by which communities struggle, adapt, and navigate their way to a state of well-being and how they negotiate, recreate, and affirm their way of life.
4. Decolonizing methodologies should be integrated in the study of resilience to address larger context issues that shape people's ability to survive and thrive.
5. Resilience processes must be anchored in the multiple subjectivities of those who face adversities; embodied voices must be part of the meaning making process, along with access and opportunity for collective coping and an outlook open to possibilities.

Notes

1. This term usually refers to people of mixed racial or ethnic ancestry, especially, in Latin America, of mixed Indigenous and European descent.
2. "As legally defined in 1503, an *encomienda* ("'to entrust'") consisted of a grant by the crown to a conquistador, soldier, or official of a specified number of Indians living in a particular area. The encomendero extracted tribute from the Indians in gold, in kind, or in labor and was required to protect them and instruct them in the christian faith. The *encomienda* did not include a grant of land, but in practice the *encomenderos* gained control of the Indians' lands and failed to fulfill their obligations to the Indian population" (*Encyclopedia Britannica*, 2019).

References

Anzaldúa, G. (1987). *Borderlands/la frontera: The new mestiza* (2nd ed.). San Francisco, CA: Aunt Lute Books.

Avila, M. (2004). Una Mirada a la vitalidad de la lengua indigena Kamentza a través de la descripcion sociolinguistica [A view of the vitality of the Indigenous Kamentza language through sociolinguist description]. *Forma y Function*, *17*, 34–56.

Bakhtin, M. M. (1990). *Art and answerability*. Austin: University of Texas Press.

Barrera, G. E. (2011). Campos de poder artesanales [Craft power fields]. *Apuntes*, *24*(2), 178–195.

Beltran Preciado, J. (2003). Territorio, colonización y diversidad cultural en el alto Putumayo [Territory, colonization and cultural diversity in the high Putumayo]. *Colombia Forestal*, *8*(16), 110–120.

Bonilla, V. D. (2006). *Siervos de Dios y amos de indios. El estado y la misión capuchina en el Putumayo* [Serfs of God and masters of Indians. The estate and Capuchino misión in Putumayo]. Bogotá, Colombia: Tercer Mundo.

Consejo Mundial de Pueblos Indígenas. (1977). *Mensaje aniversario* [Anniversary message]. Retrieved from http://servicioskoinonia.org/agenda/archivo/obra.php?ncodigo=125

Córdoba, A. (1982). *Historia de los Kamsá de Sibundoy:desde sus orígenes hasta 1981* [History of the Kamsa of Sibundoy: From their origins to 1981]. Bogotá, Spain: Pontificia Universidad Javeriana. Facultad de Ciencias Sociales. Departamento de Historia y Geografía.

De Sousa Santos, B. (2012). *Una Epistemología del Sur: La reinvención del conocimiento y la emancipación social* [An epistemology of the South: The reinvention of knowledge and social emancipation]. Buenos Aires, Argentina: Siglo XXI Editores.

Deloria, V. (2006). *The world we used to live in*. Golden, CO: Fulcrum.

Denborough, D. (2014). *Retelling the stories of our lives. Everyday narrative therapy to draw inspiration and transformation experience*. New York, NY: W. W. Norton.

Education project owned by the Kamentza [Proyecto de educación propia del Pueblo Kamëntsá. Sibundoy Putumayo]. (2013). Unpublished document, Sibundoy Putumayo.

Encyclopedia Britannica. (2019). Encomienda. Retrieved from www.britannica.com/topic/encomienda#ref45100
Escobar, A. (2008). *Territories of difference: Place, movements, life, redes.* Durham, NC: Duke University Press.
Escobar, A. (2018). *Designs for the pluriverse.* Durham, NC: Duke University Press.
Fikret, B., & Ross, H. (2012). Community resilience: Toward an integrated approach. *Society and Natural Resources: An International Journal, 26*(1), 90–115.
Fonseca-Cepeda, V., Idrobo, C. J., & Restrepo, S. (2019). The changing chagras: Traditional ecological knowledge transformations in the Colombian Amazon. *Ecology and Society 24*(1), 8. doi:10.5751/ES-10416-240108
Glidden, L. M. (2011). *Mobilizing ethnic identity in the Andes.* Lanham, MD: Lexington Books.
Gómez López, A. J. (2005). El Valle de Sibundoy: El despojo de una heredad. Los dispositivos ideológicos, disciplinarios y morales de dominación [The Sibundoy valley: The dispossession of an inheritance. The ideological, disciplinary and moral devices of domination]. *Anuario Colombiano de Historia Social y de la Cultura, 32*, 51–73.
Gonzalez, J. J. (1989). *Geopolítica de la violencia* [Geopolitics of the violence]. *Analísis Politíco, 2,* 43–47.
Grosfoguel, R. (2005). Decolonial approach to political economy: Transmodernity, border thinking and global coloniality. *Kult, 6,* 10–29.
Harrod Buhner, S. (2014). *Plant intelligence and the imaginal realm.* Rochester, VT: Bear & Company.
Jacanamejoy, J. (2015). *Plan de vida. Kamentza life plan.* Retrieved from https://porlatierra.org/docs/5ce7a92094c2b423b80b430d846b23a4.pdf
Jaramillo Guerrero, J., & Davila Zambrano, L. (2013). *Esteticas convergentes. Sincretismo cultural en el Becsnate Kamentza de Sibundoy Putumayo* (Master's thesis). Universidad de Narino, Colombia.
Jupp, J. C., Berumen, F.C., & O'Donald, K. (2018). Advancing Latino testimonio traditions in educational research: A synoptic rendering. *Journal of Latinos and Education, 17*(1), 18–37. doi:10.1080/15348431.2016.1270212
Kirmayer, L. J., Dandeneau, S., Marshall, E., Phillips, M. K., & Williamson, K. J. (2011). Rethinking resilience from indigenous perspectives. *La Revue Canadienne de Psychiatrie, 56*(2), 84–91.
Kovach, M. (2010). *Indigenous methodologies. Characteristics, conversations, and contexts.* Toronto, ON: University of Toronto Press.
Life Plan. (2015). *Kamentza life plan.* Retrieved from https://porlatierra.org/docs/5ce7a92094c2b423b80b430d846b23a4.pdf
Lionnet, F., & Shih, S. (2005). *Minor transnationalism.* Durham, NC: Duke University Press.
Mann, C. (2005). *1491: New revelations of the Americas before Columbus.* New York, NY: Vintage Books.
Masten, A. S. (2011). Resilience in children threatened by extreme adversity: Frameworks for research, practice, and translational synergy. *Development and Psychopathology, 23*(2), 493–506.
Maturana, H., & Varela, F. (1980). *Autopoiesis and cognition: The realization of the living.* Boston, MA: Reidel.
Maturana, H., & Varela, F. (1987). *The Tree of Knowledge: The biological roots of human understanding.* Boston, MA: Shambhala/New Science Press.
Medina, C., & Tellez, M. (1994). La violencia parainstitucional en Colombia [The parainstitutional violence in Colombia]. Bogotá, Spain: Rodriguez Quito Editores.
Mendenhall, E., & Wooyoung, A. (2019). How to fail a scale: Reflections on a failed attempt to assess resilience. *Culture, Medicine and Psychiatry, 43*(2), 315–325. doi:10.1007/s11013-018-9617-4
Mignolo, W. (2011). Geopolitics of sensing and knowing: On (de)coloniality, border thinking and epistemic disobedience. *Postcolonial Studies, 14*(3), 273–285.
Mignolo, W., & Walsh, C. (2018). *On decoloniality.* Durham, NC: Duke University Press.
Mohanty, S. (2003). *Feminism without borders.* Durham, NC: Duke University Press.
Musalem Nazar, P. (2017, June). *Redes indígenas del yagé: Historia y poder* [Yajé Indigenous networks: History and power]. Paper presented at the XVI Latin American Anthropological Association Congreso De la Asociación Latinoamericana de Antropologia, Bogotá, Colombia.
Perez, E. (1999). *The decolonial imaginary: Writing Chicanas into history.* Bloomberg: Indiana University Press.
Perez, E. (2003). Borderland queers: The challenges of excavating the invisible and unheard. *Frontiers: A Journal of Women's Studies, 22*(3), 122–131.

Polanco, M. (2011). Autoethnographic means to the end of decolonizing translation. *Journal of Systemic Therapies, 30*(3), 42–56. doi:10.1521/jsyt.2011.30.3.42

Preciado Beltran, J. (2003). Territorio, colonization y diversidad cultural en el Alto Putumayo. *Colombia Forestal, 8*(16), 108–128. doi:10.14483/udistrital.jour.colomb.for.2003.1.a09

Quijano, A. (2000). Coloniality of power, Eurocentrism, and Latin America. *Nepantla, 1*(3), 533–580.

Reynolds, V. (2013). "Leaning in" as imperfect allies in community work. *Conflict and Narrative: Explorations in Theory and Practice, 1*(1), 53–75.

Rivera Cusicanqui, S. (2014). *Hambre de huelga: Ch'iximacax Utxiwa y otros textos*. Queretaro, Mexico: La Mirada Salvaje.

Rivera Cusicanqui, S. (2014). *Oppressed but not defeated: Peasant struggles among the Aymara and Quechua in Bolivia*. United Nations Research Institute for Social Development.

Rocha Vivas, M. (2012). *Palabras mayores, palabras vivas* [Major words, words alive]. Buenos Aires, Argentina: Taurus.

Sharma, K. (2015). *Interdependence: Biology and beyond*. New York, NY: Fordham University.

Tapias Mealla, L. (2002). *La condición multisocietal: Multiculturalidad, pluralismo, modernidad* [The multisocietal condition: Multiculturalism, pluralism, modernity]. La Paz, Bolivia: Muela del Diablo Editores: CIDES-UMSA.

Theron, L., & Liebenberg, L. (2015). Understanding cultural contexts and their relationship to resilience processes. In L. C. Theron, L. Liebenberg, & M. Ungar (Eds.), *Youth resilience and culture: Commonalities and complexities* (pp. 23–36). New York, NY: Springer.

Tuhiwai Smith, L. (2012). *Decolonizing methodologies*. London, UK: Zed Books.

Ungar, M. (2011). The social ecology of resilience: Addressing contextual and cultural ambiguity of a nascent construct. *American Journal of Orthopsychiatry, 81*(1), 1–17.

Ungar, M. (2018). Systemic resilience: Principles and processes for a science of change in contexts of adversity. *Ecology and Society, 23*(4), 34. doi:10.5751/ES-10385-230434

Varela, F. J., Thompson, E., & Rosch, E. (2016). *The embodied mind: Cognitive science and human experience* (rev. ed.). Cambridge, MA: MIT Press.

Varela, F. J. (1979). *Principles of biological autonomy*. New York, NY: Elsevier.

Wade, D. (2007). Culture, anthropology, and sacred plants. In P. Harpignies (Ed.), *Visionary plant consciousness* (pp. 39–55). Rochester, VT: Park Street Press.

Walsh, F. (2016). Family resilience: A developmental framework. *European Journal of Developmental Psychology, 13*(3), 313–324. doi:10.1080/17405629.2016.1154035

Wright, M. O., & Masten, A. S. (2015). Pathways to resilience in context. In L. C. Theron, L. Liebenberg, & M. Ungar (Eds.), *Youth resilience and culture: Commonalities and complexities* (pp. 3–22). New York, NY: Springer.

Zavaleta, R. M. (1990). *Bolivia: Hoy*. Cochabamba, Bolivia: Amigos del Libro.

18

A Socioecological Developmental Systems Approach for the Study of Human Resilience

Ingrid Schoon

Introduction

Within a systems approach of human development, the notion of resilience generally describes the process of avoiding adverse outcomes or doing better than expected when confronted with major assaults on the developmental process (Luthar, Cicchetti, & Becker, 2000; Masten, 2016). It refers to the capacity to anticipate, adapt, and reorganize itself in the face of adversity enabling the maintenance of or return to effective functioning (Folke, 2016; Ungar, 2019). Resilience is understood as an interactive concept, which cannot be directly measured, but has to be inferred from individual variations in response to significant levels of stress or adversity. It can manifest in various ways, such as maintaining stable functioning (sustainability), recovery after an initial stress response (bouncing back), and adaption to or transformation of existing structures (Ungar, 2019). Although resilience is evident in individual behavior, it is not a personality characteristic. Without exposure to a risk there can be no evidence of resilience.

Resilience is a process, which emerges through the ongoing interactions between a developing individual and a changing context, reflecting the capacity to maintain or regain effective functioning in the face of adversity and constant change (Schoon, 2006, 2012). Which interactions are a likely catalyst for resilience depends on the nature of the adversity encountered, the level of response under study, the timing of their co-occurrence, and the wider context in which these interactions occur. For example, individuals might respond differently to exposure of distinct risks, such as the experience of parental divorce, depending on whether parents had been quarrelling a long time before breaking up, the length and intensity of exposure to these quarrels, the age at which the child witnessed the events, and the role of significant others in their lives, such as siblings, relatives or peers, as well as the wider sociocultural context (Amato, 2010).

As such, the study of resilience requires a socioecological and developmental systems approach, taking into account characteristics of the individual as well as characteristics of the individual's wider context, the processes of person–context interactions, their timing, and their development over time. The idea of socioecological developing systems is informed by theoretical biology and approaches to differentiate living from nonliving (or mechanical) matter. Living systems are understood as a unified whole (von Bertalanffy, 1968), where different levels of influence are interrelated and each characterized by self-activity and historicity. The aim of this chapter is to introduce a socioecological developmental systems approach for the study of human resilience, specifying the different layers of influence and their interactions over time and in context.

Resilience: A Multilevel, Relational, and Dynamic Process

The dynamics and interactions of a multisystemic model of resilience are depicted in Figure 18.1. The primary focus of the model is individual-level adjustment, which is shaped by individual characteristics as well as influences from within the family context, neighborhoods, social institutions, the wider sociohistorical context, and the natural environment. These layers define the "action field" in which individual development takes place (Heckhausen &

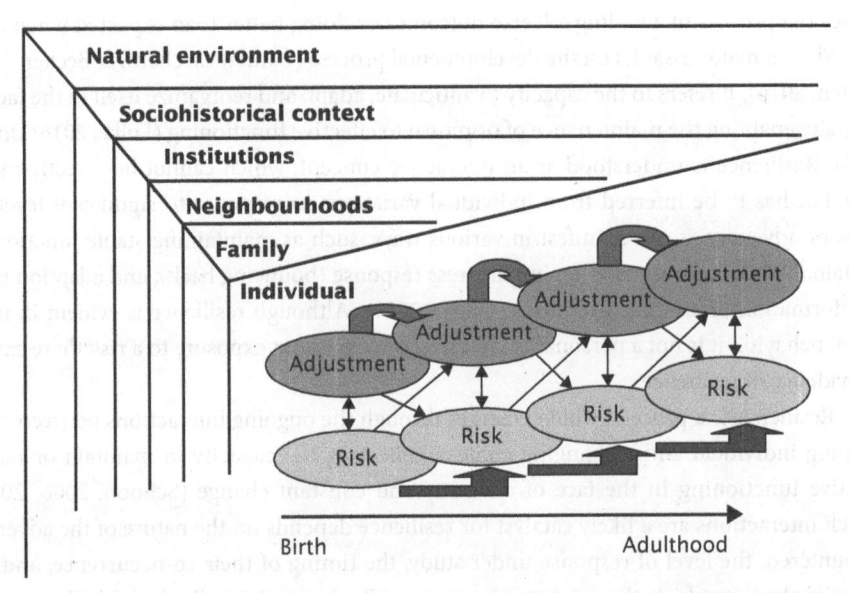

FIGURE 18.1 A socioecological developmental systems model of resilience. Adapted from Schoon (2006).

Buchmann, 2018). The model captures the transactional nature of development over time, focusing on the reciprocal interactions and feedback loops between risk experiences and individual adjustment over time and in context (Schoon, 2006).

Multiple Levels of Influence

Individual and context are understood as self-regulating, interdependent, and developing systems, where multiple levels of influence shape individual functioning and development. Each of the layers can be conceptualized as a system and further reduced to their component parts to get a proper understanding of a given system. For example, individual-level systems are composed of genetic, biological, cognitive, social, emotional, and motivational aspects. Social systems are characterized by different actors, organization, and institutions; shared norms and values; social roles and functions; and processes of interaction, regulation and control. Yet, the properties of each of these systems cannot be determined or explained by the sum of their component parts alone. Instead, the general system as a whole determines how the parts behave. For example, countries differ in their sociodemographic composition (such as the size or the age of the population) and the regulations of access to healthcare, child care, education, or housing. Focusing just on Europe (Esping-Anderson, 2002), social welfare in Scandinavian countries is orientated toward the individual, granting rights and benefits as universal entitlements. In many Anglo-Saxon countries (i.e. the United Kingdom, Ireland, or, for that matter, the United States) the social welfare state is based on the belief in the efficiency of the market and minimal state interference. In Southern European countries such as Spain, Italy, or Greece, a meager or nonexistent safety net (e.g., unemployment benefits), implies that the state shifts responsibility for support to the family and kinship networks who have to take a major role in protecting their members against economic and social risks. In contrast, the coordinated market economy in Germany and German-speaking countries (Austria, Switzerland) is characterized by major interventions into free market mechanisms, ensuring that families are protected against serious decline in living standards and that a family's social status is protected. These social structures shape the demands on individuals and their ability to respond to major shocks to the system, such as the experience of an economic downturn.

Studies comparing the experiences of young people coming of age in different countries in the aftermath of the 2008 Great Recession (Schoon & Bynner, 2017, 2019b) showed that young people in Southern Europe have been hit hardest by the recession, suffering the highest levels of youth unemployment (between 30 and 55%), while those in German-speaking countries were least affected. This was mostly due to the efficient use of vocational training programs, strong linkages between education and the labor market, and pre-existing economic conditions. These findings illustrate that individual behavior and action cannot be fully understood without consideration of the wider social and ecological context in which it is embedded and how individual and context are related (Schoon & Heckhausen, 2019). Patterns of adjustment vary depending on when and where one lives (e.g., in rural versus urban areas) in the northern or southern hemisphere or specific historical periods.

The socioecological and developmental systems approach for the study of human development presented here draws on theories from across disciplines, recognizing that complex problems, such as minimizing the impact of economic hardship and poverty and improving health, well-being, and attainment for all, require the input from different fields (Schoon, 2015; Schoon & Bynner, 2003). The systems approach is informed by social-ecological models (Bronfenbrenner, 1979; Bronfenbrenner & Morris, 2006) specifying interactions from genetic to wider sociocultural contexts; life-course models stressing the importance of time and timing and the wider sociohistorical context in which development takes place (Elder, 1998); the assumptions of human plasticity (Baltes, 1987; Lerner, 1984, 1996) and human agency (Bandura, 2006; Eccles & Wigfield, 2002; Heckhausen, Wrosch, & Schulz, 2010) specifying individual-level developmental processes and their interaction with a wider social context; and ecological theory (Folke, 2016; Preiser, Biggs, De Vos, & Folke, 2018) emphasizing the embeddedness of people, communities, economies, societies, and cultures in the biosphere. Bronfenbrenner's (1979) conceptualization of context differentiates between the proximal environment, which is directly experienced by the individual (e.g., as a lack of economic resources in the family context) and more distal cultural and social value systems that have an indirect effect on the individual, such as an economic slump, which is often mediated by experiences in the more proximal context, but can also have direct effects. Bronfenbrenner's model did not specify a layer referring to the natural environment, yet human development cannot be separated from the environmental context in which it takes place, the biosphere that sustains it (Folke, 2016). Without critical ecological resources such as clean air and safe drinking water individual lives cannot succeed.

The socioecological developmental systems approach integrates individual, social, and bioecological systems theories, recognizing that the nonreductionist analysis of individual behavior requires the simultaneous description of several spheres of influence, thereby moving beyond simple cause-and-effect explanations of behavior. For example, while young people in Germany have weathered the Great Recession quite well, there is a risk that they can become "locked" into a highly structured education system offering unequal learning opportunities and subsequent path-dependent career chances, which has shown to undermine individual agency, in particular, self-concepts (Chmielewski, Dumont, & Trautwein, 2013; Holtmann, Menze, & Solga, 2017; Marsh, Trautwein, Lüdtke, Baumert, & Koller, 2007). In contrast, in countries with more flexible and permeable transition systems, such as the United Kingdom or the United States, beneficial effects of high levels of agency are more readily manifest (Evans, 2002; Heckhausen & Chang, 2009), as are the risks of unstructured transitions pathways. There are thus no unidimensional answers to questions of how individuals respond to and adapt to changing conditions.

Co-Regulation

It is assumed that individuals and their environments are potentially malleable, whereby individuals actively shape their environment, which in turn influences them. Individual and context are understood to mutually constitute each other through processes of "co-regulation" (Sameroff, 2010; Schoon, 2012). The notion of co-regulation emphasizes the crucial role of regulation by others, which can include significant others, such as parents, peers, or teachers, as well as influences from other layers of the overall system (i.e., from institutions, the wider sociocultural and historical context, and the natural environment).

Moreover, it implies that individuals are not passively exposed to external influences but aim to gain control, to adapt and reorganize in the face of adversity, or to anticipate future goals to strive for. The goal-directedness of self-active systems, in turn, is historically situated in time and place, and comprises the adaption to and accommodation of, external conditions and internal needs at the same time (Schoon, 2006; Schoon & Heckhausen, 2019). For example, while 30 to 40 years ago the majority of young people (in the Western world) left education after the completion of secondary school (around age 16), over the past decades there has been a huge expansion of higher education institutions coupled with shifts in the occupational structure toward higher-qualified jobs and the use of new technologies (Schoon & Bynner, 2017, 2019b). These social changes exerted substantial pressure on young people to attain higher educational degrees, and nowadays most young people expect to go to university (Rosenbaum, 2011; Reynolds & Johnson, 2011), as do their parents (Schoon, 2010). Indeed parental support for higher education participation is a crucial factor, enabling young people (in particular those from less privileged background) to succeed in achieving their goal (Franceschelli, Schoon, & Evans, 2017; Mortimer, Zhang, Wu, Hussemann, & Johnson, 2017; Sacker, Schoon, & Bartley, 2002).

Timescales

Another important dimension of the socioecological developmental system is time and timing. Crucially, each of the different layers of the system change and interact on a range of timescales (Biggs et al., 2012), involving slow variables that determine the underlying structures and fast variables that respond to the conditions created by the slow variables. For example, social systems, such as legal or educational systems and shared traditions can be conceptualized as slow variables, while individual preferences and resulting actions can be understood as fast variables. The dynamics of the system typically arise from interactions and feedback loops between fast and slow variables. Resilience is a process of sustaining effective functioning in the face of adversity and constant change. Current experiences and level of functioning are influenced by prior experiences (the past) and anticipation of the future. Early experiences and the meaning attached to them are carried forward into subsequent situations. Early adjustment patterns influence later adjustment, and early risk experiences are linked to experience of risk at later life stages. Yet, lifelong development may also involve processes that do not originate at birth or early childhood, but are concurrent or emergent at later periods. For example, unexpected or nonnormative events, such as changes in family structure or death of a parent, or exposure to economic boom or bust, civic upheaval, war or ecological disaster can all cause a change in the conditions that impact human development for better or worse. Changes in conditions can be caused by catastrophic or sudden events as well as through gradual change, such as changes in the ecosphere.

In the following sections of this chapter I will provide broad definitions of key aspects of the interlinked systems and their interactions. These will be illustrated by examples of my own research on the factors and processes at different systemic levels that promote a smooth transition from dependent childhood to independent adulthood. The transition to independent adulthood is a key developmental task for young people, characterized by the assumption of new social roles and responsibilities against the background of increasing uncertainty and precarity. Young people have to navigate into unfamiliar territory, adjust to new challenges, and forge new pathways and responses to demands that are as yet unknown.

Positive Adaptation

There has been some controversy regarding the identification of positive adaptation. Adaptation can be assessed by focusing on the absence of deficits or psychopathology or through the study of competence or mastery in navigating crucial developmental tasks encountered at different life stages (Masten, 2014). Throughout the life course, the developing individual has to negotiate different developmental demands—such as learning to walk or talk during infancy, succeeding at school, establishing stable relationships, or accepting physical decline in old age. These tasks comprise processes of physical, cultural, and psychosocial maturation that represent benchmarks of adaptation in different domains and at specific developmental periods (Schoon, 2012; Ungar, Ghazinour, & Richter, 2013). Positive adaption has to be understood as a multidimensional construct, involving cultural-specific variations (Kirmayer, Dandeneau, Marshall, Phillips, & Williamson, 2011; Franceschelli et al., 2017).

Multidimensionality

Every developmental period has its own developmental challenges resulting from specific constellations of biological changes, role transitions, and common life events (Erikson, 1959; Heckhausen, 1999; Levinson, 1986). Coping adequately well with these changing developmental demands is considered to be a measure of adaptive functioning. It is now widely accepted that successful adaptation under adverse circumstances does not require extraordinary achievements or resources but results from "ordinary," normative functions such as cognitive resources, self-regulation, and access to social networks (Masten, 2014). In addition, a comprehensive understanding of positive adaption requires the recognition that human development occurs across multiple domains. For example, it is possible that a child experiencing socioeconomic hardship shows good academic performance and behavior adjustment, but at the same time develops emotional problems (Flouri et al., 2018; Schoon, 2006). Unless multiple domains of adjustment are assessed, only a partial picture of adaptation can be formulated. Adjustment in a particular domain cannot be assumed to generalize to other domains. Resilience is not an all-or-nothing phenomenon.

Culture-Specific Variations

Moreover, the criteria used to identify effective functioning are culturally determined and differ between social, developmental, and historical contexts (Kirmayer et al., 2011; Schoon, 2006, 2012, 2017; Ungar et al., 2013). For example, there are country-specific informal norms and expectations regarding appropriate behavior and adjustment, such as the consumption of alcohol or smoking or gendered stereotypes of behavior. Within countries, these norms can differ for different subgroups of the population, defined for instance by age, gender, social background, ethnicity, or religion. These norms also concern the timing of transitions, such as age at leaving school or becoming a parent, and are associated with positive or negative sanctions that can potentially influence individual attitudes and behaviors. Such social norms are however not universal, as subcultural norms might differ from the majority culture, and they can vary due to a changing sociohistoric context. For example, a study examining the socioemotional adjustment of three cohorts of Chinese elementary school children (assessed in 1990, 1998, and 2002) found that shyness was associated with social and academic achievement in 1990, while in 1998 the associations became weaker or nonsignificant (Chen, Cen, Li, & He, 2005). Furthermore, shyness was associated with peer rejection, school problems, and depression in 2002, illustrating the role of a changing social context. While shyness was positively associated with positive adaptation in the 1990s, in the aftermath of massive economic reforms and increasing marketization in China, shyness was associated with adjustment problems.

Furthermore, there are country-specific age-related formal (i.e., legal) norms regarding the completion of key transitions (such as age at school entry, leaving full-time education, entry into paid employment, or getting married). For example, as already mentioned, 30 years ago the majority of young people in the United Kingdom left school at compulsory minimum school leaving age (age 16) to enter full-time employment, while today nearly all 16-year-olds aspire to continue in further or higher education, although there are still variations by social background (Croll & Attwood, 2013; Schoon & Lyons-Amos, 2017). Normative, or on-time transitions, are culturally prepared by socialization and institutional arrangements and are understood to be psychologically salutary. Those who are "off-time" (too early or too late) are thought to be the target of negative social sanctions and to experience psychological strain (Heckhausen, 1999; Salmela-Aro, Kiuru, Nurmi, & Eerola, 2014; Sacker & Cable, 2010; Schulenberg & Schoon, 2012). Thus, the identification of positive adjustment is tied to normative expectations and judgments relating to particular outcomes. Given that these norms can vary for different subgroups in the population, a crucial issue in the identification of positive adjustment is the question, Resilience for whom? To avoid that certain values become reified, that the notion of resilience is abused to maintain the persistence of an existing status quo, researchers must specify the values and context-dependency of criteria underlying the identification of "successful" adjustment and evaluate their significance for representatives of different segments of society (Schoon, 2006, 2014, 2017).

Risk and Adversity

The notion of risk used in resilience research stems from epidemiological studies identifying expected probabilities of maladjustment (Cicchetti, 1993; Rutter, 2006). Risks can comprise genetic, biological, psychological, environmental, or socioeconomic factors that are associated with an increased likelihood of adjustment problems (Luthar & Cicchetti, 2000). Risks can stem from either within or from outside the individual system. They can comprise the genetic risk of a particular disorder, or external risks such as exposure to a natural disaster, the experience of a major economic recession, or death of a parent.

Risk factors do not exert their effect in isolation but interact with other influences—and very often risk begets risk, as expressed in the notion of cumulative adversity (Dannefer,

2003; Gutman et al., 2019; Schoon et al., 2002; Schoon & Melis, 2019). Vice versa, advantages and privileges also tend to cumulate, leading to conditions of increasing polarization and inequality. Risks tend to co-occur and to accumulate over the life course, and the relationship between any single risk factor and subsequent outcomes tends to be weak. Usually many variables are involved in determining an outcome, and serious risk emanates from the accumulation of risk effects (Rutter, 2012).

In my own research I focus on how individuals and families cope with exposure to socioeconomic hardship and adversity at key transition points, such as entry into school or the transition to the labor market. Indicators of adversity, such as the experience of income poverty, tend to co-occur with other risks such as low parental education, parental worklessness, family instability, poor housing, and area deprivation (Schoon, Cheng, Jones, & Maughan, 2013; Schoon, Jones, Cheng, & Maughan, 2012; Schoon & Melis, 2019). Each of these factors shows independent risk effects (i.e., each factor is associated with indicators of child adjustment). Moreover, each additional risk factor is associated with a decrease in effective functioning. Generally, the higher the number of risks, the higher the levels of adjustment problems (Duckworth & Schoon, 2012; Evans, Li, & Whipple, 2013; Ng-Knight & Schoon, 2017). For example, children born into less privileged families show lower levels of academic attainment (Pensiero & Schoon, 2019; Schoon, 2010, 2020), self-confidence and educational achievement motivation (Duckworth & Schoon, 2012; Schoon, 2014) than their more privileged peers; they are leaving education earlier and are less likely to continue in higher education (Schoon & Lyons-Amos, 2017). These associations can be amplified in times of a global economic downturn, such as the 2008 Great Recession (Schoon & Bynner, 2017, 2019b, b; Schoon & Lyons-Amos, 2016).

The findings furthermore suggest that there is heterogeneity in risk effects. For example, while poverty is most strongly associated with cognitive development, family disruption is a more salient risk factor for socioemotional adjustment (Schoon, 2020; Schoon, Hope, Ross, & Duckworth, 2010). To gain a more comprehensive understanding of risk effects, it is thus necessary to study more than one outcome. Moreover, it is necessary to not only examine cumulative risk exposure but also to examine constellations of risk (i.e., if economic risk is accompanied by family risk or mental health problems; Schoon & Melis, 2019).

In addition, the timing and duration of risk exposure matter. For example, risk effects appear to be strongest during the preschool and early school years (Schoon et al., 2002; Schoon, Sacker, & Bartley, 2003), although there can also be concurrent and latency effects (Gutman, Joshi, & Schoon, 2019). Concurrent risk effects imply that current exposure to risk can add to pre-existing pressures, while latency effects imply that risk effects do not manifest immediately, but occur at a later stage. Risk experiences in early childhood can set up a vicious cycle of cumulating disadvantage across domains, although this does not necessarily have to be the case (Gutman et al., 2019; Schoon, 2006, 2012). Generally, persistent risk exposure is associated with stronger adverse effects than short-term or intermittent risk (Schoon, 2020). There might however also be habituation, or so-called steeling effects (Rutter, 1987; Schoon, 2014), indicating that individuals and families can learn to cope with persistent risk exposure (if the risks are not overpowering). It might however also be the case that individuals show resilience at one particular time point but not at another, pointing to so-called sensitive or critical periods of development and the capacity for resilience can change over time.

Developmental Processes

Developmental adaptation can be considered as the progressive and mutual accommodation between a developing individual and the changing properties of the immediate and wider sociocultural and ecological context. Development comprises evolving states of being, where outcomes or consequences are themselves precursors to subsequent experiences and events (Bronfenbrenner, 1979). Within resilience research, current levels of adaptation are viewed as the product of past experiences, which, in turn can become predictors for future developmental outcomes. The assumption of such hierarchical integrative processes asserts consistency and coherence of individual development as it implies that future developmental outcomes can be predicted from knowledge of earlier adaptation patterns (Sroufe, 1979). For example, a child performing poorly in primary school is often expected to also manifest problems in later educational settings (Heckman, 2006). Yet, the very definition of resilience predicates changes in trajectories and deviation from predicted relationships. A longitudinal study of children with language problems at school entry showed that the majority of children with early receptive language problems develop into competent readers by age 10 (Parsons, Schoon, Rush, & Law, 2011). Factors promoting positive language development included parental support and, more important, a good school environment. It might also be possible, for example, that school performance had become disrupted due to the experience of a family trauma or parental divorce coinciding with school entry, only to return to "normal" levels of adjustment after some time. To capture such dynamics in adjustment, it is necessary to understand why certain individuals succeed and maintain positive functioning or return to "normal" behavior despite exposure to a significant adversity. What is needed is a model of development that takes into account both consistency and change. Key aspects of such a developmental model of resilience comprise nonlinearity, hierarchical integration and differentiation, and the time and timing of events.

Nonlinearity and Multidirectionality

Human development has been conceptualized by two contrasting positions, either describing development as a continuous growth process or as a discontinuous series of stages, where each stage requires a qualitative reorganization of the previous one (Gottlieb, 1992; Werner, 1957). While the continuous model assumes that development is predetermined from the outset, the discontinuous model recognizes the possibility of novel and emergent developmental patterns (Lerner, 1996). Both models have been used to describe the processes by which individual organisms develop from fertilization to adulthood. While some argue that the organism is preformed from the outset, persistent empirical evidence points to emergent properties through reciprocal interactions among all parts of the organism, including organism x environment co-actions. Within such an epigenetic, nonlinear, and staged model of development the emergence of new structures has been characterized as experience dependent (i.e., as based on the transactions between a developing individual and a changing context; Sameroff, 2010).

Developmental stages can be used as a descriptive concept, focusing attention on the average achievements at a particular age (Erikson, 1959; Levinson, 1986), or as a theoretical concept, conceptualizing a developmental stage as a period of stability of functioning following the transition from a structurally different period of stability (Sameroff, 2010). There are reasons to be weary of staged process models when they imply an invariant sequence. Evidence from previous research suggests substantial variations among persons or among subgroups in the population regarding the ordering, timing, and duration of adjustment to changing developmental tasks. For example, studies examining the transition from adolescence to independent adulthood show that young people do not move through life in tandem, but follow their own time table (Schoon, Chen, Kneale, & Jager, 2012; Schoon & Lyons-Amos, 2016, 2017). Some leave education directly after the completion of secondary school, while others continue in higher education before entering the labor market. Some combine work and study, others even work, study, and start a family of their own. This diversity in role combinations and associated social and economic resources, in turn, shape the context in which development and resilience are embedded. It is also of note, that what sometimes looks like self-generated stages of adjustment or coping may represent a sequence determined by external demands and constraints (Lazarus & Folkman, 1984). For example, early school leaving is often associated with lack in socioeconomic resources and the need to earn a living (Schoon & Duckworth, 2010), but also problems within the school context, mental health problems, or the need to escape an abusive home environment (De Witte, Cabus, Thyssen, Groot, & van den Brink, 2013).

In this regard, the notions of equifinality and multifinality, derived from systems theory, are relevant to a better understanding of risk and resilience processes. Equifinality refers to varied pathways leading to similar outcomes, and multifinality assumes that a single component or risk factor may act differently depending on the organization of the system in which it operates (Bronfenbrenner, 1979; von Bertalanffy, 1968). As just pointed out, the reasons for early school leaving can be manifold, as are the resulting consequences. Not all young people leaving school early fail to achieve financial independence (Schoon & Duckworth, 2010) or life satisfaction (Schoon & Lyons-Amos, 2017). Changes in development are possible at many points across the life course, illustrating the potential diversity in ontogenetic outcome, regardless of similarity in the risks that are experienced (Lerner, 1996; Schoon, 2006, 2012, 2017).

Hierarchical Integration and Differentiation

Developmental adaptation can be considered as the progressive and mutual accommodation between a developing individual and the changing properties of the immediate and wider sociocultural context (Bronfenbrenner, 1979). Functioning well in age salient developmental tasks during one developmental period establishes the foundation for doing well in future tasks (Masten, 2016), while failure to master a developmental task in early life can initiate a vicious cycle of maladjustment. Moreover, there is evidence of developmental cascades, where achievements or failures in adaptation spread over time, from one domain to another

(Blumenthal, Silbereisen, Pastorelli, & Castellani, 2015; Weeks et al., 2016), and potentially even across generations (Masten & Cicchetti, 2010). For example, according to the family stress model economic hardship can trigger stress in the family system and compromise the effectiveness of parenting and family relationships, which in turn can contribute to adjustment problems in children (Conger, Conger, & Martin, 2010). Any point in the life span can be understood as the consequence of past experience and as the launch pad for subsequent experiences and conditions, although developmental cascades can also alter the course of development. Lifelong development may involve processes that do not originate at conception, birth, or early childhood but in later periods. The nonlinear nature of human development is characterized by the reorganization and differentiation of behavior and experience, leading to the emergence of new structural and functional properties and competencies, which result as a consequence of ongoing interactions between the multiple structures or spheres of previously described influence.

Time and Timing

Time is another essential category in conceptualizing resilience. The notion of time concerns individual aspects such as the physiological changes and processes of maturation that occur with aging, as well as aspects of the wider social context that are external to the individual. Time is often treated as synonymous with chronological age, providing a temporal frame of reference for the study of change. As children get older, they may react differently to environmental risks and may be more able to determine and evaluate how that change will influence them. As shown by Elder (1974) in his well-cited study "Children of the Great Depression," the impact of economic hardship on young people's adjustment can vary by context, age, and the timing of adverse experiences. For example, the effects of poverty and hardship experienced by families were less severe for young men who were already adolescents when the Great Depression hit, compared to those who were still children. The older boys were already involved in adult life tasks, such as helping out with the family economy and aspired to become autonomous adults, while younger boys were less hopeful, less self-directed, and less confident about their future. Likewise, in a more recent study of young people's development in the 2008 Great Recession, the timing of the recession mattered (Schoon & Bynner, 2017, 2019b, 2019b). For example, while younger cohorts experienced increased difficulties in gaining entry to the labor market, older cohorts were at an increased risk of insecure and temporary employment. However, while the psychological well-being of adolescents appeared to be relatively unaffected by the Great Recession, older cohorts (aged 18–25) were more vulnerable to its psychological impact. The findings suggest a shift in the critical time window with younger children being possibly better protected by their families or institutional structures than young adults. I will come back to this point later.

Furthermore, factors that may confer resilience at one time point or for one outcome may increase vulnerability at another time or in another context. Thus, resilience cannot be fully explained by restricting analysis to specific life stages, such as mid-childhood, adolescence or old age. It is only by following individuals over time and in context that we can chart their developmental trajectories and pathways. Beyond individual maturation processes, human lives are shaped by the particular social worlds and historical period encountered. For example, the birth year locates people in specific birth cohorts and, accordingly, to particular social changes. Young people making the transition to adulthood during the 1980s witnessed a very different sociocultural context than those coming of age today. There had been massive changes, including rapid technological advances, a changing labor market and an expanding educational system, many regional conflicts, mass migration, and economic and natural disasters. Also at the more proximal level of the family environment there have been massive changes, with increasing number of children being born to cohabiting or single parents or being exposed to experiences of family break-up and instability. Changes in the proximal and wider social context pose new situational demands and bring with them changing opportunities and obstacles, influencing lives and developmental trajectories, as for example through changing expectations regarding the timing of developmental transitions. It is thus important to replicate studies in changing socio-historical contexts to assess the generalizability of evidence.

For instance, since the 1970s the transition to adulthood has on aggregate become more prolonged due to extended education participation and delayed entry into employment and family formation (Schulenberg & Schoon, 2012). Extended transitions characterized by participation in higher education and subsequent employment are considered to be "optimal," while early transitions (such as early school leaving or parenthood) have been associated with problems in establishing oneself in the labor market or making the transition to independent living (Sacker & Cable, 2010; Schoon et al, 2012). The timing of transitions is thus important in determining their meaning and implications. Yet, not all young people are able to participate in higher education, and there is persistent evidence to suggest that the preparation for adulthood has been elongated especially for those who can afford to invest in their education, while young people from less privileged backgrounds are leaving education earlier and are less likely to continue in higher education than their more privileged peers (Schoon & Lyons-Amos, 2016, 2017).

Moreover, evidence suggests that early transitions do not necessarily bring with them negative outcomes, and in certain circumstances early transitions can be beneficial for certain individuals (Booth, Rustenbach, & McHale, 2008), especially if they offer a fit to individual preferences and resources. For example, some young people succeed to make the transition to continuous employment and financial independence after leaving school early—either through learning on the job or participating in vocational training or further education—and they report high levels of satisfaction with their lives (Schoon & Lyons-Amos, 2017). Likewise, the effects of early parenthood on well-being depend on marital status as well as other circumstances in life (Nomaguchi & Milkie, 2003). Indeed, a considerable number of young people are able to turn around an initially problematic transition, such as early school leaving (Schoon & Duckworth, 2010) or early parenthood (Furstenberg, 2003; Schoon & Polek, 2011); avoid financial dependence; and lead a happy and satisfied life. Change for better or worse can occur across the entire life course and is shaped by continuous interactions between a developing individual and a changing context. Each transition can offer opportunities for change and renewal (Elder, 1998; Schoon, 2006, 2012, 2017).

Critical Windows of Opportunity

Developmental timing also plays a key role in resilience-based theories and the effective design and implementation of interventions. Research on naturally occurring resilience suggests that there are critical windows of opportunity for change, especially when developmental processes, context, and available opportunities converge to provide an opening for change (Masten, 2014). In particular, early childhood and the preschool years have been identified as a period of high plasticity with great importance for the development of capabilities, laying the foundations for successful maturation (Masten, 2016). Another example is the transition to adulthood, when brain development, motivation, mentoring, training, the assumption of new social roles, and other opportunities can provide opportunities to support positive redirection of the life course (Steinberg, 2014). Life transitions into different environments can facilitate a process of readjustment, a transformation or potential turning point, allowing for new opportunities and a change in behavioral patterns or existing structures (Salmela-Aro, 2009). Regarding interventions this implies that support is needed during key transition phases, not just during the early years—a sustainable scaffolding that enables positive development across time.

Resilience Processes

The socioecological developmental systems perspective assumes that different factors and processes can promote effective adaptation in the face of adversity. After more than 50 years of research on resilience, there has been a striking degree of consistency regarding a core set of factors associated with the manifestation of resilience across different studies, involving different populations of children, adolescents, and adults, in different risk situations and with different outcomes. These include characteristics of the individual, the family, and of the wider community (Masten, 2014). These factors are also understood as indicators of basic adaptive systems that protect human development under many different circumstances. In addition, previous empirical research has identified different resilience processes, linking experiences within and across systems. Within the socioecological developmental systems perspective these processes are conceptualized as aspects of developmental co-regulation, emphasizing the relational and interactive nature of resilience (Schoon, 2012, 2017). This approach implies a move away from a focus on individual characteristics, or personality traits, toward a better understanding of person × environment interactions bringing about positive adaptation in the face of adversity. These processes comprise compensatory, protective, and steeling effects and can involve resilient integration, turning points (or transformations) and meaning-making. Furthermore, the developmental focus acknowledges that resilience is a process that extends over time and has to be continuously supported or facilitated.

Compensatory Models

Compensatory models of resilience accounts for the availability of resources within the individual and the context that can counterbalance or neutralize the negative effects associated with risk exposure. As already mentioned, resource factors (or developmental assets) can include characteristics of the individual (such as self-regulation, life planning, self-efficacy, or cognitive competences), characteristics of the family (such as effective parenting, family cohesion, family rules and routines, collaborative problem-solving), the wider social context (including effective schools and effective neighborhoods), and social policies (Lerner, Lerner, & Benson, 2011; Masten, 2014; Schoon, 2012, 2017). Regarding youth transitions, it is in particular the role of social institutions and structural arrangements that matter, including aspects of the education and training system, the labor market, and the welfare system that shape transition opportunities and can provide a buffer against unexpected events, such as a sudden economic downturn (Schoon & Bynner, 2019a, 2019b). These resource factors show an equally beneficial effect for those that are exposed and those who not exposed to adversity and show their beneficial effect in low- as well as high-risk conditions. According to a cumulative effect model (sometimes also referred to as main effects or additive effects model), the accumulation of assets or resources will outweigh the risks. Increasing the diversity, quality, or number of protective resources could theoretically offset the negative effects of risk or adversity or improve positive adjustment in general. Such compensatory processes are also referred to as "resource substitution," where one resource can substitute for another or can fill the gap if the other is absent, and worst outcomes are predicted for those with low-levels of resources (Schoon & Lyons-Amos, 2016, 2017).

Protective or Moderating Effect Models

Within a protective or moderating effect model of resilience, exposure to a protective factor or process should have beneficial effects only for those individuals who are exposed to the risk factor, but not benefit those who are not exposed (i.e., there should be an interactive relationship between the protective factor, the risk exposure, and the outcome; Rutter, 2006). For example, there is evidence to suggest variability in response to childhood maltreatment based on the gene encoding the neurotransmitter-metabolizing enzyme monoamine oxidase A (Rutter, 2013). Children with high levels of monoamine oxidase A are less likely to develop antisocial problems in response to maltreatment, suggesting that genotypes can moderate children's sensitivity to environmental insults. Moreover, it has been argued that behavioral and morphological phenotype change can be instigated by change in developmental conditions, such as changes in rearing styles or shifts in the physical or psychosocial environment (Gottlieb, 1992; Kular & Kular, 2018; Turecki & Meaney, 2016).

However, resilience is not just a feature of gene × environment interactions and adaptive response to adverse situations can be triggered by numerous other circumstances. For example, in a study examining processes promoting academic resilience in the face of socioeconomic adversity, parental involvement with the child's education as well as social integration were identified as protective factors that were particularly important for children growing up in a high-risk environment, in addition to and above the influence of academic ability or parental education (Schoon, 2012, 2017). These resource factors facilitated the building of bridges between different systems (i.e. the family and the school system or between the individual and significant others in the neighborhood). More generally, within interactive, or moderating effect models of resilience protective factors show a buffering or ameliorative influence and are especially important if the risk level is high. Protective or moderating influences may lead to a reduction of risk effects and prevent negative chain reactions, instigating a positive chain reaction or creating opportunities to experience self-efficacy (Rutter, 2006; Schoon, 2012, 2107).

Challenge Models

The challenge model of resilience suggests that resistance to risk may come from exposure to low-level risk, or risk exposure within controlled circumstances rather than avoidance of risk altogether. Exposure to low-level risk experiences, or controlled risk exposure, may have beneficial or "steeling effects" (Rutter, 1987), providing a chance to practice problem-solving skills and to mobilize resources (Elder, 1999; Schoon, 2014; Seery, Holman, & Silver, 2010). The risk exposure must be challenging enough to stimulate a response, yet must not be overpowering. For example, a series of studies on the impact of the 2008 Great Recession on young people's achievement orientation suggest that young people tend to hang on to their ambitions even in times of economic hardship (Schoon & Mortimer, 2017), unless socioeconomic conditions are overpowering (Schoon, 2014), or changing circumstances such as the availability of new employment opportunities require them to change the course of their behavior and associated aspirations (Schoon & Bynner, 2017). The crux of the challenge model is that moderate levels of risk exposure open up opportunities for experimentation and learning of how to overcome adversity or to transform existing conditions. From a developmental perspective, the challenge model can also be considered as a model of inoculation, preparing the developing person to overcome significant risks in the future (Rutter, 2012).

Resilient Integration

To describe successful adaptation after a prolonged period of disruption or stress, the term *resilient integration* has been used (Kumpfer, 1999). The capacity for resilience is seen as developing over time, through the integration of constitutional and experiential factors in the context of a supportive environment (Oshri, Duprey, Kogan, Carlson, & Liu, 2018; Schoon, 2012). Certain attributes or circumstances that are generally associated with positive adjustment may not necessarily show immediate benefits, but may be predictive of positive adaptation later in life. Similar to the notion of sleeper effects, where beneficial effects are not detected until a period of time has elapsed, resilient integration requires protective attributes or circumstances to be stored up for later use. Moreover, developmental "reserve capacity" may not necessarily be utilized immediately but can be drawn upon when required (Baltes, 1987). For example, a study examining factors and processes involved in overcoming a potentially problematic transition such as early school leaving showed that in addition to cognitive competences, young people from a socioeconomically disadvantaged family background who actually enjoyed school and learning but had to leave education early to make a living, succeeded to maintain financial independence (i.e., they were not dependent on social benefits), and remained attached to the labor market nearly 20 years later (Schoon & Duckworth, 2010). They were also more likely to return to education later in their lives to obtain additional qualifications (Sacker & Schoon, 2007). These findings highlight the importance of building up positive attitudes and to support integration into institutions, as these factors can have long-term beneficial effects.

Turning Points

Delayed recovery may also stem from positive experiences, or "turning point" experiences in later life (Elder, 1998; Rutter, 2006). Substantial and enduring change in life course development often occurs during transition periods, such as entry into school, work, or family formation. These events are characterized by the assumption of new social roles and change of context. For example, in a follow-up study of teenage delinquents growing up in low income areas in Boston, Laub and Sampson (2003) showed that the step into a supportive marriage can instigate a beneficial turning point effect. It is however not only just one factor, such as the effect from a secure intimate relationship, that made a difference. The step into marriage also involved the "knifing-off" of the past, and the benefits of a new extended family network and friendship groups, as well as the informal controls exerted by the spouses that prevented contact with the delinquent peer group. It is this complex mix of influences that contribute to positive adjustment in the face of adversity, which also was apparent in Elder's (1974) study of young people growing up during the Great Depression of the 1920s. The evidence of turning points in human lives illustrates the potential for plasticity, which can occur across the entire lifespan, enabling individuals to turn around an initially problematic transition, such as early school leaving (Schoon & Duckworth, 2010), early parenthood (Schoon & Polek, 2011), leaving residential care (Schofield, Larsson, & Ward, 2017), or delinquency (Laub & Sampson, 2003). Increasing age imposes constraints on potential responsiveness and one's ability to act upon the environment, yet there is persistent evidence of individual capability to meet and handle adversities and to maintain or regain levels of effective functioning even in old age (Charles & Carstensen, 2010; Staudinger, Marsiske, & Baltes, 1993).

Meaning Making and Sense of Coherence

Individuals are not passively exposed to external risk experiences—they interpret and process the information, bringing order and meaning to a changing world, and produce a set of expectations about how experiences fit together. The power of meaning for human life in the face of overwhelming suffering has been described by Victor Frankl (1946/1984) in his account of daily life in a Nazi concentration camp. Frankl identified the "will to meaning" as the primary motivational force to sustain efforts to survive in horrific circumstances. The wish for meaning and coherence of what is going on in the world and one's own, often contradictory experiences of the world, has also been conceptualized as "sense of coherence" (Antonovsky, 1987). For example, a study with a group of working class adults born in 1958, who participated in higher education in a context where most people from the same socioeconomic backgrounds did not, identified different therapeutic narratives that were used to come to terms with the ambivalence produced by social mobility (Franceschelli, Evans, & Schoon, 2016). These narratives reflect a general sense of resilience, which enabled respondents to overcome their disadvantaged start in life by drawing on the hardworking ethic apparent in working-class families. In another study Black Caribbean parents in London were studied to understand how they prepare their children for the challenges ahead–including anticipated discrimination (Franceschelli et al., 2017). Through the use of family case studies different narratives were identified, linking individual experiences to family and community histories, and by drawing on the struggles of a collective past, parents passed on a sense of resilience and achievement motivation to their children. It has been argued that the cognitive restructuring involved in meaning-making requires considerable capacity for thought and reflection and is more likely to be important as people grow older (Masten & O'Dougherty Wright, 2009). However, as Ungar (2004) points out, when resilience is viewed through a constructionist lens the way individuals create meaning of their behavior and the context in which this takes place are key aspects of a resilient response at any age. Similarly, Rutter (1990) considers variations in cognitive processing and appraisal, leading to acceptance rather than denial of challenges, as a crucial protective mechanism.

Conclusion and Outlook

The socioecological developmental systems approach to the study of resilience avoids simplistic individual-focused conceptualizations, which do not account for the wider social and ecological context in which the developing individual is embedded. It takes a holistic approach, considering the multidimensional forces and relationships between individuals, their families, their neighborhoods, and wider social and ecological context. It accounts for the multidimensionality of positive adjustment, requiring attention to multiple domains, and the recognition that resilience is socially and culturally contingent. It recognizes that risk factors cumulate over time and in context, making it difficult to pinpoint one single factor or causal mechanism. It highlights the importance of time and timing of effects, which have important implications for the design of developmentally appropriate and sustainable interventions. Change for better or worse can occur across the entire life course, suggesting that it is never too early or too late to intervene. In addition, the recognition that developmental processes are profoundly affected by the wider social context draws attention to the role of public policies and practices that influence the nature of the environment and define the "action field" in which individual development takes place. Providing clean air, safe drinking water and housing condition are basic requirements for families, children, and young people to thrive, as is the provision of effective health and childcare, education, and employment opportunities. There is not one major factor that enables individuals to cope with adversity. What is important is the combination of multiple and diverse influences that make a difference and social policy and structures that create opportunities and resources, optimizing the life chances for all.

The socioecological developmental systems approach provides a framework that is generic enough to identify distinct layers of influence and to conceptualize the processes interlinking them. These processes involve compensatory, protective, challenging, and transformative effects, as well as the role of "reserve capacities" and meaning-making. The focus is on cultivating the capacity to sustain development in the face of adversity and constant change (Schoon, 2006, 2012, 2017).

While previous studies have focused mainly on development within single layers, there is a need for more concerted synergies from different disciplines regarding the conceptualization and integration of knowledge in specifying a multisystemic approach for the study of resilience. A particular focus should be directed at the interactions between individual, social, and environmental conditions. Previous evidence suggests that noise pollution, air pollution, and lack of greenspace are associated with cognitive development and health of children (Stansfeld & Clark, 2015; Sunyer et al., 2015) and adults. There is an increasing understanding of the associated epigenetic mechanisms by which exposure to pollutants mediates its negative effects (Godfrey, Costello, & Lillycrop, 2015), but less is known about how to translate findings into effective interventions that might involve changes in attitudes, in living conditions, policies to reduce exposure to harmful substances, and effective reinforcement and control. Within this context the notion of resilience could serve as a bridging concept and facilitate discussion of complex systems among experts from different disciplines, providing a platform for potentially innovative theoretical and methodological insights and approaches. The emphasis on improving conditions for all implies a distinct focus on normative expectations guiding public policies and power relations in the management of resources.

Moreover, there is a need for more longitudinal studies, moving away from single snapshots and short-term follow-up studies (often of highly selected samples) to gain a better understanding of how resilience emerges and how it can be sustained over time and in context. This requires good quality data and appropriate measures of risk and adaption, and of relevant process variables. The use of administrative data, such as information on health, education, and employment might be helpful, in particular in combination with linked geocodes enabling the inclusion of area specific information on socioeconomic and ecological resources and indicators of deprivation. In this connection, there are however issues of research ethics and limitation of access to be considered, as well as the availability of relevant background and process data.

There is potential in using "natural experiments," that is, situations such as policy changes, economic boom or bust, cultural upheaval or natural disasters that create opportunities to observe continuity and change in behavior and adjustment. Such an approach is particularly effective if there is pre-existing data on patterns of adjustment across key domains, such as in ongoing cohort or panel data. Generally, the use of national representative longitudinal data would be advantageous, enabling the comparison of adjustment processes in different subgroups in the population or different local areas. Comparing evidence across different countries would bring additional insights into similarities and variations by sociocultural conditions and thus on the generalizability of findings. The availability of harmonized data, collected across different countries, would furthermore facilitate the task of obtaining comparable data across different contexts and outcomes.

In addition to improving the quality of the empirical database, there is also a need for mixed-method approaches, using qualitative case studies to gain better insights into the endogenous and social dynamics of the system. Aiming to understand the complex and dynamic nature of the social-ecological system requires the development and adoption of diverse theoretical and methodological approaches and openness to the perspectives of diverse interest groups.

Key Messages

1. The idea of socioecological developmental systems is informed by general systems theory (Bertalanffy, 1968), conceptualizing living systems as a unified whole, where different levels of influence are interrelated and each level is characterized by self-activity and historicity.

2. Individual-level resilience is not a personality trait. It is a relational, dynamic, and multi-level process, linking the individual to a range of sociocultural, historical, and ecological influences and thereby sustaining effective functioning, recovery after an initial stress response, or transformation of ill-fitting conditions.
3. The socioecological developmental systems approach recognizes that the nonreductionist analysis of individual behavior requires the simultaneous consideration of several spheres of influence, thereby moving beyond simple cause-and-effect explanations of behavior. Moreover, it emphasizes the role of developmental processes, involving consistency and change in behavior, and the need to consider the importance of time and timing of events.
4. It is assumed that individuals and their environments are potentially malleable and mutually constitute each other through processes of co-regulation.
5. From an individual-level perspective, co-regulation can comprise a range of processes involving compensatory, protective, steeling, transformative effects, and meaning-making.

Acknowledgments

The preparation of this manuscript is supported by a Research Professorship awarded to the author by the Berlin Social Science Center (WZB), Germany, and a grant from the British Economic and Social Research Council (ESRC), Grant Number ES/J019135/1 for the Centre for Learning and Life-chances in the Knowledge Economies (LLAKES, Phase II).

References

Amato, P. R. (2010). Research on divorce: Continuing trends and new developments. *Journal of Marriage and Family, 72*(3), 650–666. doi:10.1111/j.1741-3737.2010.00723.x

Antonovsky, A. (1987). *Unraveling the mystery of health: How people manage stress and stay well* (1st ed.). San Francisco, CA: Jossey-Bass.

Baltes, P. B. (1987). Theoretical propositions of life-span developmental-psychology on the dynamics between growth and decline. *Developmental Psychology, 23*(5), 611–626. doi:10.1037/0012-1649.23.5.611

Bandura, A. (2006). Toward a psychology of human agency. *Perspectives on Psychological Science, 1*(2), 164–180. doi:10.1111/j.1745-6916.2006.00011.x

Biggs, R., Schluter, M., Biggs, D., Bohensky, E. L., BurnSilver, S., Cundill, G., . . . West, P. C. (2012). Toward principles for enhancing the resilience of ecosystem services. *Annual Review of Environment and Resources, 37*, 421–448. doi:10.1146/annurev-environ-051211-123836

Blumenthal, A., Silbereisen, R. K., Pastorelli, C., & Castellani, V. (2015). Academic and social adjustment during adolescence as precursors of work-related uncertainties in early adulthood. *Swiss Journal of Psychology, 74*(3), 159–168. doi:10.1024/1421-0185/a000159

Booth, A., Rustenbach, E., & McHale, S. (2008). Early family transitions and depressive symptom changes from adolescence to early adulthood. *Journal of Marriage and Family, 70*(1), 3–14. doi:10.1111/j.1741-3737.2007.00457.x

Bronfenbrenner, U. (1979). *The ecology of human development: Experiments by nature and design.* Cambridge, MA: Harvard University Press.

Bronfenbrenner, U., & Morris, P. A. (2006). The bioecological model of human development. In R. M. Lerner (Ed.), *Handbook of child psychology: Theoretical models of human development* (6th ed., Vol. 1, pp. 793–828). Hoboken, NJ: Wiley.

Charles, S. T., & Carstensen, L. L. (2010). Social and emotional aging. *Annual Review of Psychology*, *61*(1), 383–409. doi:10.1146/annurev.psych.093008.100448

Chen, X., Cen, G., Li, D., & He, Y. (2005). Social functioning and adjustment in Chinese children: The imprint of historical time. *Child Development*, *76*(1), 182–195. doi:10.1111/j.1467-8624.2005.00838.x

Chmielewski, A. K., Dumont, H., & Trautwein, U. (2013). Tracking effects depend on tracking type: An international comparison of students' mathematics self-concept. *American Educational Research Journal*, *50*(5), 925–957. doi:10.3102/0002831213489843

Cicchetti, D. (1993). Developmental psychopathology: Reactions, reflections, projections. *Developmental Review*, *13*(4), 471–502. doi:10.1006/drev.1993.1021

Conger, R. D., Conger, K. J., & Martin, M. J. (2010). Socioeconomic status, family processes, and individual development. *Journal of Marriage and the Family*, *72*(3), 685–704. doi:10.1111/j.1741-3737.2010.00725.x

Croll, P., & Attwood, G. (2013). Participation in higher education: Aspirations, attainment and social background. *British Journal of Educational Studies*, *61*(2), 187–202. doi:10.1080/00071005.2013.787386

Dannefer, D. (2003). Cumulative advantage/disadvantage and the life course: Cross fertilizing age and social science theory. *Journal of Gerontology: Social Sciences*, *58*(6), S327–S337. doi:10.1093/geronb/58.6.S327

De Witte, K., Cabus, S., Thyssen, G., Groot, W., & van den Brink, H. M. (2013). A critical review of the literature on school dropout. *Educational Research Review*, *10*, 13–28. doi:10.1016/j.edurev.2013.05.002

Duckworth, K., & Schoon, I. (2012). Beating the odds: Exploring the impact of social risk on young people's school-to-work transitions during recession in the UK. *National Institute Economic Review*, *222*, 38–51. doi:10.1177/002795011222200104

Eccles, J. S., & Wigfield, A. (2002). Motivational beliefs, values, and goals. *Annual Review of Psychology*, *53*(1), 109–132. doi:10.1146/annurev.psych.53.100901.135153

Elder, G. H. (1974). *Children of the Great Depression: Social change in life experience*. Chicago, IL: University of Chicago Press.

Elder, G. H. (1998). The life course as developmental theory. *Child Development*, *69*(1), 1–12. doi:10.2307/1132065

Elder, G. H. (1999). *Children of the Great Depression: Social change in life experience* (25th Anniversary Edition). Boulder, CO: Westview Press.

Erikson, E. H. (1959). *Identity and the life cycle: Selected papers*. New York, NY: International Universities Press.

Esping-Anderson, G. (2002). *Why we need a new welfare state*. Oxford, UK: Oxford University Press.

Evans, K. (2002). Taking control of their lives? Agency in young adult transitions in England and the New Germany. *Journal of Youth Studies*, *5*(3), 245–271. doi:10.1080/1367626022000005965

Evans, G. W., Li, D., & Whipple, S. S. (2013). Cumulative risk and child development. *Psychological Bulletin*, *139*(6), 1342–1396. doi:10.1037/a0031808

Flouri, E., Papachristou, E., Midouhas, E., Joshi, H., Ploubidis, G., & Lewis, G. (2018). Early adolescent outcomes of joint developmental trajectories of problem behavior and IQ in childhood. *European Child & Adolescent Psychiatry*, *27*(12), 1595–1605. doi:10.1007/s00787-018-1155-7

Folke, C. (2016). Resilience (republished). *Ecology and Society*, *21*(4), 44. doi:10.5751/es-09088-210444

Franceschelli, M., Evans, K., & Schoon, I. (2016). "A fish out of water?" The therapeutic narratives of class change. *Current Sociology*, *64*(3), 353–372. doi:10.1177/0011392115595064

Franceschelli, M., Schoon, I., & Evans, K. (2017). "Your past makes you who you are": Retrospective parenting and relational resilience among Black Caribbean British young people. *Sociological Research Online*, *22*(4), 48–65. doi:10.1177/1360780417726957

Frankl, V. (1984). *Man's search for meaning*. New York, NY: Washington Square Press. (Original work published in 1946)

Furstenberg, F. F. (2003). Teenage childbearing as a public issue and private concern. *Annual Review of Sociology*, *29*(1), 23–29. doi:10.1146/annurev.soc.29.010202.100205

Godfrey, K. M., Costello, P. M., & Lillycrop, K. A. (2015). The developmental environment, epigenetic biomarkers and long-term health. *Journal of Developmental Origins of Health and Disease*, *6*(5), 399–406. doi:10.1017/s204017441500121x

Gottlieb, G. (1992). *Individual development and evolution*. Oxford, UK: Oxford University Press.

Gutman, L. M., Joshi, H., & Schoon, I. (2019). Developmental trajectories of conduct problems and cumulative risk from early childhood to adolescence. *Journal of Youth and Adolescence, 48*(2), 181–198. doi:10.1007/s10964-018-0971-x

Heckhausen, J. (1999). *Developmental regulation in adulthood: Age-normative and sociostructural constraints as adaptive challenges.* Cambridge, UK: Cambridge University Press.

Heckhausen, J., & Buchmann, M. (2018). A multi-disciplinary model of life-course canalization and agency. *Advances in Life Course Research, 41,* 100246. doi:10.1016/j.alcr.2018.09.002

Heckhausen, J., & Chang, E. S. (2009). Can ambition help overcome social inequality in the transition to adulthood? Individual agency and societal opportunities in Germany and the United States. *Research in Human Development, 6*(4), 235–251. doi:10.1080/15427600903281244

Heckhausen, J., Wrosch, C., & Schulz, R. (2010). A motivational theory of life-span development. *Psychological Review, 117*(1), 32–60. doi:10.1037/a0017668

Heckman, J. J. (2006). Skill formation and the economics of investing in disadvantaged children. *Science, 312*(5782), 1900–1902. doi:10.1126/science.1128898

Holtmann, A. C., Menze, L., & Solga, H. (2017). Persistent disadvantage or new opportunities? The role of agency and structural constraints for low-achieving adolescents' school-to-work transitions. *Journal of Youth and Adolescence, 46*(10), 2091–2113. doi:10.1007/s10964-017-0719-z

Kirmayer, L. J., Dandeneau, S., Marshall, E., Phillips, M. K., & Williamson, K. J. (2011). Rethinking resilience from Indigenous perspectives. *The Canadian Journal of Psychiatry, 56*(2), 84–91. doi:10.1177/070674371105600203

Kular, L., & Kular, S. (2018). Epigenetics applied to psychiatry: Clinical opportunities and future challenges. *Psychiatry and Clinical Neurosciences, 72*(4), 195–211. doi:10.1111/pcn.12634

Kumpfer, K. L. (1999). Factors and processes contributing to resilience: The resilience framework. In M. D. Glantz & J. L. Johnson (Eds.), *Resilience and development: Positive life adaptations* (pp. 179–224). New York, NY: Kluwer Academic.

Laub, J. H., & Sampson, R. J. (2003). *Shared beginnings, divergent lives: Delinquent boys to age 70.* Cambridge, MA: Harvard University Press.

Lazarus, R. L., & Folkman, S. (1984). *Stress, appraisal, and coping.* New York, NY: Springer.

Lerner, R. M. (1984). *On the nature of human plasticity.* New York, NY: Cambridge University Press.

Lerner, R. M. (1996). Relative plasticity, integration, temporality, and diversity in human development: A developmental contextual perspective about theory, process, and method. *Developmental Psychology, 32*(4), 781–786. doi:10.1037/0012-1649.32.4.781

Lerner, R. M., Lerner, J. V., & Benson, J. B. (2011). Positive youth development: Research and applications for promoting thriving in adolescence. In R. M. Lerner, J. V. Lerner, & J. B. Benson (Eds.), *Advances in child development and behavior* (Vol. 41, pp. 1–17). Amsterdam, The Netherlands: Elsevier.

Levinson, D. J. (1986). A conception of adult development. *American Psychologist, 41*(1), 3–14. doi:10.1037/0003-066X.41.1.3

Luthar, S. S., & Cicchetti, D. (2000). The construct of resilience: Implications for interventions and social policies. *Development and Psychopathology, 12*(4), 857–885. doi:10.1017/S0954579400004156

Luthar, S. S., Cicchetti, D., & Becker, B. (2000). The construct of resilience: A critical evaluation and guidelines for future work. *Child Development, 71*(3), 543–562.

Marsh, H. W., Trautwein, U., Lüdtke, O., Baumert, J., & Koller, O. (2007). The big-fish-little-pond effect: Persistent negative effects of selective high schools on self-concept after graduation. *American Educational Research Journal, 44*(3), 631–669. doi:10.3102/0002831207306728

Masten, A. S. (2014). *Ordinary magic: Resilience in development.* New York, NY: Guilford Press.

Masten, A. S. (2016). Resilience in developing systems: The promise of integrated approaches. *European Journal of Developmental Psychology, 13*(3), 297–312. doi:10.1080/17405629.2016.1147344

Masten, A. S., & Cicchetti, D. (2010). Developmental cascades. *Development and Psychopathology, 22*(3), 491–495. doi:10.1017/s0954579410000222

Masten, A. S., & Wright, M. O'D. (2009). Resilience over the lifespan: Developmental perspectives on resistance, recovery, and transformation. In J. W. Reich, A. J. Zautra, & J. S. Hall (Eds.), *Handbook of adult resilience* (pp. 213–237). New York, NY: Guilford Press.

Mortimer, J. T., Zhang, L., Wu, C. Y., Hussemann, J., & Johnson, M. K. (2017). Familial transmission of educational plans and the academic self-concept: A three-generation longitudinal study. *Social Psychology Quarterly, 80*(1), 85–107. doi:10.1177/0190272516670582

Ng-Knight, T., & Schoon, I. (2017). Can locus of control compensate for socioeconomic adversity in the transition from school to work? *Journal of Youth and Adolescence, 46*(10), 2114–2128. doi:10.1007/s10964-017-0720-6

Nomaguchi, K. M., & Milkie, M. A. (2003). Costs and rewards of children: The effects of becoming a parent on adults' lives. *Journal of Marriage and Family, 65*(2), 356–374. doi:10.1111/j.1741-3737.2003.00356.x

Oshri, A., Duprey, E. B., Kogan, S. M., Carlson, M. W., & Liu, S. (2018). Growth patterns of future orientation among maltreated youth: A prospective examination of the emergence of resilience. *Developmental Psychology, 54*(8), 1456–1471. doi:10.1037/dev0000528

Parsons, S., Schoon, I., Rush, R., & Law, J. (2011). Long-term outcomes for children with early language problems: Beating the odds. *Children & Society, 25*(3), 202–214. doi:10.1111/j.1099-0860.2009.00274.x

Pensiero, N., & Schoon, I. (2019). Social inequalities in educational attainment: The changing impact of parents' social class, social status, education and family income, England 1986 and 2010. *Journal of Longitudinal and Life Course Studies, 10*(1), 87–108. doi:10.1332/175795919X15468755933380

Preiser, R., Biggs, R., De Vos, A., & Folke, C. (2018). Social-ecological systems as complex adaptive systems: Organizing principles for advancing research methods and approaches. *Ecology and Society, 23*(4). doi:10.5751/es-10558-230446

Reynolds, J. R., & Johnson, M. K. (2011). Change in the stratification of educational expectations and their realization. *Social Forces, 90*(1), 85–109. doi:10.1093/sf/90.1.85

Rosenbaum, J. E. (2011). The complexities of college for all: Beyond fairy-tale dreams. *Sociology of Education, 84*(2), 113–117. doi:10.1177/0038040711401809

Rutter, M. (1987). Pyschosocial resilience and protective mechanisms. *American Journal of Orthopsychiatry, 57*(3), 316–331. doi:10.1111/j.1939-0025.1987.tb03541.x

Rutter, M. (1990). Psychosocial resilience and protective mechanisms. In J. Rolf, A. S. Masten, D. Cicchetti, K. H. Nuechterien, & S. Weintraub (Eds.), *Risk and protective factors in the development of psychopathology* (pp. 181–214). New York, NY: Cambridge University Press.

Rutter, M. (2006). Implications of resilience concepts for scientific understanding. *Annals of the New York Academy of Science, 1094*(1), 1–12. doi:10.1196/annals.1376.002

Rutter, M. (2012). Resilience as a dynamic concept. *Development and Psychopathology, 24*(2), 335–344. doi:10.1017/s0954579412000028

Rutter, M. (2013). Annual research review: Resilience—Clinical implications. *Journal of Child Psychology and Psychiatry, 54*(4), 474–487. doi:10.1111/j.1469-7610.2012.02615.x

Sacker, A., & Cable, N. (2010). Transitions to adulthood and psychological distress in young adults born 12 years apart: Constraints on and resources for development. *Psychological Medicine, 40*(2), 301–313. doi:10.1017/s0033291709006072

Sacker, A., & Schoon, I. (2007). Educational resilience in later life: Resources and assets in adolescence and return to education after leaving school at age 16. *Social Science Research, 36*(3), 873–896. doi:10.1016/j.ssresearch.2006.06.002

Sacker, A., Schoon, I., & Bartley, M. (2002). Social inequality in educational achievement and psychosocial adjustment throughout childhood: Magnitude and mechanisms. *Social Science & Medicine, 55*(5), 863–880. doi:10.1016/s0277-9536(01)00228-3

Salmela-Aro, K. (2009). Personal goals and well-being during critical life transitions: The four C's—Channelling, choice, co-agency and compensation. *Advances in Life Course Research, 14*(1–2), 63–73. doi:10.1016/j.alcr.2009.03.003

Salmela-Aro, K., Kiuru, N., Nurmi, J. E., & Eerola, M. (2014). Antecedents and consequences of transitional pathways to adulthood among university students: 18-year longitudinal study. *Journal of Adult Development, 21*(1), 48–58. doi:10.1007/s10804-013-9178-2

Sameroff, A. J. (2010). A unified theory of development: A dialectic integration of nature and nurture. *Child Development, 81*(1), 6–22. doi:10.1111/j.1467-8624.2009.01378.x

Schofield, G., Larsson, B., & Ward, E. (2017). Risk, resilience and identity construction in the life narratives of young people leaving residential care. *Child & Family Social Work*, 22(2), 782–791. doi:10.1111/cfs.12295

Schoon, I. (2006). *Risk and resilience: Adaptations in changing times*. Cambridge, UK: Cambridge University Press.

Schoon, I. (2010). Planning for the future: Changing education expectations in three British cohorts. *Historical Social Research*, 35(2), 99–119. doi:10.12759/hsr.35.2010.2.99-119

Schoon, I. (2012). Temporal and contextual dimensions to individual positive development: A developmental-contextual systems model of resilience. In M. Ungar (Ed.), *The social ecology of resilience: Culture, context, resources, and meaning* (pp. 143–156). New York, NY: Springer.

Schoon, I. (2014). Parental worklessness and the experience of NEET among their offspring: Evidence from the longitudinal study of young people in England (LSYPE). *Longitudinal and Life Course Studies*, 6(6), 129–150. doi:10.14301/llcs.v5i2.279

Schoon, I. (2015). Let's work together: Towards interdisciplinary collaboration. *Research in Human Development*, 12(3–4), 350–355. doi:10.1080/15427609.2015.1068050

Schoon, I. (2017). Making it against the odds: Diverse strategies and successful adaptation. In A. C. Peterson, S. H. Koller, F. Motti-Stefanidi, & S. Verma (Eds.), *Positive youth development in global contexts of social and economic change* (pp. 62–81). New York, NY: Routledge.

Schoon, I. (2020). The wellbeing of children in the face of socio-economic deprivation and family instability. *Revue des Politiques Sociales et Familiales*, 131-2(4), 51–65.

Schoon, I., & Bynner, J. (2003). Risk and resilience in life course: Implications for interventions and social policies. *Journal of Youth Studies*, 6(1), 21–31. doi:10.1080/1367626032000068145

Schoon, I., & Bynner, J. (2019a). Entering adulthood in the Great Recession: A tale of three countries. In A. D. Park & G. H. Elder, Jr. (Eds.), *Children in changing worlds: Sociocultural and temporal perspectives* (pp. 57–83). Cambridge, UK: Cambridge University Press.

Schoon, I., & Bynner, J. (2019b). Young people and the Great Recession: Variations in the school-to-work transition in Europe and the United States. *Longitudinal and Life Course Studies*, 10(2), 153–173. doi:10.1332/175795919X15514456677349

Schoon, I., & Bynner, J. (Eds.). (2017). *Young people's development and the Great Recession: Uncertain transitions and precarious futures*. Cambridge, UK: Cambridge University Press

Schoon, I., Bynner, J., Joshi, H., Parsons, S., Wiggins, R. D., & Sacker, A. (2002). The influence of context, timing, and duration of risk experiences for the passage from childhood to midadulthood. *Child Development*, 73(5), 1486–1504. doi:10.1111/1467-8624.00485

Schoon, I., Chen, M., Kneale, D., & Jager, J. (2012). Becoming adults in Britain: Lifestyles and wellbeing in times of social change. *Longitudinal and Life Course Studies*, 3(2), 173–189. doi.org/10.14301/llcs.v3i2.181

Schoon, I., Cheng, H., Jones, E., & Maughan, B. (2013). *Wellbeing of children: Early influences*. Retrieved from http://www.nuffieldfoundation.org/well-being-children-early-influences

Schoon, I., & Duckworth, K. (2010). Leaving school early—And making it! Evidence from two British birth cohorts. *European Psychologist*, 15(4), 283–292. doi:10.1027/1016-9040/a000063

Schoon, I., & Heckhausen, J. (2019). Conceptualizing individual agency in the transition from school to work: A socio-ecological developmental perspective. *Adolescent Research Review*, 4(2), 135–148. doi:10.1007/s40894-019-00111-3

Schoon, I., Hope, S., Ross, A., & Duckworth, K. (2010). Family hardship and children's development: The early years. *Longitudinal and Life Course Studies*, 1(3), 209–222. doi:10.1136/jech.2010.121228

Schoon, I., Jones, E., Cheng, H., & Maughan, B. (2012). Family hardship, family instability, and cognitive development. *Journal of Epidemiology and Community Health*, 66(8), 716–722. doi:10.1136/jech.2010.121228

Schoon, I., & Lyons-Amos, M. (2016). Diverse pathways in becoming an adult: The role of structure, agency and context. *Research in Social Stratification and Mobility*, 46(Part A), 11–20. doi:10.1016/j.rssm.2016.02.008

Schoon, I., & Lyons-Amos, M. (2017). A socio-ecological model of agency: The role of structure and agency in shaping education and employment transitions in England. *Longitudinal and Life Course Studies, 8*(1), 35–56. doi:10.14301/llcs.v8i1.404

Schoon, I., & Melis, G. (2019). Intergenerational transmission of family adversity: Examining constellations of risk factors. *PLOS One, 14*(4), e0214801. doi:10.1371/journal.pone.0214801

Schoon, I., & Mortimer, J. (2017). Youth and the Great Recession: Are values, achievement orientation and outlook to the future affected? *International Journal of Psychology, 52*(1), 1–8. doi:10.1002/ijop.12400

Schoon, I., & Polek, E. (2011). Pathways to economic well-being among teenage mothers in Great Britain. *European Psychologist, 16*(1), 11–20. doi:10.1027/1016-9040/a000028

Schoon, I., Sacker, A., & Bartley, M. (2003). Socio-economic adversity and psychosocial adjustment: A developmental-contextual perspective. *Social Science & Medicine, 57*(6), 1001–1015. doi:10.1016/S0277-9536(02)00475-6

Schulenberg, J. E., & Schoon, I. (2012). The transition to adulthood in the UK, the US, and Finland: Differential social role pathways, their predictors and correlates. *Longitudinal and Life Course Studies, 3*(2), 164–172. doi:10.14301%2Fllcs.v3i2.194

Seery, M. D., Holman, E. A., & Silver, R. C. (2010). Whatever does not kill us: Cumulative lifetime adversity, vulnerability, and resilience. *Journal of Personality and Social Psychology, 99*(6), 1025–1041. doi:10.1037/a0021344

Sroufe, L. A. (1979). The coherence of individual development: Early care, attachment, and subsequent developmental issues. *American Psychologist, 34*(10), 834–841. doi:10.1037/0003-066X.34.10.834

Stansfeld, S., & Clark, C. (2015). Health effects of noise exposure in children. *Current Environmental Health Reports, 2*(2), 171–178. doi:10.1007/s40572-015-0044-1

Staudinger, U. M., Marsiske, M., & Baltes, P. B. (1993). Resilience and levels of reserve capacity in later adulthood: Perspectives from life-span theory. *Development and Psychopathology, 5*(4), 541–566. doi:10.1017/S0954579400006155

Steinberg, L. (2014). *The age of opportunity: Lessons from the new science of adolescence*. Boston, MA: Houghton Mifflin Harcourt.

Sunyer, J., Esnaola, M., Alvarez-Pedrerol, M., Forns, J., Rivas, I., Lopez-Vicente, M., . . . Querol, X. (2015). Association between traffic-related air pollution in schools and cognitive development in primary school children: A prospective cohort study. *PLOS Medicine, 12*(3), 1–24. doi:10.1371/journal.pmed.1001792

Turecki, G., & Meaney, M. J. (2016). Effects of the social environment and stress on glucocorticoid receptor gene methylation: A systematic review. *Biological Psychiatry, 79*(2), 87–96. doi:10.1016/j.biopsych.2014.11.022

Ungar, M. (2004). A constructionist discourse on resilience. Multiple contexts, multiple realities among at-risk children and youth. *Youth & Society, 35*, 341–365.

Ungar, M. (2019). Systemic resilience: Principles and processes for a science of change in contexts of adversity. *Ecology and Society, 23*(4), 34. doi:10.5751/ES-10385-230434

Ungar, M., Ghazinour, M., & Richter, J. (2013). Annual research review: What is resilience within the social ecology of human development? *Journal of Child Psychology and Psychiatry, 54*(4), 348–366. doi:10.1111/jcpp.12025

von Bertalanffy, L. (1968). *General system theory: Foundations development applications*. New York, NY: Braziller.

Weeks, M., Ploubidis, G. B., Cairney, J., Wild, T. C., Naicker, K., & Colman, I. (2016). Developmental pathways linking childhood and adolescent internalizing, externalizing, academic competence, and adolescent depression. *Journal of Adolescence, 51*, 30–40. doi:10.1016/j.adolescence.2016.05.009

Werner, H. (1957). The concept of development from a comparative and organismic point of view. In D. B. Harris (Ed.), *The concept of development: An issue in the study of human behavior* (pp. 125–148). Minneapolis: University of Minneapolis Press.

SECTION 6

Recovery and Resilience in Humanitarian Settings

19

Resilience Humanitarianism and Peacebuilding

Catherine Panter-Brick

Introduction

In the fields of resilience humanitarianism and peacebuilding, the systemic transformation of political, economic, and social systems is a pressing, present-day agenda. How do we build the foundations for more resilient systems in response to complex, protracted crises? How do we link together individual, social, and structural resilience to achieve sustained changes across generations? In this chapter, I provide three examples of systems-level thinking on resilience that have structured the architecture of the humanitarian and peacebuilding agenda: efforts to strengthen the social compacts between state and civil society in contexts of fragility, conflict, and global refugee displacement; efforts to link violence prevention and social cohesion to household food security and biopsychosocial health; and efforts to globally build cultures of peace by calling attention to the science of early child development. In doing so, I note three issues with resilience-building approaches with respect to theory, measurement, and intervention. First, there are challenges to strengthening structural and social resilience in ways that achieve a systems-level theory of change. Second, there is a need for operationalizing the parameters and pathways of resilience in ways that link the individual and collective dimensions of human experience. Third, contextual analyses require careful cultural grounding and an understanding of the political economy of resilience to make research, policy, and practice more contextually relevant.

Structural and Social Resilience

Let us start with examples of efforts to build structural and social resilience to evaluate conceptual frameworks that make resilience-building at the level of states and society an explicit intervention goal. In international policy circles, resilience has emerged as a key concept for guiding systems-level intervention in fragile and conflict-affected states. A lens on resilience provides a way of theorizing and explaining why some states have "the ability to *withstand* shocks and stressors, while others tip into spirals of fragility and violence" (van Metre & Calder, 2016, p. 2). Many think-tank institutions thus specifically focus on the drivers of state fragility and resilience to understand the tipping points that lead some societies to cycles of electoral violence, sectarian violence, or violent extremism. They look to new approaches to mitigate state fragility and to build *systems-level resilience* and violence prevention. Such approaches support interventions that mediate the space between society and state, through institutional reforms and social programs that engage with social expectations and strengthen social compacts.

Resilience in the Social Compact

One good example of a systems-level approach is detailed in the *Fragility and Resilience* policy brief (van Metre, 2016), written by a study group working on issues of international peace and U.S. strategic interests at the Carnegie Endowment for International Peace, the Center for a New American Security, and the United States Institute of Peace. This policy brief defines resilience as "the ability of a state and society to absorb, adapt, and transform in response to a shock or long-term stressor" (van Metre, 2016, p. 1). Given the goal of transformational interventions for sustainable, positive institutional changes in conflict-affected states, the brief sees resilience as a practice, in policy, of tapping into the existing capacities of the state and civil society to address the forces of fragility. It highlights that "a central feature of resilience is a strong social compact between the state and society on their respective and mutual roles and responsibilities" (van Metre, 2016, p. 1). The essence of this compact are the interactions between state and civil society—the formal and informal mechanisms that can ensure confidence and stability during crises. A social compact sets the conditions for social relations, trusted frameworks, and group collaborations that can act "as an immune system, or resilience, to internal and external stress and shock" (van Metre, 2016, p. 1).

In international circles, new policy approaches to mitigate state fragility thus encourage a focus on social cohesion and local leadership, systematically learning from local actors how they might take collective action to adapt in the wake of crises. International policy experts look to resilience capacities in civil society organizations to engage with local partners who have demonstrated a capacity for agency and collective action. In Kenya, for example, they have analyzed the ways local communities resist the rise of violent extremism in their midst and, in Iraq, how they were able to withstand sectarian violence: what turned local communities away from violence was the action of community businesses and community associations, organizing themselves to effect change (van Metre, 2016). Civil society is seen as a key stakeholder for the effective prevention of violence and extremism—to the extent that international actors have changed their funding paradigm to specifically bolster the role of civic institutions, such as labor organizations, to redirect grievances in ways that strengthen state–society relations and make local governments more accountable (Erdberg & Moix, 2019).

Contextual Analyses

Mercy Corps is one of the international nongovernmental organizations, which has adopted an explicit focus on resilience in complex crises. In contexts of poverty, conflict, and disaster, its mandate is to partner with local people to put bold ideas into action, helping to overcome adversity and build stronger communities (www.mercycorps.org). Mercy Corps emphasizes the importance of contextual analysis to identify "what gets in the way" of building resilience at scale. In one if its report—*Cracking the Code*—it offers the kind of analysis that showcases the lessons learnt in building multi-system interventions (those bridging both development and humanitarian needs) in conflict-affected countries (Mercy Corps, 2015).

In Lebanon, for example, contextual analyses sought to identify who were the first responders on the front lines of a refugee crisis—these are often municipalities, which is why there should be no missed opportunities for working with cities and local government to strengthen their capacities to accommodate to large influxes of urban refugees. In the Democratic Republic of Congo, the main challenges to sustainability and transformation were: working against the grain of humanitarian systems of international assistance, characterized by the need for speed which precluded robust analyses of the drivers of conflict; a priority given to internally displaced populations rather than host communities also affected by conflict; and the lack of funding to address the root causes of vulnerability, such as intercommunal violence and competition over land and other scarce resources (Mercy Corps, 2015). In Uganda, building resilience continued to "elude development practitioners and their programs" (Mercy Corps, 2015, p. 35)—it was not anchored into national and regional government planning and short-term economic gains were not translated into social stability. The report concluded, "Building resilience requires we design interventions across multiple systems" (p. 42), at economic, social, political, and ecological levels and that we transform the architecture of humanitarian systems, such that responses to protracted conflict are transformative and sustained, rather than achieved within humanitarian silos.

Systems-Level Responses

Indeed, the *Fragility and Resilience* Policy Brief argued:

> Resilience brings the entire political-societal system into focus and moves interventions away from discrete conflict problems and project-based responses. The key question becomes what intervention or accumulation of interventions will tip the conflict system to a nonviolent system that is improving over time, which requires a systems-level, not a project-level, theory of change. (van Metre, 2016, p. 3)

This theory of change adopts systems-level interventions to achieve synergistic (greater than the sum) impacts through strengthening the interactions between international organizations, state policies, and civil society action. In simpler terms, "resilience is the maintenance of the social contract and the ability to reconcile citizen and state expectations in the midst of sudden change or long-term stressors" (van Metre & Calder, 2016, p. 19).

This emphasis on a social and structural resilience is also seen in international migration policy in response to the global refugee crisis, the most significant crisis to challenge social, economic, and political systems since the Second World War. We see renewed international efforts to establish and strengthen social compacts to set out a comprehensive refugee response framework. This includes the Global Compact for Safe, Orderly, and Orderly Migration, the first intergovernmentally negotiated agreement on migration (United Nations, 2018), and the Global Compact on Refugees, endorsed by the United Nations General Assembly in December 2018 to strengthen the international response and increase the sharing of responsibilities in protracted refugee situations. The existing architecture of international assistance and humanitarian aid has to be rethought entirely: persistent, protracted crises demand concerted, sustainable solutions. There are pressing demands to expand the basic, classic humanitarian mandate: to move beyond saving lives and alleviating suffering, by addressing the "right to have rights" with respect to education, work, and citizenship, and by working toward peace and social cohesion. Business and civic society organizations are also called upon to make long-term investments in refugee employment and education, as worldwide, the number of forcibly displaced people has risen to over 70 million and the global refugee crisis has been linked to political failures to prevent conflict, promote tolerance, and lay the foundations for lasting peace (Grandi, 2019; United Nations High Commissioner for Refugees, 2018). Such international and community-level efforts require walking a fine line between diverse and contested political and social expectations, identifying local capacities and leadership, and strengthening social compacts between state and civil society to build multilevel, intersectoral agreements between international, state, and municipal institutions. Concerns for state fragility, financial responsibility, collective action, peacebuilding, and human dignity here come to the fore.

Challenges

Approaches to building resilience in sociopolitical systems are not without criticisms. They can be code for *disengagement*, leaving local institutions to take local action without support and investment. The everyday reality of humanitarian action is that partnerships with local institutions, while key, are difficult to sustain and build equitably, given that humanitarian responses remain highly structured around project-level deliverables, funded with short-timeframes, and respond to priorities that remain set by donors and delivered by implementing organizations. The existing system of international assistance is built on a "largely unidirectional process that is a far cry from the systemic approach" and never adds up to "peace writ large," or from a resilience perspective, a systemic transformation from conflict to social cohesion (Van Metre, 2016, pp. 3-4). While experts currently emphasize conceptual approaches that encompass notions of a humanitarian ecosystem (rather than a humanitarian system) and calls for humanitarian action that builds stronger bridges with development assistance and peacebuilding (Hilhorst, 2018), there is hardly any specific guidance provided with respect to building long-term, equitable partnerships.

The dangers of disengagement are increasingly evident in debates around international migration. Here the special status of refugees, who cross state boundaries and have rights to protection, gets buried in generalized debates about state security, sovereignty, and the nonrights of people engaged in mixed forms of migration (Hilhorst, 2018). This situation severely tests the principles, practices, and policies *of classic humanitarianism* (whereby intervention is predicated on emergency responses to crisis, driven by the moral imperative of humanitarian principles). By contrast, *resilience humanitarianism* favors interventions that will work to support states and local services, driven by contextual and pragmatic analyses of local capacities and leadership. "A major question is how the aid game will evolve in resilience humanitarianism that still walks a fine line between support and abandonment" (Hilhorst, 2018, p. 47). Specifically, Hilhorst (2018) cautioned that as refugees rapidly become indistinguishable from the urban poor, with no "linkages to the formal parts of society—nor as wage earners, nor as consumers and not as politically significant members of an electorate," there is "a real risk that the politics of resilience towards refugees turns instead into a politics of abandonment" (p. 40). And in rendering crises-affected populations responsible for their own survival and governance, the humanitarian ecosystem often operates on ill-tested assumptions.

Pathways to Systemic Resilience: Wealth, Health, and Peace

So how do we build the foundations for more resilient social, economic, and political systems? Where should we start? Is it best to build wealth to raise communities out of poverty, or best to focus on the health and well-being of individuals affected by loss or trauma, or best to promote peace, security, and stability at institutional levels? And how do we link together structural, social, and individual resilience to foster livelihoods, well-being, and peacebuilding? These are important, strategic decisions, which often prove conceptually and logistically tricky in the context of humanitarian crises.

Linking Peace to Wealth and Food Security

A lens on resilience provides a useful framework with which to connect the dots between the humanitarian needs (e.g., security) and development needs (e.g., livelihoods) of conflict-affected populations. For example, building resilience is now a primary development aim in the Horn of Africa, where recurrent droughts gravely affect household food insecurity, competition over resources, and ethnic conflict. Here systemic-thinking can be found in resilience-based approaches that foster, synergistically, the goals of improving precarious livelihoods through peacebuilding initiatives.

A proof-of-concept example is found in research investigating how peacebuilding efforts might contribute to drought resilience among pastoralist groups in the region (Mercy Corps, 2015). A two-pronged focus on the management of conflict (peacebuilding) and the management of food insecurity (resilience to drought) proved useful research to inform policy recommendations for populations experiencing persistent vulnerability to climate- and market-related shocks. An explicit theory of change examined two different pathways of intervention: the first was at the level of social cohesion (strengthening community-level safety nets, for example, such that community members help each other out during times of stress), and the second was at the level of institutional environments (enabling influential leaders to reach consensus-based agreements for access to resources, where groups habitually conflict). These two pathways to drought resilience were examined over time with data on intraethnic and interethnic disputes, household-level reports of food insecurity, and social norms pertaining to conflict and conflict resolution. The case study supported the conclusion that building resilience through peacebuilding efforts could support food security goals (Mercy Corps, 2015).

Similarly, building economic resilience through financial inclusion is also an explicit priority for many businesses and policymakers to help low-income households prepare for shocks in ways that encourage them to hold insurance, accumulate precautionary savings, and access social protection. But financial products such as consumer credit, money transfers, and insurance payouts are not often specifically designed as part of a climate change response program or as part of a regional resilience strategy for migrant populations (Moore, Niazi, Rouse, & Kramer, 2019). And there is little evidence of the long-term impacts of health financing in fragile and conflict-affected settings, which aspire to achieve financial protection, equity in access, and efficiency in resource allocation (Bertone, Jowett, Dale, & Witter, 2019).

Linking Peace to Biopsychosocial Health

An important example of systemic efforts to improve health and sustain peace, through resilience, comes from international and regional responses to the wars in Syria and Iraq. Insufficient or ineffective interventions have grave consequences, especially for children and adolescents: with exposure to violence, profound stress can negatively affect decision-making, social behaviors, learning abilities, and even future earning capacities. Much of the work undertaken on behalf of conflict-affected children emphasizes either the profound consequences of toxic stress in the wake of war and forced displacement (Save The Children, 2017) or a counternarrative of refugee resilience and agency in moving life forward (Underwood, 2018). What matters, over and above a tug-of-war between the dominant paradigms of refugee risk and resilience, is to put people—not projects—at the heart of humanitarian responses. This entails a different definition of success in humanitarian work: not just meeting short-term goals of project efficacy with respect to protection, health, or education, but building sustained partnerships to improve the life chances of individuals and social cohesion in their communities.

In response to the Syria and Iraq crises, several nongovernmental organizations thus joined forces to launch the No Lost Generation initiative, a platform for multiple donors to fund a number of child- and youth-focused interventions. This initiative was strategic at two main levels: it focused on adolescence, a key time for protecting the next generation and building its future, and it served both refugee and host communities to build trust and social cohesion. Following calls to strengthen the evidence base on health impacts in humanitarian crises, a research consortium of Western and Jordanian institutions evaluated one such program: a brief (eight-week-long) psychosocial intervention of structured, group-based activities for 8- to 15-year-olds, implemented by Mercy Corps in Jordan, Lebanon, Iraq, and Syria. Key elements of this program, known as Advancing Adolescents, were common to other psychosocial interventions, including group-based sessions to build technical, vocational, and socioemotional skills, under the supervision of trained local community volunteers. The program emphasized stress management, trusting social relationships, and personal goal achievement.

This brief intervention aimed to alleviate profound stress, strengthen resilience and learning skills, and build social cohesion, thus explicitly linking individual health with social peacebuilding outcomes: three levels of intervention (protection of children and youth in safe spaces; skills-building; relationships with mentors and peers) would lead to changes in to three measurable outcomes (reducing profound stress, building resilience, and fostering social cohesion through refugee–host community interactions) and three longer-term potential outcomes for individual and collective life (risk behavior reduction, educational and economic attainment, social stability). To evaluate this theory of change, the research consortium evaluated biopsychosocial health outcomes (the impacts of stress alleviation on the body, the mind, the brain, and sociality), conducting a randomized controlled trial with both Syrian refugees and Jordanian peers, with mixed methods that included stress biomarkers, psychometric assessment of mental health, experimental tests of cognitive function, and reports of community-level cohesion (Panter-Brick, Eggerman, Ager, Hadfield, & Dajani, 2020; Panter-Brick, Kurtz, & Dajani, 2018). Youth who participated in the Advancing Adolescents program showed significant changes in levels of hair cortisol, a useful biomarker of chronic physiological stress, and improvements in mental health and feelings of insecurity—benefits indicating a pathway to recovery, sustained over the period of one year (Dajani, Hadfield, van Uum, Greff, & Panter-Brick, 2018; Panter-Brick et al., 2017). More unexpectedly, given the stated goals to boost resilience, there were no changes in levels of resilience for program participants, relative to their peers. While a brief, structured intervention could significantly improve mental health and alleviate feelings of profound stress and insecurity, boosting the resilience levels of conflict-affected youth would need more than individual-level approaches; it would need interventions that targeted not only psychosocial health, but also family-level and society-level environments.

One methodological challenge of this impact evaluation was to operationalize the relevant dimensions of human experience in conflict-affected settings. This required meaningful measurement of stress, trauma, insecurity, resilience, and social cohesion, and necessitated developing culturally relevant, yet brief and valid metrics that nongovernmental organizations could then use at scale. Specifically, the research consortium developed the Arabic-language Child Youth Resilience Measure (Panter-Brick et al., 2017), for use in both Syrian refugee and Jordanian host populations, to assess young people's resilience—a word locally translated to *muruuna* (lit: "flexibility"). This metric built upon previous cross-cultural work (Ungar & Liebenberg, 2011) to measure the extent to which children and adolescents feel strong as individuals, in their relationships with others, and in their community. The challenge, in the field, was contextual relevance to achieve face validity, construct validity, and psychometric reliability. Specifically, the Child Youth Resilience Measure scores the extent to which respondents agree with pre-specified statements that characterize individual, relational, and cultural dimensions of resilience. Several items of the original, English-language scale needed specific attention. Statements regarding "having fun with friends," "enjoying one's traditions," and "feeling proud as citizens" were modified, as refugees pointed out that "fun" and "enjoyment" were inapplicable to their current circumstances and that some families had no citizenship status in Jordan. A statement such as "My parents watch me closely," which meant to convey close caregiving, had negative connotations, as it implied, for girls, a form of surveillance. The statement "I am proud of my traditions" could be asking whether refugees felt more Syrians than they did Jordanians (Panter-Brick et al., 2017). These nuances show the importance of fine-grained analyses of language and cultural meanings, namely, the vocabulary that expresses facets of lived experience.

Linking Peace to Early Childhood Development

Can systemic resilience-building approaches even be fostered at a global level to achieve lasting change? At the United Nations, several states have called for a U.N. resolution on the culture of peace, as a way of achieving lasting global security, with the General Assembly proclaiming 2001–2010 as the *International Decade for a Culture of Peace and Non-Violence for the Children of the World*. A culture of peace posits that the traditional ways of addressing conflict—mediation, humanitarian intervention, and diplomacy—are insufficient: building peace requires widespread societal change, a shift toward peaceful values and behavior, the elimination of social inequality, and the promotion of tolerance and solidarity. But how to link this global resolution with social change at ground level? A think-tank group of scholars and practitioners called attention to early child development and family-based interventions as ways to permeate not just individual homes, but entire communities, providing a bottom-up approach to create cumulative change in societies.

This group asked: Do the ways we raise children have implications for reducing violence and promoting peace in society (Leckman, Panter-Brick, & Saleh, 2014)? It reviewed the science on early child development that shows that the early years of human life are instrumental for laying out a foundation for healthy adulthood. Evolutionary biology teaches us that the biobehavioral systems associated with social bonds shape many of the behaviors and dispositions that pertain to trust, cooperation, empathy, or violence: caregiver–infant attachment, socioemotional stimulation in childhood, and early life skills have important and demonstrable implications for the developing brain, in terms of structure and function, while violence and socioemotional deprivation can have profound negative impacts on child and adolescent health and development. Economic modeling has shown that, in terms of dollars saved for every dollar spent on interventions over the life course, from in utero to early adulthood, investments in early childhood enrichment programs provide the greatest potential economic and human returns (Heckman, 2006). Because early life experiences are built into our bodies, in ways that affect the developing brain, the cardiovascular and immune systems, and metabolic regulatory controls (Garner & Shonkoff, 2012), childhood adversities and childhood enrichment programs can have multiple, synergistic effects on development, behavior, and sociality over the life course. This scientific evidence argues for a clear entry point in building a culture of peace: to begin with children and their families to provide foundational support for early child development.

The *ecology of peace* framework is helpful for conceptualizing how families, in their roles as caregivers, are instrumental in connecting biology, behavior, and society: they help connect the developing brain to socioemotional competencies, the developing child to the family and parenting across generations, and family-level interactions to social cohesion in the community. Families are an essential starting point for raising children with a disposition to peace: children who grow up with a disposition to act and think in ways that show empathy, maintain harmonious relationships, and promote the notions of nonviolence, equity, and social justice (Leckman et al., 2014). Importantly, group-based interventions can bring together families across ethnic or social divides, improving social cohesion as the same time as they build communication skills and nonviolent parenting. This was noted in Turkey during the implementation of a parenting enrichment program initiated by a nongovernmental organization with institutional state support. Society-wide interventions can then be layered onto these foundations, as seen in conflict-settings such as Afghanistan, Northern Ireland, and South Africa, where media initiatives and school-based interventions to promote peace education built upon family-level initiatives of violence prevention; the sustainability of change, however, remains very challenging (Abu-Nimer & Nasser, 2014; Christie et al., 2014; Leckman et al., 2014). Strong funding investments are needed for measurable progress toward systemic change. For example, in 2018, the MacArthur Foundation funded a remarkable partnership between the International Rescue Committee and Sesame Street to create *Ahlan SimSim* for war-affected children in the Middle East region, effectively supporting the largest early childhood intervention program in the history of humanitarian responses.

Early childhood development as a pathway to peace also asserts that family-level interventions will have transgenerational consequences. Children raised with a disposition to peace will raise their own children with parenting skills, social competencies, and the social, political, economic, and legal expectations of nonviolence and global citizenship. Just as violence and trauma can cascade across generations, so can peace and competencies cascade from one generation to the next. The concept of resilience is here helpful, allowing us to focus attention on the developmental and cultural leverage points that allow for transformative change (Leckman et al., 2014). This is one reason why the research on parenting and caregiving has blossomed in the fields of humanitarian interventions and peacebuilding. To give one striking example, the Luxembourg Peace prize was awarded in 2019 to Promundo, an international organization with initiatives focused on creating a world free from violence by engaging fathers in issues directly related to caregiving, non-violence, and gender equity.

Resilience as an Everyday Practice

Efforts to identify pathways to systemic resilience need to be carefully grounded in behavior, culture, history, and politics. For communities living in contexts of poverty, insecurity, and violence, resilience is an everyday practice, one that requires active steps to achieve goals and orient behaviors. Much of the cross-cultural work on resilience to date has highlighted an experiential dimension of resilience, embedded in the lived experience of social suffering. In reflecting on cross-cultural resilience, for example, Mendenhall and Kim (2019) cited important research among the Inuit, who talk of *niriunniq*, or hope as a life-giving force (Kirmayer, Dandeneau, Marchall, Phillip, & Williamson, 2011), and research among Tibetan Buddhists, who practice *lojong*, or mind-training, to cultivate compassion for others and be accepting of lifelong suffering (Lewis, 2018). However, resilience is also agency and action—it can be transformative of social and political systems. To have power as an analytical construct, the narrative of resilience needs to move beyond the narrative of social suffering in contexts of social oppression and structural violence (Panter-Brick, 2014). It draws attention to the practices that help transform society. For example, resilience can be expressed in a practice of solidarity, as in the communal support of "holding hands" (*nguyu*) that proved critical to the reintegration of formal child soldiers in Rwanda (Betancourt et al., 2011). We are not, however, to equate the practice of resilience with passive coping and relative imperviousness: for example, rather than develop resilience against the oppressive forces of racism or sexism, people might fight to see racism and gender discrimination eliminated. We must also be mindful that culturally scripted strategies of resilience can turn to vengeance or violence, rather than to empathy, peace, and nonviolence. Indeed, there can be a dark side to resilience, one that is usually overlooked in theorizing and operationalizing this construct.

Cross-cultural research demands a careful normative understanding of resilience as an everyday practice, one that reflects specific world views and orients personal and collective behaviors. Why is an emphasis on everyday practice important? It avoids sidelining key aspects of the lives of local, regional, and international communities. For example, international humanitarian efforts have often adopted a largely positivist, secular approach, one that pays attention to culture without much analytical depth and one that pays very little attention to faith-based responses: religion is often "left outside the humanitarianism frame of legitimacy" (Ager & Ager, 2015, p. 49). What we have learnt, however, from local actors is that faith and culturally scripted moral values cannot be sidelined in humanitarian responses. Faith is often an integral part of how individuals and communities rise to the challenges of adversity (Marie, Hannigan, & Jones, 2018), while moral choices loom large in efforts to make sense of life when confronting danger and uncertainty (Kleinman, 2006). These normative dimensions are one reason why cross-cultural measurement of resilience can be difficult (Mendenhall & Kim, 2019), and why sophisticated models of resilience, resistance, or coping tend to be limited to mapping functional outcomes (Bonanno & Diminich, 2013; Masten, 2011; Masten & Narayan, 2012). Paying attention to both the normative and functional dimensions of resilience is one of the better ways to help improve the relevance of theory, methods, and interventions.

The Political Economy of Resilience

Importantly, a lens on resilience as an everyday practice helps to identify synergies for taking action at the political and economic level. For example, work in Afghanistan has illustrated a remarkable example of social suffering, collective resilience, and policy implications. After decades of war, Afghans could articulate a forceful message about the need for multi-level resource provision. For Afghan families, there is no health without mental health, no mental health without family unity, no family unity without work, dignity, and a functioning economy, and no functioning economy without good governance (Ager, Annan, & Panter-Brick, 2014; Eggerman & Panter-Brick, 2010). Working systemically across sectors of health, the economy, and political governance is thereby the difference between surviving in misery and flourishing in dignity. What emerges here is an analysis of the political economy of resilience: where people are trapped in poverty, insecurity, or violence, our conceptual frames need to go well beyond a focus on individual-level functional outcomes (i.e., coping), to focus—at social, economic, legal, and political levels—on institutional power and community agency.

A political economy of resilience strives for critical analyses of the power dynamics and structural contexts that orient agency, transformation, or stasis. It gives us a political understanding—more than a functional understanding—of the trade-offs that are made in terms of personal lives, social goals, and policy interventions. It builds upon earlier work, focused on socioecological analyses of resources or transactional analyses of agency (Panter-Brick, 2014; Ungar, 2012), pushing us to ask more complex questions, including: how, when, and for whom does resilience-building work, in what contexts, over what time frame, at what scale, under which testable assumptions, and involving which actors and sectors? Pathways to systemic resilience are essential to social and political transformation: they describe how nations actively build themselves anew, after decades of neoliberal policies that transformed all levels of cultural, political, and economic life (Hall & Lamont, 2013). They are defined by political ideology and socioeconomic realities. For example, in Palestine, the notion of *sumud* (holding steadfast to the land) guides personal and collective understandings of resilience as everyday resistance against violent occupation (Marie et al., 2018), fueling survival tactics and goals for social justice.

Conclusion

Resilience is a key construct animating research and policy approaches to achieve systemic changes in the wake of crises. Seeking to achieve transformative, sustainable changes, the fields of resilience humanitarianism and peacebuilding have examined pathways to resilience in areas of violence prevention, food security, stress alleviation, child development, and social cohesion. In a sense, these approaches strive to develop three-dimensional views on resilience (linking wealth, health, and peace), moving away from a one-dimensional view on resilience as the ability to thrive or the absence of negative health outcomes.

Working toward systems-level resilience necessitates a simultaneous strengthening of structural, social, and individual resilience. This demands a careful normative understanding of the everyday practice and the political economy of resilience, which for crisis-affected communities, is rooted in agency, resistance, and transformation. It also necessitates conceptual clarity, meaningful measurement, and the cultural grounding of scalable interventions. What matters now is for research, policy, and practice to steer away from the three "sins" of resilience work: being conceptually hazy, methodologically lame, and empirically light (Panter-Brick & Leckman, 2013). I argue that critical analyses of moral, political, social, and historical contexts are essential to guard us against superficial views of resilience, against a politics of abandonment toward the people who are caught in the forks of humanitarian crises, and against a politics of laissez-faire that expects all coping to be done at an individual level without much strengthening of resources at a social and structural level. Critical analyses help us test our normative assumptions, identify the critical turning points for systemic transformation, and establish sustained partnerships for effective action.

Key Messages

1. In international policy circles, resilience-building approaches emphasize theories of change based on a social compact between state and society. They make partnerships with local actors the key to pressing global issues such as violence prevention.
2. Good examples of resilience-building interventions in humanitarian crises are those that foster wealth, health, and peace to reach synergistic impacts on livelihoods, well-being, and social cohesion.
3. Resilience is an everyday practice for crises-affected communities and can be transformative of social and political systems. Achieving systemic change requires working on the political economy of resilience, social action, and structural transformation.
4. Resilience-building approaches demand careful work with respect to theory, measurement, and intervention.

References

Abu-Nimer, M., & Nasser, I. (2014). Linking peacebuilding and child development: A basic framework. In J. Leckman, C. Panter-Brick, & R. Salah (Eds.), *Pathways to peace: The transformative power of children and families* (pp. 323–337). Cambridge, MA: MIT Press.

Ager, A., & Ager, J. (2015). *Faith, secularism, and humanitarian engagement: Finding the role of religion in the support of displaced communities.* New York, NY: Palgrave Macmillan.

Ager, A., Annan, J., & Panter-Brick, C. (2014). *Resilience: From conceptualization to effective intervention— Policy brief for Humanitarian and Development Agencies.* The Conflict, Resilience, and Health Program, Yale University, New Haven, CT.

Bertone, M., Jowett, M., Dale, E., & Witter, S. (2019). Health financing in fragile and conflict-affected settings: What do we know, seven years on? *Social Science & Medicine, 232,* 209–219. doi:10.1016/j.socscimed.2019.04.019

Betancourt, T. S., Meyers-Ohki, S., Stulac, S. N., Barrera, A. E., Mushashi, C., & Beardslee, W. R. (2011). Nothing can defeat combined hands (Abashize hamwe ntakibananira): Protective processes and resilience in Rwandan children and families affected by HIV/AIDS. *Social Science & Medicine, 73*(5), 693–701. doi:10.1016/j.socscimed.2011.06.053

Bonanno, G., & Diminich, E. (2013). Positive adjustment to adversity: Trajectories of minimal-impact resilience and emergent resilience. *Journal of Child Psychology and Psychiatry, 54*(4), 378–401. doi:10.1111/jcpp.12021

Christie, D., Panter-Brick, C., Behrman, J., Cochrane, J., Dawes, A., Goth, K., . . . Tomlinson, M. (2014). Healthy human development as a path to peace. In J. Leckman, C. Panter-Brick, & R. Salah (Eds.), *Pathways to peace: The transformative power of children and families* (pp. 273–302). Cambridge, MA: MIT Press.

Dajani, R., Hadfield, K., van Uum, S., Greff, M., & Panter-Brick, C. (2018). Hair cortisol concentrations in war-affected adolescents: A prospective intervention trial. *Psychoneuroendocrinology, 89,* 138–146. doi:10.1016/j.psyneuen.2017.12.012

Eggerman, M., & Panter-Brick, C. (2010). Suffering, hope, and entrapment: Resilience and cultural values in Afghanistan. *Social Science & Medicine, 71,* 71–83. doi:10.1016/j.socscimed.2010.03.023

Erdberg, L., & Moix, B. (2019). *How civil society can help prevent violence and extremism—And what the international community can do to support it*. Analysis, Task Force on Extremism in Fragile States, United States Institute of Peace.

Garner, A. S., & Shonkoff, J. P. (2012). Early childhood adversity, toxic stress, and the role of the pediatrician: Translating developmental science into lifelong health. *Pediatrics, 129*(1), e224–e231. doi:10.1542/peds.2011-2662

Grandi, F. (2019). *A world of pain in three stories: This is the refugee crisis today*. World Economic Forum.

Hall, P. A., & Lamont, M. (Eds.). (2013). *Social resilience in the neoliberal era*. Cambridge, MA: Cambridge University Press.

Heckman, J. (2006). Skill formation and the economics of investing in disadvantaged children. *Science, 312*(5782), 1900–1902. doi:10.1126/science.1128898

Hilhorst, D. (2018). Arenas. In T. Allen, A. Macdonald, & H. Radice (Eds.), *Humanitarianism: A dictionary of concepts* (pp. 30–51). Routledge: Taylor & Francis.

Kirmayer, L. J., Dandeneau, S., Marchall, E., Phillip, M. K., & Williamson, K. J. (2011). Rethinking resilience from Indigenous perspectives. *Canadian Journal of Psychiatry, 56*(2), 84–91.

Kleinman, A. (2006). *What really matters: Living a moral life amidst uncertainty and danger*. Oxford, UK: Oxford University Press.

Leckman, J., Panter-Brick, C., & Saleh, R. (2014). *Pathways to peace: The transformative power of children and families*. Cambridge, MA: MIT Press.

Lewis, S. (2018). Resilience, agency, and everyday Lojong in the Tibetan Diaspora. *Contemporary Buddhism: An Interdisciplinary Journal, 19*(2), 342–361. doi:10.1080/14639947.2018.1480153

Marie, M., Hannigan, B., & Jones, A. (2018). Social ecology of resilience and Sumud of Palestinians. *Health, 22*(1), 20–35. doi:10.1177/1363459316677624

Masten, A. S. (2011). Resilience in children threatened by extreme adversity: Frameworks for research, practice, and translational synergy. *Development and Psychopathology, 23*(2), 493–506. doi:10.1017/S0954579411000198

Masten, A. S., & Narayan, A. J. (2012). Child development in the context of disaster, war, and terrorism: Pathways of risk and resilience. *Annual Review of Psychology, 63*, 227–257. doi:10.1146/annurev-psych-120710-100356

Mendenhall, E., & Kim, A. W. (2019). How to fail as scale: Reflections on a failed attempt to assess resilience. *Culture, Medicine and Psychiatry, 43*, 315–325. doi:10.1007/s11013-018-9617-4

Mercy Corps. (2015). *Cracking the code: Enhancing emergency response & resilience in complex crises*. DR Congo, Lebanon, Syria, Uganda, Mercy Corps.

Moore, D., Niazi, Z., Rouse, R., & Kramer, B. (2019). *Building resilience through financial inclusion: A review of existing evidence and knowledge gaps*. Innovations for Poverty Action.

Panter-Brick, C. (2014). Health, risk, and resilience: Interdisciplinary concepts and applications. *Annual Review of Anthropology, 43*, 431–448. doi:10.1146/annurev-anthro-102313-025944

Panter-Brick, C., Dajani, R., Eggerman, M., Hermosilla, S., Sancilio, A., & Ager, A. (2017). Insecurity, distress and mental health: Experimental and randomized controlled trials of a psychosocial intervention for youth affected by the Syrian crisis. *Journal of Child Psychology and Psychiatry, 59*(5), 523–541. doi:10.1111/jcpp.12832

Panter-Brick, C., Hadfield, K., Dajani, R., Eggerman, M., Ager, A., & Ungar, M. (2017). Resilience in context: A brief and culturally-grounded measure in Syrian refugees and Jordanian host-community adolescents. *Child Development, 89*(5), 1803–1820. doi:10.1111/cdev.12868

Panter-Brick, C., Kurtz, J., & Dajani, R. (2018). What strong partnerships achieve: Innovations in research and practice. *Humanitarian Exchange, 72*, 15–19.

Panter-Brick, C., & Leckman, J. F. (2013). Resilience in child development: Interconnected pathways to wellbeing. *Journal of Child Psychology and Psychiatry, 54*(4), 333–336. doi:10.1111/jcpp.12057

Save The Children. (2017). *Invisible wounds: The impact of six years of war on the mental health of Syria's children*. Retrieved from savethechildren.net.

Underwood, E. (2018). Lessons in resilience: In war zones and refugee camps, researchers are putting resilience interventions to the test. *Science, 359*(6379), 976–979. doi:10.1126/science.aat4488

Ungar, M. (Ed.). (2012). *The social ecology of resilience: A handbook of theory and practice.* New York, NY: Springer.

Ungar, M., & Liebenberg, L. (2011). Assessing resilience across cultures using mixed methods: Construction of the child and youth resilience measure. *Journal of Mixed Methods Research, 5*(2), 126–149. doi:10.1177/1558689811400607

United Nations. (2018). *Social compact for migration and refugees.* United Nations.

United Nations High Commissioner for Refugees. (2018). *Global trends—Forced displacement in 2018.* Geneva, Switzerland: Author.

van Metre, L. (2016). *Fragility and resilience.* United States Institute of Peace. Fragility Study Group. Policy Brief No.2.

van Metre, L., & Calder, J. (2016). *Peacebuilding and resilience: How society respond to violence.* Peaceworks 119. United States Institute of Peace.

20
Toward a Multisystemic Resilience Framework for Migrant Youth

Qiaobing Wu and Ying Ou

Introduction

Resilience has gained increasing popularity in migration and youth studies. As a concept widely used in a variety of disciplines and research fields, resilience offers an appropriate lens to understand the development of children and youth in the face of adversity, to identify the risk and protective factors working in concert to influence developmental outcomes, and to unveil the mechanism through which these factors operate. Recent research on migrant youth has witnessed a growing number of examples employing the concept of resilience to decode the adaptive outcomes against the anticipated negative consequences of migration and resettlement (Motti-Stefanidi & Masten, 2017). However, an integrative framework that takes into account the functioning of multiple systems that foster resilience in migrant youth does not exist and has yet to be developed. It remains a key question in this field of research to explore: What constitutes and promotes resilience for the development of migrant youth, and how do these mechanisms work?

To address the previous question, this chapter first reviews the definition of resilience in different social science disciplines and seeks to develop a definition that is particularly suitable for use in migrant youth research. Following the review and refinement of a definition of resilience for migrant youth, the chapter continues to investigate how resilience has been manifested and studied in multiple systems in existing research, namely, the intrapersonal microsystem, the interpersonal mesosystem, and the institutional macrosystem, as well as how these multiple systems may interact with each other while exerting effects on the development of migrant youth. The chapter concludes by proposing a potential Multisystemic

Resilience Framework for migrant youth and envisions the implications of this potential framework for research, policy and practice.

Definition of Resilience in Migrant Youth Research

With the original meaning "rebound," the term *resilience* was used to describe elasticity of materials in natural sciences and then borrowed by social sciences in the 1950s. As a perfect term bridging the gap "between (dynamic) adaptation and (static) resistance," resilience has attracted increasing attention from various disciplines (Alexander, 2013, p. 2714).

In social sciences, resilience has gained a multitude of definitions and usages across a range of disciplines. From the ecological perspective, it refers to the capacity of a socioecological system coping with external stresses and barriers in the changing environment (Folke et al., 2010; Holling, 1973). In the field of developmental psychopathology, it mainly refers to the capacity of successful coping in a stressful environment in child development, particularly with a focus on the avoidance of or resistance to psychosocial adversity (Cicchetti & Cohen, 1995; Garmezy,1991; Nigg, Nikolas, Friderici, Park, & Zucker, 2007; Rutter, 1999). From the perspective of positive psychology, resilience refers to positive personality traits such as hardiness and invulnerability (e.g., Anthony, 1974; Florian, Mikulincer, & Taubman, 1995; Seligman & Csikszentmihalyi, 2000). As a broad umbrella concept, resilience not only refers to multiple systems (e.g., a person, a group, or a community), but has also been used to represent the interactions across different systems, especially interactions between risk and protective factors (Olsson, Bond, Burns, Vella-Brodrick, & Sawyer, 2003). Despite no consensus on the definition of resilience among researchers in this field, it has been generally acknowledged that resilience is composed of two core components—adversity and positive adaptation (Cosco et al., 2017).

Guided by this general understanding, a large number of studies on the resilience of children and youth have been conducted to date. Although resilience remains conceptually multifaceted in these studies, its interpretations have predominantly focused on two directions—the outcome of adaptation to adversity and the processes/mechanisms that facilitates adaptation to adversity (Olsson et al., 2003). On the one hand, these studies have contributed to introducing resilience into the general conceptual map of risk and coping. Resilience has been applied in various circumstances of adversity faced by youth at-risk, including chronic adversities, trauma, migration, cumulative life events, and specific experiences (Masten & Obradović, 2006). On the other hand, much less attention has been given to variations in the living contexts wherein different subgroups of youth grow and develop.

Recent advances in resilience studies have pointed out that considerable differences exist in the adaptation process of youth in different groups and societies, both empirically and theoretically (Masten, 2014; Tol, Song, & Jordans, 2013). For instance, stresses and challenges encountered by youth experiencing migration are different from those encountered by youth experiencing abuse, violence, or other traumatic events. For youth in the context of migration, which involves significant life transitions and multifaceted changes of environment, challenges brought to children and youth as a consequence of movement and resettlement (i.e., migration) include language and communication barriers, disrupted family dynamics, shifts in role responsibilities, broken social networks, relationship with people in the mainstream, lack of social support, and restricted access to social welfare and other services (Qin, 2006; Sodowsky, Lai, & Plake, 1991; Yeh et al., 2008; Wong, Li, & Song, 2007). These challenges have been documented in research on children and youth in contexts of both international migration and internal migration such as the rural–urban migration in China (Whyte, 2010). Therefore, migration constitutes a unique risk situation, or adversity, that is anticipated to trigger negative outcomes for youth development. However, despite the risks and challenges, some youth in the migration context adapt well. There are youths who can function better than others when fighting against the negative outcomes expected to appear as a result of migration. In other words, they demonstrate resilience in this particular risk situation. Therefore, it is the aim of this chapter to explore what fosters resilience of migrant youth by discussing the multiple systems they live with in a holistic and dynamic way. As some scholars contend, time-specific and context-specific protective factors should be identified to protect youth "in specific life contexts" "against specific risks" (Schoon & Parsons, 2002, p. 268; Masten, 2014; Tol et al., 2013). With a particular focus on migrant youth, we aim to explicate the concept and refine the understanding of resilience specifically in the context of migration and youth studies.

The adversity or risk situation faced by migrant youth can be generally decoded into challenges brought about by two transitions. On the one hand, migration involves transition of geographical and sociocultural environment from the place of origin to the place of destination. It is fraught with stresses and challenges derived from the daily interactions between the individual and socioecological systems (e.g., family, school, neighborhood) as well as various cultural encounters (Berry, 2006; Wu, Tsang, & Ming, 2014). On the other hand, migrant youth also experience a transition of developmental stage. Youth development arouses shifts in personal identity and social roles. Instability and dysfunction during this transitional period may exert negative influences on individual well-being (Cicchetti & Rogosch, 2002). As a consequence, these two transitions intertwine with each other to place migrant youth in a uniquely challenging situation that requires both inner strength and external resources to facilitate healthy adaptation and maintain positive development.

Grounded on this understanding, to provide a definition of resilience particularly for youth in the context of migration, we define resilience as positive adaptation and development despite the challenging environmental changes and life transitions resulting from migration. Resilience refers to the process of migrant youth striving for a certain standard of well-being by constantly mobilizing resources from and interacting with multiple systems, including the intrapersonal microsystem, interpersonal mesosystem, and institutional macrosystem. The remainder of this chapter will show how resilience presents and functions in multiple systems, which leads to positive developmental outcomes for migrant youth.

Resilience in the Intrapersonal Microsystem

From the ecological perspective, resilience in the microsystem traditionally refers to individual psychological advantages, such as self-control or self-organization (Cicchetti &

Rogosch, 1997; Moffitt et al., 2011). Such a view is still prevalent among helping professionals (e.g., social workers, nurses, psychologists, etc.) who seek to design resilience-based intervention programs for children and youth. However, it is noteworthy that the rapid development of epigenetics and neurobiology have updated resilience researchers' thinking on human adaptation to the environment (Greenberg, 2006; Liu, Reed, & Girard, 2017; Rutter, 2013). With cumulative empirical evidence from the previous two fields, there is increasing awareness that biological factors should be taken into account while studying the resilience of migrant youth. Hence, in this section, we will discuss potential intrapersonal factors protecting migrant youth from negative biological, psychological, and social consequences of the adversities experienced during the dual-transition in migration.

Emerging research on epigenetics has transformed our thinking on the mechanism by which the human body adapts itself to the environment at the most microlevel (Gershon & High, 2015). Genetic studies on resilience are relatively common in the field of child abuse and neglect. Existing literature has documented several protective gene expressions associated with positive adaptation outcomes. One of these is the oxytocin receptor (OXTR). In general, growing evidence suggests that OXTR polymorphisms are influential in affect regulation, social interaction, self-esteem, and empathy (Lucht et al., 2009; Milaniak et al., 2017; Saphire-Bernstein, Way, Kim, Sherman, & Taylor, 2011). OXTR DNA methylation also predicts resilience in specific domains, such as the conduct-problem domain of children aged between 4 and 13 (Milaniak et al., 2017). Other genotypes like polymorphisms of the serotonin transporter gene have also been reported to relate to resilience through moderating gene–environment interactions (Hornor, 2017). These genes help mitigate the risk/adversity encountered throughout the life course.

Advances in neurobiology suggest that resilience also manifests in one's nervous system, working in concert with genetic protective factors. Most studies on resilience in this field focus on psychological disorders like major depressive disorder or posttraumatic stress disorder (PTSD). Initial findings on protective factors (i.e., resilient phenotype) in this dimension include dehydroepiandrosterone (reducing PTSD symptom and associated with better coping with PTSD), neuropeptide Y (functioning as a buffer against stress), Hypothalamic–pituitary–adrenal axis (related to stress responses), and testosterone (enhancing positive mood and social connectedness; Rasmusson, Vythilingam, & Morgan, 2003; Rasmusson, Schnurr, Zukowska, Scioli, & Forman, 2010; Russo et al., 2012). However, despite this fast growing research field, most of these studies are limited to correlational studies. The mechanisms underlying these linkages still remain vague (Russo, Murrough, Han, Charney, & Nestler, 2012). Moreover, findings on some of the previous factors (e.g., hypothalamic–pituitary–adrenal axis) are mixed, sometimes even contradictory (Meewisse, Reitsma, De Vries, Gersons, & Olff, 2007).

Clearly, the previously discussed protective factors in genetic and neurological dimensions provide us with a unique angle to understand individual resilience. Most of the empirical evidence was obtained from children confronted by specific adversities (e.g., child abuse). Related studies are notably scarce in the context of migration. However, considering that genetic and neurological processes may function similarly when children and youth experience similar environmental change to what migration usually brings, they are presumably indispensable intrapersonal resources that contribute to resilience in the microsystem. In fact, the theory of neural plasticity also infers that genetic polymorphisms are likely to be associated with better adaptation to a supportive environment among migrant youth (Rutter, 2013). Much more work is needed to further explore these two dimensions.

Compared to genetic and neurological factors, psychological factors have received much more attention in the extant research. Developmental psychology contributes significantly to our understanding of resilience. A large number of studies have identified at least the following three groups of factors regarding personal characteristics/personality traits. In terms of mental features, protective factors include planning, self-reflection, determination, self-confidence, and self-control (Moffitt et al., 2011). Likewise, competence and ability, intelligence or scholarly competence, and general problem-solving abilities have also proved to predict positive developmental outcomes (Dumont & Provost, 1999; Masten et al., 1999; Werner, 1993). Among all these factors, self-esteem and positive self-image appear widely in many research findings (e.g., Cicchetti & Rogosch, 1997; Dumont & Provost, 1999). As for cognitive aspects of resilience, mental flexibility in cognitive operations and emotional regulation play critical roles in psychological resilience (Cicchetti & Rogosch, 1997; Flores, Cicchetti, & Rogosch, 2005; Qouta, El-Sarraj, & Punamäki, 2001).

Concerning migrant youth in particular, the current research evidence delineating the effects of genetic, neurological, and psychological factors highlights the significance of inner resources for the fostering of resilience. A longitudinal study spanning over 20 years on youth development with a school-cohort sample in the United States found some adaptive resources as protective factors of life-transition (Masten et al., 2004). The results indicate that adaptive resources at intrapersonal dimension are crucial for the healthy adaption of children and youth, including planfulness, autonomy, future motivation, and coping skills. Relevant to the focus of this chapter, self-esteem has also been identified as an important indicator of refugee youth's well-being (Correa-Velez, Gifford, & McMichael, 2015; McCarthy & Marks, 2010).

In summary, looking at resilience in the microsystem, genetic, neurological, and psychological factors could all play critical roles in the positive adaptation of migrant youth. Instead of functioning alone; however, these factors interact with each other. Mounting evidence has suggested that resilience is not determined by one single factor and does not manifest in one single dimension or exerts influence over just one adaptive outcome (Greenberg, 2006; Liu et al., 2017). Not only do resilience factors interact with one another, there is also complex interplay between these intrapersonal factors and the surrounding environment in which youth live. Furthermore, when a child is exposed to a challenging environment, whether these factors function in positive or negative ways may depend on the specific domain of adaptation and the interactions between the intrapersonal characteristics and the environment (Lengua & Wachs, 2012; Shiner & Masten, 2012). An increasing number of studies suggest that context moderates the impact of individual differences on adaptive function and development (Belsky, Bakermans-Kranenburg, & van IJzen-doorn, 2007; B. J. Ellis & Boyce, 2011). Some protective factors in youth resilience are culturally and contextually specific (Ungar, 2008). Therefore, it is important to look beyond the intrapersonal factors in the microsystem and take into consideration the interpersonal and institutional factors in the meso- and macrosystems to reach a fuller understanding of resilience among migrant youth.

Resilience in the Interpersonal Mesosystem

Research in the field of migration, particularly on migrant children and youth, mostly approaches resilience in the mesosystem (the system formed when individuals interact with one another). In these studies, application of the resilience framework is often coupled with an ecological or multisystemic perspective. Attention has been given to the risk and protective factors across a range of social contexts in the ecological system wherein children and youth grow and develop, typically including the family, school, neighborhood, and community (Bronfenbrenner, 1989; Fraser, Kirby, & Smokowski, 2004). There has also been a paradigm shift in the recent resilience literature, which encourages more focus on the strengths of an individual that can be mobilized to overcome adversity and achieve personal growth (Michaud, 2006), rather than on the adversity that creates barriers and challenges. As a consequence, research of resilience in the mesosystem has put considerable efforts into examining the protective factors that may enhance an individual's capacity to transcend life difficulties (Michaud, 2006). This focus is thus often built into theories investigating the effects of social resources (i.e., protective factors) on the various developmental outcomes of youth. One such intersection is the use of social capital theory in studying the health, education, and psychological well-being of children and youth. Much of the lead author's research on children and youth in the Chinese context of migration showcases such a research direction (Wu, 2017; Wu, Lu, & Kang, 2015; Wu & Palinkas, 2012; Wu, Palinkas, & He, 2010, 2011; Wu et al., 2014).

For example, rural–urban migration in China since the mid-1980s has featured a phenomenal large scale population flow from the rural to urban areas driven by people's hopes to seek better employment opportunities and living conditions. However, given the long-established household registration system in China, which assigns each individual a *hukou* (identity) at birth that is tied to birth place, rural migrants and their children usually have restricted access to social welfare and public services in the city because they do not possess the legitimate *hukou* status, or the urban residency necessary to enjoy welfare benefits and services in that city. For example, children from migrant families may not be able to attend public schools unless they can prove the stability of their working and living conditions in the city by presenting a considerable number of documents, or paying extremely high tuition fees, both of which are difficult for migrant families to provide. This creates a uniquely adverse situation for youth in this migration context. Moreover, despite migrating within their own country, the geographic span of China results in huge disparities in economic development and cultural norms across different regions and provinces. Therefore, the environmental changes and life transitions that migrant youths experience are no less than those found in international migration.

Wu's research applies the resilience framework, treating migration as the risk and social capital as protective factors, and investigates the influences of social resources embedded in a range of social contexts on various development outcomes of migrant youth (i.e., educational achievement, psychosocial adjustment and mental health). Following Coleman (1990), social capital is defined as "social resources inherent in social relationships that facilitate a social outcome" (p. 302). Social capital embedded in each domain of the social ecology constitutes resilience in the mesosystem, including family social capital (i.e., the bonds between parents and children reflected in the time and attention spent interacting with children and monitoring their activities; Coleman, 1990), school social capital (i.e., relational quality between all stakeholders in the school environment, such as interactions between students and teachers, between peer groups, and communications between school and family; Roffey, 2010), peer social capital (i.e., quality of peer relationships in terms of density, range, intimacy, and level of trust) (Ream, 2005), and community social capital (i.e., social connectedness among resident adults and youths, reflected by social networks, norms, trust, a sense of belonging to the neighborhood, and civic engagement; Coleman, 1988; Putnam, 2000). These various social contexts are especially important for migrant youth because the process of migration and resettlement usually involves breaking and rebuilding social networks and adapting to changed relational dynamics in all these social domains. Therefore, Wu has constructed an integrative framework to take into account social resources inherent in all of the previous dimensions, organized under the umbrella concept *social capital*, and reveals the mechanism by which these factors operate independently, jointly, and interactively. For instance, one study focusing on the psychosocial adjustment of Chinese migrant youth suggests that that interpersonal resources in all four social domains facilitate better psychosocial outcomes (Wu, 2017). Moreover, social capital in the family, school, and peer dimensions have also been found to mediate the effects of community social capital on psychosocial adjustment, meaning that one specific dimension could have an influence on other dimensions, which further leads to differential outcomes in migrant youth. In other research (Wu et al., 2011), community social capital was also found to serve as a moderator, indicating that when greater social resources are present in the neighborhood, resources embedded in the family sphere exert stronger effects on the promotion of psychosocial adjustment among migrant youth. In other words, the protective function of one social domain (e.g., family) for the adaptation and well-being of migrant youth relies on the resourcefulness and support of another domain (e.g., community). These findings provide solid evidence of the interactive nature among multiple social domains at the mesosystemic level. The next section will explore the potential main factors that contribute to resilience of migrant youth in the macrolevel institutional system.

Resilience in the Institutional Macrosystem

Factors in the macrosystem constitute another set of critical elements essential for promoting resilience but are addressed less often in the literature, even though they may affect the sustainability of positive adaptation at the individual level (Ungar, 2018). In the context of migration, supportive social environments can act as protective factors to facilitate resilience (Correa-Velez et al., 2015; Edge, Newbold, & McKeary, 2014; Fazel, Reed, Panter-Brick, &

Stein, 2012). Young migrants and their families are influenced by the culture, economics, and politics of receiving societies in regard to both their short-term adaptation and long-term development (Portes & Rumbaut, 2001; Dryden-Peterson, 2016; Suárez-Orozco, Abo-Zena, & Marks, 2015). For instance, numerous studies have suggested that acculturative stressors have negative influence on the mental health of various subgroups of migrant youth (e.g., refugees, overseas students, rural-to-urban migrants, etc.), which implies a critical role for culture and related macrolevel factors in the process of migrant adaptation (e.g., Berry, 1992, 2006; B. H. Ellis, MacDonald, Lincoln, & Cabral, 2008; Sonderegger & Barrett, 2004; Wen & Hanley, 2015; Schachner, He, Heizmann, & Van de Vijver, 2017). For example, a longitudinal study in the United States suggests that perceiving greater exposure to acculturative stress is significantly associated with internalizing mental health symptoms (i.e., withdrawal, anxiety, depression, and somatic symptom) among urban-residing high school students with first or second generation immigration backgrounds (Sirin, Ryce, Gupta, & Rogers-Sirin, 2013). Another U.S. study on English-speaking Somali adolescent refugees also found that acculturative stressors predict greater PTSD symptoms after accounting for trauma, demographic, and immigration variables (B. H. Ellis et al., 2008). In this section, we focus on three potential protective factors in the macrosystem that may promote resilience of migrant youth: culture, policy and religion.

Culture affects the meaning system that influences resource allocation (Ungar, 2015). For migrant youth, the process of adapting to a different culture is widely acknowledged as a key variable mediating emotional difficulties (e.g., Roebers & Schneider, 1999). Two distinct aspects of culture are worthy of special attention. First, the inclusiveness of mainstream culture matters for nurturing resilience among migrant youth. It has been demonstrated that environments that value cultural diversity are facilitative for the adaptation and well-being of migrant youth and result in their enhanced sense of belonging (Ward & Geeraert, 2016). For instance, research suggests that in a school context valuing diversity and cultural sensitivity, Latino students are more likely to engage in academic activities and have desirable academic outcomes (Bryan & Atwater, 2002; Richards, Brown, & Forde, 2007). On the contrary, feeling unwelcomed or alienated by the host culture prevents migrant youth from being better integrated and better adapting to a new environment. Berry, Phinney, Sam, and Vedder (2006) found perceived discrimination to be strongly and negatively associated with both psychological and sociocultural adaptation.

Second, the concordance/discordance between the culture of origin and culture of destination also influences the coping and development of young migrants during their acculturation process. The extent to which the original and host cultures share similar values and favor similar behaviors determines whether culture-related factors will create more barriers or facilitate the adaptation process of migrant youth. Research on discordant acculturation preference between two cultural groups suggests that less discordance is associated with less in-group bias, more tolerance, better intergroup relations, and less perceived threat (e.g., Pfafferott & Brown, 2006; Rohmann, Piontkowski, & van Randenborgh, 2008; Zagefka & Brown, 2002). In sum, the inclusiveness of the mainstream culture in the host society and the concordance between the culture of origin and destination constitute one critical macrofactor in the resilience of migrant youth.

Social policy may have significant impact on the development of migrant youth too. A specific social policy could impede or promote resilience for a particular subgroup of young migrants. Some existing social policies or institutional settings contribute negatively to the development of youth with a migrant background. Taking education as an example, which plays a critical role in youth development, less positive outcomes have been reported among unauthorized migrants (in comparison to peers with authorized status) across various societies (e.g., the United States, China, Europe; Bean, Brown, Bachmeier, Brown, & Bachmeier, 2015; Gonzales, 2011; Levels, Dronkers, & Kraaykamp, 2008; Wen & Hanley, 2015). Such negative impacts remain even after influential factors like ethnicity and socioeconomic status (SES) are controlled for (e.g., Hall, Greenman, & Farkas, 2010). In China, barriers to attending public schools by migrant youths given their lack of legitimate urban residency under the household registration system is an example of how social policy shapes the adaptation and development of migrants. In addition to education, the policy impact on migrant youth can also be observed in the context of healthcare. For example, in the United Sates, the eligibility criteria for immigrant children to be covered by the State Children's Health Insurance Program restricts their access to healthcare (Androff, Ayon, Becerra, & Gurrola, 2011). It was rooted in the increasingly punitive enforcement of immigrant policy and the welfare reforms of the 1990s, which had rendered restricted eligibility of immigrants for health insurance. Later changes in Obama's policy released the restrictions and expanded medical coverage for those previously excluded immigrant children through the issuing of a new children's health insurance bill. This example indicates that social policy can be detrimental or beneficial for the adaptation and development of migrant youth, depending on whether the policy orientation is for or against migrants.

Religion constitutes another critical factor in the macrosystem. As an abstract value system, religion per se has a significant influence on the psychology and spirituality of individuals. Considerable empirical evidence indicates that religious beliefs have positive impacts on the resilience of migrant youth at the macrosystemic level as well. First, the existence of religious faith may be critical for the survival and adaptation of young immigrant. A study comparing changes in religiosity among new immigrants with Catholic and Islamic beliefs in Germany suggests that in places with a clear symbolic boundary against migrants' origin culture, new immigrants may count more on religious stability for better adaptation (Diehl & Koenig, 2013). In Ireland, Ní Raghallaigh and Gilligan (2010) conducted a qualitative study with local unaccompanied minors (i.e., young immigrants under the age of 18 and separated from primary caregivers). They point out that these unaccompanied teenagers' coping strategies toward the challenging and changing environment center on religious faith (belief in God) and is manifested in multiple coping forms. In the extreme case of asylum-seeking unaccompanied minors, when facing a challenging and changing environment with different culture and without adequate social support, religion becomes a "relatively available" and "relatively compelling" resource for coping and surviving (Ní Raghallaigh & Gilligan, 2010, p. 233). Furthermore, contents of a specific religion may buffer the pressure and distress brought by the migration process. For example, a study by Holleran and Waller (2003) found that religion may act as a critical source for the resilience of Mexican adolescents who migrate to the United States. For Mexican Americans, the core beliefs of their religion are acceptance of hardship, suffering, and death as an inevitable and essential part of life, which is closely related to their attitudes toward adversities and life transitions. Another study in India found that Muslim adolescents who put their religious belief and knowledge into action achieve a high level of resilience (Annalakshmi & Abeer, 2011). It is noteworthy that religion often functions via individuals (i.e., personal faith) and institutions (i.e., churches), yet itself is far beyond the micro- and mesosystem.

To summarize, culture, policy, and religion are potential protective factors in the macrosystem that promote resilience of migrant youth. We acknowledge that this list of factors is not exhaustive. Furthermore, macrosystem factors are intertwined with one another and do not function independently (i.e., social climate and social policy are mutually dependent). Policymakers who make settlement policies are influenced by the climate in the host society, while social policies also shape the attitudes of the public toward immigrants. Likewise, religion genuinely interacts with culture, politics, and corresponding migration policies (Mavelli & Wilson, 2016). As suggested by intersectionality theory, immigrants' well-being is shaped by culture, structural discrimination, immigration policies, and the like (Viruell-Fuentes, Miranda, & Abdulrahim, 2012). Worthy of note, the previously discussed macrosystemic factors do not always act as protective factors for migrant youth, especially given the tense climate toward certain types of displaced population (e.g., refugees) in Western countries. Attitudes toward the religion of immigrants vary greatly in different host societies, too (Foner & Alba, 2008). However, despite all these limitations, it is commonly acknowledged that factors in the macrosystem cannot be overlooked while investigating the adaptation and well-being of migrant youth. To some extent, appropriate advocacy for tolerance in areas like culture, policy, and religion might enable social institutions to become migrant-friendly and contribute to the resilience of migrant youth.

A Multisystemic Resilience Framework for Migrant Youth

There have been previous efforts to construct an integrative framework of resilience with multiple systems and factors taken into account. For instance, Motti-Stefanidi and Masten (2017) propose an integrative resilience development framework that incorporates acculturative and social-psychological variables to investigate "who among immigrant youth adapt well and why" (p. 19). Another recent paper also calls for advancing resilience through an integrative approach and proposes a model of resilience consisting of intra-individual, interpersonal, and socioecological systems (Liu et al., 2017). These earlier proposed models, however, tend to place intrapersonal factors at the core position while underestimating the importance of other systems, thus failing to truly achieve the goal of building an integrative multisystemic framework of resilience. No resilience framework has been developed specifically for migrant youth.

Building upon what has been previously discussed, we propose a new comprehensive multisystemic framework to understand the resilience of migrant youth (Figure 20.1). This framework consists of three core systems wherein resilience could be fostered through different channels and fulfill different functions. In an effort to present the nature of resilience as

Adversities/challenges →

Sociocultural transition

Migrant youth as active agents

Developmental transition

Microsystem — Genetic factors, Neurological factors, Psychological factors
Mesosystem — Family resources, Community resources, School resources
Macrosystem — Policy-related factors, Religion-related factors, Culture-related factors

Resilience

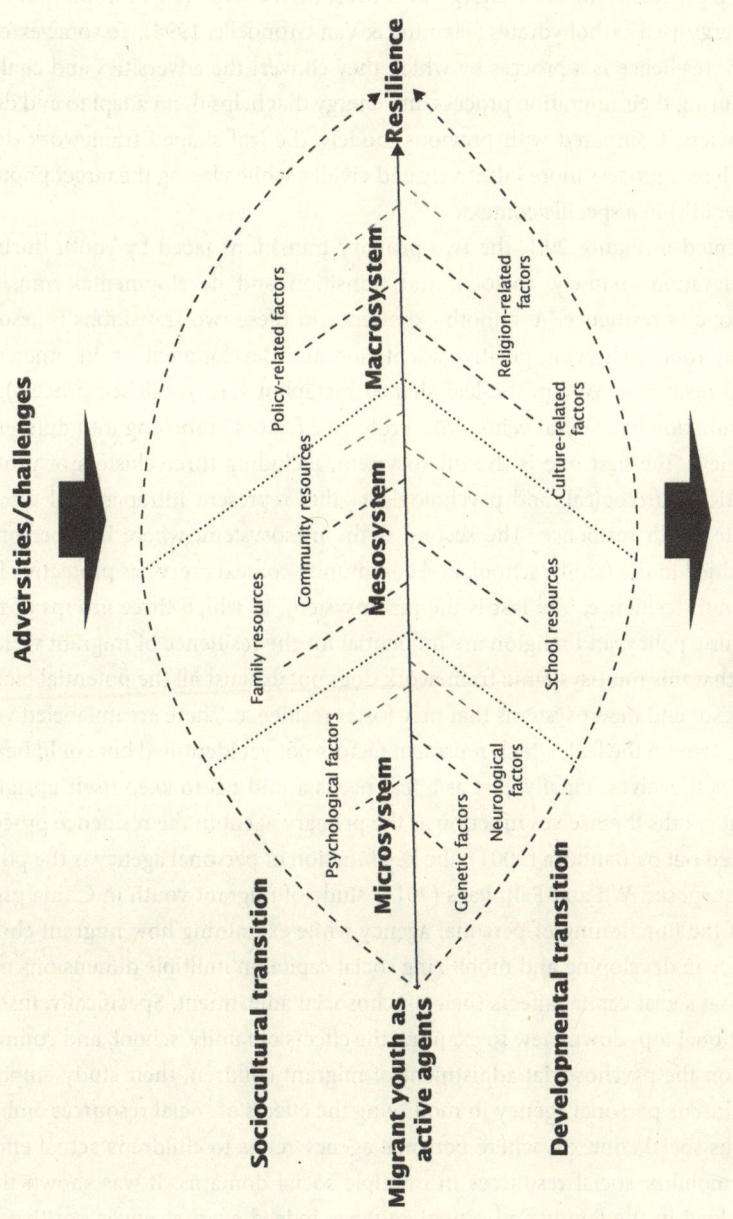

→ **Positive adaptation & development**

FIGURE 20.1 A multisystemic resilience framework for migrant youth.

a dynamic process shaped by interactions with and across multiple systems, which can hardly be exhibited in the classic structure of concentric circles commonly used for illustrating ecological models (e.g., Bronfenbrenner, 1994), we construct a leaf-shaped figure to demonstrate the Multisystemic Resilience Framework. The figure is inspired by the photosynthesis of green plants—a process using solar energy to convert light energy (e.g., carbon dioxide and water) into energy-rich carbohydrates (Fleming & Van Grondelle, 1994). To some extent, for migrant youth, resilience is a process by which they convert the adversities and challenges experienced during their migration process into energy that helps them adapt to and develop in the host society. Compared with previous models, the leaf-shaped framework demonstrates the resilience process more intuitively and vividly, while placing the target population (i.e., migrant youth) in a specific context.

As presented in Figure 20.1, the two primary transitions faced by youth during the process of migration—namely, sociocultural transition and developmental transition—defines the scope of resilience. A smooth experience in these two transitions is associated with a migrant youth achieving positive adaptation and development or, in other words, demonstrating resilience. Within the leaf-shaped metaphor (i.e., resilience process), three core systems function like lateral veins, with protective factors branching into different systems like veinlets. The first one is the microsystem, including three clusters of protective factors—genetic, neurological, and psychological—that represent intrapersonal resources, which facilitate youth resilience. The second is the mesosystem, where interpersonal resources embedded in the family, school, and community contexts serve as protective factors to promote youth resilience. The last is the macrosystem, in which three groups of factors related to culture, policy, and religion are influential for the resilience of migrant youth. We acknowledge that this multisystemic framework does not exhaust all the potential factors in the micro-, meso- and macrosystems that may foster resilience. There are unlabeled veinlets within each system on the leaf, which represent factors not yet identified but could be added to the model as it evolves. Finally, just as a leaf needs a mid-rib to keep itself upright and stable, migrant youths themselves function as the primary agent in the resilience process.

As pointed out by Bandura (2001), the key function of personal agency is the power to act for given purposes. Wu and Palinkas's (2014) study of migrant youth in China provides an example of the functioning of personal agency while examining how migrant children's personal agency in developing and mobilizing social capital in multiple dimensions moderates the way that social capital affects their psychosocial adjustment. Specifically, instead of taking a traditional top–down view to examine the effects of family, school, and community social capital on the psychosocial adjustment of migrant children, their study emphasizes the role of children's personal agency in modifying the effects of social resources embedded in these various social contexts, where personal agency refers to children's actual efforts to generate and mobilize social resources in multiple social domains. It was shown that resources embedded in the family and school contexts indeed exert stronger positive effects on children's psychosocial adjustment when migrant children present higher degrees of personal agency. This showcases one potential mechanism by which multiple systems interact with each other in the resilience process.

Another form of interaction between systems is found in the complex interplay between multiple systems as occurs when resources in the mesosystem—say, those embedded in the family, school, and neighborhood—promote the inner strength of individuals reflected as the personality trait of resilience, which, in turn, leads to more favorable outcomes for youth development. In other words, the microsystem of resilience serves as a mediator between the mesosystem and youth development. Wu and colleagues' (2014) research on the educational outcomes of migrant children in China provides an example of this type of cross-system interaction in resilience functioning. In that study, resources derived from the mesosystem (i.e., family social support and community social capital) promote the resilience (assessed as a personality trait) of migrant youths, which further results in enhanced educational outcomes. On the other hand, the microlevel resilience system, be it expressed as personality traits or resilient genes, may act as a moderator that modifies the function of resilience at the mesosystemic level. For instance, the interpersonal resilience resources may function most effectively for youths with greater resilience trait in protecting them from the negative influences of risk factors and promoting their development outcomes. Or, vice versa, the resilience resources in the interpersonal system work better for youths with weaker resilience trait, thus exhibiting a compensatory effect that mobilize contextual resources to combat the challenges brought about by insufficient inner strength in the face of risks. To elaborate more specifically, for example, social capital embedded in the family context may be most effective in promoting the life satisfaction of youths with greater resilience trait, while playing a less important or even nonsignificant role for youths with weaker resilience trait. It could also happen in a reverse direction. Social capital inherent in the family sphere may compensate for the insufficiency of intrapersonal resources thus having stronger positive effect on the life satisfaction of youths with weaker resilience trait. Whereas for youths who are internally resilient, family social capital may not exhibit such a significant effect. In both situations, the two different levels of systems are intertwined and interact with each other in their functioning on youth development through the youths themselves as the focal agents. Taken together, this Multisystemic Resilience Framework allows us to not only examine the impact of multiple systems, but to also take into account their intersections and interactions when exerting effects on youth development.

The last type of cross-system interactions in the Multisystemic Resilience Framework is achieved by manipulating the levels of analysis using different forms of variables representing different systems. For example, as Motti-Stefanidi and Masten (2017) suggest, the influence of SES, as a society variable, can be examined as an individual level variable if each person is given an SES score or be examined as an interpersonal level variable if giving the SES scores to schools or neighborhoods instead of individuals. By doing so, the same resilience factor can actually exist at different levels in different variable forms, which makes a unique channel for cross-system interactions in the multisystemic resilience model.

Implications of the Multisystemic Resilience Framework for Research, Policy and Practice

As a model developed for a specific youth population exposed to unique challenging transitions during the migration process, the Multisystemic Resilience Framework contributes to the growing body of literature on resilience and has potential implications for research, policy, and practice.

First, the Multisystemic Resilience Framework advances our understanding of the complex mechanisms by which multiple systems influence the adaptation and development of migrant youths. Typical investigations of resilience focus on independent effects of a single factor, a single dimension, or a single system on youth development. The framework calls for studies that take into account the potential interaction patterns across different systems to gain a comprehensive understanding of the resilience process. The Multisystemic Resilience Framework also stresses the critical role of migrant youths as active agents that mobilize resources embedded in each system and enable the concurrent functioning of multiple interacting systems.

Second, for policymakers and advocates, the Multisystemic Resilience Framework indicates the importance of nurturing a migrant-friendly environment as the foundation to foster resilience. Traditional policy adjustments regarding migrants usually focus on resource allocation while overlooking the role of social policy in shaping a migrant-friendly climate. Policymaking might be one of the most powerful and effective means in changing and guiding a social climate to be free of discrimination, deprivation, marginalization, and alienation. For instance, it is commonly reported that public narratives portray migrants as either victims or criminals. Such narratives could be changed if more efforts were devoted to the macrosystem, directing the policy and cultural environment to be more accommodating of migrants. Building a resilient macrosystem may influence the functioning of other systems in positive ways as well. Furthermore, previous research has demonstrated that the government has the potential power to foster migrant youth's agency in policy formulation (e.g., Hlatshwayo & Vally, 2014; Thompson, Torres, Swanson, Blue, & Hernández, 2019). Some policy sectors in Europe have started to involve migrant youth in immigration courts (Kanics, Hernández, & Touzenis, 2010). Increasing the participation of migrant youth in the policy process could be a potential strategy to promote their resilience.

Lastly, the Multisystemic Resilience Framework also provides some valuable insights for helping professionals in their development of intervention programs targeting resilience. Most existing interventions emphasize the importance of the microsystem in fostering resilience of young migrants, which leads to overemphasis on intrapersonal factors in program design. The intrapersonal factors are inarguably important, but not all resources in all systems are subject to change by programs with this exclusive focus. Some resources are more likely to increase (e.g., interpersonal resources in the mesosystem) than others (e.g., intrapersonal resources such as genetic and neurological factors). The Multisystemic Resilience Framework suggests that for interventions to be more effective, targeting more changeable factors in the interpersonal mesosystem and the institutional macrosystem could be a more effective strategy. Additionally, the framework also informs the development of intervention programs tapping into multiple systems in their design and utilizing the synergy across multiple systems to maximize the intervention effects. Moreover, helping professionals may also empower migrant youths to become active agents and navigate resources embedded in multiple systems for their positive adaptation and development. In a word, informed by the Multisystemic Resilience Framework, when it comes to fostering resilience in migrant youth, interventions should focus on factors beyond the individual level, initiate a chain of transformations across multiple systems, utilize the synergic effects across multiple systems as one system changes another, and enhance the agency of youths themselves to navigate to resources in multiple systems.

Conclusion

This chapter proposes a Multisystemic Resilience Framework for migrant youth. It first provides a definition of resilience particularly for youth in the context of migration. By developing an integrative framework and constructing a leaf-shaped model that represents the resilience process, the chapter contends that it takes multiple systems, including the intrapersonal microsystem, interpersonal mesosystem, and institutional macrosystems, to foster resilience in migrant youth. It understands resilience from a dynamic and resource-based perspective, considering resilience as fostered through the concurrent functioning of intrapersonal, interpersonal, and institutional resources embedded in multiple systems. Moreover, these multiple systems are not independent of one another, but interact through various mechanisms to facilitate resilience-enhancing processes, ensuring youths in the challenging situation of migration achieve healthy adaption and development. In addition, the Multisystemic Resilience Framework emphasizes the significant role of migrant youths as active agents in mobilizing resources from and facilitating interactions across the multiple systems. Grounded in this integrative framework, the chapter concludes by discussing the framework's potential implications for future research, policy, and practice. We acknowledge that the proposed multisystemic resilience framework is a comprehensive but far less than complete model that does not exhaust all potential systems and factors. More factors will need to be identified and incorporated that enrich the multiple systems affecting the resilience of youth migrants. The value of this framework, however, is as a general guide and reference for research, practice and policy development related to migrant youth.

Key Messages

1. For migrant youth, resilience refers to a process toward positive adaptation and development despite the challenging environmental changes and life transitions brought about by migration.
2. The resilience process for migrant youth is shaped by the complex interplay and synergistic effects of three interactive systems—the intrapersonal microsystem, interpersonal mesosystem, and institutional macrosystem.
3. Migrant youths act as active agents in the resilience process to mobilize resources from and facilitate interactions across multiple systems.

References

Alexander, D. E. (2013). Resilience and disaster risk reduction: An etymological journey. *Natural Hazards and Earth System Sciences, 13*(11), 2707–2716. doi:10.5194/nhess-13-2707-2013

Androff, D. K., Ayon, C., Becerra, D., & Gurrola, M. (2011). US immigration policy and immigrant children's well-being: The impact of policy shifts. *Journal of Sociology & Social Welfare, 38*, 77–98.

Annalakshmi, N., & Abeer, M. (2011). Islamic worldview, religious personality and resilience among Muslim adolescent students in India. *Europe's Journal of Psychology, 7*(4), 716–738. doi:10.5964/ejop.v7i4.161

Anthony, E. J. (1974). The syndrome of the psychologically invulnerable child. In E. J. Anthony & C. Koupernik (Eds.), *The child in his family: Children at psychiatric risk* (pp. 201–230). New York, NY: Wiley.

Bandura, A. (2001). Social cognitive theory: An agentic perspective. *Annual Review of Psychology, 52*(1), 1–26.

Bean, F. D., Brown, S. K., Bachmeier, J. D., Brown, S., & Bachmeier, J. (2015). *Parents without papers: The progress and pitfalls of Mexican American integration*. New York, NY: Russell Sage Foundation.

Belsky, J., Bakermans-Kranenburg, M. J., & Van IJzendoorn, M. H. (2007). For better and for worse: Differential susceptibility to environmental influences. *Current Directions in Psychological Science, 16*(6), 300–304. doi:10.1111/j.1467-8721.2007.00525.x

Berry, J. W. (1992). Acculturation and adaptation in a new society. *International Migration, 30*, 69–85.

Berry, J. W. (2006). Acculturative stress. In P. T. P. Wong & L. C. J. Wong (Eds.), *Handbook of multicultural perspectives on stress and coping* (pp. 287–298). Boston, MA: Springer.

Berry, J. W., Phinney, J. S., Sam, D. L., & Vedder, P. (2006). Immigrant youth: Acculturation, identity, and adaptation. *Applied Psychology, 55*(3), 303–332. doi:10.1111/j.1464-0597.2006.00256.x

Bronfenbrenner, U. (1989). *Ecological systems theory: Annals of child development*. Cambridge, MA: Harvard University Press.

Bronfenbrenner, U. (1994). Ecological models of human development. *Readings on the Development of Children, 2*(1), 37–43.

Bryan, L. A., & Atwater, M. M. (2002). Teacher beliefs and cultural models: A challenge for science teacher preparation programs. *Science Education, 86*(6), 821–839. doi:10.1002/sce.10043

Cicchetti, D., & Cohen, D. J. (1995). *Developmental psychopathology, Vol. 2: Risk, disorder, and adaptation*. New York, NY: John Wiley.

Cicchetti, D., & Rogosch, F. A. (1997). The role of self-organization in the promotion of resilience in maltreated children. *Development and Psychopathology, 9*(4), 797–815.

Cicchetti, D., & Rogosch, F. A. (2002). A developmental psychopathology perspective on adolescence. *Journal of Consulting and Clinical Psychology, 70*(1), 6–20.

Coleman, J. S. (1988). Social capital in the creation of human capital. *American Journal of Sociology, 94*, S95–S120.

Coleman, J. S. (1990). *Foundations of social theory*. Boston, MA: Harvard University Press.

Correa-Velez, I., Gifford, S. M., & McMichael, C. (2015). The persistence of predictors of wellbeing among refugee youth eight years after resettlement in Melbourne, Australia. *Social Science & Medicine, 142*, 163–168. doi:10.1016/j.socscimed.2015.08.017

Cosco, T. D., Kaushal, A., Hardy, R., Richards, M., Kuh, D., & Stafford, M. (2017). Operationalising resilience in longitudinal studies: A systematic review of methodological approaches. *Journal of Epidemiology and Community Health, 71*(1), 98–104. doi:10.1136/jech-2015-206980

Diehl, C., & Koenig, M. (2013). God can wait—New migrants in Germany between early adaptation and religious reorganization. *International Migration, 51*(3), 8–22. doi:10.1111/imig.12093

Dryden-Peterson, S. (2016). Refugee education: The crossroads of globalization. *Educational Researcher, 45*(9), 473–482. doi:10.3102/0013189X16683398

Dumont, M., & Provost, M. A. (1999). Resilience in adolescents: Protective role of social support, coping strategies, self-esteem, and social activities on experience of stress and depression. *Journal of Youth and Adolescence, 28*(3), 343–363. doi:10.1023/A:1021637011732

Edge, S., Newbold, K. B., & McKeary, M. (2014). Exploring socio-cultural factors that mediate, facilitate, & constrain the health and empowerment of refugee youth. *Social Science & Medicine, 117*, 34–41. doi:10.1016/j.socscimed.2014.07.025

Ellis, B. H., MacDonald, H. Z., Lincoln, A. K., & Cabral, H. J. (2008). Mental health of Somali adolescent refugees: The role of trauma, stress, and perceived discrimination. *Journal of Consulting and Clinical Psychology, 76*(2), 184–193. doi:10.1037/0022-006X.76.2.184

Ellis, B. J., & Boyce, W. T. (2011). Differential susceptibility to the environment: Toward an understanding of sensitivity to developmental experiences and context. *Development and Psychopathology, 23*(1), 1–5. doi:10.1017/S095457941000060X

Fazel, M., Reed, R. V., Panter-Brick, C., & Stein, A. (2012). Mental health of displaced and refugee children resettled in high-income countries: Risk and protective factors. *The Lancet, 379*(9812), 266–282. doi:10.1016/S0140-6736(11)60051-2

Fleming, G. R., & Van Grondelle, R. (1994). The primary steps of photosynthesis. *Physics Today, 47*(2), 48–57.

Flores, E., Cicchetti, D., & Rogosch, F. A. (2005). Predictors of resilience in maltreated and nonmaltreated Latino children. *Developmental Psychology, 41*(2), 338–351. doi:10.1037/0012-1649.41.2.338

Florian, V., Mikulincer, M., & Taubman, O. (1995). Does hardiness contribute to mental health during a stressful real-life situation? The roles of appraisal and coping. *Journal of Personality and Social Psychology, 68*(4), 687–695.

Folke, C., Carpenter, S., Walker, B., Scheffer, M., Chapin, T., & Rockström, J. (2010). Resilience thinking: integrating resilience, adaptability and transformability. *Ecology and Society, 15*(4), 20. Retrieved from http://www.ecologyandsociety.org/vol15/iss4/art20/

Foner, N., & Alba, R. (2008). Immigrant religion in the US and western Europe: Bridge or barrier to inclusion? *International Migration Review, 42*(2), 360–392. doi:10.1111/j.1747-7379.2008.00128.x

Fraser, M. W., Kirby, L. D., & Smokowski, P. R. (2004). Risk and resilience in childhood. In M.W. Fraser (Ed.), *Risk and resilience in childhood: An ecological perspective* (pp. 13–66). Washington, DC: NAWS Press.

Garmezy, N. (1991). Resiliency and vulnerability to adverse developmental outcomes associated with poverty. *American Behavioral Scientist, 34*(4), 416–430.

Gershon, N. B., & High, P. C. (2015). Epigenetics and child abuse: Modern-day Darwinism—The miraculous ability of the human genome to adapt, and then adapt again. *American Journal of Medical Genetics, 169*(4), 353–360. doi:10.1002/ajmg.c.31467

Gonzales, R. G. (2011). Learning to be illegal: Undocumented youth and shifting legal contexts in the transition to adulthood. *American Sociological Review, 76*(4), 602–619. doi:10.1177/0003122411411901

Greenberg, M. T. (2006). Promoting resilience in children and youth: Preventive interventions and their interface with neuroscience. *Annals of the New York Academy of Sciences, 1094*(1), 139–150. doi:10.1196/annals.1376.013

Hall, M., Greenman, E., & Farkas, G. (2010). Legal status and wage disparities for Mexican immigrants. *Social Forces, 89*(2), 491–513. doi:10.1353/sof.2010.0082

Hlatshwayo, M., & Vally, S. (2014). Violence, resilience and solidarity: The right to education for child migrants in South Africa. *School Psychology International, 35*(3), 266–279. doi:10.1177/0143034313511004

Holleran, L. K., & Waller, M. A. (2003). Sources of resilience among Chicano/a youth: Forging identities in the borderlands. *Child and Adolescent Social Work Journal, 20*(5), 335–350. doi:10.1023/A:1026043828866

Holling, C. S. (1973). Resilience and stability of ecological systems. *Annual Review of Ecology and Systematics, 4*(1), 1–23.

Hornor, G. (2017). Resilience. *Journal of Pediatric Health Care, 31*(3), 384–390. doi:10.1016/j.pedhc.2016.09.005

Kanics, J., Hernández, D. S., & Touzenis, K. (Eds.). (2010). *Migrating alone: Unaccompanied and separated children's migration to Europe*. Paris, France: UNESCO.

Lengua, L. J., & Wachs, T. D. (2012). Temperament and risk: Resilient and vulnerable responses to adversity. In M. Zentner & R. L. Shiner (Eds.), *Handbook of temperament* (pp. 519–540). New York, NY: Guilford Press.

Levels, M., Dronkers, J., & Kraaykamp, G. (2008). Immigrant children's educational achievement in western countries: Origin, destination, and community effects on mathematical performance. *American Sociological Review, 73*(5), 835–853. doi:10.1177/000312240807300507

Liu, J. J., Reed, M., & Girard, T. A. (2017). Advancing resilience: An integrative, multi-system model of resilience. *Personality and Individual Differences, 111*, 111–118. doi:10.1016/j.paid.2017.02.007

Lucht, M. J., Barnow, S., Sonnenfeld, C., Rosenberger, A., Grabe, H. J., Schroeder, W., . . . Rosskopf, D. (2009). Associations between the oxytocin receptor gene (OXTR) and affect, loneliness and intelligence in normal subjects. *Progress in Neuro-Psychopharmacology and Biological Psychiatry, 33*(5), 860–866. doi:10.1016/j.pnpbp.2009.04.004

Masten, A. S. (2014). Global perspectives on resilience in children and youth. *Child Development*, 85(1), 6–20. doi:10.1111/cdev.12205

Masten, A. S., Burt, K. B., Roisman, G. I., Obradović, J., Long, J. D., & Tellegen, A. (2004). Resources and resilience in the transition to adulthood: Continuity and change. *Development and Psychopathology*, 16(4), 1071–1094.

Masten, A. S., Hubbard, J. J., Gest, S. D., Tellegen, A., Garmezy, N., & Ramirez, M. (1999). Competence in the context of adversity: Pathways to resilience and maladaptation from childhood to late adolescence. *Development and Psychopathology*, 11(1), 143–169.

Masten, A. S., & Obradović, J. (2006). Competence and resilience in development. *Annals of the New York Academy of Sciences*, 1094(1), 13–27. doi:10.1196/annals.1376.003

Mavelli, L., & Wilson, E. K. (Eds.). (2016). *The refugee crisis and religion: Secularism, security and hospitality in question*. Washington, DC: Rowman & Littlefield.

McCarthy, C., & Marks, D. F. (2010). Exploring the health and well-being of refugee and asylum seeking children. *Journal of Health Psychology*, 15(4), 586–595. doi:10.1177/1359105309353644

Meewisse, M. L., Reitsma, J. B., De Vries, G. J., Gersons, B. P., & Olff, M. (2007). Cortisol and post-traumatic stress disorder in adults: Systematic review and meta-analysis. *The British Journal of Psychiatry*, 191(5), 387–392. doi:10.1192/bjp.bp.106.024877

Michaud, P. A. (2006). Adolescents and risks: Why not change our paradigm? *Journal of Adolescent Health*, 38(5), 481–483. doi:10.1016/j.jadohealth.2006.03.003

Milaniak, I., Cecil, C. A., Barker, E. D., Relton, C. L., Gaunt, T. R., McArdle, W., & Jaffee, S. R. (2017). Variation in DNA methylation of the oxytocin receptor gene predicts children's resilience to prenatal stress. *Development and Psychopathology*, 29(5), 1663–1674. doi:10.1017/S0954579417001316

Moffitt, T. E., Arseneault, L., Belsky, D., Dickson, N., Hancox, R. J., Harrington, H., . . . Sears, M. R. (2011). A gradient of childhood self-control predicts health, wealth, and public safety. *Proceedings of the National Academy of Sciences*, 108(7), 2693–2698. doi:10.1073/pnas.1010076108

Motti-Stefanidi, F., & Masten, A. S. (2017). A resilience perspective on immigrant youth adaptation and development. In N. J. Cabrera & B. Leyendecker (Eds.), *Handbook on positive development of minority children and youth* (pp. 19–34). Basel, Switzerland: Springer International.

Nigg, J., Nikolas, M., Friderici, K., Park, L., & Zucker, R. A. (2007). Genotype and neuropsychological response inhibition as resilience promoters for attention-deficit/hyperactivity disorder, oppositional defiant disorder, and conduct disorder under conditions of psychosocial adversity. *Development and Psychopathology*, 19(3), 767–786. doi:10.1017/S0954579407000387

Ní Raghallaigh, M., & Gilligan, R. (2010). Active survival in the lives of unaccompanied minors: Coping strategies, resilience, and the relevance of religion. *Child & Family Social Work*, 15(2), 226–237. doi:10.1111/j.1365-2206.2009.00663.x

Olsson, C. A., Bond, L., Burns, J. M., Vella-Brodrick, D. A., & Sawyer, S. M. (2003). Adolescent resilience: A concept analysis. *Journal of Adolescence*, 26(1), 1–11. doi:10.1016/S0140-1971(02)00118-5

Pfafferott, I., & Brown, R. (2006). Acculturation preferences of majority and minority adolescents in Germany in the context of society and family. *International Journal of Intercultural Relations*, 30(6), 703–717. doi:10.1016/j.ijintrel.2006.03.005

Portes, A., & Rumbaut, R. G. (2001). *Legacies: The story of the immigrant second generation*. Berkeley: University of California Press.

Putnam, R. D. (2000). Bowling alone: America's declining social capital. In L. Crothers & C. Lockhart (Eds.), *Culture and politics* (pp. 223–234). New York, NY: Palgrave Macmillan.

Qin, D. (2006). "Our child doesn't talk to us anymore": Alienation in immigrant Chinese families. *Anthropology & Education Quarterly*, 37(2), 162–179. doi:10.1525/aeq.2006.37.2.162

Qouta, S., El-Sarraj, E., & Punamäki, R. L. (2001). Mental flexibility as resiliency factor among children exposed to political violence. *International Journal of Psychology*, 36(1), 1–7.

Rasmusson, A. M., Schnurr, P. P., Zukowska, Z., Scioli, E., & Forman, D. E. (2010). Adaptation to extreme stress: Post-traumatic stress disorder, neuropeptide Y and metabolic syndrome. *Experimental Biology and Medicine*, 235(10), 1150–1162. doi:10.1258/ebm.2010.009334

Rasmusson, A. M., Vythilingam, M., & Morgan, C. A. (2003). The neuroendocrinology of posttraumatic stress disorder: New directions. *CNS Spectrums*, 8(9), 651–667.

Ream, R. K. (2005). Toward understanding how social capital mediates the impact of mobility on Mexican American achievement. *Social Forces, 84*(1), 201–224.

Richards, H. V., Brown, A. F., & Forde, T. B. (2007). Addressing diversity in schools: Culturally responsive pedagogy. *Teaching Exceptional Children, 39*(3), 64–68.

Roebers, C. M., & Schneider, W. (1999). Self-concept and anxiety in immigrant children. *International Journal of Behavioral Development, 23*(1), 125–147.

Roffey, S. (2010). *Changing behaviour in schools: Promoting positive relationships and wellbeing*. Los Angeles, CA: SAGE.

Rohmann, A., Piontkowski, U., & van Randenborgh, A. (2008). When attitudes do not fit: Discordance of acculturation attitudes as an antecedent of intergroup threat. *Personality and Social Psychology Bulletin, 34*(3), 337–352. doi:10.1177/0146167207311197

Russo, S. J., Murrough, J. W., Han, M. H., Charney, D. S., & Nestler, E. J. (2012). Neurobiology of resilience. *Nature Neuroscience, 15*(11), 1475–1484. doi:10.1038/nn.3234

Rutter, M. (1999). Resilience concepts and findings: Implications for family therapy. *Journal of Family Therapy, 21*(2), 119–144. doi:10.1111/1467-6427.00108

Rutter, M. (2013). Annual research review: Resilience–clinical implications. *Journal of Child Psychology and Psychiatry, 54*(4), 474–487. doi:10.1111/j.1469-7610.2012.02615.x

Saphire-Bernstein, S., Way, B. M., Kim, H. S., Sherman, D. K., & Taylor, S. E. (2011). Oxytocin receptor gene (OXTR) is related to psychological resources. *Proceedings of the National Academy of Sciences, 108*(37), 15118–15122. doi:10.1073/pnas.1113137108

Schachner, M. K., He, J., Heizmann, B., & Van de Vijver, F. J. (2017). Acculturation and school adjustment of immigrant youth in six European countries: Findings from the Programme for International Student Assessment (PISA). *Frontiers in Psychology, 8*, 649. doi:10.3389/fpsyg.2017.00649

Schoon, I., & Parsons, S. (2002). Competence in the face of adversity: The influence of early family environment and long-term consequences. *Children & Society, 16*(4), 260–272. doi:10.1002/chi.713

Seligman, M. E. P., & Csikszentmihalyi, M. (2000). Positive psychology: An introduction. *American Psychologist, 55*(1), 5–14. doi:10.1037/0003-066X.55.1.5

Shiner, R. L., & Masten, A. S. (2012). Childhood personality as a harbinger of competence and resilience in adulthood. *Development and Psychopathology, 24*(2), 507–528. doi:10.1017/S0954579412000120

Sirin, S. R., Ryce, P., Gupta, T., & Rogers-Sirin, L. (2013). The role of acculturative stress on mental health symptoms for immigrant adolescents: A longitudinal investigation. *Developmental Psychology, 49*(4), 736–748. doi:10.1037/a0028398

Sodowsky, G. R., Lai, E. W. M., & Plake, B. S. (1991). Moderating effects of sociocultural variables on acculturation attitudes of Hispanics and Asian Americans. *Journal of Counseling & Development, 70*(1), 194–204. doi:10.1002/j.1556-6676.1991.tb01583.x

Sonderegger, R., & Barrett, P. M. (2004). Patterns of cultural adjustment among young migrants to Australia. *Journal of Child and Family Studies, 13*(3), 341–356. doi:10.1023/B:JCFS.0000022039.00578.51

Suárez-Orozco, C., Abo-Zena, M. M., & Marks, A. K. (Eds.). (2015). *Transitions: The development of children of immigrants*. New York, NY: NYU Press.

Thompson, A., Torres, R. M., Swanson, K., Blue, S. A., & Hernández, Ó. M. H. (2019). Re-conceptualising agency in migrant children from Central America and Mexico. *Journal of Ethnic and Migration Studies, 45*(2), 235–252. doi:10.1080/1369183X.2017.1404258

Tol, W. A., Song, S., & Jordans, M. J. (2013). Annual research review: Resilience and mental health in children and adolescents living in areas of armed conflict—A systematic review of findings in low-and middle-income countries. *Journal of Child Psychology and Psychiatry, 54*(4), 445–460. doi:10.1111/jcpp.12053

Ungar, M. (2008). Resilience across cultures. *The British Journal of Social Work, 38*(2), 218–235. doi:10.1093/bjsw/bcl343

Ungar, M. (2015). Resilience and culture: The diversity of protective processes and positive adaptation. In L. C. Theron, L. Liebenberg, & M. Ungar (Eds.), *Youth resilience and culture* (pp. 37–48). Dordrecht, The Netherlands: Springer.

Ungar, M. (2018). Systemic resilience: Principles and processes for a science of change in contexts of adversity. *Ecology and Society, 23*(4). 34. doi:10.5751/ES-10385-230434

Viruell-Fuentes, E. A., Miranda, P. Y., & Abdulrahim, S. (2012). More than culture: Structural racism, intersectionality theory, and immigrant health. *Social Science & Medicine, 75*(12), 2099–2106. doi:10.1016/j.socscimed.2011.12.037

Ward, C., & Geeraert, N. (2016). Advancing acculturation theory and research: The acculturation process in its ecological context. *Current Opinion in Psychology, 8*, 98–104. doi:10.1016/j.copsyc.2015.09.021

Wen, Y., & Hanley, J. (2015). Rural-to-urban migration, family resilience, and policy framework for social support in China. *Asian Social Work and Policy Review, 9*(1), 18–28. doi:10.1111/aswp.12042

Werner, E. E. (1993). Risk, resilience, and recovery: Perspectives from the Kauai Longitudinal Study. *Development and Psychopathology, 5*(4), 503–515. doi:10.1017/S095457940000612X

Whyte. M. K. (Ed.). (2010). *One country, two societies: Rural–urban inequality in contemporary China.* Cambridge, MA: Harvard University Press.

Wong, D. F., Li, C. Y., & Song, H. X. (2007). Rural migrant workers in urban China: Living a marginalised life. *International Journal of Social Welfare, 16*(1), 32–40. doi:10.1111/j.1468-2397.2007.00475.x

Wu, Q. (2017). Effects of social capital in multiple contexts on the psychosocial adjustment of Chinese migrant children. *Youth & Society, 49*(2), 150–179. doi:10.1177/0044118X14530133

Wu, Q., Lu, D., & Kang, M. (2015). Social capital and the mental health of children in rural China with different experiences of parental migration. *Social Science & Medicine, 132*, 270–277. doi:10.1016/j.socscimed.2014.10.050

Wu, Q., & Palinkas, L. A. (2012). Social capital and psychosocial adjustment of migrant children in China: The role of children's personal agency. In C-C. Yi (Ed.), *The psychological well-being of East Asian youth* (pp. 281–309). Dordrecht, The Netherlands: Springer.

Wu, Q., Palinkas, L. A., & He, X. (2010). An ecological examination of social capital effects on the academic achievement of Chinese migrant children. *British Journal of Social Work, 40*(8), 2578–2597. doi:10.1093/bjsw/bcq051

Wu, Q., Palinkas, L. A., & He, X. (2011). Social capital in promoting the psychosocial adjustment of Chinese migrant children: Interaction across contexts. *Journal of Community Psychology, 39*(4), 421–442. doi:10.1002/jcop.20443

Wu, Q., Tsang, B., & Ming, H. (2014). Social capital, family support, resilience and educational outcomes of Chinese migrant children. *British Journal of Social Work, 44*(3), 636–656. doi:10.1093/bjsw/bcs139

Yeh, C. J., Kim, A. B., Pituc, S. T., & Atkins, M. (2008). Poverty, loss, and resilience: The story of Chinese immigrant youth. *Journal of Counseling Psychology, 55*(1), 34–38. doi:10.1037/0022-0167.55.1.34

Zagefka, H., & Brown, R. (2002). The relationship between acculturation strategies, relative fit and intergroup relations: Immigrant-majority relations in Germany. *European Journal of Social Psychology, 32*(2), 171–188. doi:10.1002/ejsp.73

21

Psychological Resilience in Response to Adverse Experiences

An Integrative Developmental Perspective in the Context of War and Displacement

Cassandra M. Popham, Fiona S. McEwen, and Michael Pluess

Introduction

The concept of resilience in psychology originated from observations of variance in the mental health outcomes of children growing up in adverse circumstances. The term *resilience*, meaning *the process of positive adaptation in the context of adversity* (Luthar, Cicchetti, & Becker, 2000), was applied to explain how some of those exposed to environments associated with negative development, such as poverty and deprivation, adapted well and grew into healthy adults (Masten & Garmezy, 1985). Research into resilience has proliferated in recent years, but the popularity of the phenomenon has led to a body of research comprised of a variety of conceptualizations, which remain to be integrated. This chapter will discuss the current state of resilience in the field of developmental psychology and propose an integrative perspective for future research, with a focus on its application in a population exposed to extreme adversity: refugee children. First, we will provide a brief account of the history of resilience research in the field of psychology and provide general definitions of key terms, before highlighting several ongoing debates in this field. We will then propose a new model that integrates the complex developmental processes involved in psychological resilience and review the literature from this perspective to demonstrate how to apply our integrative model of resilience in practice.

Cassandra M. Popham, Fiona S. McEwen, and Michael Pluess, *Psychological Resilience in Response to Adverse Experiences* In: *Multisystemic Resilience*. Edited by: Michael Ungar, Oxford University Press (2021). © Oxford University Press.
DOI: 10.1093/oso/9780190095888.003.0022

The History of Resilience Research in the Field of Psychology

Resilience is a central concept in many areas of psychology but has its original roots in developmental psychopathology. Early individual and collaborative work between key researchers such as Michael Rutter, Emmy Werner, and Norman Garmezy led to the emergence of the original concept on the back of empirical research on individual differences in the developmental response of at-risk children (Garmezy & Rutter, 1983; Masten, Best, & Garmezy, 1990; Werner, 1992). Their research on childhood adversity in large cohort studies found that individuals showed substantial heterogeneity in their outcomes despite equivalent childhood risk (Werner, 1992). A large proportion of individuals thought to be at risk due to socioeconomic disadvantage or parents with mental health problems developed better than expected, leading such children to be labeled as *invulnerable* (Anthony, Koupernik, & Chiland, 1978). However, it was soon recognized that invulnerability was an inappropriate term, as it implied an absolute resistance to adversity in all possible circumstances, as the function of a stable characteristic intrinsic to the individual. Rutter (1993) argued this could not be the case, as the effects of adversity tend to be cumulative and individuals who are resistant to one type of stress may not be resistant to others. Additionally, research showed that some individuals that had been exposed to adversity in childhood and initially displayed development of maladaptive behaviors recovered over time and seemed to function well in adulthood (Werner, 1992). In other words, they appeared to *bounce back*, most likely due to specific environmental or individual characteristics that exerted a protective function on their development. Hence, the term *resilience* came into use and the research focus shifted from risk to protective factors.

The rich and substantial body of research on resilience in the field of psychology can be divided into four distinct eras or waves (Masten, 2007): (a) descriptive, (b) process-focused, (c) intervention-based, and (d) multilevel. Following the first wave of investigation into predictors of the differing outcomes in adversity-exposed children, the second wave began the task of investigating the underlying processes that could explain the relationship between resilience and the variables associated with it. This included taking a longitudinal perspective of resilience, drawing on the rich literature of developmental psychology. The third wave focused on the practical implications of resilience, and research on the subject was carried out via prevention and intervention studies. The fourth wave, within which the field currently resides according to Masten (2007), aims to integrate the various research findings and study resilience across multiple levels from wider socioecological systems to the individual cellular level (Ungar, 2018).

Definition of Terms

The concept of resilience rests on the existence of some type of adversity that an individual, or system, can be *resilient to*. The nature of the adversity must therefore be understood in addition to the resilience process. Adversity can vary in terms of severity, complexity, causality, temporal characteristics, and the interpretations and relevance specific to the individual's context and culture (Ungar, 2015). To infer resilience, this adversity needs to be sufficiently contextually severe to threaten usual functioning. While we do not have an established adversity threshold in developmental psychology, Ungar (2015) has argued that a resilience "diagnosis" needs to take into account the characteristics of the adversity in addition to the outcomes. Therefore, the nature of the *risk* context, as well as specific *risk* factors, are important to understanding resilience. The word *risk* is often used interchangeably with adversity or stress as well as in terms of risk factors, which are environmental or individual factors that make an individual more likely to develop psychological problems in response to adverse experiences. *Protective* factors, on the other hand, describe those characteristics that have the opposite effect and protect, or buffer, an individual from the negative effects of adverse experiences (Rutter, 1990). The term *promotive* factors is also used to describe characteristics that promote positive adaptation irrespective of the exposure to adversity (Sameroff, 2000). Importantly, the use of the word *factor* was criticized by Rutter (1987), who argued that resilience processes are not determined by stable factors with consistent effects across contexts. Instead, he suggested that using the term *mechanisms* is more accurate. The literature has since generally accepted that resilience occurs via and is influenced by adaptable mechanisms rather than stable factors (Masten, 2007), but many papers continue to refer to factors, with the underlying understanding that this concerns specific aspects of environmental and individual characteristics that can have risk or protective *functions* in specific contexts.

Long-Standing Debates

The working definition of resilience in psychology—the *process* of adaptation in the context of adversity to continue the *successful functioning* of a system (Luthar et al., 2000; Ungar, 2018)—is sufficiently vague that how to define and measure resilience itself continues to be debated. The key points of contention are whether resilience should be considered a *trait* or a *process* and what should be considered *successful functioning*. The resulting lack of consensus is limiting progress as varying definitions make it hard to compare and conduct meta-analyses on research even within the discipline of developmental psychology. Here, we will discuss these points and some other outstanding questions to be addressed before moving on to how these might be considered in our integrated model of resilience.

Process Versus Trait

Whether to conceptualize resilience as a process or trait is an ongoing debate in the developmental psychology literature. Although early work proposed that resilience is a process that needs to be measured longitudinally to understand adaptation to adversity (Masten, 2007), some continue to define resilience as a stable trait (Hu, Zhang, & Wang, 2015). Similar to the problems with invulnerability raised by Rutter (1993), conceptualizing resilience as a trait is problematic as it implies that a person will either be resilient or not, which is both inaccurate and risks placing the culpability for a person's mental health entirely on the individual (Masten, 2012). Moreover, adversity in the context of developmental psychology is often chronic. For example, an underprivileged home environment, parental abuse, or displacement and resettlement are chronic adversities existing worldwide that put children at risk for the development of problematic outcomes. An individual's resilience, therefore, is better understood and studied in terms of the *process* of adaptation to these ongoing risks across development.

Certain individual traits, such as hardiness and ego-resiliency, reflect internal capacities that appear to overlap with the trait understanding of resilience (Hu et al., 2015). These traits have occasionally been equated with resilience itself, as they promote positive adaptation. Although these traits may reflect important mechanisms internal to the individual that influence their resilience to stressors, a process-based perspective incorporating the interactions between various systems is required to address the complexity of dynamic responses to adversity. To add a further source of divergence, some define resilience in terms of outcomes, while others include protective resources that are both internal (e.g., self-esteem) and external (e.g., social support) to the individual (Ungar, 2015). While it remains up for debate how to measure and classify resilience, we would argue that such scales measure important psychosocial resources rather than resilience itself. Furthermore, although various genetic, physiological, cognitive, and social factors have been implicated in resilience (Fazel, Reed, Panter-Brick, & Stein, 2012; Russo, Murrough, Han, Charney, & Nestler, 2012), it remains to be understood how these interact over time in the process of adaptation to adversity.

Positive Adaptation

While positive adaptation after exposure to adversity is the main, and perhaps the most obvious, element of defining resilience, it is open to a variety of interpretations ranging from the absence of disorder to the development and presence of clearly positive behaviors and traits (Luthar et al., 2000). Consequently, it remains uncertain what specific outcomes should be considered; some researchers rely on absence of psychopathology (i.e., minimal anxiety and depression scores) as evidence for resilience (e.g., Aitcheson, Abu-Bader, Howell, Khalil, & Elbedour, 2017) while others have considered scores on standardized measures of social, emotional, behavioral, and academic performance (e.g., Cicchetti & Rogosch, 2007). Furthermore, the question remains what level of positive adaptation is required to identify an individual as resilient. Some have argued that the resilience threshold should be defined using comparisons of outcomes with low-adversity groups (Sattler & Gershoff, 2019), while others place a threshold at better than expected given the adversity context (Amstadter, Moscati, Maes, Myers, & Kendler, 2016).

Importantly, individuals show different psychological trajectories following exposure to risk, meaning that a negative response at an earlier point does not necessarily mean an individual cannot be resilient in the longer term. As summarized by Masten (2012), stress resistance, posttraumatic growth, and recovery (Figure 21.1) are three different trajectories that have been recognized as types of resilience in the literature. Stress resistance describes a process of steady and positive development despite exposure to high cumulative risk. Posttraumatic growth describes an individual resisting stressors and becoming stronger from their experiences. This idea of thriving in adversity was a challenge to the initial view of resilience as successful homeostasis, suggesting that individuals can learn and grow from their experiences (O'Leary & Ickovics, 1995). Recovery describes the process of "bouncing back" to former functioning following a disruption caused by adversity. A disruption without

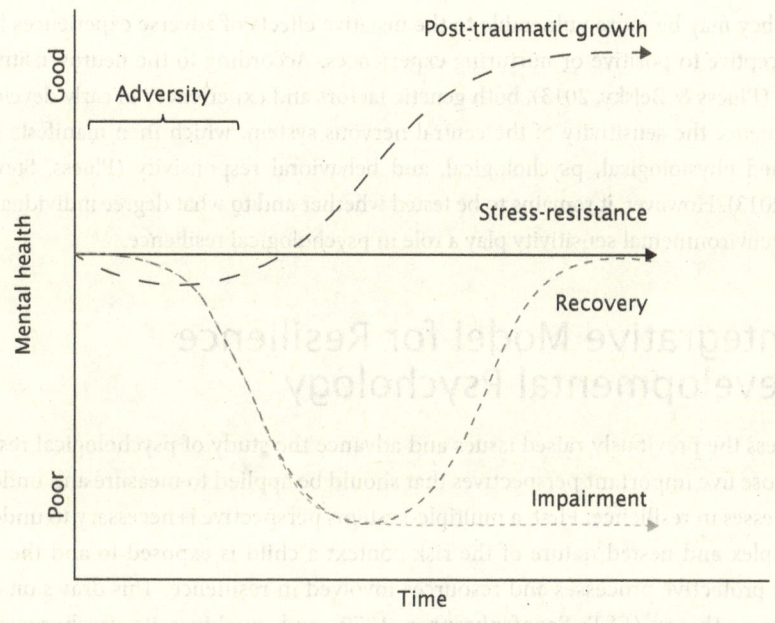

FIGURE 21.1 Three resilience trajectories and one of impairment. Adapted from Masten and Narayan (2012).

consequent recovery is known as impairment and is an example of a nonresilience trajectory. Positive adaptation is therefore not a static process that is identical across individuals. Differences in individual's trajectories may be explained by the specific resources or risk factors they are exposed to, as well as the influences of time and development.

Individual Differences in Environmental Sensitivity

A key point that as yet has not been considered in research on resilience is that some people may be more affected by both negative and positive contextual factors than others (although some factors are consistently predictive of mental health there is often considerable variation in their effect on individuals). The perspective of *environmental sensitivity* (Pluess, 2015) provides a theoretical framework for why some seem more sensitive to their experiences. According to this theory, individuals differ in the extent to which they perceive and process aspects of their environment. This includes sensitivity to physical aspects of the environment, as well as social and emotional influences. Sensitivity can be understood both in terms of *developmental plasticity* (i.e., to what extent the early environment shapes developmental trajectories) and in terms of sensitivity as a relatively stable characteristic of the individual. Environmental sensitivity builds on the traditional diathesis–stress concept, which showed that stressors lead to the development of psychopathology in the presence of some inherent vulnerability (Monroe & Simons, 1991). The environmental sensitivity framework, which encompasses, besides diathesis–stress, the concepts of *sensory processing sensitivity* (Aron & Aron, 1997), *differential susceptibility* (Belsky & Pluess, 2009), *biological sensitivity to context* (Boyce & Ellis, 2005), and *vantage sensitivity* (Pluess & Belsky, 2013), suggests that some individuals are more affected by their experiences due to heightened environmental sensitivity.

Hence, they may be more vulnerable to the negative effects of adverse experiences but also more receptive to positive or nurturing experiences. According to the neurosensitivity hypothesis (Pluess & Belsky, 2013), both genetic factors and experiences in early development may influence the sensitivity of the central nervous system, which then manifests itself in heightened physiological, psychological, and behavioral responsivity (Pluess, Stevens, & Belsky, 2013). However, it remains to be tested whether and to what degree individual differences in environmental sensitivity play a role in psychological resilience.

An Integrative Model for Resilience in Developmental Psychology

To address the previously raised issues and advance the study of psychological resilience, we propose five important perspectives that should be applied to measure and understand the processes in resilience. First, a multiple-systems perspective is necessary to understand the complex and nested nature of the risk context a child is exposed to and the various risk and protective processes and resources involved in resilience. This draws on ecological systems theory (EST; Bronfenbrenner, 1979) and combines its psychosocial focus with bioecological factors (Figure 21.2). Second, individual differences in environmental

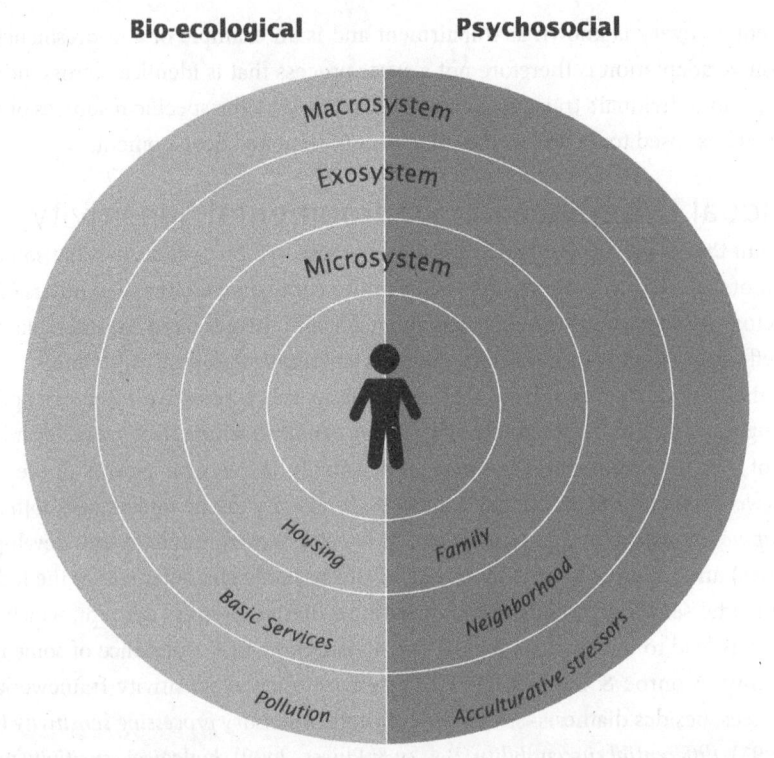

FIGURE 21.2 Representation of the individual nested within multiple systems combining psychosocial factors from ecological systems theory (Bronfenbrenner, 1979) with bio-ecological factors, with examples of factors in each system.

sensitivity may play an important role regarding the relationships between resilience processes and explain variation in outcomes beyond that predicted by environmental factors. Third, a multilevel approach should be applied to understand resilience processes and outcomes at different levels of analysis from the genetic, through physiological, to psychological and behavioral levels. Fourth, to consider the multifaceted manifestations of resilience, we need to apply a multidimensional approach to outcomes. A multidimensional approach requires consideration of various outcome dimensions beyond symptoms of psychopathology. We argue that behavioral, somatic, and academic dimensions are influenced by resilience and should be assessed from multiple points of view. Finally, a longitudinal perspective in conjunction with these four other facets is necessary to enable a cohesive picture of the resilience process and how time, development, and multiple systems influence it.

All five elements are key to understanding resilience from a perspective that integrates different contexts, systems, levels, mechanisms, and outcomes. Hence, our conceptual model (Figure 21.3) is characterized by the consideration of:

1. *Multiple systems.* Various factors throughout the psychosocial and bioecological systems impact the individual and have risk and protective functions in the context of adversity.
2. *Individual differences in environmental sensitivity.* Individuals may be more or less sensitive to the effects of both negative and positive experiences and environmental factors. This environmental sensitivity moderates the impact of environmental factors on the individual.
3. *Multiple levels of analysis.* A multilevel perspective is required to understand processes and outcomes at molecular, physiological, and psychological levels.
4. *Multiple dimensions of positive adaptation.* Resilience can manifest in children in different patterns across different dimensions with consequences for measuring resilience.
5. *Life course perspective.* Resilience should be considered as a process over time and a developmental perspective is important to understand the resilience process and children's transactions with their environment.

Review of Empirical Evidence

To assess the evidence for the different aspects of our integrated resilience model, we will consider the framework we have proposed in relation to refugee children, in which the main source of adversity is war exposure and forced displacement. One of the most pressing issues of the time is the global refugee crisis, which has exposed millions of children to extreme adversity (United Nations High Commissioner for Refugees, 2019). In what follows, we will consider current evidence for resilience in refugee children through the lens of the five facets of our integrated model. It is important to note that, due to the inconsistency of definitions of resilience in the literature, some studies that professed to investigate resilience may not fit our definition of this concept. We will therefore discuss results in terms of the specific outcomes measured and apply these to our evaluation of resilience as we define it.

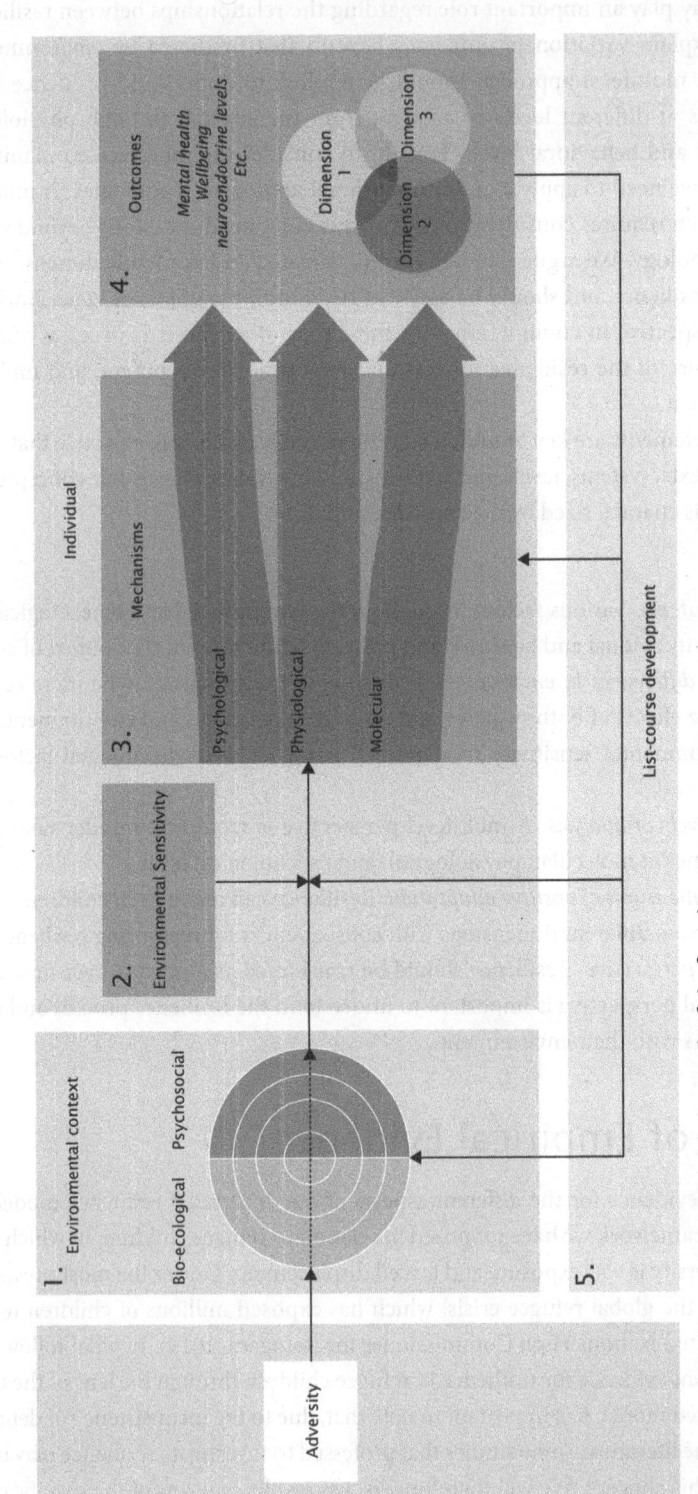

FIGURE 21.3 An integrative model, labeling each of the five elements.

Facet 1: The Multisystemic Nature of Psychological Resilience

According to EST (Bronfenbrenner, 1979), child development is influenced by multiple nested systems, as represented in Figure 21.2. The systems identified by Bronfenbrenner (1979) are the *individual* (e.g., psychological and biological factors), *microsystem* (close social systems e.g., the family), *mesosystem* (interactions between the microsystems), *exosystem* (proximal environment e.g., neighborhood), *macrosystem* (wider social context), and *chronosystem* (time). Research on resilience in refugee children has shown involvement of factors from each system. More practical environmental factors beyond these psychosocial systems, such as housing conditions or access to services, also interact with psychological and social factors as well as directly influencing an individual's well-being. All these systems are individually important, but also by nature so intertwined that interactions between them can lead to varying effects. Taking a multiple systems perspective of resilience is particularly important to understand the influence of the system contexts on the functions of resilience factors in the specific individual.

The individual. Research on risk and protective factors, and specifically research with refugee children, has identified several psychological factors, such as self-regulation and coping skills, that are associated with better mental health (Aitcheson et al., 2017; Howell et al., 2015). Cognitive resources may protect individuals or promote adaptive development by enabling them to cope with environmental stressors. For example, use of positive types of coping is associated with lower posttraumatic stress (PTS) and emotion dysregulation in refugee children, whereas avoidance strategies such as wishful thinking and social withdrawal predict greater problems on these measures (Khamis, 2019). Interestingly, Khamis (2019) found that adaptive strategies, such as cognitive restructuring and seeking social support (but not active problem-solving), were significantly associated with better mental health outcomes. This may be a result of the type of adversity that refugee children face. The participants in Khamis's study were Syrian refugees aged 7 to 18 years living in Jordan and Lebanon. As such, the stressors they faced from war, displacement, and ongoing stressors such as poverty may be particularly difficult to problem-solve. If these are the key stressors predicting psychopathology, which they generally are in such populations (Bronstein & Montgomery, 2011), the adversity may be so great that problem-solving is insufficient to make a difference as it might in less challenging contexts. This highlights the concept that certain resilience-promoting resources may only be available or effective depending on the characteristics of the adversity being faced (Ungar, 2015).

The microsystem: Family. Aspects of the family and home life are some of the most consistently reported factors associated with outcomes in children facing adversity. The family environment, relationships, and parenting style can directly influence a child's experiences and how secure they feel and (directly or indirectly) teach them ways to cope with stressors. In terms of parent–child interactions, parenting style plays a key role in resilience. For example, having at least one authoritative parent (i.e., high in behavioral control, parental knowledge, and support, and low in harsh punishment and psychological control) was associated with better academic performance, fewer internalizing symptoms, and less norm breaking in a sample of Arab refugee adolescents (Smetana & Ahmad, 2018). Parental support also seems to be important by itself; according to a systematic review of displaced and refugee children, perception of high parental support was associated with better psychological outcomes (Fazel et al., 2012).

Parents can also indirectly influence the resilience of their children. A parent's trauma experience and psychopathology are associated with their child's mental health, sometimes more so than the child's own traumatic experiences (Fazel et al., 2012). This is an example of how external influences can propagate through the ecological systems to impact the individual and a reminder that individuals should be considered in context. While trauma experiences are an important factor in mental health, children, particularly when very young, do not necessarily remember them or do so unreliably (Panter-Brick, Grimon, Kalin, & Eggerman, 2015). Children's experience and memory of war and displacement may therefore be shaped by their parents' own experiences. Parental perspectives give somewhat more objective accounts of children's adversities, while also providing a view into parental functioning and the child's home context.

The exosystem: Wider community. The exosystem describes other social systems in the community beyond the family. This may represent a collection of systems such as school, the neighborhood, or other social groups the child or family are part of. These can remain isolated from other groups within this system, or interact with one another as well as with the family environment and individual. One specific social system that is very important for child refugees with access to it is school (Trentacosta, McLear, Ziadni, Lumley, & Arfken, 2016; Wiegersma, Stellinga-Boelen, & Reijneveld, 2011). Greater positivity about school was associated with fewer PTS symptoms in children of Iraqi refugees (Trentacosta et al., 2016), while one study reported that simply attending school was associated with better mental health among asylum-seekers (Wiegersma et al., 2011). School attendance can provide a protective effect in multiple ways. Receiving education helps children to learn and develop both academically and socially, which in turn provides them with more hope and options for the future. For example, sense of school belonging is associated with lower depression and greater self-efficacy among adolescent refugees (Kia-Keating & Ellis, 2007). Additionally, school attendance can help develop individual strengths such as self-regulation and coping strategies outside the family environment.

The macrosystem: Cultural, national, and global factors. Social systems such as family and neighborhood are nested within the context of the macrosystem. Political and cultural contexts shape the functioning of social systems, while often being removed enough that individuals do not necessarily recognize the effects these macrolevel forces have on their lives. Some examples of factors or systems at the macrolevel that might affect refugees are religion, cultural norms, attitudes toward migration, social policies, economic states, and environmental factors (Aitcheson et al., 2017; Ellis, MacDonald, Lincoln, & Cabral, 2008; Montgomery, 2008; Sim, Fazel, Bowes, & Gardner, 2018; Ungar, 2015). Due to the nested nature of the ecological systems (Bronfenbrenner, 1979), macrosystem factors necessarily influence individuals largely through effects on more immediate systems, making it difficult to consider them as single effects. They are also investigated less often in the psychological literature than effects within or proximal to the individual such as cognitive processes and family dynamics. We will therefore discuss them here mainly in terms of the interactive nature of the multiple systems involved in resilience.

Religion, for example, is a factor that might influence an individual's emotions and cognitive factors, and provide another social group or influence in the micro- or exosystem (Ungar, Ghazinour, & Richter, 2013). However, religion is also a major factor on a global scale as it applies not only to personal beliefs but is upheld by and entwined in cultural systems and traditions (Masten, 2014). For example, for a sample of Middle Eastern adolescent refugees in Europe, belonging to a small, persecuted religious group or having left or changed religions was associated with greater internalizing symptoms compared to adolescents who had been and continued to be Muslim or Christian (Montgomery, 2008). The wide-ranging popularity and power of both mainstream Islam and Christianity provide greater sociopolitical protection and larger in-groups in countries where they are the majority, compared to smaller or more marginalized religions.

Just as religious identities might be a source of protection or vulnerability, other cultural identities have also been implicated in resilience. A strong national identity was predictive of less anxiety and depression among adolescents in Gaza refugee camps (Aitcheson et al., 2017). It may be that such factors are particularly important to young people who experience displacement, by helping them to maintain a sense of belonging once the social structures that reinforce belonging have been disrupted. However, as with the other factors at the macrolevel, sense of identity might also work more at a lower systems level, such as the microsystem, by improving feelings of belonging to a heritage culture.

Ecological factors. In addition to the psychosocial factors covered in EST, ecological factors of a more physical nature can have a great impact on refugee's well-being across different systems. For example, the experience of displacement confronts individuals with practical stressors and insecurities such as lack of food, water, shelter, healthcare, and education (Al-Rousan, Schwabkey, Jirmanus, & Nelson, 2018). Beyond limited access to basic sustenance, perhaps one of the most salient challenges for those displaced by war is housing insecurity (Sabin, Cardozo, Nackerud, Kaiser, & Varese, 2003; Ziersch & Due, 2018). Living in refugee camps, informal settlements, or poor quality housing, and the associated experiences that come with that can affect both physical and mental health. Among people in refugee camps, lack of housing or shelter (Feyera, Mihretie, Bedaso, Gedle, & Kumera, 2015), and poor housing conditions (Carta et al., 2013) are associated with greater depression and PTS symptoms. Individuals resettled in more permanent housing also experience challenges; crowding, stability, and satisfaction with housing are all associated with mental health outcomes (Ziersch & Due, 2018). Issues such as stability may be particularly pertinent for displaced children, as instability can contribute to a sense of ongoing potentially traumatic risk (Sabin et al., 2003). A holistic approach to resilience in refugee children must therefore consider the practical stressors occurring in the child's life, including built and natural environments.

Interactions between the systems. To understand the roles these varied systems play in resilience, it is critical to consider how they impact one another. For example, wider macrosystem factors such as culture or economic factors can affect coping strategies and parenting styles. In the Middle East, parenting is often thought to be very authoritarian, although different countries within that region report differing levels of authoritarian and permissive parenting (Dwairy et al., 2006). Meanwhile, in Western countries such as the United States, there tends to be a greater expectation for parenting to be permissive (d'Abreu, Castro-Olivo, & Ura, 2019; Smetana & Ahmad, 2018). Although parenting style is not homogenous even within cultures, beliefs about parenting might influence the styles that parents use and how children feel about these styles. The results reported by Khamis (2019) showing that children's use of problem-solving was not associated with their mental health could be explained by parenting style. If parents are more authoritative, meaning they have more behavioral control over their children (Smetana & Ahmad, 2018), the tendency and expectation, particularly for young children, to independently problem-solve will be less (Aroian et al., 2009). When refugees settle in host countries that are culturally different from their countries of origin, these interactions may become further complicated (d'Abreu et al., 2019). The gap between parenting expectations in the heritage and host culture can change children's perceptions and reduce parent's feelings of control, thereby creating another potential source of conflict in the family (Betancourt et al., 2015). While it is difficult to disentangle the interactions between such factors across the different systems, it is necessary to consider all of them to understand the complex processes influencing resilience to war and displacement among refugee children.

Facet 2: Applying the Theory of Environmental Sensitivity

Environmental sensitivity (Pluess, 2015) provides a conceptual model for why some children are more responsive to and affected by adversity as well as protective factors. As a relatively new perspective, very little research has investigated how sensitivity might be involved in refugee children's responses to risk and protective factors. Studies with nonrefugee children suggest that physiological (e.g., respiratory sinus arrhythmia and salivary cortisol) reactivity to social, cognitive, and emotional challenges is associated with different outcomes according to levels of adversity in young children (Obradović, Bush, Stamperdahl, Adler, & Boyce, 2010). Those with higher stress reactivity showed more adaptive outcomes if they lived in conditions of low adversity, but more maladaptive outcomes if they had high family adversity. If cortisol and respiratory sinus arrhythmia responsivity are markers of heightened environmental sensitivity, then it follows that those with greater stress reactivity would be more sensitive to negative effects of adversity as well as the positive effects of protective factors. Consistent with this hypothesis, children with *low* adversity and *high* reactivity were generally the best adapted group, which supports the idea that high sensitivity enables children to benefit more from positive environments in the absence of adversity (Obradovic et al., 2010). Recently, results from the first study to look specifically at the environmental sensitivity of refugee children were published (Karam et al., 2019). Karam et al. (2019) found evidence that sensitivity moderated the relationship between exposure to war events and posttraumatic stress disorder (PTSD) symptom severity with more sensitive children being more affected by war exposure. This supports our theory that environmental sensitivity moderates the effects of environmental factors on mental health outcomes, suggesting further investigation of this area is worthwhile.

Facet 3: Applying a Multilevel Perspective to Psychological Resilience

Within the individual, resilience processes occur at multiple levels of analysis, including genetic, epigenetic, biochemical, neurological, physiological, and psychological. For example, research suggests that there is a heritable component to resilience (Amstadter et al., 2016), and that neurophysiological factors influence how children respond to stressors (Russo et al., 2012). Moreover, the little neuroimaging research in this area thus far has found associations between the volume of brain regions such as the right prefrontal cortex and competence in adversity (Burt et al., 2016). Therefore, investigation of resilience mechanisms at multiple levels of analysis is crucial to identifying processes associated with individual differences in the response to adversity.

The concept of *allostasis* may help to understand the role of resilience processes at the physiological level. Allostasis describes the biological responses that allow physiological adaptation in the context of environmental changes or stressors (Karatsoreos & McEwen, 2011). Ongoing exposure to stressors can have a cumulative effect on the body by creating *allostatic load* or overload, if the system is required to continuously make allostatic responses or if they are not sufficiently well regulated. Therefore, the functioning of an individual's physiological systems involved in allostasis can have a crucial impact on how that individual responds to trauma and can also be impacted by the environment. This may have long-term effects particularly in children exposed to early life stress, due to their developing state, and potentially results in neurobiological vulnerability to subsequent stress (Heim & Nemeroff, 2001). For example, chronic stress may create chronic sensitization of the central nervous system and other neurotransmitter systems, having long-term consequences on stress reactivity. The mechanisms involved in allostasis include the activity of stress-responsive hormones within the hypothalamic–pituitary–adrenal axis, such as cortisol and dehydroepiandrosterone. These have been implicated in responses to war trauma and resilience to adversities in general, although results are varied and little research has been conducted in children displaced by war (Russo et al., 2012). While some studies of the long-term effects of trauma show hypocortisolism, others have found increased cumulative cortisol levels (Steudte et al., 2011). In fact, research into refugee adolescents showed no significant difference in cortisol levels according to trauma but did show cortisol dysregulation (Dajani, Hadfield, van Uum, Greff, & Panter-Brick, 2018).

Results are further complicated as the role of these hormones in resilience differs by gender, the diurnal cycle, the type of adversity exposure, age, and environmental and genetic factors (De Bellis & Zisk, 2014). While there is as yet no research looking at the genetics of resilience specifically for refugee children, various studies have found associations between genetic polymorphisms, early life stress, and psychological outcomes. Polymorphisms in receptors important to hypothalamic–pituitary–adrenal axis function, CRHR1 and FKBP5, have been found to interact with maltreatment during childhood to predict later psychological outcomes such as depression, PTSD, and neuroticism (Binder et al., 2008; Bradley et al., 2008; DeYoung, Cicchetti, & Rogosch, 2011). Such gene × environment interactions may influence stress responses via effects on neuroendocrine function. For example, variations in CRHR1 were associated with cortisol dysregulation in a sample of maltreated children (Cicchetti, Rogosch, & Oshri, 2011). Although we generally separate our discussion into resilience processes and outcomes for the sake of simplicity, the example of neuroendocrine involvement in adversity is a good demonstration of how in some cases they may be one and the same. Cortisol functioning can be used as an outcome measure by representing the stress impact of adversity on the body, but it may also mediate between genetics and experience to impact a child's subsequent functioning and stress response. As a dynamic, ongoing process, resilience involves many mechanisms that are both influenced by stress and influence the response to stress and adversity. This complexity emphasizes the need to investigate the interactions between different systems at different levels of analysis over time.

Interactions between different levels of analysis. As mentioned before, the exact relationship between biological processes and resilience remains somewhat unclear. Perhaps one of the reasons for this is the interactions between neurobiological factors and factors at the individual and social level. The little research that has been done on this with refugee children suggests that there are associations between exposure to adversity, maternal cortisol and immune function, child cortisol and immune function, and child mental health (Obradović et al., 2010; Yirmiya, Djalovski, Motsan, Zagoory-Sharon, & Feldman, 2018). For example, Yirmiya et al. (2018) identified three pathways from war exposure to anxiety in a sample of adolescents via maternal factors. The two biological pathways showed a mediating effect of the mother's cortisol levels (and immune function) between exposure and their child's cortisol levels (and immune function). Increase in both maternal factors was associated with increase in their child's, leading to increases in adolescent anxiety. These biological paths interacted with a third, social pathway. War exposure was associated with less supportive parenting from the mother, which was associated with lower adolescent social collaboration and subsequently greater anxiety. The authors interpreted this as evidence that maternal functioning can influence child adaptation to stress via mechanisms at multiple levels of biological and social systems.

Facet 4: The Multidimensional Nature of Psychological Resilience

As mentioned earlier, positive adaptation in the context of exposure to adversity should be conceptualized as multidimensional rather than unidimensional. Outcomes after trauma can manifest in many dimensions such as emotional, behavioral, academic, and somatic domains (Fazel et al., 2012; Infurna & Luthar, 2017). Children may be affected differentially across each (Luthar et al., 2000) depending on their personal resources and the specific nature of the adversity they experience. Additionally, assessment of adaptation is likely influenced by societal values and the priorities of the assessors (Schwarz, 2018). For example, a child may be performing well academically but behaving poorly at home. Therefore, a combination of objective (e.g., school grades) and subjective (e.g., depressive symptoms) measures across a range of dimensions may be required to assess resilience. In fact, Infurna and Luthar (2017) have shown that rates of resilience differ across measurement dimensions, such as life satisfaction, positive and negative affect, and physical functioning, with only 8% of their sample classified as resilient in all dimensions. Although this result was from adults, studies of psychopathology in refugee children show a similar story; in a sample of Syrian refugee children, 52.1% and 46.8% scored below the clinical cut-offs for depression and anxiety, respectively, but only 17% of the sample had scores below both cut-offs (Kandemir et al., 2018). Hence, measuring single dimensions of functioning will likely lead to overinflated estimates of resilience. It is therefore crucial to consider multiple dimensions to obtain a comprehensive view of how a child is functioning and accurate prevalence estimates for both psychopathology and resilience.

Not only is a multidimensional approach important to properly determine whether an individual is resilient; it is also important to understand the mechanisms promoting positive adaptation. Results showing that different factors (i.e., family cohesion, parental education) are predictive of different outcomes (i.e., PTS and behavioral problems) demonstrate that different dimensions of mental health and resilience may involve separate processes (Fazel et al., 2012). An understanding of how to operationalize the multiple dimensions of resilience is therefore crucial to getting an accurate idea of the resilience process. Furthermore, resilience in one domain may influence resilience in others. For example, in terms of academic resilience, early mathematics ability of children living in poverty in the U.S. predicted later literacy (Sattler & Gershoff, 2019). The involvement of multiple dimensions of functioning should therefore be considered both in terms of resilience mechanisms as well as outcomes.

Facet 5: A Developmental Perspective of Resilience

The developmental section of our model accounts for both the immediate process of transactions between individuals and their environment and the overall influences of personal and environmental development over time. Longitudinal research is crucial to investigate the highly dynamic and complex process of resilience, as well as the developmental factors that might affect mechanisms related to children's resilience. At the immediate transactional level, children are not only influenced by but also have influence on their environment, whether consciously or unconsciously. Bidirectional child–environment transactions affect their exposure to environments or events within the microsystem. For example, the individual-level factor of self-regulation might protect children from engaging in risky social situations (Gardner, Dishion, & Connell, 2008). Within the family, a child's behaviors can also influence the parent–child interactions they experience. In a study of anger within refugee families, parents often cited their child's misbehaviors as the reason for their anger (Hinton, Rasmussen, Nou, Pollack, & Good, 2009). Particularly among refugees where the whole family might be traumatized by their premigration and migration experiences, parents might be more easily triggered to become angry, harsh disciplinarians, or violent toward their children. Children who are traumatized are also more likely to show behavioral problems (e.g., Eruyar, Maltby, & Vostanis, 2018; Hodes & Vostanis, 2018). In this way, parental psychopathology can interact with children's behavior, the family dynamic, and the parent–child relationship as a consequence of the feedback loop shown in Figure 21.3 (Section 5).

These patterns have the capacity to develop or sustain maladaptive mental health outcomes over time (Timshel, Montgomery, & Dalgaard, 2017).

At the larger, life-course scale, one of the most replicated predictors of mental health outcomes among refugee children is age, with many studies finding increasing mental health problems with older age (Eruyar et al., 2018). The greater ability to process trauma that comes with age could lead to more negative responses as individuals are better able to understand their past experience. However, as suggested by Eruyar et al. (2018), as children age they may also be more able to develop better coping strategies. Indeed, both older age and greater use of coping skills were associated with fewer mental health problems among Palestinian adolescents (Aitcheson et al., 2017). Child development is a complex process even outside of the context of trauma and resilience. Several considerations point to early development as a crucial stage for the development of sensitivities, experiences, and coping mechanisms. The idea of steeling effects, or stress inoculation, supports the idea that early exposure to a manageable dose of adversity can help a child develop the capacity to deal with adversity in the future (Rutter, 2012). Although there is a lack of research as yet on the concept in refugee children, some evidence from human and non-human (primate) adults supports the theory that challenging but not overwhelming stress can increase resilience to subsequent stress (Daskalakis, Bagot, Parker, Vinkers, & de Kloet, 2013; Edge et al., 2009; Lyons, Parker, Katz, & Schatzberg, 2009; Seery, Holman, & Silver, 2010). However, this also works the other way, such that failure to cope with stress can have a cumulative effect and decrease capacity to cope over time (Daskalakis et al., 2013).

The concept of developmental cascades is helpful in explaining such results. Developmental cascades refer to the way in which the effects of early life experiences can be accumulated by spreading across multiple levels, systems, and domains as a result of interactions between developing systems (Masten & Cicchetti, 2010). According to the theory, cascades can flow both upwards and downwards through levels of function, so that they can have effects on the epigenetic, physiological, and psychological levels. Cascades can manifest in both negative and positive ways, such that competence in one domain early on can provide the building blocks for positive adaptation in other higher order domains, while negative experiences can increase vulnerability (Masten & Cicchetti, 2010). Therefore, in contrast to steeling effects there exists the potential for a developmental cascade of increased vulnerability. For example, war trauma could interact with genetic factors to increase sensitivity or stress reactivity and lead to changes in neurobiological and cognitive development that increase vulnerability to subsequent adverse experiences. The psychological well-being of a child at different time points is therefore a crucial factor to consider in a resilience framework.

Implications

While we have mentioned several areas in which resilience research needs further development, there is much that we already know. Psychological resilience involves and affects multiple systems; can be investigated across multiple levels of analysis; manifests in multiple dimensions, the relationships of which are influenced by the individual's environmental sensitivity; and develops over time along with developmental processes. Potential implications of this understanding apply both to research and to interventions for populations, such as refugee children, who are at great risk. Specifically, resilience cannot be understood or promoted by focusing on single systems or factors. Instead, we need to consider how factors work together. In terms of interventions, this provides support for a more holistic approach. While we accept that there are certain factors that are more challenging to change, such as exposure to war traumas, it may be the case that we should focus on changing the odds rather than trying to beat them (Seccombe, 2002). For example, psychological interventions targeting the whole family or providing children with alternative sources of social support can create a better environment for children. More immediate strategies such as improving behavioral or cognitive strategies for promoting resilience might be more successful if children have a supportive social environment. Cooperation at different levels of society could help to provide a more integrated approach to resilience more suitable for its complexity. For example, stressors for refugee children and parents such as discrimination in the host country can be tackled at each ecological level. At the macrosystem level, political changes such as reversing hostile environment policies (Liberty, 2018) can make the environment less institutionally discriminatory. Journalism and public campaigns could improve the host community's perceptions of its refugee population, while interventions at the microsystem such as in schools and workplaces could improve the behavior of hosts toward refugees. A greater feeling of community acceptance in addition to practical changes to the environment and the promotion of refugees' rights could make a difference to the mental health of parents and children and facilitate better patterns of adaptation.

Conclusions and Future Directions

In this chapter we have reviewed evidence of the complex nature of psychological resilience in the context of development during war and displacement. The evidence suggests that resilience involves multiple systems, requires investigation at multiple levels of analysis, needs to be considered across multiple dimensions of positive adaptation, and is a longitudinal, dynamic process that is affected by developmental processes and sensitivity to the environment. Although the processes that contribute to resilience are highly complex, some aspects may be more relevant to developmental outcomes in specific contexts and can be targeted with interventions. For example, alleviating external sources of stress by improving housing or supporting asylum claims or providing mental health support for parents have the potential to create environments that are more conducive to children's adaptive coping, and subsequently improve the efficacy of psychological treatment for the child. Holistic research integrating the different facets proposed in our model, in addition to reaching more consensus on the conceptualization of resilience, will significantly advance the field.

Key Messages

1. We define resilience as positive adaptation in the context of adversity. According to this definition, resilience is a dynamic process and cannot be observed in the absence of adversity.

2. Resilience processes, which occur at multiple levels of functioning (e.g., neurological and cognitive levels), manifest in multiple dimensions (e.g., emotional, behavioral, physiological). Studies of resilience must therefore consider multilevel and multidimensional approaches.
3. Resilience processes in the context of adversity are influenced by a range of additional factors with specific risk or protective functions across the different psychosocial and bioecological systems.
4. People differ substantially in their sensitivity to both negative and positive aspects of the environment. Resilience research needs to take differences in environmental sensitivity into account when investigating the variance of outcomes in children exposed to adversity but also in response to protective factors.
5. Given resilience is a process, longitudinal perspectives are necessary to capture how individuals and their environments change over time and how they adapt to adversity.

Acknowledgments

The work that went into this chapter was supported by the Eunice Kennedy Shriver National Institute of Child Health and Human Development (NICHD) of the National Institutes of Health (NIH) under grant number R01HD083387. The content is solely the responsibility of the authors and does not necessarily represent the official views of the National Institutes of Health.

The writing of this chapter has also been supported by Elrha's Research for Health in Humanitarian Crises (R2HC) program (Project 28371), which aims to improve health outcomes by strengthening the evidence base for public health interventions in humanitarian crises. R2HC is funded equally by the Wellcome Trust and the UK Government (DFID). Visit www.elrha.org/r2hc for more information about Elrha's work to improve humanitarian outcomes through research, innovation, and partnership.

References

Aitcheson, R. J., Abu-Bader, S. H., Howell, M. K., Khalil, D., & Elbedour, S. (2017). Resilience in Palestinian adolescents living in Gaza. *Psychological Trauma: Theory, Research, Practice, and Policy, 9*(1), 36–43. doi:10.1037/tra0000153

Al-Rousan, T., Schwabkey, Z., Jirmanus, L., & Nelson, B. D. (2018). Health needs and priorities of Syrian refugees in camps and urban settings in Jordan: Perspectives of refugees and health care providers. *Eastern Mediterranean Health Journal, 24*(3), 243–253. doi:10.26719/2018.24.3.243

Amstadter, A. B., Moscati, A., Maes, H. H., Myers, J. M., & Kendler, K. S. (2016). Personality, cognitive/psychological traits and psychiatric resilience: A multivariate twin study. *Personality and Individual Differences, 91*, 74–79. doi:10.1016/j.paid.2015.11.041

Anthony, E. J., Koupernik, C., & Chiland, C. (Eds.). (1978). *The child in his family: Vulnerable children.* New York, NY: Wiley.

Aroian, K., Hough, E. S., Templin, T. N., Kulwicki, A., Ramaswamy, V., & Katz, A. (2009). A model of mother–child adjustment in Arab Muslim immigrants to the US. *Social Science & Medicine, 69*(9), 1377–1386. doi:10.1016/j.socscimed.2009.08.027

Aron, E. N., & Aron, A. (1997). Sensory-processing sensitivity and its relation to introversion and emotionality. *Journal of Personality and Social Psychology, 73*(2), 345–368. doi:10.1037/0022-3514.73.2.345

Belsky, J., & Pluess, M. (2009). Beyond diathesis stress: Differential susceptibility to environmental influences. *Psychological Bulletin*, *135*(6), 885–908. doi:10.1037/a0017376

Betancourt, T. S., Abdi, S., Ito, B. S., Lilienthal, G. M., Agalab, N., & Ellis, H. (2015). We left one war and came to another: Resource loss, acculturative stress, and caregiver-child relationships in Somali refugee families. *Cultural Diversity and Ethnic Minority Psychology*, *21*(1), 114–125. doi:10.1037/a0037538

Binder, E. B., Bradley, R. G., Liu, W., Epstein, M. P., Deveau, T. C., Mercer, K. B., . . . Ressler, K. J. (2008). Association of FKBP5 polymorphisms and childhood abuse with risk of posttraumatic stress disorder symptoms in adults. *JAMA*, *299*(11), 1291–1305. doi:10.1001/jama.299.11.1291

Boyce, W. T., & Ellis, B. J. (2005). Biological sensitivity to context: I. An evolutionary-developmental theory of the origins and functions of stress reactivity. *Development and Psychopathology*, *17*(2), 271–301. doi:10.1017/S0954579405050145

Bradley, R. G., Binder, E. B., Epstein, M. P., Tang, Y., Nair, H. P., Liu, W., . . . Ressler, K. J. (2008). Influence of child abuse on adult depression: Moderation by the corticotropin-releasing hormone receptor gene. *Archives of General Psychiatry*, *65*(2), 190–200. doi:10.1001/archgenpsychiatry.2007.26

Bronfenbrenner, U. (1979). *The ecology of human development: Experiments by nature and design*. Cambridge, MA: Harvard University Press.

Bronstein, I., & Montgomery, P. (2011). Psychological distress in refugee children: A systematic review. *Clinical Child and Family Psychology Review*, *14*(1), 44–56. doi:10.1007/s10567-010-0081-0

Burt, K. B., Whelan, R., Conrod, P. J., Banaschewski, T., Barker, G. J., Bokde, A. L. W., . . . Garavan, H. (2016). Structural brain correlates of adolescent resilience. *Journal of Child Psychology and Psychiatry*, *57*(11), 1287–1296. doi:10.1111/jcpp.12552

Carta, M. G., Oumar, F. W., Moro, M. F., Moro, D., Preti, A., Mereu, A., & Bhugra, D. (2013). Trauma- and stressor related disorders in the Tuareg refugees of a camp in Burkina Faso. *Clinical Practice & Epidemiology in Mental Health*, *9*(1), 189–195. doi:10.2174/1745017901309010189

Cicchetti, D., & Rogosch, F. A. (2007). Personality, adrenal steroid hormones, and resilience in maltreated children: A multilevel perspective. *Development and Psychopathology*, *19*(3), 787–809. doi:10.1017/S0954579407000399

Cicchetti, D., Rogosch, F. A., & Oshri, A. (2011). Interactive effects of corticotropin releasing hormone receptor 1, serotonin transporter linked polymorphic region, and child maltreatment on diurnal cortisol regulation and internalizing symptomatology. *Development and Psychopathology*, *23*(4), 1125–38. doi:10.1017/S0954579411000599

d'Abreu, A., Castro-Olivo, S., & Ura, S. K. (2019). Understanding the role of acculturative stress on refugee youth mental health: A systematic review and ecological approach to assessment and intervention. *School Psychology International*, *40*(2), 107–127. doi:10.1177/0143034318822688

Dajani, R., Hadfield, K., van Uum, S., Greff, M., & Panter-Brick, C. (2018). Hair cortisol concentrations in war-affected adolescents: A prospective intervention trial. *Psychoneuroendocrinology*, *89*, 138–146. doi:10.1016/j.psyneuen.2017.12.012.

Daskalakis, N. P., Bagot, R. C., Parker, K. J., Vinkers, C. H., & de Kloet, E. R. (2013). The three-hit concept of vulnerability and resilience: Toward understanding adaptation to early-life adversity outcome. *Psychoneuroendocrinology*, *38*(9), 1858–1873. doi:10.1016/j.psyneuen.2013.06.008

De Bellis, M. D., & Zisk, A. (2014). The biological effects of childhood trauma. *Child and Adolescent Psychiatric Clinics of North America*, *23*(2), 185–222. doi:10.1016/j.chc.2014.01.002

DeYoung, C. G., Cicchetti, D., & Rogosch, F. A. (2011). Moderation of the association between childhood maltreatment and neuroticism by the corticotropin-releasing hormone receptor 1 gene. *Journal of Child Psychology and Psychiatry and Allied Disciplines*, *52*(8), 898–906. doi:10.1111/j.1469-7610.2011.02404.x

Dwairy, M., Achoui, M., Abouserie, R., Farah, A., Sakhleh, A. A., Fayad, M., & Khan, H. K. (2006). Parenting styles in Arab societies: A first cross-regional research study. *Journal of Cross-Cultural Psychology*, *37*(3), 230–247. doi:10.1177/0022022106286922

Edge, M. D., Ramel, W., Drabant, E. M., Kuo, J. R., Parker, K. J., & Gross, J. J. (2009). For better or worse? Stress inoculation effects for implicit but not explicit anxiety. *Depression and Anxiety*, *26*(9), 831–837. doi:10.1002/da.20592

Ellis, B. H., MacDonald, H. Z., Lincoln, A. K., & Cabral, H. J. (2008). Mental health of Somali adolescent refugees: The role of trauma, stress, and perceived discrimination. *Journal of Consulting and Clinical Psychology, 76*(2), 184–193. doi:10.1037/0022-006X.76.2.184

Eruyar, S., Huemer, J., & Vostanis, P. (2018). Review: How should child mental health services respond to the refugee crisis? *Child and Adolescent Mental Health, 23*(4), 303–312. doi:10.1111/camh.12252

Eruyar, S., Maltby, J., & Vostanis, P. (2018). Mental health problems of Syrian refugee children: The role of parental factors. *European Child & Adolescent Psychiatry, 27*(4), 401–409. doi:10.1007/s00787-017-1101-0

Fazel, M., Reed, R. V, Panter-Brick, C., & Stein, A. (2012). Mental health of displaced and refugee children resettled in high-income countries: Risk and protective factors. *The Lancet, 379*(9812), 266–282. doi:10.1016/S0140-6736(11)60051-2

Feyera, F., Mihretie, G., Bedaso, A., Gedle, D., & Kumera, G. (2015). Prevalence of depression and associated factors among Somali refugee at Melkadida camp, Southeast Ethiopia: A cross-sectional study. *BMC Psychiatry, 15*(1), 171. doi:10.1186/s12888-015-0539-1

Gardner, T. W., Dishion, T. J., & Connell, A. M. (2008). Adolescent self-regulation as resilience: Resistance to antisocial behavior within the deviant peer context. *Journal of Abnormal Child Psychology, 36*(2), 273–284. doi:10.1007/s10802-007-9176-6

Garmezy, N., & Rutter, M. (1983). *Stress, coping, and development in children.* New York, NY: McGraw-Hill.

Heim, C., & Nemeroff, C. B. (2001). The role of childhood trauma in the neurobiology of mood and anxiety disorders: Preclinical and clinical studies. *Biological Psychiatry, 49*(12), 1023–1039. doi:10.1016/S0006-3223(01)01157-X

Hinton, D. E., Rasmussen, A., Nou, L., Pollack, M. H., & Good, M.-J. (2009). Anger, PTSD, and the nuclear family: A study of Cambodian refugees. *Social Science & Medicine, 69*(9), 1387–1394. doi:10.1016/j.socscimed.2009.08.018

Hodes, M., & Vostanis, P. (2018). Practitioner review: Mental health problems of refugee children and adolescents and their management. *Journal of Child Psychology and Psychiatry, 60*(7), 716–731. doi:10.1111/jcpp.13002

Howell, K. H., Kaplow, J. B., Layne, C. M., Benson, M. A., Compas, B. E., Katalinski, R., . . . Pynoos, R. (2015). Predicting adolescent posttraumatic stress in the aftermath of war: Differential effects of coping strategies across trauma reminder, loss reminder, and family conflict domains. *Anxiety, Stress, & Coping, 28*(1), 88–104. doi:10.1080/10615806.2014.910596

Hu, T., Zhang, D., & Wang, J. (2015). A meta-analysis of the trait resilience and mental health. *Personality and Individual Differences, 76*, 18–27. doi:10.1016/J.PAID.2014.11.039

Infurna, F. J., & Luthar, S. S. (2017). The multidimensional nature of resilience to spousal loss. *Journal of Personality and Social Psychology, 112*(6), 926–947. doi:10.1037/pspp0000095

Kandemir, H., Karataş, H., Çeri, V., Solmaz, F., Kandemir, S. B., & Solmaz, A. (2018). Prevalence of war-related adverse events, depression and anxiety among Syrian refugee children settled in Turkey. *European Child & Adolescent Psychiatry, 27*(11), 1513–1517. doi:10.1007/s00787-018-1178-0

Karam, E. G., Fayyad, J. A., Farhat, C., Pluess, M., Haddad, Y. C., Tabet, C. C., . . . Kessler, R. C. (2019). Role of childhood adversities and environmental sensitivity in the development of post-traumatic stress disorder in war-exposed Syrian refugee children and adolescents. *The British Journal of Psychiatry, 214*(6), 354–360. doi:10.1192/bjp.2018.272

Karatsoreos, I. N., & McEwen, B. S. (2011). Psychobiological allostasis: Resistance, resilience and vulnerability. *Trends in Cognitive Sciences, 15*(12), 576–584. doi:10.1016/j.tics.2011.10.005

Khamis, V. (2019). Posttraumatic stress disorder and emotion dysregulation among Syrian refugee children and adolescents resettled in Lebanon and Jordan. *Child Abuse & Neglect, 89*, 29–39. doi:10.1016/j.chiabu.2018.12.013

Kia-Keating, M., & Ellis, B. H. (2007). Belonging and connection to school in resettlement: Young refugees, school belonging, and psychosocial adjustment. *Clinical Child Psychology and Psychiatry, 12*(1), 29–43. doi:10.1177/1359104507071052

Liberty. (2018). *A guide to the hostile environment.* Retrieved from https://www.libertyhumanrights.org.uk

Luthar, S. S., Cicchetti, D., & Becker, B. (2000). The construct of resilience: A critical evaluation and guidelines for future work. *Child Development, 71*(3), 543–562.

Lyons, D. M., Parker, K. J., Katz, M., & Schatzberg, A. F. (2009). Developmental cascades linking stress inoculation, arousal regulation, and resilience. *Frontiers in Behavioral Neuroscience, 3.* doi:10.3389/neuro.08.032.2009

Masten, A. S. (2007). Resilience in developing systems: Progress and promise as the fourth wave rises. *Development and Psychopathology, 19*(03), 921–930. doi:10.1017/S0954579407000442

Masten, A. S. (2012). Resilience in children: Vintage Rutter and beyond: Revisiting the classic studies. In A. Slater & P. Quinn (Eds.), *Developmental psychology: Revisiting the classic studies* (pp. 204–221). London, UK: SAGE.

Masten, A. S. (2014). Global perspectives on resilience in children and youth. *Child Development, 85*(1), 6–20. doi:10.1111/cdev.12205

Masten, A. S., Best, K. M., & Garmezy, N. (1990). Resilience and development: Contributions from the study of children who overcome adversity. *Development and Psychopathology, 2*(4), 425–444. doi:10.1017/S0954579400005812

Masten, A. S., & Cicchetti, D. (2010). Developmental cascades. *Development and Psychopathology, 22*(03), 491–495. doi:10.1017/S0954579410000222

Masten, A. S., & Garmezy, N. (1985). Risk, vulnerability, and protective factors in developmental psychopathology. In B. B. Lahey & A. E. Kazdin (Eds.), *Advances in clinical child psychology* (pp. 1–52). Boston, MA: Springer.

Masten, A. S., & Narayan, A. J. (2012). Child development in the context of disaster, war, and terrorism: Pathways of risk and resilience. *Annual Review of Psychology, 63*(1), 227–257. doi:10.1146/annurev-psych-120710-100356

Monroe, S. M., & Simons, A. D. (1991). Diathesis-stress theories in the context of life stress research: Implications for the depressive disorders. *Psychological Bulletin, 110*(3), 406–425.

Montgomery, E. (2008). Long-term effects of organized violence on young Middle Eastern refugees' mental health. *Social Science & Medicine, 67*(10), 1596–1603. doi:10.1016/j.socscimed.2008.07.020

O'Leary, V. E., & Ickovics, J. R. (1995). Resilience and thriving in response to challenge: An opportunity for a paradigm shift in women's health. *Women's Health, 1*(2), 121–42.

Obradović, J., Bush, N. R., Stamperdahl, J., Adler, N. E., & Boyce, W. T. (2010). Biological sensitivity to context: The interactive effects of stress reactivity and family adversity on socioemotional behavior and school readiness. *Child Development, 81*(1), 270–289. doi:10.1111/j.1467-8624.2009.01394.x

Panter-Brick, C., Grimon, M.-P., Kalin, M., & Eggerman, M. (2015). Trauma memories, mental health, and resilience: A prospective study of Afghan youth. *Journal of Child Psychology and Psychiatry, 56*(7), 814–825. doi:10.1111/jcpp.12350

Pluess, M. (2015). Individual differences in environmental sensitivity. *Child Development Perspectives, 9*(3), 138–143. doi:10.1111/cdep.12120

Pluess, M., & Belsky, J. (2013). Vantage sensitivity: Individual differences in response to positive experiences. *Psychological Bulletin, 139*(4), 901–916. doi:10.1037/a0030196

Pluess, M., Stevens, S. E., & Belsky, J. (2013). Differential susceptibility: Developmental and evolutionary mechanisms of gene–environment interactions. In M. Legerstee, D. W. Haley, & M. H. Bornstein (Eds.), *The infant mind: Origins of the social brain* (pp. 77–96). New York, NY: Guilford Press.

Russo, S. J., Murrough, J. W., Han, M.-H., Charney, D. S., & Nestler, E. J. (2012). Neurobiology of resilience. *Nature Neuroscience, 15*(11), 1475–1484. doi:10.1038/nn.3234

Rutter, M. (1987). Psychosocial resilience and protective mechanisms. *American Journal of Orthopsychiatry, 57*(3), 316–331. doi:10.1111/j.1939-0025.1987.tb03541.x

Rutter, M. (1990). Psychosocial resilience and protective mechanisms. In J. Rolf, A. S. Masten, D. Cicchetti, K. H. Nuchterlein, & S. Weintraub (Eds.), *Risk and protective factors in the development of psychopathology* (pp. 181–214). New York, NY: Cambridge University Press. doi:10.1017/CBO9780511752872.013

Rutter, M. (1993). Resilience: Some conceptual considerations. *Journal of Adolescent Health, 14*(8), 626–631, doi:10.1016/1054-139X(93)90196-V

Rutter, M. (2012). Resilience as a dynamic concept. *Development and Psychopathology, 24*(2), 335–344. doi:10.1017/S0954579412000028

Sabin, M., Cardozo, B. L., Nackerud, L., Kaiser, R., & Varese, L. (2003). Factors associated with poor mental health among Guatemalan refugees living in Mexico 20 years after civil conflict. *JAMA, 290*(5), 635–642. doi:10.1001/jama.290.5.635

Sameroff, A. J. (2000). Developmental systems and psychopathology. *Development and Psychopathology, 12*(3), 297–312. doi:10.1017/s0954579400003035

Sattler, K., & Gershoff, E. (2019). Thresholds of resilience and within- and cross-domain academic achievement among children in poverty. *Early Childhood Research Quarterly, 46*, 87–96. doi:10.1016/j.ecresq.2018.04.003

Schwarz, S. (2018). Resilience in psychology: A critical analysis of the concept. *Theory & Psychology, 28*(4), 528–541. doi:10.1177/0959354318783584

Seccombe, K. (2002). "Beating the odds" versus "changing the odds": Poverty, resilience, and family policy. *Journal of Marriage and Family, 64*(2), 384–394. doi:10.1111/j.1741-3737.2002.00384.x

Seery, M. D., Holman, E. A., & Silver, R. C. (2010). Whatever does not kill us: Cumulative lifetime adversity, vulnerability, and resilience. *Journal of Personality and Social Psychology, 99*(6), 1025–1041. doi:10.1037/a0021344

Sim, A., Fazel, M., Bowes, L., & Gardner, F. (2018). Pathways linking war and displacement to parenting and child adjustment: A qualitative study with Syrian refugees in Lebanon. *Social Science & Medicine, 200*, 19–26. doi:10.1016/j.socscimed.2018.01.009

Smetana, J. G., & Ahmad, I. (2018). Heterogeneity in perceptions of parenting among Arab refugee adolescents in Jordan. *Child Development, 89*(5), 1786–1802. doi:10.1111/cdev.12844

Steudte, S., Kolassa, I.-T., Stalder, T., Pfeiffer, A., Kirschbaum, C., & Elbert, T. (2011). Increased cortisol concentrations in hair of severely traumatized Ugandan individuals with PTSD. *Psychoneuroendocrinology, 36*(8), 1193–1200. doi:10.1016/j.psyneuen.2011.02.012

Timshel, I., Montgomery, E., & Dalgaard, N. T. (2017). A systematic review of risk and protective factors associated with family related violence in refugee families. *Child Abuse & Neglect, 70*, 315–330. doi:10.1016/j.chiabu.2017.06.023

Trentacosta, C. J., McLear, C. M., Ziadni, M. S., Lumley, M. A., & Arfken, C. L. (2016). Potentially traumatic events and mental health problems among children of Iraqi refugees: The roles of relationships with parents and feelings about school. *American Journal of Orthopsychiatry, 86*(4), 384–392. doi:10.1037/ort0000186

Ungar, M. (2015). Practitioner review: Diagnosing childhood resilience: A systemic approach to the diagnosis of adaptation in adverse social and physical ecologies. *Journal of Child Psychology and Psychiatry, 56*(1), 4–17. doi:10.1111/jcpp.12306

Ungar, M. (2018). Systemic resilience: Principles and processes for a science of change in contexts of adversity. *Ecology and Society, 23*(4), 34. doi:10.5751/es-10385-230434

Ungar, M., Ghazinour, M., & Richter, J. (2013). Annual research review: What is resilience within the social ecology of human development? *Journal of Child Psychology and Psychiatry, 54*(4), 348–366. doi:10.1111/jcpp.12025

United Nations High Commissioner for Refugees. (2019). *Syria regional refugee response*. Retrieved from https://data2.unhcr.org/en/situations/syria

Werner, E. E. (1992). The children of Kauai: Resiliency and recovery in adolescence and adulthood. *Journal of Adolescent Health, 13*(4), 262–268. doi:10.1016/1054-139x(92)90157-7

Wiegersma, P. A., Stellinga-Boelen, A. A. M., & Reijneveld, S. A. (2011). Psychosocial problems in asylum seekers' children: The parent, child, and teacher perspective using the strengths and difficulties questionnaire. *Journal of Nervous and Mental Disease, 199*(2), 85–90. doi:10.1097/nmd.0b013e31820446d2

Yirmiya, K., Djalovski, A., Motsan, S., Zagoory-Sharon, O., & Feldman, R. (2018). Stress and immune biomarkers interact with parenting behavior to shape anxiety symptoms in trauma-exposed youth. *Psychoneuroendocrinology, 98*, 153–160. doi:10.1016/j.psyneuen.2018.08.016

Ziersch, A., & Due, C. (2018). A mixed methods systematic review of studies examining the relationship between housing and health for people from refugee and asylum seeking backgrounds. *Social Science & Medicine, 213*, 199–219. doi:10.1016/j.socscimed.2018.07.045

22
The Assessment of Multisystemic Resilience in Conflict-Affected Populations

Alexandros Lordos and Daniel Hyslop

Introduction

Violent social conflict occurs within a web of negative feedback loops and maladaptive societal trajectories, which taken together constitute a cascade of stressors and shocks that can entirely overwhelm individuals, households, communities, and institutions. Violent social conflict is both driven by and contributes to interethnic hostility, extreme poverty, food insecurity, and exclusion from services and opportunities, as well as failure of governance at the local and national level (United Nations & World Bank, 2018). In the aftermath of violent conflict, populations are additionally called to address the challenges posed by destruction of productive capacity, forced displacement, posttraumatic distress of civilians and combatants, and disrupted developmental trajectories of children, adolescents, and young adults who found themselves near the epicenter of hostilities (Betancourt & Khan, 2008; Fazel et al., 2012). The incidence and intensity of violent social conflict have both been on the rise in recent years. This upsurge can primarily be attributed to a sharp increase in conflicts between nonstate actors, which grew from just under 30 active nonstate conflicts in 2010 to more than 70 in 2016 (see Figure 22.1; United Nations & World Bank, 2018). Furthermore, the number and diversity of nonstate actors that have been participating in each violent conflict have also been rising significantly since 2010 (Allansson, Melander, & Themner, 2017; Sundberg, Eck, & Kreutz, 2012), including, among others, an expanding range of militias, rebel groups, violent extremist groups, and armed trafficking groups. Partly as a result of the complexity of such multisided conflict systems, which are deeply rooted in the interaction of social, economic, and cultural forces, conflicts have also become more protracted. While the average

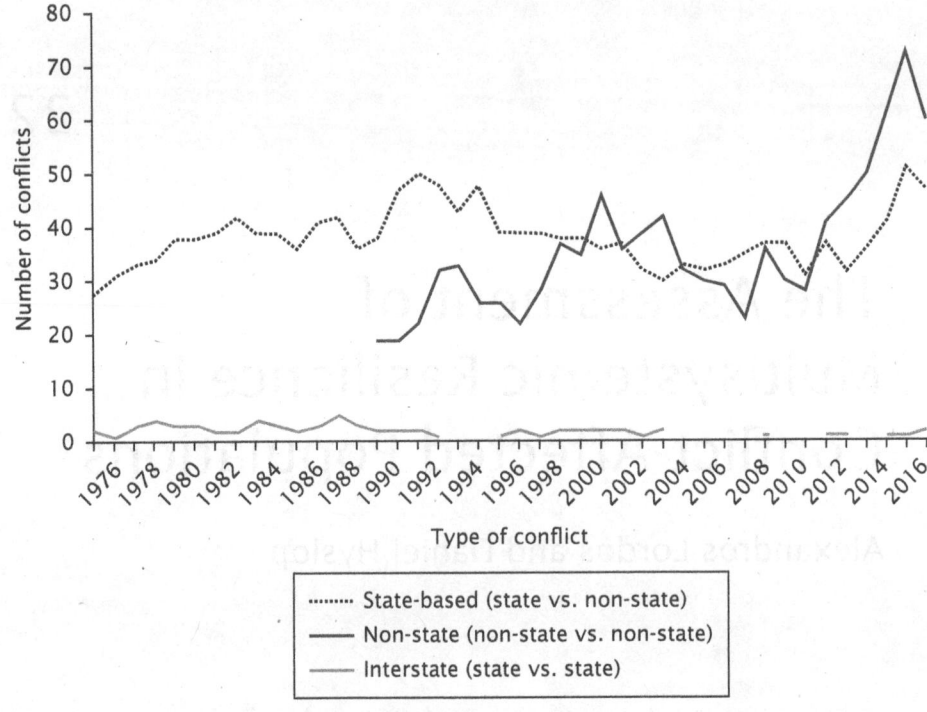

FIGURE 22.1 Trends in violent conflict, 1975–2016. Reprinted from Pathways for Peace Report (United Nations & World Bank, 2018) under Creative Commons License CC BY 3.0 IGO. Sources: For interstate and state-based conflicts, data from Uppsala Conflict Data Program (UCDP) and Peace Research Institute Oslo (Allansson, Melander, & Themner, 2017; Gleditsch et al., 2002); for nonstate conflicts, data from UCDP (Sundberg, Eck, & Kreutz, 2012; Allansson, Melander, & Themner, 2017).

duration for conflicts ending in 1970 was approximately five years, this has jumped to an average of 20 years for conflicts ending in 2015 (see Figure 22.2; United Nations & World Bank, 2018).

The increased severity and frequency of violent social conflicts, and the inability of countries to resolve such domestic arenas of contestation underlines a key challenge that the global community is gradually coming to terms with—namely, that the conflict prevention and mitigation toolkit that had been instituted after two world wars and that revolved around building harmonious relations between states through diplomacy, trade, and international norms is no longer fit for purpose in addressing emergent forms of asymmetric conflicts, hybrid conflicts, and civil wars. As these become protracted through lack of effective resolution, they are joined by newly emergent conflicts, which, taken together, are overwhelming the capacities of humanitarian response systems. Notably, it is estimated that 85% of aggregate demand for humanitarian emergency assistance currently comes from conflict-affected countries (Development Initiatives, 2018). While the core mandate of humanitarianism has always been to provide short-term relief through the process of recovery, such organizations are now finding themselves to be staying in emergency contexts for much longer, with the distinctions between emergency relief, long-term assistance, and maladaptive aid dependency increasingly becoming blurred.

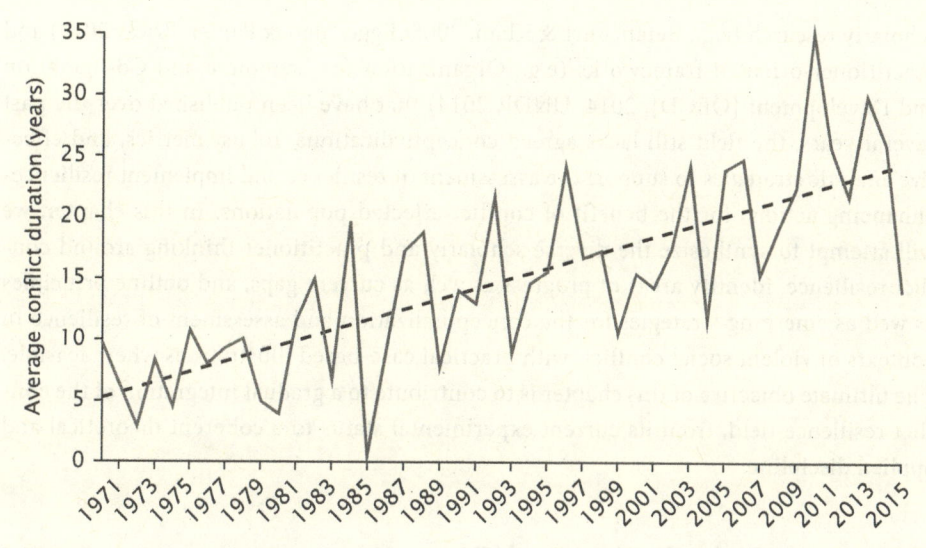

FIGURE 22.2 Average duration of conflicts worldwide, 1970–2015. Reprinted from Pathways for Peace Report (United Nations & World Bank, 2018) under Creative Commons License CC BY 3.0 IGO. Source: Uppsala Conflict Data Program (UCDP) and Peace Research Institute Oslo (Allansson, Melander, & Themner, 2017; Gleditsch et al., 2002).

In the context of these stressors to the international system for peace consolidation and humanitarian support, a transformative policy agenda that places resilience at center stage is gradually replacing traditional institutional responses. If violent social conflict, in its contemporary manifestation, is a "wicked problem"—defined as a problem that is difficult or impossible to solve because of incomplete, contradictory, or changing requirements that are often difficult to recognize (McCandless, 2013)—then persisting with linear thinking and traditional planning tools is unlikely to have adequate impact on peace and development outcomes. In contrast, systems thinking, complexity theory, resilience and social-ecological models of adaptation are all concepts that have, in the past decade, been gaining traction. From a humanitarian perspective, the promise of resilience lies in the possibility of building local capacity and agency for emergency response and return to normality, in ways that will gradually reduce dependence on external aid (Hilhorst, 2018). From a peacebuilding perspective, nurturing of resilience capacities can constitute a positive agenda for transformative social change around which multiple societal, civic, and institutional stakeholders can convene (Simpson et al., 2016). Likewise, from a development perspective, investments in resilience contribute to curtailing economic and human losses in the event of a crisis, thus protecting development gains while reducing human suffering (United Nations, 2019). The upside of such approaches is widely accepted: By investing in resilience, it will become possible to reduce long-term spending on emergency humanitarian response and free resources to strengthen prevention-oriented spending elsewhere that can help mitigate the crises of the future.

While much of this thinking was acknowledged at the World Humanitarian Summit in 2016 and captured in that summit's maxim "Change People's Lives: From Delivering Aid to Ending Need" (United Nations General Assembly, 2016), and despite substantial scholarly research (e.g., Betancourt & Khan, 2008; Eggerman & Panter-Brick, 2010) and practitioner-oriented frameworks (e.g., Organization for Economic and Co-operation and Development [OECD], 2014; UNDP, 2014) that have been published over the past several years, the field still lacks agreed conceptualizations, robust metrics, and effective analytic strategies to support the assessment of resilience and implement resilience-enhancing actions for the benefit of conflict-affected populations. In this chapter, we will attempt to synthesize the diverse scholarly and practitioner thinking around conflict resilience, identify areas of progress as well as current gaps, and outline principles as well as emerging strategies for the conceptualization and assessment of resilience in contexts of violent social conflict, with practical case-based illustrations where feasible. The ultimate objective of this chapter is to contribute to a gradual integration of the conflict resilience field, from its current experimental status to a coherent theoretical and applied discipline.

Existing Scholarly and Practitioner Efforts to Assess Resilience in Conflict-Affected Populations

To capture the diversity in the existing literature on conflict resilience, two distinct search strategies were used. First, a scholarly search engine (SCOPUS) was used to identify peer-reviewed papers which included in their titles, abstracts or keywords, the words *conflict* and *resilience*, and second, a focused search was undertaken of the official websites of international organizations and development agencies that are known to be working in conflict-affected countries for resilience assessment frameworks. As a result of these complementary search strategies, 41 scholarly papers were reviewed and deemed to be representative of diverse methods, strategies, and subpopulations under the chapeau of conflict resilience while six practitioner frameworks for the conceptualization and/or assessment of resilience were similarly considered. Findings of the two reviews reveal a heterogeneous field, with diverse conceptualizations regarding stages of the conflict (i.e., resilience before a conflict has occurred, while a conflict is ongoing, or in the aftermath of conflict), the system level, which is the focus of analysis (i.e., whether one refers to the resilience of individuals, households, communities, institutions, or the state as a whole), the understanding of what might constitute a resource for resilience (e.g., personal attributes, social capital, material assets, institutional practices), and the assessment methods that are recommended or demonstrated (e.g., participatory, quantitative, qualitative, framework-guided case study).

At the broadest level, the scholarly literature on conflict resilience was found to be divided into two primary strands: studies that conceptualize resilience as the capacity to prevent violent conflict by maintaining collaborative strategies as community stressors increase (e.g., Carpenter, 2012; Ratner et al., 2013); and studies that conceptualize resilience as the capacity of individuals, communities, and institutions to cope with the consequences of violent conflict that has already erupted, without deterioration of mental health, social functioning or essential institutional capacities (e.g., Ager et al., 2015; Betancourt & Khan, 2008; Eggerman & Panter-Brick, 2010; Zraly & Nyirazinyoye, 2010). Figure 22.3 summarizes these two broad strands of the literature, along with their substrands, on a continuum from preconflict (resilience for conflict prevention) to ongoing and postconflict (resilience to the consequences of conflict).

PRE-CONFLICT
- Community resilience to prevent conflict through inter-ethnic tolerance (e.g. Carpenter, 2012)
- Community resilience to prevent conflict through resource co-management (e.g. Ratner et al., 2013)

ONGOING CONFLICT
- Resilience of children in conditions of chronic conflict (e.g. Eggerman & Panter-Brick, 2010)
- Institutional resilience in conditions of conflict (e.g. Ager, er al., 2015)
- Community resilience in conditions of chronic conflict (e.g. Ben-Atar, 2018)
- Civilian preparedness for eruption of hostilities in conflict-prone countries (e.g. Bodas, et al., 2015)

POST-CONFLICT
- Post-conflict resilience of adult civilian populations (e.g. Zraly & Nyirazinyoye, 2010)
- Post-conflict resilience of war-affected children (e.g. Betan court & Khan, 2008)
- Post-conflict resilience of refugees (e.g. Fazel, et al., 2012)
- Post-conflict community resilience for reconciliation and reconstruction (e.g. Chandler, 2015)
- Post-conflict resilience of former combatants (e.g. Elder & Clipp, 1989)

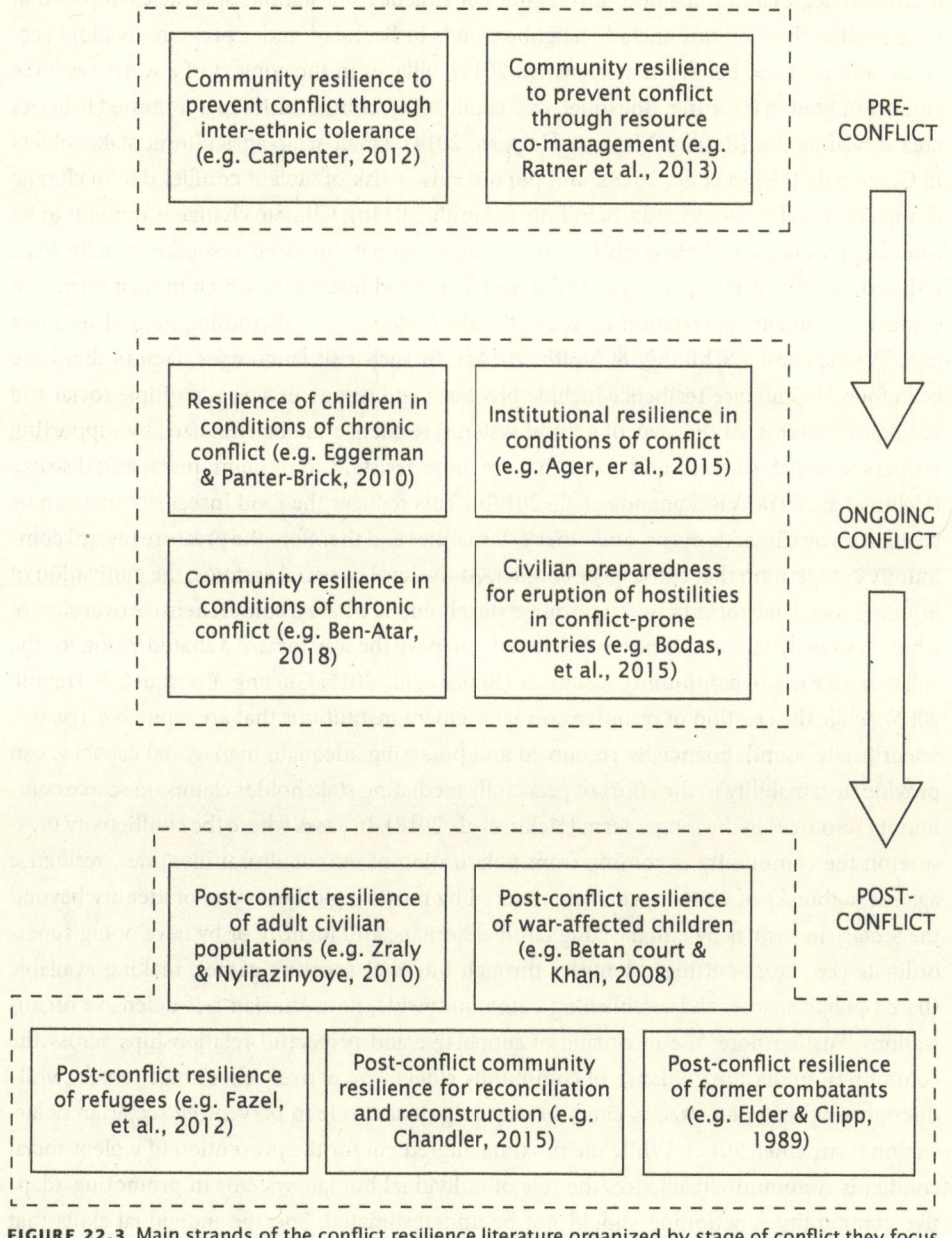

FIGURE 22.3 Main strands of the conflict resilience literature organized by stage of conflict they focus on, with illustrative publications in each category.

Investigations Into Resilience for Conflict Prevention

Studies that focus on resilience for conflict prevention mostly originate from a social-ecological research tradition, and typically focus on the level of community as the primary unit of analysis. Risk is understood as exposure to broader ethnocultural tensions and/or scarcity of natural resources, which put pressure on a community to abandon prior collaborative strategies and transition into regimes of violent contestation. Specific examples that were cited in the literature include neighborhoods in Baghdad under pressure to adopt sectarian attitudes and behaviors (Carpenter, 2012), villages in the context of a water resource conflict in Bhutan (Gurung, Bousquet, & Trebuil, 2006), communities in a contested fisheries area in Cambodia (Ratner, Mam, & Halpern, 2014), small-scale agricultural stakeholders in Guatemala (Hellin et al., 2018), and populations at risk of violent conflict due to climate change in Nepal (Vivekananda, Schilling, & Smith, 2014b). Climate change is thought to be associated with conflict through the mediation of climate-induced resource scarcity (e.g., reduced rainfall affecting crop yield) that results in food insecurity, which in turn forms the context for violent contestation by societal stakeholders over a dwindling natural resource base (Vivekananda, Schilling, & Smith, 2014a). In such risk landscapes, factors that have been found to enhance resilience include processes and resources across multiple social and ecological systems. At the level of natural systems, resilience can be enhanced by supporting farmers to switch to seeds and crops that are more resistant to draught, pests, and diseases (Hellin et al., 2018; Vivekananda et al., 2014b). This reduces the food insecurity that can be brought on by climactic events and other externalities and therefore the pressure toward community competition that can trigger conflict. At the level of social systems, the cultivation of bridging social networks between resource stakeholders, where a comprehensive overview of whole system dynamics can be co-developed, can pave the way toward a shared vision for the collaborative use of community resources (Butler et al., 2015; Gurung, Bousquet, & Trebuil, 2006), while the creation of resource co-management institutions that are reputable, trusted, scientifically sound, financially resourced and possesing adequate managerial capacity, can provide sustainability to the effort of peacefully mediating stakeholder claims on scarce community resources in the longer term (Hellin et al., 2018). In cases where the conflictivity pressure on the community is coming from polarization of ethnocultural identities, resilience against outbreaks of violence can be enhanced by nurturing other layers of identity beyond the sectarian, such as by emphasizing familial heritage and identity or by developing superordinate (i.e., cross-cutting) identities through intersect sporting games, making available shared public spaces, and establishing communitywide, nonsectarian self-defensive organizations. Furthermore, the nurturing of supportive and respectful relationships across the community, under the guidance of community elders who actively encourage respect while discouraging sectarian attacks, can also play a significant role in preventing sectarian polarization (Carpenter, 2012). While the proximal ingredient for the prevention of violent social conflict is community resilience, the role of individual human systems in promoting adaptive community functioning should not be underestimated. Specific individual skills that have been found to underpin resilience for conflict prevention include: the ability to adopt another person's perspective, the capacity to learn effectively from experience, being able to deal flexibly with new situations, and possessing skills to effectively lead groups through processes of transformation (Butler et al., 2015; Folke et al., 2005; Gurung, Bousquet, & Trebuil, 2006). On the basis of such skills, individuals can take on complementary roles within institutional or multi-stakeholder processes, for instance as knowledge retainers, visionaries, interpreters, inspirers, innovators, experimenters, followers, or reinforcers (Folke et al., 2005), thus contributing to adaptive community functioning in times of resource scarcity or ethnocultural tensions.

Investigations into Resilience to the Consequences of Violent Conflict

In contrast to the "resilience for conflict prevention" field that was previously briefly summarized and that is driven by social-ecological thinking, the literature on "resilience to the consequences of conflict" derives most of its inspiration from the disciplines of psychological science and social anthropology. Relevant studies have been taking place in contexts that are suffering from conditions of chronic conflict, such as Israel (e.g., Shoshani & Stone, 2016), Palestine (e.g., Nguyen-Gillham et al., 2008), and Afghanistan (e.g., Panter-Brick et al., 2011); countries where intense violent conflict occurred in their recent history such as Liberia (e.g., Levey et al., 2016) and Rwanda (e.g., Zraly & Nyirazinyoye, 2010); and among populations that have been displaced from their country of origin in the aftermath of violent conflict (e.g., Siriwardhana et al., 2014) or are attempting to reintegrate in their home countries as former combatants (e.g., Segovia et al., 2012). In such studies, risk is understood as exposure to violent conflict, which can lead to a cascade of negative feedback loops through death or disability of family members, disrupted social networks, loss of livelihoods, institutional failure, and mental health problems among exposed populations. Resilience, in such contexts, is typically conceptualized as maintaining individual, community and institutional survival, and adaptive functioning under conditions of extreme duress while the conflict is ongoing, while embarking on trajectories of full recovery and normalization once hostilities have ceased.

Several factors at the individual, household, community, and institutional levels have been empirically found to contribute to such positive adaptation in the context of exposure to violent conflict. At the individual level, resilience to conflict has been associated with different life skills and character strengths, including: executive skills, cognitive flexibility and persistence; emotion regulation, acceptance, self-expression, and cognitive reframing; temperance and self-control; capacity for sense-making; a hopeful outlook and optimism; social intelligence and collaborative skills; tolerance of diversity and interdependent values; sense of responsibility and commitment; capacity to appreciate resources and successes; personal agency; creativity; and a growth mindset (Ben-Atar, 2018; Betancourt & Khan, 2008; Bodas et al., 2017; Brodsky et al., 2011; Cummings et al., 2017; Eggerman & Panter-Brick, 2010; Hobfoll et al., 2012; Lavi & Stone, 2011; Levey et al., 2016; Lordos et al., 2019; Segovia et al., 2012; Shoshani & Stone, 2016; Tol, Song, & Jordans, 2013; Zraly & Nyirazinyoye, 2010). Various aspects of community support have also been extensively investigated as potential sources of resilience in war-affected populations. Experiencing connectedness, social warmth, social support, and a sense of cohesion in the various microsystems that individuals participate in, such as the family, the workplace, or school, appears to be a general protective factor during conflict-related adversities (Ager et al., 2015; Betancourt & Khan, 2008; Cummings et al., 2017; Eggerman & Panter-Brick, 2010; Fazel et al., 2012; Levey et al., 2016; Lordos et al., 2019; Nguyen-Gillham et al., 2008; Panter-Brick et al., 2011; Siriwardhana et al., 2014; Slone & Shoshani, 2017; Zraly & Nyirazinyoye, 2010). Looking into more specific community-level protective factors, several studies have identified the importance of acceptance by the community as a source of resilience for former combatants who are otherwise at risk of experiencing a negative feedback loop between stigmatization and self-exclusion (Barber, 2001; Betancourt et al., 2013; Cummings et al., 2017; Tol et al., 2013), while processes of monitoring and coaching, whether by peers at work, parents, or elders in the community, seem to play an important role in protecting community members that might be faltering under the burden of adversities (Barber, 2001; Slone & Shoshani, 2017; Tol et al., 2013; Witter et al., 2017). Additional community-based sources of resilience include ensuring that caregivers themselves possess adequate mental health to be able to support their children in times of distress (Betancourt & Khan, 2008; Fazel et al., 2012; Tol et al., 2013), a spirit of intergenerational partnership and collaboration (Eggerman & Panter-Brick, 2010), having access to spiritual resources (Barber, 2001; Betancourt & Khan, 2008; Eggerman & Panter-Brick, 2010; Fazel et al., 2012; Siriwardhana et al., 2014; Tol et al., 2013), and the normalizing effect of daily life in the community, whether than involves play (Nguyen-Gillham et al., 2008) or a focus on educational and professional pursuits in defiance of the abnormality and unpredictability that come with chronic and violent conflict (Eggerman & Panter-Brick, 2010; Levey et al., 2016; Nguyen-Gillham et al., 2008).

While individual characteristics and elements of community cohesion dominate the literature on sources of resilience among conflict-affected populations, it is notable that these two research questions—namely, which individual characteristics and which community resources contribute to resilience—remain largely disconnected. The tendency of the literature is to generate evidence for specific resilience factors, at one or the other level, which are then aggregated into lists of promising entry points for resilience-enhancing interventions. Studies that empirically investigate the interaction between resilience factors across different systems and levels have yet to emerge in the conflict resilience literature, although they could contribute to answering policy-relevant research questions, such as, Which aspects of community-based support can contribute to the development of specific individual characteristics that are associated with resilience in times of conflict? To what extent do individual characteristics and community characteristics exercise their effects separately, or co-act to produce resilience? And, which individual characteristics play a role in the emergence of community-based resilience factors? The field of conflict resilience could benefit from a thorough investigation of such research questions in future studies.

Beyond the mainstream literature on conflict resilience that has been previously summarized, which emphasizes the role of psychosocial factors as sources of resilience in times of conflict, other emerging approaches highlight the role of more concrete and functional sources of resilience, such as possessing appropriate material resources, having access to relevant information, possessing technical know-how, or utilizing adaptive organizational procedures (Ager et al., 2015; Alameddine et al., 2019; Ben-Atar, 2018; Bodas et al., 2015; Brodsky et al., 2011; Cummings et al., 2017; Fazel et al., 2012; Glass et al., 2014; Panter-Brick et al., 2011; Tol et al., 2013; Witter et al., 2017). In most cases, these studies go beyond the person as unit of analysis to focus on the resilience of households or of critical institutions and infrastructures that are under threat in conflict-affected countries. For instance, studies have been conducted to evaluate war preparedness of households, which requires owning essential equipment such as a fire extinguisher, emergency flashlight, first aid kit, radio with batteries, gas masks, and adhesive tape and nylon to seal the family's safe room; preparing and practicing a family emergency response plan; and maintaining stocks of canned foods and bottled water (Bodas et al., 2015). Such emphasis on more concrete sources of household preparedness is not in competition with psychosocial approaches to resilience. In a follow-up study, which considered the role of individual characteristics as predictors of household preparedness, it was found that optimism, rationality, and reduced level of anxiety as well as of denial coping were all found to contribute to increased household preparedness, in the sense of making sure to own the appropriate equipment and stockpiles of supplies, as previously described (Bodas et al., 2017).

Other literature strands have focused on the resilience of health services in conflict-affected countries, a critical system on which the resilience of several downstream human and social systems depends. Specifically, health system resilience in times of violent conflict was found to depend on numerous factors, including staff solidarity, mental preparation of staff before going to work, support from senior managers; reconfiguration of staff roles, introducing systems to improve patient registration process, decentralization of drug supply, educating staff on infection prevention and control, and dual professional practice by health system staff to maintain livelihoods whenever external funding is disrupted due to the conflict. In this case, psychosocial factors such as family support, sense of responsibility, spirituality, and a hopeful outlook were also found to complement the more "concrete" factors as previously described, to further enhance the resilience of staff in conflict-affected health systems (Alameddine et al., 2019; Witter et al., 2017).

This fledging literature on household and institutional resilience in times of conflict holds great promise to add new impetus to the conflict resilience field, but more research is needed in additional domains of household and institutional functioning under conditions of conflict-related adversity, for instance, through studies to understand factors that contribute to the livelihoods of households during times of conflict (i.e., how food and economic security of households can be maintained despite conflict exposure), as well as the resilience of other critical institutions whose integrity is at risk in times of violent conflict, such as the education system, the food production and distribution system, water and sewage systems, energy generation and distribution systems, the security and justice system, and local administrative authorities.

Approaches and Methods for the Investigation of Conflict Resilience

Regarding the methods and approaches for investigating conflict resilience, we discern two divergent approaches in the scholarly literature. The social-ecological research tradition explores multi-stakeholder dynamics from the lens of systems theory to achieve a holistic understanding of resilience to stressors that might potentially trigger conflict, while the psychological and social anthropological traditions are more interested to understand how specific agents at specific levels of the social system are reacting to conflict-associated adversities. These differences are underpinned by distinct epistemological assumptions: psychologists, and social anthropologists are looking for ways to measure the perspectives, intentions, actions, and characteristics of specific agents, whereas social ecologists attempt to organize and interpret observed processes and events from the lens of systems theory. Thus, the research methods that the two traditions use in studying conflict resilience diverge significantly. Social-ecological investigations of conflict resilience focus on case studies of discreet events, people, and interactions across diverse temporal and spatial scales, as they attempt to negotiate the challenges posed by a potential conflict. Such studies typically superimpose an analytic framework over the case as an interpretive lens (Hellin et al., 2018; Mitra et al., 2017; Ratner, Mam, & Halpern, 2014) and may or may not include primary data collection to verify specific elements of the system's structure and function, before proceeding with system analysis. Primary data collection in social-ecological studies can involve focus group discussions at the community level, as well as in-depth interviews with key decision makers or clandestine community informants (Carpenter, 2012; Mitra et al., 2017; Vivekananda et al., 2014a). Often, stakeholders to the conflict are incorporated as active agents in the process of interpreting empirical findings and conducting a system analysis, with the hope that more holistic understanding of the system's properties will encourage affected stakeholders to select cooperative strategies (Butler et al., 2015; Gurung, Bousquet, & Trebuil, 2006). When stakeholders are included in such a manner, the social-ecological research process can additionally be described as participatory and action oriented.

In contrast, psychological and social anthropological studies of conflict resilience tend to be extractive rather than participatory in the way they approach knowledge generation. The emphasis is typically placed on understanding a specific agent or class of agents within a conflict system (e.g., war-affected children, health workers, refugees, former combatants) through the use of empirical research methods—quantitative or qualitative—to investigate which specific conflictivity shocks and stressors are threatening an agent's functioning and which sources of resilience are being drawn upon to cope. Qualitative and quantitative methods are highly complementary in the specific field. While qualitative methods contribute to rich insight and novel hypotheses about the assets and resources that conflict-affected agents utilize to enhance their resilience, quantitative methods make it possible to actually test such hypothesized mechanisms, detect additional naturally occurring resilience mechanisms that are beyond the perceptual threshold of study participants, and develop an awareness of the prevalence of resilience-promoting assets and resources in diverse segments of a conflict-affected population.

All qualitative studies of conflict resilience utilize one or other technique for collection of narrative data, such as in-depth interviews (Ager et al., 2015; Alameddine et al., 2019; Brodsky et al., 2011; Levey et al., 2016; Witter et al., 2017; Zraly & Nyirazinyoye, 2010), open-ended questions in surveys (Eggerman & Panter-Brick, 2010), transcripts of focus groups (Nguyen-Gillham et al., 2008), or transcripts of media communications (Ben-Atar, 2018). Such texts are then processed using thematic analysis, which involves text coding to detect emerging themes around the phenomenon of conflict resilience. While some qualitative inquiries utilize a problem-and-response template for data collection and analysis, asking participants what problems they typically face and how they respond to them (Eggerman & Panter-Brick, 2010), other studies construct a life history of participants to understand trajectories of adversity and adaptation they experienced at different stages in their life and since the conflict commenced (Witter et al., 2017). Most such qualitative studies conclude with a grounded theory of resilience in the specific conflict-affected population, which typically sheds new light within the field in terms of salient features of resilience and their interrelationships (Brodsky et al., 2011; Levey et al., 2016).

In contrast, quantitative studies of conflict resilience investigate a predefined shortlist of potential resilience factors, which are converted into quantifiable indicators using psychometric and/or sociometric principles, with data collected from a sufficiently large sample of the population to permit use of inferential statistics. Most cross-sectional quantitative studies of conflict resilience use moderation analysis to identify assets and resources, which, when present, nullify the association between exposure to conflict adversity and maladaptive system transition (Barber, 2001; Lavi & Stone, 2011; Lordos et al., 2019; Glass et al., 2014; Shoshani & Stone, 2016; Slone & Shoshani, 2017). Longitudinal quantitative studies of conflict resilience attempt to answer more sophisticated research questions where the variable of time is of critical significance, for instance, what trajectories of adaptation can we discern in different segments of a population affected by conflict and how can we further investigate correlated dimensions to understand direction of causality between different assets, resources, and aspects of adaptation. Methodologies that have been used to answer such questions include general growth mixture modeling followed by logistic regression analysis to explore trajectories of post-conflict adaptation in Sierra Leonean youth (Betancourt et al., 2013) and cross-lagged structural equation modeling to confirm the direction of causality between cognitive social capital and social networks in the context of preventing mental health problems among conflict-affected youth in Burundi (Hall et al., 2014).

Each of these scholarly methods for the assessment of resilience in conflict-affected populations displays notable strengths, but all have significant limitations when practiced in isolation. Qualitative studies, when done properly through diligent coding of themes and construction of grounded theories, can provide richly textured insights into the coping strategies people and institutions employ in times of conflict-related adversity but do not provide evidence as to whether these strategies effectively contribute to resilience. Quantitative studies use rigorous statistical modelling to verify resilience hypotheses and provide actionable evidence for policy design but typically measure only a handful of potential sources of resilience, with selection of indicators usually based on international literature rather than a grounded, ecological, and multisystemic understanding of the specific conflict context. In addition, both quantitative and qualitative studies tend to be extractive in their approach and typically do not integrate methods to provide feedback to study participants so that resilience-enhancing action can be locally enabled. Social-ecological studies are better at appreciating the complexity of multisystemic interactions in a specific conflict context and involving stakeholders as active participants in the research process but tend to use rudimentary empirical methods—if at all—to explore the capacity and intentionality of specific agents within the system.

With these distinct profiles of strengths and limitations in quantitative, qualitative, and social-ecological approaches, the argument in favor of methodological integration is intuitive. Studies of conflict resilience conducted within a social ecological framework would benefit by initially relying on qualitative research to develop a grounded theory of resilience across different levels and scales of the social system, then follow up with rigorously designed quantitative studies to empirically validate emerging theoretical perspectives, with stakeholders to the conflict being included as active participants in the research design, data analysis, and policy generation process. Combined, these methods would undoubtedly constitute a promising approach toward an integrated science of resilience for conflict-affected populations.

Practitioner Frameworks for the Assessment of Conflict Resilience

In contrast to the diverse landscape of conflict resilience scholarly studies, practitioner frameworks for the assessment of resilience in conflict affected populations display much greater homogeneity and provide consistent guidance to field specialists, which is broadly inspired by systems theory. Reflecting the growing interest in resilience across the humanitarian, peacebuilding, and development nexus, several international organizations and development agencies have recently formulated their own resilience assessment frameworks. These include, among others, the United Nations (2019) Common Guidance on Helping Build Resilient Societies, the OECD (2014) Guidelines for Resilience Systems Analysis, the UNDP Community Based Resilience Analysis (CoBRA; UNDP, 2014); the GOAL Analysis of the Resilience of Communities to Disasters (ARC-D; McCaul & Mitsidou, 2016); USAID's Resilience Measurement Practical Guidance (Vaughan & Henly-Shepard, 2018); and Interpeace's Frameworks for the Assessment of Resilience (Simpson et al., 2016). Table 22.1 briefly summarizes the definition of resilience each framework is operating under, levels of the social system that are the focus of analysis, and the approach to assessment which is proposed in each case. An integrative definition of resilience, based on synthesis of largely convergent definitions provided by each framework, could be as follows: resilience is the ability of agents at different levels (i.e., individuals, households, communities, institutions, nations) in a complex social system to respond to stressors and shocks in timely and effective ways, without compromising long-term prospects to achieve sustainable development and inclusive growth, reduce chronic vulnerability, prevent new conflict, sustain peace and security, promote human rights, and ensure that means of living and well-being are enjoyed by all.

TABLE 22.1 Overview of Practitioner Frameworks to Guide the Assessment of Resilience in Conflict-Affected Countries and Other Humanitarian or Development Contexts

Framework	Definition of Resilience	System Levels Addressed	Assessment Approach
UN Common Guidance on Helping Build Resilient Societies (United Nations, 2019)	Resilience is the ability of individuals, households, communities, cities, institutions, systems and societies to prevent, resist, absorb, adapt, respond and recover positively, efficiently, and effectively when faced with a wide range of risks, while maintaining an acceptable level of functioning and without compromising long-term prospects for sustainable development, peace and security, human rights, and well-being for all	Indicators can be chosen at different levels depending on targeted systems, including household, community, regional, and national	Secondary analysis of existing assessment results and official statistics to support collaborative resilience analysis by UN agencies, followed by integration of insights into mainstream planning tools such as the Development Assistance Framework, Humanitarian Response Plans, Integrated Strategic Frameworks, and Disaster Recovery Frameworks.
OECD Guidelines for Resilience Systems Analysis (OECD, 2014)	The ability of households, communities, and nations to absorb and recover from shocks, while positively adapting and transforming their structures and means for living in the face of long-term stresses, change, and uncertainty	Indicators can be chosen at different levels depending on targeted systems, including individual, household, community, provincial, national	Secondary analysis of existing data of all types on the basis of a scoping question, leading to preparation of briefing packets on risks, shocks, and capacities, leading to a multi-stakeholder workshop to define a resilience roadmap
UNDP Community Based Resilience Analysis (CoBRA; UNDP, 2014)	An inherent as well as acquired condition achieved by managing risks over time at individual, household, community, and societal levels in ways that minimize costs, build capacity to manage and sustain development momentum, and maximize transformative potential	Household, community	Community-level focus groups to develop and score contextualized indicators of resilience, interviews with households designated as resilient based on contextualized indicators to understand in-depth factors, which drive resilience, utilization of results as a decision support tool for policy stakeholders in the assessment area
GOAL Analysis of the Resilience of Communities to Disasters (ARC-D; McCaul and Mitsidou, 2016)	The ability of communities and households living within complex systems to anticipate and adapt to risks, and to absorb, respond and recover from shocks and stresses in a timely and effective manner without compromising their long-term prospects, ultimately improving their well-being	Community	Community-level focus groups to score the community's readiness to respond to a preselected hazard scenario, on 30 predefined indicators that cover several dimensions of social and institutional functioning, with data uploaded on a global dashboard to inform resilience planning in the assessment area

(continued)

TABLE 22.1 Continued

Framework	Definition of Resilience	System Levels Addressed	Assessment Approach
USAID Resilience Measurement Practical Guidance (Vaughan and Henly-Shepard, 2018)	The ability of people, households, communities, countries, and systems to mitigate, adapt to, and recover from shocks and stresses in a manner that reduces chronic vulnerability and facilitates inclusive growth	Individual, household, community	Initial planning to determine purpose and scope of assessment, identification of knowledge gaps leading to research plan to respond to key questions, primary and/ or secondary data collection, and quantitative and qualitative analysis using best practices from psychological science and social anthropology (e.g. regression, moderation, positive deviance analysis, life history analysis, social network analysis). Results are used to design evidence-based theories of change, monitoring, and evaluation frameworks and resilience-enhancing programmatic strategies
Interpeace Frameworks for the Assessment of Resilience (Simpson, et al., 2016)	Resilience for peace refers to the diverse endogenous attributes, capacities, resources, and responses that potentially enable individuals, communities, institutions, and societies to deal peacefully with the impact of past conflict and violence, as well as to prevent new and emerging patterns of conflict and violence	Individual, household, community, institutions, state and society; with special emphasis on what connects the different systems and levels	An inclusive, participatory and stakeholder-led process, beginning with contextualization through the help of country experts, then mixed methods research though focus groups, key informant interviews and surveys, leading to integrated insights into processes of resilience at multiple system levels, to inform the design of peacebuilding strategies that build on the endogenous resilience of the population

Resilience becomes manifested in a variety of responses of agents within complex systems, depending on the temporal relationship with the stressor (i.e., prevention before the stressor; resistance during the stressor; recovery after the stressor) and the level of innovation embedded in the response (i.e., whether it is absorptive, adaptive, or transformative).

As to the specific capacities that contribute to a resilient response, several assessment approaches cite the sustainable livelihoods framework (Scoones, 1998) as a practical rubric for a holistic understanding of assets and resources that might be available to different agents within a social system. Specifically, the sustainable livelihoods framework incorporates five types of capitals that agents may or may not possess, contributing to their resilience: human capital, which includes the skills and competencies that individual persons possess; social capital, which includes the social networks and institutions to which people belong; physical capital, which refers to all manmade assets such as tools, houses, and roads that people own or have access to; natural capital, which refers to biophysical elements that people can utilize for their livelihoods such as water, sunlight, and livestock; and financial capital, which is a convertible asset that symbolically stores value and serves as a medium of exchange. Capital can be leveraged to meet threats or benefit from opportunities and, in that sense, can be a source of resilience, but only if it is actually accessible and utilized to this end. The attractiveness of the sustainable livelihood framework as a lens to understand resilience capacities lies in that it is multidisciplinary and versatile, covering the full spectrum from human to material assets. Types of capital can be converted or traded for one another (e.g., converting financial capital to human capital by purchasing access to education), while a combination of types of capital can be used to generate a third type of capital (e.g., using human skills and natural capital, such as access to stone and woodlands, to generate physical capital, in the form of a built home). From this perspective, the sustainable livelihoods framework can contribute to a multisystemic understanding of sources of resilience.

Having said that, the sustainable livelihoods framework and its application in conflict resilience assessment is not without its limitations: References to human and social capital tend to be simplified and generic, for instance by referring in general terms on the importance of education while overlooking the rich literatures on life skills (UNICEF, 2017), social cohesion (Cox & Sisk, 2017), and adaptive management (Allen et al., 2011) that scholarly studies discussed in this chapter suggest are salient to conflict resilience. Furthermore, some have argued that access to information should be considered a type of capital in its own right, alongside human, social, natural, physical, and financial (Odero, 2006).

While the practitioner-oriented resilience assessment frameworks that emerged in recent years have undoubtedly been contributing to a mindset shift toward systems-and-resilience thinking among policymakers and field practitioners, they have at the same time been less successful in providing concrete guidance on how resilience assessment can take place in practice. Despite the call of most frameworks to situationally assess risk exposure and resilience capacities at multiple levels of the social system, very little concrete guidance is provided as to the expected risk landscape of specific subpopulations at specific system levels in the context of conflict, as these are known from the scholarly literature (e.g., the challenges faced by war-affected youth, threats posed to critical institutions in times of active hostilities, pathways from ethnocultural tensions and resource scarcity to violent conflict). Thus, every new conflict resilience assessment is expected to start from first principles, with a resilience analyst or stakeholder group making basic inquiries to determine what should be assessed by following the rubric "whose resilience, against which adversities, and to what end," disregarding the cumulative scientific progress that could have made the research process more efficient.

As to assessing sources of resilience, while the sustainable livelihoods framework does provide some basic guidance as to what type of variables to look for, limited insight is offered on how exactly to conceptualize or measure indicators within each dimension and what to do if an indicator is found to be at a low or high score. In some of the authors' own past work, such as the Social Cohesion and Reconciliation Index (Centre for Sustainable Peace and Democratic Development & UNDP, 2015) and the Positive Peace Index (Institute for Economics & Peace, 2017), we conceptualized and developed metrics to assess various aspects of positive societal and institutional functioning in conflict-affected countries, but without explicitly contextualizing these dimensions within a framework of resilience assessment.

Having said that, lessons learned from such efforts, could usefully be leveraged to more effectively operationalize the assessment of resilience in conflict-affected populations.

Principles and Guidelines for an Integrated Science of Conflict Resilience

The review of scholarly studies and practitioner frameworks for the assessment of resilience in conflict-affected populations has revealed a vibrant field of inquiry that aspires to be multisystemic but still lacks the conceptual and methodological sophistication to rise to the status of a coherent and integrated science of resilience for conflict-affected populations. While achieving such integration is a broader challenge and aspiration in the study of resilience (Masten, 2015; Ungar, 2018), making progress in the specific field of conflict resilience is contingent on bridging gaps and integrating perspectives between: scholars and practitioners; investigators utilizing social-ecological, psychological, and anthropological approaches; qualitative, quantitative, and participatory methodologies; studies of conflict resilience at the individual, household, community, and institutional levels; studies that primarily focus on psychosocial systems versus studies that focus on material systems as sources of resilience; and approaches that investigate resilience for conflict prevention, resilience for mitigation of conflict consequences, and resilience for postconflict recovery and reconciliation. Building on the current literature and anticipating emerging trends, we propose in the following discussion a set of assessment principles with the hope that these will stimulate a conversation among scholars and practitioners, ultimately leading to multisystemic studies of conflict resilience that build toward an integrative and cumulative science.

Principle 1: Integrate a System-Wide Perspective With Agent-Focused Research

Violent social conflicts are characterized by exposure to a complex cascade of stressors and shocks at different levels and sub-systems, which sequentially put pressure on downstream systems that can either adapt successfully or transition into dysfunctional states. The first step in resilience assessment should be to develop a systemwide understanding of the dynamic risk landscape that the population is exposed to, through a process of participatory modelling (see Figure 22.4), which includes diverse local stakeholders that are knowledgeable about various aspects of the conflict. Such modelling would reveal several specific risk pathways within the broader conflict system, affecting different segments of the population at different stages of the conflict and levels of the social system. These specific risk pathways can then be reconceptualized into targeted, agent-specific, and resilience-oriented research questions, which can be the focus of systematic empirical inquiry (see Table 22.2) using the tools of qualitative and quantitative social research. It should be emphasized that agent-focused research does not necessarily imply emphasis on the resilience of individuals. Institutions, communities, and families can also be considered as agents in a conflict and peace system, that can be the focus of empirical research if appropriate methods and tools are utilized.

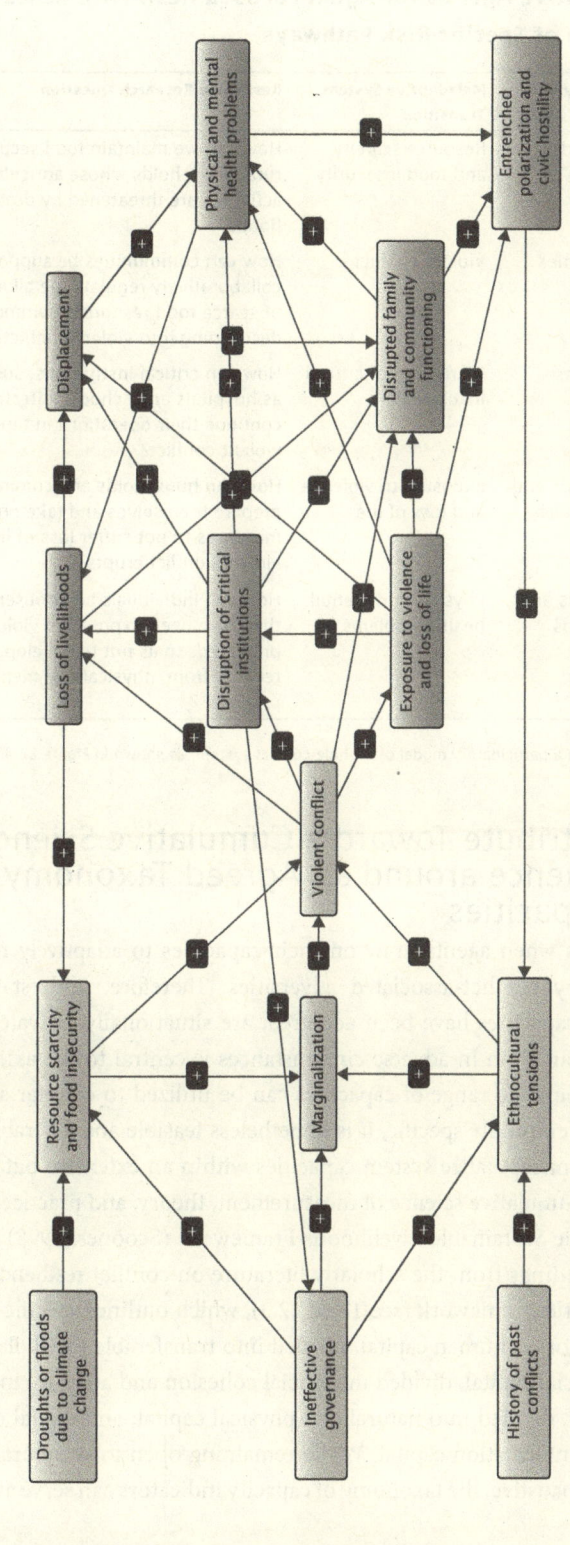

FIGURE 22.4 Conceptualization of a generic conflict system, outlining risk pathways, and feedback loops that precipitate or perpetuate violent conflict, its drivers (color-coded as orange), and its consequences (color-coded as green). Visualization was created using Mental Modeler (www.mentalmodeler.org), a participatory modeling tool that enables stakeholders to collaboratively represent their assumptions about a system in real-time. This conceptualization is intended as an illustration. Specific conflicts and their actual parameters can be modeled in a similar way through a local participatory process, to enable a prioritization of specific research questions regarding which risk pathways to focus on from a resilience perspective.

TABLE 22.2 An Illustrative Agenda for Agent-Focused Resilience Research, Based on Prioritization of Specific Risk Pathways

Stressor	Affected System Agents	Maladaptive System Transition	Resilience Research Question
Droughts or floods due to climate change	Households	Resource scarcity and food insecurity	How can we maintain food security of rural households whose agricultural activities are threatened by droughts and floods?
Resource scarcity and food insecurity	Communities	Violent conflict	How can communities be supported to collaboratively regulate the allocation of scarce food resources, without descending into violent conflict?
Violent conflict	Institutions	Disruption of critical institutions	How can critical institutions, such as hospitals and schools, effectively continue their operations in times of violent conflict?
Violent conflict	Households and communities	Exposure to violence and loss of life	How can households and communities prepare themselves and take protective measures to not suffer loss of life when violent conflict erupts?
Exposure to violence and loss of life	Individuals and households	Physical and mental health problems	How can individuals and households that have been exposed to violence be protected, so as not to develop, or to recover from, physical and mental health problems?

Note: Pathways were selected from a participatory model of a whole-conflict system, as shown in Figure 22.4.

Principle 2: Contribute Toward a Cumulative Science of Conflict Resilience around an Agreed Taxonomy of Resilience Capacities

Conflict resilience occurs when agents draw on their capacities to adaptively respond to challenges brought on by conflict-associated adversities. Therefore, understanding the extent to which diverse capacities have been acquired, are situationally activated, and effectively contribute to adaptation in adverse circumstances is central to the assessment of conflict resilience. While a wide range of capacities can be utilized to counter adversities, with some of these being culturally specific, it is nonetheless feasible and desirable to build on existing literature to conceptualize system capacities within an extensive but finite taxonomy, around which a cumulative science of measurement, theory, and practice can begin to emerge. Building on the Sustainable Livelihoods Framework (Scoones, 1998) while also incorporating relevant findings from the scholarly literature on conflict resilience, we propose an integrated capacities framework (see Table 22.3), which outlines specific indicators under the following categories: human capital, divided into transferable life skills and task-specific competencies; social capital, divided into social cohesion and adaptive institutional practices; material capital, divided into natural and physical capital; and digital capital, divided into financial and information capital. While remaining open to structural revisions and not intended to be exhaustive, the taxonomy of capacity indicators can serve as a starting

TABLE 22.3 Integrated Capacities Framework, to Assess Aspects of Human, Social, Material and Digital Capital That Might Potentially Contribute to Resilient Responses in Different Scenarios of Conflict-Associated Adversity

Human Capital		Social Capital		Material Capital		Digital Capital	
Transferable Life Skills	Task-Specific Competencies	Social Cohesion	Adaptive Institutional Practices	Natural Capital	Physical Capital	Financial Capital	Information Capital
Emotion Regulation	Food growing	Inclusive sense of identity	Mission clarity	Agricultural land	Fire extinguisher	Income from work or wealth	Information about threats
Distress Tolerance	Shelter construction	Respect of diversity	Service orientation	Fertile soil	First aid kit	Bank savings	Information about opportunities
Implementation Persistence	Providing first aid	Gender equality and partnership	Problem-solving orientation	Suitable seeds	Stocks of canned food	Remittances	Access to general education
Sense-making	Sterilization and preventing infection	Inter-generational partnership	Institutional versatility	Livestock	Access to computer or smartphone	Insurance plans	Access to technical training
Critical Thinking	Palliative treatment of common mental health problems	Family coherence	Culture of empowerment	Grazing land	Access to electricity	Access to e-banking	Access to diagnostic information
Flexibility	Palliative treatment of common physical ailments	School Connectedness	Functional Redundancy	Rivers and waterholes	Access to medication	Access to loans	Information about personal strengths and weaknesses
Growth mindset	Preparedness for emergency response	Community dialogue	Institutional preparedness	Land for habitation	Access to sanitation	Access to grants	Information about other people and their capacities
Creativity	Parenting skills	Community solidarity	Science-based practices	Access to drinking water	Farming and construction tools	Access to charitable support	Information about institutions and services they provide
Perspective taking	Conflict mediation skills	Participation opportunities	Reflective management	Community forest	Access to means of mobility	Access to social protection nets	Information about rights and duties
Negotiation	Mentoring and coaching	Local-national collaboration	Future orientation	Community biodiversity	Access to a community hub	Access to markets	Information about historical events

Note: The list of capacities within each category is not intended to be exhaustive.

point for developing a cumulative science on how resilience-promoting capacities can be effectively assessed and nurtured in times of conflict. Ongoing dialogue between scholars and practitioners, underpinned by open sharing of methods, data, and findings, is an essential prerequisite for the development of such a cumulative science of conflict resilience.

Principle 3: Become Versatile in the Use of Appropriate Qualitative and Quantitative Methodologies

The study of conflict resilience is a youthful discipline, with several still unknown or unverified processes. In this context, versatility in research methodologies can significantly contribute to advancing our collective understanding. Qualitative studies, and, more specifically, use of the life history approach (Zeitlyn, 2008) and construction of grounded theories (Charmaz, 2014), can shed new light on previously unknown processes of adaptation, while quantitative studies that, at the very least, incorporate factor analysis (Brown, 2015) and moderation analysis (Hayes, 2018) can contribute to verifying the potential effectiveness of specific resilience-enhancing strategies. Leveraging the distinct advantages of qualitative and quantitative approaches through mixed method study designs, for instance, by selecting or constructing quantitative indicators for adversity exposure and resilience capacities after establishing a grounded theory of resilience in the specific conflict context, would significantly contribute to advancing the science of conflict resilience.

Principle 4: Develop distinct Research Protocols and Approaches for the Assessment of Individual, Household, Community, Institutional, and National Resilience

Resilience in times of conflict is a property of systems at diverse levels of scale, including the individual, household, community, institutional, and national levels. To operationalize this understanding in the way we assess resilience, distinct research protocols need to be developed for assessment at each level of the social system. While qualitative research, through interviews and focus groups, can easily be adapted to investigating the resilience of different system levels, quantitative multilevel assessment requires a more thoughtful approach. This can include population surveys for the individual level, but collaborative scoring approaches for other system levels, as showcased for instance in the CoBRA (UNDP, 2014) and ARC-D (McCaul & Mitsidou, 2016) assessment frameworks. Importantly, nested sampling strategies should be utilized, keeping in mind the interconnectedness of different system levels, for genuine multilevel and multisystemic analysis to be possible (Sastry et al., 2003). Individuals, for instance must be assessed as members of their households and institutions, while households and institutions must be assessed as constituent members of their communities. As for national resilience, this can be assessed using a case study approach, after combining and synthesizing the quantitative and qualitative findings of all other in-country resilience assessments. Recent literature on applying the concept of the social contract as a path to resilience in conflict-affected countries (Lordos & Dagli-Hustings, 2018; McCandless et al., 2018) provides relevant guidance on how such case studies could be approached.

Principle 5: Leverage Analytic Methods That Are Suitable for Detection of Cross-Systemic Linkages

To investigate connections and pathways between diverse resilience capacity dimensions and system levels, advanced analytic methodologies are required, and in this respect the conflict resilience field will be required to experiment and innovate in coming years. Verification of specifically hypothesized risk pathways, before proceeding with resilience analysis, can be done through structural equation modeling where multiple risks and multiple outcomes that might be experienced within the population are put to the test simultaneously (Kline, 2015; Lordos et al., 2019). Investigating effects across system levels can benefit from the rich methodological literature on multilevel modeling (Hox, Moerbeek, & van de Schoot, 2018; Lazega & Snijders, 2019) that has already been utilized extensively in educational and management research. Exploring connections between dimensions of resilience capacities, for instance, to investigate which specific life skills are associated with which specific types of social support, can be approached through complex network analysis methodologies (Sayama, 2015; Zinoviev, 2018) or more simply through correlation analysis. Investigating the potential co-action of diverse capacities in promoting resilience would first require calculating a resilience statistic using the residuals approach (Miller-Lewis et al., 2013) to use as an outcome in statistical models, then testing mediation and moderation models to investigate the interaction between capacities in predicting resilience. Running such analyses properly, however, would require large samples and possibly use of machine learning and data mining techniques (Attewell & Monaghan, 2015; Kelleher, Mac Namee, & D'Arcy, 2015), since the number of potential interactions rises geometrically with each additional resilience capacity being considered.

Principle 6: Engage with Stakeholders Across Multiple Systems and Levels, to Maximize Resilience-Enhancing Insight, Planning, and Action

For impactful resilience-enhancing action, assessors of resilience in a conflict setting need to be aware that change in a complex adaptive system cannot take place through top–down processes only. From a systems perspective, individuals, households, communities, and institutions are understood to be mutually evolving and adapting in meeting oncoming challenges through processes that can best be described as panarchic (Allen et al., 2014). To achieve systemwide resilience would require that diverse layers of society, from the individual level all the way up to communities and institutions, are each empowered with appropriate capacities, as described earlier, that can be drawn upon as needed in times of adversity. Consequently, ownership and agency over the reflection, planning, and decision-making process needs to be distributed across all system levels (i.e., individuals, households, communities, institutions). In practice, this would involve creating systems for individuals and households to self-assess their own resilience, while encouraging participatory approaches for community, institutional, and national reflection based on resilience assessment findings. Furthermore, resilience-enhancing action can be promoted by integrating resilience assessment metrics into the monitoring and evaluation systems of humanitarian, peacebuilding, and development organizations.

Principle 7: Adjust Resilience Assessment Priorities as the Conflict and Peace System Evolves over Time, and as Local Understanding of Resilience Processes Matures

Resilience assessment in conflict contexts should always be focused on addressing the challenges posed by active risk pathways. As a system of conflict and peace evolves, previous risk pathways might become deactivated while others grow in salience. The research questions that underlie the resilience assessment process (e.g., as per Table 22.2) should be modified to reflect such shifts in the risk landscape, with concomitant downstream modifications also made to research protocols, analytic approaches, and stakeholder engagement strategies. Assessment priorities should additionally be modified as insight into sources and systems of resilience matures over time. For instance, a study of resilience at the level of individuals may reveal an important community or institution-level protective factor, which could, in turn, trigger an interest to focus investigations onto the resilience of that higher-level system.

Assessment of Multisystemic Resilience in Conflict-Affected Eastern Ukraine: A Case Study

Violent conflict erupted in Eastern Ukraine in spring 2014, after antigovernment protests in Donetsk and Lugansk oblasts (administrative regions) rapidly escalated into an armed insurgency by pro-Russia separatist groups, who took control of both oblasts, the industrial base of each region and Donetsk International Airport. These acts were met by a vigorous government counteroffensive, but after heavy fighting throughout the summer and autumn of 2014, the situation on the ground gradually stabilized into a simmering conflict which left the Donetsk and Lugansk region divided into government-controlled and separatist-held areas. Sporadic fighting along a grey zone that separates the two areas has since been ongoing. The conflict has led to more than 5,000 casualties, significant internal displacement, exacerbation of sociocultural divisions, disruption of infrastructure and economic activity in the region, and depopulation in areas proximal to the grey zone. Meanwhile, a generation of children and adolescents have been deeply affected by the conflict and its consequences, including through death of parents, siblings, or other relatives; disrupted family functioning; poverty and economic distress; exposure to soldiers and armaments; and frequent and unpredictable shelling of communities, homes, and schools.

Our research group at the Centre for Sustainable Peace and Democratic Development was invited to Ukraine in the Autumn of 2015 to conduct assessments that might inform the international community's response to the unfolding crisis in the east. Our study was conducted in accordance with several—although not all—of the principles outlined earlier. We sought to integrate a system-wide perspective with agent-focused research by commencing the study with a process of participatory modeling in which representatives of several UN agencies, including UNICEF, UNDP, and the International Organization for Migration contributed their perspectives for a more holistic understanding of risk pathways, based on which specific agent-focused research questions were formulated. Such questions included, among others, the following: How can residents of Eastern Ukraine be made resilient against the pressure to abandon the region, while the conflict is ongoing? What factors can contribute to ongoing intergroup harmony and a peaceful civic orientation among citizens of Eastern Ukraine, in spite of the polarizing narratives and conflict experiences that are driving communities apart? And, how can the mental health and broader psychosocial adaptation of adults and young people in the region be protected, in a context of ongoing insecurity and traumatizing events? To answer these resilience-oriented research questions, we incorporated in the study several types of capacities from among those included in the proposed taxonomy, although with a greater emphasis on human capital and social capital. Project stakeholders and partners actively contributed in the conceptualization and design of specific capacity indicators based on their knowledge of the local context.

Based on the study's conceptualization, we collected data from specific segments of the population (community adolescents; community adults; residents of nongovernment-controlled areas), although almost all the data we have collected so far is at the level of individuals, which restricts our capability to assess the resilience of other system levels and formulate recommendations accordingly. Incorporating additional layers to the data collection, for instance, by collecting school-level data along with adolescent-level data, or community-level data along with citizen-level data, is currently being considered in collaboration with the study's stakeholders. Even with data collected at a single level, it is still possible to detect cross-systemic effects if appropriate analytic methods are used, as will be illustrated using the example of the most recent data collection with adolescents ($n = 7,834$ girls and boys, aged 12 to 17). Specifically, factor analysis was initially utilized to develop a nuanced understanding of potential detrimental outcomes of conflict exposure, looking beyond mental health to also investigate social and civic dimensions of adaptation (see Table 22.4). Based on identified detrimental outcome dimensions, structural equation modeling was used to empirically identify risk pathways (see Figure 22.5).

To the extent that conflict and other associated adversities were found to affect multiple systems of functioning, and since resilience is the ability to interrupt the impact of a specific risk pathway to prevent a maladaptive transition, we can consider that an agent—in this case, an adolescent—would need to possess multiple resiliencies to interrupt pathways from adversity exposure to each of the detrimental outcomes. To detect these resiliencies, we regressed each outcome (e.g., emotional problems, social hostility) against the various types of adversities (i.e., conflict hardship, violence in the microsystem, sociodemographic adversity) and then took the residual of the regression—that is, the difference between actual score of the detrimental outcome versus predicted score of the detrimental outcome—as a continuous statistic of resilience (Miller-Lewis et al., 2013). In this manner, we constructed five resilience variables, namely, emotional resilience—maintaining emotional well-being despite conflict exposure and associated adversities; behavioral resilience—resisting paths to delinquency in times of conflict adversity; resilience against suicidality—resisting the contemplation of suicide or self-harm in times of extreme adversity; resilient peacefulness—remaining peaceful, prosocial and committed to human rights and intergroup harmony

TABLE 22.4 Factor Analysis of Detrimental Adolescent Outcomes Revealing Five Distinct Dimensions of Psychosocial and Civic Maladjustment

	Emotional Problems	Risk-Taking and Aggressive Behaviors	Suicidality and Self-Harm	Social Hostility	Social Disengagement
Anxiety	0.91				
Depression	0.68				
Posttraumatic stress disorder	0.50				
Conduct disorder		0.75			
Oppositional defiant disorder		0.54			
Bullying		0.53			
Substance use		0.53			
Aggression		0.50			
Unsafe sexual behavior		0.49			
Readiness for political violence		0.27			
Suicidality			0.74		
Self-harm			0.71		
Multicultural outlook (R)				0.65	
Endorsement of human rights (R)				0.62	
Feelings to outgroups (R)				0.47	
Gender equality mindset (R)				0.37	
Sense of well-being (R)					0.53
Self-Esteem (R)					0.45
Academic performance (R)					0.41
Readiness for civic participation (R)					0.36
School dropout tendency					0.22

Note: Analysis is based on a sample of 7,834 adolescents in Ukraine. Extraction method: maximum likelihood. Rotation method: Promax with Kaizer normalization.

despite conflict exposure; and resilient participation—continuing to participate in school and civic life and experience a sense of purpose, despite accumulated challenges and adversities. With these resilience variables in place, we then proceeded to screen several candidate sources of resilience across the human capital and social capital capacity indicators we assessed to see whether they are associated with resilience, and if so which type (see Tables 22.5 and 22.6 for detailed findings). Importantly, divergent capacities appear to contribute to the different types of resiliencies. As an example, emotional resilience is predicated on skills such as emotion regulation, distress tolerance, and planning, alongside social capital elements such as paternal involvement and teacher support whereas resilient peacefulness is contingent on a totally different repertoire of skills, which includes communication, negotiation, critical thinking, kindness, and respect for diversity, with maternal involvement,

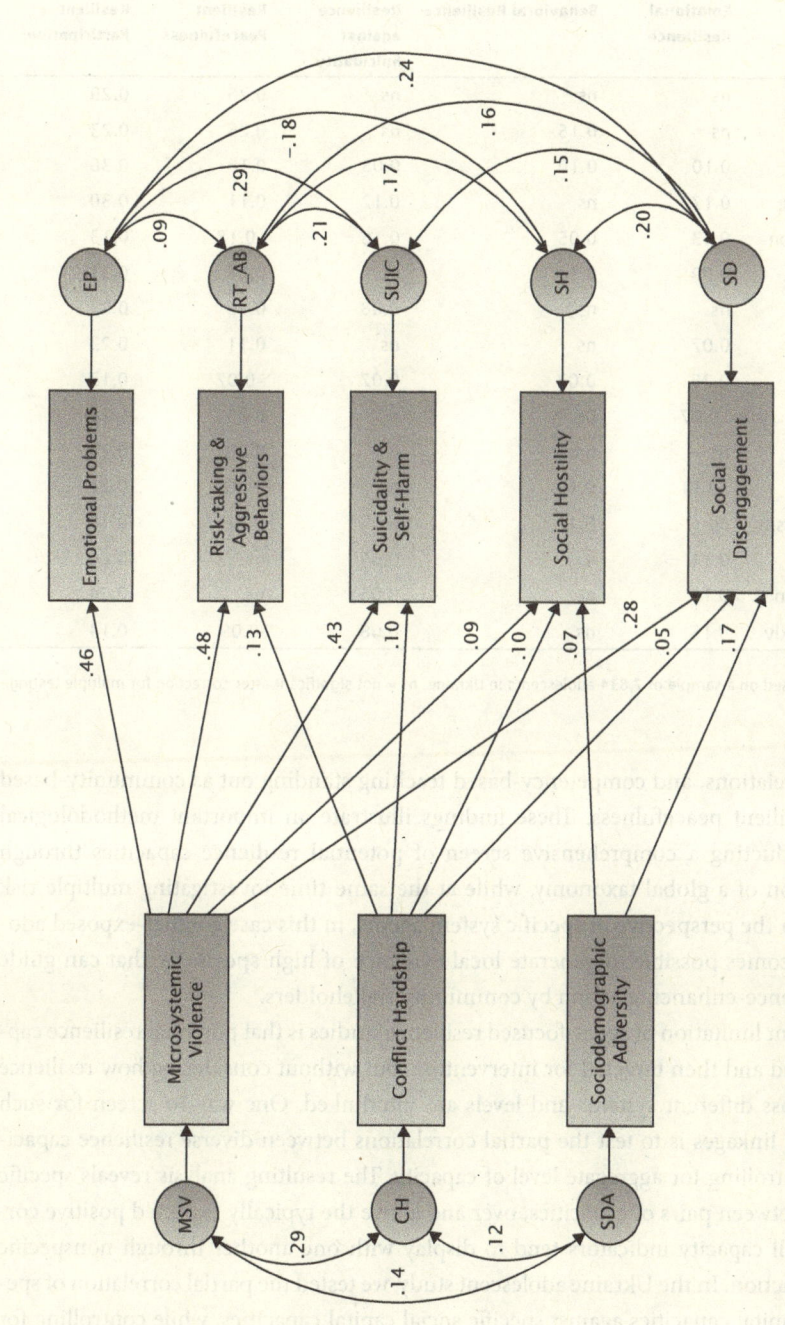

FIGURE 22.5 Structural equation model of risk pathways from conflict hardship and other associated adversities, to psychosocial and civic adolescent detrimental outcomes. Analysis is based on a sample of 7,834 adolescents in Ukraine. Model fit indices: Chi Square = 52, df = 5, comparative fit index = 0.996, root mean square error of approximation = 0.035, standardized root mean square residual = 0.013.

TABLE 22.5 Correlations of Resilience Dimensions with Specific Human Capital Capacities

	Emotional Resilience	Behavioral Resilience	Resilience against Suicidality	Resilient Peacefulness	Resilient Participation
Communication	ns	ns	ns	0.26	0.29
Negotiation	ns	0.15	ns	0.25	0.23
Cooperation	0.10	0.10	0.08	0.16	0.36
Distress tolerance	0.17	ns	0.12	0.11	0.30
Emotion regulation	0.43	0.05	0.16	−0.18	0.13
Self-management	0.09	0.11	ns	0.08	0.31
Problem-solving	ns	ns	0.08	0.15	0.25
Decision making	0.07	ns	ns	0.11	0.22
Planning	0.25	0.07	0.07	−0.07	0.13
Critical thinking	−0.07	ns	ns	0.25	0.18
Creativity	ns	0.07	ns	0.20	0.24
Kindness	−0.11	0.19	ns	0.26	0.22
Respect for diversity	ns	0.19	ns	0.31	0.18
Aerobic exercise	0.11	ns	0.05	ns	0.20
Balanced nutrition	0.15	ns	0.06	ns	0.24
Sleep hours weekly	0.15	ns	0.08	−0.09	0.14

Note: Analysis is based on a sample of 7,834 adolescents in Ukraine. ns = not significant after correction for multiple testing.

positive peer relations, and competency-based teaching standing out as community-based sources of resilient peacefulness. These findings illustrate an important methodological point: by conducting a comprehensive screen of potential resilience capacities through local adaptation of a global taxonomy, while at the same time investigating multiple risk pathways from the perspective of specific system agents, in this case conflict-exposed adolescents, it becomes possible to generate local evidence of high specificity that can guide targeted resilience-enhancing action by community stakeholders.

A frequent limitation of agent-focused resilience studies is that potential resilience capacities are listed and then targeted for intervention, but without considering how resilience capacities across different systems and levels are interlinked. One way to screen for such cross-systemic linkages is to test the partial correlations between diverse resilience capacities, while controlling for aggregate level of capacity. The resulting analysis reveals specific associations between pairs of capacities, over and above the typically expected positive correlation that all capacity indicators tend to display with one another through nonspecific virtuous interaction. In the Ukraine adolescent study, we tested the partial correlation of specific human capital capacities against specific social capital capacities, while controlling for aggregate human capital and aggregate social capital, which at their level display strong correlation (human capital with family-based social capital: $r = 0.35$, $P < 0.001$; human capital with community-based social capital: $r = 0.39$, $P < 0.001$). Findings of the partial correlation

TABLE 22.6 Correlations of Resilience Dimensions With Specific Social Capital Capacities

	Emotional Resilience	Behavioral Resilience	Resilience against Suicidality	Resilient Peacefulness	Resilient Participation
Maternal involvement	0.05	0.12	0.11	0.20	0.23
Maternal warmth	ns	0.08	0.12	0.14	0.19
Maternal monitoring	0.05	0.19	0.10	0.22	0.23
Paternal involvement	0.12	0.06	0.07	ns	0.17
Paternal warmth	0.09	0.07	0.08	0.05	0.17
Paternal monitoring	0.13	0.10	0.08	0.05	0.18
Family connectedness	0.06	0.08	0.09	0.18	0.25
Peer support	0.09	0.05	ns	0.20	0.22
Emotional connection to school	0.15	0.10	0.05	0.12	0.32
Teacher support	0.14	0.09	0.05	0.10	0.28
Competency-based teaching	ns	0.11	ns	0.20	0.28
Safe physical school Environment	ns	0.10	ns	0.09	0.19
Safe psychosocial school Environment	ns	0.11	ns	0.17	0.27
Participatory and inclusive School governance	0.08	0.11	ns	0.16	0.29
Child-friendly city	0.08	0.09	0.05	0.24	0.29

Note: Analysis is based on a sample of 7,834 adolescents in Ukraine. ns = not significant after correction for multiple testing.

analysis (see Tables 22.7 and 22.8) reveal interesting differential associations between specific capacities. For instance, critical thinking is associated with competency-based teaching, family connectedness, and maternal warmth while emotion regulation is associated with teacher support, paternal monitoring, and emotional connection to the school. Some aspects of social capital have both positive and negative associations with aspects of human capital. For instance, supportive peer relations are associated not only with improved communication skills, cooperation skills, and kindness, but also with poorer self-management skills, reduced sleep hours, and less balanced nutrition. It is important to note that the cross-sectional nature of the specific study does not permit making causal inferences as to the directionality of such associations and from there on to a firm understanding of multisystemic processes that contribute to conflict resilience. Having said that, discovering and verifying such associations, initially through cross-sectional data, are important steps toward the construction of more sophisticated causal hypotheses that can eventually be investigated through longitudinal and possibly multilevel research.

As mentioned earlier, studies of resilience in conflict affected populations must go beyond knowledge generation to engage stakeholders at diverse levels of the social system who are the ones that can take up the responsibility of resilience-enhancing action. In accordance

TABLE 22.7 Partial Correlations Between Human Capital Capacities and Family-Based Social Capital Capacities, after Controlling for Aggregate Levels of Both Capacity Dimensions, Age, and Gender, to Detect Specific Associations Between Specific Pairs of Capacities When All Else Is Held Equal

	Maternal Involvement	Maternal Warmth	Maternal Monitoring	Paternal Involvement	Paternal Warmth	Paternal Monitoring	Family Connectedness
Communication	0.07	0.04	ns	−0.05	ns	−0.07	ns
Negotiation	ns	ns	ns	ns	ns	ns	ns
Cooperation	ns	ns	ns	ns	ns	ns	ns
Distress tolerance	ns	ns	ns	ns	ns	−0.04	0.04
Emotion regulation	−0.07	−0.04	ns	ns	ns	0.07	ns
Self-management	ns	ns	ns	ns	ns	ns	ns
Problem-solving	ns	ns	ns	ns	ns	ns	ns
Decision-making	ns	ns	ns	ns	ns	ns	ns
Planning	ns	ns	ns	ns	ns	0.04	ns
Critical thinking	0.04	0.04	ns	ns	ns	ns	0.04
Creativity	ns	ns	ns	ns	ns	ns	ns
Kindness	0.05	ns	0.05	−0.05	ns	−0.05	ns
Respect for diversity	ns	ns	0.04	−0.05	ns	ns	ns
Aerobic exercise	ns	ns	ns	ns	ns	ns	ns
Balanced nutrition	ns	ns	ns	ns	ns	ns	ns
Sleep hours weekly	ns	ns	ns	0.04	ns	ns	ns

Note. Analysis is based on a sample of 7,834 adolescents in Ukraine. ns = not significant after correction for multiple testing.

with this principle, we have been working with stakeholders to consider the study's implications for policies and programs that aim to promote cohesion and stability in Eastern Ukraine. Specifically, we have been working with UNICEF and the Ukrainian Ministry of Education and Science, to incorporate the study's recommendations for enhancing adolescent resilience into the ongoing process of educational reform; with USAID, to tailor the allocation of microgrants to local nongovernmental organizations on the basis of study insights; and with several peacebuilding and civic action initiatives to integrate the study's capacity metrics into their monitoring and evaluation frameworks. Resilience-enhancing impact of the study would be even greater if we could devise methods to provide direct feedback to individuals, households and communities based on their own resilience self-assessment, but this requires overcoming several technical and methodological challenges. From a multisystemic perspective, the study's findings are raising new questions about other system levels that were not the focus of inquiry so far and that can best be addressed through multilevel research. Specifically, more focused investigations into the resilience of families, teachers and schools, local authorities, and local peacebuilding nongovernmental organizations would contribute to a more holistic and multisystemic understanding of conflict resilience in Eastern Ukraine.

Conclusion

The concept of resilience has recently become very popular among humanitarian, peacebuilding, and development practitioners. If used outside of a multisystemic lens, however, the interest in resilience is unlikely to lead to better outcomes and may even cause more harm than good. Examples of inappropriate use would include overly prioritizing the resilience of a specific system level (e.g., only focusing on individuals or only focusing on communities) or a specific type of capacity as a source of resilience (e.g., only considering the role of human capital or only considering the role of material capital). Such narrow approaches to resilience would fail to leverage its true potential, which is to integrate policies and programs across systems and levels, thus providing policy coherence to conflict prevention and peace consolidation efforts. Furthermore, narrow approaches to resilience could actually cause harm, if used as an excuse for denial of needed support on the argument that individuals and communities can draw on their own strengths to prevent conflict or recover from it (Hilhorst, 2018). Thankfully, "narrow resilience" does not appear to be the direction in which the conflict resilience field is taking. All practitioner frameworks acknowledge the multisystemic nature of resilience, while organizations that specialize in different subdomains within the humanitarian, peacebuilding, and development nexus are leveraging opportunities offered by the resilience lens to build cross-sectoral bridges.

The scholarly community has an important role to play in this emerging and multidisciplinary field of conflict resilience. While practitioners in the humanitarian, peacebuilding, and development nexus are strongly motivated to incorporate resilience-based approaches in their work, they are struggling with several conceptual and methodological challenges, including how to conduct a system-wide social ecological analysis; how precisely to conceptualize risk, adaptation, and resilience capacities; how to measure all these at diverse levels

TABLE 22.8 Partial Correlations Between Human Capital Capacities and Community-Based Social Capital Capacities, After Controlling for Aggregate Levels of Both Capacity Dimensions, Age and Gender, to Detect Specific Associations Between Specific Pairs of Capacities When All Else Is Held Equal

	Peer Support	Emotional Connection to School	Teacher Support	Competency-Based Teaching	Safe Physical School Environment	Safe Psychosocial School Environment	Participatory and Inclusive School Governance	Child-Friendly City
Communication	0.11	−0.04	−0.07	ns	−0.04	ns	ns	ns
Negotiation	ns	ns	−0.04	ns	ns	0.04	ns	ns
Cooperation	0.09	0.06	−0.05	ns	−0.07	ns	ns	ns
Distress tolerance	ns	ns	−0.04	ns	ns	ns	ns	ns
Emotion regulation	ns	0.06	0.09	−0.06	ns	−0.05	ns	ns
Self-management	−0.06	ns	ns	ns	ns	ns	ns	ns
Problem-solving	ns	−0.04	−0.04	ns	ns	0.04	ns	ns
Decision-making	ns	ns	ns	ns	ns	ns	ns	ns
Planning	ns	ns	0.05	ns	ns	ns	ns	ns
Critical thinking	ns	ns	0.05	0.04	ns	ns	ns	ns
Creativity	ns	ns	ns	ns	ns	ns	ns	ns
Kindness	0.05	ns	−0.05	ns	ns	ns	ns	ns
Respect for diversity	ns	−0.04	−0.04	0.04	ns	ns	ns	ns
aerobic exercise	ns	ns	ns	ns	ns	ns	ns	0.04
Balanced nutrition	−0.04	ns	ns	ns	ns	ns	ns	ns
Sleep hours weekly	−0.07	ns	0.04	ns	0.05	ns	ns	ns

Note: Analysis is based on a sample of 7,834 adolescents in Ukraine. ns = not significant after correction for multiple testing.

of the social system; how to analyze qualitative and quantitative data to empirically discover or verify processes of adaptation and resilience; and how to capture methodological and substantive discoveries and innovations in the context of a cumulative science. Scholars of resilience can make important contributions in meeting these challenges through scholar-practitioner partnerships. Such partnerships require flexibility and a readiness for experimentation from both sides, as the scholarly emphasis on conceptual and methodological rigor engages with the practitioner emphasis on practical utilization of study results within a complex multi-stakeholder environment.

Key Messages

1. There is strong interest within the humanitarian, peacebuilding, and development sectors to integrate resilience thinking into their work on conflict prevention and postconflict recovery.
2. Resilience in conflict is widely accepted to be multisystemic and to require an integrative understanding of adaptation processes at the individual, household, community, and institutional levels, which draw on resources across dimensions of human, social, material, and digital capital.
3. Effectively assessing resilience in contexts of conflict would require an integration of social-ecological, psychological, and anthropological approaches, utilizing qualitative, quantitative, and participatory methods of inquiry.
4. The ultimate end-goal of resilience assessment in any given conflict context should be to enhance the capacity of agents across all system levels to take effective resilience-enhancing action.
5. Scholar–practitioner partnerships can contribute to addressing existing gaps in the conflict resilience field.

References

Ager, A., Lembani, M., Mohammed, A., Ashir, G., Abdulwahab, A., de Pinho, H., . . . Zarowsky, C. (2015). Health service resilience in Yobe State, Nigeria in the context of the Boko Haram insurgency: A systems dynamics analysis using group model building. *Conflict and Health, 9*, 30. doi:10.1186/s13031-015-0056-3

Alameddine, M., Fouad, F., Diaconu, K., Jamal, Z., Lough, G., Witter, S., & Ager, A. (2019). Resilience capacities of health systems: Accommodating the needs of Palestinian refugees from Syria. *Social Science & Medicine, 220*, 22–30. doi:10.1016/j.socscimed.2018.10.018

Allansson, M., Melander, E., & Themner, L. (2017). Organized violence, 1989–2016. *Journal of Peace Research, 54*(4), 574–587. doi:10.1177/0022343317718773

Allen, C., Angeler, D., Garmestani, A., Gunderson, L., & Holling, C. (2014). Panarchy: Theory and application. *Ecosystems, 17*(4), 578–589. doi:10.1007/s10021-013-9744-2

Allen, C., Fontaine, J., Pope, K., & Garmestani, A. (2011). Adaptive management for a turbulent future. *Journal of Environmental Management, 92*, 1339–1345. doi:10.1016/j.jenvman.2010.11.019

Attewell, P., & Monaghan, D. (2015). *Data mining for the social sciences: An introduction*. Oakland: University of California Press.

Barber, B. (2001). Political violence, social integration and youth functioning: Palestinian youth from the intifada. *Journal of Community Psychology, 29*(3), 259–280.

Ben-Atar, E. (2018). On-air under fire: Media and community resilience in post-heroic wars. *Israel Affairs*, 24(4), 593–614. doi:10.1080/13537121.2018.1478781

Betancourt, T., & Khan, K. (2008). The mental health of children affected by armed conflict: Protective processes and pathways to resilience. *International Review of Psychiatry*, 20(3), 317–328. doi:10.1080/09540260802090363

Betancourt, T., McBain, R., Newnham, E., & Brennan, R. (2013). Trajectories of internalizing problems in war-affected Sierra Leonean youth: Examining conflict and post-conflict factors. *Child Development*, 84(2), 455–470. doi:10.1111/j.1467-8624.2012.01861.x

Bodas, M., Siman-Tov, M., Kreitler, S., & Peleg, K. (2015). Assessment of emergency preparedness of households in Israel for war. *Disaster Medicine and Public Health Preparedness*, 9, 382–390. doi:10.1017/dmp.2015.56

Bodas, M., Siman-Tov, M., Kreitler, S., & Peleg, K. (2017). Psychological correlates of civilian preparedness for conflicts. *Disaster Medicine and Public Health Preparedness*, 11, 451–459. doi:10.1017/dmp.2016.163

Brodsky, A., Welsh, E., Carrillo, A., Talwar, G., Scheibler, J., & Butler, T. (2011). Between synergy and conflict: Balancing the processes of organizational and individual resilience in an Afghan women's community. *American Journal of Community Psychology*, 47, 217–235. doi:10.1007/s10464-010-9399-5

Brown, T. (2015). *Confirmatory factor analysis for applied research*, (2nd ed.). New York, NY: Guildford Press.

Butler, J., Young, J., McMyn, I., Leyshon, B., Graham, I., Walker, I., ... Warburton, C. (2015). Evaluating adaptive co-management as conservation conflict resolution: Learning from seals and salmon. *Journal of Environmental Management*, 160, 212–225. doi:10.1016/j.jenvman.2015.06.019

Carpenter, A. (2012). Havens in a firestorm: Perspectives from Baghdad on resilience to sectarian violence. *Civil Wars*, 14(2), 182–204. doi:10.1080/13698249.2012.679503

Charmaz, K. (2014). *Constructing grounded theory*, (2nd ed.). Thousand Oaks, CA: SAGE.

Cox, F., & Sisk, T. (Eds.). (2017). *Peacebuilding in deeply divided societies: Toward social cohesion?* Basingstoke, UK: Palgrave Macmillan.

Cummings, M., Merrilees, C., Taylor, L., & Mondi, C. (2017). Developmental and social-ecological perspectives on children, political violence, and armed conflict. *Development and Psychopathology*, 29, 1–10. doi:10.1017/S0954579416001061

Development Initiatives. (2018). *Global humanitarian assistance report 2018*. Bristol, UK: Author.

Eggerman, M., & Panter-Brick, C. (2010). Suffering, hope and entrapment: Resilience and cultural values in Afghanistan. *Social Science & Medicine*, 71, 71–83. doi:10.1016/j.socscimed.2010.03.023

Fazel, M., Reed, R., Panter-Brick, C., & Stein, A. (2012). Mental health of displaced and refugee children resettled in high income countries: Risk and protective factors. *The Lancet*, 379, 266–282. doi:10.1016/S0140-6736(11)60051-2

Folke, C., Hahn, T., Olsson, P., & Norberg, J. (2005). Adaptive governance of social-ecological systems. *Annual Review of Environmental Resources*, 30, 441–473. doi:10.1146/annurev.energy.30.050504.144511

Glass, N., Perrin, N., Kohli, A., & Remy, M. (2014). Livestock/animal assets buffer the impact of conflict-related traumatic events on mental health symptoms for rural women. *PLoS ONE*, 9(11), e111708. doi:10.1371/journal.pone.0111708

Gleditsch, N., Wallensteen, P., Eriksson, M., Sollenberg, M., & Strand, H. (2002). Armed conflict 1946–2001: A new dataset. *Journal of Peace Research*, 39(5), 615–637. doi:10.1177/0022343302039005007

Gurung, T., Bousquet, F., & Trebuil, G. (2006). Companion modeling, conflict resolution, and institution building: Sharing irrigation water in the Lingmuteychu Watershed, Bhutan. *Ecology and Society*, 11(2), 36.

Hall, B., Tol, W., Jordans, M., Bass, J., & de Jong, J. (2014). Understanding resilience in armed conflict: Social resources and mental health of children in Burundi. *Social Science & Medicine*, 114, 121–128. doi:10.1016/j.socscimed.2014.05.042

Hayes, A. (2018). *Introduction to mediation, moderation and conditional process analysis: A regression-based approach*. New York, NY: Guildford Press.

Hellin, J., Ratner, B., Meinzen-Dick, R., & Lopez-Ridaura, S. (2018). Increasing social-ecological resilience within small-change agriculture in conflict-affected Guatemala. *Ecology and Society*, 23(3), 5. doi:10.5751/ES-10250-230305

Hilhorst, D. (2018). Classical humanitarianism and resilience humanitarianism: Making sense of two brands of humanitarian action. *Journal of International Humanitarian Action*, *3*, 15. doi:10.1186/s41018-018-0043-6

Hobfoll, S., Johnson, R., Canetti, D., Palmieri, P., Hall, B., Lavi, I., & Galea, S. (2012). Can people remain engaged and vigorous in the face of trauma? Palestinians in the West Bank and Gaza. *Psychiatry*, *75*(1), 60–75. doi:10.1521/psyc.2012.75.1.60

Hox, J., Moerbeek, M., & van de Schoot, R. (2018). *Multilevel analysis: Techniques and applications* (3rd ed.). New York, NY: Routledge.

Institute for Economics & Peace. (2017). *Positive peace report 2017: Tracking peace transitions through a systems thinking approach*. Report No. 54. Retrieved from www.visionofhumanity.org/reports

Kelleher, J., Mac Namee, B., & D'Arcy, A. (2015). *Fundamentals of machine learning for predictive data analytics: Algorithms, worked examples, and case studies*. Boston, MA: MIT Press.

Kline, R. (2015). *Principles and practice of structural equation modeling* (4th ed.). New York, NY: Guildford Press.

Lavi, I., & Stone, M. (2011). Resilience and political violence: A cross-cultural study of moderating effects among Jewish- and Arab-Israeli youth. *Youth & Society*, *43*(3), 845–872. doi:10.1177/0044118X09353437

Lazega, E., & Snijders, T. (Eds.). (2019). *Multilevel network analysis for the social sciences: Theory, methods and applications*. New York, NY: Springer International.

Levey, E., Oppenheim, C., Lange, B., Plasky, N., Harris, B., Lekpeh, G., . . . Borba, C. (2016). A qualitative analysis of factors impacting resilience among youth in post-conflict Liberia. *Child and Adolescent Psychiatry and Mental Health*, *10*, 26. doi:10.1186/s13034-016-0114-7

Lordos, A., & Dagli-Hustings, I. (2018). *Social contract-building for peace: Dissonant duello of subnational social contracts in Cyprus*. Wits School of Governance Working Paper Series.

Lordos, A., Morin, H., Fanti, K., Lemishka, O., Guest, A., Symeou, M., . . . Kontoulis, M., & Hadjimina, E. (2019). *An evidence-based analysis of the psychosocial adaptability of conflict-exposed adolescents and the role of the education system as a protective environment*. Ukraine: United Nations Children Fund.

Masten, A. (2015). Pathways to integrated resilience science. *Psychological Inquiry*, *26*, 187–196. doi:10.1080/1047840X.2015.1012041

McCandless, E. (2013). Wicked problems in peacebuilding and statebuilding: Making progress in measuring progress through the New Deal. *Global Governance*, *19*, 227–248. doi:10.1163/19426720-01902005

McCandless, E., Hollender, R., Zahar, M., Schwoebel, M., Menochal, A., & Lordos, A. (2018). *Forging resilient social contracts: A pathway to preventing violent conflict and sustaining peace*. Oslo, Norway: United Nations Development Programme.

McCaul, B., & Mitsidou, A. (2016). *Analysis of the resilience of communities to disasters: User guidance manual*. Dublin, Ireland: GOAL.

Miller-Lewis, L., Searle, A., Sawyer, M., Baghurst, P., & Hedley, D. (2013). Resource factors for mental health resilience in early childhood: An analysis with multiple methodologies. *Child and Adolescent Psychiatry and Mental Health*, *7*, 6. doi:10.1186/1753-2000-7-6

Mitra, S., Mulligan, J., Schilling, J., Harper, J., Vivekananda, J., & Krause, L. (2017). Developing risk or resilience? Effects of slum upgrading on the social contract and social cohesion in Kibera, Nairobi. *Environment & Urbanization*, *29*(1), 103–122.

Nguyen-Gillham, V., Giacaman, R., Naser, G., & Boyce, W. (2008). Normalizing the abnormal: Palestinian youth and the contradictions of resilience in protracted conflict. *Health and Social Care in the Community*, *16*(3), 291–298. doi:10.1111/j.1365-2524.2008.00767.x

Odero, K. (2006). Information capital: 6th asset of sustainable livelihood framework. *Discovery and Innovation*, *18*(2), 83–91.

Organisation for Economic and Co-operation and Development. (2014). *Guidelines for resilience systems analysis*. OECD Publishing.

Panter-Brick, C., Goodman, A., Tol, W., & Eggerman, M. (2011). Mental health and childhood adversities: A longitudinal study in Kabul, Afghanistan. *Journal of the American Academy of Child & Adolescent Psychiatry*, *50*(4), 349–363. doi:10.1016/j.jaac.2010.12.001

Ratner, B., Mam, K., & Halpern, G. (2014). Collaborating for resilience: Conflict, collective action and transformation on Cambodia's Tonle Sap Lake. *Ecology and Society*, *19*(3), 31. doi:10.5751/ES-06400-190331

Ratner, B., Meinzen-Dick, R., May, C., & Haglund, E. (2013). Resource conflict, collective action, and resilience: An analytical framework. *International Journal of the Commons, 7*(1), 183–208. doi:10.18352/ijc.276

Sastry, N., Ghosh-Dastidar, B., Adams, J., & Pebley, A. (2003). *The design of a multilevel survey of children, families and communities: The Los Angeles Family and Neighborhood Survey.* Office of Population Research Princeton University, Working Paper No. 2003-06.

Sayama, H. (2015). *Introduction to the modeling and analysis of complex systems.* New York, NY: Open SUNY Textbooks.

Scoones, I. (1998). *Sustainable rural livelihoods: A framework for analysis.* IDS Working Paper No. 72. Brighton, UK: Institute of Development Studies.

Segovia, F., Moore, J., Linnville, S., Hoyt, R., & Hain, R. (2012). Optimism predicts resilience in repatriated prisoners of war: A 37-year longitudinal study. *Journal of Traumatic Stress, 25,* 330–336. doi:10.1002/jts.21691

Shoshani, A., & Stone, M. (2016). The resilience function of character strengths in the face of war and protracted conflicts. *Frontiers in Psychiatry, 6,* doi:10.3389/fpsyg.2015.02006

Simpson, G, Makoond, A., Vinck, P., & Pham, P. (2016). *Assessing resilience for peace: A guidance note.* Geneva, Switzerland: Interpeace.

Siriwardhana, C., Ali, S., Roberts, B., & Stewart, R. (2014). A systematic review of resilience and mental health outcomes of conflict-driven adult forced migrants. *Conflict and Health, 8,* 13. doi:10.1186/1752-1505-8-13

Slone, M., & Shoshani, A. (2017). Children affected by war and armed conflict: Parental protective factors and resistance to mental health symptoms. *Frontiers in Psychiatry, 8,* 1397. doi:10.3389/fpsyg.2017.01397

Centre for Sustainable Peace and Democratic Development & United Nations Development Programme. (2015). *Predicting peace: The social cohesion and reconciliation index as a tool for conflict transformation* (2nd ed.). Nicosia, Cyprus: United Nations Development Programme.

Sundberg, R., Eck, K., & Kreutz, J. (2012). Introducing the UCDP Non-State Conflict Dataset. *Journal of Peace Research, 49*(2), 351–362. doi:10.1177/0022343311431598

Tol, W., Song, S., & Jordans, M. (2013). Annual research review: Resilience and mental health in children and adolescents living in areas of armed conflict—A systematic review of findings in low- and middle-income countries. *Journal of Child Psychology and Psychiatry, 54*(4), 445–460. doi:10.1111/jcpp.12053

Ungar, M. (2018). Systemic resilience: Principles and processes for a science of change in contexts of adversity. *Ecology and Society, 23*(4), 34. doi:10.5751/ES-10385-230434

UNICEF. (2017). *Reimagining life skills and citizenship education in the Middle East and North Africa: A four-dimensional and systems approach to 21st Century skills.* Amman, Jordan: Author.

United Nations. (2019). *UN common guidance on helping build resilient societies.* New York, NY: Author.

United Nations Development Programme. (2014). *Community based resilience analysis (CoBRA): Conceptual framework and methodology.* Retrieved from https://www.undp.org/content/undp/en/home/ourwork/global-policy-centres/sustainable_landmanagement/resilience/cobra/

United Nations General Assembly. (2016). *Outcome of the World Humanitarian Summit: Report of the secretary-general.* A/71/353. Retrieved from undocs.org/A/71/353

United Nations, & World Bank. (2018). *Pathways for peace: Inclusive approaches to preventing violent conflict.* Washington, DC: World Bank.

Vaughan, E., & Henly-Shepard, S. (2018). *Resilience measurement practical guidance note series.* Mercy Corps, Resilience Evaluation, Analysis and Learning (REAL) Associate Award. Retrieved from https://spark.adobe.com/page/rSG16suIleW7d/

Vivekananda, J., Schilling, J., & Smith, D. (2014a). Climate resilience in fragile and conflict-affected societies: Concepts and approaches. *Development in Practice, 24*(4), 487–501. doi:10.1080/09614524.2014.909384

Vivekananda, J., Schilling, J., & Smith, D. (2014b). Understanding resilience in climate change and conflict-affected regions of Nepal. *Geopolitics, 19,* 911–936.

Witter, S., Wurie, H., Chandiwana, P., Namakula, J., So, S., Alonso-Garbayo, A., . . . Raven, J. (2017). How do health workers experience and cope with shocks? Learning from four fragile and conflict-affected health systems in Uganda, Sierra Leone, Zimbabwe and Cambodia. *Health Policy and Planning, 32*(3), 3–13. doi:10.1093/heapol/czx112

Zeitlyn, D. (2008). Life-history writing and the anthropological silhouette. *Social Anthropology, 16*(2), 154–171. doi:10.1111/j.1469-8676.2008.00028.x

Zinoviev, D. (2018). *Complex network analysis in Python*. Raleigh, NC: Pragmatic Bookshelf.

Zraly, M., & Nyirazinyoye, L. (2010). Don't let the suffering make you fade away: An ethnographic study of resilience among survivors of genocide-rape in southern Rwanda. *Social Science & Medicine, 70,* 1656–1664. doi:10.1016/j.socscimed.2010.01.017

SECTION 7

Organizational Processes

23

The Multisystem Approach to Resilience in the Context of Organizations

Monique Crane

Introduction

In the context of organizations, employee resilience is related as much to intrapersonal capacities and resources as it is the organizational system and the interaction between the two. Organizations are complex collections of different systems, performing different functions at different levels. Thus, it is unsurprising that multiple systems need to be considered to capture the complexity of employee resilience. With the rising popularity of resilience training within organizations, the role of organizational factors that contribute to employee resilience has been a somewhat neglected area of scholarship. This chapter will outline a multisystemic approach to resilience in the occupational context. First, I will define resilience and explore theoretically why investigations of employee resilience need to consider multisystemic approaches to the subject. Second, I will describe organizational resource models of employee well-being and resilience that highlight the organizational and team-level factors that contribute to the likelihood that employees will experience a resilient outcome. Finally, the multisystem approach to employee resilience will be applied to a real-world case example.

Defining Resilience

As the chapters in this volume show, there is no shortage of definitions of resilience. However, most authors have settled on a definition that distinguishes between resilience as an *outcome* observed in the context of risk and the *capacity* for resilience, which is the cluster of ingredients that increase the likelihood that resilience will be observed. An accepted definition of resilience as an outcome is provided by Kalisch et al. (2017), who defined resilience as: "the maintenance or quick recovery of mental health during and after exposure to significant stressors" (p. 786). In the occupational context, the experience of significant stressors often reflects chronically high workload, organizational change, job insecurity, or potentially traumatic events in the case of military personnel and first responders (for review, see Kleim & Westphal, 2011). Resilience as an outcome is most often operationalized by the absence of depression, anxiety, or posttraumatic stress disorder despite significant risk exposure (Bonanno, Westphal, & Mancini, 2011) and cannot be measured in the absence of risk (Kalisch et al., 2017).

The capacity for resilience reflects the cluster of resilience-supporting qualities, resources, and skills that are available and used by an individual to address stressors that emerge. The investigation of these resilient capacities reflects the first wave of resilience enquiry. Over many years, such investigations have yielded a list of factors and processes that enable a resilient outcome in the face of risk (Lent, 2004; Richardson, 2002). Potential resilience capacities are many and varied and include: environmental supports (e.g., Pietrzak, Johnson, Goldstein, Malley, & Southwick, 2009), the regulation of positive affectivity (Tugade & Fredrickson, 2007; Tugade & Fredrickson, 2004), cognitive appraisal approaches (e.g., Major, Richards, Cooper, Cozzarelli, & Zubek, 1998), and flexible coping and emotion regulatory strategies (e.g., Bonanno & Burton, 2013; Cheng, Hui, & Lam, 2000; Galatzer-Levy, Burton, & Bonanno, 2012) to name a few. Important to this chapter is the role that organizational and work team systems play in extending or constraining individual capacities and resources.

Research in the field of organizational psychology has been demonstrating the importance of fit between the demands imposed on individuals and the resilience capacities or available resources. For example, a recent longitudinal study explored patterns of military personnel coping in the context of a low-control and low-autonomy workplace (Britt, Crane, Hodson, & Adler, 2016). In this low-control and low-autonomy context, the most consistently effective form of coping was acceptance, rather than other strategies typically reported to be adaptive such as problem-solving and social support seeking. Other work suggests that the resources available need to be relevant to reducing the demands imposed by particular stressors. This is referred to as the matching hypothesis (de Jonge & Dormann, 2006). The principle of the matching hypothesis is that demands in different domains (e.g., cognitive, emotional, or physical) are most effectively addressed by resources in similar domains. For example, cognitive demands, related to load on cognitive processes, are most effectively addressed by cognitive resources such as task clarity (de Jonge & Dormann, 2006). De Jonge and Dormann (2006) found that the presence of physical resources (i.e., instrumental supports) reduced the relationship between physical demands (i.e., strain on the musculoskeletal system) and physical strain. Moreover, emotional demands (i.e., emotional labor required to achieve organizational goals) were addressed by emotional resources (i.e., supervisory support) reducing emotional strain. However, other studies have found limited support for the matching hypothesis (van den Tooren, de Jonge, Vlerick, Daniels, & van de Ven, 2011).

The mixed findings in support of the matching hypothesis may reflect the nuanced capacity of certain resources to alleviate demands that are difficult to capture with broad measures of resources or demands (e.g., cognitive, emotional, physical demands). For example, a cognitive stressor may be mentally exacting work imposing demands on concentration, but the cognitive resources measure used includes aspects that may not alleviate strains particular to concentration. In this way, the broad categories do not capture the nuanced fit between specific cognitive demands and specific cognitive resources. Further, it may also be the case that some capacities are global in their beneficial effects (e.g., coping efficacy, perceived support), whereas the utility of other resources is more related to their ability to reduce the load imposed by one specific demand. For example, perceived coping self-efficacy (the perceived belief that one can manage situational demands) is likely to be applicable to a context where stressors are dynamic or constantly changing (Sandler, Tein, Mehta, Wolchik, & Ayers, 2000). In contrast, workplace specific know-how may be effective for addressing highly demanding time-sensitive workplace stressors, but less applicable to managing family conflict. Thus, certain resilience capacities may be more versatile and broadly adaptive than others.

Within a systems conceptualization of resilience, the focus is on the dynamic interplay between intra-individual characteristics, social psychological elements (e.g., group cohesion, norms), and the ecological context (e.g., organizational culture). For employee resilience, the social and ecological context in which employees find themselves is very much a core part of determining the available capacities for resilience and therefore the likelihood of resilient outcomes. Given that the outcome of resilience depends on the interaction between the capacities and resources that individual has and the demands of the situation, a person who demonstrates resilience in one setting may not necessarily demonstrate resilience in another. The situational demands and resilient capacities and coping resources available in the system at any one-time point are dynamic. For example, when employees move abroad for employment it is likely certain demands will change, as will their access to certain resources (e.g., support networks). In this way, the likelihood of resilience is not a trait or stable characteristic of a person, but modifiable over time via the accumulation or constraint of certain capacities or resources. Thus, the system in which individuals find themselves has important implications for the resilient capacities and coping resources present at any one point in time.

Many studies have focused on attributes that characterize resilient individuals and equip them to handle organizational change and other negative events (Shin, Taylor, & Seo, 2012; Tugade & Fredrickson, 2004). Such research has had two implications for organizations. The first is an interest in hiring practices that seek to screen individuals for their resilience. The second is that organizations are being encouraged to develop the capacity of employees to show resilience on the job. Arguably, the first implication is problematic for the previously discussed conceptual reasons. To summarize, the capacity for resilience can change, so past resilience may not necessarily predict future resilience, particularly in the context of new demands where the previously used strategies may not apply to the new demand. The second implication with respect to the organization's role in the resilience of employees is more in line with conventional wisdom and acknowledges the potential organizational and team role for increasing the likelihood of a resilient outcome when exposed to risk. In response to this second implication, there has been emerging interest in resilience training that has been implemented in the hope of developing individual level coping capacities (for review, see Robertson, Cooper, Sarkar, & Curran, 2015). However, *usage of coping strategies* is only one of three broad clusters of modifiable capacities for resilience identified in the literature (Crane, Searle, Kangas, & Nwiran, 2019). Others also include the availability of *coping resources* that may be derived from the environment, and *resilience beliefs* (e.g., self-efficacy), which are also affected by environmental features.

Understanding Employee Resilience: The Role of Job Design

Historically, models considering the role of job design primarily focus on explaining the manifestation of employee burnout and promoting job engagement. Yet, a similar analysis may be applied to understanding the emergence of a resilient outcome. The organizational and intrapersonal inputs into workplace systems for preventing burnout contribute to the clusters of resilience-supporting capacities. Moreover, there is the potential for a dynamic interplay between these organizational and intrapersonal inputs, whereby the organizational factors seem to influence capacities considered to be intrapersonal (e.g., motivational orientation, resilient beliefs), and vice versa.

One dominant approach to understanding employee burnout is the job demands-resources (JD-R) model whereby employee well-being and mental ill health can be explained by the existence of two factors: job demands and job resources (Demerouti, Bakker, Nachreiner, & Schaufeli, 2001). Job demands are work-related tasks that require effort, and vary by task complexity, emotional labor demands, and physical strain. Job resources are work-related assets that can be accessed to meet job demands. Job demands and resources are organizational inputs that effect resilience. Job demands tax the employee's resources creating exhaustion, whereas low resources affect motivational processes that are related to the withdrawal of effort and emotional disengagement (Demerouti et al., 2001). The combination of prolonged high demands and low resources eventually lead to burnout. Burnout is characterized by a sense of exhaustion, a lack of efficacy, and a psychological detachment from work. Examples of job resources are decision-making autonomy, emotional support from leaders, and technical equipment, all resources that could also be understood as resilience promoting resources for the workplace. The original conceptualization of the JD-R model, however, focused primarily on the role of job design, rather than individual-level characteristics to explain why employees experience burnout. Specifically, it has been proposed that high job demands will have a negative effect on employee well-being unless workers have sufficient job resources to deal with their demanding jobs. According to the JD-R model, burnout is likely in any profession where the job resources are outweighed by the job demands.

Although organizational-level inputs are important, there are also individual-level inputs into the system that have been identified to support resilience at work. In recent years, these models have been extended to include the role of individual resources (e.g., self-efficacy, optimism). Personal resources are thought to moderate the relationship between job demands and negative outcomes. For example, Van Yperen and Snijders (2000) explored the role of personal resources in buffering the effects of job demands in bank employees in the Netherlands. These authors found that general self-efficacy moderates the relationship between job demands and psychological health symptoms. Similarly, in Finnish employees

(25–59 years) under demanding work conditions, optimistic employees were found to experience lower psychological distress compared to their less optimistic counterparts (Mäkikangas & Kinnunen, 2003). Such research suggests that employees with high-levels of intrapersonal resilient capacities are able to deal more effectively with job demands. In this way, there are a set of individual level inputs into the system that also have a role in buffering the effects of workplace related risk.

The Dynamic Interplay Between Organizational and Individual-Level Resources

The previous examples present a picture of an almost passive comparison between demands and resources with resilience emerging when resources outweigh demands. However, the picture is not that simple. Recent research suggests that job resources may even contribute to capacities traditionally considered intrapersonal (Xanthopoulou, Bakker, Demerouti, & Schaufeli, 2007). Such findings have shown that job resources actually trigger personal resources that enable the enhanced likelihood of resilience to job demands. Job resources are likely to affect the motivational system of the individual, as outlined in the JD-R model, by promoting resilience beliefs such as agency and optimism regarding future positive outcomes. Thus, individual-level capacities for resilience are potentially susceptible to changes in the workplace environment. The story, however, does not end there. There is also evidence to support the suggestion that employees who are higher in certain resilient capacities are also more likely to make use of resources to facilitate goal attainment. For example, employees with good interpersonal skills may be better equipped to ask for what they need and get it. A person–environment system such as this also receives feedback in the form of goal attainment, recognition from others, positive affect that reinforces resilient beliefs and has opportunities to use certain resilient capacities—motivating more of the positive behavior. Negative feedback may also be received that can increase maladaptive beliefs (self-limiting beliefs) or contribute to reductions in problem-solving.

Job Demands Are Not All Created Equal

A further complexity is that job demands are not always viewed as detrimental and do not all yield the same negative outcomes. The challenge-hindrance stressor framework (Cavanaugh, Boswell, Roehling, & Boudreau, 2000) is one model that may present a useful way of delineating stressors that contribute to the capacity for resilience versus those that erode it. Hindrance stressors (e.g., bureaucracy, role conflict), are classed as barriers to goal accomplishment and are therefore considered obstacles to personal growth. In contrast, challenge stressors are job demands that create an opportunity for personal growth and development. Research exploring challenge and hindrance stressors demonstrate that both increase the experience of psychological stress (Boswell, Olson-Buchanan, & LePine, 2004), although challenge stressors may also have positive outcomes. This idea extends Selye's (1956) distinction between positive and negative forms of stress, referred to as *eustress* and *distress*, respectively. Eustress and distress both engage the stress system; however, eustress involves a sense of positive challenge contributing to extending oneself and growth, whereas distress promotes negative affectivity and dysfunction. In the organizational domains, challenge stressors (e.g., time pressure, high workload) are considered to also deplete energy leading to exhaustion and stress, but at the same time increase personal capabilities (Van den Broeck, De Cuyper, De Witte, & Vansteenkiste, 2010). For example, a two-wave longitudinal study of working Australians across a variety of sectors demonstrated that a greater frequency of challenge stressors at Time 1 was related to a greater perceived resilience at Time 2. In contrast, Time 1 hindrance stressors were positively predictive of strain at Time 2 and negatively related to Time 2 perceived resilience (Crane & Searle, 2016). Thus, there is some evidence that job demands are not all the same and while both result in initial increases in stress, some workplace stressors lead to positive outcomes.

The Role of Individual Appraisals

Although the challenge-hindrance stressor framework suggests that job demands may be subject to a priori classification, other research has demonstrated variability in the way individuals perceive (appraise) these demands and the link between these appraisals and job performance. Searle and Auton (2014) suggest that categorizing job demands into challenge and hindrance stressors makes assumptions about how these stressors are interpreted. These authors apply the transactional model of stress and coping (Lazarus & Folkman, 1984) to describe how appraisal of the same job demand may vary from person to person. Searle and Auton (2014) demonstrated that even after controlling for the effects of challenge and hindrance stressors, challenge appraisals were positively related to positive affect, while hindrance appraisal was positively related to negative affect. Moreover, there was some evidence that appraisals mediated the relationship between job demands and outcomes, such that both challenge and hindrance stressors demonstrated an indirect relationship to positive affect, anger and task appraisal via challenge appraisal. Challenge stressors were related to greater challenge appraisal and thereby more positive outcomes, while hindrance stressors were related to lower challenge appraisal that in turn predicted greater negative outcomes. This research demonstrates that appraisals are important to the experience of affective outcomes that may, if experienced chronically, have implications for resilience on the job. However, the mediations demonstrate that work related demands also play a role in influencing the appraisal process.

The nature of job demands, therefore, seem important to appraisal and in turn well-being. However, job related resources may also have similar effects. Previous work exploring the JD-R model has proposed the motivational nature of access to job resources (Demerouti, et al., 2001), but there is an under considered role for job resources in the appraisal process. Job resources such as supportive colleagues and appropriate feedback from one's superiors increases the likelihood of being successful in achieving one's work goals. Thus, the perception of accomplishment is also likely to enhance perceived challenge appraisals as opposed to threat of failure or loss. Furthermore, previous work has demonstrated that personal resources, like optimism, could compensate for low work resources (Riolli & Savicki, 2003). However, this idea must be considered in practical terms. For example, an employee may be *generally* optimistic that goals will be accomplished, but if he or she is chronically underresourced to achieve those goals (e.g., lacks equipment), it is likely that such optimism will be eroded. Considering the necessity to have resilient capacities that fit the demands placed on individuals and systems, available resources to achieve a task are going to be an essential aspect of an employee's resilient toolkit when coping with workplace stressors. It is even possible that job resources may also compensate for lower individual-level resources, but this is a relationship that has yet to be explored.

From the previous analysis of job design models, it is clear that there is a complex interaction between individual-level factors and the work environment. Studies exploring job design models consistently demonstrate that employees have the greatest likelihood of resilience when there are challenging work demands and they are well-resourced to meet those demands (Bakker & Bal, 2010; Demerouti & Cropanzano, 2010). Collectively, this research suggests that the resources organizations provide is essential to their employees' resilience. For example, leadership approaches can influence employees' job demands and resources (Nielsen, Randall, Yarker, & Brenner, 2008), and may indirectly influence employee engagement via promoting employee optimism (Tims, Bakker & Xanthopoulou, 2011). Job resources need to be sufficient, however, and include feedback, social support, and skill variety. Perhaps most interesting is the way organizational resources may affect individual-level resilience capacities, such that better equipping employees in their roles has the potential to increase their private resilience capacities.

Frameworks of Organizational Resources and Demands

In practice, it can be challenging to identify the resources that organizations need to provide to support employee resilience. In response to this practical challenge, specific models of organizational job-related resources have been developed. For example, the health services workplace environmental resilience (HSWER) model describes the environmental factors in the workplace that promote nurses' resilience (Cusack et al., 2016). Building nurses' resilience to complex and stressful practice environments has the potential to draw new people into the nursing profession and retain experienced professionals with well-developed skills, thereby ensuring safer patient care. Cusack et al. (2016) identified a number of protective environmental workplace characteristics emerging as important for nurses, such as mentoring, clinical supervision, education and training, staffing levels, personal safety, and self-care. From these themes, two overarching concepts emerge relating to support and development. Support was characterized as interventions and resources that allow nurses to endure the demands of their role. Development refers to interventions that empower nurses to enhance their potential (Cusack et al., 2016). In addition, support and development can be applied in three domains: (a) personal (related to individual well-being), (b) professional (relating to the values and expectations of the profession), and (c) practice (relating to work related skills and knowledge). In this way, six areas of need emerge as presented in Table 23.1. Resources can be provided in each of these domains to support resilience. Although the HSWER model provides a framework for supporting nursing staff specifically, these workplace attributes are relevant to other organizational sectors as well. Therefore, Table 23.1 adapts the themes emerging in Cusack's work for a number of different organizations.

TABLE 23.1 Modified Health Services Workplace Environmental Resilience Model

Domain	Support	Development
Personal	Interactions between colleagues that promote psychological safety Adherence to policies that support staff well-being and the immediate actioning of resolutions to issues A culture of support for adequate breaks and respect for appropriate recovery practices Leadership or supervisory support for self-care practices Access to assistance when required for mental health concerns	Resources that allow the development of skills to reduce stress or cope effectively Activities that promote the capacity to support colleagues in the workplace Development of personal self-awareness regarding mental health concerns
Practice	Clearly articulated expectations of the role that are suitable for skill level or experience Access to necessary supervision or training to facilitate skills development Access to related policies and guidelines that relate to one's work Provision of resources that enable work to be undertaken successfully Collaboration between colleagues allowing the transition of knowledge and skill	Structures that support the development of role-specific knowledge related to tasks Opportunities for the safe reflection on mistakes that enable learning
Professional	Clear processes that facilitate communication between management and employees Supportive and responsive supervision Access to decision-making support Positive interactions among colleagues that is supportive of new ideas and innovation	Mentoring programs that promote career development Performance reviews that allow a scaffolded and stepped approached to skill development Leadership support for professional development activities

Adapted from Cusack et al. (2016).

A second framework intended for broad application is the ASSET framework for identifying and understanding the sources of pressure and support in the workplace (Cartwright & Cooper, 2002; Cooper, Flint-Taylor, & Pearn, 2013; Johnson, 2009). This framework identifies six key factors pertaining to sources of workplace pressure and support: (a) resources and communication, (b) control, (c) work-life balance and workload, (d) job security and change, (e) work relationships, and (f) job conditions. The ASSET framework proposes predictable relationships between potential sources of pressure at work and individual health and job outcomes (e.g., job satisfaction). These factors not only contribute to negative sources of stress and demand, but may also be resources that support positive workplace outcomes.

The Resilient Work Systems Framework (Figure 23.1) is based on my work in occupational resilience, the existing frameworks thus far described (e.g., JD-R model, HSWER model, and the ASSET framework) and the existent scholarship on workplace stress. The Resilient Work Systems Framework articulates eight work-related dimensions that may

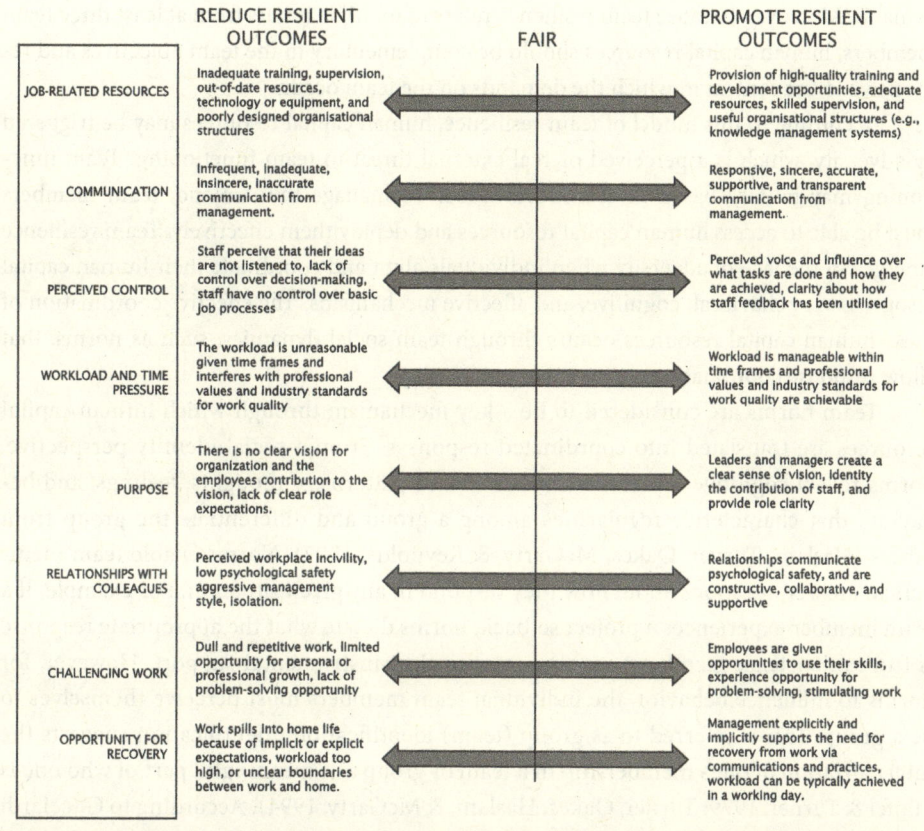

	REDUCE RESILIENT OUTCOMES	FAIR	PROMOTE RESILIENT OUTCOMES
JOB-RELATED RESOURCES	Inadequate training, supervision, out-of-date resources, technology or equipment, and poorly designed organisational structures	←——→	Provision of high-quality training and development opportunities, adequate resources, skilled supervision, and useful organisational structures (e.g., knowledge management systems)
COMMUNICATION	Infrequent, inadequate, insincere, inaccurate communication from management.	←——→	Responsive, sincere, accurate, supportive, and transparent communication from management.
PERCEIVED CONTROL	Staff perceive that their ideas are not listened to, lack of control over decision-making, staff have no control over basic job processes	←——→	Perceived voice and influence over what tasks are done and how they are achieved, clarity about how staff feedback has been utilised
WORKLOAD AND TIME PRESSURE	The workload is unreasonable given time frames and interferes with professional values and industry standards for work quality	←——→	Workload is manageable within time frames and professional values and industry standards for work quality are achievable
PURPOSE	There is no clear vision for organization and the employees contribution to the vision, lack of clear role expectations.	←——→	Leaders and managers create a clear sense of vision, identity the contribution of staff, and provide role clarity
RELATIONSHIPS WITH COLLEAGUES	Perceived workplace incivility, low psychological safety aggressive management style, isolation.	←——→	Relationships communicate psychological safety, and are constructive, collaborative, and supportive
CHALLENGING WORK	Dull and repetitive work, limited opportunity for personal or professional growth, lack of problem-solving opportunity	←——→	Employees are given opportunities to use their skills, experience opportunity for problem-solving, stimulating work
OPPORTUNITY FOR RECOVERY	Work spills into home life because of implicit or explicit expectations, workload too high, or unclear boundaries between work and home.	←——→	Management explicitly and implicitly supports the need for recovery from work via communications and practices, workload can be typically achieved in a working day.

FIGURE 23.1 The Resilient Work Systems Framework for assessing organizational contributors to the reduction or promotion of employee resilient outcomes.

either reduce or increase the likelihood of employee resilience. Each of the eight dimensions includes anchors at either pole that describe the characteristics of that dimension. For each dimension, an organization may be classed as either low (contributing to a reduction in the likelihood of a resilient outcome) or high (promoting the likelihood of a resilient outcome). Ideally, practices and policies that promote resilient outcomes at both the organizational level and the immediate team level occur consistently.

Multilevel Model of Team Resilience

The resilience literature concerned with work team functioning is a recent, albeit rapidly developing area. A recent model of team resilience highlights the connections between both individual and team level factors that contribute to the emergence of team resilience (Gucciardi et al., 2018). This model proposes that team resilience emerges from combinations of human capital resources that are relevant to the objective of the team. Individual-level knowledge, abilities, skills, and other capacities (i.e., human capital resources) remain relevant to team outcomes in terms of resilience in so far as they are related to a specific on-the-job task or demand. Moreover, because team resilience refers to multiple inputs from at least three team members, human capital resources should be complementary to the team objectives and responsive to the context in which the demands on the team occur.

According to this model of team resilience, human capital resources may be triggered by adversity, which is a perceived or real external threat to team functioning. Team functioning may be task-based or teamwork-based. To manage the demand, team members must be able to access human capital resources and deploy them effectively. Team resilience emerges in the face of adversity when individuals align and coordinate their human capital resources via behavioral, cognitive, and affective mechanisms. The effective coordination of these human capital resources occurs through team social dynamics, such as norms, that allow response coordination.

Team norms are considered to be a key mechanism through which human capital resources are translated into coordinated responses. From a social identity perspective, norms reflect cognitive representations of shared patterns of thoughts, feelings, and behaviors that characterize regularities among a group and differentiate the group from others (Haslam, Turner, Oakes, McGarty, & Reynolds, 1997). Norms enable team members to answer questions about how they respond in any given situation. For example, if a team member experiences a project setback, norms dictate what the appropriate response is from other team members, such as emotional or instrumental support. However, for norms to influence behavior, the individual team members must perceive themselves to be a group. This is referred to as group (team) identification. Identification suggests the internalization of one's membership in a team or group as a meaningful part of who one is (Tajfel & Turner, 1979; Turner, Oakes, Haslam, & McGarty, 1994). According to Gucciardi et al. (2018), the combination of team norms that encourage the effective coordination of human capital resources and team identification enable the emergence of processes that increase the likelihood of a resilient outcome. Other critical ingredients for team resilience are planning, processes for pre-empting challenges (Alliger, Cerasoli, Tannenbaum, & Vessey, 2015), and team-based reflective practices (also known as after action or activity reviews) that allow learning to take place. Planning relates to the identification of desired behaviors or outcomes in advance (e.g., goals, implementation strategies). Pre-empting challenges is part of the planning process and enables the identification of barriers to the achievement of goals and contingency plans. Reflection plays a critical role in team resilience by enabling learning from failures and success by unpacking the reasons for outcomes, exploring alternative ways outcomes could have been achieved, identifying processes requiring change, or actions that should be sustained (Ellis, Carette, Anseel, & Lievens, 2014). The reflective practice has the capacity to enable the ongoing development of team processes, but also potentially encourages employees to think about setbacks, failures, and demands as an opportunity for growth, rather than threat, promoting individual-level resilient outcomes (Crane et al., 2019). The multilevel model of team resilience suggests a complex interaction between both individual-level inputs into the system and social dynamics that allows these inputs to be synthesized and purposefully directed to team-related tasks. A key leverage point in this dynamic process is the role of leadership, which has been a critical area of interest in the occupational resilience scholarship.

The Critical Role of Leadership in Employee Resilience

Leaders and leadership behavior, as a key determinant of team and employee resilience, is well documented (see Alliger et al., 2015; Gomes, Borges, Huber, & Carvalho, 2014). Leadership is commonly defined as a person who is able to influence the behavior of followers to the achievement of desired goals (Dartey-Baah, 2015). However, just as leaders may influence goal achievement, they also have an influence over the well-being and resilience of employees in their charge. This influence may transpire in several ways. Apart from the direct interpersonal relationship that leaders have with their employees, leaders also influence other systems that are related to the quality of the employee's experience at work with important implications for resilience. Given that leaders are often responsible for resource allocation, in the context of job design and team models of resilience, leadership has an important role in cultivating the resources, as identified in Figure 23.1, and buffering employees from resilience depleting demands. Leaders are also critical for establishing norms that contribute to team functioning and supportive colleague interactions (e.g., psychological safety; Gucciardi et al., 2018).

Several lines of research speak to the potential role of leadership behavior in fostering positive and supportive interactions among teams. For example, a number of international studies have found that supportive leadership promotes better morale among soldiers (Britt, Dickinson, Moore, Castro, & Adler, 2007) and junior officers (Langkamer & Ervin, 2008). Moreover, lower conflict and less role ambiguity (both related to lower job demands) emerge in teams with supportive leadership (Britt, Davison, Bliese, & Castro, 2004). Transformational and servant leadership approaches are credited with the capacity to create co-operative employee relationships given that these approaches model behaviors that demonstrate concern for employees and consideration to their ideas promoting norms of concern for others and mutual respect (Kirkbride, 2006). Transformational leadership occurs when leaders broaden and elevate the goals and interests of their employees, generate acknowledgement and acceptance of group-based goals, and encourage group members to look beyond self-interest to the advancement of group purpose (Bass, 1985). Transformational leadership is commonly thought to comprise four dimensions: (a) idealized influence (leaders behave as role models and gain their followers' trust and respect), (b) inspirational motivation (leaders hold high expectations and communicate a compelling vision of the future), (c) intellectual stimulation (leaders encourage their followers to consider different perspectives and empower them to contribute novel ideas), and (d) individualized consideration (leaders display genuine care and concern for their followers by recognizing their individual needs; Bass & Riggio, 2006).

Servant leadership styles that emphasize service to others, team consensus, and the personal development of individuals have been shown to be related to cooperative conflict management (Wong, Liu, Wang, & Tjosvold, 2018).

Another way leaders can promote resilience in the workplace is via their capacity to inject purpose and meaning in work. For example, empowering leadership involves delegating to subordinate staff, providing opportunities for decision-making autonomy, encouraging employees to participate in mentoring, and fostering responsibility and confidence (Kim & Beehr, 2018). Recent research demonstrates how empowering leadership may have downstream effects on meaningful work and psychological well-being outcomes. In a group of 347 fulltime employees, empowering leadership was shown to have an effect on the promotion of meaningful work. Moreover, perceptions of meaningful work resulted in lower levels of emotional exhaustion and higher levels of life satisfaction (Kim & Beehr, 2018). The take-home message is that leadership approaches have implications for the demands experienced and resource availability that employees have access to and this has a considerable influence on employee resilience.

Beyond the effects of leadership approaches on demands and resources available to employees, there is some evidence that particular leadership styles contribute to employee resilience via their contribution to the trust developed between an employee and leader. Kelloway, Turner, Barling, and Loughlin (2012) demonstrated that transformational leadership was negatively related to employee psychological distress, but employee trust in leadership fully mediated the relationship between transformational leadership and employee psychological ill-health. This indicates that it is employee trust in the leader, developed by transformational leadership that is a key mechanism that supports employee well-being.

Although there is often an emphasis on leadership styles in the corporate sector (e.g., laissez-faire leadership, authentic leadership), discrete leader behaviors also have a measurable effect on positive employee outcomes. Support for the idea that leader behaviors are critical comes from work demonstrating that transformational leadership behaviors fluctuate daily, contrary to the idea that transformational leadership is a stable style (Breevaart & Bakker, 2018). It has been shown that on the days that transformational leadership is high, daily challenge demands have a positive relationship to work engagement. However, when transformational leadership is low, daily hindrances have a greater negative association with employee engagement (Breevaart & Bakker, 2018).

To date, considerable research has demonstrated the relationship between supervisor behavior and employee well-being. Foundational work by Gavin and Kelley (1978) demonstrated a positive association between the self-reported well-being of underground miners and their perceptions of how considerate their supervisors were. Similarly, studies in the 1980s demonstrated that nurses whose supervisor rated low in consideration and high in structure (i.e., tasks and processes highly structured) were most likely to report symptoms of burnout (Duxbury, Armstrong, Drew, & Henly, 1984). Martin and Schinke (1998) found that for psychiatric workers and family and child mental health workers, harsh criticism delivered by supervisors was positively associated with greater burnout. Conversely, organizational leaders with high state hope (i.e., a sense of personal agency and knowledge of pathways to goal achievement) had significantly better work unit performance, subordinate retention, and employee satisfaction outcomes than low hope leaders (Peterson & Luthans, 2003). Potentially, leaders high in state hope may be more likely to communicate clear workplace goals, intentions to achieve those goals, and pathways to goal attainment to employees. Importantly, despite the objective challenges of mental health work and the emotional demands on the workforce, leaders were able to have a significant effect on the resilience of the employees. Gilbreath and Benson (2004) add support to previous studies showing, across a range of occupational types, associations between supervisor behavior, and employee well-being. This work also demonstrated that leader behaviors contributed significantly to the prediction of burnout over the contribution of demographic variables and support from other sources (e.g., home, others at work). Wegge, Shemla, and Haslam (2014) suggest that leaders who are cognizant of employee health, particularly when dealing with exhausted employees, and model good health behaviors also influenced the health behaviors of employees. Thus, leader behaviors appear to make a robust and unique contribution to the psychological well-being of employees across a range of industries. The practical importance of this work is that leaders can be trained in behaviors that are more likely to support the well-being of employees. For example, leaders can be trained to be considerate of employee health, demonstrate concern for the well-being of their subordinates, communicate vision and meaning, and ensure that employees are intellectually stimulated and empowered.

The Application of Multisystem Thinking to Employee Resilience during Organizational Change

Organizational change is a normal part of working life. It is not only organizations and teams that are required to change, but individual employees are also expected to change and adapt to new working conditions (Anderson, 2013). Change fatigue is particularly common in the healthcare sector and the rapid and frequent pace of change within health organizations is well acknowledged (Camilleri, Cope, & Murray, 2018). In the healthcare sector, change is being driven not only by a greater public demand for services but also a shift in the needs of medical services as new public health issues emerge (e.g., COVID-19) and others become treatable (e.g., changes in the needs of HIV sufferers with the development of antivirals). However, organizational change is disruptive and a significant contributor to employee job demands, particularly as employees experience uncertainty with respect to changes to their roles, routines, or uncertainty about ongoing employment (Rafferty & Griffin, 2006). Organizational change often bears a relationship to problematic employee health outcomes such as burnout (Dubois, Bentein, Mansour, Gilbert, & Bedard, 2014). From a multisystem perspective, organizational change is likely to result in a complex interplay between individual, team, and/or organizational-level systems that determine the outcomes for employee resilience. In this way, when attempting to support the resilience of employees during periods of organizational change, it is necessary to target several systems at once for intervention. A case example follows.

The XY Hospital: Background

The XY Hospital was experiencing significant and rapid change. This change took place very quickly and meant that staff were expected to adjust to large-scale change in less than 12 months. Several voluntary redundancies, transfers and resignations occurred as a consequence of the change. Change was being driven by several factors including (a) it was no longer perceived as necessary to have several wards with specific functions (change resulted in the merger of several wards resulting in modifications of work routines, communication and IT systems, and job roles); (b) there was change in the hospital director who was seeking to save operating costs; and (c) there had been previous calls for voluntary redundancies that resulted in more than 30 employees leaving the organization. Management reported concerns about the well-being of staff given increased absenteeism, evidence of low morale, and growing cynicism. As is common in such situations, the initial solution considered by management was to provide staff with resilience training to enhance individual-level coping capacities of employees. Resilience training can contribute to the resilience supporting capacities of individual staff members (Vanhove, Herian, Perez, Harms, & Lester, 2016). However, as noted throughout this chapter, there are many ways that organizations as a whole and specific work teams (both higher order systems that play a role in positive functioning when workplaces experience atypical amounts of stress) can have significant positive effects on both employee and organizational resilience.

At the outset, understanding employee resilience in this dynamic and paying attention to context can seem overwhelming and complex. However, frameworks for assessing supports and demands such as the Resilient Systems Framework (Figure 23.1) allow the identification of possible leverage points for optimizing individual resilience and the co-design of interventions at the individual, team, and organizational levels.

Diagnosis of Organizational Sources of Demand at XY Hospital and Approaches to Intervention

Core issues for this team included:

- *Perceived lack of opportunities for development.* Staff raised concerns about educational and development resources, specifically the lack of formal clinical supervision that was contributing to concerns about deskilling. As identified previously, clinical supervision is a key area of importance for staff in the hospital sector (Cusack, et al., 2016).
- *Communication about organizational change.* Staff reported concerns that management were not transparent about the change process. Communication is vital to the effective implementation of organizational change (DiFonzo & Bordia, 1998). In the context of this organization, the lack of communication was increasing the level of uncertainty among employees. During the change process, there is often uncertainty regarding the aims of change, how change will occur, and what the outcomes of change will be for the individual

employees (Buono & Bowditch, 1993). Employee uncertainty during the change process has significant implications for well-being and readiness for change.

- *Control over decision-making.* The main concern was the perceived lack of involvement in the change process. Specifically, staff felt that their feedback as to how changes are integrated into the workplace (particularly relating to quality of care) failed to be acknowledged. Actively involving employees in the change process has important implications for employee support for change (Sharif & Scandura, 2014). Moreover, job control and autonomy has been conceptualized as a job resource. Job control can help employees deal more effectively with job demands, buffering the negative implications of job demands (Bakker & Demerouti, 2007). The end result in this context was that employees felt frustrated about their ability to affect change, influence events, and avoid negative outcomes.
- *Workload and value conflicts.* Understaffing is an issue for many organizations when there is pressure to streamline the workforce and reduce costs. In the context of XY Hospital, workload was an issue for two reasons. First, during periods of crisis staff were often required to work overtime to manage the crises, a pattern that was highly unpredictable but that was occurring more often. Second, the main concern appeared to be the impact workload had on perceived quality of care. Frustration was expressed about the limited ability of staff to engage in patient care in a way that was meaningful (e.g., not having sufficient time to support patients and their families). This is a common observation in studies of nursing. Higher workloads and long work hours can appear to conflict with real or perceived quality of care and significant role responsibilities (Peter, Macfarlane, & O'Brien-Pallas, 2004) and can take a significant toll on the well-being of nurses. At times, this conflict takes an ethical form and can result in moral distress (McAndrew, Leske, & Schroeter, 2018), defined as "the experience of psychological distress that results from engaging in, or failing to prevent, decisions or behaviors that transgress, or come to transgress, personally held moral or ethical beliefs" (Crane, Bayl-Smith, & Cartmill, 2013, p. 6).
- *Problematic recovery from work.* High levels of exhaustion and high levels of workplace spillover into family life can indicate excessively high workplace expectations and the blurring of work–life boundaries. It can also mean that individuals lack strategies to recover from workplace stress effectively. Research demonstrates that daily recovery from work is associated with enhanced well-being, work engagement, and next-day job performance (Sonnentag, 2003; Sonnentag & Fritz, 2007; Totterdell, Spelten, Smith, Barton, & Folkard, 1995). Conversely, failure to recover from work leads to the chronic accumulation of stress and has implications for longer-term physical and mental health (e.g., Brosschot, Gerin, & Thayer, 2006; Geurts & Sonnentag, 2006). Fortunately, it is not the time available for recovery that is critical, but rather the characteristics of the rest experience (Westman & Eden, 1997) that can be encouraged via training and supportive leadership.

Table 23.2 outlines the possible team and individual-level interventions that address the issues identified in the previous case study as part of a multisystemic approach to intervention. Ideally, issues are addressed at different levels within the system to achieve the most sustainable outcomes.

TABLE 23.2 Team- and Individual-Level Interventions to Address Issues Identified in the XY Hospital

Issue	Team-Level Intervention	Individual-Level Intervention
Perceived lack of opportunities for development	Develop a list of self-appointed mentors that can be sought out for career support and practice advice Promote a learning culture within the organization by identifying ward expertise and champions of particular skills on the ward Provide staff with information about the developmental opportunities already within the hospital (e.g., seminars) Managers modeling self-directed learning With staff consultation, determine strategies for staff development that would be most desired and then empowering a lateral thinking approach to meeting this demand (i.e. developing contacts both within and external to the ward/hospital)	Develop staff to be proactive about self-development and seeking mentors Assist staff in the development of realistic and achievable goals for their career Increase problem-solving behavior around competency development Encourage effective use of social support and mentoring within the hospital
Communication	Provide staff with feedback about what suggestions have been received and why a particular decision has been made (i.e., reasons behind decision-making). This could be in the form of a verbal general meeting or in a weekly update notice that outlines issues that have been received and their responses from management Be clear about what decisions staff may have a level of influence over Develop a framework with staff that allows greater upward and downward communication between staff and management Develop a standardized feedback process collaboratively with staff to pass information to management	Develop individual communication and inter-personal skills that allow them to communicate their concerns effectively Assist staff to take a management perspective when it comes to communication and negotiation
Control over decision-making	Create opportunities for staff to get involved in decision-making Allow staff to provide open solutions to problems without a preferred management driven solution being put up front	Assist staff to exercise control via the way they view and respond to a situation Assist staff to develop a greater tolerance for uncertainty and frustration in the workplace Help staff to focus on aspects within a situation that are controllable
Workload and value conflicts	If there is scope for influence, present staff with opportunities to come up with cost-neutral strategies for addressing perceived issues with workload and skill mix.	Normalize the challenges of workload that effect the health sector Help staff to balance the importance of meeting professional standards within the limitations of the hospital system

TABLE 23.2 Continued

Issue	Team-Level Intervention	Individual-Level Intervention
Recovery from work	Explicit support from management for routine breaks. Support a team-culture that values downtime and uses breaks effectively. Ensure that there is not implicit or explicit messages that communicate expectations to staff of a requirement to be available beyond work hours	Help staff understand the barriers to detaching from the workplace during breaks and evening rest periods. Help staff understand how to get the most from rest periods involving absorbing and enjoyable activities that are detached from the workplace

Conclusion

In recent years, there has been greater recognition of the role job design, workplace ecology, and leadership play in the resilience of employees. However, there are several areas in need of further exploration in terms of the role of job resources in influencing individual level event appraisals or their role in compensating for a lack of individual level resources. This is an underexplored area that could have significant implications for the way we think about the dynamic interplay between environmental and individual resilient capacities in organizational settings. Moreover, research exploring team resilience is still in the early stages of development, with efforts to understand team resilience only emerging within the last decade (e.g., Alliger, et al., 2015; Edson, 2012; Gucciardi, et al., 2018). Thus, research is required to both develop an understanding of the dynamic mechanisms at play and the leverage points where interventions may be meaningfully applied. At the organizational level, empirical investigations are required that explore the costs and benefits of various human-resource management practices on employee resilience. Human-resource management approaches to employee resilience can be reactive and driven by what is in vogue at various points in time with limited evidence of their effectiveness. On the surface, such approaches may seem intuitive with a level of face validity for their effectiveness but provide no measurable benefit. These tendencies can be curbed by the delivery of proactive evidence-based strategies and practical advice to human resource managers regarding how to support employee resilience.

Australian entrepreneur Sir Richard Branson is credited with the maxim: "Learn to look after your staff first and the rest will follow." The question that this chapter has addressed is *how* to look after your staff. The answer is via a multisystemic approach to staff resilience. I discourage the overreliance on resilience training and encourage consideration of organizational and team systems as ways to develop and sustain employee resilience. Where systematic issues of employee well-being and resilience occur, changes to job design, job demands, leadership behaviors, and available resources to cope with stress, especially during periods of organizational change, are likely to be key. Such initiatives not only sustain the resilience of employees, but also contribute to high performing organizations.

Key Messages

1. The role of organizational- and team-level factors in influencing individual-level resilience is a rich area of investigation. There are several questions yet to be answered regarding the level of fit required between certain resources and demands, and the role of job-based resources in effecting individual-level capacities for resilience.
2. Organizational and work team systems play a crucial role in extending or constraining individual capacities and resources relevant to maintaining employee resilience. Thus, better equipping employees in their roles has the potential to increase intra-individual resilience capacities.
3. Leaders and leadership behavior have been identified as a key determinant of team and employee resilience. In particular, leader behaviors make a robust and unique contribution to the psychological well-being of employees across a range of industries.
4. Leaders can be trained in behaviors that are more likely to support the resilience of employees.
5. Interventions that seek to support employee resilience need to move beyond resilience training and explore organizational and team systems as ways to develop and sustain employee resilience.

References

Alliger, G. M., Cerasoli, C. P., Tannenbaum, S. I., & Vessey, W. B. (2015). Team resilience: How teams flourish under pressure. *Organizational Dynamics*, 44(3), 176–184. doi:10.1016/j.orgdyn.2015.05.003

Anderson, D. L. (2013). *Organization development: The process of leading organizational change* (2nd ed.). Thousand Oaks, CA: SAGE.

Bakker, A. B., & Bal, P. M. (2010). Weekly work engagement and performance: A study among starting teachers. *Journal of Occupational and Organizational Psychology*, 83(1), 189–206. doi:10.1348/096317909X402596

Bakker, A. B., & Demerouti, E. (2007). The job demands-resources model: State of the art. *Journal of Management Psychology*, 22(3), 309–328. doi:10.1108/02683940710733115

Bass, B. M. (1985). *Leadership and performance beyond expectations*. New York, NY: Free Press.

Bass, B. M., & Riggio, R. E. (2006). *Transformational leadership* (2nd ed.). Mahwah, NJ: Lawrence Erlbaum.

Bonanno, G. A., & Burton, C. L. (2013). Regulatory flexibility: An individual differences perspective on coping and emotion regulation. *Perspectives on Psychological Science*, 8, 591–612. doi:10.1177/1745691613504116

Bonanno, G. A., Westphal, M., & Mancini, A. D. (2011). Resilience to loss and potential trauma. *Annual Review of Clinical Psychology*, 7, 511–535. doi:10.1146/annurev-clinpsy-032210-104526.

Boswell, W. R., Olson-Buchanan, J. B., & LePine, M. A. (2004). Relations between stress and work outcomes: The role of felt challenge, job control, and psychological strain. *Journal of Vocational Behaviour*, 64(1), 165–181. doi:10.1016/S0001-8791(03)00049-6

Breevaart, K., & Bakker, A. B. (2018). Daily job demands and employee work engagement: The role of daily transformational leadership behavior. *Journal of Occupational Health Psychology*, 23(3), 338–349. doi:10.1037/ocp0000082

Britt, T. W., Crane, M., Hodson, S. E., & Adler, A. B. (2016). Effective and ineffective coping strategies in a low-autonomy work environment. *Journal of Occupational Health Psychology*, 21(2), 154–168. doi:10.1037/a0039898

Britt, T. W., Davison, J., Bliese, P. D., & Castro, C. A. (2004). How leaders can influence the impact that stressors have on soldiers. *Military Medicine, 169*(7), 541–545. doi:10.7205/milmed.169.7.541

Britt, T. W., Dickinson, J. M., Moore, D., Castro, C. A., & Adler, A. B. (2007). Correlates and consequences of morale versus depression under stressful conditions. *Journal of Occupational Health Psychology, 12*(1), 34–47. doi:10.1037/1076-8998.12.1.34

Brosschot, J. F., Gerin, W. & Thayer, J. F. (2006). The perseverative cognition hypothesis: A review of worry, prolonged stress-related activation, and health. *Journal of Psychosomatic Research, 60*(2), 113–124. doi:10.1016/j.jpsychores.2005.06.074

Buono, A., &Bowditch, J. (1993). *The human side of mergers and acquisitions: Managing collisions between people, cultures, and organizations.* San Francisco, CA: Jossey-Bass.

Camilleri, J., Cope, V., & Murray, M. (2018). Change fatigue: The frontline nursing experience of large-scale organisational change and the influence of teamwork. *Journal of Nursing Management. 27*(3), 655–660. doi:10.1111/jonm.12725

Cartwright, S., & Cooper, C. L. (2002). *ASSET: An organisational stress screening tool: The management guide.* Manchester, UK: Robertson Cooper.

Cavanaugh, M. A., Boswell, W. R., Roehling, M. V., & Boudreau, J. W. (2000). An empirical examination of self-reported work stress among US managers. *Journal of Applied Psychology, 85*(1), 65–74. doi:10.1037/0021-9010.85.1.65

Cheng, C., Hui, W., & Lam, S. (2000). Perceptual style and behavioral pattern of individuals with functional gastrointestinal disorders. *Health Psychology, 19*(2), 146–154.

Cooper, C., Flint-Taylor, J., & Pearn, M. (2013). *Building resilience for success: A resource for managers and organizations.* Hampshire, UK: Palgrave Macmillan.

Crane, M. F., Bayl-Smith, P., & Cartmill, J. (2013). A recommendation for expanding the definition of moral distress experienced in the workplace. *The Australasian Journal of Organisational Psychology, 6,* e1. doi:10.1017/orp.2013.1

Crane, M. F., & Searle, B. J. (2016). Building resilience through exposure to stressors: The effects of challenges versus hindrances. *Journal of Occupational Health Psychology, 21*(4), 468–479. doi:10.1037/a0040064

Crane, M. F., Searle, B. J., Kangas, M., & Nwiran, Y. (2019). How resilience is strengthened by exposure to stressors: The systematic self-reflection model of resilience strengthening. *Anxiety, Stress, & Coping, 32*(1), 1–17. doi:10.1080/10615806.2018.1506640

Cusack, L., Smith, M., Hegney, D., Rees, C. S., Breen, L. J., Witt, R. R., . . . Cheung, K. (2016). Exploring environmental factors in nursing workplaces that promote psychological resilience: Constructing a unified theoretical model. *Frontiers in Psychology, 7*(600), 1–8. doi:10.3389/fpsyg.2016.00600

Dartey-Baah, K. (2015). Resilient leadership: A transformational-transactional leadership mix. *Journal of Global Responsibility, 6*(1), 99–112. doi:10.1108/jgr-07-2014-0026

de Jonge, J., & Dormann, C. (2006). Stressors, resources, and strain at work: A longitudinal test of the triple-match principle. *Journal of Applied Psychology, 91*(6), 1359–1374. doi:10.1037/0021-9010.91.5.1359

Demerouti, E., Bakker, A. B., Nachreiner, F., Schaufeli, W. B. (2001). The job demands-resources model of burnout. *Journal of Applied Psychology, 86*(3), 499–512. doi:10.1037/0021-9010.86.3.499

Demerouti, E., & Cropanzano, R. (2010). From thought to action: Employee work engagement and job performance. In A. B. Bakker & M. P. Leiter (Eds.), *Work engagement: A handbook of essential theory and research* (pp. 147–163). New York, NY: Psychology Press.

DiFonzo, N., & Bordia, P. (1998). A tale of two corporations: Managing uncertainty during organisational change. *Human Resource Management, 37,* 295–303.

Dubois, C. A., Bentein, K., Mansour, J. B., Gilbert, F., & Bedard, J. L. (2014). Why some employees adopt or resist reorganization of work practices in health care: Associations between perceived loss of resources, burnout, and attitudes to change. *International Journal of Environmental Research and Public Health, 11*(1), 187–201. doi:10.3390/ijerph110100187

Duxbury, M. L., Armstrong, G. D., Drew, D. J., & Henly, S. J. (1984). Head nurse leadership style with staff nurse burnout and job satisfaction in neonatal intensive care units. *Nursing Research, 33*(2), 97–101.

Edson, M. C. (2012). A complex adaptive systems view of resilience in a project team. *Systems Research and Behavioral Science, 29*(5), 499–516. doi:10.1002/sres.2153

Ellis, S., Carette, B., Anseel, F., & Lievens, F. (2014). Systematic reflection: Implications for learning from failures and successes. *Current Directions in Psychological Science, 23*(1), 67–72. doi:10.1177/0963721413504106

Galatzer-Levy, I. R., Burton, C. L., & Bonanno, G. A. (2012). Coping flexibility, potentially traumatic life events, and resilience: A prospective study of college student adjustment. *Journal of Social and Clinical Psychology, 31*(6), 542–567. doi:10.1521/jscp.2012.31.6.542

Gavin, J. F., & Kelley, R. F. (1978). The psychological climate and reported well-being of underground miners: An exploratory study. *Human Relations, 31*(7), 567–581. doi:10.1177/001872677803100701

Geurts, S. A. E., & Sonnentag, S. (2006). Recovery as an explanatory mechanism in the relation between acute stress reactions and chronic health impairment. *Scandinavian Journal of Work, Environment and Health, 32*(6), 482–492. doi:10.5271/sjweh.1053

Gilbreath, B., & Benson, P. G. (2004). The contribution of supervisor behaviour to employee psychological well-being. *Work & Stress, 18*(3), 255–266. doi:10.1080/02678370412331317499

Gomes, J. O., Borges, M. R., Huber, G. J., & Carvalho, P. V. R. (2014). Analysis of the resilience of team performance during a nuclear emergency response exercise. *Applied Ergonomics, 45*(3), 780–788. doi:10.1016/j.apergo.2013.10.009

Gucciardi, D. F., Crane, M., Ntoumanis, N., Parker, S. K., Thøgersen-Ntoumani, C., Ducker, K. J., . . . Temby, P. (2018). The emergence of team resilience: A multilevel conceptual model of facilitating factors. *Journal of Occupational and Organizational Psychology, 91*(4), 729–768. doi:10.1111/joop.12237

Haslam, S. A., Turner, J. C., Oakes, P. J., McGarty, C., & Reynolds, K. J. (1997). The group as a basis for emergent stereotype consensus. *European Review of Social Psychology, 8*(1), 203–239. doi:10.1080/14792779643000128

Johnson, S. (2009). Organisational screening: The ASSET model. In S. Cartwright & C. L. Cooper (Eds.), *Oxford handbook of organizational well-being* (pp. 133–158). Oxford, UK: Oxford University Press.

Kalisch, R., Baker, D. G., Basten, U., Boks, M. P., Bonanno, G. A., Brummelman, E., . . . Kleim, B. (2017). The resilience framework as a strategy to combat stress-related disorders. *Nature: Human Behaviour, 1*(11), 784–790. doi:10.1038/s41562-017-0200-8

Kelloway, E. K., Turner, N., Barling, J., & Loughlin, C. (2012). Transformational leadership and employee psychological well-being: The mediating role of employee trust in leadership. *Work & Stress, 26*(1), 39–55. doi:10.1080/02678373.2012.660774

Kim, M., & Beehr, T. A. (2018). Organization-based self-esteem and meaningful work mediate effects of empowering leadership on employee behaviors and well-being. *Journal of Leadership & Organizational Studies, 25*(4), 385–398. doi:10.1177/1548051818762337

Kirkbride, P. (2006). Developing transformational leaders: The full range leadership model in action. *Industrial and Commercial Training, 38*(1), 23–32. doi:10.1108/00197850610646016

Kleim, B., & Westphal, M. (2011). Mental health in first responders: A review and recommendation for prevention and intervention strategies. *Traumatology, 17*(4), 17–24. doi:10.1177/1534765611429079

Langkamer, K. L., & Ervin, K. S. (2008). Psychological climate, organizational commitment and morale: Implications for army captains' career intent. *Military Psychology, 20*(4), 219–236. doi:10.1080/08995600802345113

Lazarus, R. S., & Folkman, S. (1984). *Stress, appraisal, and coping.* New York, NY: Springer.

Lent, R. W. (2004). Toward a unifying theoretical and practical perspective on well-being and psychosocial adjustment. *Journal of Counseling Psychology, 51*(4), 482–509. doi:10.1037/0022-0167.51.4.482

Major, B., Richards, C., Cooper, M. L., Cozzarelli, C., & Zubek, J. (1998). Personal resilience, cognitive appraisals, and coping: An integrative model of adjustment to abortion. *Journal of Personality and Social Psychology, 74*(3), 735–752.

Mäkikangas, A., & Kinnunen, U. (2003). Psychosocial work stressors and well-being: Self- esteem and optimism as moderators in a one-year longitudinal sample. *Personality and Individual Differences, 35*(3), 537–557. doi:10.1016/S0191-8869(02)00217-9

Martin, U., & Schinke, S. P. (1998). Organizational and individual factors influencing job satisfaction and burnout of mental health workers. *Social Work in Health Care, 28*(2), 51–62. doi:10.1300/J010v28n02_04

McAndrew, N. S., Leske, J., & Schroeter, K. (2018). Moral distress in critical care nursing: The state of the science. *Nursing Ethics, 25*(5), 552–570. doi:10.1177/0969733016664975

Nielsen, K., Randall, R., Yarker, J., & Brenner, S.-O. (2008). The effects of transformational leadership on followers' perceived work characteristics and psychological well-being: A longitudinal study. *Work & Stress*, *22*(1), 16–32. doi:10.1080/02678370801979430

Peter, E. H., Macfarlane, A. V., & O'Brien-Pallas, L. L. (2004). Analysis of the moral habitability of the nursing work environment. *Journal of Advanced Nursing*, *47*(4), 356–364. doi:10.1111/j.1365-2648.2004.03113_1.x

Peterson, S. J., & Luthans, F. (2003). The positive impact and development of hopeful leaders. *Leadership and Organizational Development Journal*, *24*(1), 26–31. doi:10.1108/01437730310457302

Pietrzak, R. H., Johnson, D. C., Goldstein, M. B., Malley, J. C., & Southwick, S. M. (2009). Psychological resilience and postdeployment social support protect against traumatic stress and depressive symptoms in soldiers returning from operations enduring freedom and Iraqi freedom. *Depression and Anxiety*, *26*(8), 745–751. doi:10.1002/da.20558.

Rafferty, A. E., & Griffin, M. A. (2006). Perceptions of organizational change: A stress and coping perspective. *Journal of Applied Psychology*, *91*(5), 1154–1162. doi:10.1037/0021-9010.91.5.1154

Richardson, G. E. (2002). The metatheory of resilience and resiliency. *Journal of Clinical Psychology*, *58*(3), 307–321. doi:10.1002/jclp.10020

Riolli, L., & Savicki, V. (2003). Optimism and coping as moderators of the relationship between work resources and burnout in information service workers. *International Journal of Stress Management*, *10*(3), 235–252. doi:10.1037/1072-5245.10.3.235

Robertson, I. T., Cooper, C. L., Sarkar, M., & Curran, T. (2015). Resilience training in the workplace from 2003 to 2014: A systematic review. *Journal of Occupational and Organizational Psychology*, *88*(3), 533–562. doi:10.1111/joop.12120

Sandler, I. N., Tein, J. Y., Mehta, P., Wolchik, S., & Ayers, T. (2000). Coping efficacy and psychological problems of children of divorce. *Child Development*, *71*(4), 1099–1118. doi:10.1111/1467-8624.00212

Searle, B. J., & Auton, J. C. (2014). The merits of measuring challenge and hindrance appraisals. *Anxiety, Stress & Coping*, *28*(2), 121–143. doi:10.1080/10615806.2014.931378

Selye, H. (1956). *The stress of life*. New York, NY: McGraw-Hill.

Sharif, M. M., & Scandura, T. A. (2014). Do perceptions of ethical conduct matter during organizational change? Ethical leadership and employee involvement. *Journal of Business Ethics*, *124*(2), 185–196. doi:10.1007/s10551-013-1869-x

Shin, J., Taylor, M. S., & Seo, M.-G. (2012). Resources for change: The relationships of organizational inducements and psychological resilience to employees' attitudes and behaviors towards organizational change. *Academy of Management Journal*, *55*, 727–748. doi:10.5465/amj.2010.0325

Sonnentag, S. (2003). Recovery, work engagement, and proactive behavior: A new look at the interface between non-work and work. *Journal of Applied Psychology*, *88*(3), 518–528. doi:10.1037/0021-9010.88.3.518

Sonnentag, S., & Fritz, C. (2007). The recovery experience questionnaire: Development and validation of a measure for assessing recuperation and unwinding from work. *Journal of Occupational Health Psychology*, *12*(3), 204–221. doi:10.1037/1076-8998.12.3.204

Tajfel, H., & Turner, J. C. (1979). An integrative theory of intergroup conflict. In W. G. Austin & S. Worchel (Eds.), *The social psychology of intergroup relations* (pp. 33–47). Monterey, CA: Brooks-Cole.

Tims, M., Bakker, A. B., & Xanthopoulou, D. (2011). Do transformational leaders enhance their followers' daily work engagement? *The Leadership Quarterly*, *22*(1), 121–131. doi:10.1016/j.leaqua.2010.12.011

Totterdell, P., Spelten, E., Smith, L., Barton, J., & Folkard, S. (1995). Recovery from work shifts: How long does it take? *Journal of Applied Psychology*, *80*(1), 43–57. doi:10.1037/0021-9010.80.1.43

Tugade, M. M., & Fredrickson, B. L. (2004). Resilient individuals use positive emotions to bounce back from negative emotional experiences. *Journal of Personality and Social Psychology*, *86*(2), 320–333. doi:10.1037/0022-3514.86.2.320

Tugade, M. M., & Fredrickson, B. L. (2007). Regulation of positive emotions: Emotion regulation strategies that promote resilience. *Journal of Happiness Studies*, *8*, 311–333.

Turner, J. C., Oakes, P. J., Haslam, S. A., & McGarty, C. (1994). Self and collective: Cognition and social context. *Personality and Social Psychology Bulletin*, *20*(5), 454–463. doi:10.1177/0146167294205002

Van den Broeck, A., De Cuyper, N., De Witte, H., & Vansteenkiste, M. (2010). Not all job demands are equal: Differentiating job hindrances and job challenges in the job demands–resources model. *European Journal of Work and Organizational Psychology*, *19*(6), 735–759. doi:10.1080/13594320903223839 van den Tooren, M., de Jonge, J., Vlerick, P., Daniels, K., & Van de Ven, B. (2011). Job resources and matching active coping styles as moderators of the longitudinal relation between job demands and job strain. *International Journal of Behavioral Medicine, 18*(4), 373-383. doi:10.1007/s12529-011-9148-7.

Vanhove, A. J., Herian, M. N., Perez, A. L., Harms, P. D., & Lester, P. B. (2016). Can resilience be developed at work? A meta-analytic review of resilience-building programme effectiveness. *Journal of Occupational and Organizational Psychology, 89*(2), 278-307. doi:10.1111/joop.12123

Van Yperen, N. W., & Snijders, T. A. B. (2000). A multilevel analysis of the demands-control model: Is stress at work determined by factors at the group level or the individual level? *Journal of Occupational Health Psychology, 5*(1), 182-190. doi:10.1037/1076-8998.5.1.182

Wegge, J., Shemla, M., & Haslam, S. A. (2014). Leader behavior as a determinant of health at work: Specification and evidence of five key pathways. *German Journal of Human Resource Management, 28*(1-2), 6-23. doi:10.1177/239700221402800102

Westman, M., & Eden, D. (1997). Effects of a respite from work on burnout: Vacation relief and fade-out. *Journal of Applied Psychology, 82*(4), 516-527. doi:10.1037/0021-9010.82.4.516

Wong, A., Liu, Y., Wang, X., & Tjosvold, D. (2018). Servant leadership for team conflict management, co-ordination, and customer relationships. *Asia Pacific Journal of Human Resources, 56*(2), 238-259. doi:10.1111/1744-7941.12135

Xanthopoulou, D., Bakker, A. B., Demerouti, E., & Schaufeli, W. B. (2007). The role of personal resources in the job demands-resources model. *International Journal of Stress Management, 14*(2), 121-141. doi:10.1037/1072-5245.14.2.121

24

Resilience Engineering for Sociotechnical Safety Management

Riccardo Patriarca

Introduction

It was October 2004, when a pool of experienced researchers sat together in the Swedish city of Soderkoping reflecting on what might have been done to further improve the field of safety management. At that time, it was acknowledged that the nature of work in modern societies called for a reconsideration of what is meant by the terms *risk* and *safety*. Technology was—and is now more than ever—evolving to deal with fast-moving and competing societal requirements. The related dynamic interactions among technical, human, procedural, and organizational aspects of work have contributed to increase the inherent complexity of pure technological systems. These latter have become even more symbiotically interrelated to human agents and organizational aspects with severe implications for safety management.

Safety is generally considered as the characteristic of a system that prevents damage to the health of people (i.e., injury or loss of life), property, or adverse consequences for the environment. Following etymology, the English word *safe* comes from the Latin word *salvus*, which means intact or whole. In organizational processes, the term *safe* refers to something as being without harm or injury or even free from related risks (Hollnagel, 2018). Risk can be considered as a situation or an event where something of human value (including humans themselves) has been put at stake with an uncertain outcome (Rosa, 1998).

Building on this understanding of safety, during the first Resilience Engineering Association Symposium held in Soderkoping in 2004 the notion of resilience and, more specifically, resilience engineering moved from the original state of consensus toward a more structured stage of knowledge generation (Dekker, 2006). To better understand the scientific meaning and relevance of resilience in the context of safety management, however, it is necessary to take a conceptual step backward.

Formally speaking, the science of safety was developed to provide the epistemically most warranted and reliable statements on the subject, which reflect the best research across multiple disciplines (Hansson, 2013). As such, safety science can be considered as being constituted by two scientific components: the acquired knowledge about safety-related phenomena and the conceptual tools for understanding, assessing, characterizing, communicating, and managing safety.

The concept of resilience in safety management, meanwhile, has come to refer to the activities taken to understand, assess, communicate, and manage safety of a system, an organization or even a society, based on knowledge products produced at both conceptual and pragmatic levels. Combined, these knowledge products have come to be known as resilience engineering with the explicit aim to consider systemic sociotechnical complexity and to understand how this complexity affects a system's behavior and performance. These systems can range from aircraft to hospitals, vessels, trains, or any system characterized by a symbiotic interaction among technological, human, and social (or even societal) elements.

This chapter will first introduce the notion of complexity for sociotechnical system analysis as a starting point for resilience research that improves system safety. Next, a description of two methods typically used in resilience engineering to improve safety will be presented: the resilience analysis grid (RAG) and the functional resonance analysis method. This chapter includes examples of both methods and their application to engineering problems. The last part of the chapter summarizes the contributions resilience engineering can make to the safety of systems and a possible research agenda.

On Complexity

The word *complex* comes from the Latin *complexus*, which means "what is woven together." In the scientific world, the word *complexity* first appears within the second law of thermodynamics, in relation to the inherent irreversibility of time and a molecule's motion (Morin, 2006). Since then, research on complexity has come to a number of multidisciplinary perspectives which hold a common interest in the analysis of diverse interacting and intertwined elements that are able to adapt or react to processes they are involved in, or which they contribute to (Arthur, 1999). In a sociotechnical system, processes are strictly dependent and interacting, through multiple hardly identifiable patterns that have the potential for dynamic, nonlinear, and unpredictable behaviors. By way of illustration, consider Alaska Airlines Flight 261. In January 2000, the MD-80 taking off from Puerto Vallarta in Mexico and headed to Seattle encountered a serious problem: the horizontal stabilizer, designed to control the aircraft's node attitude during cruise, appeared to be jammed. The problem led to a disaster: 2 pilots, 3 cabin crewmembers, and 83 passengers on board were killed when the airplane was destroyed on impact. Even though an investigation identified a broken part (the jackscrew-nut assembly that held the horizontal stabilizer), the final accident report included a complex intertwined muddle of factors related to organizational practices, strategic decisions, regulatory gaps, and lack of proper redundancy strategies, which over years were progressively accepted as normal but created patterns that were the basis for the disaster itself. A critical and detailed analysis of the event has been proposed by Dekker (2011).

Epistemologically, *complex* is not a synonym for *complicated* (Dekker, Bergström, Amer-Wåhlin, & Cilliers, 2013): a system is complicated if it is ultimately knowable by a set of rules (more or less difficult to define and understand) that are able to capture its functioning, while a complex system is never fully knowable, with the impossibility to attain a complete fixed or exhaustive description (Cilliers, 2010; Heylighen, Cilliers, & Gershenson, 2007). To Illustrate these differences, Figure 24.1 describes two systems: System A, whose tight links make it a complicated system (under the hypothesis that there are no more hidden links present), and System B, whose complexity is ascribed to multiple degrees of freedom that make it impossible to predict the system's behavior and evolution precisely. In more general terms, System B would be more complex than System A, since some of the degrees of freedom of System A are constrained (Goldratt, 2008). The scientific field of resilience engineering acknowledges that complexity is not considered a thing per se, rather it is a situation to be investigated (Rasmussen, 1979).

Following a broader perspective, a sociotechnical system can be interpreted as a type of complex adaptive system whose analysis might benefit of insights from a complexity management viewpoint. Complexity can be thus managed according to three different perspectives: the algorithmic complexity, the deterministic complexity, and the aggregate complexity (Manson, 2001). Algorithmic complexity refers to computational efforts necessary for solving a problem. Deterministic complexity is grounded in chaos and catastrophe theory for the determination of major effects in output variables coming from minor changes in a set of initial variables, with high potential to become prone to crumble for large systems. Deterministic complexity relies on mathematic equations and strict assumptions of how systems behave to make equations credible.

On the contrary, aggregate complexity aims at gaining a holistic representation of a system, not forcing a strict mathematical correspondence. In this context, a complexity-oriented perspective is more focused on relationships than on constituent elements (Hollnagel, 2012a). Specifying the scope of the aggregate complexity notion, a system analysis needs to acknowledge three dimensions: the world in which the system acts, the involved elements, and the representation utilized in the observation of the system, which contributes

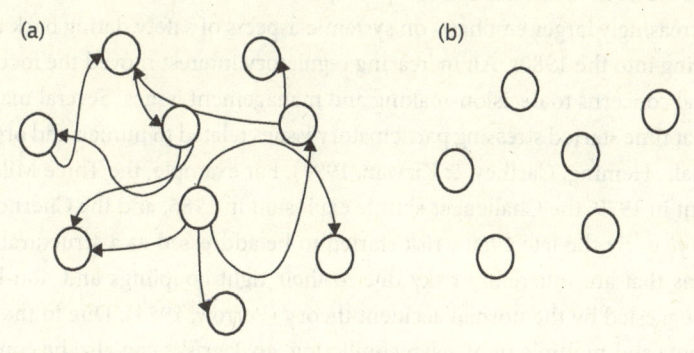

FIGURE 24.1 Complicated System A versus complex System B.

to complexity itself (Woods, 1988). A system representation is a certain model that is developed to offer a representation of a system, which has to inherently capture the dynamicity and intertwined nature of the system at hand.

It is then possible to define a set of common characteristics of complex sociotechnical systems (Pavard & Dugdale, 2006). These include

- *Limited functional decomposability*: The intertwined nature of sociotechnical systems does not ensure that the decomposed system in static stable parts keeps the same properties of the system as a whole.
- *Nondeterminism*: It is hardly possible to anticipate precisely the behavior of a complex system even though the functioning of its constituents is completely known.
- *Distributed nature of information and representation*: Some cognitive properties of the system are distributed among agents rather than assigned individually, leading to uncertain, ambiguous, incomplete, or unavailable data.
- *Emergence and self-organization*: A system property is considered emergent if it cannot be anticipated from knowing the system's components functioning. It may emerge due to local interactions between distributed actions of individual or collective sociotechnical agents.

These assumptions on complexity, as well as the ones on the nature of safety management, have been acknowledged as the theoretical foundation for the definition of the scientific field of resilience engineering (Patriarca, Di Gravio, & Constantino, 2017).

Resilience Engineering as a Paradigm Shift

In Kuhnian terms, resilience engineering constitutes a paradigm shift for safety management. It focuses on systems capability to continuously cope with the complexity arising from balancing productivity with safety in everyday work (i.e., being resilient; Hollnagel, 2006). It was early acknowledged that the discipline of resilience engineering needed to be inherently systemic by nature, focused on the complexity of the system as a whole, rather than summing oversimplified individualistic analyses of a system's constituent parts. The acknowledgement of the need for an explicit complexity-oriented viewpoint in safety science comes from the increasingly larger emphasis on systemic aspects of safety dating back to the 1970s and continuing into the 1980s. An increasing regulatory interest moved the focus from specific technical concerns to decision-making and management issues. Several major accident reports at that time started stressing participatory issues related to human and organizational activities (Hale, Heming, Carthey, & Kirwan, 1997). For example, the Three Mile Island nuclear accident in 1979, the Challenger shuttle explosion in 1986, and the Chernobyl disaster in the same year. By the late 1980s, risk started to be addressed as a structural problem of those systems that are inherently risky due to their tight couplings and non-linear interactions, as suggested by the normal accident theory (Perrow, 1984). Due to the presence of multiple agents and multiple tight, even conflicting, goals, risks can also be considered as a controllable problem to maintain a system's performance within the metaphorical boundaries of safety, economy, and workload (Rasmussen, 1997).

According to an aggregate complexity perspective, safety in a sociotechnical system cannot be represented as "a product of" or to "reside within" one or more of the social and/or technical perspective of a system (Hettinger, Kirlik, Goh, & Buckle, 2012). Given the dynamic nature of sociotechnical systems, safety is not a constant or permanent property of a system; it rather emerges from the interactive properties of the system and the environment's constituent components (Yang, Tian, & Zhao, 2017).

In this context, resilience has been shown to be related to the concept of adaptation (Amalberti, 2006), summarized as four cornerstones: responding (knowing what to do), monitoring (knowing what to look for), anticipating (knowing what to expect), and learning (knowing what has happened; Hollnagel, 2011). More recently, another theoretical perspective focused on the idea of rebound, robustness, graceful extensibility, and adaptability, has been proposed in line with awareness of the impossibility for addressing some general features of resilience, which are valid for engineering purposes (Woods, 2015).

All these definitions mostly agree with defining resilience as a system feature that allows the system itself to respond to an unanticipated disturbance and then to resume normal operations quickly and with minimum decrement in the system's performance. In formal terms, then, resilience has been defined as the intrinsic ability of a system to adjust its functioning prior to or following changes and disturbances to continue working in the face of continuous stresses or major mishaps (Hollnagel, Woods, & Leveson, 2006; Nemeth, Wears, Woods, Hollnagel, & Cook, 2008). Consequently, Resilience Engineering can be advanced as a complexity-oriented holistic discipline aimed at providing systems with the means for managing, experiencing, and enhancing resilience in response to external and internal perturbations. The discipline acknowledges that managing resilience—and safety—implies managing the dynamics and evolution of risks that may contribute to system breakdowns. In this sense, resilience engineering, like other models of resilience found throughout this volume, requires accounting for risk exposure to fully understand the adaptative capacity of the specific qualities of the mechanisms that enhance a system's resilience.

In traditional safety management, it is usually possible to identify for accident analyses or forecast for risk assessment a typical path to disaster starting from an individual failure, often linked to human actions (i.e., human error). This idea is rooted in an interpretation of risk that is focused on a system's energy (i.e., a dangerous build-up of energy, unintended transfers, or uncontrolled releases). This energy has to be contained by metaphorical and physical barriers that can stop or at least limit its propagation. Examples of barriers are a procedure, an effective management decision, a regulation, an automated feedback system, or a training action (see Figure 24.2).

Energy, however, is not always a threat and barriers can even generate unintended side effects, contributing to increase the complexity, and thus the nonintelligibility of a system and the potential for emergent risks. Such linear perspectives become progressively questionable for modern sociotechnical systems, where identifying the origin of a path's propagation becomes extremely difficult, or even impossible, due to the inherent complexity of the system itself.

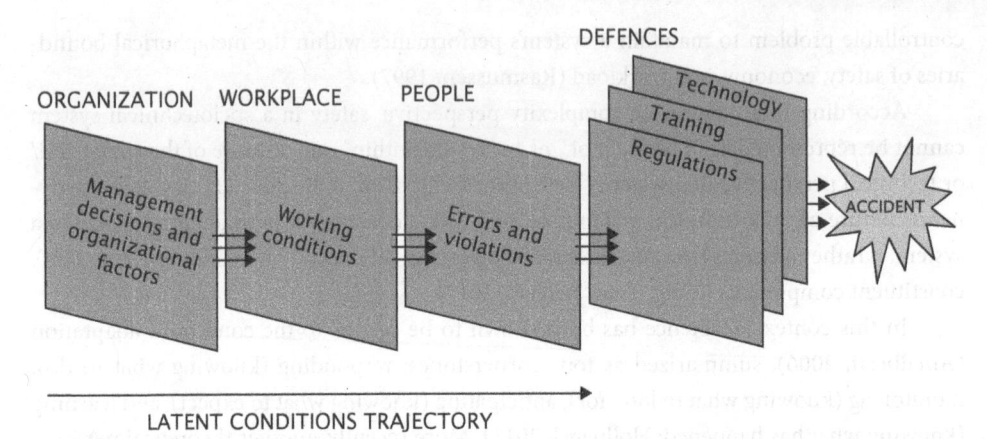

FIGURE 24.2 Swiss cheese model as an example of a barrier-based model Inspired by Reason et al. (2006).

Furthermore, systems generally behave dynamically, and thus their descriptions should be dynamic by nature, rather than oversimplified and only oriented at a constructivist viewpoint (Wrigstad, Bergström, & Gustafson, 2017). This latter refers to the WYLFIWYF principle (What you look for is what you find): causes are not found; they are chosen and selected (Lundberg, Rollenhagen, & Hollnagel, 2009). The organizational perspective cannot give an overall representation of a system's complexity, but it can be integrated with local analyses that account for human–technical interactions. The inherent complexity of systems does not allow defining a static structural cause–effect link among processes and activities that are inherently variable to cope with different operating scenarios.

The theory of resilience engineering, which acknowledges the positive effects of performance variability, is intended to provide the means for safety management of nontrivial sociotechnical systems, encompassing the hypotheses that systems are incompletely understood, descriptions can be complicated and system changes are frequent and irregular rather than infrequent and regular. Such hypotheses lead to the following principles, which are typical of resilience engineering and expressions of complexity science:

1. Systems cannot be decomposed in a meaningful way (highlighted as a main feature of a complex sociotechnical system).
2. System functions are not bimodal (functioning vs. nonfunctioning) but everyday performance is flexible and variable.
3. Human performance variability leads to success as well as failure.
4. Even though some outcomes can be interpreted as a linear consequence of other events, some events are the result of coupled performance variability.

The need to focus on performance variability rather than bimodality motivates the interest of safety for work-as-done (rather than work-as-imagined), looking at how the performance of the whole system varies (Morel, Amalberti, & Chauvin, 2009). Work-as-done represents the inherent adaptation of a system to remain productive under normal circumstances as well as

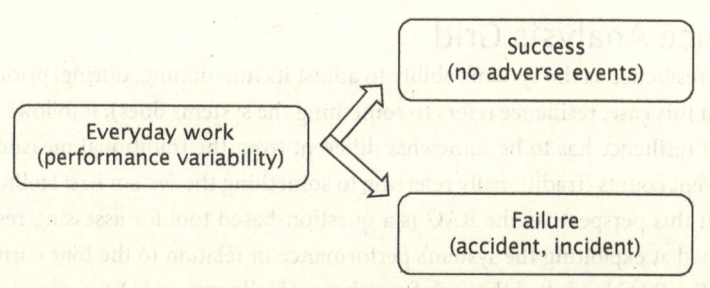

```
        ┌─────────────────┐
        │    Success      │
        │ (no adverse     │
        │    events)      │
        └─────────────────┘
               ↗
┌──────────────────┐
│  Everyday work   │
│  (performance    │
│   variability)   │
└──────────────────┘
               ↘
        ┌─────────────────┐
        │    Failure      │
        │   (accident,    │
        │    incident)    │
        └─────────────────┘
```

FIGURE 24.3 Resilience engineering point of view, acknowledging the limitedness of bimodal perspective for system functioning: success and failures come from the same source, performance variability.

under hazardous influences (see Figure 24.3). In this sense, the system is engineered to show resilience under the expected conditions in which it is used.

On Methods for Resilience Engineering

Resilience engineering offers a way of viewing processes from different angles, with the purpose of systematically understanding, extracting, or even engineering the potential of a system to self-design to match operational scenarios. In terms of methods, the approaches available in the literature range from individual, process, and systemic modeling to progressively fill the gap between the theoretical aspects of the discipline and its applicability in real contexts. These methods aim at exploring the resilience potential of a system, unveiling its strengths and weaknesses, and refining and enhancing adaptation strategies (if any).

To measure the resilience of sociotechnical systems, there are several ways to assess elements that contribute to resilience at different conceptual levels, organizing them along temporal dimensions, hierarchically (Herrera, Hollnagel, & Håbrekke, 2010; Huber, Gomes, & De Carvalho, 2012). In this context, the RAG (see following discussion) represents one of the most widely used methods for assessing resilience potential through the use of a semistandardized framework based on Hollnagel's (2011) four cornerstones of resilience (i.e., responding, monitoring, anticipating, and learning).

In terms of modeling resilience, system dynamics and causal loop diagrams have been used in several industrial applications (Salzano, Di Nardo, Gallo, Oropallo, & Santillo, 2014). Other specific models have been developed starting from graph theory mainly for technological aspects (Johansson & Hassel, 2010) or through fuzzy cognitive maps (Azadeh, Salehi, Arvan, & Dolatkhah, 2014), or benefit–cost–deficit (BCD) models (Ouedraogo, Enjalbert, & Vanderhaegen, 2013). For qualitative approaches, the functional resonance analysis method (FRAM) has become increasingly popular for modeling complex sociotechnical systems. The FRAM allows for a multidisciplinary analysis of processes, taking into account technical, human, and organizational aspects of work (Hollnagel, 2012b).

The remainder of this section provides more details on RAG and FRAM, both methods of particular interest for assessing and modeling features of sociotechnical systems related to their resilience abilities.

Resilience Analysis Grid

Looking at resilience as the system's ability to adjust its functioning, during, prior to, or after an event (in this case, resilience refers to something the systems does), it follows that the assessment of resilience has to be somewhat different from the traditional measures of safety based on event counts (traditionally referring to something the system has; Hollnagel, 2009). In line with this perspective, the RAG is a question-based tool for assessing resilience potentials aimed at exploiting the system's performance in relation to the four cornerstones of resilience. The RAG is applied through four phases (Hollnagel, 2011):

- *Phase 1. Define and describe a system's structure, boundaries, time horizon, people, and resources.* This phase refers to restricting the application field to the relevant scope of the analysis.
- *Phase 2. Select the relevant questions for correspondent relevant items of the studied system.* Even though there are some standard questions available in standard RAG theory, at this phase it become necessary to adapt them for the context at hand to generate a manageable survey. Such adaption usually consists of an iterative procedure involving subject matter experts (i.e., people with working knowledge of the system).
- *Phase 3. Rate the questions for each cornerstones.* Once the survey is finalized, a pool of people working in the system should be identified as respondents. A preliminary training on the survey and on the nature of the questionnaire is generally advisable to create the proper context for a healthy, nonjudgmental reporting of the system's functioning.
- *Phase 4. Combine the ratings.* Once concluded the data-gathering process, it is generally recommended to present the information in a star plot, where each axis corresponds to the variable used to rate each cornerstone.

The RAG has been applied in several domains, customizing a series of standardized questions depending on the features of the domain itself. For example, it has been applied to rail traffic management (Rigaud & Martin, 2013), air traffic management (Pasquini, Ragosta, Herrera, & Vennesland, 2015; Patriarca, Di Gravio, & Costantino, 2016), and in healthcare settings (Darrow & Eseonu, 2017; Patriarca, Falegnami, Costantino, & Bilotta, 2018). The traditional RAG's star plot does not present a measure of resilience per se; it rather depicts how the resilience abilities of a system have been rated at a specific moment in time (its temporal dimension). The star plot is a snapshot of organizational resilience under specific conditions. Therefore, the RAG can be used to determine what is the initial resilience potential and then to explore the gap between the achieved status and the planned ideal conditions. Finally, it can be used to understand how the system may reach a target status in the future.

Figure 24.3 shows an example of RAG outcomes, combined into a star plot for research conducted in a neuroanesthesiology department (Patriarca, Di Gravio, Costantino, Falegnami, & Bilotta, 2018). The figure shows a distinction between the scores obtained by two classes of respondents, staff and resident neuroanesthetists. Example of questions that were rated on a five-point Likert scale (none, not much, enough, more than enough, completely) include "How frequently have you been involved in a project designed to improve perioperative patient management?" and "How much are you interested and informed about

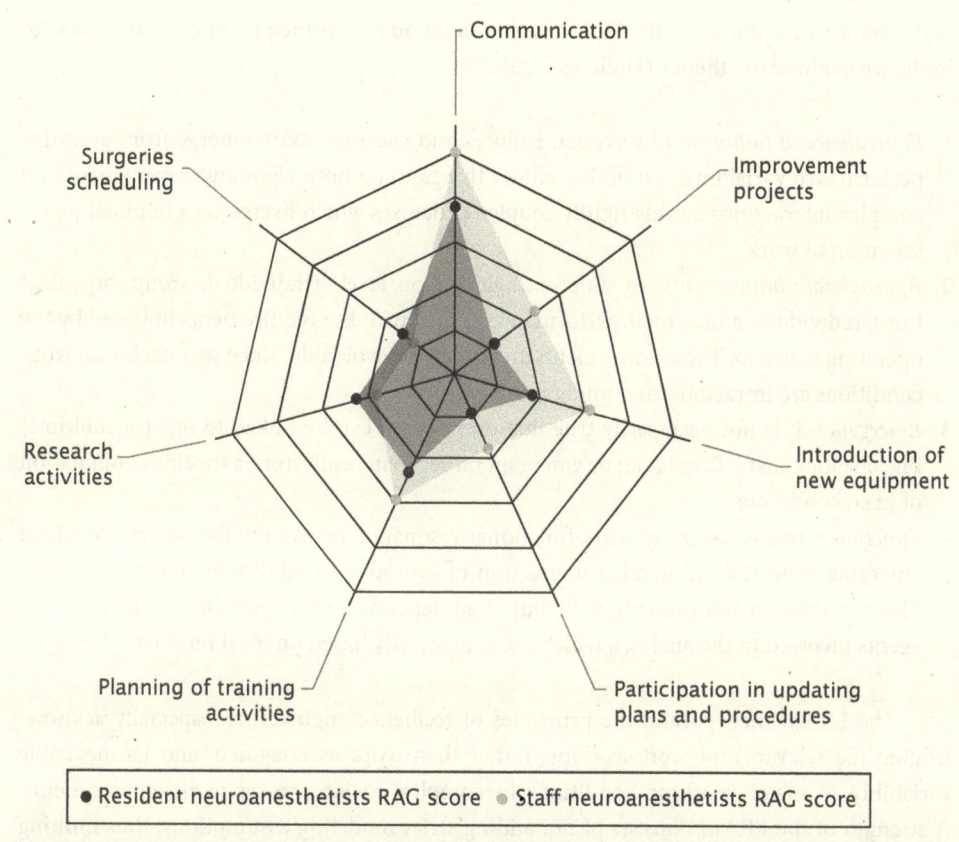

FIGURE 24.4 RAG outcomes with respect to seven questions related to the resilience ability "anticipating" of the system. The radar chat emphasizes different score for two groups of respondents: resident (black) versus staff (grey) neuroanesthesiologists.

research projects in your specific clinical setting?" When used in this way, the RAG provides a meaningful relative assessment, favoring discussions and comparison, to uncover hidden criticalities and motivate the need to acquire best practices among respondents. Exploring Figure 24.4, one can see that the RAG score is higher for resident neuroanesthetists than staff on a question related to involvement in research activities, confirming observations that the neuroanesthetists generally play a major role in trials and experimental projects but that staff do not perceive themselves as often in such functions of the department. This involvement, including an inherent continuous knowledge update on related research, is the cause for the difference. Such knowledge update is inherently considered capable of increasing a medical resident's potential to be resilient (i.e., to anticipate some possible perturbation in the provision of service).

Functional Resonance Analysis Method
The FRAM provides an approach to model complex sociotechnical systems using the concept of functional resonance, as a phenomenon arising from the variability of everyday

performance. Like the RAG, the FRAM is also based on four principles that are aligned with resilience engineering theory (Hollnagel, 2012b):

1. *Equivalence of failures and successes.* Failures and successes both emerge from everyday performance variability. Variability allows things to go both right and wrong, based on complex interactions among tightly coupled processes which overcome a bimodal representation of work.
2. *Approximate adjustments.* At different aggregation levels (individual, group, organization), individuals adjust their performance to deal with the requirements imposed by the operating scenario. These adjustments are usually unavoidable, since sociotechnical work conditions are intractable and underspecified.
3. *Emergence.* It is not necessarily true that every event can be linked to one (or multiple) linear static causes. Events can be emergent rather than result from a specific combination of fixed conditions.
4. *Functional resonance.* A system's functional resonance represents the detectable signal emerging from the unintended interaction of everyday variability for multiple signals. This variability is not random at all, but often depends on recognizable behaviors of the agents involved in the analysis, which act dynamically based on local rationality.

The FRAM incorporates the principles of resilience engineering, especially acknowledging the relevance of work-as-done, rather than work-as-imagined, and its inevitable variability to match working conditions in complex sociotechnical work environments. A strength of the FRAM consists of not adding strict modeling assumptions, thus limiting the bias of the representation. As acknowledged by Hollnagel (2012b), the FRAM is a *method sine model*, rather than a *model cum method*. Such observation implies that a detailed description of everyday system functioning is the necessary foundation for understanding a specific development of actions, actual or hypothetical, and modeling them.

The basic element of a FRAM model is a hexagon, which represents one function characterized by six different aspects (one for every corner; Hollnagel, Hounsgaard, & Colligan, 2014):

- *Input (I).* What starts the function.
- *Output (O).* What is the result of the function.
- *Precondition (P).* What must exist before a function can be carried out.
- *Resource (R).* What is necessary or consumed while the function is carried out.
- *Time (T).* The temporal constraints of relationships for the function.
- *Control (C).* What controls or monitors the function, with the potential for changing its outputs.

The FRAM has been adopted in a large set of sociotechnical system assessments, with a predominant initial focus in aviation. The first FRAM models referred to accident analyses for the study of systemic socio-technical inter-relatedness leading to plane crashes (De Carvalho, 2011; Sawaragi, Horiguchi, & Hina, 2006). Later, interest in using the FRAM model expanded to other work domains, such as industrial plants (Shirali, Ebrahipour, & Salahi, 2014), maritime operations (Praetorius, Hollnagel, & Dahlman, 2015), and healthcare settings (Sujan & Felici, 2012).

An example of a FRAM model used in a healthcare domain is included in Figure 24.4. To contrast FRAM with RAG, this case example also refers to a context where anesthetics are used, perioperative delivery. The model confirms the complexity of the work domain under analysis, in terms of a high number of links and functions. The FRAM is therefore helpful describing the nature of a work domain and supporting the identification of criticalities in the relationships between functions and processes.

The model in Figure 24.5 refers to the management of a perioperative patient's pathway for a neurosurgery and includes actions performed mainly by anesthetists. The figure highlights as hexagons some upstream and downstream connections of an exemplar function: for example, "Extubate patient" (the act conducted by an anesthetists to remove a tube from patient's airway). This latter generates one output that becomes a precondition for the function "Fill in postsurgery anesthesiology report" (the report can be filled in only after the extubation is completed), as well as other outputs connected to other downstream functions.

As Figure 24.5 shows, the FRAM model is intended to support analysis of how the variability in one function; for example, "Extubate the patient," can generate variability in related functions and how this variability propagates throughout the system, following a tight network of reinforcing or dampening relationships.

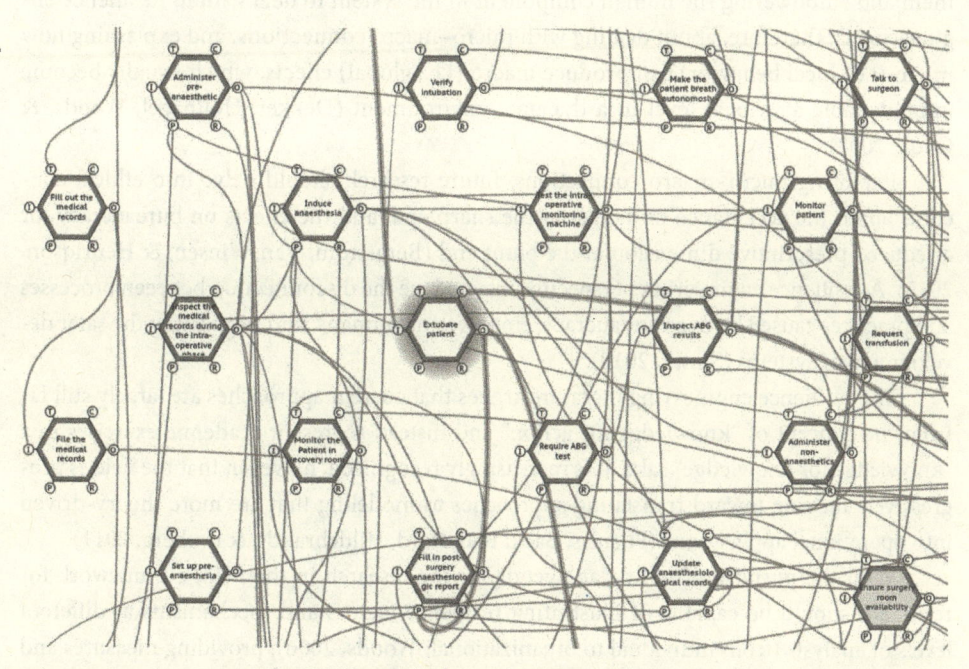

FIGURE 24.5 An excerpt of a FRAM model of a neurosurgery perioperative pathway. Hexagons and edges represent, respectively, functions and functional relationships among functions, following six different aspects (input, output, precondition, resource, control, time).

Therefore, a FRAM model remains consistent with the resilience engineering principles: it inherently supports the analyst to conduct back-and forth analyses, rather than a linear unidirectional focus (like traditional engineering mechanistic approaches). Once built, the FRAM model facilitates analysis that focuses on the couplings among functions rather than on the functions themselves. It thus remains possible to analyze multiple functions that may refer to different activities and multiple intertwined relationships but still maintain the coherence and consistency of a systemic perspective (Patriarca, Di Gravio, & Costantino, 2017).

With reference to both RAG and FRAM, and building on the evidence from research, one could argue that even if both models follow resilience principles, RAG may be more suitable for measuring resilience capabilities, or at least deviations in capabilities at an organizational level, while the FRAM may be a support tool for analyzing the details of a process, its deviance from ideal actions, and the potential source of resilience and brittleness.

Conclusion

Engineering resilience is about nonlinearity and dynamism; for example, understanding how an infinitesimally small change in initial conditions like an assumption in a software line of code can lead to huge consequences for a system as a whole (e.g., an involuntary release of energy that causes a spacecraft to crash; Leveson, 2002). Resilience provides a way of understanding variability and diversity, acknowledging the benefits arising from them and empowering the human component in the system to deal with it. Resilience engineering is, therefore, about dealing with micro–macro connections, and explaining how micro (i.e., local behavior) can produce macro (i.e., global) effects, which usually become unpredictable at a local level in a dynamic environment (Dekker, Hollnagel, Woods, & Cook, 2008).

Exploring micro–macro connections, future research should delve into ethical concerns about the acceptance of danger at the sharp end, and the effects on bureaucracy for a reduced prescriptive dimension at the blunt end (Bergström, Van Winsen, & Henriqson, 2015). A resilience engineering perspective may reduce the disconnection between processes and practices caused by overbureaucracy, empowering humans, and supporting the safer development of systems (Smith, 2018).

The resilience engineering literature argues that current approaches are largely still far from the concept of "knowledge for action" and instead represent academic exercises in a "knowledge for knowledge" sake. It is increasingly recognized, however, that the field is progressively moving toward translating approaches to modeling that are more theory-driven into operational applications (Furniss, Back, Blandford, Hildebrandt, & Broberg, 2011).

With the purpose of setting an agenda for the research in the field, a framework for resilience should be capable of illustrating resilience factors and mechanisms at different levels of analysis (from individual to organizational; Woods, 2006), providing measures and guidelines to improve the overall performance (not necessarily safety) within and across organizational domains (Patriarca, Bergström, Di Gravio, & Costantino, 2018). The framework should also be flexible enough to be used at different organizational levels, conjugating and coordinating operational and managerial resilience capabilities.

In terms of methods, it is worth noting that the traditional RAG theory can be enhanced by means of advanced analytic aspects aimed at defining more properly the relationships among the abilities, even considering the analytical effects of their interrelatedness. (Patriarca, Di Gravio, et al., 2018).

Traditionally, the FRAM is a pure qualitative method. Its qualitative nature, however, may become soon ineffective for large systems, which do not allow for manual analyses of couplings and interactions. In such contexts, researchers are investigating the possibility to combine the qualitative evaluation with a quantitative assessment through the use of simulation techniques (Patriarca, Falegnami, et al., 2018) and model verification tools (Zheng, Tian, & Zhao, 2016).

In terms of data gathering, for both FRAM and RAG, alternative ways for data gathering are needed, for example, by means of gamified techniques, which may in turn also increase the quality of the knowledge elicitation process.

In this regard, this chapter has shown the scientific progress made in the area of resilience engineering by means of a multidisciplinary perspective.

Key Messages

1. Modern sociotechnical systems are inherently complex and require innovative management approaches.
2. The discipline of resilience engineering is introduced for risk and safety management of complex sociotechnical systems.
3. The analysis of processes in terms of work-as-done is acknowledged of primary interest for sociotechnical safety management.
4. Two methods, the FRAM and the RAG, are discussed at a theoretical level and through two examples.

References

Amalberti, R. (2006). Optimum system safety and optimum system resilience: Agonistic or antagonistic concepts? In E. Hollnagel, D. D. Woods, & N. Leveson (Eds.), *Resilience engineering: Concepts and precepts* (pp. 253–272). Aldershot, UK: Ashgate.

Arthur, W. B. (1999). Complexity and the economy. *Science, 284*(5411), 107–109. doi:10.1126/science.284.5411.107

Azadeh, A., Salehi, V., Arvan, M., & Dolatkhah, M. (2014). Assessment of resilience engineering factors in high-risk environments by fuzzy cognitive maps: A petrochemical plant. *Safety Science, 68*, 99–107. doi:10.1016/j.ssci.2014.03.004

Bergström, J., Van Winsen, R., & Henriqson, E. (2015). On the rationale of resilience in the domain of safety: A literature review. *Reliability Engineering & System Safety, 141*, 131–141. doi:10.1016/j.ress.2015.03.008

Cilliers, P. (2010). Difference, identity and complexity. In P. Cilliers & R. Preiser (Eds.), *Complexity, difference and identity: An ethical perspective* (pp. 3–18). Dordrecht, The Netherlands: Springer. doi:10.1007/978-90-481-9187-1

Darrow, L., & Eseonu, C. I. (2017). Development of a resilience analysis grid survey tool for healthcare. In K. Coperich, H. B. Nembhard, & E. Cudney (Eds.), *Proceedings of the 2017 Industrial and Systems Engineering Conference* (pp. 1163–1168). Pittsburgh, PA: Institute of Industrial Engineers.

De Carvalho, P. V. R. (2011). The use of functional resonance analysis method (FRAM) in a mid-air collision to understand some characteristics of the air traffic management system resilience. *Reliability Engineering & System Safety*, 96(11), 1482–1498. doi:10.1016/j.ress.2011.05.009

Dekker, S. (2006). Resilience engineering: Chronicling the emergence of confused consensus. In E. Hollnagel, D. D. Woods, & N. Leveson (Eds.), *Resilience engineering: Concepts and precepts* (pp. 77–94). Aldershot, UK: Ashgate.

Dekker, S. (2011). *Drift into failure: From hunting broken components to understanding complex systems*. Aldershot, UK: Ashgate.

Dekker, S., Bergström, J., Amer-Wåhlin, I., & Cilliers, P. (2013). Complicated, complex, and compliant: Best practice in obstetrics. *Cognition, Technology and Work*, 15(2). doi:10.1007/s10111-011-0211-6

Dekker, S., Hollnagel, E., Woods, D., & Cook, R. (2008). *Resilience engineering: New directions for measuring and maintaining safety in complex systems*. Lund, Sweden: Lund University School of Aviation.

Furniss, D., Back, J., Blandford, A., Hildebrandt, M., & Broberg, H. (2011). A resilience markers framework for small teams. *Reliability Engineering & System Safety*, 96(1), 2–10. doi:10.1016/j.ress.2010.06.025

Goldratt, E. M. (2008). *The choice*. Great Barrington, MA: North River Press.

Hale, A. R., Heming, B. H. J., Carthey, J., & Kirwan, B. (1997). Modelling of safety management systems. *Safety Science*, 26(1–2), 121–140. doi:10.1016/S0925-7535(97)00034-9

Hansson, S. O. (2013). Defining pseudoscience and science. In M. Pagliucci & M. Boundry (Eds.), *Philosophy of pseudoscience: Reconsidering the demarcation problem* (pp. 61–78). Chicago, IL: University of Chicago Press.

Herrera, I. A., Hollnagel, E., & Håbrekke, S. (2010, June). *Proposing safety performance indicators for helicopter offshore on the Norwegian Continental Shelf*. Paper presented at the 10th International Conference on Probabilistic Safety Assessment and Management 2010, Seattle, WA. Retrieved from https://pdfs.semanticscholar.org/3324/c1b89745c0ee1388c2c447f9f77fac4b67b0.pdf

Hettinger, L. J., Kirlik, A., Goh, Y. M., & Buckle, P. (2012). Modeling and simulation of complex sociotechnical systems: Envisioning and analyzing work environments. *Ergonomics*, 58(4), 1–42. doi:10.1080/00140139.2015.1008586

Heylighen, F., Cilliers, P., & Gershenson, C. (2007). Complexity and philosophy. In J. Bogg & R. Geyer (Eds.), *Complexity, science and society* (pp. 117–134). Oxford, UK: Radcliffe.

Hollnagel, E. (2006). Resilience: The challenge of the unstable. In E. Hollnagel, D. D Woods, & N. Leveson (Eds.), *Resilience engineering: Concepts and precepts* (pp. 9–17). Aldersho, UK: Ashgate.

Hollnagel, E. (2009). The four cornerstones of resilience engineering. In C. P. Nemeth, E. Hollnagel, & S. Dekker (Eds.), *Resilience engineering perspectives. Volume 2: Preparation and restoration* (pp. 117–134). Aldershot, UK: Ashgate.

Hollnagel, E. (2011). Epilogue: RAG—Resilience analysis grid. In E. Hollnagel, J. Pariès, D. D. Woods, & J. Wreathall (Eds.), *Resilience engineering in practice: A guidebook* (pp. 275–296). Aldershot, UK: Ashgate.

Hollnagel, E. (2012a). Coping with complexity: Past, present and future. *Cognition, Technology and Work*, 14(3), 199–205. doi:10.1007/s10111-011-0202-7

Hollnagel, E. (2012b). *FRAM: The functional resonance analysis method—Modelling complex socio-technical systems*. Aldershot, UK: Ashgate.

Hollnagel, E. (2018). *Safety-II in practice—Developing the resilience potentials*. New York, NY: Routledge.

Hollnagel, E., Hounsgaard, J., & Colligan, L. (2014). *FRAM—The functional resonance analysis method: A handbook for the practical use of the method*. Centre for Quality, Southern Region of Denmark.

Hollnagel, E., Woods, D. D., & Leveson, N. (2006). *Resilience engineering: Concepts and precepts*. Aldershot, UK: Ashgate.

Huber, G. J., Gomes, J. O., & De Carvalho, P. V. R. (2012). A program to support the construction and evaluation of resilience indicators. *Work*, 41(Suppl. 1), 2810–2816. doi:10.3233/WOR-2012-0528-2810

Johansson, J., & Hassel, H. (2010). An approach for modelling interdependent infrastructures in the context of vulnerability analysis. *Reliability Engineering & System Safety*, 95(12), 1335–1344. doi:10.1016/j.ress.2010.06.010

Leveson, N. G. (2002). *System safety engineering: Back to the future.* Boston, MA: Massachusetts Institute of Technology.

Lundberg, J., Rollenhagen, C., & Hollnagel, E. (2009). What-you-look-for-is-what-you-find: The consequences of underlying accident models in eight accident investigation manuals. *Safety Science, 47*(10), 1297–1311. doi:10.1016/j.ssci.2009.01.004

Manson, S. M. (2001). Simplifying complexity: A review of complexity theory. *Geoforum, 32*, 405–414. doi:10.1016/S0016-7185(00)00035-X

Morel, G., Amalberti, R., & Chauvin, C. (2009). How good micro/macro ergonomics may improve resilience, but not necessarily safety. *Safety Science, 47*(2), 285–294. doi:10.1016/j.ssci.2008.03.002

Morin, E. (2006). Restricted complexity, general complexity. In C. Gershenson, D. Aerts, & B. Edmonds (Eds.), *Worldviews, science and us* (pp. 5–29). Toh Tuck Link, Singapore: World Scientific. doi:10.1142/9789812707420_0002

Nemeth, C., Wears, R., Woods, D., Hollnagel, E., & Cook, R. (2008). Minding the gaps: Creating resilience in health care. In K. Henriksen, J. B. Battles, M. A. Keyes, & M. L. Grady (Eds.), *Advances in patient safety: New directions and alternative approaches* (pp. 1–13). Rockville, MD: Agency for Healthcare Research and Quality.

Ouedraogo, K. A., Enjalbert, S., & Vanderhaegen, F. (2013). How to learn from the resilience of human-machine systems. *Engineering Applications of Artificial Intelligence, 26*(1), 24–34. doi:10.1016/j.engappai.2012.03.007

Pasquini, A., Ragosta, M., Herrera, I. A., & Vennesland, A. (2015). Towards a measure of resilience. In *Proceedings of ATACCS 2015—5th International Conference on Application and Theory of Automation in Command and Control Systems* (pp. 121–128). Deep Blue Piazza Buenos Aires 20, Rome, Italy. doi:10.1145/2899361.2899374

Patriarca, R., Bergström, J., Di Gravio, G., & Costantino, F. (2018). Resilience engineering: Current status of the research and future challenges. *Safety Science, 102*, 79–100. doi:10.1016/j.ssci.2017.10.005

Patriarca, R., Di Gravio, G., & Costantino, F. (2016). Resilience engineering to assess risks for the air traffic management system: A new systemic method. *International Journal of Reliability and Safety, 10*(4), 323–345. doi:10.1504/IJRS.2016.10005344

Patriarca, R., Di Gravio, G., & Costantino, F. (2017). A Monte Carlo evolution of the functional resonance analysis method (FRAM) to assess performance variability in complex systems. *Safety Science, 91*, 49–60. doi:10.1016/j.ssci.2016.07.016

Patriarca, R., Di Gravio, G., Costantino, F., Falegnami, A., & Bilotta, F. (2018). An analytic framework to assess organizational resilience. *Safety and Health at Work, 9*(3), 265–276. doi:10.1016/j.shaw.2017.10.005

Patriarca, R., Falegnami, A., Costantino, F., & Bilotta, F. (2018). Resilience engineering for socio-technical risk analysis: Application in neuro-surgery. *Reliability Engineering & System Safety, 180*, 321–335. doi:10.1016/j.ress.2018.08.001

Pavard, B., & Dugdale, J. (2006). The contribution of complexity theory to the study of socio-technical cooperative systems. In A. A. Mina & A. M. Y. Bar-Yam (Eds.), *Unifying theories in complex systems* (Volume IIIB, pp. 39–48). Berlin, Germany: Springer.

Perrow, C. (1984). *Normal accidents: Living with high risk technologies.* New York, NY: Basic Books.

Praetorius, G., Hollnagel, E., & Dahlman, J. (2015). Modelling vessel traffic service to understand resilience in everyday operations. *Reliability Engineering & System Safety, 141*, 10–21. doi:10.1016/j.ress.2015.03.020.

Rasmussen, J. (1979). *On the structure of knowledge: A morphology of mental models in a man-machine system context.* Roskilde, Denmark: Research Establishment Risoe.

Rasmussen, J. (1997). Risk management in a dynamic society: A modelling problem. *Safety Science, 27*(2–3), 183–213. doi:10.1016/S0925-7535(97)00052-0

Rigaud, E., & Martin, C. (2013). Considering trade-offs when assessing resilience. In I. Herrera, J. M. Schraaden, J. van der Vorm, & D. Woods (Eds.), *Resilience Engineering Association: 4th international symposium* (pp. 115–120). Soesterberg, The Netherlands: Resilence Engineering Association.

Rosa, E. A. (1998). Metatheoretical foundations for post-normal risk. *Journal of Risk Research, 1*(1), 15–44. doi:10.1080/136698798377303

Salzano, E., Di Nardo, M., Gallo, M., Oropallo, E., & Santillo, L. C. (2014). The application of system dynamics to industrial plants in the perspective of process resilience engineering. *Chemical Engineering Transactions, 36*, 457–462. doi:10.3303/CET1436077

Sawaragi, T., Horiguchi, Y., & Hina, A. (2006). Safety analysis of systemic accidents triggered by performance deviation. In *2006 SICE-ICASE International Joint Conference* (pp. 1778–1781). IEEE Xplore. doi:10.1109/SICE.2006.315635

Shirali, G. A., Ebrahipour, V., & Salahi, L. M. (2014). Proactive risk assessment to identify emergent risks using functional resonance analysis method (FRAM): A case study in an oil process unit. *Iran Occupational Health, 10*(6), 33–46.

Smith, G. (2018). *Paper safe: The triumph of bureaucracy in safety management.* Independently published.

Sujan, M., & Felici, M. (2012). Combining failure mode and functional resonance analyses in healthcare settings. *Lecture Notes in Computer Science (Including Subseries Lecture Notes in Artificial Intelligence and Lecture Notes in Bioinformatics), 7612 LNCS*, 364–375. doi:10.1007/978-3-642-33678-2_31

Woods, D. D. (1988). Coping with complexity: The psychology of human behaviour in complex systems. In L. P. Goodstein, H. B. Andersen, & S. E. Olsen (Eds.), *Task, errors and mental models* (pp. 128–148). Bristol, PA: Taylor & Francis.

Woods, D. D. (2006). Engineering organizational resilience to enhance safety: A progress report on the emerging field of resilience engineering. In *Proceedings of the Human Factors and Ergonomics Society Annual Meeting* (Vol. 50, pp. 2237–2241). doi:10.1177/154193120605001910

Woods, D. D. (2015). Four concepts for resilience and the implications for the future of resilience engineering. *Reliability Engineering & System Safety, 141*, 5–9. doi:10.1016/j.ress.2015.03.018

Wrigstad, J., Bergström, J., & Gustafson, P. (2017). One event, three investigations: The reproduction of a safety norm. *Safety Science, 96*, 75–83. doi:10.1016/j.ssci.2017.03.009

Yang, Q., Tian, J., & Zhao, T. (2017). Safety is an emergent property: Illustrating functional resonance in air traffic management with formal verification. *Safety Science, 93*, 162–177. doi:10.1016/j.ssci.2016.12.006

Zheng, Z., Tian, J., & Zhao, T. (2016). Refining operation guidelines with model-checking-aided FRAM to improve manufacturing processes: A case study for aeroengine blade forging. *Cognition, Technology and Work, 18*(4), 777–791. doi:10.1007/s10111-016-0391-1

25

Transformative Social Innovation and Multisystemic Resilience

Three Case Studies

Katharine McGowan and Francis Westley

Introduction

When an early (and hypothetical) 17th-century chambermaid working in Amsterdam used her life savings to purchase a share in a sea-going venture, she likely did not think about the wider system shifts that had to happen for this opportunity to emerge, or how her actions (and those of her fellow Dutch [wom]en) would trigger their own cascade of system shifts. Whatever her hopes for her investment (which was likely huge to her but was very small compared with others), she was probably not thinking about economic experimentation in England, governance and taxation crises in Spain, and theological debates across Europe—as well as the long-standing and limiting parameters of the tightly coupled Dutch agricultural economy and sociopolitical system—all of which made her investment possible. It was perhaps slightly more likely that she gave thought to a future world—one where her investment paid dividends—and where people like her had access to markets, allowing them to improve their social, economic, and even political condition. This would be a world transformed from medieval communalism and the divine rights of kings to individual capitalist democracies: A completely different set of systems arrangements, relationships, myths/sense-making and outcomes (McGowan, 2017a).

The case of the Dutch East India Company's rapid scaling of the joint stock company model is not commonly discussed in the context of social innovation, but it illustrates the importance of systems thinking and multisystem resilience in understanding how the world has changed, and how we can continue to experiment with social innovation to address social, economic, and environmental changes as they occur. This ongoing dynamic of experimentation and reflection is a critical dynamic of social innovation as we understand it. For us, social innovation encapsulates new programs, policies, processes, products, and designs that fundamentally shift authority and resource flows, which over time make systems more resilient and inclusive (Westley et al., 2011). To engage in social innovation is therefore to work toward greater systems resilience.

This chapter is a reflection on two decades of work on social innovation and resilience, focused on the output of the Waterloo Institute for Social Innovation and Resilience. However, unlike many such survey chapters, we are overlapping two generations of scholarship to consider how one generation (Westley) can define the key questions that the other (McGowan) explores. Rather than summative, this chapter is a snapshot of interwoven and interrelated research agendas, brought together by a common space and shared interest in what social innovation *is*, *has been*, and *can be*, and how social innovation contributes to (and even undermines) resilience.

This chapter will discuss some of the key conclusions we have reached related to multisystem resilience, with particular focus on how studying the drivers, processes, agency, and outcomes of social innovation have informed how we understand resilience as both a goal and an analytical framework. In this discussion we rely on several cases we have observed in real time, as well as several historical examples. We will focus here on the cases of the internet, the national parks in the United States, and the intelligence test.

Social Innovation and Resilience: A Linked Approach

To contextualize our approach to both social innovation and multisystem resilience, it is necessary to frame our specific use of both concepts and to link that frame to their respective intellectual traditions. Social innovation has been framed as broadly as innovations that are social "in both their ends and means" (European Commission, 2013, p. 9) to the significantly more organizationally and operationally specific: "Social innovation refers to innovative activities and services that are motivated by the goal of meeting a social need and that are predominantly diffused through organizations whose primary purposes are social" (Mulgan, 2006, p. 146). This breadth has inspired a small but interesting strain of scholarship that explores the origin of social innovation as an analytical term and its relatively persistent fuzziness. Ayob, Teasdale, and Fagan (2016) and Edwards-Schachter and Wallace (2017) found that the concept had a robust history in scholarship through at least the latter half of the 20th century, with a relatively high level of mutual comprehensibility if not explicitly shared definitions, and Godin (2012) argues convincingly that it can be traced to the late 19th century and the interest in social processes and social change.

However, and important in the conversation about definitions, Pol and Ville (2009) charge that social innovation may be dismissed as a normative buzz term in both the popular and academic literature. Ergo it is important to explicitly define what we mean by social innovation, as a product, process, program, policy, or design that seeks to fundamentally shift resource and authority flows and tip a system into greater resilience, inclusion and sustainability (Westley, Zimmerman, & Patton, 2006; Westley et al., 2011). This definition allows us to be relatively agnostic (the previous list is quite broad and covers many possible forms), while acknowledging both the aspirations, processes, and outcomes in which social innovators may engage over time—and time emerges as a key dynamic if the analyst seeks to measure disruption. Similarly, the use of the term allows for the inclusion of social innovations that fail—fail to scale, fail to disrupt, or fail to contribute to greater resilience, inclusion, or sustainability.

Our definition of social innovation explicitly references resilience, which is based for us on the social-ecological systems approach of the adaptive cycle, a concept that first arose in ecology (Holling, 1973) to model the dynamic resilience of an ecosystem. Holling and Gunderson (2002) elaborated the resilience dynamic by the introduction of the concept of panarchy. Adaptive cycles build resilience at all scales in an ecological system, but the transformation or continuity of the whole is linked to cross-scale dynamics. These dynamics can result in "revolt," where small fast changes cascade up to change higher scales or change at lower scales may be repressed by "snap back" or remembrance, originating at higher scales. The adaptive cycle as a model stood in sharp contrast to previous conceptualizations of static equilibrium and identified four general phases: release, reorganization, exploitation, and conservation (Holling & Gunderson, 2002). Classically mapped over a forest fire, when the forest burns, resources are released and biodiversity is low (release); as new life grows, these newly freed resources are widely distributed (reorganization); competition shrinks some of this biodiversity as some organisms beat out others and accumulate biomass (reorganization); and eventually, matures as a new forest (conservation).

The adapted cycle can be illustrative in both mapping the social innovation process and the systems in which they emerge and seek to disrupt: in release comes "the collapse of rigid, powerful rule and institutions . . . [which] may also involve new interactions and is the most likely site for create (re)combinations of ideas" (Moore, Westley, Tjornbo, & Holroyd, 2011, pp. 92–93). This is followed by reorganization which is about sense-making and coalition-building around key ideas that are forming into innovations, and in exploitation groups that leverage resources to scale, which when successful represents the conservation phase (Antadze & Westley, 2010; Moore et al., 2011). Within this heuristic is the interplay between innovation and system—social, social-political, and economic systems need to be "adaptable, flexible, and able to learn" to be resilient, or risk rigidity and vulnerability to external shock (Moore et al., 2011, pp. 91).

While the internet for instance is not a social-ecological system in a traditional sense, and we do not simply map it across the adaptive cycle; we map it across scales, using the panarchy heuristic to focus on the process of transformative innovation. Rather than treating innovation as a novel idea alone, we have studied the dynamics and process of transformation, including the importance of combination and recombination. We have used the panarchy cycle, specifically its focus on constants and change within a system, mixtures of old and new elements, and risks of rigidity and traps (Holling & Gunderson, 2002) to structure our analysis of how social innovation can disrupt a set of arrangements and possibly transform a system or multiple systems (Westley et al., 2006).

This process of bricolage (Westley, McGowan, Antadze, Blacklock, & Tjornbo, 2017)—both of the old and the new and of different systems—is critical if we wish to build "innovative solutions that take into account the complexity of the problems and then foster solutions that permit our systems to learn, adapt, and occasionally transform without collapsing" and "build the capacity to find such solutions over and over again" (Westley, 2013, p. 29). To understand the relationship between social innovation and resilience is to understand how transformative social innovation, through a necessary process of engaging across scales, includes social, economic, political, and ecological systems. The divide between these systems, from a resilience perspective, is and will continue to be artificial (Berkes & Folke, 1998; Biggs, Schlüter, & Schoon, 2015). Indeed, attempts at segmentation may be self-defeating, as "focusing primarily on wealth and inequality or social resilience while remaining ignorant about and disconnected from the biosphere and its stewardship is not a recipe for long-term sustainability for people on Earth" (Folke, Biggs, Norström, Reyers, & Rockström, 2016, p. 41).

As such, the basis of our work has been to bring together social innovation and resilience approaches, as observers have framed Waterloo Institute for Social Innovation and Resilience's approach as "focused squarely on the role of social innovation in transforming intractable problem domains and on institutional or systems change" (Olsson, Moore, Westley, & McCarthy, 2017, p. 31). While we are not alone in connecting social innovation to resilience theory (see also Howaldt & Schwartz, 2010), and we build upon a line of argument that dates to at least the 1970s, which emphasizes the importance of addressing "unmet social needs encompassing the long history of narratives about our survival (the current 'grand challenges') and the construction of a more sustainable world" (Edwards-Schachter & Wallace, 2017, p. 73). Our focus has expanded beyond unmet social needs to include a wider range of explorations of the adjacent possible, including the discovery/description of new social facts (Arthur, 2009).

The development of the internet is an example of a disruptive technology that has led to the discovery of these new social facts. The initial technical idea that gave birth to the internet, packet-switching, was devised by Paul Baran when he sought to create a survivable network. While important for the resilience of the information network more generally, this design also challenged wider telecommunications regimes' centralized architectures and monopolies (as in the United Kingdom). While the Royal Mail chose to maintain its centralized system, the U.S. Advanced Research Projects Agency (ARPA) created its own packet-switching–based network, ARPANET, in 1967. It is through ARPANET that the U.S. military worked directly with university researchers committed to open architecture in their designs over several decades (Tjornbo, 2017).

This focus on openness appeared multiple times during the development of early networks like ARPANET and throughout the creation of the modern internet. It was often the deciding factor in any given skirmish over access and design. For example, in 1984 the American Telephone and Telegraph Company began charging for the use of its programming language Unix, inciting a popular revolt among the hundreds of thousands who used it and the eventual release of software like the General Public License. Similarly, Tim

Berners-Lee made his World Wide Web system available for free and encouraged existing hypertext communities to use it. Lastly, since browsers compatible with World Wide Web were user-friendly compared to the alternatives, they became ubiquitous, creating a latticework for a massive public platform that has supported a cascade of experimentation and disruptive innovations across multiple domains, scales, and, ultimately, whole systems (Tjornbo, 2017).

The internet's disruptions are still ongoing and unfolding, from its challenge to traditional media, to new distributed sources of economic activity, to the serious and growing challenges to democratic institutions and healthy social interaction; these disruptions are collectively products of those initial starting questions: How do we design a network that does not rely on one node, and how can we support the creation of a free, uninhibited flow of information? From the point of view of the internet's creators, both of these concerns were focused on building resilience in specific conditions and from certain perspectives. Yet the end result may or may not have increased resilience from a wider multisystemic perspective (general resilience). A globally linked social system and increasingly tightly coupled economic and governance systems could potentially make these adjacent systems brittle and vulnerable to collapse, even while the communication system itself remains resilient to shocks (Walker & Westley, 2011).

Resilience and Transformation

Taking a systems perspective and acknowledging the complexity of any question or problem is critical to the process of social innovation and transformation. This is both an analytical observation and a deeply held belief we share with many researchers studying resilience in the Anthropocene—our era of human influence (Stone-Jovicich, Goldstein, Brown, Plummer, & Olsson, 2018), To fail to appreciate the complexities of the social systems involved in any wider multisystemic analysis is a risk done at the peril of the analyst and actor alike (Fabinyi, Evans, & Foals, 2014).

Important in our perspective is the shift from a focus on social entrepreneurs to systems entrepreneurs (Antadze & McGowan, 2017; Westley, 2013), specifically the role of brokers who can link ideas to resources, build or enhance networks, and identify when windows of opportunity will open and how to navigate through them. Consider the case of John Muir, Sierra Club founder and passionate advocate for conservation and the American National Parks at the end of the 19th and beginning of the 20th centuries. Muir did not create the idea of a park, nor was he their first advocate, but he correctly identified the importance of building popular support for conservation, reducing the barriers for new legislation, as well as courting key actors who could create new parks through federal legislation (Antadze, 2017). He connected those with key capacities to act with the spaces and places he sought to protect. Beyond building this elite network, Muir wrote prolifically in the popular press to build the case for parks. Muir made a deliberate effort to reorient the American mindset away from expansion and cultivation/economic development toward conservation.

Muir acted as a system entrepreneur, linking ideas with those capable of realizing them, and helping open/keep open a window of opportunity to create those parks by building popular support around conservation. This learning from system structure can be categorized as systems reflectivity, which has been described as including looking for windows of opportunity to introduce and scale ideas (Moore et al., 2018). Muir, for instance, correctly identified the emergence of a key systems ally in Theodore Roosevelt, who became president of the United States after the assassination of his predecessor, William McKinley. Roosevelt was both a passionate outdoorsman (who sought psychological refuge in ranch work after the death of his first wife) and a reformer (who introduced the Square Deal and sought to break up the Gilded Age's business monopolies).

Roosevelt was energetic and entrepreneurial; Muir saw Roosevelt's personal attributes and outlooks as a potential window of opportunity and took the president on a camping trip in Yosemite National Park in 1903 to demonstrate the potential beauty of the many new parks he wanted to create. Roosevelt used his powers through the newly passed (1906) National Monuments Act to create five such parks in the last two years of his administration (and nine total from 1903 to 1916), compared with the one-time creation of Yosemite and Yellowstone parks decades earlier. Importantly, the creation of a Parks Service, with the bureaucratic structure and permanence of government legislation, required significant bottom-up and top-down work by Muir and others. While Congress created Yosemite in 1864 and Yellowstone in 1871, the idea was stuck in a relative poverty trap with too few social, political, and economic resources and social networks to move the idea out of these niches. It wasn't until the end of the 19th and beginning of the 20th century that key systems shifted their focus and created the substantial transformative momentum needed to dramatically increase the number of national parks.

Before and after he met with Roosevelt in 1903, Muir wrote hundreds of articles aimed at a popular audience. His proposal was that rather than viewing the wilderness as an untapped economic good to be exploited, it should be viewed as a critical social, patriotic, and moral good and as such should be left undisturbed (Antadze & McGowan, 2017). His viewpoint had appeal and as the growing railroads made travel easier and the genocidal violence of the American state against American Indian tribal nations in the West ended (resulting in the forced isolation and impoverishment of these peoples), tourism began in earnest. As more people came to nature, they created formal organizations such as the Appalachian Mountain Club and Sierra Club, who then in turn engaged in both sense-making around the value of conservation and advocated for more parks and conservation generally.

Similar to Muir, businessman-turned-conservationist Stephen Mather sought to build networks among the powerful to advocate for more parks: in Mather's case businessmen and politicians. In 1915, he paid for a carefully selected group, whom he felt were open to his ideas (specifically a new park at Giant Forest and broadly a more structured and robust park system) and capable of acting to achieve his aims, to travel on a lavish train trip to the northern Sierra Nevada. He even convinced *National Geographic* magazine to devote their April 1916 issue to the national parks. Ultimately, he succeeded on both counts. Congress purchased the land for Giant Forest and created the National Parks Service in 1916, with Mather as the first director. As this case makes clear, transformative social innovation requires agency that is multiphase and multirole (Westley et al., 2013).

The parks system has been correctly criticized for erasing Indigenous peoples from the landscape and their voices from American history in favor of a romantic, unscientific, and ahistorical concept of pristine nature. Exporting this perspective of nature abroad has exacerbated racial and class conflicts in a modern enclosure movement. Yet this is a reminder of the importance of how innovations are conceived, how tensions are rarely resolved, and how yesterday's transformative innovations that may have increased the resilience of one system (natural environments in a quickly industrializing America) can create new problems. The systems reflexivity Muir and others displayed is remarkable. It helped to muscle a new regime that linked ecological conservation, American political systems and national identity with tourism and specific conceptions of history, shifting each system in turn. When filmmaker Ken Burns described the parks and parks system as "America's Best Idea" (as quoted in Antadze, 2017, p. 18), he highlighted these systems entrepreneurs' success in convincing future generations this was a shared project, something natural, normal, and preferable to an absence of parks. It cannot, however, be denied that this transformative social innovation, and the resilience of ecological systems that it contributed to, also had its shadow.

Social Innovation, Resilience, and the Shadow—Emerging Realizations

The need to think systemically in social innovation is not a minor caution; the very success that appears to build resilience in one system can lead to significant devastation across multiple interrelated systems. Tunnel vision or single-minded focus on our preferred solution can lead us to solutions that pose more and even greater problems (e.g., the commitment to replacing fossil fuels with biofuels has imperiled food security [Westley, 2013] and failed to address our economic reliance on greenhouse gas–producing energy consumption and dispersed urban development). Some of this may be attributable to the difference between specific and general resilience (Walker & Westley, 2011), so that projects and processes aimed at maintaining the forms, relationships and/or outcomes within one subsystem fail to take into account the impact of change in that subsystem on the resilience of co-occurring systems as a whole (Carpenter et al., 2015; Holling et al., 1998) and on the adjacent but linked subsystems.

This is the shadow side of social innovation, ideas that take hold and scale, but ultimately bring more harm to those systems they seek to help. Multisystemic resilience is not so much a moving target as an evolving one: as preferences change, information evolves, old asymmetries disappear, and new ones emerge. What was once a logical and generally acceptable response to a commonly conceived issue may later seem ill-formed, ill-conceived, or possibly a horrid example of social engineering either in the initial diagnosis of a problem, the solution, or some combination of both (McGowan & Westley, 2015). What previously seemed like a problem requiring a swift and surefooted response may fade in importance or, on second consideration, not qualify as a "problem" at all. This, in turn, triggers the need to respond to the initial intervention.

One case that encapsulates some of the risks embedded in social innovation conversations is that of the intelligence test. Beginning in the last quarter of the 19th century, with a specific act of bricolage between the theory of evolution and a moral veil on socioeconomic hierarchy (that the Industrial Revolution–driven multitiered social hierarchy was morally right, representing not just economic circumstances but the moral value of those in the middle class especially, and the descending moral value of those who find themselves below the middle class), the concept of social Darwinism was born (McGowan, 2017b).

The urban poverty and social issues similarly associated with the Industrial Revolution combined with the perspectives of social Darwinism to create moral panic over feeblemindedness—that there were a large number of people at the bottom on the social and economic ladders not because of economic conditions or other social factors but because these people were cognitively and morally inferior—and because of this, they would both commit crimes and have many children, who would inherit this terrible genetic legacy that would doom them to repeating this same cycle.

Contemporaneously, the emerging field of psychology was exploring intellectual capacity: what is it, can it be measured, and is it a fixed trait of the individual? These were critical questions that experimental psychologist Charles Spearman felt were a necessary part of the greater effort to leverage experiments: "Most of [the results] are like hieroglyphics awaiting their deciphering Rosetta stone" (Spearman, 1904, p. 204). The emergence of the dominant term *intelligence quotient*, over other theories such as the much more elusive and suggestively named *g*, necessitated some form of measurement. Multiple models and methods were designed, including one by Alfred Binet who designed a test for school children to determine general categories of intelligence (Binet published his method with his student Theodore Simon in 1905).

Those worried about the risks of the feebleminded could thus look to the emerging field of experimental psychology, as Binet and Simon sought to apply their test to facilitate the instruction of "defective children" (Binet & Simon, 1916). Similarly, those working with those deemed feebleminded enough to merit institutionalization desperately wanted a seemingly objective test for their patients (evidence strongly suggests that they sought to diagnose many different conditions with one test, hence their perpetual frustration). These individuals included Henry Herbert Goddard of the Vineland Research Laboratory, who discovered the Binet–Simon test in 1906 and became one of a series of psychologist advocates for the test in the United States. It also fell in the hands of those engaged in engineering other social phenomena, including immigration and race relations, always in the service of white supremacy (one anti-immigration crusader who administered the test *exclusively in English* to newly arrived immigrants at Ellis Island in 1913 declared them all feebleminded).

As with so many historical social innovations that came to prominence in the United States, a massive external shock across multiple scales—in this case, the United Sates joining the Allied Forces in the First World War—catalyzed the emerging innovation. The American government needed to build a large professional army to join a war already very much in progress and sought out new, hopefully more accurate (and certainly more rapid) means of identifying possible officers than relying on a small pool of already trained upper-class individuals. The relatively young (founded in 1892) American Psychological Association, which had a subgroup committed to the advancement of the intelligence test, saw this window of opportunity. In a matter of weeks they had a copy of the test and evidence from a nearby ally—Canada—of the need for effective officers on the U.S. Surgeon General's desk.

While ultimately there was little evidence the test actually helped identify potential officers more *effectively* than other methods, it definitely did so more *efficiently*. With relatively little training one officer could administer dozens of tests at a time (and 1.5 million over the course of America's war). In the aftermath, *The Lancet* declared the test's application had given "clear indications of their future value in the work of human selection and vocational training" ("Intelligence Test," 1919, p. 539). The test was integrated into schools more rapidly than before the war. Unfortunately, but not unexpectedly, the test reinforced racist perceptions of children's capacity.

Even worse, the test provided a seemingly scientific basis for forced sterilization of those it deemed feebleminded. This was a legal-medical boon for the eugenics movement in the United States and Canada, veiling their views under the guise that this was for the best of the individual who wouldn't be burdened with children and who would receive the appropriate care and support. Meanwhile, society would be spared the curse of the feebleminded. The horrors of the Second World War began to push these same countries away from scientific racism and toward a more meritocratic approach to education and testing. This change, however, is far from complete, given the persistence of such views on the internet and, depressingly, by men like James D. Watson, co-describer of the double helix model of DNA and a proponent of scientific racism.

We should not wrap ourselves in the comfort of our own enlightenment and relegate the lessons of these failures to the dustbin of history: the psychologists of the previous centuries who advocated for the intelligence test and forced sterilization felt equally confident of the scientific foundation for their actions. In many ways, they believed their efforts would make their society more resilient, better able to cope with a rapidly changing world. Yet in this certainty they misunderstood the complexity of both poverty and cognition, and certainly imposed the far too simple solution of sterilization (McGowan & Westley, 2015). In addition, those who supported the idea of intelligence tests as enlightened and efficient processes to improve and customize training and education failed to explore the shadow side of these assumptions: that once separated from empathy, this orientation toward empiricism was used to justify inhuman cruelty and oppression. In a very real sense, efforts to make one or more systems resilient through social innovation can have disastrous, even genocidal, consequences for other systems.

Emerging Principles of Social Innovation and Multisystemic Resilience

Based on our historical case examples of the Internet, the U.S. Parks Services, and the intelligence test, five principles emerge that should guide the continued study of social innovation and resilience:

1. Social innovation and resilience are linked, but the relationship is contextual and complex. Social innovations can both trigger shifts toward greater resilience within one system or across systems, but they can also undermine the resilience of adjacent systems, making the whole more vulnerable and brittle.

2. Social innovation is a paradox of process and context. To bring an idea to fruition, it involves a process of constant imaging, exploring strange attractors and combining/bricolage as one seeks a path to the hypothesized adjacent possibles. However, rarely does an idea entirely escape its prophetic context, initial assumptions, or perceptions. This consistency not only makes the innovation itself more resilient but can also result in unanticipated consequences as the context in which the innovation is enacted evolves.
3. Transformative social innovations are rarely pursued by those for whom the status quo satisfies their needs. The scholar in search of possible transformations needs to look beyond the shining hubs of excellence in the current order to see where disruption in social systems will emerge. It is often at the fringes, where deeper questions about alternatives and adjacent possibles take root. To have influence on mainstream institutions (an important and definitional stage of transformative social innovation) requires active and sustained agency on the part of all actors that are involved and the capacity to see the potential for new patterns of behavior to emerge when systems are linked.
4. Transformation takes time, but windows of opportunity can open and close quickly: transformative social innovation requires thinking about different systems at multiple speeds and with multiple skill sets over multiple time periods. The successful social innovator is always part of a team.
5. Transformative social innovations will cast their own shadow. In direct proportion to their impact on the linked systems that they influence, social innovations can undermine general resilience as often as it increases it. This shadow cannot be entirely avoided, but it can be ameliorated through early awareness of the fact that intervention is systemic. In the context of seeking to understand role of social innovation and its relationship to multisystemic resilience, the importance of treating all innovation as an experiment, one that reveals much about the complex system that the social innovators are seeking to transform, is vital. A constant evaluation of the path being forged, the fitness of the landscape with which that path is interacting, and the realization of the goals and values informing the innovation in each new social, economic, political, cultural, and ecological landscape will be pivotal to whether any social innovation increases or diminishes the resilience of systems as a whole.

Conclusion

Social innovation is a process, and rarely a smooth or linear one; it challenges our expectations and how decisions get made. It forces us to think about systems and can uncover critical barriers to change and opportunities for collaboration. While this is complex, and therefore often surprising, it is not wholly unpredictable. As the experiment continues, the systems that are affected will respond and react, offering critical information to parts of the system, and co-occurring systems, seeking change. Often these responses go unheeded, at the peril of both the innovation and the innovators.

In conclusion, then, let us return to our Dutch chambermaid as an illustration. Were this 1630, she may have made some money, lost some money, but ultimately only participated peripherally in a human experiment involving an economic system that was quickly evolving. Yet a few years later, many of her co-nationals would lose everything in the first financial bubble, the tulip craze of 1636–1637. New houses for the newly wealthy in the rapidly growing city of Amsterdam had gardens that would have been largely impossible within the old Medieval walls. These new private green spaces drove a general passion for gardening and flowers, none so prized as the Turkish rarity, the tulip. Quickly bulb prices rose exponentially and rapidly traded hands between initial seller and eventually planter, sometimes a hundred times. Bulb sales were carefully choreographed, done in the open air and with promises to donate a portion of the price of the bulb would be given to charity—all reliant on the mutual agreement that that bulb or bulbs would bloom into a specific color or set of colors. Such early financial experiments were based on sharing risk and a mutual agreement to do so. Once a few people questioned if this risk was shared by doubting the value of a flower, things quickly fell apart. Yet the stock market survived and not only achieved normalcy but now calls out for new disruptive innovations to address inequality, brittleness, and a lack of sustainability; disruptive innovations are rarely smooth or evenly experienced across multiple systems.

Key Messages

1. Social innovation and resilience are linked, but the relationship is contextual. Social innovations can both trigger shifts toward greater resilience within one system or across systems, but they can also undermine the resilience of adjacent systems, making the whole more vulnerable and brittle.
2. Social innovation is a paradox of process and context.
3. Transformative social innovations are rarely pursued by those for whom the status quo satisfies their needs.
4. Transformation takes time, but windows of opportunity can open and close quickly: transformative social innovation requires thinking about different systems at multiple speeds and with multiple skill sets over multiple time periods.
5. Transformative social innovations will cast their own shadow; social innovations can undermine general resilience as often as it increases it. This shadow cannot be entirely avoided, but it can be ameliorated through early awareness of the fact that intervention is systemic.

Acknowledgments

We thank Professor Ungar for his feedback on the chapter. We also owe a significant debt of gratitude to our former and current colleagues at the Waterloo Institute for Social Innovation and Resilience, especially Ola Tjornbo, Nino Antadze, Sean Geobey, Erin Alexiuk, Jaclyn Blacklock, and Dan McCarthy. Special thanks for their insight on this and other projects also to Michele-Lee Moore and Per Olsson of the Stockholm Resilience Centre.

References

Antadze, N. (2017). National parks in the United States. In F. Westley, K. McGowan, & O. Tjornbo (Eds.), *The evolution of social innovation: Building resilience through transitions* (pp. 18–39). London, UK: Edward Elgar.

Antadze, N., & McGowan, K. A. (2017). Moral entrepreneurship: Thinking and acting at the landscape level to foster sustainability transitions. *Environmental Innovation and Societal Transitions, 25*, 1–13. doi:10.1016/j.eist.2016.11.001

Antadze, N., & Westley, F. (2010). Funding social innovation: How do we know what to grow? *The Philanthropist, 23*(3), 343–356.

Arthur, B. W. (2009). *The nature of technology: What it is and how it evolves*. London, UK: Penguin Books.

Ayob, N., Teasdale, S., & Fagan, K. (2016). How social innovation "came to be": Tracing the evolution of a contested concept. *Journal of Social Policy, 45*(4), 635–653. doi:10.1017/S004727941600009X

Berkes, F., & Folke, C. (Eds.). (1998). *Linking social and ecological systems: Management practices and social mechanisms for building resilience*. Cambridge, UK: Cambridge University Press.

Biggs, R., Schlüter, M., & Schoon, M. (2015). *Principles for building resilience: Sustaining ecosystem services in social-ecological systems*. Cambridge, UK: Cambridge University Press.

Binet, A., & Simon, T. (1916). *The development of intelligence in children (the Binet–Simon test)*. (Trans. Elizabeth Kite). Baltimore, MD: Williams & Wilkins.

Carpenter, S. R., Booth, E. G., Gillon, S., Kucharik, C. J., Loheide, S., Mase, A. S., . . . Wardropper, C. B. (2015). Plausible futures of a social-ecological system: Yahara watershed, Wisconsin, USA. *Ecology and Society, 20*(2), 10. doi:10.5751/ES-07433-200210

Edwards-Schachter, M., & Wallace, M. L. (2017). "Shaken, but not stirred": Sixty years of defining social innovation. *Technological Forecasting and Social Change, 119*, 64–79. doi:10.1016/j.techfore.2017.03.012

European Commission. (2013). *Empower people, driving change: Social innovation in the European Union*. Retrieved from http://ec.europa.eu/enterprise/policies/innovation/policy/social-innovation/index_en.htm

Fabinyi, M., Evans, L., & Foals, S. J. (2014). Social-ecological systems, society diversity and power: Insights from anthropology and political ecology. *Ecology and Society, 19*, 4. doi:10.5751/ES-07029-190428

Folke, C., Biggs, R., Norström, A. V., Reyers, B., & Rockström, J. (2016). Social-ecological resilience and biosphere-based sustainability science. *Ecology and Society, 21*(3), 41. doi:10.5751/es-08748-210341

Godin, B. (2012). Social innovation: Utopias of innovation from c. 1830 to the present. Project on the Intellectual History of Innovation: Working Paper No. 11.

Holling, C. S. (1973). Resilience and stability of ecological systems. *Annual Review of Ecology and Systematics, 4*(1), 1–23.

Holling, C. S., & Gunderson, L. (2002). Resilience and adaptive cycles. In L. Gunderson & C. S. Holling (Eds.), *Panarchy: Understanding transformations in human and natural systems* (pp. 3–22). Washington, DC: Island Press.

Holling, C. S., Berkes, F., & Folke, C. (1998). Science, sustainability and resource management. In F. Berkes & C. Folke (Eds.), *Linking social and ecological systems: Management practices and social mechanisms for building resilience* (pp. 342–362). Cambridge, UK: Cambridge University Press.

Howaldt, J., & Schwarz, M. (2010). *Social innovation: Concepts, research fields and international trends*. Studies for Innovation in a Modern Working Environment 5: International Monitoring. Aachen, Germany: IMA/ZLW.

Intelligence test. (1919). *The Lancet, 193*(4987), 489–540.

McGowan, K. (2017a). "A fever for business": Dutch joint stock companies. In F. Westley, K. McGowan, & O. Tjornbo (Eds.), *The evolution of social innovation: Building resilience through transitions* (pp. 196–217). London, UK: Edward Elgar.

McGowan, K. (2017b). The intelligence test. In F. Westley, K. McGowan, & O. Tjornbo (Eds.), *The evolution of social innovation: Building resilience through transitions* (pp. 40–57). London, UK: Edward Elgar.

McGowan, K., & Westley, F. (2015). At the root of change: The history of social innovation. In A. Nicholls, J. Simon, M. Gabriel, & C. Whelan (Eds.), *New frontiers in social innovation research* (pp. 52–68). London, UK: Palgrave Macmillan.

Moore, M. L., Olsson, P., Nilsson, W., Rose, L., & Westley, F. R. (2018). Navigating emergence and system reflexivity as key transformative capacities. *Ecology and Society, 23*(2).

Moore, M.-L., Westley, F., Tjornbo, O., & Holroyd, C. (2011). The loop, the lens and the lesson: Using resilience theory to examine public policy and social innovation. In A. Nicholls & A. Murdock (Eds.), *Social innovation* (pp. 89–113). London, UK: Palgrave Macmillan.

Mulgan, G. (2006). The process of social innovation. *Innovations 1*(2), 145–162.

Olsson, P., Moore, M.-L., Westley, F. R., & McCarthy, D. D. (2017). The concept of the Anthropocene as a game-changer: A new context for social innovation and transformations to sustainability. *Ecology and Society, 22*(2), article 31.

Pol, E., & Ville, S. (2009). Social innovation: Buzz word or enduring term? *The Journal of Socio-Economics, 38*(6), 878–885.

Spearman, C. (1904). General intelligence: Objectively determined and measured. *American Journal of Psychology, 15*, 201–292. doi:10.2307/1412107

Stone-Jovicich, S. G., Goldstein, B. E., Brown, K., Plummer, R., & Olsson, P. (2018). Expanding the contribution of the social sciences to social-ecological research. *Ecology and Society, 23*(1), 41. doi:10.5751/ES-10008-230141

Tjornbo, O. (2017). The Internet: A dynamic history. In F. Westley, K. McGowan, & O. Tjornbo (Eds.), *The evolution of social innovation: Building resilience through transitions* (pp. 116–132). London, UK: Edward Elgar.

Walker, B., & Westley, F. (2011). Perspectives on resilience to disasters across sectors and cultures. *Ecology and Society, 16*(2), 4.

Westley, F. (2013). Social innovation and resilience: How one enhances the other. *Stanford Social Innovation Review, 11*(3), 28–39. Retrieved from https://ssir.org/articles/entry/social_innovation_and_resilience_how_one_enhances_the_other.

Westley, F., McGowan, K. A., Antadze, N., Blacklock, J., & Tjornbo, O. (2017). How game changers catalyzed, disrupted, and incentivized social innovation: Three historical cases of nature conservation, assimilation, and women's rights. *Ecology and Society, 21*(4), 13. doi:10.5751/ES-08811-210413

Westley, F., Tjornbo, O., Schultz, L., Olsson, P., Folke, C., Crona, B., & Bodin, Ö. (2013). A Theory of transformative agency in linked social-ecological systems. *Ecology and Society, 18*(3), 27. doi:10.5751/ES-05072-180327

Westley, F., Olsson, P., Folke, C., Homer-Dixon, T., Vredenburg, H., Loorbach, D., Thompson, J., Nilsson, M., Lambin, E., Sendzimir, J., & Banerjee, B. (2011). Tipping toward sustainability: Emerging pathways of transformation. *AMBIO: A Journal of the Human Environment, 40*(7), 762–780.

Westley, F., Zimmerman, B., & Patton, M. (2006). *Getting to maybe: How the world is changed*. Toronto, ON: Vintage Canada.

SECTION 8

Legal, Policy, and Economic Systems

26

Resilience of Legal Systems
Toward Adaptive Governance

J. B. Ruhl, Barbara Cosens, and Niko Soininen

Introduction

Although there are numerous offerings, a good working definition of resilience as used in natural and social sciences, and appropriate for legal systems as well, is "the capacity of a system to experience shocks while retaining essentially the same function, structure, feedbacks, and therefore identity" (Walker et al., 2006, p. 14). This chapter explores how to contextualize these concepts for legal systems, recognizing that legal systems are situated within a vast co-evolving system of systems, and outlines a vision of new forms of governance that focus not only on how to design and manage the resilience of legal systems, but also on how legal systems can manage the resilience of other natural and social systems with which they co-evolve. With problems on a massive global scale looming large on the horizon, such as climate change and biodiversity loss, there is no more pressing set of challenges for legal system theory and practice in our time (Fischman, 2019).

Legal System Resilience: Of What, to What, and for What?

Translating the definition of resilience into legal systems research requires an understanding of the function, structure, feedbacks, and therefore identity of legal systems (the *of what*) and the kind of shocks they experience (the *to what*). Because legal systems both govern and co-evolve with other systems in large-scale complex social-ecological systems, they can contribute to, or diminish, the resilience of these other systems (Ruhl, 2011). Resilience in legal systems is, thus, often used to facilitate normative social purposes fulfilled through other social systems (the *for what*). In this section we chart out these three foundational questions of resilience theory as applied to law in general, and environmental law in particular.

Resilience of What?

The question of what it is about legal systems that could and should be resilient begs the question, What is a legal system? An easy response is that it is the system that creates, implements, and enforces formal rules governing society. This typology contains both the institutions tasked with creating and applying legal rules, as well as legal instruments, such as laws and regulations. But that answers very little for purposes of thinking of law as a *system* and what constitutes and contributes to its resilience. How does it behave? What are its boundaries? What is its input and output? Why does it sometimes fail? How will it look in one year? In 10 years? How should we use it to make change in some other aspect of social life? These are obvious questions, yet, of the tens of thousands of references to the legal system in legal literature, few authors say anything about it *as a system*. Even in the subset of this literature devoted to legal philosophy, little attention is given to the *system* half of the "legal system" (Ruhl & Katz, 2015). Furthermore, even when the system "half" of the law is studied, the analysis often proceeds on the assumption that law is a closed and self-referential system with fairly simple operating principles (Luhmann, 2004).

Going further, many legal scholars describe the legal system as complex without saying much about what *complex* means. So, for example, Conley (2007) claims that intellectual property rights law "has radically evolved since the nineteenth century when there was no structure, to the present where there are complex legal systems and rules in place" (p. 210). Other authors even go so far as to refer to "massively complex legal systems," suggesting that they "require a great deal of constituting" (Young, 2007, p. 417). As accurate as these statements may be, beyond conjoining "complex" and "legal system," they offer no insight into what makes a legal system *complex*. Although some legal scholars use the term *complexity* in discussing legal frameworks, the term often refers to nothing more than legal indeterminacy that is caused by the law regulating a complicated topic (e.g., multiple sectors of society) and expanding onto a wide vertical landscape ranging from the international to the local level (Kades, 1997). Despite these attempts to understand the complicated nature of legal systems, no scientific understanding of law's complexity has been forthcoming. Resilience thinking and the related field of complexity science—the study of complex adaptive systems—offer much insight in this regard.

Starting with complexity science, its key premise is that there is a difference between complexity in the sense of "complicatedness" and complexity in the sense of how a system is constructed and behaves. Few dispute that law is complicated; whether it is complex in this systems sense is another matter. Miller and Page (2007) explain the distinction, which goes to the essence of complexity science theory:

> In a complicated world, the various elements that make up the system maintain a degree of independence from one another. Thus, removing one such element

(which reduces the level of complication) does not fundamentally alter the system's behavior apart from that which directly resulted from the piece that was removed. Complexity arises when the dependencies among the elements become important. In such a system, removing one such element destroys system behavior to an extent that goes well beyond what is embodied by the particular element that is removed. (p. 9)

The focus of complexity science is this kind of complexity found in systems "in which large networks of components with no central control and simple rules of operation give rise to complex collective behavior, sophisticated information processing, and adaptation via learning or evolution" (Mitchell, 2009, p. 13). Attributes of such systems include aspects of self-organization, network structure, emergence (the whole is different than the sum of its parts), feedback (both negative, which has a stabilizing effect, and positive, which has a destabilizing effect), the possibility of nonlinear behavior, contextualization (i.e., the application of the same approach in a different setting may not have the same results), and uncertainty (Mitchell, 2009).

Much of the work applying complexity science to legal systems has focused on mapping key concepts of complexity science onto legal systems (Ruhl & Katz, 2015). This work starts with the general definition of a complex adaptive system as previously mentioned: a large network of components with no central control and simple rules of operation giving rise to complex collective behavior, sophisticated information processing, and adaptation via learning or evolution. This framework is intuitive for anyone with training in law to map onto the legal system. The components of the legal system comprise a broad diversity of institutions—the organizations of people who make, interpret, and enforce laws—and of instruments—the laws, regulations, cases, and related legal content the institutions produce. These components are interconnected and interactive. Institutions are interconnected through structures and rules such as hierarchies of courts and legislative creation and oversight of agencies, and they interact in forums such as judicial trials, legislative hearings and debates, and agency rulemakings. The instruments are also interconnected through mechanisms such as code structures, and they interact through cross-references and other devices (Ruhl, Katz, & Bommarito, 2017).

The highly interconnected architecture of such a system drives the way it behaves over time (Ruhl & Katz, 2015). An agency adopts a rule, which prompts another agency to enforce a different rule, which leads to litigation before a judge, who issues an opinion overruled by a higher court, which prompts a legislature to enact a new statute, and so on. The institutional agents follow procedural and substantive rules, but there is no central controller pulling all the strings. There are hierarchies for various institutions (e.g., tiers of courts), yet there is no master agent controlling the *system*. Such systemic organization of law without a single master is one of the foundational elements of many legal systems, particularly those relying on a separation between the legislative, executive, and judicial branches. Through the separation of powers and other mechanisms, such as procedural safeguards, the rule of law seeks to secure a system in which no one institution would have all the keys to control the development of law (Dicey, 1979; Soininen, 2018; Thoma, 1978; Waldron, 2010). We recognize, of course, that there are other forms of governance, such as those of authoritarian regimes, and that they too can exhibit complexity attributes.

There is now wide acceptance of the model of legal systems as complex adaptive systems (Murray, Webb, & Wheatley, 2019). This being the nature of legal systems, what about their resilience? Resilience of complex adaptive systems has become a large research agenda in many fields (Fraccascia, Giannoccaro, & Albino, 2018). Legal scholars have also long used terms like *resilient* and *resilience* to describe qualities of a legal system. A classic example is from Karl Llewellyn (1960), who observed that "an adequately resilient legal system can on occasion, or even almost regularly, absorb the particular trouble and resolve it each time into a new, usefully guiding, forward-looking felt standard-for-action or even rule-of-law" (p. 513). Although not articulating any formal theory of resilience, this and similar descriptions seem to mean what ecologists, social scientists, and complex systems researchers mean—that a resilient legal system enjoys consistency in overall behavioral structure notwithstanding continuous change of exogenous and endogenous conditions (Ruhl, 2011). Much as legal scholars have done for complexity science, therefore, how might we map the principles of resilience theory onto legal systems to better understand when they are and are not resilient?

Resilience theorists use the metaphor of a bowl and a ball rolling around its basin to illustrate key themes (Gunderson, 2000). The legal system, like any system, can be defined by its structure (e.g., division of powers between legislatures and courts) and processes (e.g., administrative decision procedures). Structure and process thus define the shape of the resilience "basin of attraction" and produce system behavior in the form of actual decisions of executives, legislatures, courts, and agencies, which is where the "ball" is in the bowl at any time. Different configurations of structure and processes—different basin shapes—can be expected to produce different behavioral outcomes in response to changes in internal and external conditions. How we design those configurations also matters for how the system stands up to changes of different quality and magnitude over time. Some configurations could rely on more rigid strategies—what resilience theorists call "engineering resilience" (Walker et al., 2006) or "static resilience" (Giannoccaro, Albino, & Nair, 2018)—to build a very efficient set of reliable structural and process components, whereas others could use the dynamic flexibility of "ecological resilience" strategies to build more capacity to adapt into the system (Cosens et al., 2017; Cosens, Gunderson, & Chaffin, 2018; Gunderson & Holling, 2002; Walker et al., 2006). Blends of these strategies can enhance "response diversity" so that the system is better prepared for new kinds of disturbances (Walker et al., 2006). These design choices take place at different scales and for different subsystems. What we call environmental law, for example, may be different in structure and process from criminal law, although they can share some legal systemic elements, such as the constitutional requirements regulating the organization of structure and processes.

Indeed, to a resilience theorist some features of a legal system surely would be interpreted as displaying strong versions of static engineering resilience strategies (Ruhl, 2011). The U.S. Constitution, for example, displays little tolerance for structural or process change. It was designed to be hard to alter in design and has proven so (Vile, 1994). Yet it is resilient. Its highly engineered structure and process design is so enduring that flips to new equilibrium states—the so-called constitutional moments—are quite rare (Sunstein, 1996). It has proven capable of amendment in the face of major shifts in social values (i.e., the 13th, 14th, and 15th Amendments following the Civil War) and reinterpretation in the face of major shifts in social economic interaction (e.g., the New Deal in response to the industrial revolution and its impacts; Dorf & Sabel, 1998), setting a high threshold for change.

By contrast, common law legal systems, which allow for the incremental development of law through case-by-case judicial opinion, offer an example of dynamic ecological resilience, in the sense they are designed with a highly dispersed structure of courts throughout the nation, all working to craft doctrine under a loose set of process rules (Ruhl, 2011). Response diversity is high, as multiple courts from different states may be working on the same new problem to arrive at a spectrum of doctrinal results. The result is a high capacity for swings in behavior in response to changing conditions without altering the system's basic structure and process design. Outcomes can move responsively to new knowledge and changed conditions, sometimes dramatically so and other times over long periods of judicial tinkering, without the system's structure and process design changing. For example, at one time the U.S. Supreme Court declared wetlands to be common law nuisances, whereas courts today have ruled the draining or filling of a wetland to constitute a nuisance (Blumm & Ruhl, 2010). The common law of nuisance has responded to the modern science of wetland ecology and changed public perceptions to make a complete 180-degree turn on the status of wetlands (Nagle, 2008), but by no means would anyone consider the common law of nuisance to have been restructured as a system to make this shift in doctrine.

Similar incremental developments are also a feature of civil law systems governed mostly through statutes. To take one example, construction of rivers for hydropower was deemed crucial from a societal perspective in 20th-century Finland, but after the arrival and formalization of ecological water quality requirements stemming from the EU, especially small-scale hydropower has been deemed societally unsustainable. Despite this, hydropower operations still enjoy strong legal protection through constitutional protection of private property, but the change in the EU legal framework has started an incremental change toward securing ecological flows in the Finnish rivers (Soininen, Belinskij, Vainikka, & Huuskonen, 2019).

It is important in this respect to distinguish between resilience of the legal system's underlying structure and processes and the stability of the substantive content of law—that is, the lifespan and durability of particular decisions by executives, legislatures, courts, and agencies. A legal system relying heavily on ecosystem resilience strategies, for example, is likely to experience flux in the substantive legal content it produces. The ball rolls far from equilibrium in such systems. There may be many reasons, however, to prefer greater stability in the substantive content of the law, finding a balance between flexibility and rigidity in legal processes (Craig et al., 2017, 2018).

This point warrants unpacking legal system resilience into two dimensions—the institutional and the instrumental. Institutional resilience pertains to the actors in the legal system and the processes they use to create and enforce laws, whereas instrumental resilience pertains to the resilience of those substantive laws. Resilience of one is not predetermined by the resilience of the other. For example, although the recent volatility of executive institutions around the world may suggest an erosion of institutional resilience, presidents and prime ministers often find it can be quite difficult to impose similar instability on the instruments over which they have authority, such as agency regulations, due to institutional resilience elsewhere in the system. On the other hand, a highly resilient institutional structure, such as an authoritarian regime, might be so powerful as to be in a position to change legal instruments on a whim.

These possibilities lead directly to the important observation that whether a legal system is or is not resilient—institutionally, instrumentally, or in both domains—implies nothing about the system normatively (Fischman, 2019). Resilience is an emergent property of a social system, but it does not make the system "good" or "bad"—that is for society to decide. To be sure, resilience might itself be desirable and considered normatively a good quality to promote in a legal system. But the presence or absence of resilience in a legal system alone does not entitle the system to any particular normative status. What modern society might consider a discredited legal system—feudalism, for example—might nonetheless be resilient (as it was for centuries). Even today, despotic rulers establish and perpetuate resilient legal systems to support their reign.

At the same time, the normative underpinnings of the legal system (e.g. rule of law and separation of powers) can affect what kind of and how much resilience the system has (functions, basins of attraction, etc.). So law's resilience is affected by normative decisions regarding the system design (e.g., the constitution), but resilience itself is a descriptive concept once the normative foundations are put in place.

Indeed, to the extent resilience is a desired quality, it may nevertheless pose trade-offs with other normative goals of a legal system (Ruhl, 2011). It may be possible to have too much resilience. If, for example, a legal system is highly resilient in the engineering sense, but it is producing outcomes that are no longer normatively acceptable to society, its resilience is a problem, not a virtue (Gunderson, Garmestani, Rizzardi, Ruhl, & Light, 2014). In such cases an extreme external disturbance or internally initiated reformation of the system may be needed to escape from the highly resilient but undesirable regime. The persistence and ultimate demise of the legal system once supporting American slavery offers an example—it took a national civil war to begin the dismantling.

In summary, resilience of legal systems at a very general level can be defined the same as it is for other social systems—broadly speaking, it is the ability of the legal institutions and the legal instruments they produce to experience shocks while retaining essentially the same function, structure, feedbacks, and therefore identity. This property exists in countless interacting legal systems operating across horizontal scales (e.g., the interactions between substates within a national system) and vertical scales (e.g., the interactions between global, regional, national, and subnational systems). To return to the original question of this section—What is a legal system?—we thus define it as a complex adaptive system comprised of numerous interacting and even nested systems of international law, regional law (e.g. the EU), as well as national and subnational systems (i.e., a system of systems), all of which exhibit varying degrees of resilience.

Because legal systems play an important role in shaping and fulfilling social norms, one must be careful to consider that legal system resilience as defined may not be a good force in society. Where it is working well on behalf of society, legal system resilience is a positive effect to be promoted and protected; where it is not, perhaps it must be overcome to facilitate legal system transformation. Both of those possibilities raise the question, Resilience to what?

Resilience to What?

The next time you take a peaceful hike through a forest, stop for a moment and consider that you are in the middle of a war zone. Species within the ecosystem are engaged in cooperative and competitive behaviors, and the system as a whole must manage natural disturbances such as floods and droughts and human disturbances such as pollution and habitat destruction. It is no wonder that ecosystems are identified as classic examples of complex adaptive systems (Levin, 2000).

Legal systems also experience disturbances from internal and external forces. Take environmental law for example. Internally, some political actors advocate for massive revision of the system, such as repealing major statutes or privatizing public lands (for examples, see Lazarus, 2004). Although calibration of regulatory impact has always been a central debate within environmental law, such radical proposals can be seen as viable threats to system resilience. Likewise, external disturbances abound from other social systems, such as financial system collapse threatening budgets of agencies implementing and enforcing environmental regulation (Nash, Ruhl, & Salzman, 2017). At the extreme, warfare, climate change, and mass human migration can have deleterious effects on the environment and environmental law. There are also legal constraints that provide resistance at the expense of adaptive capacity, thereby diminishing system resilience, such as strong property rights regimes that exist in some nations, the United States being a glaring example. In short, legal systems like environmental law can be thought of as much like natural ecosystems, constantly working out conflicts in internal dynamics while battling off threats from outside. The difference, of course, is that legal systems are entirely the invention of, and controlled by, humans. Legal systems have normative purposes chosen by society, leading to the third fundamental resilience question: for what purpose is legal system resilience intended?

Resilience for What?

What is the legal system's role in society? Generally speaking, the purpose of legal systems is to provide a stable and equitable framework for attaining normative goals in the overall social-ecological system. To do so, legal systems interact with other social systems in such a way as to provide a stable platform for their operation (e.g., so that the financial system can function over time), but in many cases also attempt to steer those other systems toward socially desired goals (e.g., to promote greater social justice in the healthcare system). Depending on society's normative choices, in some cases the relationship between legal and other social systems is positive and in others it is antagonistic—legal systems generally promote the healthcare system and fight criminal networks. Generally, legal theorists have defined what constitutes a "good" legal system as one exhibiting and promoting legitimacy, accountability, and justice (Cosens et al., 2017, 2018). As Lon Fuller (1969) famously articulated, this would entail (a) denial of ad hoc (purely contextual) decisions, (b) public promulgation of laws, (c) denial of retroactive legislation, (d) clarity of laws, (e) denial of contradictory rules, (f) laws that do not require actions beyond the capabilities of the affected parties, (g) nonfrequent changes to the legal system, and (h) legal norms that are implemented and enforced as they are announced. In societies that value these attributes, legal system resilience is both built upon and promotes them (Cosens et al., 2017, 2018).

It is important in this respect to distinguish between resilience of the legal system and resilience of other natural and social systems the law is aimed at addressing. Environmental law, for example, might focus on how law can promote resilience of ecosystems, and banking law might focus on how to make the financial system more resilient, but that is not the same as asking how to design resilience in law. Nor does it necessarily follow that if law is successfully designed to be resilient that it will promote (or undermine) the resilience of any other social system.

These design choices, moreover, operate at multiple scales within and across the vast domain of the legal system. Resilience theory does not posit that a system as complex as law is entirely one kind of "bowl." Rather, it is more a set of landscapes over which we find engineering and ecological resilience strategies mixing in different blends to form topographies of various contours depending on where in the system we look. Some resilience theorists refer to this multiscalar complex of topographies as a panarchy. Allen and Holling (2010) explain:

> For resilience theory, it is critical to understand the scales of interest and the scale of analysis because one level of a panarchy may collapse and cascade to lower levels, but the system as a whole may be maintained.... Resilience is a property that can exist at any scale in a panarchy. A given level may not be very resilient, but the larger system may be. (p. 3)

Environmental law, for example, has many facets, not all of which use the same blend of resilience strategies. Environmental law in turn is nestled with many other fields of regulation in the larger scale system of administrative law, which in turn is embedded within a system of constitutional law, each with its own resilience landscape. Similarly, in common law nations, administrative law operates alongside the common law, which likely has different resilience properties. Thus, administrative law uses checks on agency process to allow delegation from a legislative body and a degree of flexibility in expert implantation, whereas common law involves a slow evolution of substantive law through an incremental process of judges and litigants learning by doing. In civil law systems, such a learning by doing mechanism might function through courts informing the legislature of a regulatory failure, and the legislature making the required adjustments, provided there is the political will to do so. The legal system, therefore, has many potential equilibrium states at many different scales, each with its own set of resilience attributes. One component of the larger system—to use an all too real recent example, the financial law system—may fail, but the legal system as a whole may continue to prove resilient.

It follows that the possibility of "flips" from one system state to another—which implies that the resilience strategies associated with the prior state did not ultimately resist change—are not necessarily undesirable in legal (or other) systems. If resilience of natural ecosystems or stability of legal decisions is our priority, it might be law's structure and process that have to shift to a new system state when change threatens those values. For example, if one were to trace the history of the environmental law system in the United States, an unmistakable transition occurred in the 1970s as statutory regimes supplanted common law regimes as the dominant system structure (Lazarus, 2004). And EU environmental law has undertaken a shift from rule-based statutory regulation to goal-based legislative frameworks with market-based instruments and self-regulation complementing formal regulation (Langlet & Mahmoudi, 2016). These were in many ways planned flips to a new equilibrium state, a process known in resilience theory as *transformability*, the "capacity to create a fundamentally new system when ecological, economic, or social (including political) conditions make the existing system untenable . . . [by] creating new stability landscapes" (Walker et al., 2006, p. 7). One of the facets of resilience theory thus focuses on how to manage systems that have multiple equilibrium states and how to flip between them under certain conditions (Gunderson & Holling, 2002).

Properties of Resilient Legal Systems: A Case Study of Modern Environmental Law

Given that we can define resilience and identify its operation in many social systems including law, an obvious question follows: "What is it that allows these systems to sustain such productive, aggregate patterns through so much change?" (Miller & Page, 2007, p. 28). A starting point is to unpack the engineering/ecology resilience distinction into a more refined typology of attributes. For example, in their deep examination of resilience in complex systems, Alderson and Doyle (2010) explain that five key features of a system contribute to the capacity to endure through surrounding change:

> *Reliability* involves robustness to component failures. *Efficiency* is robustness to resource scarcity. *Scalability* is robustness to changes to the size and complexity of the system as a whole. *Modularity* is robustness to structured component rearrangements. *Evolvability* is robustness of lineages to changes on long time scales. (p. 840; italics in original)

Of these five qualities, reliability and efficiency appear most in keeping with engineering resilience strategies, whereas scalability, modularity, and evolvability match up more closely with ecological robustness (Gunderson & Holling, 2002; Anderies, Janssen, & Ostrom, 2004). As such, it is likely that trade-offs will be encountered and force difficult decisions about system design. A system that is highly efficient in using scarce resources, for example, might as a consequence have less response diversity because of lower reliability in important system components (Alderson & Doyle, 2010). A recurrent system design question, therefore, is how to balance these properties, which, as previously observed, is driven in large part by the normative decisions a society has made regarding its goals for the legal system (Ruhl, 2011).

Modern environmental law offers many examples of how these properties both contribute to legal system resilience but must be balanced. Although institutions and instruments aimed at regulating human behavior toward the environment, such as laws protecting parks, have been in place in many nations for over a century, the highly articulated architecture of modern environmental law, relying on dozens of legislative acts, administrative agencies and their regulations, and judicial oversight dates back no more than a few decades in most nations (Lazarus, 2004). The core purpose of this style of environmental law is to regulate how humans treat the environment. The two principal goals are to protect what we care about in the environment itself (species, ecosystems, wetlands) and to protect human health and welfare given our dependency on the environment (antipollution, waste controls). This is a tall order. For one thing, the environment itself is a massive complex adaptive system in its own right. And there are multiple social systems, including other legal systems, acting in ways that promote or undermine the environment's resilience and which environmental law must therefore engage. Trade-offs are inevitable, as the real or imagined jobs-versus-environment debate has persisted for decades as an example. In short, environmental law as a legal system is embedded in a massive and monstrously complex social-ecological-technological system. Managing its reliability, efficiency, scalability, modularity, and evolvability is a full-time job for a large army of policymakers and practitioners.

Reliability

Modern environmental law systems consist of many institutions and instruments. Reliability means that when one of these components fails, the system as a whole does not substantially diminish in resilience. Of course, failure is often in the eyes of the beholder—some people consider the environmental law system to have failed because it regulates too much and others, because it regulates too little. Either way, in most nations that moved to the modern environmental law model beginning in the 1970s, the system remains largely intact despite many component failures along the way. In the United States, for example, every one of the suite of federal statutes enacted in the 1970s—the Clean Water Act, Endangered Species Act, Clean Air Act, National Environmental Policy Act, and a host of others—remains in place today, if not augmented through amendments over time.

Despite what Lazarus (2004) describes as a pathological series of pendulum swings in American politics, bashing environmental law in one direction, then building it back up in the other, and so on, the system has persisted. To a large extent this can be attributed to structural checks-and-balances features found in many legal systems, where shared authority reduces the propensity for any one institution, such as the executive, to move too far in one direction without other institutions, such as the judiciary, weighing in. Legitimacy and accountability of governing authorities also must necessarily factor into the type of resilience the system can deploy in this regard, promoting the ecological resilience underpinning reliability.

To be sure, the modern environmental law system has failed many times and at many places. But it is mostly a success story. Many rivers are cleaner, the air is healthier in many places, contaminated sites have been remediated, species have been protected, the loss of wetlands has been stemmed in many nations, and so on. The modern environmental law system is, in other words, largely intact and working in many nations. There are, of course, many pockets of the world where this is not the case, and the international legal system faces many environmental challenges at the global scale, such as climate change, loss of biodiversity, and massive plastics pollution in the oceans. The environmental law agenda is far from completed, and faces some problems of unprecedented scale and intensity, but the environmental law system has demonstrated immense reliability to component failure over time.

Efficiency

In most nations, the modern environmental law system ramped up quickly and without overriding attention to efficiency. This was out of necessity—the environment was in dire shape and getting worse, so strong regulatory measures were needed. The U.S. Endangered Species Act is a prime example, as it requires species to be designated for protection without regard to economic impact. The Finnish Nature Conservation Act portrays similar characteristics. It was also the case that environmental law began by relying heavily on administrative agencies to promulgate and enforce strong regulations, which itself demanded large staffs and significant expenditures.

Over time, however, environmental law systems have introduced more efficiency-conscious instruments. Many regulatory programs must at least conduct cost-benefit and technological feasibility analyses (Revesz, 1999; Hahn & Sunstein, 2002) or at least contain legal provisions to exempt certain societally desired activities from inefficient regulation. Moreover, modern regulatory programs have brought to the fore an array of new forms of instruments, such as cap-and-trade pollution programs and habitat offset banking, which rely on market forces and self-regulation to produce more efficient system operation (Esty, 2019; Gunningham & Grabosky, 1999).

Institutional efficiency is also a factor. Budgets for environmental agencies have been held static or reduced in many nations, driving a "more for less" scarcity of resources that has forced agencies to be more efficient (Nash et al., 2017). There is intense debate over how far to go in this direction but enhancing efficiency of administration and efficiency of outcome has been an unmistakable trend in modern environmental law systems, particularly in comparison to their earliest forms.

Scalability

Modern environmental law includes many mechanisms to promote robustness to changes to the size and complexity of the system as a whole. The air pollution problem, for example, operates at many scales from local to global, and environmental law systems have scaled accordingly. Some air pollutants are regulated for their local impacts as well as for their nationwide ambient impacts, and laws like the U.S. Clean Air Act include different mechanisms for each. Environmental law systems have also massively scaled in scope without falling apart, particularly as new environmental problems arise. The EU's environmental law system, for example, did not exist 50 years ago but today is considered one of the most expansive, complex, and intensive regulatory interventions found in law (Langlet & Mahmoudi, 2016). A multitude of other bilateral and regional treaties exists to manage environmental issues such as water regimes and trade (de Chazournes, 2013). On the other hand, environmental law has had less success maintaining viability at global scales. There are some success stories, such as the reduction of ozone precursor chemicals, but less traction has been gained on problems like climate change and ocean plastics pollution. There are many reasons for this beyond the capacity of environmental law systems, but it does appear that scalability becomes a severe problem for environmental law once it moves beyond regional scales.

Modularity

Environmental law's robustness to structured component rearrangements has varied largely due to broader background governance structures of relevant jurisdictions. For example, in theory at least, the federalist structure of nations like the United States allows one level of authority to step in to address a regulatory problem when other levels do not. One argument for a strong federal role in U.S. environmental law was to counter the perceived race to the bottom by states as they prioritized economic development (Lazarus, 2004), which has also been a justification given for the development of robust EU level law in Europe (Langlet & Mahmoudi, 2016). On the other hand, U.S. states like California and Oregon have often outpaced the federal government in pursuing environmental protection through their environmental law systems. There are also oftentimes multiple agencies and other entities working across the same level of authority, with overlapping and complementary roles (Freeman & Rossi, 2011; Salzman & Ruhl, 2010). This system of systems has built extensive modularity in the United States and other federalist environmental law systems employing the same kind of cooperative federalism. Modularity also allows for smaller scale experimentation, which is less risky in the face of uncertainty than large scale (as well as easier to adjust if it proves wrong). One criticism of the strong federal role in environmental law is that it does not provide sufficient space for local innovation, even when designed as so-called cooperative federalism. More centralized systems may trade off modularity in favor of efficiency or scalability, as keeping the cooperative federalism model running imposes redundancies and coordination costs.

Evolvability

As previously noted, modern environmental law is in many ways an evolutionary story, tracing its roots back over a century in many nations. It is as well an ongoing system of evolution, as new institutions and instruments appear, and some disappear, over time to adjust to new challenges and calibrate to new ways of governing. The 1970s saw the statutory revolution in the United States and the creation of the EU's system, and both have since incorporated new techniques, such as market-based approaches and goal-based framework regulation, and taken on new problems such as climate change. Some even argue that environmental law is undergoing yet another evolutionary era as private environmental governance structures such as supply chain management present potential gains on environmental quality that would be difficult to realize using only public governance mechanisms (Vandenbergh & Gilligan, 2017). Yet, there is growing concern that the type of wicked problems operating at global scales, such as climate change and biodiversity loss, are moving at so rapid a pace that environmental law may not have the adaptive capacity to keep up.

Future Research Pathways for Resilient Legal Systems: The Adaptive Governance Frame

The rise of complexity science and resilience thinking as serious and influential disciplines has helped put meat on the bones of the claim that legal systems are complex and resilient, and resilience thinking's analytical framework for studying social-ecological systems situates legal systems within the larger system of systems (Fischman, 2019). Future application of resilience thinking to legal systems, therefore, must start with the recognition that law is but one mechanism of governance within large-scale social-ecological systems (Drahos & Krygier, 2017; Gunningham & Grabosky, 1999). Legal system resilience might obstruct overall governance resilience, such as by crowding out or prohibiting innovative private actor solutions or by suppressing progressive cultural norms. Or legal system resilience may be absolutely necessary to serve social goals, in which case the challenge of balancing reliability, efficiency, scalability, modularity, and evolvability will be ever present. Ultimately, though, most policy decisions require at least some legal framing, so legal system resilience is rarely not a concern (Black, 2012). Choices about legal system resilience—how much of it to have and how to achieve that goal—are thus part of a broader governance regime facing questions like these across many social systems (Frohlich, Jacobson, Fidelman, & Smith, 2018; Lebal, Anderies, Campbell, & Hatfield-Dodds, 2006; Sellberg, Ryan, Borgstrom, Norstrom, & Peterson, 2018).

Reflecting this awareness, in recent years legal system resilience has been taken up as part of a more comprehensive research agenda focused on adaptive law to support adaptive governance. Adaptive law refers to the design of legal systems, institutions, and instruments intended to facilitate flexibility, resilience, and dynamism in the management of complex social-ecological systems. It has emerged in theoretical literature and practical implementation largely as a response to perceived inadequacies of conventional regulatory law, particularly law governing environmental and natural resources management.

Conventional regulatory regimes, often referred to as the command-and-control approach, rely on centralized regulatory institutions, rigid rules and standards, permitting programs demanding extensive front-end assessment of an action's impact, extensive postdecision litigation, and limited opportunity at the back end for administrative adjustment of those decisions (Craig & Ruhl, 2014). While credit is due to such approaches for the immense progress they have achieved in improving environmental and natural resources conditions (Lazarus, 2004), there is a growing perception among scientists and policymakers that the major challenges on the horizon, such as climate change, biodiversity degradation, and widespread ecological disturbance, are so complex, evolving, interconnected, and large in scale that different governance approaches are needed. Recognizing that social and ecological systems are linked in a system-of-systems dynamic, legal theorists and practitioners of adaptive law embrace law as part of social-ecological systems. Legal regimes must therefore not only consider the complex adaptive qualities of social-ecological systems, but also must themselves achieve appropriate resilience and adaptive capacity.

Broadly speaking, adaptive law is one component of the mesolayer fitting between adaptive governance at the macrolevel and adaptive management decision-making at the microlevel. Adaptive governance integrates adaptive law, and adaptive law integrates adaptive management. To understand adaptive law, therefore, requires some attention to the concepts of adaptive governance and adaptive management, their historical development, and their relation to adaptive law in theory and practice.

Adaptive governance has been defined as "governance that allows emergence of collective action capable of facilitating adaptation to change and surprise as well as the capacity itself to evolve" (Cosens et al., 2018, p. 6). Governance is composed not only of government institutions but also of private and other social actors influencing social-ecological system policy through markets and other social networks (Chaffin, Gosnell, & Cosens, 2014; Vandenbergh & Gilligan, 2017). Adaptive governance focuses on increasing cross-scale interactions and social networks among stakeholders within the governance system (Frohlich et al., 2018; Karpouzoglou, Dewulf, & Clark, 2016). Adaptive governance encourages matching the scales of government and nongovernmental authorities to the scales of the social-ecological system being governed by employing multiple units of power, operating at multiple scales, to create partially redundant and overlapping public and private authorities to act. This polycentric structure enables decision-making to operate closer to the social or environmental issue demanding an action, by increasing local authority management capacity while retaining networks across horizontal, vertical, and diagonal dimensions within the network of governance actors. As such, the polycentric model can actually enhance modularity, scalability, and efficiency at the same time, since it is not only highly inefficient to create a formal entity at the scale of every problem, in the face of uncertainty, it is impossible to do so. Thus, through the self-organization of responding networks the scaled response must emerge rather than be designed.

Adaptive law facilitates adaptive governance. Although there are other mesoscale components necessary to achieve the promise of adaptive governance, such as social norms and financial capital, law in both its private and public forms is central to operationalizing adaptive governance. Adaptive law searches for arrangements of legal institutions and instruments, operating in public, private, and hybrid spheres, that optimize the opportunities for adaptive capacity at macroscales of social-ecological system management.

Adaptive law traces its roots to critiques of conventional command-and-control regulatory models, emerging in the 1980s, that advocated greater reliance on market-based and information-based instruments, such as habitat credit banking, pollution cap-and-trade programs, and pollution emission disclosures (Stewart, 2001). These so-called next-generation approaches, however, were intended primarily to *reduce* the need for expert administrative decision-making at microscales by leveraging the dynamic forces of market mechanisms and information disclosure (Bevir, 2012; Craig & Ruhl, 2014; Dorf & Sabel, 1998). Statutes and regulations established the market and information disclosure regimes, which were broadly overseen by administrative authorities, but turned over ultimate decision-making in the field to market transactions and the reputational and network impacts of information disclosure.

By the mid-1990s, it had become increasingly apparent that even these innovations in decision-making, while producing some very positive outcomes, were not up to the task of supporting adaptive governance of complex social-ecological systems or increasingly complex, globalized social systems in general (Dorf & Sabel, 1998). The coupled concepts of goals-based ecosystem management and its decision-making methodology of adaptive management became a focus for theoretical design and practical implementation for these large scale social-ecological system management challenges (Williams & Brown, 2014). Contrary to the market and information mechanisms, adaptive management *increases* the decision-making engagement of expert agencies; but also, contrary to the command-and-control approach, does so in a way that encourages a learning-by-doing culture by allowing agencies responsible for social-ecological system management to set goals, test hypotheses, implement planned actions, monitor results, and adjust approaches without undergoing the heavy procedural burdens of conventional regulatory regimes (Craig & Ruhl, 2014).

Adaptive management principles were quickly embraced by resource management agencies around the globe (Frohlich et al., 2018; Williams & Brown, 2012). At the same time, increasing concern over the global-scale impacts of climate change, biodiversity degradation, and large-scale ecological impairment led to greater attention for building more robust social-ecological system resilience and adaptive capacity. Efforts to implement adaptive management within the traditional technocratic framework failed in application to large-scale systems including the Florida Everglades (Gunderson et al., 2014) and the Columbia River (Lee, 1999; Volkman & McConnaha, 1993). Legal scholars began to focus on the governance regime in which adaptive management of complex social-ecological systems might work (Cosens et al., 2018; Cosens & Gunderson, 2018). Whereas adaptive management focuses on *instrument* design for decision-making at the microscale, this new movement focused on *governance* design to promote adaptive capacity at the macroscale of social-ecological system management more broadly. Early manifestations, sometimes referred to by legal scholars as the "new governance" movement, emphasized polycentric, redundant, interdisciplinary governance institutions, as well as reliance on flexible regulatory instruments including adaptive management and market and information based instruments and increased public–private interaction (Cosens et al., 2018). Over time, other research disciplines including political science, sociology, ecological economics, and natural resources management began emphasizing adaptation and resilience as qualities of governance necessary to manage complex social-ecological system. They referred to this new configuration of institutional design and capacity as adaptive governance, which is generally the more accepted term today for new governance that includes flexibility and learning by doing (Chaffin et al., 2014).

Although achieving adaptive governance does not necessitate employing adaptive management and employing adaptive management does not guarantee achieving adaptive governance, most theorists and practitioners suggest that the two are reinforcing and should go hand in hand (Folke, Hahn, Olsson, & Norberg, 2005). What sits between and connects them at the mesoscale includes, principally, legal systems such as environmental law. Environmental law can support adaptive governance and utilizes adaptive management to do so. Yet, it had grown increasing apparent by the early 2000s that environmental law, after decades of command-and-control regime implementation, had become deeply embedded with the rigid attributes of conventional resource management law, as previously described, and was an obstacle to both implementing adaptive management and facilitating adaptive governance. In particular, conventional resource management regimes traditionally have relied on siloed authorities conducting purportedly comprehensive predecision impact assessment and subjecting those authorities' decision processes to extensive opportunity for public intervention and probing postdecision judicial review (Bevir, 2012; Dorf & Sabel, 1998; Soininen et al., 2019). Although each of these design features responds to central goals of good governance, such as transparency, legitimacy, and accountability, each also impedes the flexibility and dynamism needed for both adaptive governance and adaptive management.

Growing increasingly aware of this inherent tension, legal, policy, and resource management scholars and practitioners have begun forging new ground in legal theory aimed toward achieving more adaptive forms of law intended on the one hand to robustly support adaptive social-ecological system governance and embrace adaptive management's iterative decision-making style, but on the other hand not to undermine the goals of transparency, legitimacy, and accountability (Cosens, 2013; Craig et al., 2017; DeCaro, Chaffin, Schlager, Garmestani, & Ruhl, 2017; Soininen & Platjouw, 2019). It is a balancing act, but one that is unavoidable. As previously noted, the premise of adaptive governance is that social-ecological systems are complex adaptive systems in which legal systems are embedded and co-evolving. The challenge for design of adaptive law therefore is to take the complex adaptive qualities of a social-ecological system into account while also taking into account that the legal system is embedded in these social-ecological systems and thus itself is a complex adaptive system.

Responding to that challenge, the building literature on adaptive law identifies several key features of what defines adaptive law and how to build it out in robust, durable forms. Adaptive law involves iterative processes that stimulate monitoring and evaluation of social-ecological systems to identify changes and/or generate new knowledge that can inform adjustments in both governance and management systems, including opportunities for legal reform (i.e., the adjustment of the legal regime of the entities involved). Importantly, it is widely agreed that there is no set formula for achieving adaptive law or that there is some optimal set of institutions and instruments that will necessarily be the most adaptive. Rather, theorists have proposed, and practitioners have tested, a broad array of strategies. What constitutes adaptive law, in other words, is an ever-evolving work in progress. Nevertheless, some core goals and principles have emerged in adaptive law theory and practice.

Synthesizing these concepts with resilience thinking, Cosens et al. (2017) identify the three governance aspects manifested through law and unpack the qualities that distinguish adaptive law from conventional regulatory models. *Structure* has to do with the way in which governance institutions are constructed, interconnected, and operationalized through law. Adaptive law promotes structure that is polycentric, integrated, and persistent. *Capacity* speaks to the resources and authority of governance to adapt. Adaptive law that is resilient promotes adaptive and participatory capacity. Lastly, *process* involves how the structure exercises its capacity. Adaptive law promotes process that is legitimate, just, problem-solving, reflective, dispute resolving, and balanced between stability and flexibility. The latter quality—the optimal trade-off between stability and flexibility that produces neither too much rigidity nor too much room for arbitrary decision-making—is perhaps the one that will be most vexing for legal theorists and practitioners to design and implement (Craig et al., 2017; Craig & Ruhl, 2014; Frohlich et al., 2018). Substantive weighing and balancing of norms, combined with procedural safeguards such as the administrative and judicial reason-giving requirement, have been proposed as partial solutions to this problem (Soininen, 2016).

Needless to say, forging adaptive governance theory is a work in progress, and applying it in real-world contexts will no doubt run into many barriers (Sharma-Wallace, Velarde, & Wreford, 2018). But the growing consensus among governance theorists is that conventional governance systems are simply not well-equipped to manage the kinds of problems facing complex social-ecological systems around the globe. Problems such as climate change, biodiversity loss, and water scarcity will test the resilience of social-ecological systems, which in turn will test the resilience of legal systems. Just as any other natural or social system must build adaptive capacity to manifest resilience, so too will a new model of adaptive law be needed, and soon.

Conclusion

Resilience thinking has profound implications for law and its capacity to support adaptive governance. Law is a complex adaptive system comprised of institutions and instruments at multiple levels ranging from international to local and regulating most aspects of human activity, either directly or indirectly. But law does not do so from outside other social systems; rather, it co-evolves with them in a system-of-systems network. As a system within a system, law has resilience features that can be characterized along the lines of general resilience theory: it exhibits properties of reliability, efficiency, scalability, modularity, and evolvability. One of law's main functions is to govern human activity so that the resilience of other systems (ecosystems, markets, cities etc.) can be managed effectively, efficiently, and legitimately. Hence, law is inherently a case multisystemic resilience—we must manage legal system resilience to manage resilience of other social systems. Adaptive governance is a theoretical framework and a set of principles for managing the resilience of systems to societally desired ends. Legal system resilience, managed properly, produces the adaptive law needed to support adaptive governance.

To be sure, these are broad and lofty principles. They chart a new direction in governance theory and practice, one aimed at bringing law in tune with the complex adaptive system qualities of social-ecological systems and of law itself. The challenges to social-ecological system resilience around the globe, on the near and distant horizons, demand nothing less of law and its resilience.

Key Messages

1. Law is a complex adaptive system comprised of institutions and instruments at multiple levels ranging from international to local and regulating most aspects of human activity either directly or indirectly.
2. As a system, law has resilience features that can be characterized along the lines of general resilience theory: (a) reliability, (b) efficiency, (c) scalability, (d) modularity, and (e) evolvability.

3. One of law's main functions is to govern human activity so that the resilience of other systems (ecosystems, markets, cities, etc.) can be managed effectively, efficiently, and legitimately.
4. Adaptive governance is a theoretical framework and a set of principles for managing the resilience of systems for socially desirable ends.

Acknowledgments

This work was the result of a pursuit funded by the U.S. National Socio-Environmental Synthesis Center (SESYNC) NS also received support from the BlueAdapt-project funded by the Strategic Research Council of Finland under funding from the U.S. National Science Foundation, NSF DBI-1052875. Portions of the text are adapted from Ruhl & Katz (2015) and Ruhl (2014).

References

Alderson, D. L., & Doyle, J. C. (2010). Contrasting views of complexity and their implications for network-centric infrastructures. *IEEE Transactions on Systems, Man, and Cybernetics, Part A: Systems and Humans, 40*(4), 839–852. doi:10.1109/TSMCA.2010.2048027

Allen, C., & Holling, C. S. (2010). Novelty, adaptive capacity, and resilience. *Ecology and Society, 15*(3), 24. Retrieved from https://www.ecologyandsociety.org/vol15/iss3/art24/

Anderies, J. M., Janssen, M. A., & Ostrom, E. (2004). A framework to analyze the robustness of social-ecological systems from an institutional perspective. *Ecology and Society, 9*(1), 18. doi:10.5751/ES-00610-090118

Bevir, M. (2012). *Governance: A very short introduction.* Oxford, UK: Oxford University Press.

Black, J. (2012). Paradoxes and failures: "New governance" techniques and the financial crisis. *Modern Law Review, 75*(6), 1037–1063. doi:10.1111/j.1468-2230.2012.00936.x

Blumm, M. C., & Ruhl, J. B. (2010). Background principles, takings, and libertarian property: A reply to Professor Huffman. *Ecology Law Quarterly, 37*, 805–842.

Chaffin, B. C., Gosnell, H., & Cosens, B. A. (2014). A decade of adaptive governance: Synthesis and future directions. *Ecology and Society, 19*(3), 56. doi:10.5751/ES-06824-190356

Conley, C. B. (2007). Parallel imports: The tired debate of the exhaustion of intellectual property rights and why the WTO should harmonize the haphazard laws of the international community. *Tulane Journal of International and Comparative Law, 16*, 189–212.

Cosens, B. A. (2013). Legitimacy, adaptation, and resilience in ecosystem management. *Ecology and Society, 18*(1), 3. doi:10.5751/ES-05093-180103

Cosens, B. A., Craig, R. K., Hirsch, S. L., Arnold, C. A., Benson, M. H., DeCaro, D. A., . . . Schlager, E. (2017). The role of law in adaptive governance. *Ecology and Society, 22*(1), 30. doi:10.5751/ES-08731-220130

Cosens, B., & Gunderson, L. (Eds.). (2018). *Practical panarchy for adaptive water governance: Linking law to social-ecological resilience.* Cham, Switzerland: Springer.

Cosens, B. A., Gunderson, L., & Chaffin, B. C. (2018). Introduction to the special feature on practicing panarchy: Assessing legal flexibility, ecological resilience, and adaptive governance in regional water systems experiencing rapid environmental change. *Ecology and Society, 23*(1), 4. Retrieved from https://www.ecologyandsociety.org/vol23/iss1/art4/

Craig, R. K., & Ruhl, J. B. (2014). Designing administrative law for adaptive management. *Vanderbilt Law Review, 67*(1), 1–88. doi:10.2139/ssrn.2222009

Craig, R. K., Garmestani, A. S., Allen, C. R., Arnold, C. A., Birgé, H. E., DeCaro, D. A., . . . Schlager, E. (2017). Balancing stability and flexibility in adaptive governance: An analysis of tools available in U.S. environmental law. *Ecology and Society, 22*(2), 3. doi:10.5751/ES-08983-220203

Craig, R. K., Garmestani, A. S., Allen, C. R., Arnold, C. A., Birgé, H., DeCaro, D. A., & Gosnell, H. (2018). Stability and flexibility in the emergence of adaptive water governance. In B. Cosens & L. Gunderson (Eds.), *Practical panarchy for adaptive water governance: Linking law to social-ecological resilience* (pp. 167–181). Cham, Switzerland: Springer.

de Chazournes, L. B. (2013). *Fresh water in international law.* Oxford, UK: Oxford University Press.

DeCaro, D. A., Chaffin, B. C., Schlager, E., Garmestani, A. S., & Ruhl, J. B. (2017). Legal and institutional foundations of adaptive environmental governance. *Ecology and Society, 22*(1), 32. doi:10.5751/ES-09036-220132

Dicey, A. V. (1979). *Introduction to the study of the law of the constitution.* London, UK: Palgrave Macmillan.

Dorf, M. C., & Sabel, C. F. (1998). A constitution of democratic experimentalism. *Columbia Law Review, 98*(2), 267–473. doi:10.2307/1123411

Drahos, P., & Krygier, M. (2017). Regulation, institutions and networks. In P. Drahos (Ed.), *Regulatory theory: Foundations and applications* (pp. 1–24). Canberra, Australia: Australia National University Press.

Esty, D. C. (Ed.). (2019). *The labyrinth of sustainability: Green business lessons from Latin American corporate leaders.* New York, NY: Anthem Press.

Fischman, R. L. (2019). Letting go of stability: Resilience and environmental law. *Indiana Law Journal, 94*(2), 689–725.

Folke, C., Hahn, T., Olsson, P., & Norberg, J. (2005). Adaptive governance of social-ecological systems. *Annual Review of Environment and Resources, 30*(1), 441–473. doi:10.1146/annurev.energy.30.050504.144511

Fraccascia, L., Giannoccaro, I., & Albino, V. (2018). Resilience of complex systems: State of the art and directions for future research. *Complexity, 2018*(3421529). doi:10.1155/2018/3421529

Freeman, J., & Rossi, J. (2011). Agency coordination in shared regulatory space. *Harvard Law Review, 125*(5), 1131–1211.

Frohlich, M. F., Jacobson, C., Fidelman, P., & Smith, T. F. (2018). The relationship between adaptive management of social-ecological systems and law: A systematic review. *Ecology and Society, 23*(2), 23. doi:10.5751/ES-10060-230223

Fuller, L. L. (1969). *The morality of law.* New Haven, CT: Yale University Press.

Giannoccaro, I., Albino, V, & Nair, A. (2018). Advances on the resilience of complex networks. *Complexity, 2018*(8756418). doi:10.1155/2018/8756418.

Gunderson, L. H. (2000). Ecological resilience: In theory and application. *Annual Review of Ecology and Systematics, 31*(1), 425–439. doi:10.1146/annurev.ecolsys.31.1.425

Gunderson, L., Garmestani, A., Rizzardi, K. W., Ruhl, J. B., & Light, A. (2014). Escaping a rigidity trap: Governance and adaptive capacity to climate change in the everglades social ecological system. *Idaho Law Review, 51*(1), 127–156. Retrieved from https://cfpub.epa.gov/si/si_public_record_report.cfm?Lab=NRMRL&dirEntryId=335840

Gunderson, L., & Holling, C. (Eds.). (2002). *Panarchy: Understanding transformations in human and natural systems.* Washington, DC: Island Press.

Gunningham, N., & Grabosky, P. (1999). *Smart regulation: Designing environmental policy.* Oxford, UK: Oxford University Press.

Hahn, R. W., & Sunstein, C. R. (2002). A new executive order for improving federal regulation? Deeper and wider cost-benefit analysis. *University of Pennsylvania Law Review, 150*(5), 1489–1552. doi:10.2307/3312946

Kades, E. (1997). The laws of complexity & the complexity of laws: The implications of computational complexity theory for the law. *Rutgers Law Review, 43*(2), 403–484.

Karpouzoglou, T., Dewulf, A., & Clark, J. (2016). Advancing adaptive governance of social-ecological systems through theoretical multiplicity. *Environmental Science & Policy, 57*, 1–9. doi:10.1016/j.envsci.2015.11.011

Langlet, D., & Mahmoudi, S. (2016). *EU environmental law and policy.* Oxford, UK: Oxford University Press.

Lazarus, R. (2004). *The making of environmental law.* Chicago, IL: University of Chicago Press.

Lebal, L., Anderies, J. M., Campbell, B., & Hatfield-Dodds, S. (2006). Governance and the capacity to manage resilience in regional social-ecological systems. *Ecology and Society, 11*(1), 19. doi:10.5751/ES-01606-110119

Lee, K. N. (1999). Appraising adaptive management. *Conservation Ecology, 3*(2), 3. Retrieved from http://www.consecol.org/vol3/iss2/art3/

Levin, S. A. (2000). *Fragile dominion: Complexity and the commons*. Reading, MA: Basic Books.

Llewellyn, K. (1960). *The common law tradition: Deciding appeals*. Buffalo, NY: Little, Brown.

Luhmann, N. (2004). *Law as a social system*. Oxford, UK: Oxford University Press.

Miller, J. H., & Page, S. E. (2007). *Complex adaptive systems: An introduction to computational models of social life*. Princeton, NJ: Princeton University Press.

Mitchell, M. (2009). *Complexity: A guided tour*. New York, NY: Oxford University Press.

Murray, J., Webb, T. E., & Wheatley, S., (Eds.). (2019). *Complexity theory and law: Mapping an emergent jurisprudence*. Oxon, UK: Routledge.

Nagle, J. C. (2008). From swamp drainage to wetlands regulation to ecological nuisances to environmental ethics. *Case Western Reserve Law Review, 58*(3), 787–812. doi:10.2139/ssrn.1346983

Nash, J. R., Ruhl, J. J., & Salzman, J. (2017). The production function of the regulatory state. *Minnesota Law Review, 102*(2), 695–759. Retrieved from https://ssrn.com/abstract=2927208

Revesz, R. L. (1999). Environmental regulation, cost-benefit analysis and the discounting of human lives. *Columbia Law Review, 99*(4), 941–1017. doi:10.2307/1123481

Ruhl, J. B. (2011). General design principles for resilience and adaptive capacity in legal systems: Applications to climate change adaptation. *North Carolina Law Review, 89*(5), 1373–1403. Retrieved from https://ssrn.com/abstract=1694187

Ruhl, J. B. (2014). Managing systemic risk in legal systems. *Indiana Law Journal, 89*(2), 559–603. Retrieved from https://www.repository.law.indiana.edu/ilj/vol89/iss2/2/

Ruhl, J. B., & Katz, D. M. (2015). Measuring, monitoring, and managing legal complexity. *Idaho Law Review, 101*(1), 191–244. Retrieved from https://ilr.law.uiowa.edu/assets/issues/volume-101-issue-1/ILR-101-1-RuhlKatz.pdf

Ruhl, J. B., Katz, D. M., & Bommarito, M. (2017). Harnessing legal complexity. *Science, 355*(6332), 1337–1338. doi:10.1126/science.aag3013

Salzman, J., & Ruhl, J. B. (2010). Climate change, dead zones, and massive problems in the administrative state A guide for whittling away. *California Law Review, 98*(1), 59–120. doi:10.2307/20743966

Sellberg, M. M., Ryan, P., Borgstrom, S. T., Norstrom, A. V., & Peterson, G. D. (2018). From resilience thinking to resilience planning: Lessons from practice. *Journal of Environmental Management, 217*(1), 906–918. doi:10.1016/j.jenvman.2018.04.012

Sharma-Wallace, L., Velarde, S. J., & Wreford, A. (2018). Adaptive governance good practice: Show me the evidence! *Journal of Environmental Management, 222*, 174–184. doi:10.1016/j.jenvman.2018.05.067

Soininen, N. (2016). *Transparencies in legality: A legal analysis of the reason-giving requirement in water management permitting in Finland*. Helsinki, Finland: Finnish Lawyers' Association. (Original in Finnish)

Soininen, N. (2018). Torn by (un)certainty: Can there be peace between the rule of law and other SDGs? In D. French & L. Kotzé (Eds.), *Sustainable development goals: Law, theory and implementation* (pp. 250–270). Cheltenham, UK: Edward Elgar.

Soininen, N., & Platjouw, F. M. (2019). Resilience and adaptive capacity of aquatic environmental law in the EU: An evaluation and comparison of the WFD, MSFD, and MSPD. In D. Langlet & R. Rayfuse (Eds.), *Ecosystem approach in ocean governance and planning* (pp. 17–79). Leiden, The Netherlands: Brill Nijhof.

Soininen, N., Belinskij, A., Vainikka, A., & Huuskonen, H. (2019). Bringing back ecological flows: Migratory fish, hydropower and legal maladaptivity in the governance of Finnish rivers. *Water International, 44*(3), 321–336. doi:10.1080/02508060.2019.1542260

Stewart, R. B. (2001). A new generation of environmental regulation? *Capital University Law Review, 29*(1), 21–182.

Sunstein, C. R. (1996). Social norms and social roles. *Columbia Law Review, 96*(4), 903–968. doi:10.2307/1123430

Thoma, R. (1978). Rechtsstaatsidee und Verwaltungsrechtswissenschaft. In M. Tohidipur (Ed.), *Der bürgerliche rechtsstaat* (pp. 177–194). Frankfurt, Germany: Suhrkamp Verlag.

Vandenbergh, M. P., & Gilligan, J. M. (2017). *Beyond politics: The private governance response to climate change*. Cambridge, UK: Cambridge University Press.

Vile, J. R. (1994). *Constitutional change in the United States*. Westport, CT: Praeger.

Volkman, J. M., & McConnaha, W. E. (1993). Through a glass, darkly: Columbia River salmon, the endangered species act, and adaptive management. *Environmental Law, 23*(4), 1249–1272.

Waldron, J. (2010). The rule of law and the importance of procedure. In J. E. Fleming (Ed.), *Getting to the rule of law* (pp. 3–31). New York, NY: New York University Press.

Walker, B., Gunderson, L. H., Kinzig, A. P., Folke, C., Carpenter, S. R., & Schultz, L. (2006). A handful of heuristics and some propositions for understanding resilience in social-ecological systems. *Ecology and Society, 11*(1), 13. Retrieved from http://www.ecologyandsociety.org/vol11/iss1/art13/

Williams, B. K., & Brown, E. D. (2014). Adaptive management: From more talk to real action. *Environmental Management, 53*(2), 465–479. doi:10.1007/s00267-013-0205-7

Young, E. A. (2007). The constitution outside the constitution. *Yale Law Journal, 117*(3), 408–473.

27
Thinking Systemically About Transitional Justice, Legal Systems, and Resilience

Janine Natalya Clark

Introduction

Legal systems are commonly judged on the basis of certain criteria: their stability, their transparency, their procedures, and the fairness of the laws they apply. These criteria might be broadly subsumed under the label *resilience*. When societies undergo change, and when they face new upheavals and crises, it is often legal systems that act as a crucial stabilizing factor. They are social structures that help to absorb the impact of stresses and shocks, while at the same time reinforcing a sense of continuity. When they function well, they can be described as resilient. This resilience, however, has boundaries. While legal systems have to adapt, they need to do so in a way that does not undermine their "own basic behavioural structure" (Ruhl, 2011, p. 1388). Therefore, thinking about resilience in the context of legal systems necessarily has wider implications because of their inter-connections with other systems. As Connell (1997) has underlined, "there is a dialectic interplay between law and society" (p. 123). The resilience of a legal system, thus, will necessarily affect the resilience of other systems. For example, legal systems can help to make societies more resilient by providing institutional structures needed for good governance and social order. Viewed in this way, part of the conceptual and empirical utility of resilience as a concept is that it opens up a space for analyzing the wider societal and systemic impact of legal systems. This broad argument is explored and developed in this chapter through a specific focus on transitional justice. Although it is important to underline at the outset that legal processes form only one part of transitional justice, they are often a very central part.

It will be shown that the multifarious goals of transitional justice implicitly encompass a resilience element; the process of dealing with the past is posited as a way of rebuilding and strengthening societies. It is striking, however, that discussions of resilience are pronouncedly absent from existing transitional justice literature. While there have been some references to resilience (e.g., Duthie, 2017; Wiebelhaus-Brahm, 2017), to date there are no systematic analyses of transitional justice within a resilience framework, or vice versa. Kastner's work (2020) is a recent exception. Approaching resilience as a systemic concept and drawing insights from dynamic systems approaches to conflict analysis, this chapter demonstrates how resilience thinking can potentially enhance the impact of transitional justice on the ground. In particular, it argues that a resilience lens can significantly contribute to the development of more ecological approaches to transitional justice that locate individuals within their broader social environments. Furthermore, by showing that transitional justice can make legal systems more resilient, especially during extreme events like war, this chapter provides the basis for thinking about legal systems as part of a matrix of interrelated systems that create the conditions for societal resilience in contexts of adversity.

Transitional Justice

Transitional justice is the complex process of dealing with a legacy of past human rights violations and abuses, through a combination of judicial and nonjudicial means. These can include criminal prosecutions, truth commissions, lustration (administrative purges of officials) and institutional reforms, reparations, memorials, and apologies. The ambitious goals associated with transitional justice are similarly diverse. Among the most frequently mentioned are delivering justice, giving victims a voice, combating impunity, strengthening the rule of law, establishing the truth and contributing to reconciliation (United Nations [UN], 2010). While the field of transitional justice rapidly continues to grow, so too does the imperative of thinking critically and pushing new boundaries. Albert Einstein once said, "Problems cannot be solved at the same level of perspective from which they are perceived to exist as problems.... Some new level of perspective must be found" (cited in Coleman, 2006, p. 346). This chapter aims to contribute a new perspective by looking at transitional justice and legal systems through the lens of resilience.

Defining Resilience

Existing scholarship on resilience is vast, and the concept is discussed and dissected in highly diverse contexts extending across multiple disciplines. Accordingly, a plethora of definitions exists. One of the consequences is that resilience has become an increasingly slippery concept that is often difficult to describe. What adds to its lubricity in this regard is the fact that, as this volume shows, resilience resides not just in individuals, but in entire systems which influence and interact with each other. Resilience is thus a dynamic concept with highly fluid boundaries. As Nguyen-Gillham, Giacaman, Naser, and Boyce (2008) underline, "resilience does not exist as a static quality or a mechanistic process but in a continuum that varies over time and context" (p. 296).

Within the field of transitional justice, resilience can be described as a latent concept in the sense that it is present in various guises. Prior to completing its mandate in December 2017, for example, the International Criminal Tribunal for the former Yugoslavia (ICTY)—which will be further discussed in the case study section of this chapter—engaged in significant capacity-building work to support and strengthen local courts in the former Yugoslavia (including Bosnia-Herzegovina, Croatia, Kosovo, and Serbia; see ICTY, n.d.b). This international-to-national transfer of knowledge and expertise in the handling of complex war crimes cases can be viewed as an example of building resilience within national legal systems. Resilience, in this regard, is the process of enabling and assisting these systems to adapt to prosecuting crimes—including genocide, massacres, and widespread acts of sexual violence—that ordinarily fall outside the remit of domestic courts. As a further example of the contribution that resilience can make to transitional justice, Wiebelhaus-Brahm (2017) notes that although proponents of transitional justice do not employ resilience language, they "claim transitional justice processes can promote such outcomes as reconciliation, trust, and the rule of law, which development practitioners associate with more resilient societies" (p. 142). The latent presence of resilience as a concept within transitional justice points to the existence of "common features" between the two (Kastner, 2020, p. 369). For example, "individuals and communities undergo significant changes in conflict and post-conflict situations; they need to adapt, find strategies to cope with various forms of violence and develop the ability to survive through and after periods of significant stress" (Kastner, 2020, p. 369). If important synergies exist, this necessarily invites crucial reflection on why the concept of resilience has rarely been explicitly discussed within the field of transitional justice. This section's point of departure is precisely to engage with that question, as a way of contextualizing the relative absence of resilience definitions within transitional justice literature.

Resilience—A Neglected Concept within Transitional Justice

There are four main reasons why transitional justice (and, indeed, the justice literature as a whole) has largely overlooked the concept of resilience. The first reason is that one of the core aims of transitional justice is to deliver justice (UN, 2010). While justice has an obvious legal dimension, involving the prosecution of indicted war criminals, it can also encompass victim-focused restorative and reparative forms of addressing the past, including truth and reconciliation commissions, compensation, and rehabilitation. Prioritizing resilience, however, can potentially result in justice trade-offs. By way of illustration, Fainstein (2015) asserts:

> Efforts to achieve resilience in relation to climate change through developing natural buffers against sea level rise will likely result in the displacement of populations. Who will be displaced and what measures will be taken to replace lost housing and community are crucial questions not captured by the term resilience. (p. 157; see also Harris, Chu, & Ziervogel, 2018)

Yet, conversely, giving more attention to resilience within transitional justice, and possible ways of fostering resilience, can potentially provide a framework for delivering more comprehensive and deeper forms of justice. The human rights abuses that trigger transitional justice processes, for example, may intersect with and build on longer-term patterns of discrimination and structural violence, including socioeconomic marginalization and deprivation of land rights. In other words, acts of episodic violence against individuals may be embedded within broader systems of oppression (Lykes, 2001). If transitional justice processes do not address these systemic injustices, the "justice" that they deliver can easily appear deficient. Highlighting this, Laplante (2008) underlines that "even with trials and reparations, if economic and social inequalities go unaddressed and the grievances of the poor and marginalized go unheard, we are left with only uncertain guarantees of non-repetition" (p. 332). Such arguments, however, have met with concerns that transitional justice risks losing its quintessential raison d'être and becoming overstretched if it is asked to do too much and to address issues such as economic and social rights (McAuliffe, 2011, p. 33; Waldorf, 2012, p. 179). From this perspective, the introduction of a resilience discourse, especially one that emphasizes the multiple systems that produce resilience, could contribute to this problematic overreach.

The second reason why resilience remains underdiscussed in the field of transitional justice is that there does not immediately appear to be an obvious place for it. Within transitional justice theory and practice, there is a strong emphasis on victims and their rights—for example, to know the truth, to have their suffering formally acknowledged, and to receive reparations. Some scholars have, therefore, called for more victim-centered ways of doing transitional justice that prioritize the needs of victims (e.g., Robins, 2011). At first glance, introducing the discourse of resilience potentially takes away part of the rationale for having transitional justice. If victims have positively adapted to the adversities they have faced, if they are coping well and managing their everyday lives, what can transitional justice offer them? This is, of course, both an erroneous and highly simplistic way of viewing the relationship between resilience and transitional justice. However, on the surface at least, the victimological dimensions of transitional justice may not be entirely compatible with the discourse of resilience. This is not to say that victims do not demonstrate resilience. The very act of testifying in court against an indicted war criminal, for example, can be a powerful act of resilience. The important point is that transitional justice has given little attention to the concept of the resilient victim or to possible ways of fostering resilience in victims and their communities. Relatedly, transitional justice processes and the expectations that they can generate on the ground potentially diminish the incentive for victims to actively negotiate for vital resources (an important part of resilience), encouraging them instead to overrely on their status as victims to get what they need. Discussing their work in northern Uganda, for example, Hollander and Gill (2014) reflect on their discomfort "as those affected [by the conflict] sought to make themselves visible by putting their bodies on display, exhibiting wounds, scars and other physical deviances" (p. 221). They observe that "the logic of this biomedical gaze implies that only by representing themselves as abject, agency-less 'victims' with extreme medical needs would they be 'entitled' to any kind of assistance" (Hollander & Gill, 2014, p. 221).

A third reason for the lack of writing connecting resilience and transitional justice may be that in a transitional justice environment where mass human rights violations have occurred, the language of resilience is problematic. It might be asked, for example, whether the resilience label places unfair demands on individuals who have endured immense suffering and trauma. Kastner (2020), for example, points out that "Transferring the responsibility to local actors to find their own solutions to past and present forms of violence also means that, thanks to their presumably commendable 'resilience', they would and should be able to continue to endure various forms of ongoing violence and suffering" (pp. 374–375). A related issue is the criteria for dividing those who are "resilient" from those who are not. Lenette, Brough, and Cox (2013), for example, pertinently ask: "Given the experience of human rights violations among refugees, who should decide what constitutes a (non)resilient response? Is it reasonable to assign some responses to human rights violations as resilient and some not resilient?" (p. 640). Resilience is a process, not an end state, and it varies across both time and space. An individual may demonstrate resilience in one part of his or her life, for example, but not in another (Wright, Fopma-Loy, & Fischer, 2005). It is important to stress, however, that many of these issues and concerns with resilience primarily arise when the concept is reductively viewed "as a personal trait" (Mohaupt, 2008, p. 67), rather than as an innately complex and multilayered concept that reflects the interactions between individuals and their environments (Hayward, 2013; Southwick, Bonanno, Masten, Panter-Brick, & Yehuda, 2014; Ungar, 2013).

A final reason for the underexplored linkages between resilience and transitional justice is that transitional justice is associated with the exceptional (van der Merwe & Lykes, 2016, p. 362). It focuses on seemingly out-of-the-ordinary crimes, such as genocide and crimes against humanity, and on regimes that commit singularly flagrant violations of human rights. Orford (2006), for example, remarks, "The literature gives the sense that large-scale human rights violations are exceptional, so that mechanisms to address them take place in a state of transition from apartheid, dictatorship, or communism to liberal democracy" (p. 861). This emphasis on the extraordinary can deflect attention from the quotidian—from the needs, challenges, and problems that individuals living in postconflict environments face in their daily lives. Resilience, as many authors have noted, is often manifested in the domain of everyday life and everyday practices (Nguyen-Gillham et al., 2008, p. 296; see also Ziervogel et al., 2017, p. 123). If interventions aimed at fostering and enhancing resilience need to align with the "life circumstances and everyday ecologies of the individuals served" (Luthar & Cicchetti, 2000, p. 878–879), the crucial point is that these everyday ecologies have not been a central focus of transitional justice practice to date.

All of the above reasons contribute to explaining why resilience remains a notably overlooked concept within the field of transitional justice. It is essential to reiterate, however, that there are important synergies between the two (and, perhaps, justice systems as a whole). To cite Wiebelhaus-Brahm (2017), "intentionally or not, transitional justice is one policy intervention that likely affects the resilience of human societies" (p. 142). Examining some of the definitions of resilience in related fields, moreover, helps to further accentuate these synergies—and the relevance of resilience to transitional justice.

The Concept of Resilience as Relevant to Transitional Justice

In their work on gender and resilience, Smyth and Sweetman (2015) underline:

> At the heart of the concept of resilience is the idea of strength in the face of adversity. Resilience-based approaches in humanitarian and development work aim to support people not only to survive and recover from current crises, but to strengthen their defences in the face of future threats. (p. 406)

This future-focused orientation finds a strong resonance in transitional justice, which is quintessentially about addressing the past to create a better future. Moreover, if resilience-based approaches in the context of development and humanitarian aid include enhancing well-being and investing in resources to help reduce risk (Smyth & Sweetman, 2015), there are obvious overlaps in this regard with transitional justice goals—and in particular with peace-building (UN, 2010; see however, Kastner, 2020, p. 374).

In the context of human security, Chandler (2012) defines resilience as "the capacity to positively or successfully adapt to external problems or threats" (p. 217). He further underlines:

> The resilient subject (at both individual and collective levels) is never conceived as passive or as lacking agency (as in the case of 1990s understandings of victims requiring saving interventions), but is conceived only as an active agent, capable of achieving self-transformation. (p. 217)

In a very different context, Pulvirenti and Mason (2011) similarly underscore the nexus between resilience and agency. In their research on female refugees experiencing domestic violence during resettlement in Australia, they argue:

> The resilience of these women is not a capacity for ongoing survival that comes with having been through so much already but, instead, a dynamic process of shifting, changing, building, learning and moving on from those violent histories to 'establish meaningful lives' now and in the future. (p. 46)

The framing of resilience as a strongly agentic concept is highly relevant to the development of more complex theorizations of victim-centered transitional justice that extend beyond the needs of individuals. In this regard, victim-centered is also about recognizing the agency of victims—and creating the space for this agency to directly shape transitional justice processes and outcomes. Highlighting this point, van der Merwe and Lykes (2016) argue, "Work to date demonstrates that victims are typically engaged in drawn-out struggles for reparations and other rights. Transitional justice mechanisms need to equip them for this and other battles" (p. 364). As an agentic process, moreover, resilience also has an important transformative dimension, which, in turn, is an intrinsic part of its dynamicity. Resilience is less about "bouncing back" and more about "bouncing forward" (Scott, 2013, p. 601; for a critique of both types of "bouncing", see Clark, 2020). It is not about returning to what was but about creating something new. According to Pulvirenti and Mason (2011), "it is the capacity to transform their lives—not just cope with violence—that makes refugee women resilient" (p. 46).

For the purpose of analyzing the relationship between resilience and transitional justice, this transformative dimension is highly significant. The concept of transformation underlines that resilience is not just about individuals but also about their wider environments—and the various interconnecting systems that constitute these environments. Focusing on these systems, the next section explores how resilience operates as a multisystemic concept within the fields of transitional justice and law more generally.

Law, Transitional Justice, and Multisystemic Resilience

The concept of resilience has received considerably more (although still limited) attention within general legal literature than it has within transitional justice literature. As an illustration, some scholars have questioned the compatibility of law and resilience—and the extent to which legal systems can in fact be resilient or foster resilience in other systems. Garmestani, Allen, and Benson (2013), for example, maintain that "a legal system that is linear and largely static is ill-suited for the nonlinear dynamics of linked social-ecological systems." They further underscore that "while the law seeks resolution, a legal system that sets a rule and does not revisit and adjust the rule following assessment of the rule's effects is incompatible with managing for resilience." In a similar vein, Odom Green et al. have pointed to possible tensions between law and resilience, noting that legal systems may operate in a way that circumscribes the scope for flexibility and adaptation. They remark:

> Our legal system is designed to promote social stability through reliance on precedent, prescriptive rules, and adherence to procedure. In theory, this ensures fair treatment among parties involved in disputes, resolves conflicts, and fosters economic investment and civil society, all of which are advantageous social goals. One disadvantage is rigidity in the face of change or new information (Odom Green et al., 2015, p. 333).

Such arguments have often been made in relation to environmental law, a subdiscipline that highlights the interconnections between legal systems and wider social systems. It is a branch of law that is concerned with the ecological environments in which individuals and societies live and with ensuring that these environments are safeguarded and protected. As one scholar has argued, "the environment is even more fundamental than human rights as it represents the natural conditions of all life including human beings" (Bosselmann, 2015, p. 173). Environmental law thus needs to be highly responsive to fulfill its core function, while also operating in the context of broader legal systems that have their own functions. Nevertheless, this does not mean that there is a tension between law and resilience.

Arnold and Gunderson (2013) maintain that it is essential to improve the adaptive capacity of environmental law. This, they argue, "will require the development of overarching systemic principles that maintain the resilience and adaptive capacity of ecological and social systems, not merely the occasional use of specific adaptive methods" (p. 10426). Viewed in this way, a more complex intersystemic relationship emerges. Laws are not resilient (adaptive) in and of themselves, but rather as elements of broader socioecological systems with which they synergistically interact. As part of this interaction, laws and legal systems can contribute to fostering systemic resilience by offering a social compass and providing stability. As Ebbesson and Hey (2013) point out, "while the notion of the rule of law may hamper the flexibility to adapt to change, the rule of law and legal certainty also foster trust and help to buffer capacity to persist, adapt and transform, when required."

As a response to mass human rights violations and abuses, many transitional justice processes have an important legal dimension. According to Teitel (2005), "in the contemporary phase, transitional jurisprudence reflects the normalization of an expanded juridicized discourse of humanitarian law associated with pervasive conflict" (p. 840). Legal aspects of transitional justice include the criminal prosecution of perpetrators, the restoration of the rule of law and the reform/creation of institutions tasked with upholding legal norms and human rights. These legal processes have a significant resilience underpinning, even if they have not been explicitly theorized within a resilience framework. In societies dislocated and torn apart by violence and armed conflict, legal processes form an important part of recreating a sense of normality and stability. Additionally, and to reiterate an earlier point, commonly stated goals of criminal prosecutions and nonretributive forms of transitional justice—such as peace and reconciliation—have an implicit resilience component. In short, "while transitional justice is only one of many possible policy interventions, it holds the potential to promote or undermine the resilience of post-conflict societies" (Wiebelhaus-Brahm, 2017, p. 142).

The process of fostering resilience in the context of transitional justice processes, moreover, is necessarily multisystemic. This is for two key reasons. First, human rights violations that catalyze transitional justice processes and activate international criminal mechanisms affect not just individuals but entire systems—families, communities, and societies. At a metasystemic level, they are crimes that "deeply shock the conscience of humanity" (International Criminal Court, 2002, p. 1). Transitional justice processes need to address these multiple layers of impact and thereby contribute to fostering resilience and adaptive capacity across these different interlocking social systems. Second, transitional justice processes do not exist in a vacuum, and the impact that they have on societies is not one way. They exist as part of broader systems, which, in turn, can critically shape the extent to which transitional justice processes are successful and achieve their stated goals. Duthie (2017) highlights "the bi-directional relationship between contexts of social and economic structures and transitional justice" (p. 24). For example, the existence of deep-seated structural inequalities within a society will potentially influence how communities engage with transitional justice processes and what they expect from them.

As an example of these structural inequalities, systems-based discussions within transitional justice scholarship have often focused on the concept of gender. The very notion of transition appears a misnomer if it leaves intact social systems and structures that perpetuate gender inequality and the marginalization of women. Discussing institutional reforms, for example, Ní Aoláin and Rooney (2007) note: "Questions about the equal representation of women, and which women are deemed 'representative' in these institutional decision-making sites, reveal how institutions embed conceptual frameworks that have forceful, concrete gendered outcomes" (p. 345; see also Rooney, 2006). Piecemeal institutional reforms that do not address wider systemic and gender issues can only take us so far. Relatedly, inclusivity requires that transitional justice processes take account of different intersectional experiences of conflict across gender, class, ethnicity, and so on. This is because these varied experiences "will produce different ideas as to the necessary ingredients for resolving the conflict" (Bell & O'Rourke, 2007, p. 31)—and, by extension, different ideas about dealing with the legacy of the human rights abuses committed.

Concerns that transitional justice processes often do not go far enough or penetrate deep enough—and not only in relation to gender issues—have led some scholars to call for a more comprehensive transformative justice (Daly, 2001; Lambourne, 2015). Transformative reparations, for example, would not only address the harm that results from experiences such as sexual violence, but would also seek to "transform the conditions that initially made them possible, such as cultural stereotypes and stigma surrounding sexual violence" (Sandoval, 2017, p. 170). The concept of transformation is highly relevant to both resilience and justice, and in this way it forms an important connective thread between the two. According to Gready and Robins (2014), "transformative justice entails a shift in focus from the legal to the social and political, and from the state and institutions to communities and everyday concerns" (p. 340). Transformative justice, thus, "is not the result of a top-down imposition of external legal frameworks or institutional templates, but of a more bottom-up understanding and analysis of the lives and needs of populations" (Gready & Robins, 2014, p. 340). This conceptualization of transformative justice, however, is too narrow because it extracts people's "lives and needs" from the broader systems of which they form an intrinsic part. This risks replicating one of the major issues with existing transitional justice practice, namely, the fact that the strong focus on individuals (perpetrators and victims) often downplays the wider social ecologies in which these men and women live and navigate their lives (Aguirre & Pietropaoli, 2008, p. 362).

Speaking about resilience in adolescents, Olsson, Bond, Burns, Vella-Brodrick and Sawyer (2003) assert that "effective interventions could be aimed at developing the individual's internal resources and skills and equally importantly changing the social environment to further promote resilience" (pp. 3-4). By extension, it is argued that effective transitional justice interventions can promote and contribute to resilience by seeking transformations that cut across interconnecting levels. Collective reparations, for example, can include housing support or the rebuilding of a school (International Criminal Court, 2017). The extent to which such developments contribute to community resilience will be limited, however, if they do not address divisive social attitudes that potentially undermine a community's resilience. Qayoom (2014) notes, for example, "Widowhood is socially stigmatized in South Asia and becoming a widow means possible isolation, loss of dignity and individual identity, since widows become dependent on their relatives. They are frequently denied inheritance and property rights" (p. 162). Relatedly, efforts to rebuild infrastructure resilience within a community will fall short if the support networks that play an elemental role in buffering shocks and strains are not themselves repaired and restored. In the Ivory Coast, for example, women who are internally displaced in the capital have described "feeling socially isolated in Abidjan and far from family and friends." As a result of this they are less likely to disclose interpersonal violence and seek help (Cardosa et al., 2016, p. 371).

Thinking explicitly about resilience in a transitional justice context, and the different systems involved in resilience, offers a framework for theorizing and developing more ecological—and transformative—pathways to doing transitional justice that address the interactions between individuals and their environments. It also provides deeper insights into how legal systems and resilience can work better together and how the balance between "legal certainty and flexibility" manifests and is resolved at different levels (Ebbesson, 2010, p. 417). Ebbesson and Hey (2013), for example, suggest that "as law moves from the local level to the national, regional, and international levels, law itself, due to the enhanced complexity of decision-making, becomes more resilient to change, and its capacity to address change, complexity, and adaptation slows down" (para. 7).

This notion of resilience to change brings forth a conceptual aspect of resilience that runs counter to ideas of adaptation and flexibility. It is the juxtaposition between change-resistant and change-enabling resilience that is central to the next section, which presents a model aimed at guiding future study of multisystemic resilience within the fields of law and transitional justice. The development of this model is informed by conflict analysis literature and, in particular, the concepts of attractors and feedback loops.

Modeling Multisystemic Resilience

Transitional justice and legal systems form part of a broader "dynamical system," which Coleman (2006) defines as "a set of interconnected elements that changes and evolves in time" (p. 327). A change in one element causes changes in the other elements. Thus, resilience thinking can contribute to enhancing the social ecological impacts and effectiveness of transitional justice and legal processes. As a starting point, it is important to recognize, however, that components within the overall dynamical system can obstruct and impede these processes. Creating friction and resisting change, these components can be described as attractors—a concept that has been used to explain the genesis and persistence of conflict.

According to Vallacher, Coleman, Nowak and Bui-Wrzosinska (2010),

> in generic terms, an attractor refers to a subset of potential states or patterns of change to which a system's behaviour converges over time. Metaphorically, an attractor 'attracts' the system's behavior, so that even very different starting states tend to evolve toward the subset of states defining the attractor. (pp. 264–265)

In other words, the existence of attractors fosters change-resistant resilience that restricts the possibilities for multisystemic change. Conversely, "in the absence of an attractor, a system can change and evolve in response to whatever influences and forces it experiences" (Vallacher et al., 2010, p. 265). These attractors are necessarily cross-systemic and may include entrenched social attitudes, deep-rooted historical grievances, the persistence of political ideologies at the state level, absence of political reforms, and embedded structural violence. Because attractors hinder change, they are "similar to the notion of equilibrium or homeostasis" (Vallacher et al., 2010, p. 265).

Transitional justice processes and legal processes, however, are not about homeostasis but about addressing the past as a way of enabling societies that have experienced mass atrocities, violence, and human rights atrocities to rebuild and move forward. These processes cannot contribute to fostering resilience to future shocks and stressors if many of the factors that underpinned or fueled past violence remain unchanged. Us–them thinking, for example, is a significant driver of conflict and violence (Staub, 2012) and may be expressed within communities, through media outlets and via state and religious institutions. The persistence of such thinking in postconflict societies can be conceptualized as a significant attractor, pulling a system back to a negative status quo and thereby obstructing transitional justice work that indirectly seeks to create community resilience by laying the foundations for trust and reconciliation.

If, as previously argued, resilience opens a space for thinking more ecologically about transitional justice processes, then a critical part of developing and building ecological ways of doing transitional justice is to look at the wider whole. Some authors have used the term *holism* in relation to transitional justice to underscore the necessity of combining different retributive, restorative, and reparative mechanisms, thus shifting from an overreliance on criminal prosecutions (e.g., Boraine, 2006; Sooka, 2006). Yet, this type of holism does not extend far enough. The peace that is discussed in the context of transitional justice is not merely a negative peace or a return to a previous state of homeostasis, defined by the end of physical violence or a return to previous patterns of social exclusion (Gautung, 1969). Rather, it is a deeper and more resilient "positive peace" that is "inherently holistic" and transformational (Sharp, 2014, p. 159). If transitional justice is to contribute to positive peace, it needs to be more "holistic" in the sense of looking at the dynamical system as a whole—and at the attractors that can derail core transitional justice goals. What is imperative is that transitional justice processes do not harden these attractors and thereby reinforce change-resistant resilience within and between systems.

In this regard, the concept of feedback loops is extremely useful. Positive and negative feedback loops form important parts of conflict dynamics, affecting whether or not those dynamics escalate and destabilize systems or make systems more resilient. According to Coleman (2006):

> a positive feedback loop (in which one element stimulates another along its current trajectory) is instrumental in bringing together the mechanisms necessary to generate and maintain an action (e.g., when a series of negative encounters with someone leads to an explicit expression of hostility). A negative feedback loop (in which one element constrains another), on the other hand, is necessary for terminating action once a threshold is reached that suggests the action is sufficient or extreme (e.g., when a parent steps in to stop a fight between siblings). (p. 328)

In terms of their impact on conflict, it is positive feedback loops that present the biggest danger, causing conflicts to escalate, while negative feedback loops help to promote conflict resolution. In short, "As long as a system is characterized by negative feedback loops, control mechanisms are available for mitigating and terminating conflict, allowing situations of conflict to be temporary and constructive rather than destructive" (Coleman, 2006, p. 328). Transposing the concept of feedback loops to a transitional justice context, one way in which transitional justice processes can potentially weaken the pull of attractors within the system is through the creation of negative feedback loops that limit the scope for individual attractors—which will often be mutually reinforcing—to spread to other levels within the system. For example, a highly unpopular court judgement can potentially strengthen a broader system attractor, such as nationalism or revisionism. In this situation, an optimal transitional justice response would be the creation of a negative feedback loop around the court judgement—for example, through engagement with local communities, the media, and religious leaders—to minimize its impact on the attractor. To reiterate, it is essential that the individual parts of the system are seen in the context of the systemic whole. Figure 27.1 summarizes this relationship between the dynamical system, transitional justice, attractors, and feedback loops.

The example of an unpopular court judgement highlights a broader issue, namely, that transitional justice processes can be highly polarizing. As Leebaw (2008) notes, "truth commissions and criminal tribunals investigate extremely divisive and violent histories" (p. 96). Their impact on the ground can be similarly divisive (Olsen, Payne, & Reiter, 2010, p. 988), potentially reinforcing attractors. Vallacher et al. (2010) suggest a possible approach for dealing with attractors that is useful in this regard. "The key," they argue, is "moving the system out of its manifest attractor into a latent attractor that is defined in terms of benign or even positive thoughts, actions, and relationships" (p. 273). One way in which transitional

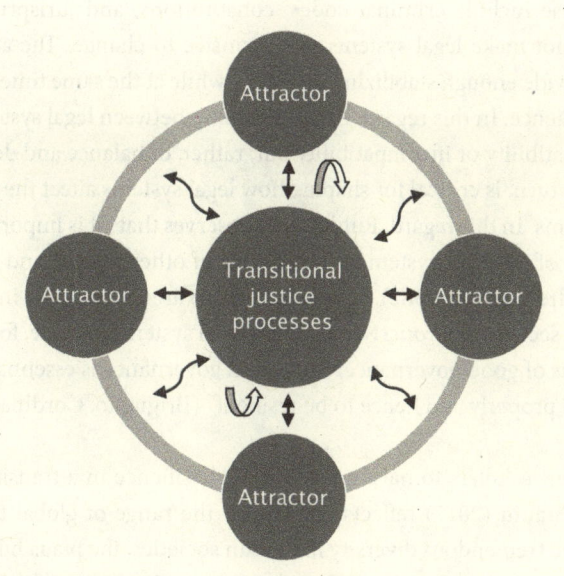

FIGURE 27.1 Attractors, feedback loops, and transitional justice processes.

justice processes might move an attractor into a latent form is by focusing people's attention on what they have in common—the desire for peace, for stability, for "normal" lives. In societies where levels of poverty, unemployment and general malaise are high, communities may struggle to see the relevance of transitional justice, particularly if they do not personally benefit from it (Clark, 2014). If people are focusing on making ends meet and getting through each day, the notion of dealing with the past to create a better future can seem highly abstract. When viewed from the ground up, it is often the case that "the normative and intellectual frame of transitional justice floats above" everyday needs and priorities (Shaw & Waldorf, 2010, p. 4).

This frame can assume a more connected and concrete form, however, through a greater emphasis on the relevance of transitional justice for shared hopes and goals relating to the present and the future, which are known elements of resilient communities (Zautra, Hall, & Murray, 2008). As the attractor fostering change-resistant resilience moves into a latent form, this in turn opens the space for transitional justice work to contribute to resilience by enabling societies to grow, positively adapt to the legacy of the past and rebuild. Bringing the everyday into focus also draws attention to important quotidian manifestations of resilience. In their work with female antimining activists in Peru and Guatemala, Jenkins and Rondón (2015) depict resilience as "an ability to survive in challenging contexts—not in the context of sudden disaster or crisis, but in relation to longer-term challenges such as mining conflict, violence, and poverty" (p. 419). Thus, a further way in which transitional justice processes (and possibly all legal processes) can assume a more grounded and locally embedded form is by enhancing resilience-supportive environments that enable individuals and communities to manage the challenges that they face.

While the aforementioned discussion has focused on transitional justice, the discussion about attractors has broader implications for the relationship between legal systems and resilience. Within all legal systems, there are attractors that create the necessary stability and certainty. These include criminal codes, constitutions, and jurisprudence. Yet, these attractors should not make legal systems unresponsive to change. The attractors, in other words, need to provide enough stabilizing resilience while at the same time allowing for sufficient adaptive resilience. In this regard, the relationship between legal systems and resilience is not one of compatibility or incompatibility but, rather, of balance and degree. The balance that is achieved, in turn, is critical for shaping how legal systems affect the resilience of other co-occurring systems. In this regard, Ruhl (2011) observes that "it is important to distinguish between resilience of the legal system and resilience of other natural and social systems the law is aimed at addressing" (p. 1382). However, the two are intrinsically interconnected. The rule of law and the security of property rights that legal systems provide, for example, are important dimensions of good governance, and "good governance is essential for an economic system to function properly and hence to be resilient" (Briguglio, Cordina, Farrigia, & Vella, 2009, p. 236).

One of the few scholars to have written about resilience in a transitional justice context, Wiebelhaus-Brahm (2017) reflects that "given the range of global transitional justice experiences and the tremendous diversity in human societies, the plausibility of diverse relationships between transitional justice and resilience is perhaps unsurprising" (p. 149). With this thought in mind, this section has outlined a model for thinking about resilience and its relationship with transitional justice through a focus on the attractors (and positive feedback loops) that maintain negative or change-resistant systemic resilience. This is an entirely novel way of both approaching transitional justice and thinking about resilience in the context of transitional justice and broader legal systems. The next section applies the model to an empirical case study, drawing on the author's fieldwork in the former Yugoslavia.

A Case Study of the International Criminal Tribunal for the Former Yugoslavia

In 1993, the UN Security Council established the ICTY. Acting under Chapter 7 of the UN Charter, it deemed that the violations of international humanitarian law taking place in the former Yugoslavia, and in particular in Bosnia-Herzegovina, constituted a threat to international peace and security (UN Security Council, 1993). The Tribunal's mandate was to prosecute crimes (specifically, violations of the laws or customs of war, grave breaches of the 1949 Geneva Conventions, crimes against humanity, and genocide) committed in the territory of the former Yugoslavia since 1991. Located in the Hague in the Netherlands, the Tribunal issued 161 indictments in total and convicted a number of high-ranking political and military figures. These included the former Bosnian Serb leader, Radovan Karadžić; the wartime commander of the Army of Republika Srpska, Ratko Mladić[1]; and the leadership of the Croatian Defence Council.

Retired judge Gabrielle Kirk McDonald, who was the ICTY's second president, has stated that when she and the other original 10 judges took their oath of office in November 1993: "We believed the judicial process would exact individual accountability instead of 'collective responsibility' and thereby contribute, albeit gradually, to a lasting peace" (ICTY, 2017b). The Tribunal's statute itself referred to the "restoration and maintenance of peace" (UN Security Council, 1993), although not specifically to reconciliation. However, reconciliation is arguably necessary for a lasting peace, particularly in communities and societies torn apart by violence and bloodshed, and over the years the Tribunal's work increasingly came to be associated with reconciliation. Giving a speech in Belgrade in 2007, for example, the then-prosecutor, Carla Del Ponte, maintained that "the Tribunal was established as a measure to restore and maintain peace and to promote reconciliation in the former Yugoslavia." She further claimed that "the Tribunal's primary contribution to peace and security, to regional stability and reconciliation is in establishing the facts and individual criminal responsibility" (ICTY, 2007). Speaking on July 11, 2016 during the annual memorial event in Potočari to commemorate the Srebrenica genocide in 1995, the then-president of the Tribunal, Judge Carmel Agius, noted, "A fundamental part of any reconciliation process is justice, which of course is where the ICTY directly plays a role." He added, "The contribution of the ICTY also helps you all to redouble your determination never to forget, and your efforts to strive for peace and reconciliation" (ICTY, 2016, p. 2).

Intrigued by the idea that an international tribunal, located outside the former Yugoslavia, might contribute to such a complex—and, in many respects, highly personal—process as reconciliation, I undertook extensive fieldwork in the former Yugoslavia to empirically explore the impact of the Tribunal's work on interethnic reconciliation (e.g., Clark,

2011, 2012, 2014). Over a five-year period from 2008 to 2013, more than 300 semistructured interviews in Bosnia-Herzegovina, Croatia, and Kosovo were conducted. That research concluded that the work of the ICTY did not make any contribution to improving or rebuilding interethnic relations (Clark, 2014). Reaching a similar conclusion, and speaking shortly before the Tribunal completed its mandate, Prosecutor Serge Brammertz commented: "It has been said that the Tribunal has not achieved reconciliation in the former Yugoslavia. It is hard to disagree" (ICTY, 2017a, p. 3). Reflecting on why reconciliation remains a significant challenge, he underlined that "the reality is that there is still no true will within the region to accept the immense wrongdoings of the past and move forward, sadly most of all among the political leadership" (ICTY, 2017a, p. 3). This lack of political will—and the culture of denial that it has contributed to fostering on all sides—can be conceptualized as a major system attractor.

The Tribunal embraced the assumption that its work would puncture denial. The facts that it established about the crimes committed in the former Yugoslavia, and about who was responsible, would make it impossible for individuals and communities to continue negating the truth. In this regard, the ICTY's (n.d.a) website expressly stated: "The Tribunal's judgements have contributed to creating a historical record, combatting denial and preventing attempts at revisionism." Such claims, however, are overly simplistic. This can be illustrated using the concept of fractals. Fractals are "complicated figures of infinite length that do not simplify when magnified, that is, whose structure repeats itself at all scales" (Post & Eisen, 2000, p. 547). What is significant is that "fractals appear to get longer and longer as the measuring stick gets smaller and smaller, and the estimated length of a true fractal diverges to infinity as e [length of the ruler] approaches zero" (Post & Eisen, 2000, pp. 549–550). The central point, thus, is that fractals have "no 'true length'" (Post & Eisen, 2000, p. 551). In the context of war crimes and transitional justice, truth can itself be conceptualized as a fractal object. It has no true length and is repeatedly contested (Clark, 2014; Mannergren Selimovic, 2015).

What is also noteworthy about fractals is that the parts replicate the whole. For example, "A fern leaf, its small leaves reflecting the shape of the leaf as a whole, is often taken as demonstrating fractal properties, as are pieces of broccoli and clouds" (Finan, 2012, p. 67). In the former Yugoslavia, the fractal truths that people cling to are pieces of broader ethnic narrative wholes that jostle and collide. These narratives act as a major system attractor, which is highly resilient (i.e., resistant) to "disconfirmatory events and information" (Vallacher et al., 2010, p. 267). The existence of this attractor, it is argued, limited the impact of the ICTY's work and in particular its contribution to interethnic reconciliation—and, by extension, resilience.

This chapter's core argument is that transitional justice must be done in a systemic way if it is to counter system attractors, restrict positive feedback loops that accentuate violence, and contribute to building societies that can cope with shocks and stressors. If transitional justice processes simply deal with the parts but not with the whole, their effects will be limited. Rather than seeking to address system attractors, the ICTY arguably reinforced them because it assumed that its work would counter denial, rather than seeking—as part of broader justice efforts—to address the factors that underpin this denial and the concomitant glorification of war criminals (Hodžić, 2010).

While the ICTY has now completed its mandate, the same trend continues. In October 2018, for example, a transitional justice conference in Sarajevo organized by the Balkan

Investigative Reporting Network had a strong focus on criminal prosecutions, and many of the speakers emphasized the need for regional cooperation between different national courts in the former Yugoslavia. What was critically overlooked were the obstacles to such cooperation—including nationalism, lack of political will relating to extradition (Mackic & BIRN Sarajevo, 2018), and denial—and how these might be addressed within a transitional justice framework. Connell (1997) underlines that "while law has the potential for fostering social transformation, law may itself also be shaped by social-cultural processes" (p. 124). Hence, efforts to use the law to (indirectly) enhance a community's resilience need to take account of wider social and cultural practices that can foster the very behaviors that fuel interethnic tensions and conflict. These are the same behaviors that the law seeks to prevent as part of its deterrent function.

Conclusion

Underlining that resilience remains a neglected concept within the field of transitional justice, this chapter has sought to demonstrate—through a combination of conceptual and empirical discussion—that resilience should be taken more seriously. It is highly relevant to transitional justice and offers a new framework in which to situate existing debates. As a way of drawing out this relevance and exploring what it means for transitional justice theory and practice, this chapter concludes by making several suggestions for future research.

First, adding a resilience lens magnifies the flaws of piecemeal approaches to transitional justice and foregrounds the need for more systemic approaches that situate processes of dealing with the past within the context of broader social-ecological systems. Fineman (2014) notes that resilience is accumulated within social systems and that "the failure of one system . . . to provide necessary resources such as a failure to provide an adequate education affects the individual's future prospects in employment, building adult family relationships, and old age" (p. 321). Taking the example of conflict-related sexual violence, transitional justice processes need to tackle the stigma that male and female victims-survivors often face (Clark, 2018). If these processes do not work to create attitudinal resources in the sense of building understanding and empathy, this will affect how victims-survivors deal with their experiences, regardless of whether their perpetrators have been prosecuted or reparations have been awarded. Future research should, therefore, explore what these systemic approaches to transitional justice might look like—and how they can be operationalized in practice.

Second, Olsson et al. (2003) argue that "where young people are well resourced within themselves, within their family and social contexts, a capacity for constructive adaptation to adversity, that is, resilience can be enhanced" (p. 6). A key question for future study is how can transitional justice processes, and legal processes more generally, enhance resilience? More specifically, to use common resilience terminology, how can these processes strengthen protective factors and minimize the impact of risk factors (Rutter, 1987)? While the language of risk and protective factors is not currently utilized within the context of transitional justice, future research should identify where these factors exist within different transitional justice contexts and how transitional justice processes can address them. Because these risk and protective factors are likely to exist across multiple levels, engaging with them is part of the process of developing more social-ecological and systemic approaches to doing transitional justice.

Third, and relatedly, while transitional justice is partly about creating better futures, communities can become disengaged from these processes when they see no benefits, and when the costs of dealing with the past appear to deflect resources away from current needs (Hayden, 2011). A resilience discourse has the potential to offer a way of addressing this. Folke (2006) maintains that resilience is partly about "the opportunities that disturbance opens up in terms of a recombination of evolved structures and processes, renewal of the system and emergence of new trajectories" (p. 259). In other words, future research should explore how the inclusion of resilience thinking into transitional justice potentially adds a new forward-looking dimension, through an emphasis on the opportunities that can be created from past shocks.

Finally, this chapter has shown that giving greater attention to resilience in the field of transitional justice has wider implications for the relationship between resilience and legal systems. Arnold and Gunderson (2013) argue that "law is brittle and maladaptive if it assumes and reinforces a static state that does not match ecological or sociological change" (p. 10427). However, if legal systems, like transitional justice processes themselves, are situated within a broader systemic framework, the key issue is not whether these legal systems are adaptive or maladaptive. Rather, what is crucial is that they provide sufficient stability to enhance adaptive capacity within the social ecologies of which they form a part, while at the same time being adaptive enough to keep up with changes within these social ecologies. In this regard, future research should explore the adaptive capacity of legal systems within a broader systemic framework and how the two interact. According to Ruhl (2011), resilience theory views legal systems as "a set of landscapes over which we find engineering and ecological resilience strategies mixing in different blends to form topographies of various contours depending on where in the system we look" (p. 1318). Giving more attention to these strategies within a systemic context can provide new insights into the resilience dynamics of legal systems.

Key Messages

1. Thinking about resilience in the context of transitional justice scholarship potentially enriches the field both theoretically and practically.
2. Individual-centered approaches to transitional justice neglect wider socioecological dynamics. Adding a resilience lens to transitional justice can contribute to the development of more ecological ways of addressing the past that situate individuals in their wider environments.
3. Resilience is a multisystemic concept that draws attention to the systemic dimensions of transitional justice processes. These processes necessarily interact with other systems, which can limit their on-the-ground impact.
4. The concept of resilience has an important transformative dimension. It is therefore useful for theoretically and empirically developing the notion of transformative justice.
5. The relationship between law and resilience is not one of compatibility/incompatibility, but rather of balance and degree between legal certainty and flexibility. How legal systems intersect with other systems critically shapes the level of balance that is achieved.

Acknowledgments
Thank you to Professor Ungar for his feedback on the chapter.

Note
1. The Mladić case is currently on appeal at the International Residual Mechanism for Criminal Tribunals (see http://www.irmct.org/en/cases).

References
Aguirre, D., & Pietropaoli, I. (2008). Gender equality, development and transitional justice: The case of Nepal. *International Journal of Transitional Justice, 2*(3), 356–377. doi:10.1093/ijtj/ijn027

Arnold, C., & Gunderson, L. (2013). Adaptive law and resilience. *Environmental Law Reporter, 43*, 10426–10443.

Bell, C., & O'Rourke, C. (2007). Does feminism need a theory of transitional justice? An introductory essay. *International Journal of Transitional Justice, 1*(1), 23–44.

Boraine, A. L. (2006). Transitional justice: A holistic interpretation. *Journal of International Affairs, 60*(1), 17–27.

Bosselmann, K. (2015). Global environmental constitutionalism: Mapping the terrain. *Widener Law Review, 21*, 171–185.

Briguglio, L., Cordina, G., Farrigia, N., & Vella, S. (2009). Economic vulnerability and resilience: Concepts and measurements. *Oxford Development Studies, 37*(3), 229–247. doi:10.1080/13600810903089893

Cardosa, L. F., Gupta, J., Shuman, S., Cole, H., Kpebo, D., & Falb, K. L. (2016). What factors contribute to intimate partner violence against women in urban, conflict-affected settings? Qualitative findings from Abidjan, Côte d'Ivoire. *Journal of Urban Health, 93*(2), 364–378. doi:10.1007/s11524-016-0029-x

Chandler, D. (2012). Resilience and human security: The post-interventionist paradigm. *Security Dialogue, 43*(3), 213–229. doi:10.1177/0967010612444151

Clark, J. N. (2011). The impact question: The ICTY and the restoration and maintenance of peace. In G. Sluiter, B. Swart, & A. Zahar (Eds.), *The legacy of the International Criminal Tribunal for the Former Yugoslavia* (pp. 55–80). Oxford, UK: Oxford University Press.

Clark, J. N. (2012). The ICTY and reconciliation in Croatia: A case study of Vukovar. *Journal of International Criminal Justice, 10*(2), 397–422. doi:10.1093/jicj/mqs017

Clark, J. N. (2014). *International trials and reconciliation: Assessing the impact of the International Criminal Tribunal for the Former Yugoslavia*. Abingdon, UK: Routledge.

Clark, J. N. (2018). Transitional justice, education and sexual violence stigma: The results of a schools-based study in Bosnia-Herzegovina. *Journal of Law and Society, 45*(4), 509–537. doi:10.1111/jols.12128

Clark, J. N. (2020). Beyond "bouncing": Resilience as an expansion–contraction dynamic within a holonic frame. *International Studies Review*. doi:10.1093/isr/viaa048

Coleman, P. T. (2006). Conflict, complexity and change: A meta-framework for addressing protracted, intractable conflicts—III. *Peace and Conflict: Journal of Peace Psychology, 12*(4), 325–348. doi:10.1207/s15327949pac1204_3

Connell, P. (1997). Understanding victimization and agency: Considerations of race, class and gender. *PoLAR: Political and Legal Anthropology Review, 20*(2), 115–143. doi:10.1525/pol.1997.20.2.115

Daly, E. (2001). Transformative justice: Charting a path to reconciliation. *International Legal Perspectives, 12*(1–2), 73–183.

Duthie, R. (2017). Introduction. In R. Duthie & P. Seils (Eds.), *Justice mosaics: How context shapes transitional justice in fractured societies* (pp. 8–38). New York, NY: International Center for Transitional Justice.

Ebbesson, J. (2010). The rule of law in governance of complex socio-ecological changes. *Global Environmental Change, 14*(3), 414–422.

Ebbesson, J., & Hey, E. (2013). Where in law is social-ecological resilience? *Ecology and Society, 18*(3), 25. doi:10.5751/ES-05750-180325

Fainstein, S. (2015). Resilience and justice. *Ijurr: International Journal of Urban and Regional Research*, 39(1), 157–167. doi:10.1111/1468-2427.12186

Finan, E. T. (2012). The "lords of life": Fractals, recursivity and experience. *Philosophy and Rhetoric*, 45(1), 68–88.

Fineman, M. A. (2014). Vulnerability, resilience and LGBT youth. *Temple Political and Civil Rights Law Review*, 23(2), 307–329.

Folke, C. (2006). Resilience: The emergence of a perspective for social-ecological systems analyses. *Global Environmental Change*, 16(3), 253–267. doi:10.1016/j.gloenvcha.2006.04.002

Garmestani, A. S., Allen, C. R., & Benson, M. H. (2013). Can law foster social-ecological resilience? *Ecology and Society*, 18(2), 37. doi:10.5751/ES-05927-180237

Gautung, J. (1969). Violence, peace and peace research. *Journal of Peace Research*, 6(3), 167–191.

Gready, P., & Robins, S. (2014). From transitional to transformative justice: A new agenda for practice. *International Journal of Transitional Justice*, 8(3), 339–361. doi:10.1093/ijtj/iju013

Harris, L. M., Chu, E. K., & Ziervogel, G. (2018). Negotiated resilience. *Resilience: International Policies, Practices and Discourses*, 6(3), 196–214. doi:10.1080/21693293.2017.1353196

Hayden, R. M. (2011). What's reconciliation got to do with it? The International Criminal Tribunal for the Former Yugoslavia (ICTY) as antiwar profiteer. *Journal of Intervention and Statebuilding*, 5(3), 313–330. doi:10.1080/17502977.2011.595597

Hayward, B. M. (2013). Rethinking resilience: Reflections on the earthquakes in Christchurch, New Zealand, 2010 and 2011. *Ecology and Society*, 18(4), 37. doi:10.5751/ES-05947-180437

Hodžić, R. (2010). Living the legacy of mass atrocities. *Journal of International Criminal Justice*, 8(1), 113–136. doi:10.1093/jicj/mqq008

Hollander, T., & Gill, B. (2014). Every day the war continues in my body: Examining the marked body in postconflict northern Uganda. *International Journal of Transitional Justice*, 8(2), 217–234. doi:10.1093/ijtj/iju007

International Criminal Tribunal for the Former Yugoslavia. (n.d.a). *Achievements*. Retrieved from http://www.icty.org/en/about/tribunal/achievements

International Criminal Tribunal for the Former Yugoslavia. (n.d.b). *Capacity building*. Retrieved from http://www.icty.org/en/outreach/capacity-building

International Criminal Tribunal for the Former Yugoslavia. (2007). *Address by Tribunal Prosecutor Carla Del Ponte to NATO parliamentary assembly in Belgrade: The ICTY and the legacy of the past*. Retrieved from http://www.icty.org/en/press/address-tribunal-prosecutor-carla-del-ponte-nato-parliamentary-assembly-belgrade-icty-and

International Criminal Tribunal for the Former Yugoslavia. (2016). *Judge Carmel Agius, president U.N. International Criminal Tribunal for the Former Yugoslavia*. Retrieved from http://www.icty.org/x/file/Press/Statements%20and%20Speeches/President/160711_president_agius_srebrenica_en.pdf

International Criminal Tribunal for the Former Yugoslavia. (2017a). *Address of Mr Serge Brammertz, Prosecutor International Criminal Tribunal for the Former Yugoslavia and Mechanism for International Criminal Tribunals to the United Nations Security Council*. Retrieved from http://www.icty.org/x/file/Press/Statements%20and%20Speeches/Prosecutor/171206-prosecutor-brammertz-address-unsc-en.pdf

International Criminal Tribunal for the Former Yugoslavia. (2017b). *Message by Judge Gabrielle Kirk McDonald on the occasion of the final ICTY symposium*. Retrieved from http://www.icty.org/x/file/Press/Events/2017/171221-legacy-symposium-kirk-mc-donald-statement.pdf

International Criminal Court. (2002). *Rome Statute of the International Criminal Court*. Retrieved from https://www.icc-cpi.int/nr/rdonlyres/ea9aeff7-5752-4f84-be94-0a655eb30e16/0/rome_statute_english.pdf

International Criminal Court. (2017). *Katanga case: ICC trial chamber II awards victims individual and collective reparations*. Retrieved from https://www.icc-cpi.int/pages/item.aspx?name=pr1288

Jenkins, K., & Rondón, G. (2015). "Eventually the mine will come": Women anti-mining activists' everyday resilience in opposing resource extraction in the Andes. *Gender & Development*, 23(3), 415–431. doi:10.1080/13552074.2015.1095560

Lambourne, W. (2015). Transformative justice, reconciliation and peacebuilding. In S. Buckley-Zistel, T. Koloma Beck, C. Braun, & F. Mieth (Eds.), *Transitional justice theories* (pp. 19–39). Abingdon, UK: Routledge.

Laplante, L. J. (2008). Transitional justice and peace building: Diagnosing and addressing the socioeconomic roots of violence through a human rights framework. *International Journal of Transitional Justice*, *2*(3), 331–355. doi:10.1093/ijtj/ijn031

Leebaw, B. A. (2008). The irreconcilable goals of transitional justice. *Human Rights Quarterly*, *30*, 95–118.

Lenette, C., Brough, M., & Cox, L. (2013). Everyday resilience: Narratives of single refugee women with children. *Qualitative Social Work*, *12*(5), 637–653. doi:10.1177/1473325012449684

Luthar, S. S., & Cicchetti, D. (2000). The construct of resilience: Implications for interventions and social policies. *Development and Psychopathology*, *12*(4), 857–885.

Lykes, M. B. (2001). Human rights abuses as structural violence. In D. J. Christie, R. V. Wagner, & D. Du Nann Winter (Eds.), *Peace, conflict and violence: Peace psychology for the 21st century* (pp. 158–167). Englewood Cliffs, NJ: Prentice Hall.

Kastner, P. (2020). A resilience approach to transitional justice? *Journal of Intervention and Statebuilding*, *14*(3), 368–388. doi:10.1080/17502977.2019.1709775

Mackic, E., & BIRN Sarajevo. (2018). *Poor cooperation leaves Balkan war crimes suspects at large*. Retrieved from https://balkaninsight.com/2018/10/01/poor-cooperation-leaves-balkan-war-crime-suspects-at-large-09-26-2018/

Mannergren Selimovic, J. (2015). Challenges of postconflict coexistence: Narrating truth and justice in a Bosnian town. *Political Psychology*, *36*(2), 231–242. doi:10.1111/pops.12205

McAuliffe, P. G. (2011). Transitional justice's expanding empire: Reasserting the value of the paradigmatic transition. *Journal of Conflictology*, *2*(2), 32–44. doi:10.7238/joc.v2i2.1297

Mohaupt, S. (2008). Review article: Resilience and social exclusion. *Social Policy and Society*, *8*(1), 63–71. doi:10.1017/S1474746408004594

Nguyen-Gillham, V., Giacaman, R., Naser, G., & Boyce, W. (2008). Normalising the abnormal: Palestinian youth and the contradictions of resilience in protracted conflict. *Health and Social Care in the Community*, *16*(3), 291–298. doi:10.1111/j.1365-2524.2008.00767.x

Ní Aoláin, F., & Rooney, E. (2007). Underenforcement and intersectionality: Gendered aspects of transition for women. *International Journal of Transitional Justice*, *1*(3), 338–354. doi:10.1093/ijtj/ijm031

Odom Green, O., Garmestani, A. S., Allen, C. R., Gunderson, L. H., Ruhl, J. B., Arnold, C.A., . . . Holling, C. S. (2015). Barriers and bridges to the integration of social-ecological resilience and law. *Frontiers in Ecology and the Environment*, *13*(6), 332–337. doi:10.1890/140294

Olsen, T. D., Payne, L. A., & Reiter, A. G. (2010). The justice balance: When transitional justice improves human rights and democracy. *Human Rights Quarterly*, *21*, 980–1007.

Olsson, C. A., Bond, L., Burns, J. M., Vella-Brodrick, D. A., & Sawyer, S. M. (2003). Adolescent resilience: A concept analysis. *Journal of Adolescence*, *26*(1), 1–11. doi:10.1016/s0140-1971(02)00118-5

Orford, A. (2006). Commissioning the truth. *Columbia Journal of Gender & Law*, *15*, 851–883.

Post, D. G., & Eisen, M. N. (2000). How long is the coastline of the law? Thoughts on the fractal nature of legal systems. *The Journal of Legal Studies*, *29*(Suppl. 1), 545–584.

Pulvirenti, M., & Mason, G. (2011). Resilience and survival: Refugee women and violence. *Current Issues in Criminal Justice*, *23*(1), 37–52. doi:10.1080/10345329.2011.12035908

Qayoom, F. (2014). Women and armed conflict: Widows in Kashmir. *International Journal of Sociology and Anthropology*, *6*(5), 161–168. doi:10.5897/IJSA2013.0512

Robins, S. (2011). Towards victim-centred transitional justice: Understanding the needs of families of the disappeared in postconflict Nepal. *International Journal of Transitional Justice*, *5*(1), 75–98. doi:10.1093/ijtj/ijq027

Rooney, E. (2006). Women's equality in Northern Ireland's transition: Intersectionality in theory and place. *Feminist Legal Studies*, *14*(3), 353–375. doi:10.1007/s10691-006-9032-z

Ruhl, J. B. (2011). General design principles for resilience and adaptive capacity in legal systems—With applications to climate change adaptation. *North Carolina Law Review*, *89*, 1373–1403.

Rutter, M. (1987). Psychosocial resilience and protective mechanisms. *American Journal of Orthopsychiatry*, *57*(3), 316–331. doi:10.1111/j.1939-0025.1987.tb03541.x

Sandoval, C. (2017). Reflections on the transformative potential of transitional justice and the nature of social change in times of transition. In R. Duthie & P. Seils (Eds.), *Justice mosaics: How context shapes transitional justice in fractured societies* (pp. 166–201). New York, NY: International Center for Transitional Justice.

Scott, M. (2013). Resilience: A conceptual lens for rural studies? *Geography Compass, 7*(9), 597–610. doi:10.1111/gec3.12066

Shaw, R., & Waldorf, L. (2010). Introduction: Localizing transitional justice. In R. Shaw & L. Waldorf (Eds.), *Localizing transitional justice: Interventions and priorities after mass violence* (pp. 3–26). Stanford, CA: Stanford University Press.

Sharp, D. N. (2014). Emancipating transitional justice from the bonds of the paradigmatic transition. *International Journal of Transitional Justice, 9*(1), 150–169. doi:10.1093/ijtj/iju021

Smyth, I., & Sweetman, C. (2015). Introduction: Gender and resilience. *Gender & Development, 23*(3), 405–414. doi:10.1080/13552074.2015.1113769

Sooka, Y. (2006). Dealing with the past and transitional justice: Building peace though accountability. *International Review of the Red Cross, 88*(862), 311–325.

Southwick, S. M., Bonanno, G. A., Masten, A. S., Panter-Brick, C., & Yehuda, R. (2014). Resilience definitions, theory and challenges: Interdisciplinary perspectives. *European Journal of Psychotraumatology, 5*(1). doi:10.3402/ejpt.v5.25338

Staub, E. (2012). The roots and prevention of genocide and related violence. *Zygon, 42*(4), 821–842. doi:10.1111/j.1467-9744.2012.01302.x

Teitel, R. (2005). The law and politics of contemporary transitional justice. *Cornell International Law Journal, 38*(3), 837–862.

Ungar, M. (2013). Resilience, trauma, context and culture. *Trauma, Violence & Abuse, 14*(3), 255–266. doi:10.1177/1524838013487805

United Nations. (2010). *Guidance note of the Secretary-General: United Nations approach to transitional justice*. Retrieved from https://www.un.org/ruleoflaw/files/TJ_Guidance_Note_March_2010FINAL.pdf

United Nations Security Council. (1993). *Resolution 827*. Retrieved from http://www.icty.org/x/file/Legal%20Library/Statute/statute_827_1993_en.pdf

Vallacher, R. R., Coleman, P. T., Nowak, A., & Bui-Wrzosinska, L. (2010). Rethinking intractable conflict: The perspective of dynamical systems. *American Psychologist, 65*(4), 262–278. doi:10.1037/a0019290

van der Merwe, H., & Lykes, M. B. (2016). Transitional justice processes as teachable moments. *International Journal of Transitional Justice, 10*(3), 361–365. doi:10.1093/ijtj/ijw019

Waldorf, L. (2012). Anticipating the past: Transitional justice and socio-economic wrongs. *Social & Legal Studies, 21*(2), 171–186. doi:10.1177/0964663911435827

Wiebelhaus-Brahm, E. (2017). After shocks: Exploring the relationships between transitional justice and resilience in post-conflict societies. In R. Duthie & P. Seils (Eds.), *Justice mosaics: How context shapes transitional justice in fractured societies* (pp. 140–165). New York, NY: International Center for Transitional Justice.

Wright, M. O. D., Fopma-Loy, J., & Fischer, S. (2005). Multidimensional assessment of resilience in mothers who are child sexual abuse survivors. *Child Abuse & Neglect, 29*(10), 1173–1193. doi:10.1016/j.chiabu.2005.04.004

Ziervogel, G., Pelling, M., Cartwright, A., Chu, E., Deshpande, T., Harris, L., . . . Zweig, P. (2017). Inserting rights and justice into urban resilience: A focus on everyday risk. *Environment and Urbanization, 29*(1), 123-138. doi:10.1177/0956247816686905

Zautra, A., Hall, J., & Murray, K. (2008). Community development and community resilience: An integrative approach. *Community Development, 39*(3), 130–147. doi:10.1080/15575330809489673

Understanding Societal Resilience

The Case for Engaged Scholarship

Rosanne Anholt, Caroline van Dullemen,
Juliana Santos de Carvalho, Joris Rijbroek,
Stijn Sieckelinck, and Marieke W. Slootman

Introduction

Since the second half of the 20th century, the concept of resilience has been gaining ground in research, policy, and practice in a wide variety of domains. In the last decade, both scholars and practitioners have increasingly added the lexicon of resilience thinking to their work. Nevertheless, what resilience actually entails remains a highly debated topic. Both scholars and practitioners have grappled with pinpointing what resilience means and defining its conceptual boundaries.

In this chapter, we argue that rather than problematizing the conceptual ambiguity surrounding the concept of resilience, we should embrace its openness and approach resilience through an open research methodology, such as action research and engaged scholarship. Such approaches take the complexity of societal issues to which resilience is being applied as a starting point and thus welcome a pluralist perspective of the problems and realities resilience-based approaches are designed to address.

Our chapter is structured as follows. In the first part we focus on theoretical issues. We address the use of the concept of resilience in social studies and discuss the various criticisms that resilience has received throughout the social sciences. We then argue that accepting the conceptual openness of resilience is necessary because of the complexity of societal concerns to which resilience is being applied. In the second part, we describe engaged scholarship as an opportunity for inclusive societal resilience. In the third part, we focus on the operationalization of engaged scholarship to understand societal resilience. We briefly introduce the Institute for Societal Resilience (ISR) at the Faculty of Social Sciences at the Vrije Universiteit Amsterdam, the Netherlands. Here, we discuss various examples of ongoing research at ISR to demonstrate the need for bridging academic and practical expertise for a better understanding of resilience. We conclude with a plea for more plural theorization of resilience that should be the conceptual seedlings to grow into further research.

Understanding Societal Resilience

The term *resilience* itself is far from new. Its roots can be traced to the Latin word *resilire*, which signifies something that rebounds or recoils. Resilience has been used by physical scientists to describe and explore the characteristics of a spring, as well as the resistance of materials to external shocks and their ability to spring back to their original shape (Davoudi, 2012). During the 1970s, the term became increasingly common in the fields of resource management, engineering, and ecology. This is especially due to the work of Canadian ecologist Crawford Stanley Holling (1973, 1986), who approached resilience as a way to explore how natural systems would—and could—reach equilibrium after unexpected and acute disturbances, as well as how these systems could transform while returning to equilibrium (Walker & Cooper, 2011).

More recently, resilience thinking has entered the social sciences as a way to better examine the response of individuals, communities, and organizations in the face of challenges (Walker & Cooper, 2011). Much like its scientific origins in the natural and physical sciences, resilience in social studies has two different, but nevertheless connected, perspectives. The first is that of *conservative resilience*, which investigates how social systems reach equilibrium after a shock. The second is referred to as *transformative resilience*, which is more focused on how these systems renew themselves while going back to normal functioning after disturbances (Brown, 2011; MacKinnon & Derickson, 2013; Pain & Levine, 2012; Walker & Cooper, 2011). Although these two approaches can be understood as two different streams, they are not airtight categories. As previously explained, the genealogy of resilience is closely related to both adaptive and transformative capacities of a system. It is, then, a concept that takes the well-known adage "Never waste a good crisis" to heart: it examines and exposes how disturbing events can trigger social systems' adaptive and restructuring functionalities.

This is well illustrated by the work of social psychologists and organizational managers in studies of the adaptation and transformation cycles in human systems (Weick & Sutcliffe, 2015). By studying cosmology episodes (Orton & O'Grady, 2016)—that is, acute disturbing events, in which "people suddenly and deeply feel that the universe is no longer a rational, orderly system" (Weick, 1993, p. 633)—these disciplines have provided insights on how individuals and organizations experience collapse—"sense-losing"—as well as how they may eventually restructure themselves to create a new normal through sense-making (Weick, 1993).

This focus on acute and unlikely disturbances to individuals and communities has not been circumscribed to social psychology and organizational management. Rather, it has increasingly gained ground across various domains that aim to understand global vulnerabilities and transnational responses. Climate change has brought about a global sense of uncertainty about the future—ranging from critical infrastructure problems to the prospect of displacement and/or total loss of livelihoods (Maldonado, Shearer, Bronen, Peterson, & Lazrus, 2013; Tanner et al., 2014). Terrorism has heightened an overall sense of insecurity, with pre-emptive security measures and policies being justified on the basis of a constant and uncertain threat of terrorist attacks (Aradau & Munster, 2007; Coaffee & Wood, 2006; De Goede, 2008). Moreover, contemporary armed conflicts have often been studied with regards to their complexity, prolonged duration, and impact beyond the immediate locality where hostilities take place (Anholt, 2017; Commission of the European Communities, 2004; Smith & Fischbacher, 2009). Contemporary humanitarian crises have also been explored in their growing complexity, interconnectedness, and protractions—characteristics that have increased the acute, unlikely, and prolonged effects of such events. (Anholt, 2017; Commission of the European Communities, 2004; Macrae & Harmer, 2004).

It is within this scenario that the concept of [resilience has rapidly proliferated in the social sciences. Departing from the observations that contemporary social issues are increasingly uncertain, prolonged, complex, and interdependent, resilience has emerged as a transdisciplinary term for investigating cycles of adaptation and transformation of social systems to the challenges of today. For this reason, resilience has, for instance, often been coupled with the notion of a culture of preparedness, whereby individuals and communities are expected to be continuously prepared to absorb and address very unlikely—but not impossible—stresses (Renn & Klinke, 2015; U.S. Department of Homeland Security, 2007; Walker & Cooper, 2011). Resilience has also been closely linked to emergency response toward more long-term goals and development assistance, as a way to curb the complex and protracted profile of crises today (Anholt, 2017; Ghorashi, de Boer, & ten Holder, 2018; Pain & Levine, 2012). Moreover, the term has also been a common background to proposals for more multilevel and transnational crisis response governance, given the growing interdependence of contemporary global issues (Aradau, 2014; Dunn Cavelty, Kaufmann, & Søby Kristensen, 2015; Pugh, Gabay, & Williams, 2013).

In parallel to this growing interdisciplinary expansion within social studies, resilience has also been increasingly met with criticism. In this regard, one of the most common critiques of the concept has been related to its conceptual openness. Despite prominently featuring in mainstream discourses of development, humanitarian aid, economy, and sustainability, the term has been considered as an "under-theorized term of art" (Walker & Cooper, 2011, p. 3). The capacity of being translatable across different disciplines has then been at the expense of more defined boundaries for the term—something that has been considered to render the concept as "evidently common sense, and yet conceptually and programmatically elusive" (Pain & Levine, 2012, p. 3).

For instance, conceptual vagueness in transformative resilience led to the critique that social change is not always positive (Brasset & Vaughan-Williams, 2015; Pain & Levine, 2012). Not only that, the elusive sense of ubiquitous uncertainty and social threat has also been considered to propel forward constant state of exceptionalism and securitization within society (Evans & Reid, 2013; Malcolm, 2013; Manyena & Gordon, 2015). Furthermore, the lack of preciseness as to how a culture of preparedness is to be achieved has been criticized, especially with regard to how it places the responsibility for insecurity on the shoulders of individuals rather than states (Brasset & Vaughan-Williams, 2015; Chandler, 2014; Howell, 2015). Moreover, the focus of resilience on the response of individuals and communities to crises—which is not necessarily met with a more concrete definition of roles, responsibilities, and solutions tested in action—has often been criticized for enabling a neoliberal model for addressing contemporary societal problems (Chandler 2013a, 2013b; Chandler & Coaffee, 2017; Duffield, 2012; Joseph, 2013; Rogers, 2013). The concept has also been critiqued for its underestimation of equity and power in human–environmental systems. Matin, Forrester, and Ensor (2018), for example, use the term *equitable resilience* instead. Based on a literature review, they identify four themes essential to understanding equitable resilience in practice: attention to subjectivities, inclusion, cross-scale interactions, and transformation. They formulate a middle-range theory that attends to the social, cultural, and political factors that distribute resilience outcomes. Along similar lines, Pelling and Manuel-Navarrete (2011) use the idea of equitable resilience and propose combining it with a sociological theory of power whereby the reproduction of social systems is based on both structure as well as agents.

In view of all this, it could be argued that the way forward would be to work toward a more precise and defined understanding of resilience. Indeed, this could help shed light on crucial programmatic issues, in an effort to standardize and improve coherence among interventions and policies (Pain & Levine, 2012). However, we submit that the closing-off of the concept is not necessarily the way to solve its conceptual and practical conundrums.

Whereas the previously delineated criticisms by and large converge their considerations toward the lack of preciseness of the term, other essential questions underlie those concerns. The argument that transformative resilience is not always positive raises the questions: *Who* benefits from social change, and *what* are the broader consequences of these transformations? When decentralized and private-based forms of governance and resilience are denounced, this asks for elaboration on the *means* by which resilient-based policies and practices are being carried out. When one underscores that the term may be underestimating equity, this is fundamentally a question of *who* is included in so-called resilient approaches to social issues and whether they benefit at all.

In view of this, it becomes clear that the current concerns are not about the conceptual openness of resilience and that the solution is not to be found in a more definite, closed definition of the term. Rather, it cuts deep into a recurrent theme in interdisciplinary studies—that of the impossibility of a universal and absolute understanding of a topic (Welch, 2011; Klein, 1996). Just as in the genealogy of resilience, interdisciplinarity departs from the realization that world phenomena are too complex to be dealt by one single perspective (Chettiparamb, 2007; Katz, 2001; Klein, 2010). Instead, the complexity of our realities calls for integrative understanding of different approaches—which should not be considered as mutually exclusive, but as complementary to each other. And this is where interdisciplinary studies show that the openness of a term is not necessarily a negative factor. Interdisciplinary researchers have been generally "tolerant of ambiguity" (Welch, 2011, p. 18), as this can allow for a more dynamic kaleidoscopic of methods for co-generating knowledge (Bromme, 2000; Hursh, Haas, & Moore, 1983).

With this in mind, we argue that the current "undefinition" of resilience is not entirely undesirable for social studies. Rather, when one sees such fluidity as a possibility for a more multidimensional approach to the term, such broadness can turn into an opportunity for inclusiveness, from which social sciences will benefit. However, which specific methodology could provide the means to benefit from such conceptual openness?

Engaged Scholarship as an Opportunity

To understand how conceptual openness can be used as an advantage for researching societal resilience, the notion of engaged scholarship (or action research) can be a useful tool. Engaged scholarship builds upon the idea that social problems are increasingly complex and that understanding and addressing them requires joint efforts between different stakeholders, including researchers, practitioners, citizens, and policymakers (Van de Ven, 2007). This approach takes into consideration that learning and producing knowledge can never be absolute, all-encompassing or universal and, consequently calls for engagement between various perspectives to provide a more comprehensive overview of certain issues. The importance of this engagement is the symbiotic relationship between academic and practical expertise: people and places outside the campus bring academia toward larger, more humane ends, while academics bring a set of organizational, methodological, and structural tools to better organize and advance scientific knowledge regarding the topic at hand (McNiff, 2013; Van de Ven, 2007).

The chaotic outlook of the conceptual openness of social resilience reverberates a scenery that is familiar for action researchers. Departing from the realization of the high complexity (i.e., multisystemic nature) of contemporary social problems, action researchers acknowledge the messy social reality whose complexity goes beyond conventional theoretical and disciplinary models (McNiff, 2013). Because of this, action research propels forward the idea of embracing this chaos and seeing it as an opportunity to break with the conventional mold and seek new solutions by going for a cogenerated knowledge across and beyond academic insights (Coghlan, 2011).

Engaged scholarship is also closely tied to the idea of research being transformative. Practical knowledge is historically rooted in a scholarship from the margins, which sought to break from the paradigms of neutrality and detachment of mainstream positivist research and engage academia with social change (Coghlan, 2011). Engaged scholars acknowledge that contrary to positivist models the production of knowledge is never detached from the social context from which it is created. Rather, it is socially constructed—and aligns with an agenda that seeks to challenge unjust and undemocratic systems. This does not make it less scientific. Engaged scholarship, or action research, has a particular focus in producing insights that can be applied to societal issues, which makes the collaboration with the most at-risk stakeholders crucial for such an aim (Brydon-Miller, Greenwood, & Maguire, 2003). This collaboration allows not only for co-generating knowledge with relevance tested in action, but also to stimulate a comprehensive and critical research approach, which is sensitive and responsive to power imbalances (McNiff, 2013). In other words, collaboration between academia and practice creates scientific understanding of the complex dynamics of the social challenges we face today and offers concrete insights on how to improve policies, methodologies, and interventions for specific problems (Bekkers, 2016).

With this in mind, we argue that resilience cannot be grasped through a fully closed definition. Instead, resilience requires open research methodologies that includes the different perspectives of multiple stakeholders, as well as practical expertise. Therefore, instead of seeing engaged scholarship as a means to understand resilience as an open and ambiguous concept, it is the complexity of the phenomena that *requires* both this openness of the concept as well as engaged scholarship.

How would this engaged scholarship translate in studies on societal resilience? How could this methodology be used to study and apply resilience to societal issues? To illustrate how this has been done in practice, the next section presents various cases in which engaged scholarship is used to study forms of societal resilience in various projects of the Institute for Societal Resilience at Vrije Universiteit Amsterdam.

Operationalizing Engaged Scholarship

Established in 2015, the ISR is embedded within the Faculty of Social Sciences at the Vrije Universiteit Amsterdam. ISR aims at identifying what makes citizens, institutions, and governance systems resilient in dealing with complex social issues—such as increased social inequality, tensions between ethnic and religious communities, new forms of (cyber) crime, and challenges to systems of care and welfare. Examples of ISR research projects follow. These include (a) transformations in urban education, (b) authoritative alliances for resilient identities, and (c) resilient responses to refugee reception.

Transformations in Urban Education

Research was conducted at an MBO school in Amsterdam (secondary vocational education) as part of a larger research project on the professionalization of education. This study focused on the student perspective on code switching and self-efficacy and connected the student perspective with that of the teachers. Central is the idea that for students to be successful and climb the school-ladder, students need to have self-efficacy and in class to switch in their behavior to adhere to certain norms or codes (e.g. to arrive in time, be attentive in class and participate actively). The project aimed to better understand students' code-switching behavior and to understand how students themselves view their needs to climb the school ladder and to compare these needs with what teachers can offer.

The project consisted of three tracks. In the first track, two researchers studied code-switching behavior through participatory observation in class settings in school as well as outside school during students' internships. In the second track, a researcher conducted semistructured interviews with students about their behavior, attitudes, motivations, and experiences in class and how these are influenced by the teacher's practices. The last track includes the teachers' perspectives, through analysis of peer review conversations between two teachers and a trainer that were part of the professionalization program.

The findings show a bright contrast between the students' behavior during internships (in which students rather smoothly adopt the professional codes) and in school, where students often refrain from switching to school codes (they come in late, shout, speak Arabic or other non-Dutch languages with fellow students, watch movies on their laptop or visit web shops on their phones during class). That they relatively smoothly adopt the professional codes during internships shifts the focus from the student's individual code-switching ability to the role of the institutional context, which we consider as one of the fundamental factors of societal resilience. It appears that in school students place the responsibility for the norms to be enforced with the teacher. In affirmation of the developed transformative teaching model, for students to experience self-efficacy, they find it important that a normative framework is effectuated while at the same time teachers should support them, with humanity and respect. Although the teachers' conversations show that most teachers do recognize these conditions, the conversations also show that these conditions are not easy to establish. They are often perceived as contrary, particularly in the interaction with "difficult" groups of students. Clearly, also teachers often lack self-efficacy.

In analogy with Ervin Goffman's metaphor of the frontstage and backstage, these results call for a strengthening of the area behind the scenes, between the stage where the primary performance takes place (the classroom or the internship) and the dressing room where informal codes dominate (teachers' lounge or the peer group). This is where teachers align their normative frameworks and where they coach and support each other. This is where the collective efficacy of the team forms, which is inducive for the self-efficacy of individual teachers (resilience). Also, students can benefit from such middle area. This area is where students are prepared—and prepare themselves in mutual interaction—for the professional stage. This where they play active roles in shaping their own roles, personality, and education and where they can unwind from the pressures they feel in their internships and life outside school (which for many students is no sinecure). Instead of informality, this area is characterized by constructive learning codes and attitudes. The strengthening of these middle areas behind the scenes calls for an engaged and actively involved school management.

The results showed three positive outcomes. First, the relationship, trust, and shared interest became a common issue and ensured the involvement of school management, which greatly facilitated access to the school. Second, the engagement of the school management led to automatic valorization and use of the gained knowledge.

Finally, the recommendations directly feed into the intervention line, strengthening the professionalization projects at the same school (and other schools). In this way, through the engaged scholarship approach, the study contributes to the strengthening of societal resilience in the Dutch education system.

The findings illustrate the advantages of an open approach, which is multidisciplinary, with the close involvement of practical stakeholders. Through the combination of sociological perspectives with didactical and psychological perspectives, concepts, and models, the academic framework capitalizes on the complementary nature of various disciplines. The actor-centered perspective was crucial. It led us to reveal unforeseen mechanisms, and hence increased the understanding of how schools can increase experiences of self-efficacy (of students, teachers and teams) and stimulate a fertile learning environment (for both students and teachers). The project showed how schools can strengthen societal resilience. (El Hadioui et al., 2019).

Crisis Governance or Governance Crisis? Resilient Responses to Refugee Reception

In 2015, many Dutch municipalities faced the sudden challenge of needing to receive and accommodate high numbers of refugees in their communities. During that year, the situation became tense, and various protests, chants, threats and other harsh expressions of resistance against arrival of refugees emerged. The arrival of refugees was framed in terms of "the refugee crisis." These tensions—closely covered by (social) media—gave the impression that the Netherlands was responding to the refugees' arrival in resentful ways. However, most of the municipalities did not witness such reactions. The responses in municipalities varied widely, in content, shape, and fierceness. While in some municipalities the arrival of refugees caused tensions and evoked harsh reactions, in other municipalities refugee arrivals did not evoke any significant reaction. In reaction, municipal executives responded differently to the issue of refugee arrival in their municipalities. What explained these various responses to the "refugee crisis"? The antagonistic reactions that occurred in some places, and especially the ferocity of them, evoked the desire to examine the differences between the municipalities. What could we learn from these diversities? The "refugee crisis" provided a window of opportunity to research the decision-making process and communication strategies on the local level in the (national) context of societal tensions around developments that many citizens perceived as a threat.

The research project had a mixed-method design, using both big data (quantitative analyses of sentiments in media coverage) and small data (qualitative interviews with municipal officials and administrators, focus groups and a public research session). Around 500,000 messages in traditional media, over 5 million tweets, and more than 800,000 messages on public Facebook pages were scraped in the period from July 2015 until July 2016. In November 2016, during a public research session local and national officials, administrators, nongovernmental organizations, and researchers reflected on the crises—supported by the data the research project presented.

The quantitative analysis of media coverage showed a strong increase in online messages, posts and reactions from August 2015 onward. This increase in (social) media attention created the perception the whole country was in turmoil although not all municipalities were involved—by far. In fact, media coverage on the refugee crises was strongly influenced by events in only a few municipalities. In only 7 of 391 total municipalities, more than 20 messages per 100 inhabitants were sent—predominantly expressing negative sentiments.

Based on the qualitative data gathered, we found that already existing networks among the municipal population played an important role in the articulation of "positive" versus "negative" voices with regard to arrival of refugees. This can be framed as a form of societal resilience with respect to the reception of refugees. Also, the type of reactions corresponded with respectively consensus or division among municipal executives. Interaction with the administrative level seemed to reinforce the dominant response of residents in the municipalities involved; the more division among municipal executives, the more negatively citizens seemed to respond. By applying this multisystemic approach to the arrival of refugees, three decision-making paths could be distinguished. First, in municipalities with a participatory tradition involving their citizens in decision-making and important developments, inhabitants predominantly showed more confidence in the local authorities and reactions were less antagonistic. In contrast, in municipalities with a less participative style of governance and where citizens were less involved in local decision-making and decisions on refugee reception were taken more top–down, citizens showed less confidence in their local government and were less satisfied with the decisions. In some of these top–down municipalities the responses of local citizen networks were extremely antagonistic. These networks took their chance to (finally) make themselves heard, unleashing years of accumulated dissatisfaction.

We found that, against the dominant media-driven public perception, and despite some serious disruptive incidents, Dutch society in general responded in a rather resilient manner to the arrival of relatively large numbers refugees. Can we conclude that the municipal decision-making process, which in many municipalities prevented escalations, would have prevented escalations in the other municipalities and would result in a similar smoothness in future crises? The results suggest that united and decisive action by local government can make a positive difference, but not in all cases. For example, unity and decisiveness can also be perceived and interpreted as a top–down imposition of (unpopular) measures. In the case of the 2015 refugee crisis, some of the municipalities could not prevent escalations. They seemed to be curbed by the decision-making processes that shaped over decennia.

The project offered participating municipalities and professionals practical lessons for resilient governance. During the public research session, stakeholders shared recommendations: (a) "invest in sustainable interactive forms of public consultation," (b) develop mechanisms to manage consequences of "unwelcome decisions," and (c) organize conditions for what in the project is called as "democracy from below." In the long term, however, it is questionable whether these recommendations are sufficient. The role of the governance dimension in such crisis-like situations should be investigated more thoroughly. Path dependencies can be bent and/or broken during crises. The 2015 refugee crisis is a case par excellence in this regard. Possible dormant dissatisfaction with local governance styles might surface in contexts where decision-making processes ran smoothly so far. Meaningful lessons might have been learned in contexts that apparently seemed problematic and—in retrospect—all commotion proved to be quite functional. It's important to continue researching the (social, administrative, and institutional) implications of the decision-making period in 2015, thus allowing us to determine which administrative practices are also resilient in the long term.

Authoritative Alliances for Resilient Identities

In 2016, during the European Union Council of Government leader's chairmanship by the Netherlands, a wave of violent extremism was washing over European soil caused by Daesh and the involvement of our countries in the Iraq–Syrian civil war. In this climate of civil and political panic over a seemingly uncontrollable threat, policymakers were demanding more legal measures, expansion of intelligence, and instrumental breach of civil rights if necessary. In this same climate, the Dutch minister and his team responsible for youth affairs decided to change course and explore a pedagogical approach to understanding and tackling violent radicalization. In the policy brief, the topic of extremism, generally approached from a legalistic–criminological point of view, was looked at from an unusual angle: the challenge of education in youth centers and the role of parents and police in building resilient identities. This opening of minds let to the current research project.

In earlier research, radicalization was often understood as a coping reaction to troubled individual, social, and political identity development. As the need for agency and radicality is characteristic of youth in socially and culturally deprived situations, programs directed at deradicalization of youth deserve more scrutiny. Sieckelinck introduced the term *reradicalization* as a strategy against extremism. Therefore, the current research project (2017–2020) is titled "Social Strategies for Resilient Identities: Authoritative Alliances as Practices of Re-Radicalization." In this research project, the schools', youth works', and religious institutions' possibilities and limits of reacting from an educative and empowering approach against (possible) radicalization is explored. Is there an alternative to the authorities' threat with force in the early stage of interest or engagement?

By taking a so-called reradicalizing approach (Sieckelinck, Kaulingfreks, & De Winter 2015), the project intends to find out what happens when young people start to identify themselves with a particular group, or movement. Then the conversation is opened up, instead of closed down.

Where strategies of surveillance—silencing antiliberal democratic voices—are generally considered effective short-term instruments of repression against political and religious extremism, its longer-term effect is unclear. Promoting resilience among marginalized youth is generally seen as an effective preventative strategy on the longer term, forming a response to radicalization and group polarization as well. Although its finesses are largely unexamined, building, boosting, and bolstering resilience is at the order of the day in policy papers targeting the social domain. All over the world, professionals are expected to build resilience against extremism, but they often feel lonely and incapable of doing this. Meanwhile, young citizens from the margins are overwhelmingly negative about their future and ask for guidance to help leading their lives and coping with their problems but—due to the moral unavailability of adults—risk finding credible moral authority in anti-social or extremist milieus.

As stated in a recent USAID report that explores the merits of a process akin to reradicalization, what we need is empowerment informed by a deep understanding of what makes radicalization so total, so quick, and so potent a path for creating transformative personal and social change.[1] Hence, the importance of creating *places of resilience* where the desire for agency and radicality is nourished, not frustrated.

Operationally, this research project is divided into three studies:

- A first study examines the impact of preventing violent extremism policies toward building resilience. It is based on document analysis and nonexperimental qualitative field work. It consists of in-depth interviews (Phase 1), Q-sorting (Phase 2), and focus groups with adult respondents in a professional role (individually and in group, online and offline).
- A second study has a descriptive and a normative leg. First, it is an examination of 15 formal and nonformal contexts of upbringing and civic education. It draws mainly on qualitative, nonexperimental fieldwork. Second, it helps practices to building resilience in

co-creation with these local partners within an action-research design. This study makes use of in-depth interviews with adult professionals (Phase 1), observations of group interactions between professionals and youth of 15 to 20 years old (Phase 2) and intergenerational focus groups (Phase 3).
- A third study examines the role for police in building resilient identities. It consists of ethnographical classroom observations (nonexperimental) of group interactions between police officers and children (10–14 years old) in the context of civic education.

Although the project, compared to standard research project, is complex in design, ethics, and operation, it benefits from an open multidisciplinary approach, with the close involvement of practical stakeholders.

The following findings recur in the field reports: authoritative alliances, it seems, lead to building resilient identities if one succeeds in setting up shared authoritative practices where youth feel at home and can air their grievances and where pedagogical confrontations are organized. Much less results are expected in contexts where these confrontations are avoided or brought to escalation. Authoritative alliances, based on this specific form of authority, increase trust and a sense of responsibility, two cornerstones of resilient identity development. (Sieckelinck, 2018; Sieckelinck, Sikkens, Kotnis, van San, & de Winter, 2017).

Conclusion

In this chapter we sketched out the current understandings of societal resilience and/or resilience in social sciences. At present, the term does not have a generally agreed-upon definition, and scholars have noted the potential dangers of its conceptual ambiguity.

This chapter argues that at present the openness of the concept of societal resilience should be considered crucial to the rightful use of resilience. As we have shown, its conceptual openness allows for taking into account societal complexities and variations in the forms of resilience studied and for the inclusion of multiple perspectives. Engaged scholarship is a productive way of doing so. As the ISR projects illustrate, engaged scholarship approaches have the potential to bridge academic with practical (societal) expertise. Academic knowledge provides the scientific rigor to comprehend and identify the notions shares among scholars of what societal resilience fundamentally consists of. Practical knowledge, in turn, adds the necessary detail and differentiation required to address complex societal issues. The symbiotic relationship that characterizes engaged scholarship approaches allows for developing balanced academically sound understandings in combination with a factual strengthening of societal resilience in various forms, in various contexts, for various stakeholders.

Key Messages

1. Resilience has been gaining ground in research, policy, and practice in a wide variety of domains; both scholars and practitioners have increasingly added the lexicon of resilience thinking to their work.

2. What resilience actually entails remains a highly debated topic. In particular, both scholars and practitioners have grappled with pinpointing what resilience means and defining its conceptual boundaries.
3. Rather than problematizing the conceptual ambiguity surrounding the concept of resilience we should embrace its openness and approach resilience through an open research methodology, such as action research and engaged scholarship.

Acknowledgments

We thank Professor Ungar for his feedback on the chapter. All authors contributed equally to this work.

Note

1. According to the report, radicalization can be seen as a destructive form of empowerment when it leads to violence. When taken alone, then, and decoupled from violence, radicalization is little more than a process of empowerment hyperfocused on specific ideological or social convictions. There are individual psychological processes that affect empowerment, and these include the need for agency, personal identity, purpose, justice, and control. These same needs that, when addressed, lead to what we call "empowerment," can also lead to acts of abuse or violence, such as terrorism.

References

Anholt, R. (2017). *Governing humanitarian emergencies, protracted crises, and (in)security through resilience*. Retrieved from https://research.vu.nl/ws/portalfiles/portal/12946141/ISR_Governing_Insecurity_Through_Resilience_Research_Report_2017.pdf

Aradau, C. (2014). The promise of security: Resilience, surprise and epistemic politics. *Resilience: International Policies, Practices and Discourses, 2*(2), 73–87. doi:10.1080/21693293.2014.914765

Aradau, C., & Munster, R. (2007). Governing terrorism through risk: Taking precautions, (un)knowing the future. *European Journal of International Relations, 13*(1), 89–115. doi:10.1177/1354066107074290

Bekkers, R. (2016, January 15). *Foundations of societal resilience*. Paper presented at Talma Lecture. Amsterdam. Retrieved from https://renebekkers.files.wordpress.com/2016/01/15_01_08_foundations-of-societal-resilience.pdf

Brasset, J., & Vaughan-Williams, N. (2015). Security and the performative politics of resilience: Critical infrastructure protection and humanitarian emergency preparedness. *Security Dialogue, 46*(1), 32–50. doi:10.1177/0967010614555943

Bromme, R. (2000). Beyond one's own perspective: The psychology of cognitive interdisciplinarity. In P. Weingart & N. Stehr (Eds.), *Practising interdisciplinarity* (pp. 115–133). Toronto, ON: University of Toronto Press.

Brown, K. (2011, September). *Rethinking progress in a warming world: Interrogating climate resilient development*. Paper presented at the EADI/DSA General Conference, University of York, UK.

Brydon-Miller, M., Greenwood, D., & Maguire, P. (2003). Why action research? *Action Research, 1*(1), 9–28. doi:10.1177/14767503030011002

Chandler, D. (2013a). International statebuilding and the ideology of resilience. *Politics, 33*(4), 276–286. doi:10.1111/1467-9256.12009

Chandler, D. (2013b). Resilience and the autotelic subject: Toward a critique of the societalization of security. *International Political Sociology, 7*(2), 210–226. doi:10.1111/ips.12018

Chandler, D. (2014). *Resilience: The governance of complexity*. London, UK: Routledge.
Chandler, D., & Coaffee, J. (2017). Contested paradigms of international resilience. In D. Chandler & J. Coaffee (Eds.), *The Routledge handbook of international resilience* (pp. 3–9). London, UK: Routledge.
Chettiparamb, A. (2007). *Interdisciplinarity: A literature review*. Southampton, UK: Interdisciplinary Teaching and Learning Group.
Coaffee, J., & Wood, D. M. (2006). Security is coming home: Rethinking scale and constructing resilience in the global urban response to terrorist risk. *International Relations, 20*(4), 503–517. doi:10.1177/0047117806069416
Coghlan, P. (2011). Action research: Exploring perspectives on a philosophy of practical knowing. *The Academy of Management Annals, 5*(1), 53–87. doi:10.1080/19416520.2011.571520
Commission of the European Communities. (2004). *Research for a secure Europe: Report of the group of personalities in the field of security research*. Retrieved from https://ec.europa.eu/home-affairs/sites/homeaffairs/files/e-library/documents/policies/security/pdf/gop_en.pdf
Davoudi, S. (2012). Resilience: A bridging concept or a dead end? *Planning Theory & Practice, 13*(2), 299–333. doi:10.1080/14649357.2012.677124
De Goede, M. (2008). The politics of preemption and the war on terror in Europe. *European Journal of International Relations, 14*(1), 161–185. doi:10.1177/1354066107087764
Duffield, M. (2012). Challenging environments: Danger, resilience and the aid industry. *Security Dialogue, 43*(5), 475–479. doi:10.1177/0967010612457975
Dunn Cavelty, M., Kaufmann, M., & Søby Kristensen, K. (2015). Resilience and (in)security: Practices, subjects, temporalities. *Security Dialogue, 46*(1), 3–14. doi:10.1177/0967010614559637
El Hadioui, I., Slootman, M., el-Akabawy, Z., Hammond, M., Mudde, A., & Schouwenburg, S. (2019). *Switchen en klimmen: Over het switchgedrag van leerlingen en de klim op de schoolladder in een grootstedelijke omgeving* [Switch and climb: On the switching behavior of students and the climb up the school ladder in a metropolitan environment]. Amsterdam, The Netherlands: Van Gennep.
Evans, B., & Reid, J. (2013). Dangerously exposed: The life and death of the resilient subject. *Resilience: International Policies, Practices and Discourses, 1*(2), 83–98. doi:10.1080/21693293.2013.770703
Ghorashi, H., de Boer, M., ten Holder, F. (2018). Unexpected agency on the threshold: Asylum seekers narrating from an asylum seeker centre. *Current Sociology, 66*(3), 373–391. doi:10.1177/0011392117703766
Holling, C. S. (1973). Resilience and stability of ecological systems. *Annual Review of Ecological Systems, 4*(1), 1–23.
Holling, C. S. (1986). The resilience of terrestrial ecosystems: Local surprise and global change. In W. C. Clark & R. E. Munn (Eds.), *Sustainable development of the biosphere* (pp. 292–317). London, UK: Cambridge University Press.
Howell, A. (2015). Resilience as enhancement: Governmentality and political economy beyond "responsibilisation." *Politics, 35*(1), 67–71. doi:10.1111/1467-9256.12080
Hursh, B., Haas, P., & Moore, M. (1983). An interdisciplinary model to implement general education. *Journal of Higher Education, 54*(1), 42–49. doi:10.1080/00221546.1983.11778151
Joseph, J. (2013). Resilience as embedded neoliberalism: A governmentality approach. *Resilience: International Policies, Practices and Discourses, 1*(1), 38–52. doi:10.1080/21693293.2013.765741
Katz, C. (2001). Disciplining interdisciplinarity. *Feminist Studies, 27*(2), 519–520.
Klein, J. T. (1996). *Crossing boundaries: Knowledge, disciplinarities, and interdisciplinarities*. Charlottesville: University Press of Virginia.
Klein, J. T. (2010). A taxonomy of interdisciplinarity. In R. Frodeman, J. T. Klein, C. Mitcham, & J. B. Holbrook (Eds.), *The Oxford handbook of interdisciplinarity* (pp. 15–30). Oxford, UK: Oxford University Press.
MacKinnon, D., & Derickson, K. D. (2013). From resilience to resourcefulness: A critique of resilience policy and activism. *Progress in Human Geography, 37*(2), 253–270. doi:10.1177/0309132512454775
Macrae, A. & Harmer, J. (2004, July). *Beyond the continuum: The changing role of aid policy in protracted crises* (Issue Brief). Retrieved from https://www.odi.org/publications/268-beyond-continuum-changing-role-aid-policy-protracted-crises
Malcolm, J. A. (2013). Project Argus and the resilient citizen. *Politics, 33*(4), 311–321. doi:10.1111/1467-9256.12021

Maldonado, J. K., Shearer, C., Bronen, R., Peterson, K., & Lazrus, H. (2013). The impact of climate change on tribal communities in the US: Displacement, relocation, and human rights. *Climatic Change, 120*(3), 601–614. doi:10.1007/s10584-013-0746-z

Manyena, S. B., & Gordon, S. (2015). Bridging the concepts of resilience, fragility and stabilisation. *Disaster Prevention and Management, 24*(1), 38–52. doi:10.1108/DPM-04-2014-0075

Matin, N., Forrester, J., & Ensor, J. (2018). What is equitable resilience? *World Development, 109,* 197–205. doi:10.1016/j.worlddev.2018.04.020

McNiff, J. (2013). *Action research: Principles and practice.* New York, NY: Routledge.

Orton, J. D., & O'Grady, K. A. (2016). Cosmology episodes: A reconceptualization. *Journal of Management, Spirituality & Religion, 13*(3), 226–245. doi:10.1080/14766086.2016.1159975

Pain, A., & Levine, S. (2012, November). *A conceptual analysis of livelihoods and resilience: Addressing the "insecurity of agency"* (Working Paper, IBSN 978-1-909464-00-1). Retrieved from https://www.odi.org/sites/odi.org.uk/files/odi-assets/publications-opinion-files/7928.pdf

Pelling, M., & Manuel-Navarrete, D. (2011). From resilience to transformation: The adaptive cycle in two Mexican urban centers. *Ecology and Society, 16*(2), 11. doi:10.5751/ES-04038-160211

Pugh, J., Gabay, C. & Williams, A. J. (2013). Beyond the securitisation of development: The limits of intervention, developmentalisation of security and repositioning of purpose in the UK Coalition Government's policy agenda. *Geoforum, 44,* 193–201. doi:10.1016/j.geoforum.2012.09.007

Renn, O., & Klinke, A. (2015). Risk governance and resilience: New approaches to cope with uncertainty and ambiguity. In U. Fra.Paleo (Ed.), *Risk governance: The articulation of hazard, politics and ecology* (pp. 19–41). Dordrecht, The Netherlands: Springer.

Rogers, P. (2013). The rigidity trap in global resilience: Neoliberalisation through principles, standards, and benchmarks. *Globalizations, 10*(3), 383–395. doi:10.1080/14747731.2013.787834

Sieckelinck, S. (2018). Towards a pedagogy of the radicalised. In P. Smeyers (Ed.), *International handbook of philosophy of education* (pp. 1375–1387). Dordrecht, The Netherlands: Springer.

Sieckelinck, S., Kaulingfreks, F., & De Winter, M. (2015). Neither villains nor victim: Towards an educational perspective on radicalisation. *British Journal of Educational Studies, 63*(3), 329–343. doi:10.1080/00071005.2015.1076566

Sieckelinck, S., Sikkens, E., Kotnis, S., van San, M., & De Winter, M. (2017). *Formers & families: Transitional journeys in and out of extremisms in Denmark and The Netherlands. A biographical approach.* Retrieved from https://www.ris.uu.nl/ws/files/15886833/end_report_formers_and_families_tcm126_610120.pdf

Smith, D., & Fischbacher, M. (2009). The changing nature of risk and risk management: The challenge of borders, uncertainty and resilience. *Risk Management, 11*(1), 1–12. doi:10.1057/rm.2009.1

Tanner, T., Lewis, D., Wrathall, D., Bronen, R., Cradock-Henry, N., Huq, S., . . . Thomalla, F. (2014). Livelihood resilience in the face of climate change. *Nature Climate Change, 5*(1), 23–26. doi:10.1038/nclimate2431

US Department of Homeland Security. (2007). *The national strategy for homeland security.* Retrieved from http://www.dhs.gov/xabout/history/gc_1193938363680.shtm

Van de Ven, A. H. (2007). *Engaged scholarship: Creating knowledge for science and practice.* Oxford, UK: Oxford University Press.

Walker, J., & Cooper, M. (2011). Genealogies of resilience: From systems ecology to the political economy of crisis adaptation. *Security Dialogue, 42*(2), 143–160. doi:10.1177/0967010611399616

Weick, K. E. (1993). The collapse of sensemaking in organizations: The Mann Gulch disaster. *Administrative Science Quarterly, 38*(4), 628–652. doi:10.2307/2393339

Weick, K. E., & Sutcliffe, K. M. (2015). *Managing the unexpected: Sustained performance in a complex world.* Hoboken, NJ: John Wiley.

Welch, J. IV. (2011). The emergence of interdisciplinarity from epistemological thought. *Issues in Integrative Studies, 29,* 1–39.

Decolonial Enactments of Human Resilience

Stories of Palestinian Families From Beyond the Wall

Devin G. Atallah

Introduction

From cellular to cultural levels, ecologically minded social scientists highlight that human phenomena should be understood systemically (e.g., Christens & Perkins, 2008). Multisystemic frameworks of resilience (e.g., Folke, 2016; Masten, 2015; Ungar, 2018) argue for the importance on studying processes and pathways ranging from individual- or organism-level systems (including biological, emotional, cognitive, behavioral, and spiritual domains) to the mesosystems (including interpersonal, family, group, and local collectivities) and to the macrosystems (social and political structures). Decolonizing perspectives, critical race theories, and transnational feminisms, however, underscore how we must contend with the messiness of relationality, as human processes do not fit neatly into ecological levels or models (Atallah, Bacigalupe, & Repetto, 2019). According to Whyte (2018), increased attention should be placed on rethinking the complexity of human relationality, which unfolds not only within human relations, but with "different relationships connecting human and nonhuman living beings (plants, animals, persons, insects), nonliving beings and entities (spirits, elements), and collectives (e.g., forests, watersheds)" (p. 126).

When constructs of multisystems, environment, or place are understood as unfolding within and in-between both human and nonhuman relations, we can create epistemological challenges to the Eurocentric, Global North dualist thinking that views humans as separate and superior and where human phenomena primarily exists within hierarchies of humanity (Atallah & Ungar, 2020; Westley et al., 2013). These constructs that mark hierarchies of humanity and separate humans from nature contribute to the idea that some people should benefit from the exploitation of the environment while others are expendable and must suffer. This tangled set of ideologies has been at the heart of settler-colonialism and the threat it poses. The result has been not only an epoch of despoiled environments (the Anthropocene), but also systemic marginalization of racialized peoples—and here I mean Black, Brown, and Indigenous peoples internationally—members of the Global South (Native peoples of the Americas, Africa, southern regions in Asia and the Middle East, and Oceania and Polynesia) who have been historically colonized by actors using European and/or Global North patterns of thinking, action, and power.

As Atallah, Bacigalupe, and Repetto (2019) argue, root causes for differential opportunities for human resilience are shaped by "patterns of inequities and social suffering, determined by life-world conditions and caused by interplays between material, psychological, and sociopolitical processes that create disproportionate adversities in marginalized communities" (p. 3). A core assumption upheld in this chapter, rooted in Global South decolonizing perspectives in psychology, is that to promote human resilience (through linked material, psychological, sociopolitical responses), there is a pressing need for solidarity and allyship, including from psychologists and mental health researchers and practitioners, to advocate for and accompany communities on the front lines of resisting settler-colonialism (Atallah, 2016). When we accompany communities in this way, we are gifted the opportunity to hear into the depths of human suffering, splitting the notion of adversity wide open, finding local as yet unnamed ways of adapting, or better, transforming systems. In the process, we name and analyze all that remains absent from the mainstream literatures on resilience. Before we explore resilience from decolonial perspectives, let us first turn toward expanding our understandings of an adversity that is present in the lives of Palestinian refugee communities where the current narratives analyzed in this chapter are rooted: settler-colonialism, which is an adversity that is not unique to Palestine but, rather, marks the lives of diverse Black, Brown, and Indigenous communities internationally. In doing so, we hope to contribute to the building of understandings useful for addressing root causes that create disproportionate adversities for Global South and racialized groups in particular, as Atallah et al. (2019) suggest, by engaging "social justice perspectives on how resilience processes are marked by inequities and by the consequences of a history of the coloniality of power, oppression, and privilege" (p. 9).

What Is Settler-Colonialism?

> The colonial world is a world divided into compartments. It is probably unnecessary to recall the existence of native quarters and European quarters, of schools for natives and schools for Europeans; in the same way we need not recall Apartheid in South Africa. Yet, if we examine closely the system of compartments, we will at least be able to reveal the lines of force it implies.
> (Fanon, 1963, p. 29)

According to Fanon (1963), a core element of colonialism is that the way we see colonialism depends on a system of compartments and, more specifically, which compartment we are in. Furthermore, it takes courage to name these systems of compartments for what they are and to work to expose the sites of structural violence that the lines, or the walls, of the compartments reveal. Maldonado-Torres (2007) describes colonialism as a complex "relation in which the sovereignty of a nation or a people rests on the power of another nation" (p. 243). However, there are many types of colonialism. Cavanagh and Veracini (2013) define *settler-colonialism* as a phenomenon whereby migrants that hold a clear sovereign capacity create policies aimed at disappearing Indigenous peoples as they themselves (the migrants/settlers) become the founders of new political systems upon conquered lands. Wolfe (2006) described settler-colonialism as centralized around a cognitive structure—a logic of elimination—which focuses on replacing Indigenous groups on their lands.

Moreover, even after peace treaties are signed, and Indigenous lands and peoples are captured, there are a multiplicity of colonial systems that continue. Quijano (2000) theorized this concept as "coloniality." Maldonado-Torres (2007) defines coloniality as the "longstanding patterns of power that emerged as a result of colonialism, but that define culture, labor, intersubjective relations, and knowledge production well beyond the strict limits of colonial administrations" (p. 243). Coloniality involves a cognitive model, a perspective on humanness, identity, and place, within which everything (and everyone) that is colonized is transformed, or racialized, as being inferior and therefore as not requiring voice or agency in shaping knowledge and human ways of being. In this way, Indigenous and colonized peoples develop new racialized identities, which result from not only the loss of land, but also the loss of identity and loss of opportunities to partake in productions of knowledge and being (Maldonado-Torres, 2007; Quijano, 2000).

Indeed, racialized and Indigenous peoples rooted in the Global South have long responded to White Eurocentric settler domination by recentering the need for decolonial praxis. *Praxis*, as defined by Freire (1970), highlights how knowledge, practices, and places are interconnected and that cycles between reflection and action are required to lead to radical productions of being that can create sustained changes in social realities. In this way, decolonial praxis underscores that the Eurocentric ontologies and epistemologies of the Global North are not the only valid sources of knowledge and being. It is this praxis, grounded in communities' decolonial enactments in daily life and in cycles of radical knowledge that emerge, that are core dimensions of resilience for racialized and Indigenous peoples. These dimensions of resilience, not surprisingly, are too often absent, even silenced, in the Eurocentric literature that theorizes what resilience looks like and how it is manifested.

Exploring Resilience from Decolonial and Indigenous Perspectives

When identifying pathways toward healing and racial justice, Davis (2019) underscores the salience of the southern African knowledge system of *ubuntu*, which can be "translated to mean 'a person is a person through their relationships,' . . . [and] emphasizes humans' interidentity and interrelationality with all dimensions of existence—other people, places, land, animals, waters, air, and so on" (p. 18). Whyte (2018) highlights how groups, such as the

Potawatomi Indigenous nation of North America that he himself is a member of, emphasize the importance of restoring customs and Indigenous institutions of sovereignty and promoting ways of thinking and action that highlight interdependence of relationships between humans and environments. Whyte argues that focusing on interdependence draws attention to the responsibility that humans have for reciprocal, nonhierarchical relationships with each other and with their ecosystems. It is these relationships that contribute to reciprocal cycles of well-being for both people and the "natural" world with which they interact.

Therefore, one way of understanding settler-colonialism (and the resulting structural violence and threats to individual and collective well-being that follow), as Whyte suggests, is by engaging the idea of *collective continuance*. Whyte (2018) translates collective continuance from a Native American concept of Anishinaabe intellectual traditions. Whyte describes collective continuance as

> an ecological system, of interacting humans, nonhuman beings (animals, plants, etc.) and entities (spiritual, inanimate, etc.), and landscapes (climate regions, boreal zones, etc.) that are conceptualized and operate purposefully to facilitate a collective's (such as an Indigenous people) adaptation to changes. (pp. 133–134)

Knowledge systems across the historically colonized communities, such as *ubuntu* or *collective continuance,* are examples of Global South understandings that recenter focus on resilience within entirely multisystemic ways of being that are tied to the quality of human relationships and bonds between peoples and places. These forms of Indigenous knowledge highlight the unique type of colonial violence that is the forced separation of families and communities and the displacement and ethnic cleansing of Indigenous peoples off of their historic lands. Addressing these fractures is one pathway to resilience, although not one typically discussed in the mainstream psychological literature.

In this light, settler-colonialism involves complex systems of domination and displacement, which methodically sever Indigenous and racialized communities' access to equitable opportunities for recovery, adaptation, and transformation (all processes synonymous with resilience; e.g., Atallah et al., 2019; Kirmayer, Dandeneau, Marshall, Phillips, & Williamson, 2011; Ungar, 2018), disrupting their relationships with their ancestral communities, lands, environments, and places of belonging (Whyte, 2018). This structural violence can take many forms, however, all of which compromise capacities of Indigenous and racialized populations to thrive. These structural violence of settler-colonialism are becoming exposed and better understood (in academic writings in English) as scholar activists and community allies explore theoretical and practice implications of critical race theory, Black consciousness, Indigenous intellectual traditions, and decolonial transnational feminisms (e.g., Atallah, 2016; Bell, Canham, Dutta, & Fernandez, 2019; Davis, 2019; Fanon, 1963; Said, 1993; Wynter & McKittrick, 2015).

In summary, ethnic cleansing and displacement that occurs within settler-colonial projects not only strips people from their lands, their histories, and their truths—it also reduces colonized peoples to a psychopolitical environment of inferiority: to zones of subhumanity (Maldonado-Torres, 2016). Within these "zones," after the colonized are displaced from their

Indigenous lands and their *collective continuance* is attacked, the fabrics of their selves and societies are ripped apart and the colonized are constructed by settler societies as segregateable, detainable, or deportable, or in the most frightful of circumstances, as enslaveable, rapeable, and killable (Maldonado-Torres, 2007). Through this settler-colonial process, the racialized groups are displaced into geographies of subhumanity, which are blended territorial–corporal–cognitive spaces where people are seen and treated as not human enough, or even, as not human at all (Maldonado-Torres, 2016; Wynter & McKittrick, 2015).

This (dis)placement of people into geographies of nonhumanness, or not human enough, sheds light on the importance of reconsidering how we think about multisystemic human resilience within places or systems where people are locked into zones of subhumanity and their identities and their Indigenous *collective continuance* threatened or even completely destroyed. As Wynter and McKittrick (2015) explain, from 1492 onward, Europeans crossed oceans not only as settlers in the pursuit of lands, safety, and prosperity, but in the ongoing conquering and ethnically cleansing acts of venturing into environments that settlers considered to be "cognitively open" (p. 62). In these new geographies, where Indigenous peoples were racialized as being less than human and therefore gave no cause for cognitive dissonance when exploited, settlers gave themselves the freedom to rule over both the land and the emplaced peoples who belonged to the newly conquered territories. As Said (1993) highlights, this process of ruling over both land and people involves creating colonial facts and truths on the ground, which together work to hide, or invisiblize, the structural violence of the settlers and colonial systems of domination. In fact, colonized communities, rather than the settler societies, frequently are seen as the violent ones, while the violence of the colonizer are obscured and normalized (Said, 1993). This is why part of resilience processes against colonialism involves making the invisible visible, decolonizing minds and cognitions, which requires epistemological resistance (Fanon, 1963; de Sousa Santos, 2018) as a strategy to restore, or restory, historical harms and create new frameworks that can make the institutionalized, normalized violence of colonialism visible and fathomable. As Maldonado-Torres (2016) theorizes,

> decoloniality refers to efforts at rehumanizing the world, to breaking hierarchies of difference that dehumanize subjects and communities and that destroy nature, and to the production of counter-discourses, counter-knowledges, counter-creative acts, and counter-practices that seek to dismantle coloniality and to open up multiple other forms of being in the world. (p. 31)

Decolonial Strategies for Restorying Resilience

Storytelling and truth-telling against settler-colonial oppression can be a means of epistemological resistance and a practice of generating rehumanizing counternarratives (Wynter & McKittrick, 2015). Furthermore, as de Sousa Santos (2018) summarizes when exploring the work of Amílcar Lopes da Costa Cabral, a Cape Verdean and Bissau-Guinean decolonial revolutionary and philosopher, "the knowledge born of struggle is the most precious of all, for it is the one in which the relation between theory and practice is the most complex"

(p. 72). Storytelling can be a powerful way to hold this complexity and shed light on the messiness of human relationality, while contesting the master narratives embedded in settler-colonial discourses, including the ones apparent or hidden within rigorous and empirical scientific studies (Atallah, Shapiro, Al Azraq, Qaisi, & Suyemoto, 2018; Bell et al., 2019; Smith, 2012; Wynter & McKittrick, 2015). Tuck and McKenzie (2015) underscore how Indigenous scholars have "extensively theorized the role of storytelling as practice of shaping and being shaped by place. . . . Stories thus carry out a labor; creating, maintaining, and/or shifting narrative about the places in which we live and how they produce us and us them" (p. 34).

Moreover, a profound example of structural violence associated with the consequences of ongoing settler-colonialism and manifold decolonial enactments of resilience with shifting narratives and resistance can be seen in places beyond the walls in colonized Palestine (Davis, 2016). Salamanca, Qato, Rabie, and Samour (2012) notice that although settler-colonialism has framed conditions of daily life for Palestinians for decades, "the creative offerings of the settler-colonial studies paradigm" (p. 4), have been undertheorized and underutilized across discourses on Palestinian experiences including in the health and social sciences literatures. Furthermore, Palestine is also one of my many homespaces, and one of the locations where my research takes place. Therefore, in this chapter, I aim to contribute to the restorying of resilience from decolonial perspectives as an act of epistemological resistance, grounded in the storytelling of displaced Palestinian families living in refugee camps in the West Bank. More specifically, I will share my reflections on resilience grounded on stories of two families who participated in a research project that I completed (see Atallah, 2015, 2017) in the West Bank, the Palestinian Refugee Family Trees of Resilience project (PRFTR). Before presenting the stories, however, I will first provide brief background information on the West Bank and the PRFTR project to help contextualize the narratives that follow.

Background on the West Bank, the PRFTR Project, and the Research Participants

The West Bank is a territory conquered by the state of Israel. There are approximately 2.79 million Palestinians living in the West Bank, and about one third are registered United Nations (UN) refugees, many living in UN camps across the occupied territory (Palestinian Central Bureau of Statistics, 2016). According to B'TSELEM (2019), the Israeli Information Center for Human Rights in the Occupied Territories, as of the end of 2017 there were 600,000 Israeli settlers in the West Bank (many of whom reside in colonies within the Israeli separation barrier—or the Wall—which means that these settlements are often in close proximity to displaced Palestinian communities. In total, there are 131 Israeli colonies recognized by Israel, and approximately 110 settlement outposts, which do not yet have Israeli government recognition; however, they do have significant sovereign capacities to soon become official colonies (B'TSELEM, 2019).

The stories explored in the following text are testimonies of displaced Palestinian families locked within territories that are inside the West Bank behind separation barriers and checkpoints—zones of subhumanity—ghettoized places behind the Wall of ongoing settler-colonial expansion. As we read through these families' statements, we bear witness to their stories of suffering associated with colonial structural violence, yet also their rehumanizing journeys as decolonial enactments of resilience.

The overarching research questions of the PRFTR project were (a) What is the resilience process of Palestinian refugee families exposed to historical trauma and continuous structural violence associated with the Israeli occupation? and (b) How do Palestinian refugee families transmit resilience across generations (see Atallah, 2017)? Thus, the PRFTR project explored how refugee families respond to and create opportunities for healing and justice within contexts of historical and ongoing settler-colonialism. PRFTR's methodology engaged a critical constructivist qualitative method of grounded theory situational analysis (Charmaz 2006; Clarke, 2005) and decolonizing strategies of community engagement (Atallah, Shapiro, et al., 2018).

Participants in PRFTR were invited to engage in the project through a partnering community-based organization, which was founded in the camp by Palestinian refugees themselves more than a decade ago. In total, 30 participants ($N = 30$) from five extended family networks residing in this camp for several generations participated in the PRFTR project. Participants ranged in age from 19 to 90 years old. All participants were Indigenous Palestinians and survivors of the *Nakba* ("disaster" in Arabic) and their descendants. *Nakba* refers to events where approximately 750,000 Palestinians were forcibly displaced during the creation of the state of Israel in 1948 (Pappe, 2006). The government of Israel refers to this event as the "War of Independence" (Israeli Ministry of Foreign Affairs, n.d.). Since the *Nakba* of 1948, displaced Indigenous Palestinian families have been living in UN refugee camps like the one where the PRFTR project took place, which is managed by the UN Relief and Works Agency for Palestine Refugees in the Near East (UNRWA). The Palestinian Authority (PA) has influence over populations in these camps as well. The Israeli Occupation of the West Bank began in 1967 and was followed by Israeli settler-colonial expansion, in addition to waves of mass Palestinian protest and resistance (UN, 2009). Therefore, the Palestinian residents of these UN camps essentially navigate three different authorities—none of which represent them: (a) UNRWA, (b) PA, and (c) the Israeli settler-colonial, occupation system. Furthermore, it is important to understand that many of the participating families in PRFTR have lived in the same refugee camp over many generations.

The PRFTR project received approval from the University of Massachusetts Boston Institutional Review Board and complied with high standards of ethical research (Atallah, 2015, 2017). Pseudonyms are used in place of the birth names of the participants from the two families presented in this chapter for the purposes of protecting their privacy. From the first family, the two pseudonyms used will be Hajj Al-Khader for the elderly father who is in his 80s and Cais for the son who is in his 30s (and who is also a father himself). From the second family, pseudonyms Hajja Rinad will be used for the elderly mother who is in her 80s, and Naila for the daughter who is in her 40s (and who is also a mother herself). Hajj, placed in front of the name of the elderly man, and Hajja, in front of the name of the elderly woman, are honorific terms showing respect. By turning to the stories shared by these two families, I do not hope to speak for them as "silenced" colonized subjects, nor are their experiences meant to represent all Palestinian family experiences living under the Israeli settler-colonial occupation system, the PA, and UNRWA. Instead, I aim to shed light on an alternatively painted language to contribute to the building of the alternative thinking on resilience, a mural of discourses inspired by Palestinian families' fluid, messy, and intersecting processes of becoming and shaping their possibilities for dignity and decolonization. Before turning to the narratives of the two participating families, however, consistent with decolonizing scholarships (e.g., Atallah, Shapiro, et al., 2018; Bell et al., 2019; Smith, 2012), it is important to engage in reflexivity and work toward attempting to make this research and writing more accountable to the people most impacted—in this case—Palestinian refugee families living in the UN camps.

Reflexivity

I would like to underscore that the PRFTR project took place in a UN refugee camp in an area of the West Bank that is directly adjacent the Indigenous village and ancestral place of my paternal ancestors. In many ways, my own family life has been shaped by settler-colonial structural violence, evidenced, in part, by the fact that my grandfather's lands are now sites of Israeli settlements. Therefore, when listening to the families' stories and offering my interpretations in this chapter, I draw not only on interview data from my qualitative research within the PRFTR project and from previously published social science literatures and decolonizing theories. I also draw from my own lived and intergenerational familial experiences of displacement, loss of lands, and the manifold of violent ways that Indigenous *collective continuance* of my native communities have been targeted, damaged, or, at times, even completely destroyed. I understand these issues not only in abstract ways, but I also feel these structural violence survived by my family and communities in my body. Due to the focus of this book, an in-depth exploration of the ways that structural violence associated with settler colonialism impacted my research in Palestine, including my working from positions of relative privilege and power as a U.S. and Chilean academic, is beyond the scope of this chapter. For more on critical reflexivity and the need for it in deconstructing and interrupting colonial relations when engaging in research as enactments of decolonial praxis, readers are encouraged to see Atallah (in press).

Two Stories of Decolonial Enactments of Resilience of (Dis)placed Palestinian Families Beyond the Wall

The first family story is about Cais, a 35-year-old man born in the refugee camp, and his father Hajj Khader, a 86-year-old elder who was born and raised in *Allar* village, which is an area that is now inside the state of Israel. Listening to stories of decolonial enactments of resilience include hearing how Cais and Hajj Khader remember and resist the charting of their lands by the settler nation-state. Decolonization is not a metaphor—it has everything to do with restoring lands and a journey of returning to places of belonging. Decolonization is a declaration of human dignity. Rather than being treated as landless, stateless, "empty" bodies placed in a refugee camp, Cais and Hajj Khader share their rehumanizing stories related to ways they have worked to affirm their humanity by reclaiming rootedness in their lands.

For example, in Cais's narrative that follows, he shares how he would frequently encounter Israeli attempts to deny his identity, to disconnect him from the land and his Indigenous village. Attacks on his humanity and dignity occurred, in part, through a process of being disjointed from the land not only by being physically removed as a child and growing up in a refugee camp, but also systematically transformed by an imposed identity separate from his ancestral homelands. Cais explains how even as a child he defiantly resisted Israeli state policies of dehumanization by developing decolonial attitudes and voicing his invisible history affirming his roots and his humanity, rather than his chronic state of exile.

> Cais: I remember at school, all the schools were under the Israeli administration during that time, the printed books would all have a map of Israel in them and would not have Palestine anywhere on it. No mention of the West Bank even, just "Judea and Samaria." So, at school, we used to erase and write over those maps and write "Palestine." Even on our birth certificates, it would say Israel. So we would actually cross out this on our birth certificates and write Palestine . . . and I remember once, when we had a demonstration outside our UN refugee school, the next day, an Israeli military officer visited the school. He came to the school because he considered us troublemakers. He came to try to speak to us kids the day after our demonstration. Every time that he tried to ask us where we were from, we wouldn't answer that we were from this refugee camp, none of us did! We'd all answer him by saying the name of our villages. Even, at one point the officer got so frustrated by this he was pulling my ear! He said to me, yanking my ear, "So, again, where are you from boy?" And I still told him, "I'm from *Allar* [which is the name of Cais's ancestral village in lands that were conquered by Israel in *Nakba* of 1948 and are now within the borders of the Israeli nation-state]" He said back to me the name of the refugee camp, but I said back to him, "*Allar*!" He kept pulling my ear but I didn't back down. This was really annoying for the Israeli officer, I was provoking him and I loved it! "I am from *Allar*!" I'd say over and over again! "I am from *Allar*!"

Cais shares how he, alongside his community, developed strong decolonial attitudes to protect his place in this world, scratching out the colonial definitions of self and community. Cais's story reminds us how one of the front lines of settler-colonial oppression incudes the mapping of lands, selves, and communities together, which are produced and sustained by colonial discourses and settler nation-state policies marking identities and citizenships. Cais challenged these front lines despite the multiplicity of ways that Israeli colonial systems attempted to school and control him, measure and mark him.

Furthermore, it is important to listen to how Cais's decolonial attitudes, as resilience, are linked to his intergenerational family trees. For example, in an interview with Cais's father Hajj El-Khader, I learned how he faced the forced separation from his village *Allar*—the lands, homespaces, and trees, which also represented a devastating loss and disconnection within his body, mind, identity, dignity, and ancestors. Hajj El-Khader described the process of returning to his Indigenous village after it was demolished during *Nakba* of 1948 and annexed into the nascent state of Israel. He described how he would return to his village and smuggle his olives across the border back into the West Bank. This was a common practice that many displaced Palestinians engaged in during the years after *Nakba*. Palestinians who transgressed the nascent border were frequently killed or imprisoned if they were caught returning to their lands by the patrolling Israeli soldiers. And yet, despite the risk, Hajj Khader continued to cross and harvest his trees. More recently, Hajj Khader has returned with his children, including Cais, showing them their lands, homes, and even the old school in the *Allar* village that Hajj Khader attended when he was a boy in the 1930s and 1940s. In the rare circumstances that they cross the border to return, just for the day, to walk in their native lands, they still do this with the risk of being shot or detained for their transgressions—moving beyond the Wall without permission by the state of Israel.

Hajj Khader: I was 14 years old during *Nakba*. Years after we were kicked off our land, I still returned. Regularly. I would smuggle myself back.... I got strength from my homeland. I depended on my homeland, on the olive trees. When I used to smuggle myself to return to my village, I used to eat the dirt of my village. I used to travel by myself, using the shelter of the night for safety... I did this for many years after *Nakba*, even though it was dangerous.

Devin Atallah: There were plenty of olives around you in the area here near the refugee camp, why did you go back to your village to pick those olives?

Hajj Khader: Because these were my olives. This was my sweat, the effort we put into our land over generations. My grandparents took care and harvested these trees! Lastly, I always wished the Israelis would find me and kill me in my village. Even now, I wish I would die in the village. Why did they demolish the village? Because at the time it was part of Arab lands, not Israeli, so they just wanted to make sure we Arabs would not come back, so they emptied the villages. To this day, my village is ruins and no one lives there. It is wilderness.... When I return, I rub the dirt on my chest.... My blood still flows even today. We were forced to leave our villages but I teach my children, and the children of my children, they should not forget *their* village ... my land my honor ... my land my nobility.

In this resilience process, I bear witness to Hajj Khader's courageous truth-telling and transgressions, his rejection of the boundaries enforced by the settler nation-state, which is also a rejection of his chronic condition of displacement and homelessness in the refugee camp. Following his footsteps, however, it is important to understand that this individual action that Hajj Khader takes is actually an enormous multisystemic action. His rejection of the imposed boundaries is a decolonial dismissal of the system of compartments—which strikes at one of the core dimensions of settler-colonialism. Hajj Khader's narrative deepens our understandings of the complexity of human relationality and multisystems and includes a story of the cultivation of radical hope and holding onto the right for self-determination, across not only borders, but across generations. And like Hajj El Khader's olive trees, which travel through time more than they travel through space, decolonial enactments of resilience are intergenerationally bound.

This envisioning of resilience links healing and justice in how father Hajj El Khader and his son, Cais, both highlighted that remembering and transgressing can be curative, as can be the dirt of the land of their Indigenous village. Hajj Khader eats and rubs this dirt upon his chest in expression of deep suffering, yet also with defiance and radical love, which together form a persisting decolonial attitude that stands up to forced displacement and destruction of their Indigenous *collective continuance*. In so many ways, El Khader's eating and rubbing of the earth on his chest calls us to rethink what it means to be human, and how humans belong to lands, perhaps even more than lands could ever belong to humans. The Palestinian resistance poet Rashid Hussein wrote:

> Tent number fifty on the left – that is my present
> But it is too crammed to contain a future
> And, 'Forget,' they say
> But how can I!
> Teach the night to forget to bring
> Dreams showing me my village
> Teach the winds to forget to carry me
> The aroma of apricots in my fields
> And teach the sky too to forget to rain
> Only then may I forget my country. (Quoted in Shahin, 2005, p. 46)

The second family story is about Naila, a 48-year-old woman born in the refugee camp, and her mother Hajja Rinad, a 81-year-old elder who was born and raised in *Al-Qabu* village, which is an area that is now a state park where Israelis can enjoy camping, picnicking, and other outdoor activities. The home that Hajja Rinad was born in has been destroyed, but the stones of the foundation are still visible, partially hidden by outgrowth of mountain sage, cactus, and thyme.

Naila is currently a social worker providing community-based mental health support to marginalized families in her community. Before becoming a mental health worker, Naila was an activist and has been imprisoned several times throughout her life thus far by the Israeli authorities. She is 1 of 11 children, and her family lived in poverty in the camp throughout her upbringing. Naila lived with her mother Hajja Rinad, her father, and her siblings (13 people in total). For Naila's early years, they all lived together in the confines of one UN unit, which includes one small room and a kitchen. As a teenager, the family moved into two UN units, which still continued the cramped and inhumane living conditions.

Naila's parents struggled to provide food for the family because of their devastating economic situation. Naila describes being frequently hungry growing up, and beginning to actively resist Israeli soldiers and settlers while she was in middle school. Naila recalls throwing stones and protesting her circumstances including the poverty, the Israeli military occupation, the historical and ongoing settler-colonialism, in addition to her father's authority.

Naila: I think that the hardest thing was to try to be sure that we had enough to eat. My mother used to complete the most strenuous tasks to make sure we had food to eat. I remember people used to go to the bakers to get their dough and bake their bread. But my mother started her own traditional oven, we call it *Taboon*, which you have a hole and you cover it with fire and then you open it and put the bread in. My mother had to do all of that by herself, going around to carpenters to get the leftover wood to cover this hole and keep it warm, even the chickens' manure, she would dry it to cover the hole and this would keep the fire going, cook and keep the oven warm for days on end, although it's smoky and smelly.... It's very hard work, believe me, just baking bread for your family. When I was like 12 or 13 years old, I was always dreaming of having a super power of changing the world and I would actually take out my anger by participating in demonstrations and just being active ... so when I was active, it's about, a mix of things: it's about the oppression, about my family, about the poverty and the situation I was living. Even at a very young age I was wanted by the Israelis for my activism. They would send a soldier to my house requiring for my father and I to report to the Israeli military compound in the city [a nearby West Bank municipality]. We would have to spend the whole day there, sometimes every day for weeks on end, sitting at the compound and my father would be lectured from the Israeli soldiers and commander about needing to control his daughter. I still remember that I used to be more afraid of my father than of the Israeli soldiers [with this Naila breaks out in laughter].

Throughout her storytelling, Naila elaborated on her fears, on her radical dreams of changing the world, and how the settler-colonial struggles intersected with her family struggles and her developmental trajectories as a youth. Her father's parenting strategies were directly negotiated in relationality with military forces and settler nation-state policies of domination, mediated through the authority of a local commander who routinely gave "advice" to Naila's father about how to control, or to rule, his unruly daughter.

Naila was imprisoned by the state of Israel for the first time when she was 19 years old. She remained in detention of three years, surviving torture and a multiplicity of tactics of domination, which Naila understood as Israel's attempts to break her. Naila explains how despite the many violence experiences of imprisonment, she grew and developed herself, learning and teaching with the other women prisoners. Naila expressed feeling profound connection with the other women on the inside, especially in their constantly reading and rising together. The literature they were reading was unauthorized by the Israeli prison authorities. This did not stop them. Naila recounts how she would smuggle readings into the prison with the support of friends who would inscribe miniature text on paper folded into tiny capsules then wrapped in plastic. Naila would swallow these writings during visitations with these friends and then they would emerge once back in her cell in the toilet. Naila shared how these writings would be passed around among the community in prison and nurtured their minds and activisms throughout years in detention and were key to her perseverance (*sumoud* in Arabic).

When released, Naila was discharged back to the refugee camp as an educated young woman, far from broken; instead, despite having survived torture and sexist gender-based violence in prison, she had worked, alongside the other women prisoners, to disentangle the colonial oppressions and how the occupation systems framed their bodies, framed their identities, framed their womanhood, framed their activisms, framed their histories, and yet ultimately, altogether failed at framing their futures. Decolonial enactments of resilience evidenced in Naila's story include her radical dreaming and her working together with other incarcerated women to create conditions for community and to develop decolonial attitudes and knowledge while healing and growing from behind the bars of settler-colonial detention. Incredibly, as a young woman, at the same age that many would be entering college, Naila describes how she partook in the creation of a collective decolonizing university, a community space within the compartments, behind the walls of prison alongside the other incarcerated women. This is evidence of resilience as the promotion of "decolonial attitudes which form the basis for creating rehumanizing praxes for healing from collective trauma. Healing from oppression's pain, with one another, could return us to a state where the self is prized and can rise in and through community" (Bell, 2018, p. 259). Naila's decolonial attitude and collective activism was strengthened in prison and only continued to rise upon her release.

Furthermore, similar to Cais and Hajj Khader's story, it is important to listen to how Naila's decolonial resilience processes are linked to her intergenerational family trees. For example, Naila highlights how her mother Hajja Rinad's perseverance through struggles to feed the family as a whole and her reconstructing the Indigenous oven (*Taboon*), really left a mark on her as a child. Furthermore, after Naila was arrested and put into prison, Israeli soldiers immediately came to their home in the UN camp and demolished it as a way to punish the whole family as a system for their daughter's defiant transgressions. Hajja Rinad's narrative that follows describes her journeys in creating a collective, healing homespace after their two UN housing units were destroyed, which emerge as a potent decolonial enactment of resilience. In so many ways, collectively rebuilding a home is a powerful practice of perseverance, almost a metaphor for defying the weight of colonial structural violence that subjects families to collective punishment and prolonged dislocation.

Hajja Rinad: The soldiers came right after they arrested our daughter Naila. They looked around just to see how they were going to demolish the house. They came at night, at ten at night, and they asked everyone to leave the house.

Devin Atallah: How many soldiers were there?

Hajja Rinad: A lot of them, it felt like the whole army was there... We had two UN units, and the Israelis demolished both of them. When the soldiers came, they allowed us to take some stuff, and we insisted on staying there and living in a tent under the olive tree, to make sure, because a lot of the houses that were demolished in the camp were not allowed to return and rebuild on the land if they had left it. They would lose their land. So, we knew that if we left and settled down somewhere else, the Israelis might not give us enough space one day to rebuild again and we would be completely homeless! So we insisted on living in a tent, on the ruins of our demolished home. We lived in the tent for a full year, and that paid off because we eventually got to rebuild our house again on that same space of land.

It is important to understand that Hajja Rinad's family lived in a tent for a year, all 12 of them (usually they were a family of 13, but Naila was incarcerated). They lived in the tent for a year not because they didn't have the means to rebuild but, instead, because it took the Israeli military a year to issue them a building permit. If Hajja Rinad's family had rebuilt a home instead of a tent without waiting for the permit, they would have risked having it labeled as an illegal structure and therefore demolished once again and more family members taken off to prison. Furthermore, it is important to understand how immediately after Hajja Rinad's and Naila's family home was demolished, the youth of the camp organized themselves and responded by making a shelter. As Hajja Rinad's story continues, she highlights how their community revealed itself as a sheltering force when responding to home demolition and the impact of forced and prolonged homelessness.

Hajja Rinad: The first night, the youth around, from the neighbors and relatives and the youth of the camp, went to a nearby factory for plastic carpets, and they got some of the debris from our demolished home, and with the plastic they made kind of like a shape of a house for us to live in until we got a tent.... I remember when my husband went to another city to get two huge pieces of fabric that would be suitable to create the tent . . . and it was like a visiting tent. People used to come over from everywhere and spend the night with us. Everybody showing solidarity. Wanting to sleep with us to show that we were not alone. People from everywhere would come, from other camps, and even from other villages, and from within the refugee camp, like the neighbors, and our relatives. Everybody. It was a real nice sense of solidarity from everybody. It was not an easy time though. When it used to rain, the water used to go under the tent, and you could see the water coming into the tent, so we used to create a small tunnel, canal, to direct the water outside the tent so the children would not get too wet.

The apparently localized, spontaneous, and informal process of families and neighbors helping each other to rebuild, emerged as a very important and multisystemic decolonial enactment of resilience. These decolonial enactments manifest in response to state-sponsored policies of home demolitions, which are violent colonial tactics, in part, for land-taking or annexing territory, which people face by persevering and seeking shelter under the strength of family bonds, community embodiments of affection, and collective reconstruction. Both Naila and Hajja Rinad's storytelling of their time apart while Naila was detailed, required decolonial enactments of resilience that wielded the power of community, decolonial attitudes, and collective reconstructing of selves and homespaces to break free from the systems of compartments that wall their lives.

Conclusion

The current chapter centers understandings of resilience on stories of two displaced Palestinian families who shared their experiences and perspectives with me during the PRFTR. In doing so, I draw on decolonial perspectives (Atallah, 2016, 2017; Bell, 2018; Dutta, 2018; Maldonado-Torres, 2007; Quijano, 2000) with the goal of contributing to the development of alternative thinking of multisystemic, embodied, and intergenerational processes of Palestinians on the front lines of surviving colonial structural violence. When reading and interpreting these stories, I asked that you accompany me in an alternative way of seeing, listening, and reading, so that we could bear witness to decolonial enactments of resilience in ways that called ourselves as readers, into accountability.

These understandings of resilience are born from stories of the silenced, yet never muted, voices of families on the front lines of a colonized, displaced place. The longitudes and latitudes of this place have long been mapped, fortified, and walled-in by colonial, structural violence. Yet, as the stories of Hajj Khader, Cais, Naila, and Hajja Rinad's demonstrate, resilience in this place has long been spoken in native tongues and poems, in the radical dreams and decolonial attitudes of refugees, in the critical knowledge housed in bodies and swallowed dirt, in the elders' stories who are living out life sentences of exile and repeated home demolitions, and in the leadership of defiant and detained women and men front liners that are continually incarcerated by militaries and memories, which no one outside the Walls ever has to return to resee or remember.

Furthermore, these stories obligate that we struggle ourselves and deepen our listening and theorizing practices—to be able to approach comprehensions of a messy multisystemic human relationality. This complex theorization of multisystemic relationality overlaps with the courageous work of transnational women of color philosophers and justice seekers (e.g., Moraga & Anzaldua, 1983), and decolonial feminists in Palestinian contexts (e.g., Shalhoub-Kevorkian, 2009). These radical women theorists and activists argue that instead of focusing exclusively on dismantling sexist *or* racist structures, systems of patriarchy should be explored within a complex web of power and relationality that includes our interrogating racism, colonialism, militarism, and other structural violence particular to the dilemmas in question—or the system of compartments (Fanon, 1963) that need to be transgressed. In this light, the contestations of patriarchal power in Palestinian social systems, the local militarization and war violence, and the global constraints on the contestations against Israeli colonial rule should be understood as linked processes that cut across scales and systems, rather than being compartmentalized into separate levels, processes, or discourses (Shalhoub-Kevorkian, 2009). To put an end to social silence, forgetfulness, and ongoing colonial dominance, resilience within conditions of settler-colonialism requires intersectional thinking, courageous remembrance, and intergenerational, decolonizing healing *and* justice (Ginwright, 2016; Grant, Marinho, & Crean, 2019; Just Healing Collective, 2014). As Atallah et al. (2019) argue,

> human resilience itself is intersectional. More specifically, resilience processes intersect with the human bodies and selves that die, survive, respond, and heal in the face of sudden catastrophes and the disasters of daily life in marginalized

communities . . . embedded in the racialized, gendered, and classed structures that enhance and/or obstruct people's responses to suffering. (p. 14)

In conclusion, when shifting, and recentering our gaze on the pressing concerns of Indigenous, racialized, colonized families and communities, such as in refugee camps in Palestine, our understandings of resilience and the possibilities for transformation are deepened. Intergenerational family resilience journeys within colonized communities can hold critical decolonial knowledge and promises. Future research that contributes to shifting thinking of human relationality in ways that afford the emergence of solutions grounded on voices of Indigenous peoples is critical to making resilience more relevant and accountable. But this goes beyond voice and includes vision. As Dutta (2018) describes, "decoloniality entails a fundamental transformation of the terms of knowledge production, striving toward a new vision of human life that is not configured by the imposition of White Euro-American societal ideals . . . [and] necessitate a fundamental shift in vantage point" (p. 273). These shifting visions and vantage points are so critical, as Bell et al. (2019) argue, because the minds and bodies of segregated and colonized front liners are the only ones who hold the knowledge of the ways toward a place outside the Wall—beyond the system of compartments. This is a desegregated and decolonized place of healing and justice. As evidenced in Hajj Khader, Cais, Naila, and Hajja Rinad's stories, their intergenerational family and community trees are also keepers of these knowledge.

Key Messages

1. Critical insights on multisystemic resilience are grounded in Global South knowledge of human relationality. These insights are rooted in colonized communities' embodied and emplaced struggles for healing and justice, for dignity and decolonization, and can be heard in the voices of Black, Brown, and Indigenous peoples.
2. The stories shared in this chapter by participants from two displaced Palestinian families living in a colonized West Bank community demonstrate that structural violence of settler-colonialism create legacies of wounds and ongoing war across generations, where participants respond through intergenerational, decolonial enactments of resilience.
3. There is a need to link resilience and justice work to address and repair the multisystemic relational harms and injustices associated with legacies of colonialism and ongoing coloniality—both historical and structural—that settle into our bodies, lands, practices, policies, and family and community lives in intergenerational, nuanced, and complex ways.
4. Psychologists, mental health workers, and transdisciplinary social scientists working within Global North institutions and Eurocentric epistemological traditions have a responsibility to disrupt colonial patterns of power, to listen to, and accompany families and communities who are on the front lines of contesting the conditions, thinking, policies, and practices that make the structural violence of settler-colonialism endure.

Acknowledgments

I would like to thank the two participating families from the PRFTR project whose stories are featured in this chapter, for so generously sharing their insights, courage, and hospitality with me throughout the research process. I also thank the community-based organization in the refugee camp that made the interviews that I recorded possible. In addition, the Arabic–English translator/interpreter working with me, Yaser Qaisi, deepened the interviews and storytelling processes on so many levels. I would also like to thank Ester Shapiro, Karen Suyemoto, and Leila Farsakh, as my mentors and now also as my colleagues, who helped guide and support the PRFTR project from beginning to end while I was still a graduate student. I would also like to thank my beloved wife/life partner and our two children who inspire and sustain me in all of my research and writings. In addition, I would like to thank the editor of this volume, Michael Ungar, for his support of my alternative writing approach, encouraging my own decolonial resolve to attempt at listening closely to narratives of Palestinian refugee families beyond the Wall. Lastly, I am also very grateful to Urmitapa Dutta for her uplifting feedback on numerous drafts of this manuscript.

References

Atallah, D. G. (in press). Reflections on racial love and rebellion: Solidarity praxis and decolonial resilience research with Palestinian and Mapuche communities in struggle. In K. Shose, S. Suffla, & M. Seedat (Eds.), *Decolonial enactments in community psychology*. New York, NY: Springer.

Atallah, D. G. (2015). *Palestinian refugee family trees of resilience: Intergenerational cultivation of resistance, return, and perseverance in response to Israel state violence and occupation* (Doctoral dissertation). Retrieved from ProQuest Dissertations & Theses Global (Order No. 3622183). University of Massachusetts, Boston.

Atallah, D. G. (2016). Toward a decolonial turn in resilience thinking in multifaceted disasters: Example of the Mapuche from southern Chile on the frontlines and faultlines. *International Journal of Disaster Risk Reduction, 19*, 92–100. doi:10.1016/j.ijdrr.2016.08.027

Atallah, D. G. (2017). A community-based qualitative study of intergenerational resilience with Palestinian refugee families facing structural violence and historical trauma. *Transcultural Psychiatry, 54*(3), 357–383. doi:10.1177/1363461517706287

Atallah, D. G., Bacigalupe, G., & Repetto, P. (2019). Centering at the margins: Critical community resilience praxis. *Journal of Humanistic Psychology*, 1–31. doi:10.1177/0022167818825305

Atallah, D. G., Shapiro, E. R., Al-Azraq, N., Qaisi, Y., & Suyemoto, K. L. (2018). Decolonizing qualitative research through transformative community engagement: Critical investigation of resilience with Palestinian refugees in the West Bank. *Qualitative Research in Psychology, 15*(4), 489–519. doi:10.1080/14780887.2017.1416805

Atallah, D. G., & Ungar, M. (2020). Indigenous communities facing environmental racism: Human rights, resilience, and resistance in Palestinian communities of the West Bank and the Mapuche of Chile. In N. Sveaass, P. Hagenaars, & T. Wainwright (Eds.), *Human rights and human rights education for psychologists*. London, UK: Routledge.

Bell, D. (2018). A pedagogical response to decoloniality: Decolonial atmospheres and rising subjectivity. *American Journal of Community Psychology, 62*(3–4), 250–260. doi:10.1002/ajcp.12292

Bell, D., Canham, H., Dutta, U., & Fernandez, J. S. (2019). Retrospective autoethnographies: A call for decolonial imaginings for the new university. *Qualitative Inquiry*. Advance online publication. doi:10.1177/1077800419857743

B'TSELEM. (2019). *The Israeli Information Center for Human Rights in the Occupied Territories: Statistics on settlements and settler population*. Retrieved from: https://www.btselem.org/settlements/statistics

Cavanagh, E., & Veracini, L. (2013). Editors statement. *Settler Colonial Studies, 3*(1), 1. doi:10.1080/18380743.2013.768169

Charmaz, K. (2006). *Constructing grounded theory: A practical guide through qualitative analysis*. London, UK: SAGE.

Christens, B. D., & Perkins, D. D. (2008). Transdisciplinary, multilevel action research to enhance ecological and psychopolitical validity. *Journal of Community Psychology, 36*(2), 214–231. doi:10.1002/jcop.20232

Clarke, A. E. (2005). *Situational analysis: Grounded theory after the postmodern turn*. London, UK: SAGE.

Davis, A. (2016). *Freedom is a constant struggle: Ferguson, Palestine, and the foundations of a movement*. Chicago, IL: Haymarket Books.

Davis, F. (2019). *The little book of race and restorative justice: Black lives, healing, and US social transformation*. New York, NY: Good Books, Skyhorse.

de Sousa Santos, B. (2018). *The end of the cognitive empire: The coming of age of epistemologies of the South*. Durham, NC: Duke University Press.

Dutta, U. (2018). Decolonizing "community" in community psychology. *American Journal of Community Psychology, 62*(3–4), 272–282. doi:10.1002/ajcp.12282

Fanon, F. (1963). *The wretched of the Earth*. New York, NY: Grove Press.

Folke, C. (2016). Resilience (republished). *Ecology and Society, 21*(4), 44. doi:10.5751/ES-09088-210444

Freire, P. (1970). *Pedagogy of the oppressed*. New York, NY: Continuum International.

Ginwright, S. (2016). *Hope and healing in urban education: How urban activists and teachers are reclaiming matters of the heard*. New York, NY: Routledge.

Grant, J., Marinho, R., & Crean, G. (2019, June). *Healing justice and community psychology praxis*. Roundtable conducted at the Society for Community Action and Research (SCRA)'s biennial conference, Chicago, IL.

Israeli Ministry of Foreign Affairs. (n.d.). *The war of independence*. Retrieved from https://mfa.gov.il/MFA/AboutIsrael/Maps/Pages/The-War-of-Independence-1948.aspx

Just Healing Collective. (2014). *Healing justice practice spaces: A how-to guide*. Retrieved from: https://justhealing.files.wordpress.com/2012/04/healing-justice-practice-spaces-a-how-to-guide-with-links.pdf

Kirmayer, L. J., Dandeneau, S., Marshall, E., Phillips, M. K., & Williamson, K. J. (2011). Rethinking resilience from indigenous perspectives. *Canadian Journal of Psychiatry, 56*(2), 84–91. doi:10.1177/070674371105600203

Maldonado-Torres, N. (2007). On the coloniality of being. *Cultural Studies, 21*(2), 240–270. doi:10.1080/09502380601162548

Maldonado-Torres, N. (2016). *Outline of ten theses on coloniality and decoloniality*. Fondation Frantz Fanon. Retrieved from http://frantzfanonfoundation-fondationfrantzfanon.com/article2360.html

Masten, A. S. (2015). Pathways to integrated resilience science. *Psychological Inquiry, 26*, 187–196. doi:10.1080/1047840X.2015.1012041

Moraga C., & Anzaldua, G. (1983). *This bridge called my back: Writings by radical women of color*. New York, NY: Kitchen Table/Women of Color Press.

Palestinian Central Bureau of Statistics. (2016). *Palestinians at the end of 2016*. Retrieved from: http://www.pcbs.gov.ps/post.aspx?lang=en&ItemID=1823

Pappe, I. (2006). *The ethnic cleansing of Palestine*. Oxford, UK: Oneworld.

Quijano, A. (2000). Coloniality of power, Eurocentrism, and Latin America. *International Sociology, 15*(2), 215–232. doi:10.1177/0268580900015002005

Said, E. (1993). *Culture and imperialism*. New York, NY: Vintage Books.

Salamanca, O. J., Qato, M., Rabie, K., & Samour, S. (2012). Past is present: Settler colonialism in Palestine. *Settler Colonial Studies, 2*(1), 1–8. doi:10.1080/2201473X.2012.10648823

Shahin, M. (2005). *Palestine: A guide*. Northampton, MA: Interlink.

Shalhoub-Kevorkian, N. (2009). *Militarization and violence against women in conflict zones in the Middle East: A Palestinian case-study*. New York, NY: Cambridge University Press.

Smith, L. T. (2012). *Decolonizing methodologies: Research and indigenous peoples* (2nd ed). London, UK: Zed Books.

Tuck, E., & McKenzie, M. (2015). *Place in research: Theory, methodology, and methods*. New York, NY: Routledge.

Ungar, M. (2018). Systemic resilience: Principles and processes for a science of change in contexts of adversity. *Ecology and Society, 23*(4), 34. doi:10.5751/ES-10385-230434.

United Nations. (2009). *Human rights in Palestine and other occupied Arab territories: Report of the United Nations fact-finding mission on the Gaza conflict* (A/HRC/12/48). Retrieved from http://www2.ohchr.org/english/bodies/hrcouncil/docs/12session/A-HRC-12-48.pdf

Westley, F. R., Tjornbo, O., Schultz, L., Olsson, P., Folke, C., Crona, B., & Bodin, Ö. (2013). A theory of transformative agency in linked social-ecological systems. *Ecology and Society, 18*(3), 27. doi:10.5751/ES-05072-180327

Whyte, K. (2018). Settler colonialism, ecology, and environmental injustice. *Environment and Society, 9*(1), 125–144. doi:10.3167/ares.2018.090109

Wolfe, P. (2006). Settler colonialism and the elimination of the native. *Journal of Genocide Research, 8*(4), 387–409. doi:10.1080/14623520601056240

Wynter, S., & McKittrick, K. (2015). Unparalleled catastrophe for our species? Or, to give humanness a different future: Conversations. In K. McKittrick (Ed.), *Sylvia Wynter: On being human as praxis* (pp. 9–89). Durham, NC: Duke University Press.

30
The Economics of Multisystemic Resilience

Gabriella Conti and Tatiana Paredes

Introduction

Children are exposed to a variety of adverse events from an early age. Most of these adversities can be traced back to poverty (understood as the lack of material resources or of other inputs in the production of child development), although in other cases they are due to human- or nature-made shocks of various kinds (Almond & Currie, 2011; Almond, Currie, & Duque, 2018; Cunha & Heckman, 2007). While eradicating poverty remains a primary policy target, one efficient way this can be achieved is by equipping children with the tools to cope with—and eventually overcome—adversity by promoting their development in a holistic manner. Preventive or remediation interventions in the early years of life, which promote children's cognitive, socioemotional, and health development, can help build resilience in children. In economics, the more recent theory of human capital formation suggests that there are certain critical or sensitive periods when the investments made to promote children's development are more productive. This means that once the opportunity to remedy the adverse effects of initial disadvantage is lost, it becomes harder to help children catch up (Heckman & Mosso, 2014).

At an aggregate level, education is a widely used tool to create competitive and resilient nations. A resilient society is one made up of individuals who, despite having disadvantaged origins, reach education and income levels that are similar to those of their more affluent peers. Such upward mobility translates into low levels of socioeconomic inequality. One efficient way to achieve this is through effective interventions that promote human capital accumulation beginning at an early age. Macroeconomic models envision this process of human capital accumulation—with a goal being to raise people's productivity over time—as a continuous knowledge exchange between members of different systems (Doepke & Tertilt, 2016).

At the microlevel, the more recent applied literature reports on studies of whether subsequent investments can help children overcome the negative effects of shocks. This literature is in its infancy, the main reason being the stringent requirements for study design. As pointed out by Almond and Mazumder (2013), it is difficult to find overlapping episodes of early life trauma and an orthogonal natural experiment that assign investments in children in a quasi-random fashion (among those exposed and not exposed to the trauma) to counteract the impact of early adversity.

On the other hand, there has been important progress in the field of macroeconomics and social mobility where family decisions and government interventions designed to boost child resilience have become central to growth theory, with more recent studies emphasizing the importance of human capital accumulation. This field is very promising since it allows us to analyze the multisystemic, economy-wide effects of interventions.

In this chapter, we review the existing evidence in support of multisystemic resilience and child development in the field of economics, from both a micro- and a macroeconomic perspective. To do this, we first review the theory of human capital development and the large body of empirical literature about prevention or remediation interventions in childhood. We then summarize the recent empirical microlevel evidence that tests whether subsequent investments can help offset the effects of early-life shocks. Next, we examine the most recent literature that incorporates endogenous human capital investments into complex macroeconomic models to understand how investment decisions in human capital at the family level affect aggregate welfare via multisystemic effects.

The remainder of this chapter is structured into the following sections: an introduction to the theory of human capital development; a review of the evidence on the long-lasting effects of early life shocks and on some key interventions, with a presentation of the more recent evidence that tests whether subsequent investments can help offset the effects of early-life shocks; a presentation of a case study of multisystemic resilience; a discussion of a macroeconomic approach to multisystemic resilience; and the conclusion.

The Theory of Human Capital Development

Human capital can be defined as the set of knowledge, skills, personality, and other endowments, including health, that constitute the assets an individual possesses to generate economic value. Human capital is now considered as multidimensional, and its different components interact with each other in ways that are just starting to be elucidated. For example, it might be possible to compensate for certain deficiencies in cognitive skills with better performance in noncognitive skills, such as motivation and persistence. Although genetics plays a role in the transmission of human capital, one of the central principles of this field of study is that abilities are not only inherited, they can also be acquired. The traditional nature–nurture distinction has been overcome, and it is now recognized that genes and environments interact in complex ways in producing human capital (Heckman & Mosso, 2014). In addition, the role that parents play is an active area of investigation. Parents can offset (or reinforce) differences in human capital among their offspring by investing more in the worse (or better) endowed ones (Almond & Mazumder, 2013).

It is useful at this point to present a simple model of investment in human capital from an economics point of view, following on the simple model by Attanasio (2015). Parents in household i choose how much to spend on their own consumption and on investment in their children's human capital. Their choice is subject to two constraints: a budget constraint, which says that they can only consume up to how much they earn,[1] and a production function of human capital, which specifies the way that various inputs are converted into output. Let us define $H_{i,t}$ as the human capital of a child of age t being raised in household i and think of it as a multidimensional vector that includes different dimensions, such as cognition (c), socioemotional skills (s) and health (h). The production function of human capital $H_{i,t+1}$ is assumed to depend on the initial level of human capital $H_{i,t}$, on background variables $Z_{i,t}$ (either fixed or time varying, representing characteristics of caregivers such as mother m, father f, and other r), on investments in human capital $X_{i,t}$ (including material M like toys and time T), and on a vector of random shocks $e_{i,t}^H$. The latter can also be interpreted as reflecting inputs in the production function that are not directly observed or considered by the researcher.

The production function in a general form can then be expressed as

$$H_{i,t+1} = g_t(H_{i,t}, X_{i,t}, Z_{i,t}, e_{i,t}^H) \tag{1}$$

The variables $H_{i,t}, X_{i,t}, Z_{i,t}$ and $e_{i,t}^H$ can be multidimensional:

$$H_{i,t} = \{\theta_{i,t}^c, \theta_{i,t}^s, \theta_{i,t}^h\}$$

$$Z_{i,t} = \{\theta_{i,t}^m, \theta_{i,t}^f, \theta_{i,t}^r\}$$

$$X_{i,t} = \{\theta_{i,t}^M, \theta_{i,t}^T\}$$

As previously mentioned, parents make choices to maximize their utility subject to two constraints:

$$\max_{\{C_{i,t}, X_{i,t}\}} U(C_{i,t}, H_{i,t+1}) \tag{2}$$

$$subject\ to: C_{i,t} + P_t^x X_{i,t} = Y_{i,t}$$

$$and\ H_{i,t+1} = g_t(H_{i,t}, X_{i,t}, Z_{i,t}, e_{i,t}^H)$$

Where $C_{i,t}$ is consumption, P_t^x is the vector of prices of investments $X_{i,t}$ and $Y_{i,t}$ is income. One implication of the previous model is that, since $H_{i,t+1}$ and $H_{i,t}$ are multidimensional vectors that include, for example, cognition, socioemotional skills, and health, the various dimensions of human capital are not only self-reinforcing (an attribute defined as self-productivity: higher stocks of skills in one period create higher stocks of skills in the next period) but also cross-fertilizing (cross-productivity). Additionally, different forms of investments can be more effective at higher or lower levels of human capital at time t to produce human capital at time $t+1$ (dynamic complementarity or substitutability).[2] Different from the traditional model of Becker and Tomes (1979), the more recent model of human capital development, starting with Cunha and Heckman (2007) considers multiple stages of childhood, which also allow for productivities, complementarities and substitutabilities among different inputs to vary over time. Coherent with this model, the recent empirical human capital development literature (for example, Attanasio, 2015; Cunha, Heckman, & Schennach, 2010) has estimated different functional forms of the production function in (1) to measure how substitutable investments are during different periods in producing skills. Intuitively, if the degree of intertemporal substitutability is small, low levels of early investment (X_1) are not easily remediated by later investment (X_2) in producing human capital, so investing in the early years becomes crucial.

Heckman and Mosso (2014) summarize some main findings of the empirical literature. First, only very early interventions (before age three) have been shown to improve IQ in lasting ways; this is consistent with the idea that early childhood is a critical period for cognitive development. Second, programs targeting disadvantaged adolescents are less effective than those targeting children, consistent with the concept of dynamic complementarity. Third, despite being less effective than early childhood interventions, there are some promising adolescent interventions—featuring mentoring and scaffolding—that can help boost resilience among adolescents.

Born to Fail, Nurture to Thrive? Shocks, Interventions, and Resilience

Shocks

A large body of research from numerous disciplines shows the persistence of early-life disadvantage in shaping later life outcomes. Several shocks of different nature have been studied in the economic literature, including income shocks (Baird, Friedman, & Schady, 2011; Bhalotra, 2010), air and water pollution (Chay & Greenstone, 2003; Currie & Neidell, 2005; Greenstone & Hanna, 2014), natural disasters (Cas, Frankenberg, Suriastini, & Thomas, 2014), nutrient scarcity (Almond, Hoynes, & Schanzenbach, 2011), poor sanitation (Watson, 2006), and influenza (Almond, 2006). With some variations, the general finding across these studies is that an early exposure to negative shocks has detrimental effects on a variety of outcomes across the life course, such as educational attainment (Cas et al., 2014; Almond, 2006) and socioeconomic status in adulthood (Almond, 2006), and is linked to higher rates of infant mortality (Baird, Friedman, & Schady, 2011; Bhalotra, 2010; Chay & Greenstone, 2003; Currie & Neidell, 2005; Watson, 2006) and physical disability (Almond, 2006). (For a complete review of the literature that studies the importance of prenatal and early childhood environments on adolescent and adult health and socioeconomic outcomes, the reader is directed to Cunha, Heckman, Lochner, & Masterov, 2006; Almond & Currie 2011; Almond et al., 2018; Conti, Mason, & Poupakis, 2019).

One important finding in this literature is that the negative impacts of early life shocks are often heterogeneous, reflecting differences in child endowments, budget constraints, and production technologies. Part of this heterogeneity is also caused by the parental responses to these shocks, which can exacerbate or mitigate their effects (Almond et al., 2018; Almond & Mazumder, 2013; Attanasio, 2015). In the remainder of this section, we review recent evidence on some of the most successful early childhood interventions meant to prevent or remediate the development gaps that appear very early among underprivileged children (Conti & Heckman, 2014). We then summarize the evidence of studies where researchers have found overlapping episodes of early life trauma and an orthogonal natural experiment meant to remediate its effects.

Policies and Interventions

Promoting the development of disadvantaged children to try to reduce inequalities from an early age and, at the same time, to increase their resilience is a pressing concern for policymakers worldwide. When gaps get perpetuated, disadvantaged children keep falling behind, becoming increasingly more vulnerable to shocks of a different nature.

Cash and in-kind transfers are one way to mitigate the impact of these shocks. Cash transfers are expected to increase both childhood investments (in particular, conditional cash transfers) and household consumption. Many recent papers examine the impact of cash transfers on child and adult outcomes. Aizer, Eli, Ferrie, and Lleras-Muney (2016) evaluated the effect of the U.S. Mother's Pension program and found that children of mothers who were accepted to the program obtained one third more years of schooling and had higher income in adulthood, with the largest effects occurring for the poorest families. Another relevant U.S. program that works like a cash transfer to lower-income working families is the Earned Income Tax Credit. Hoynes, Miller, and Simon (2015) exploited variation in the generosity of the program in the mid-1990s and found that the likelihood of low birth weight decreased among mothers who benefited from the expansion of the program during pregnancy. The possible mechanisms for the changes in infant health include more prenatal care and less negative health behaviors (smoking). Dahl and Lochner (2012) also exploited the expansions of the Earned Income Tax Credit in the late 1980s and 1990s to identify the effects of family income on child achievement and found that increases in family income improve test scores, particularly among children from more disadvantaged backgrounds. Conditional cash transfers, including child-care subsidies and child allowances, have also been found effective at improving child cognitive development (Black, Devereux, Løken, & Salvanes, 2014; Milligan & Stabile, 2011). Lastly, having access to the U.S. Food Stamps program in childhood has been found to reduce the incidence of metabolic syndrome in adulthood and to increase economic self-sufficiency among women (Almond et al., 2011).

Some interventions target primarily health (among the dimensions of child development), for example, health insurance expansions and policies that promote medical care. Bharadwaj, Løken, and Neilson (2013) examined infants in Chile and Norway and used data showing that infants below the 1,500-g threshold cut-off for very low birth weight received more intensive medical services than those just above this threshold. Their data show that more intensive medical care increases adult wages by 2.7% in Chile and by 1.8% in Norway. Most studies of U.S. Medicaid rely on the fact that the expansions of this program were phased in at different rates across states. Cohodes, Grossman, Kleiner, and Lovenheim (2016) found that expanding health insurance coverage for low-income children increases the rate of high school and college completion. Not surprisingly, access to Medicaid is also beneficial to participants' long-term health (Miller & Wherry, 2018).

One widely advocated policy deemed effective at reducing gaps in child development that are evident by the time children start school is quality child care. Some of the strongest evidence comes from the iconic Perry Preschool program in the United States, a randomized trial that targeted 123 disadvantaged, low IQ African American children aged three to four during the 1960s. Heckman, Moon, Pinto, Savelyev, and Yavitz (2010), and Conti, Heckman, and Pinto (2016) showed that the Perry program significantly enhanced adult outcomes, including better education, employment, earnings, health, and lower rates of criminal activity. Importantly, Conti et al. (2016) show that improvements in child development in the early years, rather than later socioeconomic status, are the main drivers of the treatment effects on adult outcomes. A more recent study by Heckman and Karapakula (2019) adds to this evidence by finding significant intergenerational treatment effects on education, employment, and crime, using 50-year follow-up data from the offspring of the original participants.

Another flagship preschool program in the United States is the Abecedarian. Beginning in 1972, the randomized trial included 111 low-income, mostly African American families. Treated children received a year-round, full-time center-based care for five years, starting in the child's first year of life. The program included individualized educational activities that changed as the children grew older and low child–teacher ratios of 3:1 for the youngest children and up to 6:1 for older children. The treatment group also received primary healthcare and provision of nutritious meals. By the time these children were five, their IQ scores were 10 points higher than scores of comparable children who did not participate in the program (Duncan & Magnuson, 2013). Furthermore, those in the treatment group earned significantly higher scores on intellectual and academic measures as young adults (aged 21), attained significantly more years of education, were more likely to attend a four-year college (Campbell, Ramey, Pungello, Sparling, & Miller-Johnson, 2002), and were in significantly better health in their mid-30s (Campbell et al., 2014). Like for the Perry Preschool, Conti et al. (2016) show for the Abecedarian that improvements in child development in the early years, rather than later socioeconomic status, are the main drivers of the treatment effects on adult outcomes.

While it is difficult to replicate at scale, the intensive small-scale interventions such as the Abecedarian and the Perry Preschool, one key policy lesson that can be learned is the importance of quality. The first attempt of a large-scale, although still targeted, program has been Head Start, a public preschool program that began in the United States in 1965 as part of the "War on Poverty." Some early studies estimated the effects of Head Start by comparing program participants to their nonparticipant siblings. Results from this research design showed positive short-term effects on test scores (Currie & Thomas, 1995; Deming, 2009) and long-term effects on educational attainment and earnings (Garces, Thomas, & Currie, 2002). More recent studies use either the randomized evaluation of Head Start (the Head Start Impact Study) or quasi-experimental variation in program assignment to show Head Start had positive impacts on test scores (Kline & Walters, 2016), problem behavior (Carneiro & Ginja, 2014), and health (Carneiro & Ginja, 2014; Ludwig & Miller, 2007).

In addition to center-based childcare programs, home-visiting programs are becoming increasingly popular to reach disadvantaged populations, as they have been shown to have positive impacts on many domains, including education, income, employment, health, and behavior (Almond et al., 2018). One of the programs with the strongest evidence base is the Nurse Family Partnership (NFP), which provides nurse home visits to pregnant mothers in disadvantageous conditions with no previous live births and is now delivered at scale in the United States. In three randomized evaluations in the United States, the NFP has been shown to improve both child and maternal outcomes, with persistent effects up to adulthood (Eckenrode et al., 2010; Olds, 2006). Randomized evaluations of the NFP have been carried out also in England (Robling et al., 2016) and Germany (Sandner, Cornelissen, Jungmann, & Herrmann, 2018; Sierau et al., 2016) where the impacts are somewhat more muted than in the original U.S.-based evaluations, possibly because of the nature of the usual care delivered to the control group.

A recent strand of the literature addresses a key question: How do different interventions interact to promote human development? Rossin-Slater and Wüst (in press) conducted one of the first studies to test whether access to a home-visiting program at birth amplifies or diminishes the positive long-term effects of early childcare in Denmark. The study uses the exogenous timing of each program's rollout in the first years of the millennium and finds statistically significant negative interaction effects between home-visiting and preschool childcare exposure, suggesting that some early childhood interventions might be substitutes and not complements when the outcome of interest is years of schooling.

The evidence reviewed in this section of the chapter shows that early childhood is a critical window of opportunity for prevention and remediation interventions that promote child development and, by extension, foster resilience in contexts of early disadvantage. However, the question of whether it is possible to achieve impacts at scale in a cost-effective manner remains; a related question is whether a targeted or universal approach to scaling up is preferable. On the other hand, some adolescent interventions that seek to foster character skills—such as self-confidence, teamwork, autonomy, and discipline, which are often lacking in disadvantaged youth—have also been shown to achieve positive impacts, although of a smaller magnitude than early interventions (Heckman & Mosso, 2014). In particular, mentoring programs in schools that provide school-aged children and adolescents with information and support have been shown to be particularly effective (Bettinger, Long, Oreopoulos, & Sanbonmatsu, 2012; Cook et al., 2014; Kosse, Deckers, Pinger, Schildberg-Hörisch, & Falk, in press).

Environmental Shocks and Interventions

There are few papers that study whether subsequent investments can help children overcome the effects of a shock. This literature to date has exploited quasi-random exposures of children to shocks and interventions in the early and later stages of their childhood to provide evidence on remediation effects.[3] Adhvaryu, Nyshadham, Molina, and Tamayo (2018) studied whether the conditional cash transfer program Progresa in Mexico mitigated the effects of rainfall shocks on cognitive test scores and years of education, measured at ages 12 to 21. They found that Progresa offsets 60% to 80% of the negative impact of rainfall shocks on child development. On the other hand, Aguilar and Vicarelli (2015) found that children exposed to rainfall shocks during the early stages of life exhibit lower cognitive development, shorter height, smaller weight, and higher anxiety levels at ages two to six, with no mitigation effect by Progresa. It is unclear whether these conflicting results are caused by subtle differences in the approaches taken; it could be the case that one can find positive long-term effects even in cases where the immediate short-term effects appear to be negligible (Almond et al., 2018).

Gunnsteinsson et al. (2019) studied whether a randomized controlled trial of vitamin A supplementation in Bangladesh protected children in the study areas devastated by a tornado in 2005. Exposure to the tornado in utero and during infancy decreased birth size and physical growth, but infants who received vitamin A supplementation, which boosts immune system functioning, were protected from these effects. Triyana and Xia (2018) further exploited exogenous variation in typhoon exposure and the introduction of a disaster relief policy to analyze the effects of early-life shocks on mortality and human capital outcomes in the Philippines. Once implemented, the disaster relief policy mitigated the mortality effect of severe typhoons; however, survivors exhibited lower educational attainment and lower probability of attaining a skilled occupation. This suggests that disaster relief efforts improved the chances of survival among the treated but were not sufficient to alleviate the long-term scarring effects among those who survived. Duque, Rosales-Rueda, and Sánchez (2016) instead analyze the interaction of weather shocks and a conditional cash transfer program in Colombia and show that the timing matters, in the sense that the impacts of the program are larger for earlier rather than later childhood exposures.

A study related to this strand of literature investigates whether birth endowments affect the degree to which individuals are affected during recessions (i.e., whether children with better health at birth are more resilient in times of crises). Bharadwaj, Bietenbeck, Lundborg, and Rooth (2019) study the economic crisis during the early 1990s in Sweden and use a twin-based design to show that early-life health is an important determinant of labor market vulnerability during macroeconomic downturns. Adults who were born with higher birth weight were significantly less likely to face job loss and go on unemployment insurance during a crisis.

An important aspect about this literature that deserves further study is the optimal temporal gap between the shock and the remediation intervention. Furthermore, we still know relatively little about the optimal timing for different interventions to affect different outcomes, considering the various ways in which skills and investments can interact with each other at different stages of development. Some interventions are designed to stimulate the development of a certain type of skill (e.g., only the development of cognitive abilities), and some others have a more comprehensive approach and seek to stimulate the development of multiple skills, including health (preschool and home-visiting programs). The evidence to date seems to suggest that earlier intervention is particularly salient for health and cognition, while noncognitive skills are still malleable during adolescence. However, it is important to keep in mind that even interventions that only attempt to stimulate one type of skill can benefit the development of other skills, given the different cross-productivities embedded in the model in the first section of this paper. In fact, several studies have found evidence of interactions, for example, between cognitive and noncognitive skills (Cunha & Heckman, 2007) and between health and cognition (Attanasio, Meghir, & Nix, 2015). All of the previous highlights the fact that we are only beginning to understand how shocks, skills, and investments interact over the life course and how interventions can help offset the negative effects of shocks by promoting resilience in children.

A Case Study of Multisystemic Resilience

Early childhood interventions have the potential to generate resilience at different levels. A policy that has proven to be effective in promoting resilience at the individual and multisystemic level through its positive impact on the community is Sure Start, a major area-based early-years initiative in England. Sure Start targets children aged zero to five. Its core offer consists of integrated early education and childcare, parental outreach, family and parenting support, child and family health services, and links with Jobcentre Plus (Conti, Mason, & Poupakis, 2019).

Scaled-up interventions like Sure Start could provide benefits through different channels, given the variety of the services offered. Conti et al. (2019) discuss some of the main direct and indirect channels through which the program might improve children's health, cognition, and behavior. First, Sure Start is expected to improve children's overall health status through an increase in health-promoting activities (e.g., because of better information), a greater willingness to use health services (e.g., due to lower stigma or increased perceived benefits), and/or better screening for conditions that might benefit from treatment. There are also a number of indirect channels through which Sure Start could affect children's health. One potentially important channel is parental employment, since Sure Start provides job-search assistance and job-related training to parents. However, the direction of this effect is not clear: a higher family income (resulting from increased employment) could allow parents to increase material investments in their children, but longer working hours might also negatively affect the time parents spend with their children. Another indirect channel through which Sure Start might promote child development is by changing the type and quality of environments that children spend time in. For example, many centers offer access to play and reading materials and so offer more stimulating environments than the ones disadvantaged children have at home. Also, through parenting classes and other forms of support, Sure Start might improve parentings skills and maternal mental health and contribute to reducing child maltreatment.

Conti et al. (2019) have found that greater access to Sure Start in the first five years of life reduces the likelihood of hospitalizations among children aged 5 to 11, with benefits growing with age. While Sure Start had few effects on hospitalizations for respiratory illness, there were big decreases in the rates of hospitalizations for infections at young ages, for injuries at every age considered (particularly fractures), and head injuries at age five, all of which are costly conditions that can cause long-term damage. Importantly, all impacts are concentrated in the poorest areas of England. The observed decline in admissions for injuries give us a hint about the possible mechanisms in place. While the available data do not make it possible to identify the mechanisms, plausible candidates are safer home environments, better parenting practices, and fewer behavioral problems in children.

Sure Start is based on the premise that children and families could be affected by the program directly via services and indirectly via community changes engendered by the program. Melhuish, Belsky, and Barnes (2010) document some improvements in community characteristics after five years of implementation (although they cannot causally link them to the program). For example, in Sure Start areas, the proportion of children under four years in workless households decreased markedly from 45% in 2000–2001 to 40% in 2005–2006. Some aspects of crime and disorder also improved, notably, burglary, school exclusions, and unauthorized school absences. Furthermore, the percentage of children identified with special educational needs or eligible for disability benefits increased, suggesting improved health screening, and there was an improvement in academic achievement among 11-year-olds (Melhuish et al., 2010).

The Macroeconomic Approach to Multisystemic Resilience

Recently, part of the macroeconomic literature has been studying micro-founded models that examine how government policies affect parental investment choices and welfare in a general equilibrium framework, as opposed to more conventional partial equilibrium treatment-effect approaches to policy evaluation. This has allowed researchers to deal with one of the limitations of small-scale empirical studies, which is that they cannot account for several indirect (multisystemic) effects of interventions. General equilibrium models are well suited to studying aggregate effects like the impact of policies on poverty reduction or aggregate welfare, but until recently they generally ignored the role of endogenous early childhood development (Daruich, 2018). A few recent studies have, however, begun to incorporate human capital investments into standard macroeconomic models (Abbott, Gallipoli, Meghir, & Violante, 2018; Daruich, 2018; Lee & Seshadri, 2019; Restuccia & Urrutia, 2004). This approach is very useful for policymakers, considering that it allows them to simulate the effect of large-scale government interventions and to estimate the indirect effects of these policies (including taxation and general equilibrium effects).

The models used in this body of literature rely on two sets of principles. The first builds on the human capital accumulation literature (Cunha et al., 2010; Heckman, 2007) where skills are determined by investments (of money and time) made during the early stages of development. The second set of principles describe a general equilibrium life-cycle framework in which these investments and intergenerational linkages are embedded (Aiyagari, Greenwood, & Seshadri, 2002; Daruich, 2018; Lee & Seshadri, 2019). The definitions and relations depicted in these models highlight the multisystemic nature of the interactions between government, firms, and households and the role that each one plays in shaping economic incentives (i.e., the returns to education) and on aggregate macroeconomic variables. For instance, if instead of being altruistic, parents were to place a higher weight on present consumption relative to the next generation's future consumption, this would dissuade savings, driving up the interest rate and modifying the investment-to-gross domestic product ratio observed in the economy (Aiyagari et al., 2002). Furthermore, general equilibrium forces explain some indirect effects of early childhood interventions, for instance, how taxes to finance additional government expenditures reduce the welfare gains of early childhood education policies by lowering the wage of college graduates and therefore the return on those investments.

This strand of the macroeconomic literature does not address the issue of resilience explicitly, but clearly describes some of the processes by which young adults can compensate for the lack of early parental investments in adulthood. In this regard, Lee and Seshadri (2019) argue, "Young parents with high-ability children are unable to invest enough in their human capital because of life cycle borrowing constraints, but these same children can quickly accumulate human capital as an adult" (p. 889).

A resilient society is made up of individuals who, despite their background, reach similar education and income levels as those of their more affluent counterparts. This translates into low levels of socioeconomic inequality and low persistence of economic status across generations. Structural micro and macro models help explain the process by which investments made in early childhood not only create more resilient children but have redistributive and multiplicative effects that spill over to the next generation (Becker & Tomes, 1979; Goldberger, 1989; Lee & Seshadri, 2019; Restuccia & Urrutia, 2004). When governments invest in early childhood education programs, they solve the problem generated by the lack of a compensation-borrowing mechanism that compensates parents for their investments.

Lee and Seshadri (2019) compare the relative effectiveness of different government interventions on the persistence of economic status across generations. Income persistence declines when both the intergenerational and life-cycle borrowing constraints faced by parents are relaxed. A similar effect is achieved by reducing taxes on parents and by providing education subsidies. This happens because these policies allow parents to invest more in the human capital of children. However, only education subsidies targeted to children aged zero to five years seem to have a sizable impact on reducing income persistence in the long run—a fact that is consistent with complementarity of investments. Consistent with the importance of early investments, Hendren and Sprung-Keyser (2019) conducted a comparative welfare analysis of 133 historical policy changes over the past half-century in the United States and found that direct investments in low-income children's health and education have historically had the highest marginal value of public funds (the ratio of the benefits provided to the recipient over the cost to the government). As they put it, "many such policies have paid for themselves as governments recouped the cost of their initial expenditures through additional taxes collected and reduced transfers" (p. 1).

Conclusion

The concept of resilience in the child development literature focuses on the capacity that individuals (in particular children) have to mitigate the impact of early life shocks. The question of how to protect vulnerable children or whether it is possible to engender resilience to shocks has been addressed by several branches of economics including family economics, the interventions literature, and, more recently, the macroeconomic literature in a general equilibrium framework.

From a theoretical standpoint, there are several advantages to using a micro-founded general equilibrium framework. First, compared to small-scale evaluations, studies that model human capital accumulation in a general equilibrium framework allow us to estimate the indirect effects of policies that promote human capital accumulation and to understand the mechanisms for the intergenerational transmission of skills. Furthermore, these studies can help explain the origins of inequality and inefficiency in parental investments that arise in the presence of incomplete markets where parents face intergenerational and life-cycle borrowing constraints. Understanding these mechanisms is crucial for the design of preventative and remediation interventions that foster child resilience.

From an applied standpoint, the economic literature studying how interventions can foster children's resilience by buffering them from the impacts of shocks is only in its beginnings. Further research is needed, particularly on the nature of shocks, which can be remediated; the most effective interventions at remediating those shocks; and on the optimal temporal gap between shocks and remediation interventions. More generally, there is still much to investigate about the optimal timing for different interventions to affect different outcomes, considering the various ways in which different dimensions of human capital and investments can complement each other at different stages of development. Future micro-oriented studies of multisystemic resilience in this field should explicitly account not only for the direct effects of interventions but also for their indirect effects to give a better idea of the mechanisms behind the observed improvements in resilience at the individual, community, and macrolevels.

Key Messages

1. Resilience in economics is centered around the concept of human capital.
2. Effective early interventions can promote child resilience and help children overcome the impacts of shocks.
3. The study of human capital in a general equilibrium framework allows us to account for several indirect (multisystemic) effects of interventions.

Acknowledgments

We acknowledge funding from the European Research Council (ERC) under the European Union's Horizon 2020 research and innovation program (grant agreement No. 819752—DEVORHBIOSHIP—ERC-2018COG).

Notes

1. No borrowing or saving is allowed in this simple model.
2. Dynamic complementarity arises when the stocks of skills acquired in the past make current investments more productive (Heckman, 2007).
3. While so far we have mostly focused on the literature from developed countries, given the paucity of studies on the interactions of shocks (mostly natural disasters) and interventions, we do not make such distinction in this paragraph.

References

Abbott, B., Gallipoli, G., Meghir, C., & Violante, G. L. (2018). Education policy and intergenerational transfers in equilibrium. Cowles Foundation Discussion Paper No. 1887R2. New Haven, CT: Cowles Foundation for Research in Economics. doi:10.2139/ssrn.3206752

Adhvaryu, A., Nyshadham, A., Molina, T., & Tamayo, J. (2018, July). *Helping children catch up: Early life shocks and the PROGRESA experiment* (Working Paper No. 24848). Cambridge, MA: National Bureau of Economic Research. doi:10.3386/w24848

Aguilar, A., & Vicarelli, M. (2015). *El Niño and Mexican children: Medium-term effects of early-life weather shocks on cognitive and health outcomes* (Working Paper). Retrieved from http://www.aguilaresteva.com/wp-content/uploads/2012/09/2018_07_17_Article.pdf

Aiyagari, S. R., Greenwood, J., & Seshadri, A. (2002). Efficient investment in children. *Journal of Economic Theory*, 102(2), 290–321. doi:10.1006/jeth.2001.2852

Aizer, A., Eli, S., Ferrie, J., & Lleras-Muney, A. (2016). The long-run impact of cash transfers to poor families. *American Economic Review*, 106(4), 935–971. doi:10.1257/aer.20140529

Almond, D. (2006). Is the 1918 Influenza pandemic over? Long-term effects of in utero influenza exposure in the post-1940 U.S. population. *Journal of Political Economy*, 114(4), 672–712. doi:10.1086/507154

Almond, D., & Currie, J. (2011). Human capital development before age five. In O. Ashenfelter & D. Card (Eds.), *Handbook of labor economics* (Vol. 4, Part B, pp. 1315–1486). Amsterdam, The Netherlands: North Holland. doi:10.1016/S0169-7218(11)02413-0

Almond, D., Currie, J., & Duque, V. (2018). Childhood circumstances and adult outcomes: Act II. *Journal of Economic Literature*, 56(4), 1360–1446. doi:10.1257/jel.20171164

Almond, D., Hoynes, H. W., & Schanzenbach, D. W. (2011). Inside the war on poverty: The impact of food stamps on birth outcomes. *The Review of Economics and Statistics*, 93(2), 387–403. doi:10.1162/rest_a_00089

Almond, D., & Mazumder, B. (2013). Fetal origins and parental responses. *Annual Review of Economics*, 5(1), 37–56. doi:10.1146/annurev-economics-082912-110145

Attanasio, O. P. (2015). The determinants of human capital formation during the early years of life: Theory, measurement, and policies. *Journal of the European Economic Association*, 13(6), 949–997. doi:10.1111/jeea.12159

Attanasio, O., Meghir, C., & Nix, E. (2015, March). *Human capital development and parental investment in India* (Working Paper No. 21740). Cambridge, MA: National Bureau of Economic Research. doi:10.3386/w21740

Baird, S., Friedman, J., & Schady, N. (2011). Aggregate income shocks and infant mortality in the developing world. *The Review of Economics and Statistics*, 93(3), 847–856. doi:10.1162/rest_a_00084

Becker, G., & Tomes, N. (1979). An equilibrium theory of the distribution of income and intergenerational mobility. *Journal of Political Economy*, 87(6), 1153–1189.

Bettinger, E. P., Long, B. T., Oreopoulos, P., & Sanbonmatsu, L. (2012). The role of application assistance and information in college decisions: Results from the H&R Block FAFSA experiment. *The Quarterly Journal of Economics*, 127(3), 1205–1242. doi:10.1093/qje/qjs017

Bhalotra, S. (2010). Fatal fluctuations? Cyclicality in infant mortality in India. *Journal of Development Economics*, 93(1), 7–19. doi:10.1016/j.jdeveco.2009.03.006

Bharadwaj, P., Bietenbeck, J., Lundborg, P., & Rooth, D.-O. (2019). Birth weight and vulnerability to a macroeconomic crisis. *Journal of Health Economics*, 66, 136–144. doi:10.1016/j.jhealeco.2019.05.001

Bharadwaj, P., Løken, K. V., & Neilson, C. (2013). Early life health interventions and academic achievement. *American Economic Review*, 103(5), 1862–1891. doi:10.1257/aer.103.5.1862

Black, S. E., Devereux, P. J., Løken, K. V., & Salvanes, K. G. (2014). Care or cash? The effect of child care subsidies on student performance. *The Review of Economics and Statistics*, 96(5), 824–837. doi:10.1162/rest_a_00439

Campbell, F. A., Ramey, C. T., Pungello, E., Sparling, J., & Miller-Johnson, S. (2002). Early childhood education: Young adult outcomes from the abecedarian project. *Applied Developmental Science*, 6(1), 42–57. doi:10.1207/S1532480XADS0601_05

Campbell, F., Conti, G., Heckman, J. J., Moon, S. H., Pinto, R., Pungello, E., & Pan, Y. (2014). Early childhood investments substantially boost adult health. *Science, 343*(6178), 1478–1485. doi:10.1126/science.1248429.

Carneiro, B. P., & Ginja, R. (2014). Long-term impacts of compensatory preschool on health and behavior: Evidence from Head Start. *American Economic Journal: Economic Policy, 6*(4), 135–173. doi:10.1257/pol.6.4.135

Cas, A. G., Frankenberg, E., Suriastini, W., & Thomas, D. (2014). The impact of parental death on child well-being: Evidence from the Indian Ocean tsunami. *Demography, 51*(2), 437–457. doi:10.1007/s13524-014-0279-8.

Chay, K. Y., & Greenstone, M. (2003). The impact of air pollution on infant mortality: Evidence from geographic variation in pollution shocks induced by a recession. *The Quarterly Journal of Economics, 118*(3), 1121–1167. doi:10.1162/00335530360698513

Cohodes, S. R., Grossman, D. S., Kleiner, S. A., & Lovenheim, M. F. (2016). The effect of child health insurance access on schooling: Evidence from public insurance expansions. *Journal of Human Resources, 51*(3), 727–759. doi:10.3368/jhr.51.3.1014-6688r1

Conti, G., & Heckman, J. J. (2014). Economics of child well-being. In A. Ben-Arieh, F. Casas, I. Frønes, & J. E. Korbin (Eds.), *Handbook of child well-being: Theories, methods and policies in global perspective* (pp. 363–401). Dordrecht, The Netherlands: Springer.

Conti, G., Heckman, J. J., & Pinto, R. (2016). The effects of two influential early childhood interventions on health and healthy behaviour. *Economic Journal, 126*(596), F28–F65. doi:10.1111/ecoj.12420

Conti, G., Mason, G., & Poupakis, S. (2019, June). *Developmental origins of health inequality* (Working Paper No. W19/17). London, UK: Institute for Fiscal Studies. doi:10.1920/wp.ifs.2019.1719

Cook, P., Dodge, K., Farkas, G., Fryer, R., Guryan, J., Ludwig, J., . . . Steinberg, L. (2014, January). *The (surprising) efficacy of academic and behavioral intervention with disadvantaged youth: Results from a randomized experiment in Chicago* (Working Paper No. 19862). Cambridge, MA: National Bureau of Economic Research. doi:10.3386/w19862

Cunha, F., & Heckman, J. (2007). The technology of skill formation. *American Economic Review, 97*(2), 31–47.

Cunha, F., Heckman, J. J., & Schennach, S. M. (2010). Estimating the technology of cognitive and noncognitive skill formation. *Econometrica, 78*(3), 883–931. doi:10.3982/ECTA6551

Cunha, F., Heckman, J. J., Lochner, L., & Masterov, D. V. (2006). Interpreting the evidence on life cycle skill formation. In E. A. Hanushek & F. Welch (Eds.), *Handbook of the economics of education* (Vol. 1, pp. 697–812). Amsterdam, The Netherlands: Elsevier.

Currie, B. J., & Thomas, D. (1995). Does Head Start make a difference? *American Economic Review, 85*(3), 341–364.

Currie, J., & Neidell, M. (2005). Air pollution and infant health: What can we learn from California's recent experience? *The Quarterly Journal of Economics, 120*(3), 1003–1030.

Dahl, G. B, & Lochner, L. (2012). The impact of family income on child achievement: Evidence from the earned income tax credit. *American Economic Review, 102*(5), 1927–1956. doi:10.1257/aer.102.5.1927

Daruich, D. (2018, October). *The macroeconomic consequences of early childhood development policies* (Working Paper No. 2018-029B). New York, NY: NYU Department of Economics. doi:10.20955/wp.2018.029

Deming, D. (2009). Early childhood intervention and life-cycle skill development: Evidence from Head Start. *American Economic Journal: Applied Economics, 1*(3), 111–134. doi:10.1257/app.1.3.111

Doepke, M., & Tertilt, M. (2016). Families in macroeconomics. In J. B. Taylor & H. Uhlig (Eds.), *Handbook of macroeconomics* (Vol. 2B, pp. 1789–1891). Amsterdam, The Netherlands: Elsevier. doi:10.1016/bs.hesmac.2016.04.006

Duncan, G. J., & Magnuson, K. (2013). Investing in preschool. *Journal of Economic Perspectives, 27*(2), 109–132. doi:10.1257/jep.27.2.109

Duque, V., Rosales-Rueda, M., & Sánchez, F. (2016, May). *How do early-life shocks interact with subsequent human-capital investments? Evidence from administrative data* (Working Paper). Colombia: CAF. Retrieved from http://conference.iza.org/conference_files/Gender_2019/duque_v27803.pdf

Eckenrode, J., Campa, M., Luckey, D. W., Henderson, C. R., Cole, R., Kitzman, H., . . . Olds, D. (2010). Long-term effects of prenatal and infancy nurse home visitation on the life course of youths: 19-year follow-up of a randomized trial. *Archives of Pediatrics & Adolescent Medicine, 164*(1), 9–16. doi:10.1001/archpediatrics.2009.240

Garces, B. E., Thomas, D., & Currie, J. (2002). Longer-term effects of head start. *American Economic Review, 92*(4), 999–1012.

Goldberger, A. S. (1989). Economic and mechanical models of intergenerational transmission. *American Economic Review, 79*(3), 504–513.

Greenstone, B. M., & Hanna, R. (2014). Environmental regulations, air and water pollution, and infant mortality in India. *American Economic Review, 104*(10), 3038–3072. doi:10.1257/aer.104.10.3038

Gunnsteinsson, S., Adhvaryu, A., Christian, P., Labrique, Sugimoto, J., A., Shamin, A. A., & West, K. P., Jr. (2019, June). *Protecting infants from natural disasters: The case of vitamin A supplementation and a tornado in Bangladesh* (Working Paper No. 25969). Cambridge, MA: National Bureau of Economic Research. doi:10.3386/w25969

Heckman, J. J. (2007). The economics, technology, and neuroscience of human capability formation. *PNAS, 104*(33), 13250–13255. doi:10.1073/pnas.0701362104

Heckman, J. J., & Karapakula, G. (2019, May). *Intergenerational and intragenerational externalities of the Perry preschool project* (Working Paper No. 25889). Cambridge, MA: National Bureau of Economic Research. doi:10.3386/w25889

Heckman, J. J., Moon, S. H., Pinto, R., Savelyev, P. A., & Yavitz, A. (2010). The rate of return to the high/scope Perry preschool program. *Journal of Public Economics, 94*(1–2), 114–128. doi:10.1016/j.jpubeco.2009.11.001

Heckman, J. J., & Mosso, S. (2014). The economics of human development and social mobility. *Annual Review of Economics, 6*, 689–733. doi:10.1146/annurev-economics-080213-040753

Hendren, N., & Sprung-Keyser, B. (2019, August). *A unified welfare analysis of government policies* (Working Paper No. 26144). Cambridge, MA: National Bureau of Economic Research. doi:10.3386/w26144

Hoynes, H., Miller, D., & Simon, D. (2015). Income, the earned income tax credit, and infant health. *American Economic Journal: Economic Policy, 7*(1), 172–211 doi:10.1257/pol.20120179

Kline, P., & Walters, C. R. (2016). Evaluating public programs with close: The case of Head Start. *The Quarterly Journal of Economics, 131*(4), 1795–1848. doi:10.1093/qje/qjw027

Kosse, F., Deckers, T., Pinger, P., Schildberg-Hörisch, H., & Falk, A. (in press). The formation of prosociality: Causal evidence on the role of social environment. *Journal of Political Economy*. doi:10.1086/704386

Lee, S. Y., & Seshadri, A. (2019). On the intergenerational transmission of economic status. *Journal of Political Economy, 127*(2), 855–921. doi:10.1086/700765

Ludwig, J., & Miller, D. L. (2007). Does Head Start improve children's life chances? Evidence from a regression discontinuity design. *The Quarterly Journal of Economics, 122*(1), 159–208. doi:10.1162/qjec.122.1.159

Melhuish, E., Belsky, J., & Barnes, J. (2010). Evaluation and value of Sure Start. *Archives of Disease in Childhood, 95*(3), 159–161. doi:10.1136/adc.2009.161018

Miller, S., & Wherry, L. R. (2018). The long-term effects of early life Medicaid coverage. *Journal of Human Resources, 54*(3), 785–824. doi:10.3368/jhr.54.3.0816.8173r1

Milligan, K., & Stabile, M. (2011). Do child tax benefits affect the well-being of children? Evidence from Canadian child benefit expansions. *American Economic Journal: Economic Policy, 3*(3), 175–205.

Olds, D. L. (2006). The nurse-family partnership: An evidence-based preventive intervention. *Infant Mental Health Journal, 27*(1), 5–25. doi:10.1002/imhj.20077.

Restuccia, D., & Urrutia, C. (2004). Intergenerational persistence of earnings: The role of early and college education. *American Economic Review, 94*(5), 1354–1378.

Robling, M., Bekkers, M.-J., Bell, K., Butler, C. C., Cannings-John, R., Channon, S., . . . Torgerson, D. (2016). Effectiveness of a nurse-led intensive home-visitation programme for first-time teenage mothers (building blocks): A pragmatic randomised controlled trial. *The Lancet, 387*(10014), 146–155. doi:10.1016/S0140-6736(15)00392-X

Rossin-Slater, M., & Wüst, M. (2020). What Is the Added Value of Preschool for Poor Children? Long-Term and Intergenerational Impacts and Interactions with an Infant Health Intervention. *American Economic Journal: Applied Economics, 12*(3), 255–286. doi:10.1257/app.20180698

Sandner, M., Cornelissen, T., Jungmann, T., & Herrmann, P. (2018). Evaluating the effects of a targeted home visiting program on maternal and child health outcomes. *Journal of Health Economics, 58*, 269–283. doi:10.1016/j.jhealeco.2018.02.008

Sierau, S., Dähne, V., Brand, T., Kurtz, V., von Klitzing, K., & Jungmann, T. (2016). Effects of home visitation on maternal competencies, family environment, and child development: A randomized controlled trial. *Prevention Science, 17*(1), 40–51. doi:10.1007/s11121-015-0573-8

Triyana, M., & Xia, X. (2018, July). *Selective mortality and the long-term effects of early-life exposure to natural disasters* (Working Paper No. 50). Stanford, CA: Stanford Asia Health Policy Program. doi:10.2139/ssrn.3166382

Watson, T. (2006). Public health investments and the infant mortality gap: Evidence from federal sanitation interventions on U.S. Indian reservations. *Journal of Public Economics, 90*(8–9), 1537–1560. doi:10.1016/j.jpubeco.2005.10.002

SECTION 9

Architecture and Urban Design

The Embodied Multisystemic Resilience of Architecture and Built Form

Brian McGrath and Dongxue Lei

Introduction

In Italian neorealist cinema, filmed within the ruins of European cities destroyed by World War II, characters are depicted inhabiting a world in which they do not know how to perceive, feel, act, reflect, or relate that which surrounds them. In scenes of returning to daily life in the aftermath of such destruction, the actors express, what French philosopher Gilles Deleuze refers to as "sensorimotor breakdowns." Deleuze utilized an "operative" history of cinema to develop philosophical insight into contemporary life. In other words, cinema is used to explain concepts of being and time developed over the 20th century, especially in relation to the European trauma of two world wars. Deleuze's use of cinema to describe the human sensorimotor system integrates the cognitive theories of Henri Bergson with C. S. Peirce's logical and pragmatic systemic classification of human habitual reasoning (Bergson, 1907/1983, 1896/1991; Deleuze, 1986, 1989; Pierce, 1998). In *Creative Evolution*, Bergson (1907/1983) states that the sensorimotor system consists of "the cerebro-spinal nervous system together with the sensorial apparatus in which it is prolonged and the locomotor muscles it controls" (p. 124).

Environmental historian and activist Jean Gardner brought the concept of embodying resilience to architectural education as an experiential teaching module that begins with the remarkable agility of the human sensorimotor system to adapt to an often uncertain world that passes by and surrounds us (Gardner, 2019). This sensorimotor system is schematized by Deleuze into cycles of perception, affection, impulse, action, reflection, and relation images. The cyclical dynamics of these images, occurring rapidly in succession, form the patterns of our habits. However, we all are familiar with sensorimotor breakdowns when experiences are new and we do not know how to act. What is of interest are historical conceptualization of the human body/organisms as an information feedback system and a way of embodying multisystemic resilience in architecture and built form (McGrath & Gardner, 2007).

Italian architect Saverio Muratori (1960; Muratori, Bollati, Bollati, & Marinucci, 1963, 1967, 1973) provides an operative history of the built environment and, like Deleuze with cinema, identifies a cognitive breakdown in postwar Europe as a crisis that interrupted the organic continuity of city building traditions and consequently social-natural relations. In three research projects, he developed what he called "studies on an operative urban history" of architecture from the scale of individual buildings and rooms to regional and continental territories shaped by civilization. His notion of an operative history is embodied in the innumerable acts of world making in city building itself, rather than contemplative and distant theorization of historical time. Muratori metaphorically conceives of the city, its neighborhoods, and its architecture, as organisms, in the sense that they are bodies with "tissues" that adapt and change over time in response to crisis and disturbance (see Figure 31.1).

Muratori's death in 1973 coincided with the landmark publication of "Resilience and Stability of Ecological Systems" by C. S. Holling, and an intellectual baton based on notions of crisis, instability, adaption, and change can be retroactively seen as traveling between the two scholars. More recently, Lance H. Gunderson teamed with Holling (2002) to coin the term *panarchy* to describe transformations in human and natural systems and to measure resilience

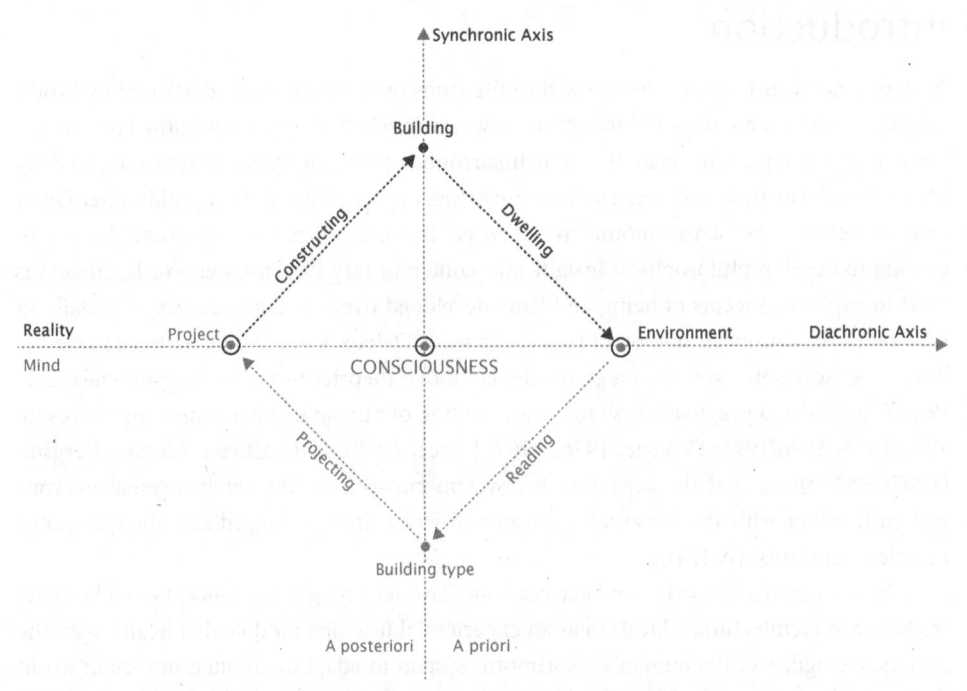

FIGURE 31.1 Muratori's building cycle. In his operative historical studies, Muratori identifies a cycle of the mental reading of the environment preceding a projection of future building, followed by the real construction of buildings and dwelling in settlements, which are, in turn, read and adapted. Adapted from Cataldi (2018).

as a dimension within nested adaptive space and time cycles. These nested scales reflect the systemic approach of Muratori's operative urban histories of neighborhoods, cities, and territories across the millennia. Panarchy establishes an important framework of multiscalar adaptive cycles consisting of phases of exploitation, conservation, release, and reorganization at different scales in space and time. Resilience is described as a "third dimension" through which to measure the expansion and contraction of adaptive cycles. Embodying resilience can be conceived as positioning the human sensorimotor system within operative histories of architecture and built form as a microcosm within the nested scales of panarchy's adaptive cycles in three physical dimensions (see Figure 31.2).

An operative panarchy integrates this continuity of thought between the disciplines of architecture and ecology to develop practices for embodying resilient processes across systems at different nested spatial and temporal scales. In ecology, these scales are described as ranging from the pine needle, to the tree crown, forest patch, and stand to the entire forest biome and regional landscape. These scales represent temporal as well as spatial disturbances from wind and thunderstorms, to fire and infestation, up to climatic forces such as el niño and global climate change itself. The built environment, likewise, is a nested system that ranges from the sensorimotor system of brief and small scales of daily encounters with objects and furniture, to generational change within rooms and buildings, neighborhoods and cities, to civilization upheavals encompassing territorial regions. In this era of the Anthropocene, the entire planet is seen as a human constructed environment confronting a new geological age.

The vast archive of resilience embodied in architecture and built form is supplemented by the innumerable cultural points of view present in the polyglot descriptions of buildings

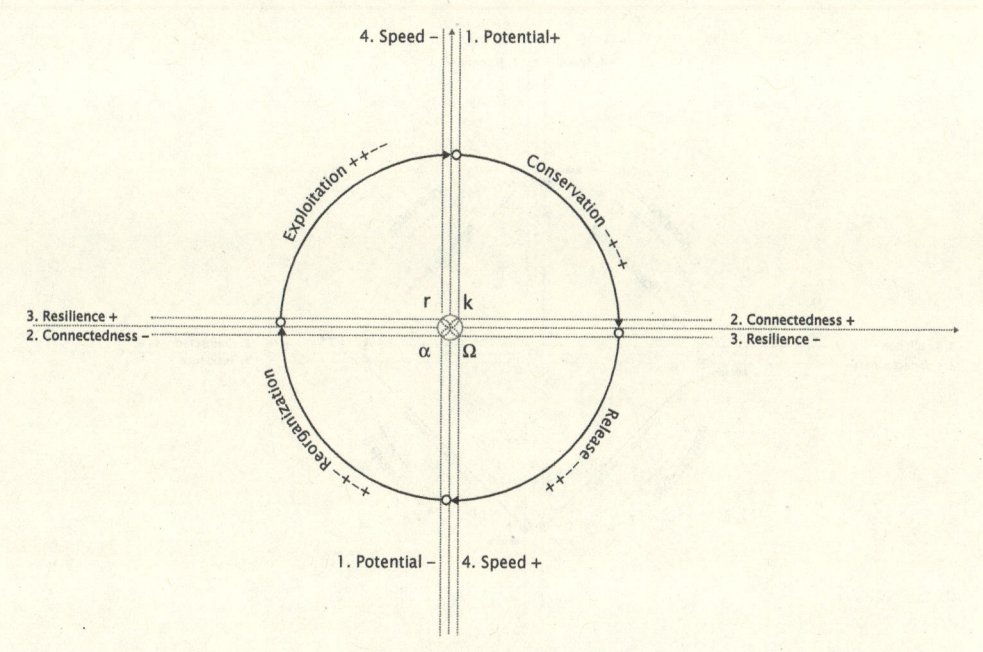

FIGURE 31.2 Adaptive cycle. The adaptive cycle with four variables: potential, connection, resilience. and speed. Adapted from Gunderson and Holling (2002).

and cities in art, literature, and film over time and around the world. Even more potential information is embedded in the living archaeological strata of buildings, cities and rural landscapes as the embodiment of world making, memory, and learning themselves. In the rush to develop contemporary practices that adopt scientific concepts such as resilience, the vast archive of historical evidence for understanding resilience from cultural vantage points is often neglected. As embodied knowledge, architecture and built form provide shared experiences, contexts, forums, and action models situating new pathways for a more inclusive debate concerned with how we collectively inhabit this planet.

Deleuze and Muratori developed their operative histories of cinema and the city in the aftermath of World War II. Likewise, the turn of the 21st century has been marked by critical breakdowns in sensorimotor, social, and ecological systems. Historically, as civilizations grew into territorial empires, vast social organizations developed intricate water, road, and food supply infrastructures along with armies to protect and spiritual beliefs to guide. Contemporary interest in the collapse of these civilizations is further fodder for considering multisystemic resilience given our present predicaments of social inequity and climate change. Embodying resilience through an operative panarchy of architecture and built form recognizes that urbanization is global in scale and climate change often seems distant in time, but that our individual and collective extended sensorimotor systems allows for ethical values and actions to achieve a just transition from an extractive to a regenerative economy here and now. We can look at the growth, shrinkage, and collapse of cities both as part of natural evolution of human learning and adaptation historically and via actions of resiliency in the present moment (see Figure 31.3).

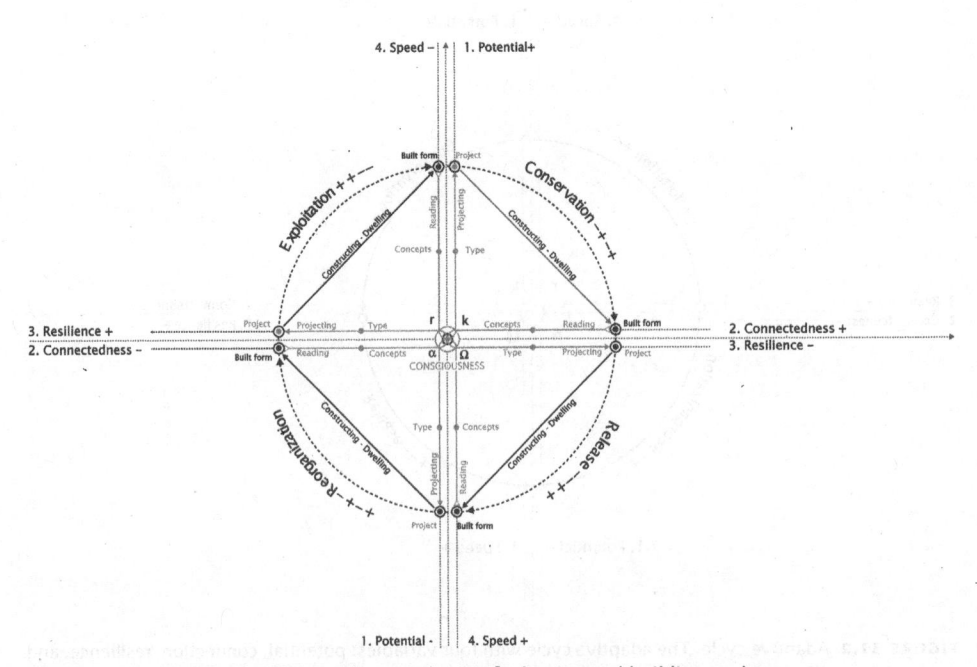

FIGURE 31.3 Adaptive building cycles: synthesis of adaptive and building cycles.

An operative panarchy considers emerging forms of multidisciplinary practices that can consider buildings, neighborhoods and cities as complex adaptive systems, which go through spatially and temporally distributed cycles of growth, crisis, reorganization, and sometimes collapse. In this chapter various scales of multisystemic resilient thinking are presented to develop a working model for analyzing architecture and built form at the intersection of historical and ecosystem studies. An operational panarchy is presented as a process of understanding various nested time and spatial scales from individual bodies structured by daily life worlds within vast regional and global networks of infrastructures of trade and migration over long time frames. Following a literature review of resilience in the built environment, this new hybrid method will be presented by integrating the operational historical method of Muratori and the model of panarchy developed by Gunderson and Holling. Finally, China will be presented as a case study situating and embodying multisystemic resilience within these nested temporal and spatial scales as it incorporates both an operational history of an ancient civilization in relation to the largest and most rapid urban development in the history of the world.

Resilience in the Built Environment

In the following examples, the literature of resilience in the built environment can be understood within three primary paradigms: first, bringing the science of resilience *to* the disciplines of architecture, urban design, and planning; second, integrating ecosystem science *with* architecture and urban design; and third, developing a way to understand the embodied resilience *of* architecture and built form. The first paradigm approaches resilience as a model constructed by scientists and engineers and applied technologically in architecture, urban design, and planning practice. The second paradigm employs resilience as a metaphor that can be shared between the disciplines of architecture and ecology. The third suggests resilience is general knowledge accumulated individually and collectively through trial and error, learning, and memory. As an example of the first paradigm, contemporary practices in the built environment, especially in high seismic or storm risk areas, incorporate resilience thinking from scientific approaches such as the physics of material and engineering resilience (Walker, Salt, & Reid, 2006). The work of the Baltimore Ecosystem Study is presented in the second example, and finally an example of "urban panarchy" from Argentina is presented to introduce the third example.

The first publication of relevance to understanding resilience and architecture is Hassler and Kohler's (2014) edited issue of the journal *Building Research & Information* titled "Resilience in the Built Environment," which focused on the connotative problems with the adoption of the term *resilience* in ecological, psychological, social, social-technical, organizational, and social-ecological systems over the last four decades. The volume is framed by a discussion of the obstacles or constraints for the application of the different meanings of resilience in the planning, design, and operation of the built environment. The editors offer a communication model from ecology that structures multidisciplinary discussions within a discursive framework around common metaphors, such as resilience, versus core definitions based on disciplinary meaning to create working models to operationalize resilience

(Pickett, McGrath, Cadenasso, & Felson, 2014). Hassler and Kohler's introduction argued that resilience-based principles can be applied to the design and long-term management of the built environment in specific areas such as disaster risk management (Bosher, 2014), resilience engineering (Hollnagel, 2014), the institutional management of building stocks, and housing quality (Nicol & Knoepfel, 2014; Pearson, Barnard, Pearce, Kingham, & Howden-Chapman, 2014). Broader themes include a discussion of resilience and cultural notions of time and politics (Moffatt, 2014; Vale, 2014). Moffatt (2014), for example, reflects on how a society thinks about time itself and how the built environment provides continuity for everyday activities and rituals from the past to the future. Vale (2014) articulated the political questions of resilience "To and of what?" and "For whom?" a notion further elaborated by Meerow and Newell (2016) in a subsequent publication.

In sum, Hassler and Kohler (2014) presented multiple physical scales and time horizons of the built environment and explored how the interaction of those different scales creates, maintains, or destroys resilience. Most of the contributions in this special journal issue were more detailed in the description of a specialist understanding of resilience than in the evidence of the built environment itself. Differently scaled urban elements are described as nested systems, mosaics, patches, or assemblages linked by multiple forms of feedback. The soft infrastructure of actors, communities, institutions, rules, governance, and values relate to what the editors refer to as "action arenas." For them, resilience in architecture, urban design, and planning practice has been generally treated as applied technology in relation to natural disasters and climate change, but there is a larger cultural role and meaning revealed in the study of the resilience of buildings and cities as comprising the change and growth to multiple systems under conditions of significant exposure to stress or adversity. The editors find a common shift among the authors in their focus on system breakdown and disorder to recovery, adaptation, or systemwide transformation after exposure to a crisis and the link between the resilience of one system and the resilience of mutually dependent co-occurring systems.

Their introduction briefly acknowledges the resilience *of* architecture and built form as traditional forms of tacit construction knowledge, such as oversizing building components and spaces, redundancy, and reparability. Hassler and Kohler (2014) stated that the urban fabric is a complex sociotechnical system encompassing different scales—building stocks, neighborhoods, cities, and regions—each with different time constants, actors and institutional regimes. They also used the term *built environment* to address the relation between the built and the unbuilt part of the environment, an artifact in an overlapping zone between culture and nature, with causation occurring in both directions. None of the essays in their edited volume, however, addressed embodied forms of resilience that come from understanding the human sensorimotor system in relation to the built environment itself in the face of both social crises and environmental breakdowns (the current volume of papers attempts to address gaps in knowledge such as this; see for example the Chapters 32 and 33).

The second publication of relevance to understanding resilience and built environments is *Resilience in Ecology and Urban Design: Linking Theory and Practice for Sustainable Cities* (Pickett, Cadenasso, & McGrath, 2013), a book that emerged from the 2007 Cary Conference titled "Urban Ecological Heterogeneity and Its Application to Resilient Urban Design." The publication intersperses chapters from scientists and designers around shared conceptual understandings of the multiple dimensions of resilience: the spatial heterogeneity of cities; the flux of organisms, water, materials, and information in the urban realm; adaptation and change in urban systems; and social actors and agents of urban change. Multiple case studies are presented, and the editors introduce the novel concept of the "metacity" as a way to locate resilience at the intersection of ecology and urban design. In the volume, resilience is defined as a foundation for both urban design and sustainability (Wu & Wu, 2013), but it is described as a dynamic and often unstable one. Key concepts of resilience in ecology that are related to urban design include multiple stable states, thresholds and regime shifts, specified and general resilience, complex adaptive systems, and panarchy. Cities are presented as nested adaptive cycles at characteristic scales in space and time. Examples of crisis in adaptive cycles include protest or revolt, urban development and its myriad of processes and institutions and levels, economic recessions, and climate change. Cross-scale dynamics of urban systems can induce phenomena that are difficult to predict, but that can be prepared for. Capacities for urban transformation, such as the capacity to overcome the obstacles of an undesirable regime to create a fundamentally new system, include connectedness, modularity, and tight feedback loops.

Concurrent with the Cary Conference, Pickett, Cadenasso, and Grove (2003) presented "resilient cities" as a metaphor for integrating ecological, socioeconomic, and planning realms. For science, metaphors are slippery figures of speech that yet have explanatory power for interdisciplinary discussion and can spur creativity around common conceptions and visions. The authors argue, however, that metaphors must be followed with the realization that terms will have different meanings across disciplines and descriptive models must be employed to make metaphors operative in real situations. Resilience is proposed as an integrative metaphor to establish links between the new nonequilibrium paradigm of ecosystem science with the dynamics of the architecture, design, and planning of cities. They argued that this new paradigm is more inclusive and open and acknowledges that ecosystems may be externally regulated; may have multiple, or no, stable state(s); and have probabilistic dynamics and disturbance. Their essay concludes with a formulation of tactics to promote resilience in the nonequilibrium sense in ecology, planning, and design: spatial heterogeneity, linked concern of structure, function or process, and temporal changes that can be exploited through watershed, patch dynamics, and human ecosystem frameworks. Human perception, actions, reflection, and learning are a part of the human ecosystem "learning loop" where dialogue and co-production of research and design choices can have ecological consequences that can be measured and communicated.

Pickett, Cadenasso, and Grove's (2003) essay grew out of a National Science Foundation program that began funding long-term ecological research in two urban areas in the United States beginning in 1997—Central Arizona–Phoenix (CAP) and the Baltimore Ecosystem Study (BES). This new approach redirected the science of urban ecology away from focusing on green spaces *in* the city to establish an ecology *of* the city as a whole (McGrath, 2018; Pickett et al., 2013). From 2002 to 2005, architecture and urban design faculty and students worked in collaboration with the BES through academic project-based design research, in essence, operationalizing patch dynamics (Cadenasso, 2013; Cadenasso, Pickett, McGrath,

& Marshall, 2013; McGrath et al., 2007; Pickett & Cadenasso, 2007). Student design projects were evaluated within the discursive traditions and research culture of ecology as the scientific study of the distribution of organisms in space, their relation to environment, and the flows and feedbacks between organisms and their environment.

The designers working with BES developed a notion of resilient practices and interconnected social-natural relations (Marshall, McGrath, & Towers, 2007). Diagrams were important design tools for translating scientific concepts, such as the dynamics between environmental and cognitive factors (Van der Leeuw & Aschan-Leygonie, 2005). Designs were seen as a way to improve resilience by providing cognitive experiences in the built environment that allowed for social dynamics to adapt to the speed and frequency of environmental change. The authors describe this as a socially adaptive transformation of design practice itself. The concluding chapter in the book "Designing Patch Dynamics" (McGrath et al., 2007) discusses positioning urban designs around community-based models of patch dynamics, not in just the scientific sense as a description of a system's structure and function but in an inclusive design sense as speculative idea or mental image of an object or form, which can be collectively initiated (McGrath, 2007). The essay correlates Paul Krugman's self-organization of the economy in space (1996) with Simon Leven's (1999) description of complex adaptive system and building resilience through the reduction of uncertainty by monitoring, spreading risks and forming groups, the expectation of surprise by adaptively managing, by building flexible response systems, maintaining heterogeneity, sustaining modularity, preserving redundancy, and tightening feedback loops, all qualities that are evident in the history of architecture and built form.

The third publication of significance to this discussion of resilience in the built environment is by Garcia and Vale (2017) who provide more direct evidence of the role architecture and the built form play in sustaining resilience in their book *Unraveling Sustainability and Resilience in the Built Environment*. Their description of resilience not only follows a familiar trajectory from early definitions in engineering related to mechanics of materials and elasticity (19th century) to Holling's (1973) description of resilience in ecology but also touches on resilience in behavioral science and environmental psychology. However, it is the authors' embrace of what they refer to as "building an urban panarchy" around adaptive cycles where "the built environment as a house sits in a neighborhood, which sits in the city, which sits in a landscape, which sits in a hydrological cycle, and so on" (Garcia & Vale, 2017, p. 52), which is, potentially, the most influential part of their argument.

Garcia and Vale (2017) provide the case study of San Miguel de Tuduman in Argentina to support their notion of urban panarchy because of its transformation from a colonial, liberal metropolis to a contemporary "borderless" city. For them, urban heritage is not conservation through old buildings but instead the continuous spatial pattern of streets, blocks, and plots and the evolution and emergence of new building types within the persistence of the urban identity. San Miguel de Tuduman's extended colonial grid remained the same through the modern development of the city center with the connection of the railway and plot subdivisions and building footprints - "sausage" types of housing within the long and thin blocks. In a context like this, change happens in long and short durations, and at big and small scales. Because of rules governing change, which allowed blocks and plots in the city center to be maintained beyond more than one cycle, the case of San Miguel de Tuduman is an example of how the resilience *of* the built environment can be measured over time. Building an urban panarchy, for the authors, involved the generation of timelines of major events and perturbances within urban histories.

Ecological resilience offers Garcia and Vale (2017) a comprehensive, systemic and methodological way of linking key concepts that are familiar to architects: complex systems, scales, diversity, connectivity, redundancy. "The idea of understanding the urban landscape of cities as an urban panarchy could be promising for both managers and designers. The adaptive cycle, panarchy and the idea of multiple stability states are all theoretical instruments with which to assess the quality and quantity of change of a system" (p. 53). They suggest that urban databases can be combined with the question of where you are in the cycle. The authors recognize that the integration and visualization of the behavior and performance of a system at multiple scales at the same time leads to a big change in urban analysis as both bottom–up and top–down forces are acknowledged. Urban panarchies introduce nonlinear dynamics into urban thinking and provide a rich context for novelty and creativity for designers and citizens alike. Their urban panarchy provides a way to look at crisis or collapse as an opportunity. The next section explores this topic in greater depth by introducing a multisystemic understanding of built form through Saverio Muratori and his notions of civic consciousness understood through operative history.

The Resilience of Architecture and Built Form

In the context of the European crisis following the destruction caused by World War II, Italian architect Saverio Muratori conducted a series of studies at successively larger scales for an "operative history" of buildings, neighborhoods, cities, and their surrounding territory (1960; Muratori, Bollati, Bollati, & Marinucci, 1963, 1967, 1973). The crisis, for Muratori, was not only the devastation from the war, but the sensorimotor disruption of modernity, which interrupted the continuous spontaneous tradition of city building that prevailed from antiquity to the enlightenment. As mentioned in the opening reference to neorealist cinema, centuries-old bodily habits, social behaviors, and individual thoughts no longer made sense. For Muratori, building is not just the assembly of inert construction materials, but a living act embodying human memory, values, and actions relating to a common, universal experience and understanding of nature as the basis for life (Tagliazucchi, 2014, 2015). In the moment of crisis in the postwar city, Muratori recognized what he referred to as a loss in an organic spontaneous civic consciousness. Civic consciouness can be maintained between historic phases of crises, where city dwellers/builders construct and adapt the cities they inherit over time without needing or requiring mediation or choice (Caniggia & Maffei, 2001). Muratori's history is an activation of a collective body of hereditary knowledge to uncover and remember a lost civic consciousness and to make it operative in the face of contemporary challenges. Urban form, structure, and function are organic aggregations of the learning, memory, decision-making, and actions that produce buildings and open spaces within nested scales of what is referred to as urban tissue or fabric, "special organisms" within the city, the city metaphorically as an organism itself, and regional territory as the human imprint on nature.

The hybrid concept of an operative panarchy links Muratori's concept of a working, activated history of civic consciousness in architecture and built form with Gunderson and Holling's nested panarchy framework for resilience. An operative panarchy comprises a multisystemic understanding of human resilience in the face of crises within cycles of historic and ecosystem transformation in the built environment. The term *panarchy* was adopted during the multidisciplinary meetings of the Resilience Alliance, which were seeking a cross-scale, interdisciplinary, and dynamic theory of adaptive change (Gunderson & Holling, 2002). The concept was developed as an integrative theory to help in the understanding of interrelated economic, ecological, social, and evolutionary changes occurring globally. Based on Holling's description of resilience and instability in ecological systems, members of the Alliance used the name of the unpredictable Greek god Pan to capture the interplay between change and persistence and between the predictable and unpredictable. Previously, Belgian journalist Paul-Emile de Puydt (1860) coined the term *panarchy* to describe a political utopia where individuals could freely choose from alternative forms of government without physically moving. De Puydt imagined a shifting mosaic of political allegiances not aligned to the geography of a nation state. An operative panarchy here specifically refers not only to the nested spatial and temporal scales of adaptive ecosystem cycles, but also conjures the radically decentered political system proposed by de Puydt (1860) (see Figure 31.4).

Like Muratori before them, Gunderson and Holling were interested in the interactions between people and nature as examples of social and environmental responsiveness and learning. In addition to examining the patterns of change at multiple scales, panarchy also suggests an analysis of the variable temporalities of change in ecological, social, and cultural systems. They argue that panarchy frees us from the trap of the expert where agencies become rigid and lose a sense of the larger whole in trying to solve immediate problems of the parts. An operative panarchy extends Muratori's method, based in the political, economic, and cultural history embodied in the architecture of the city, to ecosystem science. Through

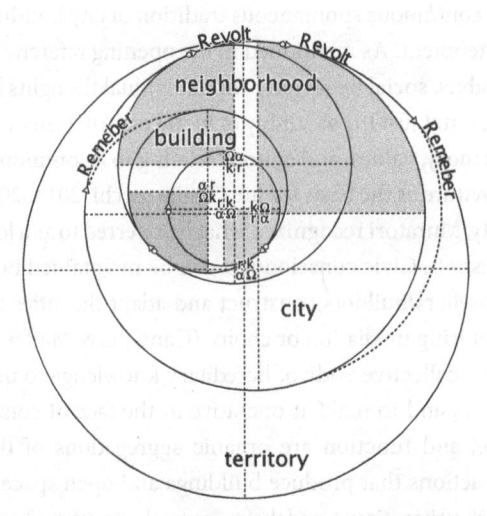

FIGURE 31.4 An operative panarchy. The shaded areas depict the phase of an adaptive cycle. A new cycle is created either by a revolt effect to a higher scale, or a remembering event to a lower scale.

an operative panarchy we can sense and read cities and territories as the result of the interactions between slow/large and fast/small moving processes and collectively govern them as nonlinear alternating states of stability and change (Gunderson & Holling, 2002). Operative historical analyses of architecture and built form embody concepts of multisystemic resilience and reveal how decisive actions made by individuals give rise to emergent features of communities and societies. An operative panarchy categorizes different scales of architecture and built form within different time cycles to stress the importance of sensing, reading, and interpreting building as a progressive, open, and inclusive system. Furthermore, it places the researcher as part of a community within the physical evidence of adaptive cycles where an embodied collective understanding of the past through an analysis of the present reality leads to a better and more resilient future.

As a critical start to his way of thinking, *Studies for an Operative Urban History of Venice* (Muratori, 1960) was the result of 10-year pedagogical project began in 1950 when Muratori became professor of Distributive Characteristics of Architecture at the University of Venice. His objective was to redirect architectural teaching away from the abstract technical lessons of modernism and toward the direct observation of human life and decision-making embodied in the distributive pattern of Venice's historical city fabric. Beginning with a close study of a single neighborhood, Muratori and his team of students identified simple changes in building construction as a method of studying the dynamics of architectural reality "from life," much like a plant ecologist's direct study of the structure of nature. The focus of their studies was a room by room survey of selected buildings and critical historical reconstructions of entire neighborhoods. The research identified phases in the continual construction process and evolution of Venice's historic building fabric separated by what are referred to as crises, taking advantage of the "precious field experiment" (p. 5) offered by the living laboratory of the city itself. Individual, anonymous building types were studied both in their own line of development and stratification, but also as part of what was referred to as the city's "tissue," which in turn comprised, for them, the urban "organism" grasped only in its historical dimension. Today we can understand that Muratori was describing the city as a complex adaptive system, and the organism in question are human agents constructing their habitat individually and collectively through sensation, experimentation, learning, remembering, and feedback (see Figure 31.5).

The seeming inert permanence of buildings belies the fact that cities grow, shrink, change, and adapt continuously over time and any new construction is a consequential response to the conditions set by the past. Surveys and reconstruction drawings were just the first step in Muratori's (1960) efforts to interpret the "irrepressible individuality of historical vision, actuality, intentionality and then the appropriate adaptation practice" (p. 5). Through an operative practice, the history of a city like Venice, Muratori's focus, was understood as constituting an ethical, social, and civil cultural heritage. Construction layers in different parts of the city revealed different phases in development of Venice's civic consciousness. The remote lagoon island of Burano was studied to discern the original process of constructing an "archipelago city" of fortified enclaves within the lagoon. Various remote neighborhoods revealed different phases in the evolutionary process of the transformation of the city's fabric. The study identified a new political economy that emerged to create the mature version of

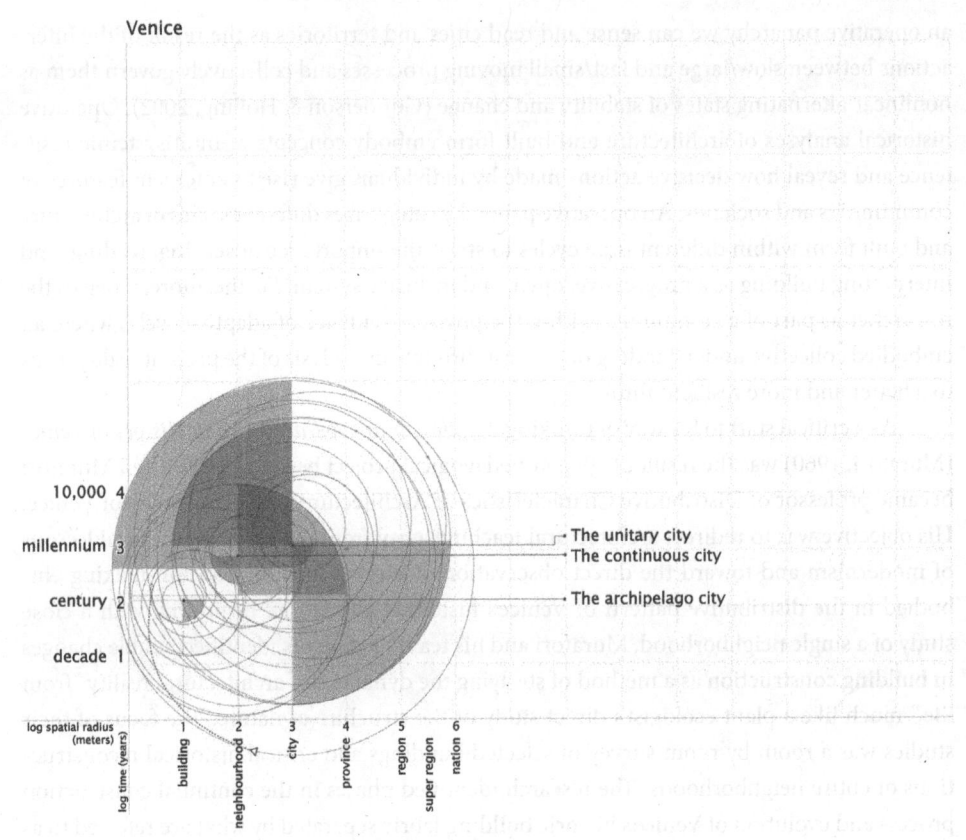

FIGURE 31.5 Venice panarchy: diagram of the adaptive cycles described in Muratori's history of Venice. The centers of the circles are located on time and space scales.

the "unitary city" that is evident today in public promenades connecting the neighborhoods around Venice's commercial center near the Rialto bridge to the religious and political center of San Marco. Muratori's study of the changing neighborhood dynamics of Venice demonstrated both the construction methods for the initial fortified inhabitation of the lagoon, followed by Byzantine and Gothic phases of reconstruction around a network of islands and canals, and the later mature development of an open and unified pedestrian and public space network after the Renaissance.

In contrast, Muratori's operative history of Rome (1963) demonstrated the longer and more dramatic adaptive cycle of civilization as he traced four phases from the origins of the city as fortified villages occupying the city's famous seven hills overlooking a crossing at the Tiber River, through their unification during the Republican age around the Forum, to extensive monumental development at the height of the empire, and its shrinkage following collapse (see Figure 31.6). Most interesting in the case of Rome, reorganization and regrowth of the city following imperial collapse occurred within its ruins. Muratori and his team of researchers created an atlas of four folios that systematically catalogued changes to routes and pathways, civic and commercial nodes, neighborhood tissue or fabric, and what he metaphorically called "special organisms," that were new building types developed to serve public

Rome

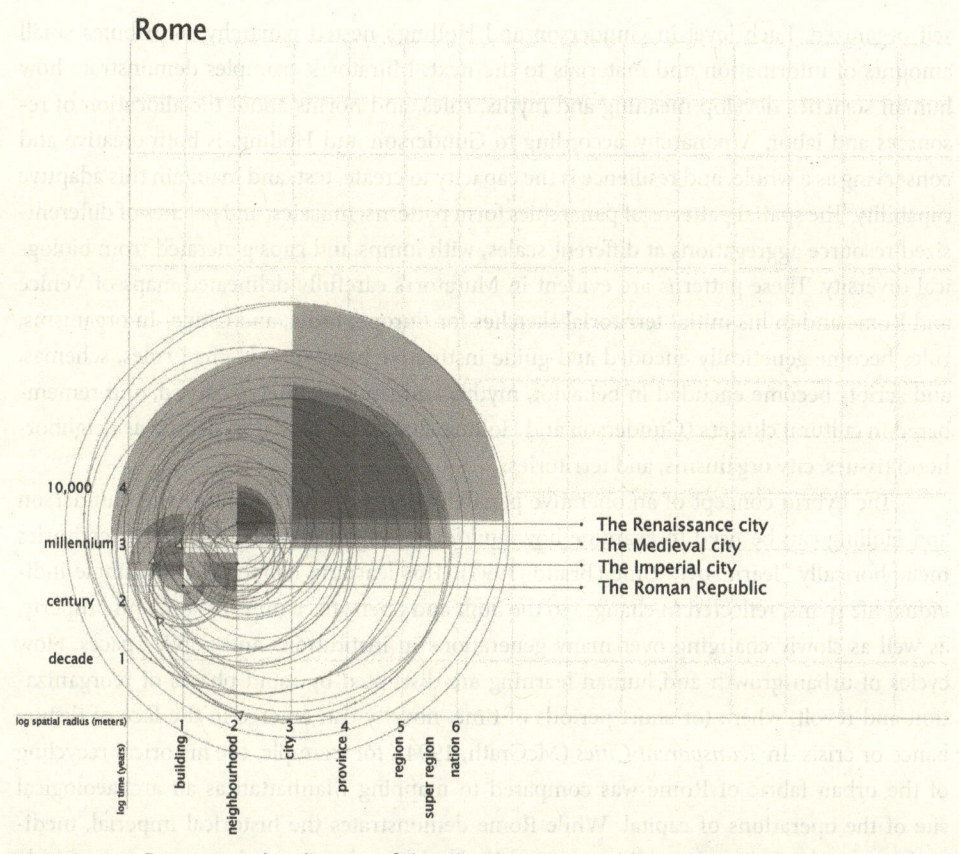

- The Renaissance city
- The Medieval city
- The Imperial city
- The Roman Republic

10,000 4
millennium 3
century 2
decade 1

log spatial radius (meters) 1 2 3 4 5 6
building neighbourhood city province region super region nation

log time (years)

FIGURE 31.6 Rome panarchy: diagram of the adaptive cycles described in Muratori's history of Rome.

and institutional needs during the four different time periods. Through his study of Rome, Muratori presented the case that architecture and built form embody a practice of civic consciousness, what we might now call multisystemic resilience, even in the face of catastrophic political and economic collapse. This study of the city of Rome overlapped with his larger unfinished final project of a comparative operative history of global civilizations and territories, including India and China, which remains especially relevant today. Noticeably absent from Muratori's histories of Venice and Rome, however, is a discussion of great buildings or famous architects. Instead his operative history focuses on the anonymous actors who construct the ordinary city and collectively transform it through economic crisis and political shifts.

An Operative Panarchy

Like Muratori's multidimensional building operations, Gunderson and Holling (2002) describe resilience as a dimension within what ecosystem science describes as the adaptive cycle. However, Muratori provides a clearer definition of embodied human consciousness, agency, and choice in successional dynamics that Gunderson and Holling often describe as self-organized. Each level in Gunderson and Holling's nested panarchy contributes small amounts of information and materials to the next. Muratori's examples demonstrate how human societies develop meaning and myths, rules, and norms about the allocation of resources and labor. A panarchy, according to Gunderson and Holling, is both creative and conserving as a whole, and resilience is the capacity to create, test, and maintain this adaptive capability. The spatial patterns of panarchies form patterns, mosaics, and patches of different-sized resource aggregations at different scales, with lumps and gaps generated from biological diversity. These patterns are evident in Muratori's carefully delineated maps of Venice and Rome and in his initial territorial sketches for Europe, India, and China. In organisms, rules become genetically encoded and guide instinctive behaviors. Human rules, schemas, and scripts become encoded in behavior, myths, and rituals gathered, stored, and remembered in cultural clusters (Gunderson and Holling, 2002) that Muratori depicts as neighborhood tissues, city organisms, and territories.

The hybrid concept of an operative panarchy derived from Muratori and Gunderson and Holling can be used to examine how buildings, neighborhoods, cities, and territories metaphorically "learn" over time (Brand, 1994). This learning happens within single individual life spans, reflected in changes to the built and open space units of land and property, as well as slowly changing over many generations in institutions and public spaces. Slow cycles of urban growth and human learning are disrupted by rapid phases of reorganization and revolt, where for short periods of time, novelty can emerge in the face of disturbance or crisis. In *Transparent Cities* (McGrath, 1994), for example, the historical recycling of the urban fabric of Rome was compared to mapping Manhattan as an archaeological site of the operations of capital. While Rome demonstrates the historical imperial, medieval and modern phases of its history, New York's urban change can be seen as successively structured by mercantile, industrial, and financial capital. In the online interactive website Manhattan Timeformations (The Skyscraper Museum, 2019), this urban archaeology was extended through three-dimensional digital modeling and the interactive user interface of a computer to explore the emergence of both the skyscraper as a building type, and the evolution of Manhattan's two business districts. Initiated by a timeline that charted the cycles of real estate booms and busts, the digital model extrudes that timeline as the third, vertical dimension in the computer-generated model. Toggling through space and time, a viewer can understand how the economic busts of the Great Depression in the 1930a and the Oil Crisis in the 1970s resulted in technological novelty in the subsequent phases of skyscraper development: the glass curtain wall, fluorescent lighting, and air conditioning in the building boom after World War II, and the use of computers in workspaces in the reorganization of the economy in the 1980s.

The Embodied Resilience of Architecture and Built Form in China

Satellites, GPS, and digital hand-held devices have extended our human sensorimotor reach. We sense the city remotely as well as close-up (McGrath & Shane, 2005). Global positioning technology traces our daily activities within a vast archive of spatial and temporal information of our journeys through an operative urban panarchy. An example may stretch from a rice farming village measuring water pollution on the outskirts of Shanghai, to the map of lowland rice cultivation in the major rice growing countries of Asia prepared by the International Rice Research Institute (Nelson & Gumma, 2015; see Figure 31.7). Lowland wet rice cultivation is the cradle of the civilizations of South, East, and Southeast Asia. The impact of colonization, independence, and the global extension of neoliberalism across Asia are three relatively recent crises and phases that have shaped a surge in urbanization, the shocking extent of which is most visceral in the data set of nighttime lights as indicator of urbanization (NASA, 2017). When we turn on our lights, our presence is registered by this constantly updated database. The superposition of these two data sets produces a striking portrait of panarchy, territory, civilization, and the planetary urban crises, as well as a framework to fulfill Muratori's operative history of territory through Gunderson and Holling's panarchy. Given access to the tools and enabling forms of governance, there is a remarkable agility of the human sensorimotor system to adapt to an often-uncertain world that passes by and surrounds us.

To illustrate, at the turn of the millennium, millions of residents of the cities of China experienced sensorimotor breakdowns similar to those experienced in postwar Europe.

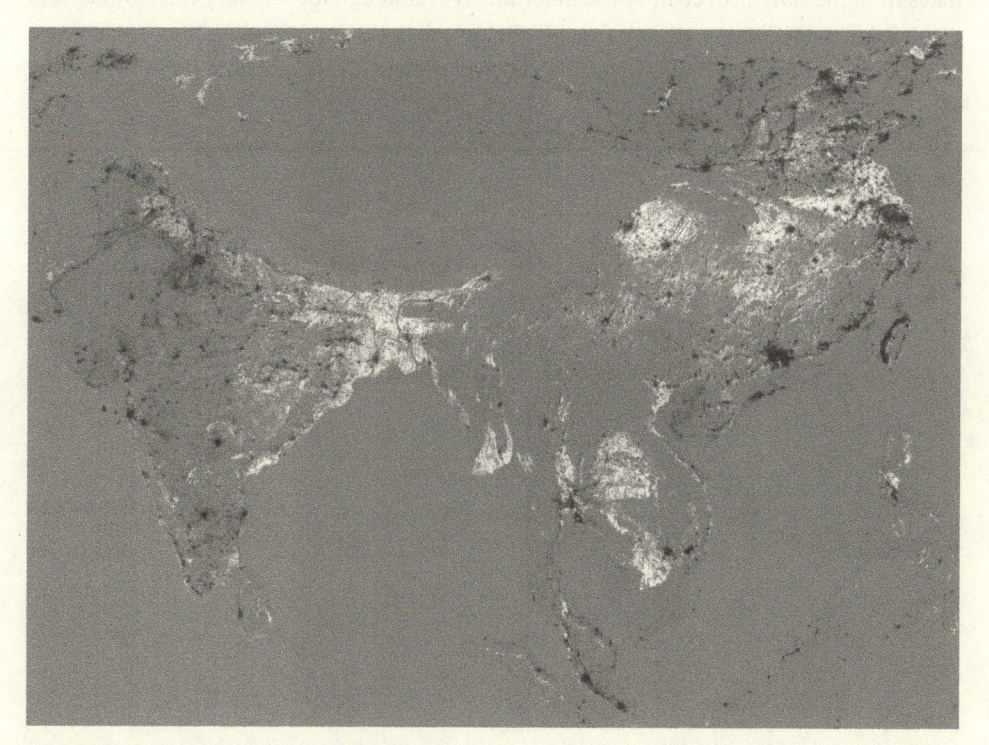

FIGURE 31.7 Asia map. This superposition of Nelson and Gumma's data of lowland rice cultivation in Asia with NOAH's nighttime lights imagery shows the explosive growth in Asia's cities on landscapes created by hand over multiple millennia.

Thousands of years of Chinese architecture and built form were suddenly transformed beyond recognition following the largest and most rapid urban transformation in the history of the world. An operative panarchy of architecture and built form in China, based both on remote-sensing and historical inquiry, can provide physical and theoretical evidence to reveal the ideals and processes of constructing buildings and cities over the millennia in relation to the goals of embodying multisystemic resilience (see Figure 31.8). As has been established, cities and buildings are complex adaptive systems based on the social organization of human organisms in relationship to territorial transformation. Furthermore, the human organism is equipped with a sensorimotor apparatus that allows for circuits of learning, remembering, and innovating. China presents a considerable challenge in testing the operative panarchy model of architecture and built form based on Muratori's unfinished operative history of territory. China contains the longest continuous tradition of built form historically constructed without the presence of the profession of architecture. The craftsmen and builders were the architects of ancient China embodying the collective consciousness of construction knowledge. This history, if operationalized, could provide further evidence of Muratori's argument about the spontaneous civil consciousness of the anonymous architecture of the city.

Uniquely, China established a collective building system that, until the fall of the Qing dynasty in 1911, had been imperially legislated, governed by bureaucrats and constructed by craftsmen according to long established handbooks and such as the *Yingzao Fashi,* which dates from the early 12th century (Steinhardt, 2014) although the territory was invaded and occupied by non-Chinese at several times. Steinhardt notes that Western self-consciousness in innovation in design had no place in the evolution of China's ancient building system.

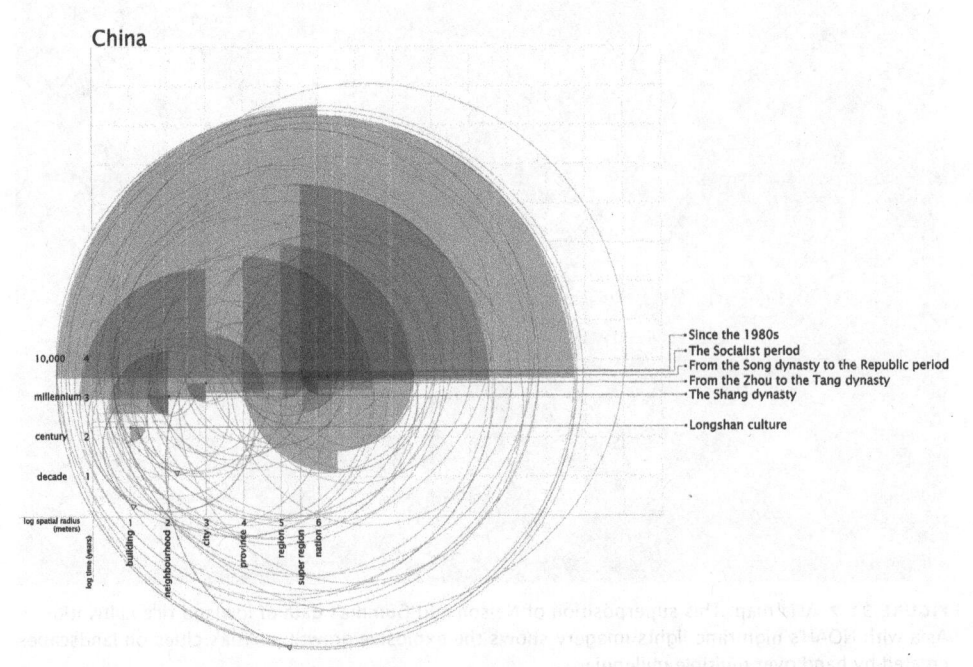

FIGURE 31.8 China panarchy: diagram of the adaptive building cycles in Chinese history.

There were no schools in which to study architecture in China until the third decade of the 20th century when the first generation of architects returned from study abroad and set out to establish a history of Chinese architecture (Steinhardt, 2014). They quickly organized schools of architecture and began to examine historical treatises and local records across the country in what Muratori would identify as the basis of an operative history. The elite first generation of architects broke with social taboos of the imperial system and explored China's countryside and engaged with the local villagers to uncover and survey old buildings, many of which were lost in the wars and upheavals of the 1940s and the Cultural Revolution from 1966 to 1976. The establishment of this slow and measured work in cities and villages across the country today is constantly hindered by urban modernization and the rural improvement movement. China continues to seek rapid economic and technological modernization, which makes it far more difficult to reconnect recent development booms to long building tradition and culture.

As Chinese architectural historian Fu Xinian (1984) argues, Chinese buildings are not merely artifacts invented by human creativity according to different geographical and climatic conditions but are also an enduring and continuous system generated across the civilization's vast territory over several millennia of innovation and synthesis. Steinhardt (2014) describes the defining feature of Chinese architecture as its recognizable identity based on many shared features that is unchanged by purpose, location, or time period of construction. These shared features include an architectural complex of interrelated buildings, courtyards, and enclosing arcades organized within a horizontal axial space enclosed within a walled rectangle extending through gates in the four cardinal directions, with one main building at the center. A modular and flexible timber post and beam system with glazed tile roofs indicates a building occupant's rank. This use of architecture and built form as a lexicon of culture and status was reproduced and persisted as a powerful symbol of Chinese civic consciousness across time and space. This tradition aligns with Muratori's argument about buildings and cities as archetypes and as part of a collective memory. But the physical evidence defies his methods of chronological classification of building cycles, as the same architectural language was continuously repeated across the world outside of his classification system of discernable temporal phases in Europe (Steinhardt, 2014).

Although there had been a significant decline in traditional urban tissue and landscape during the Republican Era (1911–1949), Gaubatz (1998) points out the continuity of key landscape elements in different eras of Chinese urban history before the 20th century. In socialist China (1950–1978), a new link between building tradition and territorial civilization was set up in through a predominant type of work unit—danwei. The intention of building the danwei system had been heavily inspired by the former Soviet Union, however, the built form of the danwei is actually a variant of the walled wards of early traditional Chinese cities (Gaubatz, 1995). The development policy since the Cultural Revolution (1966–1976) emphasized rural development and the role of small and medium-sized traditional cities. The old administrative cities had been gradually transformed into a hierarchical urban network of local work units of industrial and agricultural production centers. Subsequently, there has been an accelerated erasure of historical Chinese cities and buildings since 1979 when China first introduced the newly created city of Shenzhen, and later transformed every major city according to a national program of rapid urbanization at a huge scale. Since the top-down emphasis on urbanization in the 1980s, the unprecedented construction behavior has led to a fundamental transformation of the country's character at all scales from buildings to cities, which is highly visible in the spectacular landscapes of megablocks encompassing urban villages and enormous gated developments of superblock dwellings.

Four recent publications point the way to an operative panarchy of architecture and built form in China. In 2010, McGrath wrote about the recent ambition of creating "Silicon Valley in Paradise" in Hangzhou, the ancient capital of the Southern Song Dynasty (McGrath, 2010). The city continues to embrace the lush public landscape of West Lake, a former scenic imperial enclave celebrated in poetry and painting for centuries, now the most visited domestic tourist spot in China. Likewise, Sharon Haar and Victoria Marshall (2012) recognize the impact of Chinese urbanization on the ecology of the "megadeltas" of China and point to solutions involving remote sensing and local feedback. Pickett and Zhou (2015) describe the territorial analysis of the Chinese "megaregion" as a new phase in urbanization following the city, metropolis, and megalopolis. Using remote satellite data, they are able to track the last 30 years of urbanization in Chinese cities as part of what they refer to a global urban continuum. David G. Shane (2015) explores Chinese "metacities" as digitally enhanced information systems. This interlinking between the social and ecological "crisis" of rapid and large-scale urbanization in China coincides with both the spread of digitally enhanced communication and information systems across the planet and a growing realization of the limits of the planet's natural carrying capacity. Combining historical inquiry with theories of ecosystem change, these authors have begun the theoretical work of recognizing the importance of embodying multisystemic resilience at the nested scales of an operational panarchy of China's megaregional territories.

Conclusion

Karl Kropf (2008) refers to Muratori's notion of crisis as both present in the mental state of involved humans and something pervasive across society. The perceived crisis today includes the feelings and thinking that have arisen in response to rapid urbanization, global warming, resource scarcity, pervasive inequality, and a global pandemic. Kropf locates Muratori's notion of crisis within a spiraling sequence of human life: crisis–response–habit-crisis–response–habit, a coarse grain version of Deleuze's human sensorimotor system. Our sensorimotor apparatus responds to difference and is disrupted by chance, variability, and diversity. Different kinds and scales of crisis contribute to different cognitive states of mind, producing resilient responses later ingrained in habits. Kropf lists stories, religion, music, visual art, the sciences, technology, and, of course, architecture and urbanism as cultural responses to this sense of overcoming crises and of overcoming sensorimotor breakdowns, the embodiment of resilience.

In related writing on the sensorimotor system, Henri Bergson (1896/1991) describes our human consciousness as split in two: there is the actor playing our role in the arenas of life, and the split self, watching as if floating above the scene. This dual sensibility is the primary question of embodying multisystemic resilience: How can we act as sentient, ethical, embodied beings in our daily lives, while having a reflective civic consciousness of the consequences our acts, above and beyond them at a planetary scale? The metacity was introduced as a concept linking this split consciousness to architecture and urban ecology to develop the cognitive capacity to become more resilient as individuals, social groups and a species in the face of the unprecedented challenges we face globally (McGrath & Pickett, 2011; McGrath & Shane, 2005). The concept resonates with new urban forms and ways of life ushered in since the introduction of the internet as a way of enabling new understandings of the heterogeneity and dynamics of both ecological and social systems. Metacities are not only nested panarchical phenomena that transform at different spatial and temporal scales (Pickett et al., 2013) but are also connected globally through shared concerns around social injustice and climate change and the ability to communicate distantly through the internet. De Puydt's (1860) political panarchy conceives of distributed governance systems, which parallel the basis of the metacity in ecological theories of metacommunity and metapopulation. Metacities are the embodiment of our digitally extended sensorimotor resilience and can also be seen within resilient panarchical governance system. Therefore, the metacity as a theoretical model and a set of principles can guide future study of an operative panarchy of embodied multisystemic resilience globally.

An operative panarchy of the metacity provides a way to respond to our current crisis through the recognition of the embodied multisystemic resilience *of* architecture and built form. An extended sensorimotor system engages cultural and scientific representation and communication through digital technologies, remote-sensing, and data-rich handheld devices. Multisystemic resilience in architecture and urban design is conceived, represented, and communicated through a civic consciousness as well as embodied and lived. A structure for responsive change that scales from architectural and urban systems begins with the sensing human body. By operationalizing panarchy, nested ecosystem scales are seen in both short and long-term durational frameworks. The human sensorimotor system is extended through the ubiquitous integration of deep data drawn from satellites, grounded instruments and handheld devices. The seamless location and spatialization of data and information exponentially increase our ability to assess, measure, and study the resilience of multiple systems of built form across scales and over time (McGrath & Shane 2005) and to collectively act on the basis of this extensive access. For all these reasons, developing an embodied understanding of multisystemic resilience, linked by an extensive and collective global sensorimotor system can help guide the future health of individuals, communities, and the planet itself through the embodiment of an operative panarchy of architecture and built form.

Key Messages

1. This chapter introduces an embodied approach to multisystemic resilience through an understanding of architecture and built form as the physical evidence of complex adaptive social-natural systems over time. Current approaches to resilience in the built environment respond to specific, immediate, and projected threats rather than a more

fundamental and universal knowledge of multisystemic resilience in architecture and built form.
2. A brief overview of the literature on resilience in the built environment demonstrates the limits of a technical focus of resilience in the professional disciplines of architecture, urban design and planning. Three recent publications are discussed that cover a broad range of applied resilience in architecture, urban design and planning, resilience as a metaphor to link ecology and urban design, and an architecturally based typomorphological basis of resilience in the built environment.
3. The hybrid concept of operative panarchy is introduced linking Saverio Muratori's concept of an operational history of architecture, city, and territory and Lance H. Gunderson and C. S. Holling's panarchy framework of human adaptation and ecosystem transformation. This hybrid concept forms the basis for establishing an array of spatial and temporal scales in which to embody multisystemic resilience in the physical reality of the built environment.
4. Following on the case study of urbanization in China, speculations on the metacity as a framework to establish a politically operative panarchy is presented. The metacity is both a set of principles and an array of models for action that can guide multisystemic resilience research through technological extensions of the human sensorimotor system.

Acknowledgments

The authors thank to Professor Ungar for his feedback on the chapter. The authors are grateful for funding from China Scholarship Council (No. 201806190192).

References

Bergson, H. (1983). *Creative evolution* (A. Mitchell, Trans.). Lanham, MD: University Press of America. (Original work published 1907)

Bergson, H. (1991). *Matter and memory* (N. M. Paul, & W. S. Palmer, Trans.). New York, NY: Zone Books. (Original work published 1896)

Bosher, L. (2014). Built-in resilience through disaster risk reduction: Operational issues. *Building Research & Information*, 42(2), 240–254. doi:10.1080/09613218.2014.858203

Brand, S. (1994). *How buildings learn*. New York, NY: Viking Press.

Cadenasso, M. L. (2013). Designing ecological heterogeneity. In B. McGrath (Ed.), *Urban design ecologies* (pp. 272–281). London, UK: John Wiley.

Cadenasso, M. L., Pickett, S. T. A., McGrath, B. P., & Marshall, V. (2013). Ecological heterogeneity in urban ecosystems: Reconceptualized land cover models as a bridge to urban design. In S. T. A. Pickett, M. L. Cadenasso, & B. P. McGrath (Eds.), *Resilience in urban ecology and design: Linking theory and practice for sustainable cities* (pp. 107–129). New York, NY: Springer.

Caniggia, G., & Maffei, G. L. (2001). *Architectural composition and building typology*. Florence, Italy: Alinea Editrice.

Cataldi, G. (2018). Towards a general theory of urban morphology: The type-morphological theory. In V. Oliveira (Ed.), *Teaching urban morphology* (pp. 65–78). Cham, Switzerland: Springer.

de Puydt, P. E. (1860). *Panarchy* (J. Zube, Trans.). Retrieved from http://www.panarchy.org/depuydt/1860.eng.html

Deleuze, G. (1986). *Cinema 1: The movement image*. Minneapolis: University of Minnesota Press.

Deleuze, G. (1989). *Cinema 2: The time image*. Minneapolis: University of Minnesota Press.
Garcia, E. J., & Vale, B. (2017). *Unravelling sustainability and resilience in the built environment*. London, UK: Routledge.
Gardner, J. (2019). *Embodying Resilience Experiential Module* [Course material]. Parsons School of Design. doi:10.13140/RG.2.2.25686.70723
Gaubatz, P. (1995). Urban transformation in post-Mao China: Impacts of the reform era on China's urban form. In D. Davis (Ed.), *Urban spaces in contemporary China* (pp. 28–60). Cambridge, UK: Cambridge University Press.
Gaubatz, P. (1998). Understanding Chinese urban form: Contexts for interpreting continuity and change. *Built Environment (1978–), 24*(4), 251–270.
Gunderson, L. H., & Holling, C. S. (2002). *Panarchy: Understanding transformations in human and natural systems*. Washington: Island Press.
Haar, S., & Marshall, V. (2012). Mega urban ecologies. In B. McGrath (Ed.), *Urban design ecologies* (pp. 141–161). London, UK: Wiley.
Hassler, U., & Kohler, N. (2014). Resilience in the built environment. *Building Research & Information, 42*(2), 119–129. doi:10.1080/09613218.2014.873593
Hollnagel, E. (2014). Resilience engineering and the built environment. *Building Research & Information, 42*(2), 221–228. doi:10.1080/09613218.2014.862607
Kropf, K. (2008). Crisis in the typological process and the language of innovation and tradition. *Urban Morphology, 10*(1), 70–73.
Krugman, P. (1996). *The self-organizing economy*. New York, NY: Blackwell.
Leven, S. (1999). *Fragile dominion: Complexity and the commons*. Cambridge, UK: Perseus.
Marshall, V., McGrath, B., & Towers, J. (2007). Introduction. In B. McGrath, V. Marshall, M. L. Cadenasso, S. T. A. Pickett, R. Plunz, & J. Towers (Eds.), *Designing patch dynamics* (pp. 4–15). New York, NY: Columbia Books on Architecture.
McGrath, B. (1994). *Transparent cities*. New York, NY: Lumen Books.
McGrath, B., & Gardner, J. (2007). *Cinemetrics: Architectural Drawing Today*. London, UK: John Wiely & Sons.
McGrath, B. (2007). Designs as models of patch dynamics. In V. Marshall, B. McGrath, J. Towers, & R. Pluz (Eds.), *Designing patch dynamics* (pp. 148–158). New York, NY: Columbia University Press.
McGrath, B. (2010). Silicon Valley in paradise: Wiring the urban waterbody in Hangzhou, China. In A. Gurung, J. Zha, & B. McGrath (Eds.), *Growing cities in a shrinking world: The challenges of India and China* (pp. 87–96). Delhi, India: Macmillan.
McGrath, B. (2018). Intersecting disciplinary frameworks: The architecture and the ecology of the city. *Ecosystem Health and Sustainability, 4*(6), 148–159. doi:10.1080/20964129.2018.1482730
McGrath, B., Marshall, V., Cadenasso, M. L., Pickett, S. T. A., Plunz, R., & Towers, J. (Eds.). (2007). *Designing patch dynamics*. New York, NY: Columbia Books on Architecture.
McGrath, B., & Pickett, S. T. A. (2011). The metacity: A conceptual framework for integrating ecology and urban design. *Challenges, 2*(4), 55–72. doi:10.3390/challe2040055
McGrath, B., & Shane, D. S. (Eds.). (2005). *Sensing the 21st century city: Close up and remote*. London, UK: John Wiley.
Meerow, S., & Newell, J. P. (2016). Urban resilience for whom, what, where, when and why? *Urban Geography, 40*(3), 309–329. doi:10.1080/02723638.2016.1206395
Moffatt, S. (2014). Resilience and competing temporalities in cities. *Building Research & Information, 42*(2), 202–220. doi:10.1080/09613218.2014.869894
Muratori, S. (1960). *Studi per una operante storia urbana di Venezia* [Studies for an operative urban history of Venice]. Rome, Italy: Instituto Poligraphico dello Stato.
Muratori, S., Bollati, R., Bollati, S., & Marinucci, G. (1963). *Studi per una operante storia urbana di Roma* [Studies for an operative urban history of Venice]. Rome, Italy: Consiglio Nazionale delle Ricerca.
Muratori, S., Bollati, R., Bollati, S., & Marinucci, G. (1967). *Civiltà e territorio* [Civilization and territory]. Rome, Italy. Centro Studi di Urbanistica.
Muratori, S., Bollati, R., Bollati, S., & Marinucci, G. (1973). *Studi per una operante storia del territorio* [Studies for an operating history of the territory]. Rome, Italy: Consiglio Nazionale delle Ricerca.

NASA. (2017). *New night lights maps open up possible real time applications.* Retrieved from https://www.nasa.gov/feature/goddard/2017/new-night-lights-maps-open-up-possible-real-time-applications

Nelson, A., & Gumma, M. K. (2015). *A map of lowland rice extent in the major rice growing countries of Asia.* Retrieved from http://irri.org/our-work/research/policy-and-markets/mapping

Nicol, L. A., & Knoepfel, P. (2014). Resilient housing: A new resource-oriented approach. *Building Research & Information, 42*(2), 229–239. doi:10.1080/09613218.2014.862162

Pearson, A., Barnard, L., Pearce, J., Kingham, S., & Howden-Chapman, P. (2014). Housing quality and resilience in New Zealand. *Building Research & Information, 42*(2), 182–190. doi:10.1080/09613218.2014.850603

Pickett, S. T. A., Cadenasso, M. L., & Grove, J. M. (2003). Resilient cities: Meaning, models, and metaphor for integrating the ecological, socio-economic, and planning realms. *Landscape and Urban Planning, 69*(4), 369–384. doi:10.1016/j.landurbplan.2003.10.035

Pickett, S. T. A., & Cadenasso, M. L. (2007). Patch dynamics as a conceptual tool to link ecology and design. In B. McGrath, V. Marshall, M. L. Cadenasso, J. M. Grove, S. T. A. Pickett, R. Plunz, & J. Towers (Eds.), *Designing patch dynamics* (pp. 16–29). New York, NY: Columbia Books on Architecture.

Pickett, S. T. A., Cadenasso, M. L., & McGrath, B. (Eds.). (2013). *Resilience in ecology and urban design: Linking theory and practice for sustainable cities.* Dordrecht, The Netherlands: Springer.

Pickett, S. T. A., McGrath, B., Cadenasso, M. L., & Felson. A. J. (2014). Ecological resilience and resilient cities. *Building Research & Information, 42*(2), 143–157. doi:10.1080/09613218.2014.850600

Pickett, S. T. A., & Zhou, W. (2015). Global urbanization as a shifting context for applying ecological science toward the sustainable city. *Ecological Health and Sustainability, 1*(1), 1–15. doi:10.1890/EHS14-0014.1

Pierce, C. S. (1998). *The essential Peirce: Selected philosophical writings* (Vol. 2, pp. 1893–1913). Bloomington: Indiana University Press.

Shane, D. G. (2015). Rapid urbanization and the informational metacity in China. *Nakhara: Journal of Environmental Design and Planning, 11,* 51–74. Retrieved from https://www.tci-thaijo.org/index.php/nakhara/article/view/104851

Steinhardt, N. S. (2014). Chinese architectural history in the twenty-first century. *Journal of the Society of Architectural Historians, 73*(1), 38–60. doi:10.1525/jsah.2014.73.1.38

Tagliazucchi, S. (2014, October). Unione tra uomo e natura: L'analisi del territorio secondo Saverio Muratori [Union between man and nature: The analysis of the territory according to Saverio Muratori]. Paper presented at the Ninth Congresso Città e Territorio Virtuale, Università degli Studi Roma Tre, Rome.

Tagliazucchi, S. (2015). *Studi per una operante storia del territorio: Il libro incompiuto di Saverio Muratori* [Studies for an operating history of the territory: The unfinished book by Saverio Muratori] (Doctoral dissertation). Università di Bologna, Italy. doi:10.6092/unibo/amsdottorato/7011

The Skyscraper Museum. (2019). *Introduction to Manhattan timeformations.* Retrieved from https://www.skyscraper.org/timeformations/intro.html

Xinian, F. (1984). *Chinese traditional architecture* (N. S. Steinhardt, Ed.). Princeton, NJ: Princeton University Press.

Vale, L. (2014). The politics of resilient cities: Whose resilience and whose city? *Building Research & Information, 42*(2), 191–201. doi:10.1080/09613218.2014.850602

Van der Leeuw, S. E., & Aschan-Leygonie, C. (2005). A long-term perspective on resilience in socio-natural systems. In H. Liljenstrom & U. Svedin (Eds.), *Micro-meso-macro: Addressing complex systems couplings* (pp. 227–264). Toh Tuck Link, Singapore: World Scientific.

Walker, B., Salt, D., & Reid, W. (2006). *Resilience thinking: Sustaining ecosystems and people in a changing world.* Washington, DC: Island Press.

Wu, J., & Wu, T. (2013). Ecological resilience as a foundation for urban design and sustainability. In S. T. A. Pickett, M. L. Cadenasso, & B. McGrath (Eds.), *Resilience in ecology and urban design: Linking theory and practice for sustainable cities* (pp. 211–229). Dordrecht, The Netherlands: Springer.

The Social Contexts of Resilient Architecture

Terri Peters

Introduction

This chapter explores the social contexts of resilience in architectural design focusing on strategies for high-performing buildings that promote happiness and health among building users. Resilience is often generally defined as the ability to become strong, healthy, or successful again after a mishap or to return to an original shape after being pulled, stretched, pressured, or bent by external forces. Depending on context, this term could relate to a person's resilience, or an object's or a material's resilience, in relation to its respective contexts. Researchers have traced a recent history of this term as it applies to the design disciplines and found that its interdisciplinary focus emerged from different fields, including psychology, engineering, and ecology (Trogal, Bauman, Lawrence, & Petrescu, 2019). The work of ecological scientist C. S. Holling is particularly relevant as it frames the concept of resilience as "a measure of the persistence of systems and their ability to absorb change and disturbance and still maintain the same relationships between populations or state variables" (Holling, 1973, p. 14). Holling's definition is often cited in texts on resilient design due to his focus on the impacts of human activity on ecosystems. Academic and professional disciplines relating to the built environment have explored more specific interpretations of resilience, for example, urban ecological resilience (Alberti & Marzluff, 2004), urban resilience (100 Resilient Cities, 2019), security and risk reduction in cities (Coaffee, 2008), and promotion of resilience through urban governance and institutions (Leichenko, 2011).

In architecture, the term *resilience* tends to be used narrowly describe a building's structural and environmental performance in quantitative terms, but can a building be called resilient if it fails to make inspiring spaces for people, promote well-being, or improve people's experience? This is the focal question to be addressed in this chapter. The chapter brings an architectural perspective to the concept of resilience and begins by exploring how the term is currently evaluated in and around buildings, through discussion of related concepts such as sustainability, passive survivability, and performance gaps. Promising new design approaches that better consider occupant comfort and well-being are introduced, in particular the behavioral design practice of 3XN, which focuses on how buildings can positively impact people's social interactions. The chapter traces the emergence of a new generation of building evaluation metrics and certification systems that are focused not solely on environmental performance but that also consider synergies between people's experience and our natural resources, such as the WELL Building Standard and Active House. Examples from the multifunctional, process-based strategies used in a series of new climate adaptation renovations in Copenhagen, Denmark, are discussed as exemplary resilient design projects that address neighborhood flooding by simultaneously improving the qualities of public spaces and better connecting people to nature. The chapter concludes with a discussion of how locally specific and socially focused designs can support more resilient environments for people.

From Resilient Buildings to Resilient Occupants

According to the U.S. National Infrastructure Advisory Council and included as guidance to building designers in the Whole Building Design Guide, resilient buildings should address four main considerations: *robustness*, both at the building scale in terms of soundness and functionality and in terms of infrastructure that allows building operations like power and thermal comfort during a crisis; *resourcefulness*, for example, prioritizing actions to control and mitigate damage and keep communications and supply chain going; *rapid recovery*, to resume normal operations and conditions as soon as possible after a crisis; and *redundancy*, which means having access to back up resources in case of a failure in normal operations (National Institute of Building Sciences, 2018). By this definition, resilient buildings are not about people and our specific emotional and cultural needs but rather about the responsibility of buildings to continually provide the bare necessities of functionality and shelter.

The social roles of buildings and how they influence our well-being are entirely overlooked—although these aspects would be particularly important in the event of a crisis. People spend more than 90% of our time indoors (Klepeis et al., 2001), and the qualities of buildings and landscapes impact our moods, well-being, social experiences, and how we behave. The American Association of Architects (AIA) brought together a working group to develop design priorities for the creation of built environments that promote health and well-being to inform design. According to their findings, the main points that designers must focus on are *environmental quality*, for example, by reduce chemicals and pollutants; *natural systems*, for example, by promoting healthy eating and social behavior; *physical activity*, by considering how the environment encourages daily movement; *safety*, by reducing changes of accidental injury and considering ways to lessen stress and anxiety; *sensory environments* that are varied and include diversity in sounds, light, smells; and *social connectedness*, by designing spaces where people like to be, to help strengthen professional and social relationships (AIA, n.d.). However, the AIA's design priorities are general and do not include spatial suggestions, nor are there any examples of best practices. These also do not include design guidelines or drawings, which limits how much practical use they can be to the profession.

One reason for the lack of prescriptive information and quantitative description could be that important concepts such as safety and sensory environments are difficult to apply in the same way to different projects. Much of the designer's role is to interpret what strategies are most needed in a specific scenario and to consider how to balance client requirements with the needs of the future building users. Due to people's cultural backgrounds, ages, and interests, and personal expectations of a space, as well as numerous other factors, people respond differently to qualities in their environments.

There are some environmental features and qualities that nearly everyone would have a positive reaction to, like daylight and connection to outdoors. Adopting principles of *biophilia*, a term coined by E. O. Wilson in 1984 referring to people's natural affinity to nature, is one way that designers can attempt to design spaces that have universal appeal (Kellert & Wilson, 1984). Studies show that biophilic design strategies, using specific spatial and sensory strategies to connect people to the natural environment, reduces people's stress and promotes well-being (Kellert, Heerwagen, & Mador, 2008). Foregrounding biophilic design strategies could also be an effective way of boosting resilience in assisting people in our adjustment to the realities of a changing climate. Currently mainstream notions of occupant comfort in buildings is based on how well the indoors seems to defy seasonal variations in temperature and humidity and assumes that people want a steady state of "comfort" indoors. Globally, people are experiencing more extreme weather and a changing climate, and our buildings could help us better understand our local context. Biophilic design strategies such as limiting floorplan depth and thereby increasing chances for daylight and natural ventilation, using effective building orientation to achieve daylighting in main spaces, as well as designing windows to give views of the sky could help people be more connected to the natural world, can be ways of encouraging people to acknowledge rather than conceal seasonal variabilities. This could lead to different expectations of comfort inside buildings. As outlined in this chapter, the current state of building performance evaluation, and how buildings are considered high performing or not, is often quantitative and removed from our social contexts. This is starting to change, as designers and clients become aware that often the strategies for positive environmental performance and benefits to human well-being are compatible or even the same (Peters, 2017).

Climate change and extreme weather are a main focus in resilient design, but largely from the perspective that minimizing a building's environmental impact will achieve better building performance and therefore require fewer scarce resources (National Institute of Building Sciences, 2018). In design, resilience is often considered alongside *passive survivability*, a term coined by Resilient Building Institute founder Alex Wilson, which he defined after studying how uncomfortable and vulnerable buildings were without power after Hurricane Katrina in New Orleans (Wilson, 2005). Over the past 100 years, people have become heavily reliant on "active" systems in buildings for their comfort, those systems that require fossil fuels to function, like typical heating, ventilation, and air conditioning systems. Given these technological advances, the ability of our buildings to serve our needs in the event of a loss of power has been tremendously compromised. Resilient design addresses these shortcomings. It is "the intentional design of buildings, landscapes, communities, and regions in response to vulnerabilities to disaster and disruption of normal life" (Resilient

Design Institute, n.d.). Passive survivability is a desirable condition where due to effective resilient design strategies, buildings maintain livable conditions in the event of extended loss of power or interruptions in heating fuel. The terms *sustainability* and *sustainable design* in buildings are also widely used, largely relating to a building's performance. In design, the term *sustainability* is borrowed from the concepts of sustainable development, relating to the goals of balancing and maintaining a relationship between built and natural environments and has within it the notion of social, environmental, and economic parameters (World Commission on Environment and Development, 1987). While sustainability seeks balance, resilience focuses on restoring the balance while accommodating future challenges.

In architectural design and urban design research and practice, there is an emerging interest in expanding the concept of resilience to better consider people and our experience inside buildings. Boone (2013) argues that any efforts to design resilient or sustainable cities must therefore take into account the "social contexts" of urbanism. This could be applied to architectural design as well. Recently, design researchers have been incorporating concepts of social justice and urban community resilience (De Carli, 2019), which explicitly considers people and our relationships to one another in the spaces we build. However, there is a missing link between this forward-thinking design research and current design practice. For example, there are few if any published examples that illustrates these principles in practice, nor are there design guidelines for social justice and architecture. Some progress is being made in terms of considering buildings and people, in particular new research is aimed at gaining a better understanding of the significant role that building users play in how a building performs compared to design intentions. The difference between user expectations and design intentions and buildings in use are known as "performance gaps" (Coleman, Touchie, Robinson, & Peters, 2018). Understanding the reasons behind the gaps, has been an area of research for the last five or so years in academia. A number of special issues of journals have picked up on this topic including a special issue of Building Research and Information journal titled, *Energy Performance Gaps: Promises, People, Practices*, in 2017. This has been reflected in the building industry with a number of building standards and metrics that seek to quantify the ways buildings impact people's health and well-being. For example, the WELL Building Standard, established in 2014 and slowly gaining momentum, is the first building standard that is exclusively concerned with people—there are no points for low energy use (International WELL Building Institute, n.d.). It is focused on quantifying how people feel in buildings and considers how a building promotes mental health, healthy nutrition, air quality, water quality, and exercise, along with other human-centered criteria. Such standards signal a noticeable shift in the building industry toward new ways of certifying green or sustainable buildings and defining and measuring building performance and resilient design. There remains, however, a lack of coordination and few built examples of how to reconcile the seemingly conflicting needs of people and our natural environment.

Design features for resilient buildings and human resilience are often the same and are most effective when considered together. People know, and numerous studies support the idea, that how we experience buildings shapes our well-being and behavior. It makes sense to focus on the building performance impacts that people can experience and care about. For example, people using a building care about how a space or room makes them feel in the moment, not necessarily the cost savings over time or environmental benefits of putting extra insulation in the walls. The concepts of resilience and sustainability in buildings needs to be reframed as offering benefits to people, promoting social sustainability and human well-being rather than focusing solely on environmental sustainability.

Two built examples are discussed in detail in this chapter, a Canadian example of an Active House that is part of the VELUX Model Homes program, and two neighborhood scale climate adaptation projects in Denmark. These examples highlight how resilient design can be an opportunity to rethink current building typologies, rather than a constraint. For example, suburban homes could be health-promoting with better environmental performance, as evidenced by several of the VELUX Model Homes projects, which focus on designing for a higher than typical quality and quantity of natural light and its impact on people's sense of well-being in the home (VELUX, n.d.). These pilot projects in this program address the issues that in and around buildings, experiential aspects such as daylight, thermal comfort, sound, privacy, comfort, and spaciousness are harder to measure than, for example, energy performance or light levels, but they impact quality of life and offer valuable benefits to people. Experiential parameters of light and air are invisible and not drawn on floorplans. For this reason, it is challenging to have a vocabulary for these experiential aspects of a building, and although people spend so much time in their homes, these aspects are often not well considered. The Active House building rating system is part of a new generation of voluntary building certification standards that have emerged in the last few years that consider well-being and experience in everyday buildings like housing, or offices, not just hospitals and care environments (Active House Alliance, n.d.). Pairing this with examples from a citywide initiative in Copenhagen that aims to address flooding and public space shows how resilient design strategies can be adapted at varied scales. Rather than individual buildings, the initiatives in Copenhagen impacts streetscapes, roads, sidewalks, parking areas, and pedestrian links in neighborhoods. These initiatives began with an overall plan and looked to identify and maximize the positive co-benefits for both the environment and for local residents as a way to increase public support for these urban renovations, which are costly and cause short-term disruptions.

New Forms of Practice: How Design Shapes Behavior

Architects believe that when they design buildings, their decisions directly and indirectly impact how people use the spaces, their health and well-being, and their interactions with others (U.S. Green Building Council, n.d.). Architects have been known to agonize over the dimensions of a window seat or the quality of the view, or the qualities of a cladding material on a building and how it will weather over the course of time and how its color will appear in different weather and seasons. Research from numerous disciplines supports the belief that people act differently depending on environmental qualities (Huisman, Morales, van Hoof, & Kort, 2012). For example, in behavioral economics researchers have measured the impacts of lighting quality on consumer spending (Summers & Hebert, 2001) and in public health researchers have studied hospital ward design and room layouts and the spread of infectious disease (Stiller, Salm, Bischoff, & Gastmeier, 2016). In architectural design, researchers have examined the impacts of various floorplan arrangements and environmental cues on people living with dementia to see how it impacts their ability to find their way around their nursing homes (Marquardt, 2011), and in environmental psychology researchers have examined the restorative benefit of nature (Kaplan, 1995). The discipline of environmental psychology is relatively new, becoming popular in the 1970s by focusing on the relationships between human behavior and the natural and built environments. Research organizations like Environmental Design Research Association, which holds international conferences on this topic and publishes proceedings, remains a leader in research into how people's environment impacts their behavior.

Environmental psychology has not greatly impacted mainstream architectural design or engineering research or practice and is not taught in the North American professional architecture curriculum. However, over the last decade, there has been a growing interest in understanding aspects of environmental psychology in the workplace, starting with questions about occupant productivity and now including occupant well-being and mental health. Over the last decade, three architectural research journals, *Health Environment Research Design*, *World Health Design*, and *Environment and Behaviour*, have been leaders in promoting evidence-based design (Lundin, 2015) to study the impacts of buildings and on occupant health and well-being beyond healthcare settings. For example, researchers have found links between people's well-being in buildings and the outdoor context and walkability, due to the opportunities for social contact and sense of community that being out in public brings (French et al., 2013). The quality of our surroundings has been shown to impact our neurological functioning as well. For example, a series of studies led by researchers at Harvard show a measurable link between fresh air and enhanced mechanical ventilation and better cognitive performance at work (Allen et al., 2016; MacNaughton et al., 2017). A sense of control over one's immediate surroundings and freedom to move around a space has been positively linked to a person's well-being and health (Ulrich, 1991).

Designing spaces that are customizable with aspects that can be personalized with color or furnishings, with local environmental controls such as operable windows, are ways that design can influence well-being. In particular the design of a person's home impacts mental health and well-being and sense of self. Housing can have a major impact on our social interactions and mental health. Among other considerations, at a minimum a home must be safe, large enough for people to have privacy and social connections, and thermally comfortable. Recent studies such as a pilot project in the United Kingdom called "Boiler on Prescription" tested assumptions about thermal performance in buildings and people's perception of their health (Burns & Coxon, 2016). This initiative found that installing new energy efficient heating systems in people's homes did more than improve their thermal comfort, people had 60% less interactions with their general practitioner doctor. This study showed a link between thermal comfort, mental well-being, and physical health (Burns & Coxon, 2016). This particular study also had economic impacts, as the new boilers were higher efficiency and cheaper to run in the long term. Given this accumulating evidence, there has been a number of design offices formally researching how and in which ways building design shapes behavior of the inhabitants they design for, then using this information as feedback in their design processes (Peters, 2018). One example, 3XN Architects in Denmark, follows.

3XN Architects

3XN is a globally successful architecture firm focused on designing buildings to encourage social connectedness, effective communication and community (GXN, n.d.). They have an in-house research office, GXN, which investigates digital design, circular design, and behavioral design. GXN's research practice informs every 3XN project, and the team carries out experiments, develops prototypes and designs research to better understand the social impacts of buildings. Their methods are interdisciplinary, drawing from environmental psychology, social sciences, humanities, and architecture. Their research team responds to changing design practice, as the architecture profession faces new challenges and professional expectations relating to sustainability, including the social aspects of how buildings make people feel. These challenges have led the team to develop and adopt new workflows, methods, and ways of representing their work. For example, they integrate PhD researchers into their team. A recent social psychology doctoral student worked on documenting and analyzing how people used some of the buildings the office designed, creating a number of postoccupancy evaluations relating to social interactions in everyday spaces (Sylvest, 2018). In these studies (Figures 32.1 and 32.2), the firm's finished buildings were compared with their design intentions. Findings focused on the social interactions that take place within buildings. For example, the 3XN is known for designing grand staircases; they have dubbed these "lazy staircases" and they are normally daylit, in an atrium, wider than usual, and encourage people to climb up (rather than take a faster elevator) to be social and have views up and through the building (3XN, 2010). For example, in their Ørestad College project, the main staircase encourages students to chat together and becomes important for social mixing, and it is designed so that people can gather around the atrium on various floors and see people walking up and down between floors. After it was built, GXN conducted formal evaluations and observations of this (see Figures 32.1 and 32.2) to understand how they worked and then used their findings as feedback for future designs.

This work draws on the history of socially focused Danish design, including the work of urban designer and researcher Jan Gehl who runs a research driven practice that focuses on people and how we respond to design (Gehl Architects, n.d; Gehl & Svarre, 2013). Gehl Architects uses methods from environmental psychology like behavioral mapping and other observational techniques to quantify people's behavior in urban spaces. Both Gehl Architects and GXN are exploring architectural resilience without using the term, and developing their designs based on research they carry out to gain an enhanced understanding of the specific social contexts of the resilient architecture they are producing. Their work is part of a new approach to sustainable and resilient design that 3XN calls "informed design" meaning that they use data and observation to lead their work, in addition to their intuition and experience in the process of building design (GXN, 2019).

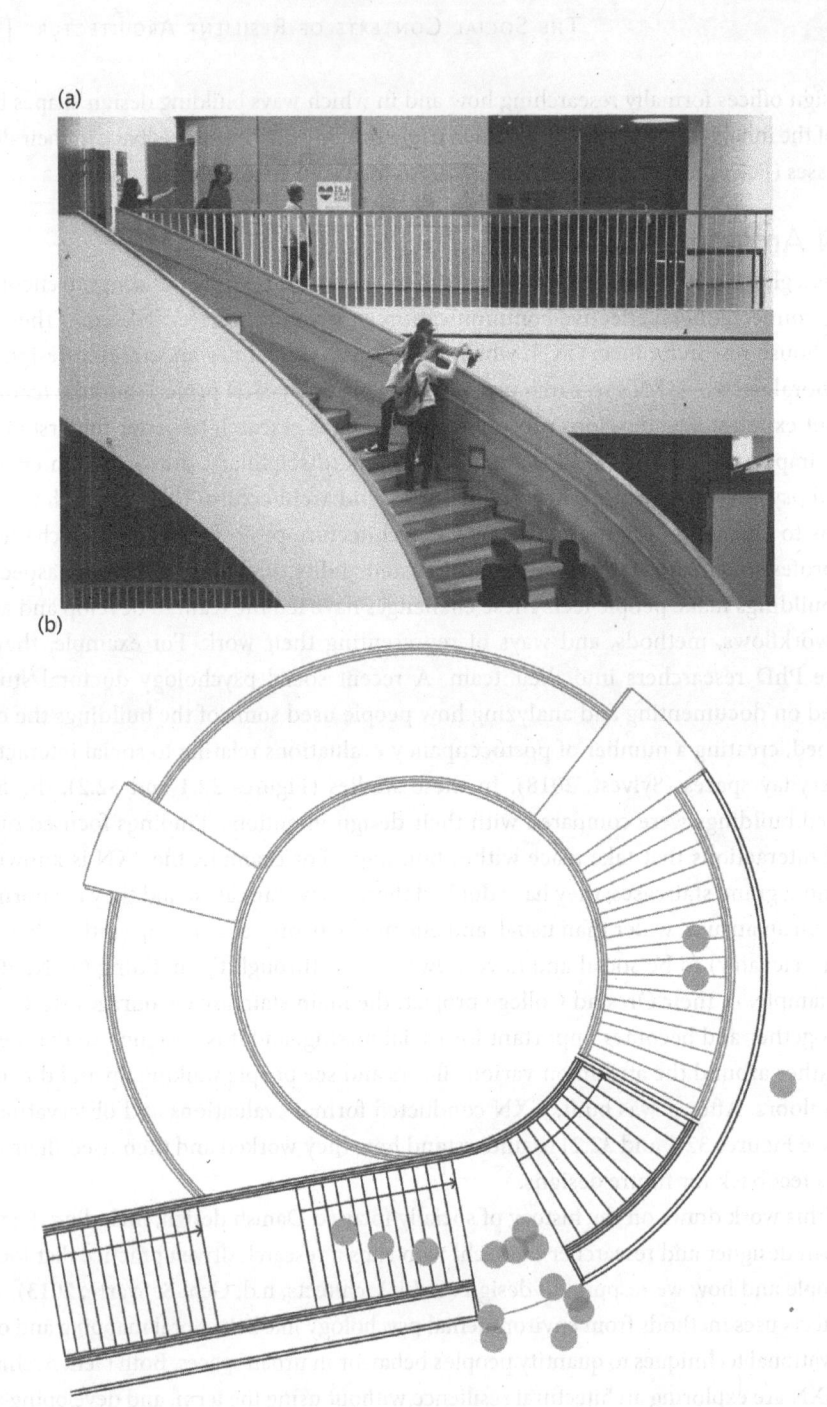

FIGURE 32.1 Behavioral Analysis of Social Uses of Staircases, Ørestad College, Copenhagen Denmark 2007 (a). GXN's behavioral design research group analyzed Ørestad College after it was built considering how people used the building (b). This diagram by researcher Mille Sylvest was part of her PhD research about the social use of spaces. She mapped people's movement around the open plan design and how the sightlines of the staircases and landings promoted social connectedness and facilitated wayfinding. Images by Mille Sylvest and GXN.

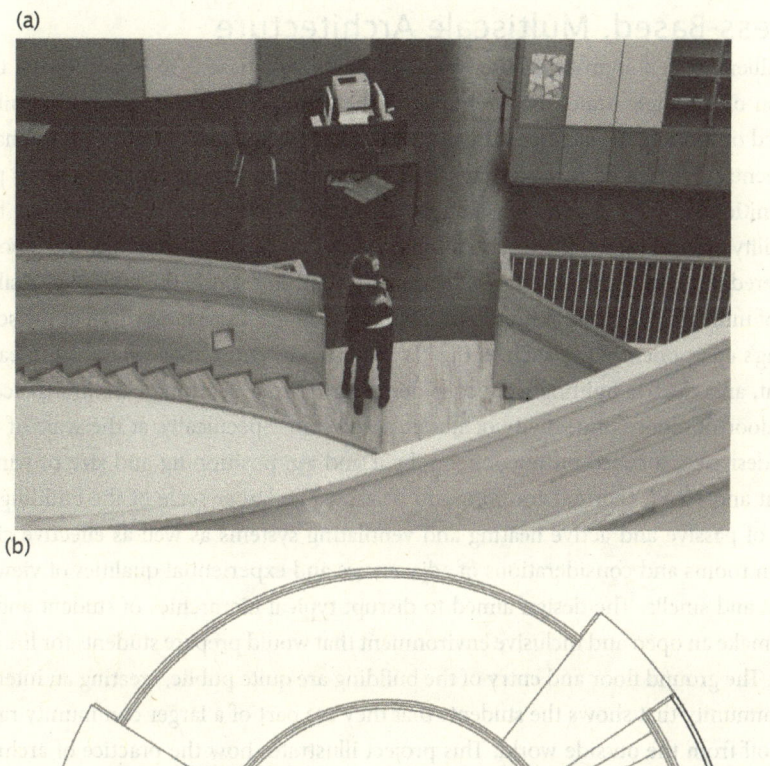

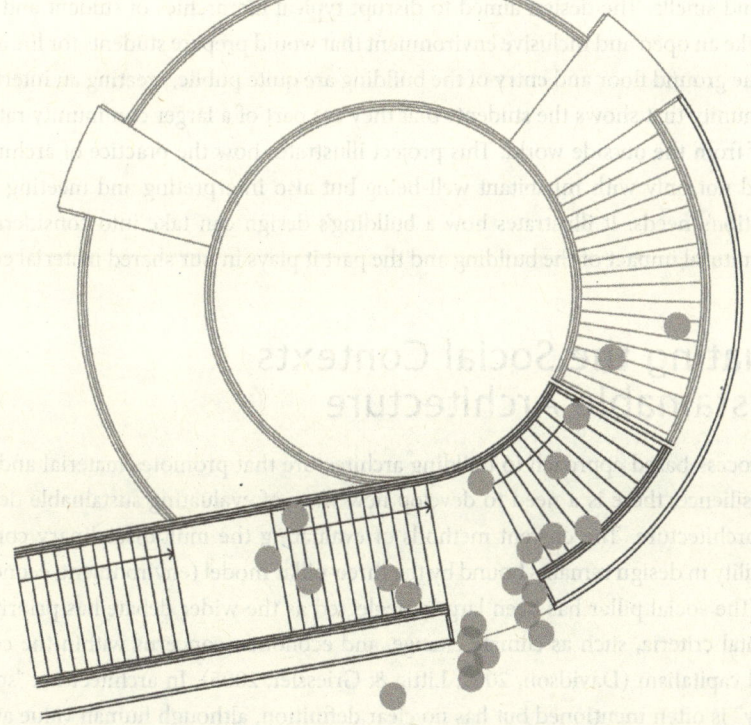

FIGURE 32.2 Behavioral Analysis of Greetings on the Staircase, Ørestad College, Copenhagen Denmark 2007 (a). This diagram (b) by GXN researcher Mille Sylvest was part of her PhD research about the social use of spaces. She mapped people's movement around the open plan design in particular she studied the nature of meetings and greetings in or around the staircase landings which she termed "social junctions." Images by Mille Sylvest and GXN.

Process-Based, Multiscale Architecture

The resilient design approaches used by 3XN are process-based. To be successful, they must function on multiple scales. For example, in the Ørestad College project, the building was arranged on the site to maximize the potential for a positive interaction with the natural environment: it is oriented toward sunlight and shade and social conditions such as proximity to amenities, views, and privacy (Poulsgaard, 2019). The relation to neighboring buildings, availability of local materials, and building systems that can use local skills and labor were all considered in the building's design and fabrication. In this sense, the building's resilience is a result of multiple decisions at multiple scales across multiple systems. Even at the scale of the building's component parts such as the classrooms and entry areas, views from each space, daylight, and electric lighting were considered for optimal learning conditions, accessibility and indoor-outdoor connectivity of students and staff. Specifically, at the scale of the classroom, designers focused on maximizing light and air, positioning and size of windows for daylight and views, thermal comfort, and privacy. The larger scale of the building required design of passive and active heating and ventilating systems as well as effective circulation between rooms and considerations of adjacencies and experiential qualities of views, sound, privacy, and smells. The design aimed to disrupt typical hierarchies of student and teachers and to make an open and inclusive environment that would prepare students for life after high school. The ground floor and entry of the building are quite public, creating an interface with the community that shows the students that they are part of a larger community rather than sealed off from the outside world. This project illustrates how the practice of architecture is concerned not only with inhabitant well-being but also interpreting and meeting a client's or institution's needs. It illustrates how a building's design can take into consideration the broader cultural impact of the building and the part it plays in our shared material culture.

Evaluating the Social Contexts in Sustainable Architecture

In this process-based approach to building architecture that promotes material and psychological resilience, there is a need to develop new ways of evaluating sustainable design and resilient architecture. The current methods of evaluating the multidisciplinary concepts of sustainability in design remains bound by the three-pillar model (environment, economy, and society). The social pillar has been largely neglected as the wider debate has prioritized environmental criteria, such as climate change, and economic concerns within the context of industrial capitalism (Davidson, 2009; Littig & Griessler, 2005). In architecture, "social sustainability" is often mentioned but has no clear definition, although human value and needs are the foundation for what the phrase means in the built environment. In architecture, practitioners and theorists work on the assumption that the design of spaces explicitly shapes the well-being and even the behaviors of people that use them (Peters, 2013). This is not necessarily easy to prove outside of the discipline, but it is nevertheless a guiding principle in theory and in practice. For example, architects do not typically require evidence that cluttered or unhygienic environments make us uncomfortable or that spacious, sunlit, varied environments put us at ease. Architects assume that we are able to impact the moods, desires, and experiences of people that inhabit the spaces we design. This is well studied in the theoretical framework of phenomenology in the classic works of Norberg-Schulz (1966) and Bachelard (1964). Since architectural design cannot take into consideration the desires of every inhabitant personally, architects intuitively assume there are certain universal needs that all people have and design for those. Culturally and professionally, however, there is little agreement about what these needs are and therefore social sustainability in architecture remains a major challenge.

Globally, the most used green building certification system is the Leadership in Energy and Environmental Design (LEED) designation. This program has been at the forefront of granting recognition for "green" buildings designed with energy conservation in mind since its development in 1993 (U.S. Green Building Council, n.d.). LEED is a points-based system whereby a candidate building or neighborhood is assessed based on its merits across a series of broad categories with points assigned based on a structure's performance in seven distinct sustainable parameters relating to:

1. *Sustainable sites*: focusing on site selection and site attributes and associated infrastructure.
2. *Water efficiency*: centered on retention and conservation measures.
3. *Energy and atmosphere*: rewarding minimization of energy consumption and on building commissioning protocols.
4. *Materials and resources*: focused on ecologic construction materiality practices and building longevity.
5. *Indoor environmental quality*: centered on air quality monitoring and non-toxic material palettes, thermal comfort and daylighting/view amenity
6. *Innovation and design process*: addressing ecologically attuned design strategies
7. *Regional priority*: relating to the building's location and context.

Scores for the lowest certification (certified) are often criticized as supporting initiatives that are easy to achieve and not very impactful, such as adding bike racks or educational displays (Frangos, 2005). This is in contrast to the highest certification (platinum), which demands that a building score extremely well in all categories. Additionally, since LEED certification is based on a design's expected energy use before it is built, rather than actual measured building performance, there have been many cases where LEED buildings do not perform any better than noncertified buildings (Newsham, Mancini, & Birt, 2009).

The first building certification system to focus on human well-being and experience was introduced in 2013. As previously mentioned, the WELL Building standard aims to measure "how design, operations and behaviors within the places where we live, work, learn and play can be optimized to advance human health and well-being" (International WELL Building Institute, n.d.). WELL is the only building certification system that does not measure energy use. It too awards points in seven categories though these differ significantly from those assessed by the LEED system and are more human-centered. They include:

1. *Air*: requiring buildings to promote clean air and reduce sources of air pollution.
2. *Water:* promoting safe and clean water through the implementation of proper filtration techniques and regular testing.

3. *Nutrition:* making available fresh, wholesome foods, limiting unhealthy ingredients and designs that encourage better eating habits and food culture.
4. *Light:* design thresholds that minimize disruption to the body's circadian system, enhance productivity, support good sleep, and provide appropriate visual acuity.
5. *Fitness:* integrating physical activity into everyday life by providing opportunities and support for an active lifestyle and discouraging sedentary behaviors.
6. *Comfort:* rewarding designs that are distraction-free, productive, and comfortable indoor environments.
7. *Mind:* designs that optimize cognitive and emotional health through technology, design strategies, and assistance programs to employees.

Rating systems like LEED have raised awareness of green buildings among clients and professionals, and now WELL is starting to shift the focus to people and how buildings can make people feel more productive and happier. Unlike LEED, WELL certified buildings must be evaluated after they are built and occupied for a period of time so they use actual performance data for aspects such as energy use, lighting levels, and air quality, and performance data must be submitted to the International WELL Building Institute to maintain their WELL certification. However, like all rating systems, on their own certification systems like these cannot create more ecological buildings. Designers, clients, and the wider community need to keep a focus on harder to measure priorities such as integrating renewable energy, improving design quality, and creating inspiring buildings and places that people want to maintain and keep over time. Not only the measurement tools but also the language and cultural aspects of nature and culture need to shift in response to architectural design imperatives.

Representative of this shift, *superarchitecture* is a term describing designs that do more than minimize harm (Peters, 2017). These designs form a special category of regenerative buildings that offer measurable and integrated positive co-benefits for environmental sustainability and human health and well-being. Superarchitecture describes building strategies that work at multiple scales, using multifunctional strategies for our physical environment and improving health. A related term is *net zero building*, defined by the World Green Building Council as a high performance building that is entirely powered by renewable energy either from the site or near it (World Green Building Council, n.d.). The even more ambitious concept, *net positive building*, is also beginning to be used although there are very few if any built examples (Cole, 2015). Net positive, like superarchitecture, is focused on improving the existing environment and doing more than minimizing harm and actually adding value to the environment (Cole & Fedoruk, 2015). Certification programs generally lag behind the new concepts and theories and LEED overwhelmingly remains the most well used building certification standard. Newer initiatives such as Passive House, which focuses on ultra-low energy strategies that minimize the need for heating and cooling (Passive House Institute, n.d.), Living Building Challenge, the most rigorous environmentally focused building performance metric that evaluates the regenerative potential of a building and site to restore its environment (International Living Future Institute, n.d.), and Active House, a building standard that focuses on measurable design strategies for occupant comfort, daylight and air strategies (Active House Alliance, n.d.). This latter program is the focus on the following detailed case study.

Active House

The Active House standard (Active House Alliance, n.d.) evaluates buildings in three main categories:

1. *Energy*: measuring how a building integrates renewable energy to positively contribute to the energy balance of the building.
2. *Indoor climate*: measuring how the building creates a healthier and more comfortable life for occupants.
3. *Environment*: measuring the positive impact on the environment

There have been several educational and housing projects built in the VELUX Model Homes initiative as prototypes for highly performing buildings (VELUX, n.d.). This program, led by VELUX, a Danish window and skylight manufacturer with an in-house research team, has seen the design and construction of a several single-family houses designed to connect environmental design and wellness in specific architectural ways. The design of these buildings has included the use of digital simulation tools to predict aspects of environmental performance including energy and daylight. A recent example in this program, is a suburban home in Toronto, Canada designed by local architects Superkul. The Active House Centennial Park became Canada's first certified Active House and used environmental simulation tools to be able to predict qualities of light and energy use in the building during design stage. The design focuses on natural daylight and ventilation for optimal indoor quality in ways that promotes sustainability and the well-being of inhabitants (Figure 32.3

FIGURE 32.3 The benefits of extra daylight in the home. Active House Centennial Park, Toronto Canada, 2016. Photograph: Eyecapture—Igor Yu.

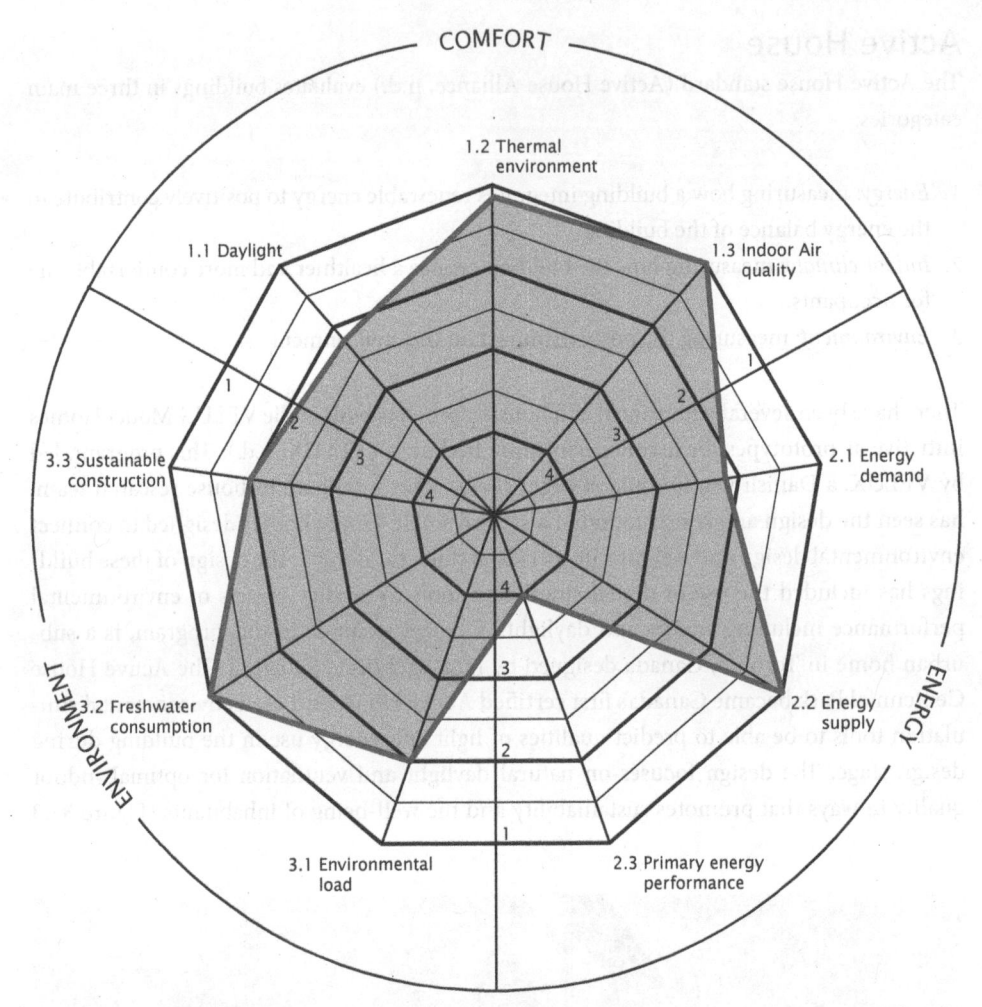

FIGURE 32.4 Active House Metric, Centennial Park Active House, 2016. The Active House metric focuses on comfort, environment, and energy, producing a score for how the building performs. This diagram shows the relationships and tradeoffs between the different parameters such as thermal comfort and energy use. Image courtesy Velux.

and 32.4). The large house has operable triple-paned windows and programmable skylights, as well as a Tesla Powerwall rechargeable lithium-ion battery system for the home that pulls electricity from its energy provider (in this case a provider whose grid is 100% renewable) during off-peak hours. From the outside, it has a similar size and shape as its neighbors, but on the inside, it is surprisingly bright with 11 skylights and the living room is two stories high, not like a typical suburban home (Active House Centennial Park, building visit, April 25, 2017; Great Gulf, n.d.a). Superkul incorporated details like an articulated side wall with windows to bring daylight into the house's middle spaces and to give the living room a sense of having a small courtyard facing the neighbor's blank side wall. After it was completed in 2016, a VELUX employee and his family moved into the house to document their experiences and blog about how it feels to live in the house and its psychological impact on their comfort and well-being as well as how easy the technologies that operate the house are to use (Great Gulf, n.d.b).

The Social Benefits of Climate-Adapted Neighborhoods

The intersections between the social and ecological aspects of resilient design have been explored at a neighborhood scale in a series of climate adaptations in Denmark. These are a series of road and public space renovations that address rising sea levels and urban flooding and are designed to encourage social and nature-based interactions among residents. The projects began in response to a serious flood event that occurred in July 2011, when more than 150 mm of rain fell in Copenhagen in only two hours causing some areas of the city to be up to a meter under water (Strickland & Divall, 2015). Many residents experienced serious flooding in their homes and damage to roads and parks, as the water overwhelmed the sewer system. Causing more than €800 million in insurance claims, with a total socio-economic loss estimated to be more than double this figure (Strickland & Divall, 2015), this particular flooding event became a catalyst for political and economic support for the development of an ambitious climate adaptation strategy for the city. Shortly after, Copenhagen adopted the Climate Adaptation Plan (City of Copenhagen, 2011) and then a Cloudburst Management Plan (City of Copenhagen, 2012), which outlined specific urban renovation projects. Over the next 10 to 20 years, 300 neighborhood design transformations will be implemented around the city to respond to local needs and current and projected flood events (City of Copenhagen, 2012; Saaby & Bauman, 2019). The mandate of the program is to improve resident quality of life using these renovations and to better connect people to each other and to nature, not solely to stop buildings and streets from flooding. The plan details that Copenhageners must be able to deal with a one-meter sea level rise over the next 100 years, and these urban design changes should help people emotionally and practically cope with the future reality of a climate changed city.

Danish office Tredje Natur was part of the team that designed the one square kilometer neighborhood masterplan for the first Climate Neighborhood in 2012 (Tredje Natur, 2015). Among its key principles, the masterplan reclaims 20% of the current road area for pedestrians, bikes, and parks, by optimizing the road infrastructure and parking lots (SLA & Ramboll, 2016). The masterplan introduces bicycle paths that act as storm water channels, water towers, green roofs, urban gardens, green houses, and canals that carry water out from the neighborhood to the harbor. These strategies were designed to simultaneously give rise to greater biological diversity in the city. Tredje Natur is known for their multiscale approach to resilience, and their ideas extended beyond neighborhood regeneration. For example, their "Climate Tile" is a rainwater management strategy but also a tactile and modular material system that improves the sidewalks in the city (Tredje Natur, 2014). The tile is designed to be used when sidewalks are demolished for infrastructure works or to widen the sidewalk. The tiles are permeable, modular, sidewalk pavers that can be installed in such a way that they drain excess rainwater to street trees and to the soil beneath for absorption.

FIGURE 32.5 Rendering of the climate adaptation of Sankt Kjelds Square and Bryggervangen in rainy weather, Copenhagen, Denmark, 2017. The climate adaptation by SLA completed in 2019 and is designed to improve people's connection to nature and address the storm water and rising sea levels in Copenhagen. This image shows the vision of the project in rainy weather. Rendering courtesy SLA.

Climate Adapted Renovation of Sankt Kjelds Square and Bryggervangen Road by SLA Architects

The first completed climate adapted neighborhood in Copenhagen focused on the redevelopment of a public square and main road by SLA architects. Finished in early 2019, the design integrated trees, plants, walking paths, and green space into this streetscape, previously dominated by hard, nonporous surfaces and a very wide circular roundabout (City of Copenhagen, 2012). The paved roads for cars was narrowed and reduced in size, and the area now has a variety of pedestrian spaces and planted areas. There 586 new trees, shrubs, and plants providing a surface for absorbing rainwater, reducing flooding, and greatly enhancing the area's natural environment. The design encourages residents to spend more time outside and to engage with nature with areas for outdoor dining, benches between the trees, and large tree trunks that children can play on and climb. During an extreme cloudburst, rainwater will be directed to the permeable areas called "rain beds" where it will slowly be absorbed and sink or drain further away to the Copenhagen harbor via a cloudburst line (Figure 32.5). The renovation is specifically designed to offer neighborhood amenities during sunny weather as well (Figure 32.6). Studies of neighborhood greenspace show that initiatives incorporating trees not only promote biodiversity, but they also positively impact people's sense of health and well-being, and quality of life for residents (Kardan et al., 2015).

Climate Adapted Renovation of Hans Tavsens Park and Korsgade, SLA Architects

The newest climate adaptation neighborhood by SLA Architects incorporates a public park and street renovation and will start construction in late 2021. The designers worked closely

FIGURE 32.6 Rendering of the climate adaptation of Sankt Kjelds Square and Bryggervangen in sunny weather, Copenhagen, Denmark, 2017. The climate adaptation by SLA completed in 2019 reduces the area of paved roads for cars and provides more shared space for neighbors. This image shows the vision of the project in dry weather. Rendering courtesy SLA.

with local residents to understand specific local needs to maximize the social and ecological improvements (SLA & Ramboll, 2016.). There will be an improvement to the dimensions and materials of the sidewalks and pedestrian areas along Korsgade street while making the built environment more resilient to sudden weather events. As with the earlier project, the redesigned street has been narrowed to reduce space for cars and has been redesigned with permeable paving materials and patterns. The street will have vegetation to absorb excess rainwater, and channels of irrigation to force the water away from the local site and into the lake. With fewer hard impermeable surfaces, city noise will be dampened, the new greenery improves biophilia, and bird and pollinators will be attracted to the site (SLA & City of Copenhagen, 2016). Combined with environmental and ecological benefits, there are a number of social sustainability features that incorporate active design principles, including new bike lanes and multifunctional minigardens to get people outside playing, tending to nature, and walking along the new streetscape (Peters, 2017). The new Hans Tavsens Park will function as a large rainwater catchment basin during storm events creating a sculptural circular pool. The pool will become a local landmark and symbol for the park and a way of making water a part of the city.

Locally Specific Approaches to Resilient Design

In each of the climate adaptation projects in Copenhagen, the focus has been on multifunctional design features that have many benefits. These projects illustrate how resilient architecture can be a process that is influenced by people's expectations and how people use buildings, not an end goal with clear boundary conditions. For example, in the areas of Copenhagen that were just described, the context of climate change and extreme weather is a focus but the designers have taken into account that water imposes varied environmental challenges (and opportunities) throughout the year. Not just flash flooding but a number of unusual weather events are impacting Copenhagen, including storm surges, blizzards, and summer dry spells. A strong feature of the urban interventions is that rather than a singular climate change vision for the city, there has been a neighborhood scale approach that has been carefully planned by Tredje Natur, with numerous designs created by different design teams (the two examples discussed here are by SLA Architects, but future design competitions have been won by different designers). Although the process of arriving at climate adaptation initiatives can and should be repeated elsewhere, the specific design solutions employed are not resilience promoting strategies that should necessarily be replicated around the world in other social or ecological contexts. The nature-based urban interventions proposed for a number of resilient neighborhoods in Copenhagen are examples of how some design studios are rethinking resilient design to maximize the social impacts of resilient design strategies.

Conclusion

Since the qualities of buildings play such an important role in how we live, there is potential to better relate to, and incorporate, concepts of resilience. As shown, terms like *resilience* and *sustainability* are often used interchangeably in architecture but in the push for new buildings to reduce their impact on the natural world, the human and social dimensions, and potential benefits of buildings are often neglected. While reducing negative impact is critical, given that buildings and their operations contribute nearly half of all harmful greenhouse gas emissions and that buildings are intensive users of nonrenewable energy and resources especially during their operational phases (International Energy Agency, n.d.), research has shown that overwhelmingly it is the operation of buildings—how, when, in which ways they are used, and by whom—that most affects the environmental performance and impacts of buildings on people and natural environments (Janda, 2011). The culture of how we use buildings and what we expect from them needs to shift to make real progress if we are to make our cities, and ourselves, more resilient. Multifunctional resilience initiatives that focus on positive co-benefits for the environment and people can lead to better collaboration from stakeholders and increased public support. The example of the Copenhagen Cloudburst program, and others, illustrate some of these challenges. There is an urgent need for deeper studies and analysis of built examples of resilient architecture. By better connecting the term *resilience* to concepts in other fields and better aligning the priorities of people to buildings, the term *resilience* will be made more relevant and adaptable to architectural design.

Key Messages

1. The social roles of buildings and how they influence our well-being are largely overlooked—although these potentially resiliency-promoting aspects would be particularly important to people in the event of a crisis. People spend more than 90% of our time indoors and the qualities of buildings and landscapes impact our moods, well-being, social experiences, and how we behave.

2. Designers have the potential to better relate to, and incorporate, concepts of resilience. This means finding better ways of evaluating the success of buildings, and challenging the narrow existing metrics of building performance. New metrics such as Active House and WELL are focusing on people and our experiences.
3. Design features for resilient buildings and human resilience are often the same, and are most effective when considered together. Multifunctional resilient design initiatives that focus on positive co-benefits for the environment and people can lead to better collaboration from stakeholders and increased public support.
4. There are some examples of forward thinking architects that are incorporating behavioral design in their work. Multidisciplinary researchers at GXN in Denmark have a behavioral design research cluster in their office that studies how people use buildings and how to design environments that promote social interactions and well-being.
5. A series of climate adaptation renovations in neighborhoods in Copenhagen Denmark offer a multifunctional approach to resilient design, addressing neighborhood flooding by simultaneously improving the qualities of public spaces and better connecting people to nature.

References

100 Resilient Cities. (2019). *Resilient cities, resilient lives: Learning from the 100RC network*. The Rockefeller Foundation. Retrieved from http://www.100resilientcities.org/wp-content/uploads/2019/07/100RC-Report-Capstone-PDF.pdf

3XN. (2010). *Mind your behavior: How architecture shapes behavior*. Copenhagen, Denmark: Actar.

Active House Alliance. (n.d.). *Active House*. Retrieved from https://www.activehouse.info/

Alberti, M., & Marzluff, J. M. (2004). Ecological resilience in urban ecosystems: Linking urban patterns to human and ecological functions. *Urban Ecosystems, 7*(3), 241. doi:10.1023/B:UECO.0000044038.90173.c6

Allen, J. G., MacNaughton, P., Satish, U., Santanam, S., Vallarino, J., & Spengler, J. D. (2016). Associations of cognitive function scores with carbon dioxide, ventilation, and volatile organic compound exposures in office workers: A controlled exposure study of green and conventional office environments. *Environmental Health Perspectives, 124*(6), 805–812. doi:10.1289/ehp.1510037

American Institute of Architects. (n.d.). *AIA's design and health initiative*. Retrieved from http://new.aia.org/pages/3461-aias-design-and-health-initiative

Bachelard, G. (1964). *Poetics of space*. New York, NY: Orion Press.

Boone, C. G. (2013). Social dynamics and sustainable urban design. In S. T. A. Pickett, M. L. Cadenasso, & B. McGrath (Eds.), *Resilience in ecology and urban design: Linking theory and practice for sustainable cities* (pp. 47–61). Heidelberg, Germany: Springer Nature.

Burns, P., & Coxon, J. (2016). *Boiler on prescription trial: Closing report*. Gentoo Group. Retrieved from https://www.housinglin.org.uk/_assets/Resources/Housing/Research_evaluation/boiler-on-prescription-closing-report.pdf

City of Copenhagen. (2011). *Copenhagen climate adaptation plan*. Copenhagen, Denmark. Retrieved from https://en.klimatilpasning.dk/media/568851/copenhagen_adaption_plan.pdf

City of Copenhagen. (2012). *Cloudburst management plan*. Copenhagen, Denmark. Retrieved from https://en.klimatilpasning.dk/media/665626/cph_-_cloudburst_management_plan.pdf

Coaffee, J. (2008). Risk, resilience, and environmentally sustainable cities. *Energy, 36*(12), 4633–4638. doi:10.1016/j.enpol.2008.09.048

Cole, R. J. (2015). Net-zero and net-positive design; A question of value. *Building Research & Information, 43*(1), 1–6. doi:10.1080/09613218.2015.961046

Cole, R. J., & Fedoruk, L. (2015). Shifting from net-zero to net-positive energy buildings. *Building Research & Information, 43*(1), 111–120. doi:10.1080/09613218.2014.950452

Coleman, S., Touchie, M. F., Robinson, J. B., & Peters, T. (2018). Rethinking performance gaps: A regenerative sustainability approach to built environment performance assessment. *Sustainability, 10*(12), 4829. doi:10.3390/su10124829

Davidson, M. (2009). Social sustainability: A potential for politics? *Local Environment, 14*(7), 607–619. doi:10.1080/13549830903089291

De Carli, B. (2019). Micro-resilience and justice in São Paulo. In K. Trogal, I. Bauman, R. Lawrence, & D. Petrescu (Eds.), *Architecture and resilience: Interdisciplinary dialogues* (pp. 88–103). Abingdon, UK: Routledge.

French, S., Wood, L., Foster, S. A., Giles-Corti, B., Frank, L., & Learnihan, V. (2013). Sense of community and its association with the neighborhood built environment. *Environment and Behavior, 46*(6), 677–697. doi:10.1177/0013916512469098

Frangos, A. (2005, October). Is it too easy being green? Eco-friendly certification is big with builders, tenants; critics see a "broken" system. *The Wall Street Journal*. Retrieved from https://www.wsj.com/articles/SB112967950603172567

Gehl Architects. (n.d.). *Gehl Architects*. Retrieved from https://gehlpeople.com/

Gehl, J., & Svarre, B. (2013). *How to study public life*. Washington, DC: Island Press.

Great Gulf. (n.d.a). *Active house centennial park*. Retrieved from https://greatgulf.com/activehouse/

Great Gulf. (n.d.b). *Meet the Ibbotsons* [Blog]. Retrieved from https://greatgulf.com/activehouse/the-family/

GXN. (n.d.). *GXN*. Retrieved from https://gxn.3xn.com

GXN. (2019). *Digital design*. Retrieved from https://gxn.3xn.com/project/digital-design

Holling, C. S. (1973). Resilience and stability of ecological systems. *Annual Review of Ecology and Systematics, 4*, 1–23. doi:10.1146/annurev.es.04.110173.000245

Huisman, E. R. C. M., Morales, E., van Hoof, J., & Kort, H. S. M. (2012). Healing environment: A review of the impact of physical environmental factors on users. *Building and Environment, 58*, 70–80. doi:10.1016/j.buildenv.2012.06.016

International Energy Agency. (n.d.). *Energy efficiency: Buildings* [Report]. Retrieved from https://www.iea.org/topics/energyefficiency/buildings/

International Living Future Institute. (n.d.). *Living building challenge*. Retrieved from https://living-future.org/lbc/

International WELL Building Institute. (n.d.). *WELL building standard version 1.0*. Retrieved from https://www.wellcertified.com/

Janda, K. B. (2011). Buildings don't use energy: People do. *Architectural Science Review, 54*(1), 15–22. doi:10.3763/asre.2009.0050

Kardan, O., Gozdyra, P., Misic, B., Moola, F., Palmer, L. J., Paus, T., & Berman, M. G. (2015). Neighborhood greenspace and health in a large urban center. *Scientific Reports, 5*, 11610. doi:10.1038/srep11610

Kellert, S. R., Heerwagen, J. H., & Mador, M. L. (2008). *Biophilic design: The theory, science, and practice of bringing buildings to life*. Hoboken, NJ: John Wiley.

Kellert, S. R., & Wilson, E. O. (1984) *The biophilia hypothesis*. Washington, DC: Island Press.

Kaplan, S. (1995). The restorative benefits of nature: Toward an integrative framework. *Journal of Environmental Psychology, 15*(3), 169–182. doi:10.1016/0272-4944(95)90001-2

Klepeis, N. E., Nelson, W. C., Ott, W. R., Robinson, J. P., Tsang, A. M., Switzer, P. . . . Engelmann, W. H. (2001) The National Human Activity Pattern Survey (NHAPS): A resource for assessing exposure to environmental pollutants. *Journal of Exposure Science and Environmental Epidemiology, 11*(3), 231–252. doi:10.1038/sj.jea.7500165

Leichenko, R. (2011). Climate change and urban resilience. *Current Opinion in Environmental Sustainability, 3*(3), 164–168. doi:10.1016/j.cosust.2010.12.014

Littig, B., & Griessler, E. (2005). Social sustainability: A catchword between political pragmatism and social theory. *International Journal of Sustainable Development, 8*(1–2), 65–79. doi:10.1504/IJSD.2005.007375

Lundin, S. (2015). In search of the happy balance—Intuition and evidence. *HERD: Health Environments Research & Design Journal, 8*(2), 123–126. doi:10.1177/1937586714567646

MacNaughton, P., Satish, U., Laurent, J. G. C., Flanigan, S., Vallarino, J., Coull, B., . . . Allen, J. G. (2017). The impact of working in a green certified building on cognitive function and health. *Building and Environment, 114*, 178–186. doi:10.1016/j.buildenv.2016.11.041

Marquardt, G. (2011). Wayfinding for people with dementia: A review of the role of architectural design. *HERD: Health Environments Research & Design Journal, 4*(2), 75–90. doi:10.1177/193758671100400207

National Institute of Building Sciences. (2018). *Whole building design guide: Building resilience.* Retrieved from http://www.wbdg.org/resources/building-resiliency

Newsham, G. R., Mancini, S., & Birt, B. J. (2009). Do LEED-certified buildings save energy? Yes, but ... *Energy & Buildings, 41*(8), 897–905. doi:10.1016/j.enbuild.2009.03.014

Norberg-Schulz, C. (1966). *Intentions in architecture.* Cambridge, MA: MIT Press.

Passive House Institute. (n.d). *Passive House.* Retrieved from https://passivehouse.com

Peters, T. (2013). Architecture shapes behavior [Monograph]. 3XN Architects. Copenhagen, Denmark: Archilife.

Peters, T. (2017). Superarchitecture: Building for better health. *Architectural Design, 87*(2), 24–31. doi:10.1002/ad.2149

Peters, T. (2018). Data buildings: Sensor feedback in sustainable design workflows. *Architectural Design, 88*(1), 92–101. doi:10.1002/ad.2263

Poulsgaard, K. S. (2019, May). *Wellbeing in the workplace.* Paper presented at Rockwool Thought Leadership Series, Toronto, ON.

Resilient Design Institute. (n.d.). *What is resilience?* Retrieved from https://www.resilientdesign.org/what-is-resilience/

Saaby, T., & Bauman, I. (2019). From city policy to the neighborhood: An interview with Tina Saaby. In K. Trogal, I. Bauman, R. Lawrence, & D. Petrescu (Eds.), *Architecture and resilience: Interdisciplinary dialogues* (p. 251). Abingdon, UK: Routledge.

SLA, & City of Copenhagen. (2016). *Climate adaptation and urban nature: Development catalogue.* Copenhagen, Denmark: SLA Architects. Retrieved from https://issuu.com/sla_architects/docs/bynatur_booklet_uk_small

SLA, & Ramboll. (2016). *Climate adaptation Copenhagen: The soul of Nørrebro.* Retrieved from https://sla.dk/files/2914/9449/3217/SLA_Ramboll_HansTavsensPark_UK.pdf

Stiller, A., Salm, F., Bischoff, P., & Gastmeier, P. (2016). Relationship between hospital ward design and healthcare-associated infection rates: A systematic review and meta-analysis. *Antimicrobial Resistance and Infection Control, 5,* 51. doi:10.1186/s13756-016-0152-1

Strickland, L., & Divall, S. (2015, June). Cloudbursts: What can we learn from Copenhagen? *Envirotecmagazine.* Retrieved from https://envirotecmagazine.com/2015/06/25/cloudbursts-what-can-we-learn-from-copenhagen/

Summers, T. A., & Hebert, P. R. (2001). Shedding some light on store atmospherics: Influence of illumination on consumer behavior. *Journal of Business Research, 54*(2), 145–150. doi:10.1016/S0148-2963(99)00082-X

Sylvest, M. (2018). *Situated social aspects of everyday life in the built environment* (Doctoral dissertation). Roskilde University, Denmark.

Tredje Natur. (2014). *Climate tile.* Retrieved from https://www.tredjenatur.dk/en/portfolio/climatetile/

Tredje Natur. (2015). *Green climate adaptation.* Retrieved from https://www.tredjenatur.dk/en/portfolio/green-climate-adaption/

Trogal, K., Bauman, I., Lawrence, R., & Petrescu, D. (2019). Introduction. In K. Trogal, I. Bauman, R. Lawrence, & D. Petrescu (Eds.), *Architecture and resilience: Interdisciplinary dialogues* (pp. 1–14). Abingdon, UK: Routledge.

Ulrich, R. S. (1991). Effects of interior design on wellness: Theory and recent scientific research. *Journal of Health Care Interior Design, 3,* 97–109.

United States Green Building Council. (n.d.). *Leadership in energy and environmental design.* Retrieved from https://new.usgbc.org/leed

VELUX. (n.d.). *Demo buildings.* Retrieved from https://www.velux.com/innovation/demo-buildings

Wilson, A. (2005). Passive survivability. *Building Green, 14*(12), 2–3. Retrieved from https://www.buildinggreen.com/op-ed/passive-survivability

World Commission on Environment and Development. (1987). *Our common future.* Oxford, UK: Oxford University Press.

World Green Building Council. (n.d.). *What is net-zero?* Retrieved from https://www.worldgbc.org/advancing-net-zero/what-net-zero

33
Resilience in Postdisaster Reconstruction of Human Settlement

An Architectural Perspective

Haorui Wu

Introduction

Diverse extreme events, varying from earthquakes to traffic accidents and mass shootings, have been taking place in every corner of society, causing catastrophic effects on human settlement and its inhabitants' overall well-being. Generally, there are three types of hazards: natural hazard, technical hazard, and terrorist attacks or other acts of intentional violence (Centre for Research on the Epidemiology of Disasters, 2009). Natural hazards are "natural processes or phenomena that may cause loss of life, injury or other health impacts, property damage, loss of livelihoods and services, social and economic disruption, or environmental damage," including massive forced displacement of people, extreme temperatures, drought, and epidemics (United Nations, 2019, para. 9). The United Nations International Strategy for Disaster Reduction defines technological hazards are "originating from technological or industrial conditions" that "may cause health impacts, property damage, loss of livelihoods," including chemical spills, transportation accidents, and industrial pollution (United Nations, 2009, p. 29).

Despite these definitions, some social science scholars suggest that "there is no such thing as a natural disaster" (Smith, 2006, para. 1). When a hazard devastates a human community, the societal characteristics, such as vulnerability, social status, and economic development, collectively contribute to the catastrophic impact of the adverse event, dramatically increasing casualties, increasing economic loss, and damaging structure and infrastructure.

These outcomes turn a hazard into a disaster. Hazards are, therefore, primary triggers of disasters. Social and humanitarian factors, however, are the fundamental generators of disasters (McFarlane & Norris, 2006). Thus, all disasters are not natural processes but, rather, human-made outcomes. Disasters affect the natural, built, and social and humanitarian dimensions of human community.

Accordingly, disaster risk reduction has become an international strategy, aiming to build capacity by successfully dealing with extreme events at individual, family, community, and societal levels (United Nations International Strategy for Disaster Reduction, 2019). This capacity to anticipate, adapt, and recover from a hazard has been interpreted as resilience. Resilience has recurrently become the core structure of a series of international policies and agreements for disaster risk reduction, such as the Hyogo Framework for Action 2005–2015 (United Nations, 2005), the Sendai Framework for Disaster Risk Reduction 2015–2030 (United Nations, 2015a), and the 2030 Agenda for Sustainable Development (United Nations, 2015b). Correspondingly, almost all nations have adopted their own resilience strategies for climate change, disaster, and other world crises, aiming to achieve sustainable development goals (Partnership for Resilience and Preparedness, n.d.).

Principles of Disaster Resilience

According to Ungar (2018), resilience is a system's capacity "to anticipate, adapt, and reorganize itself under conditions of adversity in ways that promote and sustain its successful functioning" (p. 34). When this concept is applied to hazards and disaster research, resilience enables a system to prepare for, respond to, adapt, and recover from extreme events (Berke & Campanella, 2006; Cutter et al., 2008). The following two definitions are among the most commonly cited regarding disaster resilience at international and national levels:

> The ability of a system, community or society exposed to hazards to resist, absorb, accommodate, adapt to, transform and recover from the effects of a hazard in a timely and efficient manner, including through the preservation and restoration of its essential basic structures and functions through risk management (United Nations, 2016, p. 24).
>
> Disaster Resilience is the ability of countries, communities and households to manage change, by maintaining or transforming living standards in the face of shocks or stresses—such as earthquakes, drought or violent conflict—without compromising their long-term prospects. (Department for International Development, 2011, p. 6)

Based on these two definitions and other related concepts and/or contributions to disaster resilience, the following five principles are clearly observed in the writings of disaster resilience experts.

- *Principle 1*: The core competence of resilience is "to absorb disturbance" and "re-organize into a fully functioning system" (Cutter et al., 2008, p. 599). The United Nations uses the phrase "build back better" to illustrate the ideal outcomes of a resilient community's postdisaster recovery, rehabilitation, and reconstruction (United Nations International Strategy for Disaster Reduction, 2017). The key issue is "build better" rather than "build back."

- *Principle 2*: Resilience should be interpreted as a process rather than an outcome (Norris, Stevens, Pfefferbaum, Wyche, & Pfefferbaum, 2008). Resilience is adaptive rather than stable (Norris et al., 2008). The ongoing process consists of: sensing, anticipating, learning, and adapting (Park, Seager, Rao, Convertino, & Linkov, 2013).
- *Principle 3*: Disaster affects almost all socioecological environments, including the economic, built, cultural, and political aspects of society. All these dimensions are closely connected to and strongly influence one another.
- *Principle 4*: Since disaster encompasses a cycle, the postdisaster response, reconstruction, and recovery from a particular disaster is the predisaster preparedness for the next one, which is essential for communities that are geographically located in hazard-prone zones (Wu & Hou, 2019). Building resilience is an ongoing process, involving long-term engagement between the local residents and their communities.
- *Principle 5*: The process of building resilience necessitates "the principles of equity, fairness, and access to resources" (Cutter, 2016a, p. 112). Since resilience is a shared capacity within a system, building resilience does not privilege one element over another. The process of building resilience reflects and supports social equality (Tierney, 2006).

Building Disaster Resilience Requires a Collaborative Approach

Currently, resilience research in the hazards and disaster field mainly concentrates on two phases of the disaster cycle: (a) predisaster preparedness, including preventing potential risks and hazards and (b) postdisaster initiatives to reduce damages and losses (Tierney & Bruneau, 2007). These two streams strengthen two aspects of resilience: inherent capacity (during the noncrisis periods as the predisaster stage) and adaptive capacity (during the postdisaster stage; Cutter et al., 2008). As previously mentioned in Principle 4, there are rarely clear boundaries between different stages within one disaster cycle and among multidisaster events. The adaptive resilience capacity developed as a consequence of previous disaster events will be converted into the inherent capacity of systems to cope with future disasters. This ongoing dynamic process is aligned with the unique characteristics of resilience.

To achieve this pattern of early preparedness and learning from past efforts to adapt, multidisciplinary engagement has become a mainstream innovative approach in hazards and disaster research to examine, measure, and evaluate community resilience (Ellingwood et al., 2016). Although academic researchers tend to stay in their own disciplinary domains, the complexity of hazards and disasters propels them to collaborate to more deeply understand resilience. Hence, resilience becomes a boundary word to connect various disciplines. For example, the civil engineering perspective of resilience focuses on the postdisaster reconstruction of the built environment, especially physical infrastructure (e.g., buildings, transportation, power, and telecommunication), which contribute to the goal of "bouncing back" to the predisaster condition (Bruneau et al., 2003). The complexity of societal issues necessitates viewing these engineering solutions within broader social and economic processes (Peek et al., 2020). To do this, cross-disciplinary cooperation must be pursued, especially between engineers and social scientists, to comprehensively evaluate contributions of the physical environment and move toward community resilience (Hassan & Mahmoud, 2019). Fiksel (2003) argues that cross-system design that builds resilience needs to "take advantage of fundamental properties such as diversity, efficiency, adaptability, and cohesion" (p. 5330), all of which are properties of both engineered and social systems (see other chapters in this volume).

Academic researchers have been qualitatively and quantitively measuring and evaluating resilience from different disciplinary perspectives (Chang & Shinozuka, 2004; Cimellaro, Reinhorn, & Bruneau, 2010; Choi, Deshmukh, & Hastak, 2019; Linkov et al., 2013; Sina, Chang-Richards, Wilkinson, & Potangaroa, 2019). Indeed, the "systems-theoretical accident model and process" was developed to analyze system accidents to advance the resilience of engineered systems (Leveson, 2004). In the field of risk management, for example, "qualitative uncertainty assessment" and "scenario building instruments" have been applied to address uncertainty and severity of terrorism risk (Aven & Renn, 2009, p. 587). From the perspective of geography, disaster resilience is measured by "the spatial, temporal scale of resilience, and attributes of hazard-affected bodies" (Zhou et al., 2010, p. 21). To date, there is no standard monodisciplinary measurement protocol for evaluating resilience of engineered and social systems, let alone pluridisciplinary approaches that are standardized.

Research aims to guide practice as well as inform policy development and the decision-making process, especially in the hazards and disaster field (Wu & Hou, 2019). Implementing the field trip, which is a widely employed research approach in hazards and disaster research, can bring many benefits but largely depends on community-based support from local residents, agencies, and different levels of government (Tierney, 2007). In turn, community-based stakeholders, such as agencies, organizations, and institutions, may request of academic researchers to provide their community-based solutions regarding disaster and emergency management. However, political and practical guarantees need to be developed to safeguard disaster risk reduction. Simultaneously, a collaborative approach, connecting "individuals, families, communities, the private sector, faith-based organizations, nongovernment organizations, academe, and all levels of government" must be established to increase resilience at individual, family, and community levels (National Research Council, 2012, p. 28). The collaborative approach was one of the main themes in the 2019 Global Platform for Disaster Risk Reduction (GP2019, Geneva, Switzerland): *Resilience Dividend: Towards Sustainable and Inclusive Societies* (United Nations Disaster Risk Reduction, 2019). In addition to the UN's global horizontal cooperation platform, the UN encourages nations worldwide to develop a vertical collaborative approach within their countries by engaging different stakeholders to sculpt a resilient community for future generations.

Indeed, immediately after the 2015 Nepal Earthquake, the National Human Rights Commission of India (NHRC; an ethical review board) was not approving international research applications that included human subjects due to concern about the potentially coercive nature of research that might burden disaster survivors. Those research projects, which were proven to be in cooperation with National Human Rights Commission of India, co-led by Nepali organizations (including local government officials and local community leaders, especially those that came from ethnic minority groups), hired local professionals from affected communities, and developed intervention-based strategies with local community-based service agencies were, however, swiftly approved. Welton-Mitchell and James (2018), two American researchers who conducted research of mental health integrated disaster preparedness (MHIDP) during that period, highly recommended the collaborative approach:

> [T]his process of co-creation, adaptation and facilitation by local staff helps to ensure that the MHIDP intervention does not challenge or undermine existing belief systems or practices—a key consideration, not only in terms of ethical practice, but also to increase the likelihood of community acceptance. (para. 7)

Resilience in Postdisaster Human Settlement Reconstruction

Postdisaster reconstruction of the built environment is the basis for other disaster initiatives, such as the social, economic, cultural, and ecological efforts to restore a community (Wu, 2014). Architects are frequently on the front lines of these initiatives, taking leadership of the built environment reconstruction, as well as coordinating with other professionals such as urban designers, planners, landscape architects, and civil engineers (Wu & Hou, 2016).

Human Settlement

Generally, extreme events have catastrophic influence on natural and built, as well as social and human, environments (National Research Council, 1999; see Figure 33.1). The natural environment, also known as the ecological environment, comprises all living and nonliving things, in contrast to synthetic things (Johnson et al., 1997). An ecological system has its own inherent resilience capacity to cope with hazards (Holling, 1973). Environment-friendly human interventions have demonstrated positive outcomes of mediating human with ecological systems, and the potential for accelerating ecological renewal (Gunderson, 2000). For instance, cities, built on the natural environment, play an essential role in tackling climate change and disaster. Increasingly, city governments worldwide have been upgrading their spatial policies in their urban regeneration plans to increase the areas of urban ecological systems (such as green spaces, water bodies, and urban farms) within their urban land use planning (Puppim de Oliveira & Balahan, 2013). These urban ecological systems not only provide recreational space, contributing to urban residents' wellness, but also reduce air pollution and flooding risks, as well as protect biodiversity. In a very specific case that took place in the Cowanus Channel, New York City, Kate Orff, a landscape architect, bundled oysters into the river bank to clean dirty water (Orff, 2010). Her urban greenspace-based intervention aimed to "links nature and humanity for mutual benefit" (Orff, 2010, para. 1). Although

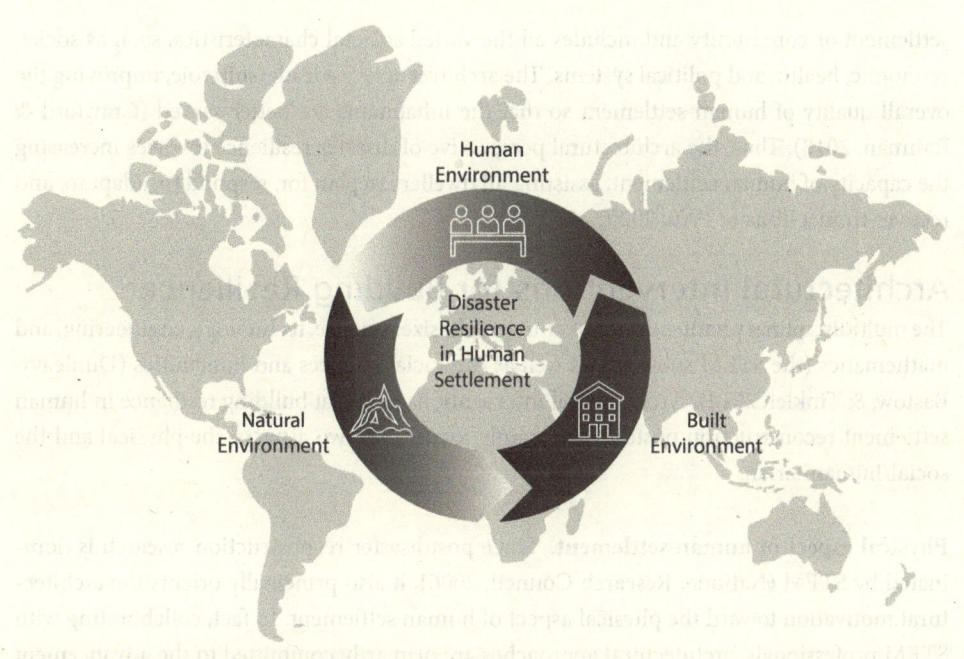

FIGURE 33.1 Disaster's influence on human settlement.

the ecological system offers a foundation for the recovery of built as well as social and human environments, none of these systems should be examined in isolation.

In the social sciences, the built environment refers to human-made physical surroundings, which create the physical foundation for human activities (Roof & Oleru, 2008). This definition is aligned with the civil engineering language of built environment, which includes structural systems (e.g., school, hospital, and recreation center) and infrastructure (e.g., water supply and drainage system, power, telecom, and road). The human–environment interplay that takes place in the built environment, such as day-to-day routines, cultural and social events, along with political and economic development, forms the social and humanitarian environment (Knight, 2015). For instance, one of public health's focuses is on health impact assessment of the built environment, especially how the built environment supports and influences inhabitants' activities as in physically active communities (The Community Guide, n.d.) to build a healthy and livable social and humanitarian environment (Centers for Disaster Control and Prevention, 2011).

Architectural intervention is one type of human–environment interplay. Hence, architects examine the living planet through two types of systems: the nonartificial one (the natural environment) and the artificial one (the built environment). Architectural approaches convert natural environment into built environments by imbedding human activities into the ecological system (Tuan, 2001). This transformational process requires balance in the design of both structures and infrastructure as well as the utilization of these structures to maintain and stimulate human activities. In other words, the architectural perception of the built environment includes dimensions from both the physical environment as well as social and human activities. This type of built environment is frequently understood as human settlement or community and includes all the varied societal characteristics, such as social, economic, health, and political systems. The architect serves a leadership role, improving the overall quality of human settlement so that the inhabitants are better served (Crawford & Rahman, 2018). Thus, the architectural perspective of disaster resilience involves increasing the capacity of human settlement, assisting all dwellers to plan for, respond to, adapt to, and recover from a disaster (Wu, 2020).

Architectural Interventions for Building Resilience

The multidisciplinary nature of architecture emphasizes science, technology, engineering, and mathematics (the STEM subjects), as well as the social sciences and humanities (Dunleavy, Bastow, & Tinkler, 2014). Architectural interventions aimed at building resilience in human settlement reconstruction postdisaster mainly focuses on two aspects: the physical and the social/humanitarian.

Physical aspect of human settlement. Since postdisaster reconstruction research is dominated by STEM (National Research Council, 2006), it also principally orients the architectural motivation toward the physical aspect of human settlement. In fact, collaborating with STEM professionals, architectural approaches are primarily committed to the advancement of the structural safety, such as improving building codes (Behnam & Ronagh, 2016), designing new structural systems and materials (Kwon & Elnashai, 2006), and protecting critical infrastructures, such as roads, power, water, and telecom systems (Ouyang, 2014). These strategies guarantee that when a disaster hits, disaster survivors' basic living requirements, such as access to water, food, and power are secured. In other words, these interventions build resilience capacity by securing disaster survivors' fundamentally physical needs.

Social and humanitarian aspects of human settlement. The social and humanitarian pillars are two critical mainstays of human settlement (UN Educational, Scientific, and Cultural Organization, 2017). During the postdisaster process, the social and humanitarian dimensions of disaster recovery must be given equal attention as the physical dimensions, which is commonly understood as social recovery (Wu, 2014). Parallel to physical reconstruction, social recovery aims to maintain and stimulate human activities in the rehabilitation of disaster survivors' social life and livelihood, so that their social wellness and overall well-being is improved by their new surroundings. Social recovery, which essentially promotes disaster survivors' resilience capacity, prepares people to respond better to the next disaster. Although STEM researchers, especially in the engineering and technology fields, have already grasped the significant lag of the postdisaster social process and have attempted to narrow the gap between physical reconstruction and social recovery by increasing cooperation among social scientists and scholars working in the natural sciences. Current political and economic forces have not given as much attention to social recovery as they have given to the rebuilding of physical structures and infrastructure (Wu, 2014).

With the onset of the 2016 European refugee crisis, Greece, especially the Greek Islands in the Aegean Sea, became the first place where the majority of refugees arrived by sea. Due to the increasingly restricted immigration policies of European Union members, the legal immigration process was dramatically delayed and the majority of these refugees had to stay on these islands for months, and even years (Vigliar, 2016). Dealing with the refugee crisis, the UNHCR (the UN Refugee Agency) cooperated with the local island governments and international organizations, such as the European Union Humanitarian Aid and Civil Protection, the Norwegian Refugee Council, and the International Organization for Migration, to provide daily meals and then engaged engineers and construction crews to build refugee camps. As time passed, the increasing violence refugees experienced pre- and postmigration propelled those sponsoring organizations to also focus on the refugees' social wellness by providing psychological support and counseling service, hiring refugees to support sponsoring organizations' daily work, operating schools, and conducting other training programs. These sponsoring organizations also coordinated volunteers with backgrounds in architecture and urban planning to collaborate with refugees to improve the refugee camps and surroundings, as not just a place to stay, but a place to live. For example, in some refugee camps on Chios Island, Greece, humanitarian workers initiated efforts to change wastelands into playgrounds, built small grocery stores and shuttlebus stations, and created gardens and farmlands. In some schools, the refuges children were invited to draw on the walls to decorate their schools.

Architectural Practice and Community Engagement

Disasters motivate disaster survivors to improve their surroundings (Cutter, 2014). Consequently, disaster survivors should participate in the design process or even the decision-making procedures related to reconstruction (Wu, 2019a). Most existing postdisaster projects are decided by politicians, governmental offices, real estate developers, and other policy and decision makers, who might not, themselves, be residents of the affected communities (Wachtendorf, Kendra, & DeYoung, 2018). Political and economic influences essentially impact and guide reconstruction. This factor, in itself, largely limits the direct input from disaster survivors (Wu, 2014).

Resilience, which is a dynamic social learning process that develops after an extreme event, is facilitated by ongoing long-term human–place interplay (Cutter, 2016b). Local residents and communities directly benefit from this learning process by profoundly understanding their surroundings, for instance, knowing what and where potential risks are and how to adapt their daily activities to avoid these risks. When a disaster happens, these place-based experiences enable the residents to take advantage of their surroundings to reach a new balance, not only of physical safety, but also social, cultural, and economic stability (Wu, 2019a).

Public interest design, a very popular current architectural approach, provides a bottom–up method that increases local residents' involvement in the design process of their own community (Abendroth & Bell, 2015). The Butaro Hospital in Rwanda is an example that reflects this human-centered and participatory approach. During the design process, the architect, Michael Murphy, lived in Butaro for over a year to understand local residents' requirements and decipher the best way to take advantage of the local ecological environment. During the construction stage, local skilled workers were hired. The whole hospital was built with local materials, and the outstanding local construction skills were also utilized (Cary

& Martin, 2012). Furthermore, during the operation of the hospital, most of the employees have come from local communities with chronic unemployment (Cary & Martin, 2012).

The architectural design not only fulfilled the building's original function by utilizing local materials and skills to harmonize with the local environment, but also provided some solutions for other societal issues, such as proving job opportunities to decrease the unemployment rate. In the postdisaster reconstruction of human settlement, architects are hopeful in the utilization of similar processes to involve local residents to cooperate with professionals to empower them with potentially vital decision-making input (Wu, 2018). This process not only achieves the goal of community empowerment by stimulating local residents' leadership (Lee, 2013), but also, more important, provides a community-driven approach when building resilience at individual, family, and community levels.

Case Studies of the Wenchuan Earthquake

Measuring 7.9 on the Richter scale, the Wenchuan earthquake occurred on May 12, 2008. It was the seventh deadliest earthquake of the 20th century worldwide (Tovrov, 2011). This earthquake devastated the rural areas of Sichuan Province in China and caused approximately 11 million people to become homeless (Hooker, 2008). As part of the Chinese Economic Stimulus Program, the Chinese central government invested US$586 billion, taking three years to rebuild the earthquake-ravaged areas (Barboza, 2008). The reconstruction was facilitated through a Counterpart Support Plan. This plan arranged for 19 provinces and municipalities located throughout the eastern and central regions of China to help with 18 counties' reconstruction in Sichuan Province (Xu & Lu, 2013). Most sponsoring provinces and/or municipalities imported their own designers, construction crews, machinery, and construction materials from their own provinces and/or municipalities to Sichuan to swiftly reconstruct villages, towns, and cities (Ge, Gu, & Deng, 2010). The speed with which the physical reconstruction was carried out did benefit disaster survivors in some ways, although the long-term impacts have been less universally positive. The enormous number of people made homeless by the earthquake were able to access housing and other resources to meet their basic living requirements within the new surroundings. China was the first country, and still is among only a few in the world, to achieve such a quick response in such a short period to a disaster of this magnitude.

The urban-style residential communities, comprised of several condominium buildings, were the commonly accepted reconstruction style by sponsoring provinces and/or municipalities to house relocated disaster survivors. However, most disaster survivors were farmers who came from villages. These disaster survivors formerly lived in hand-built houses surrounded by gardens and orchards, in close proximity to their farmlands. In the new residential communities, each family was given one apartment in a condominium, no doubt much smaller than their original home. Furthermore, any open spaces, such as plaza, family gardens, and other spaces for creative activity, were extremely limited in the new communities. As the example illustrates, top–down government-led reconstruction projects predominantly concentrated on the reconstruction of structural systems and infrastructure, largely ignoring the social dimensions and limiting the bottom–up input directly from local residents (Wu, 2019b). The side effects of this situation have continued to reveal themselves during the long-term recovery stage as the disaster survivors have continued to live in and have remained deeply engaged within their new the urban-style communities. The limitations of the new environmental structures, such as no public space afforded for socialization with their neighbors, along with the survivors being unable to keep doing their original farming activities, have proven that this urban-styled community to not be effective in supporting survivors' recovery in social, economic, and other related areas. These structures even significantly interrupted residents' recovery.

Physically, the urban-style residential communities fit urban land use situations and their inhabitants' lifestyle. The planners of the expedited reconstruction after the Sichuan earthquake did not sufficiently consider the difference between urban and rural people and did not effectively collect data about local rural dwellers' requirements. Relocation provided the dwellers with physical shelters, rather than having considered their social needs. Furthermore, the condominium-style buildings did not encourage the farmers who relocated there from adjacent villages to meet each other, to repair their social connections and social networks. This directly resulted in people expressing a desire to move back to their villages immediately, even if it meant giving up their new condominiums. As the example illustrates, limited consideration of social factors postdisaster can result in little support for the re-establishment of people's social networks or the resumption of their social lives.

Furthermore, without thorough consideration of disaster survivors' livelihoods, builders of new built environment may inadvertently cause the survivors to not be able to support their long-term economic recovery, which directly influences their basic living requirements. Survivors described themselves as "farmers without farmland."

There were other significant social and economic losses for the population as well. The traditional architectural style in the earthquake-hit rural areas of Sichuan is mud-stone foundation with a wooden structure on top. The sponsors built modern-style concrete buildings only. The traditional architecture had become a famous local cultural heritage, attracting multitudes of tourists annually who enjoyed exposure to the rural lifestyle, including fresh local produce and the leisurely rural life. This type of tourism could no longer be supported by the new communities. The economic loss had the same negative affect on the local residents livelihood as did the end of farming practices.

Conclusion

Architecture is unavoidably social (Wood, 2015). When basic living requirements are no longer unachievable, the architectural approach must also contribute to other dimensions of recovery and rehabilitation, such as social, economic, and cultural. The multidisciplinary nature of disaster recovery and reconstruction determines the systemic nature of disaster resilience. The example of post-earthquake Sichuan province clearly indicates the interplay between the physical quality and social, economic, and cultural qualities of resilience. Obviously, there are other aspects as well that are strongly associated with the built environment of most concern to architects, such as political and ecological factors. According to the barrel principle, the shortest bar determines the capacity of a barrel (Frank, 2010). Different dimensions of disaster resilience could be designated as different bars. No matter how strong the physical bar is, the capacity of resilience is ultimately measured by the shortest one, which is typically the social dimensions of those who are forcibly displaced. Building disaster resilience requires the raising of the capacity of all the various dimensions of people's lives.

It is understood that multidisciplinary and multi-stakeholder engagement has already become a trend in the field of hazards and disaster research and practice and has begun to augment a better understanding of building resilience at individual, family, community, and societal levels. Within hazards and disaster practice, multi-stakeholder engagement and collaboration aims to build resilience by minimizing disaster's impact on human settlement. The collaborative approach, especially in building cross-organizational partnerships, is an appropriate strategy for disaster practitioners to more effectively address the complexity of human settlement reconstruction. It also generates the question: Who can best facilitate various stakeholders becoming engaged in the reconstruction process? Such a question, in both research and practice, orients the prospective of disaster resilience initiatives.

Disaster resilience, as a whole, illustrates the systemic connections among various factors across multiple scales which influence resilience. The reconstruction, recovery, and rehabilitation of human settlement creates the foundation so that other social and engineering processes can unfold smoothly, all heading toward the refinement of a population's capacity for resilience the next time they experience a disaster.

Key Messages

1. The interdisciplinary academic nature of architectural research and education, as well as the collaborative nature of architectural practice, position architects as leaders of multidisciplinary and multi-stakeholder engagement processes for building postdisaster resilience.
2. The multidisciplinary nature of disaster research and practice necessities that, in the course of building disaster resilience, all societal factors need to be simultaneously and comprehensively balanced.
3. Disaster resilience in human settlement reconstruction requires a seamless synthesis of short-term physical reconstruction with long-term social and humanitarian recovery.
4. Building disaster resilience is an ongoing learning process. Community engagement is one of the most effective strategies to strengthen resilience at individual, family, and community levels.
5. Hazards and disaster research and practice inescapably involve multidisciplinary and multi-stakeholder engagement. Leadership needs to be established for harmonious facilitation of engagement of professionals' and other stakeholders' engagement, to build affected communities' resilience.

References

Abendroth, L. M., & Bell, B. (Eds.). (2015). *Public interest design practice guidebook: SEED methodology, case studies, and critical issues*. Public Interest Design Guidebooks. Abingdon, UK: Routledge.

Aven, T., & Renn, O. (2009). The role of quantitative risk assessments for characterizing risk and uncertainty and delineating appropriate risk management options, with special emphasis on terrorism risk. *Risk Analysis, 29*(4), 587–600. doi:10.1111/j.1539-6924.2008.01175.x

Barboza, D. (2008, November 9). China plans $586 billion economic stimulus. *The New York Times*. Retrieved from https://www.nytimes.com/2008/11/09/business/worldbusiness/09iht-yuan.4.17664544.html

Behnam, B., & Ronagh, H. R. (2016). Firewalls and post-earthquake fire resistance of reinforced-concrete frames. *Proceedings of the Institution of Civil Engineers: Structures and Buildings, 169*(1), 20–33. doi:10.1680/stbu.14.00031

Berke, P. R., & Campanella, T. J. (2006). Planning for post-disaster resiliency. *Annals of the American Academy of Political and Social Science, 604*(1), 192–207. doi:10.1177/0002716205285533

Bruneau, M., Chang, S. E., Eguchi, R. T., Lee, G. C., O'Rourke, T. D., Reinhorn, A. M., . . . von Winterfeldt, D. (2003). A framework to quantitatively assess and enhance the seismic resilience of communities. *Earthquake Spectra, 19*(4), 733–752. doi:10.1193/1.1623497

Cary, J., & Martin, C. E. (2012, October 7). Dignifying design. *The New York Times*. Retrieved from https://www.nytimes.com/2012/10/07/opinion/sunday/dignifying-design.html?pagewanted=all

Centers for Disease Control and Prevention. (2011). *Impact of the built environment on health*. Retrieved from https://www.cdc.gov/nceh/publications/factsheets/impactofthebuiltenvironmentonhealth.pdf

Centre for Research on the Epidemiology of Disasters. (2009). *General classification*. Retrieved from https://www.emdat.be/classification

Chang, S. E., & Shinozuka, M. (2004). Measuring improvements in the disaster resilience of communities. *Earthquake Spectra, 20*(3), 739–755. doi:10.1193/1.1775796

Choi, J., Deshmukh, A., & Hastak, M. (2019). Seven-layer classification of infrastructure to improve community resilience to disasters. *Journal of Infrastructure Systems, 25*(2). doi:10.1061/(ASCE)IS.1943-555X.0000486

Cimellaro, G. P., Reinhorn, A. M., & Bruneau, M. (2010). Framework for analytical quantification of disaster resilience. *Engineering Structures, 32*(11), 3639–3649. doi:10.1016/j.engstruct.2010.08.008

Crawford, T. W., & Rahman, M. K. (2018). Settlement patterns. *Comprehensive Remote Sensing, 9*(10), 106–122. doi:10.1016/B978-0-12-409548-9.10419-1

Cutter, S. L. (2014). What makes events extreme? *Journal of Extreme Events, 1*(1), 1402001. doi:10.1142/S2345737614020011

Cutter, S. L. (2016a). Resilience to what? Resilience for whom? *The Geographical Journal 182*(2), 110–113. doi:10.1111/geoj.12174

Cutter, S. L. (2016b). The landscape of disaster resilience indicators in the USA. *Natural Hazards, 80*(2), 741–758. doi:10.1007/s11069-015-1993-2

Cutter, S. L., Barnes, L., Berry, M., Burton, C., Evans, E., Tate, E., & Webb, J. (2008). A place-based model for understanding community resilience to natural disasters. *Global Environmental Change: Human and Policy Dimensions, 18*(4), 598–606. doi:10.1016/j.gloenvcha.2008.07.013

Department for International Development. (2011). *Defining disaster resilience: A DFID approach paper*. Retrieved from https://assets.publishing.service.gov.uk/government/uploads/system/uploads/attachment_data/file/186874/defining-disaster-resilience-approach-paper.pdf

Dunleavy, P., Bastow, S., & Tinkler, J. (2014). *The contemporary social sciences are now converging strongly with STEM disciplines in the study of "human-dominated systems" and "human-influenced systems."* Retrieved from https://blogs.lse.ac.uk/impactofsocialsciences/2014/01/20/social-sciences-converging-with-stem-disciplines/

Ellingwood, B. R., Cutler, H., Gardoni, P., Peacock, W. G., van de Lindt, J. W., & Wang, N. Y. (2016). The Centerville virtual community: A fully integrated decision model of interacting physical and social infrastructure systems. *Sustainable and Resilient Infrastructure, 1*(3–4), 95–107. doi:10.1080/23789689.2016.1255000

Fiksel, J. (2003). Designing resilient, sustainable systems. *Environmental Science & Technology, 37*(23), 5330–5339. doi:10.1021/es0344819

Frank. (2010, September 14). The barrel principle [Blog post]. Retrieved from http://4wise.blogspot.com/2010/09/barrel-principle.html

Ge, Y., Gu, Y. T., & Deng, W. G. (2010). Evaluating China's national post-disaster plans: The 2008 Wenchuan earthquake's recovery and reconstruction planning. *International Journal of Disaster Risk Science, 1*(2), 17–27. doi:10.3974/j.issn.2095-0055.2010.02.003

Gunderson, L. H. (2000). Ecological resilience—In theory and application. *Annual Review of Ecology and Systematics, 31*, 425–439. doi:10.1146/annurev.ecolsys.31.1.425

Hassan, E. M., & Mahmoud, H. (2019). Full functionality and recovery assessment framework for a hospital subjected to a scenario earthquake event. *Engineering Structures, 188*, 165–177. doi:10.1016/j.engstruct.2019.03.008

Holling, C. S. (1973). Resilience and stability of ecological systems. *Annual Review of Ecology and Systematics, 4*, 1–23. doi:10.1146/annurev.es.04.110173.000245

Hooker, J. (2008, May 26). Toll rises in China quake. *The New York Times*. Retrieved from https://www.nytimes.com/2008/05/26/world/asia/26quake.html

Johnson, D. L., Ambrose, S. H., Bassett, T. J., Bowmen, M. L., Crummey, D. E., Isaacson, L. S., . . . Winter-Nelson, A. E. (1997). Meanings of environmental terms. *Journal of Environmental Quality, 26*(3), 581–589. doi:10.2134/jeq1997.00472425002600030002x

Knight, C. G. (2015). Human-environment interactions: Case studies. In J. D. Wright (Ed.), *International encyclopedia of the social & behavioral sciences* (2nd ed., pp. 405–409). Boston, MA: Elsevier. doi:10.1016/B978-0-08-097086-8.91006-7

Kwon, O. S., & Elnashai, A. (2006). The effect of material and ground motion uncertainty on the seismic vulnerability curves of RC structure. *Engineering Structures, 28*(2), 289–303. doi:10.1016/j.engstruct.2005.07.010

Lee, A. (2013). Casting an architectural lens on disaster reconstruction. *Disaster Prevention and Management, 22*(5), 480–490. doi:10.1108/DPM-10-2013-0178

Leveson, N. (2004). A new accident model for engineering safer systems. *Safety Science, 42*(4), 237–270. doi:10.1016/s0925-7535(03)00047-x

Linkov, I., Eisenberg, D. A., Bates, M. E., Chang, D., Convertino, M., Allen, J. H., . . . Seager, T. P. (2013). Measurable resilience for actionable policy. *Environmental Science & Technology, 47*(18), 10108–10110. doi:10.1021/es403443n

McFarlane, A. C., & Norris, F. H. (2006). Definitions and concepts in disaster research. In F. H. Norris, S. Galea, M. J. Friedman, & P. J. Watson (Eds.), *Methods for disaster mental health research* (pp. 3–19). New York, NY: Guilford Press.

National Research Council. (1999). *The impacts of natural disasters: A framework for loss estimation*. Washington, DC: National Academies Press.

National Research Council. (2006). *Facing hazards and disasters: Understanding human dimensions*. Washington, DC: National Academies Press.

National Research Council. (2012). *Disaster resilience: A national imperative*. Washington, DC: National Academies Press.

Norris, F. H., Stevens, S. P., Pfefferbaum, B., Wyche, K. F., & Pfefferbaum, R. L. (2008). Community resilience as a metaphor, theory, set of capacities, and strategy for disaster readiness. *American Journal of Community Psychology, 41*(1–2), 127–150. doi:10.1007/s10464-007-9156-6

Orff, K. (2010, December). *Reviving New York's rivers—with oysters!* [Video file]. Retrieved from https://www.ted.com/talks/kate_orff_oysters_as_architecture#t-21098

Ouyang, M. (2014). Review on modeling and simulation of interdependent critical infrastructure systems. *Reliability Engineering & System Safety, 121*, 43–60. doi:10.1016/j.ress.2013.06.040

Park, J., Seager, T. P., Rao, P. S. C., Convertino, M., & Linkov, I. (2013). Integrating risk and resilience approaches to catastrophe management in engineering systems. *Risk Analysis, 33*(3), 356–367. doi:10.1111/j.1539-6924.2012.01885.x

Partnership for Resilience and Preparedness. (n.d.). *About*. Retrieved from https://www.prepdata.org/about

Peek, L., Tobin, J., Adams, R., Wu, H., Mathew, M. (2020). A Framework for Convergence Research in the Hazards and Disaster Field: The Natural Hazards Engineering Research Infrastructure CONVERGE Facility. *Frontiers in Built Environment, 6*, 110. doi:10.3389/fbuil.2020.00110

Puppim de Oliveira, J. A., & Balahan, O. (2013). Climate-friendly urban regeneration: Lessons from Japan. *Our World*. Retrieved from https://ourworld.unu.edu/en/climate-friendly-urban-regeneration-lessons-from-japan

Roof, K., & Oleru, N. (2008). Public health: Seattle and King County's push for the built environment. *Journal of Environmental Health, 71*(1), 24–27.

Sina, D., Chang-Richards, A. Y., Wilkinson, S., & Potangaroa, R. (2019). A conceptual framework for measuring livelihood resilience: Relocation experience from Aceh, Indonesia. *World Development, 117*(C), 253–265. doi:10.1016/j.worlddev.2019.01.003

Smith, N. (2006). There's no such thing as a natural disaster. *Social Sciences Research Council: Items*. Retrieved from https://items.ssrc.org/understanding-katrina/theres-no-such-thing-as-a-natural-disaster/

The Community Guide. (n.d.). *Combined built environment features help communities get active*. Retrieved from https://www.thecommunityguide.org/content/combined-built-environment-features-help-communities-get-active

Tierney, K. (2006). Social inequality, hazards, and disasters. In R. J. Daniels, D. F. Kettl, & H. Kunreuther (Eds.), *On risk and disaster: Lessons from hurricane Katrina* (pp. 109–128). Philadelphia: University of Pennsylvania Press.

Tierney, K. (2007). From the margins to the mainstream? Disaster research at the crossroads. *Annual Review of Sociology, 33*(1), 503–525. doi:10.1146/annurev.soc.33.040406.131743

Tierney, K., & Bruneau, M. (2007). Conceptualizing and measuring resilience: A key to disaster loss reduction. *TR News, 250*, 14–17.

Tovrov, D. (2011, September 11). 10 Deadliest earthquakes in the past century. *International Business Times*. Retrieved from https://www.ibtimes.com/10-deadliest-earthquakes-past-century-315356

Tuan, Y. (2001). *Space and place: The perspective of experience*. Minneapolis: University of Minnesota Press.

Ungar, M. (2018). Systemic resilience: Principles and processes for a science of change in contexts of adversity. *Ecology and Society, 23*(4), 34. doi:10.5751/ES-10385-230434

United Nations. (2005). *Hyogo framework for action 2005-2015: Building the resilience of nations and communities to disasters*. Retrieved from https://www.unisdr.org/we/inform/publications/1037

United Nations. (2009). *2009 UNISDR terminology on disaster risk reduction*. Retrieved from http://www.saludydesastres.info/index.php?option=com_docman&task=doc_download&gid=388&Itemid=

United Nations. (2015a). *Sendai framework for disaster risk reduction 2015-2030*. Retrieved from https://www.unisdr.org/files/43291_sendaiframeworkfordrren.pdf

United Nations. (2015b). *Transforming our world: The 2030 agenda for sustainable development*. Retrieved from https://www.un.org/ga/search/view_doc.asp?symbol=A/RES/70/1&Lang=E

United Nations. (2016). *Report of the open-ended intergovernmental expert working group on indicators and terminology relating to disaster risk reduction*. Retrieved from https://www.preventionweb.net/files/50683_oiewgreportenglish.pdf

United Nations. (2019). *Risk and disasters*. Retrieved from http://www.un-spider.org/risks-and-disasters

United Nations Disaster Risk Reduction. (2019). *Global platform for disaster risk reduction*. Retrieved from https://www.unisdr.org/conference/2019/globalplatform/home.

United Nations Educational, Scientific, and Cultural Organization. (2017). *Human settlements*. Retrieved from http://www.unesco.org/new/en/natural-sciences/environment/water/wwap/facts-and-figures/human-settlements/

United Nations International Strategy for Disaster Reduction. (2017). *Build back better in recovery, rehabilitation, and reconstruction*. Retrieved from https://www.unisdr.org/files/53213_bbb.pdf

United Nations International Strategy for Disaster Reduction. (2019). *What is the international strategy?* Retrieved from https://www.unisdr.org/who-we-are/international-strategy-for-disaster-reduction

Vigliar, V. (2016, November 25). In Greece, lack of legal aid leaves migrants and refugees guessing. *Devex*. Retrieved from https://www.devex.com/news/in-greece-lack-of-legal-aid-leaves-migrants-and-refugees-guessing-88964

Wachtendorf, T., Kendra, J. M., & DeYoung, S. E. (2018). Community innovation and disasters. In H. Rodríguez, W. Donner, & J. Trainor (Eds.), *Handbook of disaster research* (pp. 387–410). Cham, Switzerland: Springer.

Welton-Mitchell, C., & James, L. (2018). *Evidence-based mental health integrated disaster preparedness in Nepal and Haiti*. Retrieved from https://odihpn.org/magazine/evidence-based-mental-health-integrated-disaster-preparedness-in-nepal-and-haiti/

Wood, A. (2015). Architecture as a social science. *Architecture and Education*. Retrieved from https://architectureandeducation.org/2015/10/27/architecture-as-a-social-science/

Wu, H. (2014). *Post-Wenchuan earthquake rural reconstruction and recovery, in Sichuan China: Memory, civic participation, and government intervention* (Doctoral dissertation). Retrieved from http://circle.ubc.ca/handle/2429/50340

Wu, H. (2018). Promoting public interest design: Transformative change toward green social work during post-Lushan earthquake reconstruction and recovery in Sichuan, China. In L. Dominelli (Ed.), *Handbook of green social work* (pp.87–98). Abingdon, UK: Routledge.

Wu, H. (2019a). Advancing post-disaster resilience: Improving designer-user communication in the post-Lushan earthquake reconstruction and recovery. In B. Kar & D. Cochran (Eds.), *Understanding the roles of risk communication in community resilience building* (pp. 198–210). Abingdon, UK: Routledge.

Wu, H. (2019b). Post-disaster reconstruction in China: The need for harmonization of physical reconstruction and social recovery after the Wenchuan earthquake. In J. Drolet (Ed.), *Rebuilding lives post-disaster* (pp. 204–225). New York, NY: Oxford University Press.

Wu, H. (2020). Airdropped Urban Condominiums and Stay-Behind Elders' Overall Well-Being: 10-Year Lessons Learned from the Post-Wenchuan Earthquake Rural Recovery. *Journal of Rural Studies, 79*, 24–33. https://doi.org/10.1016/j.jrurstud.2020.08.008

Wu, H., & Hou, C. (2016). Community social planning: The social worker's role in post-earthquake reconstruction and recovery planning, Sichuan China. *Social Dialogue, 4*, 26–29.

Wu, H., & Hou, C. (2019). Utilizing co-design approach to identify various stakeholders' roles in the protection of intangible place-making heritage: The case of Guchengping Village. *Disaster Prevention and Management: An International Journal*. doi:10.1108/DPM-09-2018-0291

Xu, J., & Lu, Y. (2013). A comparative study on the national counterpart aid model for post-disaster recovery and reconstruction: 2008 Wenchuan earthquake as a case. *Disaster Prevention and Management, 22*(1), 75–93. doi:10.1108/09653561311301998

Zhou, H. J., Wang, J. A., Wan, J. H., & Jia, H. C. (2010). Resilience to natural hazards: A geographic perspective. *Natural Hazards, 53*(1), 21–41. doi:10.1007/s11069-009-9407-y

SECTION 10

Technology and Human Systems

34

Design and Engineering of Resilience for Networked Computer Systems

David Hutchison, Mark Rouncefield, Antonios Gouglidis, and Tom Anderson

Introduction

Networked computer systems that are designed for resilience form the bedrock of many enterprises and activities in the modern world, from telecommunications (telephone, broadband) through utility networks (electricity, water, gas, etc.) to banking, commerce, government, and all sorts of organizations including those in areas of healthcare and transportation. These systems are composed of nodes (computers) and links (communication paths, which may be wired or wireless), interconnected in some topology or arrangement of links (e.g., mesh, star, or tree). It is convenient to represent networked systems as a number of services running on top of the communications topology (see Figure 34.1). Each is a combination of software and hardware. One reason for this representation is that it allows designers to separate the concerns of the communication topology from those of the services.

Modern networked systems definitely need to be reliable and trustworthy. In other words, the operators and, ultimately, the users need to know that the service they receive will be what they expect and also what they have paid for. Put simply, networked systems need to show resilience when strained. The subject of QoS has been a highly active research topic for many years and is still perhaps the most important aspect of any system because the service the user receives is its essential purpose.

In recent years, it has become evident that modern networked systems are critical infrastructures (and services), because of the reliance that users put on them. Not only that, if some of these systems fail to provide their expected service (perhaps a prolonged downtime),

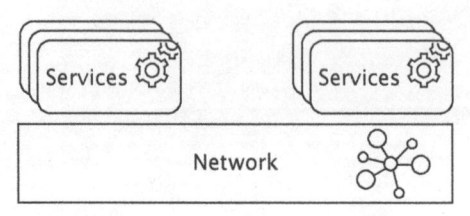

FIGURE 34.1 Networked system: topology and services.

then losses will occur in terms of time and money, and in extreme cases there may be damage and even loss of life. Critical infrastructures comprise of assets and systems that maintain societal functions, including health, safety, security, and the economic and social well-being of people. Supervisory control and data acquisition (SCADA) and industrial control systems (ICS) are particular examples of critical infrastructures for the monitoring, control, and automation of operational plants of various sorts, such as utility networks. SCADA systems monitor and control infrastructures including power plants, water utility, energy networks, and gas pipelines, which makes them highly critical. Providing protection in terms of security, safety, and resilience in such networks is inherently considered to be of vital importance. Traditionally, most of these systems were air-gapped (physically isolated) from other unsecured networks, but in several cases, access to these devices may still be available over a public network (e.g., the Internet) as a requirement to improve usability via providing operators with the potential to remotely access devices (Shirazi, Gouglidis, Farshad, & Hutchison, 2017).

While automation and interconnectivity increase the efficiency of these computer systems and reduce operational costs, they expose these systems to new threats. For instance, the existence of a vulnerability in a system on the top layers of the Purdue model, a way of modeling multiple layers and stages of the architectural life cycle (Obregon, 2015), may allow attackers to exploit them and to gradually take control of systems or devices that operate at the lower levels, such as SCADA systems; this could cause failure and hence serious disruptions. In recent times, there has been a significant increase in the functional demands upon utilities, for example, resulting in an increased rate of automation in networked controls and interconnections, as well as an increase in dependencies between diverse infrastructures. Consequently, utility networks are now more susceptible to sophisticated attacks including advanced persistent threats (König, Gouglidis, Green, & Solar, 2018). Additionally, new challenges arising from system complexity, overloading, unanticipated human behavior, and vulnerabilities from third-party sources must also be considered. Needless to say, providing protection in terms of security, safety, and resilience in such networks is vitally important. Research on the emerging area of security in critical infrastructures has resulted in rules, legislation, and good-practice guidelines that we will outline later in this chapter.

The sources of challenges for networked systems can include natural disasters such as flooding, weather events leading to failure of electrical power, overdemand for the services of the system, software bugs and consequent failures, hardware component faults, complexity leading to errors by a human operator, and cybersecurity attacks (Esposito et al., 2018;

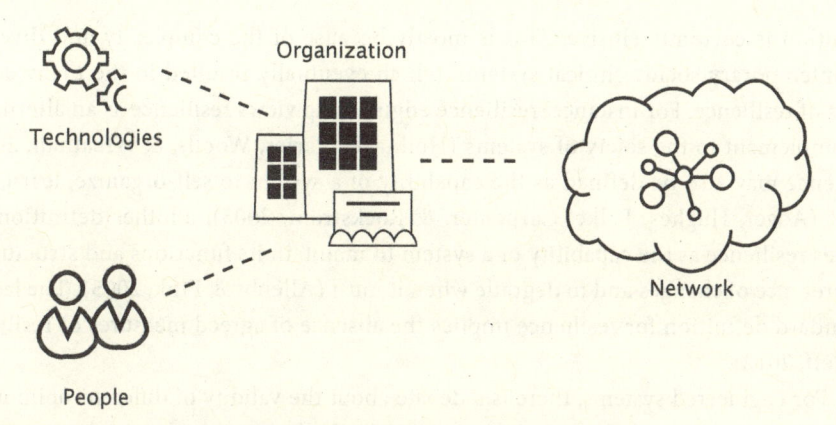

FIGURE 34.2 Technology, organization, and people in networked systems.

Machuca et al., 2016). Networked systems need to be able to continue to offer a satisfactory QoS no matter what challenge they experience—this is our definition of *resilience*. In this chapter we explain our approach to engineering resilience into such systems (Hutchison & Sterbenz, 2018).

Networked systems are generally complex, and they have three aspects that need to be considered in combination when building resilience into them: these are technology, organizations, and people, as illustrated in Figure 34.2.

We start by looking at the technology aspect, which is where we started in our own research. In later sections we consider organizations and people, by means of a case study based on work we did with utility networks. Originally, our work on resilience was in the context of future telecommunication systems, and we wanted to explore the extension of traditional QoS concerns (performance—throughput and delay in particular) to make sure these systems could be relied on, not only at the level of recovering from the failure of a node or link but also at the services level.

Our early research (Sterbenz et al., 2010) reviewed the related terminology (including fault, error, failure, fault tolerance, trustworthiness, etc.) and we described in some detail the relationship of our definition of resilience with prior and related work; this is often understood differently in disciplines other than our own area of information and communication technologies (ICT).

Resilience and Related Terminology for Engineered Systems

The term *resilience* has been used in the past several decades in different ways to describe the ability of materials, engineered artefacts, ecosystems, communities, and other built and biological systems to adapt to changes and is also adopted by diverse sciences (e.g., in the discipline of psychology) and organizations (e.g., as a description of business continuity lifecycles; Hollnagel, Woods, & Leveson, 2006). Although the etymology of resilience clearly refers to the capacity to recover from difficulties, a single agreed, precise, definition is currently elusive. This is mostly because of the complexity and diversity of contemporary sociotechnical systems, which eventually resulted in the many definitions of resilience. For instance, resilience engineering views resilience as an alternative or complement to the safety of systems (Hollnagel, Paries, Woods, & Wreathall, 2010); resilience may also be defined as the capability of a system to self-organize, learn, and adapt (Adger, Hughes, Folke, Carpenter, & Rockström, 2005); another definition describes resilience as the capability of a system to maintain its functions and structure in the presence of changes and to degrade when it must (Allenby & Fink, 2005). The lack of a standard definition for resilience implies the absence of agreed measures of resilience (Moteff, 2012).

For engineered systems, there is a debate about the validity of different opinions in the communities interested in quantifying resilience. In the context of networked computer systems, which arguably forms the basis of an increasing number of critical infrastructures, we define resilience as "the ability of a network or system to provide and maintain an acceptable level of service in the face of various faults and challenges to normal operation" (Sterbenz et al., 2010). The overall resilience strategy, which we have labeled as D^2R^2+DR, is depicted in Figure 34.3. This definition resulted from research conducted in ResumeNet (Bruncak et al., 2011), a Seventh Framework Programme European Union–funded Future Internet project and was subsequently adopted by the European Union Agency for Network and Information Security (ENISA; Górniak et al., 2011). Based on the previous references, it is clear that there exists no single, agreed definition of resilience, and current definitions rely on the specific area of application. However, there is clearly a common thread in all of the definitions. We propose to use the above, broad, ENISA definition, as it is sufficiently general and encompasses the elements that apply to the resilience of critical infrastructures.

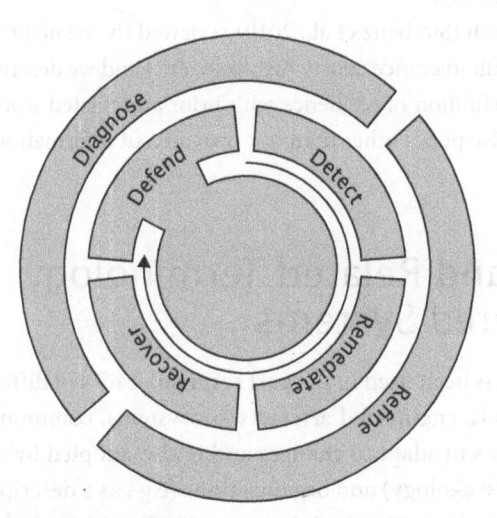

FIGURE 34.3 The D^2R^2+DR resilience strategy.

Engineering Resilience Using the Resilience Strategy

To design and build or adapt networked systems to be resilient, we adopt the D^2R^2+DR strategy, which is essentially two sets of steps organized in two "loops" as shown in Figure 34.3. The inner loop, D^2R, is intended to operate in real time (or as fast as possible) to detect and correct anomalies, whereas the outer loop, DR, can act more sedately (initially offline, mediated by a human expert, but ideally in the future it will function autonomously with the help of a machine expert; Smith et al., 2011). Each component of the model requires its own explanation if one is to grasp the complexity of their interactions.

Defend

Initially, a thorough system analysis needs to be carried out to decide how best to build defensively against perceived threats and vulnerabilities; this includes a risk assessment to prioritize the assets in the system—which of them needs to be protected and which of these, most urgently. Building resilience into a system inevitably incurs costs, and these need to be carefully weighed. As a result of the system analysis, the system designer will propose a range of actions including: building defensive walls (e.g., firewalls to defend against cyberattacks); adding some redundant links and nodes into the communications infrastructure; and at runtime, making appropriate adjustments such as firewall rules and resources.

Detect

The detect phase requires a monitoring system. Essentially, the network and/or networked system needs to be "instrumented" so that the effects or symptoms of any challenge to the system's normal operation can be rapidly observed. This is sometimes called "anomaly detection" or "intrusion detection," and it has been the subject of much research in past decades (Chandola, Banerjee, & Kumar, 2009). Nevertheless, it is difficult to distinguish the root cause of a challenge, and the detection may have to proceed without actually knowing for sure what is causing the problem. Typically, detected anomalies are classified and using this classification allows the next phase to be carried out.

Instrumenting the system implies knowing what (and where) to measure some artefact of the system that will indicate there is a threat. In a network it is usual to measure network traffic (i.e., the packets of information that are passing across it) to assess whether some variation indicates abnormal behavior. What is measured is often referred to as a "metric"; deciding which metrics to observe to estimate the resilience of a system remains an important topic of research.

Remediate

Remediation (or "mitigation" as used by some resilience researchers; Sedgewick, 2014) is the phase whereby some action is carried out to remove or improve the symptoms of a challenge or threat. In networked systems, it is typical to use traffic engineering to improve the situation—for example, to remove or redirect a particular stream of information packets that come from a suspicious source in the network and that is adversely affecting a destination in the network such as a server that may be saturated with this traffic. Ideally, remediation should be done in real time, and it should be done autonomously—that is, the resilience management mechanism makes the decision what to remediate and how, and carries this out without human intervention. This is still a sensitive topic, and in existing systems the remediation will usually be carried out under the supervision of a human expert.

To make autonomous operation more feasible and trustworthy, it is important to get as much context as possible about the source and nature of the anomaly or challenge. Given that root cause analysis is likely to take too much time, a situational awareness (SA) subsystem could be employed to gather and assess contextual data about the environment or conditions surrounding the networked system. This can potentially provide enough information to assist the appropriate remediation decision to be made. For example, context data may be able to tell whether a web server is being saturated because of some malicious activity or, by contrast, if it is a national holiday or there is a surge of bookings for a new event and therefore not a denial of service cyberattack. SA is still a key research topic.

Recover
In the recovery phase, the aim is to return the networked system to normal behavior if possible, and to try to make sure that the system takes account of the conditions that caused the anomalies. This implies some form of machine or human learning to improve the system's resilience. The recover activity should, of course, be carried out once the source of the challenge has been removed. Policies for high-level guidance may be used in this phase (Gouglidis, Hu, Busby, & Hutchison, 2017).

Diagnose and Refine
The outer loop of the resilience strategy is an underexplored research area. The idea is that in future there will be a machine learning phase that steadily learns from previous experiences and builds up a body of expert knowledge on which to draw to improve the remediation and recovery activities and the resilience model that underlies them both. This requires providing real historical data for a DR prototype and, in turn, the development of resilience subsystems that are subsequently deployed in the field. This raises an important ethical question—whether, for networked systems that operate critical infrastructures and services, there will or should always be a human in the loop.

System Risk

Risk is defined by ENISA as "the chance of something happening that will have an impact upon objectives. It is measured in terms of impact and likelihood." (ENISA Glossary, 2019). Therefore, a cyber risk can be conceived as a risk in the context of ICS and/or ICT systems. In addition, an operational cyber security risk can be defined as "operational risks to information and technology assets that have consequences affecting the confidentiality, availability, or integrity of information or information systems" (Cebula & Young, 2010, p. 1). They classify the taxonomy of operational cyber security risks into four main groups: (a) *actions of people* is considered with actions taken or not taken by individuals in a given situation; (b) *systems and technology failures* refers to technology assets and specifically in their problematic, abnormal or unexpected functioning; (c) *failed internal processes* refers to needed or expected performance of internal processes and associations with problematic failures; and (d) *external events* refers to external events that might affect an organization's control. Therefore, to consider how a system's risk is affected when various type of changes apply to a system, it is required to examine the system under organization, technology, and individual (OTI) viewpoints (Gouglidis, Green, et al., 2016). The organization viewpoint is concerned with the groups of people who work together in an organized way for a shared purpose as well as any type of policies, processes, and procedures in the organization. The technology viewpoint references the implemented technologies in a system including the software, hardware, and network components, as well as any type of communication among them. The individual viewpoint brings awareness of a single person or entity and how it acts or behaves in a particular situation or under particular conditions. We have already covered the technology viewpoint sufficiently in previous sections of this chapter, so we move directly now to address the organizations and individual (people) aspects. It is also noteworthy that the last of these three viewpoints is able to enhance the awareness of the state of a system. In subsequent sections of this chapter, we consider the organization and individual (people) aspects, having already addressed the technology parts.

More specifically, the application of OTI (three viewpoints) may provide awareness of all the previously discussed four categories since system risks in external events may be identified by the organizational viewpoint. Likewise, system risks due to system and technology failures, or failed internal processes may be identified by the technological viewpoint. Similarly, system risks regarding actions of people might be identified by the individual viewpoint. Therefore, the application of OTI as a first point of contact toward an architecture capable of protecting ICS is capable of identifying in a timely manner various type of threads, and simultaneously considering current, evolving, or potential system risks due to a feedback process.

The components of the D^2R^2+DR resilience strategy can be used as an overarching process in the context of a wider risk management framework to provide the indicators and measurements to ensure an ongoing and effective monitoring of the networked systems. In the context of ISO 31000 (2009), a resilience framework may operate as part of the "monitoring and review" component (Schauer, 2018). The latter is responsible to provide indicators, progress measurement of conducting the risk management plan, risk reports, and reviews of design and effectiveness of the applied risk management measures implemented as an ongoing effectiveness monitoring of the complete framework (Austrian Standards Institute, 2010, Section 19). This component includes a constant feedback loop, taking the main and partial results from each step and evaluating their effectiveness. Risk-related information may be provided by other components of the framework, which could include the general organizational structure coming from "establishing the context" up to the estimation of the consequences and likelihood for identified threats under "risk analysis."

Situation Awareness and Resilience

SA is defined by the Committee on National Security Systems (2010) as "within a volume of time and space, the perception of an enterprise's security posture and its threat environment; the comprehension/meaning of both taken together (risk); and the projection of their status into the near future" (p. 69). In addition, cyber SA can be defined as the part of SA that is concerned with the cyber environments (Franke & Brynielsson, 2014). Here we present related work with regards to the application of SA in ICS and elaborate on cyber SA in utility networks.

Utility networks are complex organizations where interactions take place among the assets of the network, the participating people and the ICS (Gouglidis, Shirazi, Simpson, Smith, & Hutchison, 2016). Any of these might be vulnerable to various types of threats, and therefore, become a risk for the network. Annual reports from agencies (e.g., ENISA) and major consultancy firms elaborate a list of threats to critical infrastructures. Nevertheless, considering the wide variety of ICS systems and their continually evolving environment, operational SA should be considered. Therefore, in the context of providing a holistic approach toward protecting utility networks, we propose the application of the OTI viewpoint-based approach as a first step toward gaining cyber SA on utility networks. Cyber SA is crucial to apply in networks to safeguard sensitive data, sustain fundamental operations, and protect infrastructures (all aspects of making the network more resilient).

Linking Technology, Organizations and People

A common approach toward conceptually understanding networks is to divide them into levels based on their function. Considering a utility network, for example, a simple three-level approach is adopted: field site, control center, and corporate (Wei, Lu, Jafari, Skare, & Rohde, 2011). Specific devices, boundaries, processes, etc. are then associated with each level, depending on the industry and network topology in question. More detailed layering approaches, such as the Purdue model, are able to provide further granularity by introducing a six-level view approach. Nevertheless, in all cases there is a clear indication of the complexity and interconnections between the levels. The application of the OTI viewpoints enables a broader view of a system (e.g., a utility network) and its levels as it can provide a representation of the whole system from the perspective of a related set of concerns—as stated before, this may help in increasing the level of threat awareness by identifying potential vulnerability-creating behaviors.

Organizations and People

The investigation of organizational aspects of networks may increase our understanding with respect to their resilience against vulnerabilities that arise from working conditions, technology affordances and social context. As Randell (2000) writes:

> how important it is to accept the reality of human fallibility and frailty, both in the design and the use of computer systems... all too often, the latest information technology research and development ideas and plans are described in a style which would not seem out of place in an advertisement for hair restorer. (p. 105)

In the context of organizations, issues of resilience are not simply technical issues resolved by technical means. Specifically, the investigation of organizational aspects will help in understanding how these create vulnerabilities in the technology (e.g., networked computer systems), how organizational aspects may help mitigate vulnerabilities in the technology, and eventually how organizational functioning becomes vulnerable to utility failures. Randell's comment about the issues of designing dependable systems illustrates that making critical infrastructure systems inherently more resilient and safer is more than a simple technical problem. Instead, what a range of studies of critical infrastructure failure have illustrated is that such complex systems also have important organizational and human components that need to be understood and integrated into design to make such systems more resilient (Clarke, Hardstone, Rouncefield, & Sommerville, 2005; Dewsbury & Dobson, 2007). Consequently, we see the prevalence of what are termed "human and organizational factors" and a range of interdisciplinary approaches as a means of developing a more nuanced understanding—in the same way as we have striven to develop more nuanced understandings of resilience and its relationship to other very similar or related (and perhaps more researched) topics like risk, trust, dependability, and sensemaking.

Resilience and the Mental Models Used in Reasoning About Risk and the Importance of Trust

As part of our attempt to understand some of the human and organizational factors involved in resilience, we conducted ethnographic observations and interviews in various utility and information organizations in different parts of Europe (Gouglidis, Green, et al., 2016). In our analysis of the ethnographic data and in trying to understand the components of individual and organizational resilience, we were interested in unpacking people's ideas about risk and how these might relate to other notions such as trust or organizational resilience. Our focus was on how organizational members modeled risk as part of their organizational roles; how different models of risk might interact or impact on each other; how the models changed in response to organizational events; and how these models might be interrelated with notions of trust—in individuals and the organization—and thereby might affect individual and organizational resilience in the face of change and the possibility of failure.

The elicitation of mental models in risk studies was aimed at uncovering deficiencies in individuals' understanding of complex risks (e.g., Bostrom, Morgan, Fischhoff, & Read, 1994)—how they understand exactly what is going on in terms of various kinds of risk. Our work used unstructured interviewing and ethnography to get a contextualized understanding of how organizational members use particular interpretive schemes, heuristics, and other forms of discursive reasoning to deal with organizational risks. We therefore developed an analysis that is closer to notions of the social construction of risk—and Hilgartner's (1992) approach where risk objects come into prominence, or recede out of prominence, in a process termed *emplacement* and *displacement*. Emplacement occurs when the consequences of a risk become magnified, or the causes of risk seem to be less manageable and more likely. Displacement occurs when risk seems to come under greater control. Our primary concern was with how people's risk models perform this process of emplacement and displacement.

From our analysis, it was clear that organizational members have a wide variety of risk models that are not generally integrated, uniform, or self-consistent representations. These risk models tend to be, or at least emerge as, fragmentary and partial, and serve as discursive resources to justify a claim as much as resources for reasoning toward a claim. The function of risk models in one utility organization, for example, appeared much more often displacement than emplacement, but more emplacement than displacement for the information systems organization. Sometimes emplacement and displacement went together. For example, a risk may be emplaced to show how the organization has taken it seriously enough to displace it with strong controls—for example, by having a clear and monitored set of processes, such as having a clear reporting structure for email phishing attacks. One of the fieldwork sites had a clear notion of actual and potential risks, meaning that the organization could acknowledge that some risk existed, but had good grounds for not devoting resources to managing it—because, for example, it was argued that even if someone obtained access to the system they would not be able to do much, such as switching people's electricity off, since this depended on a different set of controls. Potential risks were in some sense theoretical and general—decontextualized and offering no reason for acting on them in this particular organization at this particular time. The fieldworker identified what appeared to be two registers of risk—the actual and the potential. At both field sites, cyber security risks were displaced by other risks—safety, usability, customer satisfaction—which were seen as substantially more important.

Different kinds of risk models were found in the analysis. Failure path models represented sequences of action that were required to bring about some kind of failure state. These enabled people to reason about how plausible different failure or cyber security scenarios were. For example, one respondent reasoned that risks were low because of the fact that an attacker would need one kind of expertise to gain access to computing devices, but a different kind of expertise to actuate physical devices. Technical boundary models involved representations of the technical system as a collection of devices that were strongly partitioned, and typically supplied by different providers. The boundaries represented boundaries of responsibility for risk and boundaries of competence. Sometimes people would say, "We can only do something about X but not Y" to indicate a residual uncertainty about a risk that was partially the responsibility of someone else and beyond their control. Experiential narrative models were stories of incidents or materialized risks of some sort. Narratives provided structured accounts of some issue or problem (in this case security risk) that had come into discourse. Often the narrative involved emplacing a risk, explaining an event in the recent past and then displacing it by reasoning about how controls had subsequently been brought in. The narrative sequence of some experienced event followed by some remedial action seemed to help people reason about security. Ordering models placed the explanation for a lack of interest in certain kinds of risk on priority—an ordering that put security risk well below other risks and other demands on resources. In the utility organization, the main risks were seen by some as being commercial, displacing cyber security risks; in the system's organization, the main risks were said to be seen as being physical. For an organizational actor, it may be less important to have a descriptive representation of risk than to have a list of actions and associated priorities. As our fieldworker remarked,

> more importance is given to safety at work due the deaths of some employees ... in the past. The fear of court cases and also bad media coverage means that more

money is invested in this area rather than in cyber-security, which is seen to be less important... it is easy to cover up cyber-security attacks. The repercussions of these breaches were also deemed to be less serious.

Cost–benefit models involved reasoning that risks were low because the costs to an attacker were high and benefits low. This was typically a risk displacement strategy. They also argued that possible risk controls were unnecessary as their cost exceeded their benefit. Abstract, or global attribute models were simple characterizations of the entire organization or some particular situation. Those of the utility organization were more optimistic. For example, some people had a simple model of sufficiency, a general belief that there were enough appropriate controls to nullify risk. In the systems organization these were more pessimistic, characterizing the organization as having a culture inappropriate to security in a number of ways.

In terms of our ideas about resilience, these different risk models could be a source of vulnerability or of resilience. It is the specific context and specific manifestation that may prove decisive. But it is instructive how wide-ranging the types of model are. They are qualitatively quite different and point to the resourcefulness of organizational members in coping with a world that is complex. Some of these demands involve having an appropriate representation of a conventional system, but others involve having an appropriate representation of other people's expectations and capacities, of norms and conventions, and so on. This means it will always be insufficient to assess mental models of security or resilience merely in terms of their technical correctness, as it will sometimes be more important how well they represent prevailing social issues and requirements. What is important is that there is an awareness within the system of how those models contribute to, or detract from, its security.

Related to ideas about risk, the fieldwork interviews and observations in the different utilities also provide insight into how workers perceive trust, and how trust is an implicit and taken-for-granted feature in the accomplishment of work and therefore a key aspect of resilience. The extent to which risk is perceived and acted upon is linked to some degree to the extent to which people, technology, and organizations are trusted. This in turn impacts on resilience, on the ability of the organization to respond to sudden change or failure. Lack of trust acts as a contributor to a range of problems—be it the poor quality of work resulting from collaboration or a failure to complete tasks at all. Trust and the degree and quality of trust existing between collaborating parties shapes the possibilities for how parties undertake and complete work. Collaboration within and between organizations presupposes trust.

Trust is generally assumed to be organizationally important and a key contributor to the prevention of organizational failure, as a number of studies have suggested. For example, the U.S. Government's Baker Report (Baker et al., 2007) highlighted lack of trust as a precursor to the 2005 explosion at BP's Texas City refinery that killed 15 people, noting that the

> single most important factor in creating a good process safety culture is trust [and] that employees and contractors must trust that they can report incidents, near misses, and other concerns—even when it reflects poorly on their own knowledge, skills, or conduct—without fear of punishment or repercussion. (p. 75)

In a similar fashion, the high reliability organization (HRO) literature sees trust as an important organizational and cultural feature of reliability. Trust is, however, an elusive and difficult to define concept since there are multiple and diverse perspectives. Contemporary research areas include reciprocating trust among teams (Serva, Fuller, & Mayer, 2005), trust in leaders (Burke, Sims, Lazzara, & Salas, 2007), and trust as a heuristics in decision-making and its effects on attitudes, perceptions, behaviors, and performance within organizational settings (Dirks & Ferrin, 2001).

Resilience as Sensemaking and Mindfulness

In this last section we consider how the topic of resilience might relate to other theoretical and empirical concepts in the organizational literature. One possible way of thinking about resilience is to compare our findings and approach with the reliability and dependability literature—specifically that connected to the idea of the HRO—or what we might perhaps want to rephrase as the "high resilience organization." Of particular interest, as far as resilience is concerned, are the concepts of sensemaking and mindfulness that are invoked when considering high reliability organizations (Snook, 2000; Weick, 1987, 2001; Weick & Sutcliffe, 2007; Weick, Sutcliffe, & Obstfeld, 2005).

An HRO is depicted as an organization that has accurate, precise, and commonly held understandings about current operations and the relationship between those operations and potential accidents (Cook & Rasmussen, 2005). A basic assumption is that accidents can be prevented through good organizational design and management and that HROs organize themselves in such a way that they are better able to notice and stop unexpected events. If they cannot halt such a development, they are resilient and able to swiftly restore the functioning of the system (e.g., Rochlin, La Porte, & Roberts, 1987). This approach is commonly contrasted with what is termed "normal accident theory" (Perrow, 1999)—although the approach to resilience may well be similar in both cases.

In terms of sensemaking for resilience and for the HRO, there is a range of research on sensemaking, across the individual, group/organizational, multiorganizational, and societal levels. Weick describes sensemaking as "a developing set of ideas with explanatory possibilities, rather than as a body of knowledge" (Weick, 1995, p. xi). Weick views the concept of sensemaking as a collective, social activity—a cognitive process that can be described through seven properties that "involves turning circumstances into a situation that is comprehended explicitly in words and that serves as a springboard into action" (Weick et al., 2005, p. 409). The seven properties of sensemaking appear equally applicable to resilience. Adapted, these properties appear as follows:

- *Social*: People do not discover resilience, rather they create it. In other words, organizational resilience is interactive.
- *Identity*: Resilience unfolds from identities. People develop identities for themselves during inexplicable events (e.g., as victim, fighter), and this identity can lock them into particular options.

- *Retrospect*: Resilience is constructed by reference to the past. Faced with the inexplicable, people often act their way out of ambiguity by talking about the past and assessing what they have said before about similar events, to discover what they should do and how they should think in the present.
- *Cues*: Resilience is developed as people deal with the inexplicable by paying attention to small cues that enable them to construct a larger story. They look for cues that confirm their analysis and, in doing so, ignore other less relevant information.
- *Ongoing*: Resilience is dynamic and requires continuous updating and re-accomplishment. Resilience requires that people stay attuned to what is happening around them—if not, they lose context and information.
- *Plausibility*: Resilience depends on robust and plausible analyses rather than fixation on a single plausible explanation of an event.
- *Enactment*: In inexplicable times, people have to keep moving. Recovery lies not in thinking and then doing, but in thinking while doing something.

Sensemaking, then, like resilience, involves the ongoing retrospective development of plausible images that rationalize what people are doing (Weick et al., 2005) and points to the need for rapid assessment of a constantly changing environment and to the constant reinterpretation of perceived reality. Taken together, these properties suggest that increased skill at sensemaking—and resilience—should occur when people are socialized to make do, to treat constraints as self-imposed, strive for plausibility, keep showing up, use the past to get a sense of direction in the present, and articulate descriptions that energize.

Ultimately for Weick et al. (2005), the language of sensemaking "captures the realities of agency, flow, equivocality, transience, re-accomplishment, unfolding, and emergence" (p. 410). The means by which this is best achieved according to Weick (2009) is by using the processes of mindfulness. According to Langer and Moldoveanu (2000), mindfulness has been used as a basis for investigating a number of research areas, including decision-making and has also been associated with organizational learning (Levinthal & Rerup, 2006). Following Langer's work, the idea of mindfulness has been extended from analysis at the individual level to analysis at the organizational level (Weick, Sutcliffe, & Obstfeld, 2008). In doing this, Weick et al. (2005) shifted the focus from individual mindfulness to collective mindfulness and "heedful interrelating" (Weick & Roberts, 1993). Heedful interrelating arises when people "act like they are under the direction of a single organizing centre... have a visualized representation of a group's meshed contributions... and bring group facts into existence" (Weick, 2009, p. 218). By analyzing data from HROs, Weick showed that individuals within these organizations collectively used five cognitive processes related to mindfulness to overcome a broad range of unexpected events.

Preoccupation With Failure

HROs are preoccupied with failures. There is a constant concern in HROs that error is embedded in ongoing day-to-day activities and that unexpected failures and limitations of foresight may amplify small errors. HROs realize that if separate small errors occur simultaneously, then the result could potentially be disastrous. Worrying about failure gives HROs much of their distinctive quality, and this distinctiveness arises from the simple fact that failures are a rare occurrence. This means that HROs are preoccupied with something that is seldom visible. To foster organization-wide concern with failure, HROs encourage personnel at all levels to report errors when they arise and make the most of any failure that is reported.

Reluctance to Simplify Operations

A common property of organizations is that their members simplify tasks—either in the way work is carried out, or in the way they perceive risk. For HROs, this simplification is potentially dangerous as it limits the precautions people take and the number of undesired consequences that they envision. Simplification increases the likelihood of eventual surprise and allows anomalies to accumulate, intuitions to be disregarded, and undesired consequences to grow more serious. To resist temptations to simplify, HROs cultivate requisite variety, which takes such forms as diverse checks and balances, including a proliferation of committees and meetings, selecting new employees with nontypical prior experience, frequent job rotation, and retraining. Redundancy also forms an important component of HROs, not only in the form of system standbys and backups, but also in the form of scrutiny of information and the inclusion of conceptual slack—defined as "a divergence in analytical perspectives among members of an organization over theories, models, or causal assumptions pertaining to its technology or production processes" (Vogus & Welbourne, 2003, p. 13).

Sensitivity to Operations

HROs are attentive to the frontline where the real work is being done. When people have well developed SA, they can make continuous adjustments that prevent errors from accumulating end enlarging. This is achieved through a combination of collective story building, shared mental representations, situation assessing with continual updates, and knowledge of physical realities of the organization's systems.

Commitment to Resilience

Weick and Sutcliffe (2001) define resilience as "the process of being mindful of errors that have already occurred and correcting them before they worsen or cause more serious harm" (p. 67). People in HROs are encouraged to make their system transparent and their operational practices widely known. This helps people to appreciate weaknesses and manage them better. People in HROs are committed to resilience and actively work to keep errors small and improvise workarounds to keep systems functioning. HROs see this "firefighting" as evidence that they are able to contain the unexpected. This is in contrast to other organizations, where managers may perceive successful firefighting as evidence that they are distracted and therefore unable to do their normal work (Weick & Sutcliffe, 2001). HROs need to have a broad repertoire of actions they can roll out when required, including informal skill and knowledge-based networks that organize themselves when potentially dangerous situations arise.

Underspecification of Structures

Weick, Sutcliffe, and Obstfeld (2008) argue that HROs are failure-free despite their orderliness, not because of it. An orderly hierarchy can amplify errors, and higher-level errors tend to amalgamate with lower level errors. This combination of errors is harder to understand when more interactive and complex. It is the very reliability that HROs cultivate that makes it possible for small errors to spread, accumulate, interact, and trigger serious consequences. To prevent this, HROs allow for underspecification of structures (also referred to as "deference to expertise"). Decisions may come from the top during normal times but during times of potential danger, decision-making migrates, and a predefined emergency structure comes into force. Decision-making can be made on the frontline, and authority is given to people with the most expertise, regardless of their rank. The decision-making structure in HROs is a hybrid of hierarchy and specialization. Decision-making authority therefore is shifted down to the lowest possible levels and clear lines of responsibility are put into place.

Mindfulness, then, is the

> combination of ongoing scrutiny of existing expectations, continuous refinement and differentiation of expectations based on newer experiences, willingness and capability to invent new expectations that make sense of unprecedented events, a more nuanced appreciation of context and ways to deal with it, and identification of new dimensions of context that improve foresight and current functioning. (Weick & Sutcliffe, 2001, p. 42)

For Weick, the five processes of mindfulness mobilize the resources for sensemaking.

Conclusion

The advance of digital technologies has substantially improved the resilience and efficiency of networked computer systems. These technologies provide various processes, including monitoring, control, and automation, to help achieve resilience. Networked systems are widely used for communication purposes and thus are essential. Yet, they face growing and evolving cyber-physical and social risks, as well as other challenges including natural disasters. These risks result not only from growing direct threats, but also from interdependencies and associated cascading effects. Ambitious investment in innovation is required to increase the resilience of networked systems, especially in the context of sensitive industrial sites and plants when protection measures against impacting events fail. The critical functions that sensitive industrial sites and plants provide, including safety and security, need to be resilient when adverse conditions present themselves. A holistic approach to resilience should include both technical and nontechnical approaches to promptly cope with cyber-physical and social-related threats to networked systems.

Our current and future work is concerned with using the technical, human, and organizational insights we have obtained from our studies of resilience and applying them to understand and develop resilient and secure industrial systems in the European and indeed the global economy. Of particular concern is the impact of cyberattacks on sensitive industrial sites as digital technologies become increasingly vital for ICS that control and monitor safety, security, and production processes. Manufacturing and industrial sites constitute a critical component for the sustainable development of economies and society. These sites constitute an interdependent network of plants and facilities. Sensitive industrial sites and other industrial plants such as nuclear facilities produce or handle hazardous materials (e.g., radioactive materials, toxic chemicals, explosive materials). An attack or challenge at one of these sites could lead to significant environmental damage including loss of life and disruption of global supply chains.

Therefore, investment in research and innovation is required to increase the resilience of sensitive industrial sites and plants when protection measures against impacting events fail. The critical functions that sensitive industrial sites and plants provide, including safety and security, need to be preserved when adverse conditions present themselves. To minimize the associated risks, measures are necessary to prevent major accidents and to ensure appropriate preparedness and response should such accidents happen. Future research needs to be concerned with enhancing the resilience of ICT systems, ICS, and associated processes. Special attention must be paid to communications and information-sharing regarding about incidents and possible precursor indicators of cascading impacts that result from neighboring events.

Key Messages

1. Modern networked systems are critical infrastructures.
2. Modern networked computer systems need to be designed and engineered to have resilience as a major property.
3. Resilience is "the ability of a network or system to provide and maintain an acceptable level of service in the face of various faults and challenges to normal operation" (Sterbenz, Hutchison, et al., 2010)
4. Modern networked systems are complex and have three aspects that need to be considered in combination when building resilience into them: these are technology, organization, and people.
5. Investment in research and innovation is required to increase the resilience of sensitive industrial sites and plants when protection measures against impacting events fail. The critical functions that sensitive industrial sites and plants provide, including safety and security, need to be preserved when adverse conditions present themselves.

References

Adger, W. N., Hughes, T. P., Folke, C., Carpenter, S. R., & Rockström, J. (2005). Social-ecological resilience to coastal disasters. *Science, 309*(5737), 1036–1039. doi:10.1126/science.1112122

Allenby, B., & Fink, J. (2005). Toward inherently secure and resilient societies. *Science, 309*(5737), 1034–1036. doi:10.1126/science.1111534

Austrian Standards Institute. (2010). *Hrsg., Risikomanagement—Grundsätze und Richtlinien*. Bd. 1. Retrieved from https://shop.austrian-standards.at/action/de/public/details/353917/OENORM_ISO_31000_2010_02_01

Baker, J. A., III., Bowman, F. L., Erwin, G., Gorton, S., Hendershot, D., Leveson, N., . . . Wilson, L. D. (2007). *The report of the BP US refineries independent safety review panel*. Retrieved from http://www.csb.gov.assets/1/19/Baker_panel_report1.pdf

Bostrom, A., Morgan, M. G., Fischhoff, B., & Read, D. (1994). What do people know about global climate change? 1. Mental models. *Risk Analysis, 14*(6), 959–970. doi:10.1111/j.1539-6924.1994.tb00065.x

Bruncak, R., Bohra, N., Simpson, S. P., Rohrer, J. P., Sterbenz, J. P., Hutchison, D., . . . de Meer, H. (2011). *Resilience and survivability for future networking: Framework, mechanisms, and experimental evaluation.* ResumeNET. Retrieved from https://pdfs.semanticscholar.org/33a2/14185f74972c9b1b6f9f296a2de1af1ee8ad.pdf

Burke, C. S., Sims, D. E., Lazzara, E. H., & Salas, E. (2007). Trust in leadership: A multi-level review and integration. *The Leadership Quarterly, 18*(6), 606–632. doi:10.1016/j.leaqua.2007.09.006

Cebula, J. J., & Young, L. R. (2010). *A taxonomy of operational cyber security risks* (No. CMU/SEI-2010-TN-028). Pittsburgh, PA: Carnegie Mellon University, Software Engineering Institute.

Chandola, V., Banerjee, A., & Kumar, V. (2009). Anomaly detection: A survey. *ACM Computing Surveys (CSUR), 41*(3), 15. doi:10.1145/1541880.1541882

Clarke, K., Hardstone, G., Rouncefield, M., & Sommerville, I. (2005). *Trust in technology: A socio-technical perspective.* Dordrecht, The Netherlands: Springer.

Committee on National Security Systems. (2010). *National information assurance (IA) glossary* (CNSS Instruction No. 4009). Retrieved from https://www.cdse.edu/documents/toolkits-issm/cnssi4009.pdf

Cook, R., & Rasmussen, J. (2005). "Going solid": A model of system dynamics and consequences for patient safety. *Quality and Safety in Health Care, 14*(2), 130–134. doi:10.1136/qshc.2003.009530

Dewsbury, G., & Dobson, J. (2007). *Responsibility and dependable systems.* Heidelberg, Germany: Springer Verlag.

Dirks, K. T., & Ferrin, D. L. (2001). The role of trust in organizational settings. *Organization Science, 12*(4), 450–467. doi:10.1287/orsc.12.4.450.10640

ENISA Glossary. (2019). *Risk management.* Retrieved from https://www.enisa.europa.eu/topics/threat-risk-management/risk-management/current-risk/bcm-resilience/glossary/p-z

Esposito, C., Gouglidis, A., Hutchison, D., Gurtov, A. V., Helvik, B. E., Heegaard, P. E., . . . Rak, J. (2018). On the disaster resiliency within the context of 5G networks: The RECODIS experience. In *European Conference on Networks and Communications 2018.* New York, NY: IEEE.

Franke, U., & Brynielsson, J. (2014). Cyber situational awareness: A systematic review of the literature. *Computers & Security, 46,* 18–31. doi:10.1016/j.cose.2014.06.008

Górniak, S., Tirtea, R., Ikonomou, D., Cadzow, S., Gierszal, H., Sutton, D., . . . Vishik, C. (2011). *Enabling and managing end-to-end resilience.* ENISA. Retrieved from https://www.enisa.europa.eu/publications/end-to-end-resilience

Gouglidis, A., Green, B., Busby, J., Rouncefield, M., Hutchison, D., & Schauer, S. (2016, September). Threat awareness for critical infrastructures resilience. In *2016 8th International Workshop on Resilient Networks Design and Modeling (RNDM)* (pp. 196–202). Halmstad, Sweden: IEEE. doi:10.1109/RNDM.2016.7608287

Gouglidis, A., Shirazi, S. N., Simpson, S., Smith, P., & Hutchison, D. (2016). A multi-level approach to resilience of critical infrastructures and services. In *2016 23rd International Conference on Telecommunications (ICT)* (pp. 1–5). Thessaloniki, Greece: IEEE. doi:10.1109/ICT.2016.7500410

Gouglidis, A., Hu, V. C., Busby, J. S., & Hutchison, D. (2017). Verification of resilience policies that assist attribute based access control. In *Proceedings of the 2nd ACM Workshop on Attribute-Based Access Control* (pp. 43–52). Scottsdale, AZ: ACM. doi:10.1145/3041048.3041049

Hilgartner, S. (1992). The social construction of risk objects: Or, how to pry open networks of risk. In J. F. Short & L. Clarke (Eds.), *Organizations, uncertainties, and risk* (pp. 39–53). Boulder, CO: Westview Press.

Hollnagel, E., Paries, J., Woods, D. W., & Wreathall, J. (2010). *Resilience engineering in practice: A guidebook.* Boca Raton, FL: CRC Press.

Hollnagel, E., Woods, D. D., & Leveson, N. (2006). *Resilience engineering: Concepts and precepts.* Farnham, UK: Ashgate.

Hutchison, D., & Sterbenz, J. P. (2018). Architecture and design for resilient networked systems. *Computer Communications, 131,* 13–21. doi:10.1016/j.comcom.2018.07.028

International Organization for Standardization. (2009). *ISO 31000: 2009 Risk management—Principles and guidelines.* Geneva, Switzerland: Author.

König, S., Gouglidis, A., Green, B., & Solar, A. (2018). Assessing the impact of malware attacks in utility networks. In S. Rass & S. Schauer (Eds.), *Game theory for security and risk management* (pp. 335–351). Basel, Switzerland: Birkhäuser.

Langer, E. J., & Moldoveanu, M. (2000). The construct of mindfulness. *Journal of Social Issues, 56*(1), 1–9. doi:10.1111/0022-4537.00148

Levinthal, D., & Rerup, C. (2006). Crossing an apparent chasm: Bridging mindful and less-mindful perspectives on organizational learning. *Organization Science, 17*(4), 502–513. doi:10.1287/orsc.1060.0197

Machuca, C. M., Secci, S., Vizarreta, P., Kuipers, F., Gouglidis, A., Hutchison, D., . . . Ristov, S. (2016). Technology-related disasters: A survey towards disaster-resilient software defined networks. In *2016 8th International Workshop on Resilient Networks Design and Monitoring (RNDM)* (pp. 35–42). Halmstad, Sweden: IEEE. doi:10.1109/RNDM.2016.7608265

Moteff, J. D. (2012). *Critical infrastructure resilience: The evolution of policy and programs and issues for congress*. Congressional Research Service Reports. Washington, DC: Library of Congress.

Obregon, L. (2015). *Secure architecture for industrial control systems*. The SANS Institute. Retrieved from https://www.sans.org/reading-room/whitepapers/ICS/secure-architecture-industrial-control-systems-36327

Perrow, C. (1999). *Normal accidents: Living with high-risk technologies* (2nd ed.). Chichester, UK: Princeton University Press.

Randell, B. (2000). Turing memorial lecture facing up to faults. *The Computer Journal, 43*(2), 95–106. doi:10.1093/comjnl/43.2.95

Rochlin, G. I., La Porte, T. R., & Roberts, K. H. (1987). The self-designing high-reliability organization: Aircraft carrier flight operations at sea. *Naval War College Review, 40*(4), 76–90.

Schauer, S. (2018). A risk management approach for highly interconnected networks. In S. Rass & S. Schauer (Eds.), *Game theory for security and risk management* (pp. 285–311). Cham, Switzerland: Birkhäuser.

Sedgewick, A. (2014). *Framework for improving critical infrastructure cybersecurity* (Version 1.1). NIST Cybersecurity Framework. doi:10.6028/NIST.CSWP.02122014

Serva, M. A., Fuller, M. A., & Mayer, R. C. (2005). The reciprocal nature of trust: A longitudinal study of interacting teams. *Journal of Organizational Behavior, 26*(6), 625–648. doi:10.1002/job.331

Shirazi, S. N., Gouglidis, A., Farshad, A., & Hutchison, D. (2017). The extended cloud: Review and analysis of mobile edge computing and fog from a security and resilience perspective. *IEEE Journal on Selected Areas in Communications, 35*(11), 2586–2595. doi:10.1109/JSAC.2017.2760478

Smith, P., Hutchison, D., Sterbenz, J. P., Schöller, M., Fessi, A., Karaliopoulos, M., & Plattner, B. (2011). Network resilience: a systematic approach. *IEEE Communications Magazine, 49*(7), 88–97. doi:10.1109/MCOM.2011.5936160

Snook, S. (2000). *Friendly fire*. Chichester, UK: Princeton University Press.

Sterbenz, J. P., Hutchison, D., Çetinkaya, E. K., Jabbar, A., Rohrer, J. P., Schöller, M., & Smith, P. (2010). Resilience and survivability in communication networks: Strategies, principles, and survey of disciplines. *Computer Networks, 54*(8), 1245–1265. doi:10.1016/j.comnet.2010.03.005

Vogus, T. J., & Welbourne, T. M. (2003). Structuring for high reliability: HR practices and mindful processes in reliability-seeking organizations. *Journal of Organizational Behavior, 24*(7), 877–903. doi:10.1002/job.221

Wei, D., Lu, Y., Jafari, M., Skare, P. M., & Rohde, K. (2011). Protecting smart grid automation systems against cyberattacks. *IEEE Transactions on Smart Grid, 2*(4), 782–795. doi:10.1109/tsg.2011.2159999

Weick, K. E. (1987). Organizational culture as a source of high reliability. *California Management Review, 29*(2), 112–127. doi:10.2307/41165243

Weick, K. E. (1995). *Sensemaking in organizations*. Thousand Oaks, CA: SAGE.

Weick, K. E. (2001). *Making sense of the organization*. Oxford, UK: Wiley-Blackwell.

Weick, K. E. (2009). *Making sense of the organization: Vol. 2: The impermanent organization*. Chichester, UK: John Wiley.

Weick, K. E., & Roberts, K. H. (1993). Collective mind in organizations: Heedful interrelating on flight decks. *Administrative Science Quarterly, 38*(3), 357–381. doi:10.2307/2393372

Weick, K. E., & Sutcliffe, K. M. (2001). *Managing the unexpected: Assuring high performance in an age of complexity*. San Francisco, CA: Jossey-Bass.

Weick, K. E., & Sutcliffe, K. M. (2007). *Managing the unexpected: Resilient performance in an age of uncertainty.* San Francisco, CA: John Wiley.

Weick, K. E., Sutcliffe, K. M., & Obstfeld, D. (2005). Organizing and the process of sensemaking. *Organization Science, 16*(4), 409–421. doi:10.1287/orsc.1050.0133

Weick, K. E., Sutcliffe, K. M., & Obstfeld, D. (2008). Organizing for high reliability: Processes of collective mindfulness. In A. Boin (Ed.), *Crisis management:* (Vol. III, pp. 31–66). London, UK: SAGE.

Patterns for Achieving Resilience in Engineered and Organizational Systems

Scott Jackson, Victoria Hailey, Keith D. Willett, Timothy Ferris, and Eric A. Specking

Introduction

This chapter introduces the concept of system resilience and provides a foundation from which to identify recurring patterns of resilience in resilient system design applicable to engineered and organizational systems. Specifically, we are concerned with how resilience in different domains is affected by the system type commonly found in those domains and the adversities encountered. This chapter focuses on how resilience is achieved in two different types of systems (engineered and organizational) and the patterns involved in achieving that resilience.

Traditionally fields like psychology, ecology, and materials science define resilience as "the capacity to recover quickly from difficulties; toughness" ("Resilience," 2018, para. 1). An assumption is the definition applies to regaining the state or functionality affected by the adversity or recovery from some functional degradation caused by the adversity. More recently researchers (e.g., Hollnagel, Woods, & Leveson, 2006) have adopted a broader definition to include anticipating, withstanding, adapting, anticipation, and avoidance. This is the definition adopted by the systems engineering community.

For engineered systems the definition of resilience is "the ability to provide required capability in the face of adversity" (BKCASE Editorial Board, 2016, para. 4). BKCASE is the Body of Knowledge and Curriculum to Advance Systems Engineering Project, which is the compendium of knowledge about systems engineering overseen by the International Council on Systems Engineering (INCOSE). Four characteristics of resilient systems (identified by

Madni & Jackson, 2009) are the ability to anticipate, absorb, reconfigure, and restore capability in the face of a threat. These characteristics apply to both engineering and organizational systems). Jackson and Ferris (2013) identify a set of design principles, which can also be called techniques for a system to achieve these characteristics associated with resilience.

Domain Characteristics and Resilience

For our purposes, a domain is a specified boundary of knowledge or activity. Following are the five characteristics of domains that influence the ability of a system to be resilient.

System Resilience

According to BKCASE Editorial Board (2016), system resilience is the ability to provide required capability in the face of adversity. By this definition, an adversity must have an effect for recovery from that effect to occur. Therefore, the concept of resilience is a response to an adverse effect. Resistance is the ability to withstand the initial impact of the adversity. Following the initial impact, the system may adapt to the adversity or it may degrade to an acceptable level of capability. If the degradation is gradual, this is called tolerance. Finally, the system may recover to an acceptable level of capability. This recovery does not necessarily imply full recovery but rather recovery to a level acceptable to system stakeholders.

To understand a system's resilience, the type of system being examined must be accounted for. According to INCOSE (2015) a system is "an integrated set of elements, subsystems and assemblies that accomplish a defined objective. These elements include products (hardware, software, firmware), processes, people, information, techniques, facilities, services, and other support elements" (p. 5). For this chapter, the systems of interest are the broadest range of systems defined by Sillitto and colleagues (2017) in which the essential characteristics of a system are any entity consisting of (a) many parts, (b) a relationship between parts, and (c) emergent properties not exhibited by the individual parts. These systems can be real or abstract.

One system type is a system of systems (SoS). This type of system is comprised of multiple component systems independently developed but acting together for a common goal. Sometimes in the SoS context the interaction between component systems makes it harder to achieve resilience. Other times the interaction enhances resilience. Jamshidi (2009) provides a comprehensive study of SoS.

Adversity

The quality of system resilience depends on how well the system responds to an adversity or adverse effect. There are many types of potential adversities. Some domains are inherently hostile, such as nature. Adversities can be human-made or natural and may originate within the system (endogenous adversity) or from without the system (exogenous adversity). Endogenous adversities include inclement weather, natural disasters, and adversaries with intelligence and intent.

In any domain, particularly in the civil domain, adversities can be either natural or human-made. In human-made domains adversities can be internal, that is, the result of internal latent faults.

Responding to an adversity may not mean fully regaining what was lost nor full recovery. If the system is human-made, the acceptable degree of recovery will depend on the expectations of stakeholders.

Capability

Central to resilience is the concept of capability. According to the INCOSE (2015) handbook, capability is the "ability to achieve a specific objective under stated conditions" (p. 262). Capability is one expression for system efficacy, that is, the system's ability to bring about a desired result. To recover is to compensate for the temporary or permanent loss. The system of interest (SoI), that is the system being addressed, may not get back what it lost even as it continues to produce desired results via compensation from other functions. In other words, part of system resilience is it *regains* what it lost or *recovers* from a loss through compensation for that loss.

Capability also includes the ability to anticipate or avoid an adversity, to withstand an adversity, to degrade gracefully following an encounter with an adversity, to recover to an acceptable level, and to remain an integral system before, during, and after an encounter with an aversity.

Central to the SoI's consistent and comprehensive ability to sustain desired capability are *patterns* that help retain efficacy, prevent the loss of ability to perform a function, regain what it lost, or recover from that loss. Patterns of robustness help the system withstand the adversity. Patterns of adaptability help the system recover or regain (e.g., return to a prior state). Patterns of tolerance allow a system to degrade gracefully to a lower but acceptable level of capability. Patterns of integrity allow a system to remain whole before, during, and after an encounter with adversity.

Timeframe

In all domains, damage by an adversity and recovery will occur over a period of time. Intervals of interest include times to prepare for the adversity, time to anticipate and detect the adversity, time to react to the adversity, and the time to recover. The capability required of a system may be constant through all the times referred to in the previous sentence, where the need is for a system, which under a very wide spanning envelope of conditions would be required to produce constant available capability. Other systems may perform roles where the necessity for available capability changes in response to *time* or some other factor.

Reviewing an operational timeline for resilience can help distinguish the nuances of the different phases. Figure 35.1 shows a general timeline for resilience that includes *before an event*, *during an event*, and *after an event*. Upon threat initiation, the SoI may be resistant to its effects. For example, a common system is a coastal community threatened by a hurricane. In the earliest phase of the timeframe a hurricane may be detected far out at sea. It is not known whether this particular hurricane will strike the community or not. However, even during this phase the coastal communities may have taken some preliminary steps such as

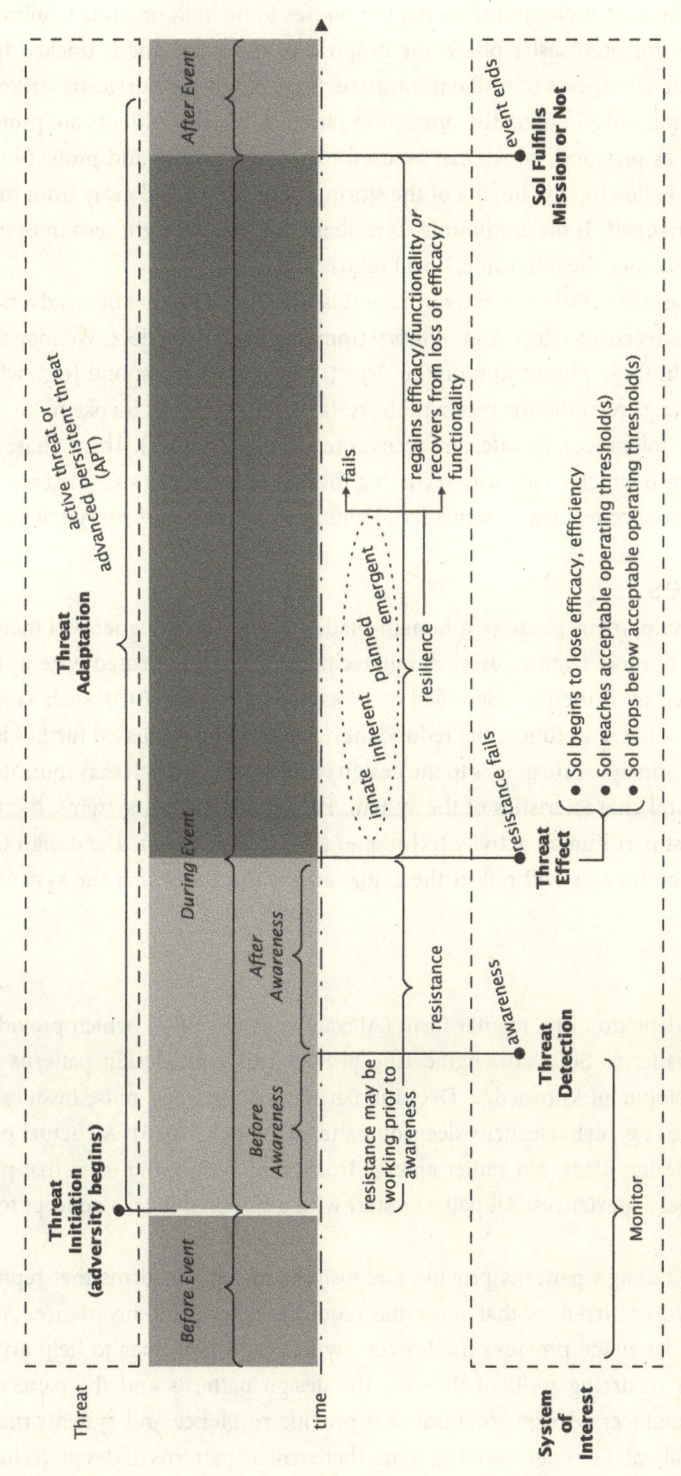

FIGURE 35.1 Resilience timeline (operational view).

providing distributed power systems (e.g., generators) to residents. Anticipating a series of such storms, many such communities require houses to be built on stilts to allow for water surges. During this predisaster phase, the progress of the hurricane is tracked using satellites and aircraft, all aspects of resilient infrastructure. When the hurricane strikes land, the system (the community) enters the protection phase in which residents are protected with materials such as plywood, which can be used to cover windows and protect homes from water damage. Following the impact of the storm, water is diverted away from the community through channels. If the community is resilient and has the right resources in place before, during, and after the hurricane, it will return to normal.

Three phases for resilience emerge from this timeline: *detection* of an adversity's effect, *response* to an adversity's effect, and *recovery* from an adversity's effect. We may then define functions within these phases to monitor, detect, triage, notify, respond (e.g., withstand or resist), change (e.g., reconfigure, reconstitute, restart), fail over (e.g., invoke redundancy), fail gracefully (e.g., tolerance), failsafe, and recover (e.g., adapt, restore). These phases provide a framework within which to identify recurring themes of resilience such that we can design guidelines to produce resilient systems (i.e., identify and codify *resilient system patterns*).

Techniques

During the development phase of a human-made system, the designer will incorporate in the design one or more features using design techniques. For engineered systems these techniques are based on principles identified by Jackson and Ferris (2013), such as absorption, physical redundancy, and functional redundancy. Each will be discussed further later in this chapter. These principles are guides to the design of the system, which may indicate the physical or behavioral characteristics of the system. For organizational systems, the techniques are for the most part human activity techniques (ISO 22301, 2012). The design features incorporated in both cases will reflect the actual adversities for which the system is able to respond.

Patterns

A *pattern* is a depiction of a regular form (Alexander et al., 1977), which provides us with architectural patterns. Software engineering provided us with design patterns to capture and reuse development knowledge. Decision patterns capture and reuse business and mission knowledge (e.g., cybersecurity decision patterns; Willett, 2016). All actual patterns are not arbitrary design ideas, but rather emerge from observation; that is, actual patterns are mined from real experiences. All patterns start with a notional idea, a concept for a particular pattern.

Resilience design patterns provide a repository of regular forms that represent real-world resilience occurrences that meet the requisite criteria for invariance. A resilience design pattern language provides the lexicon, syntax, and grammar to help articulate the abstractions of recurring resilient themes. The design patterns and the pattern language help systems engineers design solutions that provide resilience and systems that have the ability to be resilient. For engineered systems, there will be patterns of design techniques that enhance resilience. For organizational systems, there will be patterns of human activity that do the same.

The Engineered System Domain

The engineered system domain consists primarily of systems that are human-made and physical, as opposed to organizational. This section describes these types of systems, their adversities, their expected capabilities, the timelines over which they encounter adversities, and the techniques they use to achieve resilience. This section also provides case studies that illustrate the application of these principles and the consequences of the failure to apply them. Some of the systems may have human operators. In those cases, these systems are called sociotechnical systems.

Systems for the Engineered System Domain

A Department of Homeland Security report (2018) identifies 16 infrastructure sectors that are critical. These sectors include chemical processing; commercial facilities, such as offices; communications, such as telephones; manufacturing, such as automobiles; dams; emergency services, such as ambulances; energy, such as electrical power generation; financial services, such as banks; food and agriculture, such as farms and food processing; government facilities, such as state and federal office buildings or military bases; the healthcare sector, such as hospitals; the information technology sector, such as databases; water and waste systems, such as water mains and sewers; nuclear reactors; and transportation systems, such as railways and airports. The systems discussed in this section are primarily civil rather than military in mission. Many of these systems are systems of systems. For example, the electrical power system, in whatever form, provides power to almost all other systems.

Techniques for the Engineered Systems Domain

Each system within the engineered systems domain has its own set of techniques that can be identified and implemented in the development phase. All of the techniques described next are abstractions; that is, they do not identify a specific solution. They only suggest an approximate form for the final solution to take. The following paragraphs describe some of the more notable techniques followed by a case study of its application.

The Absorption Technique

This technique protects the system from forces or stresses to a predicted design level (it absorbs the stress to maintain functioning). This level is accompanied by an acceptable margin of strength and an acceptable level of degradation. Almost every domain has an absorption level to which the system is designed. For example, in the aviation domain, all commercially certified aircraft have to meet the bird strike requirement. This is the requirement that the engines of an aircraft should be able to *absorb* the impact of a bird of a certain weight without loss of power. According to the Federal Aviation Administration (2015), this weight is about four pounds. This does not mean that the requirement will not be exceeded. If they are, as was the case with US Airways Flight 1549 that was forced to land on the Hudson River in New York after striking a flock of Canada geese (Pariès, 2011), the aircraft will have to rely on other techniques such as *functional redundancy* described in the following text to maintain capability.

The Physical Redundancy Technique

This is one of the most widely recognized techniques in engineering. It simply states that the system should be designed with two or more identical and independent branches. If one of the branches fails, the other branch will be able to sustain the predicted load despite adversity. Following the failure of the U.S.–Canada power grid in 2003, the U.S.–Canada Task Force (2004) issued a report that called for "backup capabilities of all critical functions" (p. 9). This is tantamount to *physical redundancy*.

The Functional Redundancy Technique

Functional redundancy is similar to physical redundancy except that the two branches are physically and functionally different. This technique has been found to be useful in many cases. The idea is that there is one branch that the system depends on for normal operation. There is a second branch with less capability but sufficient to maintain an adequate level of capability. In the case of US Airways Flight 1549 the primary branch was the engines designed with the *absorption* technique in mind. When that system failed (shut down), the secondary branch consisted of internal power provided by a ram air turbine and control by the pilot, the latter constituting the *human in the loop* technique described next. These two techniques provided the secondary capability for the aircraft to land in the river and save the lives of the 155 passenger and crew, thus achieving functional redundancy.

The Human in the Loop Technique

This technique states that the system should be designed to allow for human cognition where needed. One of the most well-known examples of the use of this technique is the Apollo 11 mission. According to Eyles (2009) computer problems on this mission forced the operator Neil Armstrong to land the module on the moon manually. It can be said that the *human in the loop* technique was critical to the success of the mission.

The Distributed Capacity Technique

This technique states that the system should be designed so that its nodes are independent such that if one or more nodes are damaged or destroyed, the remaining nodes will continue to operate. For example, following a hurricane, the electrical power system employs this technique by installing portable generators in critical structures, such as hospitals. An example of the use of this technique was the deployment of generators during the engagement timeframe as described by Mendoça and Wallace (2006) to restore power in New York after the 9/11 attacks. Distributed systems are usually expected to be enduring, perhaps with replacement of assets which form parts of the system. In the case of 9/11, the distributed systems were stored for emergency use and then deployed as needed. Distributed systems allow the entire system to degrade more gradually when it encounters an adversity.

Organizational Systems Domain

Organizations are systems, satisfying the various definitions of resilience through their form and function: they have interrelated elements—people, processes, technology, information, data, and feedback loops—that are interdependent and produce more than the sum of their parts. By nature, organizational systems are comprised of multiple systems or SoS. Each individual employed in an organization is, by nature, both a system as well as a system element. A division of a corporation may be a self-sustaining system within a larger organizational system. The relationships formed by the SoS structures are virtually infinite in their range, making control over such systems challenging.

Organizations rarely follow an engineering process during their early formation and development. People form relationships, more or less formally, that develop into new organizations, which are usually allowed to evolve organically toward a shared goal. For example, as most people know, Apple was the result of a working partnership between college buddies Steve Jobs and Steve Wozniak that coalesced around an idea to popularize personal computing.

Organizational processes, as qualities of systems, function similarly in bee or ant colonies: each is a superorganism whose shared goals, means, and opportunities translate into shared objectives, tasks, and processes. Likewise, the United Nations, as an international organization, shares the same characteristics as the local neighborhood recycling collective: both share the same general behavioral patterns that people (and some insects) follow when collectively organizing to accomplish a specific purpose or goal.

It takes time and effort for organizational teams to form, storm, norm, and then perform. Once formed, the system's components—people and other resources—are constantly changing, even as their processes stabilize. This dynamic aspect of organizational behavior is apparent in any commercial corporation: its people, structures, processes, products, services, suppliers, and customers are always changing and intentionally evolving to a level of performance capability that can provide a return for corporate investors.

Individual elements, as well as their composition, can and must be replaceable for the organization to meet its customer needs consistently, as a measure of its quality performance. When viewed in this way, the organization can be seen to be continually undergoing change, with that undercurrent of constant activity challenging the limits of its control and efficacy in perpetuity.

When viewed through a resilience lens, one of the critical prerequisites for achieving organizational capability to recover is having the required level of *process* capability already well established in the event of a disruption. For example, organizations often believe they are resilience-capable because they have documented policies, processes, procedures, and job descriptions, but are surprised to learn they also need adequate resources to execute production processes. To recover from a potentially catastrophic event, the organization needs to be able to reproduce its own set of derived or designed processes when the need arises, together with the resources, whether material or human, to execute a recovery plan. When the twin towers were attacked on 9/11, the stark reality was that those organizations housed in only one location, and without distributed resources, perished. Those with distributed plans, resources, policies, procedures, and the resources to use them, were able to recover.

Whether sales, finance, operations, management, or governance, each set of processes has its own key resources that become essential elements for recovery that, while unique, can be replicated, if and when needed. However, not all organizational processes should be prioritized as essential to begin recovery. For example, to prioritize sales over operations as the first recovery target in the midst of a disaster could be viewed by existing customers as disloyal, or worse, profiteering, when it appears that a corporation is ignoring its operational responsibilities to its customers.

The unpredictability and complexity of organizational systems take root in the dynamic nature of one of its main system elements: people who, by nature, tend to resist change, are unpredictable and perpetually fail to understand their own biases and limitations, including learning from history (Kahneman, 2011). These aspects of human nature make it more difficult to predict with any certainty that outcomes can be achieved without specific plans, accountabilities, and responsibilities in place to orchestrate events.

Sometimes, organizational systems are not designed or engineered with a purpose in mind, instead evolving into their operational forms. Organizations that spontaneously materialize, such as grassroots citizen movements that evolve into formalized activist groups, demonstrate that direction, purpose, and goals are not always defined or even understood. The emerging entity forms around a shared belief or vision. Greenpeace emerged from an ad hoc citizen's group called the "Don't Make a Wave Committee" whose members protested underground nuclear testing. Over time, its members formalized the Canadian nonprofit, nonviolent environmental protest group, with its name representing the unity of the peace and ecology movements (Greenpeace, 2019).

Organizations seeking resilience as an inherent system characteristic need to be cognizant that the pursuit of this attribute often implies a return or recovery to a former operational state prior to the adversity. To build resilience requires having a target capability defined. Without defined, organized, and structured organizational systems in place, the recovery target can remain undefined, and recovery cannot be assured. The various components of the organization must be identified to do so. Given that each organization is different and that the recovery context will be derived from the organizational context, all the elements that are comprised by the "organization," whether permanent or variable, must be identified if they are to be targeted to be a vital system element needing to be recovered.

In addition to such elements as people, systems, processes, policies, procedures, and relationships, there is an endless array of system elements that contextualize each system's recovery efforts, such as buildings, locations, market capitalization, materials, reputation, and intellectual property. The value and priorities for recovery for each of these, as elements of that organizational system, must be determined if resilience is to be achievable when needed.

But what about situations in which resilience is achievable, but a return to a former state is neither possible nor desirable? For example, all organizations, including governments, corporations, businesses, and cooperatives, large and small, urban and rural, are facing the uncertainties of climate change. It may not be possible for recovery to a former state, for example, when hurricanes and monsoons leave a wake of geophysical changes in coastlines, landscapes, and waterways. Instead, recovery may mean adaptation to a new and different state where continuity is once again possible.

Consider, then, those organizations expecting to achieve climate resilience when faced with weather-related disasters. They must understand their operational processes in their current state—their inputs, activities, and outputs—and, in doing so, bring into focus considerations of such issues as whether to source from local or national or global suppliers in the face of disruptive climate events. Interactions between systems and process interdependencies must also be understood if plans for a successful recovery strategy are to be successful, especially when supply chain reliability affects critical infrastructure.

Identifying existing vulnerabilities and threats to recovery is key to understanding, and eliminating, the potential failure points when recovery plans are triggered into action. A full understanding of the current physical and operational states before, during, and after impact requires a precautionary approach when identifying weaknesses, so that realistic recovery plans can be developed to achieve a specified future recovery target. When this step is omitted, results can be catastrophic, and the planned recovered state can be unachievable. For example, regulators' assumptions about Fukushima's vital cooling systems capabilities were wrong when faced with an earthquake-induced 50-foot tsunami. By failing to recognize, and plan for, the nuclear facility's actual, as opposed to perceived, vulnerabilities: "Three of the six reactors melted down, with their uranium fuel rods liquefied like candle wax, dripping to the bottom of the reactor vessels in a molten mass hot enough to burn through the steel walls and even penetrate the concrete floors below (Fackler, 2017, para. 7). It took officials six and a half years to move from "disaster" to "clean-up," with full recovery never being achieved, and the facility undergoing decommissioning instead.

Priorities help with decisions concerning the deployment of scarce and urgent resources. Decisions, made by appropriate authorities, should determine the necessary course of action at the moment of impact: who should do what, when, where, and how, with the *why* having become the trigger to act. Stimulus–response type decisions, similar to automated systems inputs/outputs, progressing through if–then–else decision logic, must also be "programmed" into organizational decision-making processes. Decisions have to be made well in advance, not at the time of impact, when the emotional human response is limited to fight, flight, or freeze.

Responsible authorities, both public and private, are the appropriate accountable parties for determining whether recovery is even possible, such as with Fukushima or with a devastating corporate loss of reputation resulting from a corruption indictment. In some contexts, perseverance is the ideal continuity strategy, whereas in other circumstances, without knowing what the desired operational state is or what it takes to achieve it, achieving expected outcomes in the face of adverse conditions becomes an impossible task.

When planning for organizational resilience, preparing to mitigate the effects of such far-reaching and all-encompassing catalysts for change, such as global warming and biodiversity loss, organizations are often criticized for being too risk-averse. However, as unwelcome as the task is, preparation for disaster is also the critical first step in determining which possible actions will best determine successful organizational outcomes—in this case, resilience in the face of disruptions.

Organizational System Adversity

Adversity in organizational systems translates to threats arising from internal and external sources. External threats to organizations are virtually infinite, from distributing malware to industrial espionage, making context and probability two key components in determining what threats to resilience need to be managed. In some cases, when external threats cannot be avoided easily, such as the location of a facility on a fault line in an active earthquake zone, other strategic safeguards are required to ensure risks are appropriately mitigated to make resilience achievable.

An organization's need to understand, for example, the multifaceted nature of climate change—an external threat—will force a different analysis of risk than a competitive analysis. The specific threats, vulnerabilities, and required safeguards each present a varied set of resilience targets to be managed, with different impacts being mitigated to achieve recovery. Each organization must be able to identify its risk sources according to its own unique context. To do so, it must evaluate the probability and severity of its critical threats and their impacts, providing an accurate assessment of existing vulnerabilities.

By way of illustration, organizations that provide critical infrastructure services, such as telecommunications and hospitals, are expected to have a recovery plan at the ready that offers seamless 24/7 service capability, even in the event of a Category 5 storm. Despite such dangers, critical infrastructure is expected to withstand unpredictable, chain reactions of hazardous events such as lightning strikes, floods, power outages, downed communications, and failures in transportation.

Each recovery context, however, needs to maintain its own unique and predetermined plans of organizational capability. Operations and communications with customers and suppliers depend on critical infrastructure to move goods and services, and even have employees report for work. An online, for-profit games developer, on the other hand, itself dependent on critical infrastructure to function, is unlikely to be expected to remain operational during such hazards.

External threats are also context specific. Generally, an organization's purpose and mode of operation are readily identifiable through commonly obtained, industry-specific threat lists that characterize those threats most likely to be experienced within a specific sector. For example, there is little value in a hospital reviewing the threats lists of a construction company. However, building resilience requires also identifying the unique risk sources. Common organizational threats, such as bad actors and natural disasters, are more obvious, while others may be unique to their own purpose, such as the inability to procure suppliers in a new industry space.

Assessment of risk is a knowledge area required by most organizations if they plan to achieve resilience. Insurance is an industry that manages resilience risk using actuarial science. Ironically, insurance customers, as the industry's primary revenue source, are also one of its biggest threats and liabilities, when too many legitimate claims require immediate payouts.

Internal threats are sometimes considered easier to identify, since they are attributable to the activities and behaviors occurring within the organization's boundaries. However, internal threats warrant equal, and in some domains even more, attention than publicly known external threats, since by nature internal threats to resilience are easier to mask outside the glare of public scrutiny. Confidentiality and nondisclosure agreements often compound the secrecy surrounding internal threats and their co-existing vulnerabilities, making them even more insidious, and potentially delaying recovery, and in doing so, increasing their negative impact.

On the other hand, some of the most challenging adversities are those that arise from within, such as fraud or intellectual property theft because they are often hidden. When internal threats materialize and go unmitigated or unnoticed, they can weaken and destroy an organization's overall capabilities to recover, especially if vulnerabilities are continually exploited and capabilities are eroded without scrutiny. For example, employees working in a toxic organizational culture are less likely to contribute productively when working for repressive, bullying bosses (Van Rooj & Fine, 2018). Internally unstable, the organization's recovery becomes increasingly uncertain as the integrity of the system itself erodes under the impact of internal threats.

Contrast this result with organizations promoting positive psychological benefits, where employees benefit and feel motivated to perform at higher levels as a consequence of feeling emotionally stronger in a positive and thriving work environment (Cameron, Dutton, & Quinn, 2003; Hargrove, Nelson, & Cooper, 2007; Luthans, 2002; Wright, 2003). In such cases, when faced with the threat of change, transformation, and uncertainty, the positive psychological benefits that enable employees to be resilient are reflected in their performance (Luthans, Avolio, Avey, & Norman, 2007). Similarly, resilience in leaders has been shown to positively affect both employees' and an organization's performance (Youssef-Morgan, 2004).

The prerequisite for recovery, then, is a clearly defined pathway forward after adversity. The organization needs to ask, and sufficiently answer, the following questions if it is to assure itself of continuity:

- What processes need to be enacted once an adversity triggers action?
- How do the system elements need to re-identify, regroup, and reprioritize to meet the recovery plan?
- Who is responsible and who is accountable for the recovery?
- When must recovery actions be triggered and complete, and what time constraints must be considered in the recovery planning?
- Where does recovery materialize and manifest?
- Why is recovery and continuity being assured?

Resilience manifests in an organization when a threat that acts on a vulnerability within the system materializes, resulting in a loss of some kind. Typically, the loss affects the organization's ability to continue to operate in some way, such as when a data center is flooded in a storm, triggering a switch to its backup systems.

Even when due diligence is practiced, and processes are consistent, the inherent stability of the organization is at risk of being compromised any time a threat is realized. Consequently, when organizational processes operate at a low maturity level, epitomized by hero employees and managers diligently putting out fires when faced with go/no-go decisions, the costs are typically born elsewhere and often in unintended consequences.

Predictability of a process to achieve its planned and intended purpose—the ability of inputs to be translated into their intended outputs—diminishes as process discipline diminishes. Lack of process capability always translates into increased process risk and, in turn, organization risk (ISO/IEC NP/TR 33015, 2014). This point illustrates why start-ups, due to their trial and error nature, lack resilience.

Predictability of process performance also becomes critical in the evaluation of the system's behavior, relative to its purpose. Organizational systems often devise their own constraints to prevent specific activities and behaviors from continuing, such as through the choice of markets, sectors, or technologies. These constraints operate as parameters for what the organizational systems *shall not* do, bound by good governance principles and policies. For example, within the bounds of civilized society, organizational systems cannot break the law, harm humans, or ignore their safety responsibilities to their employees, without being held accountable.

Resilience requirements, or *shall not* constraints, often serve to protect the integrity of the system itself by establishing priorities. They provide insight into managing resource capability, as well as the specification of acceptable and unacceptable recovery activities. This specification narrows the recovery requirements such that system boundaries are visible or can be established in a way that enables recovery to occur: what is in the system and prioritized as needing resilience capability and what is out of the system and of little value or interest?

Organizations that decide what not to do become better at what they are capable of doing because they avoid resource conflicts by providing clarity of focus. Organizations that fail to do so bring truth to the ancient adage, "Jack of all trades, master of none."

When resources operate in a consistent state of reactive behavior and fail to adhere to the rigors of process discipline—communication, documentation, records, monitoring, traceability, accountability—decisions are made without all the data and evidence necessary for consideration, and mistakes are commonplace. Such errors tend to be proportionate to the degree of complexity of the project underway, such as a company's decision to go live with a facial or emotion recognition technology system whose artificial intelligence hasn't learned how to identify and mitigate racial and gender biases, causing more harm than benefit when false readings occur (Rhue, 2019).

Organizational Processes

The complexity of organizational systems is exacerbated by their inherent nature. As a systems of systems structure, the ability to reliably predict system outcomes is no longer a matter of design, but of risk management of the less reliable system elements—humans—which require constant scrutiny through vigilant monitoring and oversight.

Organizational resilience requires a high degree of organizational maturity to be effective. The inherent process capability of each of the processes used to achieve resilience becomes a measure of risk in determining whether or not resilience can be achieved (ISO/IEC NP/TR 33015, 2014). As a general principle, when confidence in expected outcomes is high, risk is perceived to be low. When confidence is low, risk is perceived to be high and potentially unacceptable. Credit ratings reflect this type of zero-sum thinking, when organizations operate at low maturity levels, making credit harder to achieve when it is needed most. This is one of the reasons that start-ups typically have to rely on investors rather than creditors.

Credit tends to be abundant when it is needed least, reflecting confidence in maturity and responsibility, both of which contribute to resilience capability.

For any organization to become resilient, it needs to first decide which processes are essential and are actually required by customers or regulators. This effort, in itself, often requires significant analysis and reanalysis to get it right. Most organizations, when they are first conceived, rarely invest the time, effort, and what are often scarce resources to formally evolve their purpose, goals, outcomes, costs, and processes. With change so rampant in the early days of an organization's evolution, processes are rarely documented until some level of reproducibility, and therefore an aspect of resilience, is required. The impetus to demonstrate a capability for resilience is often triggered by customers requiring their suppliers to provide evidence-based confidence in the supplier's capacity to continue.

The capability of the organizational system to design for, and achieve, resilience is a direct measure of the maturity of its processes. Beneficial outcomes associated with maturity include self- and other-awareness (of other organizations, stakeholders, competitors, etc.) consistency, reliability, discipline, evidence-based decision-making, plans, resources, and leadership—all necessary components for building the capability to survive adversity (Ungar, 2018). Whether natural disasters, fluctuating market conditions, or such opaque threats as internal mistakes and fallible human judgment, mature organizations possess the functional capability to understand how to replicate their priority operations and enable them to recover.

These patterns are similar for engineered systems. When computer or physical systems are built to be resilient, the specification of required target recovery levels must be precise enough to flow through the subsequent inputs and activities as outputs, since any errors will flow through the process—thus, the euphemism, "Garbage in, garbage out." These errors affect the next downstream process and often impact upstream processes as well, such as customer service, when a complaint is reported.

Processes also need to be relatively consistent and predictable if they are to become reproducible (imagine trying to build an assembly line based on a prototype that is always changing). In many cases, it does not make sense for organizations to try to engineer for resilience while they are still evolving, especially entrepreneurial organizations whose limited resources are completely devoted to initial commercialization. Investing time, money, effort, and procedures to support recovery for a business that is still launching would make even the most conservative entrepreneur regret such critical resource mismanagement.

For these reasons, specified degrees of formalization are required, depending on the context, and only then does resilience become possible. Similar to any other system, resilience can be designed and engineered into the organization's performance characteristics.

Organizational System Capability

Organizations, as purpose-based systems, are driven to achieve their intended outcomes through a sharing of purpose, goals, strategies, and objectives. Whether processes are ad hoc or formal and documented, together as a system, they serve to satisfy organizational goals.

Organizational systems, being people-based, are rarely engineered as precisely as other systems. People-based systems face far more challenges to retaining cohesion and control than systems whose components can be engineered to a level of predictable precision.

Humans, as a dynamic and unpredictable element of systems behaviors, together with general resistance to being controlled, introduce management system engineering challenges that are constantly changing and evolving, especially given how little agency organizations have over their actors.

Organizations with externally imposed recovery targets, including those prescribed for critical infrastructure or bureaucracies, such as power companies, are accountable for service levels to regulators and customers. Resilience in these cases is an externally imposed requirement on utilities to ensure that formal recovery policies, processes, procedures, records, and identified resources are capable of providing a predictable level of stability and consistency, both in planning and execution.

Recovery goals are inherent within the organization's target resilience capability level. They provide the degree of reliability and integrity precision necessary to rely on not only the processes required to orchestrate the recovery effort, but also on any plans that were developed. In turn, those plans require the assurance that planning processes were followed with sufficient discipline and formality.

A dilemma eventually presents itself for organizations when considering the cost of loss versus the investment costs necessary to exercise prepared and planned recovery options. Where safety is concerned, risk-averse options always dominate. However, investments into full recovery option scenarios may not always be possible, especially if costs of recovery are less than the costs of starting over and absorbing all losses. If a business is worth US$2 million, but its ideal recovery plan costs $4 million, the decision becomes clear.

Organizational capabilities, when not entrenched in process knowledge and consistency, are harder to recover. Founders' knowledge, experienced-based team competencies, and relationships with customers are all areas of capability that contribute to organizational maturity but are virtually impossible to capture and measure. Similar to the concept of "good will," intangible social assets, such as high-performance teams, should also comprise aspects of organizational resilience that, depending on its criticality, should be replicable.

The risk of loss of long-term employees who have years of experience and broad knowledge of the organization must be measured against the organization's dependency on, and subsequent cost of the loss of, those critical resources. Losing a founder can be ruinous if no one shares their knowledge, but with a well-informed, well-trained, and well-performing team, the loss of a founder may be beneficial, if change is the objective.

To be effective, organizational resilience requires basic communication elements: policies, processes, procedures, records, and skilled resources, prioritized and assessed, are the simple building blocks of an effective recovery plan. Any deviation in process or behavioral dynamics that fails to undergo the rigor of change management risks becoming ad hoc and disruptive. Any such deviation becomes a precursor to uncontrolled change, where a significant degree of uncertainty and negative risk usually enter the resilience equation.

People are, therefore, constituent elements of organizational systems. However, by virtue of being human, people have an elevated status or worth when compared to other organizational resources. This understanding of basic human rights forces organizations to adopt a different perspective and approach to understanding their resilience resource requirements.

Skilled personnel, while replaceable and reproducible, are not expendable or disposable. A unique, one-of-a-kind prototype, such as a manufactured product, can be commissioned, created, replicated, dismantled, and thrown away. An individual person, by virtue of having intrinsic value in and of himself or herself may become part of, but still remain separate and distinct from, the organizational system of which the individual is a part. This fact constrains how resilience is achieved and requires a significant degree of flexibility and interoperability for recovery procedures to be effective.

Parallels may be drawn in the adoption of certain resource management principles, such as recycling, which can be applied to materials or to skills. However, beyond such similarities, people have special resource status. The cost of a human life is incalculable, placing even greater responsibility on the system to protect and preserve itself and its human elements. Humans as components of an organizational system present more constraints than perhaps other systems in the pursuit of available resilience options.

Despite these constraints, designing for organizational resilience should follow the same process as designing any other system requirement to fulfill its intended outcome. The development of an organization's resilience capabilities should follow the same systems engineering processes used to reliably enable any system capability. Once the organization's unique constraints are considered, it must engineer its systems to meet its own unique resilience requirements for its resilience-building recovery efforts to be successful in the face of adversity. This means designing resilience into all significant organizational processes and enabling them to deliver predictable outcomes. Engineering for resilience is similar to engineering systems for safety and reliability in the design of a jet engine, a medical device, or a software application: each step in the design follows a rigorous, tested process.

Organizational resilience is a non-functional organizational system requirement that organizations must engineer into their management system components—their processes— to benefit from the essential behaviors, activities, relationships, and information flows at the time they are needed (even if they are never used). Internal and external systems and processes interface, cross, and co-mingle at various systems boundaries. These exchanges often become critical vulnerabilities when organizations, as a result of low maturity and/or ineffective communication, fail to identify and manage their risks.

Unique Techniques

As with any system type, assuring the capability to resist and recover from adversities requires establishing plans, well in advance, that are able to script and orchestrate the necessary sequence of activities that must occur for a resilient state to be realized. Risk assessments that project as much foreknowledge and experience as possible into test scenarios also need to track changing priorities against risk tolerances. Responsible teams, also subject to change, are required to remain vigilant and aware of the changing threat environment, including accounting for and monitoring evolving threat agents and triggers that could initiate a response. Hospitals are examples of proceduralized systems that require the establishment of a variety of standby plans, each of which can be invoked on demand.

If resilience is a response to a stressor, then organizational resilience must be a response that plans for recovery to be feasible. The process of engineering resilience into an organization's systems and processes as a means of recovery assurance requires a systematic deployment of actions and decisions that contribute to recovery, as and when needed. Like an army at the ready, embedding resilience into organizational processes includes the assurance that activities, such as the following are performed consistently and competently:

- Analyzing the threat landscape according to the organization's unique context, from proximity to hazardous land features that precipitate natural disasters to unreliable data as input to critical decisions.
- Mapping out the organization's processes and systems that prioritize critical core processes and subsystems to differentiate them from supporting, noncritical systems.
- Determining where the organization's vulnerabilities are, such as targeted takeover bids.
- Estimating the probability of occurrence of the adverse event.
- Assessing and analyzing the impact to the organization and its customers or stakeholders.
- Determining and specifying the required target recovery capability.
- Planning for various recovery scenarios, based on the need for full or partial recovery.
- Providing assurance of the expected capability against required capability.
- Reporting on any expected changes in recovery potential.
- Maintaining readiness to achieve target levels of required capability including readiness to respond, training capabilities, job competencies, and materials and equipment availability.

Organizational Resilience through Management Systems Standards

On April 24, 2014, during the UN's deliberations on its own resilience capability, the High Level Committee on Management chair opened their meeting by "noting that the Organizational Resilience Management System (ORMS) was approved by the General Assembly as the emergency management framework for the organization." (UN, 2014, para. 1). They had determined the need for and the criticality of systematizing the process of becoming resilient so that, through testing, they can be resilient in the face of a calamitous event.

To become resilient, the organization's approach must be systematic, like the UN's. Achieving a required level of resilience that enables a successful recovery from an adverse event is dependent on fully comprehending the risks facing the organization. There's no point buying sandbags to ward off rising waters for a location in the desert.

Once risks are understood, they can be managed, and leadership can adopt a resilience framework, such as ISO 22301 or the UN's Organizational Resilience Management System. Frameworks, such as those provided by international consensus-based standards, provide a structured approach to achieving resilience that supports the discipline of assuring organizational ability, and subsequent capability, to survive adversity.

Systematic planning often leads to the recognition and adoption of resilience as an organizational priority, with that decision triggering the development of a business continuity plan. Engineering resilience into organizational systems is similar to the injection of any other nonfunctional requirement into a system's capability: the new capability—resilience—must be conceived of, planned for, understood, resourced, designed, developed, documented, tested, and monitored. Confidence in its execution through verification and validation can assure the system's recovery. This systematic approach serves as a specification of the organization's required operation capability to recover.

The degree to which an unprepared organization, comprised of unprepared humans, will have the capability and capacity to react to stressors and adversity, and to ultimately recover, will depend on how much advanced preparation is invested into the task. Assessing this capacity is part of the process of making engineered systems and organizations resilient. Proactivity is a necessary step that organizational system must undertake to overcome humans' natural tendencies to resist, to procrastinate, and to negate the possibility that disasters can and do happen.

Conclusion

This chapter provides insights into the resilience of engineered and organizational systems. These domains contain both overlapping and unique resilient features. Each domain includes unique systems with necessary capabilities that face a variety of adversities at some point in time. These adversities can be due to internal, external, and/or environmental causes. Certain techniques are implementable to help improve system resilience. These techniques could be physical architectural, design principles, system attributes, fundamental objectives/means, or inherent system characteristics.

There are a few points to take away from this chapter that are reflected in Table 35.1. First, the main difference between engineered systems and organizational systems is that engineered systems are for the most part physical, while organizational systems are human intensive. This difference leads to several major differences in purpose and resilience:

TABLE 35.1 Comparisons of Domains With Respect to Resilience Aspects

Aspect	Engineered Systems	Organizational Systems
System type	Primarily physical systems: utilities, transportation, infrastructure, buildings.	Primarily human-intensive systems: enterprises, government. Generally more vulnerable than engineered systems.
Adversities	Natural: earthquakes, hurricanes. Human-made: terrorist attacks. Internal threats: reliability failures; software errors.	Bad actors; natural disasters.
Capability	Speed, range, power, etc.	Organizational goals, human resources, etc.
Time frame	Anticipation, withstanding, adaptation, gradual degradation, recovery.	Same as engineered systems.
Techniques	Physical and behavior architecture responses.	Human activity responses.
Patterns	Timeline patterns from anticipation to recovery; use of detection and adaptation techniques.	Vulnerability to physical adversities; same timelines as engineered systems; advantage of human cognition.

- Engineered systems will have intrinsically different goals. Engineered systems will have technical goals, while organizational systems will have organizational goals.
- While engineered systems will differ in their vulnerability, organizational systems will be physically more vulnerable than engineered systems.
- Organizational systems have one major advantage over engineered systems, namely, that organizational systems consist of human beings whose cognizance contributes to their resilience.
- If there is a common pattern to both engineered and organizational system resilience, it is the timeline pattern. All systems will have to transit through the same timeline from anticipation to recovery. Nevertheless, the physical differences between the two types of systems will lead to differing amounts of recovery time depending on the adversity.

Regardless of the type of system, the key to achieving resilience is the capability of that system to resist, withstand, and recover from whatever stressors it faces, at the time that they are faced. That achievement depends on mature processes.

Key Messages

1. All domains examined revealed similar patterns in maintaining capability, recovery from an adversity, timeline of interaction with the adversity, and techniques to achieve resilience.
2. Engineering system resilience is dependent on system architecture and the adaptability of that architecture.
3. Organizational system resilience is dependent on the dynamics of human interaction.

References

Alexander, C., Ishikawa, S., Silverstein, M., Jacobson, M., Fiksdahl, I., & Angel, S. (1977). *A pattern language: Towns, buildings, construction*. New York, NY: Oxford University Press.

BKCASE Editorial Board. (2016). *Systems engineering body of knowledge (SEBoK)*. Retrieved from https://www.sebokwiki.org/wiki/System_Resilience

Cameron, K. S., Dutton, J. E., & Quinn, R. E. (2003). An introduction to positive organizational scholarship. In K. S. Cameron, J. E. Dutton, & R. E. Quinn (Eds.), *Positive organizational scholarship* (pp. 3–13). San Francisco, CA: Berrett-Koehler.

Department of Homeland Security. (2018, 18 August). *Critical infrastructure sectors*. Retrieved from https://www.dhs.gov/critical-infrastructure-sectors

Eyles, D. (2009, July 18). 1202 computer error almost aborted lunar landing. *MIT News*. Retrieved from http://njnnetwork.com/2009/07/1202-computer-error-almost-aborted-lunar-landing/

Fackler, M. (2017, November 19). Six years after Fukushima, robots finally find reactors' melted Uranium fuel. *The New York Times*. Retrieved from https://www.nytimes.com/2017/11/19/science/japan-fukushima-nuclear-meltdown-fuel.html

Federal Aviation Administration. (2015). *Bird strike requirements for transport category airplanes*. Retrieved from https://www.federalregister.gov/articles/2015/07/20/2015-17404/bird-strike-requirements-for-transport-category-airplanes

Greenpeace. (2019). *About Greenpeace*. Retrieved from https://www.greenpeace.org/usa/

Hargrove, M. B., Nelson, D. L., & Cooper, C. L. (2007). *Generating eustress by challenging employees: Helping people savor their work* (Vol. 42). Washington, DC: American Psychological Association.

Hollnagel, E., Woods, D. D., & Leveson, N. (2006). *Resilience engineering: Concepts and precepts*. Aldershot, UK: Ashgate.

International Council on Systems Engineering. (2015). *Systems engineering handbook: A guide for system life cycle processes and activities*. Seattle, CA: Wiley.

International Standards Organization. (2012). *Societal security: Business continuity management systems—Requirements. ISO 22301*:Retrieved from www.iso.org

International Standards Organization. (2014). *Information technology: Process assessment—Guide to process related risk determination*. ISO/IEC NP/TR 33015. Retrieved from www.iso.org

Jackson, S., & Ferris, T. (2013). Resilience principles for engineered systems. *Systems Engineering*, 16(2), 152–164. doi:10.1002/sys.21228

Jamshidi, M. (Ed.). (2009). *System of systems engineering: Innovations for the 21st century*. Hoboken, NJ: John Wiley.

Kahneman, D. (2011). *Thinking fast and slow*. New York, NY: Farrar, Straus and Giroux.

Luthans, F. (2002). Positive organizational behavior: Developing and managing psychological strengths. *Academy of Management Perspectives*, 16(1). doi:10.5465/ame.2002.6640181

Luthans, F., Avolio, B. J., Avey, J. B., & Norman, S. M. (2007). Positive psychological capital: Measurement and relationship with performance and satisfaction. *Personnel Psychology*, 60(3), 541–572. doi:10.1111/j.1744-6570.2007.00083.x

Madni, M. A., & Jackson, S. (2009). Towards a conceptual framework for resilience engineering. *Institute of Electrical and Electronics Engineers (IEEE) Systems Journal*, 3(2), 181–191. doi:10.1109/JSYST.2009.2017397

Mendoça, D., & Wallace, W. (2006). Adaptive capacity: Electric power restoration in New York City following the 11 September 2001 attacks. In E. Hollnagel & E. Regaud (Eds.), *Second Resilience Engineering Symposium* (pp. 209–219). Juan-les-Pins, France: Mines Paris.

Pariès, J. (2011). Lessons from the Hudson. In E. Hollnagel, J. Pariès, D. D. Woods, & J. Wreathhall (Eds.), *Resilience engineering in practice: A guidebook* (pp. 9–27). Farnham, UK: Ashgate.

Resilience. (2018). *Oxford Dictionaries*. Retrieved from https://en.oxforddictionaries.com/definition/resilience

Rhue, L. (2019, January 3). Emotion-reading tech fails the racial bias test. PHYS.ORG. Retrieved from https://phys.org/news/2019-01-emotion-reading-tech-racial-bias.html

Sillitto, H., Dori, D., Griego, R. M., Jackson, S., Krob, D., Godfrey, P., . . . McKinney, D. (2017). Defining "system": A comprehensive approach. *INCOSE International Symposium*, 27(1), 170–186. doi:10.1002/j.2334-5837.2017.00352.x

Ungar, M. (2018). Systemic resilience: Principles and processes for a science of change in contexts of adversity. *Ecology and Society*, 23(4), 34. doi:10.5751/ES-10385-230434

United Nations. (2014). *Action on the UN system Organizational Resilience Management System*. Retrieved from https://www.unsystem.org/content/organizational-resilience-management-system-orms

US-Canada Task Force. (2004). *Final report on the August 14, 2003 blackout in the United States and Canada: Causes and recommendations*. Washington, DC, Ottawa, ON.

Van Rooj, B., & Fine, A. (2018). Toxic corporate culture: Assessing organizational processes of deviancy. *Administrative Sciences*, 8(3), 23. doi:10.3390/admsci8030023

Willett, K. D. (2016, November). *Cybersecurity decision patterns as adaptive knowledge encoding in cybersecurity operations*. Poster presented at the 4th Annual SERC Doctoral Students Forum and 8th Annual SERC Sponsor Research Review, Washinton, DC. Retrieved from http://docplayer.net/156473866-Cybersecurity-decision-patterns-as-adaptive-knowledge-encoding.html

Wright, T. A. (2003). Positive organizational behavior: An idea whose time has truly come. *Journal of Organizational Behavior*, 24(4), 437–442. doi:10.1002/job.197

Youssef-Morgan, C. M. (2004). *Resiliency development of organizations, leaders and employees: Multi-level theory building and individual-level, path-analytical empirical testing* (Doctoral dissertation). Retrieved from https://digitalcommons.unl.edu/dissertations/AAI3131572/

SECTION 11

Social Ecological Systems

Social and Ecological Systems Resilience and Identity

Francois Bousquet, Tara Quinn, Clara Therville, Raphaël Mathevet, Olivier Barreteau, Bruno Bonté, and Chloé Guerbois

Introduction

For several decades now, researchers have been examining the resilience of social and ecological systems (SES; Folke, 2006) ranging in scale from forests, towns, fisheries, and lakes through to planetwide systems. Given the number of rapidly changing SES and their implications for global health and well-being, there is an impetus to examine how resilient they are in the face of global changes. Here we outline what a SES is, and we give an overview of the history of interdisciplinary encounters that has led to the evolution in definition of SES resilience. Subsequently, we will focus on the process of identification and distribution of vulnerability, and we propose (using the empirical example of the experience of four cities) a new lens through which SES processes can be conceived that helps to identify the potential resilience of a system.

Plants, animals, humans, water, and social, natural, and physical infrastructures interact, and observers, actors, and analysts identify an SES through the definition of its boundaries, the components, and the important interactions. After this first task the observers look at the properties, the functions of the SES (to provide goods, to secure services), and they try to understand whether the SES they have identified is resilient, which means whether the components, the interactions, the properties, and the functions are maintained when the SES faces adversity and shocks. Thus, resilience is a process and not a trait. The resilience process is inextricably shaped by the vulnerabilities embedded in the SES. A forest largely dominated by one species is vulnerable to a disease affecting that species; a town built on a river can be vulnerable to floods if the inhabitants are not prepared; etc. Each SES has embedded in it both a distribution of vulnerabilities together with the means to cope with these vulnerabilities. Time passes by, components of the SES will disappear, new ones will be included, and interactions will change but the properties and the function is maintained: for the observers, the SES is the same despite the changes. Or, to the contrary, the properties and the functions have changed, and for the observers, this is not the same SES. For instance, after a large forest fire, trees have regrown, but new species are dominating the diversity. Previous inhabitants have left and people with different lifestyles settle in the forest and make use of it. For the observers it is not the same SES as the previous one. It has not the same identity. We will argue in the second part of this chapter that the study of the resilience needs, in parallel to the analysis of modifications of components and their interactions, to look at the identity of an SES and the embedded vulnerabilities.

In one of his recent synthesis papers on SES resilience, Carl Folke (2016), a leading researcher in this field, defines the resilience of SESs as: "the capacity of a system to absorb disturbance and reorganize while undergoing change so as to still retain essentially the same function, structure, and feedbacks, and therefore identity, that is, the capacity to change in order to sustain identity" (para. 21). When an SES faces events and adversity (e.g., storms, diseases, invasions, droughts, pollution) resilience is the process that enables an SES to maintain its identity (forest/fishery/town/catchment remains the "same"). But what does the identity of an SES exactly mean? How can an observer say that this forest/town/fishery has been resilient and retained its identity or that, on the contrary, it has lost its identity? From a complexity science perspective an SES is an organization/configuration made up of plants, animals, humans, infrastructures, and entities—parts of the SES or external observers of the SES—internalize this organization through their perceptions, attitudes, and actions and the identity of the SES can consequently be reinforced or transformed. The identification process is the bundle of construction processes that ascribes an identity to a SES, either confirming the previous one or declaring a new identity (e.g., the Amazon forest was formerly identified as the "green hell" and is now identified as "the planet's lung"). At any given time in the identification process, the declared identity of the system reflects the dominant perception of the organization of the SES and reveals its capacity to deal with its vulnerabilities.

In a complex multisystemic organization such as a SES, the modification of one relationship within the system leads to modifications in other parts of the system (Anderies & Janssen, 2011). Due to external shocks, adversity, or internal modification of relationships, the distribution of vulnerabilities within the SES evolves. An entity that was formerly vulnerable is not anymore but has transferred its vulnerability to another entity, maybe at another scale; therefore, a new type of vulnerability has emerged affecting a group of entities. For example, when the Amazon was identified as a green hell, the vulnerable entities were the people settling there (not the Indigenous peoples), while now, as a green lung, the vulnerable entities are the trees, the Indigenous peoples, and the region's biodiversity. The boundaries of the system have also changed, the green lung being a fragile part of a larger planetary body. The transformation, the disruption of the relationship between natural and social entities, leads to transfers of vulnerability and a new distribution of vulnerabilities. The identification process leads to a new distribution of vulnerabilities among the entities of the SES and the means to cope with them.

In summary, in the SES resilience domain, it is assumed that SES continuously reorganize while undergoing change. Resilience is not a question of whether a SES can come back to a former state but rather whether the SES remains the same or has become something else. To address this question, we use the body of research on identity, which tells us that identity results from a continuous identification process that reveals but also contributes to SES change and distribution of vulnerabilities. Consequently, our main thesis is that to study and qualify the resilience of a SES, there is a need to study the intertwined processes of SES change and identification.

An Overview of SES Resilience

A chronological look at research on SES resilience shows that the SES concept has been defined after the process which is at stake—resilience. Having been dominated in the 1970s and 1980s by the studies of researchers in ecology, the focus of the concept evolved in the 1990s with the growing weight of work on social dynamics: the object of resilience gradually moved from ecosystems to SESs. Here, we define the concept briefly and paint the story of the evolution of the (SES) resilience concept.

What Is a Socioecological System?

As indicated by Brondizio, Solecki, and Leemans (2015) in their reflection on the history of SES, decades of study on the relationship between ecology and society preceded the emergence of the SES concept. More recently, Colding and Barthel (2019) published a paper on the SES concept attributing the first definition of a SES to the Russian microbiologist B. L. Cherkasskii (1988) who described it as

> consisting of two interacting subsystems: the biological (epidemiological ecosystem) and the social (social and economic conditions of life of the society) subsystems where the biological subsystem plays the role of the governed object and the social acts as the internal regulator of these interactions. (p. 321)

Almost at the same time in 1989 (referring to a paper written in 1986), the Argentinian ecologist Gilberto Gallopin (Gallopin, Gutman, & Maletta, 1989) framed socioecological systems "in terms of a set of causal circuits and of relevant questions to be asked, rather than as a set of subsystems (other than the obvious—and still somewhat arbitrary—splitting of the whole into social and ecological subsystems)" (p. 385).

In the early 1990s, Berkes and Folke (1994) introduced this concept into their resilience research. Unlike Gallopin, they framed socioecological system as the integration of humans and their actions into ecological systems. Several years later, Ostrom published in *PNAS* (Ostrom, 2007) and *Science* (Ostrom, 2009), two articles proposing a framework of analysis for socioecological systems that put humans at the center of analysis as users of natural resources. Her research focused on the coevolution of ecological dynamics and management rules.

François Bousquet

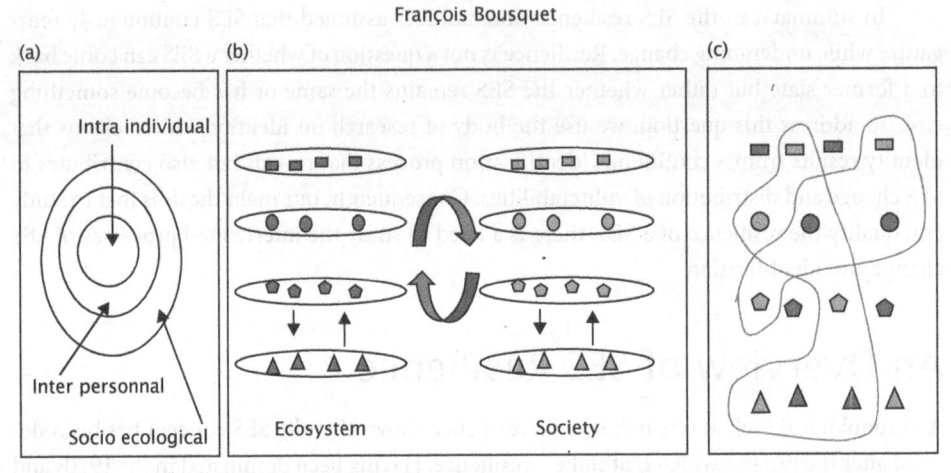

FIGURE 36.1 Different conceptualizations of an SES.

Schoon and Van der Leeuw (2015) brought new epistemological dimensions to the SES concept. For them, SES proposes a new ontological approach that includes (a) an integration of the social and ecological into a fully coupled SESs perspective; (b) a holistic view of scientific phenomena requiring a transdisciplinary approach to its study; and (c) the refutation of a purely equilibrium-based understanding of systems.

Figure 36.1 illustrates different conceptualizations of SES. Figure 36.1A presents the idea of nested systems, the individual being embedded in a group, which itself is embedded in a socioecological set of processes (Liu, Reed, & Girard, 2017). Figure 36.1B presents the SES as composed of two interacting systems, an ecological and a social one. Each system is viewed as a hierarchy of dynamic subsystems (i.e., individuals, households, institutions, and organizations on the social side; individuals, populations, and ecosystems on the ecological side). This is the model that prevails in the ecosystem services literature. Figure 36.1C present the view of complex systems where human, nonhuman entities, institutions, and organizations interact in many ways across scales and categories. A tree can interact with a state; an individual, with a fish population; and so forth.

The Development of the SES Resilience Concept

Inspired by Folke's 2006 paper we outline here a story of the emergence and trajectory of this concept.

From Equilibrium to Multiple Stable States

In the late 1960s and early 1970s, ecologist Crawford S. Holling worked on population interactions, such as predator–prey relationships, using a combination of mathematical models and experiments. Researchers in ecology were interested in the notion of equilibrium. The work of Holling and his colleagues showed that there is not just one but in fact several states of equilibrium between these populations. This discovery transformed how the concept of resilience was applied in research (Holling, 1973). Resilience had previously been defined by the return time to a unique equilibrium for which Holling spoke of "engineering resilience"; here the world is perceived as predictable and the aim is to understand the system's return to an initial state after a disturbance. With the conception of a world of multiple equilibria, Holling introduced the "ecological resilience" concept, defined as the amount of disturbance a system is able to receive before moving to another state. He then used the metaphor of the ball and the landscape (see Figure 36.2 for an illustration by Mathevet and Bousquet, 2014) to illustrate what he calls the different "myths" of nature, each image representing different ways of seeing the world.

The ball represents the system and is placed on a line that represents the landscape, the context in which the system evolves. If the landscape is flat, a small disturbance will make it evolve erratically; the myth of a "flat nature." If the ball is placed in a hole (Figure 36.2a), small disturbances will not make it change because it will fall back into the depression; it is in a stable state; the myth of an "equilibrium nature" and reflecting the concept of resilience in engineering. If the ball is placed on a hump (Figure 36.2b), a tiny disturbance will have great effects; it is the myth of an "anarchic nature." The last situation corresponds to a landscape with multiple equilibria; there are several holes and several humps corresponding to different equilibria. This is the myth of "resilient nature" in the sense of ecological resilience. The landscape changes and hollows and bumps are transformed (as illustrated by (Figure 36.2c–e). Research efforts switched to a focus on understanding change instead of stability. How and under what conditions does the system pass from one state to another, cross thresholds, and tipping points? What are the slow and fast processes that modify the landscape? In the 1970s

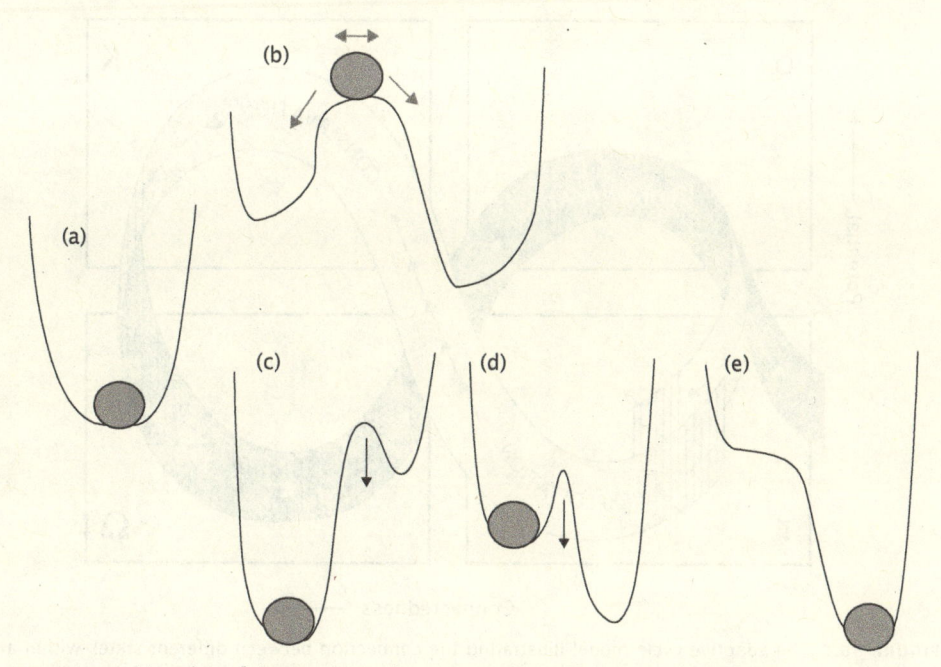

FIGURE 36.2 Metaphor of the transitions between states (Mathevet & Bousquet, 2014).

and 1980s, Holling and the researchers working with him studied these shifts, always combining field data analysis and mathematical modeling.

The Transition From a Focus on States to a Focus on Trajectories and Cycles

After laying the foundations of this new perspective in the 1970s, researchers expanded the number and types of cases they studied. Then, rather than simply focusing on transitions from one state to another, they proposed a general model of transitions between states (Holling, 1986). Figure 36.3 shows the model of adaptive cycles that provides a framework for thinking about the trajectories of ecosystems.

Building on this previous model, in the early 2000s researchers proposed the concept of panarchy, which incorporates the idea of different levels of organization within a SES (Gunderson & Holling, 2002; see Figure 36.4).

The trajectory at a given scale influences interactions at other scales. The lower scales, whose dynamics are faster, invent and test new ways of life or new practices; the higher scales, whose dynamics are slower, gradually integrate tests where results have been conclusive (such as technological innovations or know-how).

In 1995, Frances Westley introduced the notion of institutions in the field of resilience. It was also at that time, in 1996, that Holling and Lance Gunderson began an active collaboration with the Beijer Institute of Ecological Economics in Sweden where Folke was developing his research. The network, called the Resilience Network and later the Resilience Alliance, promoted meetings and collaborations of researchers. At that time, Elinor Ostrom who won Nobel prize for economics in 2009 was collaborating with other scientists that were

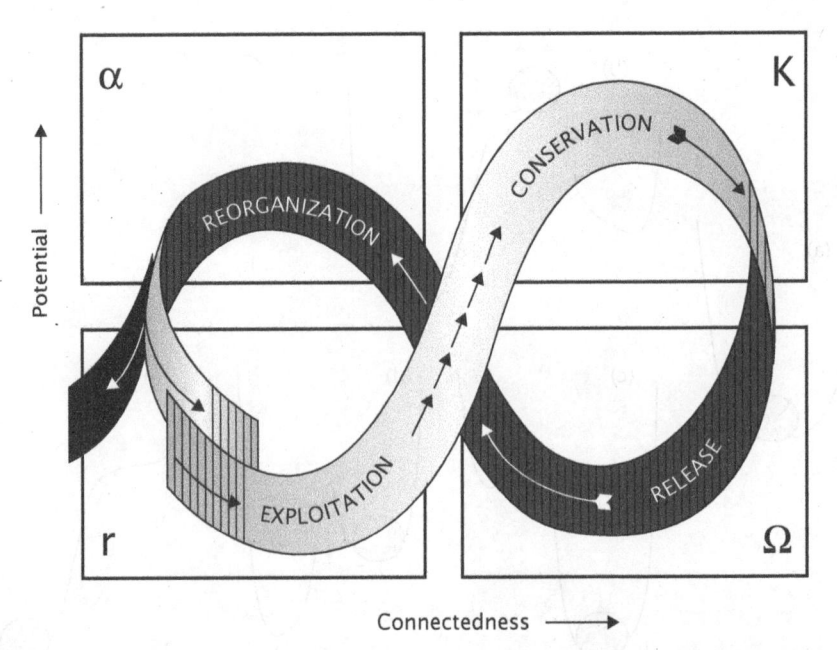

FIGURE 36.3 The adaptive cycle model illustrating the connection between different states within a system.

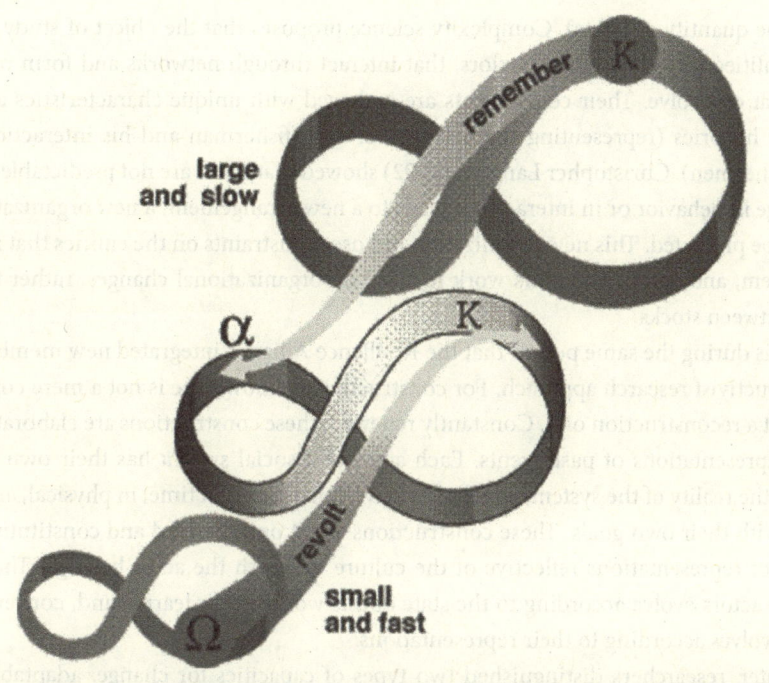

FIGURE 36.4 The panarchy model showing the multiple scales at which SES resilience can be measured, and the connections between these.

studying management of the commons. Her work in political science provided a scientific basis for a pragmatic collective action approach during adaptive management workshops, transforming a practice into a subject for scientific research. Fikret Berkes, an ecologist, also played an important role in the evolution of thinking about resilience, both for his work on institutions, but also because he has greatly contributed to the recognition of the importance of local knowledge for land management. An environmental social scientist, Neil Adger, also posed the question of how resilient institutions are in environmental management by introducing the concept of social resilience that defines the ability of a social group to cope with a disruption or external stress resulting from social, political, or environmental change (Adger, 2000). This period of interactions with social scientists took resilience thinking a step further by integrating the idea that actors and social groups adapt and transform themselves in interaction with ecosystem changes.

From Resilience to Transformability

In the late 1990s and early 2000s, encounters between researchers active in the field of complexity science also contributed to the changing thinking on frameworks of resilience. The systemic vision, the bedrock of resilience research in the 1970s, consisted of identifying stocks (of matter, energy, information) and flows between these stocks, or by measuring the positive and negative influences that variables exert on each other. One simplified example of such an approach would be to analyze a fishery by modeling the interactions between fish stocks (the variable being the number of fish) and the capital of the fishermen (the variable being the quantity of boats). Complexity science proposes that the object of study is made up of entities with different behaviors, that interact through networks and form organizations that co-evolve. Their components are endowed with unique characteristics and bear singular histories (representing the behavior of each fisherman and his interactions with other fishermen). Christopher Langton (1992) showed that states are not predictable a priori. A change in behavior or in interactions leads to a new arrangement, a new organization that cannot be predicted. This new organization imposes constraints on the entities that make up the system, and so on. Langton's work focused on organizational changes, rather than the flows between stocks.

It is during the same period that the Resilience Alliance integrated new members with a constructivist research approach. For constructivism, knowledge is not a mere copy of reality, but a reconstruction of it. Constantly renewed, these constructions are elaborated from older representations of past events. Each actor of a social system has their own point of view of the reality of the system, which they have constructed in time, in physical, and social space, with their own goals. These constructions are at once derived and constitutive of the system of representations reflective of the culture to which the actor belongs. The visions of these actors evolve according to the state of this world—they learn—and, conversely, the world evolves according to their representations.

Later, researchers distinguished two types of capacities for change: adaptability and transformability. Adaptability is the ability to react to stress or disturbance without modifying the structure and functioning of the system. A transformation stems from the observation that the functioning of a system is not desirable and must be changed. The transformability is the ability to create untried beginnings from which to evolve a new way of living when existing ecological, economic, or social structures become untenable (Walker, Holling, Carpenter, & Kinzig, 2004).

Critiques of a Systems Approach

There are a number of critiques of the SES resilience concept. We propose here a brief synthesis and look at how these critiques have been taken into account in recent research.

Some researchers emphasize that a systems approach erases the diversity of perspectives, the complexity of processes, the balance between different positions. Stedman (2016) suggests that the "SES perspective may relatively neglect the subjective human agent as an active perceiver and interpreter of social-ecological change and stability" (p. 892). In addition, an extension of the systemic approach to the social system, generally carried out by ecologists, supposes an analogy between nature and society, which meets fierce disputes (Cote & Nightingale, 2012; Foster & Clark, 2008).

Another critique of a systemic approach is the need to define the limits to the system. What is part of the system and what is not? How to define them, and who defines them? Olsson, Jerneck, Thoren, Persson, and O'Byrne (2015) published a social science critique and analyzed core concepts and principles in resilience theory that cause disciplinary tensions between the social and natural sciences (system ontology, system boundary, equilibria and thresholds, feedback mechanisms, self-organization, and function).

A third objection emphasizes that the systemic approach tends to neglect relationships between individuals, the role of power and structural arrangements (Hatt, 2012) for the benefit of a more functional design based on consensus. A theory of resilience would propose a simplistic analysis of the institutions or arrangements between actors that does not adequately integrate the issue of power (Nadasdy, 2007).

And, finally, there is a concern about the strategic use of the resilience concept in policies and governance (Bousquet et al., 2016; Brown, 2015). For Leach, Raworth, and Rockström (2013), resilience narratives represent a powerful storyline that assigns responsibility and blame and underpins, justifies, and legitimates action. For instance, the application of a resilience perspective at the global level favors the recognition of the "Earth system" and "safe operating space" as legal entities that could legitimize supranational resilience governance and threaten to become "a pervasive idiom of global governance" (Walker & Cooper, 2011). For Joseph (2014), the resilience project is part of a broader strategy that seeks to govern from a distance and regulate the conduct of states.

A New Stage in SES Resilience Research

After this period of criticism, which mainly related to the charge of the imperialism of natural sciences and market forces over social sciences, it seems that new perspectives are emerging. Evidence-based investigations into the differences between approaches have been experimented with leading to nuanced conclusions and a plea for pluralism in approaches and methods (Bousquet, Robbins, Peloquin, & Bonato, 2015). Stone-Jovicich, Goldstein, Brown, Plummer, and Olsson (2018) present new social science perspectives that stress the complex, dynamic, and multiscalar interconnections between biophysical and social realms in explaining social-environmental change and that place both the social and ecology center stage in their analyses. They identify integrative and hybrid approaches that share with social-ecological resilience thinking a focus on the interdependent and dynamic ways in which biophysical and social processes shape our world. Olsson and Jerneck (2018) suggest that combining field theory and systems thinking can assist resilience scientists and others in integrating the best available knowledge from the natural sciences with that from the social sciences. Endress (2015) discusses the sociohistorical construction of resilience from a sociological point of view guided by four central analytical dimensions: normative neutrality, temporality, perceptivity, and power. Rampp (2019) proposes the use of Norbert Elias's concept of figuration to understand the resilience of SES (Elias, van Krieken, & Dunning, 1997).

Social and Ecological System Identification

The story of the SES resilience concept is a story of trajectories between persistence and change. In this section we use a hybrid approach to look at the dynamics of SES identity.

From Identity to Identification

In 2005, Cumming and Collier (2005) wrote the first piece of work on identity we know of by an SES researcher. It deals with the question of identity in complex systems with a focus on SESs, paying particular attention to the ecosystem element. Recently Rampp (2019) posed the question of sociological identity in research on the resilience of SESs.

With regard to systems research, it is common to distinguish between an essentialist vision and a constructivist vision. Cumming and Collier (2005) propose a rather essentialist vision arguing that "the challenge of determining the identity of the system is to establish the natural properties of the system that constitutes identity conditions over time and space" (para. 6). They make an equivalence between identity and unity:

> System identity resides in the continued presence, in both space and time, of key components and key relationships . . . the following should be included: (1) the system components, which may be defined in varying degrees; (2) the relationships between system components; (3) the location and spatial dimension, where the definition is applicable and the importance, or lack thereof, of spatial constancy; and (4) the temporal scale, which is applicable to the author's perspective on identity through time. (para. 11)

In this instance identity is defined by the perspective of the author (the observer, the analyst). A decade later Cumming and Peterson (2017) proposed an updated definition of identity that reflects a constructivist epistemology:

> Identity is defined by key components and relationships that must be maintained through time and space for the system to be considered the same system. Identity is subjectively defined according to the properties in which an observer, who may also be part of the system, is interested. Although subjective, it is not arbitrary; it requires establishment of (and agreement on) key criteria. (p. 699)

The position of most of the social sciences is resolutely constructivist. Identity is a matter of perception and ascription at the intrapsychic, interpersonal, and intergroup levels. At the internal psychological level, for Erikson (1972), the identity of the individual is the subjective and tonic feeling of personal unity and temporal continuity. At the external sociological level, identity comes from everything that makes it possible to identify the subject from the outside and refers to the status that the subject shares with the range of groups they belong to. For Tajfel (1974) identity is the emotionally significant self-image of an individual, which is derived from their membership in social groups (called in-groups). Researchers are more interested in the identification process than in the concept of identity. Identification is therefore made up of a number of processes:

> Identity has to be understood in this context (never final, but always contingent and continuously contested) result of various, interrelated processes of construction. Processes of construction—and thus empirical realizations of identity—are deeply rooted in the respective social, spatial, and temporal context and they are related to manifest issues of power. (Rampp, 2019, p. 63)

The identification process is therefore a dance between interiorization and exteriorization: as long as it is not internalized and recognized externally, an identity has not emerged yet, although an identification process can be ongoing.

Identification as a Processual, Relational, and Strategic Approach to Resilience

If the approaches to identity vary, they converge on certain issues: The relationship between continuity and change and the importance of a relational understanding.

- *Continuity and change.* To tackle the question of identity requires attention to the relationship between continuity and change. As previously discussed, in the field of SESs resilience research, the prevailing model of change is the tryptic of coping, adaptation, and transformation. Only the model of transformation would correspond to a change of identity, as the entities of the system consider the ecological, economic, or social structures untenable. But how do we know if we are in a situation of transformation? For Cumming and Collier (2005), a loss of identity occurs when there is spatial or temporal separation of a system from its predecessor, where one exists. In social sciences, the question of an identity shift passes by the question of the process of identification: at a given moment of the process how does a new crystallized order emerge, how do individuals internalize it and reproduce it? Generated over time, what makes a new continuity tangible, conceivable, or even legitimate?
- *Relationships.* Identity is defined through relationships, relations between social and ecological elements within the system and external relations with other entities. For Cumming and Collier, it is about identifying the relationships that make the system. Which relations are relevant to the system is an empirical question that varies for each type of dynamic system. Following Barth (1969) and other social scientists, the question of identity lies in the definition of "we" and "them" at the border between these two groups. It is the examination of the interactions that characterize the differences between two groups rather than the attempt to define what is the essence of a group. And these boundaries are continually readjusted. The identification process is always contingent, contested, and negotiated between several construction processes. The construction processes are rooted in contextual, temporal, relational contexts.

A constructivist approach leads to the question of why identities are constructed and described. Identification is linked to a question of power and normativity. A positive identity is the product of confidence in the continuity of self and in-groups and a sense of self-efficacy, distinctiveness, and self-esteem (Breakwell, 2015). It is a key factor in people's behavior as they seek to maintain a positive self-image by behaving in ways that are consistent with the norms of their in-groups. Identity can be purposively used to create action, to assign rights, to empathize, or to exercise control. Bousquet and Mathevet (2019) outline an example on the dynamics of these negotiated identities through the study of a Spanish festival in southern France as an example of festivals that mobilize the representation of nature.

The processes of identification and distinction are inseparable. Identity is a relative notion that can be built on a balance of power, which means that the resilience of one unit implies the vulnerability of another (Endreß & Rampp, 2015; Sondershaus & Moss, 2014). "Human systems, environmental systems, and the built environment interact to produce antecedent conditions which contain both inherent vulnerabilities as well as inherent resilience" (Cutter, 2014, p. 66). Thus, there is a need to identify the probable winners and losers (Keck & Sakdapolrak, 2013) of resilience in the process of analyzing the figurations in which identities are being socially constructed.

Out of a diversity of perceptions, meanings, ideologies, practices, attitudes, and power tensions, new patterns of SES emerge and become "common sense" for the individuals and the collective. These new patterns integrate visible and invisible vulnerabilities. Bourdieu notes that every established order tends to produce the "naturalization" of its own arbitrariness (Stedman, 2016). In this sense, the identification process contributes to the crystallization of a new distribution of vulnerabilities among the entities of the SES.

Understanding the Resilience of SES Through an Analysis of Identification Processes: The Tale of Four Towns

In this section we consider two case studies, one of two German cities facing climate change taken from the literature and our own research in two French cities facing similar flood risks. We first outline how these SESs cope with change, and we describe the associated identification process. We then take our analysis a step further with our French site and unpack how the identification processes reshaped the distribution of vulnerabilities within the SES and consider what this ultimately means for a system's resilience.

The Changing Identity of Towns in Response to Climate and Global Change

Rostock and Lübek, Germany. Christman, Balgar, and Mahlkow (2014) have analyzed using discourse analysis of local publications the constructions of vulnerability and resilience in the context of climate change relying on two German cities, Rostock and Lubeck, and their reactions to climate change. With a distance of 100 kilometers between them, the cities are similar with regard to their geographic position on the coast: they have comparable natural conditions, and according to predictions by natural scientists, they will have experience similar climate-related developments, including sea level rise. They are port cities and, more specifically, Hanseatic cities (an historical alliance of ports in the Northern and Baltic sea). However, each of the cities have distinct histories.

Central to Lübek's history is the reputation of being a culturally important city. This is a vital part of Lübeck's urban identity and also frames its approach to climate change. What is essential for the local population is the preservation of the old buildings, the cultural heritage of the city, and the inner city itself. At the same time, however, Lübeck is portrayed in the publications as a city that has always defied the biggest challenges in its long Hanseatic history and has traditionally been well-equipped to cope with the threats to come. Local media points to centuries-old traditions and extensive experience of dealing with the dangers of the sea. Lübeck's actors trust in their own competence; they believe that they are up to the climate change–induced challenges of the future. The old town is viewed as being threatened and worthy of being preserved, whereas the sea together with storm surges as well as heavy rain are seen as threatening elements. Although possible vulnerabilities emanating from climate change point to devastation in the (distant) future, the debate on climate change stands under the wider umbrella of the city's history: it is the narrative of the Hanseatic tradition and of the centuries-old experience with hazards that is dominant. This narrative implies that over a long period of history, the city has had a high coping capacity on which one can rely on in the future (Christmann et al., 2014).

In Rostock, by contrast, vulnerability perceptions are primarily focused on the urban economy, high unemployment, and increasing emigration. With regards to vulnerabilities due to climate change, it is the sea that is seen as being vulnerable because fish stocks are changing. Urban actors anticipate that, as a consequence, former fishing methods will not be suitable anymore, which will also call the economic utilization of the sea into question and will further weaken the economic situation of the city. The central narrative, thus, is the problematic economic situation (Christmann et al., 2014). The coastal area is constructed as being vulnerable because various fish stocks will probably disappear. This unit of analysis, however—which is a material factor—is not the only salient element of the system's identity. Other units of the relational network are the structurally weak economy and rising temperatures, as well as an anticipated growth in the tourism sector. The structurally weak economy is seen as threatening and the whole city as being threatened (unemployment, emigration). According to the Rostock rationale, global warming can help to build resilience. Warm and long summer periods promote tourism, which will improve the economic situation. As already mentioned, in Rostock we can find very few historical references in the context of climate change issues. The past is largely eclipsed, be it the Hanseatic tradition, which remains weak, or the recent history of the former German Democratic Republic from which residents distance themselves. Rather, attention is given to the future and to the hope of becoming a "climate winner" (Christmann et al., 2014, p. 154).

Sommières and Lattes, France. Another study compares the response to global change of two towns in the south of France interrogating their relationship with water (Quinn, Bousquet, Guerbois, Heider, & Brown, 2019). The study comprised surveys in both towns ($n = 400$) and a number of interviews with public authorities and risk management organizations. Half a century ago, the two towns of Lattes and Sommières, approximately 30 kilometers apart, were similar in the way they managed autumnal river floods (the hydrological regimes are similar). The different perceptions of the acceptability of floods by public authorities, informed by prevailing urban planning, though, has led to different flood adaptation trajectories in the two towns.

Sommières, a town built partly on the riverbed since the Roman era, has a long history of flooding, and residents and authorities have developed adaptive strategies to deal with autumnal floods, such as monitoring the upper watershed, warning systems, and rapid transfer of their belongings to the upper floors of their homes. The river Vidourle, often personified by residents, floods the city every year, and the river's rhythm has been considered by the city's population as a natural event for centuries and is generally accepted as part of Sommières life. For survey respondents in Sommières, the river meanings are often positive, either for the relationships it enhances or the services it provides. However, it is important to note that of the responses given, approximately 15% of those surveyed in Sommières associated the river with a danger meaning. In the recent past Sommières has developed an identity of a town that "lives with floods." Policymakers and residents in Sommières continue to claim to have a "living with risk" culture as they have for centuries. Risk can be responded to quickly through warnings and solidarity.

Lattes, a former agricultural town whose population used to accept the risk of living with floods, became part of the greater urban area of Montpellier city in line with an urban planning strategy in the 1960s, and national and local governments (department and regional) targeted this area for the expansion and location of large infrastructure. Decision makers in Lattes reoriented their management approach toward that of "protection from risk," which started in the late 1980s with investments in costly hard infrastructures (e.g., dykes, canals) to protect the population from flood risk. As evident in local flood management documents where the focus of planning moved from coping to flood prevention, floods are no longer an acceptable risk in Lattes. This shift was highlighted by an elected official, who described how the development of infrastructure is changing knowledge in risk management: "Now in Lattes we have lost this culture of risk. If something happens, no-one is prepared." Work by Durand (2014) analyzed how the river Lez in the town of Lattes has been represented in a local newspaper over 30 years. The personalized relationship with the river typified in the earlier period of this study contrasts with the apparent paring back of the relationship to the river in recent times. The representations of the river in the local paper have become more homogenized, and the river Lez has become an object of leisure (see Table 36.1).

Through the example of Lübeck and Rostock on one side and Lattes and Sommières on the other, we have illustrated the framing of a local construction of continuity and change, transformation and identity. It emerges that the differences are rooted in very specific local cultures with their own narratives, rationales, and temporal structures and the relationship with nature and its dynamics. In Lübeck and Sommières, it is the strong historical relationship between the population and water that frames the change issue, whereas in Rostock and Lattes it is problems and a transformation in society which shapes how change is framed.

In terms of SES identity, as previously discussed we can examine the two stories according to the two dimensions, continuity and change on the one hand and the relational aspect on the other. As observers, we can say that in Lubeck and Sommières the core relationship between society and water dynamics has been conserved. The floods and the risks associated with it and the coping and adaptations that were adopted are claimed as part of the local culture. In addition, the inhabitants themselves claim these relationships as part of their identity, and they position this identity in long-term local traditions. The actual identification process which is composed of many potential identities is dominated by an historical identity (respectively, Hanseatic and Roman).

TABLE 36.1 Dimensions of Identification Process in the Four Towns

	Lattes	Sommières	Rostok	Lubek
Continuity or Disruption	Disruption	Continuity	Disruption	Continuity
Relationships	Leisure relationship with the river, new composition of inhabitants, new relationship with neighboring towns	Personalized relation with the river, spatial separation of risk (different areas), local solidarity in case of disaster	Value of the sea to attract tourists and reinforce economy, political shift from former system	Hanseatic traditional relationship with the sea, value of history and culture
Purpose of the identification process	Attract entrepreneurs and wealthy people	Maintain a lifestyle, an aesthetics and a culture	Shift to a new economic model	Maintain a lifestyle, an aesthetics and a culture
Distribution and transfers of vulnerabilities	Risk of flood transferred downstream, indebtment, poor people have to leave, dependence on infrastructure providers, loss of sense of place, agricultural and ecological processes depend on frequency of floods	Neighborhoods at risk of floods, tensions between poor and rich, isolation from the global growth model	Fisheries and fishers activity disappear, unemployment, loss of sense of place	Neighborhoods at risk, self confidence in capacity to cope

As observers, we can say that in Rostock and Lattes the core relationship between society and water dynamics has changed. An active and voluntary transformation process (large-scale building of dykes) has separated the inhabitants of Lattes from the river in terms of landscape, practices, and representations. Agriculture does not exist anymore and the size of the temporary wetland ecosystem has been reduced. With climate change the relationship of Rostock inhabitants to the sea, which was based on fish exploitation, is moving to a leisure relationship. Therefore, fisheries and fish population dynamics are changing. The infrastructures in Lattes and the climate in Rostock are considered as opportunities for transformation attracting new people who will have new relationships with water. Therefore, we claim here that there is an ongoing identification process at stake, composed of many interacting forces, which is leading to a novel SES identity.

As discussed by Rampp (2019), the identification process is strategically used to strengthen the power and the resilience of a SES. For instance, if we compare the two towns of Lattes and Sommières we observe that their claim for a given identity corresponds to positions taken within the watershed and power relations with other SES. Lattes uses its identity of a "town that controls the risk" to attract entrepreneurs, wealthy residents, and hard public infrastructures for transportation or leisure. Sommières officials uses its identity as a "town that lives with the risk" to become "a model of thousands of years adaptation" and attract tourists and residents for the culture and natural dimension of the city. It also uses this identity to reject hard infrastructures upstream and their associated side effects, which would not be compatible with this identity. Both attitudes imply transfer of vulnerability to other SES or to other components of the SES, leading to new distributions of vulnerabilities.

Resilience, SES Identification Process, and Distributions of Vulnerabilities

Adopting a complex system perspective on a SES means that an SES is composed of many interacting entities (Figure 36.1C) and that its resilience should be studied through hybrid approaches. Any SES is subject to adversity and changes, and there are permanent modifications of the entities composing the SES and modifications of the relationships among these entities. SES resilience research studies and conceptualizes these changes and the persistence of regime shifts (Rocha, Peterson, & Biggs, 2015). The contribution of this chapter is to complement this body of research with an analysis of the identification process. The analysis of resilience of a SES questions whether the SES remains the same (it keeps its identity) or it becomes something else (its identity has changed). The identity is ascribed by people within or from outside the SES, crystallizing for a moment the organization between humans, nonhumans, and infrastructures. Therefore, there are two intertwined processes: the process of change and the process of identification. The examples of Rostock, Lubeck, Sommières, and Lattes demonstrate that these towns are facing challenging events and adversities. For two of them (Rostock and Lattes), we see that there is a change in the relationship between the ecological component and the social one. This leads to a reorganization within the system, new dependences, and new identities that will be declared (Lattes, a former garden agriculture village became a rich suburb; Rostock, a former fishing center, has become an attractive tourist city and a "climate change winner"). In contrast, for the two towns where the relationship between the ecological and social components were not changed, their identity was kept constant (the Roman town for Sommières and the Hanseatic city for Lubeck). The previously described examples also show that the changes to the SES and the crystallization of an identity are associated with a distribution of vulnerabilities, which is key for the resilience of the SES. The identity, as it is ascribed by people, reveals and defines vulnerabilities. For instance, the town's living with the previously described risk identity assigns the responsibility of risk coping to the individuals and causes an internal segregation while the town's living against the risk identity assigns the responsibility of risk coping to the infrastructure providers and creates vulnerabilities outside the SES.

Figure 36.5 presents an illustration of this complex set of processes. Resilience of an SES is a process and not a trait. The resilience process has to be studied through the modification of systems as well as the identification process, which both create the capacity to deal with change. In Figure 36.5, a given SES exists with a given identity. It is composed of human and nonhuman entities (green and red, respectively) at different scales that interact. If the ecological and social connection are disrupted (slowly or rapidly) a reorganization can result of the interactions among entities, and vulnerabilities are transferred. A new distribution of vulnerabilities is then defined; the SES includes some entities and excludes some other (the boundaries are not the same) at a given time. The new identity reflects the

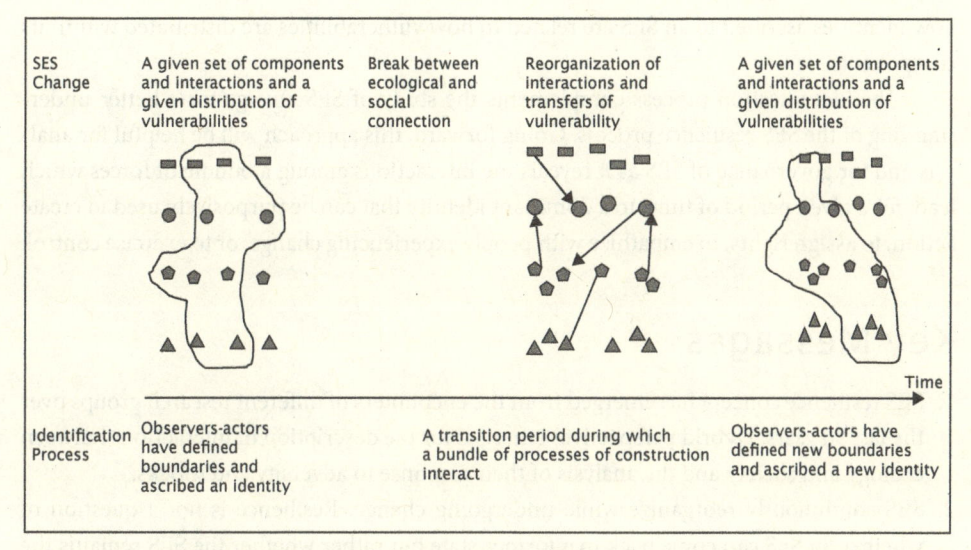

FIGURE 36.5 Interrelated processes of change and identification after a disruption between ecological and social components of an SES.

dominant perception of the organization of the SES and reveals its capacity to deal with its vulnerabilities.

This study of resilience through the identification process is consistent with the transition between the conservation, the release, and reorganization phase of the adaptive cycle model (Figure 36.3). Our contribution here is to orient the research on the identification process, which leads either to the conservation of the previous identity or to a new identity because the SES has been transformed and is not the same as it was before.

Conclusion

In this chapter we have introduced the notion of SES resilience. We have traced the history of the two concepts (SES and resilience), which are interdependent, narrating the interactions between groups of researchers who study the interactions between social and ecological processes. Different concepts, approaches, tools, principles to analyze and manage social, and ecological interactions emerged. From the diverging stances new perspectives also emerged or were reinforced. The core of the conflict was (and still is partly) the criticism of the systems approach that was used by natural sciences to integrate social processes into a pre-existing ecological scientific perspective. Hybrid perspectives are emerging for the description of interactions between ecology and society and the analysis of their response to adversity and shocks.

In the second part of the chapter, we used an approach that combines a complexity lens and a social science analysis of continuity and change. We looked at the specific question of the identity of a SES and how it persists or changes. We examined the meaning of this concept through a literature review, which led us to look at the identification process rather than identity as a trait. We used empirical examples and proposed two narratives to illustrate how identities ascribed to an SES are related to how vulnerabilities are distributed within its components.

The identification process complements the study of SES change for a better understanding of the SES resilience process. Going forward, this approach will be helpful for analysis and for governance of SES as it reveals the interactions among a bundle of forces which lead, for a given period of time, to a dominant identity that can be purposively used to create action, to assign rights, to empathize with people experiencing change, or to exercise control.

Key Messages

1. SES resilience concept has emerged from the encounters of different research groups over the last 50 years. Hybrid perspectives emerged for the description of interactions between ecology and society and the analysis of their response to adversity and shocks.
2. SES continuously reorganize while undergoing change. Resilience is not a question of whether an SES can come back to a former state but rather whether the SES remains the same or has become something else. Identity results from a continuous identification process that not only reveals but also contributes to SES change.
3. The identity of an SES and the resilience process are inextricably shaped by the vulnerabilities embedded in the SES.
4. The disruption of the relationship between natural and social entities that compose a SES leads to a new distribution of vulnerabilities among the entities and a new identity.
5. Identification is as a processual, relational, and strategic approach to change and resilience.

References

Adger, W. N. (2000). Social and ecological resilience: Are they related? *Progress in Human Geography, 24*(3), 347–364. doi:10.1191%2F030913200701540465

Anderies, J. M., & Janssen, M. A. (2011). The fragility of robust social-ecological systems. *Global Environmental Change, 21*(4), 1153–1156. doi:10.1016/j.gloenvcha.2011.07.004

Barth, F. (1969). *Ethnic groups and boundaries: The social organization of culture difference.* Oslo, Norway: Universitetsforlaget.

Berkes, F., & Folke, C. (1994). *Linking social and ecological systems for resilience and sustainability.* Beijer Discussion Paper Series No. 52, Stockholm, Sweden.

Bousquet, F., & Mathevet, R. (2019). Cultural resilience as the resilience of a distinctness. Distinctness from what? For what? In B. Rampp, M. Endreß, & M. Naumann (Eds.), *Resilience in social, cultural and political spheres* (pp. 305–321). Wiesbaden, Germany: Springer Fachmedien Wiesbaden.

Bousquet, F., A. Botta, L. Alinovi, O. Barreteau, D. Bossio, K. Brown, . . . Staver, C. (2016). Resilience and development: Mobilizing for transformation. *Ecology and Society, 21*(3), 40. doi:10.5751/ES-08754-210340

Bousquet, F., Robbins, P., Peloquin, C., & Bonato, O. (2015). The PISA grammar decodes diverse human–environment approaches. *Global Environmental Change, 34,* 159–171. doi:10.1016/j.gloenvcha.2015.06.013

Breakwell, G. M. (2015). *Coping with threatened identities.* London, UK: Psychology Press.

Brondizio, E. S., Solecki, W., & Leemans, R. (2015). *Climate change: A virtual special issue with commentary for COP21: Current Opinions in Environmental Sustainability.* Amsterdam, The Netherlands: Elsevier. Retrieved from https://www.elsevier.com/connect/climate-change-a-virtual-special-issue-with-commentary-for-cop21

Brown, K. (2015). *Resilience, development and global change.* Abingdon, UK: Routledge Press.
Cherkasskii, B. L. (1988). The system of the epidemic process. *Journal of Hygiene Epidemiology Microbiology and Immunology, 32*(3), 321–328.
Christmann, G. B., Balgar, K., & Mahlkow, N. (2014). Local constructions of vulnerability and resilience in the context of climate change. A comparison of Lübeck and Rostock. *Social Sciences, 3*(1), 142–159. doi:10.3390/socsci3010142
Colding, J., & Barthel, S. (2019). Exploring the social-ecological systems discourse 20 years later. *Ecology and Society, 24*(1), 2. doi:10.5751/es-10598-240102
Cote, M., & Nightingale, A. (2012). Resilience thinking meets social theory: Situating social change in socio-ecological systems (SES) research. *Progress in Human Geography, 36*(4), 475–489. doi:10.1177/0309132511425708
Cumming, G. S., & Collier, J. (2005). Change and identity in complex systems. *Ecology and Society, 10*(1), 29. Retrieved from https://www.jstor.org/stable/26267756
Cumming, G. S., & Peterson, G. D. (2017). Unifying research on social-ecological resilience and collapse. *Trends in Ecology & Evolution, 32*(9), 695–713. doi:10.1016/j.tree.2017.06.014
Cutter, S. L. (2014). What makes events extreme? *Journal of Extreme Events, 1*(1), 1402001. doi:10.1142/s2345737614020011
Durand, S. (2014). *Vivre avec la possibilité d'une inondation? Ethnographie de l'habiter en milieu exposé... et prisé* (Doctoral dissertation). Aix-Marseille Université. Retrieved from https://hal.archives-ouvertes.fr/tel-01470592/document
Elias, N., van Krieken, R., & Dunning, E. (1997). Towards a theory of social processes: A translation. *The British Journal of Sociology, 48*(3), 355–383. doi:10.2307/591136
Endress, M. (2015). The social constructedness of resilience. *Social Sciences, 4*(3), 533–545. doi:10.3390/socsci4030533
Endreß, M., & Rampp, B. (2015). Resilienz als perspektive auf gesellschaftliche prozesse. In M. Endreß & A. Maurer (Eds.), *Resilienz im Sozialen* (pp. 33–55). Wiesbaden, Germany: Springer.
Erikson, E. (1972). *Adolescence et crise: La quête de l'identité.* Paris, France: Champs essais.
Folke, C. (2006). Resilience: The emergence of a perspective for social-ecological systems analyses. *Global Environmental Change, 16*(3), 253–267. doi:10.1016/j.gloenvcha.2006.04.002
Folke, C. (2016). Resilience (republished). *Ecology and Society, 21*(4), 44. doi:10.5751/ES-09088-210444
Foster, J. B., & Clark, B. (2008). The sociology of ecology: Ecological organicism versus ecosystem ecology in the social construction of ecological science, 1926–1935. *Organization & Environment, 21*(3), 311–352. doi:10.1177/1086026608321632
Gallopin, G. C., Gutman, P., & Maletta, H. (1989). Global impoverishment, sustainable development and the environment: A conceptual approach. *International Social Science Journal, 121,* 375–397.
Gunderson, L., & Holling, C. S. (2002). *Panarchy: Understanding transformations in systems of humans and nature.* Washington, DC: Island Press.
Hatt, K. (2012). Social attractors: A proposal to enhance "resilience thinking" about the social. *Society & Natural Resources, 26*(1), 30–43. doi:10.1080/08941920.2012.695859
Holling, C. (1973). Resilience and stability of ecological systems. *Annual Review of Ecological Systems, 4,* 1–23. doi:10.1146/annurev.es.04.110173.000245
Holling, C. (1986). Resilience of ecosystems: Local surprise and global change. In W. Clark & R. Munn (Eds.), *Sustainable development of the biosphere* (pp. 292–317). Cambridge, UK: Cambridge University Press.
Joseph, J. (2014). The EU in the horn of Africa: Building resilience as a distant form of governance. *Journal of Common Market Studies, 52,* 285–301. doi:10.1111/jcms.12085
Keck, M., & Sakdapolrak, P. (2013). What is social resilience? Lessons learned and ways forward. *Erdkunde, 67*(1), 5–18. doi:10.3112/erdkunde.2013.01.02
Langton, C. G. (1992). Life at the edge of chaos. In C. G. Langton, C. Taylor, J. D. Farmer, & S. Rasmussen (Eds.), *Artificial life II* (pp. 41–91). Boston, MA: Addison-Wesley.
Leach, M., Raworth, K., & Rockström, J. (2013). Between social and planetary boundaries: Navigating pathways in the safe and just space for humanity. In ISSC & UNESCO (Eds.), *World social science report 2013, changing global environments* (pp. 84–89). Paris, France: OECD Publishing and UNESCO Publishing.

Liu, J. J. W., Reed, M., & Girard, T. A. (2017). Advancing resilience: An integrative, multi-system model of resilience. *Personality and Individual Differences, 111*, 111–118. doi:10.1016/j.paid.2017.02.007

Mathevet, R., & Bousquet, F. (2014). *Résilience et environnement: Penser les changements socio-écologiques.* Paris, France: Buchet.

Nadasdy, P. (2007). Adaptive co-management and the gospel of resilience. In D. Armitage, F. Berkes, & N. Doudleday (Eds.), *Adaptive co-management: Collaboration, learning and multilevel governance* (pp. 208–227). Vancouver: University of British Columbia Press.

Olsson, L., & Jerneck, A. (2018). Social fields and natural systems: Integrating knowledge about society and nature. *Ecology and Society, 23*(3), 26. doi:10.5751/es-10333-230326

Olsson, L., Jerneck, A., Thoren, H., Persson, J., & O'Byrne, D. (2015). Why resilience is unappealing to social science: Theoretical and empirical investigations of the scientific use of resilience. *Science Advances, 1*(4), e1400217. doi:10.1126/sciadv.1400217

Ostrom, E. (2007). A diagnostic approach for going beyond panaceas. *PNAS, 104*(39), 15181–15187. doi:10.1073/pnas.0702288104

Ostrom, E. (2009). A general framework for analyzing sustainability of social-ecological systems. *Science, 325*(5939), 419–422. doi:10.1126/science.1172133

Quinn, T., Bousquet, F., Guerbois, C., Heider, L., & Brown, K. (2019). How local water and waterbody meanings shape flood risk perception and risk management preferences. *Sustainability Science, 14*(3), 565–578. doi:10.1007/s11625-019-00665-0

Rampp, B. (2019). The question of "identity" in resilience research: Considerations from a sociological point of view. In B. Rampp, M. Endreß, & M. Naumann (Eds.), *Resilience in social, cultural and political spheres* (pp. 59–76). Wiesbaden, Germany: Springer.

Rocha, J. C., Peterson, G. D., & Biggs, R. (2015). Regime shifts in the anthropocene: Drivers, risks, and resilience. *PLoS One, 10*(8), e0134639. doi:10.1371/journal.pone.0134639

Schoon, M., & Van der Leeuw, S. (2015). The shift toward social-ecological systems perspectives: Insights into the human-nature relationship. *Natures Sciences Sociétés, 23*(2), 166–174. doi:10.1051/nss/2015034

Sondershaus, F., & Moss, T. (2014). Your resilience is my vulnerability: "Rules in use" in a local water conflict. *Social Sciences, 3*(1), 172–192.

Stedman, R. C. (2016). Subjectivity and social-ecological systems: A rigidity trap (and sense of place as a way out). *Sustainability Science, 11*(6), 891–901. doi:10.1007/s11625-016-0388-y

Stone-Jovicich, S., Goldstein, B. E., Brown, K., Plummer, R., & Olsson, P. (2018). Expanding the contribution of the social sciences to social-ecological resilience research. *Ecology and Society, 23*(1), 41. doi:10.5751/es-10008-230141

Tajfel, H. (1974). Social identity and intergroup behaviour. *Social Science Information, 13*(2), 65–93. doi:10.1177/053901847401300204

Walker, B., Holling, C. S., Carpenter, S. R., & Kinzig, A. (2004). Resilience, adaptability and transformability in social-ecological systems. *Ecology and Society, 9*(2), 5. Retrieved from http://www.ecologyandsociety.org/vol9/iss2/art5/

Walker, J., & Cooper, M. (2011). Genealogies of resilience: From systems ecology to the political economy of crisis adaptation. *Security Dialogue, 42*(2), 143–160. doi:10.1177/0967010611399616

Adaptive Management of Ecosystem Services for Multisystemic Resilience

Iterative Feedback Between Application and Theory

Katharine F. E. Hogan, Kirsty L. Nash, and Elena Bennett

Introduction

Society and the natural world are irrevocably intertwined forming social-ecological systems. One set of interactions between society and ecosystems relate to the reliance people place on the environment to provide critical ecosystem services (ES). ES are broadly defined as "the benefits people obtain from ecosystems" (Millennium Ecosystem Assessment, 2005) and include provisioning (e.g., food, water, and fiber), regulating (e.g., climate regulation and pollination), cultural (e.g., spiritual, aesthetic, and recreational value), and supporting (e.g., soil formation) services. These services were valued at US$125 trillion globally per year in 2011 and are critical to human well-being (Costanza et al., 2014).

However, ecosystems' capacity to support and provide ES is under pressure, with important implications for the ongoing delivery of services on which society relies; the value of ES is estimated to be declining at a rate of US$4.3 trillion to US$20.2 trillion per year due to environmental change (Costanza et al., 2014). In light of ongoing global climate change, increased population and resource extraction, and environmental degradation (Steffen et al., 2015), it is crucial that society effectively manages social-ecological systems to support ES delivery now and in the future.

Some ES can be replaced by engineered solutions, for example, storm barriers, levees, and dams can be used to provide protection from storm surges. Similarly, water purification traditionally provided by wetlands that filter out pollutants or excess nutrients may be replaced by water treatment facilities. However, technology can only replace some ES and only to a limited extent. Thus, managers require tools to work within social-ecological systems supporting the ecosystems from which ES are derived, and the people and communities that use these services.

In this chapter we synthesize research, both theoretical and applied, that has led to the development of these management tools. First, we provide a brief overview of historical management approaches. Next, we examine the theoretical underpinnings of ecological resilience in social-ecological systems, covering topics ranging from complex adaptive systems to adaptive cycles and panarchy. We then discuss the adaptive management model for ES management that will support multisystemic resilience of social-ecological systems and that draws on this body of theory. We conclude with a discussion of emerging and future research directions that will directly influence our capacity to support the multisystemic resilience of social-ecological systems.

Historical Management Paradigm

Historically, management of ES has focused on a single service such as grazing and made decisions using an equilibrium-based thinking, where an ecosystem follows a single, linear predictable trajectory of succession and is ecologically "recoverable" following disturbance, regardless of size of the area or the nature of the disturbance (Twidwell, Allred, & Fuhlendorf, 2013). This approach supports the assumption that small, isolated ecosystem remnants provide the same ES as large, intact ecosystems and can be managed in perpetuity for maximum yield of single benefits (such as food production like corn and soybeans). Associated management interventions tend to focus on controlling the system and maintaining the status quo (Holling & Meffe, 1996). In reality, ecosystems are dynamic and nonlinear across space and time, sometimes experiencing seemingly sudden or catastrophic shifts in structure and function becoming new, unrecognizable systems (Anderson et al., 2009; Gunderson, 2000). As a result, these command-and-control type management approaches often result in unintended consequences for ES delivery and the social-ecological system as a whole (Holling & Meffe, 1996). The inconsistent outcomes provided by historical management of ES has led to the development of new management approaches for social-ecological systems, focusing on complex adaptive systems, multisystemic resilience, and adaptive management, which we explore in this chapter.

Theoretical Underpinnings for Managing Social-Ecological Systems

The notion of complex adaptive systems is fundamental to social-ecological systems. A complex adaptive system has (a) independent, interacting components; (b) selection process(es) at work among and between components; and (c) variation and novelty through changes in components (Levin, 1998). This leads to a system in which a change in one part of the system can, through a series of feedbacks, lead to adaptation of the entire system. Another level of complexity is added when we consider scale, which is defined in ecology as "the spatial extent and temporal frequency, of a specific set of processes or structure" (Angeler & Allen, 2016, p. 620). Management results within social-ecological systems can become maladaptive if social (i.e., individual, organizational) and ecological (i.e., patch, ecosystem) scales are mismatched, creating process dysfunction, inefficiency, or loss of system components (Cumming, Cumming, & Redman, 2006).

Social-ecological systems are linked, interacting human and ecological communities that must be considered and managed together. These coupled systems change across scales of time and space in complex ways, which cannot necessarily be predicted. In such complex adaptive systems, long-term sustainability of ES is reliant on acknowledging, learning from and working with this change rather than trying to suppress it (Biggs et al., 2012; Walker & Salt, 2006). This is a fundamentally different way of managing ES from the one taken traditionally, which more typically manages ecosystems to suppress variability and change to provide a reliable and consistent stream of products, such as food or timber at often arbitrary scales (Gunderson et al., 2017; Holling & Meffe, 1996).

Resilience

Resilience thinking is central to managing complex adaptive systems. Resilience, in this context, is commonly defined as the capacity of a system to cope with stressors and perturbations yet retain the same structure and functions (Holling, 1973). In other words, resilience is the capacity for the system to absorb disturbance and reorganize such that it retains the same function, structure, identity, and feedbacks (Walker, Holling, Carpenter, & Kinzig, 2004). Unlike in traditional equilibrium-based management, these definitions imply the possibility of more than one system state. A clear lake switching to a turbid lake provides an ecological example of multiple states.

Managing social-ecological systems effectively requires an understanding of the dynamics and resilience trajectories of different components of the system (both social and ecological; Hicks, Crowder, Graham, Kittinger, & Cornu, 2016). As a result, resilience in social-ecological systems is inherently multisystemic. For example, in the context of ES, a loss of ecosystem resilience can lead to rapid shifts or volatility in the provision of critical services, such as crop production. Thus, there is a clear link between the resilience of an ecosystem and its capacity to provide ES. However, a resilient social system that uses these ES may have the capacity to cope with rapid shifts in crop production through increased production in other areas or food systems. Thus, there is also a clear link between the resilience of society and its capacity to respond to changing ES (Tanner et al., 2014). Furthermore, an ecologically resilient system (in a desirable state) may support a more resilient society. Critically, as the resilience of a social-ecological system declines, there is greater chance of switching to a new state. An expanding body of literature now suggests that building resilience into both human and ecological systems, as well as into integrated social-ecological systems may be an effective way to cope with environmental change characterized by future surprises or unknowable risks (Cumming et al., 2014; Tanner et al., 2014; Tompkins & Adger, 2004).

Fast and Slow Variables

In exploring and managing the dynamics of social-ecological systems, it is useful to differentiate between external forces that impact on a system, and characteristics inherent to the system. Internal changes are driven by a combination of "fast" and "slow" variables (Crépin, 2007). Ecosystem services tend to be fast variables and are the focus of traditional management. However, their dynamics are influenced by other variables that tend to change more slowly over time. The dynamics of these slow variables must be accounted for to effectively manage ES delivery, as ignoring these changes may lead to perverse outcomes such as increased system vulnerability and brittleness (Gunderson & Holling, 2002). For example, crop production, a fast variable, is an important ES. The impact of external perturbations such as rainfall variability, on crop production, is mediated by organic matter levels in the soil, a slow variable (Walker, Carpenter, Rockstrom, Crépin, & Peterson, 2012). Focusing management on crop production rather than accounting for the dynamics of the soil may lead to short-term gains in yield but drive unforeseen outcomes in the long-term, such as switch between ecosystem states, known as a regime shift.

Regime Shifts

While regime shifts are often triggered by a sudden large external impact, it is the underlying changes of the "slow" variables that are typically preparing the system for such a change long before the external impact occurs (Scheffer & Carpenter, 2003). Such gradually changing conditions may create situations of reduced resilience, increasing the vulnerability of a system to smaller disturbances that it might otherwise have been able to cope with. For example, in Caribbean reef social-ecological systems, a shift from coral to algal-dominated reefs occurred following the impacts of hurricanes and a sea urchin pathogen. However, this shift was driven by the previous slow loss of herbivorous fish due to prolonged high levels of fishing by local communities focused on maximizing their access to a key provisioning ES—food. Algal growth had been controlled by herbivorous fish; however, over time, fishing had severely impacted on the herbivorous fish community and the grazing function it provided. The loss of these herbivores was largely masked by expanding sea urchin populations that became dominant in grazing on and controlling algal cover. However, a loss of corals from hurricane damage combined with a sea urchin pathogen that dramatically reduced the now-widespread urchins meant grazing rates were insufficient to control algal growth leading to a shift from coral- to algal-dominated reef systems (Hughes, Graham, Jackson, Mumby, & Steneck, 2010).

The shape of the relationship between fast and slow variables in a social-ecological system will impact the dynamics of the system over time, the outcome of declining resilience and the potential options for management of ES (Figure 37.1). Linear relationships show stepwise impacts of any external disturbance (Figure 37.1, black line). In contrast, nonlinear relationships may result in tipping points between ecosystem states (Figure 37.1, red and blue

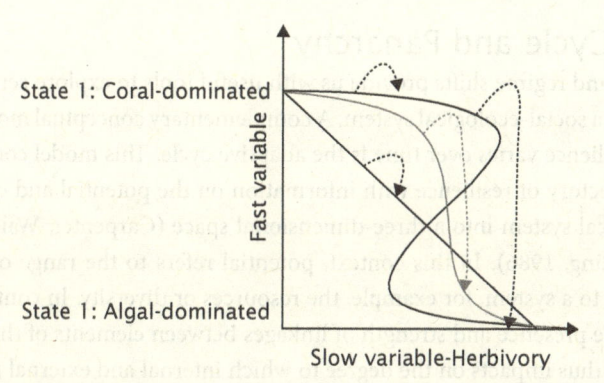

FIGURE 37.1 The relationship between fast and slow variables in social-ecological systems and the impact of external disturbance on state of the system.

lines). Where external disturbances impact resilient ecosystems, little change occurs in ecosystem state. As resilience is eroded (system moves closer to the tipping point), an external disturbance can shift the system into a new, radically different state, in a move known as a regime shift. Where more than one system state can occur for the same value of the slow variable, the system is said to have alternate stable states.

Ecologists use "ball and cup" diagrams to illustrate alternative states in ecosystems (Figure 37.2). In these diagrams, the state of the system is represented by a ball, which can roll into any of several "cups" (valleys). The depth and width of the valley determine the system's capacity to remain in its current state or retain its current identity, despite disturbances (i.e., the resilience of the system; Cumming et al., 2005; Gunderson, 2000). External disturbances shake the ball and create opportunities for it to move to a new valley. The shape of valleys can change over time due to changes in the larger social-ecological system (Gunderson, 2000). In the previously described case of the coral reef, one valley represents the coral-dominated state, and the other, the algal-dominated state. The shape of the valleys is determined in part by the amount of fishing of herbivorous species. Disturbances such as hurricanes removing coral and urchin disease causing high mortality of grazing urchins catalyze the regime shift between states, with implications for both provisioning ES such as fisheries and cultural ES such as tourism.

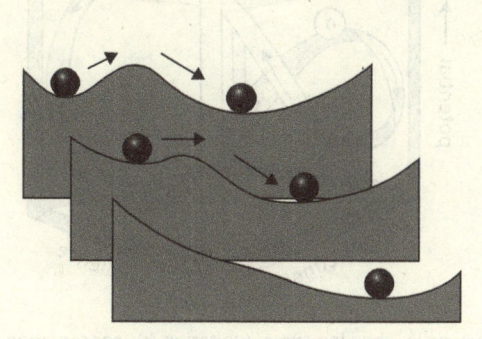

FIGURE 37.2 Ball and cup model. Modified from Gunderson (2000).

Adaptive Cycle and Panarchy

Tipping points and regime shifts provide us with useful tools to explore certain characteristics of change in a social-ecological system. A complementary conceptual model that explores how system resilience varies over time is the adaptive cycle. This model combines information on the trajectory of resilience with information on the potential and connectedness of a social-ecological system into a three-dimensional space (Carpenter, Walker, Anderies, & Abel 2001; Holling, 1986). In this context, potential refers to the range of possibilities or capital inherent to a system, for example, the resources or diversity. In contrast, connectedness refers to the presence and strength of linkages between elements of the complex adaptive system and thus impacts on the degree to which internal and external forces impact on system behavior (Gunderson & Holling, 2002). Critically, understanding where a system is in the adaptive cycle allows decision makers to choose appropriate management interventions (Walker & Salt, 2012).

The model describes the dynamics of social-ecological systems in four phases (Figure 37.3). The first two phases of the cycle describe the slow front loop of relatively predictable system dynamics. These are a growth and exploitation phase (r) and the conservation phase (K). The r phase is characterized by low potential and connectedness and high resilience. During the K phase, resilience declines, the system is less flexible, more rigid and more responsive to external shocks. External shocks that overcome the resilience of the system in K state trigger a move into the back loop, with the collapse and release phase (Ω). During the Ω phase, there is a release of the energy and potential that accumulates within the system during the K phase. Following collapse and release, there is the reorganization (α) phase, during which innovation and new opportunities are possible and resilience is increasing (Figure 37.3; Holling, 2001). During the α phase, the state of the system may change to a new state. It is at this stage, that links can be drawn to the concept of regime shifts, with reorganization leading to a new regime (Walker & Salt, 2012).

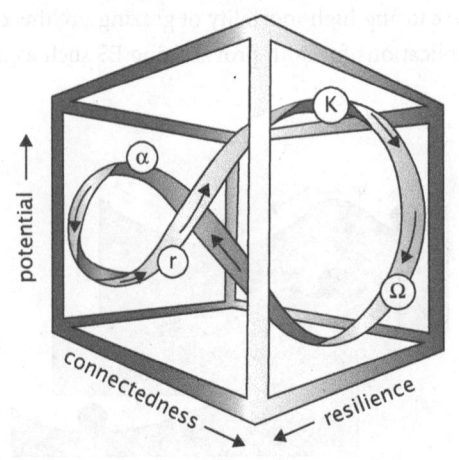

FIGURE 37.3 The adaptive cycle, showing the exploitation (r), conservation (K), release (Ω) and reorganization (α) phases in the three dimensional space provided by system potential, connectedness and resilience. Reproduced from Gunderson and Holling (2002).

The adaptive cycle has largely been used to conceptualize the behavior of social-ecological system. However, there are emerging empirical examples of a range of different types of systems following the adaptive cycle (Sundstrom & Allen, 2019). For example, phytoplankton communities in the Baltic Sea have been demonstrated to reliably follow patterns of growth, organization, and conservation and collapse over time (Angeler & Allen, 2016). It is, however, important to note that while the adaptive cycle is often visually displayed as a predictable route, the reality is that systems can move among the phases in a variety of ways, both forward and backward (Burkhard, Fath, & Müller, 2011). Furthermore, many of these cycles will interact within and across systems at multiple scales, leading to dynamic cross-scale effects on the behavior of social-ecological systems in what is known as a panarchy.

Panarchy introduces cross-scale dynamics by connecting multiple adaptive cycles in a nested hierarchy (Figure 37.4; Gunderson & Holling, 2002). The smaller, faster adaptive cycles invent, experiment, and test, while the larger, slower levels stabilize and conserve accumulated memory of system dynamics. In this way, the slower and larger levels set the conditions within which faster and smaller levels function. These cross-scale linkages are related to the within-scale system position within the adaptive cycle (Allen, Angeler, Garmestani, Gunderson, & Holling, 2014). That is, during reorganization at one scale, conservative structures at larger scales provide a form of memory that encourages reorganization around the same structures and processes rather than a different set (i.e., rather than a new regime). During the Ω (release) phase at a one scale, "destructive" processes can affect larger scales, sometimes leading to revolt and release at these scales as well (Allen et al., 2014).

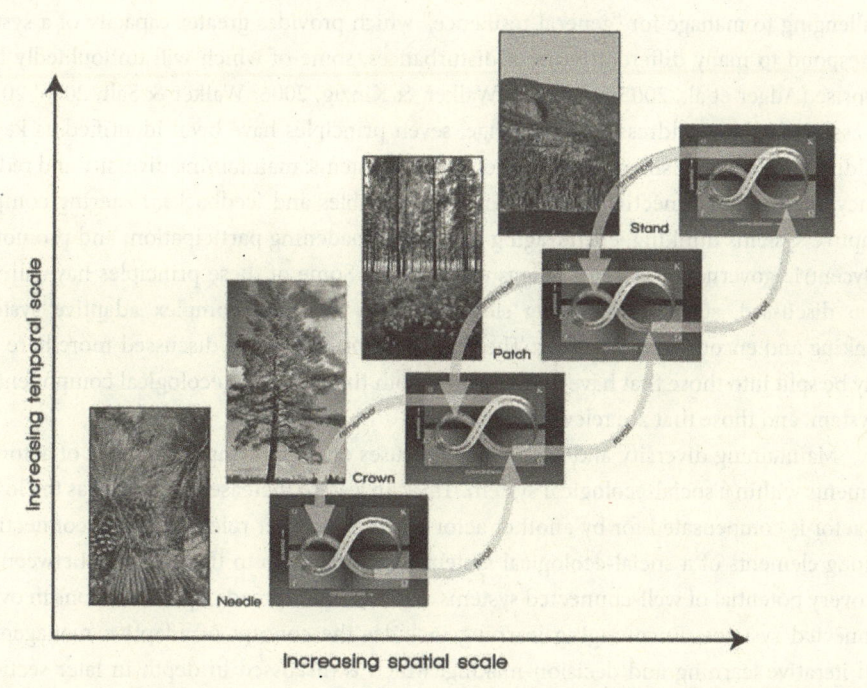

FIGURE 37.4 A conceptual diagram showing the relationship between scales of ecological structure and the nested adaptive cycles comprising a panarchy for a pine dominated forest ecosystem. Adapted from Allen et al. (2014).

Managing for Resilience

Resilience thinking, and the theoretical foundations, as previously discussed, have fundamentally changed the framing of sustainability science from seeking to achieve and maintain a static optimal state toward managing for change and accounting for tipping points (Selkoe et al., 2015; Walker et al., 2004). Nevertheless, while resilience, the adaptive cycle and panarchy are often used as metaphors to help us conceptualize ecosystem management, there is increasing interest in operationalizing these ideas (Gunderson et al., 2017), such that managers of social-ecological systems are able to translate these concepts into management approaches and practices on the ground. In this section, we first discuss broad principles of resilient systems that suggest management actions that may support the desired state of a system. We then explore a whole approach to management that enables learning in the face of uncertainty and change.

Characteristics of a Resilient System

Where managers have an understanding of the specific types of disturbances they are likely to face, they may be able to put in place targeted measures to increase the system's resilience to these disturbances (Adger, Hughes, Folke, Carpenter, & Rockström, 2005). For example, if one knows that flooding is a problem, resilience can be increased by better information about storm systems, reducing building in the flood zone, adding wetland areas to absorb some storm surges. This type of management approach focuses on "specific resilience" (i.e., resilience of a specific system state to a specific set of disturbances). It is considerably more challenging to manage for "general resilience," which provides greater capacity of a system to respond to many different types of disturbances, some of which will undoubtedly be a surprise (Adger et al., 2005; Anderies, Walker, & Kinzig, 2006; Walker & Salt, 2006, 2012). To assist managers address this challenge, seven principles have been identified as key to building the general resilience of social-ecological systems: maintaining diversity and redundancy, managing connectivity, managing slow variables and feedbacks, fostering complex adaptive systems thinking, encouraging learning, broadening participation, and promoting polycentric governance systems (Biggs et al., 2012). Some of these principles have already been discussed, such as managing slow variables, fostering complex adaptive systems thinking and encouraging learning. The remaining principles are discussed more here and may be split into those that have an impact on both the social and ecological components of a system, and those that are relevant to society.

Maintaining diversity and redundancy focuses on supporting the variety of actors or elements within a social-ecological system. This can lead to increased resilience as the loss of an actor is compensated for by another actor playing a similar role. Managing connectivity among elements of a social-ecological system pays attentions to the trade-off between the recovery potential of well-connected systems and the rapid spread of perturbations in overly connected systems. Encouraging learning includes the concept of adaptive management and iterative learning and decision-making, which is discussed in depth in later sections. Broadening participation focuses on the benefits derived from a diverse group of people being involved in management processes as this can support the development of trust and a richer, more integrated understanding of the system (Biggs et al., 2012). Finally, polycentric governance systems are collections of decision-making bodies that are connected informally (Ostrom, 2010). Promotion of this type of governance system is thought to support collective action and provide redundancy in decision-making, just as maintaining diversity supports redundancy in both social and ecological elements of a system.

These principles provide managers with potential tools to manage for resilience within social-ecological systems. However, it should be noted that resilience of a system state is not inherently desirable. Certain states may be highly resilient but have negative implications for social-ecological systems or for certain groups within a system (Glaser et al., 2018). For example, international food retailers ensure the resilience of their supply chains by developing production hubs in multiple territories, thereby reducing the risk of production losses from extreme weather events. However, this has led to the acquisition of large areas of land in developing, food insecure countries (European Environment Agency, 2015). In this context, the resilience supporting economic returns of global companies is extremely detrimental to vulnerable communities (Oliver et al., 2018). As a result, effective management requires the development of an understanding of the system configuration one wants to support. Where systems are in a desirable state, the focus will be on supporting the current state. In contrast, where a system is in an undesirable state, managers may focus on eroding resilience and using disturbances to shift the system into a more desirable state (Graham et al., 2013).

Adaptive Management and Ecosystem Services

The previously discussed principles inform potential management actions to support resilience, but they do not necessarily provide a framework for learning in the face of social-ecological change. We currently know little about how the dynamic natural systems that provide ES will influence the resilience of social-ecological systems, and the inherent complexity of social-ecological systems makes generalization difficult (Palomo, Felipe-Lucia, Bennett, Martin-Lopez, & Pascual, 2016). This, coupled with increasing global stressors and change (Steffen et al., 2015), makes improving our ability to sustainably manage ES across scales and systems even more critical. Historical single-state ecosystem management has struggled to address these stressors and complexity, as there is no inherent framework within the philosophy for acknowledging and embracing the inevitability of surprise, uncertainty, and change. In recent decades, the philosophy of adaptive management has emerged as a way to improve our understanding and ability to manage ES for resilience, while acknowledging and accounting for unknown sources of variability. Adaptive management (AM) provides a way for managers to explore system resilience and dynamics while continuing to addressing management objectives by using purposeful experiments that improve learning and lessen uncertainty over time (Allen, Fontaine, Pope, & Garmestani, 2011).

AM is a structured, iterative process through which natural resource and ES management decisions can be made and lessons learned (Holling, 1978; Walters & Hilborn, 1978). Critically, AM follows a purposeful structure, whereby predefined objectives are used to assess management progress and lessons learned in a defined but iterative learning loop: plan, do, monitor, and learn (Stankey, Clark, & Bormann, 2005; Webb, Watts, Allan,

& Warner, 2017). It is unique in that it explicitly assumes incomplete knowledge and the inevitability of uncertainty and follows decision with action by increasing knowledge of the system under management, thereby also decreasing uncertainty in future management actions (Allen & Gunderson, 2011). AM also makes consideration of trade-offs explicit and critical when assessing how management actions will impact the complex relationships between different ES (Birgé, Bevans, et al., 2016; Rodriguez et al., 2006), which we will discuss later in this chapter. Early work in fisheries (Beverton & Holt, 1957) first discussed the process of adaptive decision making as a potential solution for overexploited fish stocks. The concept was later formalized into AM as a framework that embraces uncertainty and surprise in complex systems (consider the Ω collapse and release phase of the adaptive cycle) and acknowledges that managers must act with incomplete knowledge while taking steps to better understand the system (Figure 37.5; Allen, Fontaine, Pope, & Garmestani, 2011).

Researchers and practitioners are increasingly interested in using adaptive management to address natural resources and ES issues (McFadden, Hiller, & Tyre, 2011; Peterson et al., 2007; Tyre et al., 2011). However, use of the AM framework over the last couple decades has been limited by ambiguities and barriers (Allen & Gunderson, 2011). Like many

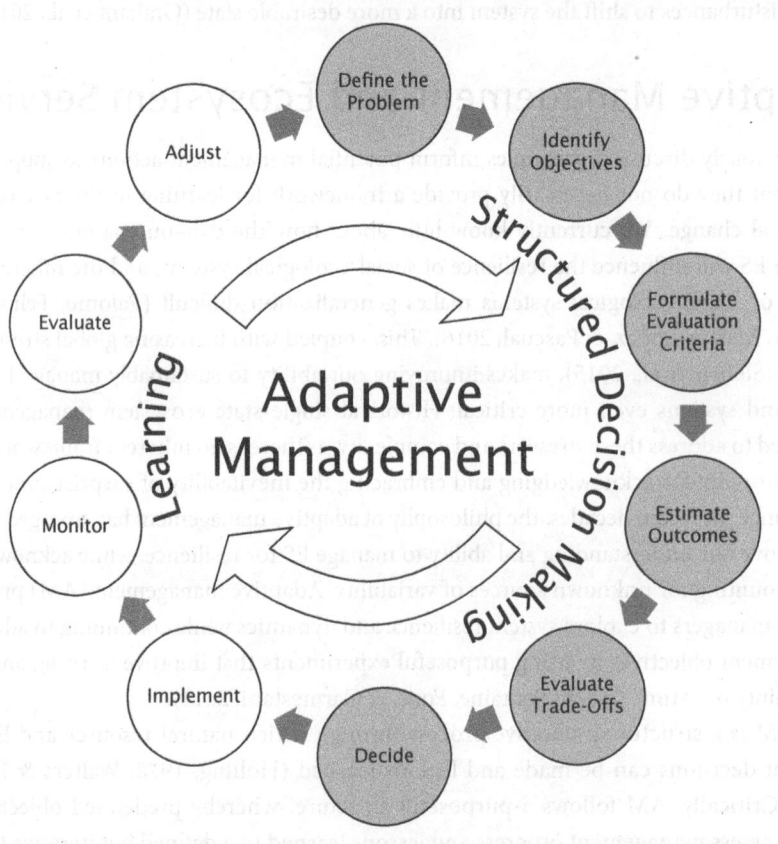

FIGURE 37.5 The adaptive management process. Used with permission from Allen et al. (2011)., available from https://www.sciencedirect.com/science/article/pii/S0301479710004226).

	Low	High
High Uncertainty	Scenario Planning	Adaptive Management
Low Uncertainty	Build Resilience	Maximum Sustained Yield

CONTROLLABILITY

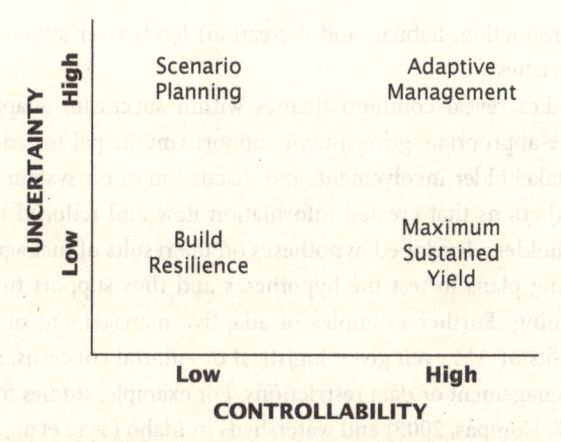

FIGURE 37.6 Different management approaches according to levels of system uncertainty and availability. Used with permission from Allen et al. (2011), available from https://www.sciencedirect.com/science/article/pii/S0301479710004226).

other proposed philosophies and frameworks, AM has been considered a silver bullet solution for any and all natural resource issues, when, in fact, it is only effective when applied at certain scales across space and time (Birgé, Allen, Garmestani, & Pope, 2016) and depends on stakeholders, researchers, and managers all being able to agree on a common vision and principles for guiding the iterative "learning by doing" process. AM is appropriate where the potential for learning is high and where the system is at a scale in space and time where it can be manipulated (Figure 37.6; Birgé, Bevans, et al., 2016). This contrasts with situations where either uncertainty is high but controllability is low (scenario planning is beneficial) or when uncertainty is low and controllability is either low (building-specific resilience is important) or high (a maximum sustainable yield approach may be suitable).

Adaptive Management in Social-Ecological Systems

The fundamental logic supporting adaptive management's modern framework has been utilized by societies that long precede modern notions of ecosystem service management (Berkes, Colding, & Folke, 2000). Furthermore, recent research suggests that this adaptive way of viewing and interacting with the natural world can improve the provision of ES critical for social-ecological systems in the 21st century (Ruhl, 2016). AM approaches to ecosystem service concerns have met with success in several areas, primarily within aquatic resources management.

The AM process has been applied in multiple watersheds in the Southeast United States where some combination of severe drought, water quality concerns, and threatened and endangered aquatic species co-occurred (reviewed in Peterson et al., 2007). Rivers are classic examples of natural resources that are prone to surprises such as drought (high uncertainty), but highly regulated by water laws that operate at multiple scales of government (high controllability). This coupled with the fact that they provide multiple ES (i.e., water quality and quantity, energy production, habitat, and recreation) lends river systems well to adaptive management approaches.

The case studies reveal common themes within successful adaptive management. These include scale-appropriate government support (municipal to federal) given the issues of concern, stakeholder involvement, and discussion of ecosystem service trade-offs, and modeling predictions that created information flow and reduced uncertainty (Allen et al., 2011). Stakeholders developed hypotheses on the results of management actions and designed monitoring plans to test the hypotheses and thus support further iterations of management planning. Further examples of adaptive management of aquatic resources highlight the benefits of AM even given logistical or cultural concerns, such as reluctance to adapt to new management or data restrictions. For example, studies focusing on marine reserves (Grafton & Kompas, 2005) and watersheds in Idaho (Tyre et al., 2011) have shown how modeling techniques can, through quantifying uncertainty, highlight and clarify both broad visions and questions of ES tradeoffs in multiuse systems, thereby alleviating certain sources of concern.

As with the inevitable ecological tradeoffs in adaptive management, there are also social, economic, and policy trade-offs when managing for sustainable ES within social-ecological systems (Craig, 2010; Polasky, Nelson, Pennington, & Johnson, 2011). Communities of scientists, managers, and decision makers can work toward more resilient social-ecological systems by leveraging both the perspectives of individual stakeholders and the collective vision of involved parties through adaptive management practices (Allen et al., 2011). One approach is through the development and use of bridging organizations, which are briefly defined as "institutions that use specific mechanisms such as working groups to link and facilitate interactions among individual actors in a management setting" (Kowalski & Jenkins, 2015, p. 1). Due to the complex, interdisciplinary nature of ES management concerns, there is a high social energy cost to building and maintaining the collaboration, communication, and trust necessary for both common vision and specific actions. Bridging organizations can help lower this cost by facilitating interactions, being a conduit for knowledge and information flow and building the social memory that is imperative for dealing with system surprise and change (Folke, Hahn, Olsson, & Norberg, 2005; Olsson, Folke, Galaz, Hahn, & Schultz, 2007).

AM can be difficult to visualize because it is by nature complex, iterative at multiple spatiotemporal scales and variables in practice within different social-ecological contexts. It is also not directly appropriate to systems that cover either very small or vast spatial and temporal scales such as individual plots as are common in field research or terrestrial systems that consist of thousands of square kilometers (Birgé, Allen, et al., 2016). These situations, where either uncertainty, controllability or both are low, are better approached by other management philosophies not covered in this chapter (see Figure 37.6).

Despite these considerations, adaptive management is a promising framework for pursuing sustainable ES management among diverse stakeholders that operate at scales where uncertainty and controllability are both reasonably high. Although AM is not a silver bullet solution for the sometimes wicked, large problems of 21st-century ES management, it is a highly flexible philosophy that facilitates working toward a common vision in complex, dynamic systems that often baffle more traditional single-state management approaches. We have outlined some situations in which application of AM principles has yielded significant learning, increased predictive capacity, and enhanced decision-making. In the following section, we outline five research and practice gaps which could greatly increase the potential of AM for sustainable management of the ES that underlie the well-being of humanity across the globe.

Future Research Directions

Management of social-ecological systems is moving away from management for steady states and toward adaptive management of dynamic systems (Bestelmeyer & Briske, 2012). Important next steps for research and management that embrace the inevitability of change include quantifying the resilience of social-ecological systems, determining if regime changes are imminent (Biggs, Carpenter, & Brock, 2009), improving knowledge exchange between researchers and managers in ways that account for the complexities managers face in their day-to-day work (Walker et al., 2002), and linking ecosystem service science with thinking on resilience (Bennett, 2017). A common thread through the research priorities we discuss here is the need for multisystemic, interdisciplinary, and collaborative action that extends beyond historical disciplinary problem-solving.

Perhaps because much scientific knowledge is disciplinary and static, research that truly informs decisions and improves environmental decision-making has been limited despite recent advances (Kirchoff, Lemos, & Dessai, 2013; Mauser et al., 2013). Some researchers are moving forward with co-development of knowledge, working directly with managers and decision makers in the process of scientific discovery to improve insights, lessons, and uptake by those who could use it to improve decision-making (Bennett, 2017; Future Earth, 2013). AM principles, applied to research, can facilitate this by necessitating involvement from stakeholders affected by decisions and policy shifts and requiring their input on which hypotheses and future actions will yield the most useful learning.

Another important area of research is detecting surprise regime shifts, which are notoriously difficult to predict (Biggs et al., 2009), but of critical importance as they typically involve undesirable changes to ES that people depend on and are costly or impossible to reverse (Scheffer et al., 2001). Recent work indicates that there may be several areas worth investigating further, including rising variance (Carpenter & Brock, 2006), changes in skewness (Guttal & Jayaprakash, 2008), and slower than normal rates of recovery in disturbed systems (van Nes & Scheffer, 2007). However, it is not entirely clear if these changes occur with enough advance warning to change management to avoid the regime shift (Biggs et al., 2009). The flexibility and iteration of AM, applied at appropriate scales and in contexts where results are controllable, could support insight on the dominant processes driving regime shifts and the spatial and temporal scales at which they could occur in larger systems.

There are other pressing questions of scale in current ecological and ES research. There is a great need to unravel the scales at which ecological processes (i.e., ES like soil nutrient cycling or vegetation regimes) actually occur in natural systems, and if they match the scales at which social-ecological systems choose to manage them. Since scale effects when and where

ES are provided, better understanding of the spatial and temporal dynamics that lead to sustainable ES is critical (Pope, Allen, & Angeler, 2014; Rodriguez et al., 2006).

Outside the realm of ecology, similar questions of scale often apply to environmental law and regulation. The scales at which laws and policies operate are often arbitrary and at a mismatch with social-ecological scales (Garmestani, Allen, & Benson, 2013). Legal systems, particularly those in the United States, do not often account for the fact that ecosystems and their services as complex, dynamic, nonlinear, and, above all, often uncertain (Allen et al., 2011). Law and policy, therefore, must develop flexibility and allow agents to adapt in the face of varying scales of change in social-ecological systems (Craig, 2010). AM and the explicit consideration of uncertainty has been effective in situations where there was support from political and regulating bodies ranging from local to federal (Peterson et al., 2007; Tyre et al., 2011). Therefore, it seems the goals of law, regulation, and adaptive management of ES are not inherently opposed; rather, the structure and support of law and policy can complement the flexibility of AM when both are approached transparently and with the goal of building trust, collaboration, and shared insight.

The quantitative frameworks necessary for learning and reducing uncertainty within the AM cycle can be highly complex and challenging due to the nuances of the social-ecological system in question (Tyre et al., 2011). Therefore, another critical area of research and practice is to develop systematic, effective teaching and training for undergraduate and graduate students in natural resources programs (Powell, Tyre, Conroy, Peterson, & Williams, 2011). Methods for accomplishing this are not well developed, but early perspectives recommend the integration of new concepts into existing coursework, including but not limited to goal-setting, complex modeling prediction, stakeholder interactions, and law and policy (Powell et al., 2011). In this way, with monitoring and evaluation of introduced curricula, the principles of AM could become more integrated into the professional research and management landscape over time.

Finally, more precise quantification of the values of ES and its connections to resilience in different social-ecological systems is critical (Polasky et al., 2011). An active area of research attempting to approach this surrounds the relationships and interactions between ES and biodiversity (Weisser et al., 2017). Although the causal relationships between biodiversity and ecosystem functioning (and therefore resilient ES) are still being investigated, there is general consensus that biodiversity does, to some extent, positively influence critical ecosystem functioning (Cardinale et al., 2012). By nature of the complex interplay among the natural, human, and built (infrastructure) capital necessary to provision humanity with ES, the approach to ES quantification must of necessity be interdisciplinary (Costanza et al., 2017; Mace, Norris, & Fitter, 2012). Therefore, the nexus of ES, biodiversity (Tscharntke et al., 2012), and the resilience of social-ecological systems (Biggs et al., 2012) is of critical importance.

Conclusion

Resilience in social-ecological systems is inherently multisystemic. Because of the interdependence of social and ecological systems, an ecologically resilient system (in a desirable state) can produce a more resilient society. Here we have reviewed the theory and practice by which the social-ecological sciences seek to sustainably manage critical ES that support human well-being. Over the last 50 years there has been significant progress in understanding the processes and feedbacks that govern change and resilience in ecosystems, but researchers and practitioners still struggle to connect this with the increasing complexity and surprises of sustainably managing the earth's resources in light of accelerating global change. We have presented a framework that will allow for the iterative testing of theory and applied practice, with each informing the other and thereby reducing uncertainty. The future research discussed in the final section are target areas for this approach, which, we believe, will produce the most critical advances in our understanding of resilient ES within social-ecological systems.

The ability of the earth system to provide the ES that confer human well-being in the face of increasingly rapid global change depends on the multisystemic resilience of the social-ecological system at multiple scales. Shifting from a static to dynamic view of systems can change the nature of ecosystem management to something much more likely to be sustainable long term, and, thus far, scientific work on resilience in social-ecological systems has developed from a need to understand the multisystemic nature of social and ecological systems to improve management. While past research has increased understanding about linked social-ecological systems and the need for flexibility and adaptability in management, there is still work to be done. In particular, we see considerable promise in research and practice focusing on feedbacks between ES and system resilience and managing resources with consideration of surprise, uncertainty, and potential system transformation.

Key Messages

1. People are dependent on the natural world to provide ES, and the ability of the earth system to provide these services in the face of increasingly rapid global change depends on the multisystemic resilience of the social-ecological system at multiple scales.
2. The multisystemic resilience of social-ecological systems is in turn affected by our ability to sustainably manage the provision of critical ES, which has historically been done by managing for maximum yield of single desired resources within ecosystems.
3. Resilience in social-ecological systems is commonly defined as the capacity of a system to cope with stressors and perturbations and yet remain in the same regime, with the same structure and functions.
4. Concepts and practices including the adaptive cycle, ball-and-cup diagrams, panarchy, scale, and adaptive management are used as key models to understand resilience by researchers and practitioners who work in social-ecological systems.
5. AM is a structured decision-making and iterative learning process by which researchers, practitioners, and stakeholders can frame hypotheses, test management actions, reduce uncertainty, and clarify further management decisions.

References

Adger, W. N., Hughes, T. P., Folke, C., Carpenter, S., & Rockström, J. (2005). Social-ecological resilience to coastal disasters. *Science, 309*(5737), 1036–1039. doi:10.1126/science.1112122

Allen, C. R., & Gunderson, L. H. (2011). Pathology and failure in the design and implementation of adaptive management. *Journal of Environmental Management, 92*(5), 1379–1384. doi:10.1016/j.jenvman.2010.10.063

Allen, C. R., Fontaine, J. J., Pope, K. L., & Garmestani, A. S. (2011). Adaptive management for a turbulent future. *Journal of Environmental Management, 92*(5), 1339–1345. doi:10.1016/j.jenvman.2010.11.019

Allen, C. R., Angeler, D. G., Garmestani, A. S., Gunderson, L. H., & Holling, C. S. (2014). Panarchy: Theory and application. *Ecosystems, 17*(4), 578–589. doi:10.1007/s10021-013-9744-2

Anderies, J. M., Walker, B. H., & Kinzig, A. P. (2006). Fifteen weddings and a funeral: Case studies and resilience-based management. *Ecology and Society, 11*(1), 21. Retrieved from http://www.ecologyandsociety.org/vol11/iss1/art21/

Anderson, B. J., Armsworth, P. R., Eigenbrod, F., Thomas, C. D., Gillings, S., Heinemeyer, A., ... Gaston, K. J. (2009). Spatial covariance between biodiversity and other ecosystem service priorities. *Journal of Applied Ecology, 46*(4), 888–896. doi:10.1111/j.1365-2664.2009.01666.x

Angeler, D. G., & Allen, C. R. (2016). Quantifying resilience. *Journal of Applied Ecology, 53*(3), 617–624. doi:10.1111/1365-2664.12649

Bennett, E. M. (2017). Research frontiers in ecosystem service science. *Ecosystems, 20*(1), 31–37. doi:10.1007/s10021-016-0049-0

Berkes, F., Colding, J., & Folke, C. (2000). Rediscovery of traditional ecological knowledge as adaptive management. *Ecological Applications, 10*(5), 1251–1262. doi:10.2307/2641280

Bestelmeyer, B., & Briske, D. D. (2012). Grand challenges for resilience-based management of rangelands. *Rangeland Ecology & Management, 65*(6), 654–663. doi:10.2307/23355256

Beverton, R. J. H., & Holt, S. J. (1957). On the dynamics of exploited fish populations. *Fisheries Investigations, 19*, 1–533.

Biggs, R., Carpenter, S. R., & Brock, W. A. (2009). Turning back from the brink: Detecting an impending regime shift in time to avert it. *PNAS, 106*(3), 826–831. doi:10.1073/pnas.0811729106

Biggs, R., Schlüter, M., Biggs, D., Bohensky, E. L., BurnSilver, S., Cundill, G., ... West, P. C. (2012). Toward principles for enhancing the resilience of ecosystem services. *Annual Review of Environment and Resources, 37*(1), 421–448. doi:10.1146/annurev-environ-051211-123836

Birgé, H. E., Allen, C. R., Garmestani, A. S., & Pope, K. L. (2016). Adaptive management for ecosystem services. *Journal of Environmental Management, 183*(Part 2), 343–352. doi:10.1016/j.jenvman.2016.07.054

Birgé, H. E., Bevans, R. A., Allen, C. R., Angeler, D. G., Baer, S. G., & Wall, D. H. (2016). Adaptive management for soil ecosystem services. *Journal of Environmental Management, 183*(Part 2), 371–378. doi:10.1016/j.jenvman.2016.06.024

Burkhard, B., Fath, B. D., & Müller, F. (2011). Adapting the adaptive cycle: Hypotheses on the development of ecosystem properties and services. *Ecological Modelling, 222*(16), 2878–2890. doi:10.1016/j.ecolmodel.2011.05.016

Cardinale, B. J., Duffy, J. E., Gonzalez, A., Hooper, D. U., Perrings, C., Venail, P., ... Naeem, S. (2012). Biodiversity loss and its impact on humanity. *Nature, 486*(7401), 59–67. doi:10.1038/nature11148

Carpenter, S. R., & Brock, W. A. (2006). Rising variance: A leading indicator of ecological transition. *Ecology Letters, 9*(3), 311–318. doi:10.1111/j.1461-0248.2005.00877.x

Carpenter, S. R., Walker, B., Anderies, J., & Abel, N. (2001). From metaphor to measurement: Resilience of what to what? *Ecosystems, 4*(8), 765–781. doi:10.1007/s10021-001-0045-9

Costanza, R., de Groot, R., Braat, L., Kubiszewski, I., Fioramonti, L., Sutton, P., ... Grasso, M. (2017). Twenty years of ecosystem services: How far have we come and how far do we still need to go? *Ecosystem Services, 28*, 1–16. doi:10.1016/j.ecoser.2017.09.008

Costanza, R., de Groot, R., Sutton, P., van der Ploeg, S., Anderson, S. J., Kubiszewski, I., ... Turner, R. K. (2014). Changes in the global value of ecosystem services. *Global Environmental Change, 26*, 152–158. doi:10.1016/j.gloenvcha.2014.04.002

Craig, R. K. (2010). Stationarity is dead—Long live transformation: Five principles for climate change adaptation law. *Harvard Environmental Law Review, 34*(2008), 9–75. Retrieved from https://papers.ssrn.com/sol3/papers.cfm?abstract_id=1357766

Crépin, A.-S. (2007). Using fast and slow processes to manage resources with thresholds. *Environmental and Resource Economics, 36*(2), 191–213. doi:10.1007/s10640-006-9029-8

Cumming, G. S., Allen, C. R., Ban, N. C., Biggs, D., Biggs, H. C., Cumming, D. H. M., . . . Schoon, M. (2014). Understanding protected area resilience: A multi-scale, social-ecological approach. *Ecological Applications, 25*(2), 299–319. doi:10.1890/13-2113.1

Cumming, G. S., Barnes, G., Perz, S., Schmink, M., Sieving, K., Southworth, J., . . . Van Holt, T. (2005). An exploratory framework for the empirical measurement of resilience. *Ecosystems, 8*(8), 975–987. doi:10.1007/s10021-005-0129-z

Cumming, G. S., Cumming, D. H. M., & Redman, C. L. (2006). Scale mismatches in social-ecological systems: Causes, consequences, and solutions. *Ecology and Society, 11*(1), 1931–1934. doi:10.5751/ES-01569-110114

European Environment Agency. (2015). *SOER 2015—The European environment—State and outlook 2015: A comprehensive assessment of the European environment's state, trends and prospects, in a global context*. Retrieved from https://www.eea.europa.eu/soer

Folke, C., Hahn, T., Olsson, P., & Norberg, J. (2005). Adaptive governance of social-ecological systems. *Annual Review of Environment and Resources, 30*(1), 441–473. doi:10.1146/annurev.energy.30.050504.144511

Future Earth. (2013). *Future Earth initial design: Report of the transition team*. International Council for Science.

Garmestani, A. S., Allen, C. R., & Benson, M. H. (2013). Can law foster social-ecological resilience? *Ecology and Society, 18*(2), 37. doi:10.5751/ES-05927-180237

Glaser, M., Plass-Johnson, J. G., Ferse, S. C. A., Neil, M., Satari, D. Y., Teichberg, M., & Reuter, H. (2018). Breaking resilience for a sustainable future: Thoughts for the Anthropocene. *Frontiers in Marine Science, 5*(34). doi:10.3389/fmars.2018.00034

Grafton, R. Q., & Kompas, T. (2005). Uncertainty and the active adaptive management of marine reserves. *Marine Policy, 29*(5), 471–479. doi:10.1016/j.marpol.2004.07.006

Graham, N. A. J., Bellwood, D. R., Cinner, J. E., Hughes, T. P., Norström, A. V., & Nyström, M. (2013). Managing resilience to reverse phase shifts in coral reefs. *Frontiers in Ecology and the Environment, 11*(10), 541–548. doi:10.1890/120305

Gunderson, L. H., & Holling, C. S. (Eds.). (2002). *Panarchy: Understanding transformations in systems of humans and nature*. Washington, DC: Island Press.

Gunderson, L. H., Cosens, B. A., Chaffin, B. C., Arnold, C. A., Fremier, A. K., Garmestani, A. S., . . . Llewellyn, D. (2017). Regime shifts and panarchies in regional scale social-ecological water systems. *Ecology and Society, 22*(1). doi:10.5751/ES-08879-220131

Gunderson, L. H. (2000). Ecological resilience: In theory and application. *Annual Review of Ecology and Systematics, 31*, 425–439. doi:10.1146/annurev.ecolsys.31.1.425

Guttal, V., & Jayaprakash, C. (2008). Changing skewness: An early warning signal of regime shifts in ecosystems. *Ecology Letters, 11*(5), 450–460. doi:10.1111/j.1461-0248.2008.01160.x

Hicks, C. C., Crowder, L. B., Graham, N. A. J., Kittinger, J. N., & Cornu, E. L. (2016). Social drivers forewarn of marine regime shifts. *Frontiers in Ecology and the Environment, 14*(5), 252–260. doi:10.1002/fee.1284

Holling, C. S. (1973). Resilience and stability of ecological systems. *Annual Review of Ecology and Systematics, 4*, 1–23. Retrieved from https://www.jstor.org/stable/2096802

Holling, C. S. (1978). *Adaptive environmental assessment and management*. Hoboken, NJ: John Wiley.

Holling, C. S. (1986). The resilience of terrestrial ecosystems: Local surprise and global change. *Sustainable Development of the Biosphere, 14*, 292–317.

Holling, C. S. (2001). Understanding the complexity of economic, ecological, and social systems. *Ecosystems, 4*(5), 390–405. doi:10.1007/s10021-00 -0101-5

Holling, C. S., & Meffe, G. K. (1996). Command and control and the pathology of natural resource management. *Conservation Biology, 10*(2), 328–337. doi:10.1046/j.1523-1739.1996.10020328.x

Hughes, T. P., Graham, N. A. J., Jackson, J. B. C., Mumby, P. J., & Steneck, R. S. (2010). Rising to the challenge of sustaining coral reef resilience. *Trends in Ecology & Evolution, 25*(11), 633–642. doi:10.1016/j.tree.2010.07.011

Kirchoff, C. J., Lemos, M. C., & Dessai, S. (2013). Actionable knowledge for environmental decision making: Broadening the usability of climate science. *Annual Review of Environment and Resources, 38,* 393–414. doi:10.1146/annurev-environ-022112-112828

Kowalski, A. A., & Jenkins, L. D. (2015). The role of bridging organizations in environmental management: Examining social networks in working groups. *Ecology and Society, 20*(2). doi:10.5751/ES-07541-200216

Levin, S. A. (1998). Ecosystems and the biosphere as complex adaptive systems. *Ecosystems, 1*(5), 431–436. doi:10.1007/s100219900037

Mace, G. M., Norris, K., & Fitter, A. H. (2012). Biodiversity and ecosystem services: A multilayered relationship. *Trends in Ecology & Evolution, 27*(1), 19–26. doi:10.1016/j.tree.2011.08.006

Mauser, W., Klepper, G., Rice, M., Schmalzbauer, B. S., Hackmann, H., Leemans, R., & Moore, H. (2013). Transdisciplinary global change research: The co-creation of knowledge for sustainability. *Current Opinion in Environmental Sustainability, 5*(3–4), 420–431. doi:10.1016/j.cosust.2013.07.001

McFadden, J. E., Hiller, T. L., & Tyre, A. J. (2011). Evaluating the efficacy of adaptive management approaches: Is there a formula for success? *Journal of Environmental Management, 92*(5), 1354–1359. doi:10.1016/j.jenvman.2010.10.038

Millennium Ecosystem Assessment. (2005). *Ecosystems and human well-being: Wetlands and water.* Washington, DC: World Resources Institute.

Oliver, T. H., Boyd, E., Balcombe, K., Benton, T. G., Bullock, J. M., Donovan, D., . . . Zaum, D. (2018). Overcoming undesirable resilience in the global food system. *Global Sustainability, 1,* e9. doi:10.1017/sus.2018.9

Olsson, P., Folke, C., Galaz, V., Hahn, T., & Schultz, L. (2007). Enhancing the fit through adaptive co-management: Creating and maintaining bridging functions for matching scales in the Kristianstads Vattenrike Biosphere Reserve, Sweden. *Ecology and Society, 12*(1), 28. doi:10.5751/ES-01976-120128

Ostrom, E. (2010). Polycentric systems for coping with collective action and global environmental change. *Global Environmental Change, 20*(4), 550–557. doi:10.1016/j.gloenvcha.2010.07.004

Palomo, I, Felipe-Lucia, M. R., Bennett, E. M., Martin-Lopez, B., & Pascual, U. (2016). Chapter six—Disentangling the pathways and effects of ecosystem service co-production. *Advances in Ecological Research, 54,* 245–283. doi:10.1016/bs.aecr.2015.09.003

Peterson, J., Moore, C., Wenger, S., Kennedy, K., Irwin, E., & Freeman, M. (2007). Adaptive management applied to aquatic natural resources. *Proceedings of the 2007 Georgia Water Resources Conference,* March 27–29.

Polasky, S., Nelson, E., Pennington, D., & Johnson, K. A. (2011). The impact of land-use change on ecosystem services, biodiversity and returns to landowners: A case study in the state of Minnesota. *Environmental and Resource Economics, 48*(2), 219–242. doi:10.1007/s10640-010-9407-0

Pope, K. L., Allen, C. R., & Angeler, D. G. (2014). Fishing for resilience. *Transactions of the American Fisheries Society, 143*(2), 467–478. doi:10.1080/00028487.2014.880735

Powell, L. A., Tyre, A. J., Conroy, M. J., Peterson, J. T., & Williams, B. K. (2011). Turning students into problem solvers: Integrating adaptive management into wildlife curricula. *The Wildlife Professional,* Summer, 74–76.

Rodriguez, J. P., Beard, T. D. Jr., Bennett, E. M., Cumming, G. S., Cork, S. J., Agard, J., . . . Peterson, G. D. (2006). Trade-offs across space, time, and ecosystem services. *Ecology and Society, 11*(1), 28. doi:10.1017/CBO9780511979095.060

Ruhl, J. B. (2016). Adaptive management of ecosystem services across different land use regimes. *Journal of Environmental Management, 183*(Part 2), 418–423. doi:10.1016/j.jenvman.2016.07.066

Scheffer, M., & Carpenter, S. R. (2003). Catastrophic regime shifts in ecosystems: Linking theory to observation. *Trends in Ecology & Evolution, 18*(12), 648–656. doi:10.1016/j.tree.2003.09.002

Scheffer, M., Carpenter, S. R., Foley, J. A., Folke, C., & Walker, B. (2001). Catastrophic shifts in ecosystems. *Nature, 413,* 591–596. doi:10.1038/35098000

Selkoe, K. A., Bleckner, T., Caldwell, M. R., Crowder, L. B., Erickson, A. L., Essington, T. E., . . . Zedler, J. (2015). Principles for managing marine ecosystems prone to tipping points. *Ecosystem Health and Sustainability, 1*(5), 17. doi:10.1890/EHS14-0024.1

Stankey, G. H., Clark, R. N., & Bormann, B. T. (2005). *Adaptive management of natural resources: Theory, concepts, and management institutions*. Gen. Tech. Rep. PNW-GTR-654. Portland, OR: US Department of Agriculture, Forest Service, Pacific Northwest Research Station 73.

Steffen, W., Richardson, K., Rockstrom, J., Cornell, S. E., Fetzer, I., Bennett, E. M., . . . Sorlin, S. (2015). Planetary boundaries: Guiding human development on a changing planet. *Science, 347*(6223), 1259855. doi:10.1126/science.1259855

Sundstrom, S. M., & Allen, C. R. (2019). The adaptive cycle: More than a metaphor. *Ecological Complexity, 39*, 100767. doi:10.1016/j.ecocom.2019.100767

Tanner, T., Lewis, D., Wrathall, D., Bronen, R., Cradock-Henry, N., Huq, S., . . . Thomalla, F. (2014). Livelihood resilience in the face of climate change. *Nature Climate Change, 5*, 23. doi:10.1038/nclimate2431

Tompkins, E. L., & Adger, W. N. (2004). Does adaptive management of natural resources enhance resilience to climate change? *Ecology and Society, 9*(2), 10.

Tscharntke, T., Tylianakis, J. M., Rand, T. A., Didham, R. K., Fahrig, L., Batáry, P., . . . Westphal, C. (2012). Landscape moderation of biodiversity patterns and processes: Eight hypotheses. *Biological Reviews, 87*(3), 661–685. doi:10.1111/j.1469-185X.2011.00216.x

Twidwell, D., Allred, B. W., & Fuhlendorf, S. D. (2013). National-scale assessment of ecological content in the world's largest land management framework. *Ecosphere, 4*(8), article 94. doi:10.1890/ES13-00124.1

Tyre, A. J., Peterson, J. T., Converse, S. J., Bogich, T., Miller, D., van der Burg, M. P., . . . Runge, M. C. (2011). Adaptive management of bull trout populations in the Lemhi Basin. *Journal of Fish and Wildlife Management, 2*(2), 262–281. doi:10.3996/022011-jfwm-012

van Nes, E. H., & Scheffer, M. (2007). Slow recovery from perturbations as a generic indicator of a nearby catastrophic shift. *The American Naturalist, 169*(6), 738–747. doi:10.1086/516845

Walker, B., & Salt, D. (2006). *Resilience thinking: Sustaining ecosystems and people in a changing world*. Washington, DC: Island Press.

Walker, B., & Salt, D. (2012). *Resilience practice: Engaging the sources of our sustainability*. Washington, DC: Island Press.

Walker, B. H., Carpenter, S. R., Rockstrom, J., Crépin, A.-S., & Peterson, G. D. (2012). Drivers, "slow" variables, "fast" variables, shocks, and resilience. *Ecology and Society, 17*(3), 30. doi:10.5751/ES-05063-170330

Walker, B., Holling, C. S., Carpenter, S. R., & Kinzig, A. (2004). Adaptability and transformability in social-ecological systems. *Ecology and Society, 9*(2), 5. Retrieved from http://www.ecologyandsociety.org/vol9/iss2/art5/

Walker, B., Carpenter, S., Anderies, J., Abel, N., Cumming, G. S., Janssen, M., . . . Pritchard, R. (2002). Resilience management in social-ecological systems: A working hypothesis for a participatory approach. *Conservation Ecology, 6*(1), 14. Retrieved from http://www.consecol.org/vol6/iss1/art14/

Walters, C. J., & Hilborn, R. (1978). Ecological optimization and adaptive management. *Annual Review of Ecology and Systematics, 9*, 157–188. doi:10.1146/annurev.es.09.110178.001105

Webb, J. A., Watts, R. J., Allan, C., & Warner, A. T. (2017). Principles for monitoring, evaluation, and adaptive management of environmental water regimes. In A. C. Horne, J. A. Webb, M. J. Stewardson, B. Richter, & M. Acreman (Eds.), *Water for the environment* (pp. 599–623). Cambridge, MA: Academic Press.

Weisser, W. W., Roscher, C., Meyer, S. T., Ebeling, A., Luo, G., Allan, E., . . . Eisenhauer, N. (2017). Biodiversity effects on ecosystem functioning in a 15-year grassland experiment: Patterns, mechanisms, and open questions. *Basic and Applied Ecology, 23*, 1–73. doi:10.1016/j.baae.2017.06.002

38

Conceptualizing Cascading Effects of Resilience in Human–Water Systems

Li Xu, Feng Mao, James S. Famiglietti,
John W. Pomeroy, and Claudia Pahl-Wostl

Introduction

Resilience was introduced to ecological research by C. S. Holling in the 1970s (Holling, 1973). Originally, the concept of resilience described the properties of an ecological system and its ability to withstand or recover from severe disturbance. This concept has had a substantial impact within ecology while also experiencing exponential growth in academic fields ranging from psychology and engineering to social sciences and interdisciplinary domains (Xu, Marinova, & Guo, 2015a). Resilience theory opens up new ways of thinking about how a system shifts from one stable state to another by investigating dynamics between thresholds of variables (how much stress they can tolerate before they must change) and external disturbances. Despite this, measuring resilience is challenging due to the complex system dynamics characterized by multiple interactions of system components both within and across scales over time and space (Quinlan, Berbés-Blázquez, Haider, & Peterson, 2016). Systemic interactions are even more complicated when social dimensions are involved in natural processes, exemplified by domains of social-ecological and socio-hydrological systems. An investigation of resilience thus requires a systematic perspective looking at not only resilience of the system of interest, but also its potential to affect the resilience of interconnected systems, which is referred to as "systemic resilience" (Ungar, 2018).

A number of questions become important when systemic thinking about resilience is applied to interconnected systems, such as cascading effects of resilience across systems. Cascading effects can be defined as the effects on one system that are generated by initial events or factors and that propagate to other systems due to the existence of interdependencies and cause-effect relationships between systems and their components (Pescaroli & Alexander, 2016). Several early studies in ecology have demonstrated clearly the existence of cascading effects in many ecological systems (see Schmitz, Hambäck, & Beckerman, 2000), and such cascading mechanisms can also occur in the connected ecological and socioeconomic systems because of threshold interactions (Kinzig et al., 2006). In systems, cascading effects could exist among thresholds, meaning that the tendency of crossing thresholds to induce the crossing of other thresholds, which could lead to changes in system states (Kinzig et al., 2006). Based on their previous syntheses, Rocha, Peterson, Bodin, and Levin (2018), for example, identified 30 types of regime shifts in social-ecological systems and found the importance of cross-scale interactions in determininig different regimes of systems. They suggested that the key for the sustainable management of future environmental change be better understanding of connections between human and natural systems.

Human actions exert pressures on water systems, while also being influenced by the changes of hydrological regimes. In examining such human and water coupled systems, there is a need to discover whether and how cascading effects occur in social and hydrological systems (i.e., how do shifts in one system's regime result in regime shifts in another?). Exploring answers to this question can help to identify ways to avoid undesirable regime shifts of systems and to reduce what may be called "systemic risks." Systemic risk describes an adverse risk to a component of a system, with the potential of spreading throughout the connected and coupled socio-hydrological system (Renn, 2016). In an extreme case, this could lead to the breakdown of the whole socio-hydrological system. In this chapter, we explore the mechanisms that explain cascading effects in coupled socio-hydrological systems and what they mean for interactions between people and water. In doing so, we propose a conceptual framework to explain how changes in resilience of any ecological system may generate cascading effects on its interconnected systems, both human and ecological. We use a case study of an agricultural drainage basin in the Canadian Prairies where extensive wetland drainage has occurred to exemplify resilience in socio-hydrological systems that are challenged by human activity and resulting climate change.

Human–Water Coupled System

While water systems are broader in definition, the hydrological system is critical for water systems as it provides essential functions to support water systems and the associated ecosystem services. In this chapter, we examine human–water relations by emphasizing the interaction between social and hydrological systems. Human and water systems are interconnected in the whole hydrological cycle (Figure 1a). The interplay between the two systems represents as two-way feedback loops that integrate both social and hydrological components and processes (Figure 1b). However, the conventional way hydrology treats humans as exogenous factors, or drivers to hydrological dynamics, overlooks contributions from the social sciences that focus on social processes and the hydrological variations that occur when water systems are exposed to exogenous constraints. The traditional research hypotheses are no longer appropriate for understanding the water cycle, in that water systems confront a myriad of threats, changes, and uncertainties brought about by anthropogenic disturbances (Wada et al., 2017). When examining water problems, Sivapalan, Savenije, and Blöschl (2012) have called for research to focus on the interface between water and social systems at the same time.

Increasing evidence has pointed to regime shifts of diverse water systems due to processes at various scales, from microscopic natural forces to macroscopic socioeconomic processes. For example, global changes in patterns of water availability, due to anthropogenic climate change and other human activities such as groundwater pumping (Rodell, Velicogna, & Famiglietti, 2009; Thomas & Famiglietti, 2019); hypoxia environments in coastal water systems, caused by excessive nutrient inputs from fertilizers or untreated sewage (Conley et al., 2009); river channel position, modified by land clearance and artificial channel widening (Knox, 2006); and the shift in freshwater lakes from clean water state to murky water state, as a result of long-term eutrophication (Carpenter, Ludwig, & Brock, 1999).

In turn, changes in hydrologic conditions (either in quantity, quality, or both) of water systems have had significant impacts on society at a number of scales. Globally, the overexploitation of groundwater has decreased the resilience of depleted regions in the face of drought events (Rodell et al., 2018). Regionally, increased water extraction has become a major force leading to changed flow regimes and groundwater levels, and therefore the increased risk of seawater intrusion and water insecurity. These patterns have been well-studied, notably in coastal regions of Australia. While data are sparse due to difficulty in monitoring, a national assessment of coastal aquifers has estimated that 47% of coastal areas in Australia had high vulnerability to seawater intrusion, and this figure is expected to increase to 57% in the future (Commonwealth of Australia, 2011). In Canada, land-use change and agricultural drainage of surface depressional storage on the Prairies have led to the dramatic loss of wetlands and increased flood risk downstream in many basins (Pomeroy et al., 2014). It is thus essential to understand how humans affect, and are affected by, water in a co-evolutionary systematic perspective (Sivapalan et al., 2012; Wada et al., 2017) with wide interdisciplinary collaboration needed to investigate more synthetic topics such as sustainability and resilience (Xu, Gober, Wheater, & Kajikawa, 2018).

Defining Resilience in the Coupled Human–Water Context

The concept of resilience is abstract, which makes it challenging to define and measure when it is fused to human–water systems because of ambiguous system boundaries. While interpretations of resilience can be diverse in different research fields (see Meerow, Newell, & Stults, 2016; Xu et al., 2015a; also see chapters in this volume), most of these definitions share principles and features that can be integrated for a clearer application to different contexts (Biggs, Schlüter, & Schoon, 2015; Brown, 2016; Ungar, 2018; Xu & Kajikawa, 2018). For example, definitions of resilience are always related to the capacity of a system to retain specific functions in the face of disturbance and change.

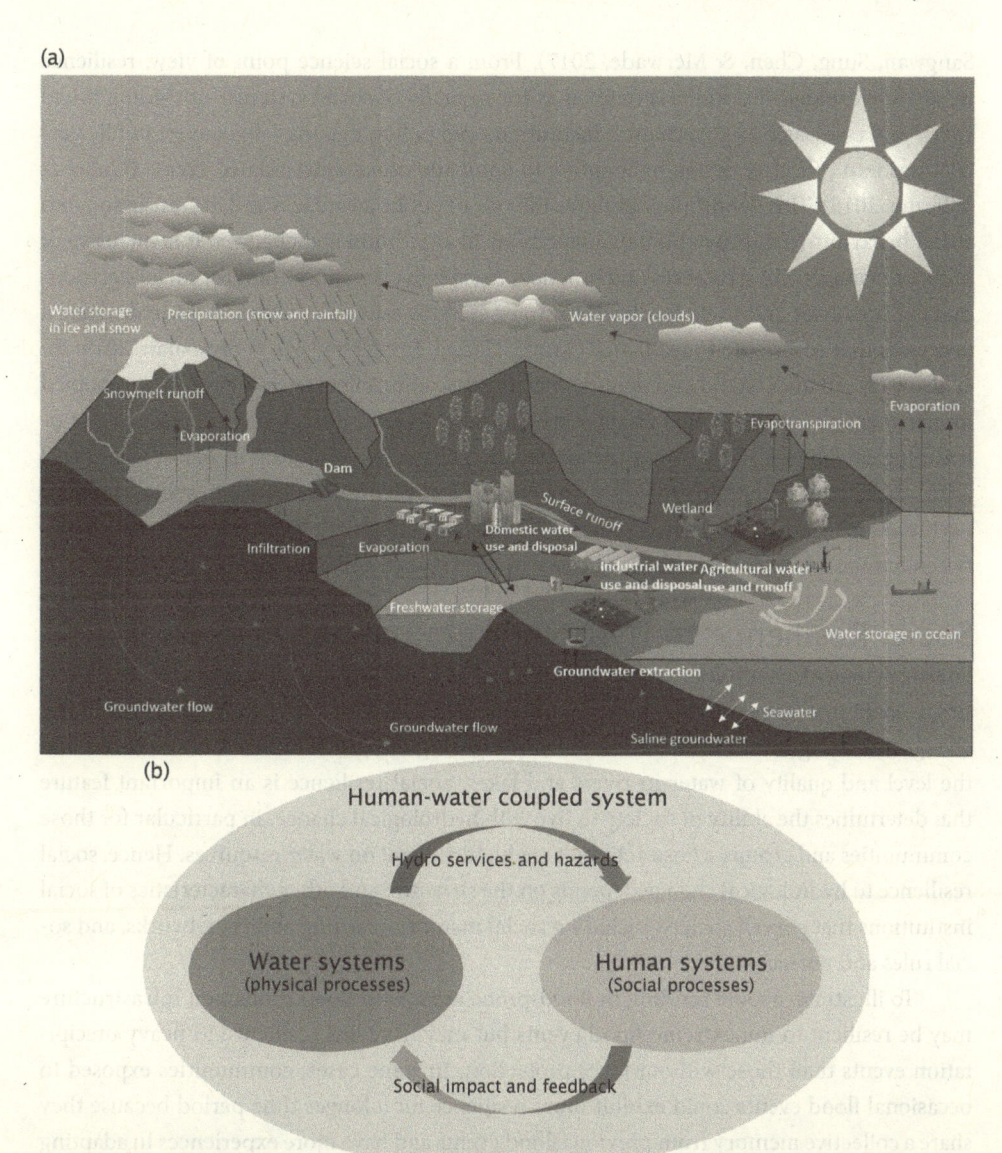

FIGURE 38.1 (a) Social and hydrologic processes in the hydrological cycle. (b) The interplay between human and water systems. *Notes:* Authors' own drawings. The Figure 38.1a was modified from the base diagram in Wikimedia for Water Cycle (https://commons.wikimedia.org/wiki/File:Water_cycle_blank.svg) under the GNU Free Documentation License. It illustrates the hydrological cycle in which some human activities are included and marked in red color.

The flexible interpretation of resilience has made the concept widely applicable to the study of the feedback between human and natural systems (e.g., social-ecological systems; Walker, Holling, Carpenter, & Kinzig, 2004). In a similar vein, resilience in sociohydrological systems has been linked to stochastic hydrological events such as drought and flood and the ability of communities, either on their own or collectively, to adapt to and recover from these events (Ciullo, Viglione, Castellarin, Crisci, & Di Baldassarre, 2017; Yu,

Sangwan, Sung, Chen, & Merwade, 2017). From a social science point of view, resilience in socio-hydrological systems is defined as the capacity of social systems—including broad social processes such as governance, institutions and policy-making—to convert public perceptions into collective action in adapting to flood and other water-related events (Gober & Wheater, 2015). This definition highlights the role of public awareness and its translation into social behaviors to improve human adaptations to environmental changes. It is inclusive of broader management structures and practices to explain even more complex social decision-making processes and their feedback to water systems when modeling socio-hydrological processes that contribute to resilience (Konar, Garcia, Sanderson, Yu, & Sivapalan, 2019; Xu et al., 2018). To understand and demonstrate the cascading effect of resilience in the coupled human–water context, in this chapter we describe three framings of resilience in socio-hydrological couplings, following the systematic perspective proposed in Mao et al. (2017) as (a) social resilience to hydrological change; (b) hydrological resilience to social (human) perturbations; and (c) socio-hydrological resilience dealing with bidirectional feedback between human and water systems in the face of disturbance and adversity.

Social Resilience to Hydrological Change

Social resilience to hydrological change is defined as the ability of individuals and communities to adapt to changed hydrological conditions or to deal with social, political, and cultural changes resulting from the alteration of hydrologic regimes, such as flow rates, volume, and the level and quality of water in rivers and lakes. Social resilience is an important feature that determines the ability of society to live with hydrological change, in particular for those communities and groups whose activities are highly reliant on water resources. Hence, social resilience to hydrological change depends on the structure and other characteristics of social institutions that govern society, including social memory, learning ability, networks, and social rules and norms.

To illustrate, people residing in flood-prone areas with flood protection infrastructure may be resilient to nonextreme flood events but may have less resilience to heavy precipitation events than those without levee protection. In some cases, communities exposed to occasional flood events could exhibit more resilience for a longer time period because they share a collective memory from previous flood events and have more experiences in adapting to flooding than those who have been protected from such events (Yu et al., 2017).

Hydrological Resilience to Social Perturbations

Hydrological resilience to social perturbations refers to the capacity of hydrological systems to absorb disturbances from human activities without losing their functions in both quantity and quality to safeguard the needs for attendant ecosystem services and human well-being. The hydrological system is a system of interconnected components involved in the natural processes of precipitation, transpiration, infiltration and flows, and infrastructure that support the management of the system. Human-created systems such as levees, dams, river canals, and irrigation ditches have significantly affected hydrologic processes and the storage of freshwater due to the reallocation of water resources in time and space. These human activities substantially disturb hydrological functions and have the potential to push water systems toward a tipping point that leads to fundamental shifts in system feedback (Dumanski, Pomeroy, & Westbrook, 2015; Falkenmark, Wang-Erlandsson, & Rockström, 2019; Famiglietti et al., 2011; Harder, Pomeroy, & Westbrook, 2015; Rocha et al., 2018; Rodell et al., 2018). As a result, losing resilience in hydrological systems will affect hydrological functions for ecosystems services that are critical to human welfare, which further result in the loss of resilience in joint social and economic systems.

Socio-Hydrological Resilience

Fusing resilience into a coupled human–water context is challenging but has become especially urgent in the era of the Anthropocene where human and water systems need to cope with disturbances from each other (Falkenmark et al., 2019). There is growing evidence that the bidirectional feedback between human and water systems worldwide results in interrelated regime shifts in social-ecological systems related to water (Rocha et al., 2018). However, when and how changes in resilience of either human or water systems react positively or negatively to another is not straightforward.

As an attempt, Mao et al. (2017) developed a conceptual framework to explain socio-hydrological resilience and argued that resilience of socio-hydrological systems could be derived from human and water interactions. Building upon their proposal, we define socio-hydrological resilience as the ability of socio-hydrological systems to maintain the feedback that keeps both human and water systems in a desired state during socio-hydrological (people and water) interactions. In such a coupled system, resilience refers to the system's ability to deal with not only external hazards resulting from environmental change but also the internal perturbations caused by the interactions of human and hydrological systems, such as competing demands for water. For instance, maintaining the complete hydrological function of a river may require a dramatic decrease in water uses in the whole basin, but it would be a significant sacrifice for many water sectors. Therefore, one critical mission to achieve a resilient socio-hydrological system is to deal with conflicts and trade-offs among individuals whose interests and preferences vary. Water governance and policy could play an important role in solving these challenges as they help to integrate management of water resources and safeguard provisions of water services at multiple levels of society to direct the resource toward a desirable state (Pahl-Wostl, 2015). However, what state can be desirable for different societal parties requires negotiation and needs to rely on wider interdisciplinary and transdisciplinary approaches engaging various stakeholders at different levels.

Systematic Understanding of Socio-Hydrological Resilience

Resilience theory offers a systematic thinking of the bifurcation of systems' stable states controlled by a critical threshold (tipping point) at which a system's state can be easily shifted to a new stability domain or a contrasting regime, or even collapse, through its self-reinforcing mechanisms or by external shocks (Scheffer et al., 2009). One example of system collapse is when high nutrient loads to freshwater lakes lead to algal blooms. The enhanced nutrient status of lakes makes them vulnerable to eutrophication, particularly in combination with warm weather, resulting in algal blooms and their concurrent social and economic problems, with implications for drinking water and human and environmental health. Understanding why and when such regime shifts occur is not straightforward because the causal mechanisms can be varied and occur at different scales. They are also sometimes hidden as most systems do not exist alone but intimately connect and interact with others (Rocha et al., 2018). This requires exploring the dynamic mechanisms that affect resilience of a system and its synergistic effects on the resilience of interrelated systems.

Systemic Resilience

Loss of resilience in a system has the potential to erode the resilience of related systems, which would increase the likelihood of regime shifts of systems and the risk of system collapse. However, this is not always the case for all systems. Even perceived positive aspects of resilience of one system may have a negative impact on the resilience of interconnected systems in different temporal and spatial scales, especially those systems that are inherently nonlinear in nature, such as ecosystems and coupled human-natural systems. This is due to the fact that the interactions between system components are complicated by a hysteresis effect on system states (Levin et al., 2013). There exist trade-offs between systems' resilience, such as resilience in the short term versus resilience in the long term, and resilience in one place versus resilience in another.

The "levee effect" phenomenon is a good example of this pattern (Di Baldassarre et al., 2013). Floodplain areas have many benefits to human well-being, such as the fertilized soil condition for farming. However, the population and development plans for these areas have to remain a safe distance from rivers where there is high flood risk. Since the construction of levees, the "safe" distance is shortened. Although engineering has increased the resilience of hydrological systems to flood events, the increasing disturbances of slow variables including human-induced interference in water processes and climate-related hydrological change could decrease social resilience in the long-term in the face of catastrophic events such as extreme flooding and bank breach. In another situation, the increase in the height of a levee on one side of a river can enhance resilience of local population but might jeopardize resilience of communities on the other bank. Accordingly, exploring the patterns of resilience across systems and scales becomes a necessary part of any study of socio-hydrological systems.

Changing Patterns of Socio-Hydrological Resilience

Resilience is a dynamic process, rather than a static trait of a system. These processes account for a system's changing behaviors (i.e., adaptation, recovery, resistance, persistence, transformation, and absorption) in response to disturbances. Previous studies have defined three system behaviors that can critically determine the resilience of a system: absorbability, adaptability and transformability (Béné, Wood, Newsham, & Davies, 2012; Organisation for Economic Co-operation and Development, 2014; Mao et al., 2017). In other words, a resilient system must be embodied with these three capacities. Other studies demonstrated that these system behaviors and capacities are affected by the performance of common characteristics represented as redundancy, diversity, connectivity, flexibility, and participation in system's components and elements (Ungar, 2018; Xu & Kajikawa, 2018). This is because these system characteristics can be attributed to the system's ability to resist and persist in the presence of a disturbance, its capacity to recover to its predisturbed state, and the ability to adjust and transition to a new desirable state after the disturbance.

More specifically, absorbability requires the system be persistent in a relatively stable state when disturbance or shock happens. Adaptability means the system should be flexible in structure and be redundant and diverse in function, which allows the system to adjust in the face of changes. Transformability enables the system to create a fundamentally new system by introducing new components and features, which means that the system is flexible when required to change (Walker et al. 2004). Social (human) and hydrological (water) systems are evolving simultaneously in dynamic ways through time and space; their resilience results from interactions between social and hydrological systems, which is described as a resilience "canvas" or "cube" in Mao et al. (2017) and Karpouzoglou and Mao (2018) (Figure 38.2a).

In Figure 38.2b, the resilience of human–water systems is defined by social resilience, hydrological resilience, as well as the integrated socio-hydrological resilience. In state A, both social and hydrological resilience are undesirably low. In this state, due to the differences in environmental conditions such as stream morphology and heterogeneous climate, the hydrological system is susceptible to anthropogenic disturbances. Meanwhile, concurrent social systems have difficulty dealing with changes in hydrological conditions because of a lack of resources. For instance, the Three Gorges Dam in China has caused the instability of flow regimes along the Yangtze River and the intensification of wet and dry conditions in its adjacent lakes and downstream ecosystem services (Fu et al., 2010). The altered flow regimes have made communities at the inlet and outlet regions of the lakes less resilient to both excessively wet and dry conditions (Xu, Marinova, & Guo, 2015b). When a system is locked in this state, management interventions are usually taken to achieve state C where both hydrological and social systems are highly resilient. However, mismanagement (e.g., management that only aims to improve either hydrological or social capacities) may lead the system to state B where there is high resilience in societal systems but low resilience in hydrological systems (B_1) or high hydrological resilience but low social resilience (B_2). In other words, improving hydrological resilience may be achieved at the expense of social resilience, or the other way around. Typically, this pattern is known as upstream–downstream trade-offs at the catchment scale (Savenije, Hoekstra, & van der Zaag, 2014). For example, the development of hydropower and irrigation systems upstream may increase the resilience of upstream regions to impacts of droughts but affects water allocation in the entire basin reducing the resilience of downstream farming systems.

We are now beginning to observe some of the emerging trends in water systems and the evidence of feedback loops between water and human systems that are important for planetary health and human well-being. Understanding what drivers trigger these changes and the interactions between drivers and variables that control a system's state is one of the most important challenges for building multisystemic resilience and ways to manage it. In this chapter, we propose that cascading analysis and ecosystem services can be the critical lens to link human and water systems and serve as the vehicle for investigating synergistic impacts

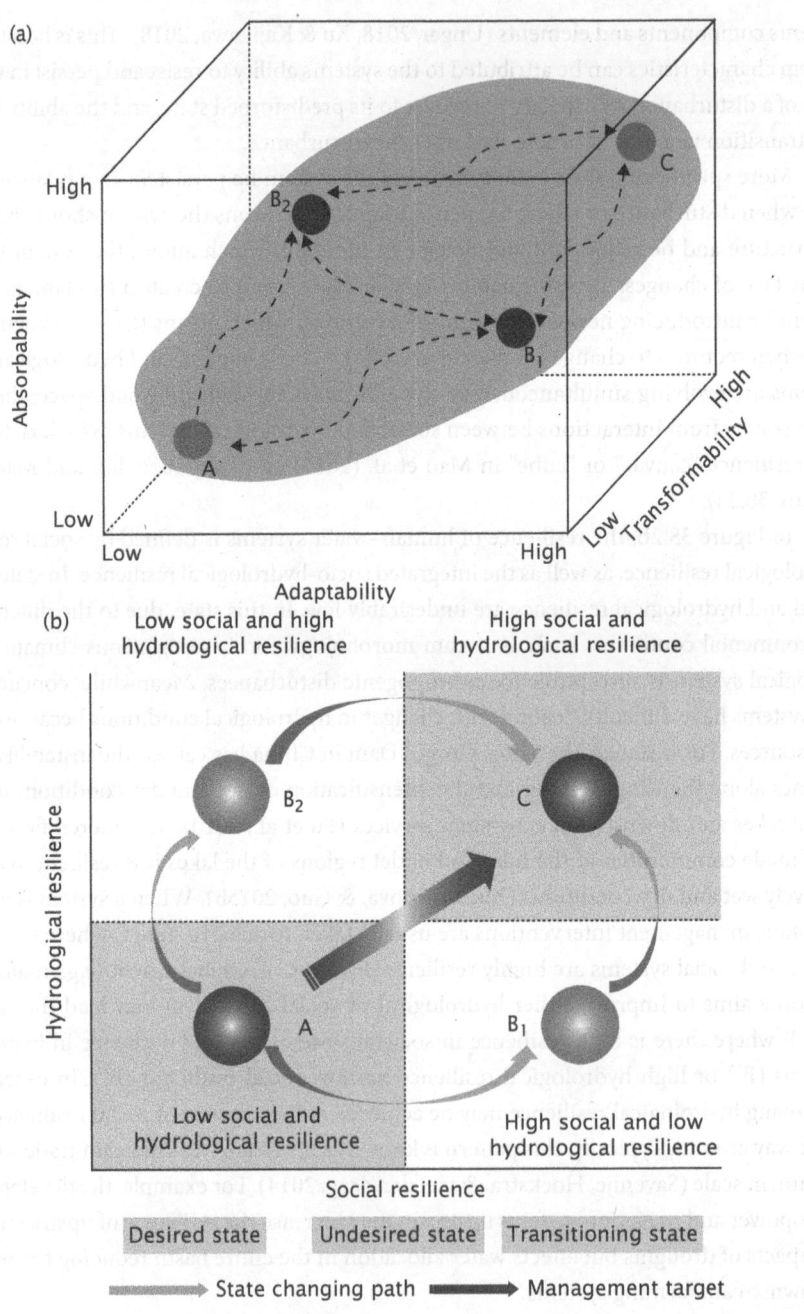

FIGURE 38.2 (a) Resilience in socio-hydrological systems and its transition between different states. (b) Resilience in human–water systems and its transition between different states. *Notes*: Authors' own figures. Figure 38.2a was modified from Karpouzoglou and Mao (2018).

of resilience across systemic levels. In the next section, we propose a conceptual framework to guide our understanding of the internal and interactive dynamics of human–water systems and the cascading effects of resilience across different system levels.

Cascading Effects in Socio-Hydrological Resilience

Cascading effects can take place once an impact on the system exceeds the system's boundary (a threshold) causing spillover effects on regimes of other interdependent systems. Likewise, changes in features of resilience of one system can increase the risk of crossing such a threshold, which can cause regime shifts of the system under shock and then alter the resilience of connected systems and their regime shifts at other spatial or temporal scales. In this chapter, we reveal that cascading effects in human–water systems could happen in three contexts. First, *cascading within the system*, meaning the synergistic impacts between components or features within the system that leads to changes in resilience itself, and then to the changes in the resilience of another through interacting dynamics of system components. Second, *cascading across systems*, meaning the effects from hydrological systems to social systems, or from social systems to hydrological systems. Third, *cascading across scales*, meaning that effects can spill over or propagate from one system to another at different temporal and spatial scales.

Cascading Effects Within the System

A system can be composed of several core subsystems (Ostrom, 2009). Each subsystem demonstrates resilience if its components help the system to deal with disturbances. The cascading effects within a system means that changes in the features of one of the subsystem's components would affect features of other components within the same system, which further affect the resilience of each interdependent subsystem. In this way, the resilience of a system is determined by the system's capacity of absorption, adaptation, and transformation, which are affected by the combined features of the diversity, redundancy, flexibility, connectivity, and openness of the system's component parts. The system is in the safe operation space if its structure and function are maintained by the combination of these features at a certain level. In turn, if the system is resilient with absorbability, adaptability, and transformability, it can nurture the features of system components to withstand disturbances. However, if this level is surpassed because of an external disturbance and internal dynamics, then the system loses its resilience making critical transition of the system state (Figure 38.3).

Water systems can be generally classified into three subsystems: surface/near-surface water, groundwater, and atmospheric water. Water moves among these subsystems through the workings of the hydrological cycle. Human systems, meanwhile, include three subsystems—production, community, and governance—which are related to water utilization. Within each subsystem, resilience is embodied with features and capacities that allow the system to avoid regime shifts. Prior to crossing the threshold, a system's state changes because of synergistic impacts between a system's features and capacities. Yet, the incremental perturbations

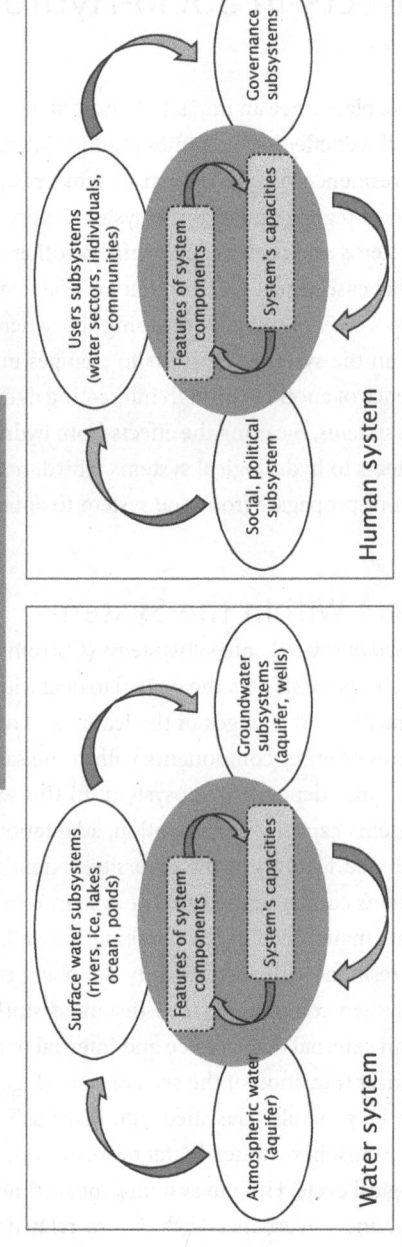

FIGURE 38.3 Cascading effects within the system. *Notes:* Authors' own figure.

(slow variables) to the subsystems can change the features of system components, affecting their capacities to withstand shocks (fast variables). Prior to a threshold being surpassed, there is strong positive feedback that maintains the system in a stable state. During the process, slow variables affect the absorptive capacity of systems while fast variables change the state of the system. Both types of variables have different impacts on a system's resilience. For example, a resilient river basin with sufficient flows of surface water can contribute to more resilient groundwater systems as it provides sufficient groundwater recharge to compensate for the impacts of climate variability (Grönwall & Oduro-Kwarteng, 2017).

Cascading Effects Across Systems

Cascading effects of resilience also occur across both human and water systems. Such effects of the two systems are usually nonlinear due to hysteresis effect determined by underlying variables and their synergies with other variables, that is, the feedback between tipping elements and between tipping and nontipping elements (Scheffer et al., 2009). In the feedback process, water can be the source of resilience, the carrier of disturbances, and the driver of change to social-ecological systems, all at the same time (Falkenmark et al., 2019). This is due to the fact that water provides benefits for ecological and social systems through multiple hydrological functions and processes. However, water can also threaten the state of social-ecological systems because of hydrological variations and crises (Figure 38.4). Defined by different attributes of quantity and quality, location, and timing of base and peak flows, water systems provides numerous hydrological ecosystem services, including a water supply for nature and different socioeconomic sectors, water damage mitigation for social-ecological systems (e.g., the reduction of flood damage, dryland salinization, saltwater intrusion, and

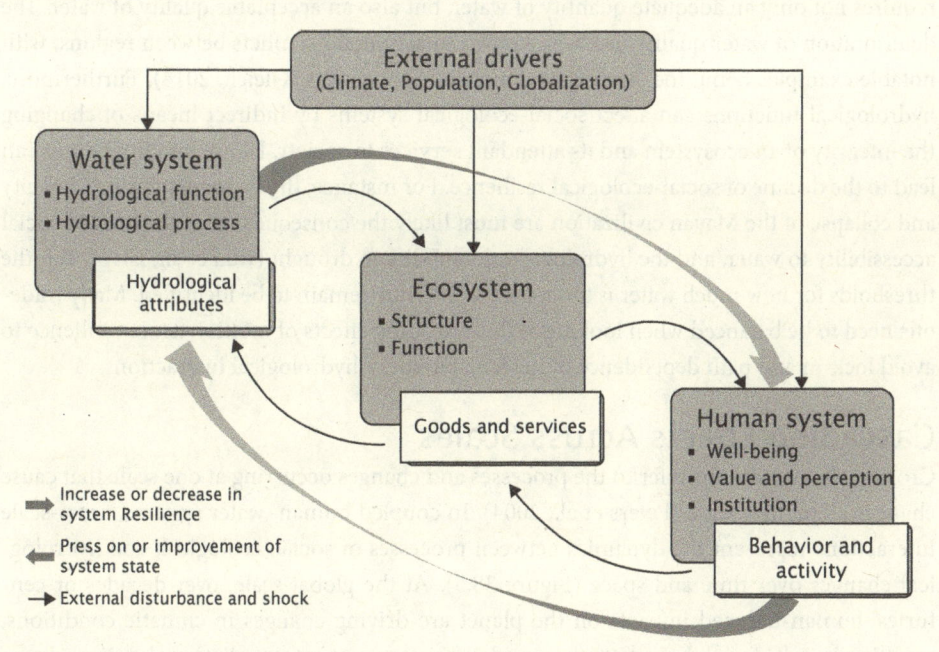

FIGURE 38.4 Cascading effects across systems. *Notes*: Authors' own figure.

sedimentation), support services for terrestrial ecosystems, and spiritual and aesthetic services for human well-being (Brauman, Daily, Duarte, & Mooney, 2007).

In a cascading way, external drivers have impacts on the water system interrupting hydrological attributes, functions, and processes. The altered hydrological systems produce effects on the structure and function of the ecosystem and its services, and changes in these services affect social well-being, people's value and perception on environmental changes, and the institutions that form human behaviors and activities. As feedbacks, social systems are resilient facing the hydrological hazards and variations, in that the society obtains experience and knowledge from the past events, which increase individuals' risk perceptions. Once effective social learning and social networks are embedded in communities, social norms and behavioral preferences in harmonizing with water can be formed, which further increases the resilience of hydrological systems.

Hydrological resilience emphasizes hydrological functions of water to safeguard ecosystem services and human utilization in the presence of human disturbances and climate variations. The failure of hydrological adaptation can jeopardize social resilience to climatic events, whereas the collapse of a water system can be a trigger for social and civilization collapse. This is because water crisis can lead to the loss of hydrological functions and services and, further, the collapse of biophysical systems on which most human civilizations rely (Falkenmark et al., 2019; Kuil, Carr, Viglione, Prskawetz, & Blöschl, 2016). However, this does not mean that the more that water is available, the more resilient a hydrological system is. On the contrary, too much water can increase the flood risks and reduce resilience of hydrological systems, particularly in engineering and social infrastructure, which may be unable to withstand heavy precipitation events. Predictability of the water supply is also crucial for the design of successful adaptations and management systems. In water supply systems, this requires not only an adequate quantity of water, but also an acceptable quality of water. The deterioration of water quality has been known to accelerate conflicts between regions, with notable examples being the Arab Spring and the Syrian War (Gleick, 2014). Furthermore, hydrological functions can affect social-ecological systems by indirect means of changing the integrity of an ecosystem and its attendant services to society. Hence, too little water can lead to the decline of social-ecological resilience. For instance, the depopulation in Tikal city and collapse of the Mayan civilization are most likely the consequences of the limited social accessibility to water, and the hydrologic vulnerability to drought (Kuil et al., 2016). Yet, the thresholds for how much water is too much or too little remain to be identified. Many trade-offs need to be balanced when looking at the cascading effects of multisystemic resilience to avoid lock-in and path dependence of unstainable socio-hydrological interactions.

Cascading Effects Across Scales

Cross-scale interactions refer to the processes and changes occurring at one scale that cause changes at another scale (Peters et al., 2004). In coupled human–water systems, cross-scale interactions represent the dynamics between processes of social, ecological, and hydrological changes over time and space (Figure 38.5). At the global scale, over decades or centuries, human-induced impacts on the planet are driving changes in climatic conditions, resulting in calls for global adaptations and mitigations. At intermediate scales, in addition

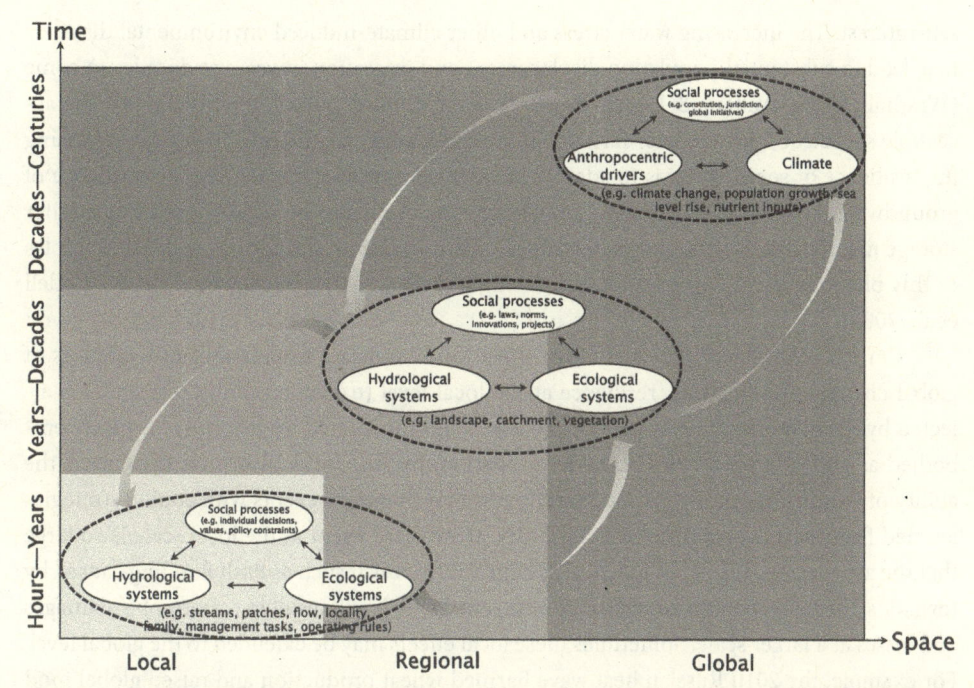

FIGURE 38.5 Cascading effects across different temporal and spatial scales. *Notes*: Authors' own figure.

to human impacts on the landscape because of land-use decisions, global changes have altered ecohydrological processes and the supply of ecosystem services (Isbell et al., 2017). These human impacts can either be immediate (such as land-use conversions from one type to another) or hysteretic over decades or even longer (e.g., land clearance for agriculture and extinctions of species; Tilman, May, Lehman, & Nowak, 1994). Small-scale hydrological processes usually happen in local streams and rivers, which affect ecosystem functions and structures in the form of patches (relatively homogeneous areas that differ from their surroundings) and are constrained to decisions of local people and policymakers. Local patchiness can lead to emergent dynamics at regional scales, and the clusters of patches can form the specific landscape at larger scales (Levin, 1992).

The observed cross-scale phenomena raise other trade-offs of systemic resilience: resilience in the short term versus resilience in the long term and resilience in one place versus resilience in another place. Resilience of a system evolves due to the interactions with other systems across different scales which have been well studied with the advantages of the analyzing approach of Gunderson and Holling's (2001) *Panarchy: Understanding Transformations in Human and Natural Systems*. The cross-scale interactions have been found to be the critical dynamics that determine the state of human and environmental systems, although the mechanism is different for each type (Rocha et al., 2018). On the one hand, given the hysteresis phenomenon, regime shifts of one system could have cascading effects on the regime shift of another system on a different time scale, sometimes from decades to centuries. For instance, the increase in global drought and land use changes may give rise to a long-term trend in landscape shifts and local changes of production due to individual risk-aversion and self-interest. The increasing water stress and other climate-induced environmental disasters may lead to substantial population displacement and migration in years or decades to come (Wrathall, Hoek, Walters, & Devenish, 2018). Furthermore, pumping wells can provide accessible source of freshwater for farmers in the short term (i.e., months to years), increasing the resilience of social systems to adapt to drought events, but threatening the resilience of groundwater systems in the longer term (decades to centuries) because of declining aquifer storage manifesting as dropping water tables. North India and California are good examples of this phenomenon (Famiglietti, 2014; Famiglietti et al., 2011; Richey et al., 2015; Rodell et al., 2009).

On the other hand, disasters at the most local levels are usually the consequences of global changes. To illustrate, resilience at the local level (e.g., community resilience) is affected by the response time of natural processes and moderated by absorptive capacity embodied as endogenous factors in the local community. The local absorptive capacity is the ability of a local community to successfully respond to hazard events with coping strategies learned from past events (Cutter et al., 2008). If a hazard event at the local scale is so large that the absorptive capacity of the local system fails to resist, such as flash flooding caused by tornados, then a certain threshold may be exceeded which will result in catastrophic damages and losses at a larger scale. Sometimes these local effects may be extended to the global level. For example, the 2010 Russian heat wave harmed wheat production and raised global food prices (Welton, 2011). Similarly, rainforest–savanna system shifts can result from local deforestation, which can cause modifications to the regional climate in the Amazon rainforest (Staal, Dekker, Hirota, & van Nes, 2015).

The previously proposed framework is, admittedly, highly conceptual in nature. It describes how cascading effects would occur in the context of multisystemic resilience. To be useful, it should be testable and scalable to different areas and across relevant temporal and spatial domains. In the next section, we make use of a basin in the Canadian Prairie as an example that demonstrates the local application of this framework for the study of cascading effects across social and hydrological systems.

Cascading Effects in Resilience of Human-Water Systems: A Case in Canadian Prairie

The Canadian Prairie is a semi-arid region characterized by a mosaic landscape formed mainly by the mixture of cropland, grassland, pastureland, and wetland. A characteristic element of the prairie landscape is the extensive occurrence of shallow depressions that lack surface water connections. These depressions were formed during the Pleistocene deglaciation of the region, and they are generally hydrologically disconnected from the stream and river networks. Wetlands and ponds have been formed in many depressions, but storage is highly varied due to the variable climate of the region (Fang et al., 2010). Agriculture is important in shaping the landscape and hydrology of the Canadian Prairies and is a major component of the economy. The region has a long history of intensive agricultural drainage, which has led to widespread loss of these depressions and associated wetlands. While research on Prairie

CONCEPTUALIZING CASCADING EFFECTS OF RESILIENCE | 759

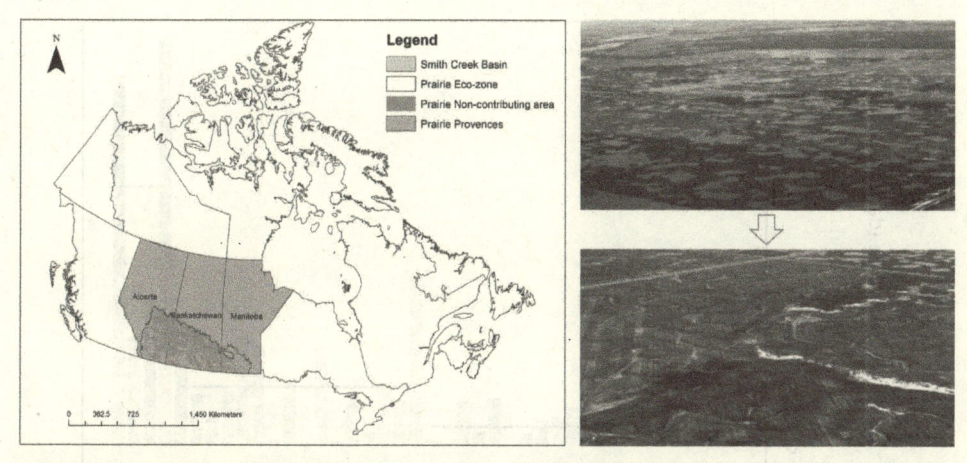

FIGURE 38.6 Human-induced alterations to landscape and water systems in the Smith Creek Basin, Canada. The right two aerial photos show two sections of land in the SCB during rapid snowmelt in April 2011. The section on the top has no artificial drainage, allowing water to pool in small and shallow natural depressions. The section on the bottom shows the impact of an artificial drainage network, which clears the land of water, increases basin connectivity and increases the flow volume downstream. *Photo credit:* Ducks Unlimited Canada.

hydrology and ecology started decades ago (Gray, 1964; LaBaugh, Winter, & Rosenberry, 1998; Pomeroy, Gray, & Landine, 1993; van der Kamp, Hayashi, & Gallén, 2003; Woo & Rowsell, 1993), the social dimensions and their coupling with water systems are relatively new (Pattison-Williams, Pomeroy, Badiou, & Gabor, 2018). In particular, the resilience of socio-hydrological systems needs to be explored given the increasing disturbances and uncertainties observed.

The Smith Creek Basin (SCB), located in southeastern Saskatchewan, Canada, is a typical prairie area which has undergone substantial drainage of depressions in recent years (Figure 38.6, left). In many parts of the basin the landscape has shifted due to the drainage activity of farmers (Figure 38.6, right). The acreage devoted to wetlands declined from 96 square kilometers (24% of the basin area) to 43 square kilometers (11% of the basin area in 2013; Dumanski et al., 2015). Benefits to farmers are offset by the social costs of agricultural drainage that include the loss of wetlands for migratory birds, increased flooding in the river basin as a whole, and reduced water quality downstream as nutrients from agricultural production are flushed downstream rather than processed in adjacent wetlands.

Changes in Hydrological Regimes and Resilience

The SCB is vulnerable to climate drivers such as floods and droughts. Millions of ponds in prairie basins absorb surges of rain, snow, and floodwaters, thus reducing the risk and severity of downstream flooding. These ponds supply water for depression-focused recharge of groundwater (Pavlovskii, Hayashi, & Cey, 2019) and provide a hedge against drought as more surface water is available to support wildlife during dry years (Wheater & Gober, 2013). These capacities maintain the hydrological resilience of the basin to climate variability. The SCB is also remarkably sensitive to the wetland drainage activity of local farmers, because

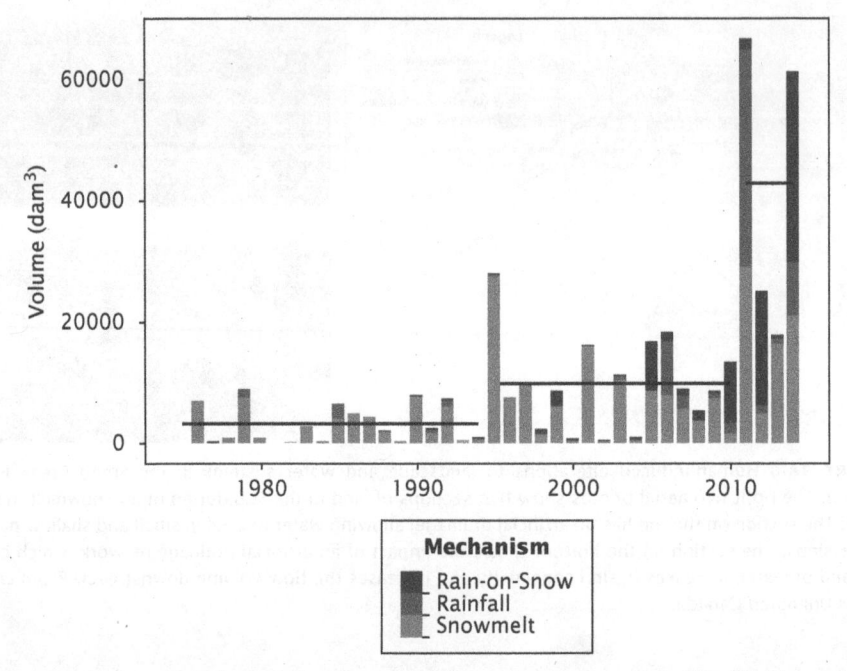

FIGURE 38.7 Changes in hydrological regimes and resilience in SCB. Figure reproduced with permission from Dumanski et al. (2015).

the drainage changes hydrological flows and self-organization capacities of the basin in dealing with floods and droughts. Specifically, drainage infrastructure opens links between noncontributing areas to the network of local streams and eventually to the Assiniboine River and Lake Winnipeg Basin. Observation and simulations show that the hydrological regime during the spring in SCB has shifted from snowmelt dominated streamflow to rainfall-runoff domination. The annual streamflow volume tripled between 1995 and 2010, a period that included a significant drought episode between 1999 and 2005 (Pomeroy et al., 2014); springtime peak flows increased causing significant flooding in 2011; and a second summer peak occurred in recent years when the creek is normally dry (Dumanski et al., 2015). Annual flow volumes from Smith Creek have increase 14-fold from the 1970s to the 2010s without a concomitant increase in precipitation (Figure 38.7). This is one of the largest increases in runoff efficiency ever measured in the world.

The drainage of depressions can increase the connectivity of surface water, but reduces the numbers of ponds on lands and the resilience of downstream areas to flooding (Figure 38.8). Hydrological modeling and observations also link farmers' drainage to the increase in flood problems and raise the potential for even more severe impacts under climate change scenarios. The complete drainage of existing wetlands would have increased the peak of a disastrous 2011 flood by 78%, and the yearly volume of stream flow, by 32% (Pomeroy et al., 2014). The combined changes in hydrological regimes and the loss of wetlands have decreased hydrological resilience in the face of climate change.

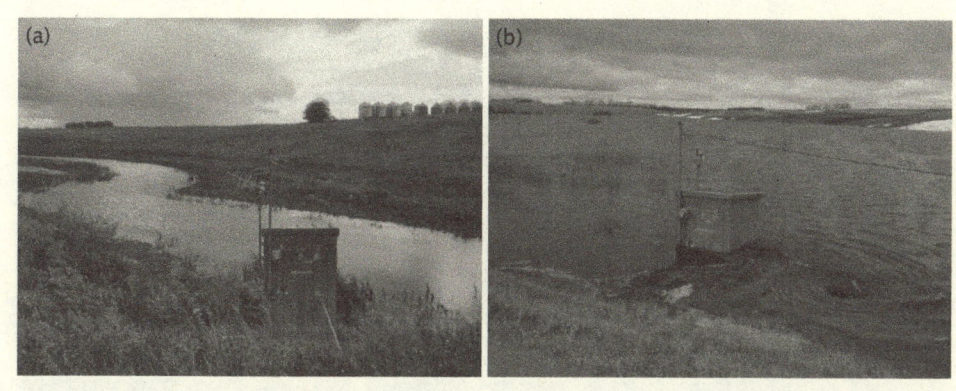

FIGURE 38.8 Less resilient hydrological system in the face of climate variations. These two photos were taken in 2011 in the same area where one of the hydrological gauges is located in the SCB: (a) shows how the stream channel appears in summer when there is no heavy rainfall—the stream flows through a culvert to the right of the station housing; (b) shows the inundation due to backwatering in the area when snow starts to melt in addition to a heavy rainfall event in late spring—the whirlpool is the streamflow entering the now inundated culvert. *Photo credit*: Nicole Seitz, Centre for Hydrology, University of Saskatchewan.

Changes in Ecosystem Services and Social Resilience

Losing hydrological resilience leads to cascading effects and a decrease in social resilience when adapting to changing hydrological regimes. Draining wetlands causes the loss of ecosystem services and social resilience to climate variability and hydrological hazards. In this case, resilience can be treated as a capital asset for both social and ecological systems (Walker et al., 2010). Changes in wetlands water storage via drainage activity will change sociohydrological resilience because of the alteration to hydrological regimes and the reduction of regulating services that wetlands provide to human and water systems such as flood control and nutrient absorption. In short, the reduction of wetland storage decreases absorptive and adaptive capacities of social-ecological systems in the face of floods and droughts (Figure 38.9). Reducing per unit of wetland stock can increase the likelihood of flood damage, and continuous loss of wetlands causes the system to become vulnerable to heavy run-off events.

Furthermore, landscape modification allowed little to no residual local storage on farmlands, and unregulated drainage ditches transported water from one local depression to another, causing flood damage to adjacent croplands and communities surrounding the terminal depression. The wet hydrological conditions caused damage to croplands because of the wet soil moisture. Local communities are able to adapt to a changed environment based on their memory and experience, but their adaptation fails when extreme hydrological events occur, such as the July 2014 flooding caused by rain in SCB. This produced the highest peak streamflow of all time at a time of year when the creek is normally dry and from rainfall run-off processes that produced only 15% of streamflow 30 years ago. Local farmers are not prepared to deal with such unexpected events. When this happens and people are negatively affected, scientific and public discussion about land and water management can contribute to improved social resilience.

FIGURE 38.9 Failure of social-ecological systems to adapt to flood events These three photos were taken in May of 2011 in the same area in SCB: (a) and (b) show how farmers protected their lands by using simple wood boards to block the water drained from their neighboring lands. However, as the water coming from upstream increased, the adaptation failed causing overtopping across the roads as shown in (c). *Photo credit:* Nicole Seitz, Centre for Hydrology, University of Saskatchewan.

Conclusion

Human influences have become a major force for change in water system dynamics. While the emerging field of socio-hydrology has made efforts to incorporate human dimensions as endogenous factors into hydrological models to simulate humans' role in the whole hydrologic cycle, the interactions and feedback between human and environmental elements of water systems have the potential to push coupled systems past critical thresholds and cause regime shifts. Hence, one key to managing human–water coupled systems is to avoid critical transitions in rapidly changing and highly uncertain environments. Resilience can be a powerful systemic way of thinking for coping with that. It emphasizes nonlinear dynamics of systems, the existence of thresholds, uncertainties, and feedback loops between human and natural systems across temporal and spatial scales (Folke, 2006). However, the integration of resilience to socio-hydrological research is still new.

When introducing resilience to socio-hydrological research, some urgent issues must be accommodated given the changes happening to river hydrology. Examples of such issues include whether or not there will be alternative regimes for farming systems if changed hydrological conditions lead to changes in farm production patterns, or even the resettlement of farmers, and whether tipping points (critical thresholds) exist between them; whether ecology should be treated as the boundary condition when it comes to socio-hydrological resilience and its modeling; whether and how different policy settings change behaviors of people, which could further affect hydrologic systems and avoid systems crossing tipping points; and how to detect early warning signs of undesirable regime shifts, which may be caused by the changing hydrology.

In addition, smart decision-making under deep uncertainty is needed, which can benefit from interdisciplinary and transdisciplinary research as well as the implementation of adaptive water governance. Managing water involves managing people and their attitudes, needs, values, and beliefs about how hydrological systems function. Continuing to foster interdisciplinary and transdisciplinary research is one possible way to adapt to this uncertainty and change. Interdisciplinary water research that brings together different disciplines will help people to understand complex human–water problems and identify uncertainties. Transdisciplinary studies that engage various stakeholders to share values and knowledge will improve people's knowledge about what the current water situation is, what the future might be, and inform science and policy-makings about the real need to live better with changing circumstances. Furthermore, adaptive water governance and management should be improved through learning processes (or cycles) and take into account different kinds of uncertainties (Pahl-Wostl et al., 2007). For example, flexible management and governance should be built to allow learning and address uncertainties in decision-making processes. This means that the governance and management systems must be flexible and adaptive to respond to new information (e.g., from experience or from prediction; Pahl-Wostl et al., 2007). The uncertainties that need to be considered stem not only from the environment, but also from economic, societal, and political changes.

To help understand these patterns and cope with uncertainties, we have introduced in this chapter the concept of socio-hydrology to investigate cascading effects of resilience in coupled human–water systems. We first defined socio-hydrological resilience and then proposed a conceptual framework to explore how changes in the resilience of either hydrological systems or human systems could impact each other. In the framework, we argued that cascading effects of multisystemic resilience could take place under three conditions: cascading effects within a system, across systems, and through cross-scale interactions. In each circumstance, we suggested that ecosystem services be the critical lens to understand how changes to the resilience of water systems can have synergistic effects on the resilience of social systems, and the other way around. We used the example of a basin on the Canadian Prairies to illustrate how hydrological resilience can be changed because of human perturbations that affect agricultural drainage and how changes in hydrological resilience can affect social resilience by altering the conditions of ecosystem services. We recommend that socio-hydrological models, such as stylized models, be built based on this framework to better describe the dynamic cascading mechanisms of human and water coupled systems and the resilience of the systems involved.

Key Messages

1. Human (social) and water systems need to be understood in a coupled context.
2. Resilience of human systems require the resilience of hydrological systems.
3. A resilient hydrological system should be capable of absorbing social disturbances.
4. Resilience of human-water systems requires investigating bidirectional feedback between social and hydrological systems.

Acknowledgments

The authors would like to acknowledge the financial support from Tri-Agency Institutional Programs Secretariat of Canada through the Canada 150 Research Chair in Hydrology and Remote Sensing; Canada Excellence Research Chair in Water Security; and Global Water Futures Program, Canada First Research Excellence Fund. The SCB research was supported by the Canada Research Chair in Water Resources and Climate Change, Ducks Unlimited Canada and the Government of Saskatchewan.

References

Béné, C., Wood, R. G., Newsham, A., & Davies, M. (2012). Resilience: New utopia or new tyranny? Reflection about the potentials and limits of the concept of resilience in relation to vulnerability reduction programmes. *IDS Working Papers, 405*(6), 1–61. doi:10.1111/j.2040-0209.2012.00405.x

Biggs, R., Schlüter, M., & Schoon, M. L. (2015). *Principles for building resilience: Sustaining ecosystem services in social-ecological systems.* Cambridge, UK: Cambridge University Press. doi:10.1017/cbo9781316014240

Brauman, K. A., Daily, G. C., Duarte, T. K., & Mooney, H. A. (2007). The nature and value of ecosystem services: An overview highlighting hydrologic services. *Annual Review of Environment and Resources, 32*(1), 67–98. doi:10.1146/annurev.energy.32.031306.102758

Brown, K. (2016). *Resilience, development and global change* (1st ed.). London, UK: Routledge. doi:10.4324/9780203498095

Carpenter, S. R., Ludwig, D., & Brock, W. A. (1999). Management of eutrophication for lakes subject to potentially irreversible change. *Ecological Applications, 9*(3), 751–771. doi:10.2307/2641327

Ciullo, A., Viglione, A., Castellarin, A., Crisci, M., & Di Baldassarre, G. (2017). Socio-hydrological modelling of flood-risk dynamics: Comparing the resilience of green and technological systems. *Hydrological Sciences Journal, 62*(6), 880–891. doi:10.1080/02626667.2016.1273527

Commonwealth of Australia. (2011). *Australian state of the environment thematic reports 2011.* Independent report to the Australian Government Minister for Sustainability, Environment, Water, Population and Communities. Canberra, Australia.

Conley, D. J., Paerl, H. W., Howarth, R. W., Boesch, D. F., Seitzinger, S. P., Havens, K. E., . . . Likens, G. E. (2009). Controlling eutrophication: Nitrogen and phosphorus. *Science, 323*(5917), 1014–1015. doi:10.1126/science.1167755

Cutter, S. L., Barnes, L., Berry, M., Burton, C., Evans, E., Tate, E., & Webb, J. (2008). A place-based model for understanding community resilience to natural disasters. *Global Environmental Change, 18*(4), 598–606. doi:10.1016/j.gloenvcha.2008.07.013

Di Baldassarre, G., Viglione, A., Carr, G., Kuil, L., Salinas, J. L., & Blöschl, G. (2013). Socio-hydrology: Conceptualising human-flood interactions. *Hydrology and Earth System Sciences, 17*(8), 3295–3303. doi:10.5194/hess-17-3295-2013

Dumanski, S., Pomeroy, J. W., & Westbrook, C. J. (2015). Hydrological regime changes in a Canadian Prairie basin. *Hydrological Processes, 29*(18), 3893–3904. doi:10.1002/hyp.10567

Falkenmark, M., Wang-Erlandsson, L., & Rockström, J. (2019). Understanding of water resilience in the Anthropocene. *Journal of Hydrology X, 2*(100009). doi:10.1016/j.hydroa.2018.100009

Famiglietti, J. S. (2014). The global groundwater crisis. *Nature Climate Change, 4*(11), 945–948. doi:10.1038/nclimate2425

Famiglietti, J. S., Lo, M., Ho, S. L., Bethune, J., Anderson, K. J., Syed, T. H., . . . Rodell, M. (2011). Satellites measure recent rates of groundwater depletion in California's Central Valley. *Geophysical Research Letters, 38*(3), 2–5. doi:10.1029/2010GL046442

Fang, X., Pomeroy, J. W., Westbrook, C. J., Guo, X., Minke, A. G., & Brown, T. (2010). Prediction of snowmelt derived streamflow in a wetland dominated prairie basin. *Hydrology and Earth System Sciences, 14*(6), 991–1006. doi:10.5194/hess-14-991-2010

Folke, C. (2006). Resilience: The emergence of a perspective for social-ecological systems analyses. *Global Environmental Change, 16*(3), 253–267. doi:10.1016/j.gloenvcha.2006.04.002

Fu, B.-J., Wu, B.-F., Lü, Y.-H., Xu, Z.-H., Cao, J.-H., Niu, D., . . . Zhou, Y.-M. (2010). Three Gorges Project: Efforts and challenges for the environment. *Progress in Physical Geography: Earth and Environment, 34*(6), 741–754. doi:10.1177/0309133310370286

Gleick, P. H. (2014). Water, drought, climate change, and conflict in Syria. *Weather, Climate, and Society, 6*(3), 331–340. doi:10.1175/WCAS-D-13-00059.1

Gober, P., & Wheater, H. S. (2015). Debates—Perspectives on socio-hydrology: Modeling flood risk as a public policy problem. *Water Resources Research, 51*(6), 4782–4788. doi:10.1002/2015WR016945

Gray, D. M. (1964). Physiographic characteristics and the runoff pattern. *Proceedings of Hydrology Symposium, 4*, 146–164.

Grönwall, J., & Oduro-Kwarteng, S. (2017). Groundwater as a strategic resource for improved resilience: A case study from peri-urban Accra. *Environmental Earth Sciences, 77*(6). doi:10.1007/s12665-017-7181-9

Gunderson, L. H., & Holling, C. S. (2001). *Panarchy: Understanding transformations in human and natural systems.* Washington, DC: Island Press.

Harder, P., Pomeroy, J. W., & Westbrook, C. J. (2015). Hydrological resilience of a Canadian Rockies headwaters basin subject to changing climate, extreme weather, and forest management. *Hydrological Processes, 29*(18), 3905–3924. doi:10.1002/hyp.10596

Holling, C. S. (1973). Resilience and stability of ecological systems. *Annual Review of Ecology and Systematics, 4*(1), 1–23. doi:10.1146/annurev.es.04.110173.000245

Isbell, F., Gonzalez, A., Loreau, M., Cowles, J., Díaz, S., Hector, A., . . . Larigauderie, A. (2017). Linking the influence and dependence of people on biodiversity across scales. *Nature, 546*(7656), 65–72. doi:10.1038/nature22899

Karpouzoglou, T., & Mao, F. (2018). What lies ahead? The future of the Earth and society as an adaptive system. In E. Chiotis (Ed.), *Climate changes in the Holocene: Impacts and human adaptation* (pp. 387–396). New York: CRC Press.

Kinzig, A. P., Ryan, P., Etienne, M., Allison, H., Elmqvist, T., & Walker, B. H. (2006). Resilience and regime shifts: Assessing cascading effects. *Ecology and Society, 11*(1), 20. Retrieved from http://www.ecologyandsociety.org/vol11/iss1/art20/

Knox, J. C. (2006). Floodplain sedimentation in the Upper Mississippi Valley: Natural versus human accelerated. *Geomorphology, 79*(3–4), 286–310. doi:10.1016/j.geomorph.2006.06.031

Konar, M., Garcia, M., Sanderson, M. R., Yu, D. J., & Sivapalan, M. (2019). Expanding the scope and foundation of sociohydrology as the science of coupled human-water systems. *Water Resources Research, 55*(2), 874–887. doi:10.1029/2018WR024088

Kuil, L., Carr, G., Viglione, A., Prskawetz, A., & Blöschl, G. (2016). Conceptualizing socio-hydrological drought processes: The case of the Maya collapse. *Water Resources Research, 52*(8), 6222–6242. doi:10.1002/2015WR018298

LaBaugh, J. W., Winter, T. C., & Rosenberry, D. O. (1998). Hydrologic functions of Prairie wetlands. *Great Plains Research, 8*(1), 17–37. Retrieved from https://www.jstor.org/stable/24156332

Levin, S. A. (1992). The problem of pattern and scale in ecology: The Robert H. MacArthur award lecture. *Ecology, 73*(6), 1943–1967. doi:10.2307/1941447

Levin, S., Xepapadeas, T., Crépin, A. S., Norberg, J., de Zeeuw, A., Folke, C., . . . Walker, B. (2013). Social-ecological systems as complex adaptive systems: Modeling and policy implications. *Environment and Development Economics, 18*(2), 111–132. doi:10.1017/S1355770X12000460

Mao, F., Clark, J., Karpouzoglou, T., Dewulf, A., Buytaert, W., & Hannah, D. (2017). HESS opinions: A conceptual framework for assessing socio-hydrological resilience under change. *Hydrology and Earth System Sciences, 21*(7), 3655–3670. doi:10.5194/hess-21-3655-2017

Meerow, S., Newell, J. P., & Stults, M. (2016). Defining urban resilience: A review. *Landscape and Urban Planning, 147*, 38–49. doi:10.1016/j.landurbplan.2015.11.011

Organisation for Economic Co-operation and Development. (2014). *Guidelines for resilience systems analysis: How to analyse risk and build a roadmap to resilience*. Retrieved from http://www.oecd.org/dac/ResilienceSystems Analysis FINAL.pdf

Ostrom, E. (2009). A general framework for analyzing sustainability of social-ecological systems. *Science, 325*(5939), 419–422. doi:10.1126/science.1172133

Pahl-Wostl, C. (2015). *Water governance in the face of global change: From understanding to transformation*. Cham, Switzerland: Springer International. doi:10.1007/978-3-319-21855-7

Pahl-Wostl, C., Sendzimir, J., Jeffrey, P., Aerts, J., Berkamp, G., & Cross, K. (2007). Managing change toward adaptive water management through social learning. *Ecology and Society, 12*(2). doi:10.5751/ES-02147-120230

Pattison-Williams, J. K., Pomeroy, J. W., Badiou, P., & Gabor, S. (2018). Wetlands, flood control and ecosystem services in the Smith Creek drainage basin: A case study in Saskatchewan, Canada. *Ecological Economics, 147*, 36–47. doi:10.1016/j.ecolecon.2017.12.026

Pavlovskii, I., Hayashi, M., & Cey, E. E. (2019). Estimation of depression-focussed groundwater recharge using chloride mass balance: Problems and solutions across scales. *Hydrogeology Journal, 27*(6), 2263–2278. doi:10.1007/s10040-019-01993-2

Pescaroli, G., & Alexander, D. (2016). Critical infrastructure, panarchies and the vulnerability paths of cascading disasters. *Natural Hazards, 82*(1), 175–192. doi:10.1007/s11069-016-2186-3

Peters, D. P. C., Pielke, R. A., Bestelmeyer, B. T., Allen, C. D., Munson-McGee, S., & Havstad, K. M. (2004). Cross-scale interactions, nonlinearities, and forecasting catastrophic events. *Proceedings of the National Academy of Sciences of the United States of America, 101*(42), 15130–15135. doi:10.1073/pnas.0403822101

Pomeroy, J. W., Gray, D. M., & Landine, P. G. (1993). The prairie blowing snow model: Characteristics, validation, operation. *Journal of Hydrology, 144*(1–4), 165–192. doi:10.1016/0022-1694(93)90171-5

Pomeroy, J. W., Shook, K., Fang, X., Dumanski, S., Westbrook, C. J., & Brown, T. (2014). *Improving and testing the prairie hydrological model at Smith Creek research basin* (Report No. 14). Saskatoon, Saskatchewan: Centre for Hydrology. Retrieved from https://www.usask.ca/hydrology/papers/Pomeroy_et_al_2014.pdf

Quinlan, A. E., Berbés-Blázquez, M., Haider, L. J., & Peterson, G. D. (2016). Measuring and assessing resilience: Broadening understanding through multiple disciplinary perspectives. *Journal of Applied Ecology, 53*(3), 677–687. doi:10.1111/1365-2664.12550

Renn, O. (2016). Systemic risks: The new kid on the block. *Environment: Science and Policy for Sustainable Development, 58*(2), 26–36. doi:10.1080/00139157.2016.1134019

Richey, A. S., Thomas, B. F., Lo, M.-H., Reager, J. T., Famiglietti, J. S., Voss, K., . . . Rodell, M. (2015). Quantifying renewable groundwater stress with GRACE. *Water Resources Research, 51*(7), 5217–5238. doi:10.1002/2015WR017349

Rocha, J. C., Peterson, G., Bodin, Ö., & Levin, S. (2018). Cascading regime shifts within and across scales. *Science, 362*(6421), 1379–1383. doi:10.1126/science.aat7850

Rodell, M., Famiglietti, J. S., Wiese, D. N., Reager, J. T., Beaudoing, H. K., Landerer, F. W., & Lo, M.-H. (2018). Emerging trends in global freshwater availability. *Nature, 557*(7707), 651–659. doi:10.1038/s41586-018-0123-1

Rodell, M., Velicogna, I., & Famiglietti, J. S. (2009). Satellite-based estimates of groundwater depletion in India. *Nature, 460*(7258), 999–1002. doi:10.1038/nature08238

Savenije, H. H. G., Hoekstra, A. Y., & van der Zaag, P. (2014). Evolving water science in the Anthropocene. *Hydrology and Earth System Sciences, 18*(1), 319–332. doi:10.5194/hess-18-319-2014

Scheffer, M., Bascompte, J., Brock, W. A, Brovkin, V., Carpenter, S. R., Dakos, V., . . . Sugihara, G. (2009). Early-warning signals for critical transitions. *Nature, 461*(7260), 53–59. doi:10.1038/nature08227

Schmitz, O. J., Hambäck, & Beckerman, A. P. (2000). Trophic cascades in terrestrial systems: A review of the effects of carnivore removals on plants. *The American Naturalist, 155*(2), 141. doi:10.2307/3078939

Sivapalan, M., Savenije, H. H. G., & Blöschl, G. (2012). Socio-hydrology: A new science of people and water. *Hydrological Processes, 26*(8), 1270–1276. doi:10.1002/hyp.8426

Staal, A., Dekker, S. C., Hirota, M., & van Nes, E. H. (2015). Synergistic effects of drought and deforestation on the resilience of the south-eastern Amazon rainforest. *Ecological Complexity, 22*, 65–75. doi:10.1016/j.ecocom.2015.01.003

Thomas, B. F., & Famiglietti, J. S. (2019). Identifying climate-induced groundwater depletion in GRACE observations. *Scientific Reports, 9*(4124), 1–9. doi:10.1038/s41598-019-40155-y

Tilman, D., May, R. M., Lehman, C. L., & Nowak, M. A. (1994). Habitat destruction and the extinction debt. *Nature, 371*(6492), 65–66. doi:10.1038/371065a0

Ungar, M. (2018). Systemic resilience: Principles and processes for a science of change in contexts of adversity. *Ecology and Society, 23*(4), 34. doi:10.5751/ES-10385-230434

van der Kamp, G., Hayashi, M., & Gallén, D. (2003). Comparing the hydrology of grassed and cultivated catchments in the semi-arid Canadian prairies. *Hydrological Processes, 17*(3), 559–575. doi:10.1002/hyp.1157

Wada, Y., Bierkens, M. F. P., de Roo, A., Dirmeyer, P. A., Famiglietti, J. S., Hanasaki, N., . . . Wheater, H. (2017). Human-water interface in hydrological modelling: Current status and future directions. *Hydrology and Earth System Sciences, 21*(8), 4169–4193. doi:10.5194/hess-21-4169-2017

Walker, B., Holling, C. S., Carpenter, S. R., & Kinzig, A. (2004). Resilience, adaptability and transformability in social-ecological systems. *Ecology and Society, 9*(2), 5. doi:10.5751/ES-00650-090205

Walker, B., Pearson, L., Harris, M., Maler, K. G., Li, C. Z., Biggs, R., & Baynes, T. (2010). Incorporating resilience in the assessment of inclusive wealth: An example from south east Australia. *Environmental and Resource Economics, 45*(2), 183–202. doi:10.1007/s10640-009-9311-7

Welton, G. (2011). *The impact of Russia's 2010 grain export ban*. Oxfam Research Reports. Retrieved from https://www-cdn.oxfam.org/s3fs-public/file_attachments/rr-impact-russias-grain-export-ban-280611-en_3.pdf

Wheater, H. S., & Gober, P. (2013). Water security in the Canadian Prairies: Science and management challenges. *Philosophical Transactions of the Royal Society A: Mathematical, Physical and Engineering Sciences, 371*(2002). doi:10.1098/rsta.2012.0409

Woo, M.-K., & Rowsell, R. D. (1993). Hydrology of a prairie slough. *Journal of Hydrology, 146*, 175–207. doi:10.1016/0022-1694(93)90275-E

Wrathall, D. J., Hoek, J. V. D., Walters, A., & Devenish, A. (2018). *Water stress and human migration: A global, georeferenced review of empirical research*. Rome, Italy: Food and Agriculture Organization of the United Nations. Retrieved from http://www.fao.org/3/i8867en/I8867EN.pdf

Xu, L., Gober, P., Wheater, H. S., & Kajikawa, Y. (2018). Reframing socio-hydrological research to include a social science perspective. *Journal of Hydrology, 563*, 76–83. doi:10.1016/j.jhydrol.2018.05.061

Xu, L., & Kajikawa, Y. (2018). An integrated framework for resilience research: A systematic review based on citation network analysis. *Sustainability Science, 13*(1), 235–254. doi:10.1007/s11625-017-0487-4

Xu, L., Marinova, D., & Guo, X. (2015a). Resilience thinking: A renewed system approach for sustainability science. *Sustainability Science, 10*(1), 123–138. doi:10.1007/s11625-014-0274-4

Xu, L., Marinova, D., & Guo, X. (2015b). Resilience of social-ecological systems to human perturbation: Assessing Dongting Lake in China. *Journal of Sustainable Development, 8*(8), 182–200. doi:10.5539/jsd.v8n8p182

Yu, D. J., Sangwan, N., Sung, K., Chen, X., & Merwade, V. (2017). Incorporating institutions and collective action into a sociohydrological model of flood resilience. *Water Resources Research, 53*(2), 1336–1353. doi:10.1002/2016WR019746

CONCLUSION

A Summary of Emerging Trends

Multisystemic Resilience

An Emerging Perspective From Social-Ecological Systems

Katrina Brown

Introduction

This volume presents remarkably rich and diverse scholarship on different perspectives on multisystemic resilience. Multisystemic resilience spans a wide range of fields, working in different domains and at different scales. This chapter sets out a perspective on multisystemic resilience from the interface of social-ecological systems and environmental social science, arguing for wider and more interdisciplinary research to account for the influence of the many different biological, psychological, social, built, and natural environmental systems that interact and influence processes of recovery, adaptation, and transformation when systems are under stress. It reviews the extent to which shared meanings and methods exist that can support systemic analysis. It explains how systems thinking has evolved and informed the development of theories of resilience and their application to practice, providing examples of how models of multisystemic resilience can be used to expand our understanding of solutions to complex human and environmental problems.

Crossing Disciplines

Resilience is a term with high levels of ambiguity. As shown throughout this volume, it is used across disciplines and fields ranging from engineering and ecology to psychology and public health. It is highly prominent in public discourse. The term, however, suffers from wide-ranging and not always compatible interpretation in lay and expert discourses. This ambiguity is, we suggest, both a good and a bad thing. On one hand, it means that different stakeholders and interests can come together and unite behind the construct of resilience;

the term has traction and meaning for diverse audiences. On the other hand, it means there is scope for ongoing mis-interpretation and contestation about precise definitions, meanings, applications, and, in turn, its measurement.

The extent to which resilience can be successfully applied within and across different systems will depend in part on the extent to which common understandings and definitions—and metrics and models—can be developed. This section, therefore, discusses the opportunities and constraints to common understandings across disciplines, reflecting on current cross-disciplinary interactions. It starts by examining where there is interaction across fields and where more cross-disciplinary approaches to resilience are evident, and how this relates to multisystemic approaches.

Disciplines and fields that routinely use resilience concepts range from social-ecological systems analysis, human development sciences, well-being and development to disasters and natural hazards. Many have used and developed the concepts over five decades or more. While having distinct epistemologies and methods, Brown and Westaway (2011) suggest that diverse disciplines share central concepts in common. They found that there are important similarities in their evolution, and in addition to shared concepts, each field had undergone paradigm shifts to integrate subjective and relational aspects with more conventional and objective measures of change. These commonalities are around issues of scale, the recognition of nonlinearities, dynamic nature of systems that show resilience, and thresholds that must be reached before systems transform. They also include concepts such as assets and capacities for adaptation and windows of opportunity (Brown, 2016). Despite the distinctiveness of the fields themselves, there are a set of tensions within and across disciplines, which are stark reminders of the heterogeneity in how resilience is understood. Reading the chapters in this volume, these tensions relate to whether resilience is, in effect, a desirable trait of a system, a static property, or a process and whether it can actually be observed as an objective reality. Other tensions include whether a system that shows resilience adapts, transforms, or bounces back or bounces forward, how resilience is socially constructed, and whether resilience is a quality of the system that makes it "normal" or exceptional. Such tensions within and between disciplines have, in effect, led to divergence on the usefulness and desirability of resilience in terms of interventions in society and for individuals.

How much do these commonalities—and tensions—affect cross-disciplinary and interdisciplinary work on resilience, and how much overlap is there currently between the different scientific fields that engage with and use resilience concepts? One means to clarify the learning between disciplines is to document cross-referencing of ideas, concepts and methods. Baggio, Brown, and Hellebrandt (2015) analyze citations networks to identify where resilience ideas are used across the most common fields and found surprisingly little cross-referencing. Five distinct scientific fields were identified: social sciences (including economics), ecology and environmental sciences, psychology, engineering, and social-ecological systems, each with different practices and patterns of learning and publishing. No surprise, then, this current volume demonstrates that there are many subdisciplines within this list that themselves have unique understandings of what resilience means. Baggio et al. (2015) sought to understand whether resilience acts as a boundary object or bridging concept; in other words, is *resilience* a term with a precise meaning within fields but also used loosely across fields or purposely to integrate different fields? The analysis by Baggio et al. (2015) found that the large majority of studies refer to and cite exclusively within their own specific field, if not subfield.

Across the fields where resilience is established, the greatest level of interdisciplinarity seems to be in analysis of social-ecological systems, where the majority of papers are cited at least 50% of the time outside of their own field, ranging from engineering to social sciences (as defined in Baggio et al., 2015). It is this pattern of multisystemic thinking, which offers clues to how other disciplines studying resilience might also advance a broader perspective of human and environmental transformation. Even within social-ecological systems studies, there remains, however, little crossover with psychology and human sciences (which themselves are quite insular in the research they cite) despite shared concepts. Such analysis of current and recent scientific practice confirms the rise of the term *resilience*, yet it shows that resilience does not seem to bridge all the scientific fields reflected in this volume where the concept of resilience is being explored.

One major issue in the use of resilience across fields is the tension between the term describing an accepted observable reality on the one hand, with its productive use as a boundary object, and its ambiguous nature on the other. Brand and Jax (2007) examine such tensions across fields of ecological and social sciences, highlighting how the distinctions between the descriptive use of resilience—originating from ecology—becomes blurred and often intertwined with more normative and extended uses to the extent that individual studies or papers often mix multiple meanings. They contend that the meaning of resilience becomes diluted and increasingly unclear in moving from a narrow ecological descriptive use to a broader normative definition, where resilience becomes a boundary object, "floating between descriptive and normative meanings" (p. 10). This has implications for development of multisystemic resilience which involves cross-disciplinary, cross-domain and cross-scale work. According to Brand and Jax (2007), the term *resilience* is used ambiguously *for fundamentally different intentions* in these contexts. They propose that the increased vagueness and malleability of resilience is in fact highly valuable to foster communications between disciplines and between science policy and practice. However, they argue for what they term "a division of labour in a scientific sense" (p. 10) between a descriptive resilience, a clear, well-defined, and measurable definition in ecological science, and social-ecological resilience as a boundary object used in a transdisciplinary approach and to foster interdisciplinary work.

What does this mean for multisystemic resilience? What key characteristics of resilience across disciplines are necessary to develop a systemic approach? What then, is multisystemic in this context? The term *system* signifies a set of interacting items or components that form an integrated whole. Multisystemic refers to interactions between multiple systems, each system itself a subordinate or supraordinate component of a co-occurring system. A genome, a family, an online community, a fishery, and a coral reef are all examples of systems that operate at different scales depending on one's point of view. A system is delineated by its spatial and temporal boundaries, surrounded and influenced by its environment, and is described by its structure and purpose and expressed in its functioning. It might be described as a set of interactions, linkages, and connections, which are often characterized by feedbacks and emergence. Feedbacks occur when outputs of a system are routed back as inputs and become part of a chain of cause-and-effect interactions that form a circuit or loop (human activity, natural ecosystems and computer networks, to name just a few different systems, all show these circuits in their behavior and structure). Emergence occurs when "the whole is greater than the sum of the parts," meaning the whole (system) has properties its individual parts do not have. Key features of systemic resilience are its focus on dynamic interactions. Distinguishing aspects then of a systemic approach would include multiple domains and components, complexity and dynamism in behavior, and cross-scalar interactions. These are key to understanding changes observed in human and environment interactions that have become increasingly complex and problematic. This means, for example, that in a systemic view, climate change is far more than an environmental problem. From the perspective of multisystemic resilience, it is also about culture, values, and identities (psychological and social processes), as well as governance (political and economic processes) and access to technology (engineered and built environments). The next section explores how the social-ecological systems field has developed a multisystemic approach to the analysis of resilience. This growing understanding of multiple systems and their role in resilience provides a potential way forward for other fields of study to broaden the systems they account for in their models of resilience.

Systemic Resilience in Social-Ecological Systems

Social-Ecological Systems: Lessons for Multisystemic Resilience

The study of social-ecological systems appears to have, as previously discussed, a higher level of learning and interface across scientific fields than many others. Analysis of social-ecological systems is inherently about phenomenon that cross multiple temporal and spatial scales and involves interaction between physical, biological, and social phenomenon and components. If such systems exhibit resilience they may, therefore, we suggest, represent a prototype set of characteristics and a role model for interdisciplinary engagement (see Chapter 36 of this volume for more details).

A social-ecological system is conceptualized as an intertwined system of humans and environment; it is a way of understanding people and the biosphere as interconnected and mutually interdependent. Resilience of social-ecological systems is generally understood to be the capacity to sustain human well-being in the face of disturbance and change, both by buffering shock and by adapting or transforming in response to change. In common with other systems, resilience involves responding to both shocks and to other types of change, and it is about persisting, adapting, and transforming—in other words about bouncing back to original states and potentially bouncing forward into new and perhaps more desirable states. These changes can occur at multiple systemic levels at the same time, or in sequence, but they seldom, if ever, affect only one system.

The concept of a social-ecological system, when first developed, represented a significant shift in thinking: traditionally, ecology and natural resources management viewed human systems as external drivers. Economics and the social sciences generally understood natural systems as nondynamic resources to be extracted for profit or to support subsistence. For 20 years or more, the benefits of social-ecological systems analysis were contested but have become now almost universally accepted in terms of their insights into why environmental degradation, inappropriate management, and such dilemmas persist (Holling & Meffe, 1996; Ostrom, 2009). Berkes and Folke (1998) represents a landmark in the development and application of social-ecological systems to analyze resilience in local natural resource management systems, involving the study the interactions and linkages between ecosystems and institutions, or the "rules-in-use" that govern them. The approach was designed to be able to understand the feedbacks between ecosystems and institutions and how best to manage them. Their framework inspired many subsequent developments and remains among the most-cited references.

The concept of social-ecological system has evolved over the past two decades to be used widely in both social and environmental sciences and in economics, psychology, arts, and humanities (Colding & Barthel, 2019). In its original conceptualization, the social-ecological system is an open system, with a number of influences on it, such as population growth, technological changes, markets, and trade. Political change and globalization were also considered important influences. From this developed the idea that the social-ecological system framework could be applied to understand how systems responded to change, and particularly their adaptability. Here, a social-ecological system became central to the analysis of resilience, in identifying how different components of a system responded to change and how novel challenges and shocks might impact on a system's ability to continue and be sustainable in the long-term.

While the original primary objective of social-ecological systems analysis was descriptive, subsequent development of the social-ecological system aimed to present a more analytical framework, which could also be used for comparative analysis. Anderies, Janssen, and Ostrom (2004) developed a simple model to analyze the robustness of social-ecological systems which aims to identify the key interactions within systems. This recognizes both the designed and self-organized components of a social-ecological system and how they interact. Ostrom (2009), for example, sets out a generic framework that could be applied and refined by scholars to clarify the structure of a social-ecological system to understand how any particular solution might affect management outcomes and sustainability and to build up a body of studies which could form the basis of large-n comparative analysis. Databases of regime shifts and marine-oriented social-ecological systems have been developed to test propositions around effectiveness of management, the propensity for major shifts, and the presence of thresholds using comparative methods (e.g., Ban et al., 2017; Rocha, Peterson, & Biggs, 2015). Ostrom further argued (Ostrom, 2009) for the need to embrace complexity and to develop better diagnostic methods to identify the combination of variables that affect the incentives and actions of different actors under diverse governance systems.

Social-Ecological Systems: Embracing Complexity

The application of systemic resilience to systems that involve people and the natural world increasingly embraces both the concept and the emerging science of complexity. This complexity has been a common theme throughout this volume, whether in discussions of computer architecture (Chapter 34, this volume) or organizations (Chapter 25, this volume) while being implicit in the analysis of biological (Chapter 2, this volume) and psychological (Chapter 6, this volume) systems. Complexity suggests a large number of components intricately related, and complexity theory has, at its core, the idea that independent components spontaneously order themselves into a coherent whole. Complex adaptive systems are therefore a set of independent agents that have the ability to learn from past experiences. Preiser, Biggs, De Vos, and Folke (2018) highlight the central notions of complexity, adaptability, and adaptation that are core to notions of systems themselves being adaptive. The principles they describe include recognition that systems are often open: their boundaries are not fixed, with components or actors being loosely or only indirectly affected by actions at the core. Further, the characterization of these systems relies on relationality—that systems are in fact characterized by interactions between components and that these agents are themselves not fixed, but defined in relation to context. Hence, for example, when adaptation of social-ecological systems such as forest landscapes to a changing climate involves feedbacks between new information, conservation goals determined by actors outside the system, and interannual climate variability, then the system itself adapts in complex ways that involve significant path dependency (Seidl & Lexer, 2013). To capture this complexity, Helfgott (2018) proposes a methodology for operationalizing systemic resilience, using insights from critical systems thinking and community operational research. This has developed from an international project to build community resilience, working across household, community and regional scales.

The features of complexity are, therefore, significant for systemic resilience analysis in a number of ways. First, the recognition of the openness and indeterminacy of system boundaries allows the incorporation and updating of analysis to bring in agents and actors that may seem peripheral. In political science, the concept of the "all affected principle" highlights that people distant in either space or time should be incorporated into decision-making, even when their representation is difficult. Future generations or future voters, for example, are not given formal recognition in representative democratic systems, a limit that leads to short-termism (Brown et al., 2019a). In systemic resilience, therefore, the recognition of agents that are not present or not directly observable in open systems presents a challenge both for how they should be incorporated, and for methods where indirect and indeterminate phenomena are affecting the systems.

A second major implication of the complexity of adaptive systems relates to notions of scale. Spatial and temporal scales are well recognized in many systems analyses, while scales of jurisdiction, the hierarchy of knowledge, or institutional scales are less well recognized (Cash et al., 2006). If systems are indeed open, then how system boundaries are defined, in effect, means that temporal, spatial, and institutional scales are in fact endogenous to the systems themselves. Who gets to define the appropriate cut-off point of the future or the jurisdictional scale? The long-standing critique of resilience science in ignoring power relations highlights this blindness to scale. So, for example, how can an economic community be resilient, when decisions about production, consumption, and the location of capital are taken in distant locations by agents never considered to be part of the system or community at hand

(MacKinnon & Derickson, 2013)? These same power dynamics are just as relevant to legal systems (Chapter 26, this volume), economic systems (Chapter 30, this volume) and health care (Chapter 4, this volume) and social justice systems for Indigenous peoples (Chapter 29, this volume). Such parallels across disciplines suggests that patterns of resilience will universally contend with dynamics of power even if disciplinary writing on resilience overlooks this dimension of positive change and development in a system over time.

Limitations of Social-Ecological System

Most representations of a social-ecological system present two sub-systems—the social and the ecological—interacting within a larger arena, the social-ecological system. Various linkages, interactions, and feedbacks between the two subsystems are posited. These are mediated by, for example, institutions such as property rights that govern people's access to and control over different components of the system. In many figures and diagrams in the literature, these are denoted as one-way and two-way arrows between the two subsystems.

Multisystemic resilience requires both realization that resilience relates to the interactions across the whole social-ecological system, rather than between specific ecological or social dimensions, and that resilience emerges from process. For example, Brown (2016) revisioned resilience to emphasize agency: that of human actors in the social-ecological system. This finds parallels with aspects of human determinism evident in psychological systems research (see Chapter 9, this volume). But agency might be extended beyond humans. For example, Dwiartama and Rosin (2014) propose that actor network theory might provide a useful starting point to extend agency to nonhumans to develop a more tightly coupled view of a social-ecological system. Christmann, Ibert, Kilper and Moss (2012) also consider actor network theory in relation to vulnerability and resilience. They view that emphasizing agency not just of individual actions, but of associations and networks as dispersed competencies, can inform and overcome social-ecological dichotomies within the social-ecological system concept.

Do nonhuman agents have agency in social-ecological systems? Dwiartama and Rosin (2014) argue that actor network theory can inform resilience analysis, by offering the opportunity of a more encompassing view of agency that extends beyond human intentionality. This focuses on the relationships in which agents participate and how these influence the shape of a network of relationships. In actor network theory agency can be extended to nonhumans, including animals, materials, ideas, and concepts. Thus diverse components of a social-ecological system, including plants and animals, minerals, and climate are system-forming entities. This enables perhaps the role of relations between humans (the social subsystem) and nonhumans (the ecological subsystems) in resilience dynamics to be viewed holistically and as an emergent property of the larger social-ecological system itself. It is this multisystemic perspective that will need further research as far too few papers account for more than one or two systems in their explanations of resilience. Indeed, even the chapters in this volume rarely manage to include human and nonhuman systems in the same models, although architects like Terri Peters (Chapter 32, this volume) and social ecologists like Katharine Hogan (Chapter 37, this volume) are making positive strides forward.

Pushing Boundaries: Emerging Perspectives on Systemic Resilience

The complex causation, emergent processes, context dependence, and dynamics of scale that characterize social-ecological systems present significant challenges for both descriptive and normative analyses. One solution to make analysis tractable is to focus on so-called middle-range theories, or contextual generalizations, that apply to a delimited set of cases rather than universal theories (Schluter et al., 2019). Perhaps an overarching theory of multisystemic resilience is unattainable—or even undesirable—and developing systemic approaches that bring together concepts from different knowledge domain and synthesize empirical findings across diverse contexts and scales might need to forge new approaches and combine methods in agile and adaptive ways. This section examines principles for managing and intervening in social-ecological systems, key elements of social-ecological resilience and how to measure them, and how to address pressing contemporary global challenges such as global change and inequality.

The underlying objective of social-ecological systems analysis is to address global scale threats and challenges to whole system integrity on which human and all life depends. Hence, key perspectives from this science are how to intervene and how to maintain system resilience in the face of both complexity of the system but the urgency of action. A desired set of system functions in the face of disturbance includes direct provision of food, fuel, and clean water; indirect services such as maintenance of soil fertility or regulation of flood and climate; and cultural services that provide spiritual, aesthetic, and recreational values. Principles for managing and intervening in social-ecological systems for resilience are categorically different for those that seek to maximize resource productivity or minimize risks to specific populations. Hence, there are apparent trade-offs between efficiency and resilience. Yet advocates point to system integrity as a long-term goal that is consistent with socially derived goals such as sustainable development (Eakin, Tompkins, Nelson, & Anderies, 2009). Principles for intervention and management are numerous: a synthesis by Biggs, Schlüter, and Schoon (2015), based on trials and a Delphi-style interrogation of researchers and managers in environmental management, identified principles such as ongoing monitoring of change, opening up system boundaries to maximize participation of all affected, and maintaining diversity, both in system structures and in ways of managing, based on principles of devolution and so-called polycentricity (Biggs et al., 2015).

A second boundary involves consilience between disciplines: a holy grail of many studies is to integrate social-ecological systems approaches to resilience with social science insights on, for example, risk, social, and cognitive psychological processes, political dynamics of power, and geographical analyses of scale and power (Brown, 2016). There are three important trends in such research. First, as the range of scientific papers throughout this volume shows, resilience is continuously becoming more mainstream and popular across many different disciplines that complement the work of social-ecological systems scholars (just as their work is now expanding the way resilience is conceptualized by human biological and social scientists): it has resonance and traction in science as well as in policy and public debate. Second, resilience is grounded in different fields of scientific inquiry, showing its theoretical, conceptual, and methodological richness (see Downes, Miller, Barnett, Glaister, &

Ellemor, 2013; Ungar, 2018). Third, there is convergence around the need for greater understanding of social dynamics of resilience, the use of narratives and constructivist approaches to understand the relationships between structure and agency, and how different factors converge and will produce different outcomes for different people in different contexts (Ungar, 2004). Constructivist approaches to understanding scale and in-depth inclusive methods, such as using narratives to study peoples' accounts, experiences, and stories to understand how they construct meanings of resilience, are all pushing boundaries for resilience research across disciplines (Brown et al., 2019a; Jones & d'Errico, 2019; Morrison et al., 2019).

When issues such as place, scale, power, and risk are incorporated into social systems, three key integrating features and boundaries emerge: resistance, rootedness, and resourcefulness (as further elaborated in Brown, 2016). Resistance recognizes agency by individuals in taking control of their destiny which often seems imposed by actors at different scales. Rootedness recognizes that context determinants of resilience—how elements are situated in place and time and how risk aversion and collective identity play out in complex systems. Resourcefulness suggests that social-ecological systems retain capacity for change, even toward radically altering or revolutionizing the system itself. This socially informed system view of resilience suggests strongly that resilience is a process by which change is negotiated and contested in complex social-ecological situations to make up every day experiences (Ungar, 2011).

New Frontiers for Resilience Science

Applications of resilience in social-ecological systems have evolved to tackle grand and thorny challenges about the future integrity of the Earth following a great acceleration of human interventions and exploitation. The varied and rich insights throughout this volume strongly suggest that resilience insights can illuminate complex issues and point to how human biological systems, social systems, and engineered and built systems need to be part of this global challenges conversation if we are to address wicked problems that will plague our generation and generations to come. This section discusses contemporary global challenges to sustainability and how a multisystemic analysis of resilience potentially brings greater insights and helps to identify potential solutions. The first illustrative challenge is around places and communities facing multiple crises that challenge the core ability of societies to function and for governments to secure their populations. A second challenge is to explain and seek to intervene in the arena of massive disparities in wealth, income, power, and ecological footprint apparent at multiple scales, from the Global North and South, through to localized inequalities within societies. These two phenomena are related, but each is complex, highly dynamic, and characterized by change at multiple scales and rates. In this way they each demand a multisystemic approach, one that crosses boundaries and pushes new science and new engagement.

Interlocking Vulnerability and Multiple Crises in Fragile Contexts

Countries, regions, and societies are on the edge of breakdown in many parts of the world. States are fragile, and in places where trust is scarce, ungoverned spaces experience organized violence and disruptions that create displaced populations and trap others in cycles of insecurity. Sometimes crises result from major ecological disruptions and extreme events, exacerbated by local state failure. For example, more than 20 million people are displaced annually over the past decade by weather-related disasters. Framed in relation to multisystemic resilience, a key shared characteristic of such crises is that of marginalization. Such dynamics occur where environmental shocks and stresses exacerbate existing economic, social, and spatial inequalities contributing to downward spirals of social and economic impoverishment, psychological and physical vulnerability, and degradation of both built and natural environments (as identified, for example, by Leach et al., 2018). Such marginalization results in traps, populations unable to move, and individuals and places trapped in poverty where long-term development opportunities are curtailed (Haider, Boonstra, Peterson, & Schlüter, 2018; Nayak, Oliveira, & Berkes, 2014). There is an increased recognition that shocks and stresses evolve from the interplay and coupling between social and ecosystem changes across multiple scales (Galaz, Moberg, Olsson, Paglia, & Parker, 2011; Rocha, Peterson, Bodin, & Levin, 2018). The outcomes of such stresses are population displacement, food insecurity, and health and livelihood declines. Resilience science should now be applied to identify and quantify the capacities necessary to escape traps and reverse marginalization dynamics. This new science has the tools to measure and analyze resilience processes from the individual to global scale and their positive and negative interactions. It needs, though, to integrate transboundary effects, such as emergencies whereby the interconnectedness of nations increases the chances of the effects of poorly managed shocks and stresses in any single country being transferred rapidly throughout the wider region (Liu et al., 2018).

What methods could be used to analyze the systemic risks linked to land use, political instability, climate change, and disaster response? Integrating methods to analyze interacting, cascading, and cross-scale effects in environmental thresholds and stresses are required (Reyers, Nel, O'Farrell, Sitas, & Nel, 2018; Rocha et al., 2018). These innovative methodologies, gleaned from across disciplines, would need to build on methods to measure resilience capacities from individual (Theron, 2016), community (Brown, 2014), and system scales (Reyers et al., 2015) to develop new multisystemic resilience understanding (Helfgott, 2018; Ungar, 2018). Understanding system dynamics and resilience capacities would, however, yield significant benefits, for early warning of crises, for conflict resolution, and for incorporating environmental dimensions into reconstruction from disasters and preventing conflict based on shared understandings of multisystemic resilience.

Inequality as a Threat to Sustainable Development

A body of work has emerged in the last decade that demonstrates how global income or wealth inequality has grown rapidly over the past century at the expense of the environment and the world's poorest nations. The seminal paper by Srinivasan et al. (2008) describes the "ecological debt of nations" and demonstrates how the costs of global environmental change associated with climate change, ozone depletion, agricultural expansion and intensification, deforestation, overfishing, and mangrove conversion are disproportionately borne by poorer nations. Furthermore, as articulated by Turner and Fisher (2008) commenting on the Srinivasan study, the benefits in terms of increased consumption, wealth generation, and enhanced well-being have overwhelmingly accrued to the richest countries. This prompts

Turner and Fisher to suggest that "we must better understand the complex relationships between ecological, social and economic systems. . . . And how and why current economic paradigm produces such inequalities; who pays the costs, and how they can be made more socially and ecologically more sustainable" (p. 1068).

Currently these issues play out in international scientific and policy debates on global climate change. An editorial in *Global Environmental Change* in 2017 Sonja Klinsky et al. (2017) argue that—rather than skirting around normative issues as some commentators and policy makers insist—we need rigorous analysis of equity and justice to inform political decisions on climate change at all scales. This is what we see emerging in policy documents and from think tanks and civil society groups around a whole range of debates about fairness, climate justice, and equity in implementing a post-Paris agenda for action.

Reflecting this emerging, multisystemic thinking, two key papers have been published that move beyond one-dimensional and linear analysis of ecological inequality. First, a review paper published by the Beijer Institute Young Scholar Group led by Maike Hamann (Hamann et al., 2018) applies a social-ecological systems perspective to explore linkages between rising inequalities and accelerating global environmental change. Most research to date has only considered one-dimensional effects of inequality on the biosphere, or vice versa. But their analysis highlights the importance of cross-scale interactions and feedback loops between inequality and the biosphere. A second paper is authored by the Future Earth Science Committee and led by Melissa Leach. The authors argue that it is no longer possible or desirable to address the dual challenges of equity and sustainability separately. They highlight the interlinkages between, and the multiple dimensions of, equity and sustainability. Again, they use a social-ecological systems lens to illustrate how equity and sustainability are produced by interactions and dynamics of coupled social-ecological systems. Their approach emphasizes equity as multidimensional, thus moving beyond an emphasis on distributional aspects of the crisis and instead examining the question of equity of what and equity between whom.

A multisystemic approach to resilience understands the relationship between inequality and sustainability as being highly dynamic, operating through a series of complex mechanisms and pathways, at different scales ranging from the psychological to the environmental, and with interacting slow and fast variables and feedbacks. This means that there is not one intervention point, but many, but how and when they are made is important. For example, interventions to effect change in patterns of consumption may have limited impact unless accompanied by changes in broader moral framings and values (Brown et al., 2019b). Yet these slow drivers—perhaps constituted as social norms—might be powerful tipping points to shift behavior (Nyborg et al., 2016).

Both of these frontier issues involve resilience embracing normative dimensions of the science, highlighting what is desirable and undesirable system features, and making explicit claims on where system boundaries are drawn and the type of disturbance identified. Recent calls to operationalize systemic resilience (e.g., Helfgott, 2018) argue strongly that resilience science should be framed by directly addressing the questions of resilience of what, to what, for whom and over what timescale. Helfgott (2018) and others are becoming more explicit that significant social and environmental challenges could and should be best addressed through building resilience at lower levels, such as facilitating local ownership of issues through iterative and reflexive processes including future visioning and building social cohesion and empathy between agents.

Conclusion

This chapter has approached multisystemic resilience from the perspective of social-ecological systems resilience, demonstrating that by taking a systems approach we are more likely to explain the processes by which systems recover, adapt and transform when stressed. Clearly, extending this understanding to many more human, biological and engineered systems can add to our understanding of the dynamic processes that create solutions to large scale issues which are challenging our world today. The more multisystemic our thinking becomes, and the more interdisciplinary our research, the more likely we are to understand how to manage multiple systems to produce the constructive changes required to save our planet and ourselves.

Key Messages

1. Multisystemic resilience can inform and expand conceptualizations of resilience and fields like social-ecological systems expand, blend and interrogate defintions across disciplines.
2. Methodological diversity is required to study resilience.
3. Significant challenges facing humanity today require new ways of thinking to identify complex multisystemic solutions that can be informed by the emerging science of resilience.
4. The chapters in this volume provide a forum for thinking multisystemically about resilience and the similarities and differences in how the concept is researched and applied.

Acknowledgments

Many colleagues have inspired and helped in development of the ideas set out in this chapter. I am especially grateful to Neil Adger for his valuable advice and support.

References

Anderies, J., Janssen, M., & Ostrom, E. (2004). A framework to analyze the robustness of social-ecological systems from an institutional perspective. *Ecology and Society*, *9*(1), 18. Retrieved from http://www.ecologyandsociety.org/vol9/iss1/art18/

Baggio, J. A., Brown, K., & Hellebrandt, D. (2015). Boundary object or bridging concept? A citation network analysis of resilience. *Ecology and Society*, *20*(2), 2. doi:10.5751/ES-07484-200202

Ban, N. C., Davies, T. E., Aguilera, S. E., Brooks, C., Cox, M., Epstein, G., . . . Nenadovic, M. (2017). Social and ecological effectiveness of large marine protected areas. *Global Environmental Change*, *43*, 82–91. doi:10.1016/j.gloenvcha.2017.01.003

Berkes, F., & Folke, C. (Eds.). (1998). *Linking social and ecological systems: Management practices and social mechanisms for building resilience*. Cambridge, UK: Cambridge University Press.

Biggs, R., Schlüter, M., & Schoon, M. L. (Eds.). (2015). *Principles for building resilience: Sustaining ecosystem services in social-ecological systems*. Cambridge, UK: Cambridge University Press.

Brand, F., & Jax, K. (2007). Focusing the meaning(s) of resilience: Resilience as a descriptive concept and a boundary object. *Ecology and Society*, *12*(1), 23. Retrieved from http://www.ecologyandsociety.org/vol12/iss1/art23/

Brown, K. (2014). Global environmental change I: A social turn for resilience? *Progress in Human Geography*, *38*(1), 107–117. doi:10.1177/0309132513498837

Brown, K. (2016). *Resilience, development and global change*. London, UK: Routledge.

Brown, K., Adger, W. N., Devine-Wright, P., Anderies, J. M., Barr, S., Bousquet, F., . . . Quinn, T. (2019a). Empathy, place and identity interactions for sustainability. *Global Environmental Change*, *56*, 11–17. doi:10.1016/j.gloenvcha.2019.03.003

Brown, K., Cinner, J., & Adger, N. (2019b). Moving Climate Change beyond Tragedy of the Commons. *Global Environmental Change*, *54*, 61–63. doi:10.1016/j.gloenvcha.2018.11.009

Brown, K., & Westaway, E. (2011). Agency, capacity, and resilience to environmental change: Lessons from human development, well-being, and disasters. *Annual Review of Environment and Resources*, *36*(1), 321–342. doi:10.1146/annurev-environ-052610-092905

Cash, D., Adger, W. N., Berkes, F., Garden, P., Lebel, L., Olsson, P., . . . Young, O. (2006). Scale and cross-scale dynamics: Governance and information in a multilevel world. *Ecology and Society*, *11*(2), 8. Retrieved from http://www.ecologyandsociety.org/vol11/iss2/art8/

Christmann, G., Ibert, O., Kilper, H., & Moss, T. (2012). *Vulnerability and resilience from a socio-spatial perspective: Towards as theoretical framework* (IRS Working Paper 45). Leibniz Institute for Regional development and Structural Planning. Retrieved from www.irs-net.de/download/wp_vulnerability.pdf

Colding, J., & Barthel, S. (2019). Exploring the social-ecological systems discourse 20 years later. *Ecology and Society*, *24*(1), 2. doi:10.5751/ES-10598-240102

Downes, B. J., Miller, F., Barnett, J., Glaister, A., & Ellemor, H. (2013). How do we know about resilience? An analysis of empirical research on resilience, and implications for interdisciplinary praxis. *Environmental Research Letters*, *8*(1), 014041. doi:10.1088/1748-9326/8/1/014041

Dwiartama, A., & Rosin, C. (2014). Exploring agency beyond humans: The compatibility of actor-network theory and resilience thinking. *Ecology and Society*, *19*(3), 28. doi:10.5751/ES-06805-190328

Eakin, H., Tompkins, E. L., Nelson, D. R., & Anderies, J. M. (2009). Hidden costs and disparate uncertainties: Trade-offs involved in approaches to climate policy. In W. N. Adger, I. Lorenzoni, & K. L. O'Brien (Eds.), *Adapting to climate change: Thresholds, values, governance* (pp. 212–226). Cambridge, UK: Cambridge University Press.

Galaz, V., Moberg, F., Olsson, E. K., Paglia, E., & Parker, C. (2011). Institutional and political leadership dimensions of cascading ecological crises. *Public Administration*, *89*(2), 361–380. doi:10.1111/j.1467-9299.2010.01883.x

Haider, L. J., Boonstra, W. J., Peterson, G. D., & Schlüter, M. (2018). Traps and sustainable development in rural areas: A review. *World Development*, *101*(C), 311–321. doi:10.1016/j.worlddev.2017.05.038

Hamann, M., Berry, K., Chaigneau, T., Curry, T., Heilmayr, R., Henriksson, P. J., . . . Nieminen, E. (2018). Inequality and the biosphere. *Annual Review of Environment and Resources*, *43*, 61–83. doi:10.1146/annurev-environ-102017-025949

Helfgott, A. (2018). Operationalising systemic resilience. *European Journal of Operational Research*, *268*(3), 852–864. doi:10.1016/j.ejor.2017.11.056

Holling, C. S., & Meffe, G. K. (1996). Command and control and the pathology of natural resource management. *Conservation Biology*, *10*(2), 328–337. Retrieved from https://www.jstor.org/stable/2386849

Jones, L., & d'Errico, M. (2019). Resilient, but from whose perspective? Like-for-like comparisons of objective and subjective measures of resilience. *World Development*, *124*. doi:10.13140/RG.2.2.13691.16162

Klinsky, S., Roberts, T., Huq, S., Okereke, C., Newell, P., Dauvergne, P., . . . Keck, M. (2017). Why equity is fundamental in climate change policy research. *Global Environmental Change*, *44*, 170–173. doi:10.1016/j.gloenvcha.2016.08.002

Leach, M., Reyers, B., Bai, X., Brondizio, E. S., Cook, C., Díaz, S., . . . Subramanian, S. M. (2018). Equity and sustainability in the anthropocene: A social-ecological systems perspective on their intertwined futures. *Global Sustainability*, *1*, e13. doi:10.1017/sus.2018.12

Liu, J., Dou, Y., Batistella, M., Challies, E., Connor, T., Friis, C., . . . Triezenberg, H. (2018). Spillover systems in a telecoupled anthropocene: Typology, methods, and governance for global sustainability. *Current Opinion in Environmental Sustainability, 33,* 58–69. doi:10.1016/j.cosust.2018.04.009

MacKinnon, D., & Derickson, K. D. (2013). From resilience to resourcefulness: A critique of resilience policy and activism. *Progress in Human Geography, 37*(2), 253–270. doi:10.1177/0309132512454775

Morrison, T. H., Adger, W. N., Brown, K., Lemos, M. C., Huitema, D., Phelps, J., . . . Quinn, T. (2019). The black box of power in polycentric environmental governance. *Global Environmental Change, 57,* 101934. doi:10.1016/j.gloenvcha.2019.101934

Nayak, P., Oliveira, L., & Berkes, F. (2014). Resource degradation, marginalization, and poverty in small-scale fisheries: Threats to social-ecological resilience in India and Brazil. *Ecology and Society, 19*(2), 73. doi:10.5751/ES-06656-190273

Nyborg, K., Anderies, J. M., Dannenberg, A., Lindahl, T., Schill, C., Schlüter, M., . . . Chapin, F. S. (2016). Social norms as solutions. *Science, 354*(6308), 42–43. doi:10.1126/science.aaf8317

Ostrom, E. (2009). A general framework for analyzing sustainability of social-ecological systems. *Science, 325*(5939), 419–422. doi:10.1126/science.1172133

Preiser, R. Biggs, R., De Vos, A., & Folke, C. (2018). Social-ecological systems as complex adaptive systems: Organizing principles for advancing research methods and approaches. *Ecology and Society, 23*(4), 46. doi:10.5751/ES-10558-230446.

Reyers, B., Nel, J. L., O'Farrell, P. J., Sitas, N., & Nel, D. C. (2015). Navigating complexity through knowledge coproduction: Mainstreaming ecosystem services into disaster risk reduction. *Proceedings of the National Academy of Sciences, 112,* 7362–7368. doi:10.1073/pnas.1414374112

Rocha, J. C., Peterson, G. D., & Biggs, R. (2015). Regime shifts in the Anthropocene: Drivers, risks, and resilience. *PLoS One, 10*(8), e0134639. doi:10.1371/journal.pone.0134639

Rocha, J. C., Peterson, G., Bodin, Ö., & Levin, S. (2018). Cascading regime shifts within and across scales. *Science, 362*(6421), 1379–1383. doi:10.1126/science.aat7850

Schlüter, M., Orach, K., Lindkvist, E., Martin, R., Wijermans, N., Bodin, Ö., & Boonstra, W. J. (2019). Toward a methodology for explaining and theorizing about social-ecological phenomena. *Current Opinion in Environmental Sustainability, 39,* 44–53. doi:10.1016/j.cosust.2019.06.011

Seidl, R., & Lexer, M. J. (2013). Forest management under climatic and social uncertainty: Trade-offs between reducing climate change impacts and fostering adaptive capacity. *Journal of Environmental Management, 114,* 461–469. doi:10.1016/j.jenvman.2012.09.028

Srinivasan, U. T., Carey, S. P., Hallstein, E., Higgins, P. A., Kerr, A. C., Koteen, L. E., . . . Norgaard, R. B. (2008). The debt of nations and the distribution of ecological impacts from human activities. *Proceedings of the National Academy of Sciences, 105*(5), 1768–1773. doi:10.1073/pnas.0709562104

Theron, L. C. (2016). Researching resilience: Lessons learned from working with rural, Sesotho-speaking South African young people. *Qualitative Research, 16,* 720–737. doi:10.1177/1468794116652451

Turner, R. K., & Fisher, B. (2008). Environmental economics: To the rich man the spoils. *Nature, 451*(7182), 1067–1068. doi:10.1038/4511067a

Ungar, M. (2004). A constructionist discourse on resilience: Multiple contexts, multiple realities among at-risk children and youth. *Youth and Society, 35*(3), 341–365. doi:10.1177/0044118X03257030

Ungar, M. (2011). The social ecology of resilience. Addressing contextual and cultural ambiguity of a nascent construct. *American Journal of Orthopsychiatry, 81,* 1–17. doi:10.1111/j.1939-0025.2010.01067.x

Ungar, M. (2018). Systemic resilience: Principles and processes for a science of change in contexts of adversity. *Ecology and Society, 23*(4), 34. doi:10.5751/ES-10385-230434

Name Index

For the benefit of digital users, indexed terms that span two pages (e.g., 52-53) may, on occasion, appear on only one of those pages.

Figures are indicated by *f* following the page number

Abdi, S., 300-1, 302-3
Acevedo, V. E., 241
Adger, N., 710-11
Adger, W. N., 21-22
Adhvaryu, A., 590-91
Agius, C., 543
Agreda, L., 325
Aguilar, A., 590-91
Ahmed, O., 309-10
Aizer, A., 588
Alderson, D. L., 517
Aldridge, J. M., 206-7
Alessa, L., 171-72
Allen, C., 516, 536
Almond, D., 585
Alt, D., 22-23
Anderies, J., 775
Anderson, T., 673
Annarelli, A., 10-11
Antonovsky, A., 156, 159-60, 183-84
Anzaldúa, G., 320
Armstrong, N., 688
Arnold, C., 537, 546
Aron, F., 182
Atallah, D. G., 565, 566, 568, 572, 579-80
Atkinson, M., 190
Attanasio, O. P., 586
Auton, J. C., 460
Avila, M., 322-23
Ayers, S., 60, 61-62
Ayob, N., 495

Bachelard, G., 634-35
Bacigalupe, G., 566
Baggio, J. A., 772-73
Bainbridge, R., 206-7
Bakhtin, M. M., 329
Balgar, K., 716
Bandura, A., 386
Banton, M., 181-82
Baraitser, L., 61-62
Baran, P., 497
Barling, J., 466
Barnes, J., 593
Barocas, B., 182
Barrera, G. E., 323
Barreteau, O., 716
Barth, F., 715
Barthel, S., 707
Becker, B., 303
Becker, G., 586-87
Bell, D., 580
Belsky, J., 593
Beltman, S., 240-41
Bennett, E. M., 727
Benson, M. H., 536
Benson, P. G., 466-67
Berger, J. M., 294-95
Bergson, H., 603, 620-21
Berkes, F., 707, 710-11, 774-75
Berners-Lee, T., 497
Bernstein, G. A., 222-23
Berry, J. W., 382

Bharadwaj, P., 588–89, 591
Bietenbeck, J., 591
Biggs, R., 775–76, 778
Binet, A., 500–1
Blair, C., 235–36
Blöschl, G., 745–46
Böbel, T. S., 15–16
Bodin, Ö., 744–45
Boksa, P., 82
Boles, K., 85
Bombardier, J.-A., 95
Bonanno, G. A., 138–39
Bond, L., 538–39
Bonté, B., 719
Boone, C. G., 628
Borieux, M., 265–66
Bottrell, D., 213–14
Bousquet, F., 8, 706, 708–9, 715
Bowlby, J., 272, 275–76
Boyce, W., 531–32
Brammertz, S., 543–44
Brand, F., 773
Breen, M. S., 137–38
Brody, G. H., 44
Brondizio, E. S., 707
Bronfenbrenner, U., 37, 44–45, 116, 183–84, 234, 278, 337–38, 403
Brough, M., 534
Brown, K., 2–3, 18, 713, 772–73, 777
Bui-Wrzosinska, L., 539
Burns, J. M., 538–39
Burns, K., 499
Bush, N., 38–39

Cabell, J. F., 27
Cadenasso, M. L., 609–10
Canton, A. N., 182
Carland, S. J., 303
Carlson, M. W., 18–19
Cavanagh, E., 566–67
Cavioni, V., 225
Cebula, J. J., 668–69
Cefai, C., 223, 225
Chandler, D., 535
Chandler, M. J., 85
Cherkasskii, B. L., 707
Christman, G. B., 716–17
Christmann, G., 777
Christmann, K., 306
Cicchetti, D., 303
Clark, J. N., 533
Clarke, A. M., 223
Cluver, L. D., 243
Coaffee, J., 295–96
Cohodes, S. R., 588–89

Colding, J., 707
Coleman, J. S., 380–81
Coleman, P. T., 539, 540
Collier, J., 713–14, 715
Conley, C. B., 510
Connell, P., 530
Conti, G., 586, 589, 592
Córdoba, A., 323
Cosens, B. A., 514, 524–25
Cox, L., 534
Cox, R. S., 25–26
Crane, M., 458
Crowley, M., 224
Culbertson, S. S., 185–86
Cumming, G. S., 713–14, 715
Cunha, F., 586–87
Cusack, L., 461
Cyran, J. F., 15–16
Cyrulnik, B., 101, 278

Dahl, G. B., 588
Dalicandro, L., 88
Davis, F., 567–68
Davis, K., 61–62
De Jonge, J., 456
Dekker, S., 478–79
Delahaij, R., 187–88
Deleuze, G., 603, 604, 606, 620
Del Ponte, C., 543
Denny, B., 61–62
de Puydt, P.-E., 612, 620–21
De Sousa Santos, B., 318–19
De Vos, A., 775–76
Diamond, A., 235–36
Dijk, A., 181–82
Dinan, T. G., 15–16
Distelberg, B. J., 265–66
Doosje, B., 297–98
Dormann, C., 456
Doyle, J. C., 517
Dozier, M., 46
Duprey, E. B., 18–19
Duque, V., 591
Durand, S., 718
Duthie, R., 537
Dutta, U., 580
Dwiartama, A., 777

Ebbesson, J., 537, 539
Edwards-Schachter, M., 495
Einstein, A., 531
Elder, G. H., 345, 350
Eli, S., 588
Elias, N., 713
Ellis, H. B., 300–1, 302–3

Endress, M., 713
Engel, G. L., 58
Ensor, J., 553–54
Erikson, E., 714
Eriksson, M., 153, 157
Escobar, A., 320–21, 326
Eyles, D., 688

Fagan, K., 495
Fainstein, S., 532
Falicov, C. J., 256–57
Famiglietti, J. S., 756
Fanon, F., 566–67
Fellow, R. S., 295
Ferrie, J., 588
Ferris, T., 682–83, 686, 690
Fikret, B., 329–30
Fiksel, J., 648–49
Fineman, M. A., 545
Fisher, B., 780–81
Fisher, P., 46
Fogarty, W., 205
Folke, C., 3–4, 18, 546, 706, 708, 710–11, 774–76
Fonseca-Cepeda, V., 325
Forrester, J., 553–54
Francis, A., 61–62
Frank, J., 188
Frankl, V., 350–51
Freire, P., 567
Fuller, L., 515–16

Gagnon, A. J., 62
Galea, S., 82–83
Gallopin, G. C., 707
Garcia, E. J., 610–11
García-Sanjuán, N., 279–80
Gardner, J., 603–4
Garmestani, A. S., 536
Garmezy, N., 114, 155, 396
Gaubatz, P., 619–20
Gavidia-Payne, S., 61–62, 69–70
Gavin, J. F., 466–67
Gehl, J., 631
Genet, J., 108
Gershon, R. R., 182
Ghazinour, M., 183–84
Giacaman, R., 531–32
Gielen, A. J., 298–99
Gilbreath, B., 466–67
Gill, B., 533
Gilligan, R., 383–84
Goddard, H. H., 501
Godin, B., 495
Goffman, E., 557
Goldstein, B. E., 713

Gooda, M., 202–3
Gottesman, I. I., 120
Gouglidis, A., 670
Grange, J. M., 16
Gready, P., 538
Grecksch, K., 172
Green, O., 536
Greenberg, M., 224
Griffin, J. D., 185–86
Grossman, D. S., 588–89
Grossman, M., 190, 295, 300–1, 302, 303, 306, 309–10
Grothmann, T., 172
Grove, J. M., 609–10
Gucciardi, D. F., 464–65
Guenther, J., 204
Guerbois, C., 722
Guerrero, A., 326
Gunderson, L. H., 18, 115, 311, 495–96, 546, 604–5, 607, 612–13, 615–17, 710–11, 757–58
Gunnsteinsson, S., 591

Haar, S., 620
Hadfield, K., 157
Hailey, V., 684–86
Hallett, D., 85
Hamann, M., 781
Hannich, H., 159
Hardy, K., 297
Hart, A., 222
Haslam, D., 236–37
Haslam, S. A., 466–67
Hassler, U., 607–8
Heaver, B., 222
Heckman, J., 125, 586–87, 589
Helfgott, A., 775–76, 781–82
Hellebrandt, D., 772–73
Hendren, N., 594
Hernandez-Wolfe, P., 241, 318–19, 321–22
Herrero Romero, R., 237–39
Hey, E., 537, 539
Hilgartner, S., 671
Hilhorst, D., 364–65
Hogan, K. F. E., 731, 777
Hollander, T., 533
Holleran, L. K., 383–84
Holling, C. S., 8, 10–11, 311, 495–96, 516, 552, 604–5, 607, 610, 612–13, 615–17, 622, 625, 708–9, 710–11, 744, 757–58
Hollnagel, E., 486
Hoogewoning, F., 181–82
Hope, A., 20
Hopkins, K. D., 206–7
Hordge-Freeman, E., 25
Hoynes, H., 588

Huffman, A. H., 185–86
Hussein, R., 575
Hutchison, D., 14, 15, 20, 665
Hyslop, D., 427–28

Ibert, O., 777
Idrobo, C. J., 325
Imhof, C. B., 185–86
Infurna, F. J., 408–9

Jacanamejoy, J., 328–29
Jackson, M., 61–62
Jackson, S., 682–83, 686
James, L., 649–50
Jamioy Muchavisoy, S., 318–19, 322, 325–26, 328, 330
Jamshidi, M., 683
Janssen, M., 775
Jax, K., 773
Jenkins, K., 542
Jerneck, A., 712, 713
Jones, D. E., 224
Joober, R., 82
Joseph, J., 713

Kajikawa, Y., 2–3
Kalisch, R., 137–41, 455–56
Kampa, M., 141
Kamphuis, W., 187–88
Karam, E. G., 406–7
Karapakula, G., 589
Karasek, R., 187
Karpouzoglou, T., 751
Kelley, R. F., 466–67
Kelloway, E. K., 466
Khamis, V., 403
Kilper, H., 777
Kim, A. W., 369–70
Kirk McDonald, G., 543
Kirmayer, L. J., 82, 119, 265–66, 328
Kleiner, S. A., 588–89
Klinsky, S., 781
Kliskey, A., 168
Kogan, S. M., 18–19
Kohler, N., 607–8
Kowatch, K. R., 90, 92–93
Kropf, K., 620

Lalonde, C. E., 85
Lambert, E. G., 188
Langer, E. J., 675
Langton, C., 711–12
Laplante, L. J., 533
Larkin, S., 204
Laub, J. H., 350

Lazarus, R., 518
Leach, M., 713, 781
Lederbogen, F., 16–17
Lee, S. Y., 594
Leebaw, B. A., 541–42
Leemans, R., 707
Lei, D., 610–11
Lenette, C., 534
Leopold, A., 175
Leven, S., 610
Levin, S. A., 744–45
Lewin, K., 12
Li, X., 182
Liebenberg, L., 329–30
Lim, S. Y., 186
Lindström, B., 153, 157
Lionnet, F., 320
Lipsey, M. J., 223
Lipsky, M., 189–90
Liu, S., 18–19
Lleras-Muney, A., 588
Llewellyn, K., 512
Lochner, L., 588
Løken, K. V., 588–89
Longstaff, P., 115
Lopes da Costa Cabral, A., 569–70
Lordos, A., 423
Lösel, F., 300–1
Loughlin, C., 466
Lovenheim, M. F., 588–89
Lowe, G., 186
Lund, J., 95
Lundborg, P., 591
Luthar, S., 155, 303, 408–9
Lykes, M. B., 535–36

Mahlkow, N., 716
Maldonado-Torres, N., 566–67, 569
Mancini, A. D., 138–39
Manuel-Navarrete, D., 553–54
Mao, F., 747–48, 749, 750, 751
Marshall, V., 620
Martin, A. S., 265–66
Martin, U., 466–67
Mason, G., 535–36
Masten, A., 3–4, 9–10, 35, 113, 155, 158, 221, 224, 243–44, 265–66, 329–30, 384, 387, 396, 398–99
Mather, S., 499
Mathevet, R., 708–9, 714, 715
Matin, N., 553–54
Maturana, H., 320–21
Mazumder, B., 585
McCalman, J., 201–2
McCraty, R., 190

McCubbin, H. I., 256
McCubbin, M. A., 256
McEwen, F. S., 405
McGill, J., 493–94
McGowan, K., 493
McGrath, B., 607, 616, 620
McKenzie, M., 569–70
McKittrick, K., 569
Meerow, S., 607–8
Melhuish, E., 593
Mendenhall, E., 318–19, 369–70
Mendoça, D., 688
Miah, S., 306
Mignolo, W., 319–20
Miller, A., 108
Miller, D., 588
Miller, G. E., 42
Miller, J. H., 510–11
Mills, M. J., 185–86
Mittelmark, M. B., 155
Moffatt, S., 607–8
Mohanty, S., 329–30
Moldoveanu, M., 675
Molina, T., 590–91
Monn, A. R., 265–66
Moon, S. H., 589
Moss, T., 777
Mosso, S., 587
Motti-Stefanidi, F., 384, 387
Muir, J., 498–99
Müller, M., 144
Munford, R., 201
Muratori, S., 604f, 604–5, 606–7, 611–12, 613–16, 614f, 615f, 617–18, 619, 620
Murphy, L. R., 186
Murphy, M., 653–54
Mushquash, C., 80

Naicker, I., 238–39
Narayan, A. J., 158, 224
Naser, G., 531–32
Nash, K. L., 736
Natur, T., 639
Neilson, C., 588–89
Newell, J. P., 607–8
Nguyen-Gillham, V., 531–32
Ní Aoláin, F., 537–38
Nind, M., 223, 224
Ní Raghallaigh, M., 383–84
Noack, A., 61–62
Nonino, F., 10–11
Norberg-Schulz, C., 634–35
Norris, F. H., 82–83, 297, 298, 301
Nowak, A., 539
Nyshadham, A., 590–91

O'Brien, G., 20
Obstfeld, D., 676–77
O'Byrne, D., 712
O'Dougherty, M., 224
Oelofse, M., 27
Okeke, C. I., 237
Oloo, W. A., 265–66
Olsson, C. A., 538–39, 545–46
Olsson, L., 712, 713
Orff, K., 650–51
Orford, A., 534
Oshri, A., 18–19
Ostrom, E., 167, 707, 710–11, 775
Ou, Y., 380–81

Page, S. E., 510–11
Pahl-Wostl, C., 764
Palinkas, L. A., 386
Panter-Brick, C., 363
Paredes, T., 586
Paton, D., 183–84
Patriarca, R., 479
Pedro-Viejo, A. B., 273
Peirce, C. S., 603
Pelling, M., 553–54
Pérez, E., 329–30
Perry, K. M. E., 25–26
Persson, J., 712
Peters, T., 629, 777
Peterson, G., 714, 744–45
Pfefferbaum, B., 297
Pfefferbaum, R. L., 297
Phinney, J. S., 382
Pianta, R. C., 236
Pickett, S. T. A., 609–10, 620
Pinto, R., 589
Pitillas Salvá, C., 275
Pluess, M., 398
Plummer, R., 713
Pol, E., 495
Pomeroy, J. W., 761
Popham, C. M., 401
Portilla, X. A., 236
Preiser, R., 775–76
Pulvirenti, M., 535
Punch, M., 181–82

Qato, M., 570
Qayoom, F., 538–39
Quijano, A., 319–20, 567
Quinn, T., 708
Qureshi, H., 188

Rabie, K., 570
Raichel, N., 22–23

Rampp, B., 713–14, 719–20
Randell, B., 670–71
Raworth, K., 713
Repetto, P., 566
Restrepo, S., 325
Richter, J., 183–84
Riedel, J., 159
Rijbroek, J., 557
Rivera Cusicanqui, S., 326
Robins, S., 538
Rocha, J. C., 744–45
Rockström, J., 713
Rolland, J. S., 279
Rondón, G., 542
Rooney, E., 537–38
Roosevelt, T., 498–99
Rooth, D.-O., 591
Rosales-Rueda, M., 591
Rosch, E., 321–22
Rosh, E., 329
Rosin, C., 777
Ross, H., 329–30
Rossin-Slater, M., 590
Rostami, A., 187
Roubinov, D. S., 43
Rouncefield, M., 668
Rubinstein, J., 181–82
Ruhl, J. B., 511, 542, 546
Rutter, M., 2–3, 35, 114, 155, 222–23, 350–51, 396, 397–98

Sabol, T. J., 236
Said, E., 569
Salamanca, O. J., 570
Sam, D. L., 382
Samour, S., 570
Sampson, R. J., 350
Sánchez, F., 591
Sanders, J., 201
Santos de Carvalho, J., 555
Saul, J., 265–66
Savelyev, P. A., 589
Savenije, H. H. G., 745–46
Sawyer, S. M., 538–39
Schafer, J. A., 187–88
Schetter, D., 68–69
Schinke, S. P., 466–67
Schlüter, M., 778
Schoon, I., 338–39
Schoon, M., 708, 778
Schore, A. N., 80
Schrödinger, E., 166
Schwab, R., 205
Searle, B. J., 460
Selye, H., 459–60

Seshadri, A., 594
Shane, D. G., 620
Sharkey, D., 238–39
Shean, M., 154, 155
Sheffield, P. E., 244
Shelley, M., 105–6
Shemla, M., 466–67
Sherrieb, K., 82–83
Shih, S., 320
Shiwaku, K., 239–40
Siebenhuner, B., 172
Sieckelinck, S., 298–99, 560
Sillitto, H., 683
Simon, D., 588
Simon, M., 501
Simon, T., 500–1
Simon, W., 265–66
Sivapalan, M., 745–46
Slootman, M. W., 560
Smith, J., 204
Smyth, I., 535
Snijders, T. A. B., 458–59
Soininen, N., 516
Sokol, B. W., 85
Solecki, W., 707
Spearman, C., 500
Specking, E. A., 691–92
Spitz, R. A., 272
Sprung-Keyser, B., 594
Srinivasan, U. T., 780–81
Stanford, C. A., 16
Stanford, J. L., 16
Stedman, R. C., 712
Steinhardt, N. S., 618–19
Sterbenz, J. P. G., 14, 15, 20
Stern, D. N., 282
Stevens, W., 297
Stewart, D., 62, 244
Stone-Jovicich, S., 713
Sun, I. Y., 185–86
Sun, J., 244
Sutcliffe, K. M., 676–77
Sweetman, C., 535
Sylvest, M., 632*f*, 633*f*

Tahiri, H., 303
Tajfel, H., 714
Tamabioy, C., 325
Tamayo, J., 590–91
Tapias Mealla, L., 326
Taylor, C. L., 206–7
Taylor, E. L., 299
Taylor, R., 223
Teasdale, S., 495
Teitel, R., 537

Theorell, T., 187
Theron, A. M. C., 237
Theron, L., 236–37, 329–30
Therville, C., 712
Thomas, P., 306
Thompson, E., 321–22, 329
Thoren, H., 712
Tomes, N., 586–87
Toombs, E., 95
Trinidad, S., 204
Triyana, M., 591
Tronick, E., 276–77
Tuck, E., 569–70
Tuhiwai Smith, L., 329
Turner, J. C., 466
Turner, R. K., 780–81
Tüscher, O., 144

Ungar, M., 9, 35, 44–45, 80–81, 154–55,
    157, 159, 160, 183–84, 221, 222, 238,
    241–42, 309–10, 319, 329–30, 350–51,
    396–97, 647

Vale, L., 607–8, 610–11
Vallacher, R. R., 539, 541–42
Van der Leeuw, S., 708
van der Merwe, H., 535–36
van Dullemen, C., 552
Van Yperen, N. W., 458–59
Varela, F. J., 320–22, 329
Vedder, P., 382
Vella-Brodrick, D. A., 538–39
Veracini, L., 566–67
Vicarelli, M., 590–91
Ville, S., 495
Violanti, J. M., 182–83
Vlahov, D., 182

Wagner, R., 105–6
Wallace, M. L., 495
Wallace, W., 688
Waller, M. A., 383–84

Walsh, C., 319–20
Walsh, F., 256, 257, 324–25
Weare, K., 223, 224
Wegge, J., 466–67
Weick, K. E., 674, 675, 676–77
Weine, S., 265–66, 300–1, 309–10
Welton-Mitchell, C., 649–50
Werner, E., 114, 155, 224, 396
Westaway, E., 772
Westley, F., 493–94, 710–11
Whyte, K., 565, 567–68
Wiebelhaus-Brahm, E., 532, 534, 542–43
Wiesmann, U., 159
Willett, K. D., 688
Williams, R., 295
Wilson, A., 627–28
Wilson, E. O., 627
Wilson, S. J., 223
Winges, M., 172
Winnicott, D. W., 277
Wolfe, P., 566–67
Wooyoung, A., 318–19
Wright, M. O. D., 158
Wu, H., 648
Wu, Q., 377, 380–81, 386–87
Wüst, M., 590
Wyche, K. F., 297
Wynter, S., 569

Xia, X., 591
Xinian, F., 619
Xu, L., 2–3, 746

Yavitz, A., 589
Young, C., 58–59
Young, L. R., 668–69

Zammit, A., 303
Zavaleta, R. M., 326
Zelazo. P. D., 114
Zhou, W., 620
Zubrick, S. R., 206–7

Subject Index

For the benefit of digital users, indexed terms that span two pages (e.g., 52–53) may, on occasion, appear on only one of those pages.

Tables and figures are indicated by *t* and *f* following the page number

ABC (Attachment and Biobehavioral Catch-Up) program, 46
Abecedarian program, 589
absence of attachment, as adversity, 272
absorbability, and socio-hydrological resilience, 750–51, 752*f*
absorption technique for engineered systems, 687–88
abstract models of risk, 673
acculturative stress, 381–82
action research. *See* engaged scholarship
active coping style, and perinatal resilience, 65
Active House standard, 629, 636–39, 637*f*, 638*f*
actor network theory, 777
acute trauma, in person-focused models, 120*f*, 121
adaptability, 712, 750–51, 752*f*
adaptation. *See also* resilience; *specific areas of resilience research*; *specific types of resilience*
  in model of multisystemic resilience, 12*f*, 13
  in person-focused models, 120*f*, 120–22, 121*f*
  positive, 340–41
  resilience as process of, 136
  as resilience-promoting process, 20
adaptation belief, 172
adaptation motivation, 172
adaptive building cycles, 606*f*, 606–7
adaptive cycles. *See also* operative panarchy; panarchy
  in development of SES resilience concept, 710*f*, 710
  in panarchy concept, 495–96, 604–5, 605*f*
  and SES resilience, 730*f*, 730–31

adaptive governance, 521–25
adaptive law, 521–22, 524–25
adaptive management (AM)
  and adaptive law, 521–22
  and ecosystem services, 733–35, 734*f*
  future research directions, 737–38
  overview, 522–24
  in social-ecological systems, 735–37
adolescents. *See specific areas of research focused on adolescents*; young people
adulthood, transition to. *See* socioecological developmental systems approach to resilience
adversity. *See also* resilience; *specific areas of resilience research*
  absence of attachment as, 272
  attachment resilience as activated under, 273–74
  developmental cascades, 124
  developmental perspective on family resilience, 257–59
  epigenetics and narrative resilience, 101–2
  mass-trauma adversities, 114–15
  narration of memories related to, 103–5
  narrative resilience, 107–9
  neurological imprint of past, 106–7
  in organizational systems, 691–94
  patterns of childhood resilience after, 36
  perinatal experience of, 57–58, 59–60
  in person-focused models, 120*f*, 120–22, 121*f*
  resilience as occurring in contexts of, 18–19
  and resilience to violent extremism, 305–6
  and salutogenic model of health, 158

adversity (*cont.*)
    socioecological developmental systems approach to resilience, 341–43
    stories surrounding victims of, 106
    in system resilience, 683–84, 699*t*
    in understanding of resilience, 396–97
    when modeling multisystemic resilience, 11
African Americans, skin-deep resilience in, 44, 45–46
age, in developmental perspective of resilience, 410
agency
    and resilience in migrant youth, 386
    in social-ecological systems, 777
agent-focused research on conflict resilience, 426–28, 432, 434*t*, 438–45
agentic concept, resilience as, 535–36
agent types, and perceptions of change in SESs, 174
aggregate complexity, 479–80
agricultural drainage, and socio-hydrological resilience, 758–60, 759*f*, 760*f*, 761*f*, 762*f*
agroecological resilience, 27
Alaska Airlines Flight 261, 478–79
algorithmic complexity, 479
allostasis/allostatic load, 40, 44, 136–37, 407
α (reorganization) phase, adaptive cycle, 730*f*, 730
alternate stable states, in systems, 728–29, 729*f*
AM. *See* adaptive management
American Association of Architects (AIA), 626–27
Analysis of the Resilience of Communities to Disasters (ARCD), GOAL, 428–30, 429*t*
analytic methods, in conflict resilience investigations, 437
ancestral lands, in resilience of Kamentza people, 325, 330–31
ANS (autonomic nervous system), 39
anthropocentric understanding of resilience, 17
antiterrorist hotlines, 305–6
anxiety, model of pregnancy, 68. *See also* stress
appraisals, link to job performance, 460–61
appraisal theory, 145–48
architecture. *See also* embodied multisystemic resilience of architecture and built form; social contexts of resilient architecture
    definition of resilience in, 9
    postdisaster human settlement reconstruction, 650–54, 651*f*
assessment of resilience in conflict-affected populations
    approaches and methods for, 426–28
    Eastern Ukraine case study, 438–45, 440*t*, 441*f*, 442*t*, 443*t*, 444*t*, 446*t*
    existing efforts, 420–21, 421*f*
    integrated science of conflict resilience, 432–38, 433*f*, 434*t*, 435*t*
    overview, 419–20
    practitioner frameworks for, 428–32, 429*t*

ASSET framework, 462
assimilation policies, 80–81
at-risk subgroups, 158
Attachment and Biobehavioral Catch-Up (ABC) program, 46
attachment resilience
    case study, 283–85, 284*f*
    characteristics of, 273–75
    components of, 275–77
    defined, 273
    ecological construction of, 278–80, 280*t*
    general discussion, 285–86
    overview, 271–72
    principles for research and intervention, 281–83
    resilience and early attachment relationships, 272–73
attractors, and transitional justice processes, 539–40, 541*f*, 541–44
atypical stress, resilience in contexts of, 18–19. *See also* adversity; stress
Australia. *See also* Indigenous education and resilience
    education system in, 203*f*, 203
    Living Safe Together strategy, 305
authoritative alliances as practices of re-radicalization, 559–61
autonomic nervous system (ANS), 39
autonomous remediation, 667–68
autopoietic systems, 321–22
ayahuasca (yajé), 327–28

babies. *See also* attachment resilience; perinatal resilience
    effect of anxiety and trauma in pregnancy on, 57–58
    narrative resilience in, 101–2, 108
backstage metaphor, 557
Baker Report, 673
"ball and cup" diagrams, 729*f*, 729
Baltimore Ecosystem Study (BES), 609–10
barrier-based models in safety management, 481, 482*f*
behavioral design, 629–34, 632*f*, 633*f*. *See also* social contexts of resilient architecture
behaviors, leader, 466–67
belief systems, in family resilience, 260, 266*f*, 266
bimodal perspective for system functioning, 482–83, 483*f*
biodiversity, 738
bioecological model of human development, 37, 38*f*
biological resilience. *See also* narrative resilience; perinatal resilience
    brief introduction to resilience, 35–36

challenges and tension in understandings
of, 47–48
in culturally sensitive framework, 44–46
developmental timing and domain, 43–44
evidence for role of neurobiology in
resilience, 40–43
general discussion, 49–50
integrative model for resilience in developmental
psychology, 407–8
intervention/reversibility, 46–47
in migrant youth, 377–80
overview, 35
principles to guide future research, 48–49
stress-relevant neurobiological systems, 39–40
understanding resilience systemically, 37–39, 38f
biological sciences, shifting focus to multiple
systems in, 26
biological sensitivity to context (BSC), 36
biomarkers of resilience. See biological resilience
biophilic design strategies, 627
biopsychosocial-ecological processes, 154
biopsychosocial health, linking peace to, 366–68
biopsychosocial model of pregnancy and birth, 58
biopsychosocial perspective on resilience, 220–21,
257. See also transactional, whole-school
approach to resilience
birth
experiences of, 58–59
overview, 57–58
resilience in, 61–66, 62f, 64t
risk and adversity in, 59–60
theoretical approaches to resilience during, 67–70
traumatic, 60–61, 63
Black Americans, skin-deep resilience in, 44, 45–46
boarding schools, supporting resilience of
Indigenous students at, 207–11, 208f, 209f
bodily (noncognitive) intrapersonal influences on
resilience, 147–48
"Boiler on Prescription" project, UK, 630–31
borderlands space, resilience in. See also Kamentza
people, resilience of
epistemology of the South, 319–22
overview, 318–19
BOUNCE program (European Commission), 298
brain
epigenetics and narrative resilience, 101–2
role in neurobiological resilience of children, 42
structural development, 13–14
bridging organizations, 736
Bryggervangen Road climate adaptation, 640f,
640, 641f
BSC (biological sensitivity to context), 36
building design shaping behavior, 629–34, 632f,
633f. See also social contexts of resilient
architecture

built environment, postdisaster reconstruction of.
See also disaster resilience
overview, 650–54, 651f
Wenchuan earthquake case study, 654–55
built form, embodied multisystemic resilience of
in China, 616–20, 617f, 618f
general discussion, 620–22
operative history of architecture and built form,
611–15, 612f, 614f, 615f
operative panarchy, 615–16
overview, 603–7, 604f, 605f, 606f
resilience in built environment, 607–11
burkinis, 306–7
burnout, employee, 458
Butaro Hospital (Rwanda), 653–54

Cabenge Bëtsknaté (Clestrinye) festivity of
Kamentza, 328
Canadian Prairie, socio-hydrological resilience in,
758–61, 759f, 760f, 761f, 762f
Canadian public health approaches. See public
health approaches to resilience
CANS (Child and Adolescent Needs and
Strengths) assessment tool, 90
capability
organizational system, 695–97
in system resilience, 684, 699t
capacities
adaptive law promoting, 524–25
for change, 712, 750–51
related to conflict resilience, 434–36, 435t, 438–
45, 440t, 442t, 443t, 444t, 446t
for resilience, 455–58
when modeling multisystemic
resilience, 12f, 12
capital. See also human capital; social capital
in integrated capacities framework, 434–36, 435t
in sustainable livelihoods framework, 430–31
caregiver–child dyads. See attachment resilience
CAS (complex adaptive systems), 165–67, 726–27.
See also social-ecological systems
cascades, developmental, 122–24, 344–45, 410
cascading effects in socio-hydrological
resilience
across scales, 756–58, 757f
across systems, 755f, 755–56
case study, 758–61, 759f, 760f, 761f, 762f
general discussion, 763
overview, 744–45, 753
within the system, 753–55, 754f
cash transfers, 588, 590–91
cause, attachment as, 272
chains of security, 281
challenge-hindrance stressor framework, 459–60
challenge model of resilience, 349

change
  organizational, employee resilience during, 467–69, 470t
  and patterns of socio-hydrological resilience, 750–53
  perceptions of in messy SESs, 171–76, 173f
  resilience as process of, 136–38
  and SES identification, 715, 718, 720, 721f
Chicago Center for Family Health (CCFH), 267t, 262–64
Child and Adolescent Needs and Strengths (CANS) assessment tool, 90
childbirth. *See* birth
child care for disadvantaged children, 589
childhood resilience
  brief introduction to resilience, 35–36
  challenges and tension in understandings of, 47–48
  in culturally sensitive framework, 44–46
  developmental timing and domain, 43–44
  evidence for role of neurobiology in resilience, 40–43
  general discussion, 49–50
  intervention/reversibility, 46–47
  overview, 35
  principles to guide future research, 48–49
  stress-relevant neurobiological systems, 39–40
  understanding resilience systemically, 37–39, 38f
children. *See also* family resilience; *specific areas of research focused on children*
  effect of anxiety and trauma in pregnancy on, 57–58
  linking peace to biopsychosocial health in, 366–68
  linking peace to early childhood development, 368–69
  macroeconomic interventions for, 593–94
  microeconomic interventions for, 587–92
  narrative resilience in, 101–6, 108
  shocks, interventions, and resilience, 587–92
  Sure Start program, 592–93
  theory of human capital development, 586–87
Child Youth Resilience Measure, 367–68
China
  embodied resilience of architecture and built form in, 616–20, 617f, 618f
  rural–urban migration in, 380
  Wenchuan earthquake postdisaster reconstruction, 654–55
chronic adversity
  integrative model for resilience in developmental psychology, 407
  in person-focused models, 121f, 121
cinema, operative history of, 603
city building. *See* embodied multisystemic resilience of architecture and built form

civic consciousness, in built form, 611, 617–18, 619
civil society, social compact between state and, 362
classic humanitarianism, 364–65
Clestrinye (Cabenge Bëtsknaté) festivity of Kamentza, 328
climate-adapted neighborhoods, social benefits of, 629, 639–42, 640f, 641f
climate change
  prevention of conflicts related to, 422–23
  and resilience of social ecological systems, 716–17, 719t
Closing the Gap policy paper (Australia), 205
Cloudburst Management Plan (Copenhagen, Denmark), 639
CLT (construal level theory), 172
CoBRA (Community Based Resilience Analysis), UNDP, 428–30, 429t
code switching, student, 556–58
co-facilitative systems, 242–44
cognitive biases, and perception formation, 172
coherence, sense of, 156–58, 350–51
cohesion, community, 189
collaborative approach to building disaster resilience, 648–50
collective continuance, 568–69
Colombia. *See* Kamentza people, resilience of
coloniality. *See also* decolonial enactments of resilience
  defined, 567
  epistemology of the South, 319–22
  Kamentza's relationship with, 325–26
  settler-colonialism, 566–67, 568–69
colonies, Israeli, in West Bank, 570
colonization, 319–23, 325–26. *See also* coloniality; decolonial enactments of resilience
commitment to resilience, in HROs, 676
Common Guidance on Helping Build Resilient Societies (UN), 428–30, 429t
common law legal systems, resilience of, 513
common pool resources, 167
communal ways of living, in resilience of Kamentza people, 325–26
communication
  in family resilience, 260, 266f 267t, 266
  role in successful organizational change, 468–69, 470t
communication topology, in networked systems, 663, 664f
community
  and ecological police resilience, 186–89
  in First Nations Mental Wellness Continuum Framework, 93
  Indigenous Australian student transition to boarding school from, 207–10, 208f, 209f

in integrative model for resilience in
developmental psychology, 404
investigations into conflict resilience,
422–23, 436
involvement in postdisaster
reconstruction, 653–54
partnerships related to family resilience, 262–64
and perinatal resilience, 66
role in decolonial enactments of resilience, 578
role in resilience to consequences of
conflict, 423–24
in salutogenic model of health, 160
Sure Start program effects on, 593
Community Based Resilience Analysis (CoBRA),
UNDP, 428–30, 429t
community cohesion, 189
community policing, 188–89
community resilience. See also Kamentza people,
resilience of; socioecological developmental
systems approach to resilience
conflict resilience, 422–23, 436
defined, 189
multifinality in, 25–26
public health as promoting, 79–83, 80t
versus resilience to violent extremism, 302–3
to violent extremism, 299–304, 308, 309, 310–11
compartments, in colonialism, 566–67
compensatory models of resilience, 347–48
complex adaptive systems (CAS), 165–67, 726–27.
See also social-ecological systems
complexity
embracing, 775–77
of legal systems, 510–12
origins of resilience, 166–69
of resilience-enabling transactions in
schools, 234–38
of resilient systems, 21–22
of social-ecological systems, 711–12, 726–27
of social problems, 552–53, 555
in sociotechnical systems, 478–81, 479f
complex systems, 166–67, 479f, 479, 708f, 708
complicated systems, 479f, 479
computing science. See also engineered system
resilience; networked computer systems;
resilience engineering
co-occurring systems and resilience, 14, 15
definition of resilience in, 9
COMT gene, 235–36
conceptual openness of resilience
engaged scholarship as benefiting from, 555–56
in social sciences, 553–55, 561
conflict-affected states. See Palestinian refugee
communities; peacebuilding, resilience-
building approaches in; refugee children,
psychological resilience in; transitional justice

conflict resilience
approaches and methods for
investigation, 426–28
Eastern Ukraine case study, 438–45, 440t, 441f,
442t, 443t, 444t, 446t
existing efforts to assess, 420–21, 421f
general discussion, 445–47
overview, 417–20, 418f, 419f
practitioner frameworks for assessment,
428–32, 429t
principles and guidelines for integrated science
of, 432–38, 433f, 434t, 435t
resilience for conflict prevention, 422–23
resilience to consequences of conflict, 423–25
connection, as characteristic of attachment
resilience, 274
connectivity, resilient systems as promoting, 22
conservation (K) phase, adaptive cycle, 730f, 730
conservation, transformative innovations leading
to, 498–99
conservative resilience, 552
Constitution, resilience of U.S., 512–13
construal level theory (CLT), 172
constructivism, 712, 714, 715
CONTEST strategy (UK), 295, 296, 297, 305
context
of education for Indigenous students, 204–5
outcomes specific to, in measurement of
resilience, 88–89
of police work, 181–82
in research on family resilience, 264–65
in resilience research versus salutogenic model
of health, 159–60, 161
social innovation as paradox of process and, 502
socioecological developmental systems model of
resilience, 336f, 336–38
contextual analysis, in conflict-affected
countries, 363
contextually specific resilience, 10
contextual processes, in programs to improve
student resilience, 224
continuity, and SES identification, 715, 718
continuous model of development, 343–44
continuous quality improvement (CQI), 210,
211–13, 214
controllability, and adaptive management,
734–35, 735f
control over decision-making, during
organizational changes, 469, 470t
co-occurring systems and resilience. See also
multisystemic resilience; specific areas of
resilience research
overview, 13–17
and studies of systemic student resilience, 242–44
trade-offs between systems, 21

Copenhagen, Denmark, 629, 639–42, 640f, 641f
coping processes. *See* resilience; salutogenic model of health; *specific areas of resilience research*; *specific types of resilience*,
co-regulation, in socioecological developmental systems approach, 338–39
cortisol, 39, 407–8
cost-benefit models of risk, 673
counterterrorism (CT). *See* violent extremism, resilience to
Cracking the Code report (Mercy Corps), 363
crises, humanitarian. *See* conflict resilience; humanitarianism, resilience-building approaches in; migrant youth, resilience in; refugee children, psychological resilience in
critical infrastructures, 663–64, 687, 692. *See also* engineered system resilience; networked computer systems
critical reflexivity, 572
critical windows of opportunity, 347
cross-cultural resilience, 369–70
cross-disciplinary interactions in work on resilience, 771–74. *See also* multisystemic resilience; *specific areas of resilience research*,
cross-scale interactions, and socio-hydrological resilience, 756–58, 757f
cross-sectional research designs, 138–39
cross-systemic linkages, detection of, 437
cross-system interaction in resilience functioning, 386–87
cultural continuity, 82, 85
cultural heterogeneity, 307
culturally appropriate care, 85
culturally sensitive framework, biological resilience in, 44–46
cultural tension between parenting models, 284, 285
culture. *See also* Kamentza people, resilience of
  centrality in understanding people, 318–19
  cross-cultural resilience, 369–70
  in First Nations Mental Wellness Continuum Framework, 91
  in integrative model for resilience in developmental psychology, 404–5, 406
  organizational, 186–87
  of peace, 368
  and perinatal resilience, 64t, 66
  and positive adaptation, 340–41
  and resilience in migrant youth, 381–82, 384
  in resilience research and salutogenic model of health, 159–60, 161
  role in experience of pregnancy and birth, 58–59
  role in narrative resilience, 105–6
cumulative science of conflict resilience, 434–36
cumulative stressors, and family resilience, 258

cyber security risks, 668–69
cyber situational awareness, 669–70
cycles, in development of SES resilience concept, 710f, 710–11, 711f. *See also* adaptive cycles; panarchy

D^2R^2+DR resilience strategy, 666f, 666–68, 669
decision-making
  in high reliability organizations, 676–77
  during organizational changes, 469, 470t
  in organizational systems, 691
Declaration on the Rights of Indigenous Peoples (UN), 202–3
decolonial enactments of resilience
  background on West Bank and PRFTR project, 570–72
  general discussion, 579–80
  overview, 565–66
  reflexivity, 572
  resilience from decolonial and Indigenous perspectives, 567–69
  settler-colonialism, 566–67
  stories of displaced Palestinian families, 572–78
  strategies for restorying resilience, 569–70
decolonizing methodology, 329–30, 331
defend phase, D^2R^2+DR resilience strategy, 667
deference to expertise, in HROs, 676–77
deficit-based approach to Indigenous development, 202–3, 205
dehumanization, in settler-colonialism, 568–69
delta (difference between perception of and measured change), 172–74, 173f
demands, relation to employee resilience, 456–57, 458–63, 462t, 463f, 468–69
Denmark, climate-adapted neighborhoods in, 629, 639–42, 640f, 641f
design, resilient. *See* embodied multisystemic resilience of architecture and built form; social contexts of resilient architecture
detect phase, D^2R^2+DR resilience strategy, 667
deterministic complexity, 479
development
  inequality as threat to sustainable, 780–82
  measuring resilience through processes of, 90–91
  needs related to, in humanitarian and peacebuilding efforts, 365–66
  opportunities for, role in employee resilience, 468, 470t
developmental cascades, 122–24, 344–45, 410
developmental perspective
  of attachment resilience, 279
  family resilience, 256–59
  in integrative model for resilience, 400–1, 409–10

developmental resilience science. *See also* integrative model for resilience in developmental psychology; migrant youth, resilience in; socioecological developmental systems approach to resilience
- definition of resilience, 115–18
- developmental cascades, 122–24
- frameworks for practice and policy, 124–25
- general discussion, 129
- key concepts in, 118–20
- models in, 120f, 120–22, 121f, 123f
- new horizons in, 128–29
- overview, 113–15, 343–46
- resilience framework for action, 125–28, 125t

developmental systems theory, 114–18, 221
developmental timing, role in neurobiological resilience, 43–44
developmental transitions, attachment relationships across, 279
diagnose and refine phase, D^2R^2+DR resilience strategy, 668
dialogue, in resilience of Kamentza people, 329
differential susceptibility (DS), 36
digital capital, in integrated capacities framework, 435t
digital technologies. *See* engineered system resilience; networked computer systems
direct instruction in resilience skills, 222–23
disaster resilience, 9–10
- case studies of Wenchuan earthquake, 654–55
- collaborative approach, need for, 648–50
- general discussion, 655–56
- overview, 646–47
- postdisaster human settlement reconstruction, 650–54, 651f
- principles of, 647–48
- of schools, 239–40
- social capital dimensions of, 301

discontinuous model of development, 343–44
disengagement, in humanitarian efforts, 364–65
displacement, forced. *See* humanitarianism, resilience-building approaches in; migrant youth, resilience in; Palestinian refugee communities; refugee children, psychological resilience in
displacement, in risk models, 671–72
distancing, technology-induced environmental, 175–76
distress, versus eustress, 459–60
distributed capacity technique for engineered systems, 688
diversity
- cultures valuing, and resilience in migrant youth, 382
- environmental, and resilience, 15–17
- microbial, 15–17, 21
- and resilience in messy SESs, 171, 173f
- resilient systems including, 23
- response, 512, 513

doing well despite adversity, 158–59. *See also* resilience; salutogenic model of health
domain characteristics and resilience, 683–87, 685f
drainage, and socio-hydrological resilience, 758–60, 759f, 760f, 761f, 762f
drought resilience, 365–66
DS (differential susceptibility), 36
Dunning–Kruger effect, 172
dynamic processes
- attachment resilience as, 275
- in family resilience, 260, 266f, 266 267t
- resilience as, 336f, 336–39

dynamic systems, resilient systems as, 21–22

early attachment relationships, resilience and, 272–73
early childhood development, linking peace to, 368–69
early childhood interventions, economic
- case study, 592–93
- microeconomic approach, 587–92
- theory of human capital development, 586–87

early intervention to improve student resilience, 224
early life shocks, impact of, 587–88. *See also* childhood resilience; *specific areas of research focused on early life*,
Earned Income Tax Credit, 588
earthquake in Wenchuan, postdisaster reconstruction after, 654–55
Eastern Ukraine, assessment of resilience in conflict-affected, 438–45, 440t, 441f, 442t, 443t, 444t, 446t
ecological aspects of resilient design, 626–29, 634–42, 640f, 641f
ecological factors, integrative model for resilience in developmental psychology, 405
ecological model of resilience. *See also specific areas of resilience research*
- attachment resilience, 278–80, 280t, 283–85, 284f
- definition of resilience in, 154
- developmental outcomes, 221
- in development of SES resilience concept, 708–10, 709f
- legal system resilience, 512, 513
- resilience in migrant youth, 380–81
- resilience to violent extremism, 308–9

ecological police resilience
  community level, 186–89
  community policing, 188–89
  family, 185–86
  individual-level factors, 184–85
  laws, 189–90
  organizational factors, 186–88
  overview, 184, 185f
ecological sciences. See also specific areas of resilience research
  integrating with architecture and urban design, 607, 608–10
  resilience as process in, 19
ecological systems. See also natural environment; social-ecological system resilience; socioecological developmental systems approach to resilience; socio-hydrological resilience
  ecology of peace framework, 368–69
economic development, role in community resilience, 82–83
economic factors in postdisaster reconstruction, 655
economics of multisystemic resilience. See also humanitarianism, resilience-building approaches in
  case study, 592–93
  co-occurring systems and resilience, 13–14
  general discussion, 594–95
  macroeconomic approach, 593–94
  overview, 584–85
  shocks, interventions, and resilience, 587–92
  theory of human capital development, 585–87
ecosystemic view of family resilience, 256–57
ecosystem services (ES). See also socio-hydrological resilience
  adaptive management, 733–37
  cascading effects in socio-hydrological resilience, 761
  future research directions, 737–38
  general discussion, 738–39
  historical management paradigm, 726
  managing for resilience, 732–33
  overview, 725–26
  theoretical underpinnings for managing SESs, 726–31, 729f, 730f, 731f
education. See also Indigenous education and resilience; student resilience; transactional, whole-school approach to resilience
  Australian system, 203f, 203–5
  barriers to resilience in Indigenous communities, 86–87
  urban, transformations in, 556–58
EF (executive function), 124, 126
efficiency, in legal system resilience, 517, 519

embodied multisystemic resilience of architecture and built form
  in China, 616–20, 617f, 618f
  general discussion, 620–22
  operative history of architecture and built form, 611–15, 612f, 614f, 615f
  operative panarchy, 615–16
  overview, 603–7, 604f, 605f, 606f
  resilience in built environment, 607–11
embryo resilience, 101
emerging challenges, and family resilience, 257–58
emotion, and narrative resilience, 103–5, 108
emplacement, in risk models, 671–72
employee resilience
  critical role of leadership, 465–67
  defining resilience, 455–58
  frameworks of organizational resources and demands, 461–63, 462t, 463f
  general discussion, 472
  multilevel model of team resilience, 463–65
  need for multisystemic approaches, 457
  and organizational change, 467–69, 470t
  overview, 455
  role of job design, 458–61
engaged scholarship
  and openness of resilience concept, 551–52, 561
  operationalizing to understand societal resilience, 556–61
  as opportunity for inclusive societal resilience, 555–56
engineered system resilience. See also networked computer systems
  domain characteristics, 683–87, 685f
  general discussion, 699–700
  versus organizational system resilience, 699–700, 699t
  overview, 682–83, 687
  processes, 695
  systems for engineered system domain, 687
  techniques for, 687–88
engineering resilience. See resilience engineering
ENISA (European Union Agency for Network and Information Security), 666, 668–69
environment. See also specific related areas of resilience research
  cultural narratives about relationship with, 21–22
  Kamentza people's view of, 320–21
  and perinatal resilience, 64t, 66
  in resilience research versus salutogenic model of health, 157–58
  when modeling multisystemic resilience, 12f, 12
environmental distancing, technology-induced, 175–76

environmental law
  multisystemic resilience concept, 536–37
  questions of scale in, 738
  resilience in, 513, 515, 516–20, 523–24
environmental performance, in architecture, 626–29, 634–42, 640f, 641f
environmental psychology, 629–30
environmental sensitivity
  individual differences in, 399–400
  in integrative model for resilience in developmental psychology, 400–1, 406–7
environmental shocks, interventions remediating, 590–92
epigenetics
  change in people who show stable mental health, 137–38
  neurological traces in preverbal world, 101–2
  and perinatal resilience, 64t
  and resilience in migrant youth, 378–80
epistemological resistance to colonialism. *See* decolonial enactments of resilience
Epistemologies of the South (de Sousa Santos), 318–19
epistemology of the South, 319–22
equifinality
  in developmental systems theory, 117
  in patterns of resilience, 23–26
  socioecological developmental systems approach, 344
equilibrium, in development of SES resilience concept, 708–10
equitable resilience, 553–54
equity, and sustainable development, 780–82
ES. *See* ecosystem services; socio-hydrological resilience
essential services, in FNMWCF, 93
Eurocentric thinking, 565–66. *See also* decolonial enactments of resilience
European Commission BOUNCE program, 298
European Union Agency for Network and Information Security (ENISA), 666, 668–69
eustress, 459–60
everyday practice, resilience as, 369–70
evolvability, in legal system resilience, 517, 520
executive function (EF), 124, 126
exosystem
  ecological model of attachment resilience, 280t, 284f
  integrative model for resilience in developmental psychology, 404
experience of buildings, architecture focused on. *See* occupants, architecture focused on experience of
experiential dimension of resilience, 369–70
experiential narrative models of risk, 672

experimentation, resilient systems as demonstrating, 22–23
expertise, deference to in HROs, 676–77
exploitation (r) phase, adaptive cycle, 730f, 730
external threats to organizations, 691–92
extra-individual factors
  in intra-individual theory of resilience, 143–44
  in positive appraisal style theory of resilience, 147–48
  in psychological resilience research, 141–43
extremism, engaged scholarship on, 559–61. *See also* violent extremism, resilience to

factor analysis of detrimental outcomes of conflict exposure, 439, 440t
failure, preoccupation with in HROs, 675–76
failure path models of risk, 672
faith, and resilience as everyday practice, 370. *See also* religion
familism, 45
family. *See also* attachment resilience; developmental resilience science
  biological resilience in culturally sensitive framework, 45
  complexity of resilience-enabling transactions, 237
  and ecological police resilience, 185–86
  in ecology of peace framework, 368–69
  influence on Indigenous student resilience, 204
  in integrative model for resilience in developmental psychology, 403–4, 406
  and narrative resilience, 105–6
  and neurobiological resilience of children, 40–41
  Palestinian Refugee Family Trees of Resilience project, 570, 571–72
  promotion of resilience among school children, 224–25
  resilience enhancement for Indigenous boarding students, 209f, 210
family resilience
  advances and challenges in research on, 264–67, 266f
  concept, 256
  cumulative stressors, 258
  developmental perspective, 256–59
  ecosystemic view, 256–57
  emerging challenges and resilient pathways over time, 257–58
  equifinality and multifinality in, 24–25
  general discussion, 267
  mapping key processes in, 260 267t
  multigenerational family life cycle, 258–59
  overview, 255–56
  practice applications, 262–64 269t

fast variables
  and ecological resilience, 308–9
  in social-ecological systems, 728–29, 729f
  in socioecological developmental systems approach, 339
feeblemindedness concept, 500–1
feedback
  and social-ecological resilience, 174
  in social-ecological systems, 165
  and transitional justice processes, 540–41, 541f
festivities, in resilience of Kamentza people, 328
financial assets, and mental health, 142. *See also* economics of multisystemic resilience
First Nations Mental Wellness Continuum Framework (FNMWCF), 91–94, 92f
flood risks, and resilience of social-ecological systems, 717–20, 719t
food, relation to resilience in Indigenous communities, 86–87
food insecurity, prevention of conflicts related to, 422–23
food security, linking peace to, 365–66
forced displacement. *See* humanitarianism, resilience-building approaches in; migrant youth, resilience in; Palestinian refugee communities; refugee children, psychological resilience in
formative resilience. *See* childhood resilience
fractals, 544
Fragility and Resilience policy brief, 362, 363
Frameworks for the Assessment of Resilience (Interpeace), 428–30, 429t
FRIENDS program, 222–23
Fukushima nuclear facility, 691
functional redundancy technique for engineered systems, 688
functional resonance analysis method (FRAM), 483, 485–88, 487f, 489
future orientation, 18–19

Gehl Architects, 631
gender issues, and transitional justice, 537–38
gene expression studies, 137–38
general equilibrium models, 593–94, 595f
generalized resistance resources, in salutogenic model of health, 156–57
general resilience of social-ecological systems, 732–33
genetics. *See also* epigenetics
  integrative model for resilience in developmental psychology, 407–8
  and neurobiological resilience of children, 42–43
  and perinatal resilience, 64t
  and resilience in migrant youth, 378–80
  and self-regulation, 235–36

global attribute models of risk, 673
global challenges, multisystemic approach to, 779–82
global change, and resilience of social-ecological systems, 717–20, 719t
Global North thinking, 565–66. *See also* decolonial enactments of resilience
global refugee crisis. *See* Palestinian refugee communities; refugee children, psychological resilience in; refugee crisis
Global South decolonizing perspectives. *See* decolonial enactments of resilience
GOAL Analysis of the Resilience of Communities to Disasters (ARCD), 428–30, 429t
good-enough mothers, 277
governance
  adaptive, 521–25
  concern about strategic use of resilience concept in, 713
  resilient, 558–59
government
  in First Nations Mental Wellness Continuum Framework, 93
  macroeconomic approach to multisystemic resilience, 593–94
  and resilience to violent extremism, 303–4, 310–11
  state resilience, 361–65
Greece, architectural interventions related to refugee crisis in, 652–53
green buildings. *See* sustainable architecture
Greenpeace, 690
growth, posttraumatic, 62–63
Guidelines for Resilience Systems Analysis (OECD), 428–30, 429t
GXN, 631

Hans Tavsens Park climate adaptation, 640–41
harm, attachment interventions focused on, 281–82
hazard types, 646–47. *See also* disaster resilience
Head Start, 589
healing practices, in resilience of Kamentza people, 326–28
health. *See also* perinatal resilience; salutogenic model of health
  and biological resilience, 45–46
  early childhood interventions promoting, 592
  in humanitarian and peacebuilding efforts, 365, 366–68
  in social context of architecture, 626–29
healthcare
  employee resilience during organizational change in, 467–69, 470t
  for Indigenous children in boarding schools, 210–11

interventions for disadvantaged children, 588–89
and resilience in Indigenous public health, 87
health services workplace environmental resilience (HSWER) model, 461, 462t
health system resilience, in conflict-affected countries, 425
Healthy Babies Healthy Children, 81
healthy organizations, 186
heedful interrelating, 675
heterogeneity
  and resilience to violent extremism, 307
  in risk effects, 342–43
hierarchical integration and differentiation, 343, 344–45
hierarchies of humanity, 565–66, 568–69
high reliability organizations (HROs), 674, 675–77
hindrance stressors, 459–60
holism, in transitional justice, 540
holistic well-being, 89–90, 91
home-visiting programs for disadvantaged children, 590
Homework Starts With Home Research Partnership, 127
horizontal integration by schools to strengthen Indigenous student resilience, 211–13, 212f
household preparedness for conflict, 424–25
household resilience, 436
HPA (hypothalamic–pituitary–adrenal) axis, 39, 407–8
human-based systems. *See* organizational system resilience
human capital
  and conflict resilience, 439–43, 442t, 444t, 446t
  in integrated capacities framework, 435t
  in multilevel model of team resilience, 463–65
  theory of human capital development, 584, 585–87
human-centered architecture, 653–54. *See also* occupants, architecture focused on experience of
human development, bioecological model of, 37, 38f. *See also* developmental resilience science
human factors, in networked computer systems, 670–77
human in the loop technique, 688
humanitarian aspects of human settlement in postdisaster reconstruction, 652–53
humanitarianism, resilience-building approaches in. *See also* conflict resilience; migrant youth, resilience in; refugee children, psychological resilience in
  general discussion, 371–72
  overview, 361
  pathways to systemic resilience, 365–69
  political economy of resilience, 370–71

resilience as everyday practice, 369–70
structural and social resilience, 361–65
humanity, hierarchies of, 565–66, 568–69
human relationality, multisystemic, 565, 579
human rights abuses. *See* transitional justice
human rights approach to Indigenous development, 202–3
human settlement reconstruction, postdisaster. *See also* disaster resilience
  overview, 650–54, 651f
  Wenchuan earthquake case study, 654–55
human-water systems. *See* socio-hydrological resilience
hydrological resilience to social perturbations, 748–49, 751, 752f, 759–60, 760f, 761f. *See also* socio-hydrological resilience
hygiene hypothesis, 16
hypothalamic–pituitary–adrenal (HPA) axis, 39, 407–8

ICS (industrial control systems), 663–64. *See also* networked computer systems
ICT (information and communication technologies). *See* networked computer systems
ICTY (International Criminal Tribunal for the former Yugoslavia), 532, 543–45
identification
  social-ecological system, relation to resilience, 705–6, 707, 713–22, 719t, 721f
  team, 464–65
immunology, and multisystemic resilience, 15–17
impairment, 398–99, 399f
inclusiveness of mainstream culture, 382
inclusive societal resilience, 555–56
income inequality, 780–82. *See also* economics of multisystemic resilience
Indigenous communities, public health approaches to resilience in
  First Nations Mental Wellness Continuum Framework, 91–94, 92f
  general discussion, 94
  overview, 78–79, 79f
  promoting community resilience across levels of care, 79–83, 80t
  resilience as multisystemic, 84f, 84–88
  resilience measurement, 88–91
Indigenous education and resilience
  case study, 207–11, 208f, 209f
  context of education for Indigenous students, 204–5
  definition of resilience, 200–1
  education system in Australia, 203f, 203
  general discussion, 211–14, 212f
  methods and measures, 205–7
  overview, 199–200
  reasons to focus on resilience, 201–3

Indigenous peoples. *See also* Kamentza people, resilience of
  decolonial strategies for restorying resilience, 569–70
  resilience from perspective of, 566–67
  settler-colonialism, 566–67
  stories of decolonial enactments of resilience, 572–78
individual assets contributing to community resilience, 80
individualized concept, definitions of resilience as, 200–1
individual level
  in conflict resilience investigations, 426–28, 432, 434t, 438–45
  ecological police resilience, 184–85
  in integrative model for resilience in developmental psychology, 403
  socioecological developmental systems model of resilience, 336f, 336–37
individual resilience. *See* psychological resilience; *specific areas of resilience research*,
individual resources, relation to employee resilience, 458–59, 460–61
individuals, in First Nations Mental Wellness Continuum Framework, 93–94
individual viewpoint, in networked computer systems, 665f, 668–69, 670–77
industrial control systems (ICS), 663–64. *See also* networked computer systems
inequality, as threat to sustainable development, 780–82. *See also* economics of multisystemic resilience
infants. *See also* attachment resilience; perinatal resilience
  effect of anxiety and trauma in pregnancy on, 57–58
  narrative resilience in, 101–2, 108
information and communication technologies (ICT). *See* networked computer systems
innovation, social. *See* social innovation and resilience
Institute for Societal Resilience (ISR), 551–52, 556–61
institutional macrosystem, and resilience in migrant youth, 381–84, 385f, 386–87, 388–89
institutional resilience, 425, 436, 513–14
instrumental resilience, 513–14
instrumenting networked systems, 667
integrated capacities framework, 434–36, 435t
integrated resilience approaches in education. *See* Indigenous education and resilience
integrated science of conflict resilience, 432–38, 433f, 434t, 435t
integration, resilient, 349

integrative framework for resilience in migrant youth. *See* Multisystemic Resilience Framework for migrant youth
integrative model for resilience in developmental psychology
  developmental perspective, 400–1, 409–10
  environmental sensitivity, 400–1, 406–7
  implications, 410–11
  multidimensional nature of, 400–1, 408–9
  multilevel perspective, 400–1, 407–8
  multisystemic nature of, 400–1, 402f, 403–6
  overview, 400f, 400–1
  review of empirical evidence, 401–10
integrative models of knowledge, 84–85
intelligence tests, 500–1
interacting systems, social-ecological systems as, 708f, 708
interactions, as component of attachment resilience, 276–77, 278, 280t, 284f
interdependence of system resilience, 119
interdisciplinary study of resilience. *See* multisystemic resilience; *specific areas of resilience research*,
interethnic reconciliation in former Yugoslavia, 543–44
interlocking vulnerability, 779–80
internal threats to organizations, 692–93
International Criminal Tribunal for the former Yugoslavia (ICTY), 532, 543–45
international migration, 364–65
international organizations. *See* humanitarianism, resilience-building approaches in
internet, development of, 497
Interpeace Frameworks for the Assessment of Resilience, 428–30, 429t
interpersonal mesosystem, and resilience in migrant youth, 380–81, 385f, 386–87, 388–89
intersubjectivity, as component of attachment resilience, 277
interventions. *See also* Indigenous education and resilience; transactional, whole-school approach to resilience
  applying multisystemic resilience concept to, 26–27, 243–44
  architectural, for postdisaster reconstruction, 652–53
  attachment resilience, 281–83, 285
  and biological resilience, 46–47
  critical windows of opportunity, 347
  developmental resilience frameworks for, 124–25
  economic, 584–85
  family resilience orientation in, 262–64
  to improve employee resilience, 468–69, 470t

and integrative model for resilience in developmental psychology, 410–11
linking peace to biopsychosocial health, 366–68
macroeconomic approach, 593–94
microeconomic approach, 587–92
promoting resilience in migrant youth, 388–89
in resilience framework for action, 127
in resilience research versus salutogenic model of health, 157–58, 161
Sure Start program, 592–93
theory of human capital development, 586–87
intra-individual theory of resilience, 141, 143–48
intrapersonal factors
relation to employee resilience, 458, 459, 460–61
and resilience in migrant youth, 377–80, 385f, 386–87
in resilience research versus salutogenic model of health, 157–58
Introduction to Manhattan Timeformations website, 616
investment in human capital, 586–87
invulnerability, 220–21, 396
ion channels expression, 137
ISR (Institute for Societal Resilience), 551–52, 556–61
Israel, settler-colonial, occupation system in, 570, 571. *See also* Palestinian refugee communities

job control, 187
job demands-resources (JDR) model, 187, 458–60
job design, role in employee resilience, 458–61. *See also* employee resilience
John Henryism, 45–46
"Jordan's Principal," 93
justice, transitional. *See* transitional justice

K (conservation) phase, adaptive cycle, 730f, 730
Kamentza people, resilience of
background of Kamentza people, 322–24
epistemology of the South, 319–22
general discussion, 331–32
interstices of, 324–28
ontological resilience, 328–31
overview, 318–19
knowledge
barriers to resilience in Indigenous communities, 86–87
co-generating through engaged scholarship, 555–56
construction of, in resilience of Kamentza people, 329
Korsgade street climate adaptation, 640–41

labor. *See* birth
land, in resilience of Kamentza people, 325, 330–31

land-based activities, and resilience in Indigenous public health, 87
Latino cultural values, and biological resilience, 45
Lattes, France, 717–20, 719t
law. *See also* legal system resilience
adaptive, 521–22, 524–25
and ecological police resilience, 189–90
multisystemic resilience concept in, 536–39
and social-ecological scales, 738
leadership
critical role in employee resilience, 465–67
management systems standards in organizational resilience, 698–99
police, 187–88
Leadership in Energy and Environmental Design (LEED) program, 635
learning, resilient systems as demonstrating, 22–23
legal system resilience. *See also* transitional justice
adaptive governance frame, 521–25
general discussion, 525–26
identity of legal systems, 509–15
multisystemic resilience concept, 536–39
overview, 509–10, 530–31
properties of, 517–20
purpose of, 509–10, 515–17
shocks experienced in legal systems, 509–10, 515
"levee effect" phenomenon, 750
life course perspective. *See* longitudinal perspective
Life Plan (Kamentza), 328–29
Living Building Challenge, 636
Living Safe Together strategy (Australia), 305
local context for resilience, 10
local leadership, in humanitarian efforts, 362, 364
locally specific approaches to resilient design, 641–42
longitudinal perspective
of attachment resilience, 279
family resilience, 256–59
in integrative model for resilience, 400–1, 409–10
longitudinal research designs, 138, 139, 140
Lübek, Germany, 716–17, 718, 719t

macroeconomic approach to multisystemic resilience, 584, 585, 593–94
macrosystem
ecological model of attachment resilience, 280t, 284f
effect on student resilience, 234, 235f, 237–38
in integrative model for resilience in developmental psychology, 404–5
and resilience in migrant youth, 381–84, 385f, 386–87, 388–89
and school disaster resilience, 239–40
MAMAS study, 47

management. *See also* adaptive management
  police, 182–83, 187–88
  systems standards, organizational resilience through, 698–99
management of ecosystem services
  adaptive management, 733–37
  future research directions, 737–38
  general discussion, 738–39
  historical approach, 726
  overview, 725–26
  for resilience, 732–33
  theoretical underpinnings, 726–31, 729f, 730f, 731f
manifested resilience, 117–18
maps, family resilience-oriented, 260 267t
marginalization related to multiple crises, 779–80
mass-trauma adversities, 114–15, 128–29
matching hypothesis, 456–57
material capital, in integrated capacities framework, 435t
maternal functioning, influence on resilience in children, 408
maternal resilience, 61–62. *See also* parents/parenting; perinatal resilience
mature narration, 106–7
meaning making
  and perinatal resilience, 63–65
  as resilience process, 350–51
meaning systems, when modeling multisystemic resilience, 12f, 13
measured change, disparity between perceptions of change and, 172–74, 173f
measures
  in resilience framework for action, 126–27
  of resilience in conflict-affected settings, 367–68
  of resilience in Indigenous Australian students, 205–7
  of resilience to violent extremism, 309–10
medical sciences, definition of systems in, 7–8
medicine, in resilience of Kamentza people, 326–28
memories
  narration of, 101, 103–5
  neurological imprint of past, 106–7
mental health, impact of housing on, 630–31
mental illness, in perinatal period, 57, 59
mental models of risk, 671–74
Mercy Corps, 363, 366–68
mesosystem
  ecological model of attachment resilience, 280t
  and resilience in migrant youth, 380–81, 385f, 386–87, 388–89
messy social-ecological systems
  perceptions of change in, 171–74, 173f
  resilience as process in, 168–71, 168t, 170f
metacities, 608–9, 620–21, 622

methods
  for assessing resilience in Indigenous Australian students, 205–7
  in resilience framework for action, 127
microbial diversity, 15–17, 21
microeconomic approach to multisystemic resilience, 585, 587–92
microsystem
  ecological model of attachment resilience, 280t, 284f
  in integrative model for resilience in developmental psychology, 403–4
  and resilience in migrant youth, 377–80, 385f, 386–87
  and student resilience, 233t
migrant youth, resilience in. *See also* refugee children, psychological resilience in
  definition of resilience, 376–77
  general discussion, 389
  in institutional macrosystem, 381–84
  in interpersonal mesosystem, 380–81
  in intrapersonal microsystem, 377–80
  Multisystemic Resilience Framework, 384–89, 385f
  overview, 375–76
migration, international, 364–65
mindfulness, resilience as sensemaking and, 674–77
mobility, and resilience in messy SESs, 171, 173f
models
  in developmental resilience science, 120f, 120–22, 121f, 123f
  of pregnancy anxiety, 68
  in resilience framework for action, 125–26
moderating (protective) effect model of resilience, 348–49
modularity, in legal system resilience, 517, 520
molecular psychosomatics, 15–16
mothers. *See also* parents/parenting; perinatal resilience
  functioning of, influence on resilience in children, 408
  maternal resilience, 61–62
multidimensionality
  of positive adaptation, 340
  of psychological resilience, 400–1, 408–9
multidirectionality of development, 343–44
multidisciplinary approach to building disaster resilience, 648–50, 656
multifinality
  in developmental systems theory, 117
  in patterns of resilience, 23–26
  socioecological developmental systems approach to resilience, 344
multifunctional approach to resilient design, 641–42

multigenerational family life cycle, 258–59
multilevel interventions related to family
      resilience, 262–64
multilevel model of team resilience, 463–65
multilevel perspective, applying to psychological
      resilience, 400–1, 407–8
multilevel process, resilience as, 336f, 336–38
multilevel resilience research, advancing,
      265–67, 266f
multiple crises in fragile contexts, 779–80
multiple stable states, in development of SES
      resilience concept, 708–10, 709f
multiple systems
   interventions to improve student resilience, 224–25
   in resilience framework for action, 127–28
multiscale architecture, 634
multisystemic resilience. *See also specific areas of
      research*
   application to research and intervention, 26–27
   case for reductionism, 141–43
   common principles of resilience, 18–23
   co-occurring systems and resilience, 13–17
   cross-disciplinary interactions, 771–74
   definitions of resilience, 6–7, 8–11
   emerging perspectives on, 778–79
   general discussion, 27–28, 782
   model of, 11–13, 12f
   new frontiers for resilience science, 779–82
   overview, 6–8, 7f, 154–55, 771
   reasons for focus on, 1–3
   resilience as tangram, 23–26, 24f
   in social-ecological systems, 774–77
   urgency of need to understand, 3–4
Multisystemic Resilience Framework for
      migrant youth
   general discussion, 389
   overview, 384–87, 385f
   research, policy and practice
      implications, 387–89
Muslim women, burkini ban applying to, 306–7
mutual regulation, as component of attachment
      resilience, 275–76

Nakba of 1948 (Palestine), 571, 573–74
narrative resilience
   developing capacity related to narrative, 100–1
   general discussion, 107–9
   of Kamentza people, 328
   mature narration, 106–7
   narration of memories, 103–5
   neurological traces in preverbal world, 101–3
   overview, 100–1
   surrounding stories, 105–6
National Human Rights Commission of India
      (NHRC), 649–50

National Infrastructure Advisory Council
      (U.S.), 626
national parks, transformative innovations leading
      to, 498–99
national resilience to conflict, 436
Native Wellness Assessment (NWA), 89–90
natural environment. *See also specific related
      subjects*
   co-occurring systems and resilience, 15–17
   cultural narratives about relationship
      with, 21–22
   and effects of disasters on human settlements,
      650–52, 651f
   Kamentza people's view of, 320–21
natural hazards, 646–47. *See also* disaster resilience
natural resource managers, 172–74
neat social-ecological systems, 167
negative feedback loops, 540–41
negotiated outcomes, as aspect of resilience, 10–11
neighborhood scale climate adaptation projects,
      629, 639–42, 640f, 641f
neodevelopmental psychology, narrative resilience
      in, 107–9
nested panarchy. *See* operative panarchy
nested systems, social-ecological systems as,
      708f, 708
net positive building, 636
networked computer systems
   application of OTI viewpoints to, 665f,
      665, 670–71
   co-occurring systems and resilience, 14
   D^2R^2+DR resilience strategy, 666f, 666–68
   general discussion, 677–78
   human and organizational factors, 670–77
   overview, 663–65, 664f
   resilience and models of risk and importance of
      trust, 671–74
   resilience and related terminology, 665–66
   resilience as sensemaking and
      mindfulness, 674–77
   situation awareness and resilience, 669–70
   system risk, 668–69
net zero building, 636
neurobiological resilience
   brief introduction to resilience, 35–36
   challenges and tension in understandings
      of, 47–48
   in culturally sensitive framework, 44–46
   developmental timing and domain, 43–44
   evidence for role of neurobiology in
      resilience, 40–43
   general discussion, 49–50
   integrative model for resilience in developmental
      psychology, 407–8
   intervention/reversibility, 46–47

neurobiological resilience (cont.)
  in migrant youth, 378–80
  overview, 35
  principles to guide future research, 48–49
  stress-relevant neurobiological systems, 39–40
  understanding resilience systemically, 37–39, 38f
neurological traces in preverbal world, 101–3
neuronal excitability, 137
New York, urban change in, 616
NHRC (National Human Rights Commission of India), 649–50
No Lost Generation initiative, 366–68
noncognitive (bodily) intrapersonal influences on resilience, 147–48
nonhumanness zones, in settler-colonialism, 568–69
nonlinearity of development, 343–45
nonstate violent conflicts, 417–18, 418f. See also conflict resilience
normalizing mental health changes to stressor exposure, 139
normative dimensions of resilience, 370
normative expectations, and positive adaptation, 340–41
norms, team, 464–65
Nurse Family Partnership (NFP), 590
nurses, promoting resilience of, 461
NWA (Native Wellness Assessment), 89–90

occupants, architecture focused on experience of
  building design shaping behavior, 629–34, 632f, 633f
  climate-adapted neighborhoods, 639–42, 640f, 641f
  evaluating social contexts in sustainable architecture, 634–39, 637f, 638f
  general discussion, 642–43
  overview, 626–29
occupational context, resilience in. See employee resilience
occupation of West Bank, 570–71. See also Palestinian refugee communities
OECD (Organization for Economic and Co-operation and Development), 428–30, 429t
ontological resilience, 328–31
open systems, resilient systems as, 21–22
operational/inherent stressors, in police work, 182–83
operations, in high reliability organizations, 676
operative history of architecture and built form, 604f, 604–5, 611–15, 612f, 614f, 615f, 616–20
operative panarchy
  adaptive building cycles, 606f, 606–7
  in Chinese architecture and built form, 616–20, 617f, 618f
  general discussion, 620–21
  operative history of architecture and built form, 612f, 612–15, 614f, 615f
  overview, 605, 615–16
opportunities, when modeling multisystemic resilience, 12f, 13
optimal stress response regulation, 144–48
optimism, and perinatal resilience, 63–65
ordering models of risk, 672–73
Ørestad College project (3XN), 631, 632f, 633f, 634
organization, technology, and individual (OTI) viewpoints
  human and organizational factors, 670–77
  linking technology, organizations and people, 670
  overview, 665f, 665
  system risk, 668–69
organizational change, employee resilience during, 467–69, 470t
organizational culture, 186–87
organizational factors, and ecological police resilience, 186–88
organizational partners, in FNMWCF, 93
organizational processes, in family resilience, 260, 266f, 266 267t
Organizational Resilience Management System (ORMS), UN, 698
organizational resources
  frameworks of, 461–63, 462t, 463f
  role of job design, 458–61
organizational support, 188
organizational system resilience
  adversity, 691–94
  capability, 695–97
  domain characteristics, 683–87, 685f
  versus engineered system resilience, 699–700, 699t
  general discussion, 699–700
  management systems standards, 698–99
  organizational processes, 694–95
  overview, 682–83, 689–91
  unique techniques, 697–98
organizational systems, in school ecologies, 232–34
Organization for Economic and Co-operation and Development (OECD), 428–30, 429t
OTI viewpoints. See organization, technology, and individual viewpoints
outcome measures, in measurement of resilience, 88–91
outcome perspective on psychological resilience, 455–56
  case for reductionism, 141–43
  general discussion, 148
  intra-individual theory of resilience, 143–45
  overview, 135–40

positive appraisal style theory of
resilience, 145–48
outcomes
attachment as, 272–73
in messy social-ecological systems, 169, 173*f*
oxytocin receptor (OXTR), 378

Palestinian Authority (PA), 571
Palestinian refugee communities
background on research in, 570–72
decolonial strategies for restorying
resilience, 570
general discussion, 579–80
settler-colonialism in, 566
stories of decolonial enactments of
resilience, 572–78
Palestinian Refugee Family Trees of Resilience
project (PRFTR), 570, 571–72
panarchy. *See also* operative panarchy
adoption of term, 612
in development of SES resilience concept,
710, 711*f*
and legal system resilience, 516
overview, 604–5, 605*f*
and P/CVE field, 311
and SES resilience, 731*f*, 731
social innovation and, 495–96
urban, 610–11
parasympathetic nervous system (PNS), 39
parental resilience, 61–62, 69–70. *See also* perinatal
resilience
parents/parenting. *See also* attachment resilience
biological resilience in culturally sensitive
framework, 45
complexity of resilience-enabling
transactions, 237
developmental cascades, 122–24
in integrative model for resilience in developmental
psychology, 403–4, 406, 408, 409–10
promotion of resilience among school children,
224–25, 226–27
role in neurobiological resilience of
children, 40–41
states of mind, 276–77
theory of human capital development, 586–87
understanding history behind in attachment
interventions, 282–83
participation, resilient systems including, 23
participatory modeling, 432, 433*f*, 438–39
Passive House standard, 636
passive survivability, 627–28
PASTOR (positive appraisal style theory of
resilience), 145–48
pathway (person-focused) models, 120*f*,
120–22, 121*f*

pathways, in developmental systems theory, 117
patterns
of socio-hydrological resilience, 750–53
system resilience, 684, 686–87, 699*t*
P/CVE (preventing/countering violent extremism).
See violent extremism, resilience to
peacebuilding, resilience-building approaches in.
See also conflict resilience; migrant youth,
resilience in; transitional justice
general discussion, 371–72
overview, 361
pathways to systemic resilience, 365–69
political economy of resilience, 370–71
resilience as everyday practice, 369–70
structural and social resilience, 361–65
people, in networked computer systems, 665*f*, 665,
668–69, 670–77
people-based systems. *See* organizational system
resilience
perceived social support, 143
perceptions of change, in messy SESs, 171–76, 173*f*
performance gaps, in architecture, 628
performance variability, in resilience engineering,
482–83, 483*f*
perinatal resilience
experiences of pregnancy and birth, 58–59
factors associated with poor, 67
future research and theory development, 70–71
general discussion, 71–72
overview, 57–58
posttraumatic growth and salutogenesis, 62–63
resilience in pregnancy and birth, 61–66, 62*f*, 64*t*
risk and adversity in pregnancy and birth, 59–60
theoretical approaches to, 67–70
traumatic birth, 60–61
Perry Preschool program, 589
persistence
as resilience-promoting process, 19
and resilience to violent extremism, 306–7
personal agency, and resilience in migrant
youth, 386
personal attributes contributing to perinatal
resilience, 63–65, 64*t*
personality
early assumptions about resilience as linked
to, 135–36
role in neurobiological resilience of children, 41
personal resources, relation to employee resilience,
458–59, 460–61
person-focused (pathway) models, 120*f*,
120–22, 121*f*
physical aspect of human settlement, in
postdisaster reconstruction, 652
physical factors related to perinatal risk and
adversity, 59

physical redundancy technique for engineered systems, 688
physiological factors. *See also* neurobiological resilience
  ecological police resilience, 184–85
  integrative model for resilience in developmental psychology, 407–8
  role in neurobiological resilience of children, 41–42
picture puzzle, resilience as, 23–24, 24*f*
plant knowledge, in resilience of Kamentza people, 326–28
PMSIF (Positive Mental Health Surveillance Indicator Framework), 88
PNS (parasympathetic nervous system), 39
police resilience
  context of police work, 181–82
  general discussion, 190–91
  multisystemic definition, 183–84
  overview, 181
  social-ecology of resilience in police work, 184–90, 185*f*
  stressors in police work, 182–83
policy
  concern about strategic use of resilience concept in, 713
  developmental resilience frameworks for, 124–28, 125*t*
  and economics of multisystemic resilience, 588–90
  macroeconomic approach to multisystemic resilience, 593–94
  and Multisystemic Resilience Framework for migrant youth, 387–89
  related to Indigenous Australian students, 205
  and resilience in migrant youth, 383, 384
  on resilience to violent extremism, 295–97
  role in community resilience, 83
  and social-ecological scales, 738
political economy of resilience, 370–71
political panarchy, 612*f*
political systems, resilience in. *See* humanitarianism, resilience-building approaches in
polyglot aphasia, 107
populations, focus on in salutogenic model of health, 158
positive adaptation. *See also* resilience; *specific areas of resilience research; specific types of resilience*
  debates over, 398–99, 399*f*
  socioecological developmental systems approach, 340–41
positive appraisal style theory of resilience (PASTOR), 145–48

positive feedback loops, 540–41
positive goals, in resilience framework for action, 125
positive mental health outcomes, in measurement of resilience, 88–90
Positive Mental Health Surveillance Indicator Framework (PMSIF), 88
postconflict societies. *See* transitional justice
postdisaster human settlement reconstruction. *See also* disaster resilience
  overview, 650–54, 651*f*
  Wenchuan earthquake case study, 654–55
postpartum period. *See* perinatal resilience
posttraumatic growth, 62–63, 124, 136–37, 398–99, 399*f*
posttraumatic stress disorder (PTSD), 57, 137–38
poverty. *See* economics of multisystemic resilience
power, relation to resilience, 10, 776–77
Power, Threat, Meaning Framework, 282–83
practice
  applications of family resilience orientation, 262–64, 265–67, 266*f*
  collaboration with through engaged scholarship, 555–56
  developmental resilience frameworks for, 124–28, 125*t*
  everyday, resilience as, 369–70
  and Multisystemic Resilience Framework for migrant youth, 387–89
practitioner frameworks for assessment of conflict resilience, 420, 428–32, 429*t*
praxis, decolonial, 567
preconception stress and resiliency pathways (PSRP) model, 68–69
predictability of process performance, 693–94
prediction of mental health outcomes, 138–39
predisaster preparedness, 648
pregnancy
  experiences of, 58–59
  overview, 57–58
  resilience in, 61–66, 62*f*, 64*t*
  risk and adversity in, 59–60
  theoretical approaches to resilience during, 67–70
pregnancy anxiety model, 68
preoccupation with failure, in HROs, 675–76
preschool programs for disadvantaged children, 589
preventing/countering violent extremism (P/CVE). *See* violent extremism, resilience to
prevention
  conflict, investigations into resilience for, 420–23
  primary, 84*f*, 85
  primordial, 84*f*, 84–85
  resilience to violent extremism as, 297–98

secondary, 84f, 85–86
tertiary, 84f, 85–86
preverbal world
    development of, 100
    neurological traces in, 101–3
PRFTR (Palestinian Refugee Family Trees of Resilience project), 570, 571–72
primary prevention, 84f, 85
Primera Alianza attachment intervention, 285
primordial prevention, 84f, 84–85
problem-solving processes, in family resilience, 260 267t
procedural aspects of community resilience, 83
process, resilience as
    attachment resilience, 275, 279
    disaster resilience, 648
    messy SES resilience, 165–66, 168–71, 170f
    overview, 19–21
    psychological resilience, 135–38
    in social-ecological systems, 705–6, 720–21, 721f
    socioecological developmental systems approach, 336f, 336–39
    versus trait definitions, 397–98
process-based, multiscale architecture, 634
process(es)
    adaptive law promoting, 524–25
    attachment as, 273
    organizational, relation to resilience, 689–90, 693–95, 697
    in resilience research and salutogenic model of health, 157–58
    SES identification as, 715–16
    social innovation as paradox of context and, 502
process measures, in measurement of resilience, 90–91
production function of human capital, 586–87
Progresa program, 590–91
promotive factors or processes, 118–20
protective (moderating) effect model of resilience, 348–49
protective factors or processes, 118–20, 303, 396–97. *See also* resilience; *specific areas of resilience research*,
PSRP (preconception stress and resiliency pathways) model, 68–69
psychological distance, in perception formation, 172
psychological factors
    ecological police resilience, 184–85
    related to perinatal risk and adversity, 59
psychological flexibility, and perinatal resilience, 65
psychological resilience. *See also* integrative model for resilience in developmental psychology; outcome perspective on psychological resilience; *specific areas of resilience research*
    defined, 183–84
    definition of related terms, 396–97
    general discussion, 410–12
    history of research on, 396
    investigations into conflict resilience, 423–24, 426–28, 436
    long-standing debates related to, 397–400, 399f
    in migrant youth, 377–78, 379–80
    overview, 395
    to violent extremism, 298–99
psychological sciences. *See also specific areas of resilience research*
    definition of resilience in, 9
    definition of systems in, 7–8
    history of resilience research in, 396
    investigations into conflict resilience, 423–24, 426–28
    resilience as occurring in contexts of adversity, 18–19
    resilience as process, 19
    shadow side of social innovation in, 500–1
psychosocial resource models, 142
PTSD (posttraumatic stress disorder), 57, 137–38
public health approaches to resilience
    First Nations Mental Wellness Continuum Framework, 91–94, 92f
    general discussion, 94
    overview, 78–79, 79f
    promoting community resilience across levels of care, 79–83, 80t
    resilience as multisystemic, 84f, 84–88
    resilience measurement, 88–91
public interest design, 653–54

qualitative methods in conflict resilience research, 426–28, 436
quantitative methods in conflict resilience research, 426, 427–28, 436
Queensland, Australia, 207–11, 208f, 209f
questionnaires, resilience, 138–39, 264–65

r (exploitation) phase, adaptive cycle, 730f, 730
racialized peoples. *See* decolonial enactments of resilience; *specific topics related to Indigenous peoples*,
radicalization, engaged scholarship on, 559–61. *See also* violent extremism, resilience to
RAG (resilience analysis grid), 483, 484–85, 485f, 488, 489
Ready? Set. Go! program, 126, 127
reappraisal processes, in PASTOR, 145–46
reconstruction, postdisaster. *See also* disaster resilience
    overview, 650–54, 651f
    Wenchuan earthquake case study, 654–55

recover phase, D^2R^2+DR resilience strategy, 668
recovery. *See also* resilience; *specific areas of resilience research*
  in model of multisystemic resilience, 12*f*, 13
  of organizational systems, 690–91, 696–97
  as resilience-promoting process, 20
  resilience to violent extremism as, 297–98
  as type of resilience, 398–99, 399*f*
  from work, importance to employee resilience, 469, 470*t*
reductionism, in resilience research, 141–43
redundancy, resilient systems including, 23
refine phase, D^2R^2+DR resilience strategy, 668
reflexivity, 572
refugee children, psychological resilience in. *See also* migrant youth, resilience in
  developmental perspective of resilience, 409–10
  environmental sensitivity, 406–7
  implications of research on, 410–11
  multidimensional nature of resilience, 408–9
  multilevel perspective, 407–8
  multisystemic nature of psychological resilience, 402*f*, 403–6
  overview, 401
refugee crisis. *See also* conflict resilience; Palestinian refugee communities
  architectural interventions related to, 652–53
  humanitarian responses to, 364–65
  resilient responses to, 558–59
regime shifts
  in social-ecological systems, 728, 729*f*, 737
  and socio-hydrological resilience, 749–50
regrettable substitutions, 15
regulation, mutual, as component of attachment resilience, 275–76
regulations, and police resilience, 189–90
rehumanizing counternarratives, 569–70, 572–78
relational developmental systems theory. *See* developmental systems theory
relationality
  Kamentza people's view of, 320–22
  multisystemic human, 565, 579
relational understanding of SES identification, 715–16, 718–19
relational view of resilience, 255–56, 324–25, 336*f*, 336–39. *See also* family resilience
relationships
  in First Nations Mental Wellness Continuum Framework, 93
  and perinatal resilience, 64*t*, 66
release (Ω) phase, adaptive cycle, 730*f*, 730
reliability
  in legal system resilience, 517, 518–19
  resilience as sensemaking and mindfulness, 674–77

religion
  in integrative model for resilience in developmental psychology, 405
  and resilience as everyday practice, 370
  and resilience in migrant youth, 383–84
remediate phase, D^2R^2+DR resilience strategy, 667–68
reorganization (α) phase, adaptive cycle, 730*f*, 730
reporting on terrorism, 305–6
representations, as component of attachment resilience, 276–77, 278, 280*t*, 284*f*
reradicalization, engaged scholarship on, 559–61
RESCUR Surfing the Waves program, 225–27
research, applying multisystemic resilience concept to, 26–27, 243–44
residential communities, in Wenchuan postdisaster reconstruction, 654–55
residential schools, in Canada, 81–82
resilience. *See also specific areas of resilience research; specific types of resilience*
  application to research and intervention, 26–27
  common principles of, 18–23
  co-occurring systems and, 13–17
  cross-disciplinary interactions, 771–74
  definitions, 6–7, 8–11
  emerging perspectives on, 778–79
  general discussion, 27–28, 782
  new frontiers for science of, 779–82
  overview, 771
  reasons for focus on, 1–3
  in social-ecological systems, 774–77
  as tangram, 23–26, 24*f*
  urgency of need to understand, 3–4
  waves of research on, 114, 128, 167–68, 396
Resilience Alliance, 612, 710–11
resilience analysis grid (RAG), 483, 484–85, 485*f*, 488, 489
resilience engineering
  complexity, 478–80, 479*f*
  functional resonance analysis method, 485–88, 487*f*
  general discussion, 488–89
  legal system resilience, 512–13
  methods for, overview, 483
  overview, 477–78
  as paradigm shift, 480–83, 482*f*, 483*f*
  resilience analysis grid, 484–85, 485*f*
resilience framework for action, 125–28, 125*t*
resilience humanitarianism, 364–65
Resilience in Ecology and Urban Design (Pickett, Cadenasso, & McGrath), 608–9
"Resilience in the Built Environment" (Hassler and Kohler), 607–8
Resilience Measurement Practical Guidance (USAID), 428–30, 429*t*

resilient design. *See* embodied multisystemic
    resilience of architecture and built form;
    social contexts of resilient architecture
resilient integration, 349
resilient school ecologies, 238–40
Resilient Systems Framework, 468
Resilient Work Systems Framework, 462–63, 463*f*
resistance
    as resilience-promoting process, 19–20
    resilience to violent extremism as, 297–98
resources
    attachment interventions focused on, 281–82
    relation to employee resilience, 456–57, 458–59, 460–63, 462*t*, 463*f*
    role in community resilience, 82
resource substitution, 347–48
response diversity, 512, 513
responses, in messy social-ecological systems, 169, 172–74, 173*f*
responsiveness, as component of attachment resilience, 275–76
restorying resilience, decolonial strategies for, 569–70, 572–78
restrictive parenting, and biological resilience, 45
reversibility of harm in biological systems, 46–47
right-wing extremism. *See* violent extremism, resilience to
risk. *See also* adversity; *specific areas of resilience research*
    and community resilience to violent extremism, 303
    mental models of, 671–74
    in networked computer systems, 668–69
    and organizational maturity, 694–95
    for postpartum PTSD, 61
    in pregnancy and birth, 57–58, 59–60
    socioecological developmental systems approach, 341–43
    in understanding of resilience, 396–97
    when modeling multisystemic resilience, 12
ritual, in resilience of Kamentza people, 324–25, 328
Rome panarchy, 614–15, 615*f*
Rostock, Germany, 716–17, 718–19, 719*t*
rupture and repair, as component of attachment resilience, 277
rural–urban migration in China, 380

SA (situational awareness), 668, 669–70
safety management, resilience engineering for
    complexity, 478–80, 479*f*
    functional resonance analysis method, 485–88, 487*f*
    general discussion, 488–89
    methods for, overview, 483

overview, 477–78
    as paradigm shift, 480–83, 482*f*, 483*f*
    resilience analysis grid, 484–85, 485*f*
salutogenesis, 63, 156–57
salutogenic model of health
    comparing resilience scholarship and, 157–60
    concept of resilience in, 153, 160–62
    definition of resilience, 154–55
    general discussion, 162
    overview, 153–54
    salutogenesis definition, 156–57
Sankt Kjelds Square climate adaptation, 640*f*, 640, 641*f*
San Miguel de Tuduman, Argentina, 610–11
SCADA (supervisory control and data acquisition) systems, 663–64. *See also* networked computer systems
scaffolded resilience-enabling school-student transactions, 238–40
scalability, in legal system resilience, 517, 519–20
scales
    cascading effects in socio-hydrological resilience across, 756–58, 757*f*
    implication of complexity of adaptive systems, 776–77
    in operative panarchy concept, 604–5, 612*f*, 612
    social-ecological, 726–27, 737–38
SCB (Smith Creek Basin), Canada, 759*f*, 759–60, 760*f*, 761*f*, 762*f*
school ecologies, and student resilience
    complexity of resilience-enabling transactions, 234–38
    overview, 232–34, 233*t*, 235*f*
    scaffolding of resilience-enabling transactions, 238–40
    trade-offs related to resilience-enabling transactions, 240–41
school resilience, 238–40
schools. *See also* Indigenous education and resilience; student resilience; transactional, whole-school approach to resilience
    in integrative model for resilience in developmental psychology, 404
    urban education, transformations in, 556–58
secondary prevention, 84*f*, 85–86
sectarian polarization, prevention of conflicts related to, 422–23
security. *See also* networked computer systems
    attachment, 272–73, 281
    as characteristic of attachment resilience, 274
    in critical infrastructures, 663–64
    resilience logics driven by, 296–97
SEL (social and emotional learning) programs, 223
self-efficacy, student, 556–58
self-regulation, student, 235–37

sensemaking, resilience as, 674–77
sense of coherence, 156–58, 350–51
sensitivity
　environmental, 399–401, 406–7
　to operations, in HROs, 676
　and resilience in messy SESs, 171, 173f
sensorimotor system, and built form, 603–4, 611, 616–18, 620–21
sensory niche, and narrative resilience, 102
servant leadership, 465–66
services, in networked systems, 663, 664f
SES. See ecosystem services; social-ecological system resilience; social-ecological systems
settler-colonialism
　overview, 566–67
　stories of decolonial enactments of resilience, 572–78
　structural violence of, 568–69
　in West Bank of Israel, 570–71
shadow side of social innovation, 499–501, 502–3
shocks, and economics of multisystemic resilience, 587–88, 590–92
short-term crises, and family resilience, 257–58
Sibundoy, Colombia. See Kamentza people, resilience of
Sichuan province earthquake postdisaster reconstruction, 654–55
simplification, HRO avoidance of, 676
situational awareness (SA), 668, 669–70
skills based, universal resilience curriculum, 223–24
skin-deep resilience, 44, 45–46
SLA Architects, 640–41
slow variables
　and ecological resilience, 308–9
　in social-ecological systems, 728–29, 729f
　in socioecological developmental systems approach, 339
Smith Creek Basin (SCB), Canada, 759f, 759–60, 760f, 761f, 762f
SNS (sympathetic nervous system), 39
social and emotional learning (SEL) programs, 223
social anthropological research on conflict resilience, 423–24, 426–28
social capital
　and conflict resilience, 439–43, 443t, 444t, 446t
　in integrated capacities framework, 435t
　and resilience in migrant youth, 380–81
　and resilience to violent extremism, 300–2
　role in community resilience, 82–83
social compact, resilience in, 362
social contexts of resilient architecture
　building design shaping behavior, 629–34, 632f, 633f
　evaluating social contexts in sustainable architecture, 634–39, 637f, 638f
　general discussion, 642–43
　occupants, focus on experience of, 626–29
　overview, 625–26
　social benefits of climate-adapted neighborhoods, 639–42, 640f, 641f
social Darwinism, 500
social determinants of health, 92–93
social-ecological resilience model
　conflict resilience, 422–23, 426–28
　Kamentza indigenous people, resilience of, 329–30
　resilience to violent extremism, 298, 302–3
social-ecological system (SES) resilience. See also ecosystem services
　agent types and perceptions of change, 174
　case studies, 716–20, 719t
　complexity of process, 720–21, 721f
　complexity theory, 166–69
　critiques of systems approach, 712–13
　defined, 727–28
　definition of SESs, 707–8, 708f
　development and evolution of concept, 708–13, 709f, 710f, 711f
　general discussion, 176, 721–22
　overview, 165–66, 705–7
　perceptions of change in messy SESs, 171–74, 173f
　resilience as process, 169–71, 170f
　SES identification, 713–16
　technology-induced environmental distancing, 175
　testing resilience process using technology as inhibitor, 175–76
social-ecological systems (SESs). See also socioecological developmental systems approach to resilience
　adaptive cycles, 495–96
　adaptive governance in, 523–24
　complexity in, 775–77
　cross-disciplinary interactions, 773
　defined, 707–8, 708f
　definition of resilience in, 8
　definition of systems in, 7–8
　emerging perspectives on multisystemic resilience, 777
　identification, 705–6, 707, 713–22, 719t, 721f
　limitations of, 777
　multisystemic approach to analysis of resilience, 774–77
　role of legal systems in, 515–16, 521
　theoretical underpinnings for managing, 726–31, 729f, 730f, 731f
social-ecology of resilience in police work

community level, 186–89
community policing, 188–89
family, 185–86
individual-level factors, 184–85
laws, 189–90
organizational factors, 186–88
overview, 184, 185f
social environment, role in resilience, 159–60, 161
social factors related to perinatal risk and adversity, 59–60
social heterogeneity, and resilience to violent extremism, 307
social innovation and resilience
emerging principles, 501–2
general discussion, 503–4
linked approach to, 494–97
overview, 493–94
resilience and transformation, 497–99
shadow side, 499–501
social mobility. *See* economics of multisystemic resilience
social perturbations, hydrological resilience to, 748–49, 751, 752f, 759–60, 760f, 761f
social policy, and resilience in migrant youth, 383, 384
social process, resilience in SES as, 165–66, 169–71, 170f
social recovery, postdisaster, 652–53, 654–56
social resilience. *See also* humanitarianism, resilience-building approaches in
to hydrological change, 748, 751, 752f, 761
systems-level approaches to, 361–65
social sciences. *See also specific areas of resilience research*
concept of resilience in, 551–55
definition of systems in, 7–8
social support
and perinatal resilience, 64t, 66
as protective factor for mental health, 142–44
social values, and biological resilience, 44–46
societal resilience
engaged scholarship as opportunity for inclusive, 555–56
general discussion, 561–62
operationalizing engaged scholarship to understand, 556–61
overview, 551–52
understanding, 552–55
sociocultural transition, 384. *See also* migrant youth, resilience in
socioecological developmental systems approach to resilience
co-regulation, 338–39
developmental processes, 343–47
general discussion, 351–53

multiple levels of influence, 337–38
overview, 335–36
positive adaptation, 340–41
resilience model in, 336f, 336–39
resilience processes, 347–51
risk and adversity, 341–43
timescales, 339–40
socioecological systems. *See* social-ecological system resilience; social-ecological systems
socioeconomic inequality. *See* economics of multisystemic resilience
socio-hydrological resilience
cascading effects in, 753–58, 754f, 755f, 757f
case study, 758–61, 759f, 760f, 761f, 762f
defined, 749
defining resilience in coupled human–water context, 746–49
general discussion, 762–64
human–water coupled system, 745–46, 747f
overview, 744–45
systematic understanding of, 749–53, 752f
sociotechnical safety management, resilience engineering for. *See also* engineered system resilience
complexity, 478–80, 479f
functional resonance analysis method, 485–88, 487f
general discussion, 488–89
methods for, overview, 483
overview, 477–78
as paradigm shift, 480–83, 482f, 483f
resilience analysis grid, 484–85, 485f
Sommières, France, 717–20, 719t
SoS (system of systems), 683, 689
spatial scales. *See* scales
specific resilience of social-ecological systems, 732
speech. *See* narrative resilience
stable states
alternate, in systems, 728–29, 729f
multiple, in development of SES resilience concept, 708–10, 709f
staff resilience. *See* employee resilience
staged process models of development, 344
staircases, social use of, 631, 632f, 633f
state resilience, 361–65
states of mind, parental, 276–77
static resilience, 512–13
steeling effect, 16, 136–37, 222–23, 410
STEP UP intervention, 210
storytelling
decolonial strategies for restorying resilience, 569–70, 572–78
developing capacity related to, 100–1
general discussion, 107–9
mature narration, 106–7

storytelling (cont.)
　narration of memories, 103–5
　neurological traces in preverbal world, 101–3
　overview, 100–1
　in RESCUR Surfing the Waves program, 226
　surrounding stories, 105–6
strategic approach to SES resilience, 715–16
strategies of intervention, in resilience framework for action, 127
street-level bureaucrats, 189–90
strengths-based approaches
　to family resilience, 260 267t
　to Indigenous development, 202–3, 205
stress
　attachment resilience as activated under, 273–74
　challenge-hindrance stressor framework, 459–60
　co-occurring systems and resilience, 16
　developmental perspective on family resilience, 257–59
　epigenetics and narrative resilience, 101–2
　model of pregnancy anxiety, 68
　neurobiological systems relevant to, 39–40
　optimal stress response regulation, 144–48
　perinatal experience of, 57–58
　in police work, 182–83
　positive appraisal style theory of resilience, 145–48
　preconception stress and resiliency pathways model, 68–69
　resilience as occurring in contexts of, 18–19
　stressor exposure reductions, 141–43
　when modeling multisystemic resilience, 11
stress immunization/inoculation. See steeling effect
stress reactivity, 406–7
stress resistance, 398–99, 399f
stress shield police resilience model, 183–84
structural coupling, by Kamentza people, 321–22
structural equation modeling, in conflict resilience investigations, 439–42, 441f
structural inequalities, and transitional justice, 537–39
structural resilience, systems-level approaches to, 361–65. See also humanitarianism, resilience-building approaches in
structural violence of settler-colonialism, 568–69
structure
　adaptive law promoting, 524–25
　underspecification of in HROs, 676–77
student resilience
　complexity of resilience-enabling transactions, 234–38
　general discussion, 244–45
　implications for research and intervention, 243–44
　overview, 232–34, 233t

　propositions based on research, 241–43, 242f
　scaffolding of resilience-enabling transactions, 238–40
　in systemic context, 232–34, 235f
　trade-offs related to resilience-enabling transactions, 240–41
students, engaged scholarship involving, 556–58. See also Indigenous education and resilience; transactional, whole-school approach to resilience
Studies for an Operative Urban History of Venice (Muratori), 613–14, 614f
subaltern groups, resilience of. See Kamentza people, resilience of
subhumanity zones, in settler-colonialism, 568–69
subjectivity, in research on family resilience, 264–65
subsystems, cascading effects across, 753–55, 754f
superarchitecture, 636
Superkul, 637–39
supervisory control and data acquisition (SCADA) systems, 663–64. See also networked computer systems
supply chain resilience, 10–11
support, organizational, 188
support systems, and perinatal resilience, 64t, 66
Sure Start program, 592–93
surveillance, public health, 88
sustainable architecture
　evaluating social contexts in, 634–39, 637f, 638f
　taking social context into account, 627–29, 642
sustainable development, inequality as threat to, 780–82
sustainable livelihoods framework, 430–31
sympathetic nervous system (SNS), 39
systemic assets contributing to community resilience, 82–83
systemic resilience. See also specific areas of research; specific systems
　application to research and intervention, 26–27
　case for reductionism, 141–43
　common principles of resilience, 18–23
　co-occurring systems and resilience, 13–17
　cross-disciplinary interactions, 771–74
　definitions of resilience, 6–7, 8–11
　emerging perspectives on, 778–79
　general discussion, 27–28, 782
　model of, 11–13, 12f
　new frontiers for resilience science, 779–82
　overview, 6–8, 7f, 154–55, 771
　reasons for focus on, 1–3
　resilience as tangram, 23–26, 24f
　in social-ecological systems, 774–77
　urgency of need to understand, 3–4
system of systems (SoS), 683, 689

system resilience
  defined, 683
  domain characteristics, 683–87, 685f
  engineered system domain, 687–88
  general discussion, 699–700
  organizational systems domain, 689–99
  overview, 682–83
systems, defining, 6–8, 7f. See also specific related topics; specific system types
system safety. See safety management, resilience engineering for
systems engineering. See engineered system resilience
systems entrepreneurs, 498–99
systems-level responses in humanitarianism and peacebuilding, 363–64
systems theory, developmental. See developmental systems theory
system-wide perspective on conflict resilience, 426, 428, 432, 433f, 438–39

Tabanok, Colombia. See Kamentza people, resilience of
tangram, resilience as, 23–26, 24f
targeted interventions to improve student resilience, 221–22, 223, 224
teachers
  complexity of resilience-enabling transactions, 234–35, 236, 237
  engaged scholarship involving, 556–58
  promotion of resilience among school children, 225, 227
  trade-offs related to resilience-enabling transactions, 240–41
team resilience
  critical role of leadership, 465–67
  multilevel model of, 463–65
technical boundary models of risk, 672
technical hazards, 646–47. See also disaster resilience
techniques for system resilience
  engineered systems, 687–88
  organizational systems, 697–98
  overview, 686, 699t
technology, and social-ecological systems, 165. See also networked computer systems; sociotechnical safety management, resilience engineering for; system resilience
technology-induced environmental distancing (TIED), 175–76
teleological view of resilience, 17
temperament, role in neurobiological resilience of children, 41
temporal scales. See scales; time
territory, in resilience of Kamentza people, 325, 330–31

terrorism. See also violent extremism, resilience to
  as multisystemic phenomenon, 293–94
  reporting on, 305–6
  resilience features in, 307–8
tertiary prevention, 84f, 85–86
theory of human capital development, 584, 585–87
3XN Architects, 631–34, 632f, 633f
thresholds. See cascading effects in sociohydrological resilience; tipping points
time
  in resilience of Kamentza people, 325–26
  in socioecological developmental systems approach, 339–40, 345–46
  in system resilience, 684–86, 685f, 699t
  in understanding of attachment resilience, 279, 280t
timing, developmental, and neurobiological resilience, 43–44
tipping points, 172–74, 728–29, 749–50. See also regime shifts
topology, in networked systems, 663, 664f
trade-offs of systemic resilience, 17, 21, 240–41, 757–58
trait definitions of resilience, 36, 47, 135–36, 397–98
trajectories, in development of SES resilience concept, 710f, 710–11, 711f
transactional, whole-school approach to resilience
  framework for, 221–25
  general discussion, 227–28
  overview, 220–21
  RESCUR Surfing the Waves case study, 225–27
transactional processes
  facilitating family resilience, 260 267t
  socioecological developmental systems model of resilience, 336f, 336–37
transdisciplinary approaches to studying resilience. See multisystemic resilience; specific areas of resilience research,
transformability, 712, 750–51, 752f
transformation. See also resilience; specific areas of resilience research
  defined, 712
  in model of multisystemic resilience, 12f, 13
  as resilience-promoting process, 20
  and SES identification, 715, 719
  and transitional justice, 535–36
transformational leadership, 465–66
transformative justice, 538–39
transformative resilience, 552, 553–54
transformative social innovation, 497–99, 502–4
transitional justice
  case study, 543–45
  defined, 531
  general discussion, 545–46

818 | SUBJECT INDEX

transitional justice (*cont.*)
   modeling multisystemic resilience, 539–43, 541*f*
   multisystemic resilience concept in, 536–39
   overview, 530–31
   resilience, defined, 531–47
   resilience as neglected concept within, 532–34
   resilience relevance to, 535–36
Transition Support Service (TSS), Australia, 207–11
Transparent Cities (McGrath), 616
transversal analysis of attachment resilience, 279
trauma. *See also* adversity; *specific areas of resilience research*
   absence of attachment as, 272
   attachment resilience as activated under, 273–74
   epigenetics and narrative resilience, 101–2
   mass-trauma adversities, 114–15, 128–29
   narration of memories related to, 103–5
   narrative resilience, 107–9
   neurological imprint of past, 106–7
   perinatal experience of, 57–58
   in person-focused models, 120*f*, 120–22, 121*f*
   stories surrounding victims of, 106
traumatic birth, 60–61, 63
Tredje Natur, 639
trust
   importance of, resilience and, 671–74
   and resilience to violent extremism, 310–11
   role in individual and organizational resilience, 671–74
turning points, 350

ubuntu, 567–68
Ukraine, assessment of resilience in conflict-affected, 438–45, 440*t*, 441*f*, 442*t*, 443*t*, 444*t*, 446*t*
uncertainty, and adaptive management, 734–35, 735*f*
underspecification of structures in HROs, 676–77
United Kingdom (UK)
   "Boiler on Prescription" project, 630–31
   CONTEST strategy, 295, 296, 297, 305
United Nations (UN)
   Common Guidance on Helping Build Resilient Societies, 428–30, 429*t*
   Declaration on the Rights of Indigenous Peoples, 202–3
   Organizational Resilience Management System, 698
United Nations Development Programme (UNDP), 428–30, 429*t*
United Nations Relief and Works Agency for Palestine Refugees in the Near East (UNRWA), 571
universal resilience programs in schools. *See* transactional, whole-school approach to resilience

Unraveling Sustainability and Resilience in the Built Environment (Garcia and Vale), 610–11
urban design. *See* embodied multisystemic resilience of architecture and built form; social contexts of resilient architecture
urban ecological systems, 650–51
urban education, transformations in, 556–58
urban Indigenous populations, 87–88
urban panarchy, 610–11
urban-style residential communities, in Wenchuan postdisaster reconstruction, 654–55
USAID Resilience Measurement Practical Guidance, 428–30, 429*t*
US Airways Flight 1549, 687–88
U.S. Constitution, resilience of, 512–13
U.S. National Infrastructure Advisory Council, 626
utility networks. *See also* networked computer systems
   application of OTI viewpoints to, 670
   cyber situational awareness in, 669–70
   resilience and mental models of risk and importance of trust, 671–74

valley of Sibundoy, Colombia. *See* Kamentza people, resilience of
value conflicts during organizational changes, 469, 470*t*
variable-focused models of resilience, 120, 122, 123*f*
VELUX Model Homes program, 629, 637–39
Venice panarchy, 613–14, 614*f*
vertical integration by schools to strengthen Indigenous students resilience, 211–13, 212*f*
vicarious resilience, 264
victim-centered transitional justice, 533, 535–36
violence of settler-colonialism, 568–69
violent extremism, engaged scholarship on, 559–61
violent extremism, resilience to
   community, 299–304
   conceptual gaps, 303–4
   general discussion, 310–12
   importance of social capital, 300–2
   individual, 298–99
   multisystemic nature of, 303–8
   overview, 293–95
   prevention, resistance, and recovery, 297–98
   principles for future study of, 308–10
   research and policy focus on, 295–97
violent social conflicts, 417–19, 418*f*, 419*f*. *See also* conflict resilience; Palestinian refugee communities; peacebuilding, resilience-building approaches in; refugee children, psychological resilience in; transitional justice
Vrije Universiteit Amsterdam Institute for Societal Resilience, 551–52, 556–61

vulnerabilities. *See also* resilience; *specific areas of resilience research*
　and community resilience to violent extremism, 303
　interlocking, 779–80
　in social-ecological systems, 705–6, 716–17, 719*t*, 720–21
　when modeling multisystemic resilience, 12*f*, 12

Ω (release) phase, adaptive cycle, 730*f*, 730
Walsh Family Resilience Framework, 260 267*t*
war. *See* conflict resilience; Palestinian refugee communities; peacebuilding, resilience-building approaches in; refugee children, psychological resilience in; transitional justice
Waterloo Institute for Social Innovation and Resilience, 494, 496–97
water systems. *See* socio-hydrological resilience
wealth. *See also* economics of multisystemic resilience
　in humanitarian and peacebuilding efforts, 365–66
　inequality as threat to sustainable development, 780–82
　and mental health, 142
weathering hypothesis, 44
well-being. *See also* resilience; *specific types of resilience*
　holistic, in measurement of resilience, 89–90, 91
　in social context of architecture, 626–29
　teacher, trade-offs related to, 240–41

WELL Building standard, 628, 635–36
Wenchuan earthquake postdisaster reconstruction, 654–55
West Bank, 570–78
White Eurocentric thinking, 565–66. *See also* decolonial enactments of resilience
Whole Building Design Guide, 626
whole-of-society approach to CT and P/CVE, 294–95
whole-school approach to resilience
　framework for, 221–25
　general discussion, 227–28
　overview, 220–21
　RESCUR Surfing the Waves case study, 225–27
work, resilience related to. *See* employee resilience
work–family conflict, in police work, 185–86
workload, during organizational changes, 469, 470*t*

yajé (ayahuasca), 327–28
young people. *See also* childhood resilience; children; *specific areas of research focused on youth*
　conflict resilience investigation involving, 438–45, 440*t*
　economic interventions targeting, 587, 590
　engaged scholarship on reradicalization, 559–61
　linking peace to biopsychosocial health in, 366–68
　narrative resilience in, 103–6
Yugoslavia, transitional justice in former, 543–45